D1557444

Handbook of
Wealth Management

Handbook of
Wealth Management

LEO BARNES, PH.D.

Professor of Banking, Finance and Investments;
Director, Center for the Study of Capital
Needs for Full Employment, Hofstra University

STEPHEN FELDMAN, PH.D.

Dean, School of Business and
Public Administration, Western
Connecticut State College

McGRAW-HILL BOOK COMPANY

New York   St. Louis   San Francisco   Auckland   Bogotá
Düsseldorf   Johannesburg   London   Madrid   Mexico
Montreal   New Delhi   Panama   Paris   São Paulo
Singapore   Sydney   Tokyo   Toronto

Library of Congress Cataloging in Publication Data
Main entry under title:

Handbook of wealth management.

   Includes index.
    1. Investments—Handbooks, manuals, etc.
2. Finance, Personal.   I. Barnes, Leo, date. II. Feldman,
Stephen.
HG4521.H237   332.6′78   77-2989
ISBN 0-07-003765-5

1234567890   KPKP   786543210987

The editors for this book were W. Hodson Mogan and Tobia L. Worth,
the designer was Naomi Auerbach, and the production supervisor
was Teresa F. Leaden. It was set in Baskerville
by University Graphics, Inc.

Printed and bound by The Kingsport Press.

DEDICATION

The editors join in dedicating this *Handbook* to their wives, Regina Barnes and Constance Feldman, without whose encouragement, understanding, patience, advice, and assistance their long and arduous task could not have been completed.

Contents

Contributors

CARL E. ANDERSEN
Senior Vice President, The Keystone Company of Boston (Chapter 45)

STANLEY APFELBAUM, LL.B.
President, First Coinvestors Inc. (Chapter 40)

LEONARD W. ASCHER, PH.D.
Professor of Finance Emeritus, University of Hawaii (Chapter 25)

LEO BARNES, PH.D.
Professor of Banking, Finance and Investments; Director, Center for the Study of Capital Needs for Full Employment, Hofstra University (Chapters 1, 5, 6, 7, 14, 16, 26, 42, 45, 56, and 57)

ROBERT E. BROWN
Consulting Publisher, Value Line, Options & Convertibles (Chapter 23)

CHARLES F. CONGDON, M.ED., M.B.A.
Associate Professor of Quantitative Methods, University of Hawaii (Chapter 25)

D. LARRY CRUMBLEY, CPA
Professor of Accounting, Texas Agricultural and Mechanical University; Editor, Oil and Gas Tax Quarterly *(Editor, Section XII; Chapter 64)*

P. MICHAEL DAVIS, PH.D., CPA
Professor of Accounting, University of Kentucky (Chapter 66)

PETER A. DICKINSON
Editor, The Retirement Letter: The Money Newsletter for Mature People *(Chapter 63)*

ROBERT E. DIEFENBACH
Director of Research, U.S. and Foreign Securities Corp. (Chapter 47)

ROBERT R. DINCE, PH.D.
Associate Deputy Controller of the U.S., Department of Economic Research and Operational Analysis (Chapter 9)

DAVID K. EITEMAN, PH.D.
Professor of Finance, University of California, Los Angeles (Chapters 10 and 12)

FRANK J. FABOZZI, PH.D.
Assistant Professor of Finance, Hofstra University (Chapter 61)

STEPHEN FELDMAN, PH.D.
Dean, School of Business and Public Administration, Western Connecticut State College (Chapters 13, 27, 28, 29, 31, and 60)

JOHN F. FERRARO
Chief Analyst, The Predictor, Incorporated (Chapter 20)

LEWIS P. FREITAS, PH.D.
Professor of Finance, College of Business Administration, University of Hawaii (Chapter 24)

SIDNEY FRIED
President, RHM Associates (Chapters 21 and 22)

MARK R. GREENE, PH.D.
Professor of Insurance, University of Georgia (Chapters 59 and 67)

MARK HANNA, PH.D.
Professor of Finance, University of Georgia (Chapter 43)

CHARLES V. HARLOW, D.B.A.
President, Cambistics Inc., Professor of Finance, California State University at Long Beach (Chapters 32, 33, 34, and 35)

RUDOLF HAUSER, M.B.A.
Financial Analyst, Institutional Research Dept., Oppenheimer and Company (Chapter 58)

JOHN E. HERZOG, M.B.A.
President, Herzog, Heine & Co. (Chapter 18)

GEORGE S. JOHNSTON
President and Chief Executive Officer, Scudder, Stevens and Clark (Chapters 1 and 44)

ROBERT KATZ, LL.M.
Assistant Professor of Accounting and Taxation, Hofstra University (Consulting Editor, Section XII)

JOEL KAUFFMAN, LL.M., CPA
Professor of Accounting and Law, University of North Florida (Chapters 17 and 62)

EDWARD J. LANDAU, J.D., CPA
Partner, Lowenthal, Landau, Fisher and Singer (Chapter 52)

ROBERT A. LERMAN, M.S.E.E.
President, The Predictor, Incorporated (Chapter 20)

JESSE LEVIN
Financial Consultant and Author, deceased (Chapter 7)

ROBERT A. LEVY, PH.D.
President, Computer Directions Advisors, Inc. (Chapters 2, 3, and 19)

ARTHUR A. MERRILL, M.B.A.
President, Merrill Analysis Inc. (Chapter 8)

EDWARD E. MILAM, PH.D., CPA
Associate Professor of Accounting, University of Mississippi (Chapter 64)

JAMES E. PARKER, PH.D., CPA
Professor of Accounting, University of Missouri-Columbia (Chapter 11)

JOSEPH PETRITZ
Director, Editorial Services, International Monetary Market Division of the Chicago Mercantile Exchange Inc. (Chapter 36)

RALPH POLIMENI, PH.D., CPA
Chairman, Department of Accounting and Business Law, Hofstra University (Chapters 48, 49, 50, and 51)

FRANK K. REILLY, PH.D.
Professor of Finance, University of Illinois at Urbana (Chapters 2, 5, and 15)

MARTIN RICHARDS, LL.M.
Tax Attorney, International, Richardson, Merrell (Chapter 52)

LEMONT K. RICHARDSON, PH.D.
Principal, Richardson Associates (Chapters 4 and 55)

KENNETH W. RIND, PH.D.
Principal, Xerox Development Company (Chapter 46)

RICHARD H. RUSH, D.C.S.
Author and President, Richard H. Rush Enterprises; Contributing Editor, The Wall Street Transcript *and* The Art/Antiques Investment Report *(Chapters 37 and 38)*

PAUL SARNOFF, M.B.A.
Director, Options Department, Conticommodity Services (Chapter 23)

MAURICE L. SCHOENWALD, J.D.
President, Accrued Equities Inc. (Chapter 39)

LEONA SELDOW, PH.D., C.P.C.U., C.L.U.
Associate Professor of Finance and Insurance, Hofstra University (Chapter 41)

KEITH V. SMITH, PH.D.
Professor of Finance, Graduate School of Management, University of California, Los Angeles (Chapters 53 and 54)

TERENCE E. SMOLEV, LL.M.
Partner, Naidich and Smolev (Chapter 65)

HERBERT L. STONE, D.B.A.
Professor of Management and Management Science, California State University at Long Beach (Chapters 32, 33, 34, and 35)

RICHARD J. TEWELES, PH.D.
Vice President, Cambistics Inc.; Professor of Finance, California State University at Long Beach (Chapters 32, 33, 34, and 35)

JAMES TURLEY, LL.M., J.D.
Assistant Vice President, Manufacturers Hanover Trust Company (Chapter 68)

DONALD E. VAUGHN, PH.D.
Professor of Finance, Southern Illinois University at Carbondale (Chapter 19)

RUSSELL WAYNE, M.B.A.
Senior Analyst, The Value Line Investment Survey (Chapter 16)

PAUL F. WENDT, MAI, CRE, CRA, PH.D.
Professor of Real Estate and Urban Development, University of Georgia (Chapter 30)

Preface

The *Handbook of Wealth Management* has been planned and designed to treat in adequate detail virtually all the areas in which capital can be profitably invested. While the initial emphasis is on equity and debt securities, our many distinguished contributors go on to analyze all areas of selection, timing, and management of real estate, commodities, gold, art, antiques, coins, stamps, livestock, oil, and other varieties of special and unusual investments and their suitability for all types of individual and institutional investors. The key aspects of tax, retirement, insurance, gift, and estate planning are also explored in detail.

Special care has been taken to ensure that the many and often far-reaching changes resulting from the Tax Reform Act of 1976 in the taxation of income, capital gain, most tax shelter investments, and gifts and estates have been fully incorporated and analyzed in the appropriate sections of the *Handbook*.

All the chapters of this work have been prepared by highly qualified authorities, so that it is our hope and belief that the *Handbook* will long serve as a professionally recognized reference guide, providing a high standard of money management for building, protecting, and perpetuating capital. A primary aim has been to blend theory and practice, on the premise that practice without theory is all too often blind, while theory without practice is all too often futile.

To all our contributors, the editors extend their deep thanks and appreciation. Great credit for the successful completion of this *Handbook* must also be given to the editors, W. Hodson Mogan, Senior Editor of Business Books, Tobia L. Worth, and Beatrice E. Eckes, as well as to Mildred Hetherington and Margaret P. DeJoy, for their administrative assistance, and other members of the McGraw-Hill team. Their encouragement, guidance, and editorial and proofreading assistance have been indispensable.

LEO BARNES *and* STEPHEN FELDMAN

Handbook of
Wealth Management

Section One

Basic Decisions of Investment Planning

Chapter 1

Basic Decisions of Family Financial Planning

LEO BARNES

GEORGE S. JOHNSTON

Relatively few investors have carefully thought-out, consistent, long-term financial, investment, and estate plans for themselves and their families. It is a prime purpose of the *Handbook of Wealth Management* to provide the basic data and techniques for such planning.

Five Keys to Family Planning

Your spouse, children, and other close members of your family should either join you in your financial planning or, as a minimum, be kept adequately and promptly informed about it. Sound family financial planning involves:

1. Providing for temporary emergencies like sickness and accidents.
2. Setting aside funds for major future outlays—a first or second home, college or professional education of children and close relatives, major travel or vacation plans, and the like.
3. Maintaining sufficient life and disability insurance for your family and dependents, a task made much more difficult by persisting inflation (see Section Eleven).
4. Providing sufficient capital and income for you and your spouse's retirement years (see Sections Two, Three, Four, Five, and Eleven).
5. Preserving and maximizing your estate for your survivors and descendants (see Section Twelve).

Determining Your Investment Objectives

Investors can be grouped in terms of their investment targets as conservative, aggressive, and speculative. The dividing lines between these objectives are not absolute, and one may, if one so decides, combine two or even all three of these approaches.

The conservative investor stresses low risk or safety above the level of return. The first consideration is preservation of capital; the second, a very safe and stable income. Holding periods for investments are on the longish side—years rather than months.

The aggressive investor is willing to take somewhat greater risks for the probability of a higher total return from a combination of capital growth and income. Such an investor will buy or sell more frequently to realize capital gains or to cut capital losses.

The speculative investor will take the greatest risks to achieve maximum capital gains, frequently at the price of capital losses, which he or she attempts to limit via various stop-loss techniques. Such an investor will buy and sell most frequently, often without regard to the long-term–gain holding period for tax purposes. There will typically be plenty of short-term losses to offset realized short-term gains.

It is often feasible for some investors to combine two or even all three of these basic investment objectives. However, if one does this, it is probably wise, if only for psychological reasons, to separate the funds concerned into different investment programs (perhaps involving different investment advisers or brokers) rather than to maintain them in a single portfolio.

Normally, it is expected that higher risks are rewarded in the long run by higher average returns. Otherwise, why take the higher risks? In practice, however, this risk-return hypothesis does not always hold true. In particular, it has not been valid during most of the inflation-ridden period since 1968, when quality bonds often fared better than risky stocks; when high-grade short-term market instruments sometimes outperformed both stocks and bonds; and when more and more investors were switching from securities to commodities, stock options, foreign exchange, gold, real estate, art, antiques, oil drilling, cattle and racehorse breeding, and other offbeat areas analyzed in Sections Five, Six, Seven, and Nine.

In this section of the *Handbook,* various concepts and applications of pretax and aftertax yield, return, reward, safety, risk, and volatility are analyzed in detail.

Who Should Handle Your Investments?

Individuals or corporate investors can either (1) do their own investing, (2) give others that responsibility in full, or (3) work out an effective combination of both methods. If you have little or no time to devote to investment analysis and timing, estate planning, and the other matters treated in the *Handbook,* you have no choice but to use professional money management. But if you can devote at least five hours a week to supervising your investments and other assets, you *may* prefer to manage part or all of your funds.

In reaching a conclusion on this basic question, the decisive consideration should always be: "After considering all expenses involved, can I *consistently* do as well (or better) on my own?" A good yardstick to use as a test of your abilities is one or more of the leading stock market indicators (see Chapter 2 for the recent statistical record of the widely used stock market indices). Has your total return (income plus net capital gain) in the last few years matched or exceeded that of the Dow Jones Industrial Average or Standard & Poor's 500-Stock Index?

Since 1969 relatively few individual investors have come even close to these averages, and increasing numbers of investors have drawn the appropriate conclusion by withdrawing from the stock market. Accordingly, you should continue to handle your own stock investments only if you have positive evidence that you can do as well as or better than the popular averages.

How to Select Advisers, Brokers, and Dealers

Sections Five and Eight of the *Handbook* analyze the major types of investing institutions, including mutual funds, closed-end investment companies, dual-purpose funds, commingled investment accounts managed by banks or insurance companies, and various types of real estate investment trusts. In addition to such institutions, in which individual investors participate by owning shares, there are investment advisers who handle individual or corporate accounts on a separate, discretionary basis. Because of the fees involved, this alternative is suited primarily to investors with substantial assets. The investment counseling profession is analyzed later in this chapter.

The first factor in your choice of an investing institution or a personal investment adviser is your basic investment attitude—conservative, aggressive, or speculative. Next is the factor of the candidates' demonstrated performance record over a representative recent time period that includes both bull and bear markets. How does the record of each possible candidate, adjusted for expenses, compare with the leading market averages in both up and down markets? Has the performance been consistently good, is it improving, or is it deteriorating? There seems to be little point in going further back than five or six years, since over a longer time period the personnel responsible for the record are apt to have left the organization.

Such past performance records are published and are readily available for mutual funds, investment companies, and real estate investment trusts. Similar data are not so easy to obtain from other investing institutions or from personal investment advisers, who are not required to make public their past results. Even if such figures are presented, you should bear in mind that their accuracy is usually not certified by a public accountant or a government agency like the Securities and Exchange Commission.

What Is Professional Investment Counsel?

The professional investment counsel industry has existed as a formalized concept since 1919. Until recent years, it retained a rather low profile. This has been interpreted by some as aloofness and by others as a mystique, but it probably is more accurately described as a direct reflection of the industry's own business standards and its self-image as a new profession. In the last few years, however, it has received more extensive publicity and has experienced a wide proliferation of participants.

The name "investment counsel" and the basic structure it denotes first came into being in the form of Scudder, Stevens & Clark in 1919. The principals of this firm, who had experience in both banking and brokerage, determined that existing vehicles did not fully satisfy many investors' requirements for objective and impartial advice. They were particularly concerned with potential conflicts of interest associated with a compensation system attached to the actual execution of transactions as well as with conflicts that might arise from commercial banking relationships between the money manager and companies in which investments were made.

After a relatively short period of trial and error and experimentation with various forms and fees, the new structure was identified as a source of investment advice through a tailor-made, individualized product, and a fee system that closely synchronized the interests of client and counsel was developed. This system consisted of a charge that represented a constant percentage of portfolio asset value as computed periodically.

In 1924 the firm of Russell, Berg was formed as the second entry in the field, and a year later A. Vere Shaw resigned from Scudder, Stevens & Clark to establish Shaw, Loomis & Sayles, now Loomis, Sayles & Co., Inc. About the same time, the firm of Haydock, Kressler & Lamson (later to become part of Scudder, Stevens & Clark) was formed in Cincinnati, and the industry was off and running.

In 1937, in an era of increasing governmental concern with the securities business in general, the Investment Counsel Association of America was established at the initiative of the industry. It articulated standards of practice and ethical guidelines for its members that underscored the professional nature of the industry's attitude toward itself and toward its relationships with clients. Many of the principles thus enunciated were used by Congress as a basis for the Investment Advisers Act of 1940, under which members of the industry with fifteen or more clients must register.

The industry today is a good deal less homogeneous, for many formerly independent firms have established corporate connections with other types of organizations. For example, Loomis, Sayles is now a subsidiary of the New England Mutual Life Insurance Company. Lionel D. Edie is associated with Merrill Lynch, Pierce, Fenner & Smith. Naess & Thomas (now Schroder Naess & Thomas) is a division of Schroder Trust Company. John W. Bristol & Company and Douglas T. Johnston and Company have become connected with the Boston Company, itself an offshoot of Boston Safe Deposit & Trust Company. Of the larger firms, very few have remained independent.

As both a symbol and a symptom of industry growth, many new firms have been organized in recent years, although the difficult stock market environment during this period and the increasing demand by clients for persistency and consistency of performance may well have led to a degree of turnover. These factors, plus the organizational changes discussed above, make it difficult to produce a meaningful estimate of the total value of portfolios supervised. As of 1974, the total could well be any figure from $50 billion to $100 billion. It is clear, however, that this fifty-year-old industry in one form or another has become a major factor in institutional and individual money management.

How Investment Counsel Firms Are Organized

The internal structures of investment counsel firms vary widely. The larger firms have their own in-house research departments that act, in a sense, as service organizations for their portfolio managers. Similarly, such firms may also have separate resident staffs that are expert in other areas associated with money management, including economics, taxation, financial planning, legal matters, and order placing.

At the other end of the spectrum, the principals of smaller firms, in addition to managing portfolios, may perform these functions themselves, drawing on brokerage firms and outside consultants for research. The bulk of the industry probably falls somewhere in between, with the distinction between research and portfolio management functions sometimes blurred and at least some of the other responsibilities performed extracurricularly.

A uniform characteristic of the industry is its avoidance of custodial services, which are generally handled by banks, brokers, or individual clients with safe-deposit boxes. The actual arrangements with clients can differ widely between firms and within firms. Some smaller firms devote themselves solely to discretionary accounts: clients authorize counsel to make investment changes without obtaining advance approval and are generally notified of the details subsequently. Other firms will accept both discretionary accounts and advisory accounts, for which recommendations are made first and action taken only if approval is received.

While advisory relationships were the rule in earlier years, discretionary arrangements are generally encouraged today since they reduce the delay between the exercise and implementation of investment judgment. Many institutional and fiduciary clients, however, are unable for legal reasons to grant unlimited authority; thus investment counsel firms have worked out many gradations of the two basic arrangements. All firms provide some form of periodic reporting of portfolio values, and many now prepare performance computations either with their own computer installations or with the aid of outside service organizations.

Investment Counsel Clients

Clients of investment counsel firms include individuals, personal trusts, estates, corporate (including insurance company) reserve funds, corporate pension and profit sharing funds, college and hospital endowments, charitable foundations, offshore investment pools, and state and local retirement funds.

Fortunes of private individuals undoubtedly comprised the backbone of the business through the 1950s. The growth in size of tax-exempt funds, particularly retirement funds, their increased emphasis on equities, and the greater willingness of these institutions to consider investment counsel as well as trust companies as candidates for prospective investment management roles have weighted the business, at least in dollar terms, in this direction in more recent years.

Some firms accept only institutional accounts. Others restrict the focus of their business even more specifically by using investment objectives and, for example, accept only aggressive accounts for which current income is not a concern. Most investment counsel firms delimit their clientele through minimum account sizes for both individuals and institutions, ranging from $500,000 to $50 million.

Investment Counsel Charges

Investment counsel fees are generally expressed in stated percentages of portfolio market values. The exact percentages vary considerably from one firm to another, and there is no clear correlation with past performance records. One 1973 study showed a range in charges for managing a $5 million account from about $6,310 per year (0.13 percent) to $50,000 per year (1 percent).

In many cases, the percentages are graded downward at indicated rising levels of portfolio value. Different schedules are often posted for institutional and individual accounts, reflecting variations in objectives, workload, tax considerations, and degree of investment and management flexibility.

The Revenue Act of 1942 permitted tax-paying clients to deduct investment counsel fees in computing their income taxes, a privilege subsequent revenue acts have not altered. This consideration is obviously of little interest to tax-exempt clients, a factor that has contributed to differences between prevailing institutional and individual fee scales.

Many firms do not incorporate their relationships with clients in formal contracts. The only tie is satisfaction with the service provided. In some cases, institutional clients request a written contract, and a few firms use contracts as a regular procedure, generally on a quarter-to-quarter basis.

Despite the many differences between investment counsel firms that make it difficult scrupulously to characterize the group, there are important common threads that justify the formal industry label. They are, in fact, implicit in each word of the designation "professional investment counsel": *professional* connotes the ethical and confidential aspects of the client relationship; *investment,* in the general sense, identifies the raison d'être of the industry and, in a more limited sense, its approach to security management; and *counsel* suggests the personal and individualized orientation with which the industry performs its basic services.

Chapter 2

How to Calculate Yields, Returns, and Rewards

Part 1. Construction and Evaluation of Market Averages and Indices

ROBERT A. LEVY

During the calendar year 1970 the stock market was up 4.8 percent. Or was it up only 1 percent? Or was it down 2.5 percent? Or did it get clipped for a 13.4 percent loss? The answers are: Yes, Yes, Yes, and Yes. The numbers represent, respectively, the changes in the Dow Jones Industrial Average, the Standard & Poor's 500-Stock Index, the New York Stock Exchange Index, and the American Stock Exchange Index. Why don't the indices agree? Which one is most revealing? Or are there other measures that can give us a better gauge of stock market behavior?

The retrospective appraisal of investment performance is partly dependent upon the availability of an appropriate standard of comparison representing "the market." Some would agree that a properly constructed yardstick would also be invaluable to forecast market direction. Accordingly, it might be worthwhile to examine some of the existing market indices and averages and to suggest possible improvements.

Dow Jones Industrial Average

The Dow Jones Industrial Average is computed by adding the prices of the thirty component securities and dividing by a figure that originally was 30 but has since been adjusted for splits and stock dividends. The adjustment of the divisor can be illustrated as follows: Consider only three stocks with prices of $20, $60, and $100 respectively. The sum of the three prices would be $180, and the average price would be $180 divided by 3, or $60. If, however, there was a 2-for-1 split of the $60 stock, the sum of the three prices would then be $150 ($20 + $30 + $100). Since nothing has occurred other than a doubling of the number of outstanding shares of one of the component stocks, to maintain an average of $60 the divisor would have to be adjusted from 3 to 2.5.

This method of computation has two weaknesses. First, it assumes that an equal number of shares of each stock is held. Thus each stock has a weight in the average that is directly proportional to its price, so that a 100 percent increase in a stock priced at $20 would have only half the effect on the average that a similar increase for a $40 stock would have.

To illustrate, let us consider a portfolio of two stocks, one of which experiences no price change during 1971 and one of which gains 20 percent:

	Price	
Stock	*Dec. 31, 1970*	*Dec. 31, 1971*
A	10	10
B	100	120
Total	110	130
Average	55	65

$$\text{Percentage change} = {}^{10}\!\!/_{55} = +18.2 \text{ percent}$$

Let us consider the same situation, reversing the performance of the individual stocks.

	Price	
Stock	*Dec. 31, 1970*	*Dec. 31, 1971*
A	10	12
B	100	100
Total	110	112
Average	55	56

$$\text{Percentage change} = {}^{1}\!\!/_{55} = +1.8 \text{ percent}$$

Clearly, the $100 stock has an overbearing effect on the average. In point of fact, in mid-1971 General Electric had about the same importance in the Dow as AT&T and General Motors combined; and Dupont had greater weight than the sum total of Allied Chemical, Anaconda, Bethlehem Steel, Chrysler, and United States Steel.

The second major weakness of a price average such as the Dow is that the influence of each stock in the average is affected by splits and stock dividends that change the price of the stock but do not change any of the stock's underlying characteristics. For example, consider the implications of a $50 stock that increases to $200 and then is split 4 for 1, thus again selling for $50. The original 150-point increase in the price of the stock would have had an influence on the average that could not be completely reversed after the split. Even if the price of the stock, postsplit, were to fall to zero, the stock would have lost only one-third of the number of points that it originally had gained.

The most obvious criticism of the Dow is that a mere thirty large blue-chip companies cannot be considered representative of the overall market. For this reason alone, many market enthusiasts prefer either the Standard & Poor's 500-Stock Index or the all-inclusive indices prepared by the New York and American stock exchanges.

Standard & Poor's 500 and New York Stock Exchange Common Stock Indices

The New York Stock Exchange and Standard & Poor's indices (consisting largely of NYSE issues) employ very similar computational methods. The price of each component stock is weighted by outstanding shares. The products of shares times price are accumulated to produce an aggregate market value, and the resultant market value is then compared with a predetermined base period value and expressed as an index. This method of computation avoids any distortion due to splits or stock dividends, since neither splits nor stock dividends cause any change in aggregate market value (that is, the increase in the number of outstanding shares offsets the decrease in market price). Even if this important advantage over the Dow is conceded, serious weaknesses remain.

First, there is substantial double counting because some corporations own shares of others. For instance, Shell Transport owns about 40 percent of Shell Oil stock; there are many similar situations. The methodology used by S&P and the New York Stock Exchange in computing their indices counts all outstanding shares, even though some are in the hands of corporations whose own shares already reflect the value of their holdings of other common stocks.

Second, both the S&P and the NYSE indices are influenced disproportionately by the price movements of a very few giant corporations. In mid-1971 there were some 1,360 common stocks on the Big Board, but just 67 of these had the same total market value as all remaining 1,293 companies. The top 136 stocks, or 10 percent of those listed, accounted for nearly 62 percent of the NYSE index, whereas the bottom 136 stocks accounted for less than 0.5 percent.

To be sure, the biggest financial institutions with billions of dollars to invest must restrict their portfolios to the largest corporations. But for many institutions and certainly for almost all individual investors, no such restrictions exist.

American Stock Exchange Index System

On September 4, 1973, the American Stock Exchange introduced a market value index system similar to that used by the New York Stock Exchange, Standard & Poor's and the National Association of Security Dealers (described below). This system replaced a price change index, in effect since April 1966, that was similar to the Dow Jones indices in that each stock had a weight exactly proportional to its price.

The ASE Market Value Index measures the change in the total market value of all the common shares, American depository receipts (ADRs), and warrants listed on the ASE (market value equals share price times the number of shares outstanding). The new indices make it easier for investors to compare market performance on the ASE with that of other markets, since all the three major markets now employ market value indices.

Sixteen subsidiary ASE market value indices cover eight industrial, seven geographical, and one foreign groupings. The ASE is the first to offer market value indices on a regional basis (determined by the location of company headquarters). The eight industrial subindices, which are somewhat different from the corresponding breakdowns on the NYSE and the over-the-counter market (NASDAQ; see below), are as follows: Capital Goods; Consumer Goods; Financial; High Technology; Housing, Construction, and Land Development; Natural Resources; Retail; and Services. More than eighty companies have such diverse operations that they could not be included in the industrial classifications.

The close of trading on August 31, 1973, represents 100.00 on the new ASE market value indices.

NASDAQ Over-the-Counter Indices

On February 8, 1971, the bid and asked quotations of 3,500 leading issues in the huge over-the-counter securities market became fully automated with the introduction of the National Association of Security Dealers automated quotation system (NASDAQ). This is a set of market value indices similar to most of the other leading indices described above.

There are six major subindices in the NASDAQ formulation, or two more than for the NYSE and two fewer than for the ASE system. In addition to the standard breakdown of industrials, transportation, and utilities, NASDAQ provides greater discrimination in the financial area by separating banks, insurance companies, and other financial companies.

See Part 2, section "Differential Long-Run Returns between Segments of the Stock Market," for a performance comparison of major market indices since 1960.

Buy-and-Hold Models

To overcome the weighting problem of either price-weighted or market value–weighted indices, many students of the market have used buy-and-hold models as a performance gauge. These models assume an equal dollar investment in each of a selected number of securities at the beginning of the period and no purchases or sales at any time thereafter. The value of the portfolio may then be computed at any time during the period and compared with the value at any previous time to determine the profitability of the portfolio. A hypothetical portfolio of three securities is illustrated below:

	Value at Beginning of Period			
Stock	*1*	*2*	*3*	*4*
A	$100	$120	$130	$150
B	100	115	120	130
C	100	95	90	80
Total	$300	$330	$340	$360

The profitability of this portfolio could be summarized in the following manner: the value increased 10 percent from the first to the second period, 3 percent from the second to the third, and 5.9 percent from the third to the fourth. Notice, however, that these results are still affected by the weighting of the investment selection. Only at the beginning of period 1 is there an equal dollar investment in each stock. Subsequent to period 1, there are substantial changes in the composition of the portfolio.

	Portfolio Composition by Stock at Beginning of Period (In percentages)			
Stock	*1*	*2*	*3*	*4*
A	33.3	36.4	38.2	41.6
B	33.3	34.8	35.3	36.2
C	33.3	28.8	26.5	22.2
Total	100.0	100.0	100.0	100.0

The result is an ever-increasing investment in the strongest stocks (A and B), coupled with a decreasing investment in the weakest stock (C). The rates of return, beginning with period 2 are not indicative of returns obtained by an unweighted portfolio. Any yardstick assigning greater weight to stocks that have shown greater relative strength is hardly appropriate as a frame of reference for gauging portfolio performance. As a matter of interest, the same criticism could also be leveled at the S&P, NYSE, ASE, and NASDAQ indices. The strongest companies are continually allocated greater weight as their market values increase. Moreover, were it not for the effect of stock splits, the Dow might be challenged on similar grounds.

Arithmetic Average of Price Relatives

In the example above, we could have minimized the disparity due to weighting simply by reequalizing the investment in component securities at the beginning of every period. If this procedure were followed, the performance would be computed by averaging arithmetically the price relatives (the ratio of the price at the end of a period to the price at the beginning) of the individual stocks. The accompanying table uses the same numbers as those for the buy-and-hold illustration.

	Period 1–2			Period 2–3			Period 3–4		
Stock	Beginning price	End price	Price relative	Beginning price	End price	Price relative	Beginning price	End price	Price relative
A	100	120	1.200	120	130	1.083	130	150	1.154
B	100	115	1.150	115	120	1.043	120	130	1.083
C	100	95	0.950	95	90	0.947	90	80	0.889
Total			3.300			3.073			3.126
Average			1.100			1.024			1.042
Performance			+10.0%			+2.4%			+4.2%

Unfortunately, the use of arithmetically averaged price relatives creates two serious problems. First, percentage increases are given greater weight than percentage decreases (that is, intraperiod weights favor the stocks that appreciate most rapidly). Second, the base date of the index cannot be shifted (that is, successive periods cannot be linked).

To illustrate the first problem, let us consider a one-year example.

Stock	Price Dec. 31, 1969	Price Dec. 31, 1970	Price Relative
A	1	2	2.000
B	2	1	0.500
Total			2.500
Average			1.250
Performance			+25.0%

The indicated 25 percent gain could have occurred only if twice as many shares of A as shares of B were held throughout the period. But if this were so, midway through the period the dollar investment in A, the stronger stock, would have exceeded the dollar investment in B, the weaker stock, and we are back to our original difficulty with weighting.

To illustrate the second problem, let us carry the example one year further:

Stock	Price Dec. 31, 1970	Price Dec. 31, 1971	Price Relative
A	2	1	0.500
B	1	3	3.000
Total			3.500
Average			1.750
Performance			+75.0%

Linking the 1970 performance (+25 percent) with the 1971 performance (+75 percent), the two-year results are $1.25 \times 1.75 = 2.1875 = +118.75$ percent. But take another look at 1971 in terms of 1969, as shown below:

Stock	Price Dec. 31, 1969	Price Dec. 31, 1971	Price Relative
A	1	1	1.000
B	2	3	1.500
Total			2.500
Average			1.250
Performance			+25.0%

The discrepancy between the linked two-year results and the table shows that it is impossible to shift the base (that is, link the periods) when using arithmetic averages of price relatives. This is, of course, a significant drawback.

Geometric Averages

The arithmetic average of price relatives assumes an equalization of the amount invested in each component stock every time that the average is computed. What may be needed is a measure that reflects continual equalization and disregards time intervals.

A geometric average weights each security equally, the investment in each security is continually evened up, and a given percentage change in the price of any stock has an identical effect on the average. To compute a geometric average, multiply all the price relatives together and take the nth root, where n is the number of stocks. A convenient shortcut is to take the antilog of the average log of the relatives. For example, the geometric average of 10, 100, and 1,000 is 100, whereas the arithmetic average is 370.

	Number	Log	Antilog
	10	1	
	100	2	
	1,000	3	
Total	1,110	6	
Average	370	2	100

$$= (10 \times 100 \times 1000)^{1/3}$$

The effect of continual equalization can be clarified by reviewing the two-year illustration presented above, but with the use of geometric averaging.

	1970			1971		
Stock	Price Dec. 31, 1969	Price Dec. 31, 1970	Price relative	Price Dec. 31, 1970	Price Dec. 31, 1971	Price relative
A	1	2	2.000	2	1	0.500
B	2	1	0.500	1	3	3.000
Geometric total (A × B)			1.000			1.500
Geometric average (total$^{1/m}$)			1.000			1.225

Note that the 1970 performance (+0 percent) linked to the 1971 performance (+22.5 percent) gives two-year results of $1.000 \times 1.225 = 1.225 = 22.5$ percent, or the same figure as that derived directly from the 1969 and 1971 prices:

Stock	Price Dec. 31, 1969	Price Dec. 31, 1971	Price relative
A	1	1	1.000
B	2	3	1.500
Geometric total (A × B)			1.500
Geometric average (total$^{1/n}$)			1.225

Thus, the important characteristics of a geometric index are that (1) it assigns equal weight to every security, (2) it *continually* adjusts the weights so that they are reequalized, and (3) it can be linked from period to period.

Major disadvantages include the following: (1) The geometric index is somewhat more difficult to compute than certain other indices. (2) It is not so widely accessible (various forms of geometric indices are published by Value Line Investment Survey in New York, American Investors Service in Greenwich, Connecticut, *Indicator Digest*, and Computer Directions Advisors, Inc., in Silver Spring, Maryland). (3) It hypothesizes an investment strategy, continual reequalization of the number of dollars invested in each security, that cannot be replicated in practice.

Combination Link Relatives

Mathematically, a geometric average of a set of numbers will always be smaller than an arithmetic average. It would, of course, be possible to compute a market index both geometrically and arithmetically and average the results. This is precisely what the Center for Research in Security Prices at the University of Chicago has done. It has created combination link relatives for all New York Stock Exchange common stocks.

These combination relatives are 56 percent determined by arithmetic averaging and 44 percent determined by geometric averaging. The percentages were chosen to produce a market index that would coincide as nearly as possible with previous studies of the Center on common stock rates of return. Two sets of combination relatives, one adjusted for the reinvestment of cash dividends and one not adjusted, were computed.

Several problems are involved in using the combination link relatives: (1) they are computed only monthly, (2) they are not available immediately at month-end, (3) they are the most difficult indices to understand and rationalize, and (4) they bear no resemblance to any practical investment strategy.

Comparative Performance Results

The accompanying table reflects the sizable disparities that existed among various market indices from 1940 to 1960. None of the figures include reinvestment of dividends.

Period	Annual rates of return (In percentages)			
	Combination relatives	Geometric index	Dow industrials	S&P 500
1940–1945	25.2	21.0	8.0	10.4
1945–1950	0.2	−1.5	4.1	3.3
1950–1955	11.0	9.6	15.7	17.4
1955–1960	4.8	3.1	4.7	5.0
1940–1960	9.9	7.7	8.0	8.9

Since 1960 disparities among market indices, especially between unweighted geometric indices and price-weighted or market valuation–weighted indices, have become even more marked. A detailed analysis of these disparities is included in a study of the comparative performance record since 1960 of major price indices of various types for different segments of the stock market, which is presented in Part 2 of this chapter.

Which Type of Index to Follow?

Since most institutional investors invest primarily in the heavily capitalized market leaders, capitalization-weighted indices provide a fairly satisfactory yardstick of their performance. By contrast, geometric averages are more suitable for individual investors who invest mainly or substantially in smaller, secondary companies.

Moreover, as we have seen, most indices apply to one exchange or market only. Just a few, such as the Value Line indices, consist of stocks from all three major market areas.

It is thus virtually impossible to pick one index that is truly representative of the market as a whole. If one had to choose such an index willy-nilly, perhaps the best practical approximation would be a simple arithmetic average of (1) a capitalization-weighted index like the Standard & Poor's 500-Stock Index or the New York Stock Exchange Composite Index, representing the institutional side of the market, and (2) a broad geometric index covering all the major markets, like the Value Line Composite, representing noninstitutional investors.

Actually, in practice it is very useful to follow several indices, including one or more geometric ones, in order to detect as early as possible significant internal market performance discrepancies, such as those occurring in 1965–1968 and 1969–1974.

Part 2. Differential Returns and Risks among Stock Market Segments

FRANK K. REILLY

In a relatively efficient capital market with risk-averse investors, one would expect a fairly consistent positive relationship between the rates of return derived from an asset and the amount of risk or uncertainty involved. Put another way, the more uncertainty or risk involved in the returns from an investment, the higher an investor's required and actual rate of return should be.

This part of Chapter 2 is concerned with a presentation of empirical data confirming or disproving this proposition in relation to common stocks. The differences in risk available, the magnitude of the differences in returns available, and the source of these alternative returns and risks are presented and discussed.

The initial section is concerned with various studies of average returns on common stocks and common stock returns by risk class, related mainly to the New York Stock Exchange. Subsequently, there is a comparison of returns on common stocks on the NYSE, the American Stock Exchange, and the over-the-counter market.

RETURNS AND RISKS ON THE NEW YORK STOCK EXCHANGE

Fisher-Lorie Studies

Probably the best-known and most highly regarded studies on the subject of returns to common stockholders are those carried out by Professors Lawrence Fisher and James Lorie at the University of Chicago for Research in Security Prices (CRSP). The center was sponsored originally by Merrill Lynch, Pierce, Fenner & Smith to conduct research on the stock market and disseminate the results. Its initial task was to create a highly useful and flexible stock price data source. This was accomplished by collecting the monthly closing prices of all common stocks on the NYSE from January 1926 to December 1960. In addition, information on trading volume, capital changes, stock splits, and dividend distributions was compiled.

Original Fisher-Lorie Study

The first major study using this data base, the Fisher-Lorie study, was concerned with accurately measuring the rates of return on investments in common stocks listed on the NYSE. It covered all common stocks listed on the NYSE and measured their rates of return during twenty-two time periods and, in contrast to most prior studies, considered taxes, commissions, and rates of return with and without reinvestment of dividends.[1]

For each of three tax brackets (tax-exempt, $10,000 income in 1960, and $50,000 income in 1960), the rates of return were computed on the assumption that the portfolio was sold at the end of the period (that is, cash to cash) and that it was retained (cash to portfolio). While it is not possible to reproduce the tables, the annual compound rate of return during the total period (1926–1960) was 8.8 percent with these assumptions: reinvestment of all dividends, a tax-exempt investor, and cash to portfolio. Under the cash to cash assumption the annual compound rate of return was 8.7 percent.

When taxes were considered with the reinvestment of dividends, investors in the $10,000 income bracket in 1960 received an annual return of 8.2 percent if they did not sell their portfolios and 7.9 percent if they did sell them. Under the same conditions investors in the $50,000 income bracket would have received a 7.2 percent return (cash to portfolio) and 6.6 percent for cash to cash.

Regarding these results the authors concluded:

> Aside from most periods ending in 1932 or 1940, the rates of return are surprisingly high. For half the twenty-two periods, the rates are above 10 percent per annum compounded annually; and for two-thirds of the periods, the rates exceed 6 percent.[2]

When rates of return were computed on the assumption that the dividends were not reinvested, the authors concluded:

> At first, one might expect the rates in Table 2 to be significantly lower than in Table 1, whereas in fact the rates are quite similar for most of the periods. This similarity merely reflects the fact that the rate of appreciation in the prices of stocks after the receipt of dividends was on the average about the same as the rate of appreciation before the receipt of dividends. When the latter rate was higher, the rates in Table 2 are lower than those in Table 1 and vice versa. The individual who reinvests his dividends is obviously wealthier at an ending date than is the individual who spends them. On the average he

---

[1] Lawrence Fisher and James H. Lorie, "Rates of Return on Investments in Common Stocks," *The Journal of Business*, vol. 27, no. 1, pp. 1–21, January 1964.
[2] Ibid., p. 6.

TABLE 2-1   Volume in Registered Exchanges

VOLUME IN SHARES TRADED

	No. of shares traded (millions)			Percent of total		
Year	NYSE	ASE	Other	NYSE	ASE	Other
1960	958.3	300.6	129.6	69.0	21.6	9.3
1961	1,292.3	525.3	192.9	64.3	26.1	9.6
1962	1,186.5	332.6	144.4	71.3	20.0	8.7
1963	1,350.9	336.3	151.4	73.5	18.3	8.2
1964	1,482.3	397.0	165.6	72.5	19.4	8.1
1965	1,809.4	582.2	195.3	69.9	22.5	7.5
1966	2,204.8	730.9	252.2	69.2	22.9	7.9
1967	2,885.8	1,290.2	327.8	64.1	28.6	7.3
1968	3,298.7	1,570.7	442.6	62.1	29.6	8.3
1969	3,173.6	1,341.0	448.8	63.9	27.0	9.0
1970	3,213.1	878.5	444.1	70.8	19.4	9.8
1971	4,265.3	1,049.3	601.1	72.1	17.7	10.2
1972	4,496.2	1,103.2	699.8	71.4	17.5	11.1

VALUE OF SHARES TRADED

	Dollar value (millions)			Percent of total		
Year	NYSE	ASE	Other	NYSE	ASE	Other
1960	37,960	4,176	3,083	83.9	9.2	6.8
1961	52,699	6,752	4,352	82.6	10.6	6.8
1962	47,341	3,648	3,743	86.5	6.7	6.8
1963	54,887	4,755	4,678	85.3	7.4	7.3
1964	60,424	5,923	5,802	83.7	8.2	8.0
1965	73,200	8,612	7,402	82.0	9.7	8.3
1966	98,565	14,130	10,339	80.1	11.5	8.4
1967	125,329	23,111	13,318	77.5	14.3	8.2
1968	144,978	34,775	16,605	73.8	17.7	8.5
1969	129,603	30,074	15,621	73.9	17.2	8.9
1970	103,063	14,266	13,579	78.7	10.9	10.4
1971	147,098	17,664	20,169	79.5	9.6	10.9
1972	159,700	20,453	23,873	78.3	10.0	11.7

SOURCE: Securities and Exchange Commission.

also has a great deal more invested in his portfolio. Thus, some rates in Table 1 are higher than the corresponding rates in Table 2; some are lower, and several are the same.[3]

These well-documented results indicated that common stock returns were higher than most individuals would have estimated over the long period considered. Also, the returns were much higher than returns attainable from other investment sources such as savings and loan associations, mortgages, and government bonds, although the risks were also greater than the alternatives in terms of the variability of returns over time.

[3]Ibid., p. 7.

Fisher Random Investment Study

Recognizing that rates of return can be influenced by the stocks selected and the time periods considered, Professor Fisher analyzed the overall effect of these variations on the returns.[4] He did this by enumerating the results for *all possible combinations of purchases and sales of individual stocks listed on the NYSE between January 1926 and December 1960.* For all stocks listed every possible holding period was considered from 1 month to 420 months if the stock was listed for the total period being considered. For the 1,715 stocks available, 56,556,538 combinations were tabulated.

The results were presented as a total frequency distribution of returns and, after brokerage commissions, were summarized as follows:

> The rates of return expressed in percent per annum, compounded annually, show extreme variation, ranging from −100 percent per annum (which, of course, means total loss) to over a trillion percent per annum (in ten cases). But the rate of return has a marked central tendency. *Seventy-eight percent of the time common stocks yielded a positive net return* [italics added]. Over two-thirds of the time the rate of return exceeded 5 percent (which is a larger rate of return than can be obtained on any sort of savings account). *The median rate of return was 9.8 percent* [italics added]. (The interquartile range is 1.8 percent to 17.3 percent.) Nearly one fifth of the time the rate of return exceeded 20 percent per annum, compounded annually.[5]

When commissions were not considered, the median rate of return for the total period increased from 9.8 percent to 10.2 percent per annum.

Subsequently, Fisher analyzed results during sixteen subperiods of economic expansion and contraction as defined by the National Bureau of Economic Research. The results were described as follows:

> Note that, since upswings last longer than downswings, purchases and sales during upswings are most frequent and purchases and sales during downswings are least

[4]Lawrence Fisher, "Outcomes for 'Random' Investments in Common Stocks Listed on the New York Stock Exchange," *The Journal of Business,* vol. 38, no. 2, pp. 149–161, April 1965.
[5]Ibid., pp. 153–154.

TABLE 2-2   Security Issues Listed at Year-End on the NYSE and ASE, 1962–1972

	Issues listed	
Year	NYSE	ASE
1962	1,559	1,018
1963	1,572	1,003
1964	1,606	1,022
1965	1,627	1,028
1966	1,665	1,038
1967	1,700	1,061
1968	1,767	1,088
1969	1,789	1,152
1970	1,840	1,222
1971	1,927	1,308
1972	2,003	1,375*

*Estimate.
SOURCE: American Stock Exchange, *Databook;* New York Stock Exchange, *Fact Book;* 1973.

frequent. For the subperiods the probability of gain varies from 0.12 (for transactions made within the period of the 1937–38 recession) to 0.99 (for transactions with purchases during the 1938–45 upswing and sales during the 1958–60 upswing). Median rates of return ranged from −59.6 percent per annum, compounded annually (for transactions during the 1937–38 downswing), to 25.6 percent (for purchases during the 1957–58 recession and sales during the 1958–60 rise in general economic activity). For holding periods of five years or more the lowest probability of gain is 0.27 (for purchases in 1928–29 and sales in 1937–38). Note that it generally makes little difference whether stocks are bought during a recession or the immediately following expansion but that *it almost always paid to sell during an upswing in the economy rather than during the previous recession* [italics added].[6]

In summarizing the results and relating the findings to the individual investor, Fisher pointed out that the probability of gain on a long-term investment would be much greater than the overall results of 78 percent, which included many short-run losses. Because the distribution for *individual* stocks was positively skewed, holding a portfolio of more than one stock would also have led to positive gains more than 78 percent of the time. Finally, holding several stocks also would have resulted in returns greater than the median return of 9.8 percent more than half of the time.

Fisher's study may be considered more acceptable by many observers than the original Fisher-Lorie study because it examined the total frequency distribution of all possible investment alternatives for individual stocks on the NYSE. The results confirmed the prior findings but also indicated a higher return of 9.8 percent as compared with the overall return of 8.8 percent of the original study for a tax-exempt investor during the period 1926–1960. Fisher noted that these results do not deny that there is still a substantial chance of loss in investing in common stocks, but they do indicate that there were few long periods when the chances of gain were not substantially greater than the chances of loss.

The Year-by-Year Fisher-Lorie Study

This third study updated the original 1964 study and provided more detailed results of the original study period.[7] Specifically, this study presented results for portfolios of all common stocks listed on the NYSE, with the assumption of equal initial investments in each stock from the end of each year to the end of each subsequent year, for the years from 1926 through 1965, or a total of 820 overlapping time periods. As in the original study, the results were presented for different tax brackets on the assumption, first, that dividends were reinvested, then, that dividends were not reinvested, and, finally, by ignoring dividends completely.

Although it is not possible to reproduce the eighteen pages of tables contained in the article, some major conclusions of the study follow:[8]

1. The average of the annual returns during the added five years 1961–1965 was 15.9 percent per annum compounded annually.

2. Of the 820 overlapping and, therefore, dependent time periods, there were only 72 periods in which there were negative rates of return. Most of the periods of negative returns were periods beginning in 1927, 1928, and part of 1929.

3. The rates of return during the last twenty years were consistently high. Specifically, there were positive rates of return during 199 of the 210 overlapping

---

[6]Ibid., pp. 155, 157.

[7]Lawrence Fisher and James H. Lorie, "Rates of Return on Investments in Common Stock: The Year-by-Year Record, 1926–1965," *The Journal of Business*, vol. 41, no. 3, pp. 291–316, July 1968.

[8]These are taken from the highlights presented in the study, p. 293.

periods, or in 95 percent of the periods. Further, there was *no* interval of more than four years when the return was less than 7 percent and no ten-year period when the return was less than 11 percent.

4. Finally, it is shown that the cumulative effect of taxes on wealth is great. The study pointed out:

> For the period January, 1926–December, 1965, the terminal wealth of a tax-exempt investor who reinvested dividends would have been 1.36 times as great as that of the investor in the lower tax bracket and 2.26 times that of the investor in the higher tax category, if they had all sold their holdings at the end of 1965. For December, 1945– December, 1965, the ratios were 1.30 and 1.97 respectively.[9]

These results provided more details and an extension and confirmation of prior results. The confirmation is found in the more detailed evidence that investors in common stocks listed on the NYSE have received positive rates of return during the great majority of periods since 1926. Also, investors have received fairly substantial positive returns during most periods even when commissions and taxes are considered.

Variability and Returns on the NYSE

While the Fisher-Lorie studies were concerned with the average rates of return of all stocks on the NYSE, Professor Shannon P. Pratt employed the Chicago stock price tapes to test the hypothesis that high-risk common stocks on the NYSE provided their owners with higher returns than low-risk stocks.[10] Return (IPR) was the total discounted return during a period of time for which dividend and capital appreciation was considered. Risk was measured by the instability of the historical rates of return, that is, the standard deviation of the logarithms of the IPRs.

The risk factor was computed for all common stocks on the NYSE for 372 monthly base dates from January 31, 1929, through December 31, 1959. The stocks were then divided into five equal groups on the basis of the risk measures for the past thirty-six months from a "base date." Risk grades were designated from Grade A (lowest) through Grade E (highest). Subsequent rates of return (IPRs) from the base date for each portfolio were computed to include all dividends, rights, and other distributions, with the assumption that all dividends were reinvested.

When the arithmetic average of the returns for all the stocks in the portfolio was computed, it was concluded:

> In all cases except the 7-year holding periods, the arithmetic mean of the IPR's for portfolios of stocks of different risk grades over time rises consistently, but at a decelerating rate, as risk grade declines.[11]

Pratt also computed a geometric mean of the returns. The results for this comparison were summarized as follows:

> However, as measured by the geometric mean, the overall average IPR's consistently "top out" at either the C or the D risk grade. In every case, the geometric mean of IPR's over time is lower for Grade E portfolios than for Grade D portfolios; in most cases the geometric mean of IPR's for Grade E portfolios is lower than for Grade C portfolios, and in five instances the geometric mean of IPR's for Grade E portfolios is even lower than for Grade B portfolios.[12]

---

[9]Ibid., p. 293.

[10]Shannon P. Pratt, "Relationship between Variability of Past Returns and Levels of Future Returns for Common Stock, 1926–1960," in E. Bruce Fredrikson (ed.), *Frontiers of Investment Analysis,* 2d ed., Int. Textbook Co., Scranton, Ohio, 1971, pp. 338–353.

[11]Ibid., p. 347.

[12]Ibid., p. 348.

Therefore, it appears that the investor in stocks on the NYSE would have received higher returns for accepting a higher risk, at least for stocks through the medium-risk class. In the high-risk categories the returns either did not increase as much as one might expect or did not increase at all. It is concluded:

> During the historical period covered by this study, the portfolio manager could have increased the expected value of his returns by accepting additional volatility of returns up to some point, . . . but . . . the expected value of his returns would not have been increased by accepting additional risk beyond that point without better than average selection and/or timing expertise.[13]

RETURNS OFF THE NEW YORK STOCK EXCHANGE

All the studies alluded to thus far have been concerned with rates of return or risk variables, or both, for stocks listed on the NYSE. It is true that NYSE-listed companies are probably the best-known firms in the economy, and the great majority of investors consider the NYSE when the term "stock market" is used. At the same time, the other segments of the stock market—the American Stock Exchange (ASE), the regional exchanges, and the over-the-counter market (OTC)—approach, and in some cases exceed, the NYSE in terms of trading volume, the value of trading activity, and the number of issues. In addition, there is evidence that these other segments of the stock market differ from the NYSE in short-run and long-run stock price movements.

Differential Volume between Registered Exchanges

Differences in trading volume can be measured either in the number of issues traded or in the value of the stock traded. Table 2-1 contains volume figures for the NYSE, the ASE, and all registered regional exchanges. It does not contain figures for the OTC market, since actual OTC volume figures were not available until the latter part of 1971. The OTC figures are discussed below.

The figures in Table 2-1 show that the NYSE is the dominant registered exchange in terms of the value of trading. At the same time, the share volume figures for the ASE are not insignificant and show that greater recognition should be given to this segment of the market, especially if short-run price movements and long-run price changes differ from those on the NYSE. While the regional exchanges have typically played a minor role among the exchanges, as a group they have enjoyed substantial growth and in 1971 surpassed the ASE in terms of the value of trading.[14] In any case, the regionals are large enough to command recognition. Because there is a substantial overlap between the stocks on the NYSE and those on the regional exchanges, it is unlikely that there would be significant price change differences in comparison with the possible differences in price change for the ASE or the OTC, where there is very little trading overlap with the NYSE except in the third market.

Differential Volume on the OTC

OTC trading volume was unknown before 1969 because of the basic fragmentation of the market and the absence of a central data collection agency. In 1969 the OTC Information Bureau, in cooperation with the OTC Clearing Corporation,

---

[13] Ibid., p. 352.

[14] For a discussion of the regional exchanges, their impact, and their problems, see Chris Welles, "The War between the Big Board and the Regionals," *Institutional Investor*, vol. 4, no. 12, December 1970; David A. Hoddeson, "Rise and Fall? Prospering Regional Exchanges May Face Tough New Rules," *Barron's*, Feb. 6, 1971.

began publishing the Share Volume Index of OTC trading.[15] While the index did not provide the actual number or value of the shares traded, it could be used to compare short-run changes, long-run growth, and variability in trading volume. Subsequently, with the introduction of the National Association of Securities Dealers automated quotation system (NASDAQ), it became possible to collect and report actual share trading volume for stocks traded on the NASDAQ system.[16] The NASD began releasing such figures on November 1, 1971. Although the NASDAQ figures are not strictly comparable with exchange volume because of different trading practices, the figures have indicated very substantial OTC trading volume. Specifically, a news release by the OTC Information Bureau dated October 30, 1972, stated:

> More than two billion shares of Over-the-Counter Securities were traded on the NASDAQ system alone during the first year such figures have been made available to the public. . . .
>
> In the 52 weeks ended October 27, 1972, NASDAQ volume totaled 2,151,007,600 shares, based upon the Bureau's compilation of aggregate weekly volume reported by NASDAQ market makers. . . .
>
> There are currently 3,450 securities in the NASDAQ system, and many times that number which are traded Over-the-Counter but which are not carried on NASDAQ. Estimates of total OTC trading indicate that it is the largest securities market in the world, accounting for approximately 75 percent of all security sales in the United States.

This 2 billion-share total may be compared with 4.2 billion shares traded on the NYSE and 1 billion shares traded on the ASE during 1971. Therefore, this portion of the OTC market has about half the trading activity of the NYSE (with many more issues, as is shown below) and twice as much trading activity as the ASE. It is contended that under such conditions the OTC market is a major stock market segment in terms of trading volume and should be considered an alternative source of investment.

Difference in Issues Traded on Alternative Segments of the Market

The number of different stock issues traded on the various segments of the market is important because it indicates the number of *alternatives available* to the investor. Table 2-2 contains the number of security issues listed at year-end on the NYSE and the ASE for the period 1962–1971. Again, comparable figures for the OTC market are not available, but some information regarding this segment will be introduced.

The figures in Table 2-2 show a consistently greater number of issues on the NYSE than on the ASE. However, the differential is probably not so great as one might expect, given the emphasis placed on the NYSE.

If the number of issues on the OTC and the number on either of the major exchanges are compared, the rankings are reversed. The fact is that *many more issues are traded on the OTC market than on either of the major exchanges alone or on the two exchanges combined.* Specifically, the NASDAQ system includes 3,400 stocks, compared with a combined total of about 3,350 issues on the NYSE and ASE. The stocks on NASDAQ are required to meet standards in terms of size, shares

---

[15]For a description of the index and a detailed analysis of the OTC compared with the NYSE and the ASE, see Frank K. Reilly, "A First Look at O-T-C Volume," *Financial Analysts Journal*, vol. 25, no. 1, pp. 124–128, January–February 1969.

[16]For a description of the NASDAQ system, see "NASDAQ and the OTC," a booklet prepared by the OTC Information Bureau in cooperation with the National Security Traders Association and the National Association of Security Dealers, 1735 K Street N.W., Washington, D.C. 20006.

outstanding, and the number of market makers. Beyond the stocks included on the NASDAQ system, the National Quotation Bureau (NQB) publishes a daily quotation service (the "pink sheets") that during a given year typically contains quotations on more than 8,000 stocks. Finally, it is estimated that more than 20,000 issues are traded on a local or regional basis.

In summary, while the NYSE is the major segment of the stock market in terms of the value of stock traded and the number of shares traded (compared with the ASE and NASDAQ), the other segments of the stock market are certainly significant. In addition, the OTC market vastly exceeds the NYSE in terms of the number of stock issues available.

Short-Run Price Changes

Obviously these differences in value of trading, number of shares traded, and issues available would matter little if there were no differences in the price movements of stock on the three segments of the market. If short-run and long-run price movements were the same on all three segments, the source of stocks would not make any difference: the three different areas would not really be different segments.

A study by the author was directed to the question of differences in short-run price changes.[17] Specifically, it analyzed daily percentage price changes on the three segments by using the following price indicator series:
1. New York Stock Exchange
    a. Dow Jones Industrial Average (DJIA)
    b. Standard and Poor's 425 Industrial Stock Index (SP425)
    c. New York Stock Exchange Composite Index (NYSECO)
2. American Stock Exchange Price Change Index (ASE)
3. National Quotation Bureau Over-the-Counter Industrial Average (NQBIA)

The Dow Jones Industrial Average (DJIA), the oldest and most widely quoted of all stock price indicator series, is an average of thirty industrial stocks listed on the New York Stock Exchange.[18] The Standard and Poor's 425 Industrial Stock Index (SP425) is an index of 425 industrial stocks listed on the New York Stock Exchange.[19] The New York Stock Exchange Index (NYSECO) is the composite index of all common stocks listed on the exchange.[20] Because figures for the NYSE industrial index date back only to December 31, 1965, the composite index was examined instead of the NYSE industrial index. The American Stock Exchange series is a price level index of all stocks and warrants listed on the American Stock

---

[17]Frank K. Reilly, "Evidence Regarding a Segmented Stock Market," *Journal of Finance,* vol. 27, no. 3, pp. 607–625, June 1972.

[18]For a detailed discussion of how the Dow Jones averages are computed, see Henry A. Latane and Donald L. Tuttle, *Security Analysis and Portfolio Management,* The Ronald Press Company, New York, 1970, pp. 154–166; Fred B. Renwick, *Introduction to Investments and Finance,* The Macmillan Company, New York, 1971, pp. 59–64; Jack C. Francis, *Investments: Analysis and Management,* McGraw-Hill Book Company, New York, 1972, pp. 138–143. For a list of the current companies in the Dow Jones averages as well as a complete list of all company changes, stock splits, and changes in the divisor since Oct. 1, 1928, see M. L. Farrell (ed.), *The Dow Jones Investor's Handbook,* Dow Jones Books, Princeton, N.J., 1975, pp. 8–12.

[19]For a detailed presentation of how the S&P series are computed and their advantages and problems, see Latane and Tuttle, op. cit., pp. 172–174; Renwick, op. cit., pp. 65–67.

[20]See Stan West and Norman Miller, "Why the NYSE Common Stock Index?" *Financial Analysts Journal,* vol. 23, no. 3, pp. 49–52, May–June 1967.

Exchange.[21] Publication of the ASE Index began in January 1966, with figures presented back to October 1, 1962. The final price indicator series examined was the NQB average of thirty-five OTC industrial stocks (NQBIA).[22] A more comprehensive OTC stock price series was created by the National Association of Securities Dealers (NASD). Unfortunately, the various NASDAQ series have been available only since February 1971 and so cannot be used to examine historical relationships.[23]

Note that there is a substantial overlap in the samples used in the various NYSE price indicator series. Specifically, all 30 of the stocks in the DJIA are included in the SP425 Industrial Index, and all 425 of the stocks in the SP425 are in the NYSE Composite Index. In contrast, there is no overlap between stocks in the ASE Index and any of the other indicators, and no overlap of stocks in the NQBIA and other price indicator series. There are, of course, numerous instances in which stock shift from the OTC to one of the listed exchanges or between the exchanges over time.

Results of Short-Run Price Change Analysis

When possible, the daily changes were compared for the period 1960–1968. The major findings were:

1. There was a very strong relationship among the three NYSE price indicator series even though the series differ significantly in terms of the number of stocks in each of them and the method of computation.

2. When the ASE series was related to the three NYSE series, the relationship was significantly weaker than the inter-NYSE relationship, or about one-half to two-thirds as strong.

3. The relationship between the OTC series and the various series for the NYSE and the ASE was almost zero when coincident daily changes were considered, mainly because the NQBIA is computed at a different time of day (noon for the OTC versus 3:30 P.M. for the exchange series). When the OTC series were compared with the exchange series for the prior day to compensate for the time differential, the relationships improved substantially and were nearly in line with the ASE-NYSE results. At the same time, they were still significantly lower than the inter-NYSE relations.

4. An analysis of price changes during past periods of rising prices and declining prices indicated significant differences in the relationships between market segments during these subperiods, with the stronger relationships occurring during declining markets.

5. A comparison of the relationships over time (year by year) did not indicate any consistent or significant trends in the coefficients (that is, the relationships are

[21]See B. Alva Schoomer, Jr., "American Stock Exchange Index System," *Financial Analysts Journal,* vol. 23, no. 3, pp. 57–61, May–June 1967. Recently there have been severe criticisms of the construction of the index. These criticisms are discussed below when the long-run results are examined.

[22]For a brief description of the average, see W. J. Eiteman, C. A. Dice, and D. K. Eiteman, *The Stock Market,* 4th ed., McGraw-Hill Book Company, New York, 1966, p. 195. For current discussion and comment, get in touch with the National Quotation Bureau, 116 Nassau Street, New York, N.Y. 10038, or the OTC Information Bureau, 120 Broadway, New York, N.Y. 10005. For a current list of the stocks in the NQBIA, see *The OTC Market Chronicle,* weekly, William B. Dana Company, 25 Park Place, New York, N.Y. 10007.

[23]For a detailed discussion of the NASDAQ series and an analysis of the short-run and longer-run relationships, see Frank K. Reilly, *An Early Report Card on the NASDAQ Over-the-Counter Stock Price Indicators,* Research Paper No. 1, University of Wyoming, Laramie, Wyo., 1972.

not getting better) but did indicate *substantial fluctuations* in the relationships between the OTC series and the exchange series.

In summary, the evidence showed significant differences between the three segments of the stock market in terms of short-run price changes.

DIFFERENTIAL LONG-RUN RETURNS BETWEEN SEGMENTS OF THE STOCK MARKET

This section is concerned with an analysis of long-run price changes that can be used to indicate alternative rates of return. Although long-run price changes cannot be strictly interpreted as rates of return since they do not consider dividends (that is, they understate the true rates of return), they can be used to compare alternative rates of return because dividend rates are typically stable over time. If the dividend rates are equal, the differential price changes would indicate the difference in the absolute rates of return. In any case, consistent differences in price changes should indicate differential rates of return available in the alternative segments of the stock market.

The price changes for the three major segments were inferred from the changes experienced by the same price indicator series used in the short-run price change analysis.

Presentation of Results

As noted above, the comparison is limited to annual percentage price changes because most of a stock's rate of return is attributable to price changes. Because the dividend payment is quite stable, the price change is the most volatile component of the rate of return. This analysis concentrates on the most important aspects of returns.

Table 2-3 contains the annual percentage change in the various price indicator series for the individual years 1960 (when available) through 1973. It also contains an average of the annual percentage changes, the standard deviation of the annual percentage changes, the percentage change for the full period, and, finally, the average annual compound rate of change implied by the total change. The computations are made for eleven- and fourteen-year periods because the ASE Index has been available only since October 1962.

Table 2-4 contains the total price changes for each series during alternative market periods: price changes during periods of generally declining stock prices or periods of rising stock prices. The author has dated the stock market peaks and troughs, and these dates have been used in other studies.[24] These periods are similar to those used by other authors.[25]

Differences in Price Changes

The figures in Tables 2-3 and 2-4 show five significant differences among the indicator series:

1. The S&P 425 Industrial Stock Index and the NYSE Composite Index show very similar results year by year, during alternative market periods, and overall. In contrast, price changes for the DJIA differed substantially from those of the other two series during several individual years and were considerably

---

[24]Reilly, "Evidence Regarding a Segmented Stock Market," loc. cit.; Frank K. Reilly and Lawrence A. Sherr, "The Shift Method: A Technique for Measuring the Differential Performance of Stocks," *Mississippi Valley Journal of Business and Economics,* vol. 9, no. 1, pp. 28–40, Fall, 1973.

[25]D. H. Bellemore and J. C. Ritchie, Jr., *Investments,* South-Western Publishing Company, Incorporated, Cincinnati, 1969, pp. 95–97; James C. Van Horne, "New Listings and Their Price Behavior," *Journal of Finance,* vol. 25, no. 4, p. 792, September 1970.

different for the long periods. While the annual changes do not show any consistency in the direction of variation, the long-term results indicate uniformly *lower* average price increases for the DJIA compared with the other NYSE series.

2. There was a significant disparity between the price changes experienced by the various NYSE price indicator series and those experienced by the ASE series. Prior to 1971 the ASE series was more volatile.

TABLE 2-3   Percentage Changes in Stock Price Indicator Series, 1960–1973

Year	DJIA	S&P425	NYSE Composite	Original ASE	New ASE	NQBIA	NASDAQ Industrial
1960	−9.34	−4.67	−3.89	. . . *	. . . †	−1.47	. . . ‡
1961	18.71	23.14	24.08	. . . *	. . . †	31.85	. . . ‡
1962	−10.91	−13.00	−11.95	. . . *	. . . †	−14.37	. . . ‡
1963	17.12	19.37	18.07	21.06	. . . †	16.97	. . . ‡
1964	14.57	13.96	14.35	19.35	. . . †	25.63	. . . ‡
1965	10.88	9.88	9.53	38.32	. . . †	30.10	. . . ‡
1966	−18.94	−13.60	−12.56	−4.47	. . . †	−1.50	. . . ‡
1967	15.20	23.53	23.10	79.12	. . . †	53.97	. . . ‡
1968	5.24	8.47	10.39	34.58	. . . †	22.17	. . . ‡
1969	−15.19	−10.20	−12.51	−19.71	−28.98	0.76	. . . ‡
1970	4.82	−0.58	−2.52	−13.40	−18.00	−13.73	. . . ‡
1971	6.11	11.71	12.34	12.48	18.86	35.39	. . . ‡
1972	14.58	16.10	14.27	3.01	10.33	30.25	13.63
1973	−16.58	−17.38	−19.63	−17.68	−30.00	−25.49	−36.88
AVERAGE OF ANNUAL CHANGES							
1960–1973	2.59	4.77	4.51	. . . *	. . . †	13.61	. . . ‡
1963–1973	3.44	5.57	4.98	13.87	. . . †	15.87	. . . ‡
STANDARD DEVIATION OF ANNUAL CHANGES							
1960–1973	13.32	13.86	14.10	. . . *	. . . †	22.19	. . . ‡
1963–1973	13.11	13.28	13.66	28.11	. . . †	22.35	. . . ‡
TOTAL PERCENTAGE CHANGE							
1960–1973	25.30	68.94	61.18	. . . *	. . . †	335.88	. . . ‡
1963–1973	30.48	65.08	53.27	202.23	. . . †	296.95	. . . ‡
AVERAGE ANNUAL COMPOUND RATE OF CHANGE							
1960–1973	1.61	3.80	3.45	. . . *	. . . †	11.04	. . . ‡
1963–1973	2.44	4.65	3.98	10.54	. . . †	13.32	. . . ‡

*Not available; price level index started in January 1966 with data back to October 1962.
†Not available; market value index started on Aug. 31, 1973, with data back to Jan. 1, 1969.
‡Not available; index started on Feb. 5, 1971, with no prior data available.

3. There was also a definite disparity between price changes for the OTC series and price changes on the NYSE. Increases in the NQBIA were typically greater than NYSE increases, and, somewhat surprisingly, the NQBIA generally *declined less* than the NYSE indicator series.

4. There were some differences between the ASE Index and the NQBIA. It appears that the ASE series was more volatile before 1970 and less volatile during 1971–1973. This apparent change in volatility can be explained in terms of the construction of the ASE series, discussed below.

5. There were obvious differences in the standard deviation of annual percentage changes. These differences followed the same general pattern as the differences in price changes.

TABLE 2-4 Price Changes on the NYSE, ASE, and OTC during Periods of Rising and Falling Stock Prices, October 1, 1962–December 31, 1973

Dates	Number of months		Percentage change in stock price indicator						
	Rising	Declining	DJIA	S&P425	NYSE Composite	Original ASE	New ASE	NQB1A	NASDAQ Industrial
Oct. 1, 1962*–Feb. 9, 1966 (P)	40.0		73.2	73.3	N/A	132.7	(1)	126.9	...†
Feb. 9, 1966–Oct. 7, 1966 (T)		8.0	−24.9	−22.4	−22.7	−23.3	(1)	−17.8	...†
Oct. 7, 1966–Dec. 3, 1968 (P)	26.0		32.4	51.2	55.2	169.8	(1)	115.5	...†
Dec. 3, 1968–May 26, 1970 (T)		18.0	−35.9	−35.8	−38.3	−40.6	(1)	−36.4	...†
May 26, 1970–Apr. 28, 1971 (P)	11.0		50.2	53.1	52.9	37.3	68.6	72.2	...†
Apr. 28, 1971–Nov. 23, 1971 (T)		7.0	−15.8	−14.1	−13.9	−12.1	−17.9	−7.2	...†
Nov. 23, 1971–Jan. 11, 1973 (P)	14.0		31.8	35.4	32.0	14.2	30.6	50.7	39.6
Jan. 11, 1973–Dec. 31, 1973*		12.0	−19.1	−19.0	−20.9	−18.7	−26.0	−27.8	−39.0

*The beginning and ending dates are neither troughs (T) nor peaks (P) but were selected on the basis of availability of data.
†Not available; figures available beginning on Jan. 1, 1969.

Discussion of Diverse Results

In the past, differences among market indicator series were explained in terms of the methods of constructing the alternative series and the biases inherent in each.[26] While there is justification for such explanations, too little consideration has been given to an examination of the *sample of stocks* included in the various market indicator series. It is felt that the differences in annual changes among the price series can be explained by considering the inherent risks of the market segments represented by the sample of stocks used.

DJIA Compared with Other NYSE Indicators

The differences in percentage changes between the DJIA and the other NYSE indicator series can be explained by the fact that the DJIA stocks are the bluest of the blue chips on the NYSE. Although the DJIA includes a broad cross section of industries, the stocks selected to represent these industry segments are, in almost all cases, the industry leaders in size, stock distribution, and financial prestige. This selection process can be justified on the basis of investor interest, but it means that the companies selected should be of lower risk. Therefore, the common stock will have a lower rate of return than a broader sample of all NYSE securities. Greater representation of NYSE stocks is accomplished by the S&P425 industrials, and complete representation by the NYSE Composite Index.

NYSE Indicators Compared with the ASE Price Change Series

The differences found between the three NYSE series and the ASE series during the period 1963–1970 can best be explained by sample differences. However, the differences during 1971–1973 require consideration of the construction of the ASE series.

The results during the 1963–1970 period, when the ASE series was more volatile, can be explained by the fact that the ASE series includes *all* stocks and warrants listed on the American Stock Exchange. This sample differs substantially from the NYSE sample because of the difference in listing requirements. The requirements established by the NYSE are extensive and ensure that the firms of listed securities are of substantial size and have wide stock distribution. Such requirements practically guarantee that stocks listed on the NYSE, on the average, will carry a lower risk than stocks on other exchanges. While the ASE requirements are certainly substantial, they are nowhere near as demanding as those of the NYSE.

It has been shown that these listing differentials are reflected dramatically in the actual firms listed on the two exchanges: the firms on the NYSE are more than 4

[26]H. L. Butler, Jr. and M. B. Decker, "A Security Check on the Dow-Jones Industrial Average," *Financial Analysts Journal,* vol. 9, no. 1, pp. 37–45, February 1953; R. B. Shaw, "The Dow-Jones Industrials vs. the Dow-Jones Industrial Average," *Financial Analysts Journal,* vol. 11, no. 5, pp. 37–40, November 1955; Lawrence Fisher, "Some New Stock Market Indexes," *Journal of Business,* vol. 39, no. 1, part 2, pp. 191–225, January 1966, Supplement; W. F. Balch, "Market Guides," *Barron's,* Sept. 19, 1966, pp. 9, 17; Paul Cootner, "Stock Market Indexes: Fallacies and Illusions," *Commercial and Financial Chronicle,* Sept. 29, 1966, pp. 18–19; E. E. Carter and K. J. Cohen, "Bias in the DJIA Caused by Stock Splits," *Financial Analysts Journal,* vol. 22, no. 6, pp. 90–94, December 1966; R. D. Milne, "The Dow-Jones Industrial Average Re-examined," *Financial Analysts Journal,* vol. 22, no. 6, pp. 83–88, December 1966; E. E. Carter and K. J. Cohen, "Stock Averages, Stock Splits, and Bias," *Financial Analysts Journal,* vol. 23, no. 3, pp. 77–81, May–June 1967; Lewis L. Schellbach, "When Did the DJIA Top 1200?" *Financial Analysts Journal,* vol. 23, no. 3, pp. 71–73, May–June 1967.

times as large as firms on the ASE in terms of sales, assets, and net income.[27] Therefore, one would expect ASE firms to carry greater risk than NYSE firms. As a result, stock price changes over market cycles would be more volatile for ASE stocks, which they were through 1970.

During the period 1971–1973 the ASE series went from being the *most* volatile series to being the *least* volatile series. It has been shown twice by S. C. Leuthold and coauthors that because of its construction the ASE Index has become seriously distorted by stock splits over time.[28] It appears that the current average price of stocks on the exchange has declined substantially over time because of stock splits and changes in the stocks listed on the exchange. Such a deviation of an index figure from the average price of stocks on an exchange is not unusual and has happened on the NYSE as well. The problem arises because daily changes in the ASE Index are an average of daily *absolute* price changes for all stocks on the exchange. The long-run distortion occurs because absolute price changes are naturally related to the average price of stocks on the exchange: higher-priced stocks experience larger absolute price changes, and lower-priced stocks smaller absolute price changes. As a result, when average prices decline for normal reasons and absolute price changes are computed, if these smaller absolute price changes are not adjusted for the change in the average price, the change as a *percentage* of the *original* base, which has not been adjusted, will be much lower than it should be. The consequence has been a less volatile series.[29]

ASE Compared with NQBIA

Contrary to expectations based upon apparent risk differentials, the ASE Index, which represents a listed segment of the market, increased on the average at a slightly greater rate than the NQBIA before 1971. These differences can be explained by a careful consideration of the two samples. The ASE Index included all stocks and warrants listed on the American Stock Exchange. In contrast, the NQBIA is an average of thirty-five nonrandomly selected OTC industrial stocks that are consistently described as the blue chips of the OTC market.[30] As such, the NQBIA is similar to the DJIA.[31] Although the NQBIA sample is representative of the OTC market in terms of the industries considered, it is probably not representative in terms of risk. Specifically, the risk inherent in the NQBIA sample is almost certainly not representative of the thousands of diverse OTC stocks. Therefore, the average risk inherent in all ASE stocks is probably greater than the average risk for the thirty-five OTC industrial blue chips. As before, this risk differential largely explains the price change differences.

The differences during the period 1971–1973 can again be explained by the construction of the ASE Index, which has caused a serious dampening in long-run price changes.

[27]Frank K. Reilly, W. A. Page, and B. L. Myers, *A Consideration of Factors That Influence Stock Market Efficiency: The New York and American Stock Exchanges Compared,* Working Paper No. 40, University of Kansas, Lawrence, Kans., 1972.

[28]The two studies analyzing the biases inherent in the system are S. C. Leuthold and C. E. Gordon II, "Margin for Error," *Barron's,* Mar. 1, 1971; S. C. Leuthold and K. F. Blaich, "Warped Yardstick," *Barron's,* Sept. 18, 1972, pp. 9, 16, 18, 30.

[29]Because of the bias, the ASE has developed a new index similar in construction to the S&P425 and the NYSE Composite Index. For a description and discussion, see "AMEX Introduces New Market Value Index System," *American Investor,* American Stock Exchange, Inc., September 1973.

[30]See *The OTC Market Chronicle,* weekly, William B. Dana Company, 25 Park Place, New York, N.Y. 10007.

[31]The NQBIA is also similar to the DJIA in method of computation.

Price Changes and Specific Risk Measures

The foregoing discussion compared alternative long-run price changes and expected differences in risk on the basis of the samples used in the various price indicator series. In this subsection we specifically measure differences in risk on the basis of differences in the variability of price changes over time. Variability is measured by the standard deviation.[32] Unfortunately, it is impossible to develop the full theoretical argument for its use.[33] The basic idea is that investors view risk as a function of *uncertainty regarding expected returns.*

An example of a risk-free investment is the ninety-day Treasury bill, for which the investor knows at the time of purchase the promised yield. As one moves away from short-run government securities to securities that are unlikely to be held to maturity (for example, long-term government bonds) or do not mature (common stocks), there is less certainty regarding the expected realized rate of return on the investment. Given that returns can vary over time for these risky investments, the greater the *past* variability in rates of return, the harder it is to predict *future* expected rates of return and, therefore, the greater the uncertainty. Empirical evidence that investors require higher rates of returns for stocks with greater variance of return is provided by Professor Pratt in the study previously discussed.[34] Evidence is also contained in a study by Arditti.[35]

In the present case, the figures contained in Table 2-3 indicate an increase in the average price changes and the standard deviation of price changes over time. The only partial exception seems to be the ASE, in which the price changes were below expectations on the basis of variability. Again, this can be explained by the very small price changes during the period 1971–1973, when typically the ASE results should have been more consistent with the NQBIA results.

Summary of Long-Run Price Changes

This comparison of long-run price changes for the three segments has shown that the returns on the ASE and the OTC market are substantially different from those on the NYSE. Specifically, there are somewhat larger price declines on the ASE and OTC market during periods of falling stock prices and *substantially higher price increases* during periods of generally rising prices. Overall, average annual compound price changes for the ASE and OTC segments were more than double the price changes for the various NYSE indicator series. Also, there was probably greater risk inherent in the ASE and OTC stocks because their firms are smaller in terms of assets, sales, and earnings. In addition, these stocks experienced greater price volatility over time.

SUMMARY AND CONCLUSION

This part of Chapter 2 has been concerned with an analysis of the returns and risk available to investors on the three segments of the stock market. The initial section discussed several studies by Fisher and Lorie that thoroughly documented the

[32]For an extensive discussion of the standard deviation as a measure of variation, see Ya-lun Chou, *Statistical Analysis,* Holt, Rinehart and Winston, Inc., New York, 1969, pp. 97–102; or any standard statistics text.

[33]For a very readable discussion of the justification, see Richare A. Brealey, *An Introduction to Risk and Return from Common Stocks,* The M.I.T. Press, Cambridge, Mass., 1969, pp. 133–139.

[34]Pratt, op. cit.

[35]Fred Arditti, "Risk and the Required Return on Equity," *Journal of Finance,* vol. 22, no. 1, pp. 19–36, March 1967.

rates of return available to investors on the NYSE for the periods 1926–1960 and 1926–1965. The results indicated that investors enjoyed between 8 and 10 percent returns over the long period, with taxes and commissions taken into account. Also, while there were periods of low or negative returns, the investor received positive returns in almost all periods of four years or more.

A study by Pratt analyzed returns for different risk classes of stocks on the NYSE and found a positive relationship between rates of returns and risk measures for the lower-risk groups. In contrast, there appeared to be a topping out of this relationship because the returns for the highest-risk classes were the same as, or in some cases lower than, the returns for the stocks in the lower-risk classes.

A subsequent analysis of the other segments of the stock market, the ASE and the OTC market, indicated that the NYSE is probably the dominant segment in terms of shares traded and value of trading but that the other segments are certainly significant and should be considered by an investor if there are differences in price movements. Finally, it was noted that the number of issues on the OTC market was substantially larger than the combined number on the two listed exchanges.

Obviously these differences would be irrelevant if there were no differences in price movements over time. A study of short-run price changes by the author indicated significant differences in short-run price changes between the three segments. There were even more substantial differences in price changes during rising and falling markets. Notably, the relationships between the segments have not improved over time.

An analysis of long-run price changes attempted to determine whether there were significant differences that would imply differences in the long-run rates of return for the three segments. The analysis showed that there were some small differences within the NYSE, with the DJIA below the other NYSE series. Of more importance, there were very substantial differences between the three NYSE series and the ASE Index or between the NYSE and the OTC series. Specifically, the ASE and OTC series increased several times as much as the NYSE during periods of rising stock prices, while the ASE and OTC declined a little more than the NYSE during falling markets. As a consequence, over the eleven- or fourteen-year periods the ASE and the OTC market experienced average annual price changes 2 or 3 times larger than comparable price changes experienced by stocks on the NYSE. These differences were at least partially attributable to the higher risk of stocks on the latter segments in terms of size, investor interest, and variability of returns over time.

Chapter **3**

Measurement of Volatility, Risk, and Performance

ROBERT A. LEVY

With the increasing emphasis on the performance of institutional portfolios, it is important to have an accurate measure of investment results—a measure applicable to both individuals and institutional investors. Accordingly, this chapter is devoted to the clarification and possible resolution of the following issues:

1. How may operating results be segregated from contributions and withdrawals of capital?

2. How may the "dollar weighting" inherent in compound rates of return be eliminated?

3. How should risk be quantified?

4. Can both risk and return be considered in one composite measure of investment performance?

5. How may regression analysis be used to determine volatility and performance?

Segregation of Operating Results

If a fund experiences no contributions or withdrawals of capital after the initial investment, the measurement of the rate of return over a specified period of time is relatively simple. For example, given a beginning investment cost (C) of $100 and an ending portfolio value (V) of $106.70, the percentage return can be computed by $V/C - 1$, or 6.7 percent. By converting this percentage into an annual rate of return, the formula becomes $r = V/C^{1/y} - 1$, where y is the time period expressed in years. Thus, in the foregoing illustration, had the time period been 73 days (one-fifth of a year), the annual rate of return would have been $1.067^5 - 1 = 38.3$ percent; and had the time period been 1,095 days (three years), the annual rate of return would have been $1.067^{1/3} - 1 = 2.2$ percent. In more general terms, $V = C(1 + r)^y$, where r is the annual rate of return compounded annually.

The problem becomes somewhat more complex if contributions and withdrawals of capital occur during the specified time period. Under these conditions the quotient V/C becomes meaningless, since C would be composed of discrete increments and decrements, some or all of which would apply to only a part of the time period. That is, if new money is contributed, it is available for investment only from the date of contribution to the end of the time period; and if capital is withdrawn, performance on that capital is possible only from the beginning of the time period to the date of withdrawal. Consider the following examples:

Month Number	Beginning of Month Contribution or (Withdrawal)	End of Month Portfolio Value
1	$100	$106
8	. . .	110
9	(50)	50
18	. . .	40
19	250	320
24	. . .	330
	$300	

The ratio of value to cost (V/C) at the end of the time period is 1.100. This does not mean that the rate of return for the two-year period was 10 percent (4.9 percent per year compounded annually). To find the annual rate of return, the interest rate that would produce sufficient profits (losses) to equalize the contributions (withdrawals) and the value of the ending portfolio must be determined. The general formula is $V = C_1 (1 + r)^{y1} + C_2 (1 + r)^{y2} \ldots + C_n (1 + r)^{ym}$, where C_i is the ith contribution (if positive) or withdrawal (if negative), and y_i is the remaining time period in years when the ith contribution or withdrawal is made.

Solving this formula is a repetitive, or iterative, process. Successive trials for r must be made, each trial more closely approximating the true return. In the preceding illustration, $300 = 100 (1 + r)^2 - 50 (1 + r)^{4/3} + 250 (1 + r)^{1/2}$. By using detailed compound-interest tables, logarithms, or an electronic computer, the correct value of r can be obtained. A trial of $r = 11$ percent yields $300 = 329.14$; a trial of $r = 12$ percent yields $330 = 331.86$. The approximate annual return is 11.3 percent; this is the rate at which the specified contributions would have had to have been invested to produce the ending portfolio value of $330 in two years, while allowing for a $50 withdrawal at the beginning of month 9.[1]

The compound-return method described above has two important advantages. First, in the case of a pension fund, it produces a rate of return that can be compared with actuarially computed requirements. Second, it necessitates only one valuation of the portfolio: at the end of the period rather than, in addition, at the date of each contribution and withdrawal.

Unfortunately, these advantages are outweighed by one disadvantage of major significance: the compound-return method does not properly weigh the impact of varying dollar amounts in a portfolio; that is, it does not segregate operating results as such. Portfolio managers usually have no control over the timing or amount of contributions to and withdrawals from a fund. The fact that the portfolio illustrated above performed exceedingly well from month 19 through month 24, when the greatest dollar amount was invested, and exceedingly poorly from month 9 through month 18, when the least dollar amount was invested, was happenstance as far as the portfolio manager was concerned. Certainly the portfolio benefited from varying dollar investments in this instance, but the benefits

---

[1]To limit the number of iterations, a useful first approximation may sometimes be obtained by dividing the profits or losses $(V - C)$ by the average investment at cost and converting the resulting percentage to an annual return. Average investment may be computed as $(C_1 Y_1 + C_2 Y_2 \ldots + C_n Y_n)/Y_1$. Applying this estimate to the above problem yields $(330 - 300)/[(100 \times 2 - 50 \times 1.333 + 250 \times .5)/2] = 30/129.167 = 23.2$ percent. A return of 23.2 percent for two years is equal to 11.0 percent per year $(1.232^{1/2})$.

should not be credited to the skill of the manager. In measuring return, some method of eliminating the effect of varying dollar weights should be utilized.

Elimination of Dollar Weights

It might be instructive for comparative purposes to consider another hypothetical portfolio also yielding an annual rate of return of approximately 11.3 percent.

Month Number	Beginning of Month Contribution or (Withdrawal)	End of Month Portfolio Value
1	$100	$110
8	. . .	130
9	(50)	90
18	. . .	120
19	250	360
24	. . .	330
	$300	

This illustration is identical to our previous example in several respects. First, the timing of contributions and withdrawals is the same; second, the dollar amounts of contributions and withdrawals are the same; third, the ending portfolio value is the same; and fourth, the compound annual return of 11.3 percent is the same. The only differences between the two examples are the interim portfolio valuations. Whereas in the initial illustration the portfolio manager fortunately performed most satisfactorily when the greatest number of dollars were invested, in the present illustration the portfolio manager unfortunately was most effective when employing the lowest amount of funds. Since the amount of capital available for investment was beyond the control of the portfolio manager, the effect of the size and timing of contributions and withdrawals (that is, dollar weights) should be eliminated.

One method of eliminating dollar weights would be to determine the rate of return each portfolio manager would realize from the several dates of each contribution or withdrawal. This can be done by "linked relatives" or by "unit accounting." In either case, the portfolio value must be determined immediately prior to each contribution and withdrawal as well as at the end of the period. The linked-relative method, as it applies to our two hypothetical portfolios, is illustrated in the accompanying tables.

	Portfolio No. 1		
	Beginning value*	Ending value	Value relative
Months 1 through 8	$100	$110	1.100
Months 9 through 18	60	40	0.667
Months 19 through 24	290	330	1.138
Cumulative relative			0.835

*Portfolio value at the end of the preceding period plus contributions or minus withdrawals.

	Portfolio No. 2		
	Beginning value	Ending value	Value relative
Months 1 through 8	$100	$130	1,300
Months 9 through 18	80	120	1.500
Months 19 through 24	370	330	0.892
Cumulative relative			1.739

To compute an equivalent annual return, the cumulative relative (R) is raised to the $1/y$ power, and the result is reduced by 1. Accordingly, for Portfolio No. 1, $r = R^{1/y} - 1 = 0.835^5 - 1 = 31.9$ percent.[2]

The important conclusion to be drawn from the tables shown above is that Portfolio Manager No. 2 has significantly outperformed Portfolio Manager No. 1, even though both portfolios yielded an identical compound annual rate of return of 11.3 percent. By using geometrically linked relatives, it was proved that Manager No. 1 would have lost 8.6 percent per year on an unchanged investment of X dollars, while Manager No. 2 would have earned 31.9 percent per year.

The technique of unit accounting, practiced by nearly all mutual funds, provides us with another method of arriving at the same comparative figures. This technique is illustrated in the accompanying tables.

Portfolio No. 1

| | Beginning of month | | | | End of month | |
Month	Contribution (withdrawal)	Value per unit	No. of units	Portfolio value	No. of units	Value per unit
	(1)	(2)	(3=1−2)	(4)	(5)	(6=4−5)
1	$100	$1.000	100.00	$106	100.00	$1.060
8	. . .	. . .	. . .	110	100.00	1.100
9	(50)	1.100	(45.45)	50	54.55	.917
18	. . .	. . .	. . .	50	54.55	.733
19	250	.733	340.91	320	395.46	.809
24	. . .	. . .	. . .	330	395.46	.835

Portfolio No. 2

| | Beginning of month | | | | End of month | |
Month	Contribution (withdrawal)	Value per unit	No. of units	Portfolio value	No. of units	Value per unit
	(1)	(2)	(3=1−2)	(4)	(5)	(6=4−5)
1	$100	$1.000	100.00	$110	100.00	$1.100
8	. . .	. . .	. . .	130	100.00	1.300
9	(50)	1.300	(38.46)	90	61.54	1.462
18	. . .	. . .	. . .	120	61.54	1.950
19	250	1.950	128.21	360	189.75	1.897
24	. . .	. . .	. . .	330	189.75	1.739

In both cases it is assumed that the portfolio is invested initially in 100 units, each with a value of $1. The portfolio value per unit is determined immediately prior to each contribution or withdrawal and again at the end of the period. It is then possible to express contributions and withdrawals in terms of portfolio units and to use these units in the computation of ending value on a per-unit basis. Note that,

[2] Note that the cumulative relative is derived geometrically (by multiplication of the period relatives) rather than arithmetically. It is tempting to conclude that the cumulative percentage change for Portfolio No. 1 should have been −9.5 percent (+ 10.0 percent − 33.3 percent + 13.8 percent). This arithmetic combination of percentages is incorrect for two reasons. First, the relatives applied to periods of different lengths. Second, even if appropriate weighting for period length is included, arithmetic cumulatives assign greater weight to increases than to decreases. For example, a stock declining from $10 to $8 and subsequently returning to $10 would have experienced consecutive percentage changes of −20 percent and +25 percent. Arithmetic combination would have produced +5 percent—clearly an absurdity.

with respect to both portfolios, division of the ending unit value by the initial unit value ($1) yields a result identical to the cumulative relative produced by the linked-relative method: 0.835 and 1.739.

Although it is mutual funds that are best known for the use of unit accounting, the method may be employed by any type of investment portfolio including individuals, partnerships, pension funds, and trusts. The assumed number of initial units is immaterial. The measurement of return is based upon the relationship between beginning and ending value per unit, and for any given portfolio, this relationship is not in any way dependent upon the number of units initially assumed. It is conventional and convenient to start with an initial unit value of $1 and to derive the number of initial units from that starting value.

Quantification of Risk

Risk may be defined in terms of the uncertainty of the rate of return (including both dividends or interest and the proceeds received upon sale). This definition, although verbally precise, is extremely difficult to express quantitatively. For the degree of uncertainty emanates in part from the investor and is not solely dependent upon the security or the portfolio in question. As an example, investors with *superior* information regarding a particular stock would be less uncertain of the outcome of their investment than investors selecting that stock at random would be. And investors with low liquidity needs or preference might be more certain of their return, knowing that forced sale under unfavorable circumstances would not be necessary.

In view of these problems, it is not possible to measure the degree of risk attributable to a given security at a given point in time. It is possible, however, to express quantitatively one objective characteristic of stocks that rational investors, in the aggregate, would probably rely upon in their determination of risk. This characteristic is the variability of past rates of return. Available empirical evidence indicates that common stock investors demand and receive a higher level of return with increased variability, thus suggesting that variability and risk are often related, though not synonymous.

The method of determining variability most widely used to date has been to divide the period over which performance is to be measured into subperiods and to compute the standard deviation of the subperiod value relatives (or rates of return). There are, however, several weaknesses of the standard deviation as a measure of risk.

First, the standard deviation measures absolute rather than relative dispersion. Greater variability may be expected to accompany higher mean returns. Without adjusting for this relationship, the standard deviations of subperiod returns for any two portfolios would be noncomparable. A simple corrective action would be to substitute the coefficient of variation for the standard deviation. The coefficient of variation is a measure of relative dispersion derived by dividing the standard deviation of a set of numbers by the arithmetic mean of the set.

Second, the standard deviation is computed by taking the square root of the average of the squared deviations from the arithmetic mean. However, as discussed above, it is the geometric mean of value relatives, not the arithmetic mean, that is the proper measure of central tendency. In this regard, repetition of our earlier example might be appropriate. A stock changing in price from $10 to $8 to $10 would have subperiod relatives of .8 and 1.25. Arithmetic averaging would produce 1.025 [(.8 + 1.25) − 2], whereas geometric averaging would produce 1.000 [(.8 × 1.25)$^{1/2}$]. Since the geometric mean is clearly the correct measure of central tendency, it should be the reference point for the computation of dispersion. And since the geometric mean is simply the antilog of the average logarithm of a set of numbers, the appropriate measure of dispersion is the standard deviation of the logarithms of the value relatives. Thus, our attention is diverted from the absolute deviations about the arithmetic mean to the relative deviations about the geometric mean (that is, the ratio of each number in the set to the geometric mean of the set).

The third and most significant weakness of the standard deviation is that it considers *all* variability, upside as well as downside, as adverse variability. A portfolio advancing in value, at a nonconstant rate (for example, +5 percent, +15 percent, +7 percent), would be given a positive risk; whereas a portfolio declining in value but at a constant rate (for example, −2 percent, −2 percent, −2 percent) would be labeled riskless. Yet if risk is to be associated with the probability of an unfavorable occurrence, the latter portfolio is clearly more risky than the former.

Therefore, the task at hand is to devise a measure of portfolio "vulnerability," a measure that treats only *unfavorable* returns as risky. For this purpose, the term "unfavorable return" is probably best defined as "loss." To be sure, it is true that a person partially financing his investment with borrowed capital would consider any return less than his explicit cost of capital as unfavorable, and that a person who had a number of alternative investments from which to choose would consider any return less than the return on the best of the alternatives as unfavorable.

Nevertheless, these definitional problems, while quite real, are impossible to resolve; each investor might well have a different interpretation of the concept of unfavorability. As a result, the only reasonable course of action is to accept the definition that unfavorable return equals loss, fully recognizing that many investors would not limit unfavorable events to losses alone, but that all losses are unfavorable (that is, the investor could always have refrained from investing).

A feasible measure of loss potential, or "downside vulnerability," is a modification of the quadratic mean. The square root of the average of the squares of the subperiod rates of return is computed, but all positive returns are considered as zero. For example, the modified quadratic mean of −10 percent, +8 percent, −5 percent, +12 percent, and +14 percent would be the square root of {[(−10 percent × −10 percent) + (0 percent × 0 percent) + (−5 percent × −5 percent) + (0 percent × 0 percent) + (0 percent × 0 percent)] − 5}, which equals 5 percent. By considering all positive returns as zero, a measure restricted to downside risk can be obtained. By squaring the negative returns, greater weight can be given to the larger subperiod losses.

In keeping with our previous discussion regarding the use of logarithms, it would be preferable to replace the modified quadratic mean of the returns with the modified quadratic mean of the logarithms of the subperiod value relatives, treating all logarithms greater than zero as zero. Converting the above subperiod returns to relatives, our numbers become .90, 1.08, .95, 1.12, and 1.14. The natural logarithms of the relatives are −.105361, .076961, −.051293, .113329, and .131028; and the modified quadratic mean of these logarithms is the square root of {[(−.105361 × −.105361) + (0 × 0) + (−.051293 × −.051293) + (0 × 0) + (0 × 0)] − 5}, which equals .052406.

Composite Measurement of Risk and Return

The separate determination of rate of return and risk is usually not sufficient to compare the performance of portfolio managers. Only when one portfolio clearly dominates another (that is, produces greater return at less risk, greater return at equal risk, or equal return at less risk) can separate measures of risk and return provide conclusive comparisons. Moreover, even under conditions of domination, it would not be possible to gauge the precise extent of the superiority of the dominating portfolio unless either risk or return happened to be identical for the two funds. Thus, it is necessary to devise a composite measure of both risk and return.

Professor William Sharpe has devised such a measure, which he calls the reward-to-variability ratio. The numerator of the reward-to-variability ratio is the difference between the arithmetic mean of the subperiod returns for a given fund and the arithmetic mean of the subperiod yields on United States Treasury bills. The Treasury bill yield is a reasonable approximation of the pure interest rate (that is, the return available to investors on a virtually risk-free basis). Therefore, the numerator represents the reward provided to the investor for bearing risk. The denominator of the reward-to-variability ratio is the standard deviation of the fund's subperiod returns. It is meant to reflect the degree of risk actually borne. The ratio is thus the reward (return) per unit of variability (risk).

Let us assume that a fund earned the following annual returns over a ten-year period: +70 percent, −30 percent, +85 percent, +50 percent, −20 percent, +65 percent, −25 percent, −20 percent, +90 percent, and +60 percent. The arithmetic mean return of an all-equity investment in this fund would have been +32.5 percent per annum, and the standard deviation of the annual returns would have been 47.2 percent. Had the investor placed all his capital in risk-free Treasury bill obligations, his annual return would have been, say, 4.5 percent, and the standard deviation of the annual returns would have been zero. Between these two alternatives are an infinite number of partly risk-bearing, partly fixed-income combinations.

As an example, if at the beginning of each year the investor had placed 70 percent of his money in risk-free securities and 30 percent in our hypothetical fund, he would have earned an average annual return of 12.9 percent for the ten years; and the standard deviation of his returns would have been 14.2 percent. The reward-to-variability ratio simply tells us how much the rate of return improves as we raise the standard deviation by 1, increasing the risk-bearing component and correspondingly reducing the risk-free component.

In the above illustration, the reward-to-variability ratio would have been .59 [that is, (32.5 − 4.5)/47.2]. However, our previous discussion indicated a preference for the geometric mean rather than the arithmetic mean and for the standard deviation of the logarithms of the value relatives rather than the standard deviation of the subperiod returns. Therefore, a preferable form of the reward-to-variability ratio is: logarithm of the geometric mean of subperiod risk-bearing relatives *minus* logarithm of the subperiod risk-free relative ÷ standard deviation of the logarithms of the subperiod risk-bearing relatives. In terms of our ten-year example, the revised reward-to-variability would have been .41.

One further revision of the return-risk relationship might be desirable. This last revision would be to replace the standard deviation of the logarithms of the subperiod relatives (as a measure of risk) by the modified quadratic mean of the logarithms of the relatives. Thus, the reward-to-variability ratio would be more aptly titled the "reward-to-vulnerability" ratio. Its numerical value in the above example would be .93, and its purpose would be to measure the return per unit of *downside* exposure.

The Use of Correlation and Regression Analysis

The Securities and Exchange Commission (SEC), in its transmittal letter to Congress accompanying the 1971 *Institutional Investor Study Report*, included these comments:

> In the past, most persons or firms have tended to equate "performance" with "price action" without adjusting in any way for the risk borne by the portfolio. The Study utilized econometric techniques to measure portfolio volatility, which often is interpreted as a proxy for the degree of investment risk displayed by managed portfolios,

and to adjust total return on such portfolios (price appreciation plus distributions) so that the portions of the return attributable to general market movements and to the portfolio's particular volatility can be separately identified. . . .

Although the techniques employed are of relatively recent origin, it appears that measures of risk adjusted investment "performance" such as employed in the Study are feasible.

The econometric technique alluded to by the SEC was correlation and regression analysis—more specifically, a study of the association between the price behavior of an individual fund and the behavior of the overall market. "Correlation" is concerned with measuring the presence or absence of a statistical relationship between two or more variables. "Regression" is concerned with determining the sensitivity of one variable (the dependent variable) to changes in other variables (the independent variables). When there is only one independent variable, we are involved with *simple* correlation and regression; when there is more than one independent variable, we refer to *multiple* correlation and regression.

In the case at hand, we are trying to determine the relationship between a fund's price variation (the dependent variable) and the market's price variation (the independent variable). Since there is only one independent variable, simple correlation and regression techniques are employed. And since we think that the relationship between the variables, when graphed as described below, could be portrayed by a straight line, the techniques that we use can be further characterized as simple *linear* correlation and regression. (If the relationship were more complicated, *curvilinear* techniques would be required.)

The Choice of Variables.   Choosing variables is a multipart problem. First, what series is adequately representative of "the market"? We suggest the Standard & Poor's 500-Stock Index, especially for institutions, because it is broad-based, readily and rapidly available, and widely accepted. (Its major fault is that it is dominated by a few giant companies, and so its volatility is far less than the unweighted average volatility of all New York Stock Exchange and American Stock Exchange stocks.)

Second, what period of time should be covered by the study? The longer the period, the less likely that random nonrecurring events ("noise") will have an overbearing effect on the statistical results. On the other hand, too long a period will fail to give sufficient weight to recent changes in the company, the industry, the market, the economy, the political environment, and so on. Accordingly, we recommend one to three years as the period over which the correlation and regression statistics are to be measured.

Third, how frequently must performance observations be recorded? A useful rule of thumb is that statistical reliability diminishes rapidly as the number of observations recedes below thirty. Thus, for a one-year span of coverage, weekly frequency would produce a sufficient number of observations. Three-year coverage would permit less frequent (that is, monthly) observations.

Fourth, what should be done about cash dividends in measuring performance? Clearly, price declines on ex-dividend dates do not reflect investor losses unless the amount of the decline exceeds the amount of the dividend. Therefore, it seems most appropriate to count all dividends in measuring performance. For computational purposes, we would adjust (multiply) all prices prior to the ex-date by a factor equal to 1 minus the dividend percentage. To illustrate, if a fund closed on Tuesday at \$50 and went ex-dividend \$2 on Wednesday, we should multiply all closing prices through Tuesday by .96 (that is, $1 - 2/50$). In the case of the S&P 500, the problem is much more complex because of the considerable task of tracking roughly 500 ex-dividend dates and amounts per quarter and making the necessary adjustment calculations. As a compromise, we could utilize the twelve-month cash dividends on the S&P 500, as reported by Standard & Poor, and assume that this amount is ex-dividend uniformly throughout the year. The assumption is of course incorrect, since there is certainly some seasonality in ex-dividend dates. However, in view of the magnitude of the problem, we believe that the approach is a reasonable one.

Fifth, what specific form should the observations take? Both the prices for individual funds and the values of the S&P 500-Stock Index are time series (that is, they are subject to trend and cyclical factors related to the passage of time). Fund prices and market index values both have a high degree of autocorrelation, meaning that today's close is very much dependent upon yesterday's close. Thus, these two variables may be closely associated only because of their common relationship to a third variable (for example, time).

Correlation studies using time series as the variables are subject to special statistical problems because of the nonrandomness of the observations. A widely used technique to overcome these problems is to compute and correlate first differences of the series rather than the series themselves. For example, instead of correlating fund prices and market index values, we would be better advised to correlate fund price *changes* with market index *changes*. The use of first differences minimizes the autocorrelation problem (for example, while it is true that a fund priced at $100 on Monday would be relatively certain to be priced near $100 on Tuesday, it is not true that a fund up $3 on Monday will probably be up about $3 on Tuesday as well).

Two steps remain before recording our final observations. First, we must convert absolute price changes into percentage price changes. Higher-priced funds tend of course to have larger absolute price changes. However, the investor's dollar can buy more shares of lower-priced funds, and so it is percentage change that is the appropriate datum. Finally, we should express both the fund returns and the market returns in "risk premium" form. We do this by subtracting from each the return on risk-free Treasury bills, thus reducing the observations to numbers reflective of the rewards attained for bearing risk.

Scatter Charts and Least Squares.   In examining the relationship between two variables, it is often instructive to prepare a scatter chart. The Y values (risk premiums for a particular fund) would be scaled along the vertical axis, and the X values (risk premiums for the S&P 500) would be scaled along the horizontal axis. The result, after plotting paired observations, would be a scatter of dots probably clustering around the origin (that is, the intersection of the X and Y axes).

It is then our task to draw the straight line that seems best to fit the scatter of the observations. This line, known as the "regression line," may be drawn visually, or it may be determined mathematically by the method of least squares. The latter technique is, of course, more objective and more adaptable to large-scale computer processing.

The equation for a straight line is $Y = a + bX$, where a is the intercept (the value of Y when X is zero) and b is the slope or regression coefficient (the change in the Y value along the regression line for each unit change in X). By using the method of least squares, the coefficients a and b are found by solving these equations:

$$b = (\Sigma XY - \overline{Y}\Sigma X)/(\Sigma X^2 - \overline{X}\Sigma X)$$

$$a = \overline{Y} - b\overline{X}$$

The quantity ΣX is the sum of the X observations; $\overline{X}$ is the average of the X observations (equal to X/N, where N is the number of observations); ΣXY is the sum of products X and Y; and ΣX^2 is the sum of squares of X.

By employing the method of least squares, we are assured that the regression line will have the following two characteristics: (1) the sum of the scatter deviations above and below the line will be zero; and (2) the sum of the squares of these deviations will be less than those for any other possible straight line.

Beta Coefficients.   The slope (b value in the regression equation) is the volatility, or beta, coefficient. It represents nondiversifiable risk, and it can be interpreted as the percentage performance of a fund that has historically accompanied a 1 percent move in the market reference average—in our case, the S&P 500. Funds that are about as volatile as the market will have a coefficient of around 1.00; those that are less volatile will show lower betas, and so on.

Why use the beta coefficient as a measure of risk? Because the beta coefficient allows us to distinguish between two components of total risk, the part due to the market's variability and the part due uniquely to the stocks within an individual fund portfolio.

For investors who can hold only the shares of one mutual fund, the *total* risk is obviously most important. But for those who can diversify by investing in other securities or other funds, the part of the total due to the market is the key element to stress.

Consider, for example, the case of two funds, both of which have a very high degree of total risk. If Fund A always shows a high return when the market posts a low one and a low return when the market is moving up, shareholders could minimize their risks simply by buying Fund A long with a representative sampling of the market. But if Fund B and the market always move in the same direction, investors would not have the same opportunity to reduce their risk by diversification.

Accordingly, even though Funds A and B might have the same total risk, represented perhaps by the standard deviation of their percentage returns, Fund A's risk can be offset by diversification, while Fund B's cannot. Reflective of this difference, Fund A would have a far lower beta coefficient than B; and the beta coefficient thus becomes a preferable measure of that component of risk with which investors should be principally concerned: market-related, or nondiversifiable, risk.

From the beta coefficient, we can compute the percentage (P) of total risk that is due to the market. The formula is as follows: $P = B^2M^2/F^2$, where B is the beta coefficient, M is the market's total risk (measured by the standard deviation of its percentage returns), and F is the fund's total risk. The resultant percentage is an excellent determinant of fund diversification, since it represents the part of the total risk that cannot be reduced by further investment in market-related assets.

Having computed both the average return for each fund and its volatility, we now combine the two measures to arrive at a volatility-adjusted performance rating. This combination is necessary, as mentioned above, because high return (a desirable performance characteristic) often goes hand in hand with high volatility (undesirable).

Alpha Coefficients.   To obtain the volatility-adjusted performance rating (sometimes called "excess return" or "alpha"), there is developed for each fund a comparison standard that has the same volatility as the fund itself. The standard is a hypothetical portfolio composed of an appropriate mix of the S&P 500 and Treasury bills (the mix is varied to produce the proper volatility). Each fund's volatility-adjusted performance is then calculated to be the amount by which its average rate of return exceeds the average for its own comparison standard.

By definition, the volatility coefficient for the S&P 500 is 1.00; for Treasury bills, it is assumed to be .00, since these bills are considered risk-free. Accordingly, to produce a comparison standard for a fund with a volatility coefficient of .75, we need only construct a portfolio that is 75 percent invested in the S&P 500 and 25 percent in Treasury bills.

The final step is to compute the return on each hypothetical portfolio and to compare it with the actual return of each corresponding fund. The hypothetical return is equal to (1) the average market return times the assumed percentage of capital invested in the market, plus (2) the average bill return times the assumed percentage of capital invested in bills (a negative number would result whenever the volatility coefficient of the fund exceeds 1.00).

If the fund's actual return is greater than its standard of comparison, its alpha coefficient will be positive; if its return is less, its alpha will be negative. Needless to say, the higher the alpha, the better the performance.

Another way of looking at the alpha coefficient is to consider that it represents the difference between the actual performance of the fund and the performance expected of the fund, given its characteristic volatility. If a fund has a beta coefficient of 2.00 and the market is up 10 percent over and above the Treasury bill return, then the fund would be expected to have outperformed Treasury bills by 20 percent. But if the fund's actual superiority were only 17 percent, then its alpha would be -3 percent. Thus, alpha equals the fund's risk premium minus its beta coefficient times the market's risk premium ($a = \bar{Y} - b\bar{X}$); and, not coincidentally, this is the formula for the a value, or intercept, of the regression equation.

So we see that both betas and alphas can be derived directly by regression analysis. They represent, respectively, volatility and volatility-adjusted performance, and they are the slope and intercept of the linear least-squares regression described above.

Betas and Alphas for Security Selection.   Betas and alphas can be computed for individual stocks as well as for portfolios of securities. Our discussion has focused on the uses of betas and alphas in the retrospective measurement of investment performance. To what extent can they be used for *prospective* appraisal of stocks or mutual funds, or both?

Investors should, of course, attempt to select securities that will have high alphas in the future (that is, securities that will do even better than their beta coefficients would indicate no matter in what direction the market moves). Regrettably, there is little available evidence indicating that alpha coefficients are stable. Alphas this period are not generally reliable estimators of alphas next period.

Quite the reverse is true of betas. A significant characteristic of beta coefficients is their relative stability over time. Extensive research has indicated that, for portfolios of fifty or so securities, the average beta for any given year can be accurately estimated from the average beta of the same securities for the prior year. This relationship prevails during successive bullish years, successive bearish years, or major market reversals.

As a result, the beta coefficient can be an extraordinarily useful stock selection tool *when coupled with accurate market timing*. If an advancing market is anticipated, high beta stocks are likely to rise at an above-average rate; and if a market decline is foreseen, the lowest betas will be the safest equity holdings.

It is, however, important to note two factors. First, betas used for security selection must be accompanied by accurate market timing. Second, large errors can occur in predicting betas for individual issues; it is only in dealing with reasonably large portfolios that opposite errors on individual issues can be expected to offset one another.

Chapter **4**

The Pleasures of Financial Security

LEMONT K. RICHARDSON

The Risk-Reward Theory

The notion that on the average investors can realize higher returns by taking greater risks enjoys wide acceptance in the investment world. Elegant theories and complex statistical studies have been developed and advanced by finance professors and investment firms in support of the "risk-reward" proposition.[1] During the second half of the 1960s, the activities of a number of performance-oriented investment funds appear to have been guided by this proposition. Moreover, reference to risk-reward relationships is a recurring theme in the investment letters of brokerage firms and financial advisory services, over-the-phone conversations between stockbrokers and their customers, and cocktail-hour and dinner discussions among both substantial and small investors.

What does the risk-reward proposition mean for the head of the household—the family breadwinner, who has primary responsibility for providing the income to pay for such current necessities as food and shelter as well as funding such major down-the-road cash requirements as college education for the children, possible support of the grandparents and other blood relatives, and, finally, the breadwinner's own retirement?

Given the basic assumption of the risk-reward proposition, that investors who take greater risks will, on the average, realize greater profits, it follows that the head of the household would stand to derive greater financial security in the long run by increasing the element of risk in his or her portfolio holdings.

[1]The risk-reward theory received full endorsement several years ago in a major study of pension fund investment performance sponsored by the Bank Administration Institute (BAI). This study, entitled *Measuring the Investment Performance of Pension Funds,* received considerable publicity when it was released in December 1968 and presumably was widely circulated among the investment managers of banks, which are trustees for pension funds both large and small. In particular, the "Management Summary" supplement of the BAI study contained the following emphatic statement with respect to risk and return: "The most important well-documented statement in the field of finance is that investors, on average, can receive a higher rate of return by assuming greater risk. . . . The committee members do not know any serious research . . . that suggests the proposition is not true" (p. 14).

In the most extreme case conceivable, the investor holding predominantly high-grade fixed-income investments such as passbook savings deposits, United States savings bonds, and Aaa-rated corporate and municipal bonds would switch to the most volatile common stocks that a broker could find. Presumably such common stocks would have evidenced, on the basis of past experience, substantially greater year-to-year price fluctuations than the market as a whole as measured by the Dow Jones Industrial Average, Standard & Poor's Composite Index of 500 stocks, or some other acceptable market index. Reference to market price volatility is significant, since proponents of the risk-reward proposition hold that the degree of investment risk associated with specific investment securities and whole investment portfolios either consists of or is measured by price instability, price volatility, or the range of fluctuations in price about the market average.

The important question is: Would investors who increased their risks by switching from high-grade fixed-income investments to the most volatile common stocks available always, or almost always, be better off in the long run because of the higher rate of return that they would presumably earn on their new portfolios of risky common stocks, compared with what they had been earning and could expect to earn on their relatively secure packages of fixed-income investments? Alternatively, would investors who sought to minimize their exposure to risks always, or almost always, earn a lower rate of return than investors who took higher risks?

Proponents of the risk-reward proposition would answer both questions in the affirmative. They would cite the conventional theory that investment returns are always directly proportional to the risks involved. They would also refer to the results of statistical studies of past investment performance which show that low-grade bonds have provided higher returns than high-grade bonds, common stock portfolios have provided greater returns than balanced or income-oriented portfolios, and speculative common stocks have produced higher returns than blue-chip stocks. On the other hand, many informed economists and investment counselors probably would answer in the negative and most certainly would caution any investor against operating on the proposition that prospective investment returns are directly proportionate to the degree of risk involved. These economists and counselors recognize both the erroneous logic of the risk-reward theory and the existence of statistical evidence which indicates that the theory has little substance in fact.

Before considering a move to shift liquid-asset holdings to riskier investments in the expectation of realizing greater profits, every investor, no matter how substantial or modest, sophisticated or unsophisticated, first should be acquainted with the many and diverse origins and facets of investment risk. Second, every investor also ought to consider carefully the basic logic of the risk-reward proposition as well as the results of a number of statistical studies on the subject of investment risk and rate of return.

An Anatomy of Investment Risk

Investment risk defies description in terms of a simple measurement standard such as price or market volatility in the case of common stocks or guarantee provisions and fixed-charges coverage in the case of bonds, debentures, and other fixed-income investments. The concept of investment risk, moreover, has many aspects that cannot be readily separated from the particular circumstances of individual investors: their needs for liquidity; their time horizon; their long-term employment security; their current and prospective financial strength, including down-the-road distributions from trusts and estates; their current and prospective fiduciary obligations; and their degree of investment sophistication, including awareness of alternative investment opportunities.

Thus, a specific investment could be appropriate for one investor but totally inappropriate for another. To illustrate, an investor with a substantial home equity, a comfortable savings account, and adequate life insurance coverage could afford to purchase common stocks, whereas one with a substantial home mortgage and little or no cash savings or insurance would generally be cautioned against buying common stocks, whether blue-chip or speculative.

Occupation is a further consideration in appraising the risk aspects of investment alternatives. Persons in highly perilous fields such as advertising or aerospace engineering would be ill-advised to place a substantial part of their liquid assets in common stocks. The multiple risks confronting them are that they might lose their jobs and be forced to liquidate their common stockholdings in a depressed market in order to pay for groceries and other essentials. It is worth noting in this regard that many advertising industry people and aerospace engineers lost their jobs during the business recession of 1969–1970, which coincided with a savage bear market that saw common stocks decline on the average by more than 25 percent. For the same reason, it would be imprudent for persons facing major down-the-road cash needs, such as the college education of their children, to place a substantial part of their savings in such illiquid investment situations as a second home or a part interest in a Florida citrus grove.

Examples of Risk in the Business World

A discussion of the causes of risk could fill a library. Consider, for a moment, the multiple sources of risk confronting a private business firm. Changes in social attitudes, technological innovations, changes in federal tax laws, shifts in Federal Reserve monetary policy, changes in the rate of inflation and deflation, war and the threat of war, political upheaval and expropriation of investor-owned enterprises, imposition of federal price and profit controls—all these are sources of risk to the business firm and, therefore, to the creditors and owners of that firm.

In the early 1970s, increased public concern about pollution of the environment loomed as a major element of risk and uncertainty for investors in electric utility common stocks. Yet who foresaw or could have foreseen even a few years earlier the dimensions of the public concern about pollution of the environment and the implications of this concern for specific industries and companies? Investor-owned electric utilities in virtually every one of the fifty states now have to comply with stringent but socially desirable air and thermal pollution control standards. The costs of complying with these new regulations are substantial and initially are borne entirely by the electric utility common stockholders. In addition, since the end of 1973 most electric utilities have suffered a more than threefold increase in primary fuel costs as a result of oil price hikes by the Arab-dominated oil-exporting nations.

Subsequent rate relief may permit passing on some or most of these added pollution control and fuel costs to users. But in those instances in which regulatory commissions refuse to grant rate relief because of political and other pressures, the electric utility common stockholders will bear the cost in the form of reduced earnings and dividends and, quite possibly, of an erosion in the market value of their common stock investments if the market capitalizes earnings of the affected utilities at a lower multiple than previously.

The chemical, oil, paper, and steel industries also are incurring substantial costs to comply with the environmental protection regulations. Brokerage firm investments reports on specific companies in these industries often devote special attention to the costs of pollution compliance and the possible effects on the companies' per-share earnings.

The impact of technological change on business and investment risk has been both staggering and fascinating. Thus, over the past 150 years of United States economic development, both the earning power and the economic salvage value of the assets of entire industries have been reduced to near zero because of technological change. During most of the first half of the nineteenth century, canals and turnpikes (some of which were owned by private investors) served as the main arteries of transportation between the East Coast and such major Midwest points as Chicago and St. Louis. By the end of the Civil War in 1865, steam railroads had become the country's dominant mode of transportation, and canals and turnpikes were abandoned. Numerous internal improvement bond issues floated by the states before the war to finance the construction of canals and turnpikes went into default. Another 100 years later, however, the railroads themselves were in a greatly weakened financial and operating condition because of the competitive inroads of faster or more flexible modes of transportation, notably the scheduled commercial airlines and the intercity motor carriers.

From about 1890 to the mid-1920s, electric streetcar railway systems, many of them privately financed, enjoyed vigorous and profitable growth by providing urban transportation needs and connecting downtown centers with newly formed suburban communities. During this period, the debt and equity securities of electric streetcar railways enjoyed considerable investment favor. With the advent of the automobile and the Great Depression, however, the era of the electric streetcar railway came to an abrupt end, as did the payment of interest and dividends on the outstanding securities of many electric railway companies. This writer, who was a young schoolboy during World War II, can recall the day when all the tracks of the electric streetcar railway systems connecting his small central Wisconsin hometown with Milwaukee and Chicago were ripped up for steel scrap to build tanks and battleships to fight the Germans and Japanese.

More recently, some informed investment analysts have pondered the implications of the application of available space satellite communications technology on the economic value and future earnings power of the Bell System's multibillion dollar investment in conventional earthbound telecommunications equipment. Could AT&T go the way of the canals and turnpikes and the electric streetcar railways? The possibility, however remote, is an element of investment risk.

The foregoing discussion spotlights an important aspect of business and investment risk which, in the judgment of this writer, does not receive adequate recognition either in college textbooks on finance or in securities analysts' reports on specific industries and companies in these industries. Companies in capital-intensive industries, in which the ratio of total capital investment and capital charges to annual sales is high and in which such capital investment is often very specialized in nature (for example, trackage and rolling stock in the case of the railroads, power-generating and transmission equipment in the case of the electric utility industry, blast furnaces and rolling mills in the case of the steel industry), are exposed to the long-run (and possibly sudden) risk of substantial economic obsolescence of their capital equipment because of technological change. Such companies simply do not have the flexibility to rechannel their capital facilities into other income-producing activities. Depreciated book values shown on the balance sheets of companies in capital-intensive industries may be less than market or replacement values today, but tomorrow the reverse could be true because of the risk of sudden economic obsolescence resulting from technological change.

A further element of risk for companies in capital-intensive industries is the sensitivity of their earnings to reductions in revenues due to recession-related declines in demand, to strikes, and to other factors. Revenues decline or stop, but capital charges in the form of interest and lease payments and depreciation continue, severely squeezing earnings and profit margins. In contrast, the earnings of companies in labor-intensive industries, in which labor costs account for a high proportion of total costs or revenues, are not so sensitive to these factors. When sales volumes decline or complete work stoppages occur, management can moderate the impact of the revenue loss on profits by sharply reducing labor costs through layoffs, reductions in overtime, and the like.

Seen in this light, companies in labor-intensive industries might well be deemed less risky than companies in capital-intensive industries because of their greater ability to adjust to adverse short-term factors (strikes and so on) and negative long-term developments such as the economic obsolescence of plant and equipment caused by technological change.

According to the economic textbooks, however, the profits and profitability of labor-intensive industries are generally considered to be more vulnerable than those of capital-intensive industries because of the inflationary nature of contract wage settlements and the disrupting effect of work slowdowns or stoppages and strikes invoked to enforce wage contract demands. Increased labor costs can readily be absorbed in capital-intensive industries by installing more efficient equipment, in effect by replacing labor with machines, thus boosting productivity. Thus, this simplistic view of risk does not correspond with real-world conditions.

Examples of Risk and Investment Yields in the Financial World

A conventional spectrum of the risk type of investments from the lowest to the highest risk would be as follows: United States government bonds, federally insured time deposits and savings accounts, high-quality corporate and municipal bonds with Ass or Aa ratings assigned by Moody's and other bond-rating services, medium-grade corporates and municipals rated A or Baa, unrated corporate subordinated convertible debentures, nonconvertible preferred or preference stock, convertible preferred stock, common stocks, common stock warrants, commodity futures contracts, and, finally, common stock options contracts.

Because of the stability of the United States government and the absolute authority of its monetary and fiscal agencies to create money and credit and levy taxes to meet all revenue requirements, its bonds are assumed to have no default risk; that is, interest payments during the life of the bonds will be met on interest due dates, and the bonds will be paid off in full at maturity. In this regard, yields on United States governments generally are viewed by bond market experts as a proxy for the "pure rate" of interest, or the time value of money in the absence of all risk. Yields on all other types of debt securities, in these circumstances, would reflect the sum of the pure rate of interest plus an added yield premium to compensate investors for the risk of possible default. Therefore, the greater the assumed risk of default on a specific debt security or class of debt securities, the higher the risk premium and total yield on such securities compared with United States governments in the same maturity range. The risk premium and total yield on Baa-rated corporate bonds obviously would tend to be higher than on Aaa-rated corporates, as shown in Table 4-1.

The pure rate of interest and the risk premium that investors may demand on selected classes of debt securities at any point in time are by no means constant, as the data presented in the table clearly indicate. The factors contributing to changes in the yield relationships among United States governments and other classes of debt securities are numerous and complex; several of the more important of these yield-affecting factors are discussed in Chapter 24. Over the broad sweep of time, however, corporate bond maturity yields have consistently averaged higher than long-term United States governments, and the yields on lower-grade corporates have exceeded those on high-grade corporates.

Common stocks rank near the bottom of the conventional spectrum of risk-type investments. The common stockholder is the residual claimant to the cash flows of a going corporation and to the assets of a failing company forced into bankruptcy and liquidation. Senior lenders such as first-mortgage bondholders and commercial banks have prior claims on the cash flows and assets of a corporation. Interest charges and scheduled loan repayments are paid first along with wages, rents, and other operating costs; what is left is available for earnings and cash dividends.

The market prices of common stocks also have tended to be more volatile, that is, subject to proportionately greater daily, weekly, monthly, and yearly price fluctuations, than United States government and corporate debt securities. Since market price volatility, as noted above, is the accepted measure of risk among the proponents of the risk-reward proposition, the greater volatility of common stock prices compared with bond prices is another reason for ranking these securities at or near the bottom of the risk spectrum.

TABLE 4-1   Illustration of the Risk Premium on Selected Categories of Corporate Bonds, 1970–1973

(In percentages)

	United States governments (Long-term)	Corporate bonds Aaa (Seasoned issues)	Corporate bonds Baa (Seasoned issues)	Corporate bond risk premium —yield differential over governments Aaa	Corporate bond risk premium —yield differential over governments Baa
1955	2.84	3.06	3.53	0.22	0.69
1960	4.02	4.41	5.19	0.39	1.17
1965	4.21	4.49	4.87	0.28	0.66
1970	6.59	8.04	9.11	1.45	2.52
1971	5.74	7.39	8.56	1.65	2.82
1972	5.63	7.21	8.16	1.58	2.53
1973	6.30	7.44	8.24	1.14	1.94

SOURCE: *Economic Report of the President,* January 1974.

It is natural to expect that rates of return on common stocks would have to be fairly high compared with fixed-income securities to compensate the common stock investor for the risks he has taken. Historically, rates of return on common stocks have, in fact, averaged substantially higher than the rates on investment-grade debt securities. A major statistical study by two University of Chicago professors of the investment performance of all common stocks listed on the New York Stock Exchange over a forty-year period, from 1926 through 1965, showed that common stocks, on the average, provided investors with an effective annual return of about 8.8 percent, as measured by the cash dividends received and market appreciation.[2] The 8.8 percent annual return realized on common stocks during this period was about twice as great as the yields realized on high-grade corporate bonds. The results of the University of Chicago study are widely disseminated by securities firms and by institutional investors interested in equities.

Other Factors Affecting Risk and Yields

Yield differentials among debt securities of varying investment quality at any time reflect the interplay of many other factors in addition to the default risk. These other yield-affecting factors include but are not limited to the following:
 ■ Differences in demand-supply relationships in particular segments of the money and credit markets.

[2]Lawrence Fisher and James H. Lorie, "Rates of Return on Investments in Common Stock: The Year-by Year Record, 1926–1965," *The Journal of Business,* vol. 41, no. 3, July 1968.

■ Differences in the degree of liquidity or marketability of particular securities, which, in turn, are a function of the size of the issue (that is, outstanding dollar value), number and types of investors holding the issue, and dealer interest in the issue. These interrelated factors determine the breadth and depth of the trading markets for specific securities.

■ Changes in investor attitudes and expectations about the future rate of inflation and deflation, federal monetary and fiscal policy, and so on.

Under normal credit market conditions, interest rates on particular types of debt securities tend to vary in proportion to their maturities because of the greater risks and uncertainties that exist in the future. Normally, therefore, yields on Treasury bills should be lower than those on long-term governments, and yields on finance paper and near-maturity corporate bonds lower than those on long-term corporates. Yield relationships prevailing since 1965–1966 suggest, however, that so-called normal credit market conditions may have become something of a rarity.

Are Investment Yields Indicative of Risks?

Because defaults among investment-grade corporate bonds have been almost nonexistent since the end of World War II, one may well question the logic behind the risk premium requirement as the basis for the continuing yield differential between United States government and investment-grade corporate debt securities. Moreover, since the historical rate-of-return performance of common stocks, as measured by the famous University of Chicago study,[3] has been so spectacular compared with the investment returns provided by high-grade debt securities (almost 9 percent on stocks versus less than 5 percent on high-grade bonds), one would think that investors might bid up the market prices of common stocks relative to bonds to a point at which the expected future yields on both types of investments would be essentially in equilibrium.

The possibility that this development may have occurred is suggested by the fact that maturity yields on high-grade corporate bonds have averaged upward of 7.5 percent since 1970. Bond maturity yields of this magnitude would appear to be quite competitive with the prospective yields on common stocks if most investors expect to be able to earn, on the average, an annual return of about 9 percent on their common stock portfolios.

Investors who consider the merits of accepting a lesser return on riskier investments in the future because of favorable past experience on risky investments should bear in mind the following circumstances. The fact that defaults among investment-grade corporate bonds have been virtually nonexistent since the end of World War II is no guarantee that defaults among such securities will not occur during the next two decades. Some investment-grade corporate bonds did default during the Great Depression of the 1930s. But it was among lower-grade and speculative corporate debt securities that the incidence of default was astoundingly high. Furthermore, during this period prices of lower-grade corporate bonds that had not yet gone into default dropped sharply, and maturity yields rose to levels of 12 percent and more. Meanwhile, maturity yields on Aaa-rated corporate bonds averaged about 4.5 percent, or less than during the late 1920s. This substantial yield differential reflected the extreme pessimism among investors during the Depression concerning the prospective "money good" aspect of all lower-grade debt securities.

The expectation among investors that (1) inflation will enable marginal companies to raise prices and thereby increase their earnings and coverage of fixed

[3]Ibid.

charges and (2) the Administration and Congress will almost always come to the rescue of large failing companies, as it did for Lockheed in 1971, may go a long way toward explaining why bond investors today are content to accept a much lower yield differential, or risk premium, on lower-grade and speculative corporate debt securities compared with high-grade debt securities. In recent years, the yield differential between lower-grade and high-grade corporate bonds has averaged between 1 and 2 percentage points, whereas during the Depression it exceeded 7 full percentage points.

The Administration and Congress, however, did not bail out the Penn Central in 1970; nor did the government come to the rescue of W. T. Grant in 1975–76. By contrast, the government did provide emergency financial assistance to New York City in 1975–1976.

Such a mixed pattern of federal rescue response in recent years should be a deterrent to the purchase of dubious debt securities of any company or municipal entity, no matter how large, on the assumption that United States government support will be forthcoming to avert default or bankruptcy.

Furthermore, an acceleration in the rate of inflation, as has happened since 1970, may serve to compound the problems confronting financially weak companies instead of easing their problems. During inflation the availability of credit tends to diminish, and its price increases. Companies with large amounts of short-term debt in the form of bank loans and commercial paper may encounter substantial difficulties in rolling over this debt or stretching it out through the sale of long-term securities. In any event, the cost of their debt load will increase substantially. A number of conglomerate-type companies such as LTV encountered this very problem during 1970–1971.

Inflation also can be accompanied by price controls that effectively limit the ability of individual companies to raise prices sufficiently to achieve full recovery of their increased operating costs. This certainly was one of the major effects of the periodic price freezes and price controls from August 1971 to April 1974 under the Economic Stabilization program.

On the basis of the foregoing considerations and in view of the likelihood that the rate of general inflation during the balance of the 1970s will average appreciably higher than during the 1960s, every investor would do well to review critically (1) the relationships between prevailing maturity yields on corporate bonds and expected annual yields on common stock investments (with the recognized 9 percent historical annual return representing a proxy for expected common stock returns); and (2) the current yield differentials between lower-grade and high-grade debt securities. The basic purpose of this review should be to reach an informed judgment concerning the broadly accepted proposition that investors who take greater risks will, on the average, realize greater profits than those who prefer to take smaller risks. The findings and conclusions of a number of major quantitative studies of investment risk and rate of return, which follow, should be helpful in this review.

THE STATISTICAL RECORD OF INVESTMENT RISK AND YIELD

Hickman Study of Corporate Bond Performance. In 1958 W. Braddock Hickman submitted a study of the investment performance of corporate bonds from 1900 to World War II.[4] This study, sponsored by the National Bureau of Economic Research, measured the performance of all "straight corporate bond flotations" of $5 million or more issued from 1900 through 1943, plus a 10 percent sample of

[4]W. Braddock Hickman, *Corporate Bond Quality and Investor Experience*, Princeton University Press, Princeton, N.J., 1958.

the issues below $5 million. Among other things, the Hickman study found that the realized yields on lower-grade or speculative corporate bonds were, on average, higher than on investment-quality corporates during the period examined. Moreover, it found a fairly close relationship between expected or promised yields at the time of issue and realized yields. The principal findings of the study, comparing the original promised maturity yields and actual realized yields on the various classes of corporate bonds in descending order of quality or rating, are shown in Table 4-2.

During the period 1900–1943, investment-grade bonds with the highest quality ratings (I through IV) were offered at original promised maturity yields ranging from 4.5 to 5.4 percent and provided actual realized yields ranging from 5 to 5.7 percent. The fact that the actual realized yields on these bonds exceeded the original promised maturity yields is attributable chiefly to the sharp decline in interest rates and the concomitant sharp rise in bond prices during the easy-credit period following the Great Depression and extending through World War II. The

TABLE 4-2   Corporate Bond Performance, 1900–1943

Quality rating	Original promised yield (percent)	Realized yield (percent)
I	4.5	5.1
II	4.6	5.0
III	4.9	5.0
IV	5.4	5.7
V–IX	9.5	8.6
Irregular offerings	12.3	13.7

SOURCE: W. Braddock Hickman, *Corporate Bond Quality and Investor Experience,* Princeton University Press, Princeton, N.J., 1958, Table 1, p. 10.

era of easy credit came to an abrupt end in 1951, when the Federal Reserve System stopped supporting the United States government bond market under the famous Treasury–Federal Reserve accord. During much of this easy-credit period, Treasury bill yields averaged less than 1 percent, and high-grade corporate bonds traded at yields averaging 3 percent or lower.

More important, however, the Hickman study showed that the yields actually realized on speculative corporate bonds (V through IX) during the 1900–1943 period, while somewhat lower than their original promised maturity yields, exceeded the yields realized on investment-grade bonds by a very substantial margin: 8.7 percent versus 5.0 to 5.7 percent. In addition, the study found that the yields realized on so-called irregular corporate bond offerings, resulting from bankruptcy reorganizations, averaged upward of 13.7 percent during the period examined, or more than double the yields realized on investment-grade corporates.

Hickman noted that the results of this study were probably affected significantly by the catastrophic default rates of the Great Depression, whereas the post-World War II period, not covered by the study, had been relatively free of defaults. On this evidence, he conjectured that if his study were updated to the 1950s, the results would show "realized yields above promised yields, and net capital gains on bonds offered since 1900."[5]

Publication of the Hickman study in 1958 created a considerable stir in the investment fraternity. Some bond portfolio managers adopted the attitude that they would be able to realize higher yields by purchasing relatively larger amounts of lower-grade corporate bonds and smaller amounts of investment-grade issues—

[5]Ibid., p. 8.

an investment attitude that was reinforced by recognition of the beneficial effects of national economic policies under the mandate of the Full Employment Act of 1946. The findings of the Hickman study also were widely cited in academic circles in support of the proposition that investors could, on the average, realize higher profits by assuming greater risk.

Fraine Study of Corporate Bond Performance.   In 1962 Harold Fraine, a retired professor of finance at the University of Wisconsin, released a study of corporate bond performance during the same period covered by the Hickman study (1900–1943). The Fraine study showed that the realized yields on investment-grade corporate bonds were substantially higher than those on speculative bonds despite the fact that the expected or original issue yields on the investment-quality corporates were in all instances lower than on the speculative issues.[6] In other words, according to Fraine, bond investors who took smaller risks realized, on the average, higher returns than those who took greater risks. The results of the Fraine study are shown in Table 4-3.

TABLE 4-3   Corporate Bond Performance, 1900–1943

Quality rating	Original promised yield (percent)	Realized yield (percent)
I	4.5	4.3
II	4.5	4.3
III	4.9	4.3
IV	5.4	4.5
V	6.3	3.5
Below V	7.6	3.7

SOURCE: Harold G. Fraine, *Valuation of Securities Holdings of Life Insurance Companies,* Richard D. Irwin, Inc., Homewood, Ill., 1962, Table 2-8, p. 46.

The major reason for the different conclusions drawn by the Fraine and Hickman studies from observation of essentially the same data is that the former concentrated on "total return," while the latter focused on ordinary interest yield only. Professor Fraine endeavored to remove the elements of "spurious" investment income before calculating the realized rates of return for the various bond categories. These elements of spurious income included (1) the market premiums or capital gains realized on bonds that were called prior to maturity; and (2) the unrealized market premium or capital gain on bonds still outstanding in the terminal year of the study. Both of these elements of spurious income resulted from the sharp decline in interest rates and concomitant rise in bond prices during the easy-money period beginning around 1933 and extending through 1943.

The significant difference between the realized yields on speculative corporate bonds shown in the Hickman and Fraine studies, respectively 8.6 and 3.7 percent, deserves special comment. During the early 1930s, default rates among low-grade speculative corporate debt securities were relatively high: more than 45 percent of such issues defaulted during this period. In many instances, the holders of these defaulted issues ultimately received another note or debenture in exchange that offered a much higher promised yield than the original bonds. Hickman's study included all such noncash offerings, while Fraine excluded them to avoid double counting. Many of these noncash offerings had risen to substantial premiums by the end of 1943 in response to the general decline in interest rates and the post-Depression revival of business confidence. This situation explains why Hickman's realized yields on speculative corporate bonds were substantially higher than Fraine's.

[6]Harold G. Fraine, *Valuation of Securities Holdings of Life Insurance Companies,* Richard D. Irwin, Inc., Homewood, Ill., 1962.

The Fraine study, which demonstrated that during the period from 1900 through 1943 corporate bond investors who took smaller risks realized higher returns, on the average, than bond investors who took greater risks, appears to be every bit as valid as the earlier Hickman study, which came to the opposite conclusion. Yet the Fraine study does not appear to have received the same recognition as the Hickman study in academic and investment circles.

A number of other points are worth noting in an overall appraisal of the practical investment policy implications of the principal findings of the Hickman study: that lower-grade corporate bonds, over the broad sweep of time, provided higher effective yields than high-grade bonds. Averages of experience over long periods of time generally tend to show favorable results (for example, growth is output, employment, wealth, and income; positive yields on stocks and bonds) and conceal all sorts of calamities. However, an investor holding a representative cross section of all corporate bonds issued before 1930 would have had a relatively high proportion of his portfolio (in terms of both number of issues and original book value) in default at one time or another during the Great Depression.

In numerous instances, moreover, the state regulatory authorities forced the banks and insurance companies subject to their jurisdiction to sell their defaulted bonds at a loss, thereby preventing these institutions from realizing positive yields on such bonds during the ensuing economic recovery and return to general prosperity. The Hickman study, in fact, noted that the average effective yield on all defaulted issues to time of default was -3.4 percent, compared with an original average promised yield of 6.4 percent, or a difference of nearly 10 full percentage points.[7]

Furthermore, many bond portfolio managers who had bought bonds issued before 1930 that later went into default or came perilously close to default lost their jobs during the Great Depression. The irony of the situation is that the original investment decisions of these dismissed portfolio managers were subsequently exonerated by the return to general prosperity and recovery in bond credit quality and bond prices.

University of Chicago Study of Rates of Return on Common Stocks.   The availability of high-speed electronic computers has greatly facilitated quantitative studies of the effective rates of return realized by common stock investors over long periods of time. The rate of return in these studies is expressed as a discount rate that equates the present value of the common stock investor's realized income stream (the cash dividends received plus the subsequent market price at the time of sale or the terminal year in the study) to the original purchase price. These historic rate-of-return studies have been performed on specific stocks and representative groups of stocks such as the Dow Jones Industrial Average, Moody's 125 Industrials, and Standard & Poor's 500-Stock Index.

The most ambitious studies of this type have been done by the University of Chicago's Center for Research in Security Prices under the direction of Professors James Lorie and Lawrence Fisher. In 1968 these gentlemen published a study of the effective annual rates of return produced by *all* common stocks listed on the New York Stock Exchange (NYSE) during any year or period of years between January 1926 and December 1965—a total of 820 possible year-to-year rate-of-return combinations.[8] A total of 1,856 stocks were used in the study. The rates of return were calculated in many different ways, including reinvestment of dividends, accumulation of dividends but no reinvestment, exclusion of dividends entirely, before deduction of federal income and capital gains taxes, and after deduction of certain specified federal tax liabilities.

---

[7]W. Braddock Hickman, *Corporate Bonds: Quality and Investment Performance,* Occasional Paper 59, National Bureau of Economic Research, 1957, p. 24.
   [8]Fisher and Lorie, op. cit.

The highlights of the study are summarized as follows:

- The average annual rate of return produced by all NYSE common stocks was 8.8 percent compounded annually, with reinvestment of dividends and before payment of any federal income taxes.

- In only 72 of the 820 possible year-to-year time periods, or less than 9 percent of the time, did common stocks yield negative returns.

- During the last twenty years covered by the study (1946 through 1965) common stock returns were consistently high. In this period, there was no interval of more than four years when common stocks produced an annual return of less than 7 percent. If the investor stayed in common stocks over any ten-year interval during this period, he would have earned more than 11 percent per year.

On the strength of this and other similar studies, the rates of return realized by common stock investors over long periods of time (about 9 percent per year, on the average) do appear to have been higher than the returns realized by investors on high-grade corporate bonds (4 to 5 percent per year, on the average, according to the Fraine and Hickman studies). Since few would dispute the argument that common stocks are riskier than bonds, the foregoing evidence probably has provided the greatest amount of credibility to the proposition that investors can, on the average, realize higher returns by taking greater risks.

Morton Study of Rates of Return on Common Stocks. In June 1971, Walter Morton, a retired professor of finance at the University of Wisconsin, published a study comparing the rates of return realized on 400 common stocks of varying risk characteristics during the period from 1965 through 1968.[9] The 400 stocks were obtained from the Standard & Poor's 425 Industrial Stock Index, and the risk characteristics of each stock were determined on the basis of their prior market price variability during the period from 1956 through 1965. The chief purpose of this study was to test the hypothesis that the investor who purchased risky stocks (on the basis of demonstrated past market volatility) would, on the average, realize higher profits than the investor who purchased less risky stocks. The actual rate of return realized on each of the 400 stocks during the period from 1966 to 1968 was determined by averaging of the rates of return that would have resulted from six different investment decisions as follows:

1. Invest on December 31, 1965, at the average 1965 price and sell on December 31, 1966, at the average 1966 price plus one year's dividends.

2. Buy on December 31, 1965, and sell on December 31, 1967, plus two years' dividends.

3. Buy on December 31, 1965, and sell on December 31, 1968, plus three years' dividends.

4. Buy on December 31, 1966, and sell on December 31, 1967, plus one year's dividends.

5. Buy on December 31, 1966, and sell on December 31, 1968, plus two years' dividends.

6. Buy on December 31, 1967, and sell on December 31, 1968, plus one year's dividends.

The result of the Morton study is that no significant relationship exists between risk taken and return realized. High-risk and low-risk stocks alike provided low as well as high investment returns. Differences in the returns realized among the 400 stocks in the study could not be explained by differences in their market or price volatility.

Thus, although the Fraine and Morton studies covered entirely different segments of the broad spectrum of available investment opportunities, corporate

[9]Walter A. Morton, "Market Price, Risk and Investor Return," *The Commercial and Financial Chronicle,* June 3, 1971.

bonds and common stocks respectively, both reached essentially the same conclusion: that the assumption of high risks does not guarantee the realization of high investment returns.

Special Factors Contributing to the High Realized Rates of Return on Common Stock Investments

As noted above, the University of Chicago study of common stock rates of return during the period from 1926 to 1965 showed that equity investors realized, on the average, much higher rates of return than holders of high-grade bonds, or about 9 percent per year versus 4 to 5 percent. Today's investor, however, should consider carefully a number of special factors that contributed to the very favorable rates of return on equities over the past forty years or so. Recognition of these factors should emphasize the perils of accepting the proposition that common stocks will continue to provide higher returns, on the average, than bonds to compensate for the difference in risk.

Between 1926 and 1965, the period covered by the University of Chicago common stock rate-of-return study, average net earnings per share of common stock, as measured by the Standard & Poor's Composite Index of 500 stocks, increased by 317 percent, from $1.24 to $5.17, or at a rate of about 3.7 percent compounded annually. Common stock prices during this period rose by 554 percent, or at a rate of about 4.9 percent compounded annually—roughly one-third again as fast as the rate of increase in average per-share earnings. The proportionately faster rate of increase in common stock prices is attributable to the secular rise in price-earnings ratios, the rate at which investors are willing to capitalize earnings, from an average of less than 11 times earnings in 1926 to slightly more than 17 times earnings in 1965. Two factors largely explain this willingness on the part of investors to capitalize common stock earnings at much higher multiples than formerly: (1) inflationary expectations fueled by the inexorable rise in the general level of prices since the end of World War I (except during the Great Depression and World War II, when price controls were in effect); and (2) recognition of the beneficial effects of post-World War II full-employment policies on the prospective stability of corporate earning power.

On this evidence, if we assume that average net earnings per share of common stock will continue to rise at the historic rate of about 4 percent per year, it is clear that average common stock price-earnings multiples must rise substantially above present levels for common stock investors to realize, on the average, the same 9 percent rate of return as they did during the forty-year period from 1926 through 1965. But how many investment analysts would be willing to recommend the purchase of common stocks when investment-grade corporate bonds offer promised maturity yields of 8 percent or more, on the expectation that common stock price-earnings ratios will rise to a range of 25 to 30 times earnings during the next thirty to forty years? An increase in price-earnings ratios from the 1965–1970 average of about 16 times to a range of 25 to 30 times by end of the twentieth century would be in proportion to the increase in earnings multiples that has occurred since the mid-1920s.

Post Mortem on the Hobson's Choice of Investment Planning: Making the Most of Risk Versus the Pleasures of Financial Security

The standard dictionary definition of Hobson's choice is a choice without an alternative. According to fact or legend, Thomas Hobson, who ran a livery stable in seventeenth-century England, required all his customers in need of a horse to take the one nearest the stable door. There is a strong flavor of Hobson's choice in the risk-reward proposition referred to throughout this chapter. Investors must either accept greater risks to earn greater profits or be satisfied with lower profits if they prefer financial security, that is, if they have a strong preference for risk aversion.

At this juncture, however, the perceptive investor-reader should be aware of some of the major theoretical limitations of the risk-reward proposition itself and of the existence of several competent statistical studies referred to above that suggest the theory is not supported in fact. In reality, there need be very little if any of the Hobson's-choice dilemma confronting investors in their personal investment planning, if we assume, of course, that the investors act rationally.

An essential starting point is a full understanding of (1) the highly arbitrary and misleading nature of the definition of investment risk in terms of relative market price volatility in the case of common stocks, yield differentials in the case of bonds, or other simple statistical standards; and (2) the self-contradictory nature of the risk-reward proposition itself. Most informed and rational investors should be, and probably are, concerned primarily with preserving and augmenting the value of their capital over the long pull, as opposed to minimizing or maximizing year-to-year fluctuations in the value of their portfolio holdings. The possibility of long-term impairment of capital values is the essence of investment risk. Such a loss could take the form of (1) an absolute decline in the value of principal, ranging all the way down to zero in the case of bankruptcy and default, or (2) a relative decline in purchasing power of, for example, bonds and savings accounts versus real estate, mineral rights, timber, and other tangible property in a highly inflationary period. This second type of loss has an opportunity cost aspect, measured by the rate of return forgone on the alternative, more profitable investment opportunity. However, either type of loss is the result of uncertain future developments. Every investor should appraise these possible future developments and establish subjective probabilities of their occurrence.

Upside Volatility Preferable to Downside Volatility

Reliance on market price volatility or any other volatility standard for measuring the investment risk of selected common stocks or entire portfolios has a rather serious shortcoming—the inability of most of these techniques to allow for the difference between upside and downside volatility. To illustrate, a common stock portfolio that rose at an average of 15 percent per year over a ten-year period could conceivably evidence greater year-to-year price volatility relative to the general market than another portfolio that declined by an average of 5 percent annually during the same ten-year period. With the wisdom of hindsight, most investors probably would conclude that the first portfolio that rose by 15 percent per year was less risky than the second that declined by 5 percent per year, even though the degree of year-to-year price volatility of the first might have been substantially greater than the second.

Cyclical-Growth vs. Hard-Times Companies

A further example of the misleading nature of the volatility standards for measuring risk would be a comparison of the earnings and market performance of a cyclical-growth company and a former stable-industry company that had fallen on hard times and was now experiencing a gradual earnings decline. In these circumstances, the cyclical-growth company might well evidence substantially greater year-to-year earnings and market price variability than the hard-times company. Yet, from the shareholders' point of view, is it reasonable to characterize the cyclical-growth company as a more risky investment than the hard-times company, as proponents of the volatility standards of risk measurement are wont to do? Common sense suggests that the factors affecting the future level and trend of earnings of a company and, therefore, its investment value relative to other companies are more important parameters of investment risk than the historical magnitude of quarterly or annual variations in market values and earnings. In the long run, the prospect of capital appreciation would appear greater for growth companies than for stable-industry companies because of the likelihood of faster earnings growth and the possibility of leverage associated with an increase in earnings multiples.

Historical Volatility vs. Future Risks

Market price and earnings volatility standards, appropriately refined, may have validity in measuring *past* investment risk *after the fact.* The real question, however, is whether such standards have any practical value in day-to-day investment decision making, the least of which lies in appraising *prospective* investment performance. The answer is clearly negative. For documentation, a case study of two specific stocks, AT&T and LTV, follows.

During the period from 1960 through 1970, the market price volatility of these two stocks differed markedly. AT&T had a high of 75 and a low of 40 during this period, while LTV had a high of 169 and a low of 8. On the basis of the market price volatility standard, LTV evidenced the greater risk and therefore should have produced the higher return over the period in question. But did it? Yes, for the investor who bought LTV at 8 and sold at 169. But what about the investor who bought LTV at the 1968 high of 169 and then subsequently had to sell out at a price of 8? Probably not. Furthermore, can one reasonably assume that a buyer of LTV at any price in the future will always do better than the buyer at AT&T at any price? Yes, according to the market price, volatility-oriented risk-reward theory. Probably not, if one considers the various factors affecting the future earnings outlook for both companies. In short, past market price and earnings volatility simply cannot ensure that the purchase of any investment security now or in the future will be profitable.

The concepts of risk measurement used to support the high-risk–high-return theory are inadequate as a guide to investment decision making because they (1) ignore the price at which an investor gets into a high-risk stock, (2) are based on after-the-fact information, and (3) do not distinguish between upward and downward movements in either prices or earnings. To judge the propriety of current and prospective investment decisions one must know what the risks are at the time the investment is made. To argue that investors would have done better in LTV than in AT&T during the past decade because they could have bought LTV lower and sold it higher is utterly meaningless unless one possesses the clairvoyance to determine these lows and highs in advance.

Earnings Trends vs. Price Variability

In making a judgment of the prospects of capital loss or capital appreciation attaching to most private-sector investment securities, especially common stocks, informed and rational investors tend to pay greater heed to the many factors affecting the level and trend of earnings of the companies they have invested in or are considering rather than the magnitude of year-to-year variability in the market prices of these companies.

For example, consider the following two investment opportunities as of the latter part of 1973: (1) a high-grade electric utility common stock with a current annual cash dividend yield of 7 percent and a price-earnings multiple of 9 times and (2) a high-grade corporate bond offering a maturity yield of close to 8 percent. Any rational decision by an investor to purchase the utility stock instead of the bond must involve some assumption as to the probable long-term rate of growth in the earnings and dividends of the utility under consideration.

In arriving at a determination of a growth factor for the utility, the investor would have to give careful consideration to a wide variety of separate and interrelated factors affecting the level and trend of the utility's earnings. These factors include but are not limited to the following:

- The competence and depth of management
- The rate of expansion of the company's rate base
- Changes in the company's capital structure
- The rate of price and wage inflation in the economy and the effect on the company's labor and fuel costs
- The posture of the state regulatory commission with respect to the company's requests for rate increases to cover rising capital and operating costs, particularly fuel costs
- Potential competitive inroads by alternative sources of energy in the markets
- The relative stringency and associated costs of complying with pollution control measures adopted by the federal, state, and local governments

A deterioration in management, for example, would adversely affect the rate of growth in the utility's projected earnings and dividends, as would an acceleration in the rate of inflation and a series of unfavorable actions by the state public service commission on the company's applications for upward rate adjustments to offset increases in capital and operating costs. The utility's projected earnings also would be adversely affected by population and industry shifts to other regions because of changes in the level and pattern of defense procurement and other factors. Since 1968, for example, a decline in total federal aerospace spending has had a material impact on the earnings position of gas and electric utilities serving such metropolitan areas as Dallas, Los Angeles, and Seattle.

On balance, the possibility of occurrence of these and other developments that could adversely affect the projected level and trend of the utility's earnings and thereby increase the chance of capital loss vis-à-vis alternative investment opportunities, notably high-grade bonds, constitutes the only real basis by which current and prospective investors in that company can evaluate investment risk. The same would apply to any other investor-owned company.

It is difficult to comprehend how these and other risk factors can be taken into account by risk measurement techniques that focus chiefly on period-to-period variability in market values, earnings, and rates of return.

If More Risk Means More Return, What Is the Risk?

The appeal of the risk-reward proposition is that investors can, on the average, realize greater profits by taking greater risks. The proposition suggests, therefore, that investors tend to get what they expect, that is, that expected and realized rates of return are identical. Naturally investors who are risk-oriented expect to realize higher returns than investors whose investment decisions are guided primarily by a preference for risk aversion. If expectations were always realized in fact, the investor in high-risk situations would, on the average, earn more than someone who took lower risks. The investor in low-grade bonds would, on the average, realize higher returns than the investor in high-grade bonds; the investor who bought speculative stocks would, on the average, do better than the investor who bought blue-chip stocks; gold and uranium ventures would, on the average, provide higher investment returns than either food-processing or utility companies; and common stock investors who bought in at the top of the market when the risks were greatest would, on the average, do better than those who dollar-averaged. Similarly, the horseplayer who always placed bets on the long shots at the track would, on the average, be better off than someone who went with the odds-on favorites.

Reflection on such examples raises serious questions about the logic of the risk-reward proposition. As Dr. Morton pointed out in an earlier study of risk, if investors always get what they expect, then all risk and uncertainty would go out the window.[10] If the risk-reward proposition had any practical validity, investment funds would pour increasingly into low-grade, high-risk securities; and relatively few investors would buy high-grade, low-risk securities unless the law and other constraints required them to hold specific amounts of such securities. Such a shift in the flow of investment funds would tend to raise the price of low-grade, high-risk securities relative to high-grade, low-risk investments. In this eventuality, the logic of the risk-reward theory would lead one to believe that such a bidding up of the price of high-risk securities would offer subsequent buyers of such securities the prospect of realizing even greater profits because of the concomitant increase in risk.

However, the fact that maturity yields on Baa-rated and other lower-grade corporate bonds continue to average significantly higher than those on AAA-rated bonds suggests that most bond investors have a practical concern about risk and uncertainty in the future and are not persuaded that the way to make greater profits is to take greater risks. The daily listings of 20 to 1 and 40 to 1 long shots on the pari-mutuel boards at racetracks across the country also suggest that horse-players see no practical merit in the proposition that betting on the long shots always pays.

Furthermore, relatively few corporate executives would be persuaded that an increase in the risks confronting their respective companies, as posed, for example, by the entry of new competitors into their established markets, relaxation of import controls, removal of tax incentives, or more vigorous antitrust enforcement, would result in higher dollar earnings and returns on capital. A total repeal of oil import quotas would increase the risks confronting domestic oil producers, as would a reduction in the depletion allowance and related oil industry tax incentives. The fact that such measures are strongly opposed by oil companies suggests that the managements of these companies see no merit in the argument that an increase in risks opens the door to increased profitability.

In fact, a significant amount of the strategic long-range planning effort of many business firms is geared toward reducing risks. Notable examples of this risk minimization effort include horizontal and vertical mergers, to the extent possible under the antitrust laws, in order to achieve greater economies of scale in operations and to protect markets and sources of supply; diversification moves, involving the acquisition of firms in unrelated industries, to offset seasonal and cyclical characteristics of their own operations and to obtain new product know-how and complementary management skills; management development and training programs to improve management competence and depth; and research and development programs to improve existing products and thereby maintain market position and to assure a continuing flow of new products that will support an expansion of sales volume and earnings.

Summary and Conclusion

The foregoing discussion should not be construed as an endorsement of the reciprocal of the risk-reward proposition: that investors will, on the average, earn high profits by taking smaller risks. The primary purpose of this discussion has been to emphasize the serious limitations of the empirical evidence cited in support of the theory and the logical inconsistencies of the theory itself. In view of

---

[10]Walter A. Morton, "Risk and Return: Instability of Earnings as a Measure of Risk," *Land Economics,* May 1969, pp. 230–231.

these limitations, the notion that investors can, on the average, realize higher profits by taking greater risks can have no practical validity in investment decision making. As it now stands, the risk-reward proposition should be viewed as a rather simple, arbitrary, academically inspired concept of what investing is all about. Rational investors, therefore, need not be confronted with a Hobson's-choice dilemma in deciding when and how to make the trade-off between risk and financial security. Their investment decisions should be based on a careful consideration of their current and prospective cash needs and the strategic factors that may affect the prospective effective returns on each of the many investment alternatives available to them. This decision-making process is what investing is all about.

Chapter 5
Investing in an Inflationary Environment

Experience confirms the fact that overcoming inflation is much easier said than done. There is no sure method that can be readily used by large numbers of investors. Even if such a method existed, making it public would typically push up the price of the recommended asset to such high levels that the inflation protection provided to most investors would be small or nonexistent. We would have still another example of the boomerang effects of too widely available knowledge.

Thus, successful asset management to overcome inflation is a complicated business. It involves selecting the right asset at the right price at the right time, using the right degree of leverage, to achieve the right aftertax return.

What is the right return? Ideally, to be a complete and fully statisfactory inflation hedge, an investment must earn during its holding period (1) the prevailing risk-free rate of return on Treasury bills or AAA bonds, plus (2) a business risk premium, plus (3) a financial risk premium, plus (4) the prevailing or projected percentage rate of inflation. Moreover, it should achieve these earnings after all applicable income and capital gain taxes. Clearly, to achieve this rigorous ideal one has to be exceedingly lucky or have considerable knowledge of alternative investment assets, and also be expert in investment timing, in the proper use of leverage, and in the optimum exploitation of all available tax benefits and shelters.

Accordingly, almost all the pages of the *Handbook* can contribute to the difficult task of overcoming inflation. Just buying and holding common stocks alone is a very poor answer, as Professor Reilly amply demonstrates in Part 1 of this chapter. But certainly above-average *timing* in the purchase and sale of common stocks (see Section Two) can provide satisfactory inflation protection. And if superior *industry selection* (see Section Three) is added to superior overall timing, the results will be even better.

In practice rather than in theory, however, it is probably necessary to settle for somewhat less rigorous standards of inflation protection than the ideal set forth above. Thus, many investors would be satisfied if their aftertax return on an investment more than kept pace with the rate of inflation, without any of the enumerated premiums. Still others would be content with a *pretax* return that matched or topped the inflation rate. And, for some investors, it may be necessary to settle for a *partial inflation hedge* that is somewhat superior to other partial inflation hedges, such as high but safe short-term money market instruments or funds, if that is the best they can do. Thus, all investors should aim at realistic inflation protection targets in terms of their capabilities, while perhaps also supporting, if not participating in, political efforts to curb the major world economic illness of the 1970s: inflation.

Part 1. Common Stocks as an Inflation Hedge

FRANK K. REILLY

Probably one of the best-preserved bits of folklore on Wall Street is that the purchase of common stocks is a good way to hedge against the effects of inflation. This part of Chapter 5 examines the belief in detail, beginning with a general definition of inflation and an examination of inflation in the United States since 1937. Subsequently, a definition of an inflation hedge and a consideration of what common stocks must do to hedge against inflation are presented. A discussion of the generally accepted folklore of common stocks as good hedges against inflation follows. Some possible problems with common stocks as inflation hedges are then considered. Finally, the results of empirical studies on the subject of common stocks as inflation hedges during periods of substantial inflation are analyzed.

INFLATION DEFINED AND DESCRIBED

Inflation is defined as *an increase in the general price level*. The series used to measure the price level, which is a matter of some controversy, is discussed in the following subsection. Inflation can also be defined as *a decrease in the value of the dollar*. Obviously, the two definitions are equivalent: if there is an increase in the general price level, a given number of dollars cannot buy as much in terms of goods and services as it could prior to the rise in prices. Therefore, the dollars (or other currency) have less value in terms of general purchasing power.

When discussing inflation, one typically talks about the *rate* of inflation. This is so because it is not very meaningful to talk about a 5-cent increase in a price or a 1-point increase in a price index. What is important is the *percentage change in prices* (that is, the 5-cent increase on a $1 item would be discussed as a 5 percent increase in price). The use of percentages makes price changes comparable for different items. Another practice is to annualize percentage changes. A change of 1 percent for one month in a price level series is considered a 12 percent annual rate of change in the price level—a 12 percent rate of inflation during the one-month period.

Inflation in the United States since 1937

In measuring the annual percentage changes in prices, there are several price series to choose from: the Consumer Price Index (CPI), the Wholesale Price Index (WPI), and the GNP Implicit Price Deflator. In the analysis of common stocks as inflation hedges for individual investors, the CPI was selected as the appropriate price index series because it reflects the inflationary forces facing the consumer; that is, it contains prices for goods consumed in the "typical household." In contrast, the WPI is concerned only with wholesale prices that are not available and items not of interest to the consumer. The GNP Deflator is intended to measure price changes in all goods and services produced in the economy and likewise contains many items not relevant to the consumer.

Several observations may be drawn from the figures in Table 5-1. First, from 1937 to 1974 there were *only four years when the price level declined* on a year-to-year

TABLE 5-1   Annual Percentage Change in Consumer Price Index, December to December, 1937–1974 (All Items)

(1967 = 100)

Year	Percent	Year	Percent	Year	Percent
1937	3.1	1952	0.9	1967	3.1
1938	(2.8)*	1953	0.6	1968	4.7
1939	(0.4)	1954	(0.4)	1969	6.1
1940	1.0	1955	0.3	1970	5.5
1941	9.8	1956	2.9	1971	3.4
1942	9.1	1957	3.0	1972	3.4
1943	3.2	1958	1.7	1973	8.8
1944	2.1	1959	1.5	1974	12.2
1945	2.3	1960	1.6		
1946	18.1	1961	0.6		
1947	9.1	1962	1.2		
1948	2.7	1963	1.7		
1949	(1.9)	1964	1.1		
1950	5.8	1965	2.0		
1951	5.9	1966	3.3		

*Parentheses indicate negative numbers.
SOURCE: U.S. Department of Labor, Bureau of Labor Statistics.

basis. Obviously, there is a general tendency for consumer prices in the United States to increase at various rates of growth. Most economists and consumers probably do not become overly concerned with a 1 or 2 percent rate of increase, but they do become concerned when the rate reaches or exceeds 3 percent. In this regard, the United States experience was a relatively low but increasing rate of growth in the CPI during the period from 1961 to 1964 followed by larger increases during the period 1965–1967, further increases to fairly high rates of inflation during 1968–1970, a slowdown in the rate of increase during 1971 and 1972 attributable to price controls, and finally, an explosion in prices in 1973 after the relaxation or lifting of most price controls.

Therefore, there seems to be a tendency of generally rising prices, including occasional periods of high rates of increase. During the last several years, the rate of price increase has been high, and it showed no tendency to decline even during the recession from November 1969 to November 1970. It appears that investors will probably have to learn to live with, and protect themselves from, a fairly regular, relatively high rate of inflation during the coming decades.

INFLATION HEDGES

A hedge is a transaction intended to safeguard an individual against a loss on another investment. A hedge against inflation, then, would be the acquisition of an asset that would safeguard the investor against an increase in the general price level. Specifically, an inflation hedge is *an asset that generates a return at least equal to the increase in the general price level.* For example, a work of art that increased in value by 4 percent during a period when the general price level increased by 4 percent would be considered an inflation hedge.

Common Stocks as Inflation Hedges

The traditional definition of an inflation hedge presented here is incomplete when applied to common stocks because it overlooks the *normal* required rate of return on an investment in common stocks regardless of the current rate of inflation. Even on the assumption that there is no inflation, investors will require some rate of return on their common stock. This normal required rate of return should compensate investors for the time period in which funds are committed and for the risk involved. The return required to compensate investors for the time period involved is the risk-free rate of return, also referred to as the pure-time value of money. In addition, common stock investors require a risk premium.

During noninflationary periods, the principal risk is the uncertainty of future operating cash flows. This uncertainty is a function of the business of the firm and is generally referred to as "business risk." In addition, if the firm has fixed obligations, common stock investors will require an increased rate of return because of the additional uncertainty of the earnings available to the common stock because of these prior debt claims. This latter uncertainty is thought of as "financial risk." Therefore, in an inflation-free world the required rate of return on common stocks is determined by the economy's prevailing risk-free rate, plus a business risk premium and a financial risk premium.[1]

When investors expect a given percentage increase in the general price level, they must consider a potential investment's "real" rate of return in comparison to their required rate of return. The real rate of return is the current-dollar, or nominal, rate of return on an investment adjusted for the current rate of inflation. The important point is that the normal required rate does *not* take inflation into account; the normal rate is an inflation-free rate of return. Therefore, for a stock to be a complete inflation hedge, *its real rate of return must be greater than its normal required rate of return.* This can be presented as follows:

$$r' \geq k$$

where r' = real rate of return. The real rate of return is the nominal rate of return during a period r, adjusted for the rate of inflation g during the period. Specifically,

$$r' = \frac{1 + \text{nominal rate of return}}{1 + \text{rate of inflation}} - 1$$

$$r' = \frac{1 + r}{1 + g} - 1$$

k = normal rate of return for the risk class of stock, assuming a zero rate of inflation.

Assume, for example, that investors in common stock have a normal required return of 8 percent ($k = 0.08$). Assume further that the general price level is increasing at 4 percent ($g = 0.04$) and that the nominal return from common stocks is 10 percent ($r = 0.10$). Under these conditions the real rate of return is 5.8 percent:

$$r' = \frac{1.10}{1.04} - 1 = .058$$

---

[1]For a more detailed discussion of this point, see James C. Van Horne, *Financial Management and Policy*, 3d ed., Prentice-Hall, Inc., Englewood Cliffs, N.J., 1971.

When the real rate of return (.058) is below the normal required rate of return (0.08), common stocks are *not* a complete inflation hedge during the period. In contrast, if the nominal return had been 14 percent, the real return would have been 9.6 percent. When this real rate of return is compared with the 8 percent normal required rate, it is seen that common stocks would have been a complete inflation hedge.

THE FOLKLORE OF COMMON STOCKS AS INFLATION HEDGES

The belief that the ownership of common stock is a good way to hedge against inflation is pervasive on Wall Street and elsewhere. The initial concept probably stems from the possibilities in stocks compared with alternatives available in the capital markets: fixed-income securities such as debentures and preferred stocks. In these cases, because the return is fixed by the instrument, the price of the security must be adjusted so that the *realized* rate of return will be acceptable during the period of inflation; that is, the price declines until the promised yield compensates for the expected inflation.

In contrast, returns on common stock are best described as a residual because the common stockholders are the owners of the company. Their returns, by definition, are highly variable. During a period of prosperity, returns to common stockholders will increase substantially, while during a period of generally depressed earnings returns to the residual common stock owners will be substantially reduced and could become negative. This potential variability is the key to the reason why common stocks are expected to be inflation hedges. With the variability of returns, the *potential* for an increase in returns is available, which is not true of the fixed-income securities mentioned above.

Given the potential for higher returns on common stock during periods of inflation, the next questions are: Why do investors believe that inflation should cause such an increase? Why should business firms gain from inflation?

Potential Reasons for Gains from Inflation

There are three generally espoused reasons why business firms might experience an increase in earnings during periods of inflation. The first is the net debtor position of business firms. It is recognized that during a period of *unanticipated* inflation individuals and companies that assume debt positions gain at the expense of their creditors because the required rate of return on the debt does not include the future rate of inflation. As an example, creditors normally requiring a 5 percent rate of interest on a loan during a period of stable prices would increase their required rate of interest to approximately 9 percent to compensate for the loss of purchasing power if they anticipated a 4 percent rate of inflation during the period of the loan. At the same time, borrowers would not object to the higher rate since they would likely expect to receive a higher rate of return on the intended investment. Obviously, if the inflation is not anticipated, lenders do not increase their required rate of interest on loans and borrowers gain at the expense of lenders because they receive the higher return on their investments yet pay only the preinflation rate. Borrowers pay off loans in dollars of lower purchasing power. In addition to the liabilities of a business firm, one should consider the firm's monetary assets (cash and accounts receivable) because the firm will naturally lose on these assets in terms of purchasing power. Therefore, during a period of inflation the firm wants more monetary liabilities on which it gains relative to monetary assets on which it loses; that is, it wants a *net debtor position* because firms that are net debtors should experience increased earnings during periods of unanticipated inflation.

The second reason why business firms may gain during periods of inflation is the possible existence of a wage-price lag. It is hypothesized that prices adjust rapidly to inflation but that wage rates are slow to adjust because of long-term wage contracts or a lack of information. In any case, if wage increases lag behind price increases, during a period of inflation real wages will decline, and business firms will experience increased earnings growth at the expense of their labor; that is, wealth will be transferred from wage earners to the business firms. There should be an increase in the firms' profit margins during the period of inflation as the prices of their products increase but wage costs remain constant.

The final possible reason for gains by business firms during inflation is that companies carry inventories or own resources that were acquired at preinflation prices. These assets are subsequently sold at inflated prices. While these gains from the sale of assets acquired before inflation may be considered the result of historical cost accounting rules, the fact remains that during the period of inflation while these resources last, business firms will experience an increase in their profit margins and increases in the rate of growth of reported earnings.

Apparently, those who espouse common stocks as inflation hedges feel that one or several of these conditions exist in corporations. They therefore expect an overall increase in returns to the companies and their stockholders during the period of inflation that will increase the wealth of the stockholders enough to offset the negative effects of inflation.

POTENTIAL PROBLEMS WITH COMMON STOCKS AS INFLATION HEDGES

Although there is a potential for corporate gains, two factors must be considered before one can expect these gains to benefit the stockholders.

Increase in Required Returns

First, investors increase their required return on investments because of the inflation. This means that the company must experience the increase in earnings; otherwise stock prices would decline similarly to bond prices. Put more simply, if companies increase their rate of earnings growth by the rate of inflation and the required rate of return increases by the same rate, there will be no change in the current price and the subsequent return on the stock will compensate for the inflation.

Existence of Corporate Gains

While there are three reasons explaining a firm's gains from inflation, there is a major question whether these conditions do in fact lead to gains and also whether they consistently exist for most companies so that firms in general will experience the required increase in growth.

Evidence on the Net Debtor Hypothesis. Several studies have considered the benefits of a net debtor position to a corporation and its stockholders. The first rigorous test was conducted by Prof. Reuben Kessel, who analyzed the shares of banks and industrial firms during periods of significant inflation and significant deflation.[2] The results confirmed the hypothesis, since the stock prices of the net debtor firms increased during inflation while the stocks of creditor firms declined in value. During deflation, the opposite occurred: the creditor stocks rose in value while the real value of the debtor stocks declined.

Subsequent to the Kessel study, a similar study by De Alessi employed more

[2]Reuben A. Kessel, "Inflation-caused Wealth Redistribution: A Test of a Hypothesis," *American Economic Review,* vol. 46, no. 1, pp. 128–141, March 1956.

extensive tests and data for the United Kingdom for the period from December 1948 through December 1957.[3] Although the results differed with the sample and the definitions used for wealth and a firm's monetary position, the general trend of the test results was quite consistent in supporting the hypothesis during the years of significant inflation, 1949–1952 and 1956–1957.

The studies by Kessel and De Alessi provided consistent support for the net debtor hypothesis in the United States and the United Kingdom. It is important to recall that, for business firms in general to gain from inflation under the net debtor hypothesis, (1) the inflation must be unanticipated, and (2) business firms in general must be net debtors. The latter point is emphasized by De Alessi in an article discussing the proportion of net debtors in the United States and United Kingdom economies.[4] The initial evidence for the United States was taken from an unpublished study by Alchian and Kessel for the period from 1915 to 1952. The figures indicated that the overall percentage of net debtor firms generally declined over the test period from 94 percent in 1915 to 55 percent in 1934, and varied thereafter, but that it generally hovered around the 55 percent figure into the 1950s. A subsequent study by Broussalian confirmed the latter results for the period 1948–1956.[5] Broussalian found that the percentage of net debtor firms varied from 42 to 57 percent but generally remained quite close to 50 percent. Also, what was true for individual firms was true for the balance sheets of all firms combined: the aggregate balance sheets were either slightly net creditor or barely net debtor.

These results indicate that even if inflation is not anticipated and even though the net debtor hypothesis is true for net debtor firms, it is questionable whether one should expect United States firms in general to gain from inflation, because *only about half of United States firms are net debtors.* Therefore, given the requirement that firms be net debtors, one would expect about half of United States firms to gain from inflation and about half to lose, and in general there would be no strong tendency for consistent gains from this source.

Evidence Regarding the Wage Lag Hypothesis.   Recall that the wage lag hypothesis contends that during periods of inflation product and service prices will rise in line with the general price rise but that wage rates will be slow to adjust because of a lack of information or the existence of long-term wage contracts. As a result, real wages decline during inflation, and business firms enjoy an increase in profit margins and earnings.

An extensive review of past evidence regarding this hypothesis and an analysis of new evidence on the subject were provided by Kessel and Alchian.[6] They contended that prior studies found a decline in real wages without ever considering other factors that could have caused the decline. Other arguments against the prior results that indicated a wage lag were concerned mainly with the specific data employed (were the data adequate or complete?), the interpretation given to the results (the results in some cases could also have been caused by other events), or the fact that other coincident events were not considered. Also, in several instances the results were heavily biased by the starting point or ending point of the examination.

[3]Louis De Alessi, "The Redistribution of Wealth by Inflation: An Empirical Test with United Kingdom Data," *The Southern Economic Journal,* vol. 30, no. 4, pp. 113–127, October 1963.

[4]Louis De Alessi, "Do Business Firms Gain from Inflation?" *The Journal of Business,* vol. 37, no. 2, pp. 162–166, April 1964.

[5]J. V. Broussalian, "Unanticipated Inflation: A Test of the Debtor-Creditor Hypothesis," unpublished Ph.D. dissertation, University of California, Los Angeles, 1961.

[6]Reuben A. Kessel and Armen A. Alchian, "The Meaning and Validity of the Inflation-induced Lag of Wages behind Prices," *American Economic Review,* vol. 50, no. 1, pp. 43–66, March 1960.

The wage lag hypothesis was tested by examining the relationship between annual wage bills and stock price changes during the total period 1939–1952. It was contended that the hypothesis implied a positive relationship between the variables. An examination of 113 firms using rank correlation indicated a *negative* relationship: a lower wage equity ratio was correlated with higher equity increases. Further tests likewise failed to support the hypothesis, which led the authors to conclude that the hypothesis was really untested and definitely could not be accepted as a certainty.

A study by Thomas Cargill attempted to test the wage lag hypothesis. By examining numerous wage and price series with spectral analysis, the study determined whether there was a consistent lead-lag relationship.[7] The data used were yearly time series during the periods 1791–1932, 1820–1965, and 1860–1965. The overall results for the United States and England indicated a moderate association in the long run but one that was reduced in short-run analysis. For the United States, the results basically indicated a mixture of leads, lags, and no differences in the wage and price series; overall, no consistent relationship manifested itself. The results for England were likewise divided. For long-run frequencies, a wage lag was manifested, but there was no lag in the short-run frequency tests. On the basis of his results, Cargill likewise argued against the uncritical acceptance of the wage lag hypothesis.

Two points should be made regarding the tests and conclusions by Kessel and Alchian and by Cargill. First, the wage lag hypothesis is concerned with the wage-price relationship during sudden, unanticipated periods of significant inflation. Therefore, it is not apparent that the analysis should cover extremely long time intervals encompassing periods of inflation, deflation, and price stability which would cloud the relationship that might exist during periods of inflation. Second, any wage lag that might exist during an inflation is probably a rather short-run phenomenon. While wages may not initially react to price changes, once the inflation has been under way for about a year, one would expect labor to require compensation for the inflation and also to ensure that future inflation would be offset in wage contracts. As a result, one would expect the wage lag to be evident only during the brief initial phase of inflation.

Some recent evidence that took these latter points into consideration was presented by the author.[8] Specifically, hourly earnings and prices for the period 1947–1972 were analyzed on an annual basis with particular attention to the pattern of changes during periods of significant inflation. The analysis of peaks and troughs in the two series indicated that *the price series either turned ahead of the wage series or was coincident with the wage series with one exception.* Beyond the initial turning points, the two series were generally consistent, which led the author to conclude that there was a tendency for prices to turn ahead of wages but that the wage lag was short-lived. This would mean that any benefit from a wage lag would be of a short-run nature.

EMPIRICAL EVIDENCE REGARDING COMMON STOCKS AS INFLATION HEDGES

Prior subsections of this part have considered the requirements for a common stock to qualify as an inflation hedge and the arguments for and against such an expectation. This section is concerned with a discussion of some prior empirical

[7] Thomas F. Cargill, "An Empirical Investigation of the Wage-Lag Hypothesis," *American Economic Review,* vol. 59, no. 5, pp. 806–816, December 1969.

[8] Frank K. Reilly, "A Theoretical and Empirical Analysis of Companies and Common Stocks as Inflation Hedges," Western Finance Association meeting, Claremont, Calif., August 1973.

work regarding common stocks as inflation hedges and the problems with the prior analysis. Then recent results for the aggregate stock market (before and after taxes) and results for individual stocks are presented.

Prior Studies of Common Stocks as Inflation Hedges

Prior studies analyzing common stocks as inflation hedges suffered from two major problems. First, they examined long time periods that included periods of significant inflation but also contained periods of stable prices and even periods of price deflation. Such a mixture of time periods makes it impossible to say what happened to investors during the periods of inflation. It is entirely possible, and quite probable, that the average returns during these long periods were dominated by the experience during the periods of price stability or price deflation. Specifically, it is likely that the returns during periods of price stability were high enough to more than offset possible low returns during periods of inflation. It is preferable to isolate periods of significant inflation and examine specifically what transpired during these particular periods. The key point is that it is precisely during periods of significant inflation that it is important to determine whether stocks are an inflation hedge; during periods of price stability it is irrelevant whether they are hedges.

The second problem with prior studies has been the tendency to ignore the normal required return on common stocks without inflation. As discussed above, investors require the rate of return on common stocks to compensate them for the time value of money (the risk-free rate of return) and also for the business and financial risks involved in common stocks. This combination of returns is the normal inflation-free required return. For common stock to be an inflation hedge, therefore, the return on the stock must increase by the rate of inflation: the required rate of return during the period of inflation must be the normal required rate plus the rate of inflation. In most of the prior analysis of common stocks as inflation hedges, the comparison generally ignored the normal return and simply compared the rate of inflation to the rate of return on stocks. In these comparisons, if the return on common stocks was greater than the rate of inflation, it was contended that common stocks were a hedge against inflation. (This approach will henceforth be referred to as the traditional inflation theory.)[9]

Recent Studies of Common Stocks as Inflation Hedges

During the past few years, several studies by the author and Professors Johnson and Smith on the subject of common stocks as inflation hedges have corrected the deficiencies of prior studies. The specific steps used in these studies were as follows:

    1. Specify periods of deflation, relative noninflation, and significant inflation.

    2. Determine the nominal rate of return on common stocks during the periods of inflation.

    3. Compute the real rates of return during the periods of inflation.

    4. Compare the real rates of return with alternative normal required rates of return.

    5. If the real rates of return were equal to or greater than the investors' normal required rate of return, stocks were a complete inflation hedge. Alternatively, if the real rates of return were less than the normal required rate for investors in common stock, stocks were not a complete inflation hedge.

---

[9]For a discussion of some of these prior studies, see Glenn L. Johnson, "A Critical Analysis of Common Stocks as Inflation Hedges," *Mississippi Valley Journal of Business and Economics*, vol. 3, no. 3, pp. 50–62, Spring, 1968.

Following a comparison of real rates and a number of alternative normal required rates, several market-specified normal rates were considered.

Designation of Periods of Inflation.   It was somewhat surprising to find that, given the extensive discussion of inflation, there is no generally recognized tabulation of periods of "significant" inflation. It was therefore necessary to examine an

TABLE 5-2   Designation of Periods as Inflation, Relative Noninflation, or Deflation in the United States, 1937–1974

Beginning date	CPI (1967 = 100)	Annual compound rate of change (percent)	Type of period	Length of period (months)
Sept. 30, 1937	43.8			
		−0.9	Deflation	42
Mar. 31, 1941	42.4			
		9.8	Severe inflation	27
June 30, 1943	52.4			
		1.6	Relative noninflation	33
Mar. 31, 1946	54.7			
		12.5	Severe inflation	30
Sept. 30, 1948	73.4			
		−2.7	Deflation	18
Mar. 30, 1950	70.3			
		7.0	Severe inflation	21
Dec. 31, 1951	79.3			
		0.3	Relative noninflation	51
Mar. 30, 1956	80.4			
		3.7	Moderate inflation	24
Mar. 30, 1958	86.4			
		1.3	Relative noninflation	93
Dec. 31, 1965	95.4			
		5.6	Severe inflation	108
Dec. 31, 1974	155.4			
Periods of moderate or severe inflation				210
Periods of relative noninflation				177
Periods of deflation				60
Total number of months				447

SOURCE: U.S. Department of Labor, Bureau of Labor Statistics.

appropriate price index and attempt to specify periods of inflation and relative noninflation.

The Consumer Price Index was selected as the appropriate price index series, in contrast to either the Wholesale Price Index or the GNP Implicit Price Deflator, for the reasons discussed in the introduction to Chapter 5. Inflationary periods were determined by examining quarterly percentage changes for the CPI series. Because dividend payments for the stock price indicator series are reported quarterly, all inflationary periods were dated March, June, September, or December, Table 5-2 contains the chronicle of periods as indicated by this examination and the rates of change for each period since 1937.

Common Stock Price Indicators Examined.   To examine a large cross section of the market, the test outlined was applied to the following stock price indicators:

- Standard & Poor's 425 Industrials
- Standard & Poor's Utilities
- Standard & Poor's Rails
- Standard & Poor's 500-Stock Composite
- Dow Jones Industrial Average

Determination of Rates of Return.   The nominal, or current-dollar, rate of return on a market indicator series for a period r was determined by finding the rate of discount that made all cash flows (including the dividends) equal to zero. Put another way, it was the rate of discount that made the present value of all dividends received and the ending price for the indicator series (the inflows) equal to the beginning price for the indicator series (the outflow).[10] Thus, the technique used included both dividends and price appreciation in determining the rate of return.

To arrive at the real rate of return r', the nominal rate of return r was discounted by the rate of general price increase g:

$$r' = \frac{1 + r}{1 + g} - 1$$

Specification of Normal Rates of Return.   Because the normal required return on any stock is very subjective, it is impossible to specify any one rate of return as normal and expect to receive universal agreement. In theory, of course, a good estimate of a stock's normal required rate of return could be the nominal return received by investors during some period of relative noninflation. Rather than attempt to specify any one rate or several rates as possible candidates for the normal rate, the real rates computed were compared initially with several possible normal required rates from 1 to 10 percent.

Net Rates of Return.   Given real rates of return during each period of inflation and alternative normal rates of return, the *net return is the real rate of return minus the normal rate of return.* If the net return as defined is positive, the stocks examined were a complete inflation hedge during that period. As an example, if the computed real return during some period of inflation was 6 percent and a normal required return of 5 percent is assumed, the net return would be 1 percent and would indicate that stocks were a complete inflation hedge during that period. On the other hand, if the real return was 6 percent and a normal required return of 8 percent is assumed, the net return would be − 2 percent and would indicate that common stocks were not a complete inflation hedge during the period.

Aggregate Market, Pretax Study

The first of several studies by Reilly, Johnson, and Smith extended from 1937 through 1968. Stocks were initially analyzed in terms of the traditional hedge theory, which holds that a stock will be an inflation hedge if the nominal rate of return is equal to or greater than the rate of inflation.[11] Thus, the traditional concept requires only that the real rate of return be equal to or greater than zero and does not require any normal required return.

[10]In solving the equations an algorithm developed by Lawrence Fisher and revised by Seymour Kaplan was used: Lawrence Fisher, "An Algorithm for Finding Exact Rates of Return," *The Journal of Business,* vol. 39, no. 1, pp. 111–118, January Supplement, 1966; Seymour Kaplan, "Computer Algorithm for Finding Exact Rates of Return," *The Journal of Business,* vol. 40, no. 4, pp. 389–392, October 1967.

[11]Frank K. Reilly, Glenn L. Johnson, and Ralph E. Smith, "Inflation, Inflation Hedges, and Common Stock," *Financial Analysts Journal,* vol. 26, no. 1, pp. 104–110, January–February 1970.

To arrive at a composite view of the results during these five periods of inflation, a weighted average of the real rates of return for the five periods was computed. The weights were the time periods in months. Table 5-3 contains updated nominal and real rates of return for the alternative indicator series for all the periods of significant inflation from 1937 through 1973 and the weighted-average results.

TABLE 5-3   Market Indicators as Inflation Hedges, Assuming Market-specified Normal Rates of Return, September 1937–December 1973

Market indicators	Nominal return (r)	Real return (r')	Net return $(r' - 8.2$ percent$)$	Estimated normal returns (k)	Net returns $(r' - k)$
	I MAR. 31, 1941–JUNE 30, 1943				
DJ Industrials	12.8	2.7	−5.5	7.4	−4.7
S&P 425 Industrials	17.6	7.1	−1.1	8.2	−1.1
S&P Utilities	6.5	−3.1	−11.3	6.0	−9.1
S&P Rails	21.3	10.5	2.3	8.0	2.5
S&P 500 Stocks	16.6	6.2	−2.0	7.9	−1.7
	II MAR. 31, 1946–SEPT. 30, 1948				
DJ Industrials	0.2	−11.0	−19.2	7.4	−18.4
S&P 425 Industrials	−0.7	−11.7	−19.9	8.2	−19.9
S&P Utilities	−5.8	−16.3	−24.5	6.0	−22.3
S&P Rails	−6.0	−16.4	−24.6	8.0	−24.4
S&P 500 Stocks	−1.5	−12.5	−20.7	7.9	−20.4
	III MAR. 31, 1950–OCT. 31, 1951				
DJ Industrials	24.9	16.9	8.7	7.4	9.5
S&P 425 Industrials	31.5	23.1	14.9	8.2	14.9
S&P Utilities	8.5	1.5	−6.7	6.0	−4.5
S&P Rails	30.1	21.8	13.6	8.0	13.8
S&P 500 Stocks	28.4	20.2	12.0	7.9	12.3
	IV MAR. 31, 1956–MAR. 31, 1958				
DJ Industrials	−2.1	−5.6	−13.8	7.4	−13.0
S&P 425 Industrials	−6.2	−9.5	−17.7	8.2	−17.7
S&P Utilities	7.2	3.4	−4.8	6.0	−2.6
S&P Rails	−16.0	−19.0	−27.2	8.0	−27.0
S&P 500 Stocks	−3.1	−6.5	−14.7	7.9	−14.4
	V MAR. 31, 1965–DEC. 31, 1973				
DJ Industrials	1.9	−2.8	−11.0	7.4	−10.2
S&P 425 Industrials	4.4	−0.4	−8.6	8.2	−8.6
S&P Utilities	−0.8	−5.3	−13.5	6.0	−11.3
S&P Rails	2.9	−1.8	−10.0	8.0	−9.8
S&P 500 Stocks	4.0	−0.8	−9.0	7.9	−8.7
	WEIGHTED AVERAGE*				
DJ Industrials	5.1	−1.6	−9.8	7.4	−9.0
S&P 425 Industrials	7.0	0.3	−7.9	8.2	−7.9
S&P Utilities	1.4	−4.9	−13.1	6.0	−10.9
S&P Rails	4.7	−1.9	−10.1	8.0	−9.9
S&P 500 Stocks	6.6	−0.1	−8.3	7.9	−8.0

*Weights equal to number of months in each inflationary period.
SOURCE: Updated results from Frank K. Reilly, Glenn L. Johnson, and Ralph E. Smith, "Inflation, Inflation Hedges and Common Stock," *Financial Analysts Journal*, vol. 26, no. 1, pp. 104–110, January–February 1970.

Analysis of Traditional Theory.   The results by period were mixed. Common stocks were generally traditional inflation hedges (that is, real returns were above zero) during the 1941–1943 period; they definitely were not hedges during the 1946–1948 period; all classes of stocks were traditional hedges during the 1950–1951 period; and, with one exception, stocks have not been traditional inflation hedges during the latest two periods of significant inflation. Therefore, during the majority of the individual periods common stocks have not been traditional inflation hedges. The composite weighted-average results were consistent with the individual period results, since they indicated that only the industrial stocks, as represented by the S&P 425, had a tendency to be hedges. Utility stocks showed the worst result (as expected because of heavy price regulation), and railroad stocks also had negative real returns.

It was subsequently assumed that investors have some required return on stocks during periods of noninflation and, therefore, that the real return must exceed this normal required return before the stock can be considered a complete inflation hedge. Because the normal return is a subjective matter for each investor, several alternative market rates of return were considered normal.

Alternative Suggested Normal Rates of Return.   Specifically, one good estimate of the market's *required* normal rate of return might be the market's *realized* rate of return during some extended period of time.[12]

The first realized rate of return considered was the nominal rate of return for any and all stocks listed on the New York Stock Exchange for the period 1926–1960. This computation by Lawrence Fisher indicated that the median rate of return for all stocks listed on the NYSE for all possible holding periods was 9.8 percent.[13] When this estimated nominal rate of return was adjusted for the long-run inflation rate of 1.5 percent during this period, the result was an estimated normal return of 8.2 percent.

A more individualized estimate of the normal return was derived from the nominal return for each indicator series for the period 1937–1973. When these nominal rates were adjusted for the inflation rate of 3.3 percent, the following estimates of normal rates were generated:

Dow Jones Industrials	7.4
S&P 425 Industrials	8.2
S&P Utilities	6.0
S&P Rails	8.0
S&P 500 Stocks	7.9

The resulting net returns employing the estimated normal returns are quite consistent because the nominal returns were relatively consistent. The results can be summarized as follows:

1. In three of the five periods of inflation all the net returns were negative.

2. During one period of inflation (1941–1943) all but one indicator series had a negative return.

3. During one inflationary period (1950–1951) all but one indicator series had a positive net return.

4. The weighted-average net returns for *all* periods of inflation were rather *large negative values.*

On the assumption that past realized rates of return are reasonable estimates of normal required rates of return on common stocks, the results indicate that for the normal investor common stocks definitely were not complete inflation hedges.

Conclusion of Initial Study.   These results indicate that during the periods of inflation from 1937 through 1973 common stocks as a group were not consistent or complete inflation hedges. This does not mean that common stocks were never complete hedges or that there were no individual common stocks that were

---

[12]This is similar to the assumption made in Fred D. Arditti, "Risk and the Required Return on Equity," *Journal of Finance,* vol. 22, no. 1, pp. 19–36, March 1967.

[13]Lawrence Fisher, "Outcomes for 'Random' Investments in Common Stocks Listed on the New York Stock Exchange," *The Journal of Business,* vol. 38, no. 2, pp. 149–161, April 1965.

complete hedges. It does mean that blanket statements made about common stocks as inflation hedges cannot be accepted.

Aftertax Analysis

Following the initial study, some readers contended that income taxes should have been considered. Therefore, an aftertax analysis was carried out.[14] The test procedure was basically the same as in the initial study, except that the rates of return were determined after taxes. The rates of return were determined by finding the rates of discount that made the present value of all dividends received (after taxes) and the ending price for the indicator series (after adjustment for the tax on capital gains or capital losses) equal to the beginning price for the indicator series. The tax rates used were those determined by Jolivet, who found that the marginal personal tax rate of investors who received dividends during the period 1955–1965 was approximately 40 percent.[15] It was also assumed that investors typically had capital gains to offset capital losses incurred, which meant that there was a 40 percent tax rate on dividends and a 20 percent rate on net capital gains.

Results.   As expected, the aftertax nominal rates of return were consistently below the before-tax rates of return. Given lower nominal rates of return and similar rates of inflation during the recent periods, the real aftertax rates of return during the periods of inflation were likewise consistently below the before-tax real rates of return. Because of the tax treatment of capital losses (there is a tax offset for part of the loss), if the before-tax real rates of return were negative, they became larger negative values, but the changes were relatively small.

In general, the real aftertax rates of return, as well as the net returns adjusted for a normal return, confirmed the previous results. The traditional theory of inflation hedges requires only a real rate of return greater than zero. In the before-tax study, ten of the twenty-five real rates of return were positive, and one of the five weighted-average real rates was positive. In the aftertax study, only eight of the twenty-five real rates were positive, and none of the weighted-average real rates of return was positive.

Results with Market-determined Normal Rates of Return.   As before, recent actual rates of return were used as estimates of normal required rates of return. The first realized rate of return considered was the aftertax rate of return derived by Brigham and Pappas.[16] Employing the tax rate derived by Jolivet,[17] Brigham and Pappas found that between 1946 and 1965 the average aftertax rate of return earned on 658 common stocks was 9.8 percent. When adjusted for the 2.1 percent rate of inflation during the period, the 9.8 percent was equivalent to a real market-determined aftertax rate of return of 7.5 percent.

An individualized estimate of the aftertax normal return for each indicator series was derived from the nominal aftertax returns for each indicator series adjusted for the 3.1 percent rate of inflation during the period. The following estimates of normal aftertax rates of return were generated: DJIA, 4.3; S&P 425 Industrials, 5.1; S&P Utilities, 3.3; S&P Rails, 3.4; and S&P 500-Stock Composite, 4.9. Table 5-4 contains the real after-tax rates of return, the net returns assuming a 7.5 percent normal aftertax rate, and the net returns assuming each of the normal rates specified above.

[14]Frank K. Reilly, Glenn L. Johnson, and Ralph E. Smith, "A Note on Common Stocks as Inflation Hedges—the After Tax Case," *Southern Journal of Business,* vol. 7, no. 4, pp. 101–106, November 1972.

[15]Vincent Jolivet, "The Weighted Average Marginal Tax Rate on Dividends Received by Individuals in U.S.," *American Economic Review,* vol. 56, no. 3, pp. 473–477, June 1966.

[16]Eugene F. Brigham and James L. Pappas, "Rates of Return on Common Stock," *The Journal of Business,* vol. 42, no. 3, p. 308, July 1969.

[17]Jolivet, *op. cit.*

The net returns employing the 7.5 percent figure indicate that *almost all net returns were negative.* The only exceptions were the rail results during the 1941–1943 period and four of the five series results during 1950–1951. When the normal returns derived from each series were used, fifteen of twenty-five net returns were negative. Finally, *all* weighted-average net returns for all periods of

TABLE 5-4   Market Indicators as Inflation Hedges, Assuming Market-specified Normal Rates of Return, September 1937–December 1971

Market indicators	Aftertax nominal return (r)	Aftertax real return (r')	Net return: real return minus 7.5	Estimated normal returns (K)	Net returns: real returns minus estimated normal returns (r' − K)
I MAR. 31, 1941–JUNE 30, 1946					
DJIA	9.1	−0.6	−8.1	4.3	−4.9
S&P 425	12.9	2.8	−4.7	5.0	−2.2
S&P Utilities	3.8	−5.5	−13.0	3.4	−8.9
S&P Rails	15.5	5.1	−2.4	3.2	1.9
S&P 500	12.0	2.0	−5.5	4.8	−2.8
II MAR. 31, 1946–SEPT. 30, 1948					
DJIA	−0.8	−11.8	−19.3	4.3	−16.1
S&P 425	−1.4	−12.4	−19.9	5.0	−17.4
S&P Utilities	−5.4	−16.0	−23.5	3.4	−19.4
S&P Rails	−5.7	−16.2	−23.7	3.2	−19.4
S&P 500	−2.1	−13.0	−20.5	4.8	17.8
III MAR. 31, 1950–OCT. 31, 1951					
DJIA	18.3	10.7	3.2	4.3	6.4
S&P 425	23.6	15.7	8.2	5.0	10.7
S&P Utilities	5.6	−1.2	−8.7	3.4	−4.6
S&P Rails	22.6	14.7	7.2	3.2	11.5
S&P 500	21.2	13.4	5.9	4.8	8.6
IV MAR. 31, 1956–MAR. 31, 1958					
DJIA	−2.6	−6.0	−13.5	4.3	−10.3
S&P 425	−5.6	−9.0	−16.5	5.0	−14.0
S&P Utilities	4.8	1.1	−6.5	3.4	−2.3
S&P Rails	−13.5	−16.6	−24.1	3.2	−19.8
S&P 500	−3.2	−6.6	−14.1	4.8	−11.4
V DEC. 31, 1965–DEC. 31, 1971					
DJIA	0.9	−3.3	−10.8	4.3	−7.6
S&P 425	3.7	−0.6	−8.1	5.1	−5.7
S&P Utilities	−0.5	−4.6	−12.1	3.3	−7.9
S&P Rails	0.8	−3.4	−10.9	3.4	−6.8
S&P 500	3.3	−1.0	−8.5	4.9	5.9
WEIGHTED AVERAGE*					
DJIA	3.5	−3.0	−10.5	4.3	−7.3
S&P 425	5.4	−1.3	−8.8	5.1	−6.4
S&P Utilities	0.8	−5.5	−13.0	3.3	−8.8
S&P Rails	2.6	−3.9	−11.4	3.4	−7.3
S&P 500	5.0	−1.6	−9.1	4.9	−6.5

*Weights equal to number of months in each inflationary period.

inflation using any of the market-determined normal rates were *rather large negative values.*

In summary, these results definitely confirmed the prior results. Specifically, they indicated that during recent periods of significant inflation common stocks as a group, after taxes, were not consistent traditional inflation hedges and definitely were not complete inflation hedges.

Individual Common Stocks as Inflation Hedges

It was noted that common stocks as a group were not consistent or complete inflation hedges, but the results did not indicate that there were no individual common stocks that were complete or partial inflation hedges. Given the several reasons why companies may hedge against inflation (net debtor-creditor hypothesis, wage lag hypothesis, and the stock-of-assets hypothesis), one would expect that firms can differ markedly with respect to each of these variables. Therefore, the stocks of alternative firms can and possibly will differ in their ability to be inflation hedges.

To consider such a possibility for individual stocks, the thirty industrial stocks that comprise the Dow Jones Industrial Average (DJIA) were examined during the three inflationary periods, 1949–1951, 1955–1957, and 1965–1968.[18] As before, each stock was analyzed by assuming a zero required rate of return as well as a normal return of 8.2 percent, which was Fisher's 9.8 percent return adjusted for inflation.[19] Subsequent to the original study it was discovered that although the individual rates of return for the individual periods were correct, the weighted-average real returns contained a computational error. Therefore, in a later paper the error was corrected and the original results updated through December 31, 1973.[20] Hence, the ensuing discussion is concerned with results from both studies.

Individual Period Results.   During the 1949–1951 inflationary period, the stocks in the DJIA generally were effective inflation hedges. If a zero normal required rate of return is assumed (the traditional theory), twenty-six of the thirty industrial common stocks (87 percent) were inflation hedges. If an 8.2 percent normal required rate of return is assumed, twenty-two of the thirty common stocks (73 percent) were complete inflation hedges.

During the 1955–1957 inflationary period, the individual stocks in the DJIA were generally not effective inflation hedges. If a zero normal required rate of return is assumed, only ten of the thirty common stocks (33 percent) had positive real rates of return. More important, if an 8.2 percent normal required rate of return is assumed, only two of the thirty common stocks (7 percent) were complete inflation hedges.

If a zero normal required rate of return is assumed, only four of the stocks in the DJIA (13 percent) were inflation hedges during the 1965–1973 inflationary period. Finally, only one of the thirty common stocks (3 percent) was a complete inflation hedge if an 8.2 percent normal required rate of return is assumed.

If a zero normal required rate of return is assumed, only three common stocks (10 percent) had zero or positive real rates of return over all three inflationary periods. Those three companies that consistently qualified as inflation hedges under traditional investment theory were Eastman Kodak, Exxon, and Procter & Gamble. If an 8.2 percent normal required rate of return is assumed, *none* of the thirty industrial common stocks was a complete inflation hedge over all three inflationary periods.

Weighted-Average Results.   Similarly to the analysis of composite stock market series, the weighted-average real rates of return were computed for each stock, using months as the weights. Finally for each stock there were derived net returns equal to the weighted-average real return minus the 8.2 percent normal return used previously. The results for the thirty stocks are contained in Table 5-5.

[18]Glenn L. Johnson, Frank K. Reilly, and Ralph E. Smith, "Individual Common Stocks as Inflation Hedges," *Journal of Financial and Quantitative Analysis,* vol. 6, no. 3, pp. 1015–1024, June 1972.
[19]Fisher, "Outcomes for 'Random' Investments."
[20]Frank K. Reilly, Ralph E. Smith, and Glenn L. Johnson, "A Correction and Update Regarding Individual Common Stocks as Inflation Hedges," *Journal of Financial and Quantitative Analysis,* vol. 10, no. 5, December 1975.

The weighted-average results indicate that only eleven of the common stocks (37 percent) were traditional inflation hedges and only two (7 percent) were complete inflation hedges. Thus, the weighted-average results definitely supported the prior results that indicated that most common stocks have not been traditional inflation

TABLE 5-5 Weighted-Average Real Rates of Return and Net Returns on Individual Common Stocks during the Three Inflationary Periods: 1949–1951, 1955–1957, and 1965–1973*

Company	Weighted-average real return	Weighted-average real return minus 8.2 percent normal return
Allied Chemical	−0.60	−8.80
Aluminum Co. of America	−1.27	−9.47
American Brands†	−2.03	−10.23
American Can	−5.72	−13.92
A.T.&T.	−1.32	−9.52
Anaconda Co.	−0.72	−8.92
Bethlehem Steel	2.92	−5.28
Chrysler Corp.	−11.23	−19.43
Du Pont	−2.82	−11.02
Eastman Kodak	7.07	−1.13
Esmark Inc.‡	−4.38	−12.58
Exxon§	9.67	1.47
General Electric	2.87	−5.33
General Foods	−4.75	−12.95
General Motors	−3.03	−11.23
Goodyear	6.25	−1.95
International Harvester	−2.77	−10.97
International Nickel of Canada	1.85	−6.35
International Paper Co.	7.37	−0.83
Johns-Manville Corp.	−1.57	−9.77
Owens-Illinois	−5.20	−13.40
Proctor & Gamble	10.25	2.05
Sears, Roebuck	−0.70	−8.90
Standard Oil of California	3.58	−4.62
Texaco	4.28	−3.92
Union Carbide	−3.95	−12.15
United Aircraft	−7.08	−15.28
United States Steel	1.30	−6.90
Westinghouse Electric	−0.43	−8.63
Woolworth, F. W.	−7.12	−15.32

*Weights equal to months during period.
†Formerly American Tobacco.
‡Formerly Swift & Co.
§Formerly Standard Oil of New Jersey.

hedges and almost no stocks have been complete inflation hedges during total periods of inflation.

To summarize, the study results indicate that *the individual common stocks in the DJIA were not consistent inflation hedges.* If an 8.2 percent normal required rate of return is assumed, *none* of the common stocks was a complete inflation hedge during the three recent inflationary periods tested. Even if a zero normal required rate of return à la traditional investment theory is assumed, only three of the thirty common stocks sampled (10 percent) were inflation hedges during all three inflationary periods. These results were confirmed by the weighted-average results, which indicate that eleven of the thirty stocks were traditional inflation hedges and only two were complete inflation hedges.

Stock Price Movements within an Inflationary Period

The prior studies reviewed have clearly shown that investors who acquired common stock at the beginning of a period of significant inflation and sold it at the end of the period did not enjoy positive real rates of return on the average and definitely did not have complete inflation hedges during the total periods of inflation. The period of inflation that began in 1966 and extended into 1976 is the longest period of significant inflation in the last sixty years and could be the longest in well over a century.[21]

Such a long period of significant inflation has made it possible to analyze what happens to stock price movements *within* a period of significant inflation. The key question is whether what is true for the total period of inflation is true for subperiods within the inflation. Therefore, an analysis of relevant economic variables was conducted for the period from 1966 into 1974.[22]

Determination of Share Prices.   It was noted above that share prices are determined by the discounted value of the future earnings stream. Therefore, share prices will move directly with changes in expectations regarding future earnings and inversely with changes in required rates of return. During inflation, if expected earnings increase, share prices will increase provided all else is the same. In contrast, if inflation causes an increase in the required rate of return on stocks and nothing else changes, stock prices will decline.

Prior Discussion of Short-Run Effect.   Two prior articles with limited empirical evidence considered the short-run effect of inflation on common stock returns. Their discussion helps pinpoint the relevant considerations. The first article, by Daniel Seligman, was rather pessimistic regarding the outlook for common stocks because of the inflationary environment.[23] The strong pessimism was attributable mainly to his heavy concentration on the adverse effect of inflation on the required rate of return, little or no consideration being given to any possibility of benefits to earnings. In fact, Seligman generally expected profit margins to decline.

Subsequently, William Freund, in a reply to the Seligman article, pointed out that during a period of sustained inflation it was necessary to be aware of *changes* in earnings patterns and in the rate of inflation.[24] Specifically, Freund asserted that, given a specified level of inflation, investors adjust stock prices to take account of the effect of the inflation on earnings and the required rate of return. Given a relatively efficient security market, this should be a rapid, one-time adjustment. If no further *changes* in inflationary expectations are assumed, one would expect stock prices to begin increasing as before, and someone who acquires stock after the adjustment should experience satisfactory returns. Freund's main point is that people would expect *continued* stock price declines only if they expect *continued*

---

[21]See Frank K. Reilly and Ralph E. Smith, *Inflation: An Historical Review,* University of Wyoming Research Paper No. 53, January 1975.

[22]The bulk of this analysis is from Frank K. Reilly, "A Theoretical and Empirical Analysis of Companies and Common Stocks as Inflation Hedges," *The Bulletin,* New York University, January 1975.

[23]Daniel Seligman, "A Bad New Era for Common Stocks," *Fortune,* October 1971, pp. 73–79.

[24]William C. Freund, "What 'Bad New Era' for Stocks?" *Fortune,* April 1972, pp. 45, 46, 48, 50, 52.

increases in the rate of inflation. Also, if there is stability in the rate of inflation, profit margins would eventually stabilize and earnings grow in line with the inflation.

Principal Considerations. Therefore, the important consideration in the analysis of returns on common stock within a period of sustained inflation is not the level of inflation but changes in the rate of inflation and changes in earnings expectations during the inflation prompted by current-earnings changes. Hence, the annual and quarterly analysis emphasized changes in stock prices over time relative to changes in aggregate earnings, profit margins, consumer prices (that is, inflation), and interest rates. A positive relationship was expected between changes in stock prices and changes in earnings or profit margins, and a negative relationship was expected between changes in stock prices and changes in consumer prices or interest rates. A major consideration was the relative impact of these changes; that is, which change was more significant in relation to stock price changes.

Annual Changes. Annual data for stock prices, earnings, and inflation are contained in Table 5-6.

TABLE 5-6   Annual Figures and Percentage Changes for Stock Prices, Corporate Earnings, Profit Margins, Consumer Prices, and Long-Term Government Bond Yields, 1965–1973

Year	S&P 425 (1) Ending price	S&P 425 (1) Percent change	Corporate earnings (2) Annual	Corporate earnings (2) Percent change	Profit margin (3) Annual	Profit margin (3) Percent change	CPI, (1967=100) (4) Ending index	CPI, (1967=100) (4) Percent change	Long-term government bond yields (5) Ending yield	Long-term government bond yields (5) Percent change
1965	98.47	. . .	5.51	. . .	5.6	. . .	95.4	. . .	4.46	
1966	85.08	−13.60	5.89	6.90	5.6	0.00	98.6	3.35	4.63	3.81
1967	105.11	23.54	5.66	−3.90	5.0	−10.71	101.6	3.04	5.43	17.28
1968	113.02	7.53	6.15	8.66	5.1	2.00	106.4	4.72	5.83	7.37
1969	101.49	−10.20	6.17	0.33	4.8	−5.88	112.9	6.11	6.91	18.52
1970	100.90	−0.58	5.43	−11.99	4.0	−16.67	119.1	5.49	6.31	−8.68
1971	112.72	11.65	6.02	10.87	4.1	2.50	123.1	3.36	5.72	−9.35
1972	131.87	16.99	6.83	13.46	4.3	4.88	127.3	3.41	5.68	−.70
1973	109.16	−17.22	8.86	29.72	4.9	13.95	138.5	8.80	6.12	7.92

SOURCE: (1) Standard and Poor's *Trade and Securities Statistics.*
(2) Earnings for S&P 425 from Standard and Poor's *Trade and Securities Statistics.*
(3) All manufacturing corporations, Federal Trade Commission.
(4) U.S. Department of Labor, Bureau of Labor Statistics.
(5) Standard and Poor's *Trade and Securities Statistics.*

In 1966, the first year of recent significant inflation, stock prices declined by 13.6 percent even though corporate earnings increased by 6.9 percent. This decline in stock prices with higher earnings can be attributed to the increase in the rate of inflation from less than 2 percent during 1965 to more than 3.3 percent during 1966.

During 1967, stock prices rebounded dramatically while earnings declined. Again, this can be attributed to a small reduction in the rate of inflation and possibly to the expectation of further declines. Stock prices probably were also affected by the higher expected earnings of 1968.

During 1968, earnings increased by almost 9 percent while stock prices increased by about 7.5 percent. This shortfall in the stock price increase can be attributed partly to an increase in the rate of inflation from about 3 to 4.7 percent.

The stock market decline of 10.2 percent during 1969 can be attributed to an increase in the rate of inflation, from 4.72 to 6.11 percent, because there was almost no change in earnings. The reverse occurred in 1970: corporate earnings declined substantially, but stock prices were basically unchanged, which was consistent with the decline in the rate of inflation.

In retrospect, 1971 was (and should have been) a good year for the stock market as earnings increased and the rate of inflation declined substantially. Again, in 1972, the stock market did well as earnings increased by about 13.5 percent and the inflation rate was almost constant.

The very significant impact of inflation can be seen in what transpired in 1973. While corporate earnings enjoyed one of the largest *increases* recorded in recent history (almost 30 percent), stock prices *declined* substantially (over 17 percent). This can be explained by the astronomical *increase* in the rate of inflation, from 3.4 to 8.8 percent, and widespread expectations of further increases or continued high rates.

Although nobody would deny the impact of current and expected changes in earnings on stock price movements, the last several years have demonstrated the equally dramatic impact of inflation on stock prices. On several occasions the stock market moved directly opposite to concurrent earnings changes, but stock prices moved consistently with expectations based upon changes in the rate of inflation.

These results demonstrate two facts. First, during a period of prolonged inflation, one can and should expect both good and bad years for the stock market on the basis of both future earnings changes and changes in the rate of inflation. Although the rate of inflation may remain high, any major declines should be considered bullish for stock prices, if one assumes that the earnings outlook does not degenerate too badly during the period.

As an example, if investors invested during every year when the rate of inflation declined or was relatively stable, they would have invested during 1967, 1970, 1971, and 1972. Given this investment policy, they would have experienced positive price changes during three of the four years, a small decline in one year, and an average annual price change of 12.9 percent.

Put another way, using this decision rule, which basically ignored earnings changes, investors would have avoided all the large price declines and missed only one year of positive price changes.

The second point is that the optimum setting for common stock investment is an environment of earnings growth and price level stability or even stability in the rate of inflation. Such a combination occurred in 1971 and 1972, and the results within a period of significant inflation were very satisfactory for common stock investors.

Quarterly Changes.   The specific data and percentage changes for the period from the first quarter of 1966 through the second quarter of 1974 are contained in Table 5-7 on page 5-22. Examination of the quarterly series confirms the discussion of annual data because there are numerous instances of a negative relationship between stock price changes and the level of inflation or changes in the rate of inflation, or both. One would hypothesize that investors are concerned with *changes* up or down in the rate of inflation, in addition to the prevailing rate of inflation. In this regard, see 1/1966, 3/1966, 4/1966, 1/1967, 1/1968, 3/1968, 1/1969, 2/1969, 2/1970, 3/1970, 1/1971, 1/1973, 2/1973, and 1/1974 in the table. In each case there was a negative relationship between changes in the rate of inflation and stock price movements.

The negative relationship between stock price changes and the level of inflation indicates that stock prices generally declined during periods of inflation exceeding 5.13 percent (the mean annualized rate of inflation during this period). If this implied rule were applied and stock price changes were examined during quarters when the annualized rate of inflation exceeded 5.13 percent (this happened during fourteen quarters), it would be found that stock prices declined during twelve of the fourteen quarters and *the average quarterly decline in stock prices was 3.77 percent,* which is about a *15.1 percent annual rate of decline.*

In contrast, stock price performance during the twenty quarters when the inflation rate was less than 5.13 percent indicated that the stock price changes were positive during fifteen of the twenty quarters and the average quarterly price change was +3.49, which is an annual rate of change of about +13.96.

Finally, if investors are assumed to have been astute enough to invest during the six quarters when the annualized rate of inflation was less than 3 percent, they would have experienced stock price increases during five of the six periods. The average price increase during these six quarters was 5.95 percent, which is an annualized increase of about 23.8 percent.

While it is difficult to deal in absolutes in a dynamic environment, the foregoing demonstrates the unique impact of the rate of inflation upon stock prices during this period. Although the general principle will probably be valid in the future, the relevant range will likely vary with the environment: one cannot expect the relevant boundaries to be less than 3 percent and more than 5.13 percent when the rate of inflation exceeds 8 or 10 percent.

The negative relationship between stock price changes and changes in the rate of inflation also implies an investment policy of investing in common stocks when the rate of inflation declines and not investing when the rate increases. Given this implied policy, of the thirty-four quarters examined, the rate of inflation declined in fifteen. During nine of these fifteen quarters, stock prices increased, and the average increase in stock prices during all such quarters was 2.54 percent, which is an annual increase of about 10.2 percent. Again, while one cannot guarantee such a decision rule, the results indicated that consideration of changes in the rate of inflation should be a very relevant investment criterion during prolonged periods of significant inflation.

To summarize the stock price movements within a period of prolonged inflation, the annual results indicated a fairly consistent negative relationship between changes in the rate of inflation and stock price changes. The relationship between stock price changes and coincident earnings changes was generally negative, but there was a positive relationship with future earnings changes. *In any case, a simple decision rule that considered only changes in the rate of inflation and implicitly ignored earnings generated an annual return of 12.9 percent.*

The quarterly results likewise indicated a negative relationship between stock price changes and the rate of inflation. Several investment decision rules that considered only the rate of inflation or changes in the rate of inflation were examined, and they all indicated the unique importance of this one variable, irrespective of earnings changes. More important for an investor, these results indicated that positive rates of return on common stocks are possible if investors can time their purchases correctly during a period of significant inflation.

SUMMARY AND CONCLUSION

This part of Chapter 5 has had several objectives, including defining inflation, describing inflation during the years since 1937, defining inflation hedges in general and as applied to common stocks, discussing why one might expect common stocks to be an inflation hedge, considering some possible problems with such expectations, and, finally, analyzing the empirical results regarding common stocks as inflation hedges during periods of significant inflation since 1937.

Inflation was defined as an increase in the general price level. It was pointed out that there has been a definite tendency for such increases during the last thirty-six years, with only brief periods of price stability or decline. More important, during

TABLE 5-7 Quarterly Values and Percentage Changes for Stock Prices, Earnings, Net Profit Margin, Consumer Prices, and Long-Term Government Bond Yields, First Quarter, 1966–Second Quarter, 1974

Quarter	S&P 425 stock prices		S&P 425 average quarterly earnings		Net profit margin		CPI (1967=100)			Long-term government bond yield	
	Ending value	Percent change	Annual rate	Percent change	Annual rate	Percent change	Index	Annual percent change	Percent change in annual rate	Ending yield	Percent change
4/1965	98.47	...	5.51	...	5.7	...	95.4	2.52	...	4.46	...
1/1966	95.51	-3.01	5.67	2.90	5.6	-1.75	96.3	3.76	40.16	4.55	2.02
2/1966	90.72	-5.02	5.79	2.12	5.9	5.36	97.1	3.32	-11.70	4.71	3.52
3/1966	81.65	-10.00	5.84	0.86	5.4	-8.47	98.1	4.12	24.10	4.78	1.49
4/1966	85.08	4.20	5.89	0.86	5.5	1.85	98.6	2.04	-50.49	4.63	-3.14
1/1967	96.71	13.67	5.72	-2.72	4.9	-10.91	98.9	1.20	-41.18	4.48	-3.24
2/1967	97.71	10.34	5.63	-1.75	5.2	6.12	99.7	3.24	170.00	5.01	11.83
3/1967	105.05	7.51	5.62	-0.18	4.7	-9.62	100.7	4.00	23.46	5.11	2.00
4/1967	105.11	0.06	5.66	0.72	5.2	10.64	101.6	3.56	-11.00	5.43	6.26
1/1968	98.20	-6.57	5.78	2.12	5.0	-3.85	102.8	4.72	32.58	5.52	1.66
2/1968	108.31	10.30	5.93	2.60	5.2	4.00	104.0	4.68	-0.85	5.23	-5.25
3/1968	112.01	3.42	6.03	1.69	4.9	-5.77	105.1	4.24	-9.40	5.14	1.72
4/1968	113.02	0.90	6.15	1.99	5.2	6.12	106.4	4.96	16.98	5.83	13.42

1/1969	110.91	-1.87	6.23	1.30	4.9	-5.77	108.0	6.00	20.97	6.20	6.35
2/1969	107.06	-3.47	6.25	0.32	5.1	4.08	109.7	6.32	5.33	6.15	-0.81
3/1969	102.49	-4.27	6.30	0.80	4.6	-9.80	111.2	5.48	-13.29	6.49	5.53
4/1969	101.49	-0.98	6.17	-2.06	4.6	.00	112.9	6.12	11.68	6.91	6.47
1/1970	98.05	-3.39	6.00	-2.76	4.0	-13.04	114.5	5.68	-7.19	6.50	-5.93
2/1970	79.89	-18.52	5.88	-2.00	4.4	10.00	116.3	6.28	10.56	7.01	7.85
3/1970	92.57	15.87	5.70	-3.06	3.9	-11.36	117.5	4.12	-34.39	6.70	-4.42
4/1970	100.90	9.00	5.43	-4.74	3.7	-5.13	119.1	5.44	32.04	6.31	5.82
1/1971	110.42	9.44	5.51	1.47	3.9	5.41	119.8	2.36	-56.62	5.63	-10.78
2/1971	109.95	-0.43	5.62	1.81	4.5	15.38	121.5	5.68	140.68	6.28	11.55
3/1971	108.77	-1.07	5.72	1.96	4.1	-8.89	122.2	2.32	-59.15	5.81	7.48
4/1971	112.72	3.63	6.02	5.24	4.1	.00	123.1	2.96	27.59	5.72	1.55
1/1972	119.26	5.80	6.14	1.99	4.0	-2.44	124.0	2.92	-1.35	5.79	1.22
2/1972	119.91	0.55	6.32	2.93	4.5	15.00	125.0	3.24	10.96	5.70	-1.55
3/1972	123.74	3.19	6.51	3.01	4.2	-6.67	126.2	3.84	18.52	5.70	.00
4/1972	131.87	6.57	6.83	4.92	4.4	4.76	127.3	3.48	-9.38	5.68	-.35
1/1973	125.00	-5.21	7.26	6.30	4.5	2.27	129.8	7.84	125.29	6.13	7.92
2/1973	116.72	-6.62	7.78	7.16	5.1	13.33	132.4	8.00	2.04	6.21	1.31
3/1973	121.58	4.16	8.31	6.81	4.6	-9.80	135.5	9.36	17.00	5.96	-4.03
4/1973	109.14	-10.23	8.86	6.62	4.7	2.17	138.5	8.84	-5.56	6.13	2.85
1/1974	105.08	-3.72	9.17	9.69	4.5*	-4.26	143.1	13.28	50.23	6.62	7.99
2/1974	97.39	-7.32	9.69	5.67	4.5*	.00	147.1	11.20	-15.66	6.60	-.30

*Estimate.

the past ten years we have witnessed continuous inflation at rates above 3 percent a year with several periods in excess of 4 and 5 percent. Given such an environment, it is important that investors determine adequate inflation hedges.

There is long-standing folklore regarding common stocks as inflation hedges, based upon the expectation that corporations will gain from inflation and that these earnings gains will be passed along to the stockholders. In theory, the gains are derived from either a net debtor position, a wage lag, or the company's stock of resources. Given these possibilities, several empirical studies have indicated that the proper net debtor conditions will benefit a company, but since these conditions do not exist for the majority of firms, one should not expect substantial benefits for corporations in general. Regarding the wage lag concept, it was shown that it does not exist over long periods and, therefore, that any benefits are relatively short-run.

Following the discussion of alternative possibilities, there was an examination of the actual performance of common stocks during periods of significant inflation. The results can best be summarized as bad news and good news. The bad news was derived from the performance of common stocks during total periods of significant inflation. The results consistently indicated that, in general, common stocks have not usually been inflation hedges under the traditional definition whereby no normal return is required. If a normal required rate of return equal to past returns is assumed, common stocks in general have definitely not been inflation hedges. This was demonstrated by the aggregate stock market indicator series (before and after taxes) and also by a group of individual stocks.

The good news was derived from an examination of the performance of common stocks within a prolonged period of significant inflation. The analysis indicated that common stocks performed quite well during specified subperiods. The positive returns came during periods in which the overall rate of inflation was relatively low or in which the rate of inflation declined.

IMPLICATIONS

There are several implications of this part of Chapter 5 for investors who recognize the erosive effects of inflation on their wealth position and would like to use common stocks in their battle against inflation. First and most important is recognition that the age-old folklore that common stocks are a good hedge against inflation is naïve at best. The empirical evidence regarding total periods of inflation simply does not support such beliefs. At the same time, the analysis of subperiods within a period of significant inflation implies that investors need not abandon common stocks during a period of significant inflation because what is true for the total period is not true for all subperiods. These latter results imply that during prolonged periods of inflation common stocks are not a lost cause, but the presence of inflation adds two very important new dimensions to the analytical process. The new dimensions are the *rate* of inflation and *changes* in the rate of inflation. Inflation becomes a main character, and investors must become aware of future moves by this character. Put another way, the investment game is the same, but a minor player, inflation, has come to center stage and must be given special attention and major billing. On the basis of hypothetical investment results, the potential returns justify the greater attention and the major billing.

Part 2. How Chronic Inflation Has Changed Bond-Stock Risk-Return Relationships—and Two Proposed Remedies

LEO BARNES

The long-term picture for common stocks was presented in Part 1 of this chapter by Frank K. Reilly. Has the chronic worldwide inflation of the late 1960s and early 1970s changed the long-term picture? It may well have, for if common stocks as a group are poor inflation hedges, how can returns from risky stocks be greater than those from safe bonds under conditions of chronic, continuing high-level inflation?

Stocks apparently offer greater returns than bonds only if inflation is relatively mild and intermittent, as it was, for example, in the United States in the twenty years from 1948 to 1967. During this period, the Consumer Price Index rose at an annual compound rate of less than 2 percent, and bond and other interest rates were relatively quite low. In such an environment, risky common stocks returning an average of more than 9 percent in dividends and capital gains combined were attractive investments compared with high-grade bonds yielding 4 to 5 percent.

But from 1967 through 1975, the Consumer Price Index advanced by over 7½ percent compounded, while high-grade bond interest rates rose correspondingly to a peak of more than 9 percent in 1974. In that environment, stock returns were low or, frequently, negative.

Geometric Stock Indices More Quickly Reveal Basic Changes

The changed relationship between stock and bond returns was not generally or quickly noticed because it did not reveal itself for some time in the popular blue-chip stock market indices, such as the Dow Jones Industrial Average (DJIA) or the Standard & Poor's 500-Stock Index. The new relationship was, however, obvious quite early in the various lesser-known *geometric* stock market indices. As pointed out in Part 1 of Chapter 2, geometric indices differ from both price-weighted indices (notably, the DJIA and the ASE Price Change Index) and capitalization- or market value–weighted indices (the S&P, NYSE, and NASDAQ indices), in that all stocks, small or large, cheap or dear, are given exactly the same weights. This means that, when measuring security price changes, equal percentage changes in prices for any and all stocks have exactly the same impact on the geometric index. Thus, superior performance by more expensive, heavily capitalized blue chips and institutional growth stocks will not overshadow poorer performance by the secondary "red chips," "white chips," and "cat-and-dog" issues.

Table 5-8 gives the box score for a dozen widely used as well as less well-known stock market indices of all three types for various periods from 1960 to 1975. It was in 1974 that the top-tier institutional market finally collapsed. In the table, the statistical category to which each index belongs is indicated.

Note how the geometric indices have consistently done far worse than either the price-weighted or the capitalization-weighted indices. This startling discrepancy is a post-1968 development. It reflects the rise of a strongly differentiated, two-tier market, with continuous institutional support sustaining the heavily capitalized and higher-priced blue chips and major growth companies while increasingly neglecting secondary issues. It also results from the steady departure of individual investors from a stock market with excessive downside volatility in many of the

TABLE 5-8 Comparative Record of Key Stock Market Indices since 1960[a]

Year	New York Stock Exchange					American Stock Exchange			Over-the-counter		All markets	
	DJIA[b]	S&P 425[c]	S&P 500[c]	NYSE Composite[e]	Indicator Digest (IDA)[d]	Price Change Index[b]	Market Value Index[e]	Indicator Digest (AIDA)[d]	NQBIA[b]	NASDAQ Composite[c]	American Investors Geometric[a]	Value Line Composite[a]
1960	−9.3	−4.7	−3.0	−3.9					−1.5		−5.7	
1961	18.7	23.1	23.1	24.1					31.9		22.3	
1962	−10.9	−13.0	−8.8	−12.0					−14.4		−23.2	−16.3
1963	17.1	19.4	18.9	18.1		21.1			17.0		11.2	13.6
1964	14.6	14.0	13.0	14.4		19.4			25.6		9.3	13.3
1965	10.9	9.9	9.1	9.5		38.3			30.1		21.9	19.0
1966	−18.9	−13.6	−13.1	−12.6	−14.0	−4.5			−1.5		−9.3	−12.3
1967	15.2	23.5	20.1	23.1	32.7	79.1			54.0		32.6	29.1
1968	5.2	8.5	7.7	10.4	18.4	34.6			22.2		20.4	19.8
1969	−15.2	−10.2	−11.4	−12.5	−28.9	−19.7	−29.0	−44.0	0.8		−26.3	−28.7
1970	4.8	−0.6	0.1	−2.5	−15.6	−13.4	−28.0	−39.2	−13.7		−15.8	−20.7
1971	6.1	11.7	10.8	12.3	9.7	12.5	18.9	1.7	35.4	19.0[e]	16.8	9.2
1972	14.6	16.1	15.7	14.3	0.5	3.0	10.3	−11.2	30.3	17.2	0.6	1.0
1973	−16.6	−17.4	−17.4	−19.6	−37.6	−17.7	−30.0	−46.3	−25.5	−31.1	−37.0	−35.5
1974	−29.0	−29.9	−29.7	−31.7	−37.3	−10.1[f]	−33.2	−25.1	−38.9	−35.1	−35.8	−33.5
1975	42.8	31.9	31.5	34.6	41.4	...	38.4	33.3	28.6	29.8	46.7	44.4
						PERCENT CHANGE						
1960–75	28.2	56.2	55.8	49.2	...	...	...	...	171.8	...	−17.8	...
1963–75	33.6	52.9	43.0	42.1	...	...	...	...	87.2	...	−7.1	−19.7
1968–75	−3.8	−4.0	−6.5	−10.7	−56.6	...	−41.6	−77.8	9.6	...	−47.9	−53.7
1971–75	2.8	−0.9	−2.1	−5.1	−39.0	...	−15.1	−51.6	3.2	−19.0	−30.3	−31.6

[a]Figures are percentage changes for calendar years, not including reinvestment of dividends.
[b]Price-weighted index.
[c]Market value–weighted index.
[d]Unweighted geometric index.
[e]First 5 1/2 weeks of 1971 estimated by the author.
[f]Index discontinued after 1974.

stocks they had been holding, a volatility that has been further increased by their departure from the stock arena.

Prior to 1968 and as far back as 1940, as shown in Chapter 2, there were rarely such startling differences between the performances of the commonly used price- and capitalization-weighted market indices and the less well-known geometric ones.

What Can Be Done to Restore Risk-Return Balance?

Can anything be done to restore the long-term risk-return relationship between common stocks and bonds, so that common stocks once again return 4 to 5 percent more per year than high-grade bonds?[25] Three options seem theoretically available, but they are either unlikely or unappetizing:

1. *Beat back inflation and therefore interest rates to the lower levels of the 1950s and 1960s.* Unfortunately, the economic and political measures required to do this seem beyond our capacities. There is no simple, single, quick solution. Inflation must be combated continuously and simultaneously on many fronts and internationally as well as nationally. The almost-exclusive reliance by most countries on tight money and high interest rates is unlikely to succeed, except perhaps temporarily as a result of the severe recessions or depressions they may provoke. Then, when government attention returns to these problems, inflation is likely to crop up again as our perpetual economic nightmare.

2. *Boost returns on stocks by substantially raising corporate dividends.* Some fortunately placed companies (as in metals, oils, and paper) can do this by raising product prices sharply, but dividend rates would have to be approximately doubled to boost average stock yields from 5 or 6 percent to 10 or 12 percent. For most industries, increasing dividend returns by this means and by this amount is economically difficult and politically impossible. Even if it could be done, raising prices in order to raise profits and dividends only accelerates inflation and thus drives interest rates even higher.

3. *Boost returns on stocks by forcing stock prices drastically lower.* Stocks would have to plummet to levels at which yields would once again be higher than bond yields, as they were in almost all years before 1958. For example, if the DJIA tumbled to between 500 and 600, average stock yields would rise to 9 or 10 percent, or quite likely a bit higher than bond and money market yields would be. This was the direction in which many stock markets seemed to be headed in 1974. But the non-Communist countries would be in economic and social chaos if such drastic "super bear markets" were allowed to develop and persist. Stockholder losses, real or on paper, would run into trillions of dollars, with money losses magnified in real terms by the shrinking buying power of stockholder assets resulting from inflation.

The Ideal Solution—Corporate Tax-Deductibility for Dividends

Is there any way out of this terrifying "trilemma"? Yes. One method by which we can make stocks promptly return more than bonds—without still more inflation, without higher corporate earnings, and without bear markets and social chaos—is for Congress to change the tax laws by *making all cash dividends on both common and preferred stocks tax-deductible for the corporations that pay them.*

With dividends tax-deductible, companies would be eager both to save taxes by paying as large dividends as possible and, as the prices of their stocks recovered, to

---

[25]Most of the following material in this part of Chapter 5 originally appeared (in somewhat different form) in *The Wall Street Journal,* Oct. 9, 1974, and in *Business Week,* May 5, 1975.

finance themselves once again, and increasingly, by means of common stock. With no increase in their earnings, corporations could boost their dividends up as much as the amount of taxes saved, or by more than 90 percent. That would completely reverse the typical stock-bond yield gap of about 3 percent in favor of bonds.

Here is how our proposal would work for a typical corporation and a typical stockholder, one with a federal top tax bracket of 35 percent. First, say that under

TABLE 5-9   Immediate Cost-Benefit Analysis

	Before	After	Percent change
Corporation gets as retained earnings	$1.08	$1.08	0
Stockholder gets in dividends	1.00	1.92	+92
Typical stockholder pays federal tax at 35 percent	.35	.67	+92
Typical stockholder keeps	.65	1.25	+92
Federal government gets in taxes:			
From corporation	1.92	1.00	−48
From stockholder	.35	.67	+92
Total	$2.27	$1.67	−26

present tax laws the company has earnings before federal taxes of $4 per share. At the 48 percent tax rate, it pays a federal income tax of $1.92 per share, leaving earnings after taxes of $2.08. It distributes as dividends a little less than 50 percent of net earnings, or $1 per share. It is thus left with $1.08 per share in retained earnings, which it can use for corporate purposes such as investment in new plant and equipment.

Under the proposed tax change making dividends tax-deductible as a business expense, the corporation could pay $1.92 rather than $1 per share in dividends and still have left the same $1.08 per share in retained earnings. The reason is that the higher dividend of $1.92 would be deducted from earnings *before* rather than after taxes. Deducting $1.92 in dividends from earnings of $4 per share reduces earnings before taxes to $2.08 per share. The federal income tax at 48 percent would take $1, leaving $1.08 per share in retained earnings. A cost-benefit analysis of the proposed tax change for the corporation, stockholder, and federal government in this example (immediately after the change) is shown in Table 5-9.

The fact that the difficulties of the stock markets in the early 1970s result in part from the federal tax laws as well as from rising inflation needs to be stressed. With businesses permitted to deduct from income all taxable interest paid but forbidden to make similar deductions for dividends, it has been much cheaper after taxes to finance their needs with bonds and other debt than with stock, and increasingly so whenever stock prices drop to lower and lower levels. Such contrasting tax treatment leads to continually rising bond, short-term bank, and commercial paper financing, which drives interest rates up higher and higher (but interest payments are always tax-deductible) and simultaneously imperils bank liquidity. As the gap between stock and bond yields widens, stock prices are depressed even further, and stock financing is further discouraged. This vicious circle can best be broken by putting dividends on a par with interest in terms of tax deductibility.

It is realized that this proposal goes against the current grain, not only politically (big corporations and their stockholders are not particularly popular) but also from the point of view of accounting orthodoxy. Dividends are treated by accountants as coming from net profits *after* taxes and so are not considered a "cost" of doing business, as interest payments are. But economists have long recognized that dividends are truly part of the business cost of capital, and accountants are beginning to see the light, too. Logically, it makes no sense to treat the interest paid on bonds and other debt capital, but not the dividends paid on equity capital, as a deductible expense. Either all costs of capital should be tax-deductible, or (perish the thought) none should be.

There is another striking example of discrimination against stockholders by United States tax laws. The rules for contributions of corporations to profit sharing plans were liberalized early in World War II. Like dividends, such contributions come out of profits and can be made only if there are profits, but they are fully tax-deductible by the corporation, up to 15 percent of total wages and salaries. If contributions from profits for the benefit of employees and ex-employees are treated as tax-deductible business expenses, why should the same treatment be forbidden for dividends paid to shareholders?

From the standpoint of accounting, the only change that would be required is the simple one of treating dividends as coming out of profits before rather than after taxes.

There would, of course, be some *immediate* revenue loss to the United States government (and also to those state and city governments that change their tax laws correspondingly) as a result of this proposed tax change. However, after a year or two the net annual loss would probably be negligible or nonexistent. The immediate loss would be due to the difference between the double tax on dividends at the corporate and individual levels and the average individual tax rate on dividends, estimated to be between 30 and 40 percent (it is taken as 35 percent in Table 5-9). As a result of this differential, the lower taxes on the reduced corporate profits due to the dividend tax deduction would not be completely offset by the higher stockholder taxes on the increased dividends paid by corporations. In addition, large sums of dividends go to completely or largely tax-exempt organizations such as pension and profit sharing funds, religious and educational institutions, and foundations. If our proposal were adopted, these organizations would receive much higher dividends but still pay little if any income taxes.

Tax Revenue Offsets Would Be Available

On the other side of the picture there are a number of ways in which government revenues would benefit from the tax proposal:

1. Making dividends tax-deductible for paying corporations would eliminate a long-standing tax inequity: the present double taxation of dividends, first as part of earnings at the corporate level and, second, as dividends at the stockholder level. Therefore, the current dividend credit of up to $100 for each of the 30 million-plus stockholders, adopted by Congress as a partial step in this direction, could be simultaneously repealed. This step would increase federal income tax revenues by a significant amount. Similarly, if dividends were made tax-deductible for paying corporations, the 85 percent tax credit for dividend-receiving United States corporations (which pay income tax on only 15 percent of either common or preferred dividends from other United States corporations) would have to be eliminated to prevent double deductions on dividends. This would be another significant tax-saving offset.

2. Our proposal would eliminate the double taxation of dividends in the most equitable possible way. Rather than making dividends another form of tax-exempt income available "equally" to both the high-bracket rich and the low-bracket poor, the plan would tax them at progressive personal tax rates. Given our progressive federal income tax structure, a sharply higher flow of dividends would

push many stockholders into higher tax brackets, and the subsequent revenue loss would thus be smaller than the original impact.

3. Any initial loss to the Treasury on corporate and dividend income taxes combined could well be more than compensated later on by much higher taxes on realized capital gains from recovering stock markets.

4. Flourishing stock markets would contribute to general prosperity by raising business sales and profits, which would be quickly reflected in higher federal, state, and municipal tax receipts of all kinds, from income to sales taxes.

5. Higher capital values in the securities markets would significantly boost federal and state inheritance and estate taxes.

All in all, the revenue loss from our proposed tax change is not a major problem. The long-term benefits far outweigh any relatively small short-term cost.

Most important, the adoption of our proposal would make the equity market available for a much larger proportion of the huge capital needs of the United States economy in the next decade. It has been conservatively estimated that raising the output of food, fuels, and other materials by the needed amounts while maintaining the quality of the environment will require a minimum of 4 to 5 trillion in capital outlays over a ten-year period. Such staggering sums cannot possibly be raised without a restored stock market to provide most of the total.

The Income Bond as Another Alternative

In the absence of congressional action to amend the tax laws by making cash dividends on all stocks tax-deductible as a business expense for the paying corporation, exactly as interest on bonds is now deductible, can anything be done to revive the fortunes of stockholders, who have suffered such severe "capital punishment" since 1968? Fortunately, there is one readily available way out of our recurrent equity trap. Many firms can help both themselves and their stockholders by *exchanging much or most of their present equity for new, superior types of higher-yielding income bonds, on which interest is tax-deductible and yet need be paid only if it is earned.*

Because of the tax deduction for interest, such a change would rechannel cash from federal tax collectors both to the new income bondholders and to the companies themselves. In addition, the remaining stockholders could benefit from larger earnings per share for the smaller number of shares outstanding. This triple advantage of income bonds far outweighs their very small additional risk to the company.

Precisely what is an income bond? It is the weakest possible form of debt and thus least risky for the issuing corporation. A very long-term bond, it is almost always subordinated to all other debt and has a very special feature: *interest payments are never mandatory but always completely contingent, payable only if earned.* If interest is not earned, a failure to pay it does not mean bankruptcy.

The income bond is thus a very lowly bond. Yet it is a worthwhile notch above equity, first because interest paid on income bonds comes before rather than after taxes, as in the case of dividends, so that interest might be paid even if dividends were not earned; and, second, because if income bond interest is earned, it must be paid, while dividends on either common or preferred stock are optional and need not be paid even if earned.

A broad capitalization shift from common and preferred stock to income bonds would enable companies and their shareholders to obtain exactly the same tax and income benefits that they would receive if dividends were made tax-deductible for the paying corporation. Widely followed, such a do-it-yourself capitalization improvement would convert stock investors into income bond investors, and stock exchanges into stock-plus-income-bond exchanges. It would also replace dividends on common and preferred stock with much larger amounts of interest from income bonds.

This proposal could also provide a broadly needed lift for much of the stock market. By dramatically lowering the number of equity shares outstanding, it would correspondingly raise earnings per share and, in most cases, stock prices as well. Thus, millions of present stockholders would benefit. Those who needed or wanted larger income would obtain it through higher-yielding income bonds. Those who preferred tax-favored capital gains would have a better chance of receiving them through the remaining common stock with higher leverage. In effect, by completely separating the income lambs from the capital gain bulls, we could do much better for both.

There is a useful precedent that can readily be checked. In the 1950s, quite a number of railroads took advantage of the same exchange technique to replace preferred stock issues with higher-yielding income bonds. With the newly available tax deductions for interest paid on the income bonds, they boosted their earnings per common share and often their stock prices as well.

In recent years, income bonds have been almost completely ignored by investment bankers because they are much too weak for powerful creditors. Most of them would be rated B or even CCC, far too low in quality for institutional or conservative individual bond investors. By the same token, they represent a slight upgrading in safety and yield from common stock and thus are ideal for swap arrangements with virtually powerless stockholders. In the process, the worthwhile tax and income benefits described above can be achieved.

How Income Bonds Can Help Avoid Debt Excesses

Let us now confront the basic objection to our proposal. Obviously, it is the charge that we are advocating and encouraging excessive corporate debt. Overall, the ratio of mandatory corporate debt to equity has more than doubled in the last decade, from 20 to more than 40 percent. So most United States companies are already burdened with mandatory debt. How can we rationally recommend that they assume still more debt by exchanging stock for income bonds?

Our justification is a multiple one. First, a change from equity to income bonds is just that: a shift within existing capital rather than the creation of additional capital, the customary way by which debt is established. This difference is decisive, because it means that no added earnings are needed to pay the interest on the new income bonds. Those interest payments come mostly from the former dividends on the exchanged stock and, as we have seen, partly from a portion of the tax savings resulting from the shift. The rest of the tax savings would be used to increase the company's retained earnings, which normally are reinvested to produce additional profits.

Thus, a switch from equity to income bonds, as distinguished from the assumption of additional debt, can strengthen, not weaken, a company's financial position. This is true as long as future earnings remain the same or rise.

But what if future earnings do not hold up? Here the decisive difference income bonds make is that payment of interest on them is not mandatory, as it is on mortgage bonds, regular debentures, and virtually all other types of debt. Typically, companies go bankrupt because they cannot pay mandatory interest, not because they cannot refinance debts at maturity. As long as they can pay interest charges without great difficulty, they can almost always refund maturing debts. Thus, from now until remote maturity, the 100 percent contingency of the interest on income bonds is a very useful escape hatch from possible bankruptcy in a risky and uncertain world.

We stress the concept of *remote* maturity, Income bonds usually are very long-term, maturing in 30 to 40 years. When offered in exchange for common or preferred stocks, which have no maturity, they could quite properly be made even longer-term, perhaps up to 100 years. Retirement or refunding then becomes an even more remote prospect, with eventual risk reduced still further by the ever-cheapening money of chronic inflation.

All in all, the replacement of equity by very long-term, subordinated income bonds, with interest on a 100 percent contingent basis, takes advantage of the benefits of leverage, but with vital differences from doing so by issuing additional standard senior debt with 100 percent mandatory interest. Accordingly, it is recommended that, for companies shifting from equity to income bonds, the approved analytical financial test of safety and credit worthiness should not be the customary ratio of total debt to total equity. Instead, because of the safeguards resulting from a purely internal capitalization shift and the additional special safety features of income bonds, the test should be a new, more appropriate ratio, that of mandatory-interest debt to equity plus nonmandatory-interest debt. Thus, the substitution of contingent income bonds for stock would not change this key credit risk ratio.

Improved Income Bond Formats Are Available

Let us turn again to the investor. As we have seen, the standard income bond can perform better than common or preferred stock for most income-seeking shareholders. Moreover, readily available improvements in format and terms can make income bonds still more valuable for all types of investors, and at little if any added cost to the issuing corporation.

Thus, interest on income bonds could be made *cumulative* (again, only if earned) for, say, three to five years. Alternatively, income bonds could be given possibly higher future income by means of *variable or floating interest rates* geared to the prime rate, Treasury bill rates, or even the Consumer Price Index (still, only if earned). Yet another alternative could be *participating income arrangements* if company earnings increased in the future. Any of these three income benefits would justify somewhat lower initial interest rates on the bonds.

Participation in rising future income would also usually improve the price performance of income bonds. For this purpose, however, the best solution would be income bonds *convertible* into the remaining common stock. For investors, this could be the most fascinating and rewarding income bond alternative available. Convertible income bonds would be particularly appropriate for the many common stocks that suffered such extraordinary capital losses in the period 1968–1974. Swap deals made at very depressed prices with nonconvertible income bonds would make much of these capital losses permanent.

Convertibility is also an appealing option for the issuing company and its remaining stockholders. For stockholders, providing convertibility would almost invariably increase the proportion of holders accepting the switch to income bonds, thus leaving fewer remaining common shares. Leverage for these shares would be greater, and so probably would be their future price appreciation (and that of the related convertible income bonds). For the company, the interest rate on convertible income bonds could usually be fixed at a significantly lower level than on nonconvertible bonds, thus lowering expenses and bolstering retained earnings. Similarly, convertibility would usually also make it possible to save money by omitting additional income bond features, such as cumulative, variable, or participating income, or the use of contingent sinking funds.

Finally, the convertibility feature makes the question of income bond repayment at maturity even more irrelevant. Almost always, convertible bonds are either converted or replaced by new convertibles. Thus, for the issuing company, a contingent, subordinated, and convertible income bond is almost as riskless as a common stock. It could quite appropriately be called an "equity bond." Companies would find it entirely feasible to issue two or even more series of income bonds in exchange for equity—for example, one series stressing high initial and rising future income through participation and the other concentrating on long-term capital gains through convertibility.

We conclude this analysis with a hope. As more and more corporations took advantage of the tax-saving and income-boosting potentials of replacing obsolete equity with new and improved forms of income bonds, Congress might be prodded into making all dividends tax-deductible at the corporate level, in line with our first, simpler recommendation. That would provide a substantial, much-needed upgrading for the nation's corporate equities, halt their obsolescence, and make further switches to income bonds unnecessary.

Section Two

Investment Timing

Chapter 6

Defining the Right Time for Stocks, Bonds, and Other Assets

LEO BARNES

Determining when to buy and when to sell can be almost as vital to investors as choosing the securities or assets to buy or sell. The stock market and other markets usually react excessively to both favorable and unfavorable influences. Perhaps half (sometimes even fewer) of the changes in stock prices result from rational or fundamental economic, monetary, and financial factors. The other half (sometimes even more) of the changes are due to fluctuations in investors' psychological expectations and feelings of confidence or uncertainty.

Thus, you can lose a good deal of money by buying even the best securities at the wrong time, and you can often make a good deal of money by buying a poor security at the right time. On the other side of the picture, billions in paper profits have been lost by not selling greatly overpriced securities at the right time. It is a profound truth about both the stock market and investors that when stock prices are really low, most people think they are too high and will avoid buying, and that when stock prices are really high, most people think they are still low and will buy avidly.

Successful overall timing can produce extraordinary results. Had one been able to time precisely all the turns on the Dow Jones Industrial Average since 1915, one could have parlayed an investment of $100 in the DJIA at the start of 1915 into more than $800,000 by the end of 1975 (not including dividends and commissions). To be sure, even approaching perfection in timing is a practical impossibility, but the figures cited reveal the great opportunities for investors who succeed in improving their overall market timing.

The timing techniques analyzed in Section Two of the *Handbook* stem from three approaches:

1. Some of the techniques rely on forecasting or anticipating the trend of stock and bond prices.

2. Some are designed only to spot and to follow the market trend as quickly as possible, without forecasting.

3. Still others completely ignore trend timing, whether by forecasting or by following the market trend. They make investment decisions by security pricing rather than by trend timing.

In timing the purchase and sale of your own investments, you must decide which of these approaches is best suited to both your investment targets and your analytical abilities.

For most investment purposes, it is not necessary to pinpoint well in advance exactly how long a stock market movement will last or exactly how high or how low it will go. Very probably, this cannot be done systematically. However, it is still useful to be able to define the basic direction in which the market is moving at any time—in advance when feasible but as soon as possible after a turn. With modern techniques, the direction can frequently be determined.

To be useful, forecasting need not be 100 percent or even 90 percent accurate. Stock market analysis and forecasting will be helpful if they merely raise your investment batting average from 50 to 70 percent or even from 40 to 60 percent. There is good reason to believe that this can be done, particularly by using a combination of previously successful "long-lead" economic indicators, plus a consensus of the more effective technical indicators, as discussed in detail in Chapters 7 and 8.

Finally, there are available useful timing techniques, such as formula plans and automatic stop-loss orders, that rely on forecasting only slightly or not at all. Instead, they depend on mechanical or semimechanical trend-following techniques or on security pricing rather than trend timing. These several techniques are discussed in Chapter 9.

At almost any time some stocks will be moving against the general stock market trend, but most of the time the prices of the majority of common stocks go up and down together in varying degrees. This is true to an even greater degree of the prices of bonds and preferred stocks, which are closely tied to changes in interest rates, resulting in part from the policies and actions of the federal government and the Federal Reserve Board.

There are four main kinds of market price movements:

1. Major bull and bear market swings, usually of two or more years' duration. Bear markets are typically faster and shorter than bull markets. Plainly, disillusion and deflation panic investors more powerfully than illusion and inflation elate them.

2. Intermediate market movements within a major bull or bear market, usually measured in months.

3. Seasonal market movements, lasting a month or so, that seem to be superimposed on intermediate swings.

4. Immediate short-term fluctuations of weeks or days.

Various investment timing techniques have been developed to attempt to spot and pinpoint all four of these market movements. Even the most conservative investors will want to call the approximate turn on major bull and bear market swings, at least for some of their funds. Less conservative investors and speculators will also want to catch many or most of the intermediate swings and also the major seasonal shifts. Only professional short-term speculators will play for the short, day-to-day fluctuations, but other investors could well consider them in estimating the best time to buy or sell a stock on which a buy or sell decision has been made.

Chapter **7**

Timing on the Fundamentals: Long-Lead and Medium-Lead Business and Stock Market Indicators

LEO BARNES

JESSE LEVIN[1]

It is by now a truism that the stock market is a better forecaster of business than business is of the stock market. As represented by Standard & Poor's 500-Stock Index, equities usually lead business peaks and troughs by an average of six to eight months. Because the stock market typically turns relatively early, there would seem to be available rather few economic indicators that have long enough lead times to be useful for effective stock market forecasting.

A main purpose of this chapter is to locate and evaluate these unusual economic and financial indicators that can serve this purpose. In the process, we shall find that the selected indicators are also quite useful in business forecasting, especially in inflationary periods like the early 1970s.

CLASSIFICATION OF LEADING INDICATORS BY LENGTH OF LEAD

The Bureau of Economic Analysis (BEA) of the Department of Commerce and the National Bureau of Economic Research (NBER) have long provided copious data on leading, roughly coincident, and lagging indicators. In this chapter, we are interested in only some of the leading indicators.

Our study of the performance data since 1948 for such indicators suggests that they are usefully classified for forecasting purposes into three major groups: long-lead, medium-lead, and short-lead. For convenience, and because most long-lead

---

[1]Mr. Levin died in January, 1974. Dr. Barnes had the privilege of working with Jesse Levin editorially for a number of years before his death. With his passing, economists and financial analysts have lost a keen mind and a prolific author.

indicators perform best prior to business peaks, we shall define these three categories in terms of such performance.

Thus, we define a "long-lead indicator" as one for which, prior to business peaks, (1) the *maximum* historical lead time since 1948 is two years (twenty-four months) or longer, *and* (2) the *average* historical lead time since 1948 is one year (twelve months) or longer.

Similarly, we define a "medium-lead indicator" as one which is not a long-lead indicator and for which, prior to business peaks, (1) the *maximum* historical lead time is one year (twelve months) or longer, and (2) the *average* historical lead time is six months or longer.

Finally, we define a "short-lead indicator" as one which is neither a long- nor a medium-lead indicator and for which, prior to business peaks, (1) the *maximum* historical lead time is six months or longer, *and* (2) the *average* historical lead time is three months or longer.

The necessity that, in all three cases, requirements (1) and (2) must both be met is responsible for the curious form our definition takes.

There are leading indicators with even shorter reported lead times than those just specified for short-lead indicators. Such indicators may, for reasons to be noted, be grouped for most practical purposes with the BEA-NBER roughly coincident indicators. Short-lead indicators, as we have here more rigorously defined them, are not very useful in either business or stock market forecasting, and accordingly no attention is paid to them in this chapter.

TRADITIONAL NEGLECT OF LONG-LEAD INDICATORS

Prior to 1975 it was customary for cycle analysts and business economists to pay less attention to long-lead indicators than to medium-lead indicators, for three main reasons:

1. Lead times of two years or more are deemed too long. We may just be coming out of a recession when we get an early-warning signal that a business peak lies somewhere ahead. Of course! But there is plenty of time before we reach that peak, and (hope springs eternal) perhaps in the meantime we can get business, the Federal Reserve Board, and federal, state, and local governments to do something to forestall the impending downturn.

2. Long-lead indicators tend to be highly variable or erratic, with substantial variations in minimum and maximum lead times from cycle to cycle.

3. In addition, the *effective* lead times for long-lead indicators are considerably shorter than their reported lead times, for much the same reasons stated below for medium-lead indicators.

These defects of long-lead indicators are real enough. Unfortunately, however, medium-lead business indicators have similar practical difficulties, to wit:

1. Their effective lead times are also much shorter than their reported lead times, and this is particularly serious because of the relatively short time lead available.

Effective lead times are shortened, first, by the time lag involved in data collection and dissemination. It takes anywhere from an hour or so (in the case of stock prices and crude material prices) to three or four months (in the case of almost all the other indicators) for the final data to become available to users. In addition, preliminary figures that are released earlier in some cases are often partial and unreliable, to be used with caution. And, to cap it all, even after so-called final figures are released, they are sometimes revised, occasionally several years later, thus changing reported lead times that had been assumed to be final.

Effective lead times are further shortened by the number of months required before a change in indicator direction can be interpreted as more than a random fluctuation and thus acquire statistical significance and forecasting usefulness. For such assurance, we must wait at least one month in the case of crude material prices, about two months for stock prices, and from three to six months for slower or more erratic indicators.

In toto, we estimate an overall effective *average* lag for leading indicators of roughly five months: a two-month average lag for collecting and reporting data, plus a three-month average lag for achieving statistical significance and forecasting usefulness. Moreover, if we wish to rely on a full consensus of a dozen or more indicators, we have to wait for the slowest indicator(s), which may sometimes require a few months beyond this five-month overall average.

The economists of the Cleveland Trust Co., in timely comments on the business downturn that began in late 1973, put it well: "Both lags in data collection and random fluctuations mean that the establishment of an index level for the NBER twelve leading indicators takes so long that the 'leading' indicators may signal a recession only with the use of hindsight"[2]

Of course, the effective lead times for long-lead business indicators are similarly reduced by at least five months on the average by the circumstances just described for medium-lead indicators. But when one has a reported lead time of up to two years or more to work with, there is still left, after such reduction, quite a comfortable and useful effective forecasting margin.

2. A second weakness of medium-lead business indicators is that the variability of their lead times is usually *relatively* large. While not, of course, as great as the lead-time variability of the more erratic long-lead indicators, the spread between the minimum and maximum historical reported lead times for many medium-lead indicators exceeds the indicator's average reported lead times. Such a degree of variability obviously further reduces the effective lead times of the indicators involved.

For a decisive illustration of these several difficulties, it is useful to examine in Table 7-1 the lead-time record of the two BEA-NBER diffusion indices of twelve leading indicators prior to the six business peaks and six business bottoms that occurred in the United States from 1948 to 1975. We utilize both the old BEA-NBER leading indicator series, in use until 1975; and the new BEA-NBER series, introduced in 1975 after the old series completely missed the November 1973 business peak as a result of a failure to adjust leading indicators stated in dollar terms for rampant inflation.

It will, of course, be noted in Table 7-1 that when we reduce the average lead times of the two sets of indicators by five months, we get *negative* lead times in five out of eight instances. In addition, uncertainty will be very high in any specific forecasting situation, because what we call the "minimax" spread of the BEA-NBER lead indicators ranges from five to twenty-eight months for the old diffusion series and from five to nineteen months for the new diffusion series.

As a business or financial analyst interested in useful forecasts, one would surely wish to improve such forecasting results, if one could, by *also* utilizing more long-lead indicators despite their erratic lead times. A finding of this chapter is that both our total knowledge and our forecasting abilities are modestly but usefully increased by such maximum use of long-lead indicators in combination with medium-lead indicators.

It is significant that, in addition to the introduction of four new lead indicators in constant-price versions, one of the major improvements in the new BEA-NBER

[2]*Business Bulletin,* Cleveland Trust Co., January 1974.

TABLE 7-1 Record of the BEA-NBER Old and New Diffusion Indices of Twelve Leading Series at Business Cycle Turning Points

BEA-NBER diffusion index	Batting average (percent)	Maximum lead time (months)	Minimum lead time (months)	Minimax spread of lead (months)	Average (and median) lead time (months)	Effective average (and median) lead time (months)	Rank for peaks or bottoms
SIX BUSINESS PEAKS, 1948–1973							
Old diffusion index, No. 811, original trend	83	20	−8	28	8.3 (10.0)	3.3 (5.0)	3
New index, original trend	100	23	5	18	13.0 (10.5)	8.0 (5.5)	1
Old diffusion index, No. 810, reverse trend	83	8	−8	16	3.7 (5.5)	−1.3 (0.5)	4
New index, reverse trend	100	23	4	19	10.5 (10.5)	5.5 (5.5)	2
SIX BUSINESS BOTTOMS, 1949–1975							
Old diffusion index, No. 810, reverse trend	100	6	1	5	3.7 (3.5)	−1.3 (−1.5)	2
New index, reverse trend	100	8	2	6	4.0 (3.0)	−1.0 (−2.0)	1
Old diffusion index, No. 811, original trend	67	6	0	6	2.2 (1.5)	−2.8 (−3.5)	4
New index, original trend	100	6	1	5	2.9 (2.0)	−2.1 (−3.0)	3

*Five months less than average lead time, for the reasons stated in the discussion of the defects of medium-lead indicators.

diffusion index of twelve leading indicators over the old index is the utilization of four long-lead indicators, instead of only two in the prior index. The old index utilized the two series on private building permits and net business formation. The new index continued the use of these two long-lead indicators and added two other long-leaders: the layoff rate in manufacturing and vendor performance (the percentage of slower deliveries).

It may also be of some significance, in considering indicator lead times, that the five new medium-lead indicators introduced into the new BEA-NBER diffusion index would appear to be of above-average length for such indicators, as we have defined them. The average of their five maximum lead times is more than seventeen months, while the average of their average lead times is nine months.

TABLE 7-2   Leading Indicator Series in New BEA-NBER Diffusion Indices, Arranged by Average Length of Lead Times at Business Peaks

Economic or financial indicator	Maximum lead time (months)	Minimum lead time (months)	Average lead time (months)
LONG-LEAD INDICATORS			
1. Private housing permits*	30	8	14.8
2. Layoff rate in manufacturing (inverted)	28	1	14.1
3. Net business formation*	26	8	13.2
4. Vendor performance (percentage of slower deliveries)	34	1	12.5
Average	29.5	4.5	13.7
ABOVE-AVERAGE MEDIUM-LEAD INDICATORS			
5. Average workweek, production workers in manufacturing*	22	4	12.8
6. Real money supply (M − 1), 1967 dollars	13	5	9.3
7. New orders, consumer goods and materials, 1967 dollars	25	1	8.8
8. Percent change in total liquid assets	16	2	8.2
9. Contracts and orders for plant and equipment, 1967 dollars	13	1	7.7
10. Net change in inventories on hand and on order, 1967 dollars	12	4	6.7
11. Percent change in sensitive wholesale prices (non-foods and feeds)	23	−7	9.0
12. Standard & Poor's 500-Stock Index†	13	5	9.3
Average	17.1	1.9	9.0

*Indicators 1, 3, and 5 were also in the old BEA-NBER diffusion indices; the other nine indicators are new.

†Stock prices gave two false turning point signals in 1961 and 1966 (see "Table 7-5: Eight Stock Market Peaks").

Details on the composition and indicator lead times for the new BEA-NBER diffusion index are shown in Table 7-2. We are, of course, glad to welcome the Bureau of Economic Analysis and the National Bureau of Economic Research aboard our long-lead indicator bandwagon, launched a long time ago by coauthor Jesse Levin in his pioneer article, "Prophetic Leaders."[3]

[3]*Financial Analysts Journal,* July–August 1970.

HISTORICAL RECORD OF THE BEST LEADING
INDICATORS AT FOUR TYPES OF TURNING POINTS

Let us now rank the best available long-lead and medium-lead indicators, as revealed by official BEA data.[4] This is done in Tables 7-3, 7-4, 7-5, and 7-6. In each of these four tables, which deal with the four different kinds of turning points, the several indicators are listed in the approximate order of their effectiveness in anticipating business or stock market peaks or bottoms, as the case may be. At the bottom of each table, the average combined results for various groupings of the most effective indicators are shown separately so that they can be compared with the average results for all the indicators. In each of the four tables, the grouping recommended for use in forecasting is italicized.

Note that most of the indicators in the tables are included in the new revised BEA-NBER diffusion indices, issued in early 1975 following the failure of their prior diffusion indices to predict the 1973–1975 recession. In each table, those of our long-lead indicators not included in the BEA-NBER indices are marked with an asterisk. All long-lead indicators, whether or not included in the BEA-NBER indices, are also identified with an *L* to distinguish them from medium-lead indicators.

The sequence of indicators in each of the four tables is based on, first, the batting-average percentage and, second, the average lead time. Also indicated in each of the tables is the variability or reliability of all the indicator lead times, in terms of applicable maximum and minimum lead times since 1948 and the resulting minimax spreads. As previously indicated, effective lead times should be calculated as approximately five months less than the actual reported leads shown in the four tables for maximums, minimums, and averages.

There is, as we have noted, considerable overlap between the two BEA-NBER diffusion indices of twelve leading series and many of the series used in our tables; thus, from one point of view, the BEA-NBER diffusion indices might have been omitted. However, they have been included wherever they are successful forecasters so that their relative effectiveness may be rated, particularly in comparison with the long-lead indicators included in the tables.

Some key conclusions that can be derived from evaluating Tables 7-3 through 7-6 are presented below. It would be helpful for the reader to refer to the appropriate table when considering these conclusions.

Table 7-3: Six Business Peaks

1. The sixteen listed indicators are most successful in forecasting business peaks. Every one of them has a batting average of 100 percent for the six business peaks from 1948 through 1975.

2. The superiority of long-lead indicators over medium-lead indicators in forecasting business peaks is clearly demonstrated. The averages in line C for the top nine indicators (of which seven are long-lead indicators) show a maximum lead time of 29.4 months, a minimum lead time of 7.4 months, and an average lead time of 16.5 months. These figures may be compared with corresponding results for all sixteen indicators in line A of 24.4 months, 5.5 months, and 13.1 months respectively. They may also be compared with the two BEA-NBER diffusion indices (line D), for which the corresponding figures are 23 months maximum, 4 months minimum, and 10.7 average.

If 5 months are subtracted from all the previous figures so as to obtain effective maximum, minimum, and average lead times, the comparative advantage of the

---

[4]The most complete source of these data is the official *Business Conditions Digest* (BCD), published monthly by the Bureau of Economic Analysis of the Department of Commerce.

TABLE 7-3   Long-Lead and Medium-Lead Indicators as Business Forecasters: Six Peaks, 1948–1975

Economic or financial indicator	Batting average (percent)	Maximum lead time (months)	Minimum lead time (months)	Minimax spread of lead (months)	Average lead time (months)
1. Percent change in money supply and deposits (M − 2); (L)*	100	33	19	14	26.2
2. Liabilities of business failures, current dollars (inverted); (L)*	100	38	11	25	23.3
3. Private housing starts (L)*	100	35	10	25	19.5
4. Private housing permits (L)	100	30	8	22	14.8
5. Layoff rate in manufacturing (inverted); (L)	100	28	1	27	14.1
6. Net business formation (L)	100	26	8	18	13.2
7. Average workweek, production workers in manufacturing	100	22	4	18	12.8
8. Vendor performance percentage of slower deliveries (L)	100	34	1	33	12.5
9. Change in unfilled orders for durable goods, current dollars*	100	19	5	14	11.7
10. New BEA index of twelve leading indicators (original trend)	100	23	4	19	10.8
11. New BEA index of twelve leading indicators (reverse trend)	100	23	4	19	10.5
12. Real money supply (M − 1), 1967 dollars	100	13	5	8	9.3
13. New orders, consumer goods and materials, 1967 dollars	100	25	1	24	8.8
14. Percent change in total liquid assets	100	16	2	14	8.2
15. Contracts and orders for plant and equipment, 1967 dollars	100	13	1	12	7.7
16. Net change in inventories on hand and on order, 1967 dollars	100	12	4	8	6.7
A. Averages, all sixteen indicators	100	24.4	5.5	18.8	13.1
B. *Averages, top three indicators (all long-lead)*	*100*	*34.7*	*13.3*	*21.3*	*23.0*
C. *Averages, top nine indicators (including seven long-lead)*	*100*	*29.4*	*7.4*	*21.8*	*16.5*
D. Averages, two BEA indices (including four long-lead)	100	23.0	4.0	19.0	10.7
E. Averages, bottom five indicators (all medium-lead)	100	15.8	2.6	12.8	8.1

*Indicators 1, 2, 3, and 9 are *not* included in the current BEA-NBER diffusion indices.
(L) denotes a long-lead indicator.
Italics for B and C indicate that these groupings are recommended for use in forecasting.

long-lead indicators is relatively magnified. Note particularly that the effective minimum lead times are negligible or negative for all sixteen indicators (line A) and for the two BEA-NBER diffusion indices (line D).

3. The superiority of the longest-lead indicators over all the other groupings of indicators in forecasting business peaks is demonstrated in the results shown in line B for the top three indicators: the percent change in money supply and deposits (M-2), the liabilities of business failures, and private housing starts. For these three select series, the maximum lead time averages 34.7 months, the minimum lead time 13.3 months, and the average lead time 23.0 months. Even when reduced by 5 months each, the resulting effective lead times are ample and practical: 30 months, 8 months, and 18 months, respectively.

It is surprising that these three highly effective long-lead indicators are not included in the BEA-NBER diffusion indices. (To be sure, the housing permits series, which overall performs a bit less successfully than that for housing starts, is included.)

4. Had these three long-lead indicators been included, the 1948–1975 results for the two BEA-NBER diffusion indices, shown in line D, would have been better. As it is, the average lead time of the diffusion indices, 10.7 months, is somewhat too close to the 8.1 months for the bottom five indicators of Table 7-3 (all medium-lead), as shown in line E. In both cases also, if the reported figures as shown are reduced by 5 months, the effective minimum lead times become negative.

5. It is recommended that both the top three indicators (line B) and the top nine indicators (line C) of Table 7-3 be used by business forecasters. The six superior indicators, to be added to the top three already cited, are (4) private housing permits; (5) the layoff rate in manufacturing; (6) net business formation; (7) the average workweek of production workers in manufacturing; (8) vendor performance; and (9) the change in unfilled orders for durable goods, in current dollars.

The first grouping of three will make the forecast of a coming business peak at the earliest possible time, while the second grouping of nine will serve to confirm the original forecast in ample time for needed action. The somewhat later confirmation by the new official BEA-NBER diffusion indices will be welcome but unnecessary.

Table 7-4: Six Business Bottoms

1. Only eleven indicators, including the two BEA-NBER diffusion indices, prove to be fairly satisfactory leaders at business bottoms, with 100 percent batting averages from 1948 through the recession bottom of April 1975. This is five fewer than the sixteen indicators for business peaks in Table 7-3.

2. Moreover, indicator lead times at business bottoms are typically considerably shorter than for business peaks. Business low points seem to arrive much more suddenly and unexpectedly than business tops. Thus, when 5 months are subtracted from the reported averages shown in lines A through D of Table 7-4, practical effective lead times frequently become inadequate, especially for minimum and average lead times.

3. Part of the same picture is the fact that the superiority of long-lead over medium-lead indicators is far less at business bottoms than at business peaks. Indeed, long-lead indicators have to be *defined* in terms of their lead times at business tops; they are not in fact long-lead indicators at bottoms.

Only three long-lead indicators in Table 7-4 for business bottoms have perfect batting averages of 100 percent, compared with seven in Table 7-3 for business peaks. They are (1) the percent change in money supply and deposits (M-2), (5) private housing starts, and (6) private housing permits. Significantly, too, the average lead time for these three long-lead indicators is only 6.4 months, just slightly superior to the average of 5.1 months for the other eight medium-lead indicators in Table 7-4.

TABLE 7-4   Long-Lead and Medium-Lead Indicators as Business Forecasters: Six Bottoms, 1948–1975

Economic or financial indicator	Batting average (percent)	Maximum lead time (months)	Minimum lead time (months)	Minimax spread of lead (months)	Average lead time (months)
1. Percent change in money supply and deposits (M − 2); (L)*	100	15	1	14	7.8
2. Percent change in total liquid assets	100	15	4	11	7.4
3. Change in unfilled orders for durable goods, current dollars*	100	13	3	10	7.2
4. Real money supply (M − 1), 1967 dollars	100	14	1	13	6.8
5. Private housing starts (L)*	100	12	2	10	6.0
6. Private housing permits (L)	100	10	1	9	5.3
7. New BEA index of twelve leading indicators (reverse trend)	100	10	2	8	5.2
8. Percent change in sensitive wholesale prices (non-foods and feeds)	100	10	2	8	4.8
9. New orders, capital goods industries, current dollars*	100	8	1	7	4.2
10. New BEA index of twelve leading indicators (original trend)	100	6	1	5	2.8
11. Contracts and orders for plant and equipment, 1967 dollars	100	6	1	5	2.2
A. Averages, all eleven indicators	100	10.8	1.7	9.1	5.4
B. *Averages, top three indicators (one long-lead)*	*100*	*14.3*	*2.7*	*11.7*	*7.5*
C. *Averages, top six indicators (including three long-lead)*	*100*	*13.2*	*2.0*	*11.2*	*6.8*
D. Averages, two BEA indices (including four long-lead)	100	8.0	1.5	6.5	4.0

*Indicators 1, 3, 5, and 9 are *not* included in the current BEA-NBER diffusion indices.
(L) denotes a long-lead indicator.
Italics for B and C indicate that these groupings are recommended for use in forecasting.

Finally, of the three best lead indicators at business bottoms, only one is long-lead, the reliable percent change in money supply and deposits (M-2). And this time it is far from being truly long-lead, with a reported minimum lead time of just 1 month.

4. Similarly to our recommendation for Table 7-3, it is essential that both the top three (line 8) and the top six indicators (line 6) be used to forecast business bottoms, in that order. The effective lead times will not be great but usually will be positive. Practical confirmation by the BEA-NBER diffusion indices will come some months later, quite possibly retrospectively.

Table 7-5: Eight Stock Market Peaks

Stock market forecasting by means of economic indicators is much more difficult and much less successful than is using such indicators for business turning points. For stock market peaks, long-lead indicators are absolutely essential even though not infallible, while medium-lead indicators are of little use.

It will be noted that eight stock market peaks are covered, as compared with six business peaks in Table 7-3. The reason is that during the 1960s two stock market peaks were not followed by full-fledged economic recessions. The severe stock bear markets of 1961–1962 and 1966 did not foreshadow recessions as defined by the National Bureau of Economic Research, that is, two successive quarters of decline in the real gross national product (GNP).

All we had in 1962 was a so-called growth recession (a decline but not a cessation in the rate of real GNP growth), while what we had in 1966 was called either a "nongrowth recession" or a "minirecession" (a brief, one-quarter cessation of real GNP growth). These two notable failures of the stock market as a cyclical economic indicator suggest that sometimes bull and bear markets are motivated primarily by emotional investor fears and hopes rather than by basic economic or financial causes.

Since it should not be expected that economic and financial indicators can accurately and consistently forecast swings in investor psychology, in Table 7-5 and also in Table 7-6 we distinguish between the six economically induced turning points in the stock market and the two noneconomic turning points and provide different figures for each category.

Some key conclusions from Table 7-5 follow:

1. Only two indicators, both long-lead, have 100 percent batting averages for stock market peaks: the percent change in money supply and deposits (M-2) and liabilities of business failures. Average lead times are ample in both cases, and they improve somewhat when only the six economic stock market peaks are considered.

2. Four other long-lead indicators have better than 50 percent batting averages for all eight stock market peaks, ranging from 75 percent down to 63 percent. They are (3) private housing starts, (4) private housing permits, (5) the layoff rate in manufacturing, and (6) net business formation. Not one medium-lead indicator comes close to these scores. All indicator batting averages are improved moderately when only the six "economic" stock market peaks are considered.

3. Only the top two and then the top four indicators should be used for forecasting stock market peaks (lines B and C). The top two indicators have a 100 percent score for both eight and six stock market peaks; the other two have 75 percent scores for eight peaks and 83 percent scores for six peaks. However, since private housing permits and private housing starts can be regarded as largely overlapping, some forecasters may prefer also to use our fifth long-lead indicator, the layoff rate in manufacturing (included in line D).

4. Table 7-5 clearly confirms the view that forecasting probabilities are significantly lower for the stock market than for the business cycle, and especially so when investor psychology is decisive. Therefore, additional stock market analysis, both fundamental and technical, would appear to be essential to increase the

TABLE 7-5   Long-Lead and Medium-Lead Indicators as Stock Market Forecasters: Eight or Six Peaks, 1948–1975

Economic or financial indicator	Batting average (percent)	Maximum lead time (months)	Minimum lead time (months)	Minimax spread of lead (months)	Average lead time (months)
1. Percent change in money supply and deposits (M − 2); (L)*	100 100	23	3	20	13.9 17.2
2. Liabilities of business failures, current dollars (inverted); (L)*	100 100	31	1	30	11.6 12.3
3. Private housing starts (L)*	75 83	29	−4	33	7.5 10.5
4. Private housing permits (L)	75 83	17	−2	19	5.5 5.7
5. Layoff rate in manufacturing (inverted) (L)	63 67	8	−9	17	4.1 5.5
6. Net business formation (L)	63 83	13	−2	15	2.0 2.4
7. Average workweek, production workers in manufacturing	50 67	10	−4	14	2.1 3.7
8. Change in unfilled orders for durable goods, current dollars*	50 67	7	−19	26	1.0 0.3
A. Averages, all eight indicators	72 81	17.3	−4.5	21.8	6.0 7.2
B. *Averages, top two indicators (both long-lead)*	*100* *100*	*27.0*	*2.0*	*25.0*	*12.8* *14.8*
C. *Averages, top four indicators (all long-lead)*	*88* *92*	*25.0*	*0.8*	*26.8*	*9.6* *11.4*
D. Averages, top five indicators (all (long-lead)	83 87	21.6	−2.2	23.8	8.5 10.2

*Indicators 1, 2, 3, and 8 are *not* included in the current BEA-NBER diffusion indices.
(L) denotes a long-lead indicator.
Italics for B and C indicate that these groupings are recommended for use in forecasting.
   NOTE: For each stock market indicator in Tables 7-5 and 7-6, the two sets of figures shown as batting-average percentages and average lead times are for (1) all eight stock market peaks or bottoms from 1948 through 1975 and (2) six peaks or bottoms only, excluding the "noneconomic" bear markets of 1961 and 1966.
   If the minimum lead time is negative, it is also, of course, the maximum lag time.

probability of a stock market forecast based, in part, on the analysis of long-lead and medium-lead indicators.

What we favor is the use of a *consensus* of mostly technical indicators. This approach is recommended for the same reason that we employ the consensus approach for economic indicators, namely, that it is supported by the principles of probability. Thus, if a forecasting method with a given batting-average percentage is combined with another method with about the same percentage of accuracy, the combination of the two methods will have a higher percentage of accuracy than either of the individual methods. And the greater the number of methods with fair reliabilities used, the higher the batting average for their combination.

All in all, the ideal composite stock market forecasting technique would seem to be one utilizing a consensus of successful economic indicators, mostly long-lead, plus a consensus of superior fundamental and technical stock market indicators, mostly technical. See also Chapter 8.

Table 7-6: Eight Stock Market Bottoms

1. Forecasting with long- and medium-lead economic indicators achieves its poorest results at stock market bottoms. In sharp contrast to the results of Tables 7-3, 7-4, and 7-5, no indicator in Table 7-6 has a batting average of even 75 percent, let alone 100 percent. Indeed, only the top three indicators achieve results of 50 percent or better for all eight stock market bottoms. Moreover, average lead times, even when reported as positive, are invariably too short for effective forecasting when our standard five-month cutoff is employed.

All too plainly, the economy and the stock market turn *up* more closely together at bottoms than they turn *down* at tops. So our previous recommendation on composite consensus stock market forecasting applies even more strongly to stock market bottoms than to peaks.

Fortunately, it is more important for investors to catch stock market peaks as promptly as possible, and thereby to avoid bear market losses, than it is for them precisely to catch stock market bottoms and thereby to profit from a bull market in its very earliest days. This is true because while a smaller profit is only disappointing, a larger loss can spell disaster.

However, because much of the profit in a bull market comes in its first year, we do not want to miss a stock market bottom by many months. Accordingly, the following advice is given:

2. Catch bear market bottoms promptly by utilizing only the top two or three indicators in Table 7-6: the percent change in money supply and deposits (M-2), the current-dollar change in unfilled orders for durable goods, and the percent change in total liquid assets. Even though each of this triad has a relatively low probability at stock market bottoms, the consensus interpretation of all three together can, as previously suggested, increase their joint reliability to a more useful level, particularly when confirmed by an additional consensus of technical and fundamental indicators.

SUMMARY AND CONCLUSIONS

In bringing this chapter to a close, the following eight key points, a few of which have not previously been touched upon, deserve emphasis.

1. We have carefully defined three categories of leading economic indicators—long-lead, medium-lead, and short-lead—in terms of specific periods of months for maximum and average lead times.

2. Our central theme has been that medium-lead economic indicators are not by themselves very useful for *practical* forecasting of business cycle and stock market turning points. For successful forecasting, they must be supplemented

TABLE 7-6 Long-Lead and Medium-Lead Indicators as Stock Market Forecasters: Eight or Six Bottoms, 1948–1975

Economic or financial indicator	Batting average (percent)	Maximum lead time (months)	Minimum lead time (months)	Minimax spread of lead (months)	Average lead time (months)
1. Percent change in money supply deposits (M − 2); (L)*	63 67	10	−7	17	3.0 3.0
2. Change in unfilled orders for durable goods, current dollars*	50 50	9	−5	14	1.4 2.3
3. Percent change in total liquid assets	50 67	10	−5	15	0.6 2.7
4. Real money supply (M − 1), 1967 dollars	38 50	10	−3	13	0.8 2.0
5. Percent change in sensitive wholesale prices (non-foods and feeds)	38 33	6	−3	9	0.1 1.0
6. Private housing starts (L)*	38 50	5	−2	7	0.8 1.0
7. Private housing permits (L)	25 33	5	−3	8	0.1 0.5
8. New BEA index of twelve leading indicators (reverse trend)	25 33	6	−2	8	0 0.3
A. Averages, all eight indicators (including three long-lead)	40.9 47.9	7.6	−3.8	11.4	0.9 1.6
B. *Averages, top two indicators (one long-lead)*	*56.5* *58.5*	*9.5*	*−6.0*	*15.5*	*2.2* *2.8*
C. *Averages, top three indicators (one long-lead)*	*54.3* *61.3*	*9.7*	*−5.7*	*15.3*	*1.7* *2.7*

*Indicators 1, 2, and 6 are *not* included in the current BEA-NBER diffusion indices.
(L) denotes a long-lead indicator.
Italics for B and C indicate that these groupings are recommended for use in forecasting.
NOTE: See applicable comments in Table 7-5.

systematically by some long-lead indicators. In general, it is better to use fewer indicators with longer average lead times than the reverse.

3. Another major theme has been that such long-lead indicators are particularly effective in forecasting turning points at stock market peaks preceding major bear markets.

4. A fourth theme is that since individual indicators can be wrong at particular turning points, there is significantly greater forecasting reliability in a consensus of usually correct medium-lead and long-lead indicators. Unlike a chain, such a consensus is stronger than its strongest component.

5. The most useful form of consensus indicator for both economic and stock market forecasting is also the simplest and quickest, namely, the ratio or percentage of the number of favorable indicators to the total number of indicators in the consensus. In other words, *it does not appear essential or particularly helpful to construct a weighted or otherwise adjusted consensus index of the indicators.*

6. For the stock market, in which the probability and the reliability of economic forecasting are both relatively low, the consensus approach should be used in a double fashion:

a. The percentage of our selected long-lead and medium-lead indicators that are favorable.

b. The percentage of reliable fundamental and technical stock market indicators that are favorable.

Such a double consensus gives us minimum feasible uncertainty and maximum feasible reliability.

7. In rating indicators as favorable or unfavorable in future situations, some attention should be given to the *rate-of-change trend* of the indicators. Thus, if expansion of an indicator is favorable, watch for a declining rate of expansion from the previous period or from the year before. Conversely, if contraction of an indicator is favorable, beware of a decreasing rate of contraction.

Such deteriorating rates of change may well imply that the indicator is losing its effectiveness, perhaps because of the workings of the "wise guy" effect (see Chapter 8).

8. In periods of above-average inflation (that is, whenever the annual rate of inflation is more than 4 percent), it is especially important that all dollar unit indicators also be evaluated in constant-dollar form to obtain more reliable deflated, or real, changes in the indicators.

Chapter **8**

Timing via Stock Market Indicators

ARTHUR A. MERRILL

This chapter lists and describes various indicators that can help investors time their purchases and sales more successfully. It covers both fundamental (economic, monetary, and financial) and technical (internal market) indicators, with somewhat greater emphasis on the latter.

Indicators sometimes are classified by time or immediacy: short-term, intermediate, and long-term. On other occasions, they are classified by source or area covered: employment, production, money and credit, and so on. Here we prefer to classify them by *purpose*. What helpful questions do the various selected indicators serve to answer? In our approach, the eleven major questions are the following:

1. How can we determine the market trend?
2. Does the market show signs of excessive speculation?
3. Is volume performance unusual?
4. Is the market overextended? Are there noteworthy disparities in performance?
5. Are prices relatively high or low in terms of earnings and yields?
6. Are there seasonal tendencies in the market? Is the calendar or the clock a useful indicator? Does the market have other habit patterns of behavior?
7. What are the clues from sophisticated market investors? What are the professionals doing?
8. What are the clues from unsophisticated investors and speculators? What are the nonprofessionals doing?
9. What are the monetary and interest rate intentions of the Federal Reserve Board?
10. What are the economic prospects for general business?
11. How can the several interpretations of the indicators be combined to reach a central, decisive conclusion?

The applicable indicators for answering each of these questions, as we have chosen them, will be analyzed in detail and evaluated statistically later in this chapter. First, some background material on the utility and applicability of the indicator approach itself may be helpful.

HOW CAN WE DETERMINE THE MARKET TREND?

In bull markets, equities such as common stocks are the best investment; in bear markets, bonds or cash equivalents are preferable. Unfortunately, the market is beset with reactions and rallies, and the current trend is usually obscure. Indicators intended to answer this question are used to interpret the *current* trend of the market, so that the investor can adopt the proper policy and take the appropriate action.

Moving Averages of Major Market Indices

A common procedure for determining trend is the "moving average." Prices during a specified period of time (a week, a month, or some other period) are averaged, and the average is then customarily charted for the period desired.

The moving average smooths or removes the short-term vibrations of the original series. It is used to determine a trend in two ways:

1. *The direction of the moving average is assumed to be the direction of its current trend.* In this simple approach, the exact moving average need not be calculated. A quick comparison of the figure for the latest period with the figure for the earlier period discarded is quite sufficient. For example, if the most recent week's figure is higher than that for eleven weeks back, then the ten-week moving average will have risen in the current week.

2. *Index figures can be compared with their own moving average.* An index usually remains above its moving average in an uptrend and below it in a downtrend. Thus, a bull market may be defined as one in which the Dow Jones Industrials are above their 200-day moving average or their six-month moving average.

When an index moves through, or penetrates, its moving average upward or downward, the corresponding change in trend is forecast. Sometimes, a required amount of penetration is specified. A popular requirement is a 3 percent penetration. The indices most widely used for trend determination are the Dow Jones Industrials, Standard & Poor's 425 Industrials, Standard & Poor's 500-Stock Index, and the New York Stock Exchange Composite Index of all NYSE stocks.

The amount of smoothing is proportional to the span of the moving average. Short-span moving averages are more sensitive, or volatile, while longer-term averages typically move quite sedately. The moving averages with the most popular durations are the 200-day (trading, not calendar days), twenty-week, twenty-six-week (six-month), thirty-week, and forty-week moving averages.

Some analysts use two averages of different time spans. Only when both the short-term moving average (four weeks, for example) and the longer-term one (six months, for example) are penetrated by the current index figure is a change of trend forecast.

A "percentage of the previous year" measure is used by some analysts for trend determination. Since it compares the most recent figure with that of a year ago, it is similar to a moving average with a one-year span. Thus, if the percentage is above 100 percent, the one-year moving average is rising.

Dow Theory Trend Indicators

Under the Dow theory, the major trend is determined by the secondary swings. The theory is most generally interpreted as follows:

1. *A bull market is signaled as a possibility* when an intermediate decline in the Dow average stops above the bottom of the previous intermediate decline.

2. A bull market is *confirmed* when, after step 1 has happened, the next intermediate rise in the Dow average goes above the peak of the last previous intermediate rise.

3. A bull market is *in progress* as long as each new intermediate advance goes higher than the peak of the previous intermediate rise and each new intermediate decline stops above the bottom of the previous one.

4. Contrariwise, *a bear market is signaled as a possibility* when an intermediate rally in the Dow average fails to break through the top of the previous intermediate rise.

5. A bear market is *confirmed* when, after step 4 has happened, the next intermediate decline breaks through the low of the previous one.

6. A bear market is *in progress* as long as each new intermediate decline goes lower than the bottom of the prior intermediate drop and each new intermediate rally fails to rise as high as the previous intermediate advance.

This method of determining trends by breakthrough has been compared aptly to the determination of tides by the extent of waves on a sandy beach. Thus, on the upside, if the farthest sweep of a wave is marked on the beach with a stick and the next wave carries past this point (a breakthrough), the tide is probably rising.

In the determination of trend, both industrial and transportation indices must be considered under the traditional Dow theory. Changes and breakthroughs by one average are not considered signals until the moves are confirmed by the action of the companion average. The confirming action need not occur on the same day.

Since Charles H. Dow did not specifically determine the size required to qualify a market swing as intermediate or secondary, the conclusions of various Dow theory interpreters sometimes disagree. The author has found a simple 5 percent requirement to be useful. Under this method, a rise or decline through a previous swing of 5 percent or more is considered a valid breakthrough and determines the trend.

Trend Lines

The use of trend lines is a graphic method of trend determination. On a chart, the high points are connected with a straight or curved line, and the low points are also connected. The price curve moves back and forth in the channel between the two trend lines. A trend line is considered more trustworthy if it connects more than two points. Similarly, a trend line connecting four points is better than one that passes through only three points.

Since the investor is interested primarily in relative percentage changes in stock prices, a geometric or semilogarithmic scale, not an arithmetic scale, should always be used on trend charts. A geometric scale shows the same *percentage* changes at any price level as spatially equal, while an arithmetic scale will, for example, show a 10-point change in an average moving from 50 to 60 as exactly equal to a 10-point change in an average moving from 100 to 110, even though the first move is a change of 20 percent and the second a change of 10 percent. When prices break out of their trend channel by penetrating the upper or lower trend line, a change in trend in the direction of the breakout is forecast.

For stock market trend analysis, the basic stock market averages described above are typically employed.

Advance/Decline Moving Averages

A long-term average (200 days) of advances less declines, which has been called a "momentum index" by the *Indicator Digest,* is useful as a nonprice, longer-term trend indicator.

Richard Russell charts a ten-day moving average of advances and another ten-day moving average of declines, which are especially sensitive to shorter trends. When one of these averages remains above the other for thirty days or more, the short-term trend is deemed to be up or down accordingly.

Bullish Percentages of Stock Groups

In this approach, the trend lines of individual stocks in a selected group are first determined. The percentage of the group in an uptrend is then calculated. If it is above 50 percent, the trend is considered upward; if below 50 percent, downward.

There are many variations of this approach. Thus, Chartcraft, Inc., performs this analysis for all NYSE stocks, for all American Stock Exchange (ASE) issues, and separately for the Dow Jones Industrials. *Indicator Digest*, defining individual trends by the direction of a five-week moving average, calculates the bullish percentage for over 230 major stocks. The author uses a group of thirty growing companies and calculates the proportion of these rated "buy."

The Merrill Analysis Indicators

In the weekly service, *Technical Trends,* published by the author, special attention is paid to the indicators shown below for determining the market trend. Also given is the record of accuracy for each indicator for the very short term (one week); the intermediate term, specified as a 5 percent swing rather than a fixed time period; and the long term, as shown by 30 percent swings. These barometer batting averages (BBAs) are based on the accuracy of actual forecasts made with the indicators during preceding ten-year periods. All the forecasts necessarily included some judgment decisions. Each indicator is also given a weight (0, 1, 2, or 3) on the basis of its historical ratio of success in this ten-year period. These weights are shown in parentheses. The purpose of the weights is to derive a weighted indicator consensus, or "technical trend balance," described below in the section "Accuracy Record of the Technical Trends Consensus."

Six-Month Average Direction (2).   To smooth the zigzags of the DJIA, the six-month (twenty-six-week) moving average is used. If the average is rising, the long-term trend is up; if it is falling, the trend is down. A typical recent ten-year accuracy record (BBA) for this barometer is:

	Percent
Short term (following week)	54.3
5 percent swings	63.4
30 percent swings	72.0

5 Percent Swing Direction (3).   A 5 percent filter is applied to DJIA price movements to eliminate minor fluctuations. After all swings of less than 5 percent have been eliminated, the direction of price movement is an excellent indication of longer-term trend (30 percent swings). A typical recent ten-year accuracy record (BBA) for this barometer is:

	Percent
Short term (following week)	50.3
5 percent swings	67.5
30 percent swings	73.4

Price Compared with Six-Month Moving Average (3).   If the DJIA is above its six-month moving average, an uptrend is forecast; if below, a downtrend is indicated. This barometer can be used to define bull and bear markets. A typical recent ten-year accuracy record (BBA) for this barometer is:

	Percent
Short term (following week)	55.1
5 percent swings	67.4
30 percent swings	75.1

New Lows or Highs for 5 Percent Swing (3).   If a 5 percent swing is extended upward by new highs, a further extension of the move can usually be expected. If a 5 percent downswing is extended by new lows, the forecast is for an extension of the downswing. A typical recent ten-year accuracy record (BBA) for this barometer is:

	Percent
Short term (following week)	52.3
5 percent swings	75.6
30 percent swings	71.1

DOES THE MARKET SHOW SIGNS OF EXCESSIVE SPECULATION?

Speculation in moderation can be salutary when it reinforces an upward trend. Thus, the indicators in this category endeavor to give warning signals of the dangerous, excessive speculation characteristic of the very top of a bull market. Most of them are *volume* clues that reveal or pinpoint such speculative activity.

Included are such measures as volume in low-priced stocks, the daily volume of the fifteen or twenty most active stocks on the NYSE, volume on the ASE compared with that on the Big Board.

Most Active Stocks: Average Price

The average price of the most active stocks is a measure of the quality of market leadership. Usually, a market dominated by high-priced stocks is considered respectable; if low-priced stocks are attracting great interest, the market is suspect. An average price below $40 is thought to be bearish; one above $50, bullish.

Lucien Hooper suggests tabulating average prices of the most active stocks in two columns, one for advancing markets and one for declining markets. The average price figure is entered in the first column if the market has advanced for the day and in the second column if it has declined. A comparison of the two columns reveals the relative quality of leadership in advances and declines. However, Hooper does not now believe that the price of the most active stocks is as important a market indicator as it was before the institutions became so dominant in the market and, correspondingly, in the most active stock categories.

Most Active Stocks: Volume

This figure is thought to be a measure of speculation because professionals try to accumulate stocks quietly. For an indicator, Walter Heiby watches the trend of the ratio of the ten-day moving-average volume of the most active NYSE stocks to the ten-day moving average of NYSE volume.

Indicators of Speculative Activity

In the weekly service *Technical Trends,* the greatest attention is given to two indicators shown below, the Option Activity Ratio and the ASE Volume Ratio, for detecting speculative activity.

In addition to the BBAs used for the indicators in the preceding section of this chapter, in this and subsequent sections we also include useful "indicator profiles" (IP) for the accuracy of indicator predictive ability in the decade 1963–1972, in terms of unusually low and unusually high values (the indicator deciles) and moderately low and moderately high values (the indicator quartiles).

Besides the accuracy percentage, a number is shown in parentheses to indicate the statistical significance of the difference between the forecasts made by the high and low values. These differences and their statistical significance are as follows:

(3) Highly significant (3 or more standard errors)
(2) Significant (2.30–2.99 standard errors)
(1) Probably significant (1.64–2.29 standard errors)
(0) Doubtful significance (1.63 or less standard errors)

In this and subsequent sections, the distribution tables show the following:

Highest decile. 10 percent of the figures during the historical period (usually 1963–1972) were above the indicated level.

Highest quartile. 25 percent of the figures were above the indicated level.

Median. 50 percent of the figures were above the indicated level.

Lowest quartile. 25 percent of the figures were below the indicated level.

Lowest decile. 10 percent of the figures were below the indicated level.

This type of distributional analysis helps answer these questions: How high is high? How low is low?

ASE Volume Ratio (3).   Stocks on the American Stock Exchange need not meet as stringent requirements as those listed on the Big Board. The companies are usually younger, with smaller capitalizations and lower and more volatile stock prices. In a growing company, the fastest growth rates occur typically in the youthful days, before the company qualifies for listing on the NYSE. For these reasons, ASE stocks are more popular with speculative investors.

A simple index of the degree of speculation, originated by the author in 1963 and now quite popular, is the ratio of weekly volume on the ASE to weekly volume on the NYSE. When this ratio is high, beware!

The 1963–1972 statistical distribution for the ASE Volume Ratio is as follows:

Upper decile	49.7 (bearish)
Upper quartile	40.6 (bearish)
Median	31.7
Lower quartile	27.2 (bullish)
Lower decile	24.2 (bullish)

The deciles of the ASE Volume Ratio have an excellent record in forecasting both short- and long-term swings. The quartiles are also significant but at a lower level.

Typical recent ten-year BBAs for the ratio are as follows:

	Deciles (Percent)	Quartiles (Percent)
Short term (following week)	63.7 (2)	57.8 (2)
5 percent swings	72.6 (3)	62.8 (3)
10 percent swings	76.5 (3)	68.2 (3)
30 percent swings	70.6 (3)	66.3 (3)

WHAT CLUES DO WE GET FROM VOLUME PERFORMANCE?

Since every security transaction involves both a purchase and a sale, most conclusions about flow-of-money trends are in error. However, the velocity of trading, or volume, has been found helpful by many analysts. Some observers believe that more time is spent by market analysts and observers on various aspects of this factor than on any other market statistic.

When prices rise with an increase in volume, almost all writings on the market agree that the signs are good for a further rise. Conversely, when prices fall with an increase in volume, almost everyone agrees that the signs are not good. In other words, as an old market adage has it, "Volume goes with the trend." Accordingly, there are two basic bullish and two basic bearish volume patterns:

Bullish. (1) *Rising volume* on market *rallies* shows market strength; investors are eager to buy. (2) So does *shrinking volume* on market *reactions;* investors are reluctant to sell.

Bearish. (1) *Rising volume* on market *declines* shows market weakness; investors are afraid that prices will go still lower. (2) So does *declining volume* on market *rallies;* investors have little faith in the higher prices.

In terms of market cycles, total volume normally increases as prices rise in a bull market and drops off during intermediate declines. At market tops, stocks sometimes tend to move horizontally with heavy volume. Some say that this "churning" is a sign of excessive speculation; others believe that it signifies that professionals are distributing their holdings.

At the beginning of a bear market, the urgency to unload drives volume up during market declines, but as the bear market continues, public interest falls off and volume drops to low levels. Sometimes the bottom of an intermediate decline is signaled by a sharp rise in volume, a so-called selling climax.

Thus, careful analysis of volume performance should provide worthwhile clues to the position and trend of prices in major market cycles.

Total Market Volume

This measure is studied in various spans: day, week, month, and year. Moving averages of volume are also calculated for spans of 10 days, 100 days, and six months. All these figures are compared with corresponding price indices or averages. As suggested, when volume parallels price, the forecast is bullish; when the two series diverge, the forecast is bearish. Some analysts consider a drop of the 10-day volume average through a longer-term volume average (for example, 100 days) an important warning signal. Of course, longer-term comparisons of total market volume must take into account the change in the number of shares listed on the several exchanges.

On-Balance Volume

This indicator is a cumulative volume curve adjusted for price trend. The day's volume is added to the previous cumulative total if prices have risen for the day; it is subtracted from that total if prices have declined. Thus, if volume is heavy on rising days, the curve rises bullishly; if it is heavy on declining days, the curve dips bearishly. This technique is often used with individual stocks as well as for total market volume.

Volume of Advancing Stocks versus Volume of Declining Stocks

These totals are calculated by Quotron (Scantlin Electronics) and reported by *The Wall Street Journal,* other daily newspapers, and *Barron's.* The data go back to June 1965.

Usually two moving averages, one of volume for advancing stocks and one of volume for declining stocks, are prepared. A ten-day moving average is popular. Larry Williams compares the ten-day averages with one-half of a ten-day moving average of total market volume. He considers a drop of "up volume" down through the half-total curve a sell signal. Other analysts chart the differential between the two curves and view a large negative differential as a bearish warning. We favor the treatment of Richard Arms, Jr., described below in the section "Arms Index."

Buying Power versus Selling Pressure

This indicator was developed by Robert Lowry. Its key terms are defined as follows:

Buying power. Total gain on all rising stocks divided by total volume of rising stocks equals gain per share traded.

Selling pressure. Total loss on all declining stocks divided by total volume of declining stocks equals loss per share traded.

If prices move up easily without requiring high volume, buying power is great, and the indicator is bullish. If buying power declines, the rise in prices is encountering resistance, and the indicator is bearish. On the other side, an increase of selling pressure is bearish, while a decline of selling pressure is bullish. A definite signal is given when the two lines cross.

This indicator is quite sensitive and is never caught for long on the wrong side of a move. For that very reason, however, it is vulnerable to "whipsaws" when the market reverses quickly or repeatedly.

Other Volume Indicators

In the author's service *Technical Trends,* attention is concentrated on the following four volume indicators.

New York Stock Exchange Volume (2).   If, in a given period such as a week, price and volume both rise or both decline, the signs are bullish. If they move in opposite directions, the prospect is bearish.

On a weekly basis, if price and volume move in the same direction four or five days of a week, we score the factor bullish. If they move in opposite directions on four or five days, we rate it bearish. If the five working days divide three to two or two to three, the finding is neutral.

Typical ten-year BBAs for this indicator are only poor to fair:

	Percent
Short term (following week)	47.5
5 percent swings	61.6
30 percent swings	65.3

Enthusiasm (1).   This measure, which was developed by the author, compares NYSE volume on recent rising days with volume on recent declining days, thus showing the direction or thrust of investor enthusiasm or lack of it. Originally, the index was a simple comparison of the NYSE volume on the last five rising days with that for the last five declining days. The index has been refined by the use of one exponential average for the rising days and another for the declining days. In both cases, the most recent day is multiplied by 25 percent and added to 75 percent of the preceding average to form the new exponential average.

The ten-year BBAs for this indicator range from poor for the short term, through somewhat better for 5 percent swings, to very good for major long-term swings. Typical BBA percentages are:

	Percent
Short term (following week)	49.1
5 percent swings	58.8
30 percent swings	70.3

Arms Index (2).   This volume index, proposed by Richard Arms, Jr.,[1] is based on the following simple formula: Average volume of NYSE stocks that declined in a day divided by average volume of NYSE stocks advancing that day. A ratio of *less* than 1.00 means that the volume of rising stocks is greater than that of declining stocks, and the indication is bullish. Conversely, an index of *more* than 1.00 means that declining stocks are showing greater volume, and the indication is bearish.

[1]*Barron's,* Aug. 7, 1967.

Over the years, with generally rising stock prices, the volume of rising stocks averages higher than that of declining stocks. From 1965, when precise volume data became available, through mid-1973, the median ratio is 0.883. For this 8½-year period, the statistical distribution is as follows:

Upper decile	1.126 (bearish)
Upper quartile	0.996 (bearish)
Median	0.883
Lower quartile	0.802 (bullish)
Lower decile	0.741 (bullish)

The 1965–1973 BBAs for the Arms Index of relative volume are as follows:

	Deciles (Percent)	Quartiles (Percent)
Short term (following week)	59.3 (1)	59.2 (2)
5 percent swings	60.4 (1)	56.4 (1)
10 percent swings	64.8 (2)	60.9 (3)
30 percent swings	57.1 (0)	53.2 (0)

Every Skip-a-Day Index (3). This indicator has been developed by Dernell Every, who maintains modified on-balance volume charts for forty-one large industrial companies, including all thirty of the Dow Jones Industrials. The total market value of these forty-one issues amounts to more than 25 percent of the total for all shares listed on the NYSE. The number of these stocks rising and in rising trends is compared with the number of them declining and in declining trends. When the former exceed the latter by a definite margin, a buy signal is given; when the latter are in excess by a definite margin, a sell signal is flashed.

The Every Index is very sensitive and in two-way, indecisive markets gives frequent alternating signals. When used as a short-term trading device in both long buying and short selling, however, it achieved a very profitable record during the 1960s and early 1970s. Its ten-year BBAs are as follows:

	Percent
Short term (following week)	55.4
5 percent swings	64.9
30 percent swings	59.5

IS THE MARKET OVEREXTENDED? ARE THERE NOTEWORTHY PERFORMANCE DISPARITIES?

Stock prices are driven up when demand for stocks exceeds their supply and down when the reverse is true. Both buying and selling surges are very contagious. Almost everyone wants to get on the bandwagon at the same time and (forgiving a mixed metaphor) to get off a sinking ship all at once. The result of this two-sided enthusiasm is that prices are typically driven too far up in upswings and too far down in downswings.

How can we know when we are in such an "overbought" or "oversold" situation? Several indicators can be used.

Extent of Advance or Decline

It has been said that when the market begins an advance, it is starting to sow the seeds for the next decline, and vice versa for declines and subsequent advances. Can one tell from the length of an advance or a decline whether it is overextended?

For the very short term, some market analysts believe that stocks rarely make more than three sharp rises in three successive days or more than three sharp drops in succession. Thus, if the number of daily consecutive advances or declines reaches five or six, chances for a near-term reversal are substantially increased.

For intermediate and longer terms, early writings on the Dow theory considered an extended advance to be corrected (but not reversed) by the following decline, and vice versa. The required size of these corrections was estimated to be from one-third to two-thirds of the preceding upswing or downswing. If the correction was more than two-thirds, the prior trend was presumed to have been reversed.

Taking a cue from the life expectancy tables used in life insurance, the author has studied the longer moves of the Dow Jones Industrial Average from 1897 to 1972. One notable finding is the following. If we apply a 5 percent filter to DJIA market swings (ignoring all changes of less than 5 percent) and review the remaining swings of more than 5 percent, the average *additional* life expectancy after a 20 percent swing in either direction is:

	Bull Market (Percent)	Bear Market (Percent)
Upward swing	11%	8%
Downward swing	5%	8%

Another measure of swing extent is the deviation from a moving average. Thus, some analysts note the distance of the DJIA above or below its long-term moving average, such as the six-month or 200-day average. If the DJIA is more than 10 percent above or more than 10 percent below the moving average, the current upswing or downswing is expected to be corrected by a reverse move.

Number of Waves in a Swing

We mention this approach for the sake of completeness. In the wave theory of R. N. Elliot, a typical bull market has five up-and-down intermediate swings, while a typical bear market has three such component swings. This theory is complicated, however, by uncertainty about the required size needed to qualify as an intermediate swing. If a 5 percent filter is used for this purpose, the author has found that bull markets have had as many as twenty-one upward moves and as few as one, while bear markets have had as many as eleven and as few as one. Thus, the effectiveness of this indicator seems dubious.

Other Disparity Indicators

Several market indicators of disparity are based on the tendency for speculative stocks to top out near the peak of a bull market before the more conservative blue chips. The usual approach is to chart an index with a speculative component and to compare it with a blue-chip average like the Dow Jones Industrials or the Standard & Poor's 500-Stock Index. Agreement is considered neutral; a downward disparity of the speculative index is bearish.

At the bottom of bear markets, speculative stocks tend to rise with or before conservative issues. Disparity indicators, therefore, are much more useful at bull market peaks than at bear market bottoms.

In *Technical Trends,* particular attention is paid to the five disparity indicators described below.

Cumulative Advance/Decline Disparity (0).   One of the most popular indicators is based on the difference between the number of NYSE stocks advancing and the number declining in a given period. This method was originated many years ago by Gen. Leonard P. Ayres of the Cleveland Trust Co.

The number of NYSE stocks advancing and declining can be found in most daily newspapers. The usual method of interpretation is to subtract the number of stocks declining in a day from the number advancing and to cumulate daily the resulting plus or minus figures. Each day the new total, if plus, is added to the preceding day's cumulative total; if the daily total is a minus, it is subtracted.

Many analysts prefer to cumulate *percentages* rather than totals. Each day the difference is calculated as a percentage of the total number of stocks traded. This percentage is then cumulated daily.

The advance/decline (A/D) total or percentage is a nondollar figure. Since it represents all NYSE stocks, including the more speculative issues, it should turn down at major market peaks before the Dow Jones Industrials, which are investment-grade issues. Different analysts have set the lead time as varying between one and sixteen months.

The customary technique is to chart the cumulative A/D figure and align it with a chart of the DJIA. If the Dow is zigzagging upward while the A/D line begins to zigzag downward, the disparity is considered a strong forecast of a reversal of at least the intermediate trend.

In *Technical Trends*, we spot this disparity in a simple way. If the Dow Jones Industrials have risen in the preceding ten weeks and, in the same period, advances have exceeded declines (so that the cumulative curve has risen), there is agreement and no disparity. If, however, the DJIA has risen in the preceding ten weeks and, in the same period, declines have exceeded advances, there is a disparity and the factor is rated bearish.

Unfortunately, typical ten-year BBAs for this indicator are poor:

	Percent
Short term (following week)	54.1 (0)
5 percent swings	44.9 (0)
30 percent swings	36.1 (0)

Advance/Decline Noncumulative (3).   Surprisingly, this indicator achieves much more useful results than the cumulative A/D indicator. It is perhaps the most popular measure of an overbought or oversold condition. We formulate it as a weekly curve of the average daily difference between the number of NYSE stocks advancing and the number of NYSE stocks declining. Then this total difference is expressed as a percentage of the number of issues traded.

Sometimes the result is smoothed by a one-week or ten-day moving average. Thus, Richard Russell uses ten-day moving averages of both advances and declines. The two curves typically cross and recross every fifteen to thirty days. However, if the advance curve remains higher than the decline curve for more than thirty days, the market is viewed as overbought. If the reverse pattern occurs, the sign is "oversold."

The usual interpretation of a simple noncumulative A/D line is to call the market overbought when the ten-day total exceeds a bench mark of about 1,200 and to call it oversold when it drops below minus 1,600. However, the author has checked this interpretation for the ten-year period 1963–1972 and found it to be more often wrong than right. Actually, in each case a high figure seems to be bullish and a low figure bearish; forecasts made on this basis work out quite well. The greatest success was obtained when the time of excess of advances over declines and the time of excess of declines over advances were used as criteria. In other words, *it takes time, not just a high or a low value, to indicate an overbought or oversold condition.*

We have found that when advances have exceeded declines for five successive weeks, the odds shift dramatically from a continuation of the intermediate trend to its reversal; that is, the market is overbought. To spot oversold markets, the runs in the reverse direction are a bit shorter. When declines have exceeded advances for four successive weeks, the probabilities shift to a reversal of the intermediate trend.

Typical ten-year BBAs for this indicator are:

	Deciles (Percent)	Quartiles (Percent)
Short term (following week)	58.3 (1)	61.5 (3)
5 percent swings	68.9 (3)	68.5 (3)
10 percent swings	68.0 (3)	66.9 (3)
30 percent swings	62.1 (3)	61.1 (3)

Percentage Change in One Year: DJIA versus S&P 425 Industrials (2).   This indicator compares the changes from one year earlier for these two widely used indices. The Standard & Poor's 425 Industrial Stock Index includes many more speculative stocks than the DJIA. On the basis of historical trends, when this indicator's curve for the DJIA is above that for the S&P 425, the probability of a bull trend is improved by a highly significant 3 standard errors.

Index of Growth Company Ratings.   We watch listed companies that have shown rapid and consistent growth in earnings per share. We rate them by various criteria, endeavoring to select the thirty leading growth companies. Some, all, or none of these thirty achieve a score justifying a "buy" rating at any given time. We divide the number of buys by 30 to obtain the percentage rated "buy" and chart the resulting percentage figure. This indicator highlights the trend of one important type of speculative stocks.

The ten-year BBA for this indicator is quite good for 5 percent swings but quite poor for very short- and very long-term swings:

	Percent
Short term (following week)	54.1 (0)
5 percent swings	64.4 (3)
30 percent swings	53.8 (0)

Stock Investors' Confidence Index.   A measure of the confidence of stock buyers, this index contrasts with another confidence index (see section "Barron's Confidence Index") that measures the confidence of bond buyers. It is closely related to the Index of Growth Company Ratings. The indicator is a ratio of the average price-earnings ratio of the same thirty rapidly growing companies to the average price-earnings ratio for the thirty Dow Jones Industrials. This ratio is thus a direct measure of the premium, if any, that stock investors are willing to pay to get growth. If they are confident of the future, they are willing to pay a premium; if they are doubtful, they prefer the more sedate blue chips of the DJIA.

Since this indicator was developed in 1972, there are not enough historical data to assess its accuracy. However, because of its close relationship to the Index of Growth Company Ratings, their BBAs should be about the same.

A similar disparity index has been in use for many years. It relates the Standard & Poor's index of twenty speculative low-price common stocks to the S&P index of twenty-five high-grade common stocks. It has had a fair measure of success.

ARE PRICES RELATIVELY HIGH OR LOW IN TERMS OF EARNINGS AND YIELDS?

Answers to this question represent a fundamental approach that emphasizes *pricing* rather than more precise timing. Using fundamentals only, this approach tries to determine when the market is in a generally low, or buy, range or in a generally high, or sell, range. Rather than look for overbought or oversold markets, as does the preceding set of indicators, it seeks out overvalued, fairly valued, or undervalued markets.

In the author's service *Technical Trends,* the following three such value indicators are continuously charted.

Coupon Cost, or the Price of $1 of Bond Interest (0)

This index shows the number of dollars one must pay to buy enough of *Barron's* High-Grade Bond Average to receive $1 per year in interest. The latest reported yield on the bond average is divided into 100 to obtain the current index. The index is a measure of the expensiveness of bonds.

There has been a downward trend in this curve through the years, since almost-continuous creeping (and not so creeping) inflation has decreased the real return on bonds. Consequently, the upper and lower deciles of this indicator are not helpful. However, the *direction* of the indicator curve is important, since bond prices tend to lead stock prices. Bond buyers are usually large investors, presumably in the sophisticated category. See also the discussion of Barron's Confidence Index below.

Dividend Cost, or the Price of $1 of Dividends (0)

This indicator shows the number of dollars one must pay to buy enough of the Dow Jones Industrials to receive $1 per year in dividends. It is the inverse of the yield percentage. The latest reported yield on the DJIA is divided into 100 to obtain the current index. The index is a measure of the expensiveness of stocks.

Some years ago, when dividend yields were high, it was popular to subtract bond yields from stock yields and express the difference as an indicator. However, the long-term uptrend in bond yields to double and more than double stock yields has made this indicator obsolete.

From the point of view of the price of $1 of dividends, stocks can be considered expensive when this index is in its upper decile and possibly in its upper quartile. Stocks can be deemed inexpensive when the index is in its lowest quartile. However, in the years 1963–1972 this indicator was without value as a timing guide.

Typical ten-year BBAs for this indicator are:

	Deciles (Percent)	Quartiles (Percent)
Short term (following week)	48.5	47.7
5 percent swings	52.4	48.8
10 percent swings	47.6	41.0
30 percent swings	45.1	39.2

Earnings Cost, or the Price of $1 of Earnings (0)

This measure is similar to the preceding one. For it we use the ratio of price to earnings for all thirty stocks in the DJIA. The index is the number of dollars one must pay to buy enough of the Dow Jones Industrials to get $1 of earnings per year. A high price-earnings ratio is cause for a bearish forecast, while a low ratio generates a bullish prognosis. But note the poor accuracy record below. This indicator was more often wrong than right in the ten-year test period, and its weight is a repeated zero, like those of all the "fundamental" indicators here analyzed.

Typical ten-year BBAs for this indicator are:

	Deciles (Percent)	Quartiles (Percent)
Short term (following week)	54.3	43.5
5 percent swing	38.1	42.7
10 percent swing	21.9	32.3
30 percent swing	20.0	29.2

WHAT SEASONAL OR OTHER HABIT PATTERNS IN THE MARKET CAN BE USEFUL?

Habit patterns are mostly short-term where they exist at all. Theories about long-term patterns have very few supporters. So let us explore first whether short-term changes in stock prices—seasonal, monthly, weekly, daily, hourly—have any discernible useful patterns.

Stock Price Changes by Month

Monthly or seasonal shifts in stock prices are not so strong and well defined that stock market averages and indices can be adjusted for seasonal variation, as is done for most business indicators. Moreover, since stock prices are in a *long-term uptrend,* so that they tend to rise more often than they fall, it follows that many a stock's low price in any month of the year will frequently be higher than its high price or average price a few months earlier. Thus, to show a valid seasonal pattern, any changes in stock prices by month must be significantly more or significantly less than the change that would result simply from the long-term uptrend in stock prices.

Monthly Seasonal Patterns in Stock Prices, June 1896–December 1973

Month	Percent advancing	Month	Percent advancing
January	64	July	66
February	48	August	69
March	58	September	45
April	55	October	55
May	51	November	59
June	46	December	72
Percent of total months advancing			58
Percent of total months declining			42

From June 1896 through September 1973, the Dow Jones Industrial Average rose in 530 months and declined in 394 months, or a favorable long-term ratio of more than 57 percent for seventy-seven years. Accordingly, for any month which the DJIA consistently tends to go up by more than 60 percent or by less than 53 percent, some small contributory seasonal bias plus or minus may be suspected.

On this basis, the figures in the accompanying table suggest these conclusions: (1) Four months are strongly bullish: December (up 72 percent of the time), August (69 percent), July (66 percent), and January (64 percent). (2) Two other months are very slightly bullish: November (59 percent) and March (58 percent). (3) Four months are definitely seasonally bearish: September (up only 45 percent of the time), June (46 percent), February (48 percent), and May (51 percent). The other two months are slightly below average: April (55 percent) and October (55 percent).

These monthly patterns in stock prices would seem to stem from such regular factors as (1) the flow of year-end dividends and bonuses into the market at the start of a new year; (2) the drain of heavy tax payments in April; (3) the summertime optimism often engendered by the normally anticipated fall pickup in business; (4) the universally prescribed tax selling and switching in November and December; and, probably most important, (5) the now-routine efforts by mutual funds and other institutional investors to dress up their performance records by buying additional shares of their favorite portfolio holdings just before the end of the standard fiscal year on December 31.

Day of the Year

By studying daily price changes over more than seventy-five years, the author has discovered some quite significant high spots and low spots for various calendar dates. In particular, *holidays* seem to have an interesting statistical impact on stock prices. Contrary to most market lore, the day before a holiday, especially before a long holiday weekend, tends to be one of rising prices. Since 1922 the DJIA has risen almost two-thirds of the time on the day before a one-day holiday and almost three-fourths of the time when a holiday is combined with a weekend. The Friday before Labor Day has an especially good batting average of about 80 percent on the plus side, or odds of 4 to 1. By contrast, the day after a long holiday weekend tends to be bearish, the DJIA having declined about 55 percent of the time since 1922.

Day of the Month

The first three days of any month have a significant bullish bias. Since 1922 these days have been rising about the following percentages of the time: first of the month, 62; second of the month, 60; third of the month, 57. The record of the other days of the month is noncommittal.

The reason for such start-of-the-month strength may be that institutional investors frequently place orders in anticipation of the expected inflow of funds on the first of the month. Usually they promptly utilize the available balance of such funds just after the start of a new month.

Day of the Week

Within any week, one is probably better off, on the average and in the long run, by making purchases just after midday on Mondays and making sales on Friday afternoons. Our study shows that since 1922 the DJIA has gone up more than 63 percent of the time on Fridays but less than 43 percent of the time on Mondays. In periods of market decline, the odds against Mondays are, of course, much greater. Thus, for the first twenty-three weeks of 1973 prices dropped nineteen times and advanced only four times. All in all, the "blue Monday" phenomenon seems to have a solid basis in fact.

The reasons for this Friday-Monday syndrome are elusive. It may, perhaps, have something to do with the timing of favorable and unfavorable government, business, and brokers' reports. It is natural to release good news while the market is open and to hold off bad news until after Friday's close.

Another possible contributing factor may be that some bullish investors are too busy to place their buy orders during the week and therfore belatedly rush to buy on Friday afternoon before going home or away for the weekend. Correspondingly, the relative leisure of the weekend provides some investors with the time for reflection, reconsideration, or consultation with spouses, all leading to a greater number of sell decisions on Monday morning.

Hour of the Day

Within any day, stock prices more often than not open strong and stay so until about 11 A.M. Then they often weaken around noon, New York time, perhaps because floor traders close out some positions before going to lunch or because

West Coast traders sometimes start their day around this time by taking available profits. Even more markedly, stock prices often decline in the last hour or so before the close, as professional traders and specialists take their day's profits or losses.

Our statistical record since 1962 shows a rising opening more than 58 percent of the time, with prices rising in the first hour more than 60 percent of the time. On the other hand, closing prices showed a rise over the previous close less than 43 percent of the time.

Five-Week Pattern

To check the short-term repetitive habits of the stock market, the author made an extensive study of more than seventy-five years of weekly patterns. He studied the direction of prices in each week, classified the five-week patterns, and counted the movements, up or down, in the week following any given pattern. For example, if prices in the preceding five weeks have moved up, up, up, down, and up, how many times has this happened in the past seventy-five years? What happened in the sixth week following the pattern? Does the sixth-week performance deviate significantly from the expected average?

Most patterns analyzed did not have a significant bullish or bearish bias. The following four, however, were found to result in statistically significant sixth-week moves, and could therefore be helpful as indicators:

Five-Week Pattern	Percentage of Rises in the Sixth Week	Sixth-Week Probability
Up, up, down, up, up	66	Up
Down, down, up, up, up	63	Up
Up, down, up, down, down	43	Down
Down, up, up, down, down	45	Down

Long-Term Stock Market Cycles

This is an arcane area that we do not propose to explore at any length, since we do not believe that these patterns are statistically dependable. For example, some analysts think that there is a notable ten-year decade pattern, with some useful regularity for years ending in the same digit (1, 2, 3, and so on). The data are intriguing, but unfortunately there are not enough decades of data to provide statistically significant conclusions (only ten decades from 1870 to 1970). Moreover, a study by the Foundation for the Study of Cycles, after an exhaustive mathematical analysis, found a significant cycle of 9.225 years, close to the presumed decade pattern. But if 9.225 years is the right figure rather than 10.000, the cycle pattern will move backward nine months in each ten-year period, making comparisons of months in years ending in the same digit fruitless.

In *Technical Trends,* two habitual time patterns are followed regularly: monthly stock price patterns and the five-week pattern. The 1963–1972 BBAs for these two indicators are as follows:

Monthly Seasonal Patterns (1)

	Percent
Short-term (following week)	54.4
5 percent swings	55.5
30 percent swings	61.6

Five-Week Patterns (2)

	Percent
Short-term (following week)	50.7
5 percent swings	64.0
30 percent swings	59.7

WHAT ARE THE CLUES FROM SOPHISTICATED MARKET BEHAVIOR?

Participants in the stock market can be grouped approximately as professional institutional, professional noninstitutional, and nonprofessional. It is very helpful to know, at any given time, exactly what each of these groups of investors is believing and doing in the market. Numerous statistics and ratios have been developed for this purpose, and many of them are examined and evaluated in this section and the section "What Are the Clues from Unsophisticated Market Behavior?" Their underlying assumption is that while both professionals and nonprofessionals are wrong a good deal of the time, the more sophisticated professionals will outperform the nonprofessionals by a sufficient margin to make it useful to follow their leads as quickly as possible while doing the opposite of the unsophisticated crowd.

Member Buying and Selling (3)

The volume of purchases and sales made by members of the New York Stock Exchange *for their own account* is reported weekly, but three weeks after the covered week. A useful indicator is a ratio of member sales to member purchases, which is similar to the odd-lot trading ratio. For our weekly *Technical Trends,* we smooth the erratic weekly ratios with exponential averages equivalent to both a four-week and a twenty-week moving average.

We have found a seasonal bias in the figures. A low ratio, indicating member buying, is often found in the last three weeks of the year, contributing to December's record as the most bullish month of the year, as noted above. Unusually high ratios, indicating member selling, are more characteristic of the first six months of the year.

The 1963–1972 statistical distribution for this indicator is as follows:

Upper decile	105.0 (bearish)
Upper quartile	103.1 (bearish)
Median	101.5
Lower quartile	99.4 (bullish)
Lower decile	97.9 (bullish)

The 1963–1972 BBAs for this indicator are:

	Deciles (Percent)	Quartiles (Percent)
Short term (following week)	54.4 (0)	47.3 (0)
5 percent swings	62.1 (2)	56.1 (1)
10 percent swings	75.7 (3)	61.5 (3)
30 percent swings	63.7 (3)	56.3 (2)

Note the excellent decile batting averages for the intermediate- and longer-term moves, especially the 10 percent swings. The quartile results are not nearly so good as those achieved by the deciles. The weekly forecasts are not significant, very likely because the original data arrive late.

Large-Block Trading

Small fry rarely if ever trade in large blocks. When such trades appear on the tape, the participants are almost always professionals or important amateurs. Thus, the average action of these large trades reflects the thinking of sophisticated professionals.

Don Worden of Fort Lauderdale, Florida, has utilized this approach extensively and has developed some useful indicators. He is especially interested in whether a large trade was made on an uptick (higher than the last price) or a downtick (lower than the previous price). If to consummate the trade the buyer had to bid prices up, he was more eager than the seller to close the transaction. On the other hand, if the trade was made on a downtick, the seller was more anxious than the buyer and had to drop his price to make the sale.

A prime example of Worden's indices is the ten-day $100,000 index, covering only transactions larger than $100,000. This is the ratio of the number of such large transactions in ten days on upticks to the number of such transactions on downticks. Opening transactions each morning are not included, because a possible accumulation of overnight orders would result in an abnormally large initial trade. A ratio of more than 100 percent indicates an excess of big-block buying, while a ratio below 100 percent shows an excess of selling pressure.

Similar indices are calculated on a thirty-day and a sixty-day basis. Worden's tests have shown these indices to be good long-term indicators.

Short-Interest Ratio

Since most short sales are made by relatively sophisticated investors, we include this indicator in this section. Nonetheless, it turns out that the sophisticated short seller is usually wrong.

Short-interest positions on NYSE stocks, which are published monthly by the exchange, provide a measure of recent bearish investor sentiment. However, since the short-interest total involves sales that have already been made and since every short sale must be covered later by a purchase ("He who sells what isn't his'n must buy it back or go to prison"), the total also represents potential buying power. Thus, a very high short-interest total is considered bullish.

Since a higher short interest is to be expected in an active market, this indicator is expressed most effectively as a relative or ratio. Ordinarily, the total short interest reported is divided by the average daily volume in the preceding calendar month. However, because of the publication date of the NYSE figures, some analysts prefer to divide by the average volume from the eleventh of the preceding month to the tenth of the current month. A few analysts prefer to concentrate on the short-interest data for the thirty Dow Jones Industrials only, thereby eliminating the numerous short transactions used only for arbitrage.

The seasonal shorting tendency at the end of the year for tax selling purposes must also be noted. Such sales are usually covered by purchases in January, and the January short interest is almost always lower than December's.

The 1963–1972 statistical distribution for this indicator is as follows:

Percent

Upper decile	1.77 (very bullish)
Upper quartile	1.56 (bullish)
Median	1.39
Lower quartile	1.20 (bearish)
Lower decile	1.11 (very bearish)

A continually falling ratio is also unfavorable, while a steadily rising ratio is considered especially bullish, most particularly when upper decile ratios have been reached.

The 1963–1972 BBAs for this indicator are:

	Percent
Short term (following week)	48.4 (0)
5 percent swings	65.8 (3)
30 percent swings	55.1 (1)

Clearly, this indicator is most useful for gauging intermediate market swings.

Short Sales by NYSE Members

Short selling is an activity in which some internal differentiation is possible. Short sales by members of the NYSE must be considered a professional clue that the prudent investor should note. Figures on these sales are made available each week by the Securities and Exchange Commission (SEC) with a statistical lag of three weeks.

Member short sales may be evaluated as a percentage either of the total short interest or of total market volume. In terms of the former, bench marks developed by Walter Heiby suggest that when member short sales are greater than 90 percent of total short sales, the prospects are bearish, and that when this ratio is less than 60 percent, the outlook is bullish.

We choose to rate short sales by NYSE members as a percentage of total market volume, in terms of which the following distributions and accuracy ratings have been derived for the period 1963–1972:

	Distribution (Percent)
Upper decile	6.365 (bearish)
Upper quartile	5.785 (bearish)
Median	5.190
Lower quartile	4.315 (bullish)
Lower decile	3.695 (bullish)

	Accuracy (Percent)	
	Deciles	*Quartiles*
Short term (following week)	50.5 (0)	52.3 (0)
5 percent swings	55.3 (0)	54.6 (1)
10 percent swings	66.0 (3)	59.5 (3)
30 percent swings	59.8 (2)	52.5 (0)

Surprisingly perhaps, the short-swing forecasts are unimpressive, but the record for the long swings is fairly good.

Round-Lot Short Sales by Nonmembers

This group includes the larger operators who deal in round lots but who are not members of the NYSE. It is commonly believed that short selling by this group is unsophisticated and therefore is a contrary signal; that is, heavy short selling by this group is bullish.

However, the record indicates that this interpretation is in error, and we have therefore promoted this group to the level of sophistication. On the record, high short selling turned out to forecast bearish swings and low short selling bullish swings. The 1963–1972 statistical distribution pattern, again stated as a percentage of total market volume, is as follows:

	Percent
Upper decile	2.63 (bearish)
Upper quartile	1.83 (bearish)
Median	1.34
Lower quartile	1.07 (bullish)
Lower decile	0.84 (bullish)

The 1963–1972 BBAs for this indicator are:

	Deciles *(Percent)*	*Quartiles* *(Percent)*
Short term (following week)	53.8 (0)	51.0 (0)
5 percent swings	56.7 (0)	53.3 (0)
10 percent swings	61.5 (3)	66.1 (3)
30 percent swings	60.2 (2)	62.1 (3)

Although the short-term forecasts are not significant, the long-term ones are good. Moreover, since the quartiles for the two longer swings turned out to be more successful than the deciles, we need not wait for extreme values as signals.

Secondary Distributions

A secondary offering is the sale through an underwriter of a large block of outstanding stock. If such a block were placed for sale in the usual way on the exchange floor, the impact would almost always drop the price. With the help of an underwriter, the disposal job can be performed more effectively.

Investors who require an underwriter to dispose of stock are not small operators. They usually have access to good information and advice. Thus, the quantity of secondaries should be a useful trend clue, and it is. To smooth short-term fluctuations, we use a four-week moving average of the data reported each week in *Barron's*.

Typical ten-year BBAs for the indicator are:

	Deciles *(Percent)*	*Quartiles* *(Percent)*
Short term (following week)	52.2 (0)	53.1 (0)
5 percent swings	70.0 (3)	69.7 (3)
10 percent swings	60.0 (2)	66.2 (3)
30 percent swings	46.7 (0)	56.6 (1)

Insiders' Purchases and Sales

Every month the SEC publishes a report of the purchases and sales made by corporate officers and directors of stock in their companies. Certainly these insiders should be well informed about future prospects for their own companies. Thus, when they buy or sell their own stock, investors should investigate.

Sometimes, of course, an officer or a director may sell his or her firm's stock simply and solely to raise cash for some urgent personal reason. But when several officers or directors begin to buy and sell, the message is plain: "Somebody knows something."

The author has constructed a simple index for the transactions by insiders of the thirty companies included in the Dow Jones Industrial Average. To form the index, the number of stocks being sold is subtracted from the number being bought.

Typical ten-year BBAs for this indicator are:

	Percent
Short term (following week)	47.4 (0)
5 percent swings	44.4 (0)
30 percent swings	39.0 (0)

Obviously, the record is unimpressive, and one would have done much better by doing the opposite of the DJIA insiders, especially for the long term.

Mutual Fund Activity

Mutual funds have been an important institutional force in the stock market, but their relative importance has decreased in recent years compared with that of other institutions, such as insurance companies and bank-managed pension funds. Nonetheless, their sales and redemptions are still important market factors.

Two key interconnected mutual fund ratios are of interest for predictive purposes: the ratio of mutual fund sales to mutual fund redemptions and the mutual funds' current cash position. The first ratio obviously influences the second, which is also affected by the funds' expectations about stock market prices. Statistics of fund accumulations and redemptions, assets, and cash are reported monthly by the Investment Company Institute.

A high ratio of mutual fund sales (that is, purchases of funds' shares by the public) to redemptions (sales by the public back to the funds) means that the public is augmenting the buying power of the funds. A low ratio, by contrast, means that the public is draining off the funds' stock-buying power and forcing them to sell more common stock to liquidate redemptions.

The more decisive ratio is that for the mutual funds' cash position. It is customary to chart their holdings of cash, plus United States governments and short-term bonds, as a percentage of their total net assets. A cash position of more than 8 percent of assets is usually regarded as bullish, while one below 5 percent is considered bearish.

Walter Heiby also calculates the ratio of mutual fund cash to the average daily NYSE volume expressed in dollars. He believes this ratio to be a good indicator of the effect on stock prices of the funds' potential buying power.

More precise ratios are provided by our 1963–1972 statistical distribution:

	Percent of assets
Upper decile	9.14 (bullish)
Upper quartile	7.71 (bullish)
Median	5.95
Lower quartile	5.31 (bearish)
Lower decile	4.93 (bearish)

Interestingly, the accuracy record for this recent ten-year period is quite poor, and our weight for this barometer is zero.

Barron's Confidence Index

This indicator monitors the opinions of bond buyers, who are substantial and usually sophisticated investors. This group has considerable capital and must have had some acumen to accumulate or control it.

The index is calculated as the ratio of the yield on *Barron's* ten highest-grade bonds to the yield on the Dow Jones forty bonds. It may be easier to understand this ratio if bond prices (the inverse of yields) are used: Confidence index equals secondary bond prices divided by primary (high-grade) bond prices. Our indicator is the ten-week moving average, which has a better record than the index for individual weeks.

Typical ten-year BBAs for this indicator are:

	Deciles (Percent)	Quartiles (Percent)
Short term (following week)	40.7 (0)	47.3 (0)
5 percent swing	38.0 (0)	51.6 (0)
10 percent swing	37.0 (0)	45.4 (0)
30 percent swing	43.5 (0)	43.4 (0)

Note the extremely poor forecasting record for these ten recent years. This indicator seems to have outlived its usefulness, thus justifying its declining popularity.

Services' Sentiment Index

Investors Intelligence of Larchmont, New York, continuously accumulates the opinions of a large number of investment advisory services, classifying them as "bulls," "bears," and "consolidation." In our version, the number of bullish services is divided by the number of bearish ones.

Should one go with the sentiment expressed by this survey or with the opposite? The opinion of the experts is decidedly mixed. Many analysts (including Investors Intelligence) hold that one should take the contrary opinion: sell when most services recommend buying, and vice versa. They are probably right for short-term trends, but the author has found that for longer trends the investor should *not* use contrary opinion on the services. Over the period 1963–1972 they seem to have been more right than wrong for 10 and 30 percent swings.

Typical ten-year BBAs for this indicator are:

	Deciles (Percent)	Quartiles (Percent)
Short term (following week)	48.5 (0)	44.6 (0)
5 percent swings	60.6 (1)	54.8 (0)
10 percent swings	63.6 (2)	66.1 (3)
30 percent swings	66.7 (3)	73.1 (3)

Net Debit Balances

These balances represent the amount borrowed on margin in brokers' accounts. Margin traders are usually more experienced than cash traders and thus are closer to the sophisticated professionals. These traders generally enter the market during a rise and leave when the majority of stocks hit their peaks. Net debit balances drop steadily in a bear market. The conclusion is that rising debit balances are bullish and declining balances bearish.

When the Federal Reserve Board relaxes margin requirements, debit balances rise and customer buying power moves up correspondingly. When the Fed tightens up, the reverse is the case. Thus, these Federal Reserve actions have been good market forecasters. Reductions in requirements, which are almost always followed promptly by market upturns, are especially good.

Stock Exchange Seat Prices

The price of a seat on the New York Stock Exchange or other exchanges is a reflection of the opinion of informed men. If prospective members are willing to bid up seat prices, they must be optimistic about the market future. The reverse is the case for declining seat prices.

In practice, however, the batting average of this indicator has been poor in recent years. Apparently, seat prices are influenced by other key factors that are much more decisive than market trends, among them the spread of negotiated commission rates and the growth of third and fourth markets.

WHAT ARE THE CLUES FROM UNSOPHISTICATED MARKET BEHAVIOR?

The indicators in this category typically consider the reverse of the factors surveyed in the preceding category. Are the smaller, unsophisticated investors and traders buying and selling? Since this group usually does not have access to the best advice, one should seriously consider a contrary opinion.

Odd-Lot Volume

The simplest measure of participation of unsophisticated persons with relatively little capital is the volume of odd-lot purchases and sales. This indicator is usually expressed as *odd-lot purchases plus odd-lot sales as a percent of total NYSE volume multiplied by 2*. Multiplication by the factor 2 is required, since total NYSE volume is the combination of all sales and all purchases.

This percentage index tends to drop off in bear markets, reflecting a lack of small-investor interest, and to pick up in bull markets. However, over the last thirty-plus years this index has exhibited a long-term downward trend. From 1920 to 1940 the odd-lot volume ratio ranged between 11 and 16 percent. In the early 1970s it was between 2 and 3 percent.

This secular shift reflects the increasing importance of institutions as well as the growing wealth of individuals. It also serves to reduce the effectiveness of this simple indicator, requiring us to look to the following more complex ones.

Odd-Lot Index (Sales-Purchase Ratio)

It makes sense that the investor who deals in larger units is, on the average, better advised, more experienced, and more acute. If the odd-lot group is buying from the round-lot crowd, the astute observer would usually be right in betting that the time is right for a sale. Fortunately, it is easy to determine the situation, since odd-lot purchases and sales are reported by many newspapers.

As the author constructs this index, odd-lot sales in the last five days (Friday through Thursday) are divided by odd-lot purchases in the same period. A ratio of more than 100 percent means that the small trader is selling on balance and therefore is bullish (that is, the round-lot trader is buying on balance). A figure of less than 100 percent shows an excess of odd-lot purchases and therefore is bearish.

December and January have shown a definite seasonal tendency. In December odd-lot sales are usually high (Christmas bills? Tax selling?). In January odd-lot buying exceeds selling, with the difference between the December high and the January low averaging about 12 percent.

The 1963–1972 statistical distribution pattern for the odd-lot index is as follows:

Upper decile	182.9 (bullish)
Upper quartile	136.9 (bullish)
Median	115.1
Lower quartile	100.2 (bearish)
Lower decile	88.8 (bearish)

The high median of 115.1 reflects the fact that the odd lotter has consistently been selling more than buying.

The 1963–1972 BBAs for this indicator are:

	Deciles (Percent)	Quartiles (Percent)
Short term (following week)	50.0 (0)	51.3 (0)
5 percent swings	55.8 (0)	51.7 (0)
10 percent swings	63.5 (2)	64.3 (3)
30 percent swings	75.7 (3)	71.0 (3)

Note the contrast between the poor accuracy record for the weekly and 5 percent swings and the good-to-excellent batting averages for 10 percent and longer swings. Clearly, for major trends, it pays to use contrary opinion with this group.

Odd-Lot Short-Sales Ratio

While the odd-lot group as a whole has a poor success record, the very few odd lotters who sell short are generally viewed as really at the bottom of the league—almost always wrong.

Odd-lot short sales are usually expressed as a percentage of total odd-lot volume. The author calculates the index by dividing the average odd-lot short sales in the last five trading days (Friday through Thursday) by the average of odd-lot purchases and sales in the same period. For the index so calculated, the 1963–1972 statistical distribution pattern is as follows:

	Percent
Upper decile	2.55 (bullish)
Upper quartile	1.54 (bullish)
Median	1.03
Lower quartile	0.78 (bearish)
Lower decile	0.61 (bearish)

The accuracy record based on deciles and quartiles is poor. Dr. Martin Zweig has had better success by setting a higher level for a signal. He uses a ten-day moving average, which he has named TOLSR (Total Odd-Lot Short Ratio). He finds that if this ratio exceeds 4 percent, the probabilities are "overwhelming that a bull market is in the offing." This happened only seven times from 1947 through 1973. For a bear market signal Zweig uses a ratio of 0.6 percent.

Free Credit Balances

These balances represent available cash in brokerage accounts. Since cash traders (especially those who leave balances unused with brokers) are usually less experienced than margin traders, this indicator is similar to the odd-lot data in reflecting the behavior of the small operator.

This inexperienced group has a tendency to rush in with purchase orders at market peaks. Consequently, a decline in these cash balances is a warning sign. On the other hand, an increasing supply of cash is a bullish sign.

Contrary Opinion

The indicators discussed in this section are all good examples of the doctrine of contrary opinion. They illustrate the general rule that whenever nonprofessional investors (the public) become extremely one-sided in their expectations about the future of stock prices, the market will usually move in the opposite direction.

Apart from the relatively precise indicators discussed above, contrary opinion is also a school of thought developed especially by Humphrey B. Neill. It is close to the spirit expressed by Goethe when he said: "I find more and more that it is well to be on the side of the minority, since it is always the more intelligent." Neill advises checking the attitudes of the investing public and mutual fund managers and trying to develop a contrary spirit. He describes the characteristic errors of the investing public in this fashion:

- Seldom bearish, but often indifferent
- Little interested when markets are low and dull but always interested during the advance
- Attracted by market activity
- More easily shaken out by inactivity than by reactions
- Ready to buy on good news and sell on bad
- Able to absorb an amazing amount of stock in the decline following an important advance

WHAT ARE THE MONETARY AND INTEREST RATE INTENTIONS OF THE FEDERAL RESERVE BOARD?

Because of the Federal Reserve Board's control over the volume of money and credit, the level of interest rates, and the margin requirements for stock purchases, the goals and intentions of its Board of Governors are of fundamental importance to the stock market. The operations of the Federal Reserve can be very complicated and typically are planned and carried out behind closed doors. However, it is possible to follow closely the two most generally accepted indicators of the Board's aims, the level and trend of member banks' free reserves and the rate of change in the money supply.

Net Free or Borrowed Reserves

This figure, which is reported in the Friday-morning papers, is equal to member banks' excess reserves minus their borrowing from the Fed. When money is tight, borrowings exceed excess reserves, and the figure is negative, showing net borrowed reserves. When money is easy, the reverse is the case, reserves are free, and the figures are positive.

If the free reserves are consistently rising, the Fed is easing money (bullish indicator). If they are steadily declining, the Fed is applying the brakes (bearish indicator). Since the weekly figures can be erratic, a five-week moving average is commonly used.

The 1963–1972 statistical distribution pattern for free reserves is as follows:

Upper decile	+$248 million (bullish)
Upper quartile	+$105 million (bullish)
Median	−$123 million
Lower quartile	−$373 million (bearish)
Lower decile	−$835 million

The 1963–1972 BBAs for this indicator are:

	Deciles (Percent)	Quartiles (Percent)
Short term (following week)	59.2 (1)	55.5 (1)
5 percent swings	61.2 (2)	60.8 (3)
10 percent swings	81.6 (3)	76.4 (3)
30 percent swings	90.3 (3)	80.9 (3)

Note the minus median figure in the distribution pattern: it indicates the prevalence of tight money in the 1963–1972 decade. Forecasts based on this indicator have an excellent record for both the short and, particularly, the long term. The decile results are consistently better than the quartiles.

Money Stock Change

One study[2] concluded that the rate of change in the money supply typically precedes changes in stock prices by an average of seven weeks. The index that the author employs in *Technical Trends* is based on the change in one month of a four-week moving average of the money stock, including net time deposits, expanded geometrically to an annual rate (percentage per year).

Its record in recent periods does not seem to be quite as good as Rudolph claims, and we give it a weight of (2). Perhaps the "wise guy" effect (see the section below, "How Can the Several Interpretations of the Indicators Be Combined to Reach a Central, Decisive Conclusion?") is at work.

WHAT ARE THE ECONOMIC PROSPECTS FOR GENERAL BUSINESS?

While the stock market almost always moves in advance of business, trends in business can be used to confirm market trends. Among the most widely used indicators of general business are the Federal Reserve Board Index of Industrial Production and the Short List of Twelve Leading Economic Indicators, based on the National Bureau of Economic Research classification. Since they are not predictive of the stock market, our weight for both these indicators is zero.

See Chapter 7 for a full discussion of the use of economic indicators in stock market (and business) forecasting.

HOW CAN THE SEVERAL INTERPRETATIONS OF THE INDICATORS BE COMBINED TO REACH A CENTRAL, DECISIVE CONCLUSION?

A study of indicators is frustrating because of the large number available. Selection becomes a problem. Another frustration is the simple fact that, at any given time, some indicators are bullish while others are bearish.

Some analysts select a few indicators that seem interesting or critical at the moment and base their conclusions on that selection. Unfortunately, almost every indicator has good spells and poor ones. All too often, the selection reflects only the most recent accuracy record.

A more objective approach would be to combine a number of indicators mathematically, using average success over a fairly long period (say, five to ten years) as the basic criterion for selection and weighting. Sometimes a number of indicators are combined into an econometric formula or model which, with the help of a computer, yields numerical and possibly useful results.

A number of methods are considered proprietary, and only the final results are revealed by their developers. This puts such methods into the "little black box" class, and deep faith in their sponsors is required before the results should be used.

Dr. Leo Barnes, editor in chief of the *Handbook*, believes that one of the best arguments for relying on a consensus is what he calls the "wise guy effect," more

---

[2]J. A. Rudolph, "Money Supply and Common Stock Prices," *Financial Analysts Journal*, pp. 19–25, March 1972.

respectably known as forecast feedback. When indicators are discovered, found to be effective, and then given publicity, shrewd investors and speculators promptly put them to use. The resulting buying and selling tend to bring about the predicted market changes faster and faster, thus shortening or even eliminating the lead time of the indicator. As Dr. Barnes puts it, "Publish *and* perish!"

Above all, the consensus approach is supported by the principles of probability. If a method with a given percentage of accuracy (or probability) is combined with another method with another percentage of accuracy, the combination will have a higher percentage of accuracy than either of the individual methods. The greater the number of methods with some reliability, the higher the accuracy of their combination.

We illustrate the mathematics involved with the simplest case: two methods. Each method has an accuracy record of about two-thirds. The resulting reliability of both methods used together is more than three-fourths:

Let a_1 = the per-unit accuracy of the first indicator

b_1 = the per-unit failure rate of the first indicator, or $1 - a_1$

a_2 = the per-unit accuracy of the second indicator

b_2 = the per-unit failure rate of the second indicator, or $1 - a_2$

Then, if both indicators agree, the accuracy of the combination is

$$A = \frac{a_1 a_2}{a_1 a_2 + b_1 b_2}$$

For example, if one indicator has an accuracy record of 62 percent and another a rating of 67 percent, the accuracy of the combination (assuming the independence of the two indicators) is

$$A = \frac{0.62 \times 0.67}{(0.62)(0.67) + (0.38)(0.33)} = 0.77$$

or 77 percent accuracy.

Here are a few examples of widely followed consensus indicators:

1. The Cleveland Trust Co. reports periodically the results of an econometric formula that combines such factors as the money supply, corporate profits, the rate of unemployment, and the gross national product.

2. Edson Gould prepares a daily trading barometer that combines advances and declines, the ratio of the DJIA to its moving average, and the volume of rising stocks versus the volume of declining stocks.

3. The *Indicator Digest* of Palisades Park, New Jersey, prepares a comprehensive composite of twelve usually reliable technical indicators.

4. James Dines reviews sixty series and counts the number that are up, down, and neutral.

Accuracy Record of the Technical Trends Consensus

Throughout this chapter, we have presented the ten-year barometer batting averages (BBAs) for many technical and fundamental indicators reported weekly or monthly in the author's weekly publication *Technical Trends*.[3] These indicators are combined in a weighted balance, or consensus, that, as suggested above, has a higher reliability or probability than the individual indicators taken separately. The weights used range from (0) to (3), in most cases being based on performance in the ten-year period 1963–1972. Shorter periods are sometimes used if data for all the back years are not available.

[3]Box 228, Chappaqua, N.Y. 10514.

In most cases, decile and quartile analysis, as described above, is employed. In other cases, only the extreme peaks and bottoms of the indicators have had to be used. In the case of the *Technical Trends* Consensus itself, instead of deciles or quartiles, the weighted percentages of bullishness or bearishness are ranked on a balance scale into extreme and moderate areas on both bullish and bearish sides.

TABLE 8-1   Indicators with Ten-Year Barometer Batting Averages of 60 Percent or Better *(Weekly Market Swings)*

Indicator	Percent
ASE/NYSE Volume Ratio (deciles)	63.7
Technical Trends Consensus (extreme areas)	63.5
Advance/decline, noncumulative (quartiles)	61.5

TABLE 8-2   Indicators with Ten-Year Barometer Batting Averages of 60 Percent or Better *(5 Percent Swings)*

Indicator	Percent
Technical Trends Consensus (extreme areas)	82.3
New lows or highs for swing	75.6
ASE/NYSE Volume Ratio (deciles)	72.6
Secondary distributions (deciles)	70.0
Secondary distributions (quartiles)	69.7
Option Activity Ratio (deciles)	68.9
Advance/decline, noncumulative (deciles)	68.9
Advance/decline, noncumulative (quartiles)	68.5
Technical Trends Consensus (moderate areas)	68.4
Price versus six-month moving average	67.4
Option type (quartiles)	67.2
Option type (deciles)	67.0
Short-interest ratio	65.8
Every Skip-a-Day Index	64.9
Index of Growth Company Ratings	64.4
Five-week pattern	64.0
Six-month average direction	63.4
Dow Jones Transportation Average	63.2
ASE/NYSE Volume Ratio (quartiles)	62.8
Member buying and selling (deciles)	62.1
NYSE volume	61.6
Net free or borrowed reserves (deciles)	61.2
Net free or borrowed reserves (quartiles)	60.8
Sentiment index (deciles)	60.6

Thus, a weighted bullish percentage of more than 75 percent is extremely bullish, and a figure of from 58 to 75 percent is termed moderately bullish. On the other side, a bullish figure below 25 percent is rated extremely bearish while a figure between 25 and 42 percent is deemed moderately bearish. The area from 42 to 58 percent is regarded as neutral territory, either slightly bullish when above 50 percent or slightly bearish when below 50 percent.

On this basis, the 1963–1972 accuracy record of the *Technical Trends* Consensus is as follows:

	Extreme Areas (Percent)	Moderate Areas (Percent)
Short term (following week)	63.5 (1)	55.4 (0)
5 percent swings	82.3 (3)	68.4 (3)
10 percent swings	89.6 (3)	80.4 (3)
30 percent swings	94.7 (3)	82.9 (3)

The consensus has a fine record, especially when the balance needle swings to the unusual or extreme areas above 75 percent or below 25 percent favorable. The moderate swings do not rate quite so well but are very satisfactory, especially for the long term.

TABLE 8-3   Indicators with Ten-Year Barometer Batting Averages of 60 Percent or Better (10 Percent Swings)

Indicator	Percent
Technical Trends Consensus (extreme areas)	89.6
Net free or borrowed reserves (deciles)	81.6
Technical Trends Consensus (moderate areas)	80.4
ASE/NYSE Volume Ratio (deciles)	76.5
Net free or borrowed reserves (quartiles)	76.4
Member buying and selling (deciles)	75.7
Option type (quartiles)	72.3
Option type (deciles)	69.9
Option Activity Ratio (deciles)	69.8
ASE/NYSE Volume Ratio (quartiles)	68.2
Advance/decline, noncumulative (deciles)	68.0
Advance/decline, noncumulative (quartiles)	66.9
Secondary distributions (quartiles)	66.2
Nonmember round-lot short sales (quartiles)	66.1
Sentiment index (quartile)	66.1
Member short sales (deciles)	66.0
Odd-lot index (quartiles)	64.3
Sentiment index (deciles)	63.6
Odd-lot index (deciles)	63.5
Nonmenber round-lot short sales (deciles)	61.5
Member buying and selling (quartiles)	61.5
Secondary distributions (deciles)	60.0

CHECKLISTS OF INDICATORS WITH HIGHEST RATINGS (60 PERCENT OR BETTER)

Tables 8-1 through 8-4 show indicators with the best records for the 1963–1972 period, covering (1) the short term (following week), (2) 5 percent swings, (3) 10 percent swings, and (4) 30 percent swings. The indicators are ranked in groups of five or fewer according to their batting averages, from the highest to a minimum of 60 percent in each table.

As one might suspect, the short-term trend for the following week is well-nigh unpredictable. Only three indicators, including the *Technical Trends* Consensus,

TABLE 8-4   Indicators with Ten-Year Barometer Batting Averages of 60 Percent or Better *(30 Percent Swings)*

Indicator	Percent
Technical Trends Consensus (extreme areas)	94.7
Net free or borrowed reserves (deciles)	90.3
Technical Trends Consensus (moderate areas)	82.9
Net free or borrowed reserves (quartiles)	80.9
Odd-lot index (deciles)	75.7
Price versus six-month moving average	75.1
5 percent swing direction	73.4
Sentiment index (quartiles)	73.1
Six-month average direction	72.0
New lows or highs for 5 percent swing	71.1
Odd-lot index (quartiles)	71.0
Option type (deciles)	70.9
ASE/NYSE Volume Ratio (deciles)	70.6
Enthusiasm	70.3
Option Activity Ratio (deciles)	69.8
Option type (quartiles)	68.6
Sentiment index (deciles)	66.7
ASE/NYSE Volume Ratio (quartiles)	66.3
NYSE volume	65.3
Member buying and selling (deciles)	63.7
Advance/decline, noncumulative (deciles)	62.1
Nonmember round-lot short sales (quartiles)	62.1
Monthly seasonal pattern	61.6
Advance/decline, noncumulative (quartiles)	61.1
Nonmember round-lot short sales (deciles)	60.2

had a batting average of better than 60 percent. By contrast, more than twenty indicators were able to top 60 percent for the 5 percent, 10 percent, and 30 percent swings.

If one wishes to concentrate on fewer indicators, a choice from among the top ten or twelve in each table is recommended.

Chapter **9**

Defensive Strategies: Formula Plans, Dollar Cost Averaging, and Stop-Loss Systems

ROBERT R. DINCE

The bulk of investment literature is preoccupied with selecting the investment vehicle. Since the whole concept of investment is concerned with the acquisition of earning assets, this emphasis is hardly misplaced. But the techniques of investment analysis are occupied almost totally with the identification of good "investments." Presumably, the analysis technique says that security A is a better investment than security B, but it does not typically state: "Sell B and buy A." Rather, the literature emphasizes buying A and ignoring B.

The special subject of defensive strategies starts with an entirely different premise. It assumes that the investor already has securities, selected skillfully or at random. Under what circumstances should these securities be sold, or, alternatively, when should one buy more of what one already owns?

While the investment texts have little to say on the subject, the traditional wisdom of Wall Street is full of apocryphal stories dealing with the problem. Wise remarks attributed to such great figures as J. P. Morgan, Bernard Baruch, or even Lord Keynes emphasize the same point: Find out what everyone is doing, and then do the opposite. One of the most avidly followed technical indicators is odd-lot volume. If small investors are buying, "Watch out!"

Essentially, the wise money in the investment community is saying that most small investors don't know what they are doing. On the other hand, the experience of large investors in various crucial market periods has shown that many of the most astute investors in bull markets are little if at all more sophisticated than the old lady from Dubuque when it comes to determining the right time to get out.

All investment analysis should emphasize the basic premise that a strong streak of irrationality runs through the investment community. For example, a fundamental concept of the theory of finance is the investor's *required rate of return,* the rate to which the investor discounts the anticipated flow of investment income to determine the investment's present value. The investor's rate of return is equal to a pure riskless interest rate plus a premium that the investor receives for risk taking. The pure rate of interest is usually measured by some average of the yield on United States Treasury bills. It is certainly volatile, changing with the demand and supply of funds and basic national economic conditions, but the risk premium is even more volatile, since it changes, up or down, with the surging tides of investor optimism and pessimism.

Because of the ebb and flow of investor confidence, there is a constant tendency for the market to overcompensate. This constantly shifting tide of investor emotion affects not only volatile stocks but also, to a lesser extent, bonds. Expectations about the future help determine both the shifting tides of equity prices and, to a lesser degree, changing bond yields. Basically, all defensive investment plans work on the premise that securities markets overreact, either on the upside or the downside, as the risk premium expands or contracts.

A period when the market is depressed (when investor expectations have driven prices down) is one of the best times to buy. When stock prices have risen precipitously, stocks should be sold. Thus, our premise is that action should be taken against the overwhelming tide of human emotion.

A major technique for doing this is lumped under the generic term "formula plans." The essence of formula planning is the substitution of a mechanistic, predetermined course of action for the investor's own volatile judgment of the size of the risk premium.

DEVELOPING THE FORMULA PLAN

All formula plans are based on the division of the portfolio into two segments: the aggressive or volatile portion, or stocks; and the defensive segment, or bonds. Correct action is taken when changes in the value of the volatile segment relative to some determinant of their value require realignment of the portfolio. Thus, when stocks are cheap, stocks are bought and bonds sold; the opposite course is followed when the reverse is true. Obviously, the problem is the determination of "cheap" and "dear."

To illustrate the operation of a formula plan, let's take the simplest possible model and trace a few transactions. Suppose that we started with a portfolio of stocks and bonds worth $100,000. For simplicity's sake, let's assume that our stock portfolio is a group of stocks called the Dow Jones Industrial Average (DJIA).[1] Because the handling of a simulated bond portfolio is quite complicated, for the time being let us assume that the defensive portfolio is invested in a savings and loan account that we shall call bonds. A sample set of transactions will now be illustrated under the two major types of formula plan.

The Constant-Ratio Plan

Constant-ratio formula planning is based upon the implicit assumption that stock prices will rise in the long run but will fluctuate cyclically in the meantime. All other possibilities are ignored. Investors must make two basic decisions in advance. First, they must decide on the proportion of stocks and bonds they want to maintain. Second, they must set a rule as to when they will trade stocks or bonds to

---

[1]Buying a diversified list is always a problem. There is an old market belief that if you can do as well as the "average," you are doing better than average. One mutual fund, Founders Mutual, exploits this belief by offering a fund that consists of the DJIA plus a few other securities. Every time this fund buys, the funds are distributed over its security list so that an equal value of each stock is purchased. Insofar as is known, this fund never sells stock.

The DJIA may not be a truly representative average, and other averages will be used as examples in the text. But since the DJIA includes only thirty stocks, it resembles in numbers a typical investor portfolio.

restore this proportion. In the present example, an adjustment is made when the selected stock index rises by 10 percent or falls by 5 percent. The results are representative and are used only to demonstrate how the plan works.

As shown in Table 9-1, our constant-ratio plan uses the constant ratio of 60 percent stocks and 40 percent bonds. Trades are made when the stock index rises by the preset percentage of 10 percent or falls by the preset percentage of 5 percent. Calculations are kept as simple as possible. Thus, fractional shares are rounded off to the nearest tenth, and brokerage costs are not considered.

TABLE 9-1   Illustration of a Constant-Ratio Plan ($100,000 Portfolio of 60 Percent Stocks and 40 Percent Bonds)

Period	Stock index	Value of stocks	Units of stock*	Bonds	Total value
1	500	$60,000	120.0	$40,000	$100,000
2a	550	66,000	120.0	40,000	106,000
2b	550	63,600	115.6	42,400	106,000
3a	610	70,516	115.6	42,400	112,916
3b	610	67,750	111.1	45,166	112,916
4a	575	63,882	111.1	45,166	109,048
4b	575	65,429	113.8	43,619	109,048
5a	545	63,021	113.8	43,619	105,640
5b	545	63,389	116.3	42,256	105,640
6a	600	69,780	116.3	42,256	112,036
6b	600	67,222	112.0	44,814	112,036
7a	660	73,920	112.0	44,814	118,734
7b	660	71,240	107.9	47,494	118,734
8a	625	67,437	107.9	47,494	114,931
8b	625	68,958	110.3	45,973	114,931
9a	590	65,077	110.3	45,973	110,050
9b	590	65,630	111.2	44,420	110,050
10a	650	72,280	111.2	44,420	116,700
10b	650	70,020	107.7	46,680	116,700

*No brokerage cost is included, and fractional shares are permitted.

Table 9-1 shows the portfolio both before adjustment (*a* lines) and after adjustment (*b* lines). For purposes of brevity this before-and-after adjustment will not be used after this first illustration. In step 2a, the stock index rises to 550, a 10 percent rise, and the total portfolio is worth $106,000. If we are going to hold 40 percent in bonds, we multiply $106,000 by 0.4, which equals $42,400. This result entails selling $2,400 of stock, or 4.4 units (rounded off), which gives us our new position, 115.6 units of stock, as shown in step 2b. All the subsequent steps are taken in the same way.

If we had started with the position shown in step 1 and had made no adjustments, the portfolio would have been worth $118,000 (120 units of stock worth $78,000 plus $40,000 in bonds). In the generally rising market assumed in Table 9-1, a simple buy-and-hold strategy would have produced a 1.1 percent better ending position than the simple constant-ratio formula plan.

The Variable-Ratio Plan

Sophisticated formula planning begins with variable-ratio plans. As one text has it, "Variable ratio plans are designed to achieve the same ends as constant ratio plans—only more so."[2] If the formula plan says that stocks are cheap, then the

[2]J. B. Cohen and E. D. Zinbarg, *Investment Analysis and Portfolio Management,* Richard D. Irwin, Inc., Homewood, Ill., 1967, p. 548.

correct policy is not to buy stocks to balance the portfolio but to buy proportionally more stocks to take advantage of their depressed prices. Similarly, when stock prices are too high, then proportionally more stocks, not just enough to balance the portfolio, should be sold. In Table 9-1, when stock prices reached 610 in period 3, the constant-ratio plan has us sell 4.5 shares. Using the variable-ratio plan shown in Tables 9-2 and 9-3, we would have sold 27.2 shares, or 6 times as many as under the constant-ratio plan.[3] The only way to be aggressive is to buy a lot of stocks when they are cheap and to sell a lot of them when they are dear. Variable-ratio planning is aggressive formula planning.

More important, variable-ratio plans imply a more formal long-term forecast of *overall* future stock price patterns than does a constant-ratio plan. For the variable-ratio plan to work rationally, investors must have a clear idea of what a "normal" price is. By contrast, the constant-ratio plan requires no estimate of normal values.

TABLE 9-2   Relationship of Percentage Difference between Hypothetical Dow Jones Industrial Average and Formula Value as Related to Zones Determining Variable Ratios of Stocks and Defensive Portion

Dow Jones as a percentage of formula value	Zones	Percent Ratio	
		Stocks	Defensive
141 or more	I	20	80
126–140	II	30	70
111–125	III	40	60
90–110	IV	50	50
75–89	V	60	40
50–74	VI	70	30
59 or less	VII	80	20

SOURCE: Marshall Ketchum, "Investment Management through Formula Timing Plans," *The Journal of Business,* July 1947, p. 159.

If the forecast of overall price patterns is wrong, it leads either to long periods of inactivity, which might prompt investors to abandon the plan, or to overcommitment in either the defensive or the volatile portion of the portfolio.[4]

As the first step in setting up a variable-ratio plan, investors must establish some norm around which they expect stock prices to fluctuate. Since the first illustration is presented for demonstration purposes, we shall keep the plan as simple as possible. Thus, we shall use a simple moving average as the basis for determining the formula value. We make the assumption that an assumed five-year average of the DJIA establishes the norm while fluctuations around this average establish the variable ratio to be used.

For example, in period 1 in Table 9-3, the actual DJIA is divided by the average given in column 3, with a resulting ratio of 100. This value is read off from the values in Table 9-2 to establish the formula plan zone and the applicable ratio of stocks to bonds. Thus, a value of 100 reads off as Zone IV, or 50 percent in stocks and 50 percent in bonds.

When the hypothetical DJIA moves to 600, the resulting percentage when divided by the moving average is 115; this signals an adjustment to Zone III, or 40 percent in stocks versus 60 percent in bonds. Similar adjustments are made as stocks rise and fall. As stock prices fall below the average price, the variable ratio calls for a more and more aggressive position in stocks. When the DJIA price falls

---

[3]By using the variable-ratio technique together with the price pattern shown in Table 9-1, the final portfolio would have been worth $137,382. This is 17.7 percent better than results under the constant-ratio plan and 16.4 percent better than with a buy-and-hold strategy.

[4]Cohen and Zinbarg, op. cit., pp. 549–550.

in step 6 to 350, or some 200 points below the moving average, the formula plan calls for a heavy investment (70 percent) in stocks.

Although this first example of a variable-ratio plan is greatly simplified, it demonstrates the main point: as actual prices fall below the norm, the investment position of the portfolio becomes more and more aggressive. Proportionally more stocks are bought when they are cheap relative to the norm, and proportionally more stocks are sold when they are dear.

Table 9-2 should be considered as nothing more than a convention, and the ratios established for the various zones are in no way recommended as proper proportions for any given investor. The table has been used by many writers as the basis for comparing the results of different types of formula plans.[5] This convention is employed here simply because of its wide use.[6] Further, the zones in the

TABLE 9-3   Illustration of a Variable-Ratio Plan, Using a Five-Year Moving Average of Assumed DJIA Prices as the Normal Price*   ($100,000 Portfolio)

Period (1)	DJIA (2)	Moving-average price (3)	Column 2 − Column 3 (4)	Zone† (5)	Stock value‡ (6)	Units of stock (7)	Bond value (8)	Total value (9)
1	500	500	100	IV	$50,000	100.0	$50,000	$100,000
2	600	520	115	III	44,000	73.3	66,000	110,000
3	735	563	131	II	35,942	48.9	83,933	119,875
4	600	570	105	IV	56,640	94.4	56,633	113,273
5	490	585	84	V	61,733	126.0	41,156	102,889
6	350	555	63	VI	59,680	170.5	25,576	95,256
7	495	507	98	IV	54,987	111.1	54,986	109,973

*No brokerage cost is assumed, and fractional shares are permitted.
†Zone values are shown in Table 9-2.
‡Stock value is shown after adjustment.

table are comparable to the famous Keystone seven-step plan, which was used by the Keystone group of mutual funds for many years as a basis for portfolio action. If investors should feel that their normal investment position was 65 percent in stocks, this should be established as the proportion for Zone IV, and all the other proportions should be adjusted accordingly.

Results in Table 9-3 should be taken as merely illustrative. The key to the plan's success can be seen in periods 3 and 6. When the hypothetical DJIA rose to 735, 70 percent of the portfolio had to be held in bonds. To raise this amount, $17,933 of stock (24.4 units) had to be sold; this action forced the taking of profits at the top of the market. Similarly, in period 6, when stock prices fell precipitously to 350, $15,580 worth of stock had to be bought (bonds sold) to readjust the portfolio to the proportion of 70 percent stock to 30 percent bonds. The acquisition of 44.5 shares provided the base for the profitable position of the portfolio in period 10. Thus, despite the fact that stock prices actually finish below the starting point, the final value of the portfolio is $9,973 greater than that of the initial portfolio.

SETTING GROUND RULES

Because the basic nature of formula planning is mechanistic, certain rules to govern future actions must be stated before operations begin. One of the biggest

[5]C. S. Cottle and W. T. Whitman, *Investment Timing: The Formula Plan Approach*, McGraw-Hill Book Company, New York, 1953.
[6]Sherman F. Feyler, *Income Growth with Security*, The Macmillan Company, New York, 1958, pp. 82–87, 162–163.

problems of formula planning is that the trading signal used may result in too much trading. Overtrading is to be avoided to reduce record-high brokerage commissions and forestall overreacting to short-term market swings. In general, limitations on overtrading are along the following lines:

1. Trading is restricted to specified limited time intervals regardless of market movements between time intervals.

2. Sometimes, limitation 1 is replaced by a restriction that trades cannot occur unless either the volatile portion changes by more than a certain predetermined percentage or the total portfolio value changes by a given percentage. Tables 9-1, 9-2, and 9-3 are based on this restriction.

3. A common restriction is that trading does not occur unless the dollar amount to be traded exceeds a given amount or percentage.

4. Another, more sophisticated trading restriction is sometimes used in variable-ratio plans. For example, in Table 9-3 stocks are never bought if the average value compared with actual price results in stock prices being in the high Zones I, II, or III. Similarly, stocks are never sold if the values lie in the low Zones V, VI, or VII.

While there is some evidence that "the less trading, the better," the evidence is not conclusive.[7] If we consider that a formula plan operates on the idea of disconnecting investors from the random vagaries of the market, complete restrictions against trading cannot be totally recommended. Investors may get so bored and restive under the tight administration of the restrictive rules that they will be psychologically unable or unwilling to follow all these restrictions. Thus, restrictions 1, 2, and 3 above are recommended, but restriction 4 is left to the individual judgment of investors. Generally speaking, however, any plan that prevents buying stocks when prices are above the norm and that prevents selling stocks when they are below the norm will yield superior results.

Some Theoretical Problems

The preceding subsection rested on the premise that developing a standard for measuring relative values is simple. However, the actuality is that the development of an intrinsic-value formula is the most difficult area of portfolio planning. Developing a model for finding normal values involves stating a workable hypothesis. But if one could be really precise at hypothesis making, security prices could be predicted consistently without error, and there would be little reason to use formula plans. Perfect knowledge of the future implies a risk-free environment, and under these assumptions the yield on stocks would be hardly more than on savings accounts. Since this is not the case, there are many possibilities for the model builder to investigate.

Models describing levels of stock market prices for formula plans are of two general types. The first is the *fundamental* model; in other words, the level of stock prices is determined by a number of fundamental outside economic factors. The model that will be described in some detail below, the Dince-Weston model, is of this type. The other basic model type is the *trend* model; this form of model claims that the past movements of the market itself give accurate indications of future movements.

Regardless of which type of model is used, each faces the same problem. An assumption is made that stock prices should be at some given level, but in fact formula values may diverge from the actual prices by substantial amounts. A

---

[7]In an earlier article, the author tested trading restrictions seven different ways. Four portfolios yielded poorer results, and three yielded better results. The best result of all portfolios tested was the one with the greatest degree of restricted trading. See R. R. Dince, "Another View of Formula Planning," *Journal of Finance*, December 1964, pp. 686–687.

divergence is the portfolio adjustment signal. However, *the model is worthless unless the market level eventually converges with the model's predicted market level.*

Essentially, a basic paradox is at work. Factors other than those used in the model might be causing the actual market to diverge from the model, but in the long run the two must converge. The word *must* is the crux of the matter. Simply stated, the model may be wrong. The model may have tracked security prices accurately for the thirty previous years, but the past is not always the best predictor of the future. There may be new factors working on the stock market that are not included in the model.

Formula planning takes as its premise that the public, responding to mass psychology with its recurring waves of euphoria and melancholy, is usually wrong in its speculative commitments.[8] The basic formulas for determining the theoretical value of a security have as a fundamental element the risk premium demanded by investors. It is the volatility of this risk premium, as it is buffeted in the recurring waves of mass psychology, that makes the formula plan, with its mechanistically imposed calm, such an attractive device. In short, investors' risk measurement, a major determinant of security prices, is often wrong.

TREND MODELS

The simplest way to determine normal prices for the stock market is to see what kind of curve or mathematical function best fits market data for some long period of time. While most of the models used in this section are fitted by computer, no such elaborate statistical apparatus is needed. Thus, the Keystone plan, which worked so well from 1940 to 1955, was simply an eye-fitted trend line plotted on semilog paper.

All such trend models suffer from the same basic fault. To make the findings statistically significant, a large number of observations must be used. But the greater the number of observations used, the greater the number of older observations included, and the less relevance the older data have to the present.

Several different statistical fits for stock price and time are typically used. Straight-line curves imply that stock prices will increase forever at some arithmetic rate. Exponential functions assume that stock prices will change in a fixed manner as determined by the exponent. Logarithmic forms assume that the values are increasing at a geometric rate.

All these curves can be extrapolated into the future with varying degrees of success. Unless the values are constantly recalculated, the relationships swiftly become outdated and are poor forecasting tools. The basic formulas can be recalculated every year, but this is expensive unless the investor has easy and low-cost access to large computers. Basically the problem is that we are using long-run relationships for short-run decision rules. One of the best mathematically and statistically oriented textbooks in investment analysis makes the overall judgment that such models are unsatisfactory.[9] This agrees with an earlier judgment of Cottle and Whitman in testing trend models for use in formula planning.[10]

Two of the following illustrative models are based on long-run relationships between stock prices and another economic variable. In that sense they are more advanced than a simple trend model with only time as the basic outside variable. But the reader should pay particular attention to the caveat already given: all the statistical relationships discussed here are subject to error either because the basic

[8]Feyler, op. cit., p. 19.

[9]H. A. Latané and D. L. Tuttle, *Security Analysis and Portfolio Management,* The Ronald Press Company, New York, 1970, p. 351.

[10]Cottle and Whitman, op. cit., pp. 96–97.

assumptions are proved wrong by changing times and events or because the data base is outdated and new relationships must be worked out.[11]

Three Formula Plans

Sophisticated formula planning determines formula plan values via some outside factor or influence that, it is believed, determines, reflects, or anticipates stock prices. There are many theories about what determines stock prices, but current theories of this type may generally be assigned to three categories. The first and, to this observer, the most logical theory is that stock prices both reflect and anticipate general economic conditions as measured by the statistic gross national product (GNP). The second is that stock prices are determined by the rate of change of the money supply. Although the leader of the neomonetarist school, Milton Friedman, makes no such claims, several of his followers have written that stock prices are functionally determined by changes in the basic stock of money. The third concept is that stock prices are determined by the comparative yields of stocks and alternative investments.

The experience of the mid-1970s seems to show that some of the relationships that had previously been thought to hold true are coming into increasing question. Stock prices have not proved to be the inflation hedges that most people thought they were. Stock prices have stagnated or declined in the face of rapidly rising money values of GNP and an ever-escalating stock of money. These relationships seem to say that stock prices are unduly depressed relative to other inflation-swollen economic variables. Yet the whole thrust of formula planning is that temporary gaps do occur between variables that otherwise have strong secular relationships. The signals of the GNP model and the money stock models are that stock prices are too low. Stock prices were also too low relative to the GNP during the 1930s and 1940s. It was these revealed discrepancies that established the possible advantages of using formula plans.

The GNP Model

On the assumption that stock price levels are not a random event (although some day-to-day changes are undoubtedly random), J. Fred Weston clearly showed the relationship between stock prices and the GNP. He demonstrated a close relationship between the GNP and aggregate sales of business enterprises. The same close relationship exists between aggregate business sales and profits before taxes. Similarly, an obvious close relationship exists between profits before taxes and dividends and, finally, between dividends and stock prices. "Thus . . . stock prices can be linked directly to gross national product leaving out the intermediate steps. Therefore as GNP grows over the years, we would expect that the total value of stock prices will grow in the same proportion."[12] He tested this concept statistically and found the following simple regression equation for the years 1868–1940:

$$\text{DJIA} = 28.20 + 0.9675 \text{ GNP} \tag{1}$$

[11] A striking illustration is the case of population projections. Nothing is measured more precisely in the United States than population. Yet, decade after decade, most population projections have proved to be wrong. Present population statistics projections for the 1970s are based on the behavior of the population in the 1960s, but family size is falling rapidly, marriage is being postponed, and abortion and birth control devices are becoming increasingly commonplace. By contrast, population growth in the 1930s was so slow that most economists felt that the United States had fallen into a *permanent* stagnation and that its population would not reach 200 million before the year 2000.

[12] J. Fred Weston, "The Stock Market in Perspective," *Harvard Business Review,* vol. 34, p. 70, March–April 1956; "A Not-So-New Era in the Stock Market," *Financial Analysts Journal,* vol. 16, pp. 57–64, November–December, 1960.

In 1964 Weston's work was updated and a later period, 1929–1962, was tested. As shown below, the updated equation was almost identical with Weston's original.[13]

$$\text{DJIA} = 22.37 + 1.001 \text{ GNP} \qquad (2)$$

With GNP in units of $1 billion, Equation 1 yields a DJIA level of 995.70; Equation 4 predicts a level of 1028.27. This is a difference of only 3.27 percent, which is amazingly close. Although the whole series has not been rerun, data ending in 1970 (quarterly data are used) apparently support the basic hypothesis that stock prices tend to increase in a secular relationship with the GNP.

This formula is easy to calculate and is readily available. The Department of Commerce releases the GNP estimates quarterly, and these can be found in the financial press or obtained directly from the Department of Commerce. The DJIA is widely published and is available at any broker's office.

The basic concept behind the Weston model is that, if stock prices are linked fundamentally to the level of the GNP, deviations from the norm as determined by the statistical relationship could be used to run a formula plan. This was done by using, first, the Weston formula only[14] and then an improved version of the formula as shown in Equation 2.[15] Both articles showed that a more modern statistical technique could be used successfully to operate a formula plan that in general yielded excellent results. For example, the results of the Dince-Weston plan were much superior to those of all plans tested by Cottle and Whitman, including the Graham-Dodd Central Value Technique.[16] The formula value of the plan increased from $100,000 at the end of 1929 to $431,249 at the end of 1962.

Operation of the Dince-Weston Model.   At the end of 1959[17] the Dow Jones Industrial Average was 679.36. The formula value of the DJIA as shown in Table 9-4 (501.3 × 1.001 + 22.37) computes to 524.17. Dividing the formula value into the actual DJIA gives the ratio of actual to formula value and the resulting zone. By consulting Table 9-2, we see that this zone calls for holding 30 percent of the portfolio in stocks and 70 percent in bonds. The formula is signaling that the stock market is too high relative to general economic conditions and that investors should adopt a cautious attitude.

As Tables 9-4 and 9-5 show, the actual operation of the formula plan maintianed an essentially conservative position until the end of 1966 (with the exception of the last quarter of 1962). Trades were made at any period if the trade called for more than a $2,000 change in the stock position. No delaying scheme was used. Only once did the stock market decline far enough to push the portfolio into the relatively extreme position of maintaining 70 percent of the portfolio in stock. This break occurred in mid-1970, when the DJIA fell to 683.53. Since mid-1969 the formula plan has held a fairly aggressive position in stocks, which implies that the DJIA must break the 1000 mark before the plan would call for a "normal" ratio of 50/50 to be held. As shown in Table 9-5, the portfolio was "under water" only three times in the second and fourth quarters of 1960 and the second quarter of 1962, and conservative gains were made.

If we had restricted trading as explained above so that stocks were never bought in Zones I, II, or III or sold in Zones V, VI, or VII, the results would have been a

---

[13]R. R. Dince, "Another View of Formula Planning," *Journal of Finance*, vol. XIX, p. 679, December 1964.

[14]R. R. Dince, "Formula Planning: Another Method of Locating Highs and Lows," *Financial Analysts Journal*, March–April 1961, pp. 59–64.

[15]Dince, "Another View of Formula Planning," p. 679.

[16]Dince, "Formula Planning," p. 63.

[17]The GNP statistic is released approximately three weeks after the end of the quarter. For simplicity's sake, the DJIA price used was always the last price reported for the same quarter.

little better. An additional restriction was placed on the portfolio: trades were not made if the plan continued in the same zone regardless of the change in prices. By following these ground rules, trades would have been made only in the second quarters of 1962, 1963, and 1964, the fourth quarters of 1966 and 1969, and the second quarter of 1970. The portfolio would have been worth $125,794, and it

TABLE 9-4   Zone Determination in the Dince-Weston Formula Plan, 1960–1973

Date* (1)	DJIA (2)	GNP (3)	Formula value of DJIA (4)	Percentage (column 2 divided by column 4) (5)	Zone (6)
4/1959	679.36	501.3	524.17	129.6	II
2/1960	640.62	505.0	527.88	121.4	III
4/1960	615.89	505.1	527.98	116.7	III
2/1961	683.96	500.8	523.67	130.6	II
4/1961	731.13	525.8	548.70	133.3	II
2/1962	561.28	522.0	544.89	103.0	IV
4/1962	652.10	565.2	588.14	110.9	IV
2/1963	706.68	579.6	602.55	117.3	III
4/1963	762.95	599.0	621.97	122.7	III
2/1964	831.50	618.6	641.97	129.5	II
4/1964	874.13	641.1	664.11	131.6	II
2/1965	868.03	665.9	688.94	126.0	II
4/1965	969.26	704.4	724.47	133.8	II
2/1966	870.10	732.3	755.40	115.2	III
4/1966	785.69	762.1	785.23	100.0	IV
2/1967	860.26	775.1	798.25	107.8	IV
4/1967	905.11	811.0	834.18	108.5	IV
2/1968	897.80	852.9	876.12	102.5	IV
4/1968	943.75	892.5	915.76	103.6	IV
2/1969	873.19	924.8	948.10	92.1	IV
4/1969	800.36	951.7	975.02	82.1	V
2/1970	683.53	971.1	994.44	68.7	VI
4/1970	838.92	989.9	1013.26	82.8	V
2/1971	890.20	1043.1	1066.51	83.5	V
4/1971	890.22	1072.9	1096.34	81.2	V
2/1972	929.03	1142.4	1165.91	79.7	V
4/1972	1020.02	1199.2	1215.76	83.9	V
2/1973	879.82	1272.0	1295.64	67.9	VI
4/1973	855.32	1334.0	1337.70	63.9	VI

*Data is as of the end of the quarter.

would have been holding 106.32 units of the DJIA as of December 1971. Whether a typical investor could have withstood the pressure of not trading from the end of 1966 until the end of 1969 is an important question. During the same period, minor changes in the unrestricted portfolio were permitted three times, as shown in Table 9-5.

As Table 9-5 indicates, the GNP model was signaling as of the end of 1973 and well into 1974 that stock prices were unduly depressed relative to the GNP. When we consider that so many investors are discouraged with the depressed state and high volatility of the stock market, it is entirely possible that the GNP in current dollars is simply the wrong variable to correlate with stock prices. To determine whether a better relationship existed between the DJIA and *real* GNP, new correlations were run by using real GNP (in constant 1958 dollars). The results show that there is no significant difference between using real and current-price-level GNP. For example, as of the end of 1973, the total value of the portfolio, obtained by employing the identical techniques but using a different regression equation, was $123,145, or a difference of 0.92 percent. (The regression formula is as follows: DJIA = −202.802 + 1.499 real GNP. The coefficient of determination was a rather high .885.) As of the end of 1973, the real GNP model dictated a Zone V relationship, or 60 percent in stocks.

TABLE 9-5   Operation of the Dince-Weston Formula Plan, 1960–1973   *(Starting Value = $100,000)*

Date*	Zone†	Stock-bond ratio‡	DJIA	Stock	Shares held§	Bonds	Total value
4/1959	II	3/7	679.36	$30,000	44.16	$70,000	$100,000
2/1960	III	4/6	640.62	39,316	61.37	58,974	98,290
4/1960	III	4/6	615.89	37,797	61.37	58,974	96,771
2/1961	II	3/7	683.96	30,285	44.28	70,663	100,948
4/1961	II	3/7	731.13	32,374	44.28	70,663	103,037
2/1962	IV	5/5	561.28	47,758	85.09	47,758	95,516
4/1962	IV	5/5	652.10	51,622	79.16	51,622	103,245
2/1963	III	4/6	706.68	43,025	60.88	64,537	107,562
4/1963	III	4/6	762.95	49,394	58.19	66,591	110,985
2/1964	II	3/7	831.50	34,493	41.48	80,483	114,976
4/1964	II	3/7	874.13	36,309	41.48	80,433	116,742
2/1965	II	3/7	868.03	36,006	41.48	80,433	116,438
4/1965	II	3/7	969.24	36,192	37.34	84,446	120,648
2/1966	III	4/6	870.10	46,235	53.76	70,161	116,936
4/1966	IV	5/5	785.69	56,200	71.53	56,200	112,400
2/1967	IV	5/5	860.26	58,867	68.43	58,867	117,734
4/1967	IV	5/5	905.11	61,937	68.43	58,867	120,804
2/1968	IV	5/5	897.80	61,526	68.43	58,867	120,393
4/1968	IV	5/5	943.75	61,724	65.40	61,724	123,448
2/1969	IV	5/5	873.19	59,415	68.04	59,415	118,830
4/1969	V	6/4	800.36	68,322	85.36	45,549	113,871
2/1970	VI	7/3	683.53	72,727	106.40	31,168	103,895
4/1970	V	6/4	838.92	72,257	86.13	48,172	120,429
2/1971	V	6/4	890.20	76,673	86.13	48,172	124,845
4/1971	V	6/4	890.22	76,674	86.13	48,172	124,846
2/1972	V	6/4	929.03	76,914	82.79	51,275	128,189
4/1972	V	6/4	1020.02	81,438	79.84	54,289	135,722
2/1973	VI	7/3	879.82	87,174	98.98	37,360	124,534
4/1973	VI	7/3	855.32	84,660	98.98	37,360	122,020

*End of quarter.
†See Table 9-4.
‡See Table 9-2.
§After adjustment. No brokerage is included.

The Money and Stock Price Model

Conceptually, the relationship between the GNP and stock prices has major difficulties. One obvious problem is that the GNP is a summary measure of the nation's annual production on a value-added basis, whereas the DJIA is a spot price at a given moment of time. The DJIA statistic could have been adjusted to make it an average that might have answered this problem, but there is an even more fundamental reason for seeking some other determinant of a formula plan's central value. Many financial observers believe that stock prices represent investors' expectations of the future; as such, they *generally* anticipate economic conditions as represented by such statistics as the GNP.[18] Therefore, it would be more appropriate to use the DJIA to predict the GNP than vice versa.

[18]G. H. Moore and J. Shiskin, *Indicators of Business Expansions and Contractions,* National Bureau of Economic Research, New York, 1967.

The major proponents of an alternative explanation are the monetarists, economists who believe that levels of spending are determined by the changes in the money supply relative to the stock of assets. Given a change in the supply of money (usually defined as currency and demand deposits), spending will change in the same direction. One of the leading monetarists in the United States, Beryl Sprinkel, went so far as to claim that since changes in stock prices anticipate levels of spending and changes in the money stock precede both, it is necessary only to find the lead-lag response between changes in money and changes in stock prices.

In 1966 Sprinkel formulated an investment rule that "a bear market in stock prices was predicted 15 months after each peak in monetary growth and that a bull market was predicted two months after each monetary growth trough was reached." He used this idea to develop a formula timing plan approach, switching from stocks into a portfolio of all bonds on the designated switch dates. Starting in August 1918 with $100,000, the capital sum increased to $11,958,622 by February 1960, or the equivalent of a 12.2 percent compounded annual growth.

Sprinkel's plan did not work so well during the 1960s. In his 1970 book, he says that, on the *average,* a downturn is predicted nine months ahead and an upturn two to three months ahead by changes in the rate at which the money stock grows.[19] Sprinkel's new position is:

> Since we do not fully understand why the leads have been of the duration recorded in the past, we cannot be certain they will be repeated in the future. Even though we cannot be sure of future time leads both theoretical arguments and empirical evidence strongly suggest that monetary changes will provide some useful guidance to future investment timing decisions.[20]

Regardless of Sprinkel's accuracy, his strong advocacy of the Friedman approach to the study of money and its effect on macroeconomic phenomena has lead other researchers to look into the question of money and stock prices.

Perhaps the most ambitious project was undertaken by Michael Keran, a research economist at the St. Louis Federal Reserve Bank. In a very sophisticated statistical examination of the factors determining stock prices, Keran found that 98 percent of the variation in stock prices could be statistically related to rates of change in real money, real output, expectations of earnings, and past stock prices. His most spectacular finding was that stock prices were inversely correlated to inflation. Expectations of increased inflation tend to raise interest rates, and this rise in turn depresses stock prices. Unfortunately, Keran's model is so complicated that his results cannot be summarized and used as a model for formula planning. Even the use of advanced computer techniques might find a replication of Keran's effort so expensive as to be impractical.[21]

Independently of Keran, two researchers at Princeton University developed a statistical technique that does relate stock prices directly to the money stock.[22] Further, their technique seems to give as good results as Keran's and is much simpler. The basic problem with their approach is the need for great accuracy by investors in forecasting the growth of the money stock. If investors could have perfect foresight, the results are spectacular. Unfortunately, typical investors (or even the Federal Reserve Board) do not have perfect foresight. Homa and Jaffee suggest two approaches. The first they call the "naïve" approach: investors assume

[19]Beryl Sprinkel, *Money and Stock Prices,* Richard D. Irwin, Inc., Homewood, Ill., 1966, p. 120; *Money and Capital Markets,* Dow Jones-Irwin, Inc., Homewood, Ill., 1970, p. 221.

[20]Sprinkel, *Money and Capital Markets,* p. 222.

[21]Michael W. Keran, "Expectations, Money, and the Stock Market," *Monthly Review,* Federal Reserve Bank of St. Louis, January 1972.

[22]Kenneth E. Homa and Dwight M. Jaffee, "The Supply of Money and Common Stock Prices," *Journal of Finance,* vol. XXIII, pp. 1045–1066, December 1971.

that the growth of the money stock will continue at the same rate as it did in the preceding quarter. The use of such naïve extrapolations gives poor results, as shown below in the test of a formula plan using their equations. However, if the United States were ever to adopt the type of monetary policy advocated by its leading monetarist, Milton Friedman, there is reason to believe that the naïve method would work better. Friedman advocates strongly that the stock of money be increased by a constant percentage. If this procedure were followed, the next quarter's money stock growth would always approximate that of the last quarter.

Homa and Jaffee's alternative approach is very much more complicated and less stable. By analyzing the relationships among unemployment, prices, the balance of payments, and the preceding period's money stock growth, the next quarter's growth can be estimated.[23] The results of this approach are almost as good as if perfect foresight were available. However, the researchers' technique implies a good deal of ex post reasoning since the estimated coefficients varied considerably over the period. To take this into account, an estimating equation was based on the preceding five-year period. In general, Homa and Jaffee's technique could be used only by someone with access to computer facilities: lacking these, investors could use the naïve technique with the indicated poorer results.

For the period from the last quarter of 1954 through the last quarter of 1969, Homa and Jaffee developed the following estimating equation:

$$SP = -26.77 + 0.61\,M + 3.14\,G + 1.46\,G_{-1} + 0.87_{u-1} \tag{3}$$

SP refers to the Standard & Poor's 500-Stock Index. M represents the money stock (demand deposits plus currency in circulation), and G refers to the money supply growth, which is calculated as $(M_0 - M_{-1})/M_0$ and is measured at a quarterly rate in percentage points. All information is readily available in any current *Federal Reserve Monthly Bulletin*.

Operation of the Homa-Jaffee Model. The nature of the exogenous variables used as the independent determinant of stock market prices has a great deal to do with how often the model is switched. In the Homa-Jaffee model, the buy-hold-switch decisions are made quarterly. There is no intrinsic reason why a formula plan cannot be run quarterly, as long as the quantity to be traded exceeds some predetermined minimum (which is always $2,000 in the examples described here). The GNP model is shown being switched twice a year (though the switch was made quarterly in the original article), and the Graham-Dodd model that follows is shown being switched annually, precisely as Graham himself recommended that it be done. In the interests of editorial space, the money supply formula plan is shown twice a year, although the actual calculations must be made each quarter,

TABLE 9-6   Stock-Bond Ratios and Zone for Formula Plan Utilizing Homa-Jaffee Money Supply Prediction

Standard & Poor's 500 as percentage of formula value	Zone	Percentage ratio, stock-bond
112.5 or more	I	20/80
107.5–112.5	II	30/70
102.5–107.5	III	40/60
97.5–102.5	IV	50/50
92.5–97.5	V	60/40
87.5–92.5	VI	70/30
87.5 or less	VII	80/20

[23]Ibid., p. 1053.

TABLE 9-7   Zone Determination for Homa-Jaffee Money Supply–Stock Price Formula Plan

Quarterly period	Standard & Poor's 500-Stock Index	Prediction	Ratio (S&P divided by prediction)	Zone	Percentage ratio, stock-bond
1/1960	58.10	56.55	104.6	III	40/60
3/1960	53.52	54.43	98.3	IV	50/50
1/1961	64.42	56.19	114.7	I	20/80
3/1961	66.73	65.07	102.6	III	40/60
1/1962	69.55	73.76	94.3	V	60/40
3/1962	56.27	58.58	96.0	V	60/40
1/1963	66.57	65.65	101.4	IV	50/50
3/1963	72.13	72.23	99.9	IV	50/50
1/1964	79.19	77.68	103.1	III	40/60
3/1964	84.21	83.42	101.0	IV	50/50
1/1965	86.20	87.83	98.1	IV	50/50
3/1965	90.02	86.39	104.2	III	40/60
1/1966	89.54	97.86	91.5	VI	60/40
3/1966	76.56	90.05	85.0	VII	80/20
1/1967	90.20	82.74	109.0	II	30/70
3/1967	96.71	94.44	102.4	IV	50/50
1/1968	90.20	99.39	90.8	VI	70/30
3/1968	102.31	103.59	98.8	IV	40/40
1/1969	101.51	106.99	94.9	V	60/40
3/1969	94.16	99.09	95.0	V	60/40
1/1970	88.65	83.22	106.5	III	40/60
3/1970	82.58	91.41	90.3	VI	70/30
1/1971	99.60	108.71	91.6	VI	70/30
3/1971	99.40	107.18	92.7	V	60/40
1/1972	107.69	110.72	96.6	V	60/40
1/1972*	109.39	120.17	91.0	VI	70/30
1/1973	112.42	127.41	88.2	VI	70/30
1/1973	105.61	120.72	87.5	VI	70/30

SOURCE: *Federal Reserve Bulletins;* Kenneth E. Homa and Dwight M. Jaffee, "The Supply of Money and Common Stock Prices," *Journal of Finance,* vol XXIII, pp. 1050, 1052, December 1971.

*Revised formula, shown in footnote 24, is used for the subsequent values.

since the estimating equation for the current quarter must include an item determined by the prediction from the previous quarter.

Calculating the series through the third quarter of 1969 was simple, as all the values were given in the article.[24] Values after the end of 1969 had to be calculated.

The Yield Technique

The basic reason for investment is the return received. The concept of a bond yield is easy to understand: the investor gets a coupon paid periodically in dollars for a contractual period, plus the maturity value of the bond at the end of the period. At any given time, the price of a bond depends upon the current market rate of interest typical for the type of bond, because the expected yield is discounted by that rate. The typical formulation for a bond is as follows: Where i is

[24]Ibid., pp. 1050, 1052. All the values calculated in Tables 9-7 and 9-8 were based on Equation 3 through the first quarter of 1972. The remaining periods used the formula $SP = -24.18 + 0.60M + 3.44\,G_{-1} + .87\,{}_{u-1}$. This formula was provided to the author by Professor Jaffee. The problem is that as the stock of money rises, the predicted level of stock prices will rise without limit. The coefficient of the money stock must be reexamined and lowered periodically.

the interest rate, Cu is the coupon interest payment, M is the maturity value, and n the number of years to maturity,

$$\text{Price} = \sum_{t=1}^{N} \frac{Cu}{(1+i)^t} + \frac{M}{(1+i)^N} \tag{4}$$

Conceptually, a stock can be viewed in the same way. A periodic yield is usually expected, a maturity value (sales price) is anticipated, and a holding period (maturity) is assumed. The major difference is that while the values for bonds are known or assumed, stock selling prices and dividends are unknown or, at best, perceived only dimly. A notation for stocks can be developed from our notation for bonds. In this case, D refers to the current expected dividend, *price* to the security price at the end of the designated period, and k to the investors' required rate of return:

$$\text{Price} = \sum_{t-1}^{N} \frac{Dt}{(1+k)^t} + \frac{Pt}{(1+k)^N}$$

The investors' required rate of return can be formulated either as a riskless interest rate plus a risk premium or as the return that they can secure on alternative investments. Whichever concept is used, it can readily be seen that the

TABLE 9-8   Operation of a Formula Plan, Homa-Jaffee Model, 1960–1973

Quarterly period	Standard & Poor's 500-stock index	Zone	Stock value*	Shares held†	Bonds	Total value
60-1	55.98	III	$ 40,000	714.54	$60,000	$100,000
60-3	53.52	IV	49,121	917.81	49,121	98,242
61-1	64.42	I	21,649	336.07	86,597	108,246
61-3	66.73	III	43,609	653.51	65,414	109,023
62-1	69.55	V	66,520	956.44	44,346	110,866
62-3	56.27	V	58,899	1046.72	39,266	98,165
63-1	66.57	IV	54,473	818.28	54,473	108,946
63-3	72.13	IV	56,748	786.74	56,748	113,496
64-1	79.19	III	47,620	601.34	71,430	119,050
64-3	84.21	IV	61,034	724.78	61,035	122,069
65-1	86.20	IV	62,476	724.78	61,035	123,511
65-3	90.02	III	50,512	561.12	75,768	126,280
66-1	89.54	VI	75,606	844.39	50,404	126,010
66-3	76.56	VII	92,040	1202.20	23,010	115,050
67-1	90.20	II	39,434	436.99	92,014	131,448
67-3	96.71	IV	67,137	694.24	67,138	134,275
68-1	90.20	VI	90,829	1007.00	38,927	129,756
68-3	102.31	IV	70,976	693.74	70,977	141,953
69-1	101.51	V	84,839	835.78	56,559	141,398
69-3	94.16	V	78,154	861.87	54,102	135,256
70-1	88.65	III	52,203	588.88	78,303	130,506
70-3	82.58	VI	88,853	1075.96	38,080	126,933
71-1	99.60	VI	101,722	1020.80	43,574	145,246
71-3	99.40	V	87,025	875.50	58,016	145,041
72-1	107.69	V	91,379	848.54	60,920	152,299
72-3	109.39	VI	107,399	983.81	46,123	153,742
73-1	112.42	VI	110,600	983.81	46,123	156,723
73-3	105.61	VI	103,900	983.81	46,123	150,023

*No brokerage fee is calculated, and fractional shares are permitted.
†After adjustment.

current value of a stock depends on the assumptions made with regard to its future price. Even more important, the value is determined by the rate of return required. If investors can secure a 9 percent yield on Aaa-rated bonds, very healthy stock price gains must be secured to make it worthwhile to buy the much less certain returns of the stock. It is this point that Seligman hit so hard in an article in *Fortune:* "Stocks will be competing strenuously with bonds—whose returns will be substantially more attractive than they were during the lush post war years. Bond yields will increasingly function as a kind of ceiling on stock prices."[25]

Seligman's statement is very similar to what Benjamin Graham said more than twenty years ago, when he showed that the "central value" of a stock index was limited by the relationship of the yield in bonds to the earnings of the stock index. In the fourth edition of their famous *Security Analysis,* Graham, Dodd, and Cottle suggested the following central-value formulation:[26]

$$\text{DJIA} = \frac{\text{EPS (DJIA average for last ten years)}}{1.33 \text{ (AAA bond yield for last three years)}} \qquad (6)$$

The model gave clear buy signals all through the 1950s, but, like so many other central-value techniques, it gave clear sell signals in the 1960s. Continued high interest rates in the late 1960s revealed that, at all DJIA levels actually reached, the stock market was in a sell phase according to this model. For example, in 1970, the average value of the earnings of the DJIA for the preceding ten years equaled $48.99. The average Moody's Aaa yield was 7.63 percent; multiplying this figure by 1.33 equals 10.17 percent. Capitalizing the earnings by 10.17 percent yields a justified level of only 481.7 for the DJIA.

Obviously, stocks are worth less and less as bonds yield more and more, but how much less? Even if we adjust the Graham-Dodd-Cottle formulation to eliminate the multiplier of 1.33 and just capitalize the average earnings by the bond yield, we come up with a justified DJIA of only 642.1. Seeking such a relationship implies that stocks and bonds have equal risk. Perhaps a sounder technique would be to leave the multiplier of 1.33 but reduce the average earnings period to five years. Doing this yields a justified DJIA of 571.58. The closing price of the DJIA in 1970 was 838.92. The obvious result of the Graham-Dodd method is that if bond yields rise faster than corporate earnings, as they did during the 1960s, the technique pushes the appraisal value of stocks down. In view of stock market behavior in the 1970s, the Graham-Dodd formulation has achieved belated justification.

Operation of the Graham-Dodd Formula Plan.   Using the advantages of hindsight, it has been possible to develop a formula plan by employing a modification of the Graham-Dodd technique.[27] In this case, trading occurs only once a year, and the five-year average (instead of the ten-year average) of DJIA earnings is capitalized by 1.33 times the three-year average of Moody's Aaa bond yield. This procedure has the advantage of increasing the earnings to be capitalized without losing the effect that stocks are riskier than bonds.

This version of the Graham-Dodd central-value approach was prophetic as a

[25]Daniel Seligman, "A Bad New Era for Common Stocks," *Fortune,* October 1971, p. 74. This is probably one of the best reviews of recent theoretical investment literature available in layman's terms.

[26]Benjamin Graham, David L. Dodd, and C. S. Cottle, *Security Analysis,* 4th ed., McGraw-Hill Book Company, New York, 1962, pp. 510–511. In the third edition, the denomination of the equation is much higher: the *current* Moody's AAA yield doubled (*Security Analysis,* 3d ed., McGraw-Hill Book Company, New York, 1951, pp. 671–672).

[27]In 1953 Cottle and Whitman found that this modified Graham-Dodd technique yielded the best results of all the central-value techniques tested (C. S. Cottle and W. T. Whitman, op. cit., p. 121). The older version of this plan multiplied Moody's Aaa bond yield by 2. A typical bond yield of the late 1930s would have been 2.85 percent.

result of its reliance on interest rates of high-quality bonds. Despite the fact that earnings of the thirty large corporations making up the DJIA increased by 66 percent during the period 1960–1971, average interest rates rose from 4.27 to 7.48 percent in the same period—a 75 percent increase. Thus, the Graham-Dodd formula value for the DJIA actually decreased during the period even though consumer prices increased by 37 percent and industrial production by 60 percent. To postulate a market worth less in the 1970s than in the 1960s implies that there are huge new risks in the market—a situation that became more evident by the mid-seventies.

TABLE 9-9   Determination of Zone for Graham-Dodd Central-Value Technique

Year* (1)	Five-year average, earnings per share, DJIA (2)	Three-year average, Moody's Aaa bond yield × 1.33 (3)	Formula value† (4)	DJIA (5)	Ratio of column 4 to column 5 (6)	Zone (7)
1960	$32.78	5.68	577.11	615.89	106.7	IV
1961	32.49	5.83	557.29	731.13	131.2	II
1962	32.56	5.80	561.38	652.10	116.2	III
1963	35.21	5.74	561.15	762.95	136.0	II
1964	37.64	5.76	653.47	874.13	133.8	II
1965	41.93	5.83	719.21	969.26	134.8	II
1966	47.08	6.22	756.91	785.69	103.8	IV
1967	50.57	6.71	753.65	905.11	120.1	III
1968	53.91	7.46	722.65	943.75	130.6	II
1969	56.02	8.30	675.05	800.36	118.6	III
1970	55.50	9.71	571.58	839.92	147.0	I
1971	54.56	9.96	547.79	889.07	162.3	I
1972	57.07	10.02	564.56	1020.02	179.1	I
1973	63.41	10.07	629.69	855.32	135.8	II

*End of year.
†Formula value equals column 2 divided by column 3 times 100.

Only once during the period from 1960 to 1971 did the formula plan drop into the central zone. In 1966 the earnings of the DJIA increased faster than interest rates while the actual market dropped (see Table 9-9). Nevertheless, with this pattern of prices and using year-end DJIA figures, the value of the portfolio as shown in Table 9-10 increased to $123,777 in 1971 (it declined slightly over the next two years). If we consider that by 1970–1971 the formula had thrown the portfolio into Zone I, this was a respectable result from an ultraconservative position. If we had followed a program of restriction with no buying in Zones I, II, and III, no selling in Zones V, VI, and VII, and no trading if the zone didn't change, the portfolio would have been worth only $119,688 in 1971.

Summary

It is interesting to note what our three formula plans signal at the end of 1973. The Graham-Dodd-Cottle plan, despite its extreme conservatism through the 1960s, signals that strong antiequity forces are still at work. High bond yields continue to depress the intrinsic value of equities. If interest yields hold in the 9 percent range, it would take a substantial increase in the earnings of the DJIA before the extremely conservative holdings (20 percent stocks, 80 percent bonds) are changed. When risk-free rates (short-term) are in the 10 to 11 percent range, stock prices must remain depressed even if corporate earnings have risen sharply.

In contrast, the Dince-Weston formula signals the exact opposite. As of the end of 1973, the formula predicted a rise in stock prices and was advocating a firm position in the holding of equities (60 percent stocks, 40 percent bonds estimated at the end of 1971).

The formula plan using the supply of money as the key determinant of stock prices is indeterminate. It was not clear that the equation we used for determining central value would hold true during the 1970s, but if so, at the end of 1973 it was signaling a heavier common stock position.

In conclusion, formula plans can be as simple or as complex as the mind of man can devise. In general, constant-ratio plans are hardly sophisticated enough to bother with, yet they emphasize the central thesis of all formula plans that profits can be made by only selling rising stocks. Central-value formula plans all work on the basic premise that there is a relationship between stock prices and outside economic variables. Therefore, the amount of stocks to be held is determined by

TABLE 9-10   Operation of Formula Plan Using Modified Graham-Dodd Central-Value Technique

Year*	Zone	Stock-bond ratio†	DJIA	Units of DJIA	Value of stock‡	Value of bonds	Total value
1960	IV	5/5	615.89	81.18	$50,000	$ 50,000	$100,000
1961	II	3/7	731.13	44.87	32,805	76,545	109,350
1962	III	4/6	652.10	64.90	42,372	63.482	105,804
1963	II	3/7	762.95	44.93	33,899	79,098	112,997
1964	II	3/7	874.13	40.48	35,381	82,555	117,936
1965	II	3/7	969.26	37.70	36,541	85,250	121,791
1966	IV	5/5	785.69	73.10	57,435	57,435	114,870
1967	III	4/6	905.11	54.62	49,439	74,159	123,598
1968	II	3/7	943.75	39.96	37,712	87,995	125,707
1969	III	4/6	800.36	59.96	47,991	71,986	119,997
1970	I	2/8	838.92	29.13	24,469	97,878	122,347
1971	I	2/8	890.22	29.13	25,899	97,878	123,777
1972	I	2/8	1022.02	25.02	25,518	102,073	127,591
1973	II	3/7	855.32	43.31	37,042	86,431	123,473

*End of year (December 31 closing price).
†See Table 9-2.
‡After adjustment.

the movement of the outside (exogenous) variable. All three of the methods used here are based on historical relationships. It is entirely possible that these relationships will not hold true in the future and that new ones must be developed.

As we have shown, formula plans yield variable results. If the basic formula has validity, the results are acceptable within the risk assumptions made. As long as the basic premise of formula planning is kept in mind, the conservative results should be acceptable. In any case, the problems of decision making under uncertainty are ameliorated once an acceptable formula plan has been chosen.

PORTFOLIO SELECTION IN FORMULA PLANS

The Stock Portfolio

Virtually all literature dealing with formula plans deliberately begs the question of portfolio selection. In some magic way, formula planners inherit their securities or, in the manner of Boston's Back Bay ladies, they don't buy their hats—they "have" hats. The testing of formula plans is always based on some security index, which is assumed to be neutral toward the problem of stock selection,[28] but only

[28]Stock indices are not neutral. During the period 1956–1959, five stocks were replaced on the DJIA. Back in March 1939, AT&T replaced IBM with rather disastrous effects on the future levels of the thirty-stock index. The only really neutral indices are the ones designed by the exchanges, which measure all listed stocks. They may be more accurate for depicting market action and direction, but they hardly represent any actual portfolio.

the largest portfolios would resemble a security index. Further, the type of portfolio chosen is a function of many things. The needs of a young well-paid chest surgeon are quite different from those of a trust set up for the permanent care of a cemetery plot.

If we try to beg the question of security selection and merely want to duplicate market action, then for small portfolios the volatile portion should be invested in some form of mutual fund.[29] The category of fund selected is immaterial, since any particular fund is assumed to be a function of each individual investor's taste and preferences. Thus, the young surgeon would pick an aggressive growth fund, while the trustee for the cemetery might choose a fund specializing in bank or utility stocks.

There is one major problem. The various studies that have been made detail the movement of some stock average relative to an exogenous economic variable. The Standard & Poor's 500-Stock Index and the thirty-stock Dow Jones Industrial Average do not necessarily move in the same way as a growth fund or a utility stock fund. But formula plan switching is based on the movement of the overall average. There is bound to be a discrepancy between the volatility of the stock average and the volatility of the actual stock portfolio. As long as we accept this and manage the portfolio and the proportions determined by the formula plan as two different matters, we are on safe ground.

Since formula plans operate by switching at regular intervals or at the time that some particular economic index changes, the investor is given an excellent opportunity to review the portfolio and make desired or recommended changes. Various possible techniques are available:

1. Several well-known brokerage houses give portfolio advice as a customer service. Once the portfolio is set up, the brokerage house can be called on to recommend switching at the required dates.

2. Several well-known investment advisory services (Value Line, Moody's, Standard & Poor's) publish typical investment portfolios. Changes in a portfolio could be accomplished by following such standardized advice.

3. The most obvious technique for running a formula plan would be to use an investment company or the common trust fund of a bank. There are many possible vehicles to accomplish this.[30] Closed-end funds are available both on the stock exchanges and in the over-the-counter market. Open-end investment funds of both the load and the no-load types are available directly or through brokers. The only problem investors would have is to be sure that the investment company minimizes its holdings of fixed-income securities. Otherwise, investors would be duplicating their defensive position in both parts of their portfolios.

4. One possibility is quite simple and is available even to small investors. They could select from the thirty stocks making up the DJIA the three to ten stocks that they consider the best investment at the portfolio review date. The technique for selection could be one of the many covered elsewhere in the *Handbook*. The

---

[29]Cottle and Whitman were ambivalent. They invested their volatile portfolio in Standard & Poor's index of ninety stocks, but the switching was determined by movements in the DJIA. Op. cit., pp. 23–24.

[30]As previously mentioned, one unusual mutual fund might be an ideal vehicle for a formula plan. Founders Mutual places all its funds in only forty securities that include the DJIA. Not only does the list of securities remain unchanged, but the flow of funds into the mutual fund is spread equally over all the securities held. There is an old market quip that says, "If you do as well as the average, you are doing better than average." Obviously an investment in this fund would never do worse than the average. The payment of the typical commission for this fund seems high, since the investment managers make no investment decisions.

investors could even sequester a certain part of their stock portfolios for fliers in highly speculative stocks if this procedure fitted their personal preferences.

5. Investors could utilize almost any other portfolio construction technique within their capabilities, as described and analyzed in Section Ten.

Summary. Portfolio selection involves the strategic decisions that must be made in selecting individual stocks that fit the objectives of investors. There is one special overriding consideration. Since almost all formula plans involve holding some bonds at all times, the equities bought should not be bought with any consideration of building in safety through the selection of certain types of stocks. In other words, utilities or bank stocks should not be bought to get stability but because they offer the best investment opportunity at the time. As for diversification, the most important point is that after a few carefully selected securities have been included in the stock portion of the portfolio, most of the gains from diversification will have been accomplished.

Selection of the Defensive Segment of the Portfolio

For many reasons, the literature of formula plans generally ignores the problem of selecting bonds. First, relatively little time is spent by investors in bond selection. Most large investors submit a potential bond purchase to a rather routine analysis that merely duplicates what has already been done by the rating services; in any case, the final decision is made on a yield basis. Second, the problem of making the bond portfolio react in the manner in which the bond market actually moves is quite difficult. As a result, formula planners showing retrospectively how their formula plan has worked ignore the price action of bonds.[31] Third, for most small investment portfolios, it is extremely difficult to trade in the odd amounts and numbers of bonds required by the portfolio shifts.

The question of bond selection creates so great a problem that Beryl Sprinkel in his book *Money and Stock Prices* showed that the yield of his portfolio could be increased by switching to cash instead of long-maturity bonds when changes in the money supply dictated a move from stocks. Generally speaking, the reason that Sprinkel advocates avoiding long-term bonds when the portfolio is switched from stocks is that during periods when economic activity increases, the money supply is up and stock prices are rising; then all these phenomena are associated with increased demand for funds and rising bond yields.[32] The mechanics of bond prices are such that rising bond yields necessarily mean that existing bonds with lower coupons will fall in price. The precise manner in which bond prices fluctuate depends on a host of factors.[33]

Certain investment policies could mitigate the problems for which Sprinkel overcompensates by using cash. The simplest and probably the most effective technique for avoiding capital losses through increasing interest rates is the "ladder" technique. In this method, the bond portfolio is broken into time segments, and equal portions of each maturity class are purchased. Thus the maturity

[31]Cottle and Whitman assumed that bonds were bought and sold at par with 4 percent of the portfolio maturing annually. Op. cit., pp. 25–26.

In the author's first article on formula plans, he ignored the price effect; in his second article, he pretended that it didn't exist by using savings and loan accounts; in his third article, he finally attempted, with great difficulty, to simulate the price effect. For the last article, see R. R. Dince, "Portfolio Income: A Test of a Formula Plan," *Journal of Financial and Quantitative Analysis,* September 1966, pp. 90–107.

[32]Sprinkel, op. cit., pp. 147–150.

[33]The most inclusive academic article depicting the causes of bond price fluctuations is B. J. Malkiel, "Expectations, Bond Prices, and the Term Structure of Interest Rates," *Quarterly Journal of Economics,* May 1962, pp. 200–216.

structure of the bond

structure of the bond portfolio is not overweighted with long bonds, which are most subject to price fluctuation.

Another possible technique is to use a weighted ladder. Let us suppose for simplicity's sake that the bond portfolio has been broken into two classes, those with maturities of less than ten years and those with maturities of more than ten years. At the time that the formula plan recommends moving into bonds (liquidating stocks), the market yield of long-term bonds should be compared which historic bond price averages. If bond yields are greater than the average, commitments should be made in longer terms. If the opposite is true, the commitment should be made in shorter-term bonds.

Let us suppose that the adjustment of the portfolio was to take place in July 1971. At that time Moody's Aaa bond average (long-term bonds) stood at 7.64 percent. Using the weighted-ladder approach and a five-year bond average, we would have bought long-term bonds, since the market yield was 98 basis points higher than the five-year average (7.64 compared with 6.66 percent). Even if a three-year average were used, long-term bonds would have been preferred to shorter maturities because the market yield of 7.64 percent was 33 basis points higher than the three-year average.

However, a purchase of bonds in July 1963 would have favored short maturities. At that time Moody's Aaa bond average was selling to yield 4.26 percent. The three-year average was 4.31 percent, and the five-year average was 4.32 percent. This difference was enough to warrant the cautious policy of buying proportionally more short-term maturities, since the sharply rising yields of the second half of the 1960s would have inflicted large capital losses on investors in long-maturity bonds. For example, a 4 percent twenty-year Aaa-rated corporate bond would have sold for $968 in 1963, but by 1966 its price would have fallen to $861. Investors would have received $120 in interest, but they would have experienced a $107 capital loss.[34] On the other hand, bond buyers investing in July 1971 would have had a capital gain of $36 at the end of 1971 on the purchase of a similar bond.

This technique may be too complicated for average investors. One way to avoid these various problems is to invest the entire defensive fund in savings bank accounts. Since none of the plans discussed here ever takes investors completely out of stocks, one part of this method might be to invest a portion of the bond segment in savings time certificates in order to get the advantage of better yields.

Another simple technique is to buy either bond funds or $1,000 bundles of diversified bonds sold by several large brokerage houses.

We have not presented an all-inclusive list of investment techniques for the bond portfolio, since there is a myriad of possibilities. Many bonds of United States government agencies are available in $1,000, $5,000, and $10,000 denominations; the yields are usually higher than on Treasury securities. Further, the bonds are available from almost any bank, and they are quoted every day in such newspapers as *The Wall Street Journal* and *The New York Times*. If the portfolio called for $43,746 in the defensive portion, the bulk of the funds could be invested in three $10,000 bonds and thirteen $1,000 denominations, and the balance placed in a savings account. Commissions on buying and selling these bonds are relatively small.

[34]Bond price indices are always calculated by positing that the current yield is converted to a price which assumes that a 4 percent twenty-year bond was selling at the current yield. Each basis point increase in yield is related to a smaller decrease in bond prices when the bond index is adjusted for maturity. See Dince, "Portfolio Income: A Test of a Formula Plan," p. 103.

Perhaps the simplest technique, that of using a savings account compounded daily with interest paid to the date of withdrawal, would be the easiest course. There are no transaction costs, adjustments can be made easily down to the last dollar, and instant liquidity is available if necessary.

DOLLAR COST AVERAGING

Perhaps the form of formula planning in widest use today is the technique known as dollar cost averaging (DCA). The methodology is so simple that anyone can follow it. The basic assumption is this: when equal *dollar amounts* of a security are purchased regularly, its weighted-average cost will be less than its average price.

The method depends on certain basic assumptions that are quite realistic:

1. The market action of most stocks is cyclical.

2. Overall stock prices may fall drastically, but they eventually return to the same level.

3. The long-run future of the United States economy is not endangered.

The wide acceptability of DCA is based on several institutional factors that create a demand for stocks to be purchased periodically. First, most investors neither are born with nor inherit an estate to be managed; their accumulation of an estate necessarily must take place over a long period of time. Second, many investors have no sophistication in investment; they either invest directly by using securities designed as ready-made portfolios for smaller investors (investment companies) or invest indirectly by contributing to pension funds that also invest periodically. Third, life insurance companies also are practitioners of DCA, since their regular contractual inflow of funds requires periodic investment.[35]

DCA is a simple investment plan that helps unsophisticated investors with investment timing.[36] As the prices of stocks fluctuate, more shares are bought when stock prices fall and fewer shares when they rise. The example in Table 9-11 demonstrates a hypothetical case in which stock prices first fall and then return to the original level while periodic equal dollar purchases are made.

The simple example demonstrates the benefits of dollar averaging. Falling stock prices allow the investor to buy proportionally more stocks at lower prices, thus lowering the weighted-average cost. The weighted-average cost $(^{8,000}/_{110.3})$ equals \$72.53 a share, as compared with an average price of \$76.25. If we had bought ten shares of stock (rather than equal dollar amounts) at each time period, the whole portfolio would have cost \$7,625 and would have been worth \$8,000. The dollar-cost-averaging technique cost \$8,000 and was worth \$11,030.

Thus, the basic assumption of dollar cost averaging is that short-term movements of stock prices are essentially unpredictable. Instead of trying to determine whether stocks are dear or cheap, investors ignore the market and merely buy at regularly stated intervals. This enables them to buy stock at different prices and results in a lower weighted-average cost.

As previously stated, another basic assumption of dollar cost averaging is that no matter what period is chosen as the base period, the long-term trend of stock prices is up. Once this assumption has been made, investors can live through any

[35]George E. Rejda, "The Role of Dollar Averaging in the Common Stock Operations of Life Insurance Companies," *Journal of Insurance,* December 1962, pp. 533–565.

[36]In his book on investments J. C. Francis criticizes DCA in a rather heavy-handed way. He states: "DCA is a type of beat-the-market scheme for investors who lack confidence in their investment skills and are willing to forego high rates of return as long as they do not have to work or take risks in their investing." *Investments Analysis and Management,* McGraw-Hill Book Company, New York, 1972, p. 582.

TABLE 9-11   Basic Example of Dollar Cost Averaging in a Cyclical Stock   *($1,000 Invested per Period)*

Period (1)	Price of stock (2)	Number of shares bought with $1,000 (3)	Total shares owned (4)	Total amount invested (5)	Current value of shares (2) × (4) (6)	Net gain or loss percentage (6) ÷ (5) (7)
1	$100	10.0	10.0	$1,000	$ 1,000	0
2	80	12.5	22.5	2,000	1,800	−10.0
3	70	14.3	36.8	3,000	2,576	−14.1
4	60	16.7	53.5	4,000	3,210	−19.7
5	50	20.0	73.5	5,000	3,675	−26.5
6	70	14.3	87.8	6,000	6,146	+2.4
7	80	12.5	100.3	7,000	8,024	+14.6
8	100	10.0	110.3	8,000	11,030	+37.9

weak market period, accepting their paper losses calmly and continuing to invest, with the knowledge that ultimately their confidence will be proved correct.

Typically, stock prices merely need regain their former levels to make them successful investors. Sometimes—notably, when declines are very severe—even this is not necessary. The DJIA hit a high of 382 in September 1929 and did not reach this level again until November 1954! However, a quarter century of buying at depressed prices would have made investors rich well before 1954, even though they had started their DCA program at the disastrously high levels of 1929.

Volatility and DCA

Volatility seems to be an essential characteristic of a successful DCA program. Without a cyclical price pattern, DCA would not produce the desired results. Constant prices would produce no advantage, and steadily rising prices would produce only a rising average cost with each additional purchase. Thus, DCA is most appropriate for cyclical stocks with secularly rising prices. The more volatile the price movement within the secular movement, the better the results.

The advantages of volatility are shown in Tables 9-12 and 9-13. Table 9-12 is

TABLE 9-12   Dollar Cost Averaging in a Growth Stock of Low Volatility   *($1,000 Invested per Period)*

Period (1)	Price of stock (2)	Number of shares bought with $1,000 (3)	Total shares owned (4)	Total amount invested (5)	Current value of shares (2) × (4) (6)	Net gain or loss percentage (6) ÷ (5) (7)
1	$ 60	16.7	16.7	$ 1,000	$ 1,000	0
2	80	12.5	29.2	2,000	2,336	+16.8
3	75	13.3	42.5	3,000	3,188	+6.3
4	90	11.1	53.6	4,000	4,824	+20.6
5	85	11.8	65.4	5,000	5,559	+11.2
6	105	9.5	74.9	6,000	7,865	+31.3
7	100	10.0	84.9	7,000	8,490	+21.3
8	115	8.7	93.6	8,000	10,764	+34.6
9	110	9.1	102.7	9,000	11,297	+25.2
10	130	7.7	110.4	10,000	14,352	+43.5

based on the assumption of a growth stock of low volatility; in this case, volatility is measured by the standard deviation (19.874) of the prices around the mean. The results of this program would yield a portfolio worth $14,352 in period 10. The same investment in the more volatile stock in Table 9-13 (standard deviation, 24.114) would yield $15,860, an advantage of 10.5 percent over the less volatile stock. Under the assumptions used, neither DCA program would have been as good as a simple buy-hold strategy. If for $10,000 investors had bought 166.7 shares of either stock, their investment would have been worth $21,671 at period 10. However, the assumption of DCA is that investors buy in at regular intervals because they do not have the wealth to pursue the buy-hold policy.

TABLE 9-13   Dollar Cost Averaging in a Growth Stock of High Volatility   ($1,000 Invested per Period)

Period (1)	Price of stock (2)	Number of shares bought with $1,000 (3)	Total shares owned (3) (4)	Total amount invested (5)	Current value of shares (2) × (4) (6)	Net gain or loss percentage (6) ÷ (5) (7)
1	$ 60	16.7	16.7	$ 1,000	$ 1,000	0
2	90	11.1	27.8	2,000	2,500	+25.0
3	60	16.7	44.5	3,000	2,670	−11.0
4	95	10.5	55.0	4,000	5,225	+30.6
5	65	15.4	70.4	5,000	4,576	−8.5
6	100	10.0	80.4	6,000	8,040	+34.0
7	70	14.3	94.7	7,000	6,629	−5.3
8	110	9.1	103.8	8,000	11,418	+42.7
9	95	10.5	114.3	9,000	10,859	+20.7
10	130	7.7	122.0	10,000	15,860	+58.6

Returning to Table 9-11, we see that no buy-hold strategy would be as successful as DCA with this cyclical price pattern.[37] What this demonstrates is that the ideal price pattern for a successful DCA program is a U-shaped price cycle.[38]

Variations on DCA

An interesting and probably profitable variant of dollar cost averaging combines the automaticity of DCA with some of the flexibility of the formula plan. Instead of investing fixed amounts at predetermined periods, variable amounts are invested according to the dictates of an outside determinant, as might be employed in a typical variable-ratio formula plan.

For example, we might assume that, over a long enough cycle of possible prices, prices are randomly and normally distributed around a mean. On this assumption, a simple plan would be to purchase amounts larger than the regular (normal) payment when the price is lower than the weighted average and to purchase

[37]If we had taken the prices shown in Table 9-11 and increased them by 30 percent after period 1, a DCA program would have yielded superior results over a simple buy-hold strategy. A buy-hold strategy would have bought eighty shares, which would have been worth $10,400 in period 8. DCA would have yielded a result of $11,323.

[38]Correspondingly, the worst possible pattern for DCA is the inverted U. If we take the prices in Table 9-11 and make them greater than $100 by the amount they are less than $100, the investor would have bought 65.8 shares worth $6,580 and costing $8,000. The inverted-U pattern is one of the reasons for the popular dillusionment with mutual fund shares since 1971. Many DCA programs were instituted in the middle 1960s by small investors; they bought their shares through an inverted-U pattern, with very poor results.

smaller-than-normal amounts when the price is above the weighted average. Thus, while total dollar purchases would tend to be about the same, the results would be proportionally better.

Using the simple rule of buying twice as much when the market price is less than the weighted-average cost and half the normal amount when the price is greater than the weighted-average cost, we get results that are significantly better than a simple DCA program. Simple DCA for a high-volatility growth stock has been shown in Table 9-13; the variation described above with the same price pattern is shown in Table 9-14. Simple DCA produces a portfolio worth 58.6 percent more than cost; the variation in Table 9-14 is worth 79.5 percent over cost.

TABLE 9-14   Variable Dollar Cost Averaging According to Formula*

Period (1)	Price of stock (2)	Number of shares bought (3)	Total shares owned (3)	Total amount invested (5)	Current value of shares (2) × (4) (6)	Net gain or loss percentage (6) ÷ (5) (7)
1	$ 60	16.7	16.7	$1,000	$ 1,000	0
2	90	5.6	22.2	1,500	2,500	+66.7
3	60	33.3	55.6	3,500	3,333	−4.8
4	95	5.3	60.8	4,000	5,778	+44.7
5	65	30.8	91.6	6,000	5,953	−0.8
6	100	5.0	96.6	6,500	9,659	+48.6
7	70	7.1	103.7	7,000	7,261	+3.7
8	110	4.5	108.3	7,500	11,911	+58.8
9	95	5.3	113.5	8,000	10,786	+34.8
10	130	3.8	117.4	8,500	15,260	+79.5

*Double purchase when price is less than weighted-average cost and half purchase when price is more than weighted-average cost.

NOTE: Same price data as in Table 9-13.

Various other formula plan modifications of basic DCA are also feasible and can produce results equal to or even better than the superior results shown in Table 9-14.[39]

As our examples have shown, dollar cost averaging is a reasonably successful technique for the small investor accumulating an estate. The only important operational factor required is that stock prices generally move in some cyclical fashion. Almost always, growth is not as important as volatility, since it is in the depressed price period that investors get the greatest opportunity to purchase stocks at much lower than the average price.[40]

Thus, investors must, as in all formula plans, operate in bad markets as well as good; indeed, this is the only essential rule to be followed. Therefore, investors must not be in a situation in which the dollar-averaging plan must be stopped or liquidated before the cycle has been completed. Unfortunately, economic or psychological reasons for liquidation invariably coincide with periods of poor stock prices and thus vitiate the plan.

Accordingly, a careful DCA investment plan should scale down the regular

[39]See Leo Barnes, *Your Investments,* Prentice-Hall, Inc., Englewood Cliffs, N.J., 1968, pp. 195–196.

[40]In the examples shown, Table 9-13 yields a better result than Table 9-12; higher volatility yields better results than lower volatility. However, *greater growth* yields even better results than *greater volatility.* (Actually, greater growth is simply greater *upside* volatility.) Compare J. J. Harrington, Jr., "The Effect of Growth Rates and Cyclical Variability on the Results of Dollar Averaging Programs," *Proceedings of the American Statistical Association,* 1963.

contractual sum to be invested to a figure that investors believe they will be able to afford at all times. Thus, a young engineer employed at Cape Kennedy in 1965, with only rosy expectations before him, may have aggressively contracted for a $200-a-month plan. But his DCA plan, to be successful, had to be able to buy stock in the depressed markets of 1970, just when the economic environment was the worst for young space engineers.

The DCA time horizon must be long enough to allow a market cycle to run its course. Essentially, DCA ignores the market level when the plan is begun; but a plan begun at the bottom of a cycle, continuing through a high and through to the next bottom (an inverted-U pattern), would yield extremely poor results. The desired goal of DCA is to achieve a low weighted-average cost relative to a potential selling price. Generally speaking, at least ten years are required to achieve this result.

Finally, the intervals between purchases should not be very long, since investors might miss low periods in the cycle. This is a very important point because bear markets are almost invariably shorter than rising markets. Thus, small monthly investments would seem to be preferable to quarterly investments 3 times as large, especially if no sales charges are involved, as for no-load mutual funds.

The Appropriate Investment Vehicle for DCA

The basic assumptions of DCA are so convincing that this technique of investing has become the foundation for investing in mutual funds, pension plans, employee profit sharing plans, and variable annuities. The sales literature of funds and investment companies is full of examples of handsome estates that would have been built up if a certain sum had been regularly invested for some period. Despite the criticism cited previously, that "dollar cost averaging plans are usually used in hopes of attaining something for nothing,"[41] the fact is that any of the above-cited investment vehicles is ideally suited for a certain type of investor.

The ideal DCA investor is one who must build up his estate from his normal income. Since the investment must be made in relatively small amounts, it is impossible to get the proper diversification through small regular payments except at very high commission rates. Further, as Francis correctly points out, many small investors are lazy and do not want to put any personal effort into selecting securities. The other side of the coin is that many contributing members of society are so busy performing their specialties that they have little time, experience, or inclination to make the necessary investment selections.

The usual DCA investment vehicles are diversified portfolios of stocks and sometimes bonds with stated investment goals similar to those that investors might select for themselves if they had the energy and knowledge to manage a diversified portfolio. There are many possible outlets for investments made in this way, but the most typical one would be either a load or no-load mutual fund. Typically, the broadly based investment company should experience a price movement similar to that of the general market, allowing the dollar-cost-average effect to work to the investor's benefit.

While the subject of evaluation of investment company performance is best discussed elsewhere (see Section Eight), there are certain obvious problems which should be considered. Whether or not a given portfolio is the best under any set of market conditions can be determined only in the long run. Unfortunately, stocks are sold in the short run. Salesmen attracted by the high commissions available in mutual funds often oversell certain funds to people whose dispositions are not capable of the self-discipline that a DCA program requires. In the drive to secure

[41]Francis, op. cit., p. 582.

these high commissions and the high management fees for managing larger and larger portfolios, many investment management firms in the "soaring sixties" oversold the idea of performance. Mutual funds were organized for the express purpose of speculation in highly leveraged and basically risky situations. The coupling of performance orientation with the wide use of the "front-load plan"[42] led to general skepticism about the future of professional investment companies.

Several investigations into the performance of professional investment companies, whether sales were made with or without high commissions, have been commissioned by the Securities and Exchange Commission and congressional committees. The results of these investigations have not been accepted as totally correct and free from bias, yet the most comprehensive and well-known investigation states: "The funds have not generally matched the performance of equally distributed random investments in New York Stock Exchange stock."[43] An obvious criticism is that an equally distributed random investment is impossible for anyone except some mythical Howard Hughes–like figure.

Because all investors have abdicated their responsibility in selecting a well-balanced portfolio, they should not abdicate their responsibility of correctly choosing an investment company. Some funds, including no-load ones, do better than random.[44] Investors have the problem of finding the fund that conforms to their point of view and actually delivers what it promises.

The *only* requirement for DCA is investing *periodically*. Nothing in the literature says that periodic investment must be made in the same company. As long as the investment is made in a fund that moves with the market, the major goals of the dollar-cost-averaging program will be served. In the words of a well-written book on mutual funds for the lay investor, "Critics, who therefore hold that mutual funds are unacceptable investment media, are as much in error as the proponents who lead an investor to believe that any mutual fund will prove to be a good investment. The desired results are obtained from a carefully selected, well managed mutual fund."[45]

AUTOMATIC TREND FOLLOWING

The variants of finding formula approaches to investing are as numerous as the supposed ways of turning lead into gold that preoccupied the ancients. One device that signals buy-sell decisions and requires little interpretation is automatic trend following, an application of the so-called filter technique.

In simple terms, a stock is bought or sold if the price changes by a certain percentage (the filter). At this point, adventurous investors can go one step further and, on the basis of the sell signal, not only sell the stock but also go short in it. The

[42]A front-load plan is so called because of a sales contract in which the total commission is collected during the early part of the contract. If an investor contracts to buy $10,000 of a fund over ten years and the commission of $800 is collected in the first two years, then the sales commission would be 40 percent if the investor canceled the contract as of the end of the second year. For an indictment of this practice, see United States Senate, Committee on Banking and Currency, *Mutual Fund Legislation of 1967*, Part 1, pp. 154–166.

[43]Irwin Friend, Marshal Blume, and Jean Crockett, *Mutual Funds and Other Institutional Investors*, McGraw-Hill Book Company, New York, 1970, p. 64.

[44]The Friend study shows that certain kinds of funds, primarily high-risk funds, did better than the random performance of the market as a whole for the period studied. Perhaps these results were a product of the period studied rather than the management ability of the investment companies. Ibid., pp. 60–68.

[45]Stuart B. Mead, *Mutual Funds: A Guide for the Lay Investor*, D. H. Mark Publications, Braintree, Mass., 1972, p. 99.

short position will be maintained as long as the stock does not rise by a certain percentage from its previous low. All the various maneuvers of buying, selling, selling short, and placing stop-loss orders can be simply handled by a broker through the use of limit orders.

To illustrate automatic trend following, let us suppose that an investor is using a 10 percent filter. The signal calls for selling the stock short at $100. A stop-loss buy order is left with the broker at $110. Time passes, and the stock falls to $90; a new stop-loss buy order is placed at $99. Using the same technique, the investor places limit orders to ensure that whenever the trend is reversed, the stock position will be reversed either to guarantee the profit earned or to prevent a further loss. Let us suppose that the stock continues to fall until it hits $80 and a new stop-loss buy order is placed at $88. The stock reverses the trend and makes $88. Since the stock has risen 10 percent, the short position is replaced with a long position, and a new stop order to *sell* the stock is put in at $79.20. Let us suppose that the stock rises to $100 (where the cycle began), and a stop-loss sell order is placed at $90. The next day, the stock falls to $90, and the investor is sold out. As a result of all these transactions, the stockholder made $12 on the short sale and $2 on the long position. In effect, the investor had stated that a 10 percent change in the stock price indicates a reversal of trend.

It is quite obvious that the selection of the filter size can affect overall results substantially. The smaller the filter, the greater the possibility of overtrading; yet a smaller filter will retain more of the profit than a larger filter. If a stock goes up 20 points, a 5 percent filter will retain more of the profit than a 10 percent filter. But if the stock tends to move around a mean by the amount of the filter, then transaction costs will tend to wipe out profits, and the smaller filter is ineffective.

If investors use a larger filter to protect themselves from overtrading, they expose themselves to being whipsawed: selling low and buying high. Let us suppose that investors use a 20 percent filter. They decide on stock X, now selling at $100. The stock cannot be bought until it rises to $120. The investors buy at $120 and set a stop-loss order at $100. The stock falls back to that point and is sold. For their pains the investors are back where they started, less $20 a share.

There is a certain simpleminded appeal to automatic trend following. Buy orders are triggered by percentage increases. Similarly, stop-loss sell orders, coupled with short-sale orders, are triggered by percentage drops. Investors need do nothing but look at their morning newspapers, calculate the percentages, and then call the broker, leaving limit orders either on the buy or the sell side. Alas, one test of an automatic-trend-following peak plan under fairly favorable circumstances showed that the profits were not quite equal to the brokerage costs of trading in and out of the securities.[46]

Another variant of automatic trend following is the use of a moving average to determine buy and sell points. The commonest measure is the 200-day moving-average trend. A 200-day moving average is calculated for a particular stock or the stock average, and the closing price of the stock is compared with the moving

---

[46]The basic problem with use of filter rules is that as most modern financial analysts using advanced statistical techniques have shown, individual stock price movements perform a "random walk" around some central price (which may or may not indicate intrinsic value). Tests have shown that runs in price changes are not significantly different from runs in a table of random numbers. According to Francis, "It seems that short-run traders who search for various types of nonrandom trends from which to earn a profit will not be able to beat a naive buy-and-hold strategy." Op. cit., p. 540. See also S. Alexander, "Price Movements in Speculative Markets: Trends or Random Walks," *Industrial Management Review*, May 1961, pp. 7–26; E. F. Fama, "Random Walks in Stock Market Prices," *Financial Analysts Journal*, September–October 1965, pp. 55–59.

average.[47] When the price of a security bottoms out after a long decline, the average will tend to be above the market price; if the price breaks through the average, this is a clear buy signal. Similarly, if the price of the stock falls through the moving average, a sell signal is given.

A similar but more complex procedure involves exponential smoothing. In the simplest terms possible, past data are examined to find a statistical formulation that will remove random variation in a time series. This is done to find the "pure" rate-of-change curve through time. Data on individual stocks are submitted for computer analysis. A "normal" price is established; the past changes are used to determine the most likely *next* change. Stocks with the greatest anticipated change upward would be likely candidates for buying. If we consider that in the short run stock prices are most likely randomly distributed around a mean, this technique is not recommended for any except the most statistically sophisticated investors who have access (preferably free) to computers.

These more sophisticated versions of automatic trend following pose the same basic problem as the simpler forms: buyers will tend to get whipsawed by repeated price reversals. Stock prices can fall through the moving averages or the exponentially smoothed price curve, only to reverse quickly and climb back through the averages.

SUMMARY AND CONCLUSION

Formula plans all emphasize the same basic approach to investment to the exclusion of alternative approaches. Essentially, they are mechanistic rules designed to solve the problems of when to buy or sell and how to allocate the investment portfolio between aggressive and defensive securities. Like all machines, they tend to break down unless they are regularly overhauled. Further, the purpose of the machine may tend to change, or the basic purpose for which the machine was built may be outdated. Many critics of formula planning argue that if investors are shrewd enough to know how to overhaul the machine, they probably don't need the machine in the first place.

The basic advantage of formula planning is that it emphasizes contrary action. When prices fall, formula plans advocate buying, and vice versa. The reason that stock prices are falling is that investors' expectations with regard to future earnings, dividends, and stock prices are falling. Thus the required rate of return is rising. Since the investors' required rate of return is the sum of a pure riskless interest rate plus a risk premium, the formula plan is saying that often the risk premium is not as large as investors think it is. Economic conditions may be buoyant while the market is falling.

All formula plans preach a sound, unemotional, noninvolved approach to the market as it moves with the tides of investor sentiment. Further, the plans imply that stock price movements are basically cyclical and that in time they will return to a norm.

Most formula plans are based on reasonably sophisticated statistical approaches to market analysis, with one exception. The one exception is the seemingly mindless but generally successful dollar-averaging technique. Either the basic assumption that stocks will always rise (typical of the mid-1960s) or the assumption that they will never rise again (as in the 1930s or, more recently, in 1970–1971) can become the foundation of successful formula planning.

[47]If making a 200-day moving average is too tedious for the average investor, a common substitute of thirty closing prices taken on Thursday can be used. Leonard T. Wright, *Principles of Investments: Text and Cases,* Grid, Inc., Columbus, Ohio, 1972, pp. 311–312.

The successful formula plan exploits the situation in which calm, uninvolved persons can keep their heads when all around them are losing theirs. Investor depression, which typically follows downturns in the market, is the psychology in which formula plans operate successfully.

Perhaps the basic fascination of a formula plan is that it involves developing a plan that exploits other people's weaknesses. When the plan is well conceived, it gives investors the wonderful feeling of euphoria that comes from knowing that they are doing better than the market with a minimum of effort. Again, we cite the old market cliché: "If you do as well as the average, you are doing better than average."

Section Three

Common Stocks and Other Equity-geared Investments

Chapter 10
Selecting Stocks for Value

DAVID K. EITEMAN

The process of selecting individual shares of common stock to hold as an investment can be divided into two separate activities: (1) identification of expected future benefits to stockholders that derive from their ownership of shares of stock and (2) the placing of a proper value or price upon the aggregation of benefits so identified. This chapter is concerned primarily with analytical approaches to identifying and analyzing expected future benefits. Chapter 12 is concerned with techniques for establishing a rational valuation of such benefits.

When an investor purchases a share of common stock, he or she receives the following specific rights:

1. *The right to a physical certificate.* In the present era, when millions of dollars may be safely and efficiently transmitted by check, wire, or computer, the notion that a physical certificate is necessary seems an anachronism from precomputer times. Certificates as we know them are hardly necessary for the proper functioning of the stock market system, and their phase-out, starting in the near future, seems inevitable.

2. *The right to transfer shares to someone else at any mutually agreed-upon price.* "Shares" in this context refers to the legal ownership position rather than the physical certificate. The corollary to the right to sell stock to others is that the corporation is under no obligation to return a stockholder's capital prior to the actual liquidation of the company. A share of stock thus has no maturity.

Excluding liquidations, which are quite rare, the terminal value of any investment operation in common stocks depends upon what some other individual might be willing to pay for the remaining future benefits. The inexactness of this concept of remaining and terminal value creates both great interest in and, at times, great unhappiness with the concept of owning common stocks.

3. *The right to receive a pro-rata share of any dividends declared.* The shareholder has no absolute right to receive dividends, only the right to receive a proportional share of any dividends decided upon by the company's board of directors. Directors need not distribute earnings as dividends if they believe that the cash can be used to better advantage within the business.

Shareholders may, however, regard undistributed earnings as their property.

The value of this latter "right" depends primarily upon whether what one owns but cannot possess is deemed a benefit, either to oneself or because another investor will pay a price to purchase the claim.

4. *Certain procedural rights.* Shareholders may vote on important corporate matters, inspect the general corporate books and records, and, in many instances, purchase their pro-rata portion of any newly issued shares of stock. Such procedural rights may be of critical value in special situations, as when merger negotiations or proxy fights are under way. As a general matter, however, they are peripheral to the main benefits that a shareholder expects to obtain from ownership of common stock.

The major benefits are future earnings and dividends, which for the moment we shall consider as a single package, and the future sales price. The future sales price, in turn, depends primarily upon earnings and dividends still further in the future and upon the value that future investors will attribute to such future earnings and dividends. In this context, the goal of this chapter may be stated more narrowly as an explanation of how one formulates expectations about future earnings and dividends, while Chapter 12 concentrates on approaches to formulating opinions about the valuation of these expected future earnings and dividends. The success of an investment undertaking depends upon accuracy in each of these separate requirements.

QUALITATIVE FACTORS IN FORMULATING OPINIONS ABOUT FUTURE EARNINGS AND DIVIDENDS

Since future dividends depend largely upon future earnings, our initial attention must be directed toward seeking out and arranging available knowledge to arrive at an informed opinion about these earnings. One body of data relevant to this decision may, for convenience, be referred to as "qualitative" because it consists of a series of inputs that, by any definition, is composed of subjective opinions. There is no finite list of qualitative factors, for every potential investment has its unique attributes. However, the following factors are typical and perhaps among the most important in many situations.

Qualitative Factors Relating to the Industry in Which a Company Operates

Industry Permanence.   A profitable industry must serve the rising needs of society. No matter how strong at present, any company in an industry whose products are in diminishing demand is in an inherently weak situation. Industry demand might diminish because of changes in consumer tastes (lack of a market for skirts for high school girls or for men's hats), because of technological innovations (electronic watches replacing conventional watches), or because of industry costs that force prices above competition (ocean cruises relative to air transportation). Although an innovative company may sometimes succeed in changing industries (for instance, W. R. Grace & Co. successfully disinvested in Latin America), as a general matter companies in declining industries are poor investment choices.

On the other hand, industries that manufacture new and innovative products for which an untapped market seems plausible tend to be good industries from which to select companies. Even the weaker companies in such expanding industries tend to develop into satisfactory investments, at least during the growth and expansion phase of the industry.

Industry Competition and Regulation.   A healthy, balanced degree of competition with minimum government regulation creates the best investment climate.

Excess competition can be self-destructive for *all* members of an industry until competition weeds out the less efficient. During such an excessively competitive period, profits of even the strongest companies tend to suffer. Too little competition, on the other hand, especially if accompanied by unduly high profits, may attract new entrants into the field and so create a surplus of competitive pressures. Government regulation, although necessary in some categories, may prevent the flexibility needed for healthy survival (as in the railroads).

Labor Relations.   Healthy survival of corporate employers is clearly not a primary policy goal of American labor. Thus, in industries in which the relative bargaining position of organized labor is strong, possibilities for a healthy industry may be severely limited. This is especially likely when technology cannot be substituted for labor or when foreign competition sets a price ceiling or quality floor from which the United States manufacturer cannot escape (except at consumer expense by seeking political protection against imports).

Qualitative Factors Influencing an Individual Company

Quality of Management.   Corporate management should be capable and imaginative and have proper procedures for ensuring its own perpetuation as individuals enter and leave the management team. In one respect, the quality of management might be judged by the financial results that it has produced. However, to say that a good earnings trend is evidence of top-quality management is to follow circular reasoning if, at some later point, good management so defined is used to forecast a good earnings trend. Rather, management potential must be evaluated separately from visible manifestations of past accomplishments.

In this context, one must determine if management has a firm grasp of key factors influencing the company and if it is keeping abreast of new trends both in products and in management techniques. Does management have both short-run and long-run plans for the company against which actual results may be measured, and is it flexible enough to adapt to unusual events?

Product Reputation.   The company's products should be highly regarded by its customers, both for quality and for assurance that the most appropriate technology has been used for each product. If service is a factor in product acceptance, adequate service facilities should be available.

Company Reputation.   Related to the reputation of the product is the reputation of the company itself. A history of forward-looking and successful product innovation, an imaginative marketing system, appropriate policies in extending credit to customers, good relations with the community and with employees, highly regarded research and development activities, lack of any currently deemed inappropriate social characteristics (such as having been identified as racially discriminatory or as an environmental polluter)—these constitute a partial list of the endless array of characteristics that influence the probable future of a company and establish the parameters within which it must be judged.

QUANTITATIVE ANALYSIS OF FINANCIAL STATEMENTS

The quantitative analysis of financial statements consists of identifying patterns in the financial history of a company and using these patterns as a portion (but not necessarily a major portion) of a forecast of the company's future. Identified patterns may be compared with patterns in similar companies (comparative analysis), or changes and trends for a single company may be assessed over a span of time (time trend analysis). For some companies and at certain times, financial statement analysis will be a major portion of the forecast, while at other times and for other companies this analysis may be of only minor significance in assessing the future. The relative importance attached to the analysis of financial statements depends, in each situation, on the analyst's or investor's judgment of the degree to which past history is a relevant guide to the future.

Financial statement analysis may also serve as a screening device to break down a list of potential investments (say, all common stocks listed on the New York Stock Exchange) into sets for (1) further immediate consideration, (2) possible consideration in the near future, and (3) rejection from further consideration. Screening by financial variables assures that no stocks with potential are overlooked, while it avoids an expenditure of time and energy on stocks not worthy of detailed evaluation. Screening characteristics can be specified to suit each investor; for example, the set of stocks for further consideration could consist of all stocks that meet the following difficult quadruple test:

    1. Rate of return on operating assets (pretax) greater than 25 percent
    2. Earnings per share growing at an average rate greater than 15 percent per annum
    3. Price-earnings ratio below 10 to 1 at the present time
    4. Labor productivity, measured by the ratio of net income to the number of employees, greater at the end of the time period than at the beginning.

A System of Financial Statement Analysis

In the pages that follow, financial statement data for a hypothetical ABC Corporation (based on a real company) are analyzed for illustrative purposes.[1] To focus attention specifically upon the analytical process, only data for 1966, 1967, 1974, and 1975 are considered. In practice, financial information for all years or even all quarters should be studied.

Any systematized approach to financial statement analysis requires a set of data inputs for a series of years, a set of desired relationships, and a processing device (computer, slide rule, or well-worn pencil and the back of an old envelope) to rearrange the inputs into meaningful outputs. Four categories of inputs are used in the illustration that follows: (1) asset items, (2) liability and net worth items, (3) income and expense items, and (4) miscellaneous data on share prices, number of shares outstanding, and number of employees. From the first three of these groups, it is possible to reconstruct the balance sheets and income statement shown in Table 10-1.

The financial statements in Table 10-1 are somewhat more abbreviated than those actually published by most companies. For example, cash is combined with marketable securities; current liabilities are shown only as a total rather than by separate category; and miscellaneous other income is combined in the income statement with miscellaneous other expenses in a single category, "other nonoperational charges." The minus sign indicates that, on a net basis, the sum of these two miscellaneous categories constituted revenue.

Every analytical system is constructed in the face of a certain dilemma. A greater volume of input data can almost always be obtained, and thus greater and more detailed output is possible. This process is limited, however, because (1) collecting and recording data are expensive, in terms of either time or money, and the benefits of the additional data may not warrant the additional cost; and (2) an overwhelming volume of output may lead to less rather than greater understanding, simply because sheer quantity and lack of focus on important variables may

---

[1] A computer program to perform the mechanics of such comparisons is described in David K. Eiteman, "A Computer Program for Financial Statement Analysis," *Financial Analysts Journal*, November–December 1964, pp. 61–68.

TABLE 10-1   Financial Statement Data for ABC Corporation, 1966, 1967, 1974, and 1975

(Thousands of dollars)

	1975	1974	1967	1966
ASSETS				
Cash and marketable securities	23,627	14,390	15,828	16,842
Accounts receivable	29,091	31,036	10,216	11,427
Inventory	49,587	44,179	23,172	20,525
Other current assets	1,758	1,327	471	599
Total current assets	104,063	90,932	49,687	49,393
Gross plant and equipment	187,664	180,376	79,792	74,888
Accumulated depreciation	−78,732	−74,622	−42,506	−39,757
Net plant and equipment	108,932	105,754	37,286	35,131
Other assets	3,778	3,707	217	217
Total assets	216,773	200,393	87,190	84,741
LIABILITIES AND CAPITAL				
Current liabilities	35,483	31,792	16,271	16,755
Long-term debt	20,016	21,159	0	0
Deferred federal income tax	10,248	8,832	1,703	565
Other liabilities	364	340	0	0
Preferred stock	994	1,124	3,191	3,374
Common stock and paid-in surplus	27,404	27,006	21,382	21,363
Retained earnings	122,264	110,140	44,643	42,684
Total liabilities and capital	216,773	200,393	87,190	84,741
INCOME STATEMENT				
Sales	312,445	293,200	152,824	150,273
Cost of goods sold (excluding depreciation)	233,882	217,161	123,290	120,649
Gross profit	78,563	76,039	29,534	29,624
Selling and administrative expenses	29,499	27,842	14,281	13,545
Depreciation expense	10,505	9,767	3,492	3,336
Operating income	38,559	38,430	11,761	12,743
Interest expense	1,150	1,234	0	0
Income taxes	19,030	19,540	5,927	6,172
Other nonoperational charges	−772	−1,310	−392	−62
Net income	19,151	18,966	6,226	6,633
Dividends on preferred stock	40	44	121	131
Net to common stock	19,111	18,922	6,105	6,502
Dividends on common shares	6,988	7,010	4,147	4,147
Net addition to retained earnings	12,123	11,912	1,958	2,355

prevent analysts or investors from fully interpreting their results. Furthermore, the analytical process is fundamentally judgmental, with quantitative analysis serving only as a foundation for further thought and investigation. Financial analysts or investors make a major error if they believe that a greater volume of output can be substituted for informed reasoning and investigation.

Common-Size Statements

The financial statement data in Table 10-1 may be reduced to percentage form, as in Table 10-2, to focus attention on changes in the proportional mix of accounts and so to identify significant variants for further attention. Such a reduction of statements to percentage form, frequently called a "common-size statement," facilitates comparison largely because growth has been extracted.

Common-size statements for ABC Corporation, portrayed in Table 10-2, reveal

TABLE 10-2   Percentage (Common-Size) Financial Statements for ABC Corporation, 1966, 1967, 1974, and 1975

	1975	1974	1967	1966
ASSETS				
Cash and marketable securities	10.90	7.18	18.15	19.87
Accounts receivable	13.42	15.49	11.72	13.48
Inventory	22.88	22.05	26.58	24.22
Other current assets	0.81	0.66	0.54	0.71
Total current assets	48.01	45.38	56.99	58.29
Net plant and equipment	50.25	52.77	42.76	41.46
Other assets	1.74	1.85	0.25	0.26
Total assets	100.00	100.00	100.00	100.00
LIABILITIES AND CAPITAL				
Current liabilities	16.37	15.86	18.66	19.77
Long-term debt	9.23	10.56	0.00	0.00
Deferred federal income tax	4.73	4.41	1.95	0.67
Other liabilities	0.17	0.17	0.00	0.00
Preferred stock	0.46	0.56	3.66	3.98
Common stock, paid-in surplus, and retained earnings	69.04	68.44	75.72	75.58
Total liabilities and capital	100.00	100.00	100.00	100.00
INCOME STATEMENT				
Sales	100.00	100.00	100.00	100.00
Cost of goods sold (excluding depreciation)	74.86	74.07	80.67	80.29
Gross profit	25.14	25.93	19.33	19.71
Selling and administrative expenses	9.44	9.50	9.34	9.01
Depreciation expense	3.36	3.33	2.28	2.22
Operating income	12.34	13.11	7.70	8.48
Interest expense	0.37	0.42	0.00	0.00
Income taxes	6.09	6.66	3.88	4.11
Other nonoperational charges	−0.25	−0.45	−0.26	−0.04
Net income	6.13	6.47	4.07	4.41
Dividends on preferred stock	0.01	0.02	0.08	0.09
Net to common stock	6.12	6.45	3.99	4.33
Dividends on common shares	2.24	2.39	2.71	2.76
Net addition to retained earnings	3.88	4.06	1.28	1.57

a sizable drop in cash and marketable securities from almost 20 percent of total assets in 1966 to only 10.9 percent in 1975. Clearly, ABC was less liquid in 1975 than a decade before. However, the quantitative analysis as such does *not* reveal whether the company was normally liquid in 1966 and was illiquid in 1975 or whether it was excessively liquid in 1966 and had evolved to a position of normal liquidity.

Here are illustrated both the basic strength and the basic weakness of quantitative analysis: differences are made apparent, but the significance of these differences must be based upon deeper insight. In this case, the liquidity of ABC might be compared with that of a competitor, or the management might be queried about the cause of the indicated trend.

Further perusal of the common-size statements in Table 10-2 reveals that current assets as a percentage of total assets declined over the decade, while net plant and equipment (including land) increased. Apparently ABC evolved into a position of greater ownership of production capacity (as evidenced by net plant and equipment) and less ownership of working capital, as evidenced by current assets. One might surmise either that new plant and equipment had been built without any attendant increase in working capital or that working capital had been depleted. The actual significance of the trend would depend upon additional information not revealed in the statements but possibly obtainable from such sources as the president's letter, which is part of the annual report.

The common-size statements of ABC Corporation reveal the following other changes worthy of further evaluation. In 1966, 19.8 percent of total capital came from short-term debt, and none was derived from long-term debt. By 1975 this proportion had changed to 16.4 percent for short-term debt plus 9.2 percent for long-term debt, or a total debt proportion of 25.6 percent. Meanwhile, common stock equity had dropped from 75.6 percent of total liabilities and capital to 69 percent, indicating that over the decade the company had shifted toward using greater financial leverage.

In the income statement, the cost of goods sold as a percentage of sales (operating ratio) dropped from 80.3 percent in 1966 to 74.1 percent in 1974 and then rose slightly to 74.9 percent in 1975. Over the entire interval, the company seems to have significantly reduced costs relative to revenue, suggesting probably improved manufacturing efficiency. Operating income and net income, as a percentage of sales, also rose during the decade, indicating that a greater proportion of sales revenue had been retained for the benefit of the stockholders.

Financial Ratios

A number of financial ratios useful in casting a perspective on particular facets of a company's financial history are calculated in Table 10-3. These are grouped by major purpose, as follows:

1. Ratios prepared to reveal changes in liquidity
2. Ratios prepared to reveal changes in efficiency
3. Ratios prepared to measure the profitability of invested funds
4. Miscellaneous ratios.

Table 10-3 also contains proportional breakdown of the components of the company's capital structure and of its current assets. These two breakdowns supplement the information prepared in the common-size statements and may be interpreted in the same general manner.

Liquidity Ratios. The five liquidity ratios are defined below. The notation n indicates data input for the year for which the ratio is calculated, while the notation $n - 1$ indicates data input for the immediately preceding year. Thus, the denominator of the cash turnover ratio is in fact *average* cash balance calculated as the mean of the year-beginning (that is, the prior year-end) and year-end cash

TABLE 10-3   Financial Ratios, ABC Corporation, 1967 and 1975

	1975	1967
LIQUIDITY RATIOS		
Current ratio (times)	2.93	3.05
Quick ratio (times)	1.49	1.60
Cash turnover (days)	21.90	38.48
Receivable turnover (days)	34.64	25.49
Inventory turnover (days)	72.16	63.80
Total working capital turnover	128.70	127.77
EFFICIENCY RATIOS		
Earning power (percent)	18.49	13.68
Operating assets turnover (times)	1.50	1.78
Operating income margin (percent)	12.34	7.70
PROFITABILITY RATIOS		
Return on debt and equity (percent)	12.30	9.11
Return on common equity (percent)	13.33	9.39
Cash flow to common equity (percent)	20.65	14.76
MISCELLANEOUS RATIOS		
Interest coverage (times)	34.20	. . .
Dividend payout (percent)	36.57	67.93
Effective tax rate (percent)	49.84	48.77
Accumulated depreciation as a percentage of gross plant	41.95	53.27
Net debt repayment ability (years)	1.07	0.05
CAPITAL STRUCTURE		
Funded debt to capital (percent)	11.73	0.00
Preferred stock to capital (percent)	0.58	4.61
Common stock to capital (percent)	16.06	30.89
Retained earnings to capital (percent)	71.63	64.50
	100.00	100.00
CURRENT ASSET STRUCTURE		
Cash and marketable securities (percent)	22.70	31.86
Accounts receivable (percent)	27.96	20.56
Inventory (percent)	47.65	46.64
Other current assets (percent)	1.69	0.95
	100.00	100.00

balances. (The use of average denominators limits the number of years for which ratios may be calculated to one less than the number of years for which data are available; for this reason, ratios are shown only for 1967 and 1975.)

$$\text{Current ratio} = \frac{\text{cash + receivables + inventory}}{\text{current liabilities}}$$

$$\text{Quick ratio} = \frac{\text{cash + receivables}}{\text{current liabilities}}$$

$$\text{Cash turnover} = \frac{\text{sales } (n)}{\dfrac{\text{cash } (n) + \text{cash } (n-1)}{2}} \text{, divided into 360}$$

$$\text{Receivable turnover} = \frac{\text{sales }(n)}{\dfrac{\text{receivables }(n) + \text{receivables }(n-1)}{2}}, \text{divided into 360}$$

$$\text{Inventory turnover} = \frac{\text{cost of goods sold }(n)}{\dfrac{\text{inventory }(n) + \text{inventory }(n-1)}{2}}, \text{divided into 360}$$

The current ratio measures the amount of liquid assets (current assets) relative to currently existing claims due within one year (current liabilities). With a current ratio of 2.93 to 1 in 1975, ABC Corporation had almost 3 times as much in liquid assets as in liquid claims. Because there was only a minor change from the 1967 current ratio, an analyst or investor could conclude that there had been no deterioration in ABC's relative liquidity.

The quick ratio, sometimes referred to as the "acid test ratio," is similar to the current ratio, but inventory has been removed from the numerator. Inventory is deemed the least liquid of current assets; for example, it might include large quantities of obsolete inventories of no value that a company has failed to write off. Thus, the current ratio could be sustained by the spurious factor of obsolete inventories; the quick ratio checks on this possibility by providing an alternative test of liquidity.

The three current asset turnover ratios show what might be referred to as the "lingering time" within the company for each category. In 1975, for example, ABC Corporation operated with a cash balance equal to almost 22 days of sales. Receivables were equivalent to 35 days of sales, indicating that on the average the company had to wait 35 days from the date of a sale until sales proceeds were received in cash. This was a significantly longer wait than had been experienced in 1967, indicating either a weaker quality of receivables or the possibility that competition or a change in product mix had forced the company to finance its customers for a longer interval.

Inventory turnover indicates the average length of time that inventory is held. For ABC, this ratio rose from 64 days in 1967 to 72 days in 1975, indicating the possibility of a longer production process or of a greater supply of material or finished goods on hand.

The sum of the three separate current asset turnover figures is 129 days, hardly different from the 128 days of 1967. The longer receivable and inventory turnovers were effectively offset by the shorter cash turnover period. As a general matter, a shorter turnover interval for any of the current asset accounts indicates greater efficiency; however, at the extreme a low ratio might indicate a risk of running out of cash or inventory or a failure to allow credit terms possibly offered by competitors.

Efficiency Ratios.   The three efficiency ratios are defined as follows:

$$\text{Earning power} = \frac{\text{operating income }(n)}{\dfrac{\text{operating assets }(n) + \text{operating assets }(n-1)}{2}}$$

$$\text{Operating asset turnover} = \frac{\text{sales }(n)}{\dfrac{\text{operating assets }(n) + \text{operating assets }(n-1)}{2}}$$

$$\text{Operating income margin} = \frac{\text{operating income}}{\text{sales}}$$

This set of ratios is related to a triumvirate frequently referred to as the "Du Pont system of financial control,"[2] although in this particular instance the ratios are calculated somewhat differently.

Earning power indicates the rate of return that the corporation is able to earn on its operating assets before taxes, interest, and miscellaneous nonoperating expenses. Operating assets consist of all assets except those not related to normal operations, such as investments. This ratio indicates that ABC Corporation successfully increased its earning power from less than 14 percent in 1967 to more than 18 percent in 1975, for a major growth in financial profitability. The ratio thus identifies a significant improvement in the corporation's profitable use of its operating assets.

The ratio may furthermore be viewed as the product of the two ratios that follow, such that

$$\frac{\text{Operating income}}{\text{Operating assets}} = \frac{\text{sales}}{\text{operating assets}} \times \frac{\text{operating income}}{\text{sales}}$$

or   Earning power = turnover × profit margin.

In the case of ABC, the rise in earning power was obtained by increasing the profit retained from each dollar of sales (income margin), from 7.7 percent in 1967 to 12.3 percent in 1975. The volume of business relative to investment (turnover) declined slightly.

Profitability Ratios.   The three profitability ratios are defined as follows:

$$\text{Return on debt and equity} = \frac{\text{net income } (n) + \text{interest expense } (n)}{\dfrac{\text{total capital } (n) + \text{total capital } (n-1)}{2}}$$

$$\text{Return on common stock equity} = \frac{\text{net to income } (n)}{\dfrac{\text{common stock equity } (n) \quad \text{common stock equity } (n-1)}{2}}$$

$$\text{Cash flow to common stock equity} = \frac{\text{net to common } (n) + \text{depreciation } (n)}{\dfrac{\text{common stock equity } (n) + \text{common stock equity } (n-1)}{2}}$$

A very useful measure of fundamental profitability is return on invested capital, as indicated in both of the first two ratios. The ratio of return on debt and equity (that is, on total capital structure) is the annual rate of return gained collectively by all permanent investors in the company, such as long-term bondholders, preferred stockholders, and common stockholders. The total investment of these three groups earned 12.3 percent in 1975, up rather substantially from 9.1 percent in 1967.

The impact of financial leverage, that is, the use of debt funds or preferred stock with an interest or preferred dividend cost below the rate that can be earned with those funds, is shown in the second ratio. Earnings to common stockholders of ABC constituted a 13.3 percent return on their investment. Because this ratio is above the 12.3 percent earned on total investment, one may conclude that the company experienced favorable financial leverage but of a relatively slight magnitude.

In many instances, the veracity of reported net income can be questioned because the depreciable life of fixed assets is altered. For example, between 1968

[2]For an explanation of the Du Pont system of financial control, see J. Fred Weston and Eugene F. Brigham, *Managerial Finance*, 5th ed., Holt, Rinehart and Winston, Inc., New York, 1975, pp. 35–38, or most other business finance textbooks.

and 1971 many major American airlines extended the depreciable lifetime of their aircraft. Let us assume that a jet aircraft originally costing $10 million was being depreciated over a ten-year life; annual depreciation expense would be $1 million (assuming no salvage). If in 1970 the aircraft was five years old, it would have a remaining undepreciated net book value of $5 million. But if in 1970 the airline extended the depreciable life of the aircraft to fourteen years, the remaining net book value would be written off over the remaining nine years at approximately $555,000 per year. Net income before taxes would be increased by the reduction in depreciation expense, or by $445,000 per year.

Depreciation expense does not require a cash disbursement; rather, it is a bookkeeping entry to reflect the allocation to a particular time period of a portion of the cost of fixed assets purchased at some earlier date. Because the amount of depreciation charged to any single year may be determined somewhat arbitrarily, as in the airline example, a helpful calculation is to add depreciation expense back to net income and label the sum "cash flow."

Even if the amount of depreciation expense has been changed from one year to another, the sum of the two is relatively constant, being affected only by the income tax differential on the altered expense. Thus the third profitability ratio, the relationship between cash flow and common equity, serves as a check on the validity of the ratio of return on common equity. In the case of ABC, the two ratios moved in parallel, suggesting that the company had not manipulated its reported earnings by changing its general depreciation policies.

Miscellaneous Ratios.   The five miscellaneous ratios are defined as follows:

$$\text{Interest coverage} = \frac{\text{net income} + \text{income taxes} + \text{interest expense}}{\text{interest expense}}$$

$$\text{Dividend payout} = \frac{\text{common stock dividends}}{\text{net to common stock}}$$

$$\text{Effective tax rate} = \frac{\text{income taxes}}{\text{net income} + \text{income taxes}}$$

$$\text{Reserve for depreciation to gross plant} = \frac{\text{reserve for depreciation}}{\text{gross plant}}$$

$$\text{Net debt-repaying ability} = \frac{\text{current liabilities} + \text{long-term debt} - \text{cash and marketable securities}}{\text{net income} + \text{depreciation expense}}$$

Interest coverage indicates the number of dollars available, before taxes, to pay each dollar of interest expense. The ratio is a measure of the safety of debt interest payments and is used to assess the quality of a company's debt. Graham, Dodd, and Cottle suggest that an interest coverage of 7 times is sufficient for industrial bonds to be regarded as of high quality.[3] By this criterion, the bonded indebtedness of ABC Corporation, interest on which was earned more than 34 times in 1975, is of excellent quality.

Dividend payout indicates the proportion of each year's earnings available to the common stockholders that has been distributed to those stockholders in the form of cash dividends. An investor seeking dividends might not be attracted to ABC in 1975 because the average payout was quite low and sharply reduced from the level of 1967. On the other hand, an investor seeking growth without large current dividends might find the company a desirable holding.

[3]Benjamin Graham, David Dodd, and Sidney Cottle, *Security Analysis: Principles and Technique,* 4th ed., McGraw-Hill Book Company, New York, 1962, p. 348.

Effective tax rate is a check ratio calculated from the public financial statements to determine whether reported income tax expenses are within a range that would seem appropriate. With a tax rate of 48 percent on corporate income above $25,000 but with possibilities for slight variations due to possible capital gains or capital losses, varying tax treatment of consolidated foreign subsidiaries, special tax credits, and so on, a general range of 45 to 50 percent is normal. Any *significant* deviation from this range should probably be investigated for the possibility that even if current levels of pretax earnings are constant, aftertax earnings might change in the future because of the expiration of a particular short-lived tax advantage.

The ratio of accumulated depreciation (from the asset side of the balance sheet) to gross plant and equipment is a surrogate ratio that gives a rough approximation of the average age of plant and equipment. As calculated for ABC, the ratio indicates that in 1975 the company had expensed 42 percent of its fixed assets, down from 53 percent of assets in 1967. This change implies that the company was adding new assets to its plant and equipment base slightly faster than old assets were expiring. Thus one may infer that, as of 1975, the fixed plant facilities of ABC were, on the average, newer and probably more modern than they were in 1967.

Net debt-repaying ability measures the magnitude of total corporate debt (both current and long-term) relative to the company's ability to repay out of existing cash balance plus annual cash flow. In 1975 ABC was carrying debt equivalent to 1.07 years of repayment ability. The importance of this ratio lies primarily in the fact that a significant increase over a short period of time may reveal that a company is approaching a debt level that might prove difficult to handle in view of present cash-generating capacity.

Per-Share Calculations

The relationship of share prices to other per-share financial data can be explored by the series of ratios shown in Table 10-4. Market price information, as well as the

TABLE 10-4   Per-Share Calculations, ABC Corporation, 1966, 1967, 1974, and 1975

	1975	1974	1967	1966
	MARKET PRICE DATA			
Stock price low	$25.250	$21.250	$14.375	$12.875
Stock price high	40.000	44.375	17.625	18.688
Average market price	32.625	32.813	16.000	15.781
Number of shares (thousands)	6,990	6,974	5,924	5,924
	PER-SHARE CALCULATIONS			
Earnings per share	$ 2.73	$ 2.71	$ 1.03	$ 1.10
Depreciation per share	1.50	1.40	0.59	0.56
Cash flow per share	4.24	4.11	1.62	1.66
Dividends per share	1.00	1.01	0.70	0.70
Book value per share	21.41	19.67	11.15	10.81
	PRICE RATIOS			
Price to earnings (times)	11.93	12.09	15.53	14.38
Dividend yield (percent)	3.06	3.06	4.38	4.44
Price to book value (times)	1.52	1.67	1.44	1.46
Price to cash flow (times)	7.70	7.98	9.88	9.50
Net current assets to price (percent)	30.07	25.84	35.25	34.91

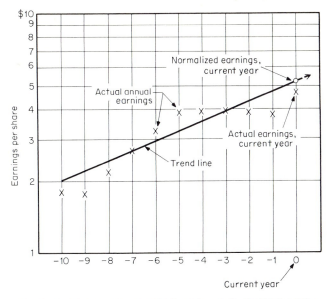

Fig. 10-1   Actual versus normalized earnings estimated by trend line.

number of shares outstanding, is shown at the top of the table, while per share calculations of such variables as earnings, depreciation, cash flow (the sum of earnings and depreciation), dividends, and book value are indicated in the center section. These per-share variables are the bench marks against which the reasonableness of present prices can be judged. Market prices (means for the year) are then related to these underlying financial characteristics in the following set of ratios: price to earnings, cash dividend yield, price to book value, price to cash flow, and net current assets (current assets less total debt) to price.

Present Normalized Earnings per Share

This measure should be earnings per share for the latest reported twelve-month period, adjusted to remove the effect of any nonrepetitive accounting charges (such as capital gains or extraordinary losses taken in the present year) and the impact of cyclical fluctuations inherent in the business. In effect, present normalized earnings per share is that measure of income for the most recent twelve-month period that assumes that this period is typical or normal and is thus the best base from which to project future earnings.

Removing the impact of cyclical fluctuations from the normalized estimate is not a precise calculation but rather is a recognition that if the most recent twelve-month period has been either unusually better or unusually worse than might have been expected over the long run, the use of actual earnings for this period as a base for estimating the future perpetuates the present position into all future years. Adjustment to achieve normalization may be accomplished by fitting a trend line to the data, as is illustrated in Fig. 10-1. The trend line point, rather than the actual point, is used as normalized earnings for the present year. For example, in the hypothetical company portrayed in Fig. 10-1, current year earnings were $4.66. However, in view of the cyclical nature of past earnings about the trend line, a good estimate of current normalized earnings is $5.18. This approach is valid only if there is no evidence to indicate that past patterns will not be repeated.

Growth Rates

Most investors seek growth in their holdings, perhaps because growth is associated in some vague way with enlarged future wealth. But "growth" in a company may refer to the growth of any of a number of variables. Table 10-5 analyzes rates of growth for seven important variables: earnings per share, net profit for the common stockholders, company net sales, dividends per share, average market price of a share of stock, book value of a share of stock, and cash flow of a share of stock.

TABLE 10-5   Growth Rates, ABC Corporation, 1966–1975

	Growth rate per annum as percentage	Correlation coefficient with time	Value of trend line	
			1966	1975
Earnings per share	13.46	0.9603	1.0297	3.2093
Net profit to common	16.09	0.9647	5.8800	22.5144
Net sales	9.34	0.9838	138.7227	309.8578
Dividends per share	4.24	0.8477	0.6402	0.9300
Average market price	10.65	0.9216	15.6948	39.0267
Book value per share	8.21	0.9912	10.2366	20.8252
Cash flow per share	13.31	0.9762	1.5585	4.7986

NOTE: Growth rate calculations are based upon annual data for all ten years, 1966 through 1975, rather than just the four years' data shown in Tables 10-1 and 10-4.

The growth rate expressed under the heading "Growth rate per annum as percentage" is the slope of the least-squares regression line that best fits the logarithms of the variables. With regard to earnings per share for ABC Corporation, a trend line fitted to the data indicates that earnings per share rose from 1966 through 1975 at an average rate of 13.46 percent, *compounded annually.*

As shown in Table 10-5, while earnings per share were increasing by an average compound rate of almost 13½ percent per annum, sales were rising at only 9.3 percent per annum. The difference was caused by the increase in relative efficiency shown in the common-size income statements in Table 10-2. On the other hand, if sales were rising only at 9.3 percent per annum, analysts and investors should hesitate to forecast a continued increase in earnings per share of more than 13 percent unless they were convinced that the company could continue to decrease the ratio of expenses to revenue. It would seem impossible to increase efficiency in this manner forever, since at some point expenses would have to decline to zero proportion of revenue, which is impossible.

The key figure to determine is the *expected average growth rate of earnings per share.* Analysts and investors must predict, as a percent per annum figure, the average annual compound growth rate of anticipated earnings per share for the period during which they expect to hold the stock. Since actual earnings per share will probably grow at varying annual rates during the period under consideration, an average growth rate is used. This may conveniently be viewed as the slope of the compound growth trend line plotted through expected earnings-per-share figures for future years. The use of an expected future compound growth rate in conjunction with present normalized earnings per share is a shortcut to defining specific earnings-per-share levels for each future year being evaluated. Given uncertainties about the future, it is probably no less accurate than an attempt to estimate earnings per share for each year separately.

Table 10-5 also indicates the correlation coefficient between each set of data and time. This enables analysts and investors to know if the growth rate is a good fit to the data. In addition, values for the first and tenth years are calculated to provide two points, so that a straight trend line may be drawn over a plotting of the data on a sheet of semilogarithmic paper, as in Fig. 10-1.

Other Calculations

The number of other calculations, ratios, or other types of relationships that might be calculated is limitless. Table 10-6 shows one set of possibilities. In an era of seemingly ever-increasing labor costs, labor productivity is a matter of concern to any investor. No matter how apparently successful a company may seem, if its labor costs tend to increase disproportionally to other variables, it will probably fail as an investment.

TABLE 10-6   Labor Productivity, ABC Corporation, 1966, 1967, 1974, and 1975

	1975	1974	1967	1966
Total number of employees	14,400	14,700	12,800	12,672
Sales per employee	$21,698	$19,946	$11,939	$11,859
Net income per employee	1,330	1,290	486	523
Net operating assets per employee	15,054	13,632	6,812	6,687
Stockholder equity per employee	10,394	9,330	5,158	5,054

Table 10-6 indicates that in 1975 ABC had invested $15,054 in net operating assets for every employee, an investment level per employee that had more than doubled since 1966. Sales per employee rose from $11,859 in 1966 to $21,698 in 1975, almost doubling; and net income per employee went from $523 in 1966 to $1,330 in 1975, an increase of 2½ times. The increased sales and profit per employee would appear to have resulted primarily from the increase in investment per employee.

SUMMARY

This chapter has suggested that the basic value of a share of stock is what an investor can derive from holding that share. For virtually all common stock investments, two potential benefits exist: dividends, which in turn spring primarily from earnings, and market price appreciation. Thus the theme of this chapter has been how to form an opinion about future earnings, dividends, and market price. The factors studied have been grouped into two categories. Investors must consider each group: reliance on only one group at the expense of the other may prove disastrous. The factors of the first group are qualitative, meaning that they are essentially subjective opinions about important aspects of the company and its products. The factors of the second group are quantitative, meaning they have been formed from calculations based on financial statements or other statistical data.

Chapter **11**

Accounting and Reporting Adjustments to Maximize Uniformity and Comparability

JAMES E. PARKER

The guiding purposes of accounting reports vary from company to company and, for any given company, for different audiences or report recipients, such as stockholders, tax collectors, and government regulatory agencies. It is useful for investors to be aware of these possible purposes so that necessary and appropriate adjustments may be made when attempting to compare two firms or several companies. Within the overall framework of generally accepted accounting principles (GAAP), the accounting and reporting options that a company selects will be governed by these basic purposes.

At bottom, a firm may seek either to maximize or to minimize its assets, earnings, market price, and taxes. Of course, it would be ideal if a company could maximize assets and earnings while minimizing both income and estate taxes for itself and its shareholders. This ideal can rarely if ever be achieved. Typically, there are three alternatives to be considered by an investor in determining the central purpose of a company's income statement, balance sheet, or other accounting report:

1. Is the company trying to maximize earnings in order to report the highest possible earnings per share or to minimize earnings and report the lowest possible earnings per share?

2. Is the company eager to maximize the current price of its shares in the stock market? Or is it seeking to promote slower but steadier growth in the price of its stock over a longer term? Or are officers or dominant shareholders trying to keep stock prices low in the near term in order to minimize family estate tax problems?

3. Is the company seeking to pay the lowest possible tax bill to the government, even at the price of lower reported earnings? Or is it ready to pay higher taxes as the penalty for higher reported earnings and, it is hoped, higher market prices for its stock?

Closely held firms are more apt to favor minimizing taxes even at the price of lower reported earnings per share and, possibly, lower stock prices. On the other hand, managements of firms with broad public ownership are apt to be interested in higher stock prices from maximum reported earnings per share, even at the cost of higher taxes.

Many companies avoid this Hobson's choice and get the best of both alternatives by keeping two sets of accounts, one for shareholders, the stock exchanges, and the public, and the other for the Internal Revenue Service (IRS). In the former, they adopt accounting procedures that maximize earnings per share and therefore report higher tax obligations, while in the latter they minimize actual taxes paid by adopting accounting procedures that permit them to report lower earnings. As of 1976, this dual procedure is entirely legal though cumbersome, but there are growing pressures to prohibit such double accounting. Thus far, however, the major restriction imposed by the Securities and Exchange Commission (SEC) is that the existence of dual accounting must be indicated in shareholder reports.

This chapter will elucidate four major areas of accounting choice that have been clarified and made more uniform by official requirements of the Accounting Principles Board (APB) of the American Institute of Certified Public Accountants (AICPA).

NET INCOME AND THE ACCOUNTING FOR EXTRAORDINARY ITEMS AND PRIOR-PERIOD ADJUSTMENTS

The measurement of business income is a complex (and loosely defined) process. Part of the difficulty is due to a lack of agreement as to the basic concept of income itself. As a result, many controversies have arisen among and between those engaged in the practice of preparing financial statements and those using such statements. In reaction to the diversity of views as to whether extraordinary items or prior-period adjustments, or both, ought to enter into the determination of net income to be reported for the period in which such items are recognized, the APB of the AICPA issued APB Opinion 9 in late 1966.[1]

Nature of the Problem

Certain gains and losses are often realized during a period or periods for which they are deemed not to have resulted from the firm's regular operations for that period. Examples of such items can be classified as follows:

1. Extraordinary items
   a. Gains or losses on sales or other disposals of fixed assets, investments, or divisions
   b. Gains or losses on changes in valuation bases of inventories, investments, or fixed assets
   c. Foreign exchange adjustments
   d. Plant expenses deemed to be nonrecurring
   e. Catastrophe losses
2. Prior-period adjustments, such as settlements of prior-year income taxes, lawsuits, and renegotiation proceedings
3. Corrections of errors in previously issued financial statements
4. Effects of changes in both accounting procedures and the estimates upon which accounting data are based
   a. Effects of changing from the straight-line to the declining-balance method of depreciation calculation (change in an accounting procedure)
   b. Effects of changing the estimate of asset life used in the depreciation calculation (change in an accounting estimate)

---

[1]Accounting Principles Board, Opinion 9, *Reporting the Results of Operations*, American Institute of Certified Public Accountants, New York, 1967.

These examples do not constitute an exhaustive listing but rather should be considered illustrative. The significance of the transactions or events labeled "extraordinary" lies (1) in their relationship to the basic operating activity of the firm and (2) in the likelihood of their recurrence in future periods. Prior-period adjustments relate, by definition, to a previous accounting period or periods, as do corrections of previous errors (the term "error" is narrowly defined to exclude mistakes in judgment).

How should each of these four classes of items be reflected in the reporting of the firm's income and earnings per share? Two opposed concepts of income developed in practice. These were the *all-inclusive concept* and the *current operating performance concept.* Under the all-inclusive concept, all items affecting the net change in owners' equity between two points in time, excepting capital transactions and adjustment, were included in the determination of the amount labeled "net income for the year" in a firm's annual financial statements. On the other hand, those following the current operating performance concept of income included none of the four types of unusual items in net income. Rather, all such items were shown as direct increases or decreases of owners' equity and hence did not appear on the income statement at all.

Arguments for each of these income concepts have long appeared in the professional literature of accountancy,[2] but there has been little success in achieving any generally acceptable solution, that is, widespread consistency in the actual preparation of published income statements. On the one hand, proponents of the all-inclusive viewpoint argue that increases in wealth during a period arise not only from normal operations but rather from the firm's total experience within its economic environment. On the other hand, advocates of the current operating performance concept stress the use of earnings figures as a guide to investors in estimating a firm's future earnings potential and therefore wish to omit any unusual gains and losses from net income and earnings-per-share amounts.

Any agreement in such a debate must be built upon an identification of the use of reported income figures. This would appear to be a hopeless task in view of the multipurpose nature of published financial statements. In addition, there has been considerable concern (with some justification, as evidenced by numerous research studies) over the potential for manipulation involved in the process of deciding which gains and losses ought to be deemed unusual and hence be excluded in the determination of earnings figures.

Perhaps, as some have suggested, there is no theoretically correct solution to the controversy concerning the reporting of unusual gains and losses. At any rate, prior to the issuance of APB Opinion 9 in 1966, one could locate authoritative support for either approach as an acceptable alternative.[3] The practical consequence of regarding either extreme as acceptable accounting procedure led to a loss of comparability among reported earnings. Many firms elected to include the unusual items in the determination of net income, while many others excluded similar items. For example, a study of 600 companies by the AICPA revealed that 250 extraordinary items were identified in annual reports for the year 1966 and that of these 143 were included in the determination of income while 107 were not.[4] This lack of uniformity in income reporting proved to be the impetus that eventually led to the arbitrary but workable compromise position set forth in APB Opinion 9.

[2]For a comprehensive discussion of the arguments involved, see Leopold A. Bernstein, *Accounting for Extraordinary Gains and Losses,* The Ronald Press Company, New York, 1967.

[3]For example, see Committee on Accounting Procedure, *Accounting Research and Terminology Bulletins, final ed.,* American Institute of Certified Public Accountants, New York, 1961, p. 63.

[4]*Accounting Trends and Techniques, 20th ed.,* American Institute of Certified Public Accountants, New York, 1966.

Provisions of APB Opinion 9

APB Opinion 9 includes a specification of the accounting treatment to be afforded to extraordinary items and prior-period adjustments, that is, items 1 and 2 on the above list. It does not cover accounting for the correction of errors (item 3) or the effects of accounting changes (item 4). However, the latter two matters are the subject of APB Opinion 20,[5] which is examined below.

With the advent of APB Opinion 9, a new income concept, often referred to as

EXHIBIT I
EXAMPLE OF INCOME STATEMENT UNDER
THE MODIFIED ALL-INCLUSIVE CONCEPT AS
PROVIDED BY APB OPINION 9

ABC Corporation
Statement of Income
for the Year Ended December 31, 1976

Net sales	$84,750,000	
Other income	90,000	$84,840,000
Expenses		
Cost of goods sold	$58,500,000	
Selling, general, and administrative		
expenses	5,400,000	
Interest expense	120,000	
Income taxes	9,200,000	73,220,000
Income before extraordinary gain		11,620,000
Extraordinary gain, less applicable		
income taxes (Note 1)		1,500,000
Net income		$13,120,000
Earnings per common share		
Income before extraordinary gain		$11.62
Extraordinary gain (Note 1)		1.50
Net income		$13.12

NOTE 1: During 1976 the company sold investments in marketable securities at a net gain of $1.5 million after applicable income taxes of $500,000.

the "modified all-inclusive concept," was advanced. Under this concept, the only exclusions in the determination and reporting of net income of the current period are items deemed to be prior-period adjustments. Examples of the formats for the income statement and the statement of retained earnings are presented in Exhibits I and II.

It will be seen in these Exhibits that prior-period adjustments are to be reported as a correction to the beginning balance of retained earnings within the statement of retained earnings (Exhibit II). On the other hand, extraordinary items of income or loss are reported within a special section of the income statement (Exhibit I) and thereby are included in the amount labeled "net income." It will also be noted that figures for earnings per share (EPS) are reported on the face of the income statement to show EPS both before and after extraordinary gains and losses.

What cannot be seen in this example are the strict definitions of "prior-period adjustment" and "extraordinary item" set forth by the APB in order to limit the events to be reported in each fashion. These definitions, which guide the accoun-

[5]Accounting Principles Board, Opinion 20, *Accounting Changes*, American Institute of Certified Public Accountants, New York, 1971.

tant in preparing financial statements, are particularly significant in that they do not correspond to the use of these terms by many members of the financial community. In short, the APB has somewhat arbitrarily identified the specific characteristics of transactions (in some instances, even specific transactions) that are to be accounted for in each manner. Thus, a reader of published financial statements is apt to be misled by the terms "prior-period adjustment" and "extraordinary gain or loss" unless he or she is aware of exactly how these terms have been defined.

According to APB Opinion 9, prior-period adjustments are "limited to those material adjustments which (a) can be specifically identified with and directly related to the business activities of particular prior periods, and (b) are not

EXHIBIT II
EXAMPLE OF STATEMENT OF RETAINED EARNINGS
UNDER THE MODIFIED ALL-INCLUSIVE CONCEPT
AS PROVIDED BY APB OPINION 9

ABC Corporation
Statement of Retained Earnings
for the Year Ended December 31, 1976

Retained earnings at January 1, 1976		
As previously reported	$45,000,000	
Adjustment (Note 1)	8,000,000	
As restated		$37,000,000
Net income for Year 1976		13,120,000
Cash dividends on common stock, $4 per share		(4,000,000)
Retained earnings at December 31, 1976		$46,120,000

NOTE 1: Retained earnings at January 1, 1976, have been restated from amounts previously reported to reflect a retroactive charge of $8 million for additional taxes settled during 1976. This settlement relates to the years 1973 and 1974. IRS audits of the company's 1975 tax return have not been completed, but management expects no additional taxes to be assessed.

attributable to economic events occurring subsequent to the date of the financial statements for the prior period, and (c) depend primarily on determinations by persons other than management and (d) were not susceptible of reasonable estimation prior to such determination.[6] The APB expected that such items would be rare in modern accounting and that, in most cases in which there was a prior-period adjustment, "the opinion of the reporting independent auditor on such prior period would have contained a qualification because of the uncertainty [then existing]."[7]

Extraordinary items are defined as being of a character significantly different from the typical business activity of the firm; thus, such items are expected to be nonrecurring in any evaluation of the ordinary operating processes of the business. Specific examples of extraordinary items named in APB Opinion 9 include material gains or losses arising "from (a) the sale or abandonment of a plant or a significant segment of the business, (b) the sale of an investment not acquired for resale, (c) the write-off of goodwill due to unusual events or developments within the period, (d) the condemnation or expropriation of properties, and (e) a major devaluation of a foreign currency."[8]

[6]Accounting Principles Board, Opinion 9, *Reporting the Results of Operations,* p. 115.
[7]Ibid., p. 116.
[8]Ibid., p. 115.

All unusual items of income or loss not meeting the definitions above are to be treated as operating items in the income statement. Examples of such special items to be included in determining operating income include (1) write-downs of receivables, inventories, and research and development costs, (2) adjustments of accrued contract prices, and (3) foreign exchange adjustments. Item 1 is deemed to fall in the class of "the normal, recurring corrections and adjustments which are the natural result of the use of estimates inherent in the accounting process,"[9] whereas items 2 and 3 are believed by the APB to be of a character typical of the firm's customary business activity.

Whether or not one agrees with the APB's designations as to which transactions and events are to be reflected in reported income figures, it remains to one's advantage to be aware of the classification system actually used in the preparation of financial statements. The basic problem lies in the difficulty of summarizing the entire economic results of a firm's operations in a single figure called "income" or "earnings." Only by being knowledgeable of the classification scheme employed can one gain insight into what any particular reported earnings figures do and do not signify.

COMMON STOCK EQUIVALENTS AND EARNINGS PER SHARE[10]

In May 1969, the APB issued Opinion 15, entitled *Earnings per Share*. The purpose of this section is twofold: (1) to direct attention to certain procedures that are employed by major United States corporations when determining per-share earnings and (2) to warn of resulting potential pitfalls for the unwary user of these data.

Under the provisions of Opinion 15, corporations with complex capital structures are required to report both "primary" and "fully diluted" EPS figures on the face of published income statements. The procedures by which each of these amounts are determined are critically examined in the following paragraphs.

Determination of Primary EPS under Opinion 15

The determination of primary EPS is based on the outstanding common shares and those, and only those, common stock equivalents that have a dilutive effect of 3 percent or more. Thus, it is important to note that a common stock equivalent may or may not be reflected in the determination of primary EPS; to be included it must have the effect of reducing EPS.

What is a common stock equivalent? To apply the test of common stock–equivalent status, it is first necessary to differentiate between (1) options and warrants and (2) convertible securities. Options and warrants "should be regarded as common stock equivalents at all times."[11] Convertible debt or convertible preferred stock "should be considered as a common stock equivalent at the time of issuance if, based on its market price, it has a cash yield of less than 66⅔% of the current bank prime interest rate."[12]

At least two characteristics of the test of common stock–equivalent status are important to anyone using amounts reported as primary EPS. First, this test is

---

[9]Loc. cit.

[10]This section is reproduced, with minor modifications, with the kind permission of the *Financial Analysts Journal,* from James E. Parker, "New Rules for Determining Earnings per Share," *Financial Analysts Journal,* January–February 1970.

[11]Accounting Principles Board Opinion 15, *Earnings per Share,* American Institute of Certified Public Accountants, New York, May 1969, p. 230.

[12]Ibid., p. 229.

made at the time of original issuance of the security in question, and once a security's status has been determined, that status never changes. Let us consider Exhibit III.

For Company B, the convertible debt *is not* considered a common stock equivalent under Opinion 15 because its cash yield (3 percent) exceeded two-thirds of the

EXHIBIT III
HYPOTHETICAL EXAMPLES OF PRIMARY EPS DETERMINATION UNDER
OPINION 15 IF CONVERTIBLE DEBT IS OUTSTANDING

	Company A	Company B
Net income for 1976	$ 4,000,000	$ 4,000,000
Common shares outstanding	1,000,000	1,000,000
Market price of common, 1976	$35	$40
Market price of common, 1966	$15	$15
Data on convertible debt		
Par value of total issue	10,000,000	10,000,000
Coupon interest rate	3%	3%
Conversion price per common share	$50	$20
Original date of issuance	Jan. 1, 1969	Jan. 1, 1959
Assumed bank prime interest rate at		
date of issuance	6%	4%
Original issue price	$100	$100
*Primary earnings per share, 1976	$3.46	$4.00

*Computation of primary earnings per share for Company A:

Net income for year		$ 4,000,000
Interest on debt (3 percent of $10 million)	$ 300,000	
Less related income taxes (50 percent)	150,000	150,000
Adjusted income		$ 4,150,000
Common shares outstanding		1,000,000
Common stock equivalent		
($10 million divided by $50)		200,000
		1,200,000
Primary earnings per share		
($4,150,000 divided by 1.2 million)		$3.46

then-current (1959) bank prime rate (4 percent). However, for Company A the convertible debt *is* considered a common stock equivalent. Yet it is Company B's debt holders who would convert at present market prices in the event of either's approaching maturity or a calling of the bonds.

Thus, the APB's belief "that the presentation of fully diluted earnings per share data adequately discloses the potential dilution which may exist because of changes in conditions subsequent to time of issuance"[13] is, in the opinion of the author, in error for at least two reasons. First, it does not allow for comparability of EPS between companies that differ in the original issuance dates of their respective convertible securities. Second, it seems internally inconsistent that the less likely "potential" dilution is reflected in primary EPS, while the more likely case of dilution is reflected only in fully diluted EPS.

A second important point regarding the test of common stock–equivalent status as set forth by Opinion 15 is that it represents a change from the previously

[13]Ibid., p. 227.

prevailing criteria of Opinion 9. Thus, there are changes for some companies in the number of shares upon which primary EPS are based. This results from reclassifications of certain convertible securities, since Opinion 15 allows for, but does not require (thus adding another potential inconsistency between companies), the classification of previously issued securities as common stock equivalents even though such securities would not have been classified as residual securities under Opinion 9.

With respect to historical data included in annual reports, it is encouraging to note that if such reclassifications of previously issued securities are made in the determination of current-year primary earnings per share, the new basis must be applied for all periods presented.

Now let us consider the determination of primary EPS when warrants are outstanding. As noted above, options and warrants are always regarded as common stock equivalents and therefore enter into the computation of primary EPS if and only if their inclusion has the effect of decreasing the per-share amount. The "treasury stock" method is specified by the APB: "Under this method, earnings-per-share data are computed as if the options and warrants were exercised at the beginning of the period (or at a time of issuance, if later) and as if the funds obtained thereby were used to purchase common stock at the average market price during the period."[14] The use of this method is limited to 20 percent of the common shares outstanding. The method is illustrated in Exhibit IV.

Historical common share market prices are not relevant to the determination of primary EPS because (1) they reflect previously held expectations, which do not necessarily bear any ordered relation to currently held expectations; and (2) the amount reported as primary EPS is intended to reflect, on a pro-forma basis, the potential dilution currently existing.

From Exhibit IV it can be noted that Companies X and Y will report different amounts as primary EPS even though all obvious financial considerations are identical for the two companies. This situation is the result of the APB's procedure of basing the dilution computation on historical common stock market prices, which may or may not approximate market prices when the investor receives the annual report and thus may or may not reflect the dilution effect then existing. Thus, before using reported primary EPS figures, the investor would be wise to determine the effect, if any, resulting from changes in market prices. In this example, using common market prices as of March 1, 1976, a recomputation of primary earnings per share yields $3.72 ($4 million divided by 1,075,000) for each company.

The procedure of basing per-share computations on the weighted average of the number of common shares actually outstanding during the period being reported is logical, since the resources received upon issuance of the additional shares during the period are available for employment for a corresponding portion of the period. Thus, if the firm continued to earn exactly the same rate of return on stockholders' equity, the past period's EPS would exactly equal the following period's EPS except for the increase due to previous earnings retained. However, there is no corresponding logical explanation for the APB's procedure of using a weighted average of the net number of shares that would have been added if the warrants had been converted, since no additional net assets would have been received. Also, it must be remembered that these are only pro-forma, or "what if," computations. Thus, it would seem logical to base such computations on the total net increase in the number of shares outstanding that would result if conversion were to take place at current market prices. This was the procedure employed in recomputing the primary EPS figure of $3.72.

[14]Ibid., p. 320.

In the past, per-share earnings figures covering a number of periods have often been used in assessing a firm's earning power and in forming opinions as to its potential. Opinion 15 introduced a new determinant of primary EPS that (for companies with warrants outstanding) reduces the appropriateness of EPS figures for this use, because changes in the level of a firm's common stock price now

EXHIBIT IV
HYPOTHETICAL EXAMPLES OF PRIMARY EPS DETERMINATION UNDER OPINION 15
IF WARRANTS ARE OUTSTANDING

	Company X	Company Y
Net income for 1976	$ 4,000,000	$ 4,000,000
Common shares outstanding	1,000,000	1,000,000
Warrants outstanding	200,000	200,000
Exercise price	$50	$50
Market price of common		
Average, first quarter, 1976	$40	$100
Average, second quarter, 1976	$40	$80
Average, third quarter, 1976	$70	$120
Average, fourth quarter, 1976	$60	$100
As of March 1, 1976	$80	$80
Average, third and fourth quarters, 1976	$65	
Average, year 1976		$100
Adjustment of shares outstanding		
Assumed issued	200,000	200,000
Proceeds (200,000 times $50)	10,000,000	10,000,000
Reacquired		
($10,000,000 divided by $65)	153,846	
($10,000,000 divided by $100)		100,000
Net increases in shares	46,154	100,000
Portion of year outstanding	50%	100%
Net adjustment	23,077	100,000
Actual outstanding	1,000,000	1,000,000
Adjusted shares outstanding	1,023,077	1,100,000
Primary earnings per share		
($4 million divided by 1,023,077)	$3.91	
($4 million divided by 1,100,000)		$3.64

directly affect the level of its reported primary EPS. Once the market price of the firm's common rises above the exercise price of any warrants outstanding, a still higher price will result in a lower reported primary EPS figure, whereas a lower price for the common will increase primary EPS.

Determination of Fully Diluted EPS under Opinion 15

The APB's stated purpose in requiring the presentation of fully diluted EPS was "to show the maximum potential dilution of current earnings per share on a prospective basis."[15] Thus, it would seem that any and all contingent issuances of additional shares, no matter how remote, must be reflected if the realization of such contingency would have the effect of reducing EPS. However, this is not true under the procedure outlined by Opinion 15 with respect to outstanding options and warrants, even though it is true with respect to convertible securities.

With respect to options and warrants, fully diluted EPS are calculated by means

[15]Ibid., p. 234.

of the treasury stock method described above, except that the market price at the close of the reporting period is used in determining the number of shares assumed to have been repurchased if such market price is higher than the average price used in computing primary EPS. Therefore, if the exercise price exceeds both the period average and period end market prices, warrants or options outstanding, or both, will have no effect in the determination of reported fully diluted EPS. On the other hand, all non-common stock–equivalent convertible preferred stock or convertible debt, or both (irrespective of conversion price), is used in determining fully diluted EPS in the manner illustrated in Exhibit III.

In summary, from the viewpoint of a potential investor, there are two undesirable aspects to fully diluted EPS figures as reported: (1) the complete omission of the potential dilution effect due to warrant or options, or both, whose exercise prices are in excess of market prices prevailing during the reporting period; and (2) the lack of any indication of the extent of remoteness associated with the dilution effects that are reflected in fully diluted EPS.

Summary

APB Opinion 15 specifies the presentation of both primary and fully diluted EPS in annual reports to stockholders. Neither of these amounts nor both of them, as determined under the procedures outlined in Opinion 15, are adequate for evaluating the past earnings performance of a business in relation to the common shares held by a single investor wherever there is a complex capital structure. However, a basic understanding of the manner in which the reported per-share amounts are determined should assist users of these data.

ACCOUNTING FOR BUSINESS COMBINATIONS

Rarely does an accounting controversy receive the attention of the business and financial community that has been accorded the question of how to account for business combinations. After two preliminary, or exposure, drafts on the issue and much controversy, the APB issued Opinions 16 and 17 in August 1970.[16,17] Prior to discussing the provisions of these opinions, we shall first discuss and illustrate the nature, magnitude, and consequences of the alternative accounting methods. In this way, we shall provide a perspective for understanding and assessing the rules that a company's accountants and auditors must follow in accounting for mergers in published financial statements.

The Problem

The seriousness of this particular accounting controversy for both accountants and nonaccountants can be attributed to perhaps four basic factors: (1) the extensive and increasing use of mergers, along with their economic impact, during the late 1960s; (2) the inability of accounting theoreticians to provide any solid basis for selecting one of two alternative views of the very nature of the merger transaction; (3) the magnitude of the dollar differences in reported figures for both assets and earnings under alternative accounting procedures; and (4) the significant self-interests perceived by many individuals and firms in the use of a particular accounting procedure under specific circumstances.

At the heart of the problem lies the inability of any group of human beings to

[16]Accounting Principles Board, Opinion 16, *Business Combinations,* American Institute of Certified Public Accountants, New York, 1970.

[17]Accounting Principles Board, Opinion 17, *Intangible Assets,* American Institute of Certified Public Accountants, New York, 1970.

identify infallibly the nature of an event as complex and involved as a modern business combination. Let us consider, for example, that even an item as simple as a doorknob has a multitude of characteristics—size, color, form, component metal, and so on—any one or combination of which could be called its nature. An individual's selection of the particular characteristics that he or she chooses to communicate might well depend upon his or her views of how the information should be used. Since any bit of data may be employed in different ways or even for different purposes, different individuals will often emphasize different characteristics of an item or event in ascertaining its nature.

Let us consider a very simple transaction involving a hypothetical business combination to illustrate the difficulty of ascertaining its "true" nature. We shall assume that, as of a given date, two companies have assets, income, and stock prices as follows:

	Company B	Company S
Cash	$100,000	$ 10,000
Other assets, at cost	500,000	100,000
	$600,000	$110,000
Liabilities	$100,000	$ 10,000
Owners' equity, 10,000 shares		
outstanding common stock at par	150,000	20,000
Retained earnings	350,000	80,000
	$600,000	$110,000
Net income	$ 50,000	$ 20,000
Earnings per share	$5	$2
Market price per share	$150	$20
Market value of other assets	$550,000	$200,000

Some comments on this data may be in order. Company B is a relatively new company in a growth industry, whereas Company S is an older firm with very little growth potential. This background should help to explain why the replacement cost of new Company B's assets has not increased over their book value to the extent that the cost of older Company S's assets has increased. It should also be noted that while the rate of return on net assets is 10 percent for Company B and 20 percent for Company S, the market, presumably because of the growth factor, has priced B's stock at 30 times earnings, whereas S's stock is priced at only 10 times earnings.

Let us consider the following transaction. Company B offers and Company S accepts 1,500 shares of Company B common stock in exchange for all assets and liabilities of Company S. Company S then distributes its only asset, B Company common stock, to S Company's stockholders. The end result is that Company B has increased its net assets, but it has also increased the number of common shares outstanding. The former stockholders of Company S now hold 1,500 shares of Company B.

What is the nature of this transaction? It is either a "purchase" of assets by Company B or a "purchase" of stock by Company S. Likewise, we could label it as either a "sale" of assets by Company S or a "sale" of stock by Company B. The point is that the spontaneous tendency to apply customary labels is of little help in transactions of this type. Traditional accounting is based upon the notions that (1) income should be recognized upon a sale and (2) purchases should be recorded at cost without the recognition of any gain or loss. Yet here we have no basis for ascertaining who is the buyer and who is the seller.

In view of this dilemma, we have little alternative but to ask what specific characteristics of the transaction are important. Some mutually exclusive possibilities are (1) the market value of the 1,500 Company B common shares, (2) the "true," or intrinsic, value of the 1,500 Company B common shares, (3) the book value of the net assets of Company S, (4) the replacement cost of the net assets of Company S, and (5) the market selling prices of the net assets of Company S. Also, is it important that all of a company's assets are involved in a single transaction? Are we concerned with whether Company B plans to operate or to resell the assets? Likewise, does it matter whether the previous stockholders of Company S plan to keep or to resell the Company B stock? All these points and many more are often mentioned in debates over the true nature of a business transaction.

The intended use of accounting data might determine which characteristics of this business combination would be employed in determining its nature. Investor Pool is interested solely in operating efficiency. For this purpose he makes year-to-year comparisons of the firm's percentage return on net assets employed. He would thus prefer that characteristic 3 above, book value, be given primary consideration. If Company B records the assets obtained at the amount shown on the Company S books and continues to use the same basis for depreciation, the total income figures of future years will be comparable with the sum of the two companies' reported incomes for previous years. Thus, Investor Pool views the transaction as a "mere exchange of ownership interests within a new accounting entity," which to him is no justification "for recognizing a hypothetical market value of the assets received." In short, the so called pooling-of-interests concept is quite suitable for his particular intended use of accounting information.

On the other hand, Ms. Purch considers financial statements to be a stewardship report by management. She observes that management issued common stock that could have been sold for $225,000 (1,500 shares times $150) in exchange for the net assets previously held by Company S. Thus, she insists that recorded assets of Company B be increased by $225,000, that is, that management must be held accountable for this amount. If the assets are sold later for, say, $150,000, a loss of $75,000 ought to be shown in the stewardship report (income statement) for the period in which the sale is made. Yet if the assets were recorded at their previous book value of $100,000, no loss would be reported. In fact, following the pooling-of-interests approach, one would actually report a gain of $50,000 in the period of sale. Hence Ms. Purch clearly favors the so called purchase method of accounting for business combinations, since this method records the entire value of the common stock issued.

The Alternatives

As indicated above, the nature of a business combination depends upon which characteristics of the event are selected for emphasis. Over the years, as we have noted, there have evolved two primary viewpoints or collections of characteristics, the purchase approach and the pooling-of-interests approach.

The purchase concept is the older approach and perhaps the simpler in concept. Any exchange transaction (including transactions involving equity securities) is deemed to be a purchase by one party and a sale by the other. The buying and selling of entire companies are held to be no different in principle from the purchase and sale of any other asset. Determination of who is buyer and who is seller would be a judgmental matter, to be based on the circumstances of each transaction considered individually. Any exchange between independent parties is held to be sufficient evidence to realize increments in asset values over original costs, that is, to recognize gains and record acquired assets at current values.

A primary element in the idea of a purchase is the changing ownership in the equity of a single ongoing firm, the buyer. None of the seller's retained earnings are carried forward; rather, the assets and liabilities are brought onto the buyer's books at current market values. If the purchase price, that is, the value of stock issued by the buyer, is greater than the present market value of the selling firm's identified assets, the excess is deemed to be the cost of an intangible asset labeled "good will." These current cost valuations for identified assets and good will then serve as the basis for determining depreciation and amortization expenses for periods after the date of merger.

The alternative viewpoint, a pooling of interests, has been defined as a business combination in which the holders of substantially all the ownership interests in the constituent corporations become owners of a single corporation that owns the assets and businesses of the constituent corporations. Here, the idea is that of a fusion of interests into a new entity, as opposed to the purchase concept of a change within a single ongoing entity. This concept is advanced only for business combinations involving issuance of equity securities, never for cash purchases.

Under the pooling concept, there is no change in ownership interest within either constituent of a business combination. Hence, no new basis of accountability arises; that is, there is no justification for recognizing current values over original costs as shown on the books of the constituent companies. Accordingly, the procedure is simply one of carrying forward the previous book values for all assets and liabilities. In this way, the combined firm will often reflect retained earnings equal to the sum of the retained earnings shown for the individual companies. Also, there is neither goodwill nor any increase in other assets recorded. Thus, there is no increase in depreciation or amortization charges for subsequent years.

To illustrate the procedures of both the purchase and the pooling-of-interests methods, the previous example of the combination of Companies B and S is recorded below under both approaches. Since Company B is the surviving legal entity, the following journal entry would be made to record the acquisition of Company S on the books of Company B:

	Under Purchase Accounting	Under Pooling-of-Interests Accounting
Cash	$ 10,000	$ 10,000
Other assets	200,000	100,000
Goodwill	25,000	. . .
Liabilities	$ 10,000	$10,000
Capital stock at par	22,500	22,500
Paid-in capital in excess of par	202,500	. . .
Retained earnings	. . .	77,500
To record the issuance of 1,500 shares of common stock in exchange for the assets of Company S		

A balance sheet for Company B prepared immediately after the combination would thus reflect the accounts as follows:

	Under Purchase Accounting	Under Pooling-of-Interests Accounting
Cash	$110,000	$110,000
Other assets	700,000	600,000
Goodwill	25,000	. . .
	$835,000	$710,000
Liabilities	$110,000	$110,000
Owners equity, 11,500 shares		
outstanding common stock at par	172,500	172,500
Paid-in capital in excess of par	202,500	. . .
Retained earnings	350,000	427,500
	$835,000	$710,000

As can be seen from these balance sheets, the difference in total assets reported under the alternative accounting procedures is $125,000 ($835,000 minus $710,-000). This represents the difference between the market value of the stock issued (1,500 shares × $150 = $225,000) used under the purchase method and the book value of net assets to Company S ($100,000) carried forward under the pooling-of-interests concept.

The differences between the two methods do not end with the balance sheet. We must also consider the relative effect of the alternative accounting procedures on reported income and earnings per share. If the assets acquired from Company S, including goodwill, have an average remaining life of twenty years, for periods subsequent to the date of combination the expenses would be greater by $6,250 ($125,000 divided by 20) if the purchase method is used. Hence, if "real" operations remain unchanged for the year after the merger, the amounts under each accounting method would be as follows:

	Under Purchase Accounting	Under Pooling-of-Interests Accounting
Company B prior income	$ 50,000	$ 50,000
Company S prior income	20,000	20,000
Increase in expense	− 6,250	. . .
Net income	$ 63,750	$ 70,000
Common shares outstanding	÷ 11,500	÷ 11,500
Earnings per share	$5.54	$6.09

We recall that earnings per share for Company B were $5 before the merger; hence, if the purchase method were used, a two-year comparative report would show:

	Under Purchase Accounting	
	Prior Year	Current Year
Earnings per share	$5.00	$5.54

This would be the case even though "real" operations remained the same. On the other hand, retroactive restatement of prior net income and earnings per share is required under the pooling-of-interests method. Thus, the following would be reported:

	Under Pooling-of-Interests Accounting	
	Prior Year	Current Year
Earnings per share	$6.09	$6.09

The data of this example should prove helpful in evaluating the arguments favoring each of the two accounting procedures. However, we should bear in mind that as long as a business combination is effected by an exchange of common stock, the legal form of the transaction is completely immaterial with regard to the selection of the accounting procedure to be used. In the above example, the exchange occurred between two corporations. Alternative legal forms that might have been used to secure the same economic results would include (1) an exchange between one corporation and the stockholders of the other corporation, (2) an exchange between a third corporation and the constituent corporations, or (3) an exchange between a third corporation and the stockholders of the two constituent corporations. In any of these cases, it is the economic substance and not the legal form of the transaction that is controlling.

Evaluating the Alternatives

Those who support pooling-of-interests accounting often base their argument upon what they view as the nature of a business combination involving the issuance of common stock. The transaction is thought of as a fusion of equity interests; that is, the fractional interests in the common enterprise are reallocated. The fundamental idea is that (1) the accounting entity is separate and distinct from the stockholders, and (2) accounting reports are concerned with the activities of the accounting entity, not those of its owners. Thus, a rearrangement of interests within the combined stockholder group does not produce activity of relevance to accounting. There has been no change in the assets or liabilities of the common enterprise. Many view this concept of the business combination as coming within the theoretical boundary of the historical cost system upon which modern accounting practice is founded.

In addition to its theoretical justification, many accountants and corporate managers favor pooling of interests on the ground of practical utility. They observe that when retroactive restatement is made for periods prior to a merger, the comparability of year-to-year earnings figures (both in toto and per share) is enhanced. Also, all assets of the combined entity are stated on a consistent basis, that is, at their original cost. These points can best be evaluated by observing the data of the example presented above.

Another point in favor of the pooling-of-interests approach is the difficulty in applying the purchase method. The fair value of common shares issued may be difficult to determine objectively. No market price may be available for unlisted or newly listed securities. Even when a quoted market price does exist, it may not be a fair value if the number of shares issued is quite large relative to normal trading activity in the security on the exchange. Furthermore, when the stock price is volatile, a serious question arises as to the exact date upon which the price should be pegged, since merger negotiations often cover a considerable time span.

Critics of the purchase method further point out that the increase in total assets recorded under that approach, which in their view is not a real asset at all, tends to be quite significant in amount. Data from a study[18] of all firms acquiring three or

---

[18]R. M. Copeland and J. F. Wojdak, "Goodwill in Merger-Minded Firms," *Financial Analysts Journal*, September–October 1969, pp. 57–62.

more firms during a selected one-year period showed a total for such assets of $1,604,993,000, or an average of $61,730,500 per acquiring company. Such asset value alone amounted to well over twice the total book value of the acquired firms. In fact, the market value of the common shares issued was more than 3 times the book value of the companies acquired. To compound the problem, there is the additional question of how to determine objectively the portion of this massive amount that should be charged to expense in each year after a merger. This question arises particularly with respect to the amount assigned to the intangible goodwill account.

Perhaps the most heated opposition to the purchase method of accounting for business combinations arises from the fear that elimination of pooling-of-interests accounting would seriously impede the merger movement.[19] It is alleged that purchase accounting would cause severe economic harm to the national economy by discouraging the formation through mergers of new businesses that result in more efficient utilization of invested capital. This concern stems from the fact that, on paper, most proposed mergers would appear to be less favorable under purchase accounting (see, for example, the data of the illustration presented above). While acknowledging abuses of the pooling concept in practice,[20] advocates of this method emphasize that the answer is to deal with such abuses directly, not entirely to eliminate pooling of interests, which they deem essential to the national (and perhaps to their own) welfare.

Now let us turn to a consideration of the arguments of those who favor the purchase method of accounting for business combinations. Their fundamental argument is that pooling of interests is not an accounting method at all but rather a technique for nonaccounting. Pooling ignores the exchange values on which the parties have traded and substitutes a wholly irrelevant figure, the amount on the seller's books. Such amounts often bear little or no resemblance to current economic values, which form the basis for all bargained exchanges between independent parties.

By not accounting for the total cost of the assets to the acquiring company, pooling often results in the reporting of false profits in subsequent years as the assets are used or sold, or both. Had the assets been acquired for cash, the buyer's cost would be the amount paid. Payment by stock should make no difference. Stock has value, and its issuance represents a cost to the issuing company. The measure of assets acquired is the economic value, not the form, of the consideration given in exchange. Whether the acquisition is for cash or for stock is strictly a matter of form, not substance. Therefore, pooling-of-interests accounting should be abolished, and all business combinations be accounted for as purchases.

In answer to the argument that it is often difficult or impossible to identify which firm is buyer and which is seller in a business combination, advocates of purchase accounting reply that in practice this is simply untrue. Such identification is usually obvious. In almost all cases, one firm is clearly the dominant and continuing entity, while control of the assets and operations of the other firm passes to this dominant entity. Ironically, evidence in support of this view has been provided by one of its critics. B. Richard Wakefield examined 391 New York Stock Exchange listing applications that related to the issuance of stock for merger or acquisition purposes. Although 82.5 percent had actually been accounted for as

---

[19]For examples of this view, see the following three articles, all of which appeared in the July–August 1970 issue of the *Financial Analysts Journal:* Herbert C. Knortz, "A Corporate Financial Officer's View"; B. Richard Wakefield, "An Investment Banker's View"; Jules Backman, "An Economist's View."

[20]For examples of such abuses, see Abraham J. Briloff, "Dirty Pooling: How to Succeed in Business without Really Trying," *Barron's*, July 15, 1968.

poolings of interests, only one of these business combinations involved constituents even remotely comparable in size.[21]

"Tell it like it is!" is the response given to those who argue that eliminating pooling will impede mergers. There is no question that, for most business combinations, purchase accounting results in lower earnings being reported in subsequent years, nor is there any doubt that the amounts of these differences are staggering. Accounting does not exist to aid or to discourage mergers but rather to account for them fairly. To set accounting principles so as to achieve social goals would destroy the credibility upon which accounting's usefulness to investors is totally dependent. Also, any such attempt would be self-defeating. In short, arguments against any accounting procedure on the basis that it fails to report "what I want to report" are not even worthy of consideration.

Provisions of APB Opinions 16 and 17

The APB ruled that some business combinations should be accounted for under the purchase method while others should be accounted for by the pooling method. However, the board also concluded that the two methods of accounting were not to be considered alternatives in accounting for the same business combination. Accordingly, the APB provided a detailed description of the circumstances under which the pooling-of-interests method is required and further specified that any other business combination must be treated as a purchase. While the procedures for applying both the purchase and the pooling methods are also included in APB Opinion 16, the accounting for the intangible goodwill arising under the purchase approach is covered in APB Opinion 17.

The conditions set forth by the APB for the use of the pooling-of-interests method are intended to ensure that the business combination is one in which the stockholder groups neither withdraw nor invest assets but, in effect, exchange voting common stock in a ratio that determines their respective interests in the combined corporation. To be accounted for as a pooling, the combination must meet the following conditions:[22]

a. Each of the combining companies must be autonomous and not have been a subsidiary or a division of another corporation within two years before the plan of combination was initiated.

b. Each of the combining companies must be independent of the other combining companies.

c. The combination must be effected in a single transaction or be completed in accordance with a specific plan within one year after the plan is initiated.

d. A corporation must offer and issue only common stock with rights identical to those of the majority of its outstanding voting common stock in exchange for substantially all the voting common stock interest of another company at the date on which the plan of combination is consummated.

e. None of the combining companies may have changed the equity interest of the voting common stock in contemplation of effecting the combination.

f. None of the combining companies may have reacquired shares of voting common stock for purposes of business combination.

g. The ratio of the interest of an individual common shareholder to those of other common shareholders in a combining company must not be changed as a result of the exchange of stock to effect the combination.

h. There must be no restrictions on the voting rights to which the common stock ownership interests in the resulting combined corporation are entitled.

i. The combination must be resolved at the date on which the plan is

---

[21]B. Richard Wakefield, "An Investment Banker's View," p. 33.
[22]Accounting Principles Board, Opinion 16, *Business Combinations*, pp. 295–304.

consummated, and there must be no provision of the plan for a pending issue of securities or other consideration.

j. The combined corporation must not agree to retire or reacquire any part of the common stock issued to effect the combination.

k. The combined corporation must not enter into any financial arrangement for the benefit of the former stockholders of a combining company that in effect negates the exchange of equity securities.

l. The combined corporation must not intend or plan to dispose of a significant part of the assets of the combining companies (other than disposals in the ordinary course of business) within two years after the combination of the formerly separate companies or to eliminate duplicate facilities or excess capacity.

In examining these conditions for a pooling of interests, it is of equal interest to note the omissions, that is, to consider some conditions that are *not* necessary in order to use the pooling-of-interests method. Notice that there are no relative-size requirement, no continuity-of-management requirement, and no limitation on the disposition of securities received by stockholders. Thus, even if General Motors acquires the assets of Joe's Garage, Inc., in exchange for GM common stock and fires Joe, while Joe sells his GM stock on the market, this transaction can still be a pooling of interests under the provisions of APB Opinion 16.

Another point that should be emphasized is the ease by which a business combination could be made not to qualify as a pooling of interests in the event that the acquiring corporation desired to report the transaction as a purchase. If even one of the dozen conditions is not met, the transaction must be treated as a purchase. Thus, for all practical purposes corporate management can still elect to report any business combination as a purchase. For example, simply extending the period over which the transaction is effected would require purchase accounting even if all other requirements were met.

APB Opinion 16 specifies the procedures for applying both the pooling and the purchase methods of accounting for a business combination. Under pooling, the recorded amounts of assets and liabilities of the separate companies become the assets and liabilities to be recorded for the combined corporation. However, when different methods of accounting (for example, depreciation methods, inventory costing methods) have been used by the separate companies prior to the combination in determining these asset and liability valuations, the amounts may be adjusted to a consistent basis. Such a change in accounting method is applied retroactively, and financial statements of the combined entity for periods prior to the combination must also be restated for all such changes.

The owners' equities of combined corporations are also combined as part of the pooling-of-interests method of accounting. However, if the par or stated value of outstanding common shares of the combined corporation exceeds the total capital stock (at par or stated value) of the separate companies, the excess is first deducted from the combined contributed retained earnings (see the example above for an application of this rule). The consequence of this requirement is that there may be a reclassification within owners' equity so as to reduce the amount shown as retained earnings for the combined company. However, there can never be an increase over the sum of the retained earnings of the separate companies.

The financial operations for an accounting period in which a pooling of interests occurs are reported as if the pooling took place at the beginning of that period. For example, a merger in December would result in reporting the financial statements for the entire calendar year on a combined basis. Similarly, any financial statements for prior years included for comparative purposes in the current annual report must also be restated on a combined basis.

In reporting the net income of a combined company under the pooling method, all expenses related to the business combination are written off as incurred; that is, no capitalization is permitted. Also, any gains of material amount resulting from abnormal dispositions of assets acquired in a pooling of interests must be separately reported as an extraordinary gain if the disposition occurs within two years of the business combination. After two years, however, no separate disclosure of such gains is required.

When the purchase method of accounting is required, the rules promulgated by the APB are essentially as follows: (1) ascertain which company is the purchaser; (2) determine the value of consideration given by the purchaser; (3) determine the value of identifiable assets and liabilities acquired; (4) record the excess of consideration given over the sum of identifiable assets as good will; and (5) depreciate the tangible assets over periods benefited and amortize intangible assets (including goodwill) over periods benefited or forty years, whichever is less.

Generally, the identification of the acquiring firm will be obvious. The single most important criterion to be employed for a noncash exchange is to note which stockholder group retains or receives the larger portion of voting rights in the combined corporation.

The cost of an acquisition is measured by the cash or other fair value of other assets given. For liabilities incurred, the measure is the present value of amounts to be paid in the future. For common stock issued, the quoted market price for a reasonable period surrounding the date of announcement is used in most cases. All direct costs of the acquisition must be included; that is, none can be charged to expense of the period in which the business combination occurs.

Identifiable assets must be recorded at current values, not the historical cost to the selling company. This requirement often necessitates the use of independent appraisals. Generally, replacement cost is used for assets intended to be used by the combined entity, while net realizable value is specified for assets to be sold. Identifiable intangible assets are recorded at appraised values, while liabilities are stated at the present values of amounts to be paid.

The excess of the cost incurred by the acquiring company over the sum of the fair values assigned to identifiable assets (less liabilities) must be recorded as goodwill. In the event that this "excess" is negative, the amounts otherwise assignable to noncurrent assets acquired (except long-term investments in marketable securities) must be reduced. No negative goodwill is recorded unless these assets are first reduced to zero value.

It should be noted that only under the purchase method can there be a recognition of goodwill resulting from a business combination. This goodwill, along with all other intangible assets, is amortized by systematic charges to income over the periods expected to be benefited. However, APB Opinion 17 requires that the period of amortization not exceed forty years. Thus, even if it is expected that an intangible asset's life is likely to be longer, published financial statements must still reflect amortization charges based on a forty-year write-off period.

A Concluding Remark

"For nearly a decade, a great corporate merger game has generated more excitement, more glamour—and probably more fortunes—than any other phenomenon in the business scene."[23] Pooling-of-interests accounting has played an integral part of this merger movement. Yet, despite its widespread acceptance in practice and its sanction by the APB, there is continued opposition to the pooling-of-interests concept. Favoring the pooling method are strong practical pressures that may be more important in explaining its acceptance than any merits of its theoretical rationale. Whether the reader agrees or not with the use of this accounting method, it remains to his or her advantage to be aware of the

---

[23]"Time of Testing for Conglomerates," *Business Week*, Mar. 2, 1968, p. 38.

procedures employed in the preparation of published financial statements, for only in this way can the significance of the reported figures be appreciated.

CHANGES IN ACCOUNTING PROCEDURES

Accounting figures are not real. They are not the actual phenomena in which an investor is usually interested but only surrogates thereof. Rather, the entire accounting process, of which financial statements are the end products, can be thought of as a system for communicating characteristics concerning some of the economic events affecting a given firm. Accounting, like any measurement process, is a means by which the events are represented through an organized set of symbols suitable for communication.

It is axiomatic that either a change in the actual events being described or a change in the accounting process by which the events are represented will cause a change in the accounting figures contained in the financial statements. Hence, accounting representation must consistently follow certain rules if it is to be convenient for the reader of financial statements to infer actual events correctly from the reported symbols.

Let us consider the effect of changing the representation rules if the financial statement user is not informed of the change. Recently, a company changed from an accelerated method of depreciation to the straight-line method. This act alone resulted in an increase in the company's reported earnings per share. An uninformed investor might have been misled to believe that the current year's real economic performance had improved over that of the preceding year, whereas in reality the change in the performance measure, earnings per share, was due merely to a change in the accounting measurement process. For this reason, it is important for the reader of financial statements to be alert to such accounting changes.

In recognition of the fact that changes in accounting may significantly affect the presentation of financial information, the APB in 1971 issued Opinion 20, defining various types of accounting changes and establishing rules by which each type is reported.[24] The board recognized that restating previously issued financial statements covering prior periods could confuse investors. On the other hand, it was held that a consistent accounting basis is often necessary if comparative financial data concerning several years are to be useful. In the process of giving consideration to each of these conflicting viewpoints, the opinion set forth a complex set of reporting requirements in which various types of accounting changes would be reported differently. The following commentary and illustrations concern the major provisions of that pronouncement.

Scope of APB Opinion 20

Opinion 20 specifies reporting procedures for each of three types of accounting changes occurring in connection with published financial statements of United States corporations. However, it does not apply to changes made in conformity with the provisions of other APB opinions, since each opinion specifies its own manner of reporting the results of any changes necessary to conform with its conclusions. This exception excludes a substantial portion of all accounting changes occurring in practice.

The three types of accounting changes are (1) change in an accounting principle, (2) change in the reporting entity, and (3) change in an accounting estimate. Although not considered an accounting change, the reporting of (4) a correction

---

[24]Accounting Principles Board, Opinion 20, *Accounting Changes,* American Institute of Certified Public Accountants, New York, July 1971.

of an error contained in previously issued financial statements is also covered by Opinion 20. Separate reporting rules are specified for each of these four situations.

Change in an Accounting Principle

A change in an accounting principle concerns a choice from among generally accepted accounting principles and the alternative methods of application thereof. Examples include changes in the method of inventory pricing, in the depreciation method for previously recorded assets, in the method of accounting for long-term contracts of the construction type, and in accounting for research and development costs.

The initial adoption of an accounting procedure is not considered a change in an accounting principle. For example, a firm might adopt a new method of determining depreciation for newly acquired assets while continuing to use another method in depreciating all previously acquired assets of the same type. This situation, according to the APB, is not a change in an accounting principle since the new depreciation method has not been applied to previously acquired assets.

Whenever a company makes a change in an accounting principle, the nature of the change and the justification thereof must be disclosed, along with the dollar effect on net income, in the financial statements of the year in which the change occurs. The investor should thus check the footnotes to the financial statements and the auditor's opinion to learn what, if any, changes in accounting principles have been made during the current year.

Most but not all such changes are recognized by including the cumulative effect of the change in the net income of the year of the change, however, prior years' income figures are presented, for comparative purposes, as previously reported. In addition, income computed on a pro-forma basis must also be shown on the face of the income statement for all periods compared. These pro-forma income figures are computed as if the new accounting principle had been in effect for the prior years. Thus, not only are the direct computational effects of the change included, but the pro-forma amounts must reflect all nondiscretionary expenses based upon income.

As an illustration of this reporting procedure, let us assume that in 1976 the ABC Corporation changes from an accelerated method to the straight-line method of determining depreciation on its plant and equipment. Both new and previously acquired assets are depreciated by the new procedure. The direct effects of this change are limited to the depreciation expense and related income taxes. We note that while such a change for book purposes only would not affect the current year's income taxes payable, both the tax expense and deferred taxes accounts appearing in the financial statements could well be affected under generally accepted tax allocation procedures. Data assumed for this illustration are:

Year	Excess of Accelerated Depreciation over Straight-Line Depreciation	Tax Effect	Direct Effect on Net Income
1971	$25,000	$12,500	$ 12,500
1972	70,000	35,000	35,000
1973	80,000	40,000	40,000
1974	60,000	30,000	30,000
1975	40,000	20,000	20,000
			$137,500

Under the terms of the company's incentive compensation plan, which provides for a fixed percentage of the firm's pretax income, this change in reported incomes would have resulted in increased compensation expenses (and related tax effects) as follows:

Year	Additional Incentive Compensation	Tax Effect	Pro Forma Effect on Net Income
1971	$2,500	$1,250	$ 1,250
1972	7,000	3,500	3,500
1973	8,000	4,000	4,000
1974	6,000	3,000	3,000
1975	4,000	2,000	2,000
			$13,750

Following the provisions of APB Opinion 20, this change in accounting principle would be reported on the firm's income statement as shown in Exhibit V.

EXHIBIT V
REPORTING A CHANGE IN ACCOUNTING PRINCIPLE

	1976	1975
Income before cumulative effect of a change in accounting principle	$200,000	$190,000
Cumulative effect on prior years (to December 31, 1975) of changing to a different depreciation method (see footnote)	137,500	. . .
Net income	$337,500	$190,000
Per-share amounts:		
Income before cumulative effect of a change in accounting principle	$ .20	$ .19
Cumulative effect on prior years (to December 31, 1975) of changing to a different depreciation method	.14	. . .
Net income	$ .34	$ .19
Pro-forma amounts assuming that the new depreciation method is applied retroactively		
Net income	$200,000	$208,000
Earnings per common share	$ .20	$ .21

FOOTNOTE: Depreciation of plant and equipment has been computed by the straight-line method in 1976. This is a change from the sum-of-the-years'-digits method used in prior years. The new method of depreciation was adopted to achieve a better matching of costs and revenues and has been applied retroactively to equipment acquisitions of prior years. The effect of the change in 1976 was to increase aftertax income by $10,000 ($.01 per share) over that which would have resulted had the depreciation method not been changed. The aftertax adjustment of $137,500 to apply the new method retroactively is included in income for 1976. The pro-forma amounts shown on the income statement have been adjusted for the effect of retroactive application on depreciation, the change in provisions for incentive compensation that would have been made had the new method been in effect, and related income taxes.

Several characteristics of the reporting procedure can be observed from this example. We notice that the effect of the depreciation change on current-year asset purchases is not shown on the face of the income statement but rather in the footnote. Thus, if the depreciation method had not been changed, there would not have been any improvement of 1976 earnings over those of 1975. A casual comparison of the top lines of the income statement is apt to convey a wrong impression, since this effect is revealed only in the footnote. We should also note that the cumulative effect included in the net income of the year of the change is not comparable with the pro-forma income figures for prior years. The pro-forma amounts include the indirect effects of nondiscretionary adjustments based on income, whereas the cumulative effect does not.

Not all changes in accounting principle are reported as illustrated above. For a few specifically identified types of changes in an accounting principle, the APB required that the financial data concerning prior years be restated. Thus for these cases no pro-forma amounts are shown, but rather the primary figures shown for prior years are restated for the direct effects of the change in accounting principle. Amounts originally reported in previously issued financial statements are not given. Also, we should notice that the restated amounts are not "pro-forma" since "indirect" effects are not included.

The changes in accounting principles for which this procedure is followed are (1) a change from last-in, first-out (LIFO) to any other method of inventory pricing, (2) a change in accounting for long-term contracts of the construction type, and (3) a change involving the "full-cost" method used in the extractive industries.

Change in the Reporting Entity

A change in the reporting entity occurs whenever there is a redefinition of the organization about which economic events are being reported. A common example involves the addition of subsidiaries in the preparation of consolidated financial statements. The use of the pooling-of-interests method of accounting for a business combination also results in a new conception of the reporting firm.

If there is a change in the reporting entity, prior years' financial data of the individual constituents making up the resulting entity are summed to restate the history of the combined firm. For example, if Firm A had sales of $100 in a prior year when Firm B had sales of $150 and the two firms are subsequently combined through a pooling of interests, prior-year sales for the combined entity would be reported as $250 to present meaningful figures for comparison with current-year sales of the present company.

The nature and reason for a change in the reporting entity must be disclosed in the year of the change. Financial statements of subsequent periods need not repeat these disclosures, although such statements would continue to reflect restated information concerning any years prior to the reorganization.

Change in an Accounting Estimate

Changes in accounting estimates are distinguished from changes in accounting principles, corrections of errors, or prior period adjustments. Accounting estimates are inputs to the measurement process, whereas accounting principles are the process itself. Changes in estimates are not deemed corrections of errors, since no mistake or error has been made; rather, a change in an accounting estimate is a revision by management based upon information not previously available. On the other hand, a prior-period adjustment is the result of a determination by someone outside the reporting entity.

The very nature of the accounting process often requires estimating the effects of future events. Since the future cannot be perceived with certainty, these estimates change as new events occur, experience is gained, or new information is obtained. Examples of accounting estimates include estimates of uncollectible accounts, inventory obsolescence, service lives and salvage values of depreciable assets, warranty costs, and recoverable mineral reserves.

In situations in which the effect of a change in an accounting estimate is inseparable from the effect of a change in an accounting principle, the entire effect of the change is treated as a change in an accounting estimate. For example, a company might change from deferring and amortizing a cost to expensing the cost as incurred (a change in an accounting principle) because future benefits of the cost have become doubtful (a change in an accounting estimate).

A change in an accounting estimate is reported prospectively, not retroactively. Unlike a change in an accounting principle, a change in an accounting estimate is not accounted for either by restating amounts reported in prior periods or by showing pro-forma amounts. Rather, a change in an accounting estimate is accounted for in the current year and, if applicable, in future years.

As an example of a change in an accounting estimate, let us assume that a firm revises its estimate of the total life of a plant asset from ten years to eight years after the asset has been in use for five years. A retroactive approach would require a determination of the depreciation error for the past five years. However, under the prospective approach required by Opinion 20, this cumulative effect must be reflected only in the income of the remaining three years of the asset's life. The procedure is simply to compute the annual depreciation by dividing the remaining 50 percent of the total asset cost by three years, the remaining asset life as revealed by the revised estimate. Thus the portion of the asset's cost charged to income under a straight-line approach would be as follows:

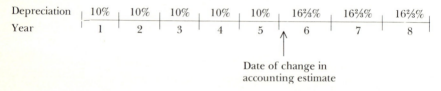

Correction of an Error

Errors in financial statements result from mathematical mistakes, mistakes in the application of accounting principles, or oversight or misuse of facts that existed at the time at which the financial statements were prepared. A change from an accounting principle that is not generally accepted to one that is generally accepted is a correction of an error, not a change in an accounting principle, for purposes of accounting.

The reporting requirement for correction of errors in previously published financial statements is the same as that described above with regard to changes in the reporting entity; that is, retroactive restatement of prior-period financial statements is required. Disclosure of the nature and effect of the error is given only in the period in which the error is discovered and corrected.

A Concluding Remark

Allegedly, the APB's objective in developing the previously described reporting procedures for various types of accounting changes was to minimize the extent of restatement of previously published financial information. It was felt that "restating financial statements of prior periods may dilute public confidence in financial statements and may confuse those who use them."[25] In summary, the resulting

[25]Ibid., p. 390.

rules are that corrections of errors and changes in the reporting entity require restatement. Changes in most accounting principles require pro-forma amounts but not restatement, while changes in a few specific accounting principles require restatement but not pro-forma amounts. On the other hand, inconsistencies in accounting information resulting from changes in accounting estimates require no adjustments at all. It is left for the reader to evaluate whether this approach is really less confusing to investors.

Chapter 12
Selecting Stocks for Growth and Future Value

DAVID K. EITEMAN

What is the value of a share of common stock in a particular company? More specifically, if an informed opinion has been established as to the probable future benefits from a share of stock, as detailed in Chapter 10, what is a reasonable price for that share? Setting a reasonable price for the bundle of expected future benefits that constitute the gain from ownership of shares of stock is the problem of *valuation*.

REASONABLE PRICE

The idea of a "reasonable price" implies that at some (presumably low) price almost every stock would be a desirable purchase, while at some other (presumably higher) price shares of the same company should not be acquired. The general idea of a reasonable price has been expressed in a variety of terms.

Graham, Dodd, and Cottle refer to "intrinsic value," which they define as an attempt "to value a stock independently of its current market price."[1] They point out that a variety of names are applied to this concept: "indicated value," "central value," "normal value," "investment value," "reasonable value," "fair value," and "appraised value."[2] Graham, Dodd, and Cottle further indicate that intrinsic value is "that value which is justified by the facts, e.g., assets, earnings, dividends, definite prospects, including the factor of management."[3] In this sense, they differentiate between intrinsic value and "market value," which denotes the price at which a stock can actually be purchased or sold in the market.

Thus is derived the basic concept underlying analysis of value in the purchase of stocks: a stock is a reasonable purchase when its intrinsic value lies below its market value. Similarly, a stock ceases to be a reasonable purchase and in fact is a likely candidate for sale when its intrinsic value lies above its market value.

[1]Benjamin Graham, David Dodd, and Sidney Cottle, *Security Analysis: Principles and Technique,* 4th ed., McGraw-Hill Book Company, New York, 1962, p. 27.
[2]Ibid.
[3]Ibid., p. 28.

Because intrinsic value is at best the subjective opinion of a particular analyst, common practice is to regard stocks as reasonable purchases only at some safety margin below one's opinion of intrinsic value. Similarly, stocks are seldom sold as soon as they climb one-eighth of a point above intrinsic value; rather they are held until some appropriate margin exists. (It should be noted that as a stock rises, there is a human tendency to revise upward previously held opinions of intrinsic value. Therefore, rising stocks are sold less often than might appear reasonable after the fact.)

Key Variables in Determining a Reasonable Price

Determining a reasonable price for a share of stock requires the formulation of opinions about some or all of a number of basic variables. These key variables, usually identified in the process of security analysis, are the following:

1. *Present normalized earnings per share.* This variable should be either primary or fully diluted earnings per share on a consistent basis, for the latest reported twelve-month period, revised to remove the effect of (*a*) extraordinary or nonrepetitive accounting charges (such as realized capital gains or losses) and (*b*) the impact of business cycles upon the firm. In effect, present normalized earnings per share is that measure of income for the current year adjusted to be typical or normal, and thus the best base from which to project earnings for future years.

2. *Expected average growth rate in normalized earnings per share.* Analysts must predict, as a percent per year figure, the average annual compound growth rate of earnings per share that they anticipate during the period in which they expect to hold the stock. Since actual earnings per share will probably grow at varying annual rates during the period under consideration, an average growth rate is used. Ideally, this may be viewed as the slope of a trend line plotted through the logarithms of the expected earnings-per-share figures for future years. Less precise but probably more convenient is the use of a simple arithmetic average of expected yearly earnings per share.

The use of an expected average growth rate in conjunction with a normalized earnings-per-share figure is a shortcut to defining specific earnings-per-share levels for each future year being considered. Given uncertainties about the future, it is probably no less accurate than an attempt to estimate earnings per share for each year separately.

3. *Expected dividend payout rate.* The dividend payout is the average annual percentage of earnings per share that is expected to be paid as cash dividends during the investment period under consideration.

4. *Expected growth period in years.* From the investment decision-making point of view, the growth period is the number of years of future growth for which investors are willing to pay at the present time. This may very well be less than the actual growth period. The question is not how long growth will continue at the expected average rate, but rather what period of growth may reasonably be incorporated into the present valuation. Thus, the limit is the *decision horizon* rather than the actual growth horizon.

5. *Price-earnings ratio at the end of the growth period.* For valuation purposes, the stock is assumed to be sold at the end of the indicated growth period, either (*a*) because analysts believe that there will be no significant growth after this period or (*b*) because they are unwilling to include in their estimate at the present time an assumption of growth beyond this period (even though it might occur). Although it may be more accurate, from a purely theoretical point of view, to anticipate an infinite stream of future cash dividends, it is more practical and realistic for analysts to estimate the value of an investment in accord with the way in which they organize their expectations for the future of the company.

6. *Desired rate of return.* This is the rate of return, expressed as a percentage

per annum, that analysts believe is desirable for investing in the security in question. A decision on a proper rate must take into account both (*a*) returns available on alternative investments of similar risk and (*b*) the level of probability that analysts assign to the expectations in items 1 through 5.

7. *Present price.* The price in today's market is the base for purchase or sell decisions. For precision, purchase price plus purchase commissions and sales price less sales commissions should be used, but for convenience the rest of this chapter will ignore commissions.

Some or all of the preceding seven key variables will be used to illustrate various approaches to the basic problem of formulating an opinion about the reasonable, or intrinsic, value of a share of stock. For convenience, the key variables plus certain related items, such as dividends per share, will generally be abbreviated as follows:

P = market price
V = value, or intrinsic value
E = normalized earnings per share
g = expected average annual growth rate of earnings per share
B = expected dividend payout rate
D = expected dividend per share
n = expected growth period in years
M = price-earnings ratio or multiplier
r = desired rate of return

Years will be indicated by subscripts: earnings per share two years hence is E_2, market price at the present date is P_0, and market price one year hence is P_1.

Relative versus Absolute Valuation

Common stock may be valued from either a relative or an absolute point of view. The relative approach attempts to answer the question: Is this stock a good buy at the present time relative to some other stock(s) that I might purchase instead? The approach attempts to direct the buyer to selecting the "best" stock at a point of time, even though the best in a relative sense might in fact be the "least worst." The failing of the relative approach, then, is that its successful application might do no more than assure that the investor loses less than he would in any other stock.

The absolute approach reduces stock selection to a process of choosing among alternative expected rates of return. It provides both relative comparison and an absolute measure which might indicate, at some point in time, that *no* stock is a good buy or that *several* stocks are good buys. If, for example, the best stock offered only an expected return of 2 percent per annum, a mental framework based upon relative approaches might have investors choose that stock (it is the "best"), but the absolute approach would suggest that they refrain from buying any stocks at the present time and perhaps place their funds in a savings institution.

The relative approach to stock selection is somewhat more popular with securities salesmen, since it always provides for a buy recommendation. (Securities salesmen seldom recommend holding funds in a savings account.) The absolute approach is thus the more logical one, but its successful implementation abounds in difficulties that, in practice, limit its appeal.

Another factor in common stock valuation is estimated risk. Risk is treated in detail in Chapters 2 (Part 2) and 3; so only brief comment is warranted here. A stock is a reasonable purchase only if potential gains offset the risks undertaken.

In general, the relative approaches to stock selection provide only a limited framework for considering risk. If stock A is ranked better than stock B, investors can do little more than ponder the question whether this "betterness" offsets any additional estimated risk for A.

By contrast, absolute approaches to valuation, if successfully implemented, permit potential buyers to apply a higher expected return for each increment of perceived risk. Thus, if stock A is expected to return 20 percent per annum and stock B only 15 percent, the investor can determine whether the added 5 percentage points of return are sufficient to offset the additional estimated risk of A.

PRICE-EARNINGS RATIOS: A RELATIVE APPROACH

The commonest valuation technique uses a price-earnings ratio. If a stock has a market price (P) of $34 and is currently earning (E) $2 per share, the price-earnings ratio (P/E) is $34/$2 = 17. Price-earnings ratios reduce stock prices to common denominators of price per dollar of earnings.

In themselves, price-earnings ratios are essentially relative valuation techniques; a stock selling at 17 times earnings is more expensive than one selling at, say, 14 times earnings. The fundamental question whether a stock is worth 17 times earnings, when another stock can be purchased for only 14 times earnings, depends upon subjective weighting of the many other variables involved in the future of that share, such as the expected future rate of growth.

The price-earnings ratio, or P/E, is the reciprocal of an earnings yield, or E/P. The earnings yield in the example above would be $2/$34 = 5.87 percent. Note, however, that the numerator, earnings per share, is not received by the investor, since only dividends are received.

Price-earnings ratios are sometimes used to relate specific stocks to levels of the stock market as a whole. Price-earnings ratio ranges for the Dow Jones Industrial Average (DJIA) since 1935 are shown in Table 12-1. If, for example, General Electric common stock is judged to be equal in quality, risk, and growth potential to the DJIA and if it can be purchased for 15 times current earnings per share while the DJIA is selling for 10 times earnings, then General Electric is overpriced relative to the average.

Price-earnings ratios are also used to indicate the relative level of the stock market as a whole. During late 1967 the DJIA sold at about 17½ times earnings, indicating that the average was then relatively high compared with its underlying earnings-generating ability. In early 1970, by contrast, the average dropped to as low as 13 times current earnings, and in 1973–1974 to below 7 times current earnings.

Dividend Variations on Price-Earnings Ratios

The use of a price-earnings ratio by itself to judge comparative values of stocks ignores several important attributes. Perhaps the two most important are dividend policy and anticipated growth. Graham, Dodd, and Cottle suggest a technique for incorporating dividend policy in the use of price-earnings ratios.[4] They refer to the price-earnings ratio itself as a multiplier and suggest that it be applied as follows:

Value = earnings multiplier × (Expected dividends + one-third expected earnings), or $V = M(D + \frac{1}{3}E)$

This approach is postulated on the observation that a "normal" stock (or a "typical" group of stocks, such as the DJIA) tends, in the long run, to pay out in dividends a sum equal to about two-thirds of its earnings. In such "typical" instances, the expression "dividends plus one-third expected earnings" is equivalent to earnings, and the entire expression is reduced to the conventional price-earnings multiplier.

However, to the extent that companies deviate from a normal two-thirds

[4]Ibid., p. 518.

dividend payout policy, the "dividends plus one-third expected earnings" formula shifts and increases or decreases the value of the stock accordingly. If payout is less than two-thirds of earnings, value is reduced; and, in the extreme case of no dividends, the value is reduced to the multiplier times one-third of earnings. Correspondingly, if dividend policy is to pay out more than two-thirds, say, 100

TABLE 12-1   Dow Jones Industrial Average, 1935–1974

Year	High closing price	Low yield (percent)	Low closing price	High yield (percent)	Earnings per share	P/E ratio High	P/E ratio Low
1935	148.44	2.69	96.11	4.14	$ 6.61	22.5	14.6
1936	184.90	3.74	143.11	4.84	9.98	18.5	14.3
1937	194.40	4.34	113.64	7.43	11.35	17.1	10.0
1938	158.41	3.25	98.95	5.20	6.17	25.6	16.0
1939	155.92	3.84	121.44	5.06	9.05	17.2	13.4
1940	152.80	4.58	111.84	6.26	10.94	14.0	10.2
1941	133.59	5.53	106.34	6.95	11.50	11.6	9.3
1942	119.71	5.45	92.92	7.02	9.18	13.0	10.1
1943	145.82	4.33	119.26	5.29	9.84	14.8	12.1
1944	152.53	4.27	134.22	4.86	10.05	15.2	13.4
1945	195.82	3.42	151.35	4.42	10.56	18.5	14.3
1946	212.50	3.53	163.12	4.60	13.63	15.6	12.0
1947	186.85	4.93	163.21	5.64	18.80	9.5	8.7
1948	193.16	5.95	165.39	6.95	23.07	8.4	7.2
1949	200.52	6.38	161.60	7.89	23.54	8.5	6.8
1950	235.47	6.85	196.81	8.20	30.70	7.7	6.4
1951	276.37	5.91	238.99	6.84	26.59	10.4	9.0
1952	292.00	5.30	256.35	6.04	24.76	11.8	10.4
1953	293.79	5.48	255.49	6.31	27.23	10.8	9.4
1954	404.39	4.32	279.87	6.24	28.40	14.2	9.9
1955	488.40	4.42	388.20	5.56	35.78	13.7	10.8
1956	521.05	4.41	462.35	4.97	33.34	15.6	13.9
1957	520.77	4.45	419.79	5.15	34.08	14.4	11.6
1958	583.65	3.42	439.89	4.54	27.95	20.9	15.7
1959	679.36	3.05	574.46	3.61	34.31	19.8	16.7
1960	685.47	3.12	566.05	3.77	32.21	21.3	17.6
1961	734.91	3.09	610.25	3.72	36.71	23.0	19.1
1962	726.01	3.21	535.76	4.35	36.43	19.9	14.7
1963	767.21	3.05	646.79	3.62	41.21	18.6	15.7
1964	891.71	3.50	766.08	4.08	46.43	19.2	16.5
1965	969.26	2.95	840.59	3.40	53.67	18.1	15.7
1966	995.15	3.20	744.32	4.28	57.68	17.3	12.9
1967	943.08	3.20	786.41	3.84	53.87	17.5	14.6
1968	985.21	3.18	825.13	3.80	57.89	17.0	14.3
1969	968.85	3.50	769.93	4.40	57.02	17.0	13.5
1970	842.00	3.74	631.16	4.99	51.02	16.5	12.4
1971	950.82	3.25	797.97	3.99	55.09	17.3	14.5
1972	1036.27	3.11	889.15	3.63	67.13	15.4	13.2
1973	1067.20	3.31	783.56	4.51	86.16	12.4	9.1
1974	904.02	4.17	577.60	6.52	96.77	9.3	6.0

SOURCE: Dow Jones Co.

percent, then the resulting value will increase. The higher the payout ratio, the higher the value.

How, then, can some commonly accepted growth stocks that pay little or no dividends command high multiples in the stock market? The answer is that if the company's earnings are expected to grow, then a higher multiple may be warranted. However, the burden of proof for justifying a higher multiple as a technique to justify a higher price depends upon a reasonable expectation of greater future earnings. Smaller dividends might contribute to such higher earnings, but small dividends per se do not automatically lead to enlarged future earnings. Thus, the rationale for a high multiple must reside elsewhere than in the lack of dividends.

Growth Adjustment of Price-Earnings Ratios

W. Edward Bell suggested a technique by which anticipated growth (in earnings per share) can be accounted for within a framework of using a basic price-earnings ratio.[5] Conceptually, such an approach may be considered a "payback" approach to common stock valuation.

In the Bell payback approach, the conventional price-earnings ratio is regarded as the number of years' earnings included in the present market price. If, for example, a stock with $2 of current earnings per share is selling at $16 and if it is not expected to grow, then eight years will be needed for the accumulation of earnings to equal the purchase price. Other stocks might be judged against this nongrowth stock.

Bell's basic table is shown as Table 12-2, in which the body indicates the number of years needed to recapture the purchase price through an accumulation of growing earnings per share. The vertical scale gives the price-earnings ratio at the time of purchase, and the horizontal scale the estimated annual growth rates for earnings per share.

For example, assume that on a given date the DJIA is selling at 18 times earnings and that investors expect earnings per share for the DJIA to grow at an average rate of 4 percent per annum for some years. The intersection of the 18 percent price-earnings ratio (left scale) and the 4 percent growth rate (horizontal scale) shows a value of 13.8 (boxed). The DJIA is thus priced at the given time to pay back through accumulated earnings (not dividends) the present price in 13.8 years.

Since the DJIA is frequently used as a general example of what an investor should be able to do in the market as a whole, specific stocks are often compared with this criterion. Suppose that a very glamorous stock in a dynamic new industry is currently selling at 30 times current earnings. Because of the expected future growth for this new industry, earnings are expected to grow at 10 percent per annum. Is this glamor issue a reasonable purchase at a price equal to 30 times its current earnings?

The intersection of the 30 percent price-earnings ratio line and the 10 percent growth column in Table 12-2 indicates that investors would need 14.5 years to recapture their purchase price through accumulated earnings. If 13.8 years is the criterion, the stock is overpriced on a relative basis. If the 10 percent growth rate is assumed to be accurate, the stock becomes a reasonable purchase only if its present price-earnings ratio should drop below about 27 times earnings (interpolating between 28 and 26 in the 10 percent column).

Bell's payback approach to common stock valuation has the advantage of considering expected growth in a consistent fashion. It works best in determining *relative* valuations in instances in which growth is expected to continue at a relatively constant rate for some time beyond the number of years needed to recapture the purchase price. As a technique, however, it makes no attempt at valuation from an absolute point of view. It is also weak in that it considers neither dividends nor possible sales prices.

---

[5] W. Edward Bell, "The Price–Future Earnings Ratio," *The Analysts Journal* (now *Financial Analysts Journal*), August 1958, pp. 25–28.

TABLE 12-2 Price–Future Earnings Ratios

	Ratio of price to future earnings													
Price-earnings ratio	Estimated annual growth rate of earnings per share (percent)													
	1	2	3	4	5	6	7	8	9	10	12	15	20	25
6	5.9	5.7	5.6	5.5	5.4	5.3	5.2	5.1	5.0					
7	6.8	6.6	6.4	6.3	6.2	6.0	5.9	5.8	5.7	5.6	5.4			
8	7.7	7.5	7.3	7.1	6.9	6.6	6.6	6.4	6.3	6.2	5.9	5.6		
9	8.7	8.4	8.1	7.8	7.6	7.4	7.2	7.0	6.9	6.7	6.5	6.1	5.6	
10	9.6	9.2	8.9	8.6	8.3	8.1	7.8	7.6	7.4	7.3	7.0	6.6	6.0	5.6
11	10.5	10.0	9.6	9.3	9.0	8.7	8.4	8.2	8.0	7.8	7.4	7.0	6.4	5.9
12	11.4	10.9	10.4	10.0	9.6	9.3	9.0	8.7	8.5	8.3	7.9	7.4	6.7	6.2
13	12.3	11.7	11.1	10.7	10.3	9.9	9.6	9.3	9.0	8.7	8.3	7.7	7.0	6.5
14	13.2	12.5	11.9	11.3	10.9	10.5	10.1	9.8	9.5	9.2	8.7	8.1	7.3	6.7
15	14.1	13.2	12.6	12.0	11.5	11.0	10.6	10.2	9.9	9.6	9.1	8.4	7.6	7.0
16	14.9	14.0	13.3	12.6	12.0	11.5	11.1	10.7	10.3	10.0	9.5	8.8	7.9	7.2
17	15.8	14.8	13.9	13.2	12.6	12.1	11.6	11.2	10.8	10.4	9.8	9.1	8.1	7.4
18	16.6	15.5	14.6	13.8	13.2	13.6	12.1	11.6	11.2	10.8	10.2	9.4	8.4	7.6
19	17.5	16.3	15.3	14.4	13.7	13.1	12.5	12.0	11.6	11.2	10.5	9.6	8.6	7.8
20	18.3	17.0	15.9	15.9	14.2	13.5	12.9	12.4	11.9	11.5	10.8	9.9	8.8	8.0
22	20.0	18.4	17.1	16.1	15.2	14.4	13.8	13.2	12.7	12.2	11.4	10.4	9.2	8.4
24		19.8	18.3	17.2	16.2	15.3	14.6	13.9	13.3	12.8	12.0	10.9	9.6	8.7
26			19.5	18.2	17.1	16.1	15.3	14.6	14.0	13.4	12.5	11.4	10.0	9.0
28				19.2	17.9	16.9	16.0	15.3	14.6	14.0	13.0	11.8	10.4	9.3
30					18.8	17.7	16.7	15.9	15.2	14.5	13.5	12.2	10.7	9.6
32					19.6	18.4	17.4	16.5	15.7	15.1	13.9	12.6	11.0	9.8
34						19.1	18.0	17.1	16.3	15.5	14.3	12.9	11.3	10.1
36						19.7	18.6	17.6	16.8	16.0	14.7	13.3	11.5	10.3
38							19.2	18.1	17.1	16.5	15.1	13.6	11.8	10.5
40							19.7	18.6	17.7	16.9	15.5	13.9	12.1	10.7
45								19.8	18.8	17.9	16.4	14.7	12.6	11.2
50									19.8	18.8	17.2	15.3	13.2	11.7
75										22.5	20.3	17.9	15.2	13.4

SOURCE: W. Edward Bell, "The Price–Future Earnings Ratio," *The Analysts Journal*, August 1958, pp. 25–28.

DISCOUNTED FUTURE CASH BENEFITS: AN ABSOLUTE APPROACH

The original theory of common stock valuation based upon discounted future benefits was developed in 1938 by John B. Williams.[6] Williams defined the investment value of a share of stock as the present worth of all the dividends to be paid upon it, noting that dividends, rather than earnings, are what the stockholder actually receives. If earnings are retained rather than distributed in dividend form, the fact of retention and reinvestment should produce later enlarged dividends. These enlarged future dividends are incorporated automatically into current value by the dividend-discounting formula. Should the retained earnings not produce enlarged future dividends, these retained earnings become in fact lost funds of no value to the stockholder.

The general model of common stock valuation in terms of this approach is frequently expressed in algebraic form as follows:[7]

$$V_0 = \frac{D_1}{1 + r_1} + \frac{D_2}{1 + r_2} + \frac{D_3}{1 + r_3} + \ldots + \frac{D_\infty}{1 + r_\infty} \tag{1}$$

where

V_0 = value of the share of stock at the time of contemplated purchase (that is, at time zero)

$D_1, D_2, D_3,$ etc. = cash dividends to be received in year 1, year 2, year 3, etc., extending to infinity

$r_1, r_2, r_3,$ etc. = discount rate desired by investors for cash receipts in year 1, year 2, year 3, etc.

From a theoretical point of view, Equation 1 is virtually a truism, since it simply says that a stock is worth the present value of all future cash receipts. To convert Equation 1 to a more practical operational form, several substitutions and changes are desirable.

Discount Rate Substitution.   Equation 1 assumes that investors have a unique discount rate for each year. Frequently, benefits expected to be received further in the future are discounted at a higher rate to reflect a greater perceived uncertainty about eventual realization of those benefits. This risk or ability-to-forecast premium is demanded in addition to the discount already implied because of the time-imposed need to wait. Although the application of differing discount rates is not illogical, we shall use a constant discount rate r, such that $r = r_1 = r_2 = r_3$, etc., because this simplifies computations, with only a limited influence upon the share values derived from discounting benefits within the relatively short time horizon actually used by most investors. Equation 1 can thus be simplified to:

$$V_0 = \sum_{t=1}^{\infty} \frac{D_t}{(1 + r)^t} \tag{2}$$

The discount rate assumed will, of course, vary with the rates of return currently available for alternative investments, including (besides stocks) high-grade bonds, medium-grade bonds, high-quality short-term money market instruments, and guaranteed savings deposits. For example, if 9 percent can be earned on high-

[6]John B. Williams, *The Theory of Investment Value,* Harvard University Press, Cambridge, Mass., 1938. Chapter 5 of this work is reprinted in Hsiu-kwang Wu and Alan J. Zakon, *Elements of Investments: Selected Readings,* 2d ed., Holt, Rinehart and Winston, Inc., New York, 1972.

[7]The development and computer formulation that follow are based upon David K. Eiteman, "A Computer Program for Common Stock Valuation," *Financial Analysts Journal,* July–August 1968, pp. 107–111.

grade bonds maturing at about the same time as the projected time of sale of the stock, one's assumed discount rate will properly be substantially higher than if the equivalent high-grade bond yield were 6 or 7 percent.

First Dividend Simplification.   Equations 1 and 2 require the forecast of dividends for each individual future year. From an operational point of view, over an extended period of time it is easier to think in terms of a present dividend growing at some *average* annual rate g. Practicing analysts may not know exactly in which year dividends will be increased, but they should have formulated some opinion as to how dividends will rise over an extended period of time. By applying the expected average growth rate for dividends to the dividend payment in the base year (the year of investment decision), Equation 2 can be rewritten as

$$V_0 = \sum_{t=1}^{\infty} \frac{D_0(1 + g)^t}{(1 + r)^t} \tag{3}$$

Second Dividend Simplification.   Although theory urges the use of dividends, today most practicing analysts and investors invariably look first at earnings in estimating the worth of a share of stock. This apparent dichotomy can be resolved by accepting anticipated earnings as the major informational factor in estimating future dividends. The process of analysis can then be directed to formulating an opinion about future earnings, supplemented by a belief about average future dividend payout rates. Future dividends can then be specified in terms of expected earnings per share E and dividend payout rate B. If, in addition, the expected average growth rate g is redefined for earnings rather than dividends, Equation 3 can be further simplified as

$$V_0 = \sum_{t=1}^{\infty} \frac{E_0 \cdot B(1 + g)^t}{(1 + r)^t} \tag{4}$$

Liquidating Dividend Simplification.   The value of a share of stock in abstract terms is the present value of all future dividends, including an eventual liquidating dividend if paid. In practice, few publicly traded companies are liquidated until after operational problems have carried them beyond the point of salvaging any value for remaining common stockholders. In addition, investors in general are seldom interested in stocks of companies likely to cease operations within the predictable future. For these two reasons, we shall ignore the possibility of liquidating dividends. (However, in such special situations as the purchase by a group of investors of a majority of shares for the express purpose of liquidating a company, the amount of the liquidating dividend would have to be included in the equation.)

Horizon Simplification.   Most investors purchase stock for a finite time horizon rather than the infinite horizon implicit in the general valuation formula. Two conceptual approaches exist by which the divergence between finite reality and infinite theory may be resolved.

One way is for actual investors to think in terms of the value of the infinite dividend stream and, by implication, to assume that they will be able to sell at the value of the remaining stream. If opinions about the actual dividend stream and about the appropriate discount rate have not changed, the investors will fare as well as they had anticipated, for they simply recover at the time of sale a cash sum equal to the value they would have placed at that time on the still-remaining dividends. Such an approach in effect places upon the investors the risk of having to sell at less than a fair value of remaining future benefits and suggests that if the investors are unwilling to take this market risk, they should perhaps not be buying common stocks. Of course, the investors might be able to sell at more than what they themselves deem a fair value, and this possibility may offset the risk of selling under adverse conditions.

A second approach is first to revise the basic equation so as to treat only a finite time horizon, over which future dividends can be predicted to the satisfaction of the investors and then to provide for a specific sales price. The proper definition of this decision horizon is that period of future growth for which the investors are willing to pay at the present time. As indicated above, this period may well be less than the actual expected growth period; that is, the question is not how long growth will continue at the expected average rate but rather what period of growth may rationally be incorporated in a present purchase price.

If this modification is made in the basic formula, the terminal sales price will most likely be forecast in terms of an expected price-earnings ratio or multiplier M likely to prevail at the time of sale. Equation 4 can now be rewritten:

Present value of stock = present value of expected + present value of expected
dividend stream for n sales price in nth year
years

or $\quad V_0 = \sum_{t=1}^{n} \dfrac{E_0 \cdot B(1 + g)^T}{(1 + r)^T} + \dfrac{M \cdot E_0(1 + g)^n}{(1 + r)^n}$ $\hspace{2cm}$ (5)

It will be noted that the final sales price is defined as the expected price-earnings multiplier M times earnings in the nth year, where earnings in the nth year are in turn defined as earnings in the base year E_0 times an expected growth factor $(1 + g)$ for n years.

Operational Implications.   Equation 5 provides a basis for determining the value of a stock by means of six variables. Using the analysis of ABC Corporation developed in Chapter 10, let us assume that we estimate these six variables as follows:

E_0 = normalized earnings per share for the present year $\qquad$ = $2.73
g $\quad$ = expected average annual growth rate of earnings per share = 11 percent
B $\quad$ = expected average dividend payout rate $\qquad\qquad\qquad$ = 60 percent
n $\quad$ = decision horizon in years $\qquad\qquad\qquad\qquad\qquad$ = 10 years
M = price-earnings multiplier expected to be in effect in the nth = 14 times
$\qquad$ year
r $\quad$ = rate of return desired by investors $\qquad\qquad\qquad\qquad$ = 15 percent

The solution of Equation 5 suggests a reasonable price of $40.38, as follows:

$$V = \sum_{t=1}^{10} \frac{(2.73)(0.60)(1.11)^t}{(1.15)^t} + \frac{(14)(2.73)(1.11)^{10}}{(1.15)^{10}} = \$40.38$$

Such a single solution is perhaps less practical, however, than a multiple solution to a series of possible variations in expected variables. Table 12-3 provides such a triple solution. First, it shows computer-generated values of the expected dividend stream for rates of growth from 5 to 17 percent per annum, these being units of 2 percentage points about the forecast 11 percent per annum rate. Second, it shows values for each decision horizon from four to sixteen years, these being variations of two years about the forecast horizon of ten years. Finally, it shows values based on selling the stock at a price-earnings multiple of from 10 to 18 times earnings, these being variations of 2 from the forecast multiple of 14 times earnings. Thus, what has been created is a three-dimensional table, with the unique solution to the forecast variable in the center of the center section (see boxed item).

TABLE 12-3   Generated Tables of Present Values for Estimated Future Cash Receipts, ABC Corporation*

Growth period (years)	Assumed growth rate (percent)							P/E ratio at time of sale (times)
	5	7	9	11	13	15	17	
4	24.22	25.95	27.77	29.70	31.72	33.85	36.09	10
6	23.05	25.41	27.98	30.77	33.82	37.13	40.72	
8	22.08	24.94	28.16	31.78	35.84	40.40	45.51	
10	21.27	24.53	28.32	32.71	37.80	43.68	50.47	
12	20.59	24.18	28.47	33.58	39.69	46.96	55.60	
14	20.03	23.87	28.60	34.39	41.51	50.23	60.91	
16	19.56	23.61	28.71	35.15	43.27	53.51	66.41	
4	28.01	30.04	32.18	34.44	36.81	39.31	41.94	12
6	26.21	28.95	31.93	35.19	38.73	42.59	46.77	
8	24.71	28.00	31.71	35.89	40.59	45.86	51.78	
10	23.46	27.18	31.51	36.54	42.38	49.14	56.96	
12	22.42	26.48	31.34	37.15	44.11	52.42	62.32	
14	21.55	25.86	31.18	37.72	45.78	55.69	67.86	
16	20.83	25.33	31.03	38.25	47.39	58.97	73.61	
4	31.81	34.13	36.59	39.18	41.90	44.77	47.79	14
6	29.38	32.49	35.89	39.60	43.65	48.05	52.83	
8	27.35	31.07	35.27	40.00	45.33	51.32	58.04	
10	25.66	29.84	34.71	40.38	46.96	54.60	63.44	
12	24.25	28.77	34.21	40.72	48.53	57.88	69.03	
14	23.08	27.85	33.75	41.05	50.05	61.15	74.81	
16	22.10	27.05	33.35	41.35	51.52	64.43	80.80	
4	35.60	38.23	40.99	43.91	46.99	50.23	53.64	16
6	32.54	36.03	39.85	44.02	48.56	53.51	58.88	
8	29.99	34.14	38.83	44.12	50.08	56.78	64.31	
10	27.86	32.49	37.90	44.21	51.54	60.06	69.93	
12	26.09	31.07	37.08	44.29	52.96	63.34	75.75	
14	24.61	29.84	36.33	44.37	54.32	66.61	81.77	
16	23.38	28.78	35.66	44.45	55.64	69.89	88.00	
4	39.40	42.32	45.40	48.65	52.08	55.69	59.49	18
6	35.70	39.58	43.81	48.43	53.48	58.97	64.94	
8	32.63	37.20	42.38	48.23	54.82	62.24	70.58	
10	30.06	35.15	41.10	48.04	56.12	65.52	76.42	
12	27.92	33.37	39.95	47.86	57.38	68.80	82.46	
14	26.14	31.83	38.91	47.70	58.59	72.07	88.72	
16	24.65	30.50	37.98	47.55	59.76	75.35	95.19	

*Market price on estimate date: $34.75. Assumptions: Normalized earnings per share (present year), $2.73; expected growth rate of earnings per share, 11 percent; expected dividend payment ratio, 60 percent; growth period, ten years; expected P/E ratio at time of sale, 14 times; discount rate, 15 percent.

From similarly constructed tables, investors can judge the sensitivity of stock valuation to changes in forecast variables. For example, let us assume that as of the date of the analysis ABC Corporation common stock was selling at $34.75 per share. This price would be justified only if, in the center section of Table 12-3, the growth rate were in fact at least 9 percent per annum. At 7 percent per annum, all other variables being held constant, the stock would be worth only $29.84. The significance of depending upon the final price-earnings multiplier can be seen by looking at the top fifth of Table 12-3, which gives values under the assumption of terminal sale at 10 times earnings. Under such conditions, the stock would have to grow for slightly more than fourteen years at an annual rate of 11 percent for value to reach the level implicit in the assumption.

The essence of the absolute approach to common stock valuation lies in the fact that a unique intrinsic value can be determined for every combination of key variables. By using Equation 5 and tables generated from it (similar to Table 12-3), investors can decide for themselves if, in the face of their personal expectations for the company, the shares are reasonably priced.

Chapter 13
Selecting Stocks for Safety

STEPHEN FELDMAN

BACKGROUND

Most investors relish the thought of quickly doubling or tripling their money in the stock market. They dream of buying a small company called Xerox at $2.25 per share and seeing it go to $295 per share or buying 100 shares of IBM at $45 per share and watching it appreciate, through stock dividends and stock splits, to almost 30,000 shares worth more than $10 million.

Although all investors desire significant capital gains, most are also acutely aware of the risks involved when they invest in stocks. Furthermore, it is often true that the stocks with the greatest opportunity for price growth may also be the most vulnerable to significant price declines. If a new company in a glamorous industry proves to be temporarily successful, its stock may temporarily increase tremendously in price. However, the mortality rate among new companies in glamour industries is quite high.

One of the most important objectives for all investors and the primary objective for many is to select stocks that have a minimum possibility of suffering severe declines in value. Investors must decide what percentage of their portfolios they wish to have in growth stocks, high-income stocks, special situations, new issues, or stocks that provide safety. (Section Ten of the *Handbook* discusses portfolio management.) However, once you have decided to place a portion of your funds in stocks that provide safety against loss, you can use the techniques discussed in this chapter to select securities that will achieve your objective.

Investors should seek protection against three types of losses. First, the economy and the stock market periodically experience cyclical downtrends that temporarily depress earnings, dividends, and stock prices. Second, and more important, is a permanent secular downtrend in the particular industry or company in which the individual has invested. Third, a firm that appears to be a growth company actually may have experienced temporary rapid growth because of a short-lived fad, and it may never be able to emerge successfully from its pioneering stage of development. Instead the firm may experience a financially painful and permanent decline.

It is impossible for any investors in the stock market to assure themselves that they will not lose money in one or more of the stocks in which they have invested. However, investors who intelligently embark on a program of investing in stocks that provide maximum protection against loss, while still providing an opportunity for a fairly good return on their investments, will probably avoid disastrous losses if a bear market should occur. In the raging bull markets that we experienced in much of the 1950s and 1960s, it was difficult *not* to make substantial profits. However, in the bear markets that were experienced in 1969–1970 and 1973–1974, many investors lost a good part or even all of their wealth. It is in this type of market that investors who have a substantial portion of their money in minimum-risk securities will be able to avoid severe financial setbacks.

CRITERIA FOR STOCK SELECTION

The investor who is interested primarily in safety may be able to select stocks on the basis of four criteria:

1. The current financial picture of a company in terms of current earnings, dividends, financial position, and market price is important for any type of stock that investors may select but is especially important for investors who are seeking safety. Promises of *future* earnings, dividends, and financial strength will not be acceptable to investors who desire safety, because any future predictions contain an element of risk. Companies with low debt-equity ratios, low price-earnings ratios, satisfactory, well-covered dividend yields, stable sales and earnings growth, and operations in a safe industry are most desirable.

2. Also significant is the historical record itself, which shows how safe specific stocks have been in the past, in terms of such desirable features as continuous payment of dividends, freedom from losses, depression resistance, price stability, and generally high quality.

3. Favorable future prospects for the company and the industry are extremely important. In selecting stocks for safety, investors are not concerned primarily with the potential growth of a company or an industry. Instead, they will desire an industry that is stable and not cyclical, presents difficult barriers to entry so that future bitter competition with young, aggressive companies is unlikely, and turns out products that will not become obsolete in the foreseeable future. Furthermore, safety-seeking investors will prefer a company that has a strong position in the industry, a stable or growing share of the market, and a progressive management team.

4. A final criterion consists of the recently recorded preferences of presumably knowledgeable professionals, primarily conservative institutional investors and sometimes inside officer-directors buying and selling shares of their own companies. It is desirable to watch the transactions of professionals in securities because they often have knowledge or insights about eroding strengths and developing weaknesses of historically strong companies that have not yet been portrayed in the financial statements.

Current Financial Position

The first of the above-mentioned methods that can be used to select stocks for safety is to analyze the current financial position of the company in question. A satisfactory, well-protected dividend yield is, of course, desirable for an investor who is seeking high current income, but, it is also extremely important for an investor whose primary concern is safety. This is true for two reasons. First, if the company is able to avoid cutting its dividends during a major stock market reversal, then as the stock declines in price, the dividend yield becomes higher. At some point the dividend yield will be high enough to support the price level of the company's stock, regardless of what conditions prevail in the stock market. This condition will often occur when the dividend yield from the stock is as high as the interest yield on bonds that are outstanding from the same company. Of course, dividend payments are less certain than bond interest, but investors may anticipate that a secure company will increase its dividends at some future point after the recession. Furthermore, they hope for increases in stock prices. These positive factors will often prevent the dividend yield from rising above the yield on corporate bonds. In addition, once the dividend yield for a high-quality company is above the yield on deposits in savings banks, investors will withdraw funds from their savings accounts and purchase stock in the company. This will further support the price level of the stock.

For example, let us assume that the stock in a company has a market price of $50 per share and pays dividends of $4 per share, which is equal to 8 percent. Let us further assume that this is a high-quality company and that its bonds pay interest of 10 percent. In a bear market, as prices begin to fall, the price of the stock will be protected by its high dividend yield. If the stock declines to a price below $44.44, it will be yielding more than 9 percent, and some investors may switch funds from a savings account into the stock. Certainly investors who own the stock will hesitate to sell because it will be hard to find a more attractive yield elsewhere with the same degree of risk. If the price were to fall to $40 per share, the yield would be 10 percent, and some investors in the corporation's bonds might switch to the stock, from which they could earn an equivalent yield with an improved opportunity for capital appreciation.

The second attractive factor about consistently adequate dividends for investors is that payouts of cash dividends are tangible proof that the company is generating enough cash to pay the dividends. Income statements can be quite misleading. A company can use different approaches to such items as inventory valuation, depreciation, the pension fund, past service liabilities, and expensing versus capitalizing outlays in such a way as to control reported net income, at least for a limited period of time. (This topic is discussed in greater detail in Chapter 10.) However, a company that is paying cash dividends must have the funds to make these payments, and this adds to the credibility of its statements.

Investors who rely heavily on dividends face the risk that these dividends can be cut at any time. However, some companies have a record of rarely, if ever, cutting dividends, and lists of such companies are available from most brokers or investment advisers.

The second and possibly most important current factor that investors will analyze is the earnings per share (EPS) and the price-earnings (P/E) ratio of a company. If either the EPS or the P/E ratio declines when the other is not rising, the price of the stock will decline. Furthermore, since the P/E ratio is largely dependent on future earnings growth, a decline in the EPS may cause a simultaneous decline in the P/E ratio, and this combination will significantly depress the price of the stock. For a glamour company with a P/E ratio of 30, 40, or 50 (in the case of companies that have been losing money or earning 1 or 2 cents per share and selling at relatively high prices, the P/E is technically infinite), the possibility of a sharp price decline is more likely than with a stable company experiencing slow but steady growth and commanding a P/E of 10 or less.

The investor should determine how a particular company's price-earnings ratio compares with those of other companies in the same industry or similar industries in the economy. Generally, a company with a relatively low P/E ratio will be less vulnerable to a severe decline in the price of its stock than will a company with a high P/E ratio. This is true because when there is a bear market or when there is bad news about a particular company, investors begin to scrutinize the company's

P/E closely. If the ratio is inflated, it may fall significantly. On the other hand, a company with a conservative P/E will experience less of a decline. However, investors should be aware that often there is a good reason for a company to have a low P/E: its earnings may be declining, or it may be losing its share of the market. In these types of cases the stock is not an attractive buy.

Investors who seek stocks with low P/E ratios must determine whether these ratios are unjustly low and the stocks are truly good buys or whether there is some underlying cause for the low ratios.

The third factor that the investor should analyze in dealing with the company's current financial position is the degree of leverage in its capital structure. A company may have experienced rapid growth of earnings per share because of a high degree of leverage. However, in a recessionary period, this type of company has high fixed charges that can cause a rapid reduction in earnings per share. Furthermore, in a period of tight money, this type of company may find it difficult to refinance its debt and be faced with either bankruptcy or the necessity of selling off assets in order to pay its liabilities. Investors interested in safety would generally be prudent to select stocks of companies with moderate amounts of debt.

A company with a record of increasing sales and earnings in recent years is a strong attraction for the safety-minded investor. This is especially true if the growth has been stable, not erratic, and if the increase in sales has occurred because of an increase in the volume of business and not merely because of a rise in the selling price. A company whose sales and earnings have been stagnant or declining will generally not be an attractive investment for investors who are concerned with safety because it may be at the beginning of a secular or cyclical downtrend. It is often hoped that a particular company will experience a rebound, or turnaround, in earnings. However, these hopes are not to be borne by safety-conscious investors.

If sales are growing and earnings are constant or declining, this is an indication that expenses are rising at a faster rate than sales, which may be an ominous sign for the future. On the other hand, if earnings are growing when sales are not, this may indicate that the company has embarked on a major cost-cutting effort. However, excess costs cannot be reduced indefinitely because eventually all the fat will be stripped away. At that point further increases in profits may be difficult to generate. For these reasons, it is most desirable to see sales and earnings grow in concert.

Sales growth that is almost totally dependent on price increases is also not desirable because this often occurs in a stagnant industry. Volume is no longer increasing, and price increases are the only means of increasing sales. Furthermore, prices cannot continue to increase indefinitely without causing an increase in competition from within the same industry, from competing industries, or from foreign corporations. This is precisely what happened to the steel industry in the early 1970s; as it increased prices, volume failed to increase, and competition from other industries and foreign companies proliferated.

Historical Performance

The second method that should be used in selecting stocks for safety is to study the historical record of the company under consideration. The investor will prefer companies that have outstanding historical performance and excellent marketability.

The ability of a company to pay dividends in every year since 1930 is an excellent test of its historical earning ability. Those years cover the Great Depression of the early 1930s and the sharp slump of 1937; the defense preparations for

World War II; the war years; the period of postwar dislocation and boom; the 1948–1949 recession; the Korean War boom of 1950–1953; and the recessions of 1953–1954, 1957–1958, 1960–1962, 1970–1971, and 1973–1975. Firms that not only survived but prospered through all these vicissitudes warrant investors' attention especially if investors are interested in regular income in addition to safety. In the event of another recession, investors have a better chance of continued dividend income from these companies than from firms that are not so well tested. In addition to paying dividends every year, many companies have a history of increasing dividends on a regular basis and of almost never reducing dividends except under extreme conditions. These companies are especially attractive because if the dividends are not cut, the dividend yield will rise as the stock price falls.

Of course, a company's past record is not an absolute guarantee of its future. Managements may change for the worse, and whole industries may decline as markets change. Therefore, before buying a stock solely on its past record, you should check the future prospects of the company and the industry.

More impressive than even the continuous dividend payers are those companies that have paid dividends since 1930 and have never shown a loss in the entire period. In other words, all or at least part of the dividends in each of the years came from current income.

Relatively few stocks are completely recession-proof, but, many companies are recession-resistant, in the sense that they operate primarily in industries with stable rather than cyclical demand patterns. Utilities, food chains, dairy products, candy companies, container companies, and finance companies are some of the types of companies that tend to be stable as opposed to cyclical.

Another standard of safety increasingly used by analytical investors is price stability, often specified in terms of low price variance or volatility. "Beta" is the term currently used to express a stock's price volatility compared with that of the market as a whole. In this approach, the accent is on the market price behavior of a stock rather than on the economic performance of the company itself. Thus, the stock of a noncyclical company could show considerable price variance for special reasons, while the stock of an essentially cyclical company could show relatively low price variance for a considerable period. Beta is discussed in depth in Chapter 3.

The stocks of even the most defensive, noncyclical companies are likely to decline sharply in price during a general bear market. In such a period the investor holding recession-resistant stocks for income must be prepared to sit through some relatively sharp, although presumably temporary, declines.

Value Line Investment Survey and other services publish price volatility measures for the stocks they evaluate, and investors who are primarily concerned with safety would generally seek issues with minimum volatility ratings.

Corporate and municipal bonds have long been rated fairly uniformly as to quality by the leading security statistical services. It is only in recent years, however, that systematic attempts have been made to rate common stocks in terms of clearly defined quality standards, in large part reflecting the safety criteria and measures previously discussed.

The complicated statistical procedures used by various services and investment advisers to obtain their stock quality ratings are far from identical. Different weights are given by the several organizations to such factors as (1) past earnings growth; (2) the consistency or reliability of such growth and its presumed implications for the future; (3) past dividend stability and growth; and (4) past price stability. As a result of these differences, the same stock can get the very highest quality rating from one service and a somewhat lower rating from another, equally reliable one. Conversely, if two or more services, using somewhat different techniques, agree that a stock is of the very highest quality, that stock clearly warrants the closest scrutiny of safety-minded investors.

Future Prospects

In addition to analyzing the current financial position of the company and its past history, it is also important to inspect its future prospects. A company may have a fine past history and a strong current financial position, but its future prospects may be rather bleak. An entire industry may be faced with a shrinking market, foreign competition, or a price-cost squeeze. An individual company may experience young aggressive competition, a declining share of the market, or obsolete management that is not developing new products or new ideas.

The first thing that investors should do is to evaluate the future of the industry. If they are interested primarily in safety, they should not be concerned mainly with finding an industry that has a potential for rapid growth. Instead, they want an industry that is almost certain to have a stable rate of growth and is unlikely to experience a decline. An analysis of future growth prospects for the industry can take place in two steps. Investors would want to know, first, what the total potential demand for the industry's products will be in the future and, second, what share of this potential demand will go to the particular industry in question and what share to competing industries. For example, the demand for travel in the United States appears to be growing with the population and the level of education. However, this does not mean that there will be more passengers in railroads, airplanes, and buses alike. The transportation industry in its broadest sense may be growing, but, the passenger railroad industry may be declining.

Another potential problem that an industry may face is a cost-price squeeze. This can be a difficult problem in a labor-intensive industry, because if labor costs are 60, 70, or 80 percent of the firm's total costs and are rising more rapidly than prices, a cost-price squeeze may develop. An investor can calculate the growth in a corporation's labor costs and the growth in its sales for the past five years. If labor costs are growing more rapidly than sales and if profit margins are declining, a cost-price squeeze may be developing.

Even if the industry appears to have a growing market and costs are rising at a moderate rate, individual companies in the industry may still be suffering from excessive competition. This competition will often be generated from one of two sources: foreign competition and new firms entering the market. If foreign producers have a small but growing share of a particular market, this can be a sign of future increased competition as these producers attempt to enlarge their share of the market. Furthermore, if there are no stringent barriers to entry, either in the form of high start-up costs, scarce patent rights, or another such obstacle, small companies may proliferate throughout the industry and cause severe competition for the well-established companies. An ideal industry for investors concerned with safety will have some immunity to foreign competition combined with difficult barriers to entry.

In addition, investors would desire a large company with a growing or stable share of a growing market. The company should also be progressive and be willing to spend money on research and development. A company can improve its short-run profit picture by skimping on R&D expenditures, but this will probably damage long-term profits.

Authoritarian Support and Insider Holdings

A fourth criterion that can be used in selecting stocks for safety is the actions of corporate insiders (officers and directors of publicly owned companies) and large institutional investors such as successful conservative mutual funds. Although this is not a fundamentally sound method of stock selection, it should not be ignored, because these professionals are often aware of information that has not yet come to the public's attention. Furthermore, corporate insiders and conservative funds usually do not buy a stock with the intention of selling it a few weeks later. When they purchase a stock, they will probably hold it for a reasonably long period of time. Therefore, this method provides average investors with a means of buying the same stock with only a minimum risk that they are buying a stock that insiders have already begun to sell. However, because of the tenuous nature of this type of selection procedure, it should always be used in concert with the methods previously described.

Probably the most popular authoritarian approach is to buy "the stocks the experts pick and the novices wish they had." The largest single group of investment experts undoubtedly consists of mutual funds and closed-end investment companies subject to public regulation. Vickers Associates, Inc., investment dealers and publishers of the *Guide to Investment Company Portfolios,* compile a quarterly box score of "the favorite fifty" stocks of more than 400 investment companies. Since 1950 prices of Vickers Associates' favorite fifty have, taken together, risen almost 3 times as rapidly as the Dow Jones Industrial Average.

To achieve similar results, investors will wish to give special attention to issues that are rising rapidly in the experts' esteem, as well as those that have entered the ranks of the top favorites for the first time. Since some investment companies may change their portfolios suddenly, investors should check the latest holdings, as shown in the companies' most recent quarterly reports.

The over-the-counter market of more than 25,000 issues, more than 5,000 of which are actively traded, is the world's largest securities market. It has long been the proving ground for many stocks that eventually are listed on the New York Stock Exchange or the American Stock Exchange and become investment favorites and institutional blue chips. For this reason, the over-the-counter issues chosen by top investment companies can provide interesting leads for safety or authoritarian investors who also want some of the zest and profit of above-average earnings growth. Vickers Associates reports the twenty-five industrial and utility common stocks traded over the counter that are most widely held, in terms of dollar value, by approximately 500 mutual funds and closed-end investment companies.

The great gap between ownership of a publicly held corporation by many thousands of individual stockholders and its management by a comparative handful of executives and directors has been widely commented upon. Many top executives in United States corporations own little or no stock of the companies they manage. How can such executives effectively hold the interest of their stockholders as paramount?

This doubt has led some investors to prefer companies whose officers and directors own a substantial number of shares in the companies they manage. Executives who are also large stockholders will probably be more conscious of stockholders' interests. Their stock ownership is also a powerful additional incentive for them to do a better management job, since their own fortunes frequently depend on it. It is usually evidence of their faith in the long-term future of their firms.

Indeed, this standard is an excellent test of a good growth stock. If a company really has good long-term growth potentialities, its top officers will surely be particularly aware of it. Thus, they should be heavy investors in their own company.

However, there are also some drawbacks to this approach:

1. Big stock ownership by a company's management may lead to stingy

dividend payments for personal tax reasons. Investors interested in income will want to watch this factor.

2. Death of an owner-executive may throw large blocks of stock on the market because of the need for cash to pay estate taxes. This could depress the price of the stock.

3. Family-managed concerns run by second-, third-, and fourth-generation descendants of the founder are often comparatively inefficient. The officers and directors may have inherited their jobs rather than won them on merit. Professional nonfamily management is usually more efficient than such later-generation family operation.

Another approach along the same line is to study changes in officer-director stockholdings as a clue to future price trends. The idea is that you will make money in stocks if you follow closely the moves of insiders, who supposedly know earliest and best what is going on in their companies. If such insiders are buying heavily, this ordinarily means that they expect the price of the stocks to rise. If they are substantial sellers, the reverse is usually true.

Since 1934 the Securities and Exchange Commission (SEC) has required monthly reports of stock purchases and sales by officer-directors of all listed companies. Since 1965 the larger unlisted companies have had to file similar reports. These reports must show purchases or sales of company stock made in the preceding month as well as the number of shares held at the end of the month. Beneficial owners of more than 10 percent of a regulated stock must also report.

Investors can now learn what the insiders of any company subject to SEC control are doing with their stock by checking a monthly SEC report, *Official Summary of Security Transactions and Holdings,* which can be obtained from the Superintendent of Documents, Washington, D.C. 20402. As republished a week or so later in *The Wall Street Journal* and in many investment letters and services, such changes in officer-director stockholdings are sometimes clues to the insiders' evaluation of future prospects for their companies. In addition, especially large sales by insiders often take the form of secondary distributions, which are announced and promoted by stockbrokers or investment bankers.

As a rule, while insiders may be well informed about what is going to develop in their own companies, they are not necessarily equally shrewd about the future behavior of either their own stock, the industry group to which it belongs, or the market as a whole. Like other investors, they also often buy or sell too soon or too late. In particular, during long bull markets, insiders, having usually acquired their shares at very low prices, often start to sell well before the top of the bull move. However, substantial blocks of stock in secondary offerings by insiders late in a bull market are pretty reliable clues to a subsequent drop in the price of the stock.

Of course, much buying and selling by insiders is of no particular significance for investors. On the buying side, a corporation executive may simply be exercising stock options. Such options are often worth exercising even if the outlook for a company is not especially bright. On the selling side, corporate insiders frequently sell small portions of their extensive holdings to raise needed cash, to gain greater investment diversification, or to carry out desirable estate planning. Such sales do not necessarily signify any expectation of a change for the worse in their companies' prospects.

Accordingly, if you follow insider transactions, you should evaluate them in terms of their size, frequency, and purpose (if ascertainable). You should also relate them to the current technical position of the stock, the industry group, and the market as a whole, particularly because reports on insider transactions often do not become public until well after they have been made.

CONCLUSIONS

Investors who are concerned primarily with selecting stocks for safety should attempt to select stocks based on four criteria: a strong current financial position, a history of stability and quality, good future prospects, and the actions of insiders and professional investors. They should avoid buying stocks based on criteria such as technical indicators, turnaround situations, an analysis of an unproven company with a potentially valuable new patent or product, and hot tips.

Chapter 14
Selecting Stocks for Income

LEO BARNES

When Even Well-to-Do Investors Should Seek Income

Many if not most investors reinvest all or most of their investment income. For them, current income should not be a major objective, even though for most people it is pleasant indeed (until income tax time comes around) to receive dividend or interest checks on a regular basis. As long as dividends and interest are taxed about twice as severely as realized long-term capital gains, investing for income will not, in the long run, provide the *maximum net aftertax return.* So why invest for income at all when it is not needed for living expenses?

The answer is suggested by the old proverb "A bird in hand is worth two in the bush." As the late sixties and early seventies have amply demonstrated, neither uninterrupted capital appreciation nor regularly realized capital gains can be relied on. So we invest for income, even though it may not be needed for daily living, in order to succeed in our investing at those times when few if any capital gains are to be realized, typically when the stock market is static, sluggish, or declining.

Who Should Almost Always Invest for Income?

Clearly, the investment objective of continuous income is most important for those investors, notably retired persons and nonworking widows, for whom securities can provide a major proportion of their current living expenses. Similarly, for preparatory purposes, individuals approaching retirement should be learning how to utilize the income approach to obtain regular and adequate income from their investments.

At the other end of the age scale, investment accounts for the benefit of minor children or students can be either tax-free or very favorably taxed and therefore can benefit from regular income receipts. Many such small investment accounts can be completely free of income tax or are taxed at the lowest rates. Moreover, in the case of a dependent who is under nineteen at the end of the parents' tax year or who, regardless of age, is a full-time student for at least five months of the year, the standard deduction can still be claimed for the child's account when figuring the tax, since it need be based only on earned income such as wages and salaries and not on investment income. Because of this tax edge, such smaller investment accounts may properly be concerned with higher-yielding income securities.

Advantages of Income Securities for Tax-exempt or Tax-favored Institutions

Because of their preferential tax position, pension and profit sharing funds, employee stock ownership plans (ESOPs), university endowments, private charitable and educational foundations, museums, and other tax-exempt institutions will often find income securities more advantageous than low-yielding growth stocks. For such institutions, above-average current income from dividends or interest can be reinvested tax-free (or nearly so), for a steadier and possibly larger long-term return than that from variable and uncertain capital gains.

This is true for private foundations also, despite the fact that they are subject to a relatively small (4 percent as of 1976) tax on net investment income.

Dividend Income Highly Tax-favored for Corporations

A corporation normally pays income tax on only 15 percent of taxable cash dividends received from other domestic corporations on either their common or their preferred stock. This means that, for large public corporations, the corporate tax (1976 rates) on such dividends is only 7.2 percent (48 percent of 15 percent). This compares with 48 percent on equivalent interest income and a flat 30 percent on long-term capital gains.

Alternative Investment Media for Income Investors

There was a time (before 1958) when stocks almost always yielded more than bonds, mortgages, certificates of deposit, short-term notes, or commercial paper. This was the case even at or near bull market peaks, when interest rates tended to be high and stock yields low. In the sixties and seventies, however, this has not been the situation, even at or near bear market lows, when stock yields are relatively high and interest rates relatively low. Apparently, the higher current yields of bonds, mortgages, and other fixed-income instruments are supposed to be more than offset by the combined prospect of (1) rising future dividends from common stocks and (2), for taxable investors, common stocks' tax-favored long-term capital gain potential.

However, many income investors have been skeptical of the likelihood of these two offsets, particularly of the second. As a result, they have increasingly settled for the safety and high yields of bonds, mortgages, and other fixed-income or fixed-asset investments. These are reviewed in other sections of the *Handbook*. So are mutual funds that specialize in such investments, whether long-term, short-term, or both. Here we analyze only the potentials and advantages of common stocks as income vehicles.

Use the accompanying work sheet to compare available current income yields from major categories of securities, mortgages, and mutual funds.

Which Combination of Income Targets Is for You?

When buying common stocks for income, investors can focus on one or several of four different targets: (1) safe, stable, and regular income, now and in the future; (2) large near-term income; (3) large long-term income; and (4) slowly but steadily rising future income. The first target is discussed in Chapter 13; the other three targets are the subject of this chapter.

WORK SHEET: WHAT AFTERTAX YIELDS ARE CURRENTLY AVAILABLE?

To determine what you can currently earn after federal, state, and local income taxes from major types of securities, fixed assets, and mutual funds, use this work sheet. Most investments are fully taxed, a few escape federal income taxes, others are free from state and local taxes, and a very few are exempt from all income taxes. Refer to Chapter 47 for details on how to figure your net marginal tax rate after paying all applicable income taxes.

Type of Investment	Approximate Current Yield Range	
	Before Tax	Net after Tax
Stocks		
Industrial common	_____	_____
Utility common	_____	_____
Transportation common	_____	_____
Preferreds (nonconvertible)	_____	_____
Preferreds (convertible)	_____	_____
Other	_____	_____
Mutual Funds		
Stock income fund	_____	_____
Taxable bond income fund	_____	_____
Tax-exempt bond fund	_____	_____
Other	_____	_____
Bonds and Fixed Assets		
United States Treasury bills	_____	_____
United States governments (short-term)	_____	_____
United States governments (intermediate)	_____	_____
United States governments (long-term)	_____	_____
Tax-exempt bonds (A-rated)	_____	_____
Tax-exempt bonds (BBB-rated)	_____	_____
United States savings bonds	_____	_____
Bank savings accounts	_____	_____
Bank certificates of deposit:		
Less than $100,000	_____	_____
More than $100,000	_____	_____
Commercial paper, 30 to 270 days	_____	_____
Corporate bonds (AAA)	_____	_____
Industrial bonds (A)	_____	_____
Utility bonds (A)	_____	_____
Transportation bonds (BBB)	_____	_____
Income bonds (BBB)	_____	_____
Real estate first mortgages	_____	_____
Real estate second mortgages	_____	_____
Ginny Mae certificates	_____	_____
Convertible bonds	_____	_____
Other	_____	_____

Utilizing Capital Gains for Additional Tax-favored Income

A dollar of realized long-term capital gain is worth somewhat more than a dollar of fully taxable income even in the lowest tax bracket and substantially, and increasingly, more in the higher tax brackets. Accordingly, capital gains, if and when available, should not be ignored or neglected by income investors. (See Chapter 56 for the relative aftertax benefits of capital gains in different tax brackets.)

It is a fact that because of technical price actions and reactions, seasonal stock market influences, and other erratic market influences most common stocks will, in any year, move up and down at least once, and often more frequently, by an amount usefully greater than their annual dividends. Alert income investors can take frequent advantage of these swings.

If you are reluctant to trade frequently or periodically, intermediate market swings can be utilized to upgrade income portfolios. When six-months-plus capital gains are available, special attention can be paid to the sale of less promising holdings, thus reaping a tax-favored capital gain in the process of upgrading.

Sometimes, too, it may be advantageous for income investors to take a capital gain instead of a dividend when a holding shows a big increase in price in the period just before its ex-dividend date. Even after paying commissions and transfer taxes, the net gain from missing the dividend will frequently be larger than the dividend and be taxable at lower capital gain rates. This technique will work best either with stocks paying dividends annually or semiannually rather than quarterly or monthly or just before an especially large special or extra distribution. Because the dividend in such cases is larger, so is the usual prior price advance. The same technique can also be used with high-yielding income bonds that pay interest only once a year.

Risk Rankings for High-yielding Stocks

In selecting common stocks for above-average yield, you should be fully alert to the risks involved. A stock returning appreciably more than the average yield is often risky and almost always worrisome. Therefore, it is useful to classify high-yielding stock options and opportunities in the following groups, listed in order of increasing risk and probable yield. Before investing in a high-yielding stock, you should be able to explain why it is selling at an above-average yield. Utilize the following fivefold classification:

1. *Neglected blue chips.* These are well-established companies that have fallen into disfavor for one reason or another, so that their yields are significantly above those of the blue-chip averages. In selecting such issues, it is wise to use additional precautionary filters, such as the following: (*a*) satisfactory coverage of the anticipated dividend, which should be less than two-thirds of the expected year-ahead earnings per share; (*b*) continuous regular payment of dividends for the past twenty or more years; (*c*) no cuts in dividends for the past five years; and (*d*) a reasonable debt-equity ratio in terms of industry averages, showing that the company is not overburdened with debt.

2. *Neglected smaller companies, or "red chips."* These are lesser-known firms with good earnings records that have been bypassed by institutional and larger individual investors, so that they sell at low P/E ratios and above-average dividend yields. They may have been founded in the forties or fifties and are thus not fully seasoned, but they are often in sound industries and will probably eventually sell at a lower yield.

3. *Companies in unfashionable industries.* Periodically, an industry will fall into disfavor with many investors and continue to be unpopular long after the original (and valid) reason has lapsed. Careful income-oriented investors are often able to take advantage of such neglect and choose from a number of high-yielding companies in the industry group. In 1974–1975, electric utilities were good examples of companies in this category.

4. *Companies with temporary sags in earnings.* If an earnings decline is deemed only temporary and if the reduced earnings still adequately cover the existing and expected regular dividend, a company in such a situation may be very attractive for its large yield. Maximum returns will come if the stock is purchased shortly

after its price has dropped sharply in anticipation of the drop in earnings or when the drop is first made public.

5. *Companies temporarily reducing dividends.* Before investing in this most risky type of situation, be certain that the dividend cut is only temporary and that the current yield from the reduced dividend is still well above average.

How to Arrange for Regular Monthly Income

A handful of companies go to the trouble and expense of paying their dividends monthly with the intention of attracting income investors, but the vast majority of companies pay dividends quarterly or semiannually. Therefore, investors who wish to regularize their dividend income must do it themselves.

The best way is probably to use a special dividend savings account that pays interest from the day of deposit to the day of withdrawal. You can write to the treasurers of the companies from which you receive dividends or bond interest and request that payments be sent directly to your bank for immediate credit to your account. The bank will promptly send you a credit notice for each payment received.

Every month, you can withdraw from this account approximately one-twelfth of the total expected annual income from your securities. (Alternatively, you might even withdraw one-fifty-second each week!) By using this technique, you may select the securities that will provide the maximum safe annual income without concerning yourself with the exact time of the year they happen to pay dividends.

Most mutual funds provide similar regular withdrawal options for their shareholders. Likewise, if your stockbroker holds your stocks for you, you can arrange to have a stipulated sum paid each month from dividends received out of your credit balance (or from your debit balance, if it is adequate under prevailing margin requirements).

Stocks That Boost Dividends Persistently for Regularly Rising Future Income or for Large Eventual Income

Steadily rising income in the years ahead has become an essential for almost everyone in an inflationary world. However, it is a particularly suitable and necessary investment target for older investors who wish to retire gradually or in several stages. Similarly, some investors wish or require a specific income starting at some future date, for example, at retirement or when a son or daughter enters college. Stocks of companies that boost their dividends persistently are ideal for both these investment purposes.

Most brokers can provide you with useful lists of regularly dividend-boosting companies that have never cut their dividends in recent years. These are the firms most likely to continue this record in the future even though, of course, their *earnings* are apt occasionally to decline from the prior year. Unfortunately, the stocks of most of these companies tend to provide a lower current return than that available from more ordinary companies, thus partly or substantially offsetting their long-term dividend uptrends.

Most companies on such lists are apt to be in growth industries, but some are in relatively cyclical industries and therefore sell at lower prices and provide higher yields. For firms in such industries to show a steady rise in dividend payments, uninterrupted by dividend cuts, suggests the presence of excellent, aggressive managements.

For many companies that boost dividends persistently, dividend increases often come with the help of stock dividends, with the prior dividend rate being continued or even raised on the increased number of shares.

Chapter 15
What to Do about New Issues

FRANK K. REILLY

THE COMMON STOCK NEW-ISSUE MARKET

New issues typically have been divided into two groups, *seasoned* new issues and *unseasoned* new issues. Seasoned new issues are sales of new stock (previously unissued) by a corporation that already has stock traded on the public market. An example would be the sale of a new issue of common stock by General Motors. The stock being sold is new, but there is a prevailing market for the firm's currently outstanding stock. In some cases, writers have even referred to the sales of outstanding stock in a secondary offering as a new issue if the stock is sold through investment banking channels.

In contrast to seasoned new issues, unseasoned new issues are new issues of companies without previously public stock. Put another way, prior to the offering there was *no public market* for the stock of this firm. The unseasoned new-issue offering can arise when a firm has been in business for several years and basically has been privately owned until the new-issue offering. The new issue can also arise because the firm needs a large amount of new capital or certain owners desire to sell some part of their holdings, or from a combination of the two reasons.

It is not necessary that the firm issuing the stock be new or unseasoned. An example of a very well-known company that "went public" after many years of business was the Ford Motor Company. Ford had been in business for more than fifty years before its first public offering in the late 1950s. When the stock was sold, it was an unseasoned new issue: prior to the offering there had been no public market for the Ford Motor Company.

The important point is that in the case of an unseasoned new issue there is *no prior public market* for the stock. As a consequence, the offering price is determined by negotiation between the issuing firm and the investment banking firm underwriting the new issue.

In this chapter of the *Handbook,* although there may be references to seasoned new issues, the major discussion will be concerned with unseasoned new issues.

WHY UNSEASONED NEW ISSUES SHOULD YIELD SUPERIOR RETURNS

There are two major reasons why investors might expect to experience superior returns from a portfolio of unseasoned new stock issues compared with a portfolio of seasoned outstanding issues. The first is that they might expect underwriters to have a downward bias in their pricing of new issues which would lead to superior returns in the short run as investors adjusted for this bias. The second reason is the higher risk involved in these new stocks.

Underwriter Pricing Strategy

As mentioned, one might expect investors in unseasoned new issues to experience superior returns in the short run because of the anticipation of a downward bias in the pricing of new stock issues by underwriters. This bias is due to the following circumstances:

1. Because of the unseasoned nature of new issues, underwriters are uncertain of the public's evaluation of the firm's past earnings stream and the corporation outlook.

2. Underwriters will tend to underprice the issue to ensure a "successful" issue. In this context, *successful* applies to an offering that is quickly sold, is possibly oversubscribed, and enjoys some increase in price soon after the offering. Such an offering results in satisfied customers for the underwriter as well as satisfied corporate stockholders.

3. A successful issue sells quickly, which is important to the underwriters since they must borrow large amounts to purchase it. Investment banking firms have relatively small capital bases for the amount of underwriting undertaken and are therefore heavily dependent on a rapid turnover of their capital. Rapid turnover, for its part, is contingent upon quick sales of all issues, especially new issues, the high-risk segment of the underwriting business.

4. Under the supervision of the Securities and Exchange Commission (SEC), underwriters are permitted to purchase and sell a new issue to stabilize the price. This stabilizing action is desirable because it reduces unnecessary price fluctuation, but it is time-consuming and ties up underwriting capital. Such stabilizing action is minimized by a successful issue that does not require support.

5. In some cases underwriters for new issues receive part of their fee in stock or are given options to purchase a block of the new-issue stock at the original offering price. Therefore, they benefit directly from a successful issue.

The only constraint on the underpricing of a new stock issue is a possible complaint by the issuing corporation that it could have received more capital from the issue. Such a concern is minimized by the following factors:

1. The new stockholders are satisfied with their purchase of the successful issue.

2. The corporate officers, like the underwriters, often receive stock options with prices close to the original offering price. Given these options, they likewise benefit directly and immediately from a successful issue that rises to a premium.

3. Corporations do not attempt to fill all their planned capital needs in the initial offering. They know that they can float future stock issues at a higher price to a satisfied stockholder group and possibly to an eager public.

Differential Risk in New Issues

Although it is not necessary that a new stock issue be issued by a new company, this is the case in many instances. Therefore, the investor in new stock issues not only is acquiring an unseasoned stock but also is acquiring a relatively unseasoned firm.

The initial stage in a firm's life cycle, sometimes labeled the "pioneer" stage, is characterized by rapid growth, but the firm is also plagued by heavy competition, and there is a high probability of bankruptcy.[1] Given this greater uncertainty of success or failure, investors should require and receive a higher than normal rate of return on the stock issues of these new firms.

EMPIRICAL STUDIES OF RETURNS ON UNSEASONED NEW STOCK ISSUES

This discussion of empirical studies will consider initially several studies that analyzed *short-run* returns on unseasoned new issues. In addition to studies that concentrated on returns during different types of market periods (rising and falling stock prices), there will be a discussion of studies concerned with how fast new-issue prices adjust and also a consideration of an alternative decision rule regarding the purchase of new issues in the short run. Then there will be a discussion of studies that examined the *long-run* returns on new stock issues.

Unseasoned New Issues in a Rising Stock Market

In recent years there has been a growing interest in the study of returns from unseasoned new issues. A study by Reilly and Hatfield examined the relative performances of fifty-three new issues sold during the period from December 1963 to June 1965.[2] The performances were tested by examining percentage price changes for the sample of new issues compared with percentage price changes in the Dow Jones Industrial Average (DJIA), the National Quotation Bureau Over-the-Counter Industrial Average (OTCIA or NQBIA), and a randomly selected sample of over-the-counter (OTC) stocks. The comparisons were made for three periods of time: (1) from the offering to the first Friday following the offering, (2) from the offering to the fourth Friday following the offering, and (3) from the offering to the Friday one year after the offering.

The DJIA and the OTCIA were employed because prior studies had indicated that short-run, as well as long-run, changes in the price indicator series for the New York Stock Exchange do *not* conform to similar changes for the major price indicator series for the over-the-counter market.[3] Therefore, since all the new issues were initially traded on the OTC market and most of them continued to be traded there during the first year, and since there are differences in price movements in the different market segments, it was considered appropriate to compare the new issues with an OTC market indicator series. Further justification was derived from correlations of monthly percentage price changes for each new issue with percentage price changes for the DJIA and the OTCIA. The correlations for the new issues with the OTCIA were always higher than the DJIA correlations and usually by substantial margins.

In addition to the greater price movement conformity, the use of the OTC

---

[1] For a discussion of the industrial life cycle, see Steven E. Bolten, *Security Analysis and Portfolio Management,* Holt, Rinehart and Winston, Inc., New York, 1972, pp. 107–114; J. B. Cohen, E. D. Zinbarg, and A. Zeikel, *Investment Analysis and Portfolio Management,* 2d ed., Richard D. Irwin, Inc., Homewood, Ill., 1973, pp. 270–274.

[2] Frank K. Reilly and Kenneth Hatfield, "Investor Experience with New Stock Issues," *Financial Analysts Journal,* vol. 25, no. 5, pp. 73–80, September–October 1969.

[3] An examination of short-run price changes is contained in Frank K. Reilly, "Evidence Regarding a Segmented Stock Market," *Journal of Finance,* vol. 27, no. 3, pp. 607–625, June 1972. Long-run price change differences are examined in Frank K. Reilly, "Price Changes in NYSE, AMEX and OTC Stocks Compared," *Financial Analysts Journal,* vol. 27, no. 2, pp. 54–59, March–April 1971.

series contributes to the solution of the risk differential problem. As noted, it is very likely that the great bulk of the new issues are sold by relatively new firms, which one would expect to be of higher risk than the blue-chip stocks included in the DJIA. Although the thirty-five OTC stocks included in the OTCIA are considered the blue chips of the OTC market, they obviously are closer in risk to the new issues than the DJIA.

The individual new issues were examined in relation to randomly selected individual OTC stocks because of the problem of comparing individual stocks to a *portfolio* of stocks, which is what averages are. Obviously the price changes for individual stocks will show much greater variation. Further, it seems somewhat intuitive that an individual investor does not consider his alternative to the purchase of a given new issue to be a portfolio of stocks (from the New York Stock Exchange or the OTC market) but rather an individual stock of commensurate

TABLE 15-1   Average Percentage Changes for New Issues Offered during a Rising Stock Market Compared with Percentage Changes in Alternative Market Indicator Series and Randomly Selected OTC Stocks

	Friday after offering	Fourth Friday after offering	Year after offering
Average percentage change in all new issues	+9.9	+8.7	+43.7
Average percentage change in the OTCIA	+0.3	+0.9	+23.1
Average percentage change in the DJIA	+0.3	+0.5	+ 6.8
Average percentage change in randomly selected OTC stocks	+0.9	+2.2	+32.5

risk. Therefore, in addition to comparing new issues with the aggregate market, the individual new issues were also compared with randomly selected stocks from the OTC market.

The results were examined in terms of the *number* of new issues that outperformed the market indicator series and the *extent* of the performance. Regarding the number of new issues, it was expected that half of the new issues would outperform the two market indicator series on a random basis. The results generally confirmed this expectation: just about half of the new issues did better than the two market indicator series, while about half did not do as well.

In addition to examining the number of new issues that gained or lost relative to the market, the extent of gain or loss relative to the market was considered. The examination of relative gains and losses of new issues compared with the indicator series revealed that while about half of the new issues did not do as well as the market indicator series, the relative percentage losses were quite small. In contrast, the relative gains for the new issues compared with the indicator series were quite substantial. The result was that the *average percentage change in price for the new issues was significantly greater than the average price change for the two market indicator series,* as shown in Table 15-1.

The comparison of the new issues and randomly selected stocks generated approximately the same results. Again, in terms of numbers there was no difference in performance. As before, the losses of the new issues relative to the randomly selected stocks were rather limited while the relative gains were substantial. As a result, the *average price change on the new issues was substantially higher than the average price change for the randomly selected over-the-counter issues,* as shown in Table 15-1.

New Issues in a Declining Stock Market

Because the time period covered by the initial study was mainly a period of rising stock prices, it was considered appropriate to examine the performance of new issues during a period of generally declining stock prices. A second study examined the relative performance of sixty-two new issues sold just prior to the 1966 market decline.[4] Therefore, the performance of the new issues during the year after the offering would be affected by the market decline. A summary of the average results for the new issues, the market indicator series, and a randomly selected sample are contained in Table 15-2.

The results shown in Table 15-2 generally confirmed those of the prior study.

TABLE 15-2   Average Percentage Changes for New Issues Offered Prior to a Declining Stock Market Compared with Alternative Market Indicator Series and Randomly Selected Stocks

	Friday after offering	Fourth Friday after offering	Year after offering
Average percentage change in all new issues	+10.2	+12.8	+20.4
Average percentage change in the OTCIA	+ 0.3	+ 3.2	+ 3.1
Average percentage change in the DJIA	+ 0.3	+ 2.1	−11.9
Average percentage change in randomly selected stocks	+ 1.1	+ 4.5	− 3.9

As before, the number of new issues that outperformed the market or the randomly selected OTC stocks was not greater than one might expect. Again, the difference was in the extent of price changes: the new issue losses were relatively limited, while some new issues that did well, did very well. As a consequence, the average price changes for the new issues were clearly superior to the price changes for the overall market and the randomly selected OTC stocks.

Because the period of market decline was relatively short (eight months from February to October 1966), the short-run results were prior to the market peak; therefore these results occurred during a rising market. The short-run results, which were almost identical to the results of the prior study, showed that the returns in the very short run (the Friday after the offering) were significantly above the market averages. During the first month after the offering there were further increases in the market averages and continued superiority for new issues.

The long-run results were heavily influenced by the declining stock market but still supported the basic hypothesis that investors in new issues enjoyed superior returns relative to the overall market. Although the new-issue price changes were not as large as in the earlier study, the absolute percentage *spread* between price changes for the new issues and price changes for the alternative market series was about the same as in the prior study.

The performance of the new issues compared with the randomly selected OTC

[4]Frank K. Reilly, *Performance of New Stock Issues during a Declining Stock Market, Working Paper No. 33,* University of Kansas, School of Business, July 1970.

stocks was likewise quite consistent with the results of the prior study. Specifically, while only about half of the new issues outperformed the randomly selected stocks, the average price change for the new issues was consistently much larger than the average of the price changes for the randomly selected stocks.

Stoll and Curley Study on New Issues

A study by Stoll and Curley[5] was concerned primarily with the adequacy of equity capital for small businesses. They analyzed this question through an examination of short-run and long-run returns for a sample of 205 Regulation A offerings by firms that sold stock for the first time during the calendar years 1957, 1959, and 1963. The rates of return for the new offerings were compared with the rates of return for the Standard and Poor's 425 Industrial Stock Index during three time periods, as follows:

    1. The time period between the date of the offering and the first market price quotation. The first market quotation was either the first March or the first September price quotation after the offering. This short-run period was typically much longer than the short run used in the studies discussed above, in which the periods were either less than one week or less than one month.

    2. The time period from the time of the first market quotation, as defined above, to the last market price quotation available. These time periods always covered several years.

    3. The entire time period available, from the offering date to the last market price quotation available. Again, this time period was generally quite long.

    The short-run results were quite consistent with those of prior tests:

> *In the short run,* the stocks in the sample showed a remarkable price appreciation. Between the initial offering date and the first market date, the average six-month rate of return for all companies in the sample, over and above the six-month rate of return on the Standard and Poor's Index, was 42.4 percent. On the average, an investor would have done almost 50 percent better per six-month period by buying new small issues *at the offering price* than by investing in a portfolio of larger stocks.[6]

Not only were the results superior, but there was consistency: only 25 percent of the new issues failed to appreciate during this initial period. It was further pointed out:

> The same results in more extreme form are observed if the immediate price change over the offering price is observed at the date of the completion of the offering. Of the 169 companies for which market prices were available near the completion of the offering, only 21 had prices lower than the offer price. The average price relative is 1.753, an immediate average appreciation of 75 percent. This result is observed despite the fact that during the offering periods observed the Standard and Poor Index decreased slightly on average.[7]

The results of the Stoll-Curley analysis of long-run returns will be considered below in the section "Long-Term Performance of New Issues."

EVIDENCE ON THE SPEED OF ADJUSTMENT OF NEW ISSUE PRICES

All the evidence thus far has been concerned with the price changes from the *offering price* to periods after the offering. On several occasions, the point has been

---

[5]Hans R. Stoll and Anthony J. Curley, "Small Business and the New Issues Market for Equities," *Journal of Financial and Quantitative Analysis,* vol. 5, no. 3, pp. 309–322, September 1970.

[6]Ibid., p. 314.

[7]Ibid., p. 314.

made to the author that the returns referred to in the studies may be correct in theory but are almost certainly not correct *in practice*. It is contended that most investors do not have the opportunity to acquire all the new issues, simply because they don't deal with all the brokers involved. Further, even if the broker were known, unless investors were preferred customers, it is unlikely that they would be able to get an equal amount of all new issues. Typical investors feel that they get all they want of the unpopular new issues but only five shares each of the "hot" issues. To examine the effects of such a contention, it seemed appropriate to repeat the prior tests using a price *subsequent* to the offering price. This postoffering price would be one that is supposedly available to everyone for a minimum of 100 shares. To determine the effect of acquiring new issues in the "aftermarket," it was

TABLE 15-3   Results Reflecting Investment in All New Issues at Postoffering Prices

	Friday after offering to year after offering		Fourth Friday after offering to year after offering	
	Declining market	Rising market	Declining market	Rising market
Average percentage change in all new issues	+ 6.3	+29.8	+ 4.9	+31.3
Average percentage change in the OTCIA	+ 2.7	+22.7	− 0.1	+22.0
Average percentage change in the DJIA	−12.2	+ 6.6	−13.7	+ 6.3
Average percentage change in randomly selected stocks	− 5.7	+31.3	− 7.4	+29.4

assumed that all the new issues from the two studies previously discussed were acquired on the first Friday and the fourth Friday after the offering and were held until the Friday one year after the offering.[8] These results were then compared with the price changes for the market indicator series and the randomly selected OTC stocks under the same assumptions. A summary of the results is contained in Table 15-3.

As before, the average price change for the new issues was always greater than the price changes experienced by either of the market indicator series, but the differentials were definitely reduced. The new-issue price changes were also better than random selection except in the case of a purchase after the first Friday in a rising market. Although these results assuming the purchase of new issues after the offering would not alter the overall conclusions of either study, this assumption did reduce the magnitude of the superior price changes. These results are consistent with the notion of an efficient stock market in which stock prices adjust rapidly to new information (that is, the underpricing of new issues).[9] In addition to supporting the notion of an efficient market, such results also show that the

[8]Reilly and Hatfield, "Investor Experience with New Stock Issues"; Reilly, *Performance of New Stock Issues.*

[9]For an extensive discussion of efficient markets and alternative tests, see Eugene F. Fama, "Efficient Capital Markets: A Review of Theory and Empirical Work," *Journal of Finance,* vol. 25, no. 2, pp. 383–417, May 1970.

substantial superior returns are available only to a limited number of investors. These results would indicate that investors who acquire the new issues after the initial offering receive returns during the first year that are above the market averages, but these returns appear to be consistent with the differential risks involved.

McDonald and Fisher Study

A study by McDonald and Fisher likewise considered the question of the purchase of new issues at postoffering prices.[10] They examined the returns for 142 new issues brought to the market during the first quarter of 1969. They then analyzed the returns for the new issues relative to the OTCIA during the following five time intervals:

0–1   Offering to first published market price in first week
1–3   First week to one year after offering
0–2   Offering to one month after offering
2–3   One month to one year after offering
0–3   Offering to one year after offering

The results indicated that the mean excess return (the "excess return" was defined as the return on the new issue minus the return during the period for the OTCIA) was significantly positive (28.5 percent) for the period 0–1, from the offering to the first published price. This is consistent with prior results that show very high short-run returns. There were also further excess returns (6 percent) during the period from the first week after the offering to the month after the offering.

Subsequent returns from the first month after the offering to the end of the year not only were not very large but were *negative*. The authors attributed these negative excess returns to the fact that the period examined was one of sharply declining stock prices and that one might expect new issues to be more volatile than the aggregate market. Therefore, the new issues would increase more than the market during a period of rising stock prices and decline more than the market during a period of falling stock prices.

In contrast to this line of reasoning is the contention that these negative excess returns were attributable to the fact that the only comparison made by McDonald and Fisher was with the OTCIA, as compared with the Reilly-Hatfield and Reilly studies that considered the DJIA, the OTCIA, and a random sample of OTC stocks.

This limitation on comparisons by McDonald and Fisher was especially unfortunate for the period of their study, which was one of generally declining stock prices that was not reflected by the OTCIA. Specifically, during the period of their study (January 1969–March 1970) the DJIA declined by more than 17 percent, the Standard and Poor's 425 Industrial Stock Index declined by 13 percent, the NYSE Composite Index declined by 15 percent, the American Stock Exchange Price Change Index declined by about 24 percent, and a randomly selected sample of OTC stocks declined by more than 30 percent, while the OTCIA declined by *only 3 percent.*

Obviously, during this period the performance by the OTCIA was not consistent with the other segments of the stock market or with the great bulk of OTC stocks. Therefore, it is entirely possible that the negative excess returns reported by McDonald and Fisher were due to the use of a poor base of comparison and that the results for the full period would have been substantially different if they had used almost any other base of comparison. Even with a more justifiable base, it

[10]J. G. McDonald and A. K. Fisher, "New-Issue Stock Price Behavior," *Journal of Finance,* vol. 27, no. 1, pp. 97–102, March 1972.

is likely that the returns after the first month would have been substantially lower than the very short-run returns derived during the first week and the first month and would still have indicated the existence of a fairly efficient market.

A Tentative Alternative Decision Rule

In contrast to the assumption of acquiring *all* the new issues at the original offering price or *all* the new issues at some postoffering price, an alternative

TABLE 15-4   Results of Investing in Initially Successful New Issues at Postoffering Prices

	Friday after offering to year after offering		Fourth Friday after offering to year after offering	
	Declining market	Rising market	Declining market	Rising market
Average percentage change in all new issues	+ 6.3	+29.8	+ 4.9	+31.3
Average percentage change in the OTCIA	+ 2.7	+22.7	− 0.1	+22.0
Average percentage change in the DJIA	−12.2	+ 6.6	−13.7	+ 6.3
Average percentage change in randomly selected stocks	− 5.7	+31.3	− 7.4	+29.4
Average percentage change in relatively "successful" new issues	+14.9	+41.6	+ 9.1	+49.3

decision rule that deserves mention has been examined on several occasions. The rule is considered tentative, since it has received only limited testing because there are some aspects of it that have not been successful and because the theoretical justification for its success is limited. The decision rule is to acquire at a postoffering price *only* the new issues that outperformed the market during the initial postoffering period. The results contained in Table 15-4 were derived when this decision rule was employed in previous studies.[11]

Because only about half of the new issues typically outperformed the market indicator series, this decision rule limited the capital requirements for the investor. Of more importance, the results indicated that the average percentage change for the successful new issues was consistently superior to random selection, to the overall market and to the purchase of *all* the new issues after the offering.

Another test of this decision rule was carried out by McDonald and Fisher, with one major change.[12] Specifically, they examined new-issue stocks that increased by more than 50 percent and by more than 100 percent during the first week and found that these did not do any better than the other new issues during the subsequent year. On the basis of their findings they concluded: "Initial price

[11]Reilly and Hatfield, "Investor Experience with New Stock Issues"; Reilly, *Performance of New Stock Issues.*
[12]McDonald and Fisher, op. cit., p. 101.

behavior did not have significant predictive value to investors making purchase decisions at the market price a short time after the offering."[13]

The difference between the McDonald-Fisher test and the previous tests discussed is that the latter examined *all* new issues that outperformed the market, whereas McDonald and Fisher looked only at the *extremely successful* new issues that had increased by 50 or 100 percent. The poor results found by McDonald and Fisher are consistent with results observed by Reilly and Hatfield and are not surprising, since these extremely successful new issues are most likely the issues that overreacted immediately after the offering. In any case, these results do point out that not all initially successful issues do well and possibly that new issues which do *extremely well* in the very short run should be avoided.

LONG-TERM PERFORMANCE OF NEW ISSUES

The discussion above of investor returns from new issues indicated consistently superior returns during the short run when the new issues were acquired at the offering price and smaller but still superior returns when issues were acquired in the aftermarket. At the same time, the tests of purchases in the aftermarket did indicate that the market was quite efficient in adjusting the price. This brings up the question whether the superior short-run returns carry over into the long run after one year.

An extensive analysis of the long-run performance of new issues was carried out by Prof. George Stigler in connection with a discussion of the *Report of the Special Study of the Securities Markets.*[14] Specifically, to test the effects of SEC activities on investor fortunes, Professor Stigler examined how investors fared before and after the SEC was given control over the registration of new issues. To accomplish this, he examined all the new issues of industrial stocks with a value exceeding $2.5 million in the period 1923–1928 and all new issues with a value exceeding $5 million in 1949–1955. The value of the new issues during the five subsequent years was compared with the offering value (all values were adjusted for relative market conditions). On the basis of the results Stigler concluded:

> In both periods it was an unwise man who bought new issues of common stock: he lost about one-fifth of his investment in the first year relative to the market, and another fifth in the years that followed. . . . With speculative new issues one would expect the one-year period to be much the most relevant, for thereafter the information provided by this year of experience would become an important determinant of the investor's behavior.[15]

A subsequent book on the topic of investment banking related to the new-issues market contained a chapter on short-run (one year), intermediate-term (one to five years), and long-run returns on seasoned and unseasoned new issues.[16] The examination of short-run price performance was confined to seasoned new issues and, therefore, is not relevant to our discussion. The intermediate-term price performance analysis for the period one to five years after issue included sixty-six issues that represented all the original nonrights, public cash sales of industrial issues of $5 million or more for the period 1949–1958. While the sample was not restricted to seasoned issues, the $5 million limit meant that it was heavily weighted

[13]Ibid., p. 102.
[14]George J. Stigler, "Public Regulation of the Securities Markets," *The Journal of Business,* vol. 37, no. 2, pp. 117–142, April 1964.
[15]Ibid., pp. 120–121.
[16]Irwin Friend and J. R. Longstreet, "Price Experience and Return on New Stock Issues," in Irwin Friend, James R. Longstreet, Morris Mendelson, Erwin Miller, and Arleigh P. Hess, Jr., *Investment Banking and the New Issues Market,* The World Publishing Company, Cleveland, 1967, Chap. 8, pp. 480–520.

by seasoned issues.[17] Unfortunately, there was no breakdown of the seasoned and unseasoned results. After analyzing the combined results the authors concluded:

> Over the ten-year period 1949–1958 the relative intermediate term price performance of large original industrial issues of common stock failed to keep pace with the market for comparable outstanding securities. Of the 50 annual mean price relatives presented . . . , only eight represented a performance better than that of outstanding issues, while the average price performance of the entire sample of new issues was consistently below that of the market.[18]

The analysis of long-run rates of return on new issues considered a sample of public issues offered for cash and included large issues of established industrials and public utilities, secondary issues of seasoned securities, mixed (original and secondary) issues of companies going public for the first time, and small issues of new companies with little demonstrated earning power.[19] Although the number of unseasoned industrial issues was only a small part of the total sample (about 10 percent), the results were examined separately, after which it was concluded:

> At least for the two periods covered, the evidence suggests that unseasoned industrial issues did not perform as well as seasoned issues in spite of a generally higher variability in return. Again the variability is so great that the differences, though sometimes quite large, are not statistically significant. However, all the differences are in the same direction.[20]

The most recent examination of long-run returns on new issues was done as part of the study by Stoll and Curley discussed above.[21] They examined 195 unseasoned new issues for the long-run period from the first market quotation to the last market price available in September 1966. They also examined these issues from the offering price to the last market price available. Overall periods differed between stocks, but all were between seven and nine years. The results indicated that in the long run investors in the new issues did not do at all well. Specifically, they showed:

> For the period first-market to last-market, average and median return relatives are less than one, for all sample years. This price performance counteracts the initial short-run price surge and is sufficiently poor to bring below one the mean and median return relatives for the period offer to last-market (except in 1957 where the median returns relative is slightly greater than one).[22]

Following a discussion of risk and transactions costs, the authors stated:

> One must conclude that, at least for the years examined, long-run rates of return in small issues were relatively low. . . . Therefore, both the bulk of the time spans and the bulk of the issues showed long-run rates of return inferior to those of large companies.[23]

Overall, the results of studies that examined long-run rates of returns on new issues were consistent in indicating that average returns on new issues were less than average returns on other common stocks in the market.

SUMMARY AND CONCLUSION

This chapter has been concerned with a discussion of why investors might expect unseasoned new issues to be underpriced at the time of issue and, therefore, why

[17]Ibid., pp. 497–498.
[18]Ibid., pp. 498–499.
[19]Ibid., p. 506.
[20]Ibid., p. 510.
[21]Stoll and Curley, "Small Business and the New Issues Market for Equities."
[22]Ibid., p. 315.
[23]Loc. cit.

they might expect to be able to derive above-average returns in the short-run relative to the market. This was followed by a consideration of empirical studies that analyzed the performance of new issues in the short run (the first year after offering) and the long run (after the first year). All the studies dealing with short-run performance were in complete agreement that *the new issues experienced very superior returns, if a purchase at the offering and a sale shortly thereafter are assumed.*

At the same time, there were indications that *a purchase at a postoffering price, while slightly superior to the overall market, generated price changes lower than the purchase at the offering price* because of the efficient nature of the market, in which prices adjust very rapidly to apparent underpricing. An alternative decision rule for the purchase of new issues after the offering was discussed, since it appeared to be moderately successful compared with the purchase of all the new issues in the aftermarket. Tests also indicated that new issues that were *extremely successful* shortly after the offering should probably be avoided, since it was entirely possible that there had been an overcompensation in the price.

Finally, the long-run performance of new issues was considered. All the studies were in agreement that *investors in new issues did not experience superior price performance in the long run.* In general, the returns for the relatively risky new issues were *below* the returns on seasoned large firms.

On the question of what to do about new issues, the evidence seems to point toward several generalizations:

1. Since all the studies were concerned with generally large samples (fifty to several hundred), the investor interested in replicating any such results should recognize that it will require the purchase of numerous new issues, that is, *portfolio* of new issues.

2. Obviously, it would be preferable to acquire the portfolio of new issues at the offering price, and the new issues typically should be sold during the first year after purchase unless subsequent analysis indicates that the stock would be a worthy addition to a seasoned portfolio.

3. If it is impossible to acquire a desired new issue at the offering price, it should be recognized that subsequent returns will be much less, but the same sale decision holds as in paragraph 2. In addition, in purchasing in the aftermarket it is probably preferable to concentrate on relatively successful new issues that have not overreacted to the underpricing.

4. While all empirical studies attempt to examine as many stocks as possible or randomly select stocks in order to be able to generalize the results, investors obviously should buy only those new issues that appear to be either correctly priced or underpriced. It is hoped that this procedure will make it possible to improve upon the results discussed in this chapter. To do this, investors interested in new issues should probably subscribe to one of the services mentioned below and attempt to analyze forthcoming new issues and acquire those that meet and exceed their normal investment criteria. Given the underpricing that appears to be so prevalent, there should be many new issues in this category.

CURRENT INFORMATION SOURCES ON NEW ISSUES

The reader interested in new issues is referred to the bibliography of studies at the end of the chapter and to the following current sources of information.

The OTC Market Chronicle. Published weekly by William B. Dana Co., 25 Park Place, New York, New York 10007. Each issue contains a list entitled "Securities Now in Registration," with an indication of which of the securities are initial public offerings. For each of the securities the list shows the date when the issue was filed, the number of shares, the approximate expected offering price, the business of the firm, the use of the proceeds, the location of the firm issuing the stock, and the name and address of the underwriter.

The paper also has a section entitled "OTC New Issue Prices," which includes most unseasoned new issues that have been sold during the prior four or five months, indicating the date of offering, the initial offering price, and a recent bid price.

Over-the-Counter Securities Review. Published monthly by Review Publishing Co., Box 110, Jenkintown, Pennsylvania 19046. Each monthly issue contains a section entitled "Initial Public Offerings," with descriptions of numerous corporations going public for the first time. Included are a detailed description of each company's business and facilities; salient balance sheet, income statement, and capital structure figures, typically for several years in the past; and underwriting facts such as the number of shares offered, the date of offering, and the offering price, as well as a recent price.

New Issues. Published annually by Review Publishing Co., Box 110, Jenkintown, Pennsylvania 19046. This brings together all the new issues reported monthly in the *Over-the-Counter Securities Review* as well as information on some new issues not previously included in it. *New Issues* contains the same information for each company as the *Over-the-Counter Review*, along with the year-end price of the stock.

New Issue Outlook, 14 Maiden Lane, New York, New York 10038. A service providing extensive advance reports on every company planning an initial public offering of SEC-registered stock. For each company there is an individual report describing its history and its current activities, its customers and competition, its officers and directors, its principal stockholders, the use of the money to be received from the offering, a comprehensive income statement covering five years if available, and a detailed balance sheet.

In addition, each week there is an eight-page computer report on the postoffering price behavior for each of the 417 most recently offered new issues from the date of offering to the date of the release. This weekly special-data report shows for each stock (1) the offering price and date, (2) the latest price, (3) dollar and percentage changes from the preceding week and from the offering price, (4) four-week and twelve-week moving-average prices, (5) the current market value of all shares outstanding and of the "float" (shares offered publicly), and (6) the latest available twelve-month per-share earnings and P/E ratio. The computer also segregates the twenty-five biggest gainers and losers in four key price movement categories.

New Issue Digest, P.O. Box 9911, Chevy Chase, Maryland 20015. Published on the first and the fifteenth of each month. It contains an analysis of selected new issues, including a brief description of each company along with its earnings and sales record. The company address and the address of the underwriter are included. For a period after the offering there is an update analysis of the firms indicating recent earnings changes.

BIBLIOGRAPHY

Brealey, Richard A.: *Security Prices in a Competitive Market,* The M.I.T. Press, Cambridge, Mass. 1971, pp. 102–107.

Friend, Irwin, James R. Longstreet, Morris Mendelson, Erwin Miller, and Arleigh P. Hess, Jr.: *Investment Banking and the New Issues Market,* The World Publishing Company, Cleveland, 1967. The section dealing with returns on new issues is Chap. 8, pp. 480–520.

McDonald, J. G., and A. K. Fisher: "New-Issue Stock Price Behavior," *Journal of Finance,* vol. 27, no. 1, pp. 97–102, March 1972.

Reilly, Frank K.: *Performance of New Stock Issues during a Declining Stock Market,* Working Paper No. 33, University of Kansas, School of Business, July 1970.

——: "Further Evidence on Short-Run Results for New Issue Investors," *Journal of Financial and Quantitative Analysis,* vol. 8, no. 1, pp. 83–90, January 1973.

—— and Kenneth Hatfield: "Investor Experience with New Stock Issues," *Financial Analysts Journal,* vol. 25, no. 5, pp. 73–80, September–October 1969.

Report of the Special Study of the Securities Markets of the Securities and Exchange Commission, 88th Cong., House Document 95, 1963, Part I, pp. 487–533.

Stigler, George J.: "Public Regulation of the Securities Markets," *The Journal of Business,* vol. 37, no. 2, pp. 117–142, April 1964.

Stoll, Hans. R., and Anthony J. Curley: "Small Business and the New Issues Market for Equities," *Journal of Financial and Quantitative Analysis,* vol. 5, no. 3, pp. 309–322, September 1970.

Chapter **16**

Profiting from
Special Situations

LEO BARNES and RUSSELL WAYNE

Many kinds of investment opportunities are reviewed in this chapter. All feature the prospect of relatively large capital gains in a relatively short time, with a relatively small risk of loss and, usually, without regard for the current market trend. Such isolation from prevailing stock or bond market conditions is often considered the distinctive characteristic of the special situation.

Who and What Make the Special Situation: Internal versus External Factors

Special situations arise from major changes or developments, typically unique and therefore nonrecurring. These can be *internal* to the company involved or *external* to it. Historically, internal, management-sponsored "workouts" or stockholder-initiated actions, such as mergers, acquisitions, spin-offs, recapitalizations, and reorganizations, have been viewed as the "true" special situations. Since about 1950, however, in part because of the paucity of such true special developments in a period in which the number of services and advisers seeking and recommending special situations was rising steadily, the concept has been broadened to include also the corporate beneficiaries of *external* developments.

Outside factors that produce special situations can arise almost anywhere. *Population* swings and shifts—overall, regional, or within different age groups—are often decisive for many companies. Such changes frequently underlie major *economic market* upheavals that can move many firms, for better or for worse, from stability, growth, or decline to the reverse. Then there are *governmental* or *political* developments and actions—legislative, administrative, or judicial, at federal, state, or local levels—that can provide new markets, tax savings, or higher income for the companies affected. Perhaps the most dramatic sources of external special situations are new *technological* or *scientific* breakthroughs that create big profit opportunities for some firms and large loss potentials for others. Finally, there are *special stock and bond market influences* that produce special situations, situations that result in either extraordinary undervaluation or extraordinary overvaluation of stocks or bonds.

Often, a timely combination of some external development with an internal management move to take advantage of it, plus favorable market conditions, produces the most profitable special situation of all.

Measuring the Special Situation Gain: Precise Projections versus Rough Estimates

An alternative interpretation of what constitutes a true special situation is based on the exactness with which the projected gain can be estimated rather than on whether this situation is isolated from market trends or is internally or externally generated. For example, a tax law change that will increase the net earnings of a particular industry by 25 percent can be deemed to produce true special situations, even though externally caused, because the expected corporate gains are mathematically predictable.

Since this is purely a matter of definition, no choice among the several alternatives need be made. In practice, precise projections of benefits usually involve internal special situations, while with external special situations we must usually settle for more approximate projections.

In the following analysis, we try to indicate, for each type of situation, the relative precision of the gain or loss potentials that are present. We conclude with a brief review of some useful investment techniques and alternatives for special-situation investors.

INTERNAL SPECIAL SITUATIONS

Acquisitions and Mergers

Capital gain potentials are similar in both acquisitions and mergers. In part, they depend on the success of the acquisition or merger in increasing profits. This situation may be designated "corporate synergism": the fact that sometimes the sum of two or more companies in a successful combination can produce greater profits than the companies could separately because of such factors as the complementary natures of the businesses, economies of scale, and other cost-cutting economies resulting from the efficiencies of the new management.

In addition to (or instead of) such corporate synergism, a merger or an acquisition often produces "investor, or stock market, synergism": the fact that sometimes two companies combined into one will promptly sell at a higher price-earnings ratio than the weighted-average price-earnings ratios of the stocks of the two companies as previously traded separately. Such stock market synergism often occurs even if there is no corporate synergism or usually well in advance of any corporate synergism that does develop.

Here is a simplified illustration of how stock market synergism can develop in an acquisition or a merger. Suppose Company Big has 1 million shares outstanding, has earned $1 million, or $1 per share, after taxes in the last twelve months, and sells on the American Stock Exchange at 15 for a current P/E ratio of 15. Its total market value is thus $15 million (1 million shares times 15).

Company Small, to be absorbed by Company Big, has 500,000 shares outstanding, has earned $500,000, or $1 per share, in the last twelve months, and sells over the counter at 5 for a current P/E ratio of 5. Its total market value is thus $2.5 million (500,000 shares times 5).

Now let us first assume that there is no stock market or corporate synergism at all. The immediate result of the merger would then be combined earnings of $1.5 million, a total stock market valuation of $17.5 million, and a resulting P/E ratio of 11⅔ ($17.5 million divided by $1.5 million). In other words, earnings of $1 million valued at 15 times, plus earnings of $500,000 valued at 5 times, equal earnings of $1.5 million valued at 11⅔ times.

Now if this were the most probable expected outcome of the combination, it probably would not occur. Stockholders of Company Big would be reluctant to approve it since they would very likely suffer a capital loss on their new shares, to the extent that stockholders of Company Small received some capital gain as an incentive for them to approve the merger. Without synergism, gain for one set of stockholders would be offset exactly by losses for the other set. As an extreme example, suppose stockholders of Company Small had to be given one new share for each old share. That would require the stockholders of Company Big similarly to receive one new share for each old share. The total market value of Company Small shareholders would then rise from $2.5 million to $5.83 million (500,000 shares times 11⅔) for a gain of $3.33 million. By contrast, the total market value of Company Big shareholders would drop from $17.5 million to $11.67 million (1 million shares times 11⅔) for an offsetting loss of $3.33 million.

Thus, either corporate or stock market synergism is required to make a corporate combination attractive. And, of course, the best special situations in this area occur when *both* corporate and stock market synergism develop. Typically, the stockholders of the company with the lower price-earnings ratio (Company Small) stand to benefit the most. Therefore, for outsider special-situation investors to benefit, they must have an opportunity to buy the shares of this company at some satisfactory level below the workout price. This usually calls for quick and early action prior to the formal announcement of the merger or acquisition. Often stock prices rise sufficiently in advance of such an announcement to eliminate most or all of the potential profit.

Of course, the major risk in this type of special situation is that the proposed deal may fall through, so that the market price of the stock acquired will decline rather than rise. To reduce the risk of such loss, *merger hedges* are sometimes employed.

Typically, in such a hedge, the stock of the larger or surviving company is bought simultaneously with the sale of the company to be acquired or merged. In this way, if the deal falls through, a profit can be made on the short sale that more than offsets any loss on the long purchase. On the other hand, if the deal is consummated, the short sale can either be quickly covered in the market to minimize loss or be covered later by the delivery of the stock of the surviving company previously purchased.

Unfortunately, the actual average profits made in such hedge operations do not seem to exceed 3 to 5 percent after all costs.[1] This is probably not a satisfactory return for the special-situation investor, however suitable it may be, on an annualized basis, for stock market members or other professional hedgers.

The best acquisition and merger candidates are newer small and medium-size firms in growth areas or markets that are selling at lower than average P/E ratios. In these ideal cases, stockholders of the candidate companies can benefit more quickly from the stock market synergism expected from the deal than from the slower buildup in their companies' P/E ratios as their growth prospects gain investor recognition.

Corporate Spin-offs

Spin-offs are the opposites of acquisitions and mergers. A company divests itself of a division or subsidiary and distributes the shares of the resulting new company to

---

[1]John P. Shelton, "An Evaluation of Merger-Hedges," *Financial Analysts Journal,* March–April 1965, pp. 49 ff.

its shareholders as of a stipulated record date. Here the hope is that stock market synergism will raise the price of the divested company by more than it lowers the price of the divesting company, so that the combined market value of the two divorced companies will be greater than the current value of the former single company.

For example, suppose Company Medium sells at 10 times earnings but has a very fast-growing subsidiary, presently accounting for 10 percent of its total earnings, which management believes could normally sell at 20 times its rising earnings were it a separate, independent Company New. The hope (and normal expectation in other than a bear market) is that any drop in Company Medium's P/E ratio after the spin-off will be small or nonexistent, while Company New rises to or approximates the expected 20 times earnings.

Of course, if there were no stock market synergism, the divestiture of Company New and its selling in the market at 20 times its earnings would be accompanied by a fully equivalent drop in the price and P/E ratio of Company Medium, now diminished in earning power by the loss of its rapidly growing subsidiary. The result would be no net gain for its shareholders from the spin-off.

In practice, however, since Company New accounts for only 10 percent of Company Medium's earnings, its spin-off will probably not reduce the P/E ratio of the parent company by much, if at all. A simplified format with which investors can approximate the profit potentials of a spin-off follows. The figures used are from the preceding example.

Case	Percent of earnings	×	Market P/E ratio	=	Index of market value
A. *The optimistic case*					
Before the spin-off	100		10		1000
After the spin-off	90		10		900
	10		20		200
					1100 (+10%)
B. *The moderately pessimistic case*					
Before the spin-off	100		10		1000
After the spin-off	90		9		810
	10		20		200
					1010 (+1%)
C. *The very pessimistic case*					
Before the spin-off	100		10		1000
After the spin-off	90		8.5		765
	10		15		150
					915 (−8.5%)

As suggested by this triple format, spin-offs are far from sure things. Because of their dependence on stock market synergism, they are almost invariably arranged in strongly rising markets, often near the peak of a bull market.

Spin-offs are relatively rare and are hard to spot in advance. A handful of companies may make a practice of periodic spin-offs, but obviously it cannot become an established habit, if only because stock market synergism is unlikely to be effective after a third or fourth spin-off.

For most investors, who do not have access to inside information or to the services of special-situation specialists, the only practical procedure in this area, after reaching a favorable decision, is to buy the parent company's stock as promptly as possible after the news of the spin-off but, of course, prior to the ex-dividend date. Another alternative that is sometimes available is to buy only the stock of the spun-off company if its initial market price is below anticipations and can be expected to rise as word gets about (for example, in the example used above, if the price were only 11 or 12 times earnings).

Reorganizations and Asset Conversions

A company can undergo internal reorganization in several ways: (1) in terms of its top and other executive personnel, as when a president or an executive vice president is replaced; (2) in terms of its basic operating targets, as when a billion-dollar automobile company decides to make only small economy cars; or (3) in terms of its basic asset structure, as when unprofitable divisions of a business are sold or written off in order to cut losses (for example, in the period 1973–1975 unprofitable computer operations were dropped by such major companies as RCA, General Electric, and Xerox, among others).

After such reorganizations of personnel, operations, or assets, the price perfor-mance of a company's securities can be expected to improve, so that purchases made at depressed prices will sooner or later pay off. Especially when tax-loss carry-forwards are available in such reorganizations, profitable asset conversion can proceed rapidly for a number of years on a tax-free or tax-sheltered basis.

Reorganizations and asset conversions almost always take time to succeed, perhaps as long as two or three years. Moreover, many do not succeed in any outstanding way; so the risk in this type of situation can be high.

Recapitalizations for Greater Profit or Lower Risk

Internal reshaping of a corporation's capital structure can be profitable if the resulting changes lower a firm's *average net cost of capital after taxes,* without too great an increase in risk because of required mandatory debt payments. For example, the substitution of convertible bonds for common stock can lower aftertax capital costs because interest charges on debt are fully tax-deductible whereas dividends on common stock are not. At the same time, stockholders who switch to convertible bonds retain part of their equity position, often with a higher income return. Of course, corporate risk may be somewhat increased, because interest on the convertible bonds is a mandatory obligation while dividends on common stock are not.

On the other side of the picture, sometimes recapitalizations are used to reduce mandatory corporate debt and risk, thus increasing the safety of a company's capital structure. Thus, if preferred stock paying a moderately higher dividend rate is substituted for bonds, the capital structure of the corporation becomes more conservative because of a lower debt-equity ratio. This procedure can facilitate the raising of additional equity at a more reasonable cost. Often; dividend rates on preferred stock can be kept at or very close to equivalent bond interest rates if the preferred stock is purchased by corporate investors benefiting from the 85 percent dividends-received credit (see Chapter 29).

Perhaps the most interesting recapitalization of all is the substitution of contin-gent income bonds for either common or preferred stock. In such a switch, tax-deductible interest replaces non-tax-deductible dividends, but with little if any increase in corporate capitalization risk, since interest on income bonds is contin-gent rather than mandatory and payable only if earned (see Chapter 5, Part 2).

In all these cases, the greater the relative magnitude of the recapitalization, usually the larger the potential profit in the resulting special situation. Similarly, the earlier the investor can take advantage of the situation, the larger the potential profit. Once again, it can be helpful to have inside information or the aid of special-situation operators in order to get on the bandwagon as early as possible.

Liquidations and Residual Stubs

A company may be "worth more dead that alive" because its net current assets per share are greater than its current market price, which may be depressed for any number of reasons. If management decides or is pressed to liquidate, a promising special situation may be in the making as the company sells its assets and distributes the proceeds to stockholders, with total distributions in excess of the stock's previous market price. In such cases, of course, liquidation is considered a more profitable alternative than selling out to some other firm. Often such a merger is simply not available at any worthwhile price, especially when the stock market is in the doldrums.

Sometimes not all the assets of a liquidating company can be advantageously sold, and what is left is reflected in a residual "stub," or certificate of participation. Occasionally, the most valuable part of such a stub may be the listing of a company on a stock exchange, especially the New York Stock Exchange or the American Stock Exchange. The value of such a listing to an up-and-coming over-the-counter firm may be substantial.

Liquidations are generally longer-term workouts than residual stubs, especially when the latter include an exchange listing. Both are usually low-risk situations in view of the excess of expected workout value over the market price. Of course, the money value of the time required for the completion of the liquidation should also be fully considered in any evaluation.

Tender Offers and Fights for Control

Offers to buy shares at above-market prices by outside interests seeking to acquire control of a corporation are a useful source of special situations. One bid may lead to competing offers at higher and higher prices as management or stockholder groups fight for control of a "bargain" company.

Special-situation investors can profit by buying the shares of the company involved at an early stage in such a contest and then either selling out for a quick short-term profit to one of the competing groups or holding on for a tax-favored longer-term capital gain, in the expectation that the long-range profit targets of the acquiring group will be realized, at least in part.

On the other hand, some special-situation operators seek to make money on the *short* side of this type of situation, by selling short the stock involved a day or two before the tender offer expires. The theory is that the demand for the stock being fought over will rapidly subside with the termination of the tender offer, so that the market price will drop significantly.

Companies Repurchasing Their Own Shares

The standard method for a company to increase the price of its common shares is by increasing earnings and passing through at least some of those increased earnings in the form of higher dividends. Another way to achieve the same result is to shrink, by stock repurchase, the number of common shares outstanding to which earnings are applicable.

Shares so reacquired, which are designated "treasury stock," are not included in outstanding stock totals used to calculate earnings per share and are not entitled to dividends. Particularly when a general market break, as in 1973–1974, depresses the price of a company's shares below book value or, even better, below net current assets, such corporate repurchases can be an excellent investment. In recent years, firms listed on the New York Stock Exchange have been buying back more of their own shares each year than the *net* purchases of *all* common stocks by *all* mutual funds in the particular year.

For companies not already overburdened with debt, it even makes sense to borrow funds for the repurchase of common shares. For example, if a company's stock were selling at about half of its book value, the company would be repurchasing $2 in assets for every $1 it borrowed. Moreover, it would save the dividends on the repurchased shares. Such saving is often sufficient to pay the interest on the loan; and if it is insufficient, the tax saving from the deduction for the interest paid on the loan usually more than makes up the difference.

Other reasons why corporations may wish to buy back their own shares include (1) obtaining shares for executive stock options or for employee pension, profit sharing, or stock ownership (ESOP) plans; (2) building a backlog of treasury stock for possible mergers or acquisitions; (3) strengthening insider voting control by reducing outside ownership; and (4) paving the way for a smaller public corporation to "go private" again, as began to happen in 1973–1974.

One customary hoped-for result of repurchasing a company's shares is to maintain or even increase earnings per outstanding share even if total company profits are level or declining. For firms in a truly declining industry, repurchasing shares may be the only path to salvation for their stockholders. A recent example is illuminating. The company involved was a heavy repurchaser of its own stock, so that in three years, from 1972 through 1974, its common stock capitalization shrank from more than 30 million shares outstanding to fewer than 19 million. As a result, although its total profits after taxes fell by 45 percent from 1971 to 1974, earnings per share dropped by only 11 percent.

The several stock exchanges provide monthly information on stock repurchases, which is widely reported in the financial press. Careful exploration of interesting companies is required, for repurchase is only one among many factors. If you come to the conclusion that you should invest in the company in any case, then repurchasing can be a persuasive clincher and profit maker. Otherwise, on the basis of the statistical record, it is possible that you can lose money in repurchase situations about as often as you can gain.

Fission Stocks: Issues Ripe for Stock Splits or Large Stock Dividends

Another internal area in which stock market synergism underlies potential special situations is that of likely stock splits or large stock dividends. The additional shares and lower prices resulting from such fission broaden the market for a stock, *sometimes* thereby boosting its typical price-earnings range of evaluation by investors. For some investors, it is psychologically more satisfying to buy 100 shares of a stock at 20 rather than 50 shares at 40 or 25 shares at 80. Also, commission costs on round lots are lower than on odd lots.

Numerous companies that have grown very rapidly over many years, like IBM or Xerox, have repeatedly split their stocks. In effect, higher and higher prices are hidden by such repeated splits.

Almost every company that splits its stock regularly or repeatedly declares large stock dividends has a normal or usual price level or price range in or around which corporate fission is carried out. The price level might be 50, 100, 200, or 500, but it is rarely less than 60 or 70.

Stock splits and large stock dividends are often the result of both good business and a strong stock market. This means that a company's earnings as well as its stock price must usually be rising before management will approve a split or a substantial stock dividend. Another important factor is the number of common shares already outstanding. Companies with a small number of common shares outstanding are likely candidates for stock splits or large stock dividends, especially when their earnings are growing steadily or rapidly. So are companies that are stingy dividend payers. Because they plow back a large part of current earnings into the company for future growth, these companies are often likely split candidates.

The price patterns of stock-split issues before and after the split are far from uniform. Much depends on how well the proposed split has been kept secret. In most cases, a split is anticipated by insiders, employees of the company, and, thanks to the resulting leaks of information, analysts and knowledgeable investors, who make shrewd guesses. In these instances, it is much more profitable to buy as long as possible before the news is out.

After the news of a split is public, there customarily is a profit-taking reaction, usually lasting for a number of weeks. Then, frequently, prices rally again until just before the split becomes effective. Whether this second peak is higher or lower than the first usually depends on the size of any dividend increase accompanying the stock split as well as on general market conditions.

Occasionally, a company may vote a stock split to distract investors from unfavorable factors in its outlook. However, the market is rarely fooled, and in these cases the split stock will usually sell at a lower price than the comparable level before the split. *Moral: before investing in any stock-split situation, be positive that the outlook for the company is favorable.*

The short-term speculator can take advantage of dubious stock splits by selling short on any significant rally before the split-up takes place.

Benefiting from Other Ways of Improving Stock Liquidity and Marketability

In addition to stock splits and large stock dividends, special situations may develop from other types of company efforts to improve a stock's market P/E ratio level, its liquidity, or its marketability. Thus, a large private company may decide to go public, or a successful company traded over the counter may conclude that it would fare better if it were listed either on the Big Board or on the American Stock Exchange.

Virtually all successful private companies eventually go public because of impending estate tax problems. In most instances, they do so well before the ultimate deadline to achieve for their principals greater liquidity, diversification, and probable capital gains resulting from above-book-value P/E ratios, especially in rising markets. Their gains usually more than compensate for the burdens of regulation and disclosure involved in going public.

Special-situation investors can often gain additional profits by keeping abreast of worthwhile large private companies well before they go public. This will enable them to give underwriters an expression of interest at the earliest possible date, thereby usually assuring all or most of the desired number of shares at the offering price. (New issues are discussed in detail in Chapter 15.)

Analogous in some ways to a private company's going public is the move of an unlisted firm to a major stock exchange as it acquires the required net worth, profitability, and number of stockholders. Over-the-counter companies in which mutual funds and other institutional investors have large holdings are prime candidates for such moves. The prevailing underlying assumption is that listed companies tend to sell at higher P/E ratios than unlisted ones. This has usually been true *on the average,* but with the development of the NASDAQ quotation system and modernized price indices (see Chapter 2) it is far from necessarily so for any particular large unlisted company with a substantial institutional following.

Similarly, it has been customary to assume that a shift from a smaller regional exchange to either the American or the New York Stock Exchange will result in at least a moderately higher P/E ratio for any given stock. Once again, there are many exceptions to the overall probability. This is also true of a shift from the ASE to the

NYSE, which is usually the most hazardous listing change in terms of probable price gain.

All in all, for the special-situation investor, either a listing or a presumed listing upgrading should be considered an additional or supplementary, rather than a decisive, selection factor.

Companies Well Supplied with Cash and Cash Equivalents

Firms amply supplied with cash and cash equivalents are interesting to special-situation investors because these highly liquid assets are apt to be used for acquisitions or investments that will produce worthwhile gains in future earnings. Such companies are also possible sources of funds for other corporations or for enterprising individuals who are long on potentially profitable ideas but short on funds. To be of interest, a company's cash and cash equivalents usually must be at least 3 times its current liabilities. A rather rare combination of an ample supply of cash and cash equivalents with a tax loss carry-forward is the most irresistible ploy of all.

Because there are considerable shifts from year to year and even from month to month among companies with excess cash and cash equivalents, you should check the latest available data.

Companies That May Benefit from Management-initiated Litigation

In recent years, many lawsuits have resulted in large windfall gains. Most of these cases have been antitrust actions against the dominant firm in an industry, such as IBM in computers. What is a relatively minor settlement for an industrial giant can be a literal bonanza for the smaller suing company. Another leading type of suit is for patent infringement damages.

This type of special situation almost always requires considerable legal and technical knowledge. Even then, the eventual legal outcome of a case can be highly problematical. Therefore, if you invest in this type of situation, choose stocks that you would be interested in holding even if the pending action does not turn out favorably.

EXTERNAL SPECIAL SITUATIONS

Lesser-Known Companies with Sustainable Earnings Growth Potential

As indicated at the beginning of this chapter, a number of external forces can create gains in earnings for various companies. What makes some selected few of these situations special is *sustainable* earnings growth potential that has not already been substantially or fully discounted in the market. In short, the accent is on *undiscounted projected earnings growth.* The crux of the matter is not the revolutionary new discovery for which relatively unknown Company X holds ironclad patent rights but rather the very substantial earnings that may accrue therefrom and the resulting sharply higher stock price for Company X.

For such a special situation, where does one look? The answer of some leading special-situation practitioners would be as follows:

Stick to industries that are up-and-coming, or limit yourself to geographic areas that are among the fastest-growing. Avoid fields that have shown cyclical characteristics in the past. Keep your hands off companies tied to the demands of economically depressed regions, such as the Pacific Northwest states during the widespread aerospace slowdown of the late 1960s and early 1970s. Place special emphasis on solid technological developments that may open up worthwhile new markets in the future. But stay away from faddish, one-shot propositions; in situations of this sort paper profits are usually eroded by unavoidably poor market timing.

One special earnings rule of thumb should be observed. Special-situation investors should seek companies whose earnings growth potential, generally arising from relatively unique developments, is of such magnitude that a broad capital gain of at least 100 to 150 percent over three to five years is likely to result.

But rapid worthwhile gains in earnings are not necessarily the whole story. Other important clues to look for are substantial increases in *revenues* or the *value of gross plant,* or both, over a few years. Sales may sometimes mushroom with no concurrent increase in profits, and this need not necessarily be a sign of weakness. Such a situation often occurs during a major expansion because start-up expenses on new ventures, especially during inflationary periods, often nip profits in the bud until the operation is running normally. Such debugging phases may last a year or more, causing the earnings trend to be undistinguished even though the sales growth is extremely impressive.

Similarly, if there is significant gearing up in the dollar level of gross plant and in its annual rate of change, noteworthy uptrends in sales and earnings may not be far behind. Admittedly, many companies have made ill-advised plant expansion decisions over the years. It is fine to set up a new 200,000-square-foot factory to turn out some thrilling new product, but it is even better to make quite sure that the company's marketing people are able to provide the customer demand necessary to justify the massive capital outlay. Experienced top management generally prefers strong marketing skill to huge output capacity. See also Chapter 12, "Selecting Stocks for Growth."

Companies Due to Benefit from Legislative or Judicial Action

If a pending change in a tax law, a regulatory act, or an administrative regulation (usually at the federal level but sometimes at the state or even the local level) would benefit either one or two companies or an entire industry, alert special-situation investors can sometimes make a worthwhile profit. An outstanding example of this situation occurred in 1960, when a new law eliminated the corporate tax on real estate investment companies that met stated requirements. Only a very few trusts were then in existence. One, the Real Estate Investment Trust of America, advanced more than 50 percent in price on the American Stock Exchange in less than a month. In the 1970s similar examples could be found in the areas of pollution control and domestic energy sources. In similar fashion, an antitrust ruling or another important court decision can benefit or injure an entire industry or particular companies in one or several industries.

Such external special situations can be unpredictable gambles, because it is usually very difficult to anticipate legislative, executive, or judicial actions, especially when different political parties are in control of the legislative and executive branches. Thus, a favorable tax measure that passes both houses of Congress can well be lost in conference or be vetoed by the President. Accordingly, if you decide to invest in a situation of this type, concentrate on companies whose stock you would be interested in holding even if the legislative or judicial action involved does not materialize.

EXTRAORDINARY STOCK MARKET UNDERVALUATION OR OVERVALUATION

Another kind of external special situation derives from the stock market itself when a truly extraordinary undervaluation or overvaluation exists, either for particular stocks, relatively few in number, or for virtually all stocks, as in an extreme bear market low such as occurred in the fall of 1974. The accent is on *extraordinary*. Most of the various shapes and forms in which such undervaluation and overvaluation may appear are reviewed below.

Stocks Selling below Net Current Assets

Sophisticated bargain hunters who want the maximum in assets for their investment dollars often look for stocks selling for less than their *net working capital* per share; that is, net *current* assets after subtracting the value of bonds, preferred shares, and other prior obligations, divided by the number of common shares outstanding.

Very occasionally, one can even find stocks selling below net *quick* assets per share (cash, cash equivalents, and accounts receivable) or even below net *cash* assets per share. Normally, very few such bargains are available, since they will usually be gobbled up by stronger companies through mergers or acquisitions.

Companies selling below their net current assets are worth more dead than alive. In effect, for such "Wall Street wallflowers," the purchaser gets plant and equipment and any remaining goodwill for nothing at a time when, thanks to continuing inflation, the cost of replacing such assets is higher than ever.

Sometimes the reason for such a low valuation of a company is temporary: a sudden management conflict, a possibly damaging lawsuit, expiration of patents, and so on. If such difficulties can be overcome by a change in management or by a shift to new product lines, the special-situation investor may find that he has picked a true bargain.

But the risk is high, and you must exercise great care in picking such "worth more dead than alive" bargains. The reason that the stocks are selling at very depressed levels is usually that their earning power and dividend-paying ability have been greatly impaired and may take a very long time to recover. So try to get at least some earnings and dividends as well substantial current assets.

The famous fundamentalist Benjamin Graham, who has fared quite well with this approach, recommends two additional qualifications for a true working-capital or "net quick" bargain. Besides a price well below net current assets per share and perhaps even below net quick assets per share, a desirable candidate must (1) be selling at less than the total of its aftertax earnings for the past five years and (2) have earnings prospects for the year or two ahead that are at least level with current earnings.

In periods of rapidly rising stock prices, the price behavior of such special situations tends to be unimpressive, since most investors are putting their funds in blue chips and glamour stocks. In more sluggish or declining markets, however, the price behavior of deflated below-current-asset situations will often be stronger than the popular averages.

Stocks Selling below Book Value Per Share

When there are relatively few issues selling under net current assets per share, some special-situation analysts use the yardstick of net *total* capital per share, or book value. While book value includes a considerable amount of nonliquid assets, these are often very conservatively stated—typically at original cost, sometimes that of many years ago, less accumulated depreciation. Thus, in an era of inflation, a stock selling at less than book value can be deemed an excellent value.

A special application of this approach is useful for corporations dealing primarily in money and credit: banks, finance companies, and savings and loan institutions. Such a company's book value or equity per share consists of more liquid assets than that of an industrial, transportation, or utility company. In periods of falling stock prices, shares of some of these liquid-asset companies frequently become available at less than book value per share.

Sold-out Stocks With Turnaround Potential

Often some stocks fall far behind the market for purely temporary reasons and then are forgotten and neglected by most investors, especially institutions. They can thus continue to be undervalued even after the original reason for their sharp decline has been eliminated.

The trick, of course, is to spot undervalued "sold-out" situations ripe for a turnaround, not just a historically very cheap stock. Locating the right laggards calls for careful investigation, including technical analysis (see Chapter 19). The number of companies that meet both fundamental and technical tests is apt to be quite small.

Bear in mind that even if a huge rebound in profits is expected for a company, many investors will not forget the fact that the stock has previously stumbled at least once, perhaps more often. The end result is a very lean market valuation of profits—the antithesis of what the special-situation investor seeks. See also Chapter 20, "Profiting from Emerging and Comeback Industries."

Companies Changing Their Lines or Going Conglomerate

A torrent of mergers and acquisitions since the early 1950s has been interrupted from time to time by bear markets, only to resume when markets have recovered. Coal producers have turned into underwear makers, washing machine manufacturers into paper producers, paper producers into oil operators, liquor companies into chemical processors, and so on. Frequently, the results of such drastic switches are higher profits, but sometimes they are bigger losses. Diversification and conglomeration are not automatically the easy road to riches they were once thought to be. The admonition "Let the cobbler stick to his last" has turned out to be as valid as the business school slogan "Our only business is making money."

Thus, extremely careful analysis is needed when selecting companies that have recently changed their lines or turned conglomerate. Some suggestions for such analysis are given below in the section "Useful Investment Approaches for the Special-Situation Investor."

Profiting from Excessive Overvaluation by Selling Short

Overvaluation as well as undervaluation can produce special situations, and here profits are made by selling short rather than by buying long. Selling short is not widely popular, however, for a number of reasons. Basically, it seems to rub against the grain of the generally prevailing American optimism. Thus, many institutional investors are forbidden by law to sell short. And, under the tax laws, long-term profits from short sales are fully taxed and do not get the favorable tax treatment received by long-term capital gains.

Nonetheless, there are times when special-situation investors can make more money by selling short than by any other technique available to them. These occasions occur at or near the peak of strong bull markets, when many stocks sell far above their typical or average valuations.

USEFUL INVESTMENT APPROACHES FOR THE SPECIAL-SITUATION INVESTOR

Earnings Valuation: The Critical Factor

Even when the special-situation investor has an excellent idea of the probable continued earnings prospects of a company, the investing equation is incomplete without a valid approximation of the range of price-earnings multiples at which the projected earnings will probably sell. The starting point for rational earnings valuation is usually the range of capitalization rates within which a stock has sold in prior years. Some approximate time trend adjustment should be considered, with recent ranges being given greater weight than more remote ones. A fair general assumption is that the stock is likely to be accorded a similar multiple in the future, as long as there is *no drastic change in the underlying fundamentals.*

But, it is hoped, in a special situation there is such a change. The development may be so new that there is no past history upon which to base future valuation estimates. Thus, the next best step is to take a *cross-sectional* approach, by determining the normal valuation rates being applied to similar companies operating in the same field.

This, of course, is somewhat more difficult because there are more variables. These include growth rates, financial structure, the debt-equity or leverage ratio, relative competitive position, and steadiness or variability of previous earnings gains. Each of these factors and possibly others require some adjustment of the typical valuation derived by the cross-sectional approach. Thus, the total modified valuation factor could be substantially more generous or leaner than the original multiplier.

For special situations, at times there is neither a meaningful history of past stock action or a representative industry or other grouping of companies with which to compare the stock in question. When this is the case, you must depend primarily on generalized guidelines.

Again, it is mainly a matter of anticipated earnings growth rates and financial strength. However, the credentials of management are often important too, since they may make it more likely that the company may succeed in reaching its goals. Previous management performance should be the paramount credential to be investigated. The scientific, educational, and other training of top officials may also be pertinent.

Potentially high growth rates, combined with sound management, are normally accorded generous price-earnings multiples. In many industries, almost any company with a respectable past record and better-than-average prospects will typically sell at 12 times earnings or better. However, firms in an industry that carries above-average economic and financial risk (apparel producers are a standard example) may be valued no more generously than average, even though superior management has enabled them to perform unusually well in the past.

On the other hand, the mere fact of participation in an acknowledged high-growth field may be enough to garner a multiple of 20 to 30 times earnings even if the company's past record is not spectacular. Drug manufacturers and business machine producers have often been examples of this type of situation.

Special financial or economic factors may necessitate further adjustment of the targeted P/E ratio. Thus, a considerable downside revision would be appropriate when (1) there is substantial potential common stock dilution from convertibles, warrants, or new stock issues; (2) the capital structure has a high leverage with mandatory debt; or (3) the company is heavily dependent on just a few major customers or suppliers. Similarly, if the situation under investigation is tied closely to government-funded projects, it is also of above-average risk and, accordingly, should be valued less generously.

There are also a few positive elements to be considered. Most noteworthy is a *proprietary product in an emerging market,* which could well assure sustained growth over a period of years. If and when it becomes clear to the investment community that this is in fact the case, a company's shares might well be bid up to a premium level in recognition of the diminished risk.

In the analysis of retail (grocery, drug, department store) chains, it is important to make comparative studies of the rate of potential growth of the city or region involved. Companies operating in high-expansion areas such as Florida, Texas, and the Southwest will be exposed to a more receptive environment providing more rapid growth, which should properly be awarded a more generous valuation.

The preceding guidelines will cover the vast majority of special situations, internal or external, but there are occasional mavericks that do not lend themselves to this sort of analysis. Such problems arise most often with companies growing faster than 25 percent per annum from internal expansion alone. In such situations, price-earnings ratios may jump to astronomical levels. Certainly, few analysts can live comfortably with capitalization rates of 40, 50, or higher. Occasionally, however, there is fundamental support.

Arnold Bernhard, the well-known investment adviser who is research chairman of the Value Line Investment Survey, believes that in these special supergrowth situations a supportable multiple can be estimated approximately by dividing 100 by the number of years needed for earnings to double. Thus, when a company's earnings growth rate is 40 percent annually, its earnings will double in about two years, so that a price-earnings multiple of 50 might not be excessive. Such a procedure may be a useful first approximation.

The Need for Balance Sheet Analysis

Only a notch lower in importance than earnings valuation is the need for special-situation investors to do a thorough job of balance sheet analysis. The traditional standards should almost always be met. On the issue of liquidity, cash and cash equivalents should at least equal current liabilities. In terms of leverage, one should be skeptical of companies that have more than 35 percent of their capital in mandatory debt.

A special factor to watch out for is the presence of deferred charges on the asset side of the balance sheet. Typically, research and development expenditures and preopening charges (as for retail operations) are hidden in this category and tend to make the current level of earnings look higher than it actually is. True, there is some basis for amortizing such outlays over a period during which they would in some way be revenue-producing. If money spent on research and development produces an item with a profitable market life of five years, it is reasonable to charge off its past development cost over that time span. But this is not the most conservative accounting practice, and it leaves a disturbing contingency, which the market abhors.

Another factor that should be checked is the amount of debt coming due in the next twelve months. It should be covered more than adequately by the company's current cash and cash equivalents.

These are simple tests, but they are often overlooked in special-situation analysis. The little time spent on them will usually pay off by screening out situations with excessive downside price risk. For additional suggestions, see Chapter 10, "Selecting Stocks for Value."

Technical Analysis and Timing

It is certainly desirable for special-situation investors to keep closely in touch with the price action of the stocks in which they are interested. A useful rule of thumb is that there should be a fairly close relationship between the prevailing fundamental and technical trends. If earnings have been going up over an extended period of time, the price movement should have been in the same direction. A glaring disparity between the two trends calls for deeper probing.

Similarly, if analysts or investors project a continuation of a persistent growth trend and the price has taken a decided turn for the worse over a period of months (apart from a deep, general bear market), this could be a sign that the fundamental judgment is in error. A disparity between the fundamentals and the technical trend means that you must ask more questions and try to locate some weakness that has been overlooked.

As for timing, of course, you will want to find special situations as early in the game as possible to obtain the maximum profit potential. At the same time, however, you should consider the need for previous development of an element of sponsorship. The choice is thus a balancing act, with two critical factors. The first is the fundamental potential. The second is *developing* recognition, evidenced by increasing upward price momentum. But what you want to avoid is the type of special situation that has already made the rounds. The familiarity factor is then very high, and the profit potential correspondingly low.

Finally, remember that "the public is right, even when it is wrong." From time to time, companies are beset by publicity which, though inaccurate or even misleading, causes their stock to drop to the depths. Some analysts are quick to explain the truth of the situation and show why the stock in question really should not have fallen at all or even should have risen in price. Their fallacy is simply that, on Wall Street, the "truth" is often what the preponderance of investors believe it to be. So, when making special-situation decisions, it is important to try to determine the potential reaction of the investment community to the company under consideration. If it is not likely to buy the company's stock, stay away. It is just no use to swim against the tide. See also Chapter 19, "Selecting the Technically Strong Stocks."

Reducing Risk by Means of Convertibles and Options

The preceding discussion has dealt with the various analytical methods of ensuring maximum profit potential in special situations with minimum exposure to risk. But risk reduction can also be managed on the *investment* level by the use of convertible securities, including options. For details, see Chapters 21, 22, and 23.

Chapter 17

Investments in Letter Securities

JOEL KAUFFMAN

Occasionally sophisticated investors are given an opportunity to invest in stock through a private placement. That is, the securities they can buy are not being offered to the public and have not been subject to registration by the Securities and Exchange Commission (SEC). By and large, offerings of this type of any size are placed with institutional investors, but sometimes individuals are invited to participate in the offering.

Obviously, the quality of securities marketed in this way, as in other ways, varies tremendously. Sometimes fantastic profits may be earned. A new company may float a small private issue to obtain capital. If the company can operate for several years with increasing profits, it may be able to sell stock to the public at a price well above the price in the private placement, thereby allowing the original investors to reap substantial rewards. On the other hand, the original investors may find themselves locked into a security that they cannot dispose of, and it becomes worthless. However, the purpose of this chapter is not to analyze investment opportunities but to describe the so-called private placement and the advantages and disadvantages of owning investment letter stock.

For a placement to be exempt from registration with the SEC, it must not be offered publicly, and it must be offered only to a small number of sophisticated investors. In practice, this restriction has generally come to mean that the securities must be offered to fewer than twenty-five offerees if the offerees consist of institutions and individuals. If the offerees are all institutions, the number may be considerably larger. The buyers are each required to supply a letter indicating that they are acquiring the securities as an investment and do not intend to sell them. As a result, the investors' rights to resell the securities have been greatly restricted.

This restriction was eased somewhat by the SEC's adoption in 1972 of Rule 144. A major advantage that Rule 144 offers to holders of letter stock is that it sets up clear standards under which such stock may be sold. These standards replaced the vague rule of thumb of a three-year holding period and a "change in circumstances" on the part of the holder, which was previously in effect.

Rule 144 permits holders to sell letter stock through a broker over the counter or on an organized exchange after they have held it for two years. However, the stock may be sold only in specified quantities, and adequate information about the financial affairs of the company must be available to the public.

The two-year holding period does not commence until the purchase price for the securities has been fully paid. Payment made by a debt obligation is not considered adequate for holding-period purposes unless the instrument provides for full recourse against the purchaser and unless the obligation is adequately secured by collateral other than the securities purchased. Moreover, if such a debt instrument has been issued for the purchase of restricted securities, the obligation must be paid before the securities may be sold under the provisions of Rule 144.

The requirement of making adequate financial information available to the public is fulfilled if the company has registered securities under the Securities Exchange Act of 1934 or has registered some securities under the Securities Act of 1933 and has filed certain requisite reports and annual statements with the SEC.

Under Rule 144 a holder of letter stock may not sell an amount in excess of 1 percent of the outstanding securities of the class being sold in any six-month period. However, if securities of the same class are listed on a national exchange, the maximum permitted to be sold in a six-month period is either 1 percent of the outstanding securities or the average weekly volume of the security traded on all exchanges during the four weeks prior to the sale, whichever is the smaller figure. For example, let us assume that a company has 100,000 shares of stock outstanding and listed on a national exchange. A holder of letter stock in this company cannot sell more than 1,000 shares in any six-month period. Furthermore, if the average weekly volume of shares of this security traded on all exchanges for the four-week period before the investor began to sell the letter stock was 800 shares, the stockholder cannot sell more than 800 shares in the six-month period.

Under Rule 144 securities may be sold only by a broker in a normal transaction. The broker may receive only the usual commission and may make no special payments in connection with the sale.

Rule 144 has greatly increased the liquidity of letter stock and, presumably, its desirability and value. Furthermore, the incidence of the rule considerably enhances the possibility that a holder may be able to use restricted securities as collateral for loans. Nevertheless, we should bear in mind that even with Rule 144 in effect holders are expected to retain securities of this nature at their own risk for a minimum period of two years. This seems to suggest that investments in restricted securities should be considered only when the securities can be obtained at a rather substantial discount from the market value of registered securities of the same class.

Chapter 18

Over-the-Counter Trading

JOHN E. HERZOG

BACKGROUND

In the stock and bond business today there are well-organized markets, brokerage firms, and trading rules. Regardless of how much we read about current problems in the securities industry, the industry is well defined, responsible, and competent when viewed against the background of the past.

It wasn't always like that. The period after the Civil War was an active one for the industry, if indeed the collection of firms and banks that participated could be called that. People with an interest in securities who were outside the major trading centers found it difficult to follow the activities of the exchanges, and the trading done was face-to-face, largely in banks. An investor with stock to sell would go to a bank and present the securities at the bank's security counter, where they would be evaluated. Subsequently, when a buyer had been found, a trade would be made.

The term "over the counter" dates from that time, and the practice continued into the twentieth century. In fact, even with the telephone there was no well-organized over-the-counter (OTC) securities market until the first sheets showing bids and offerings were published in 1918. These are what we know today as the "pink sheets" of the National Quotation Bureau.

As brokers began to be identified with certain types of stocks and bonds, the reputations of their firms became fixed in the minds of the order clerks whose job it was to locate the right market and the best price for a given security. One firm became known as a foreign bond house, another for bank stocks, and a third for utility issues. On these early reputations were based the businesses of some of the major trading firms we know today, even though most brokers now handle a wide variety of securities and provide a number of investor services.

While much misunderstanding has surrounded the over-the-counter markets in the past, there now seems to be a vastly increased interest in this segment of the securities industry. Because of this new interest, the mystery is fast disappearing, and a clear picture of the nature of over-the-counter trading is becoming a part of the general investing community. In this chapter we shall examine the way in which this trading operates.

TYPES OF SECURITIES TRADED

Simply stated, the over-the-counter market is all the buying and selling activity in securities that does not take place on a stock exchange. All new issues of any security offered to the public for the first time are traded in the OTC market, and secondary distributions of large blocks of stock, whether exchange-listed or not, usually are offered to the public at a fixed price in the OTC market. Since open-end investment company shares (mutual funds) are considered new issues under law, these are also sold within the OTC market structure.

In addition to these securities, the stocks of most of the banks and insurance companies throughout the United States are traded over the counter—a tradition, established long ago, that has persisted. A large number of exchange-listed securities of the largest companies in the country are also traded over the counter, and this group comprises what is known as the "third market."

The total volume of daily trades in all these securities across the United States is a tremendous dollar figure, greater than that of all organized exchanges, although it is one that is never published or fully apparent. In fact, it would be difficult to construct the figure. However, the volume should be borne in mind, for its size alone is very important. Since the introduction of NASDAQ (see subsection "NASDAQ" below), however, the total volume for all NASDAQ issues is available daily and cumulatively.

Some investors and casual followers of the financial pages assume that if a security isn't listed on a stock exchange, it is of inferior quality. This is certainly far from the truth. The OTC market offers investors a broad variety of issues, ranging from little-known, unproven, speculative stocks to some of the gilt-edged giants of American industry.

Many investors, analysts, and institutional managers interested in growth are constantly searching the OTC market to find special-situation companies that show unusual potential for future expansion. Many of the glamour stocks of today grew up in the OTC market, which has been called the spawning ground for the IBMs and Xeroxes of the future.

A study conducted by the trade publication *Over-the-Counter Securities Review* indicated that, in terms of common stocks alone, the OTC market had a minimum value of $150 billion as of the end of December 1971. The same publication also reported that there were 6 OTC companies whose stocks had a market value exceeding $1 billion each (the leading company's stock was valued at $2.2 billion). There were about 20 companies with a market value of more than $500 million each and almost 200 with a market value of more than $100 million each. These figures were still valid in 1977.

SYSTEM OF TRADING

NASDAQ

In over-the-counter trading, it frequently happens that men and women who have traded together for years have never met; people in different cities develop relationships based solely on the business that has been consummated. On all the exchanges, trades may be made only between members, in a face-to-face transaction on the trading floor. Here is a major difference between the two kinds of trading. Whereas exchange members are usually located in one city, over-the-counter traders are found all over the country, in firms of all sizes, banks, trust companies, and other institutions.

All over-the-counter trades are made over the telephone or, perhaps, by teletype machines. While exchange members write advices of each trade they make face-to-face, no written confirmation of an over-the-counter trade is sent until the next day at the earliest. Usually, this advice, which is called a "comparison," is mailed to the other broker.

A dealer who is making a market in a particular security will maintain an inventory of the security and be ready to buy or sell it at any time. Thus, a market maker plays a role similar in many ways to that of a specialist on a stock exchange. However, there are often three, four, five, or more competing market makers bidding for and offering a particular over-the-counter security.

Indeed, it is dealer competition in market making that acts as a balance wheel for the OTC securities market. Even though dealers are not physically together, they are in constant communication, and prices seldom drift far apart. The NASDAQ (National Association of Securities Dealers) communications system, which now ties together almost all retail firms and OTC market makers, has added the missing link to this competitive structure by providing instant trader access to up-to-the-minute quotations of all market makers in a particular stock, regardless of their physical location. If a dealer's quotations are out of line, other competing dealers find it profitable to sell to or buy from that dealer until the out-of-line quotations are adjusted.

Auction versus Negotiated Markets

On a stock exchange, the quotations given on the stocks traded are continuous. This type of market is known as an "auction market." By contrast, in traditional over-the-counter trading, a quotation is given on a particular stock each time the telephone rings, and the market for that stock is not advertised in the interim. This type of market, in which persons wishing to buy or sell give indications of their interest or leave firm orders to buy or sell at prices different from the quotation, is known as a "negotiated market." The trader negotiates the purchase or sale with the other broker, amending the price if necessary, on the basis of the number of shares offered and the overall supply-and-demand situation in the stock.

This was the nature of *all* over-the-counter trading until early 1971, when the Automated Quotation system of the National Association of Securities Dealers (NASD) was introduced. A real-time computer-based system, the NASDAQ system allows brokers across the country to see the markets and the market makers in about 3,000 stocks. Since the prices on this system must be good for the 100-share unit of trading, NASDAQ has changed the entire character of trading.

Each of the 3,000 stocks included in the NASDAQ system is required by NASD to have $1 million in assets, 500 or more shareholders, a minimum of 100,000 shares outstanding, and at least two brokers or dealers registered as market makers and continually quoting the stock in the system. NASDAQ companies must also meet the Securities and Exchange Commission (SEC) reporting and disclosure standards established for exchange-listed stocks.

The 3,000 stocks on NASDAQ number almost as many as those listed on the New York and American stock exchanges combined. Most of the stocks now in the system are OTC stocks, but a number of securities listed on major exchanges also are carried. These listed stocks, handled by nonexchange market-making OTC dealers and traded off the floors of the exchanges, are the stocks that comprise the so-called third market.

How the NASDAQ System Works

To make sound decisions, investors, OTC traders, and market-making dealers need information, which they obtain from NASDAQ. And since the information needs of these three groups are somewhat different, NASDAQ provides information in three separate formats, or levels, that are specially tailored to the requirements of each of them.

As the system is organized, Level I service is designed to serve individual investors who are clients of the retail branches of brokerage firms. It takes the quotations of all dealers making a market in a stock and delivers current representative bid and asked prices. These are actually median quotations representing the middle points of the quotations of all the dealers. Since any NASDAQ stock has a minimum of two market makers and some have as many as twenty-five or thirty, such a quotation will fairly reflect the existing market.

Level II terminals are specially designed units with TV-type screens to serve the needs of two kinds of users, (1) brokers or dealers retailing OTC securities to the public and (2) large-scale professional order executors. By pressing a few buttons on the keyboard of a Level II unit, a trader can see immediately all the current quotations of the market makers in a specific stock in the NASDAQ system. The quotations of only five market makers, ranked according to the best prevailing bids or offers at that time, are displayed on the screen. If there are additional quotations, they can be retrieved in groups of five by pressing a special "more" button.

Approximately 600 market-making dealers are equipped with Level III units. These are similar to Level II equipment except that they have features that enable dealers to enter and change or update quotations on the stocks in which they make markets.

Executing an Order

Investors accustomed to receiving a confirmation of a trade executed on a stock exchange might notice a difference in an over-the-counter trade. Exchange trades are always confirmed to the client, with the broker acting as agent, and appropriate commissions are charged. In over-the-counter trades, you may find that the confirmation does not have any commission. You may actually have bought your stock from the broker in a transaction in which the broker has acted as a principal.

In many cases of this sort, the client may see a notation on the confirmation that the broker is also a market maker in the security. Thus, the customer does not know what the broker paid for the stock, since it may have been bought at any time, either immediately before the sale to the customer or days or weeks earlier, and at a price that may differ widely from the price at which the customer has bought the stock.

These inventory trades constitute a large and important part of the OTC trading volume with investors. Naturally, many OTC trades also are executed on an agency basis, just as exchange trades would be.

When OTC trades are executed on an agency basis, the brokerage commission is very similar to the commissions charged on trades taking place on a major exchange. When the broker acts as a principal, the customer cannot be charged a price more than 5 percent greater than the prevailing offering price. For example, if a stock is quoted "18 bid, 20 offered," the broker acting as principal cannot charge more than $21 per share.

Since the OTC is a negotiated market and the market maker must act as a principal, on occasion there will be a significant spread between the bid and asked prices. For example, a stock may be "8 bid, 10 offered." In this instance a wise investor who wishes to buy or sell the stock will enter a limit order, such as "buy at 9¼." The investor will not get the stock immediately, however, if another investor enters a limit order to sell the stock at 8¾. The market maker could then simultaneously buy the stock at 8¾ and sell it at 9¼, keeping the ½ point as its commission. The market maker thus eliminates the risk, and both investors get a better price.

Prices and Size of Markets

It is not practicable to introduce investors to all the intricacies of OTC trading here. However, the bare outlines of trading practices can be enumerated, so that investors new to this part of the industry will have some foreknowledge.

Because many over-the-counter stocks are those of smaller and less seasoned companies, their prices are likely to change more rapidly than those of most listed stocks. Securities in these companies are not so widely held, and sizable orders to buy or sell may have a greater-than-normal effect on their quotations. Because investor interest in many OTC stocks is not so great as for stocks traded on the major exchanges, the prices quoted are generally firm only at the time at which they are quoted by the trader. Frequently, traders will attempt to honor markets they have given earlier, on a "call-back," but the rule is that the trader may change the market on each call or request for a quotation. Indications of buying or selling interest may also change the quotation, although this is not always the case.

NASDAQ has altered this practice to some extent, since markets shown are supposed to be good for 100 shares of stock as long as they remain unchanged on the system, but this is the first change in a trading practice that has been in use for about fifty years. If a security is traded on NASDAQ, the broker need not call for a quotation, since he or she may simply interrogate the system and see the markets of several market makers, knowing that the market of each of them will be firm for 100 shares when the broker is ready to execute an order.

All exchange markets contain a size of the market, such as "$28\frac{1}{4}$ bid, offered at $28\frac{3}{4}$, 400 by 1,000," meaning that the bid will be paid for 400 shares and that 1,000 shares are available at the offering price. Over-the-counter markets do not have sizes automatically. Indeed, although every market must be valid for the 100-share unit of trading, the order clerk who asks for the size of the market when requesting the quotation is thereby obligated to trade at least 100 shares of stock.

Traders will frequently indicate the size of the market they are making, but they are not obligated to do so. This concept is important to remember. There may be many market makers for a given security over the counter, while on an exchange there is one specialist, and that specialist is in a position to see all the inquiries on the stock being traded. The over-the-counter trader who has several competitors sees only a portion of the total number of inquiries on the stock in which a market is being made.

HOW TO OBTAIN ADDITIONAL INFORMATION

Now that the industry has matured, a number of organizations have been formed to serve investors, and many others have been modified to enable them to answer the questions that continually arise. There follow some of these organizations and a brief description of what they do.

The O-T-C Information Bureau.   The office of the bureau is at Two Broadway, New York, New York 10004; its telephone number is (212) 952-4058. The organization was formed originally by the National Security Traders Association to answer the questions of individual investors, researchers, brokerage firms, and the financial press. It will either find the information you want about the over-the-counter market or direct you to someone who can get it for you. The bureau publishes quarterly statistical reports comparing the popular market indices with the NASDAQ averages.

National Association of Securities Dealers, Inc.   NASD's New York office is at Two Broadway, New York, New York 10004; its telephone number is (212) 952-4100. There are also offices in Washington, D.C., and across the country. NASD is the industry's self-regulatory association, to which most of the OTC brokers in the country belong. The association establishes rules for trading, handling of customer's accounts, and receiving and delivering securities, as well as for a wide variety of other subjects. It arbitrates differences between brokers and also attempts to solve problems between customers and their brokers.

Securities and Exchange Commission. SEC's New York office is at 26 Federal Plaza, New York, New York 10007; its telephone number is (212) 264-1612. There are also offices in Washington, D.C., and other major cities. The SEC is the federal agency responsible for regulating the securities industry under the provisions of the Securities Act of 1933 and the Securities Exchange Act of 1934. The Commission investigates various problems of the industry and monitors the trading activity in stocks. It also files complaints against brokers who have not adhered to the rules of the industry and may prosecute them in the courts.

Chapter **19**

Selecting the Technically Strong Stocks

In this chapter Dr. Robert A. Levy presents his strong theoretical case for technical analysis, together with a related critique of the practical usefulness of the fundamental, or intrinsic-value, approach. He follows with empirical evidence of the usefulness of relative-strength technical analysis and of thirty-two varieties of 5-point chart patterns (those with two highs and three lows or two lows and three highs).

Then Dr. Donald E. Vaughn completes the chapter by tracing in great detail how bar charts, point-and-figure charts, and line charts can be used effectively in practice as analytical and forecasting tools.

Part 1. Basic Principles of Technical Analysis

ROBERT A. LEVY

Technical analysis, far from being a mystical approach to security price forecasting, has theoretical and empirical foundations. This chapter will attempt to set forth the principles underlying technical analysis, to discuss the implications of the random-walk theory, and to present the key evidence, pro and con, for technical analysis.

TECHNICAL VERSUS FUNDAMENTAL ANALYSIS

There are two major schools of security analysis: the fundamental school and the technical school. Stock market fundamentalists rely upon economic and financial statistics and information. They investigate corporate income statements, balance sheets, dividend records, management policies, sales growth, managerial ability, plant capacity, and competitive forces. They look to the daily press and trade publications for evidence of future business conditions. They analyze bank reports and the voluminous statistical compilations of the various government agencies.

Then, taking all these factors into account, they project corporate earnings and apply a satisfactory earnings multiplier (price-earnings ratio or capitalization rate) to arrive at the intrinsic value of the security under observation. Finally, they compare this intrinsic value with the existing market price; if the former is sufficiently higher, they regard the stock as a purchase candidate.

The term "technical" in its application to the stock market means something quite different from its ordinary dictionary definition. It refers to the study of the market itself as opposed to the external factors reflected in the market. Technical analysis is, in essence, the recording of the actual history of trading, including both price movement and the volume of transactions, for one stock or a group of equities and the deducing of the future trend from this historical analysis.

Numerous tools of technical analysis have evolved over the years. Space limitations preclude a discussion of them, and the interested reader is encouraged to consult one or more of the cited publications for more complete information.[1]

Technical theory can be summarized as follows:

1. Market value is determined solely by the interaction of supply and demand.

2. Supply and demand are governed by numerous factors, both rational and irrational. Included in these factors are those that are relied upon by the fundamentalists as well as opinions, moods, and guesses. The market weighs all these factors continually and automatically.

3. Disregarding minor fluctuations in the market, stock prices tend to move in trends that persist for an appreciable length of time.

4. Changes in price trends are caused by shifts in supply-and-demand relationships. These shifts, no matter why they occur, can be detected sooner or later in the action of the market itself.[2]

The basic assumption of technical theorists is that history tends to repeat itself. In other words, past patterns of market behavior will recur in the future and can thus be used for predictive purposes. In statistical terminology, stock market technicians rely upon the dependence of successive price changes.

The assumption of fundamental analysts is quite different. They believe that each security has an intrinsic value which depends upon its earning potential and that actual market prices tend to move toward intrinsic values. If their belief is correct, determining the intrinsic value of a security by capitalizing future earnings is equivalent to predicting the security's future price.

THE CASE FOR TECHNICAL ANALYSIS

By contrast, Robert D. Edwards and John Magee, two outspoken advocates of the technical school, argue:

> It is futile to assign an intrinsic value to a stock certificate. One share of U.S. Steel, for example, was worth $261 in the early Fall of 1929, but you could buy it for only $22 in June of 1932! By March, 1937, it was selling for $126 and just one year later for $38. . . . This sort of thing, this wide divergence between presumed value and actual value, is not

[1]See particularly *Encyclopedia of Stock Market Techniques,* Investors Intelligence, Inc., Larchmont, N.Y.; Garfield A. Drew, *New Methods for Profit in the Stock Market,* The Metcalf Press, Boston, 1954; Joseph E. Granville, *A Strategy of Daily Stock Market Timing for Maximum Profit,* Prentice-Hall, Inc., Englewood Cliffs, N.J., 1960.

[2]Robert D. Edwards and John Magee, *Technical Analysis of Stock Trends,* J. Magee, Inc., Springfield, Mass., 1958, p. 86.

the exception; it is the rule; it is going on all the time. The fact is that the real value of a share of U.S. Steel common is determined at any given time solely, definitely and inexorably by supply and demand, which are accurately reflected in the transactions consummated on the floor of the New York Stock Exchange.

Of course, the statistics which the fundamentalists study play a part in the supply-demand equation—that is freely admitted. But there are many other factors affecting it. The market price reflects not only the differing value opinions of many orthodox security appraisers but also all the hopes and fears and guesses and moods, rational and irrational, of hundreds of potential buyers and sellers, as well as their needs and their resources—in total, factors which defy analysis and for which no statistics are obtainable, but which are nevertheless all synthesized, weighed and finally expressed in the one precise figure at which a buyer and seller get together and make a deal (through their agents, their respective brokers). This is the only figure that counts. . . .

In brief, the going price as established by the market itself comprehends all the fundamental information which the statistical analyst can hope to learn (plus some which is perhaps secret from him, known only to a few insiders) and much else besides of equal or even greater importance.

All of which, admitting its truth, would be of little significance were it not for the fact, which no one of experience doubts, that prices move in trends and trends tend to continue until something happens to change the supply-demand balance.[3]

Technical analysts justify their activities in several ways:

1. They contend that short-term market fluctuations are more important than long-term trends if importance is judged by the profit potential in trading. Certainly traders who buy at the bottom of each short-term movement and sell at its top will realize greater profits than investors who benefit only from the major trend.

2. Technicians contend that information on fundamental conditions comes too late for maximum profit. Fundamentalists are forced to wait for statistics on sales, orders, earnings, dividends, and similar factors. By the time information of this sort is made publicly available, the market may already have discounted its effect and commenced a substantial upward or downward move. Technical traders, however, can act instantaneously on any change in stock prices whether or not the news underlying the change has been made public. Technicians believe that the movement of the market *precedes* the movement of other economic series rather than vice versa. In this regard, they have the support of the National Bureau of Economic Research, which in its study of business cycles has invariably listed stock market prices as one of the generally reliable leading indicators (see Chapter 8).

3. Business conditions, present and future, are not the only factors that determine stock prices. It is freely admitted by technicians that some fundamental analysts may be able to forecast the trend of business quite accurately; they may even know exactly what present economic conditions are and what future conditions will be; moreover, they may be absolutely correct in their earnings projections for a given company. Yet, even assuming all this to be true, their projections of stock market action could be grossly in error. It is only technical analysis that can detect the buying and selling pressures caused by psychological and emotional, rather than economic and financial, factors. Only the market action itself reflects the existence of inside information not made publicly available. This important fact, which all technicians have relied upon, is discussed by George A. Chestnutt, Jr., the manager of a mutual fund that depends heavily on technical methods:

There are so many factors, each having its own effect on the price fluctuations of any individual stock, that it is practically impossible to analyze them separately and give each its proper weight in an attempt to estimate the stock's future market action. Often the essential information is known only to insiders. It is not released to the public until it is too late to act upon it.

[3]Ibid., pp. 5–6.

Fortunately, we do not need to know why one stock is stronger than another in order to act profitably upon the knowledge of the fact. The market itself is continually weighing and recording the effects of all the bullish information and all the bearish information about every stock. No one in possession of inside information can profit from it unless he buys or sells the stock. The moment he does, his buy or sell orders have their effect upon the price. That effect is revealed in the market action of the stock.[4]

The argument of the technical analyst, in a nutshell, is that stock price moves are caused by the interaction of supply and demand and that the flow of funds into and out of various securities is first detected by the various technical market indicators, not by the analysis of fundamental economic and financial statistics.

A CRITIQUE OF THE INTRINSIC-VALUE APPROACH

Technicians agree that trends and patterns evolve in large part as a result of market action taken by persons who have, or think they have, superior knowledge of underlying fundamental factors. The obvious corollary, which fundamentalists are quick to point out, is that the possessors of this superior knowledge are in the best position to maximize their profits from stock market transactions. Since fundamental knowledge, so the argument goes, is the stuff upon which even technical analysts must ultimately rely to produce the trends and patterns that they study, it must be a superior foundation for security appraisal.

In fact, there is little justification for denying that accurate and *timely* fundamental analysis is superior to technical analysis, for technicians must wait until persons with critical information that others do not have make their move in the market. Even though technical analysts may be able to act before critical information is publicly available, they will be later in their actions than insiders who are first aware of the underlying fundamental factors. The conclusion, therefore, must be that investment analysis will be most successful when analysts are among the first to gain and correctly evaluate the necessary superior knowledge.

But technicians still have strong arguments. First, it is possible that even the best fundamental analysis could lead to unsatisfactory investment results. Why? Because the opinions of fundamentalists regarding the intrinsic value of a given security, even if correct, must be shared by other investors who control substantial financial resources and are willing to place these resources in the marketplace. Only when opinions are converted into action and a sufficient amount of capital is involved will the market price move toward intrinsic value. Thus, fundamental analysts may find themselves heavily invested in a security for a considerable length of time before market support develops. Of course, this lowers their overall rate of return by tying up funds that could have been invested elsewhere. Technicians, however, purport to avoid this potential problem by delaying their investments until market support for a particular stock has already appeared. It is conceivable that the sacrifice in profits resulting from later selection by technicians is no greater than the opportunity cost of unproductive capital arising from premature selection by fundamentalists.

Second, and of greater importance, how many investors are able to engage successfully in fundamental analysis? How many are capable of being among the first to recognize and evaluate critical information? How many have the necessary nonmonetary resources (primarily time and reliable statistical information)?

Let us assume, for the sake of argument, that all investors are capable and that they have sufficient time to analyze the economic and financial factors affecting any given security. These investors will then attempt to project the earnings of a

[4]George A. Chestnutt, Jr., *Stock Market Analysis: Facts and Principles,* American Investors Corporation, Larchmont, N.Y., 1965, p. 19.

particular company and capitalize these earnings to arrive at some estimate of intrinsic value. The most important of the statistical data upon which the investors will rely are the company's financial statements. Under these circumstances, how successful will fundamentalists be in their analysis? The question could be posed in an alternative, more specific fashion: How complete and reliable are the corporate financial reports that are the major source of information for fundamental analysts?

Inadequancy of Financial Reports

The purpose of an annual report is to convey information to present and prospective stockholders about the operations of the corporation. This information should include all that is relevant (both qualitatively and quantitatively) to enable investors to make a rational and informed judgment of the investment worth of the company. Consequently, published annual reports should be designed for the use of skilled financial analysts. Only then can they possibly include information in volume and detail sufficient to permit the efficient allocation of capital resources through investment selection.

Among the data that are badly needed in published reports but are seldom available are (1) production in units; (2) sales in units; (3) rate of capacity operated; (4) breakdown of operations into domestic and foreign categories; (5) division of sales between intercompany and outsider transactions; (6) wages, wage rates, hours worked, and number of employees; (7) state and local taxes paid; (8) amount and details of selling and general expenses; (9) amount and details of maintenance expenditures; (10) details of capital expenditures; (11) details of inventories; (12) details of properties owned; (13) number of stockholders; (14) sales by product line and by consuming industry; (15) research and development costs; (16) details of long-term lease arrangements; (17) details of stock option and pension plans; (18) more complete disclosure of depreciation policies; and (19) orders booked and unfilled orders.[5] And this is by no means an all-inclusive list.

The sparse quantity of information is only one of the problems of fundamentalists. Of equal importance is the question of reliability. Presumably, when the financial statements of a company are accompanied by the unqualified approval of independent certified public accountants, investors and creditors may be assured of the fairness and integrity of the reports. The auditors' report indicates whether they feel that the financial position of the company and the results of its operations are presented fairly, in conformity with generally accepted accounting principles. The audit supposedly eliminates, or at least discloses, unintentional errors by corporate accountants, bias on the part of corporate management, deviations from generally accepted accounting principles, and deliberate falsification. The audit also determines whether the financial statements have been prepared on a basis consistent with that of the prior year and whether they fully disclose all material facts.

In practice, there are many reasons why the auditors' certificate is of less-than-desirable significance. First, the auditors' examination is limited to a program of tests that are not infallible in detecting errors. Second, such concepts as "fairness," "materiality," "full disclosure," and "consistency" are subjective in nature and cannot be objectively verified. Third, and fortunately of rather rare occurrence, there may be outright dishonesty by the independent auditors or collusion between the accounting firm and its corporate client. Fourth, and of greatest importance, there are no truly generally accepted accounting principles. The accounting profession has been and continues to be in a state of flux. In some cases

---

[5]Benjamin Graham, David L. Dodd, and C. S. Cottle, *Security Analysis,* 4th ed., McGraw-Hill Book Company, New York, 1962, pp. 80–82.

there are a multiplicity of acceptable procedures, while in other cases principles that have been applied for many years are now being subjected to reanalysis and skeptical reevaluation.

The major problem areas include asset valuation, treatment of leases, business combinations, adjustments for changes in price level, and pensions. In each of these areas there is considerable doubt as to the propriety of presently employed accounting principles (particularly as to the appropriateness of historical cost valuations).

Additional accounting problems exist in the following areas: (1) matching revenues and expenses (for example, direct versus absorption costing, installment sales, long-term construction contracts, stock options, depreciation, the investment credit, and deferred taxes); (2) distinguishing between several acceptable accounting methods and determining the effect of using one as opposed to another (for example, depreciation, the investment credit, and inventory valuation); and (3) estimating various factors that are relevant to the accounting process (for example, depreciable lives and bad-debt expense).

Financial ratios, while potentially useful to fundamentalists, can be no better than the figures from which they are derived. And these figures, in turn, are only as good as the underlying accounting principles. Year-to-year comparisons and trends are suspect because the flexibility of accounting procedures permits manipulation of the financial data. Intercompany comparisons also are often unreliable because of the wide choice of permissible accounting methods. The end result is that analysts, using publicly available information, have an extremely difficult task in trying to reconstruct a corporation's financial statements to get a picture of the company's earning power.

Nor do the analysts' problems terminate upon the evaluation of recent financial statements. This only provides them with an approximation of current and historical earnings. Now they must project these into the future—and much further than the next year. As stated in a widely respected text on fundamental analysis:

> Typically, these . . . studies rest on a careful but too abbreviated forecast of probable future earnings for a company—covering generally only the next twelve months or less. . . .
> While such a measurement is important, it is hardly sufficient for an investment recommendation, since value cannot soundly be established on the basis of earnings shown over a short period of time.[6]

How Is a Proper Capitalization Rate to Be Determined?

And these are not all of the fundamentalists' trials and tribulations. Determining current and historical earnings is a difficult task indeed. Projecting these earnings for a number of years into the future is even more difficult. But now comes the most difficult job of all: selecting an appropriate price-earnings multiple (or capitalization rate). The problems inherent in this last step are reflected in the following statement by Graham, Dodd, and Cottle, commenting upon a 1953 estimate by the Value Line Investment Survey of the 1956–1958 prices of the stocks in the Dow Jones Industrial Average:

> Although the earnings estimates were wide of the mark in several instances . . . the aggregate earnings estimate for the 29 stocks was very close to the actual. . . . By contrast, the aggregate market value estimate for 1956–1958 was significantly less accurate— missing by more than 22 percent the three-year mean price. . . . This tends to confirm our view that earnings can be predicted with more confidence than can the capitalization

[6]Ibid., p. 434.

rate or multiplier, which to a major degree will reflect the market psychology existing at the time.[7]

Reference to the historical relationship between market price and current earnings is to no avail. Graham, Dodd, and Cottle compared, over the twenty-five-year period 1935–1959, the quarterly earnings (on an annualized, seasonally adjusted basis) of the companies represented in Standard & Poor's Composite Index of 500 stocks with the quarterly average stock price index. They found that, in 46 of the 100 quarters, stock prices moved counter to the change in earnings; that is, earnings increased while prices declined, or vice versa.[8]

Granville emphasizes the same important point by demonstrating the lack of correlation between prices and earnings as uncovered in his examination of hundreds of stocks. He found that price-earnings ratios fluctuated widely and that this fluctuation "dilutes the widely held belief that good earnings are a necessary accompaniment to advancing stock prices."[9]

With all of these difficulties (determining current earnings, projecting future earnings, and selecting an appropriate capitalization rate), it might be expected that even the best fundamental analysts can be far wide of the mark. This expectation is amply justified by the facts. For example, the 1965 range of the Dow Jones Industrial Average was 840.59 to 969.26, and the average of the 1963–1965 DJIA annual high-lows was 813.60. But in March 1961 Naess and Thomas projected the 1965 average at 688; and Value Line, in January 1961, suggested that the mean for 1963–1965 would be 705.[10]

Errors of this size have not been unusual. As a result, Graham, Dodd, and Cottle, in the 1962 edition of their book *Security Analysis,* stated that "careful consideration of this problem . . . led us to increase our 1951 valuation standards by an arbitrary 50 percent."[11] Such arbitrariness certainly bespeaks a basic unreliability.

It is clear that fundamental analysis, even when performed by experts, can be quite inaccurate. There remains the question whether technical analysis offers any better possibilities. One prominent author, Garfield A. Drew, states why he believes that it does:

> There have been frequent occasions when technical analysis was the *only* thing that could possibly have given the correct answer to the future trend of the market. This was true, for example, in the spring of 1946. If any investor had then possessed a crystal ball which would have shown him what corporate earnings were to be a year later, he could only have concluded that stock prices would be considerably higher. Instead, they were substantially lower in the face of record earnings and dividends.
>
> There was nothing in the "fundamentals"—either in 1946 or 1947—to explain why prices had collapsed in the meantime. But there was considerable evidence of a weak *technical* situation in the market beforehand. . . . The investor who acted on technical grounds did not need to concern himself with *why* the market should seem to be acting irrationally, whereas the analyst of business facts and probabilities—unable to find a "reason"—was forced to conclude that the market could not do what it actually did. . . .
>
> In a broad sense, the experience of the past ten years has very clearly demonstrated that the price-to-earnings ratio is a much more important factor than the actual level and/or trend of earnings themselves. Since the ratio is determined by investment

[7]Ibid., p. 439.

[8]Ibid., p. 719.

[9]Joseph E. Granville, *New Keys to Stock Market Profits,* Prentice Hall, Inc., Englewood Cliffs, N.J., 1963, p. 21.

[10]Graham, Dodd, and Cottle, op. cit., p. 418.

[11]Ibid., p. 421.

psychology, the study of technical market action has, on the whole, been more fruitful than fundamental analysis.[12]

MAJOR CRITICISMS OF TECHNICAL ANALYSIS

There are at least four major criticisms of technical analysis. The first three are closely interrelated. First, it is contended that the behavior of the stock market in the past may not be indicative of its behavior in the years to come. This is to say, even if we assume that technical analysis was successful over the last decade, there is no guarantee that it will be successful over the next decade. Typical of the response to this criticism is the following denial by Edwards and Magee:

> All the new controls and regulations of the past several years, the new taxes which have placed a heavy handicap on successful investors, the greatly augmented and improved facilities for acquiring dependable information on securities, even the quite radical changes in certain portions of our basic economy, have not much altered the "pattern" of the stock market.[13]

The second contention of the critics is that technical traders acting on the results of their studies tend to create the very patterns and trends that they have predicted, in a self-fulfilling prophecy. In other words, the market action may be a reflection of the chartists' actions rather than the reverse.

Technicians recognize this possibility. However, they argue that the habits and evaluative methods of individuals are so deeply ingrained that the same kinds of events continually produce the same kinds of market responses. Since these habits and methods are extremely durable and since fundamental analysts outnumber technicians, it is unlikely that technical trading alters the response of the fundamentalists to external factors. Hence the actions of technicians probably do not have a decisive influence on the behavior of a competitive market.

This second criticism inevitably leads to a third. If technical analysis is even generally successful, an influx of technical traders will neutralize whatever profit potential exists. An analogy can be offered in the field of horse racing. If someone perfected a system of wagering on horses and publicized it so that it was available for everyone's use, the amount of betting on the highest-rated horses would change the odds sufficiently to offset the profitability of the system.

There are several reasons why this criticism is not fatal to the art of technical analysis: (a) It is quite possible that extremely successful technical "systems" have been developed but, for the reason stated above, have not been publicized or made available for general use. (b) It is likely that most of those who are not engaged in technical analysis would be reluctant to believe the claims of successful technicians. (c) To the extent that technical analysis may depend in part upon the use of electronic computers and sophisticated mathematical techniques, both the expense and the requisite training and knowledge will prevent its exploitation by the majority of the investing public other than institutions. Along these lines is the following argument of Granville:

> There is no danger that the revelation of new techniques will so enlighten the masses as to render them [the techniques] useless. The application of such things requires time and work, and human nature is such that most people will neither have the time, patience or desire to do the work necessary to achieve the results which might be had when these things are done.[14]

Finally, the fourth major criticism of technical analysis is its subjectivity. Advo-

---

[12]Drew, op. cit., pp. 242–244.
[13]Edwards and Magee, op. cit., p.1.
[14]Granville, *New Keys to Stock Market Profits*, p. 11.

cates of the technical school contend that their methods preclude the somewhat arbitrary determinations that accompany fundamental analysis (for example, selection of a capitalization rate). Critics, however, maintain that the technician's favorite tool, the chart of stock price movements, is subject to a wide variety of interpretations. Without debating the validity of this criticism, it may be noted that the recent use of the computer for purposes of analyzing price and volume movements would tend to reduce the subjectivity that otherwise might be inherent in technical analysis.

The Theory of Random Walks: Background

The most critical indictment of technical analysis, thereby giving indirect support to the fundamentalists' side of the debate, is the so-called random-walk theory. This theory restates the above-mentioned criticisms in a slightly different context. It argues that the activities of chart readers, if successful, would help to produce independence of successive stock price changes. But this independence, once established, renders chart reading an unprofitable activity. On the other hand, fundamentalists who consistently evaluate the effect of new information on intrinsic values will be able to realize larger profits than those who cannot. As one advocate of the random-walk theory, Dr. Eugene F. Fama, puts it:

> There is nothing . . . which suggests that superior fundamental or intrinsic value analysis is useless in a random walk–efficient market. In fact the analyst will do better than the investor who follows a simple buy-and-hold policy as long as he can more quickly identify situations where there are non-negligible discrepancies between actual price and intrinsic values than other analysts and investors, and if he is better able to predict the occurrence of important events and evaluate their effects on intrinsic values.
>
> If there are many analysts who are pretty good at this sort of thing, however, and if they have considerable resources at their disposal, they help narrow discrepancies between actual prices and intrinsic values and cause actual prices, on the average, to adjust "instantaneously" to changes in intrinsic values.[15]

The random-walk theory, while seeking to refute the concepts of technical analysis but neither proving nor disproving those of fundamental analysis, presents an empirical challenge to both schools of thought. The challenge to technicians is a direct one. If the random-walk model is valid, as suggested by most empirical evidence to date, then future price movements cannot be predicted by studying the history of past price movements alone. Consequently, the work of chartists may be useless. To vindicate themselves, technicians should not restrict themselves to talking about trends and patterns; rather, they should demonstrate the predictive significance of the trends and patterns empirically. The challenge to fundamentalists, while still empirical, is less direct. The random-walk theory is based on the premise of an "efficient" market in which actual stock prices at any given time are likely to be close approximations of intrinsic values. Fundamental analysts must therefore demonstrate that their methods consistently result in the detection of discrepancies between actual prices and intrinsic values when these discrepancies exist.

The Theory of Random Walks: Methods of Testing

Technicians contend that the stock market is oligopolistic in nature and that there is thus an unequal distribution of critical information in the marketplace. As the awareness of critical information gradually spreads, influencing the actions of market traders, recurring patterns and continuing trends in price movements are produced.

---

[15]Eugene F. Fama, "Random Walks in Stock Market Prices," *Financial Analysts Journal,* vol. XXI, no. 5, p. 58, September–October 1965.

To the contrary, the random-walk hypothesis states that the stock market is not oligopolistic, but rather that it is efficiently competitive and that there are enough well-informed analysts operating within a free market to produce an instantaneous adjustment of price to value. Now, in fact, if price does adjust instantaneously to value, then successive security price changes would be statistically independent. In other words, you could not use past prices to forecast future prices. In simple terms, technical analysis would be a useless preoccupation.

Fortunately, there are several methods of testing the random-walk hypothesis to find if technical analysis is a desirable method of earning income in the stock market. Two of these methods are statistical in nature. First, serial correlation studies attempt to measure the relationship between successive first differences in security prices; and second, runs analysis attempt to compare the actual lengths of runs with mathematically determinable expected lengths. (For this purpose, a run is defined as any consecutive series of price changes of the same sign, plus or minus, and a run is terminated whenever the current price change is of a sign opposite to the previous price change. If the actual length of a run exceeded the expected length by a statistically significant amount, it would be decided that the stock market was a nonrandom phenomenon.)

Academicians who have performed these two types of statistical tests have been virtually unanimous in their conclusions. They have contended that the stock market does follow a random walk; thus, technical analysis cannot be used to produce profits greater than those that would be produced by random selection.[16] However, there are several serious weaknesses in the statistical tests:

1. They are not able to detect nonlinear patterns that the chartists claim exist.

2. With respect to runs analysis, the tests are too inflexible. A run is terminated whenever the current price change is of the opposite sign to the previous price change without regard for the *size* of the change.

3. Statistical tests are very difficult to interpret. Just how large must a serial correlation coefficient be to determine that technical analysis can produce satisfactory profits? By how much must the actual length of a run exceed the expected length of the run to determine that the market is sufficiently nonrandom to allow a profitable forecasting of future prices based upon past prices? (Indirectly connected with this problem of interpretation is the inability of the statistical tests to account for brokerage commissions. It would be far better to produce results in terms of dollars and cents rather than in terms of serial correlation coefficients and related statistical measures.)

4. The statistical tests do not consider the element of risk.

5. The tests fail to correct for the comovement of stock prices—that is, the tendency for the entire market to move as a whole and, in particular, for industry groups to move together. Only if tests are based upon relative strength can this comovement be filtered out.

6. Statistical tests often are not understood by market practitioners who do not have an extensive background in statistics and mathematics.

There is a method of testing the random-walk hypothesis that avoids these weaknesses of statistical tests. This method is known as simulation. It requires the use of a computer, since the amount of data to be handled is voluminous and the number of computations to be made is extensive. In performing simulation tests, the computer actually employs an investment strategy, computes the results of employing this strategy, and compares these results to results that would have been achieved by employing random investment selection.

[16]An extensive collection of articles on the random-walk hypothesis has been compiled by Paul H. Cootner (ed.), *The Random Character of Stock Market Prices,* The M.I.T. Press, Cambridge, Mass., 1964.

Simulation has these advantages: (1) It can test a wide variety of strategies actually utilized by market practitioners; (2) it can detect nonlinear patterns; (3) it can test for relative strength, thus filtering out the comovement of stock prices; (4) it can take into account brokerage commissions; (5) it can express results in terms of dollars and cents; and (6) it can yield a measure of risk.

Relatively little work has been done in the area of simulation. Professor Cootner of MIT has tested moving-average trend indicators,[17] and Sidney Alexander has tested a device known as the filter technique.[18] Their conclusions have been similar: these technical strategies can produce profits greater than the profits that would be produced by a naïve buy-and-hold policy, *but these superior profits are not sufficient to cover transaction costs.*

Cootner's and Alexander's tests were certainly far from exhaustive. In fact, *the random walk hypothesis cannot be proved* either by statistical testing or by simulation. All that can be indicated is that the specific strategies investigated do not yield profits greater than those that would be yielded by a random method of selection. It is, of course, impossible to investigate every conceivable technical strategy.

EMPIRICAL EVIDENCE IN SUPPORT OF TECHNICAL ANALYSIS

Some empirical evidence has been offered in support of technical analysis. One of the important tenets of technical analysis is that historical relative price strength for individual securities tends to persist for significant periods of time. Technicians claim that the purchase of stocks with comparatively strong price trends will yield superior investment results.

Use of Relative Strength Analysis for Portfolio Upgrading

If relative strength is a valid criterion for investment selection, an investment strategy of portfolio upgrading should prove successful. Portfolio upgrading (or letting profits run and cutting losses short) involves the sale of securities when they become relatively weak and their replacement in the portfolio with securities that are relatively strong. Thus, portfolio upgrading and relative-strength continuation are closely related concepts. On the other hand, there is an opposite axiom on Wall Street: "You can't go broke taking a profit." Which strategy is more profitable?

To investigate the issue, the author conducted an extensive array of computer simulations.[19] The data file was composed of the weekly closing prices of 200 actively traded New York Stock Exchange securities over the period from October 1960 through October 1965. These securities were distributed by industry group in about the same proportion as the securities in the S&P Index.

From this data file two measures were constructed for investment selection. To measure relative strength, the ratio of current price to the average of the preceding twenty-six weeks' closing prices was determined. To measure volatility of price movements for individual securities, the coefficient of variation was computed. The coefficient of variation is simply the ratio of the standard deviation of a set of numbers to the mean of the set. In this case, the relevant set of numbers was the

[17] Paul H. Cootner, "Stock Prices: Random vs. Systematic Changes," *Industrial Management Review,* vol. III, no. 2, pp. 24–25, Spring, 1962.

[18] Sidney S. Alexander, "Price Movements in Speculative Markets: Trends or Random Walks," *Industrial Management Review,* vol. II, no. 2 pp. 7–26, May 1961; "Price Movements in Speculative Markets: Trends or Random Walks, No. 2," in Paul H. Cootner (ed.), *The Random Character of Stock Market Prices,* pp. 338–372.

[19] Robert A. Levy, *The Relative Strength Concept of Common Stock Price Forecasting,* Investors Intelligence Inc., Larchmont, N.Y., 1968.

weekly closing prices of a given security for the current week and the preceding twenty-six weeks.

As a strategy, portfolio upgrading proved to be far superior to profit taking, as one might expect if, in fact, the principle of relative-strength continuation is valid. The purchase of securities that are both relatively strong and relatively volatile and the sale of these securities when they become relatively weak produced results up to 29.1 percent per year. Moreover, this 29.1 percent was net of 3 percent per year in brokerage fees. The average holding period for the securities held as a result of employing this strategy was eight months, indicating that the investor can profit from the long-term capital gains provisions of the federal income tax laws. The 29.1 percent per year net of commissions would have been earned at a time when random selection, as measured by the geometric average of the 200 securities in the data file, would have produced 10.6 percent per year and the Standard & Poor's Index with reinvestment of dividends would have produced 11.2 percent per year.

Notwithstanding the greater profitability of the technical strategy, its risk as measured by the variation in month-by-month rates of return was far greater than for random selection. In an effort to reduce this risk, it was decided to introduce bonds into the portfolio, the timing of the introduction to be consistent with the relative-strength principle.

To accomplish this purpose, variable-ratio formula plan models were constructed and tested. These models were very similar to the variable-ratio formula plans described in Chapter 9, with one very important exception. This is that there was to be an *increase* in the stock ratio after a strong market, whereas conventional variable-ratio plans involve a *decrease* in the stock ratio as the market rises.

This reversal of conventional variable-ratio plans was, as desired, consistent with previous findings that strength continues. The reversed variable-ratio formula plan models were combined with portfolio upgrading. This meant that securities that were both relatively strong and relatively volatile would be purchased. They would be sold when they became relatively weak. The portfolio would consist of both stocks and bonds, the ratio of one to the other progressively favoring stocks as the market moved higher and bonds as the market declined. This combination strategy produced up to 23.1 percent per year net of commissions. More important, the risk (again, as measured by the variation in month-by-month rates of return) was less than would have been produced by random selection. The combination of greater-than-random profits and less-than-random risk provided some evidence that the random-walk theory was not valid.

This evidence, affirming the value of certain technical concepts, applies, of course, only to the period covered (1960–1965). Tests of technical methods for later periods have not turned out so successfully. Moreover, the evidence has not gone uncontested. Most of the criticism has centered in the methods of taking risk into account and the possibility of sampling error and selection bias. The interested reader is referred to the articles cited at the foot of the page.[20]

Evaluation of Five-Point Chart Patterns

More recent work by the author has focused on another of the technicians' most prized tools, the chart of individual security price movements. Technicians con-

[20]Michael C. Jensen, "Random Walks: Reality or Myth: Comment," *Financial Analysts Journal,* vol. XXIII, no. 6, November–December 1967; Robert A. Levy, "Reply," *Financial Analysts Journal,* vol. XXIV, no. 1, January–February 1968.

See also Michael C. Jensen and George A. Bennington, "Random Walks and Technical Theories: Some Additional Evidence," Frank C. Jen, "Discussion," and Eugene F. Fama, "Efficient Capital Markets: A Review of Theory and Empirical Work," *Journal of Finance,* vol. XXV, no. 2, May 1970.

tend that certain price patterns (head and shoulders, triangles, channels, flags, pennants, double bottoms, and the like) recur frequently and that price direction subsequent to the formation of these patterns is predictable.

Unfortunately, little rigorous research has been addressed to the significance of the various chart patterns. This lack of research may be attributable to one or more of the following factors: (1) the scarcity of adequate computer-readable data bases; (2) the difficulty in designing an experiment; (3) the inability of standard statistical techniques to reflect satisfactorily the complicated nonlinearity of most price formations; (4) the unwillingness of many technicians to define their methods in precise, unambiguous terms; and (5) the fear of exposing the extraordinary

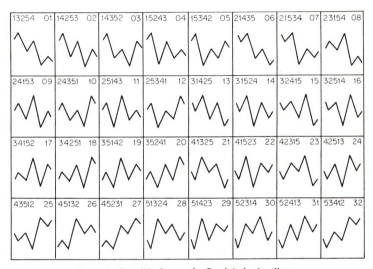

Fig. 19-1 Possible forms of a 5-point chart pattern.

success or the extraordinary failure of a rather mysterious art.

The purpose of our study was to overcome some of these obstacles; to study selected chart patterns in a systematic and scientific manner; and to measure empirically the results of chart following so that these results may receive the praise, scorn, or further study which they deserve.

Figure 19-1 illustrates the thirty-two possible forms of a 5-point chart pattern (that is, a pattern with two highs and three lows or two lows and three highs). In the right-hand corners of the boxes, the patterns are numbered from 01 through 32. In the left-hand corners, the patterns are assigned five-digit identifiers in which the digits, from left to right, represent the rank (in descending sequence) of the respective reversal points. The charts are arranged in order of these five-digit identifiers.

Avid chartists will recognize, among the thirty-two patterns, several variations of channels, wedges, diamonds, symmetrical triangles, head and shoulders, triple tops, and triple bottoms. Each of these formations allegedly reflects underlying supply-and-demand and support or resistance conditions with implications for future price behavior. A common belief among chartists is that the appearance of certain patterns followed by a "breakout" gives a profitable buy or sell signal.

Our data file consisted of daily closing prices (fully adjusted for splits, cash dividends, rights, and other distributions) for 548 New York Stock Exchange securities. The time period covered was July 3, 1964, through July 4, 1969—a span of five years. The period included one major bear market (1966), part of another (1969), an oscillating market of the type that astute traders prefer (1968), and 2½ years of strongly advancing prices (1964, 1965, and 1967). This variety of environments is, we believe, helpful in appraising the applicability of our results to diverse market conditions. A total of 19,077 patterns were detected. Of these, 9,383 patterns, with an average formative length of 149.6 weekdays, were followed by a breakout and were processed further.[21] Investment results, ignoring commissions, were measured week by week for one through twenty-six weeks subsequent to the breakout.

When investment results were summed by type of pattern, some patterns were found to precede performance that was better than average or better than the market, while others performed worse. This is hardly surprising: different investment rules, even if nonsensical, will produce different investment results. But neither the best nor the worst of these thirty-two rules performed very differently from the market. As a result, after taking trading costs into account, *none of the thirty-two patterns showed any evidence of profitable forecasting ability in either the bullish or the bearish direction.* Not one of the patterns for any holding period, from one through twenty-six weeks, produced an indication of significantly better-than-average purchase or short-sale opportunities, except for persons or firms who were able to buy and sell free of commissions. Moreover, the most bullish results tended to be generated by patterns classified as bearish in the standard textbooks on charting, and vice versa.

Of course, the omission of daily trading volume may be a deficiency. Some technicians, principally those who use bar charts, rely heavily on volume patterns to confirm the price formations we have studied. Certainly, worthwhile additional research that included this potentially important consideration could be performed. Some additional research and evidence are provided by Dr. Vaughn in Part 2 of this chapter.

Part 2. Bullish and Bearish Chart Patterns and Clues

DONALD E. VAUGHN

The technical approach to the evaluation of a security's short-run market performance is an adaptation of the Dow theory to individual issues. Under the tenets of the Dow theory, when the DJIA breaks an old intermediate high and this signal is confirmed by the transportation average, a bull market signal has been given. Likewise, when an intermediate low is broken by a subsequent low and confirmed by the transportation average, a bear market signal has been given.

---

[21]For further details regarding this study, see Robert A. Levy, "The Predictive Significance of Five-Point Chart Patterns," *The Journal of Business,* vol. XLIV, no. 3, July 1971. For pro and con evidence regarding a different type of chart pattern, see Robert A. Levy and Spero L. Kripotos, "An Empirical Investigation of Chart Consolidation Patterns," *Securities,* vol. I, no. 10, October–November 1970.

In the technical approach, similar reasoning is applied to an individual issue. Thus, when a previous intermediate high market price for an issue is broken significantly (3 percent or more is a frequently recommended rule), a bull (or buy) signal has been given. Conversely, when a previous low has been broken, a sell signal has been sounded. Rising market prices on heavy volume, with declines on relatively heavy volume, with mild recoveries on light volume, indicate a further decline in market prices of individual issues.

Astute speculators have observed that certain price and volume patterns that appear on the charts for individual issues are almost always bullish, while others are almost always bearish. Still other patterns are not trustworthy and are generally classified as uncertainty patterns. Technicians have a wide range of chart services from which to choose. They may choose among bar charts, point-and-figure charts, and line charts.

We undertake in this part of Chapter 19 a comparison of vertical bar charts, point-and-figure charts, and line charts. Interpretation of formations, estimation of probable moves, support and resistance zones, and likely reasons for securities to move in the fashion in which they usually do are discussed. The effectiveness of charts as individual price predictive devices is then considered.

One inherent danger associated with stock speculation based on technical selection is that a politically motivated market (often driven by war news, international monetary speculation, and the like) may whipsaw market prices, thus leading to trading losses for speculators. Once the charting technique begins to fail more often than to call profitable trading signals, stock speculators are advised to (1) retreat to the sidelines, thus preserving their capital, or (2) begin to play the commodity futures markets with their charts (see Section Six). When a longer-term direction is detected in stock price averages, they can return to stock speculation with reasonable chances for successful trading.

Another necessary precaution: with the growing emphasis on portfolio performance, many institutional investors have turned toward the management of stock portfolios (selection and monitoring) with electronic data processing (EDP) models. Numerous stock chart services are posted electronically, among them Compugraph, Selectrend, Chart Service Institute Charts, and Mansfield Stock Chart Service. Programs have been designed to show technical buy and sell signals such as breaking resistance or support and penetration of the forty-week moving averages. Large block trades by performance-minded institutions that are EDP-attuned to the market often lead to very rapid swings in thinly traded issues. Thus, speculators must monitor their stock positions *daily* to detect such sudden shifts in supply and demand.

VERTICAL BAR CHARTS

Construction

Vertical bar charts may be prepared on arithmetic or semilogarithmic paper. They are designed to show the price range for a stipulated period of time, such as the daily price range, the weekly price range, or the monthly price range. The volume of trading is usually reflected in bar chart form at the base of the chart immediately underneath the price trading range. Quite frequently, a small horizontal tick represents the closing price of the issue during the time period.

Small or large gaps sometimes appear on the charts. These occur when the trading range for one day or another period does not overlap the trading range for the previous day or period. An upside gap reflects strong demand, with buyers willing to bid a high price to acquire the issue. Conversely, if gaps appear on the downside, supply has at least temporarily overcome demand for the issue. This may be caused by unexpectedly poor earning news or other events concerning the stock market in general or the company in particular. It may also be the result of a shift in sentiment for no apparent reason.

In general, vertical bar chart formations may be divided into bullish formations, uncertainty patterns, and bearish formations. These widely recognized formations are described and illustrated below.

Bullish Patterns

The "saucer" pattern, or the "rounded bottom" frequently precedes an extensive upside move by an issue. In a true saucer pattern, the shape of the price and also the volume should be concave upward. On both ends of the saucer, the volume should be heavier than near the base of the formation. Frequently, a small handle is built on the formation, making it resemble a cup.

After the market price breaks above a few previous highs, there is typically a small pullback for a few days. This shake-out often precedes a major move in the issue. The extent of the upward move from this type of formation is usually extensive, amounting to a distance equal to three-fourths of the radius of the saucer formation in a weak market and to 2 or 3 times this magnitude in a strong market.

The "inverted head-and-shoulders" formation is very similar to the saucer formation. In this formation, three wavelike movements are formed by the price oscillation of the issue. The first movement represents the left shoulder, the second the head, and the third the right shoulder. The inverted head usually makes a slightly deeper penetration than the left or the right shoulder does. The third waveline movement, or right shoulder, completes the pattern when it breaks the neckline (a line extended from the highest penetrations of the left and right shoulders, adjacent to the head) by 3 percent or more.

In a true inverted head-and-shoulders formation, the volume is usually heavy on the downside of the left shoulder, declines with the completion of the left shoulder, is fairly light on the formation of the head, has light volume on the formation of the downside of the right shoulder, but is very heavy on the breakout, particularly on the breakthrough of the neckline. Quite frequently, the price "gaps" through the neckline. It usually pulls back to the neckline for a few days before beginning its upward move. The extent of the move is about the same as for the saucer pattern.

Whereas saucers usually appear in very low-priced issues, the inverted head-and-shoulders formation may appear in low-priced, medium-priced, or high-priced stocks. Chart formations have a tendency to repeat in individual issues; so an issue may form a series of inverted heads and shoulders on its upward move while other issues may form a series of saucer-shaped formations.

In their upward move, prices often move back and forth between two clearly defined channels. This is reflected in Fig. 19-2c. It is generally believed that the longer the movement within a given channel, the greater the likelihood of its continuance.[22] But not all technicians accept this hypothesis.

A majority of the vertical bar chartists believe that a price rise on heavy volume is bullish and that a price decline on light volume is also bullish. Conversely, a price decline on heavy volume is bearish, while a price rise on light volume is also bearish. Sudden volume declines on price rallies and increased volumes on reactions are often signals of a major price reversal.

Frequently, a buying or selling blowoff may carry the price of an issue far outside its upward or downward channel for a short time. The stock then usually moves back through the channel and continues in its new direction. Often the

---

[22]See, for example, William L. Jiler, *How Charts Can Help You in the Stock Market*, Commodity Research Publications Corporation, New York, 1962.

blowoff may be headed by a one-, two-, or three-day "island reversal." The island reversal appears where gaps on the upside and the downside are separated by a few days of trading activity. In this formation, the volume is usually extremely heavy on both the upward and the downward phases of the blowoff. Frequently, other gaps may occur near the island reversal. An issue may make a mild recovery attempt or a second assault on the previous high. This is usually unsuccessful, however, and the stock begins to drift downward in almost a mirror pattern of the upward movement. When a blowoff occurs, traders should be alert to a possible instantaneous change in direction and sell the issue before it falls drastically.

Quite frequently, small "pennants" and "flags" appear in an upward price

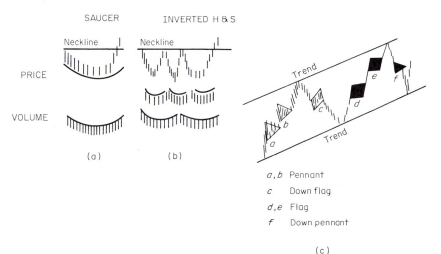

Fig. 19-2 Bullish bar chart patterns.

movement for an issue. The staffs of the pennants and flags are pointed upward, while the flag portions should be tightly formed and pointed downward. The volume pattern should be extremely heavy on the formation of the staff, fairly heavy on upward price movements, and relatively low on the decline in prices within the pennant and flag formations. These formations are usually continuation patterns of the previous upward move.

Bearish Formations

Bearish formations are not illustrated in Fig. 19-2 because they are simply the inverse of the bullish formations. Thus, the price pattern of a "rounded top" or an "inverted saucer" has a shape opposite to that of the bullish saucer pattern. In this bearish formation, the pattern should be concave downward for the price but concave upward for the volume. This type of formation usually signifies an extensive price decline for the individual issue, generally by 50 percent or more.

The "downtrend" is another bearish pattern. Instead of the trend line's being drawn underneath the wavelike motions, for the downtrend the imaginary line is usually drawn across the tops of the formation.

The "head and shoulders" is a bearish formation in which the last shoulder is a wavelike motion that does not reach as high as the second wavelike motion forming the head. The right shoulder usually does not extend as high as the head but may extend as high as or slightly higher than the left shoulder. A neckline extended from the low points between the left shoulder and the head and the right shoulder and the head shows that the formation has been completed. If the price breaks through the neckline by more than 3 percent, the down formation is usually reliable. Frequently, there is a rally to the neckline, providing a good short-selling location, prior to a rapid descent in price.

"Down pennants" and "down flags" (or inverted consolidation patterns) may also occur during the downtrend of an issue. In a down flag, the staff of the flag points downward, but the flag itself hangs upward. The "descending wedge" (sometimes mistaken for pennants or triangles) is more often than not bullish, but an "ascending wedge" is usually bearish. The wedge is very similar to the flag, but one of the ends is slightly wider than the other, and both sides are rising or declining rather than one being horizontal.[23]

Uncertainty Formations

A number of formations are uncertainty patterns. Chartists cannot accurately forecast the direction of the stock immediately after it breaks out of the formation but must wait until much of the breakout has occurred. These uncertainty patterns, which include the "triangle," the "wedge," the "rectangle," the "box," and the "diamond," are illustrated in Fig. 19-3. Usually, the volume is not much stronger on the upside than on the downside of the price movement. Frequently, when an issue's price moves to the extreme tip of a symmetrical triangle or has moved upward and downward several times within a triangle or a box and when the move does not extend all the way to the base before reversing its direction, an upside breakout may be indicated. After a breakout on heavy volume, a mild reaction usually will pull the price of the issue back to the edge of the formation pattern before the issue begins its true upward move. In a very strong market the pullback may be minor.

These uncertainty formations are much less reliable than the bullish formations described above are. Quite frequently they will give false breakout signals. Uncertainty formations sometimes appear as consolidation patterns within an upward or downward price adjustment. These formations record the relative balance between supply and demand for an issue. Until a favorable earnings report or some other favorable or unfavorable news that will upset the balance between supply and demand at a given price is publicized, the market value of the stock oscillates upward and downward within a narrow trading range.

Support and Resistance Levels

A congested trading area frequently constitutes a support as well as a resistance level. Once the market price of the stock rises above the congested trading area, the price becomes a support level. On the other hand, after an issue falls below a congested trading area, it may have difficulty in penetrating this resistance barrier.

If we consider the personal attitude of the individual investor and multiply this by thousands of shareholders for the issue involved, the reason for this double role becomes self-evident. For example, an investor may have bought a stock at $35 a share. The market price of the stock declines to $31. The buyer makes a mental note to sell the issue at $35 and thus break even. When enough people do this, the old holders of the stock will shift out of the issue so that much of the floating supply of the stock changes hands. Once the issue has broken above this congested trading range, however, individuals who did not buy at that price (or who sold there) resolve to buy the stock if it drops back to $35 or $36. This additional buying pressure keeps the issue from falling through the congested trading area.

---

[23]Because of the brevity of this subsection, only the most widely recognized chart patterns can be described. Serious chartists who are interested in pursuing the matter should read Robert D. Edwards and John Magee, *Technical Analysis of Stock Trends,* 4th ed., J. Magee, Inc., Springfield, Mass., 1964.

In addition to support and resistance levels being set by previous lows and highs, respectively, "trend lines" and "moving-average lines" also act as such barriers. Uptrend lines are usually drawn along major bottoms, while downtrend lines are drawn across intermediate tops. Moving-average lines may be weekly closing prices for the past ten, twenty, or thirty weeks and appear to offer support or resistance for many stocks.

Estimating the Move

Technicians who use vertical bar charts have developed numerous ways of estimating the distance of an expected move. When a formation breaks out of a rectangle

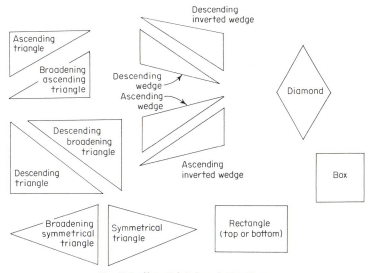

Fig. 19-3   Uncertainty bar chart patterns.

or a triangle, the expected move *averages* the base of the triangle or rectangle; however, this distance can vary from ¾ to 2 times the base in weak and strong markets, respectively.

Moves that originate from an inverted head and shoulders or a saucer average about the distance of the radius of the saucer or the depth of the head below the neckline, although any particular move is greatly influenced by the strength of the overall market. A majority of the upward moves occur in three approximately equal legs rather than in only one, with consolidations in the form of pennants, flags, triangles, or wedges.

One additional method for estimating the probable move of an issue involves the location of gaps. Quite frequently a breakaway gap will carry the price out of a particularly strong bullish formation, such as the saucer or the inverted head and shoulders. A measuring gap (frequently more than one) is often located about halfway up the expected move. Quite frequently there is an exhaustion gap near the end of a runaway move. Upside gaps occurring on very strong volume are almost always bullish, while downward gaps occurring on very strong volume are bearish.

Some individual issues decline and fill the gaps within a few trading days, but for others the gaps remain open for an extended period. The patterns are usually repeated, however, and an issue that usually fills gaps within a week or two can be expected to do so again and again after other gaps are formed. Therefore, when an upside gap is sighted, patient investors may wait until the stock has declined to or through this gap before placing their buy orders; or they may place a limited order to buy the stock at that price. Conversely, if a gap is sighted on the downside and the issue has a tendency to fill a gap, a limited order to short the issue at a price approximately equal to the gap may be placed by short sellers and will usually provide a short-term profit. Except for major bear market moves, many downside legs usually last two months or less; so shorts are usually covered after a few weeks.

Although the use of charts may seem strange to many investors and although many individuals may prefer to buy only issues with strong fundamentals, to a large extent charts do measure the demand for and supply of a stock at any given price. The use of charts will facilitate trading by speculators as well as improve the timing for purchase or sale by long-term investors.

POINT-AND-FIGURE CHARTS

Construction

The point-and-figure chart is constructed on arithmetic graph paper, the price being indicated on the vertical scale in alternating rows of rising and falling prices. Some services use *X's* to denote price advances and *O's* to denote declines.

Suppose that we begin by plotting an individual common stock issue at $10 per share with squares assigned a value of 50 cents. *X's* are placed above one another as long as the stock continues to rise in price. Some point-and-figure technicians use a single, whole square reversal technique, while others use two- or three-square reversal rules. That is, the trend is not reversed until the price of the stock has changed direction by at least 3 full points.[24]

Another publisher of a point-and-figure chart service, Morgan, Rogers, and Roberts, Inc., uses the single-full-point reversal system. In addition, this chart service places importance upon interday runs, upward and downward, as well as on the overall trading range for any given day, which is picked up from the ticker tape on charted stocks.[25]

Technicians may adopt whatever scale they please. One useful scale standard is to let each square represent 25 cents for a stock trading below $6, each square represent 50 cents for a stock trading between $6 and $20, each square represent $1 for a stock trading between $20 and $100, and each square represent $3 for a stock trading over $100.

When individuals wish to chart the Dow Jones Industrial Average or some other popular average, they may use a five-square or a three-square reversal movement, with each square representing 5 points or 3 points respectively. A scale that appears convenient to the user should be adopted. The charting of the Dow Jones Industrial Average or some other popular average may give technicians an indication of a probable change in direction of the market as a whole.

If technicians wish to indicate the time period during which the pattern is formed, they may substitute the first letter of each month for the first position within a given month, or they may substitute the numbers 1 through 12 to represent the beginning location for the first of each month.

Chart Patterns

Not all points-and-figure technicians acknowledge exactly the same patterns, nor do they agree exactly upon the names of the patterns. Some of the more important

[24]Chartcraft, Inc., uses the three-square reversal method. See A. W. Cohen, *The Chartcraft Method of Point and Figure Trading,* Chartcraft, Inc., Larchmont, N.Y., 1961.

[25]See, for example, Alexander H. Wheelan, *Study Helps and Point and Figure Technique,* Morgan, Rogers, and Roberts, Inc., New York, 1954.

configurations suggested by Alexander Wheelan and A. W. Cohen, which appear in Figs. 19-4 and 19-5, are adequate for describing reversal patterns.

Perhaps the most easily recognized chart patterns are the "bullish signal" formation and the "bearish signal" formation. These patterns closely resemble an ascending triangle and a descending triangle respectively. When a previous high has been broken, a bullish signal formation indicates a buy signal. A new low signifies a sell signal. Variations of these patterns may occur, but about the only difference is that the triangle is not quite so regular. Thus, instead of the decline stopping 1 full point above the previous column, the descent is either to the same square or to two or three squares above that position.

Instead of having a double top, as usually appears in a bullish signal formation, the configuration may form a "triple top." Sometimes even more than three runs may be taken to break out of a formation. The triple top may be flat, as shown in Fig. 19-4, or slightly ascending. Once a previous high has been broken, the formation becomes bullish.

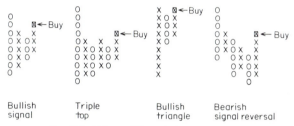

Fig. 19-4   Point-and-figure bullish patterns.

When the supply and demand for a stock are relatively in balance, a triangle may be formed. It is not possible to tell which direction the move will take until either a new high or a new low has been formed. The completion of this formation results in a bullish or a bearish triangle.

A formation very similar to the triple top (or "triple bottom") is the "spread triple top." One or two rows of the X's or O's do not extend as high or as low, respectively, as the other rows that constitute the top.

A combination of the bullish signal and triple-top patterns sometimes occurs. The bottom of the formation appears similar to the bullish signal formation, or an ascending triangle (Fig. 19-4), while the top of the formation is a triple top. The opposite of this formation (to see it, turn Fig. 19-4 upside down) results in a sell signal, or a bearish formation.

A "bearish signal reversal" appears when a new high is reached after a series of new lows have occurred. The "bullish signal reversal" is formed in opposite fashion when, after a series of new highs, a new low is made. These two formations signify buy and sell signals, respectively, and are similar to the inverted head-and-shoulders and head-and-shoulders formations, respectively, that appear on vertical bar charts.[26]

Trend Lines

The method of establishing a trend line differs slightly in the Wheelan and Cohen methods. Wheelan suggests that the bottoms of major stock movements, or support levels, be joined to form the upward trend line. Drawing a line across the tops establishes the downward trend line. Cohen, in contrast, suggests that a trend line be drawn along the diagonals of the chart squares, starting from a peak or a bottom. The trend of the stock usually follows this line. When the Cohen diagonal

[26]For a more complete analysis of these chart patterns, see Cohen, op. cit., pp. 12–26.

method is used, the trend line, up or down, always appears to be at a 45-degree angle, which is generally steeper or deeper than the trend line established by using Wheelan's method. Another reason for this is that Cohen uses the 3-point reversal signal rather than the single, whole-point square reversal; thus the point-and-square formation for a stock under his method is squeezed together much more closely than under the Wheelan method.

Wheelan believes that his method is superior to other methods, especially because it permits more accurate counts and estimates of the probable move for an individual issue. However, the use of this method would almost necessitate subscribing to a chart service. By contrast, an individual could follow fairly well the methods suggested by Cohen by using the daily or weekly trading range as it appears in the financial section of a newspaper. Under either method, the buying and selling signals are usually valid. Under the Cohen method, however, the extent of the move may be more difficult to determine.

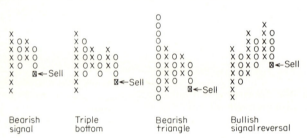

Fig. 19-5   Point-and-figure bearish patterns.

As long as the market price of a stock remains above its uptrend line, the buy signals for the stock are usually valid. Once the market value of the stock moves below the uptrend line, however, the buy signals are frequently false. Similarly, sell signals given above the trend line are often less reliable than those given below it.

Most technicians, whether they are using point-and-figure or vertical bar charts in trying to determine when an issue is about to move upward or downward, suggest trading with the general direction of the market.[27] It is easier to locate bullish price formations when the general trend of the market is upward. Conversely, good short-sale candidates appear more frequently when the market is in a downward trend. In addition, the signals are more frequently correct when they are in the same direction as the trend of the general market. The sell signals are usually more reliable when the market level is falling, and the buy signals more reliable when the general market level is increasing.

Support and Resistance Levels

A congested area of trading represents a support or resistance level. When the price of an individual issue is below the congested area of trading, the area represents a resistance level. Once the buying pressure has caused the price of the issue to rise above this point, it becomes a support level. For this reason, it is difficult for the market price of a stock to break below a triple top once it has broken out above it. This congested trading area represents a support level.

Technicians may use support and resistance levels for setting limit orders to buy or sell a stock. For example, if an issue breaks above an intermediate triple top and if it appears that the stock will run into additional overhanging supply a certain number of squares above the breakout point, this would be a strategic place for

---

[27]This topic is covered in Chapter 8.

setting a limit order to sell. Once the market price reaches this level, some selling pressure will usually take place, causing the stock's price to decline to a lower support zone.

Trading Strategies

Some technicians suggest that chartists be satisfied with a 10 or 15 percent profit. Accordingly, after locating an issue that is about to break out or one that has already given a buy signal, persons may place a limit order to sell the issue at a level that would provide a 10 or 15 percent profit on the transaction. But other technicians suggest that the issue be held until a valid sell signal has been indicated. Following the former rule would result in selling some issues before a move is completed. However, it would free capital for other investment opportunities.

Either of these methods, if followed consistently by point-and-figure chartists, will often outperform the market when applied to issues with high beta functions (those that oscillate widely relative to the popular stock averages). However, these methods do require a great deal of work and subscription to one or more chart services.

Estimating the Move

When the three-square reversal method rather than the single-square reversal method is used, the chart width of the bullish formation should be multiplied by 3 to determine the approximate number of squares upward that the issue will ultimately move. This move will not be exact and should be modified by chartists to take into consideration any support and resistance levels. At a resistance level, selling pressure may cause a pullback equal to one-third to two-thirds of the previous advance when a consolidation pattern is formed. Triangles or bullish signal patterns are common. Once the previous high has again been broken, the market price of the stock will usually carry to another resistance level.

With the 1-point reversal method, the width of the formation should be used as the probable extent of the move. The proper starting point for the move count is the row of the formation with the fewest unoccupied squares.[28]

Neither of these methods produces exact predictions of the move, but both give rough approximations. Neither offers any clues to the time period during which the move will probably take place. Consolidation movements generally take the form of a bullish or a bearish triangle on the point-and-figure chart.

LINE CHARTS

Instead of plotting the price of an issue in the form of vertical bars (representing daily, weekly, or monthly price trading ranges) or using rows of *X's* and *O's* (showing advances and declines) on point-and-figure charts, chartists may simply show closing prices with dots and join them with a line. The key price of the issue is assumed to be its final closing price for the period covered (day, week, or month).

Volume is usually recorded on a line chart in one of two ways. In Fig. 19-6 the cumulative upside-downside volume, weighted by the session's turnover and showing a plus or minus, depending on whether the session closed up or down (no-change closings are disregarded), is shown immediately below the price line. When cumulative upside volume is rising more rapidly than the issue (Fig. 19-6*a*), when price declines more rapidly than cumulative upside-downside volume (*b*), or when a breakout occurs on the volume line before the price line (*c*), the issue is interpreted as showing accumulation. The opposite tendencies show distribution and generally lead to further price declines.

[28]See A. H. Wheelan, op. cit., p. 15.

Volume may also be recorded as in Fig. 19-7, with horizontal bars weighted by trading turnover adjusted for time, since more distant trading provides less important resistance and support levels than nearby trading. Thus, trading during the current year may be weighted with a 5, trading during the previous year with a 4, and so on for the previous five years. Similarly, weights of 5, 4, 3, 2, and 1 could be assigned for trading during the current stock cycle, the previous one, and those more distant respectively. The long bands of trading (at their respective prices) shown in the figure represent resistance and support zones, with price moves coming very rapidly in the areas of little recent trading. One service refers to the price line as the "zip line" because it has a tendency to move very rapidly between zones.

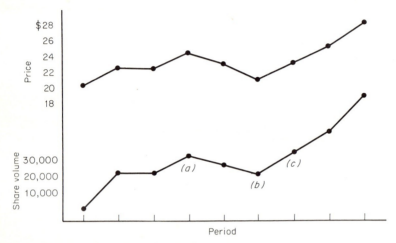

Fig. 19-6   Line chart showing cumulative upside and downside volume.

Line charts appear to have less of a following than either bar charts or point-and-figure charts, although they are simple to maintain and are designed to accomplish the same purpose: to detect accumulation and distribution.

EFFECTIVENESS OF CHARTS AS FORECASTING TOOLS

Certain formations that appear on one type of chart are similar to those on another. For example, the formation of a head and shoulders or an inverted head and shoulders, if the formation is large enough, will appear on the point-and-figure chart as the same pattern. If point-and-figure chartists use a three-square reversal, however, they may not be able to detect a head and shoulders or an inverted head and shoulders. Though they may look different, the point-and-figure configuration and the vertical bar chart patterns are of about equal forecasting ability in the hands of skilled technicians.

In general, a downside reversal movement is signaled on the vertical bar chart and on the point-and-figure chart at approximately the same time. The bullish formations that appear on the two types of chart are somewhat different. The three more common types of bullish reversal patterns are the bearish signal reversal formation, the triple top, and the bullish signal pattern. These patterns appear on the vertical bar chart as an inverted head and shoulders, a saucer, or a triangle. Astute chartists may detect the reversal signal by using either of the chart methods. To the author, more numerous and clearer buy signals appear to be formed on the point-and-figure chart than on the vertical bar chart, although much of the total move has already occurred when the point-and-figure buy patterns are complete. Line chart patterns resemble bar chart formations.

It is frequently easier to spot an upside reversal movement on a vertical bar chart or a line chart than on a point-and-figure chart. Before a true reversal signal is indicated on the point-and-figure chart, the market price may have declined by a substantial amount.

Both the vertical bar chart and the point-and-figure methods offer an approximation of the extent of the move. The vertical bar chart method uses the base of the rectangle, the halfway or one-third–distance consolidation triangle, or the distance between gaps. The distance across the consolidation formation is important on the point-and-figure chart. Of course, neither method is 100 percent

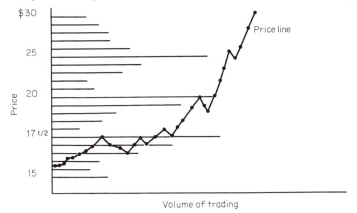

Fig. 19-7   Line and trading zone charts.

accurate in forecasting the extent of a move, although a combination of the two methods generally provides fair forecasting ability.

The shift in volume on the vertical bar chart or the line chart may indicate a probable reversal in trend long before a bearish signal is completed on the vertical bar chart or the point-and-figure chart. However, the investor must watch the issue closely, charting the volume and price range daily to detect a possible change in direction. Buy signals are reflected more clearly than sell signals on the line chart and the point-and-figure chart, while sell signals appear earlier and more clearly on the vertical bar chart, in the author's opinion. Neither of the methods is completely accurate in estimating the extent of the move, the error being influenced largely by the overall trend in the market. See also Dr. Levey's sobering evaluation of the nonusefulness of 5-point line charts in Part 1 of this chapter.

In conclusion, the effective use of either the vertical bar chart, the line chart, or the point-and-figure chart depends upon the charting experience of individuals as well as upon the amount of time that they devote to this endeavor. Valid buy and sell signals are usually in evidence on all three chart types if users can discern them. For best results, one should trade with the trend of the overall market rather than against it.

BIBLIOGRAPHY

Cootner, P. H. (ed.): *The Random Character of Stock Market Prices,* rev. ed., The M.I.T. Press, Cambridge, Mass., 1964.

Edwards, Robert D., and John Magee: *Technical Analysis of Stock Trends,* 5th ed., J. Magee, Inc., Springfield, Mass., 1972.

Freeman, George K.: "The 10 Percent Rule: It Furnishes a Simple Formula for Catching Broad Market Swings," *Barron's,* vol. 39, no. 11, p. 9, March 16, 1959.

Haas, Albert, Jr., and Don D. Jackson, M.D.: *Bulls, Bears and Dr. Freud,* The World Publishing Company, Cleveland, 1967.

Jiler, William, *How Charts Can Help You in the Stock Market,* Commodity Research Publications Corporation, New York, 1962.

Latané, Henry A., and Donald L. Tuttle: *Security Analysis and Portfolio Management,* The Ronald Press Company, New York, 1970, chap. 14, pp. 353–378.

Levy, Robert A.: "Conceptual Foundations of Technical Analysis," *Financial Analysts Journal,* vol. 22, no. 4, pp. 83–89, July–August 1966.

Seligman, Daniel: "Playing the Market with Charts," *Fortune,* vol. 65, no. 2, pp. 113–115, 178–186, February 1962.

Vaughn, Donald E., "The Reliability of Vertical Bar Charts and Point and Figure Charts," *Proceedings, Southwestern Finance Association, April 16–17, 1965,* University of Texas Bureau of Business Research, Austin, 1965, pp. 1–40.

———: "Combining the Undervaluation, Fundamental, and Technical Approaches to Security Selection," *Southwestern Social Science Quarterly,* vol. 48, no. 1, pp. 79–85, June 1967.

———: *Survey of Investments,* Holt, Rinehart and Winston, Inc., New York, 1967, pp. 312–402.

Chapter **20**

Profiting from Emerging and Comeback Industries

JOHN F. FERRARO and ROBERT A. LERMAN

This section of the *Handbook* is based upon a very simple premise: the basic idea behind investing is to make money—not to own a share of America, not to provide for forced or systematic savings, not to secure a hedge against inflation. Our subject is narrowed down to making money in *emerging and comeback industries:* how to find them, how to analyze them, and, most important, how to profit from them.

Importance of Industry Analysis

Whether you invest for the preservation of capital, liberal current income, or growth potential, sooner or later the fundamental consideration that must be faced is the outlook for the industry in which you seek to invest. Some analysts begin their study with a particular company and then turn to the industry it serves; some begin with the industry and then study companies within that industry. But careful investment analysis includes at least an overall view of the industry (preferably a detailed study), its position within the general economy, its growth prospects in relation to the gross national product, its state of development, and the outlook for the markets to which it addresses its products or services. Within this analysis, individual companies are studied to define their position in the industry, their market share, and their expected share in the industry's growth potential.

Investment profits can be realized in a good number of well-known and highly visible industries. Fortunes have been made in computers, oils, automobiles, and chemicals, and in all likelihood new fortunes will be made through investments in these industries in the future. In this chapter we shall focus on a lesser-known technique of investing: profiting from emerging and comeback industries.

EMERGING INDUSTRIES

How to Find Them

A recent magazine cartoon showed a scientist examining an apparently clear laboratory surface and announcing that he had just made an important break-through, if only he could find it. To persons in the more rarefied strata of scientific evolution such a scene is not apt to appear wholly humorous. Products today can be so minuscule that their shipping containers are marked "Not empty"; and as science advances to the point at which individual molecules can be put to work, it may be more difficult to "find" scientific or technological breakthroughs after they have been discovered.

The investor seeking to profit from emerging industries has an equivalent task. In all cases, the breakthroughs either are already there or are being formulated; the trick is to find them.

Even though emerging industries are, by their very nature, different from more highly visible and well-recognized industries, they are generally subject to the same tests as orthodox industries. Investors seeking to profit from emerging industries can identify them by asking the following questions:

1. Is there a need for their products or services?
2. Can the need be filled?
3. Can the need be filled profitably?
4. Is now the right time to invest?

Determining the Product or Service Need

The first step in determining whether an industry can truly be classified as emerging is to determine, insofar as possible, whether there is a need for the product or service that the emerging industry proposes to deliver. This may seem trivial, but it is at the heart of investors' search for an emerging industry. "Need" implies much more than the desirability or usefulness of a product; it means that, aside from other niceties, there must be a *market* for the proposed new venture.

We are reminded of the physician who invented a new type of stethoscope by utilizing a very sophisticated array of microelectronic circuitry. This particular stethoscope not only detected heartbeats but simultaneously provided various lung tests, breath analysis, rates of blood flow, and a host of additional information. Desirable? Yes. Useful? Of course. But was there a need? No. Our doctor friend had overlooked one simple fact. Physicians simply were not willing to spend $900 for a new, improved stethoscope. The stethoscope was an intriguing idea but one without a market. There wasn't a true need.

In short, alert investors must utilize the best information they can gather to determine, before proceeding further, whether there is a need for the product or industry in which they intend to invest.

Filling the Need

Once it has been determined that a true need exists, the next factor to be analyzed is the feasibility of filling the need. For example, it is well and good to say that there is a need for an artificial heart. But is there a reason to believe that the technology required to build this artificial heart is available now or soon will be available? It is likely that you can name dozens of ideas which would meet the test of need, but these ideas will die aborning unless they can be translated into really workable devices. If you doubt this, make some inquiries at the U.S. Patent Office as to why it no longer accepts patent applications for perpetual motion machines. Such a machine is a great idea, but the technology simply isn't available. The need cannot be filled.

The Profit Picture for Filling the Need

Having found a product or a service for which there is a need, and having convinced yourself that the need can be filled, you are well on the way to uncovering an emerging industry. Now only one test remains, and it concerns profitability. This is perhaps the most difficult test of all. It must be determined that the need can be filled profitably. The best technology in the world, combined with a product evidencing the greatest possible need, will still fail the test of creating an emerging industry unless the product can be marketed profitably.

For example, there is available today a rather remarkable machine that serves as an artificial kidney. For many persons afflicted with kidney disease, this machine often spells the difference between life and death. Clearly this machine meets the test of need. It also meets the test of technology. Through the miracle of modern science, man has been able to duplicate the chemical processes involved in the kidney function. Unfortunately, this technology has a price, and in the case of the artificial kidney machine the price is approximately $40,000 per machine. At this price only well-endowed hospitals, charitable organizations, and a few wealthy individuals can afford the remarkable kidney machine. So the simple fact is that the machine cannot be manufactured profitably and sustain an industry. Individual kidney machines can be manufactured profitably, but with existing price levels the market is too severely limited to support mass production. And since no industrial enterprise can exist for very long unless it makes profits on its product lines, it is obviously premature to consider the manufacture of artificial kidney machines as an emerging industry.

Similar reasoning can be applied to other ideas and devices. There is a need, the technology exists, but the test of profitability fails.

Investment Timing for Emerging Industries

This brings us to a vital factor in the search for new and emerging industries: the question of timing. The approach to timing may be analyzed through a discussion of an emerging industry that has already come to fruition, the mobile home industry. In the early 1940s mobile homes were considered little more than temporary shelter for people who could not afford permanent housing, but even then there clearly was a need for good low-cost housing. The need for sound low-cost shelter unquestionably existed even long before the 1940s, but the advent of World War II housing needs, particularly in the larger metropolitan areas, became so acute that temporary quarters were in great demand.

An analysis of the mobile home industry as a potential emerging industry in the 1940s would have yielded the following facts. There was a need. The technology was available to produce mobile homes, although clearly not on the scale of today's production. Finally, the homes could be produced profitably. As in the case of artificial kidney machines, however, the market for mobile homes was simply not great enough at the time to permit manufacturers to set up mass production facilities. So, although mobile homes could be produced profitably on an individual basis, the mass market was absent, and they could not pass the test of total profitability, as opposed to profitability on an individual basis.

When a specific situation meets the first three tests of an emerging industry— need, available technology, and profitability on an individual basis—but not the test of profitability *on a mass production basis,* investing in the emerging industry becomes a matter of timing. From an investment point of view, it is of little comfort to know that you have found an emerging industry, only to wait for years, perhaps decades, for the investment to pay off. So our analysis must now involve the question of timing.

It is possible, of course, to find an emerging industry, invest in it, and simply wait for the industry to realize the potential that your analysis suggests. The danger here is that while you are waiting, there may appear a different product, concept, or service that fills the need, has the technology available, and can be produced profitably, thereby leapfrogging the original concept and bypassing the emerging industry. So, from the investment point of view, finding an emerging industry implies finding one in which the time period between discovery and eventual profits will not be unduly long.

Divide Before You Decide

One of the major brokerage houses has a slogan that says: "Investigate, then invest." This is a sound concept, but in searching for an emerging industry we would add "Divide before you decide." We are referring to price-earnings multiples as an aid in determining suitable timing for an emerging industry. The test itself is simple: take the stock's current price, and divide by the earnings reported by the company during the most recent twelve months. This gives the price-earnings multiple, which is the first part of the test.

Now consider the second and more important part of the test: *The higher the price-earnings multiple, the more likely it is that you have found a security in an emerging industry ready to blossom forth.* This statement is probably quite contrary to what might be considered "normal" investment advice, but remember that there is nothing normal in seeking an investment in an emerging industry. We are not trying to minimize risk but are purposely accepting risk as a necessary by-product of well-above-average appreciation potential. And then we are trying to determine, insofar as is practicable, the proper timing from the investment point of view in order to capitalize on this emerging industry. The "divide before you decide" test is perhaps more useful than any other easily performed method of analysis in the matter of timing.

A high price-earnings multiple implies that a goodly number of investors are convinced that future earnings prospects for this particular security or industry are so substantial that they are willing to accept a high multiple of current earnings to have representation in the emerging concept. If the industry truly is emerging, this concept makes sense, since in most cases earnings will not have had a fair opportunity to begin multiplying.

Of course, if you have the patience of a Job and the wisdom of a Solomon, you can perform your investment analysis, be convinced that you are smarter than anyone else around, invest in an emerging industry, and then simply sit back and wait for everyone else to discover it. Most people have neither the wisdom nor the patience to do this.

Therefore, to maximize profit potential from an investment in an emerging industry, you must buy a security at some time between its embryonic stage and the point at which its future growth potential becomes discounted several years into the future. This is the time when the "divide before you decide" test will find its greatest application.

Note, however, that limitations and pitfalls are built into this tool. Since it is mathematically impossible to divide anything by zero and arrive at a rational number, some earnings must be present before you can apply the test. This means that "concept" companies, brand new start-ups, and other firms with little or no operating history, in which bottom-line earnings have not yet been generated, will not conveniently fit into the category of emerging industries. They may be turnaround situations, they may be special situations, or they may even be genuinely good investments; but they are not emerging industries as we define them. To meet the tests of need, technology, and profitability, emerging industries must also meet the test of timing, and the test is meaningless when deficit earnings are involved.

Securities in emerging industries typically sell at price-earnings multiples of about twice the current P/E multiple for the Dow Jones Industrial Average when their investment characteristics are most attractive. At these multiples, investors are putting their money on the line and saying: "Here is an industry or a security with emerging growth potential." If the multiple approaches 3 times that of the DJIA, investors have started to overdiscount future prospects. At multiples of 1½ times the DJIA or less, growth potential is not yet well defined or is not widely

A case study of the philosophy expressed above may be found by returning to our example of the mobile home industry. Skyline Corporation, as a leading factor in the field, sold at price-earnings multiples of around 6 times earnings during the early 1960s, or far below the DJIA P/E multiple. As is now evident, the mobile home industry even then met all the tests of an emerging industry, but the "divide before you decide" test would have shown an investment at this point to be premature. The stock's price during this period, registering only minor fluctuations, would have shown the wisdom of a decision not to invest as yet.

During the period from 1964 through 1967 the multiple began rising as more investors became aware of the growth potential inherent in the emerging mobile home industry. Price-earnings multiples during these four years ranged up to 17 times earnings, and there were early indications that the stock was preparing to move higher. Yet even by the end of 1967 Skyline was trading at only $6.50 per share.

By 1968 the investing public finally began to believe that the mobile home industry was an emerging industry, and for the first time in the company's history the price-earnings multiple crossed 40 and was more than twice that of the DJIA. At this point, Skyline Corporation would have qualified in every sense, including the test of timing, as an attractive security investment in an emerging industry. During 1968 Skyline's stock price surged to $32.625, eclipsing all the points gained during the previous seven years. If an investor had purchased Skyline Corporation stock when its P/E multiple first rose to more than twice that of the DJIA, the investment timing would have been virtually perfect. Years of watching investment funds sitting idle with relatively little price movement would have been avoided.

Investors who purchased Skyline Corporation stock at any time between 1969 and 1970 managed to double their money (or quintuple it if they happened to catch the low) over the next few years, which in the annals of stock market history were surely not the kindest time period to invest.

This raises a point to keep in mind. Emerging industries and the securities in those industries do not produce one brief flurry of excitement and then die out, never to be heard from again—not if they are true emerging industries, not if they have met the tests outlined above, not if you divide before you decide and the industry meets the test of timing.

Once you have found an emerging industry that meets these tests, do not rush to take your profits. Conversely, do not allow general market weakness to cause you to waver. Remember the tests outlined above, and apply them faithfully. If you do, the rewards should be more than satisfying.

When to Sell Emerging Industries

Sooner or later, even the best investment opportunities reach the pinnacle of their growth. The ideal course of action is then to sell the securities and move into the next (or another) emerging industry. However, it is much easier to theorize about this course than to carry it out. You must allow market fluctuations to occur without disturbing your position in the securities. On the other hand, when a company or an industry becomes mature, its earnings trend tends to level out, and investors do not long pay a premium price-earnings multiple for securities that do not continue to exhibit a superior rate of profit potential. So the price-earnings multiple will begin to fall, and with it your hard-earned profits.

Selling, unfortunately, is often more difficult than buying. Psychological factors play a big role. Once you have expended the effort required to find an emerging industry and have seen your analysis bear fruit, it is extremely difficult to recognize the time to sell. It takes courage, and it takes rules. Which rules apply? The same rules you used to find the emerging industry in the first place:

1. Is there *still* a need for the industry's products or services?
2. Can the need *still* be filled?
3. Can the need *still* be filled profitably?

It will become evident at some point in every industry's development that whereas the answer to all these questions was originally an unqualified "Yes," it may now be "I think so" or "Maybe." Remember that we are not interested in "Maybe." The risks involved in investing in an emerging industry are substantial enough to reject the questionable summarily while screening for the quintessential. Buggy whips were a great concept in their time, but in various stages of the buggy whip industry's development it became obvious that the need was diminishing and that the product could no longer be mass-produced profitably. The time for selling, therefore, comes when an answer to any of the three questions posed above is anything other than a firm, unqualified "Yes." When you get your first "Maybe," sell.

You will get encouragement at such times neither from your broker nor from persons who may be advising you. You'll have to rely largely upon your own initiative, using the same techniques of analysis that you employed to find the emerging industry in the first place. If you contemplate the word *initiative* for a while, you'll begin to understand how great fortunes have been amassed in the stock market.

Final Thoughts on Emerging Industries

It is sometimes possible to let others do the hard work for you in discovering an emerging industry. When this happens, apply some of the same tests of an emerging industry, but commence with the test of timing. When you divide before you decide, what you are doing is trying to find securities for which investors are willing to pay a premium multiple. It is possible, therefore, to approach an analysis of an emerging industry through the back door, by first investigating individual securities that meet the timing test.

To do this, you must find a list of securities trading between 2 and 3 times the current P/E multiple for the Dow Jones Industrial Average. Numerous statistical sources regularly list securities' price-earnings multiples. Now list the securities that fall into this category, and next to each of them note the industry or industries the company serves. Scan your list of candidates and pay particular attention to common bonds of interest. If you do not find such bonds, attribute the high multiples to excessive speculation, scattered pockets of strength, or any other qualification that comes to mind. Do not make the error of assuming that you have found an emerging industry. You have not, and you should not force one to appear.

If you have found a common concept or thread between several of the securities (it is hoped, many of them) selling in the desired price-earnings multiple band, reclassify the industry in your own words. If you are going to find an emerging industry, you must understand the concept. If the securities fall into the general area of building, for example, what is the specific aspect of building? Commercial? Residential? Low-income? Urban? Suburban? Permanent? Temporary? Vacation? Resort? Made of plastic? Facing the east? Ask all these questions, and more. Finally, you will have narrowed the area of interest.

Now apply the remaining tests: Is there a need? Can the need be filled? Can the need be filled profitably? If the answer to each of these questions is an unqualified "Yes," you have probably found an emerging industry, your timing is likely to be correct, and it is appropriate to take action.

COMEBACK INDUSTRIES

The last gambler we met who lost money on an invention had participated in an attempt to perfect a toothpaste tube that would leapfrog Stripe by emitting a white dentifrice with the word *smile* recurring once per squeeze in red mouthwash. It is probably a toss-up whether more money has been lost by investing in emerging or in comeback industries, but the odds against success in either type of venture must be recognized as substantial. We mention this fact again only because the risk in emerging and comeback industries is considerably higher than risks in the more conventional approaches to investing.

It is also true, however, that risks and rewards usually are closely related. You rarely achieve above-average rewards unless you are willing to assume above-average risks. Thus, while this chapter outlines a method of investing that is not recommended for widows and orphans, it does present an analytical technique that may be quite suitable for investors willing to risk a portion of their investment capital in what is commonly referred to as the more speculative area of the stock market. It is with this thought in mind that we now discuss a technique of investing that is closely allied with the emerging industry concept, that of the comeback industry.

Some Basic Comeback Concepts

Virtually any logical approach to the evaluation of a security in any type of industry—emerging, comeback, or somewhere in between—requires as primary information an estimate of the company's probable growth in earnings power, either in absolute terms or in relation to the growth of similarly situated companies.

Experience clearly indicates that the best way to begin to estimate future developments is to examine what has happened in the past. Investors first become familiar with the historical data—with the actual record of sales growth, earnings growth, management shifts, and related matters—and then try to learn *why* the past record was what it was. As they begin to understand the conditions that created the past trends, they then ask whether these conditions are likely to persist in the future. In the case of a comeback industry, the industry must have something to come back to. Therefore the first part of this study, dealing with records of sales and earnings growth and related matters, must be favorable. If it is not, investors are very unlikely to find a comeback industry.

Once you have learned not only *what* but *why* the past record was what it was, the next step is to find out what happened to cause a change. Did certain key patents expire? Was there a shift or a change in management? Does the market still exist? Is it growing? Did competition change?

The answers to such questions will furnish the basic reasons for an interruption in growth and help you determine whether the industry in question can begin to be considered a comeback industry. If the conditions that created the past problems seem likely to persist in the future, you have not found a comeback industry. But if, instead, you believe that certain past conditions may be altered in form or disappear entirely, you will then try to estimate the impact of the changes and allow for them in your projection of future trends.

Once you have progressed this far, you should ask yourself the following questions:

1. Is there a need for the industry's products or services?
2. Can the need be filled?
3. Can the need be filled profitably?
4. Is now the right time to invest?

Are these questions familiar? Of course they are. They are precisely the questions you ask when looking for an emerging industry. And perhaps it is not surprising after all, when you consider that a comeback industry, in effect, is really just a special case of an emerging industry. Therefore, be sure that you are familiar with the detailed definitions of these questions presented above before proceeding.

A Historical Comeback Example

To apply the four questions to the securities you are considering as potential investment candidates in the comeback industry category, you must have a starting point. In the section on emerging industries we explained various techniques for finding emerging securities with which you could begin your analysis. In the case of comeback industries, you must apply these tests somewhat differently, because you are looking not for first emergence but essentially for reemergence of growth in an existing industry.

As an example, you may look at the airline industry, whose market action as a group is due primarily to a profit breakthrough produced by a combination of circumstances. In the industry's earlier days, individual companies never really were known to make money despite the emerging-industry label appended by most investors. The first big earnings surge occurred in the mid-1960s, when the industry began its transition from propeller to jet aircraft. With the airlines' substantial debt leverage, even small changes in the number of passengers carried were translated into fairly substantial changes in the overall profit picture. And when big changes took place, profit margins were magnified accordingly. Increasing consumer acceptance of travel on the new aircraft, combined with expanding business travel and generally lower operating costs, tended to magnify the earnings increase even further. At this point, the airline industry could legitimately have been classified as an emerging industry. If you had applied the "Divide before you decide" test, you would also have found the timing appropriate and, accordingly, would have invested in the airline industry in the mid-1960s. The results would have been more than gratifying, if you assume that you also paid attention to the subsection of this chapter entitled "When to Sell Emerging Industries." In brief, you needed to ask:

1. Is there *still* a need?
2. Can the need *still* be filled?
3. Can the need *still* be filled profitably?
4. Is the time right to sell?

The answer to question 1 was obviously "Yes." The need still existed. The answer to question 2 was also "Yes," but not quite so positively as it was before. The answer to question 3 clearly was no longer "Yes." It may not have been "No," but at best it was "Maybe." And as we mentioned earlier, when you get your first "Maybe," sell.

Subsequently, the airline industry was afflicted by a combination of adverse factors that tended to bring its fortunes and the individual companies' associated stock prices tumbling down. Business began to slump, and air travel on both business and pleasure levels was curtailed. Interest rates began climbing higher, and because of the airline industry's huge debt structure leverage began working in a negative fashion, penalizing earnings. Overcapacity soon emerged as the biggest problem, with empty seats decreasing the passenger load factor. The fact that all these factors hit at the same time removed airline shares from the emerging-industry category.

If you had subsequently applied the tests of a comeback industry, you would have been sorely disappointed until the beginning of the 1970s. At that point many of the negative factors began to fade into the background, and the answers to questions 1, 2, and 3 were no longer quite so negative. The airline industry was going through a cycle from emergence to depression to reemergence for at least a few years—in short, it was a comeback industry. As soon as investors could get an unqualified "Yes" to the questions stated above, they would have identified airlines as a comeback industry worth investigating. Again the "Divide before you decide" test would have given valuable insight into proper timing, and again the results would have been more than gratifying.

Chapter **21**

Convertible Securities

SIDNEY FRIED

The virtues of the well-selected convertible have become somewhat better known in the last decade as the number of convertibles issued by a wide range of companies has climbed to an all-time high. However, the most important virtue of well-selected convertibles is almost universally ignored. We shall get to that point (explaining our belief that understanding convertibles has a potential for actually increasing market profits by several hundred percent) after a step-by-step dissection of what a convertible is, how it typically behaves in its relation to its common stock, and why we have always vigorously projected this admonition: *Never* buy a common stock until you have found out whether there is a *convertible* trading for the same company.

UNDERSTANDING CONVERTIBLES

What Is a Convertible?

A convertible is a senior security of a company, a bond or a preferred stock, that, in addition to possessing the usual attributes of a bond or a preferred stock, is also convertible into (exchangeable for) a specific amount of common stock of the company for a specified period of time.

An Example of a Convertible Bond

The Aluminum Company of America, the leading aluminum producer in the United States, has a convertible bond outstanding that is trading on the New York Stock Exchange as the 5¼s of 1991 or, by the shorthand always used by traders, the 5¼s-'91. The "bond" feature tells us that it pays a total of $5.25 in interest for each $100 face-value certificate each year and that the Aluminum Company of America has promised to redeem the bond when it matures in 1991, paying the holder $100 in cash for each $100 bond certificate.

The bond has the usual protection of a senior security. It receives its stated interest *before* the common stock can receive any dividends, and in the event that bond interest fails to be paid on time, there are usually provisions for bondholders to take over at least part of the management of the company or to protect their interests in some other efficacious manner. Furthermore, if things get so bad that bankruptcy is at hand and the company's assets must be liquidated, each $100 bond certificate must be paid off with $100 in cash before the common stock can get 1 cent. Even at this point, one can readily see why the senior security of a company, such as a bond, will hardly ever go down in value as quickly as its common stock when the company's fortunes suffer. We are already approaching the major point for understanding the convertible.

Nonetheless, to make the Aluminum Company of America 5¼s-'91 a convertible bond (in addition to giving it the typical attributes of any bond, which we have just described), each $100 face value of this bond may be exchanged, if the holder so desires and *whenever* the holder so desires, for 1.176 shares of Aluminum Company of America common stock, this conversion privilege staying in effect until the maturity of the bond, that is, until 1991.

An Example of a Convertible Preferred Stock

Allegheny Ludlum Industries, the giant steel producer, has a $3 convertible preferred stock trading on the New York Stock Exchange. Each share of stock must receive $3 in dividends before the common stock can get 1 cent in dividends. Protective provisions for the preferred stockholders typically exist in the event that preferred dividends are missed, just as we explained for bondholders, and again, in the event of bankruptcy and dissolution of the company, each share of the $3 preferred stock must receive $65 from assets before the common stockholder can receive anything. All these rights of a preferred stockholder usually rank *behind* those of the bondholder. In the typical security pecking order, the bondholder usually comes first, the preferred stockholder second, and the common stockholder last in the payment of interest or dividends and in rights to assets in the event of liquidation.

To make the Allegheny Ludlum Industries $3 preferred a *convertible* preferred stock, each share of preferred may be exchanged, if the holder so desires and whenever the holder so desires, into one share of Allegheny Ludlum Industries common stock without time limits, there being no expiration date for the conversion privilege.

A CASE STUDY IN CONVERTIBLES

In 1950 the author published a full-length study in the field of convertibles, entitled *Investment & Speculation with CONVERTIBLE Bonds & Preferreds*. At the time of its writing there were only about 90 actively traded convertible bonds and convertible preferred stocks. Since 1950 the number of actively traded convertibles has quickly grown, picking up momentum in the past ten years, to the point at which more than 1,000 convertibles are trading.

Our experience with convertibles tells us a very significant point: We can use *one* example of a convertible and follow it through all its important characteristics which have the potential for moving you in the direction of profits, and this one example will be relevant for *all* convertibles that have traded in previous markets and *all* that are currently trading. For the principles of convertibles' trading remain intact throughout and are as true of one convertible as of another. Through rising markets and declining markets, tight money and easy money, knowing these principles will open up many more investment possibilities for you.

By following the history of a convertible, you will be better able to understand the principles behind convertibles. Let us begin then, in August 1970, with our example, the Eckerd Corp. convertible bond, the 4¾s-'88.

Eckerd Corp. Convertible Bond

In August 1970 investors were actively trading the common stock of Eckerd Corp. around the 12 level on the New York Stock Exchange. Eckerd Corp. was, and is, a drugstore chain in Florida whose fast growth in both revenues and earnings seemed to dwarf the low price of its common stock. But at that time a host of common stocks were on the bargain counter, as later markets were to demonstrate, and Eckerd was hardly alone in being low-priced and undervalued. (This is, indeed, the keystone of our later major point about convertibles, but we do not wish to get ahead of our story.)

Now, on that same New York Stock Exchange other investors and a fair number of professionals were also taking positions in Eckerd, but they were not buying Eckerd common stock. Instead, they were buying the convertible bonds of Eckerd, the 4¾s-'88.

The buyers of Eckerd common were throwing money out the window in three different ways by a lack of knowledge of the alternative available in the Eckerd convertible bonds and probably were hurting themselves even more by not being able to use the entire range of available convertibles for their stock market planning. The mistakes these investors were making would be true of all common-convertible relationships of a similar nature in yesterday's market and in today's market. Because of the truly punishing nature of those mistakes, let us follow each point carefully by examining the arithmetic of the two available choices in August 1970, Eckerd common and Eckerd convertible bonds:

Choice A. Buy 400 shares of Eckered common at 12; cost, $4,800.

Choice B. Buy $5,000 face amount of Eckerd convertible bonds, the 4¾s-'88, the price of 96 being paid for each $100 certificate; cost, $4,800.

The total cost, $4,800, has been the same. In one case we have 400 shares of Eckerd common, and in the other we have Eckerd convertible bonds in the face amount of $5,000, or to put it in the $100 denominations in which bonds are quoted in all markets, we have fifty $100 bond certificates of the convertible 4¾s-'88.

Half of the Convertible Equation: the Upside

Each $100 bond certificate of the Eckerd 4¾s-'88 was convertible into (exchangeable for) 8.012 shares of Eckerd common whenever the holder of the bond wished to make the exchange, the conversion privilege continuing through to the maturity of the bond in 1988. The exchange would be made by the company itself. When holders of $100 bond certificates decided to convert, they would simply give such instructions to their brokers, and the wheels would begin to turn. The $100 certificates would be handed in to Eckerd Corp., and 8.012 shares of Eckerd common stock be given in return for each of them.

Let us recall now that Eckerd common stock was selling at 12 in August 1970. Moreover, 8.012 shares at 12 were worth about 96, and the Eckerd convertible bond was selling at 96 on the New York Stock Exchange while the common stock was selling at 12. The term used to describe this situation is "conversion parity." It characterizes any convertible *whose market price is equal to the value of the common stock for which it can be exchanged.*

One-half of an important convertible equation is in view. It states that whenever a convertible is selling at conversion parity and the company's common stock advances, the convertible must also advance by an exactly equal percentage, dollar for dollar invested.

Let us consider a hypothetical advance in Eckerd common from that initial starting point of 12. We assume that Eckerd common would double to 24. The initial investment of $4,800 in 400 shares of Eckerd common purchased at 12 would now be worth 400 times 24, or $9,600. (For simplicity we are ignoring commissions throughout this example and those that follow).

The $4,800 that went into choice B, $5,000 face amount of Eckerd convertible bonds, will now have what minimum value with the common stock at 24? Remember that each $100 face value of bond is convertible into 8.012 shares of common stock. With the common stock selling at 24, each $100 certificate must be worth 24 times 8.012, or slightly more than 192. Fifty $100 bond certificates are then worth 50 times 192, or $9,600.

Thus, you have $9,600 in market value for Eckerd common and $9,600 in market value for Eckerd convertible bonds. The advances are exactly equal and *had* to be. For, whatever 400 shares of Eckerd common might do on the upside, the $5,000 in face value of the convertible bond is itself exchangeable for the same 400 shares of Eckerd common, and no further calculations are necessary. The common stock cannot outstrip the convertible bond on the upside.

The Other Half of the Equation: the Downside

To define the other half of our equation, we assume that Eckerd common had declined by 50 percent, from 12 to 6. The 400 shares originally purchased at 12 for $4,800 are now worth only $2,400, having lost half of their value.

At 6, the conversion value of each $100 face value of bond is 6 times 8.012, or slightly more than 48. Each $100 face value of bond is worth about 48 in the market value of the common stock and therefore cannot sell below that figure. Fifty $100 bonds must be worth 50 times 48, or $2,400. Thus, we again have a value of $2,400 for the common stock and $2,400 for the convertible bonds, with an equivalent decline in both. Can the $5,000 face value in convertible bonds drop to a lower value than the 400 shares of common stock? No, never. The $5,000 face value of bonds is always convertible into 400 shares of common stock, and the value of the convertible bonds cannot drop below the market value of the common stock. This gives us the second half of our important convertible equation, which stated as a whole is as follows: Whenever a convertible is selling at conversion parity, the convertible must do as well as the common stock on the upside, dollar for dollar, and cannot do any worse than the common stock on the downside.

We are later going to demonstrate the truly vital point that while the convertible cannot do worse than the common stock on the downside, it very often does *better* than the common stock; that is, it falls far less on a percentage basis.

Our immediate job is to demonstrate that an investor who took choice A and bought 400 shares of Eckerd common threw money out the window, in comparison with the far wiser investor who took choice B and bought $5,000 face amount of the Eckerd convertible bonds for the same $4,800 investment.

Throwing Money out the Window

Part 1. In August 1970, Eckerd common stock was paying a tiny dividend, amounting to 7½ cents per share. Thus, the $4,800 invested in 400 shares of common earned a dividend return of only 0.9 percent. The same $4,800 invested in $5,000 face value of Eckerd convertible bonds, with each $100 certificate paying interest of $4.75 per annum, produced a yield of 5 percent.

In this case, buying the common stock rather than the convertible bond was simply throwing away the higher yield to no purpose, since the common stock was in no way superior to the convertible bond. Indeed, quite the contrary, as we shall soon see.

To obtain data of this type about currently trading convertibles, the reader can go to one of several investment services specializing in convertibles. By using an illustration from an investment service of which this writer is an editor, R.H.M Convertible Survey,[1] the relevant points will be quickly highlighted. See Table 21-1.

[1]R.H.M. is a weekly investment service devoted exclusively to intensive convertible coverage.

TABLE 21-1 Selected Convertible Bonds

Outstanding (in millions)	Issue	Rate (percent)	Maturity	Conversion Price ($)	Conversion Rate (shares) to maturity	Year conversion expected	Price Common	Price Bond	Common convertible value	Premium over conversion parity (percent)	Investment value	Indicated common Dividend	Indicated common Yield	Current bond yield
30.0	Columbia Pictures	5.750	94	31.55	3.170	94	11.4	60.0	36.1	66		.60	5.3	9.6
5.5	Combined Communications	8.000	90	10.50	9.524	90	11.2	105.0	106.7	0		.00	.0	7.6
0.9	Combustion Engineering	3.375	81	15.00	6.667	81	51.8	345.4	345.4	0	55	1.30	2.5	1.0
1.1	Commercial Alliance Corp.	6.250	88	6.25	16.000	88	6.4	102.4	102.4	0		.00	.0	6.1
5.0	Commercial Alliance Corp.	6.500	89	8.75	11.428	89	6.4	74.0	73.1	1		.00	.0	8.8
20.0	Commercial Solvents	4.500	91	68.00	1.470	91	16.9	54.8	24.8	121	43	.40	2.4	8.2
20.0	Commonwealth Oil Refining	4.250	92	29.50	3.389	92	16.5	69.5	55.9	24	50	.60	3.6	6.1
4.0	Commonwealth Telephone Pa	6.750	89	26.25	3.809	89	24.4	100.5	92.9	8		1.38	5.7	6.7
5.8	Commonwealth Telephone Va	7.250	90	25.00	3.922	90	42.8	162.5	167.9	0		.00	.0	4.5
50.0	Computer Sciences Corp.	6.000	94	27.00	3.704	94	9.4	53.8	34.8	55		.00	.0	11.2

Look at the column headed "Premium over conversion parity," which tells us the premium being paid for any particular convertible. The conversion value of the convertible is computed by multiplying the current common stock price by the conversion rate (the number of shares into which each convertible may be exchanged). The conversion value divided into the current market price of the convertible gives us the premium. If the premium is zero or very close to zero, the attention of the investor must then go to the common stock yield versus the convertible yield, computed on a weekly basis using current prices, the stated bond interest rate, and the indicated twelve-month dividend payout on the common stock. When the yield on the convertible is *higher than that obtained for the common stock* and the convertible is selling *at or near conversion parity,* purchasing the common stock rather than the convertible means accepting a lower rate of return to no purpose.

To reiterate, the purchaser of Eckerd common in August 1970 received an 0.9 percent return on the investment and not the 5 percent that would have been received had the investor bought the convertible, which was selling at zero premium.

Part 2.   It is very much a fact of stock market life that buying common stocks is much more expensive than buying any bonds, per dollar invested, with respect to the cost of commissions. As of the time of this writing, if you invest $1,000 in 200 shares of stock selling at 5, you pay a commission of $32.80. If you invest $1,000 in 100 shares of stock selling at 10, you pay a commission of $25. If you invest $1,000 in 50 shares of stock selling at 20, you pay a commission of $23, and so on.

On the other hand, buying $1,000 face value of any bond carries a commission cost of $5. Let us translate this into the alternative choices of common stock and convertible:

Choice A. Buy 400 shares of Eckerd common at 12 for $4,800 and pay a total commission of $89.20.

Choice B. Buy $5,000 face amount of Eckerd convertible bonds at 96 for the same $4,800 and pay a total commission of $25.

Thus far, purchasers of Eckerd common, by failing to have knowledge of the Eckerd convertible bond, not only have accepted a yield of 0.9 percent on their investment rather than 5 percent but have paid a far higher commission for the privilege of taking this loss!

The above two factors alone should convince one never to buy a common stock without first checking to see whether there is a convertible for the same company, for whenever such a convertible is selling at conversion parity or even close to it and pays a higher return than the common stock, one is simply wasting money by buying the common stock. Additionally, with respect to convertible bonds, the purchaser will always pay a substantially higher commission rate on a common stock purchase than on equivalent funds invested in convertible bonds. On convertible preferred stocks, their usually higher price also typically ensures that the common stock commission rate will be higher.

Even these two cases of financial mishandling pale in significance when we consider the third means of throwing money out the window by ignoring a potential convertible alternative.

Part 3.   From this most important point of all we lead directly into the manner in which well-selected convertibles, intelligently utilized, have the potential for increasing an investor's profits by several hundred percent in a turnaround market or during any of its recovery-boom phases. The basic point centers in the fact that while a convertible selling at conversion parity cannot decline to any *greater* percentage degree than its common stock during a falling market, it need not fall to *as great* a degree. Put another way, if we assume that a common stock falls by 25 percent during a general market decline, a convertible bond of the same company, selling at direct conversion parity, cannot itself fall by more than 25 percent during the same period of time but may fall by only 20 percent, or 15 percent, or even 10 percent.

The result will be that the convertible develops a premium over conversion value—sells for more than the market value of the common stock into which it can be converted. The fact is that in most cases in which a convertible is selling below par value ($100 in the case of a convertible bond), the convertible will develop a premium during a common stock decline of significant proportions. This means that investors who buy the common stock rather than the convertible selling at conversion parity not only will lose the higher yield that they might obtain by choosing the convertible, but they will have to pay higher commission rates, and they will also needlessly risk the danger of greater percentage downside losses—all told, a very ill-conceived action.

We can see this very clearly with Eckerd convertible bonds. During a period in 1970 before August, Eckerd common dropped to a low of 8. At that time, the Eckerd convertible bond had a straight conversion value of 8 times 8.012, or about 64. On the New York Stock Exchange, however, the Eckerd convertible bond was not selling at its straight conversion value of 64. Rather, it was selling at 89, the lowest price for which it sold at any time in 1970. If we transpose these figures to our two alternative investments, choice A and choice B, we find the following:

Choice A. Buy 400 shares of Eckerd common at 12, costing $4,800. When Eckerd common drops to 8, the 400 shares are worth $3,000, for a loss of $1,600.

Choice B. Buy $5,000 face amount of Eckerd convertible bonds at 96 for the same $4,800.

When the bonds drop to 89 (at the same time that the common is falling to 8), the $5,000 face value of bonds is worth $4,450, for a loss of $350. Put another way, Eckerd common stock showed 4.6 times as much loss as Eckerd convertible bonds in this example.

Eckerd convertible bonds performed far better than Eckerd common stock in preserving the safety of capital during a market decline. And yet, had Eckerd gone up in a rising market, we have already seen that the Eckerd convertible would have had to have moved ahead just as much as Eckerd common, dollar for dollar invested. The buyer of Eckerd common stock (choice A) not only had a far smaller yield on his investment than the buyer of Eckerd convertible bonds (choice B) and paid a higher commission rate to boot but also ran a far greater risk to capital on the downside, to no purpose whatever.

ADVANTAGES OF CONVERTIBLES

Stocks

We have reached one of the most important points in understanding the superior merit of the convertible; so we pause to look further into this particular aspect of the common-convertible relationship. Leaving aside for the moment the convertibility feature of the typical convertible, how do straight, that is, nonconvertible bonds and preferred stocks fluctuate in the marketplace in comparison with their respective common stocks? We all know from experience that many common stocks have a wide range indeed, running up to double their price or dropping to one-half of their level in the course of, perhaps, a twelve-month period.

Not so with nonconvertible senior securities. They are typically purchased for *yield,* and yield alone; so the major factor affecting them is the general level of interest rates. When money gets tighter, interest rates tend to rise all along the line, and the way to make yields go up is for the senior security to fall! After all, the interest or dividend rate is *fixed;* so a lower price for the same face-value certificate means a higher yield. But even in wide swings in interest rates (in 1969–1970, for example), straight nonconvertible senior securities still moved quite staidly when compared with common stocks of the same companies.

Regardless of how low the price of the common stock may decline, the convertible bond will not fall below its straight bond value. Consequently, if investors purchase convertible bonds selling at a price that is not significantly above their value as straight bonds, then the investors are limiting their downside risk. Of course, a rise in interest rates can cause the value of the straight bonds to decline. However, these declines will generally not be severe. For example, let us assume that a bond pays interest of $100 per year, will mature in ten years, is yielding 10 percent, and is selling for $1,000. If the yield to maturity for this bond would increase by 2 full percentage points to 12 percent, the value of the bond would fall only to $887.

Why Some Convertible Bonds Increase in Price More Rapidly Than Their Common Stocks

The ratio of the convertible bond price to the conversion ratio of the bond times the market price of its stock is the best indicator that the author has found for evaluating the upside potential of the convertible bond. For example, if a convertible bond is selling for $990 and is convertible into twenty shares of the common stock and the stock is selling for $45 per share, then the ratio is 110 percent ($990 − 20 × $45).

A convertible bond can never sell for less than its conversion ratio times the market price of its stock. This is true because if it were to fall below this point temporarily, arbitrage would occur as investors would buy the bonds, convert into stock and sell the stock. Consequently, when a convertible bond is selling at a price that is exactly equal to its conversion ratio times its stock price, any rise in the price of the stock will at least be matched by an equivalent percentage rise in the price of the convertible. The limited downside risk afforded by a convertible combined with its comparatively high interest yield often causes the bond to sell at a premium above its conversion parity (conversion ratio times stock price). As the stock is rising, the convertible must rise at an equal percentage rate; however, if a premium develops, the stock is actually rising at a more rapid rate.

We shall demonstrate this concept with a chart that this writer first developed in the late 1940s; so let us take a few paragraphs to explain how our "conversion ratio chart" is created and why it is so useful in following convertibles. Following this quick explanation, we shall pick up the thread of the important point under discussion.

Using the Conversion Ratio Chart in Evaluating a Convertible.   In Fig. 21-1 for the convertible 5¾s-'94 and the common stock of Zurn Industries, the common stock (heavy line) is plotted by using the right-hand scale in the normal manner, and the convertible (thin line) is plotted on the left-hand scale in a similarly normal manner. But because each point on the left-hand (convertible) scale is the opposite point on the common scale, multiplied by the conversion factor given on the lower left of the chart, the chart shows the common and the convertible in exact relationship to one another. When there is little or no gap between the heavy line (common) and the light line (convertible), the convertible is selling at or near conversion parity, and any rise in the common must produce a corresponding percentage rise in the convertible because of its conversion privilege. When there is a considerable gulf between the two lines, the convertible is selling at a premium over its straight conversion value: the wider the gulf, the larger the premium.

According to the Zurn Industries conversion ratio chart, in 1971 the company's common stock fell to 16, but the convertible bond sold no lower than 82, holding far above straight conversion value. The same had happened in 1970. A strong rise in Zurn Industries common in early 1972 saw the common catch up with the convertible on the chart, and thereafter they moved in concert to a top of 37 for the common and 130 for the convertible bond, or just about exact conversion parity. Let us suppose that Zurn Industries common had not topped out at 37 but had continued to higher levels. The convertible 5¾s-'94 would have moved along

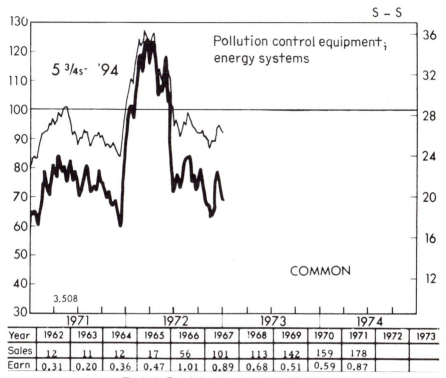

Fig. 21-1   Zurn Industries convertible 5¾s-'94.

with the common, dollar for dollar, because it was selling at direct conversion parity.

When Zurn Industries common did top out and commence to move sharply lower, the convertible bond fell rather easily to par (100) but then parted company with the common stock on the chart. The open space on the chart between the light and heavy lines measures the premium over conversion value that was developing for the 5¾s-'94. The final result for 1972 was that Zurn Industries common dropped to 17⅛, where its convertible bond had a straight conversion value of 17.12 times 3.508, or 60.05. But the convertible bond sold no lower than 86, demonstrating how much better it had safeguarded the investor's capital in a declining market.

Why didn't the Zurn Industries convertible 5¾s-'94 fall as far as the common, or down to its straight conversion value of 60.05? The immediately significant answer is that at 60.05 it would have been yielding 9.57 percent, or much too high a percentage for a senior security of a quite sound and substantial company such as Zurn Industries and much too high a percentage in comparison with the straight senior securities of comparable companies.

When Zurn Industries 5¾s-'94 was up at 130, it was acting mostly like a convertible and was rising and falling exactly like its common stock because its interest yield was far less than that of comparable nonconvertible bonds. But when the 5¾s-'94 dropped into the 90s, it began to act more like a senior security, a bond of Zurn Industries, and in view of the fact that the conversion privilege represented a right to buy the common stock until 1994, the convertible bond simply refused to decline at the same rate as the common stock.

Additional Examples from the 1972 Market.   Shown in Figs. 21-2 and 21-3 are charts of companies whose common stocks have an active following. They both

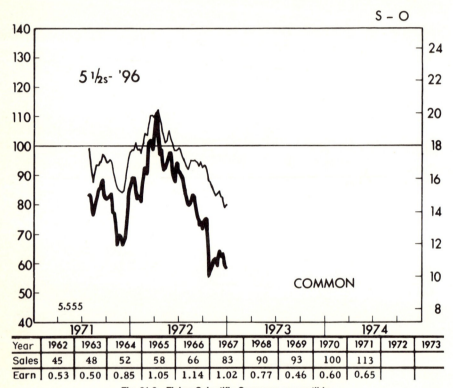

Year	1962	1963	1964	1965	1966	1967	1968	1969	1970	1971	1972	1973
Sales	45	48	52	58	66	83	90	93	100	113		
Earn	0.53	0.50	0.85	1.05	1.14	1.02	0.77	0.46	0.60	0.65		

Fig. 21-2   Fisher Scientific Company convertible.

demonstrate the same typical and vital point: the holding power of the typical convertible when it drops down to a level at which yield and its long-term conversion privilege combine in attractiveness to slow its potential decline relative to the common stock. The result in both cases was for the common stock to suffer far more than its convertible on a percentage basis, as is shown quickly and clearly in these two conversion ratio charts.

It should also be noted that in each case the common and the convertible were very close on the chart at their higher levels, indicating a quite small premium over conversion value. This ensured that had a further rise in the common stock taken place instead of a decline, the convertible would have turned in exactly as much profit, dollar for dollar invested, or very close to it.

Summary.   Thus far we have learned that a convertible—any convertible— selling at direct conversion parity, that is, at a price equal to the market value of the common stock into which it can be converted, *must* show at least as much percentage rise as its common stock, and *cannot* show any greater percentage decline than its common stock. Since convertibles often have a higher yield than their common stocks and cost far less in commissions to buy and to sell, choosing the common stock over the convertible is simply accepting a lower yield and higher commission costs with nothing on the plus side to balance these often-painful minuses. When we add the indisputable fact that at conversion parity the upside profit potential is at least *equal* to that of the common but that the downside risk to capital is typically *smaller,* often far smaller, then choosing the common stock over

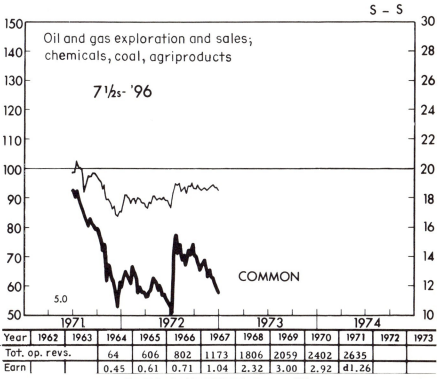

Year	1962	1963	1964	1965	1966	1967	1968	1969	1970	1971	1972	1973
Tot. op. revs.			64	606	802	1173	1806	2059	2402	2635		
Earn			0.45	0.61	0.71	1.04	2.32	3.00	2.92	d1.26		

Fig. 21-3   Occidental Petroleum convertible.

such a well-situated convertible (one at or near conversion parity) can only be termed self-injury of a high order.

The Greatest Advantage of Well-situated Convertibles

Convertibles in a Declining Market. The obvious and completely visible advantages of many convertibles compared with alternative common stock investments have been outlined above. On the basis of those advantages alone, investors who do not check to see whether there is a convertible available for the company whose common stock they are considering purchasing are wasting and even misusing their financial resources.

When we move to the next step and realize that most convertibles selling at or under their par value will hold up better than their common stocks in a declining market and often far better, then a far greater advantage for considering convertibles evolves. We shall demonstrate that, in addition to the purely negative factor of avoiding loss, the proper understanding of this premier advantage of the well-selected convertible has a most important *positive* role. This role focuses on the malady suffered by so many investors of excessive enthusiasm at the top of a market move and equally excessive pessimism at the bottom of a market move.

Falling markets breed pessimism, and when enough suffering has been endured and losses taken and when the market is ready to turn around and begin a recovery, the pessimism is typically difficult to shake. Many investors will sit worriedly on the sidelines with only token commitments or none at all, while the market makes the substantial gains typical of an important reversal of the market cycle or even merely an intermediate rise.

Turn this situation around, and you have the same bad result. Rising markets breed optimism; when investors have seen enough profits made by friends and associates and enjoyed profits themselves, their appetite begins to grow larger and larger exactly as the market moves into an area of greatest danger, and when one should reasonably be lightening one's commitments, most investors are "selling the family furniture" to enlarge their holdings, with typically punishing results as a market cycle turns to the downside with an often-breathtaking tumble, leaving little opportunity to get out.

What an impressive and rewarding role is played by the well-situated convertible for investors who have come to a true understanding of what convertibles can accomplish! Very simply, knowledge that the downside risk of a convertible in the proper convertible-common price relationship is considerably less than that of the respective common stock better enables investors to counteract timidity and paralyzing hesitancy when a market shows promise and enables them to take worthwhile positions. If their estimate of a turn proves wrong and the potential market upturn fails, the safety factors of the well-situated convertible come into play.

Convertible losses will also occur in these downside moves, but with prior intelligent selection they should be appreciably less than what would have resulted from the same amount invested in common stocks. Again, if a true market recovery has commenced, a well-considered selection of convertibles should be producing substantial profits on almost or exactly the same scale as if one were holding the risk-filled and timidity-inducing roster of common stocks.

Similarly, at the top of a sustained market rise, where doubts about continuance of the rise are reasonable and limitation of risk makes sense, one's natural desire to reach for still more profits can be expressed through well-situated convertibles, with promise of just as much upside profit if the market does continue moving up but sharply reduced capital loss if a turn to the downside eventuates instead.

Several examples will serve to make these all-important points, and the value of the conversion ratio chart will become clear in illustrating them.

Alaska Interstate. Early 1972 was a time of both worry and pessimism but also of the emergence of positive factors. Let us suppose that investors were considering entering the market but were uncertain about the timing and then became aware of some good opportunities to invest in convertibles, one of which was Alaska Interstate 6s-'96. They would have made a wise move in buying the company's convertible.

In Fig. 21-4 the arrow points to a logically strategic area in which to make a purchase of the convertible bond. The holding power of the convertible had been well demonstrated since its issuance in 1971. At the low of 14¾ for the common, the conversion value of the convertible bond was only 56.72, but it sold no lower than 89. Now in early 1972 the common stock had risen to the 30 mark, and the convertible bond was perfectly positioned at 116, selling almost at exact conversion parity. On the upside, the convertible bond had to show exactly as much profit as the common stock, dollar for dollar. And the 6s-'96 yielded 5.17 at 116, while the common stock yielded zero. On the downside, if an anticipated further gain in Alaska Interstate did not materialize but instead a sinking spell back to the late-1971 lows took place, the convertible bond position would show a loss of more than 25 percent, but the loss in the common would be almost twice as great, or more than 50 percent.

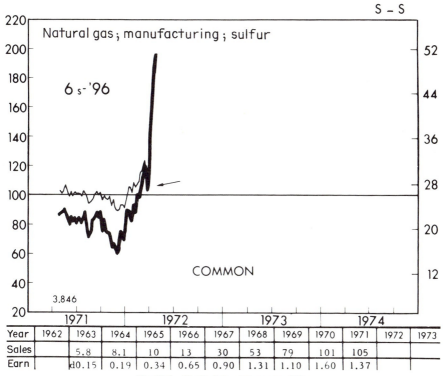

Fig. 21-4   Alaska Interstate convertible.

Year	1962	1963	1964	1965	1966	1967	1968	1969	1970	1971	1972	1973
Sales		5.8	8.1	10	13	30	53	79	101	105		
Earn		d0.15	0.19	0.34	0.65	0.90	1.31	1.10	1.60	1.37		

With knowledge of the company and use of the conversion ratio chart, would not such a realization of the substantial protection against downside loss enable investors to make a purchase? Or if they previously would have intended to make only a small purchase, wouldn't they be wise to make a larger purchase because of the diminished risk in the convertible?

Obviously, when Alaska Interstate common ran up to 54⅛ and the 6s-'96 to 208, with exactly the same percentage profit, our investors would have been most happy that knowledge of convertibles had triumphed over timidity.

Pan American Bancshares.   The same early period in 1972 found Pan American Bancshares common and Pan American Bancshares 6½s-'91 together on the conversion ratio chart (see Fig. 21-5), telling us that there was little or no premium over conversion value for the convertible bond. The common stock was paying no dividends at all, but the 6½s-'91 was yielding 6.98 percent at 93 in early April 1972 with zero premium over conversion value. The convertible bond was almost certain to hold up better than the common stock on the downside, yet it promised just as much percentage appreciation as the common stock on the upside. The subsequent run-up, with common and convertible following each other up on the chart, illustrates this fact quite graphically. An adequate knowledge of these factors could certainly have persuaded uncertain investors to make a larger commitment in the Pan American Bancshares convertible 6½s-'91 than they would have considered taking in the admittedly more risky common stock.

Curtiss-Wright and the Wankel Engine.   Early in 1972 newpaper stories about a potential substitute for the standard Detroit automobile engine began to appear in the financial press. The reportedly more efficient, less polluting engine was the

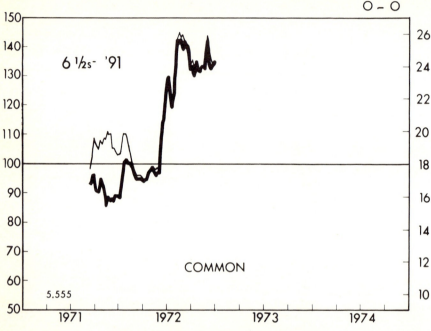

Fig. 21-5 Pan American Bancshares convertible.

Wankel engine, and an American company, Curtiss-Wright, held important patents for the engine in the United States. Here was a highly speculative gamble that would have made even aggressive investors hesitate: such speculations have unhappy outcomes more often than profitable outcomes. But suppose these investors had knowledge of an alternative to the risk-filled Curtiss-Wright common stock in the form of a convertible preferred A stock (see Fig. 21-6), each share of which was convertible into 1.25 shares of common stock without a time limit? The $2 annual dividend on this preferred stock had recently been passed as the company's earnings sagged, but prior to this dividend passing there had been an uninterrupted $2 annual dividend since 1936. Dividend payments on the preferred stock were noncumulative, but they would have to be resumed before the common stockholders could get any return, and in all the previous market history of common and convertible preferred the latter had always maintained a comfortable premium over the common stock at lower levels.

The convertible preferred stock was clearly a better choice than the common stock and, once again, could better have enabled unsure, sideline-staying investors to make commitments. This would have been a happy decision in view of the tripling of common stock and convertible preferred in the few months that followed.

Allied Artists Pictures and Union Corp.   Anyone following Allied Artists Pictures in late 1971 knew that, despite the company's losses in 1970 and 1971, the year 1972 could be different because of the potential for an Allied Artists film production of the Broadway smash hit *Cabaret*. Although risk elements were still very large, the 8¾s-'90 was yielding almost 10 percent at the beginning of 1972 (zero

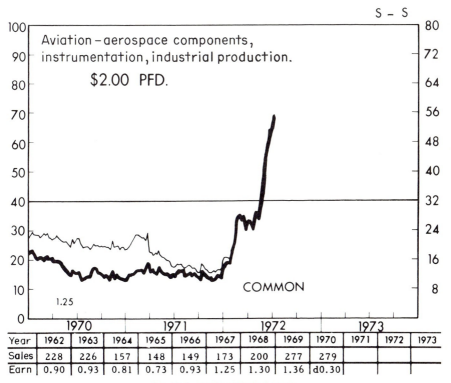

S – S

Aviation – aerospace components, instrumentation, industrial production.

$2.00 PFD.

1.25

COMMON

Year	1962	1963	1964	1965	1966	1967	1968	1969	1970	1971	1972	1973
Sales	228	226	157	148	149	173	200	277	279			
Earn	0.90	0.93	0.81	0.73	0.93	1.25	1.30	1.36	d0.30			

Fig. 21-6   Curtiss-Wright A stock.

for the common), the premium over conversion value was near zero, and the holding power of the convertible on the downside was quite visible on the chart in Fig. 21-7.

A similar potential existed with another speculative company, Union Corp. (see Fig. 21-8), whose "soft" lens in the hot contact lens market was capable of causing some market excitement. The careful and cautious investor might certainly have had many justified qualms about purchasing the common stocks of either Allied Artists Pictures or Union Corp., but their high-yielding convertible bonds (Union Corp. common also had a zero yield) had demonstrated their holding power on the downside.

Cabaret did draw favorable reviews and good public acceptance, which helped move the price of Allied Artists common up, but the good results were also enjoyed dollar for dollar by the convertible bond. In the case of Union Corp., recurring excitement about soft contact lenses was booming the giant Bausch & Lomb but also was booming the much smaller Union Corp. It produced a fair-sized run-up in 1971 and an even greater one in 1972; common stock and convertible bond both showed a 100 percent advance in a few weeks. Union Corp. was a very speculative investment medium, but its convertible bond proved to be a much better investment with its high yield (against a zero yield for the common stock) and its potential to hold up much better than the common stock on the downside.

THE SPECIAL ATTRACTION OF WELL-SITUATED CONVERTIBLES ON LOW-PRICED STOCKS

To illustrate this discussion on convertibles, we could have chosen many companies, including blue chips and other higher-priced issues, but we have rather

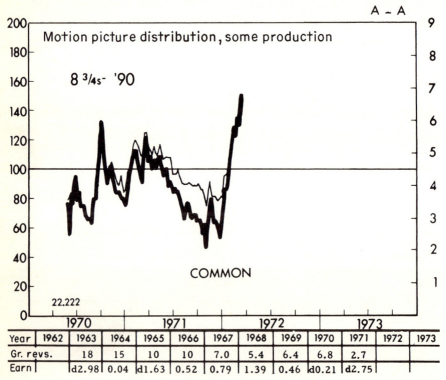

Year	1962	1963	1964	1965	1966	1967	1968	1969	1970	1971	1972	1973
Gr. revs.		18	15	10	10	7.0	5.4	6.4	6.8	2.7		
Earn		d2.98	0.04	d1.63	0.52	0.79	1.39	0.46	d0.21	d2.75		

Fig. 21-7 Allied Artists Pictures convertible.

deliberately given examples involving lower-priced stocks because with correct timing they have especially good potential.

With respect to low-priced stocks in a recovering market, the author studied 4,218 common stocks listed in the January 1968 edition of Standard & Poor's *Stock Guide,* an authoritative compendium of almost every common stock with a public market. It was found that from the 1966 lows to the 1967 recovery highs, 935 common stocks had shown a 200 percent or greater appreciation. Of these 935 stocks, 706, or 75 percent, started their move when selling under $10 per share.

When we narrowed the analysis down to those of the 935 stocks that had moved up 300 percent or more, the preponderance was weighted even more heavily in the direction of low-priced stocks, for 521 stocks gained 300 percent or more, and of these, 434, or 83 percent, started their move under $10 per share. The $10 to $20 price range also outstripped the higher-priced categories by a wide margin.

We should note that the 1966–1967 action only corroborated the conclusions we had reached in earlier studies. The invariable outcome of each statistical study was to demonstrate that, among stocks that showed the widest appreciation during market upturns, the lower the stock price group at the start, the greater the percentage they represented of the later group showing the widest percentage gains.

With more than 1,000 convertibles actively trading today, there are always a substantial number of promising low-priced stocks that have well-situated convertibles available as an alternative speculative medium. Typically, these convertibles

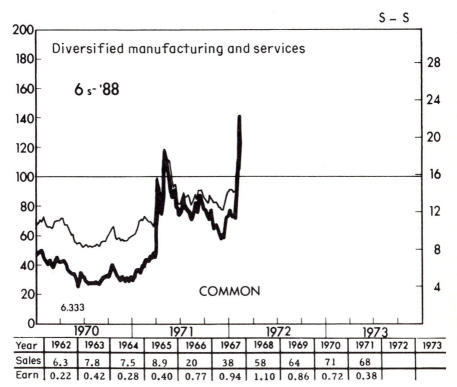

Fig. 21-8   Union Corp. convertible.

Year	1962	1963	1964	1965	1966	1967	1968	1969	1970	1971	1972	1973
Sales	6.3	7.8	7.5	8.9	20	38	58	64	71	68		
Earn	0.22	0.42	0.28	0.40	0.77	0.94	1.10	0.86	0.72	0.38		

will have a far higher yield than their respective common stocks (most low-priced common stocks pay no dividends), and we have seen how premiums tend to develop at lower levels for so many convertibles, illustrating their superior holding power relative to their common stocks during steep declines.

These factors should enable the cautious-to-timid investor to make commitments in specific convertibles during potential market turns because of the important protective features of such well-positioned convertibles. This is true of convertibles of low-priced stocks and of convertibles of higher-priced stocks too, and it all adds up to what we consider to be the most important plus factor for the convertible: the ability to inspire greater confidence in investors who have been excessively saddled with pessimism because of losses during a previous market decline and, therefore, cannot bring themselves to act even when they feel that the market looks ready to turn, because their fears of further losses are too great.

Finally, let us look at the over-the-counter market for convertibles. Many outstanding companies get their start on the over-the-counter market in convertibles when their growth rates may be at their highest. Many bank and insurance companies trade over the counter, and a goodly number of first-rate companies of significant size simply prefer to have their securities traded over the counter.

SELECTING A CONVERTIBLE BOND

An investor who is considering purchasing a convertible bond should consider the following five factors:

1. *The outlook for interest rates should be fairly stable or down.* In a period of tight money and rising interest rates, the straight value of the bond may decline rather rapidly. The protection afforded by the convertible therefore will be reduced, and if the stock price declines, the convertible may decline in equal proportion.

2. *The minimum value of the convertible as a straight bond must not be too far below the current selling price of the bond.* A maximum of 25 percent would seem reasonable. This spread is the maximum loss that the investor would incur, regardless of what happens to the common stock price, as long as the straight value of the bond does not decline because of higher interest rates or a decline in the quality of the bond.

3. *The current price of the common stock must not be too far below conversion parity.* A maximum of about 15 percent would be desirable. If the stock price is too far below conversion parity, the investor will not receive the full benefit of an increase in the price of the stock.

4. *The potential price of the stock must be well above conversion parity.*

5. *The current yield on the bond should compare favorably with the dividend yield on the common stock.*

Chapter 22
Stock Warrants

SIDNEY FRIED

A warrant is an option to buy a stated number of shares of a stock at a stipulated price during a specified period. Usually it has a time limit, generally measured in years. Sometimes, however, the life of a warrant is not limited. Such "perpetual" warrants are particularly popular.

Warrants differ from rights in that no new stock is issued simultaneously with the warrant. From the point of view of the issuing corporation, the purpose of a warrant is not to sell additional stock but to avoid issuing stock. For this reason, the price at which the warrant holder can acquire stock is invariably fixed *above* the market price of the stock at the time that the warrant is issued, frequently well above the market.

Warrants represent no direct equity in a company, have no voting rights, and receive no dividends. The commission costs involved in buying and selling them are relatively high. Nevertheless, when warrants are properly bought or sold short, the potential speculative gain is very large compared with the possible loss.

How to Compute the Value of a Warrant

When the price of a common stock with a related warrant is *below* the price at which the warrant could be exercised (the subscription price), the warrant has only speculative value. It is worth whatever speculators or investors are willing to pay at any given time for the possibility that the stock will, sometime in the future, rise to the subscription price.

But when the price of a stock with a related warrant rises above its subscription price, the warrant thereby acquires a minimum tangible value, which any owner of the warrant can quickly realize in the market by acquiring the stock at its subscription price with the warrant and immediately selling the stock at its higher market price. (A more sophisticated way of doing this, which eliminates the danger of a decline in the price of the stock in the interval between the date on which the warrant is exercised and the date on which the stock is received, is to sell the stock short and cover the short sale a few days later by delivery of the stock acquired via the warrant.)

Such minimum realizable value of a warrant is its "exercise value." A warrant's exercise value (E) can be calculated by the formula $E = n(P - S)$. Here P is the current price of the stock, S the subscription price per share of the stock at which the warrant can be exercised, and n the number of shares of stock that one warrant entitles you to buy. For example, when ABC Corporation common is selling at $12 and the subscription price at which the warrant can be exercised is $3.75, the exercise value, or minimum realizable value, of an ABC warrant is $8.25 [1 ($12 − 3.75) = $8.25].

If a warrant entitles you to buy more than one share of stock, the calculation of its exercise value follows the same formula. For example, one XYZ Company warrant entitles you to buy 2.54 shares of XYZ common at a subscription price of $8.88 per share (for a total payment of $22.555). Accordingly, when XYZ common is selling at 25, the exercise value of the warrant is $40.94 [2.54 (25 − 8.88) = 40.94].

A warrant never sells *below* its minimum realizable or exercise value, since dealer arbitrage would immediately close any such gap, and very rarely exactly at its exercise value. The excess of a warrant's price over its exercise value is its premium, or speculative value. The more optimistic warrant investors are about the future of the related stock, the larger such a premium is.

The Leverage Advantage

In November 1970, Tenneco Corp. wished to sell 6 million shares of common stock to raise more than $100 million, but money was tight, pessimism about common stocks was deep, and the success of such an issue was far from assured. As a result, the company decided to attach common stock warrants to the proposed issue. What were finally sold were *6 million shares* of common and *6 million warrants,* in units of one share of common stock plus one warrant. Each warrant represented the right to buy one share of Tenneco Corp. common stock from the company itself, upon payment of $24.25 per share, with the warrant's life due to expire on November 1, 1975.

A central point to realize about the creation of an actively trading warrant is that once an issue is sold with warrants "attached," almost immediately the warrant becomes "detached" and begins trading separately from the common stock, preferred stock, or bond to which it had initially been joined for purposes of the sale. The warrant now has a life of its own.

Tenneco common stock was at the bottom of a slide that had started in December 1968 at a top of 32¾ and, in November 1970, was selling at 19⅜ while Tenneco warrants were trading in the over-the-counter market around the 3 level.

You can gain a quick insight into the nature of opportunities in warrants by asking the seemingly logical question: Why should anyone pay $3 for a warrant that confers upon you the right to buy a share of common stock for $24.25 from the company when you can immediately buy that same share of stock in the open market for $19.37? If you buy the stock through the warrant, you pay $3 for the warrant plus $24.25 for the purchase price to the company, or $27.25 for one share of Tenneco common stock. If you buy the stock in the open market, you pay only $19.37 plus a small commission. It certainly does appear that you would be throwing away more than $750 if you attempted to acquire 100 shares of Tenneco common stock via the warrants in November 1970.

What was being overlooked in this approach, of course, was that the right to exercise the warrant had a *five-year life.* Suppose that some months or even years later Tenneco common were to double in price, from 19⅜ to 38¾? At 38¾, the right to buy this share of stock for 24¼ must be worth a minimum of $38.75 minus $24.25, or $14.50. The warrant could sell for *more* than 14½, at a premium above its straight exercise value, but it couldn't sell for *less,* or perhaps a tiny fraction less.

The arbitrager in Wall Street, who makes a living by taking advantage of just such disparities, would quickly buy a warrant selling appreciably under its straight exercise value, sell the applicable common stock short, exercise the warrant and make delivery, pocketing his or her riskless profit. This circumstance serves to keep a warrant selling very close to its exercise value at the worst, while in most cases in which a warrant still has a considerable life, a premium will exist for the warrant.

Let's examine the figures given above. A move from 19⅜ to 38¾ for Tenneco common would produce a profit of 100 percent, but a move of the Tenneco warrant from 3 to a minimum of 14½ would produce a profit of 383 percent.

The Risk-Reward Relationship

Given the above figures, we have no choice but to conclude that if we were looking for maximum appreciation, we would have to buy the Tenneco warrant rather than Tenneco common, but what would happen on the downside? Here we come to the very heart of the consideration of the value of any individual warrant. The question we must ask is always two-sided: If the common stock moves up X percent in price, how much will the warrant move up in percentage; and if the common stock moves down X percent in price, what will be the percentage loss for the warrant?

If the potential percentage gain on the upside far exceeds the potential percentage loss on the downside for an equal move in the common stock, you probably have a good warrant purchase. If the warrant promises to suffer a percentage decline on the downside equal to the anticipated percentage advance on the upside, there is no advantage to buying the warrant. Moreover, if a warrant promises to show a greater percentage loss on the downside than the gain it expects to show on the upside for an equal move in the common stock, not only do you wish to avoid purchase, but you may consider short-selling the warrant or hedging such a short sale for additional safety.

In our first calculation, we determined that for a doubling in price of Tenneco common over its November 1970 level of 19⅜, the Tenneco warrant must advance 3.83 times faster than the common stock by virtue of its exercise privilege, at a minimum, given the $3 market price of the Tenneco warrant at that time. What if the price of Tenneco common were not to double but be halved?

The answer that we derive here must be less than scientific and not a *necessary* answer, which our first calculation was. The reason is that if Tenneco common had dropped 50 percent, from 19⅜ to 9⅝ ($9.625), there would be no necessary value for the warrant. For when a common stock is selling below the price at which the warrant is exercisable, the immediate market value of the warrant is zero.

With the approximately 400 warrants trading today, we can state from experience that the approximate level of a warrant can be estimated for any price of its common stock, taking into consideration the important questions of (1) the duration of the warrant's life, (2) the speculative interest in the common stock, (3) the state of the general market, and (4) a number of other variables. We're sorry that we cannot make this basis of estimation any simpler, despite the hopes of those who feel that a programmed computer can give such an answer for each warrant. However, so much judgment is involved in these variables that to a quite considerable extent the answer must remain geared to the observer's experience.

We can get immediate guidance in the question of the Tenneco warrant by realizing that if Tenneco common were to decline by 50 percent, fiom 19⅜ to about 9⅝, the Tenneco warrant could also decline by 50 percent, from 3 to 1½, without showing any greater percentage loss. The question then becomes: With Tenneco common at 9⅝, would the Tenneco five-year warrant sell below 1½? More than two decades of experience in the evaluation of warrants by the author say "No."

To illustrate, A-T-O warrants are the right to buy at $30 to October 15, 1973, and then at $35 to October 15, 1978, when the warrants expire. At the time of writing, the common stock is selling at 12⅞, or considerably less than half of its exercise price of 30, putting it in a similar relation to the Tenneco situation at 9⅝, but the A-T-O warrant is selling at a robust 5⅝. The Bangor Punta warrant is the right to buy 1.038 shares of common stock at $53 per share until March 31, 1981. The duration is almost twice that of the Tenneco warrant, but the common stock price of Bangor Punta is far less than half of its exercise price, as we write, selling at 16.50. Again the warrant is selling at a substantial 4½.

On the basis of the author's experience, if Tenneco common had dropped to 9⅝, for a 50 percent decline from 19⅜, the Tenneco warrant would certainly not have dropped more than 50 percent, or to less than 1½ from the $3 price at which it started. Indeed, our estimate is that the Tenneco warrant, with the common at 9⅝, would have sold at about 2, suffering less than the 50 percent decline in the common.

If you accept this estimate, a rather startling fact emerges about the Tenneco warrant in November 1970, when it was selling at 3 with the common stock at 19⅜. The Tenneco warrant promised to advance at least 3.83 times as fast as the common stock on the upside but to decline no faster, or quite possibly to a lesser percentage degree, than the common stock on the downside. The Tenneco warrant not only was a much better bet than the common stock for appreciation but was actually *less speculative*, promising less downside loss.

Historical Evidence

In the above arithmetic of the Tenneco warrant, we worked with hypotheses, namely, that if Tenneco common were to double in price, from 19⅜ to 38¾, the Tenneco warrant must at a minimum move from 3 to 14½, producing a 383 percent gain for the warrant against a 100 percent gain for the common. Illustrating the fact that most warrants with more than one year of life remaining sell at some kind of premium over actual exercise value (often a large premium for varying reasons), when Tenneco common actually ran up to a 1971 high of 30⅛, the Tenneco warrant also ran up to its high of 11⅛. At 30⅛ for the common, the actual exercise value was 30.125 minus 24.25, or 5.875 (5⅞), so that the warrant was selling at a substantial premium of 5¼ points over the exercise value.

This is usually what happens when a common stock becomes buoyant. The warrant becomes the darling of the speculators and tends to sell at unrealistic premiums. The percentage results for Tenneco were as follows: Tenneco common moved from its November 1970 price of 19⅜ to 30⅛, up 55 percent, while Tenneco warrants moved from 3 to 11⅛, up 270 percent. The Tenneco warrants in actuality advanced 4.9 times as fast as Tenneco common.

The All-Important Expiration Date

In 1966 a Mack Trucks warrant was good to buy 1.47 shares of Mack Trucks common for a total price of $50 to the company. In February of that year Mack Trucks common was selling at 54¾. The right to buy 1.47 shares of a stock selling for 54¾ (a market value of 80.48) for 50 must be worth a minimum of 80.48 minus 50, or 30.48. The Mack Trucks warrant was selling at a 4⅛-point premium over that exercise value, or 34⅝.

This particular Mack Trucks warrant was due to expire on September 1, 1966. What would be the effect on the warrant in percentage terms if the common stock went down 50 percent, or from 34⅝ to about 17⅜? We shall find that the answer would have to be 100 percent. By the time that the actual expiration day arrived for the Mack Trucks warrant, its common was selling at 33. The 1.47 shares at 33 are worth 48.51, and a warrant that gives you the right to buy 48.51 in market value of stock for 50 has an immediate value of zero, and that is where the warrant ended its life, moving from 34⅝ to zero in six months.

It has been our experience that the time to start paying very close attention to a warrant's approaching expiration date is when about two years of life remain. This doesn't mean that we do not give large importance to the number of years that the warrant privilege runs in evaluating a warrant, but serious downgrading by the marketplace of the warrant's value does not make itself felt with real impact until the two-year point. If a common stock is selling not too far above the exercise price for the warrant (or worse, below that exercise price), damaging erosion often will begin in the premium being paid for the warrant. Purchasers of such a warrant must justify their position by (1) liking the common stock very much for anticipated appreciation, (2) liking the general market itself for an upside trend, and (3) finding that the upside percentage leverage of the warrant is quite high. If all three factors are amply present and if full recognition is given to the speculative element imparted by the shrinking life of the warrant, such a purchase may be justified. But the major point is that you must be very careful in considering a warrant with an approaching expiration date.

Hedging with Warrants

Whenever two different securities tend to move *in relation to one another*, market professionals known as arbitragers will look for ways to exploit any disparities in such a movement by going long one security and short the other, in varying amounts to accomplish different purposes. Here we shall describe one type of hedging in which the investor is long the warrant and short the common, and a little later we shall discuss quite another type of hedging in which the investor is doing the reverse.

A word about short selling to begin with. When you sell short, you sell a security you do not own. Your broker makes delivery for you by borrowing the security from another broker. You make your profit when the security you sold short goes down in price, whereupon you purchase it at the lower price and cover your short sale by delivering the security to the broker from whom you had borrowed. When you buy a security and later sell it at a higher price, you have made a profit the long way. Making that profit on the short side is simply to reverse the order of events, accomplishing the sale first. There are additional factors to understand about short selling, of course, but this bare outline is sufficient for our present purpose. To illustrate hedging with warrants, let's study the following hypothetical case.

Let us assume that one warrant in the XYZ Company gives the investor the right to purchase one share of stock in the corporation for a price of $70 and that the common stock is selling for 53 and the warrant for 4½. The investor can sell short 100 shares of stock at 53 for an investment of $5,300 and buy 588 warrants at 4½ for $2,646, making a total investment of $7,946.

Situation No. 1. The XYZ Company common moves up 100 percent, from 53 to 106. The 100 shares of common stock sold short at 53 show a $5,300 loss. But at 106 for the common, the warrant at a minimum must sell at 36, as we have seen, and 588 warrants at 36 are worth $21,168, for a net profit of $18,522. Deduct the loss of $5,300 on the short sale from profit of $18,522 on the warrant long position, and the hedge has put you ahead by $13,222.

Situation No. 2. The XYZ Company common has been halved in price, dropping from 53 to 26½. The 100 shares of common stock sold short at 53 show a profit of $2,650. If we assume that the warrant also declined by 50 percent, from 4½ to 2¼, the original $2,646 investment has shrunk to $1,323, producing a $1,323 loss; a $2,650 gain minus a $1,323 loss leaves us with a $1,327 gain. Would the XYZ Company warrant have held at 2¼? The answer to this question cannot affect our general thesis. For the warrant could go to zero without producing a net loss on the hedge. The $2,650 gain on the short sale is equal to the entire cost of 588 warrants purchased at 4½, and a drop of the warrants to zero could wipe out that entire cost and still not cause the hedge to suffer a net loss. The hedge position we have described had to produce a profit on an upside move for XYZ Company common, and it could not produce a net loss on a downside move.

We conclude this subsection with a general rule. Any warrant that is attractive for purchase, particularly when it has heightened leverage following a market drop, is also amenable to a hedge position. Such a position has the effect of giving up some of the potential percentage appreciation of a simple warrant purchase for downside insurance.

Short-Selling Warrants with Approaching Expiration Dates

We have just illustrated a hedge with warrants in which an investor was long the warrants and short the common stock. This hedge aimed at profits with an *undervalued* warrant and used the short sale of the common stock to limit the potential loss sharply. Now we turn this situation around and consider short-selling a warrant that is *overvalued*, again using the corollary position, in this case a long position in the common stock, to reduce the risk factor.

Of course, we have one other factor, and a most important one: an approaching expiration date. When we say "approaching," we do not mean two weeks or even two months. As we mentioned previously, the two-year point is when we begin to pay close attention to the expiration date. This is about the time that a hedged short sale of the warrant can be found to make the greatest sense, too.

Let us assume that one warrant in the XYZ Company gives an investor the right to purchase one share of stock in that corporation for a price of 20, that the warrant will expire in two years, that the stock is selling at 20, and that the warrant is selling at 10, which is a very high premium. The high premium and short maturity date would make this warrant an attractive security for a short sale.

Let us also assume that the investor sold short 100 warrants at 10 and purchased 50 shares of common stock at 20. If on the expiration date of the warrants the price of the common rises to 39, each warrant is worth 19 (39−20=19). The short sale of 100 warrants at 10 shows a 9-point loss at 19, or a total loss of $900. The 50 shares of common, purchased at 20, show a profit of $950. If the stock were selling at 39 (the break-even point), the losses on the investment would exactly equal the gains, and the investor would break even. Any point below 39 would show a profit on the hedge position; above 39 a net loss would begin to develop.

If the common dropped to zero, there would be a $1,000 profit on the short sale of the 100 warrants at 10. There would also be a $1,000 loss on the 50 shares of common purchased at 20; so the $1,000 profit would cancel the $1,000 loss.

What these figures tell us is that a hedged short position in the XYZ Company common and warrants, with the common selling at 20 and the warrants at 10, could see the common stock go up to 39 or down to zero before showing any net loss on the position. Any point in between represented a profit. The only risk involved in the hedge was that the stock might almost immediately start a big upside run, say, to 40 or 50. Even such a move would see only a small loss because the long position in the common would continue to develop profits while the premium on the warrants sold short would continue to diminish. Thus, if we assume that the common is at 50 at the expiration date, the 50 shares purchased at 20 would show a 30-point profit, or $1,500. The warrants would be worth 30 with the stock at 50, and the 100 warrants sold short at 10 would show a 20-point loss, or $2,000. With a gain of $1,500 and a loss of $2,000, we have a small net loss of $500 on an improbable run in the common from 20 to 50.

Generally, a warrant that has one or two years remaining before its expiration date is a good possibility for a short sale. However, if the common stock is selling at a high multiple of the warrant price and you feel that a good rise could develop in the common stock, the warrant may still be attractive provided you recognize the highly speculative qualities of a warrant due to expire in so short a time, especially if the stock is selling at a price that is significantly below the exercise price of the warrant.

Canadian Warrants

As the number of warrants trading in the United States grew, there was a proportional growth in the number of Canadian warrants until, in the early 1970s, the number with appreciable public markets exceeded 50. Many are long-term warrants of such major companies as Canadian Pacific Investments, Husky Oil Ltd., Interprovincial Pipe Line, Reichhold Chemical (Canada) and Trans-Canada Pipe Lines, and new industries are represented by Canadian Cable Systems, National Nursing Homes, and a fair number of realty companies.

Superlatively rich in timber, minerals, oil, and natural gas, Canadian markets will no doubt write quite a bit of market history as a growing world population reaches more insistently for these resources, and Canadian warrants will reflect that history in their own unique leveraged manner. For American investors, however, there would appear to be two stumbling blocks to full participation in Canadian warrants. Luckily, the word *appear* accurately describes the situation, for the author feels that there is no real barrier once the various elements are understood.

First, almost all Canadian warrants cannot be exercised by American citizens. This means that if you purchase 100 warrants giving you the right to buy 100 shares of Acres Ltd., a Canadian company trading on the Toronto Stock Exchange, for $1,900 ($19 per share) and you take those warrants to Acres Ltd., the company will not be able to give you stock. Even if the company will do so, neither Canadian brokers with branches in the United States nor American brokers will help you transact this exchange.

The reason is simple. The United States Securities and Exchange Commission will not permit stock to be sold to Americans without being registered in this country in the prescribed manner. If a Canadian company wishes to sell stock to Americans, it must follow the same rules. Most Canadian companies do not do this because of the considerable expense involved and because they have no difficulty in selling their entire issue to Canadians and foreigners without such restrictions. Nevertheless, this peculiarity applies only to new issues. Once an issue of stock has been sold, it can be purchased and sold freely by Americans through any broker they choose, whether in Canada or in the United States. In the same way, Americans can buy or sell any Canadian warrants, but they still cannot exercise them because the stock that the company will give them is new stock, still unissued and, therefore, still unregistered.

We already know that virtually all warrants with any appreciable life remaining will sell at a premium above their exercise value. This being the case, no one really buys a warrant to exercise it; it's bought with the expectation of selling it at a higher price, following a hoped-for run-up in the common stock. Since this expectation probably applies to 95 percent of all warrant transactions, any hindrance to exercise of the warrant by actually tendering the warrant with payment to the company has no real meaning. In addition, if a common stock is selling so far above the exercise price of the warrant that the premium is zero, Canadian arbitragers are always in the market to buy these warrants at a very slight discount. Thus we can ignore this seeming obstacle. Americans can buy or sell any Canadian warrant without hindrance, and that is the important factor.

The second problem stems from such an unlikely source as the United States balance-of-payment difficulties, evolving from the fact that we have generally been buying more abroad than we have been selling, thus producing an unfavorable balance of trade. Washington looked for ways to cut the flow of dollars from the country, and one way that seemed appealing was to make it more difficult for American citizens to pay dollars for foreign securities by taxing them through the interest equalization tax. Precise definitions of the tax are not in order here, but we shall simply report that an American who purchases a Canadian security pays a tax of 11¼ percent of the full purchase price.

Prior to the enactment of the interest equalization tax, American interest in Canadian securities was far greater than it is today. Thus, the lack of American buying pressure in such securities means that they are selling at a lower price than would be the case if Americans were buying. If the price is more that 11¼ percent lower, the tax actually gives the buyer a *bonus*. Thus, let us assume that a certain Canadian warrant would be selling at 3 if Americans were in the buying arena as forcefully as they had been before the tax. With most Americans out, if the warrant is selling at 2½, isn't that less than 3 even if we add the 11⅓ percent? Of course it is, and that is why Canadian warrants should be evaluated on the basis of the current market price in Canada plus the 11¼ percent tax. If the final price is still an attractive one, you should go ahead and buy the warrant.

Exercising Warrants with Senior Securities at Full Face Value

Certain warrants that were issued in conjunction with a bond issue allow the investor to use the associated bond at full face value, rather than the requisite number of dollars, in exercising the warrant. The potential importance of this privilege can be appreciated when we consider a hypothetical example. Warrant XYZ is the right to buy XYZ common at $30 per share for the next five years. The warrant was originally sold attached to a bond issue of XYZ, the 5½s of 1985, and the original prospectus stated that the XYZ 5½s of 1985 could be used at full face value in exercising the warrants in lieu of cash. The warrant and bond trade separately after issuance, and we find the bond selling at 75. This means that for $75 you can purchase $100 in face value of the 5½s of 1985 in the marketplace. The *effective* exercise price of the warrant thus is no longer $30 but ⁷⁵⁄₁₀₀ of $30. The arithmetic works out as follows:

On a straight cash basis, if you wanted to exercise 100 XYZ warrants and receive 100 shares of XYZ common, you would deliver $3,000 in cash with the 100 warrants. By using the bond privilege, you could employ $3,000 face value of the 5½s of 1985 instead of the cash, and with the bond selling at 75 you could purchase $3,000 face value in the market for $2,250.

It is obvious that when the bond sells at 75, the effective exercise price for the warrant is 30 if you are using cash but 22½ if you are using the bond in lieu of cash. In addition, whenever the bond sells below 100, or par, it is distinctly worth your while to utilize this privilege. If the bond sells above 100, you ignore the privilege and use cash instead. Bonds fluctuate constantly in the marketplace, exactly as stocks do, although typically in a narrower range, the major determinant for most bonds of substantial companies being fluctuation in the level of general interest rates.

At this writing there are several dozen warrants with the privilege of using senior securities for their exercise in lieu of cash. With many of them it makes a decided difference because the applicable bonds are selling appreciably below par. It is thus necessary to keep abreast of the changing market levels of such bonds when appraising the value of their warrants. A list of warrants with this privilege is shown in Table 22-1.

TABLE 22-1   Corporate Bonds with Warrant Privileges

Bond traded*	Warrant	Coupon	Bond price	Exercise price per share	Effective exercise price
A	Allegheny Airlines 1987	5½s-'87	59.50	17.31	10.30
S	Allied Products	7s-'84	81.00	58.00	46.98
A	Altec Corp.	6¾s-'88	58.50	17.00	9.95
O	American Metal Climax†	8s-'86	No market	47.50	47.50
O	Associated Mortgage Inv.	10s-'73	No market	28.25	28.25
O	Atico Mortgage Inv. "C"	6¾s-'82	No market	23.00	23.00
	Atlas Corp.	$1 preferred	No market	6.25	6.25
S	Avco Corp.	7½s-'93	83.62	56.00	46.83
	Barnett Mortgage Trust				
O	1976	6¾s-'91	No market	28.50	28.50
S	Braniff Airways	5¾s-'86	70.50	23.62	16.65
O	Brown Company	9s-'95	78.50	16.50	12.95
S	Budget Industries	6s-'88	65.75	14.00	9.21
A	Daylin	5s-'89	71.00	22.50	15.98
A	E-Systems (LTV Aero.)	6¾s-'88	65.00	16.42	10.67
O	FBT Bancorp of Indiana	9s-'86	103.75	12.00	12.45
A	Frontier Airlines	5½s-'87	58.50	12.06	7.06
S	Fuqua Industries 1973	7s-'88	83.00	38.84	32.24
O	General Host	7s-'94	69.43	40.00	27.77
O	Gondas Corp.	6s-'78	No market	9.75	9.75
A	Guardian Mortgage Inv.	6¾s-'86	86.50	37.00	32.00
A	Jones & Laughlin Ind.	6¾s-'94	62.25	57.99	36.10
S	LTV Corp. $115	5s-'88	50.62	73.04	36.97
A	Leasco 1987	5¾s-'87	71.25	16.50	11.76
S	Loew's Theatres (Corp.)	6⅞s-'93	84.62	35.00	29.62
O	NVF Co.	5s-'94	50.50	18.22	9.20
S	Northwest Industries	7½s-'94	89.25	25.00	22.31
A	Omega-Alpha Inc.	6½s-'88	53.00	70.00	37.10
S	Pacific Southwest Airlines	6s-'87	75.50	23.40	17.67
A	Rockwood Computer	8½s-'79	76.00	39.15	29.75
O	SSI Computer (ITEL)	6¾s-'89	No market	26.00	26.00
O	Security Mortgage Inv.	6s-'82	No market	16.00	16.00
O	Starr Broadcasting 1976	9s-'76	100.00‡	10.50	10.50
S	Tenneco Corp.	6s-'79	92.25	30.07	27.74
S	Trans World Airlines	6½s-'78	85.50	22.00	18.81
S	United Brands 1978	6¾s-'88	76.75	34.50	26.48
O	Zapata Offshore	6½s-'77	No market	15.00	15.00

*S is New York Stock Exchange, A is American Stock Exchange, and O is over the counter.
†Each $108 face value equals $100 in cash.
‡Bid only; no bonds offered.
SOURCE: *R. H. M. Warrant and Stock Survey,* 220 Fifth Avenue, New York, N.Y. 10010.

GROWING USE OF WARRANTS

When the author first published *The Speculative Merits of Common Stock Warrants* in 1949, only about six warrants of real interest were trading. By 1952 there were about 20 warrants; by 1970 the number had risen to 200, and by 1973 to 400. Warrants were added as sweeteners to new bond issues and also to new issues of preferred and common stock, while merger and acquisition plans more and more also began to include warrants as part of the package being offered to various classes of stock and bond holders.

Thus, whatever the scope of opportunities warrants offer for leveraged profit and for leveraged loss, the potential has been enormously widened simply by the multiplication in the number of warrants trading. With this increase in number has come an expansion in the *types* of companies issuing long-term warrants. For a good part of the 1950s and 1960s, mostly secondary, speculative companies issued warrants. But as the 1970s came into view, the old barrier melted away, and warrants came into being for such companies as American Metal Climax, Avco, Carrier Corp., Commonwealth Edison, Gould, Gulf & Western, Louisiana Land & Exploration, Mobil Oil, Tenneco, Western Pacific Industries, and many others of similar stature. The culmination from the point of view of the size of the issue involved and the prestige of the company came in 1970, when AT&T sold an issue of common stock carrying 31.3 million warrants. These warrants broke down another long-standing barrier when the New York Stock Exchange agreed to list the warrants for the first time. This was followed by the listing of other warrants on the NYSE, while the American Stock Exchange and regional stock exchanges also began to see a larger and larger number of actively traded warrants in their rosters of securities.

Appendix

A Further Demonstration of the Fact That a Well-situated Warrant Can Be Less Speculative Than Its Common Stock

In recounting the applicable figures for the Tenneco warrant, we had to fall back on the reader's acceptance of our judgment that in a 50 percent decline in Tenneco common, from 19⅜ to about 9⅝, the Tenneco warrant would not have suffered more than the 50 percent decline, or, in other words, that it would not have suffered a greater decline than from 3 to 1½.

It is November 1970 and Tenneco common is selling at 19⅜, and the new Tenneco warrant at 3. You are considering purchasing 100 shares of Tenneco common at 19⅜ for $1,937. But there is the alternative of buying Tenneco warrants at 3. Which is better? Let's look at both alternatives. In alternative A you purchase 100 shares of Tenneco common at 19⅜, which cost $1,937. In alternative B you purchase 300 Tenneco warrants at 3, which cost $900.

It did not take long for Tenneco common to make a quick recovery in the early 1971 market. Indeed, three months later the common was selling at 28½, up 47 percent. Tenneco warrants did much better, as we would expect from our previous explanations. The warrants sold at 10¼ at the same time that the common was selling at 28½, having advanced 241 percent as compared with the 47 percent advance. A glance at the actual dollar results clearly demonstrates the superiority of the warrant over the common in November 1970.

In alternative A, the $1,937 investment in 100 shares of common was worth $2,850 with the stock at 28½, for a gain of $913. In alternative B, the $900 investment in 300 Tenneco warrants was worth $3,075 with the warrant at 10¼, for a gain of $2,175. An investment of only $900 in the warrants had shown a $2,175 profit, while the much larger $1,937 investment in the common had shown only a $913 profit. How clear the superior profit potential of the Tenneco warrant was on the upside!

When we turn to the downside, we find a vivid confirmation of the fact that the Tenneco warrant was less speculative than the common in November 1970, with the common at 19⅜ and the warrants at 3. For let us consider the effect in alternative A of common declining by 50 percent, from 19⅜ to 9⅝. At 9⅝ the 100 shares would be worth $962, for a loss of $975 from the original $1,937 investment. Turning to alternative B, the $900 investment in 300 warrants, what loss would appear here with a 50 percent decline in the common? We have already presented our belief that the warrants would probably sell no lower than 2. In this case, the loss would be 1 point on 300 warrants, or $300, far less than the $975 loss on the common stock investment. Going further, a drop to 1½ for the warrants, matching the 50 percent decline in the common on a percentage basis, would show a 1½-point drop for the 300 warrants, or a loss of $450, still less than half the $975 loss in the common. But let's go even further—indeed, all the way—and assume that the Tenneco warrants would drop to zero on the 50 percent drop in the common. If this were the case, the entire $900 invested in 300 warrants would be lost, but this total $900 loss would still be less than the $975 loss in Tenneco common.

Inevitable Conclusion. The $900 invested in the warrants at 3 in November 1970 would in three months show more than twice the profit shown by the $1,937 invested in

Tenneco common at 19⅜, but it could not possibly have shown a greater loss on the downside. When investment B must show greater profit that investment A on the upside and cannot show a greater loss on the downside, then B must be considered less speculative than A. Thus, it is logically necessary to conclude that Tenneco warrants were actually less speculative than Tenneco common in November 1970.

We have treated these points in rather fine detail to lead the way to a basic factor in warrant evaluation. Let us now return to the highs for the common and warrants in 1971 and see how the arithmetic at that time compared with what we have just analyzed. The 1971 highs were 30⅛ for the common and 11⅛ for the warrants. Let us assume that the common had then moved ahead another 50 percent, to 45³⁄₁₆. Since the warrants constituted the right to buy at 24¼, their minimum value would be 45.18 minus 24.25, or 20.93. Premiums tend to shrink as we approach higher price levels, so that a substantial premium would not be expected with the warrant above the 20 mark. If we allow a premium of about 1⅜ points, it would bring the warrants up to about 22¼, for a 100 percent advance from their 11⅛-point starting mark.

A 50 percent move for the common would have produced a 100 percent move for the warrant. Not only was this a far smaller percentage advantage for the warrant than obtained when the common was 19⅜ and the warrant 3, but when we look at the downside potential, the picture becomes even more informative. Let us assume that, at the 3⅛ common level and 11⅛ warrant level, Tenneco common did not advance 50 percent but instead fell back to its 19⅜ low, with the Tenneco warrant also retreating to its low of 3. In dropping from 30⅛ to 19⅜, Tenneco common would have suffered a decline of 35 percent, but in dropping from 11⅛ to 3 the Tenneco warrant would have suffered far more—a 73 percent decline. The decline in the warrant would be about twice that for the common, and thus we arrive at the doubtful evaluation for a warrant of potential risk equaling potential gain. A 50 percent gain for Tenneco common would produce about twice the gain for the Tenneco warrant, but a 50 percent decline for the common would produce twice the loss for the warrant.

Not only was the upside leverage of the warrant in the upper reaches exceeded somewhat by its downside leverage, but it would no longer be true that the warrant was less speculative than the common. Now it was indubitably more speculative, because a steep drop in the common would produce a much steeper decline in the warrant. A basic truth emerges here: when a stock is declining and pessimism is growing, you are likely to find the potential for an opportunity-filled warrant. When the stock has been rising for some time, however, and speculative fervor is increasing, you are likely to find the warrant in a less advantageous position. Naturally, when the warrant is hitting bottom, no one wants it, and when it is far higher, demand increases. This, of course, is the story of the market itself, but it is even more relevant for warrants.

Cities Service–Atlantic Richfield Oil Warrants: An Expiring Warrant

The logic of what we have been describing is accurately mirrored by these warrants. The difficulties that corporations encountered in securing needed financing in the 1969–1970 tight-money squeeze spawned many ingenious plans to attract investors. Under one type of plan, a company that owned a block of stock of another company added warrants to a bond issue that gave rights to buy some of that stock. Thus, in 1969 Cities Service Company wanted to sell $100 million in bonds—a challenging proposition for the investment bankers in a far from robust bond market. The answer was found in a large block of Atlantic Richfield Oil owned by Cities Service.

The $100 million in bonds was easily sold when it carried 500,000 warrants, each good to buy one share of Atlantic Richfield Oil at $110 to September 1, 1972, when the warrant would expire. It would be Cities Service that would satisfy the claim of the warrant holders from its own holdings of Atlantic Richfield Oil common stock. Of course, if Atlantic Richfield Oil common stock was selling below $110 per share when the warrant expired, none of the warrants would be exercised, and Cities Service would have enjoyed the assistance of the warrants in selling its $100 million bond issue while, in the end, retaining all its Atlantic Richfield Oil common stock. And if that common stock should move up above $110, Cities Service management decided in advance that it didn't mind getting that price for its holdings.

Let us now look at the yearly ranges for Atlantic Richfield Oil common stock and the Cities Service–Atlantic Richfield Oil warrant, shown in Table 22-2, and the picture of an expiring warrant becomes crystal-clear to us and painfully clear to anyone who was holding it during that period. Earlier in 1969 Atlantic Richfield Oil had hit an all-time high of 135¾, setting up the warrant for an enthusiastic reception. When the common stock recovered after a decline to 118⅞ in August 1969, the warrant sold at a high of about 47.75. It was all downhill after that. In 1970 Atlantic Richfield Oil never sold above 90⅜; indeed, in 1972 the stock never

TABLE 22-2   Atlantic Richfield Oil Common and Cities Service Atlantic Richfield Oil Warrants Yearly Price Ranges

Year	Atlantic Richfield Oil common		Cities Service–Atlantic Richfield Oil warrants	
	High	Low	High	Low
1972	73.00	47.62	3.00	.03
1971	78.25	57.37	11.37	2.62
1970	90.37	44.87	22.62	6.75
1969*	118.87	72.50	47.75	18.00

*High and low for July–December 1969.

sold above 73. The Cities Service–Atlantic Richfield Oil warrant went to the pennies level by mid-1972. The idea is that the stock can be moving *sideways,* while as time passes and the expiration day comes nearer, the warrant will be moving steadily *downward.* It is this type of logically expected action that makes possible a hedge position aimed at short-selling the warrant and buying insurance against any too robust rise in the common stock by carrying a long position simultaneously in the common stock.

Chapter 23
Successful Option Trading

Part 1. The Changing World of Options

PAUL SARNOFF

Traditionally, the option business began during the Dutch tulipomania in the early seventeenth century. Options on securities subsequently became popular in London. Later they were listed on its stock exchange, where puts and calls, known as "privileges," are still traded. The practice soon spread to exchanges on the Continent, where options became normal adjuncts to their markets.

In the United States, puts and calls practically grew up with the stock market itself. After the New York Stock Exchange went indoors in 1817, the vending of options became part of the *modus operandi* of brokers and traders. By the time American financial markets had weathered the disastrous panic of 1857 and the Civil War, speculation in stock option contracts, popularly called "papers," had become an integral part of the Wall Street scene.

With the formation of the Put and Call Brokers and Dealers Association, Inc., and its acceptance in 1934 by the Securities and Exchange Commission (SEC) as a self-governing body controlling the put and call business, the vast majority of options issued for the forty years between 1934 and 1973 were endorsed or guaranteed by member firms of the New York Exchange on behalf of option-writing accounts. The actual options were obtained for their buyers at brokerage firms through the good offices of specialized financial intermediaries, who were mainly members of the Put and Call Brokers and Dealers Association, and were guaranteed by the member firms at which the option sellers (writers) maintained their accounts.

Although the options business was a highly specialized field controlled by fewer than a dozen dealers, about seventy-five New York Stock Exchange member firms maintained costly options departments. By the 1960s, the managers of these departments realized that something was fundamentally wrong with the option business in the United States. First, both option buyers and option writers had to support middlemen, the put and call dealers, who made an intervening profit on each transaction. In addition, there was no liquidity for either buyer or writer unless and until a particular option expired or was exercised by calling or putting the related stock. Finally, the tax aspects for option writers were somewhat obscure, in contrast to the clarity of those for buyers.

As a result, key figures among the New York Stock Exchange firms maintaining option departments began a campaign to establish exchange or public trading in options. Their hope was that an exchange marketplace for options would help the brokerage business in general through increased commissions from greater buying and selling of listed shares as well as options.

Their dream came to fruition in April 1973. With the start of trading of calls on sixteen selected securities, a revolution struck the option business. Because of the ease of obtaining adequate markets, because of fair dealing and a lack of price and volume secrecy, because of instant liquidity for both buyers and writers, and because of a special new tax treatment for option writers, trading in listed options has forcibly pushed trading in unlisted (popularly called "conventional") options into virtual discard. About the sole exception was trading in conventional puts on stocks selected as suitable for listed option trading. The reason for this major exception is that, as explained below, only buyers of puts can achieve tax-favored long-term capital gains. This sole exception will no longer exist when, following SEC approval, puts as well as calls are publicly traded on securities exchanges.

The major strategies available to buyers and writers of calls and puts are briefly summarized here.

Call buyers risk their funds to:

1. Control price action of 100-share lots of a stock for a set period of time, profiting from a rise and limiting their exposure during that time period to the cost of the calls.

2. Correct the market error of selling too soon in a rising market. Investors sell their stock and simultaneously buy calls. If the price rises, they can replace their sold shares at the price at which they sold them, plus the cost of the calls.

3. Withdraw capital while keeping a similar position. Investors liquidate and replace their positions at a fraction of their value with calls.

4. Protect a short sale. Short sellers buy calls while selling a similar amount of stock short. If the market collapses, they profit on the short sales and chalk up the cost of the worthless calls to "insurance." If the stock instead soars, they can exercise their calls and deliver stock to cover at the price at which they went short, plus, of course, the cost of the calls.

Call writers risk their funds to:

1. Earn money premiums on stock or cash reserves by writing options if the stocks remain stagnant or decline slightly.

2. Presell long positions for more than the current market.

3. Make money in a down market without going short.

Put buyers risk their funds to:

1. Profit from a down market while limiting their risk and possible loss if the market soars to the cost of their puts.

2. Insure long positions against downside deterioration in price during the life of the puts.

3. Get long-term capital gains during a market decline. Since successful short sellers cannot get long-term capital gains, even if they hold their positions for a year, the only way to establish long-term gains in a down market is to buy puts for longer than nine months' duration (twelve months' duration after 1977) and *resell* the successful puts for more than their cost.

Put writers risk their funds to:

1. Buy stock possibly below the current market. Since the Internal Revenue Service (IRS) permits put writers to consider the premiums they receive as reductions in the basis of the cost of any shares put to the writers, it follows that an investor seeking to buy 100 RC at 20 who instead writes a put at 20 for three months for $300 has contracted to buy that stock at 17 while it is actually trading at 20 if the stock declines. If it rises,

2. The writer will pocket the put premium and earn money on money.

Finally, if we think in terms of options and bullish and bearish price movements, speculators or traders who are *bullish* can (1) buy calls, (2) write calls against existing long positions, (3) write puts on stocks that they think will rise by putting up cash deposits (normally 50 percent), or (4) buy stock and protect their purchases simultaneously from downside risk by buying puts.

Traders who are *bearish* can (1) buy puts for short- or long-term gains in a down market with limited risk, (2) write naked (uncovered) call options against cash deposits (normally 50 percent for conventional options and 30 percent for listed ones), or go short on stock and simultaneously buy calls to protect their positions against unforeseen upside traumas.

The advent of public trading in options has led to numerous innovative strategies for making profits in all kinds of markets. These are analyzed in Part 2.

Part 2. A Guide to Publicly Traded Option Strategies for Buyers and Sellers[1]

ROBERT E. BROWN

THE BASICS OF PUBLICLY TRADED OPTIONS

Call options have been trading on the Chicago Board Options Exchange (CBOE) since April 1973, on the American Stock Exchange (Amex; ASE) since January 1975, and on the Philadelphia-Baltimore-Washington (PBW) Stock Exchange since June 1975. From the initial list of options on just 16 stocks, the exchanges expanded rapidly. Within 2½ years, 79 stocks were represented on the CBOE, 40 on the Amex, and 10 on the PBW. Within three years the number of optionable stocks rose to nearly 200, with well over 1,000 available options. This experience will be substantially duplicated when listed transactions in put options begin.

These options are designated "marketable" because there is a secondary market; that is, they can be bought or sold at any time prior to expiration in much the same way as listed stock. The prices appear daily in *The Wall Street Journal* and many local newspapers. A summary of the week's trades appears in *Barron's*.

[1]The contents of this part of Chapter 23 are based largely on material from the *Value Line Convertible Survey*, published by Arnold Bernhard & Co., Inc., of New York, of which the author has been the editor.

What Are Call Options?

A single call option generally gives the owner the right to buy 100 shares of a specific stock at a specified price (called the "striking price") at any time prior to a specified date (called the "expiration date"). The price of the option (often called the "premium") as quoted in a newspaper is generally one-hundredth of the price of the option in dollars; that is, a quoted price of 3 means that one option on 100 shares of stock costs $300.

A call option, from the standpoint of the buyer of the option, closely resembles a short-term warrant. And, as with a warrant, the primary appeal of a call option to the buyer is leverage: if the stock rises dramatically during the life of the option, the percentage gain in the option's price can be far greater than the percentage gain in the price of the stock. Conversely, of course, buyers of call options can lose 100 percent of their investment if the stock is at or below the striking price when the options expire. So even the most risk-oriented investors should never put more than a small fraction of their capital in call options.

Options Also Have Conservative Uses

Although the purchase of call options is the easiest option transaction to understand, we emphasize that options can also be used to reduce risk. Certain option strategies entail significantly less risk than simply owning the underlying stock. These risk-reducing strategies could be of interest even to very conservative but financially sophisticated investors.

How Options Are Identified

Each option is identified by three pieces of information: the stock that it is an option to buy (for example, IBM), the month when the option expires (each option expires on the Saturday immediately following the third Friday of the month of expiration), and the striking price (for example, $200). For instance, an IBM January/200 option would give the holder the right to buy 100 shares of IBM at $200 a share at any time between now and the Saturday following the third Friday of January. The striking price is not adjusted for ordinary cash dividends that may be paid during the life of the option.

For a given stock, three different expiration months are available at any time; these expiration months are always spaced three months apart. For example, in August there would be IBM options expiring in October, January, and April; after the October options expire, July options would be introduced. Therefore even the most distant option expires in nine months or less. About half of the stocks have been assigned January-April-July-October (JAJO) expiration months, while the other half have a February-May-August-November (FMAN) expiration cycle.

Where Do Options Come From?

Unlike common stocks, warrants, or most other securities that are issued in a fixed amount by corporations, call options are in effect created by investors themselves. Every option purchased by an option buyer must be created by another investor called the option writer. As an example, let's consider an IBM October/160 call option, and let's suppose that the price of IBM stock is 188. The price, or premium, of the option is 42 (that is, $4,200). An investor who bought this option would be paying $4,200 in the hope that IBM would rise substantially in price during the nine months remaining until the option expires. The investor who sold or wrote this option would receive $4,200 for agreeing to sell 100 shares of IBM at $160 a share at any time that the buyer wanted to exercise the option prior to its expiration.

Although there must be a writer for each new option issued to a buyer, the buyer and the writer do not deal directly with each other. Rather, both the buyer and the writer, through their respective brokers, deal with a special clearing corporation that has been set up to act as the middleman. The clearing corporation is the issuer of each option, and writers are obligated contractually to the clearing corporation. If and when buyers decide to exercise their options, they notify the clearing corporation through their brokers, and the clearing corporation notifies the brokers of writers chosen at random. The writers are then obligated to deliver the shares to their brokers for delivery to the brokerage firms representing the buyers. The clearing corporation, as issuer and obligor of each option, assures that the shares will be delivered to the exercising buyers.

The great advantage of this arrangement is that a specific writer is not tied to a specific buyer. As a result, both the buyer and the writer are free to close out their positions whenever they wish. For example, let's suppose that IBM stock rose to 220 by May. The October/160 option would then be selling for at least 60 ($6,000), since the price of the stock would be 60 points above the striking price of 160. At that point buyers might wish to take their profits; perhaps they're concerned that the stock may decline. They do not have to exercise their options to realize their profits. Instead, they can simply sell the options for $6,000 to some other investors, just as they might sell common stock. And the option writers can eliminate their obligation by repurchasing (that is, buying back) the options for $6,000. Since there is a continuous market in these options, buyers are able to sell even if the particular writers who created the options do not wish to terminate their obligations. And the writers can terminate their obligations even if the original buyers have no desire to sell. All this is possible because the clearing corporation acts as middleman and because the CBOE, Amex, and PBW maintain continuous markets.

Factors That Affect the Price of a Call Option

Although in the final analysis the price of a call option is determined by supply and demand, the price that buyers are willing to pay and writers are willing to accept is primarily a function of five factors: the exercise, or striking, price of the option, the time remaining before the option expires, and the price, volatility, and yield of the underlying stock. By varying one factor at a time, we can see that a lower striking price and a longer life increase the value and hence the price of an option. And a higher price for the underlying stock also increases the value of the option. Because the market price of an option reflects the probability of a significant rise in the price of the underlying stock, options on volatile stocks cost more in percentage terms than options on stable stocks. And because CBOE, Amex, and PBW call options are not adjusted for ordinary cash dividends, options on high-yielding stocks tend to sell for less than comparable options on low-yielding stocks. Many readers will recognize that these are the same factors that influence the price of a warrant.

Getting a Feel for the Market

We suggest that readers choose one or two optionable stocks and start watching the price movements of the respective options on a daily basis. Since daily quotations in newspapers don't show the high and low or the net change, your broker's quotation machine can be considerably more useful for this purpose than newspaper quotations. Therefore it's helpful to know how the quotation machine symbols are constructed.

Although the exact sequence of symbols varies with different brands of quotation machines, the basic ingredients are the ticker symbol for the underlying common and a two-letter "suffix code." The first letter of the two-letter suffix indicates the type of option and the month of expiration as follows:

First Letter	Month	First Letter	Month
A	January	G	July
B	February	H	August
C	March	I	September
D	April	J	October
E	May	K	November
F	June	L	December

The second letter of the suffix code indicates the striking price as follows:

Second Letter	Striking Price	Second Letter	Striking Price
A	5 or 105 or 205	K	55 or 155 or 255
B	10 or 110 or 210	L	60 or 160 or 260
C	15 or 115 or 215	M	65 or 165 or 265
D	20 or 120 or 220	N	70 or 170 or 270
E	25 or 125 or 225	O	75 or 175 or 275
F	30 or 130 or 230	P	80 or 180 or 280
G	35 or 135 or 235	Q	85 or 185 or 285
H	40 or 140 or 240	R	90 or 190 or 290
I	45 or 145 or 245	S	95 or 195 or 295
J	50 or 150 or 250	T	100 or 200 or 300

OPTION WRITING

Do you want to reduce the risk of your portfolio without selling your current holdings? If your stocks are well-known blue chips, the conservative strategy of writing options against your portfolio can help you achieve this objective and may produce significant tax savings as well. As for tax-exempt institutions, a federal law approved in September 1976 made it clear that such institutions may write call options on common stocks in their portfolios without losing their tax exemption.

Should You Consider Writing Options?

Whereas option buying is best left to individuals who can withstand sudden and very dramatic losses, writing options on a portfolio of stocks is a low-risk investment strategy. The appeal of this technique has much in common with the appeal of low-risk convertible debentures and preferreds: reduced downside risk vis-à-vis the alternative of simply holding the common stock. Of course, as with most convertibles, the writer of an option against a long position sacrifices some of the upside potential of the underlying equity. But the ability to close out a position on one of the option exchanges can be used to preserve much of the upside potential and generate significant tax savings as well.

The aim of our discussion is to present an introduction to option writing. We shall show how writing options against a long position in the stock can lower the risk of the investor's overall position. We'll explain some of the considerations involved in selecting an expiration month and a striking price. And we'll show how paper profits can be turned into real tax savings.

The Option Writer's Position

As we have seen, call options are created when an investor, called the option writer, enters into a contractual agreement with the options clearing corporation to deliver the underlying shares if the option is exercised; the options clearing corporation then issues the option to the option buyer. The writer, therefore, must be prepared to deliver the underlying shares if and when the option is exercised.

This may be done either by delivering the shares from the writer's account or by buying the necessary shares on the market (for immediate delivery) and then delivering them. However, since the vast majority of options are never exercised, writers will generally either find their written options expiring unexercised or, more frequently, will close out their positions prior to the expiration date and prior to exercise by repurchasing the equivalent options.

An Example of Option Writing

Let's consider the writer of an IBM July/180 option when the stock was at 177¼ on November 29. We assume that the writer owned 100 shares of IBM. He or she would have received a premium of 28 ($2,800) for writing the option. By a month later, on December 27, IBM had sunk to 162¼, and the option had dropped to 19⅜. How had the writer done thus far? There was a paper loss of $1,500 on the stock and a paper profit of $862 on the option. So overall the writer had a paper loss of $638. We see that when the stock dropped 8.5 percent in a month's time, the option writer lost only 3.6 percent on the overall position. This is fairly typical: on a short-term drop, the paper profit from the short position in the option offset about half of the paper loss on the stock.

By a month later, on January 31, IBM had rallied to 188¼, and the option was selling at 23¾. So the writer had a paper profit of $1,100 on the stock and a paper profit of $425 on the option. Why was the option selling at a lower price even though the stock had advanced? Because the option at that point was only six months from expiration in contrast to the original eight months. This is rather typical when the stock rises by a relatively small percentage and the option is significantly closer to expiration.

Now let's suppose that IBM had quickly advanced to 200 (which it did) and that the option had risen to 35 (even though the actual price of the option was then about 30). At that point the writer would have a $2,275 paper profit on the stock and a $700 paper loss on the option. In this instance the paper loss on the option offset about one-third of the paper gain on the stock: the writer's overall position was up 8.9 percent on a 12.8 percent rise by the stock.

It is quite true that on a much larger gain by the stock the writer would have received a smaller percentage of the stock's gain. And on a more massive drop by the stock, the writer would have suffered a more substantial loss than in our example. Remember, however, that the writer need not maintain his or her position in the option. It may be more advantageous to buy back the option and write an option with a different striking price or with a different month of expiration.

Choosing among Options for Writers

In general, among options with the same striking price, the one with the most distant expiration date will provide the greatest downside protection. We illustrate with this hypothetical example:

IBM	First Date	Second Date	Point Change	Percent Change
Common	180	160	−20	−11
October/180	18	9	−9	−50
July/180	15	7	−8	−53
April/180	10	4	−6	−60

We see that although the options with the closer expiration dates fell further in percentage terms, they fell to a smaller extent in terms of points. Therefore covered option writers who wrote one option against each 100 shares of stock in their portfolios would have lost the least on their overall positions if they had written options with the most distant expiration date.

Among options with the same expiration date, the one with the lowest striking price provides the greatest downside protection:

IBM	First Date	Second Date	Point Change	Percent Change
Common	180	160	−20	−11
October/200	10	4	−6	−60
October/180	18	9	−9	−50
October/160	30	16	−14	−47

We see that although the option with the highest strike, the one that is furthest out of the money, fell to the greatest extent in percentage terms, it fell to the least extent in terms of points. The covered writer gets the greatest downside protection from options that are into the money, that is, have a strike below the price of the stock. But these options also provide the smallest potential profit and the greatest risk of exercise. We think the best compromise of reasonable downside protection plus meaningful upside potential is achieved with options struck close to the current price of the stock.

When the stock moves substantially away from the striking price of the option that has been written, it is generally advisable to buy back the option and write another option struck closer to the current market. This procedure preserves the balance between upside potential and downside risk and thus tends to keep the risk of the overall position relatively stable. A writer following this type of strategy will rarely have an option either expire or be exercised. Rather, in the vast majority of cases the writer will buy back the option long before either of those events could occur.

TAX CONSIDERATIONS FOR OPTION TRADERS

Fundamental Problems

Tax considerations are much more important for option transactions than for stock or bond transactions. A pretax loss can sometimes become an aftertax profit, and a pretax profit can become an aftertax loss.

Option trading is a new technique for most investors, and with it come a host of new tax considerations. The tax problems are, as one might expect, quite different for buyers and writers of listed call options. A basic understanding of the tax considerations of option trading can influence one's trading decisions. We shall show how, for example, certain timely transactions can provide investors with sorely needed tax relief in bull markets.

Option Traders Have Substantial Control

Buyers of listed call options have complete control over when and how their positions will be closed; writers have less than full, but still very substantial, control over the fate of their positions. In both cases, the decision to close a position and the timing of the close depend primarily on the fundamental prospects for the position: its remaining profit potential measured against its risk. There will often be instances, however, when tax considerations will influence one's thinking; in certain instances, tax consequences could in fact be the dominant consideration. The degree to which this is so will depend upon one's tax bracket, but since we all operate with the Internal Revenue Service, the IRS, figuratively looking over our shoulders, it's wise to know how we can lessen its bite.

Tax Rules for Option Buyers

The rules we are about to outline for option buyers bear a striking similarity to those for warrant buyers. This is not surprising since call options and warrants represent essentially the same thing to their holders: the right to purchase a specified amount of stock at a specified price at any time prior to a specified date.

When an investor sells a previously purchased call, a capital gain or loss results that is long-term if the option has been held for more than nine months and short-term if it has been held for nine months or less (starting in 1978, for twelve months in both cases).

The lengthening of the long-term holding period under the Tax Reform Act of 1976 from the previously prevailing six months is an upsetting change for many option holders. It means that unless more option trading becomes available for contracts of more than nine months in 1977 and of more than twelve months thereafter, gains and losses of option holders in very large measure will be short-term and thus subject to less favorable tax rates.

In contrast, the exercising of a call is not a taxable transaction. When the call is exercised, the cost basis of the call plus the sum required to exercise the call (including commissions) becomes the cost basis for the stock received. The holding period is measured from the exercise date. If a call is allowed to expire unexercised, the holder realizes a capital loss equal to the price paid for the call including commissions; the holding period is from the date of acquisition to the date of expiration. Thus a call that expires unexercised is treated as though it were sold at a price of zero on the expiration date.

Tax Rules for Option Writers

The Tax Reform Act of 1976 specifies that either on a closing option transaction or on the lapse of an option without exercise the option writer realizes a *short-term* gain or loss on any excess over the premium received by the writer. This change does not apply to any broker or trader who buys and sells options in the ordinary course of his or her business. Here the preexisting rules apply, as described below.

Prior to the Tax Reform Act of 1976, the applicable IRS rules were much more favorable for option writers, permitting the difference between the amount paid out in a closing transaction and the premium received to be treated as an ordinary gain or loss, to be added to or subtracted from other ordinary income.

Tax Strategies for the Buyer

The buyer of call options is generally one with a speculative bent. Because of the high leverage inherent in the holder's position, profits and losses can come and go very quickly. Therefore, most decisions to close out a position will be based solely upon investment fundamentals. There may be times, however, when tax considerations can influence a decision. The key objective, from a tax standpoint, is to make gains long-term and losses short-term whenever possible.

The decision whether to sell or to exercise a call should include a consideration of the loss of the holding period that exercising entails. A holder of a profitable call that has been held more than six months (a long-term holding) would, by exercising, wind up with a short-term holding of the stock. Had the holder instead sold the call, there would have been a desirable long-term gain. So if the investor thinks that he or she might sell the stock within six months anyway, it might be better to sell the call and realize a long-term capital gain. But if the investor plans to hold the stock for more than six months, he or she should defer the gain by exercising the option.

A call option that is out of the money can either be sold or allowed to expire, either alternative resulting in a capital loss. It is a good idea for holders of calls that are likely to expire worthless to consider selling them just prior to the six-month mark if the expiration date is more than six months from the purchase date. If the call has some tangible value but is worth less than the cost basis, a potential long-term loss on the option can be turned into a short-term loss by exercising the call and immediately selling the shares received upon exercise. The need to put up additional cash plus the added commission costs should be weighed against the potential tax benefit before such a move is made.

Treatment of Wash Sales

The capital loss realized on the sale of a security is generally deferred if the seller reacquires or enters into a contract or option to reacquire the security within a period beginning thirty days before the sale and ending thirty days after the sale. Although a loss on the *sale* of a call may not be subject to this wash sale rule, investors should be aware that the purchase of a call would result in a wash sale if the underlying stock had been or will be sold at a loss within the designated period.

A wash sale would probably also occur if a call option is sold at a loss and the same option is reacquired within thirty days. Although we cannot say with certainty, it is likely that no wash sale would occur if the two options differed with respect to either striking price or expiration date.

OPTION TRADING MARGIN RULES

Part of the appeal of call options is the relatively small sum of money that is usually required to establish a position. This applies both to the purchase of options (even though options cannot be purchased on margin) and to more esoteric strategies such as "spreading" that are made feasible by realistic margin requirements.

Maximizing Return with Debt

The appeal of a particular investment strategy can vary greatly according to the amount of money that the investor is required to put up. Initial margin requirements (the amount of cash that must be deposited to establish a position) can thus be a crucial factor when it comes to weighing the merits of a proposed transaction. A knowledge of the margin rules also allows astute investors a broader degree of freedom, for the use of credit in varying degrees is one more tool at their disposal.

Thus an understanding of the relevant margin rules is very important to all who make use of listed call options, whether the individual is an aggressive trader purchasing or writing naked calls, or both, or a conservative investor writing only covered positions. Indeed, as we shall note below, certain strategies such as spreading (the purchase of an option while at the same time writing an option of the same or shorter length on the same stock) would not be feasible at all were it not for realistic margin rules. These liberal margin rules improve the efficiency of the market by providing a mechanism by which price discrepancies can be corrected.

Increased Risk

As with other types of investment vehicles, the use of credit in option transactions enhances one's potential return but also increases the risk. Before using margin, investors should carefully weigh the overall risk of the margined position to determine whether it is appropriate in view of their investment objectives and financial resources.

Margin Rules for the Buyer

Regulation T of the Federal Reserve Board requires that the purchase of a call option be made with 100 percent margin. In other words, no credit may be extended by the broker for the cost of the purchase. Long option positions may therefore be carried either in one's general margin account or in a cash account. Unlike warrants, however, options carried in the margin account are not recognized for margin purposes as securities exchangeable or convertible into the underlying stock. This means that long option positions may not be used for purposes of margining short positions in the common. Such a position requires the full current margin requirement for the shorted stock.

Margin Rules for Naked Calls

The initial margin requirement for writing a naked (uncovered) call is 30 percent of the market value of the underlying stock, based upon the preceding day's closing price and adjusted by the difference between the striking price and the price of the common. The premium received may be applied toward meeting this requirement.

For example, let's suppose one were to write a naked call on 100 shares of XYZ Corp. The striking price of the call is 50, and the premium received is $250. If the stock closed at 50 on the previous evening, the initial margin requirement is $1,500 (30 percent of the value of the common) less the $250 premium, or $1,250. If the stock instead were at 45, the margin requirement would be computed by subtracting $500 (the difference between the value of the stock at the striking price and its current market value) from 30 percent of the stock's market value and then deducting the premium received. If the stock were above the striking price, this difference would have been added rather than subtracted.

The maintenance requirement for a listed naked call is 30 percent of the market value of the common plus (if the stock is above the striking price) or minus (if the stock is below the striking price) the difference between the value of the common at the striking price and its current market value. This is subject, however, to a $250 minimum maintenance margin for each naked call. Since there is no cushion between initial and maintenance requirements, margin calls can come very rapidly.

It is important for investors to realize that the maintenance requirement for a naked option position rises faster than the price of the underlying stock. In the preceding example, the maintenance margin is initially $1,500 (30 percent of the stock value), satisfied by the $1,250 initial margin and the $250 premium. Now let's suppose that the price of XYZ Corp. common rose to 55. We compute the new maintenance requirement by adding $1,650 (30 percent of the market value of the stock) plus $500 (the difference between the market value of the stock and its value at the striking price) to get $2,150. So the maintenance margin requirement has risen by $650 ($2,150 minus $1,500) on only a 5-point rise by the common. Except when the $250 minimum maintenance margin comes into play, the required maintenance margin will change $130 for each 1-point change in the price of the underlying stock.

Margin Rules for Covered Written Calls

In establishing a covered writing position, the premium received on the call can be applied directly toward the initial margin requirement on the stock (currently 50 percent of the cost). For example, let's suppose that an investor wishes to purchase 100 shares of XYZ Corp. common at 50 (total cost, $5,000) and write one call (with a striking price of 50) against that position. Let us also suppose that the premium received is $300. The initial margin requirement is $2,500 (50 percent of the cost of the common) less the $300 premium, or $2,200. The call position itself requires no margin. After establishing the position and depositing the required margin, the account has a market value of $4,700 (market value of long position minus market value of short position), a debit balance of $2,500, and equity of $2,200. If an investor already has a position in the common stock and wishes to write a call on that stock, no additional margin is required.

In computing the maintenance requirements for a covered writing position, the stock is priced at the lower of its market price and the striking price. In the preceding example, if the price of the common rose to 60, all computations would still be based upon a price of 50 (the striking price) for the stock. If, however, the common fell to 40 and the option fell to $1, the debit balance would still be $2,500, and the equity would be $1,400. The total maintenance requirement is always 30 percent of the long stock (in this case $1,200) because the stock margins the written call for maintenance as well as initial margin purposes.

Margin Rules for Writing against Convertible Securities

Investors may choose to write options against a position in a security convertible into common. The margin requirement for the short call portion of such a position is the lower of either the requirement for the uncovered option or the amount by which the money required to convert the long position exceeds the cost of exercising the option. Let's suppose that one is long 100 warrants to purchase 100 shares of XYZ Corp. common at 50 with the stock selling at 40. The investor writes an option with a striking price of 40, receiving a $250 premium. Thirty percent of the value of the underlying stock is $1,200 (30 percent of $4,000), the margin required for the uncovered option since the stock is at the strike. The amount by which the money required to convert the long warrants ($5,000) exceeds the cost of exercising the option ($4,000) is $1,000; the lower of the two is $1,000. Since $250 has been received in premiums, only another $750 is required. If the price of XYZ common falls to 30, then 30 percent of the underlying stock (30 percent of $3,000), minus the amount by which the stock is below the strike ($1,000), is less than zero. As a result, no margin is required for the naked option.

Margin Rules for Spreads

Spreading is a technique that has gained popularity with many investors, largely as a result of the very favorable margin requirements (see below, "Spreading: Profits and Risks"). Essentially a spread is the simultaneous purchase of a call option and the writing of a different option, with the same or an earlier expiration date, of the same company.

If the striking price of the long option is the same as or lower than that of the short option, no margin is required for the option written. If the striking price of the long side is higher than that of the short side, the initial and maintenance margin for the option written is the lesser of (1) the difference between the striking prices and (2) the margin requirement for the short side as a naked option.

Let's consider the case of an investor who buys an XYZ Corp. April/50 option for $200 and writes an XYZ Corp. January/45 option for $600. The common stock is trading at 50. This qualifies as a spread, since the option purchased expires later than the option written. The difference between the striking prices is $500; 30 percent of the value of the stock ($1,500) plus the 5 points into the money ($500) is $2,000. The lesser of the two is $500. So the amount of money that must be put up for the overall position is the $500 margin for the option written plus the cost of the option purchased ($200) minus the proceeds from the option written ($600); therefore, only an additional $100 (plus commissions) is required from the investor.

A butterfly spread (the purchase of options with high and low striking prices and the writing of two options with a middle striking price, all with the same expiration date) is broken down, for margin calculations, into two spreads. For example, let's suppose that an investor purchased one April/40 call and one April/60 call and wrote two April/50 calls. This is broken down into one spread in which the premium on the buy side exceeds the premium on the short side (buy the April/40 and write the April/50) and one spread in which the reverse is true (buy the April/60 and write the April/50). The margin requirements are then calculated according to the preceding example.

There is virtually an unlimited number of conceivable spread combinations that can be concocted by a sophisticated investor, involving options with different striking prices or expiration dates, or both. A few general rules provide guidelines for matching the components of any overall position.

First, long stock is matched against calls written with the longest expiration. Any remaining stock is then matched with calls written in the next most distant month, and so on, until either the stock or the calls run out. Within any expiration month, the calls with the lowest striking prices are used first.

When the stock is used up first, long calls with the earliest expiration are matched against written calls with the earliest expiration, provided the written call expires at the same time as or earlier than the long call. If a written option expires later than any of the remaining long calls, it must be regarded as a naked option. The matching is continued (within each month the lowest striking price comes first) until all calls have been matched or one side runs out. If any written calls remain unmatched, they must be regarded as naked calls. This matching process will result in a series of positions each of which is margined in the ways outlined in previous examples.

A Final Word of Caution

The margin rules outlined above represent our understanding of minimum requirements as set by the exchanges with the acquiescence of the Federal Reserve Board. However, individual brokerage firms may (and some, in fact, do) set higher requirements for their customers. Investors should be fully aware of all the rules that may apply to their accounts. Because the margin rules are complex, we strongly recommend that investors discuss the margin requirements with their brokers before executing an option transaction.

OPTION ORDERS

A working knowledge of the various types of available orders can help an investor maximize the efficiency of any option-buying or option-writing program. This section also explains how options are executed on the floors of the exchanges.

The Chicago Board Options Exchange deserves much credit not only for its pioneering spirit in opening a whole new and promising field to all investors but also for its ability to set up, right at the beginning, the mechanics of an orderly market. The Chicago Board has borrowed proven principles and practices from several existing markets. The manner in which option transactions are executed on the floor of the Amex and PBW more closely resembles the way in which listed stocks are traded. Both procedures are outlined below.

Types of Orders

The profit potential and risk of an option position are a function not only of the company's prospects but also of a delicate price relationship between the option and the underlying common stock. Since these relationships, and hence the evaluation of the option, are likely to change very quickly, it is often advisable to make use of certain types of orders that can protect you against sudden changes.

Although some of these more sophisticated orders may sometimes make it more difficult to acquire a position, the benefits quite frequently outweigh the drawbacks.

A good way to begin this discussion is with a set of definitions of the various types of orders that may be placed:

1. *Market order.* This is simply an order to buy or sell a stated number of options at the best price obtainable. The placing of a market order generally assures that the transaction will be completed, although not necessarily at desirable prices. This type of order should be used only with very actively traded options.

2. *Limit order.* This is an order to buy or sell a stated number of options at a specified price or better. Such an order insures the investor against execution at prices that he or she considers disadvantageous, but of course there is no assurance that execution will take place at all.

3. *Contingency order.* A contingency order is any one of several types of orders that become either market or limit orders only if certain conditions are met. Types of permitted contingency orders include:

a. Market-if-touched order. A buy order of this type becomes a market order when the option trades or is offered at or below the order price. A market-if-touched sell order becomes a market order when the option trades or is bid at or above the order price.

b. Stop order. Also called a "stop-loss order," a buy order of this type becomes a market order when the option trades or is bid at or above the stop price. A sell stop order becomes a market order when the option trades or is offered at or below the stop price. The acceptability of such orders by the American Stock Exchange on option transactions is apparently a major difference in its handling of stock and option trading: stop orders on common shares are not permissible. Because the execution price can be much less favorable than the stop price, we advise against using stop orders. A stop-limit order with a separate stop and limit, described below, can serve the same purpose with less risk.

c. Stop-limit order. A stop-limit order to buy becomes a limit order when the option trades or is bid at or above the stop price. A stop-limit order to sell becomes a limit order when the option trades or is offered at or below the stop price. An investor may (and often should) make the stop price (the price which activates the order) different from the limit (the least favorable price that the investor will accept).

4. *Spread order.* This is an order to buy a particular call option and to write (sell) another option of the same company. A spread order is typically designated in terms of a desired difference in the premiums of the two sides (for example, buy one July/60 and sell one July/80, 2 points apart). Spread orders may be used even if the two options don't qualify as a spread for margin purposes. Spread orders can be a valuable tool not only for those entering into spreads but also for buyers and writers. They can be a convenient way of switching out of one option and into another. Let's suppose that you have written an XYZ Corp. October/40 option and now feel that the October/60 option offers more potential. A spread order to buy one October/40 and sell one October/60, if executed, would accomplish the desired switch.

5. *Not-held order.* This is an order that gives the floor broker wide discretion as to time or price at which the order may be executed. It is useful with orders involving the purchase or sale of large blocks.

6. *One-cancels-the-other order.* This consists of two or more orders treated as a unit. The execution of any one causes the others to be canceled. For example, an investor might wish to buy either a July/40 or an October/60 option but not both. With this kind of order, the purchase of one option cancels the buy order on the other.

An all-or-none order, in which an order to purchase or sell a given number of options is considered effective only if the entire order is executed, is not permitted.

The CBOE Floor

As we indicated, the Chicago Board Options Exchange has created a blend of practices that have been in use at existing securities and commodity exchanges. The CBOE does not use the specialist system that is the basis of trading on the nation's major stock exchanges. Instead, the responsibilities that would normally fall on specialists are divided among board brokers and market makers.

Trading is done at posts, each manned by a "board broker," an exchange member who is responsible for options on one to four stocks, depending upon trading activity. Board brokers serve as brokers' brokers, holding market and limit orders placed with them for execution by floor brokers and member firms. They earn the full floor commission (about $2 per contract) on each transaction that they execute. They may not trade for their own account but are responsible for overseeing the performance of the market makers. Board brokers must at all times maintain a display board with firm bid and asked quotation as well as the latest prices for the options under their authority. In addition, they have the responsibility of setting opening and closing prices or quotations for each of their options.

Bids and offers made by board brokers have priority over all others at the same price. For example, if a seller (either a market maker or a floor broker) comes to a post with five XYZ Corp. April/60 options and finds, for example, that the board broker and a market maker are both bidding the same for that option, the seller must first satisfy the board broker's bids completely and then, if any options are left, sell them to the market maker. The bidding market maker, however, can move ahead of the board broker in priority by increasing the bid. The priority of the board broker was established in order to give public customers preferential execution.

"Market makers" are the only persons on the exchange floor who can trade for their own account. Each market maker will be responsible for options on one or more stocks, depending upon volume; at least two market makers are appointed for each stock. Market makers perform essentially the same functions as market makers in the over-the-counter stock market. They may trade for short-term profits, or they may establish longer-term positions in the options for which they are responsible. It is their duty, however, to add to the liquidity of the market by maintaining bids and offers no more than $\frac{1}{2}$ point apart for options selling under $20, no more than 1 point apart for higher-priced options, and no more than 1 point away from the last trade price except in unusual circumstances. When called upon by a board broker, a market maker must make firm bids and offers for at least one contract. The market maker may also act as a floor broker.

"Floor brokers" are exchange members who may execute orders for nonmember customers. They may act on options in all stocks. They have the discretion of executing market or limit orders, thereby earning floor commissions or they may give those orders and their commissions to board brokers. The responsibility of executing other types of orders (spreads, contingencies) falls on floor brokers. All the trading skills of floor brokers are called on in attempting to execute orders of these types. It is up to them to satisfy contingency orders at the best possible prices when contingency conditions activate orders. Spread orders can be particularly difficult to execute because both sides must be executed simultaneously. The two options could conceivably trade only a few moments apart within the specified limits of an order, and still the spread might not be executed.

The Amex and PBW

Unlike the CBOE, the Amex and the PBW do not utilize competing market makers. Instead, option trading has been incorporated into the long-standing specialist system used for the trading of common stocks and warrants.

The specialist, in effect, combines the roles and responsibilities of the board broker and the market maker. What is not present in this system is the potential for competition between two or more market makers that could, at least in theory, result in increased liquidity and better prices for investors. As in the CBOE system, the execution of often-difficult contingency and spread orders is dependent upon the trading skills of the floor broker. Under both systems, the quality of execution on complex orders depends critically on the skill of the floor broker representing the brokerage firm.

SPREADING: PROFITS AND RISKS

A sophisticated form of option trading, spreading can be rewarding if it is handled properly. The transition from theory to practice, however, is full of potential pitfalls. The technique should not be attempted unless you are sure that you are fully aware of all the risks.

Why Spread?

Spreading involves the simultaneous purchase and writing of one or more contracts of two different calls on the same stock. The appeal of option spreading has been greatly enhanced by the adoption of margin rules that require relatively small cash outlays to enter into a position. To qualify as a spread for margin purposes, (1) the option written must expire no later than the option purchased, and (2) the number of contracts written must not exceed the number of contracts purchased. As a result of the high profit potential and relatively limited risk involved, many investors have jumped into spreading without a full awareness of the pitfalls.

Proceed with Caution

Our purpose in this discussion is twofold: we shall explain the techniques of option spreading, showing how to evaluate fully a prospective spread position; and we shall lay bare the dangers of such a program. For readers who feel that they are sufficiently sophisticated and wish to use spreading in their investment program, this is designed to serve as a useful guide. For all others, this discussion should serve as a red flag, indicating that the dangers may be too great for them to proceed.

Calendar Spreads

A calendar spread is a spread in which the options written and purchased differ in expiration date. For example, let's assume that an investor buys one ABC Corp. October/50 option and writes one ABC Corp. July/50 option with the common trading at 50. Let us further assume that the premium on the October call is $800 and the premium on the July call is $500. No margin is required for the option written since the striking price of the long position is not greater than that of the short option (CBOE rules). The total cash outlay is the cost of the option purchased ($800) minus the proceeds from the option written ($500), or $300 (plus commissions).

Is this calendar spread attractive? A good approach toward the answer of that question is to see how the value of the overall position is likely to change for different price changes by the underlying common stock. Here is where many of the potential pitfalls that we alluded to begin to enter the picture.

First, to do the necessary calculations one must estimate the prices at which the two options will sell for various levels of the common. But time is a crucial element that cannot be ignored here. Do we assume an instantaneous move by the common or a move over a period of three months, or do we use some other time period? The results could be dramatically different in each case. Let us see what would be expected to happen, at various prices for the common, by the expiration date of the shorter (July) option.

What range of common prices shall we consider? Let's suppose that we look at 45 (down 10 percent), 50 (unchanged), and 55 (up 10 percent). A 10 percent drop by the stock would leave the July option worthless (for a $500 profit on the short side) at its expiration date; the October call might be worth about $350 (a $450 loss). The net result is a $50 gain before commissions. If the stock remained unchanged at 50, the July option would still be worthless at maturity, but the October call would probably be worth about $500 (a $300 loss); the total profit would be $200 before commissions. The maximum profit is usually attained when the stock is at the striking price. A 10 percent gain by the common to 55 would result in a value of $500 (no gain or loss) for the July option at expiration and a value of about $850 ($50 gain) on the October call, for an overall profit of $50 before commissions.

If we stop here and look at what we have, we would probably conclude that this calendar spread is a pretty attractive investment, generating profits regardless of whether the common stock price rises, falls, or remains the same. The problem, however, is that we haven't considered all the possibilities. Most calendar spreads generate profits only within a fairly narrow trading range for the stock. Wider swings, in either direction, can result in either very small gross profits that are eaten up by commissions or even substantial losses. For example, if the stock in our example fell to 40, the $500 profit on the July call would be more than offset by a loss of about $600 on the long side. A similar experience would occur if the stock rose to 60. Wider swings would result in greater losses. So perhaps this calendar spread is not so attractive after all, especially if commissions are taken into account.

We summarize these results as follows:

		Price of Common When July/50 Expires				
30	**40**	**45**	**50**	**55**	**60**	**70**
		Price of July/50 at Expiration				
0	0	0	0	5	10	20
		Price of October/50 at End of July				
1	2	3½	5	8½	12	20
		Profit on July/50 Written at 5				
+$500	+$500	+$500	+$500	0	−$500	−$1,500
		Profit on October/50 Purchased at 8				
−$700	−$600	−$450	−$300	+$ 50	+$400	+$1,200
		Overall Profit before Commissions				
−$200	−$100	+$ 50	+$200	+$ 50	−$100	−$300

Commission Expense

−$ 75	−$ 75	−$ 75	−$ 75	−$100	−$103	−$126

Overall Profit after Commissions

−$275	−$175	−$ 25	+$125	−$ 50	−$203	−$426

On a precommission basis, we see that the maximum profit is about $200 and the maximum loss is $300 (the difference between the initial prices). And it appears that the spread would be profitable as long as the stock remained within about 10 percent of its initial price. But that's before we deduct commissions. In the computation above, we've used the worst possible case, in which only a single contract was employed on each side of the transaction. In this case, the expenses are devastating. The spread will already be unprofitable on a 10 percent move by the stock. The maximum profit is only $125, while the loss could be over $400 if the stock spurts to 70. And we should remember that the $125 maximum profit will be gained only if the stock ends up exactly at 50—not a very probable occurrence.

Now admittedly we've stacked the odds against this spread by assuming that only one contract was used on each side. But this does bring home the important point that the small-time spreader is almost certain to lose money. To have a reasonable chance of success, a minimum of several thousand dollars should be committed on each side of a spread.

Investors interested in establishing calendar spreads should look for situations that allow them to take advantage of a material undervaluation or overvaluation on one of the options. This can result in a much more favorable performance. For instance, in the preceding example, if the July call had originally sold for $600 (instead of $500), the profit and loss calculations would have been materially improved (by about $100 in each case).

Price Spreads

A price spread involves the purchase of a call option and the simultaneous writing of one or more options having a different exercise price but with the same expiration date. The analysis is the same as with a calendar spread, and the dangers are similar too.

Let's assume that we wish to consider a potential spread involving the purchase of an October/50 call and the writing of an October/60 call with the stock at 50. The results of our profit and loss calculations will vary greatly, depending upon the time frame that we select. And the apparent attractiveness of the position will vary depending upon the range of stock prices that we look at.

Let us see what profits or losses the position might generate at expiration (the last Monday in October). Let's assume that the initial premium on the long side is $800 and on the short side is $400. The initial cash outlay is $400 plus commissions. At all stock prices below 50 on the expiration date, both options are worthless; so we get a gain of $400 on the short side and a loss of $800 on the long side, for an overall loss of $400 before commissions. At a price of 60, the October/60 call is still worthless, but the October/50 option is worth $1,000. The overall result is a gain of $600 before commissions. The gain would be the same for all common prices above 60. The maximum profit always occurs at the striking price of the option written ($60 in this case), and the maximum profit (before commissions) always equals the difference in the striking prices ($1,000) minus the difference in the initial premiums ($400), or $600. The maximum loss is the difference in the premiums ($800 − $400 = $400). We summarize these results below:

Price of Common at Expiration

50 or below	55	60 or above

Overall Profit before Commissions

−$400	+$100	+$600

Now let's consider the same example but with the stock initially at $60. Let's suppose that we buy the October/50 for 13 and write the October/60 for 9. The initial cash outlay is $400 plus commissions. We then have the following situation:

Price of Common at Expiration

50 or below	55	60 or above

Overall Profit before Commissions

−$400	+$100	+$600

We see that the results for this example are identical to those for the preceding example. But there's one major difference: If we established the spread when the stock was at 50, we'd need a 20 percent gain in the price of the stock to reap the maximum gain from the spread. But if we established the spread when the stock was at 60, we would get the maximum gain as long as the stock stayed at or above its initial price. Obviously we would be more likely to reap the maximum profit in the latter case.

A caveat: Even though the latter spread will be profitable (before commissions) down to 54 if held until expiration, the spread is likely to lose money on any near-term decline in the price of the common.

Again, the appeal of a price spread may be greatly enhanced by the undervaluation or overvaluation of one side. Investors interested in establishing price spreads should keep an eye open for these situations. A call may, for example, be temporarily trading at or near its tangible value even though it has several months to run and is not too far into the money. This is obviously a case of an undervaluation that one may take advantage of by establishing a spread. It is sometimes possible to establish spreads that can be expected to outperform the underlying common over a broad range of stock prices.

Price spreads of the type we have discussed, in which we write the option with the higher striking price, are bullish spreads, in the sense that the maximum profit will be obtained when the price of the stock is at or above the higher strike. The reverse situation, in which we write the option with the lower strike, would be a bearish spread, in that the maximum profit would occur when the price of the stock was at or below the lower strike. For example, using the same contracts as before, let's suppose that we write the October/50 (at 8) and buy the October/60 (at 4) when the stock is at $50. Since the option written has a lower strike, $1,000 margin is required for the short side; so altogether we must put up $600 ($1,000 + $400 − $800). At any price at or below 50, both contracts will be worthless, giving us a profit of $400 before commissions. Here are the overall results:

Price of Common at Expiration

50 or below	55	60 or above

Overall Profit before Commissions

+$400	+$100	−$600

In a declining market, this type of bearish spread can be much more attractive than a short sale of the underlying stock, although the tax consequences may be even less favorable.

Other Considerations for Spreaders

An important consideration for any spread position is the time at which to close it out. There are several alternatives available: you can close out both positions simultaneously prior to expiration by selling the long option and buying back the option written, you may allow one or both to expire (if they have the same expiration date), or you may lift a leg by closing out only one side. Of course, lifting a leg exposes the investor to the high risk of a naked long or a naked short position. And there is always the risk of an unexpected early exercise that could destroy a spread.

The decision to close a spread will generally be based upon an analysis of the remaining profit potential and risk. Often an undervaluation or an overvaluation that made the position attractive in the first place will work itself out prior to expiration or even reverse itself (for example, a previously undervalued call may later become overvalued). The timing of a closeout and the manner in which it is handled may often be influenced by tax considerations. We therefore urge all investors interested in spreads to review the section "Tax Considerations for Option Traders" above, since an otherwise-unappealing spread can look quite different after taxes have been taken into account.

Another serious problem facing spreaders is the difficulty of executing spread orders. As we explained in the section "Option Orders," a spread order requires that both sides be executed simultaneously. The successful execution of such an order depends upon the skills of the floor trader. It is possible that both options could trade just a few moments apart at the specified differentials and the order still might not be filled.

Despite the difficulty of execution, the use of spread orders as opposed to two separate buy and sell orders is advised. In this way you can be assured of acquiring both sides in the desired relationship or nothing. Without the use of spread orders, you could easily find yourself in the undesirable and very risky position of either a long option holder or a naked writer.

Spread orders may also be used in disposing of a spread position. The order stipulates the purchase of the shorted option and the sale of the long option. In this way you can get out without inadvertently lifting a leg even for a short time.

AN OPTION RANKING SYSTEM

In 1972 Value Line Investment Survey extended its ranking system for common stocks, in effect since 1965, to convertible debentures, convertible preferreds, and warrants. This made it possible for the ordinary investor to manage a portfolio of convertible securities in a systematic and disciplined way. Similarly, in 1975, Value Line announced an extension of its ranking system to listed options, for both the buyer and the writer.

Needed: An Objective Guide

Whether you are a conservative or an aggressive investor, the objective of any investment program is to maximize your reward-risk ratio. Any position worthy of the commitment of your hard-earned money must offer the probability of a superior performance compared with alternative investments of similar risk. And that position should be maintained only as long as it holds out above-average prospects. What is needed, then, is an objective indication of the relative reward-risk ratios of various investment vehicles.

Ranking Option Positions

The ranking system is now being applied for the first time to all listed call options. A separate performance rank is computed and published each week for both the option buyer's position and the covered writer's position. The performance ranks, ranging from 1 (highest) down to 5 (lowest), are entirely consistent in meaning with Value Line's common stock and convertible security ranking systems.

Of course, not every security performs in accordance with its rank. And no system can guarantee a profit or eliminate the possibility of losses. But the ranking system has worked well since its inception for both common stocks and convertibles in both market upswings and declines. Although no one can guarantee future results, the fact that the option ranks are merely an extension and refinement of established objective principles that have stood up well thus far inspires confidence that they can help you tilt the investment odds significantly in your favor.

Background on the Ranks

Value Line Investment Survey introduced the common stock ranking system in April 1965. Each week nearly every one of the stocks covered by the service (now approximately 1,600) is assigned a rank indicating its probable relative performance over the coming year. The top 100 issues are assigned a rank of 1 (highest), the next 300 are ranked 2 (above average), the next 800 are ranked 3 (average), 300 are ranked 4 (below average), and 100 are ranked 5 (lowest). In December 1972, *Value Line Convertible Survey* extended the ranking system to include nearly all the 705 convertible securities that it covers.

A general definition of performance rank is as follows: The rank of any security summarizes Value Line's assessment of the probable investment performance of that security compared with other securities of similar risk.

This definition is sufficiently broad so that it can be applied to virtually any type of investment vehicle, facilitating comparisons between alternative but unlike securities. The term "investment performance," as used here, includes dividend or interest return as well as probable price changes. In other words, we are using the concept of "total return." Other securities of similar risk are used as the basis of comparison because profit potential and risk go hand in hand. And as long-time subscribers of Value Line are well aware, we measure risk in terms of "relative volatility": a relative volatility of 100 means that the security is about as risky as the typical common stock, a relative volatility of 50 means that it is half as risky as the typical common stock, and so forth. So a call option with a relative volatility of 1,000 would be 10 times as risky as the typical common stock. Another important point is that the ranking system is designed to predict relative rather than absolute performance prospects. Even most issues ranked 1 would decline in a sharp bear market, although the size of the decline would be less for low-risk than for high-risk issues.

Readers should have little trouble in conceptualizing the meaning of the option buyer's rank if they have been using the convertible ranking system. Remember that to the buyer an option is virtually the same as a very short-term warrant. And, as is the case with a warrant, the buyer's rank of an option is determined from the rank of the underlying stock and our model, which takes into consideration such factors as the volatility and yield of the common, the quality of the company's fixed-income securities, the remaining life of the warrant or option, and existing price relationships.

In general, we would expect most fairly valued options to carry the same rank as the underlying common stocks. Most significantly overvalued options (those selling for more than their estimated norm price) would normally be expected to carry a rank that is the same as or worse than the common rank; and most deeply undervalued warrants would probably be ranked the same as or better than the underlying stock. Although this is in fact the case, there are occasional discrepancies.

For example, let's consider an option on a high-yielding common stock. Let's suppose that the option is so far into the money (the common price is well above the striking price) that the option is selling at a tangible value. It is very possible that this option could be ranked worse than the stock even though the option clearly is not overpriced. This is so because the holder of the option is sacrificing the income that could have been obtained had the stock been held. In addition, we would expect the price of the option to drop suddenly when the stock goes ex dividend.

The rank for the writer's position is also consistent in meaning with our general definition. The unique consideration here, however, is that the rank indicates the probable performance not of one security but of an overall position consisting of two positions (in two different securities) that will generally be moving in opposite directions. For example, let's suppose that an investor buys 100 shares of XYZ Corp. at 50 (total cost, $5,000) and writes one XYZ Corp. July/50 option with a premium of $300. If the stock were to fall to 45, the option premium might decline by $200 (from $300 to $100). The investor then has a $500 paper loss on the stock and a $200 gain on the written option. The overall position has declined by $300.

The rank of the writer's overall position is a function of the ranks of the two component securities: Ideally, one would like, for example, to buy a 1-ranked stock and write an overvalued option ranked 2. Let us remember that we are talking about "covered writing": the investor owns 100 shares of stock against which he or she writes one option. This position is always moderately bullish in the sense that the investor does best if the stock rises. The relative importance of the common rank and the option buyer's rank in determining the option writer's rank varies as prices change.

For example, when the option is far out of the money (that is, when the striking price of the option is far above the current market price of the stock), its small premium provides little cushion against declines by the stock. Any change in the overall position would not be very different from the change in the stock position alone. So we would expect that the stock's rank would be the prime factor in determining the rank of the writer's overall position.

On the other side of the coin, if the option is far into the money (that is, if the price of the stock is far above the striking price of the option), the rank and valuation of the option play a more significant role in determining the rank for the overall position.

Using the Ranks

The performance to date of the common stock and convertible ranking systems inspires confidence that the option ranking system will also be a valuable investment tool. Whether an individual is a prospective buyer or a prospective writer, we strongly suggest that new commitments be restricted to positions ranked 1 (highest) for performance potential. Each position may then be maintained as long as its rank is at least 2 (above average); a drop in the rank to 3 (average) is a signal to consider liquidating the position after taking into account the tax considerations and transaction costs that apply to the investor's particular position. By following such a program, we believe that an investor can expect to reap a return that is above average for the amount of risk assumed.

Section Four

Fixed-Income and Fixed-Asset Investments

Chapter **24**

Bonds as Investments

LEWIS P. FREITAS

Corporations, units of government, and other organizations borrow money in a variety of ways. However, the most popular method of securing long-term loans is by issuing bonds. Bonds are long-term borrowing obligations that generally require the payment by the issuer of a fixed amount of interest at specified intervals and the payment of a principal amount at a specified maturity date. Most commonly, interest payments are made twice a year, and at maturity the bondholder is entitled to receive the principal, or face value, generally $1,000, in a lump sum. The maturity of bonds is usually fifteen to thirty years from the date of issuance.

A specific issue of bonds is referred to by the name of the issuer, the percentage of face value determining the amount of interest to be paid each year, and the year in which the issue matures. For example, AT&T 7s of 2000 are bonds issued by AT&T paying 7 percent of the $1,000 face value in interest each year and maturing in the year 2000. For further details about the issue, such as the specific dates on which interest is paid, the frequency with which interest is paid during the year, and provisions of the issue affecting the safety of the investment (see below, "Provisions of Bonds"), investors would consult one of the standard investment manuals such as Moody's or Standard & Poor's.

Bonds are generally viewed as conservative financial investments because the risk associated with investing in bonds is low relative to the risk of investing in stocks. That is true because investors who buy bonds know precisely how much interest they will receive and how often, and if they plan to hold the bonds until maturity, they can predict how much principal they will get back. There is still risk in that the issuer may be unable to pay interest or principal when due (a condition defined as being in default), but the incidence of default has been quite low in publicly traded bonds, especially since World War II. Forecasting interest and principal payments for the next twenty or thirty years is a lot easier than forecasting dividend payments on a given stock for even the next few years or the expected sales price of a stock.

Because the risk of bond investments is lower than the risk of stock investments, the rate of return that investors can generally expect is lower for bonds than for stock or other riskier investments.

ISSUERS OF BONDS

The classification of bonds by type of issuer is useful to investors since the risk characteristics and, in one case, the tax treatment differ between groups of issuers. Corporate bonds (those issued by corporations) are subdivided into public utilities, transportation companies, and industrials because of the economic similarities within each of these groups and the economic differences between them. Bonds issued by the United States government or a number of its agencies are referred to as "governments"and are treated as a class by themselves because of the absence of any risk of default. Bonds issued by states, cities, school districts, or other governmental subdivisions are called "municipals" and are unique in that the interest earned on them generally is not subject to federal income taxes.

In recent years, about 20 to 30 percent of all corporate bond issues have been issued by public utilities. Public utilities in general are able to support high levels of debt because of their relative stability of output, their technology, and state regulation of the rates that they charge their customers.

Transportation companies formerly consisted almost exclusively of rail and water carriers, but motor and air carriers have been growing in importance. Like public utilities, the transportation industry has a heavy commitment in long-lived assets. In recent years, the volume of bond issues by transportation companies has been about one-fourth as large as that of public utilities. Economic regulation of transportation companies has been limited largely to the federal government and has not been as successful as state utility regulation in minimizing risk to bond investors. The difficulties of both railroads and airlines in sustaining profits have provided ample evidence of this fact.

The term "industrials" is used loosely to cover all other corporate issuers, although some analysts prefer to subdivide these into manufacturing, commercial, communications, and real estate and financial categories. The fundamental economic characteristics of these industries do differ, and it is generally useful for investment selection purposes to define each industry separately. For example, sales finance companies as a group have a great deal of long-term debt outstanding, and that specific industry should be the starting point for an economic analysis of sales finance company bonds. Industrials have a wide range of risks that cannot usefully be generalized. However, industrial issuers tend to finance lower proportions of their capital requirements by debt than utilities do.

The most important characteristic of United States government debt is that it is free from the risk of default. Because government bonds are risk-free, they provide a lower interest yield than other types of debt. Marketable governments are available in three forms according to maturity at the time of issue. United States Treasury *bills* have a maximum maturity of a year, but most bills mature in three or six months. Bills do not bear interest in the usual way; they are sold at a discount and mature at par with the discount providing a return to investors in place of interest. Bills are not generally considered part of the bond market because of their short maturity. Federal debt issues with original maturities of one to five years are in the form of *notes,* and issues with original maturities longer than five years are in the form of *bonds.* For the investor this difference is not significant except for the fact that Congress has imposed ceilings on the interest rate that the Treasury can pay on bonds. The consequence at times has been that the Treasury has not been able to sell bonds because the market rate has exceeded the ceiling; at such times, bills and notes have had to be relied on to finance the national debt.

State governments and their subdivisions sell bonds to finance a variety of capital improvements such as schools, roads, airports, water and sewer works, and public housing. As mentioned above, this class of bonds is unique in that interest earned on them is not subject to federal income taxes. The consequence is that market rates of interest are lower for municipals than for corporates of similar risk. For example, investors in the 40 percent tax bracket would earn as much with a 4.2 percent interest rate on a tax-free municipal bond as they would with a 7 percent taxable corporate bond.

This favorable tax treatment led many municipalities to use tax-free bonds as a means of competing for companies choosing factory sites and thus of boosting employment in their areas and increasing personal tax revenues. This was accomplished by financing the construction of factories with tax-exempt bond issues called "industrial revenue bonds" and then leasing the factories to companies at favorable rentals reflecting the lower interest rates paid on municipal debt. The bonds were frequently salable not because of the credit standing of the community but of the standing of the lessee. The widespread abuse of the tax exemption was largely eliminated in 1968, when a law revoking the exemption of interest on industrial revenue bonds except for very limited amounts was passed.

Another characteristic of municipals is that issues do not have a single maturity date. Instead, serial bonds in which part of the issue matures each year for a number of years are issued. The interest rate varies by maturity date, but investors have a wide choice of maturity options.

The ability of states and their political subdivisions to sell bonds is based essentially on their power to levy taxes and user charges. An analysis of that power is necessary to appraise the investment risk of municipals.

PROVISIONS OF BONDS

The specific provisions of a bond issue regarding the rights and responsibilities of issuer and investor are detailed in a contract called an "indenture." In addition, a prospectus must be made available in the case of issues subject to regulation by the Securities and Exchange Commission (SEC). Some of the areas included in most indentures that would be of interest to investors are discussed in the following subsections.

Interest Payments

The specific dates on which interest is to be paid should be known especially for bonds that require investors to request their interest checks. Such bonds are called "coupon bonds" because as each interest payment becomes due, the appropriate coupon must be clipped off and sent to a designated agent of the issuer to receive the interest payment.

The alternative to coupon bonds is "registered bonds," for which ownership is registered with an agent of the issuer just as in the case of stock certificates. With a registered bond issue, the issuer knows who should receive the interest payments, and investors need take no action.

Coupon bonds are also called "bearer bonds" because possession is accepted as ownership. Thus there is a somewhat greater risk than with registered bonds because in the event of theft bearer bonds are still negotiable. On the other hand, bearer bonds are a little easier to sell because a transfer agent is not required.

Security

Sometimes specific assets are pledged as security for bond issues. For example, a "mortgage bond" is a bond for which certain real property has been pledged. If the issuer cannot meet interest or principal payments, the bondholders have first claim to the pledged assets to satisfy the debt. Sometimes financial assets are pledged as security, or an issuer may get another organization to guarantee repayment of the debt. In this way a parent corporation may guarantee the debt of subsidiaries. When one company acquires another company that has a bond issue outstanding, it frequently will assume responsibility for continuing interest and principal payments.

Generally a word or a phrase is used in the title of the bonds to indicate the nature of any security. In the cases just cited, the words would usually be *mortgage* for pledged real assets, *collateral* for pledged financial assets, and *guaranteed* or *assumed* for bonds whose repayment is secured by another organization. A bond issue without specific security is referred to as a "debenture" or an "unsecured bond."

Sinking Funds

Because paying off an issue of bonds at one time, the maturity date, can strain the financial resources of the issuer, it is common to spread the cost of retiring the issue over a period of years. This is usually accomplished through a sinking-fund payment that the issuer turns over to a trustee representing the interests of the bondholders. The trustee may use the money to retire some of the issue by buying up bonds in the marketplace or by calling a portion of the issue for retirement, or the trustee may set the money aside for the ultimate maturity of the bonds. A sinking-fund call is a notice that part of an issue should be presented for redemption and will no longer bear interest after the call date. The specific bonds called are selected at random; in the case of bearer bonds, the numbers of the called bonds are announced in the financial press.

Investors whose bonds are called for sinking-fund purposes receive a small premium to offset the loss of future interest. A schedule of call prices is included in the indenture, indicating the size of the premium that would be paid for each year in which bonds may be called. Generally, bonds are not called for sinking-fund purposes in the first few years of an issue's life, and thereafter the call premium declines as the issue approaches the maturity date.

Calls for Refunding

If interest rates fall after an issue of bonds has been sold, it frequently is to the issuer's advantage to sell a new issue at the lower rate available and use the proceeds to retire the old issue in advance of the scheduled maturity date. Such an action is called a "refunding operation."

From the point of view of investors, a refunding call is undesirable because their principal is returned earlier than they wished and at a time when reinvestment opportunities are available at lower rates of interest. To protect investors from such refundings, noncall provisions in bond indentures have become increasingly common. Such a provision prohibits calling the issue for the purpose of refunding until a specified period, frequently five or ten years after issuance, has passed.

As in the case of sinking-fund calls, a refunding call requires the issuer to pay a premium over the normal redemption price. The size of the premium generally declines over the life of the issue. For example, a 7 percent bond issued in 1970 and maturing in 1990 may be callable in 1976 for $1,075, in 1977 for $1,070, in 1978 for $1,065, and thereafter by prices decreasing at a rate of $5 per year until the maturity date.

Investors in callable bonds should be prepared with reinvestment alternatives when the market price of their bonds exceeds the call price by a significant margin.

Seniority

The priority of claims on income and assets varies between debt and equity claims and also between different classes of debt. A claim on assets by bondholders gives them a chance to recover all or part of their investment if the issuer cannot meet its obligations and must declare bankruptcy. In its simplest form, the proceeds from the liquidation of pledged assets are first made available to the holders of the secured debt. If those proceeds are inadequate to meet that claim, the remainder of the claim is grouped with other unsecured claims in a priority of claim against unpledged assets. If the proceeds exceed the claim, there may be a secondary claim to the same assets (for example, a second mortgage) and even a third level of claims.

For example, let us assume that a $10 million bond issue is secured by a first mortgage on the factory of a company and the company goes into bankruptcy. If the factory is sold for $8 million, the bondholders definitely receive 80 percent of their money, and they have an unsecured claim for $2 million against the other assets of the company that is grouped with the other unsecured claims. If the factory is sold for $11 million, the bondholders are paid in full and the remaining $1 million is paid against the claim of the second mortgage, if one exists, or distributed to the general creditors.

In the case of debentures (unsecured bonds) there may also be priorities of claims on assets. In some industries there are three levels of priority: senior debentures, subordinated debentures, and junior subordinated debentures. The highest-level creditors must be fully paid before any claims of the next group of creditors can be satisfied.

SPECIAL TYPES OF BONDS

Thus far bonds have been discussed as if they all have the same kind of fixed but limited return in the form of interest and principal. There are special classes of bonds without these characteristics. The commonest exception is the convertible bond that carries the option to exchange the bond for shares of stock (see Chapter 21). In addition, there are bonds with varying interest claims and bonds without maturity.

Income Bonds

A major exception to the fixed-interest claim of bonds is provided by income bonds. With such bonds interest is payable only if earnings are available. If earnings before interest and taxes are zero or negative, the interest will not be paid. Obviously, the method of measuring earnings is of great importance, and the indenture of an issue of this type should restrict management's powers in such crucial areas as depreciation and inventory evaluation. Another protection for the investor in income bonds should be a cumulative feature; with such an indenture provision, unpaid interest claims carry forward to subsequent periods when earnings may recover.

Income bonds are similar in some respects to preferred stocks, but the tax deductibility of interest payments provides a great advantage to the issuer over preferred stock. For investors the income bond has a senior claim to income and assets over preferred stock but presents a greater risk than standard bonds. Because of the increased risk income bonds generally offer a higher rate of interest.

Purchasing Power Bonds

Interest and frequently principal payments of this group of bonds vary as price levels (purchasing power) change. Such bonds have been issued only once in the United States but have been used many times in other countries, including Finland, Sweden, Iceland, Israel, France, and Mexico. In most cases the rate of payment of interest and repayment of principal has been tied to a price level index such as the Consumer Price Index in the United States or a specialized index of prices in a specific industry. There have been occasional proposals in Congress to authorize the issuance of such bonds by the United States Treasury for the protection of retirement income, but until the federal government decides that it cannot or will not control inflation, it is unlikely that such bonds will be available in this country.

Bonds without Maturity

Great Britain issued bonds after the Napoleonic Wars without maturity. Since the proceeds were used to pay off many smaller issues or to consolidate debts, the issue was called "British consols." It is unlikely that investors will find such bonds available in the future. There have been issues of bonds in the United States with a maturity of 100 years, which was almost the same as no maturity at all, but they were not available to the public and they could be converted to a maturity of twenty years at the option of either the issuer or the investor. The investors, primarily life insurance companies, exercised their option to convert to the shorter maturity on all such issues because of the subsequent rise in interest rates.

MEASURING BOND YIELDS

The major factors determining bond yields are the purchase price, the coupon rate, the length of the period in which the bond is held, the sale or redemption price, and any taxes that may be incurred. A correct calculation of the rate of return or yield to the investor must take into account all these variables, but frequently the sale price and the holding period are not known, some risk may be involved, and the tax rate varies from investor to investor. The true rate of return should be calculated by techniques that make allowance for both how much money will be received and when it will be received. Unfortunately the most practical way of calculating yields is by computer analysis, and most investors do not have access to such equipment. Alternatively, several approximation methods are commonly used, although these may produce substantial errors in estimating true rates of return.

Computerized Yields

The use of computers to calculate yields is limited to two groups, persons with direct access to computers and those who use the services of others who have access to computers. Investors with access to computers can acquire canned programs or programs built to specifications from a variety of sources. All the calculated yields in this chapter were derived from computer programs developed at the University of Hawaii's College of Business Administration.[1]

For those with access to computers, the basic solution technique is given by the following formula:

$$P = \left[\sum_{t=1}^{2h} (cF/2)(1 - T_n)(1 + k/2)^{-t} \right] + \left[S(1 + k/2)^{-2h} \right] - \left[(S - P)(1 - T_c)(1 + k/2)^{-2h} \right]$$

where P is the purchase price, c is the coupon rate, F is the face value, t is time in increments of half a year, h is the holding period in years, S is the expected proceeds from sale or redemption, T_n and T_c are the investor's marginal tax rates for regular income and capital gains respectively, and k is the aftertax annual yield on the investment. The first part of the right-hand side of the equation is the present value of the expected stream of income receipts, the second part is the

---

[1] Various computer programs were developed by Professor Charles Congdon at the College of Business Administration, University of Hawaii.

present value of the sale price or redemption value, and the third part adjusts for the tax effects of any gain or loss. The equation assumes that interest is paid semiannually and that long-term capital gains and losses generally receive preferential tax treatment. Transaction costs are ignored, although purchase price and sale price can be adjusted for commissions and any other transaction costs.

Nominal Yield

The nominal yield is the coupon rate of a bond issue. Thus a 5 percent bond has a nominal yield of 5 percent regardless of its purchase price, holding period, sale price, or taxes. This provides a correct measure of yield if the purchase price and sale price both equal the face value and if taxes are ignored. As a practical matter, if bonds are purchased near par (face value) and are expected to be held to maturity, the nominal yield is a good approximation of the pretax yield. The aftertax yield can be approximated by multiplying the pretax yield by 1 minus the tax rate. For example, a 5 percent bond purchased at par and expected to be held to maturity by a taxpayer with a 30 percent marginal tax bracket would yield an aftertax annual rate of 3½ percent (70 percent of 5 percent). The greatest drawback to this method is that bonds are frequently bought and sold at prices far removed from par.

Current Yield

The ratio of annual interest income to current market price is called "current yield." For example, a 5 percent bond bought at 80 ($800) would have a current yield of 6¼ percent (5 percent divided by 80, or $50 divided by $800). Aside from ignoring taxes, this measure of yield does not consider the gain or loss that will be realized if the sale price of the bond is very different from the purchase price. In the example cited, if the bond is purchased at 80 and held to maturity when the principal of 100 is received, there will be a $200 capital gain.

Yield to Maturity

This is the commonest measure of bond yields. It assumes that the designated interest will be received each year and that the bond will be held until maturity, when the investor will receive the face value. No allowance is made for income taxes. The reason for the widespread use of this measure is that it does make proper allowance for the purchase of bonds at prices above or below face value.

The yield to maturity of a bond can be found in published bond yield books, given the coupon rate, the years to maturity, and the price paid. A very condensed version would look something like Table 24-1. Bond yield books present much greater detail in all the variables and can run to hundreds of pages. In the table investors can see that if they purchase a bond with a 5 percent coupon rate that will mature in ten years, at a price of $800, the yield to maturity will be 7.9 percent.

To see how the price of a bond affects its yield separately from considerations of risk, we can assume a risk-free bond, that is, a bond on which interest and principal

TABLE 24-1   Illustration of Bond Yield Table

Years to maturity	5 percent coupon				6 percent coupon			
Price	1	5	10	20	1	5	10	20
70	45.6	13.4	9.8	8.0	46.9	14.7	11.0	9.3
80	29.5	10.2	7.9	6.9	30.7	11.4	9.1	8.0
90	16.2	7.4	6.4	5.9	17.3	8.5	7.4	6.9
100	5.0	5.0	5.0	5.0	6.0	6.0	6.0	6.0
110	...	2.8	3.8	4.3	...	3.8	4.7	5.2

payments are 100 percent guaranteed. Consider a hypothetical issue of bonds, Detco 6s of 1993. Upon checking the details of the issue, you find that the face value is $1,000, the interest is payable on June 30 and December 31 of each year, and the bond matures on December 31, 1993. From these facts, you can determine that as a result of buying this bond, you can expect to receive $30 each June 30 and December 31 while you own the bond until December 31, 1993, at which time you would receive the $1,000 of principal.

If you bought this bond on January 1, 1973, for $1,000 and held it to maturity, you would have earned an annual rate of return of 6 percent before taxes. If you paid less than $1,000 for exactly the same rights to interest and principal, you obviously would have earned a rate of return greater than 6 percent. Conversely, for a price in excess of $1,000, the yield would be less than 6 percent.

For example, by paying a price of $950, your yield to maturity would be 6.45 percent. This rate could be found in a bond yield book or calculated with a computer. Essentially, allowance is made for the fact that the maturity value is $50 larger than the price paid; so instead of getting just $60 of interest each year, the benefit of the extra $50 is spread over the twenty years.

In effect, investors are earning an additional $2.50 per year for each of the twenty years. However, they do not actually receive the $2.50 each year. Instead, they leave this profit in the bond until it matures, at which time they will receive the full $50. Therefore, although investors invested only $950 originally, they are investing $2.50 of their profits each year in the bond. After two years the investment in the bond will be $955, after six years $965, and after sixteen years $990. The average investment in the bond over a twenty-year period would be $975. This amount can be quickly determined by adding the initial investment to the par value of the bond and dividing by 2. The annual income was $62.50 ($60.00 plus $2.50), and the average investment was $975; therefore, the yield to maturity was approximately $62.50 divided by $975, or 6.41 percent. The following formula can be used to approximate the yield to maturity:

Approximate yield to maturity

$$= \frac{\text{annual coupon interest} + \dfrac{\text{par value} - \text{purchase price}}{\text{years to maturity}}}{(\text{par value} + \text{purchase price}) \div 2}$$

In comparison with this approximate yield of 6.41 percent, it was stated above that the yield to maturity would be 6.45 percent. This difference of .04 percent, or 4 basis points (basis points are hundredths of a percent), is attributable to the fact that the $2.50 is not really received each year and the average amount invested is not really $975. Generally, the bigger the difference between purchase price and maturity value, the greater this error will be. However, longer maturities also affect the size of the error.

Table 24-2 gives examples for different purchase prices, coupons, and maturities. Notice that in the case of bonds bought at a premium the premium must be spread out over the life of the issue and in effect reduces the annual income. For bonds bought at a premium, the approximate method consistently overstates the yield to maturity; for bonds bought at a discount, the yield is consistently understated. The significance of a tenth or a third of a percentage point varies from investor to investor.

The only major drawback to the yield-to-maturity measures that are so widely used is that no allowance is made for income taxes payable by investors. If interest and capital gains and losses are subject to the same tax rates, the aftertax yield to investors can be calculated by multiplying the before-tax yield by 1 minus the investors' marginal tax rate. For example, a 6 percent yield to maturity for an investor in the 30 percent marginal tax bracket would yield 4.2 percent after taxes: 6 percent $(1 - .3) = 4.2$ percent. Taking into account long-term capital gain rates, the aftertax yield would be greater than 4.2 percent if the bond were bought at a discount, and the greater the discount, the greater the aftertax yield.

The section "Tax Factors in Bond Investments" below should be consulted for greater detail. Table 24-3 shows how aftertax yields can vary when long-term capital gain tax rates are applied to investments in discount bonds.

Yield to Call

When a bond issue is called before maturity, a premium that can equal as much as one or two years of interest generally is paid. When a bond issue has a noncall provision for a period of years and the market price has risen to a significant

TABLE 24-2 Sample Estimated and Actual Yields

Price	Coupon (percent)	Maturity (years)	Approximate yield* (percent)	Actual yield † (percent)	Error (basis points)
$ 875.25	4	5	6.92	7	−8
679.67	4	20	6.66	7	−34
958.42	6	5	6.97	7	−3
893.22	6	20	6.90	7	−10
1,041.58	8	5	7.02	7	+2
1,106.77	8	20	7.08	7	+8

*Derived from the following formula: annual interest plus or minus amortization of discount or premium divided by average investment.
†Derived by computer by using the bond yield book method.

premium over the call price, it is useful to measure the yield to the earliest call date.

Measuring bond yields to the earliest call date indicates the assured yield of a bond even if interest rates fall and the issue is called for refunding purposes. If interest rates rise, a call of the issue is unlikely, since the issuer can retire it less expensively by buying the bonds in the market.

If the call price exceeds the market price, yield to call will be greater than yield to maturity. For example, a 7 percent bond, bought for 105, with twenty years to maturity, would have a 6.5 percent yield to maturity. However, if the bond is called in five years at 107, the yield would be 7 percent; if it is called in ten years at 107, the yield would be 6.8 percent.

Riding the Yield Curve

At most times, interest rates are higher on long-term bonds than on short-term bonds. The differences are caused by supply-and-demand factors including investors' liquidity preferences, speculation, the outlook for inflation, Federal Reserve operations, and the need for funds by various sectors of the economy.

The relationship between yield to maturity and maturity is called the "yield curve." Because differences in risk also affect bond yields, only United States government securities are analyzed in most yield curves. Figure 24-1 shows some yield curves at various points in time. The commonest shape of the yield curve is the one shown for March 24, 1971, that is, an upward-sloping curve over most of the maturity range. It is the upward-sloping portion of the curve that makes riding the yield curve possible.

If the yield curve of March 24, 1971, remained stable, investors desiring a two-

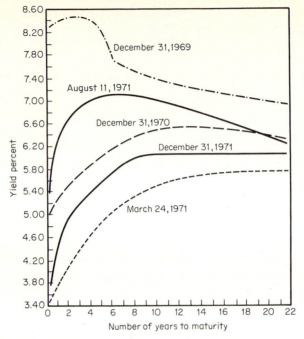

Fig. 24-1   Yields on United States government securities. [*Federal Reserve Bank of New York,* Monthly Review, *January 1972, p. 11.*]

year holding period would ordinarily consider buying bonds with a two-year maturity. However, they would get a superior yield by buying a five-year–maturity bond and selling it in two years. The same would be true for any other two-year holding period in the upward-sloping part of the yield curve. This procedure is called riding the yield curve.

The reason for this outcome is that the price of the bond must appreciate to reduce its yield as the maturity date approaches with the passage of time. In the case of discount bonds, the price would have to increase merely to keep the yield to maturity constant, but to have a decrease in the yield to maturity the price of the bond must increase even more. Under such circumstances, it is possible to achieve a higher yield than any point on the yield curve by riding part of the yield curve.

The big risk in this technique is that the whole yield curve may shift upward; that is, interest rates as a whole may increase, as they did in the months following March 1971. The result will be a decline in bond prices instead of the expected rise. The assured yield on the two-year–maturity bond would not be subject to that risk because, instead of an uncertain sale price, the investor would receive face value at maturity.

Because of the risk of fluctuating interest rates and bond prices, riding the yield curve is generally restricted to the short-term end of the curve, where price fluctuations are not so great. For example an investor desiring a six-month holding period may consider investing in a twelve- or fifteen-month maturity and plan on selling the bond after six months rather than holding it to maturity.

The opportunities to profit from changes in bond prices as interest rates change are explained in Chapter 25.

TAX FACTORS IN BOND INVESTMENT

Of course, income taxes should be taken into account in investment decisions. Tax-free interest on municipal bonds is a special case. The most important other tax factors in bond investments are that interest is taxed at regular income tax rates but that capital gains and losses, measured by the difference between purchase price and sale price (or maturity value, if held to maturity), may be subject to special capital gains tax rates. If the bond is held for at least six months, a gain qualifies for long-term capital gains tax rates, generally one-half of the normal income tax rate. Because of the differing tax brackets of investors, bond yield books cannot provide each investor with the aftertax yield to maturity. For taxpayers with net long-term capital gains, bond yield books understate the relative desirability of bonds bought at a discount.

If a 7 percent bond is bought at par (that is, 100), each year the investor will receive $70 of taxable interest. If we assume a 40 percent marginal tax bracket, interest after taxes would equal $42 per year. At maturity the investor would receive the face value, and there would be no taxable gain or loss. The aftertax yield to maturity would be 4.2 percent. If a discount bond with a yield to maturity of 7 percent were purchased instead, the tax consequences and aftertax yield would differ. For example, a 4 percent coupon bond issued ten years ago and maturing twenty years from now would have to sell at $679.67 to yield 7 percent to maturity before taxes. Each year the investor would receive $40 in taxable interest and, with the same marginal tax rate of 40 percent, would have $24 per year of interest after taxes. But at maturity the investor would receive $320.33 more than the original investment (that is, $1,000 minus $679.67). If the investor had net long-term capital gains, this gain would be taxed at only 20 percent, leaving a $256.26 gain after taxes. The combination of interest and gain after taxes would provide a yield of 4.4 percent after taxes, as opposed to 4.2 percent from the bond purchased at par.

Table 24-3 compares aftertax yields on a group of bonds with a before-tax yield to maturity of 7 percent. With deeper discounts, the aftertax yield is higher. For investors with a higher marginal tax bracket, the advantage of discount bonds is even greater; the converse is true for investors in lower tax brackets.

Capital losses offset capital gains and may be used to a limited degree to offset other income. If a long-term loss offsets long-term capital gains or income other than capital gains, the capital gains tax applies in calculating tax savings from the loss. But if long-term losses are used to offset short-term gains, the normal tax rate applies. Another complicating factor is that bond premiums may be amortized, a

TABLE 24-3   Comparison of Yields to Maturity and Aftertax Yields

Price	Coupon (percent)	Maturity (years)	Yield to maturity* without taxes (percent)	Aftertax yield† (40 percent tax bracket)
$ 679.67	4	20	7	4.42
875.25	4	5	7	4.29
893.22	6	20	7	4.26
958.42	6	5	7	4.23
1,000.00	7	any	7	4.20

*Derived by computer by using the bond yield book method.
†Capital gains taxed at one-half of the specified tax rate.

procedure that is generally desirable because it provides a current deduction against ordinary income.

Another tax consideration is that not all long-term gains on the sale of bonds qualify for long-term capital gains tax rates. In the case of corporate bonds issued at a discount after May 27, 1969, gains to the extent of that discount are taxed as ordinary income over the life of the bond. In effect, the difference between the original purchase price of less than $1,000 per bond and a maturity value of $1,000 is treated for tax purposes as if it were received each year along with interest. The tax basis of the bond is adjusted accordingly each year. The result is that taxes must be paid on income that is not received and at regular income tax rates. On bonds issued before 1969, the gain resulting from an original discount was taxed only when realized (at sale or maturity), and within fairly broad limits it qualified for the more favorable long-term capital gains tax treatment.

LEVERAGE IN BOND INVESTMENT

The margin requirement for bonds has often been as low as 25 or 30 percent. Let us assume that good-quality bonds are available with a yield to maturity of 7 percent at a time when the prime rate is 5 percent. We further assume that investors can borrow money on margin at 1 percent above prime. If they purchase $30,000 worth of 7 percent bonds at par, they will receive annual interest of $2,100. They can invest $9,000 in cash and borrow $21,000 on margin, with a margin requirement of 30 percent. They will pay interest of 6 percent on the $21,000 that they borrow, for total annual interest payments of $1,260. Their income before taxes will be $840 ($2,100 minus $1,260) on an investment of $9,000, for a return of 9.3 percent.

Individuals investing in bonds in this manner incur three potential risks. First, there is the possibility that the company will go bankrupt before the bonds mature. This is very unlikely if investors choose bonds from good-quality companies, and even if bankruptcy does occur, they may ultimately recover a large portion of their investment. Second, if long-term interest rates rise, the price of the bonds will fall. Even though the bonds will ultimately mature for $1,000 each, investors may be asked to invest additional cash to cover this margin if the bonds are temporarily driven down in price. This risk can be minimized by purchasing bonds that mature in approximately ten years or less, because these bonds are less likely to fall significantly in price even if interest rates do rise. However, investors receive a smaller return when they invest in bonds that mature in a relatively short period of time. The return is greater on long-term bonds, but so is the risk. Third, another risk is that short-term rates will rise, causing an increase in the interest rate that must be paid on the money borrowed on margin. This would decrease the current yield that investors would receive.

RISK FACTORS

Calculated yields on bonds generally assume that interest and principal will be paid as promised, but only bonds issued by the United States government are considered to be risk-free; that is, there is no risk of the interest or principal, or both, not being paid in the amounts and at the times specified. (The saying that nothing is certain except death and taxes is relevant to this risk-free judgment; the certainty of taxing power guarantees the interest and principal.) As doubt increases about the amount or timing of interest or principal that will be received on a bond, its price decreases and its apparent yield increases.

Analysis of Risk

The risk of a bond is the risk that the issuer may be unable to meet interest or principal payments when they are due. The ability of the issuer to meet these payments depends on its continued profitability relative to the size of the payments required.

To appraise the continued profitability of an issuer, investors should first evaluate the outlook for the profitability of the industry and then make some judgments about the issuer's ability to compete successfully over the life of the bond issue. Past profitability is most widely accepted as evidence of future profitability, but as conditions change in an industry or company that have a bearing on future profit potential, investors should reevaluate the risk before it is confirmed by declining future profits.

The calculation of profits starts with revenues, and then deductions are made for the cost of the goods that are sold and selling and administrative expenses. What is left at that point is referred to as operating income. The remaining deductions are interest and income taxes, but interest expense takes precedence over income taxes. The relationship between operating income and interest expense is regarded as one of the best measures of risk to bondholders. If an issuer, year after year, has operating income consistently much larger than interest expense, the risk would be regarded as low. Usually the adequacy of this ratio is judged by comparison with industry averages. One caveat is in order at this point. Companies use different accounting procedures for items such as depreciation, inventory evaluation, and pension funds, and often this circumstance can make it extremely difficult to compare the relationships between income and interest expense for different companies.

An alternative measure of the protection of interest that will give about the same results is the ratio of profits before tax plus interest to interest expense. The interest expense of a bond issue does not rise or fall with sales, but profits do. The more variable a firm's profits, the lower the tolerance for interest expense. Thus utilities with relatively stable revenues and operating expenses can support more debt than a firm producing consumer durables or luxury goods.

Other risk measures of a firm include the debt ratio, the availability of cash flow to meet sinking-fund obligations, the adequacy of working capital, and the ability of the issuer to meet other financial obligations, such as long-term leases. Preferred dividends do not constitute a legal obligation, as interest expense does, and they are not so important. The adequacy of all these measures is generally judged by reference to industry averages.

Another important set of risk factors consists of the added protections in the bond indenture such as limits on incurring added debt, limits on payment of dividends, assets pledged as security, and restrictions on the acquisition or disposition of major assets.

In the case of municipal bonds, the tax revenue capacity of the issuer is a key concern. Analysis should include the outlook for the economic base of the community and the relative fiscal responsibility of the governing bodies as evidenced by levels of debt and the amount of debt service requirements (interest and principal) relative to available tax revenues.

Bond-Rating Agencies

No one knows precisely how to measure the risk of default in bond issues, but estimates must be made. The two largest and best-known risk evaluators of bonds are Moody's and Standard & Poor's. Their analysts appraise the risk of individual bond issues along the lines suggested in the preceding subsection and classify them into groups of similar risk. Most investors rely on the ratings of these agencies for risk evaluation.

For a complete description of the ratings used by Moody's and Standard & Poor's, consult their latest publications. Generally the top two grades (Aaa and Aa or AAA and AA) are high-grade bonds without present or foreseeable default risk. The next two grades (A and Baa or A and BBB) are considered to have some future risk. Grades below the top four are considered to have significant *speculative characteristics* and not to be of investment quality.

The significance of bond ratings can be judged by the yield differentials between ratings. For example, in 1970, when bond yields were setting record highs, the average yield for the year on Aaa-rated corporate bonds was 8.04 percent, and the average on Baa-rated bonds was 9.11 percent. The corresponding figures for municipals were 5.22 and 5.89 percent. Such averages are compiled by Moody's Investors Service and published in many financial periodicals and reference books.

The availability of ratings does not eliminate the need for judgment in selecting securities. There is significant variation in yields within a rating class, and ratings change over time.

Financial institutions such as life insurance companies and banks buy most of the bonds issued in the United States. State laws have regulated these institutions in many respects, including the valuation of securities in which they invest. In the case of both banks and life insurance companies, bonds in the four highest rating grades are considered of investment quality and receive the most favorable valuation treatment. One consequence of this use of ratings is to reduce the level of demand substantially for bonds below the first rating grades. Another consequence has been that corporate managers wishing to sell bonds tend to conduct their financial affairs in ways that will result in an investment-quality rating. The overwhelming majority of bonds issued since World War II have been in the top four rating grades.

Profit Potential of Risk

If the bond market adjusted perfectly for risk, in the long run investors would net about the same return from investments in governments as they would from corporates of varying risk. The apparent extra risk would be offset by defaults, and in a perfect market the offset would be exact. A very extensive study[2] of just that point concluded that the yield spreads between the first four risk classes have been larger than experience would justify. In other words, loss rates did not completely eliminate the higher rates on lower-rated bonds. That study did not cover the postwar years, but later studies have not disproved the findings.

BOND MARKETS

Corporate bonds are traded on the major stock exchanges as well as over the counter, and quotations appear in the major periodicals that publish stock prices and quotations. Brokerage houses that deal in stocks generally deal in bonds as well. The issuance of publicly available bonds takes place through investment bankers and brokerage houses. For issuers subject to SEC regulation, a prospectus containing most of the same kinds of information as in a prospectus for a stock offering is issued.

A large proportion of bonds are unavailable to the public because they are sold directly to a limited number of financial institutions, primarily insurance companies and pension funds. These direct sales are referred to as private placements.

[2]W. Braddock Hickman, *Corporate Bond Quality and Investor Experience,* National Bureau of Economic Research, Princeton University Press, Princeton, N.J., 1958.

A round lot of bonds for trading purposes is defined as five bonds, or $5,000 of face value. Commissions are modest, around $5 per $1,000; so there is little incentive for brokers to be aggressive sellers of bonds.

Municipal bonds are sold mostly by a few investment banking houses and brokerages that specialize in this part of the market. These serve as wholesalers insofar as most private investors who deal with their regular brokers are concerned. United States government securities can be purchased through member banks of the Federal Reserve System or through brokerage offices.

The traditional view of bonds as essentially conservative investments is reevaluated in periods of high interest rates such as the early 1970s. Opportunities for unusual profit potential do arise periodically, and bonds have a well-established role in balanced portfolios.

BIBLIOGRAPHY

Books and Articles

Atkinson, Thomas R.: *Trends in Corporate Bond Quality*, National Bureau of Economic Research, Columbia University Press, New York, 1967.

Brigham, Eugene F.: "An Analysis of Convertible Debentures: Theory and Some Empirical Evidence," *Journal of Finance*, vol. XXI, pp. 35–54, March 1966.

Collier, Robert P.: *Purchasing Power Bonds & Other Escalated Contracts*, Buffalo Book Co., Ltd., Taipei, Taiwan, 1969.

Donaldson, Gordon: *Corporate Debt Capacity*, Harvard University Graduate School of Business Administration, Division of Research, 1961.

———: "New Framework for Corporate Debt Policy," *Harvard Business Review*, March–April, 1962.

Hempel, George H.: *The Postwar Quality of State and Local Debt*, National Bureau of Economic Research, General Series 94, Columbia University Press, New York, 1971.

Hess, Arleigh P., Jr., and Willis J. Winn: *The Value of the Call Privilege*, University of Pennsylvania, Philadelphia, 1962.

Hickman, W. Braddock: *Corporate Bond Quality and Investor Experience*, National Bureau of Economic Research, Princeton University Press, Princeton, N.J., 1958.

Jantscher, Gerald R.: *The Effects of Changes in Credit Rating on Municipal Borrowing Costs*, Investment Bankers Association of America Occasional Paper No. 1, Washington, 1970.

Data Sources

Moody's Investors Service, Inc.: *Moody's Bond Record*, monthly.

———: *Moody's Bond Survey*, weekly.

———: *Moody's Manuals of Investments*, annually, plus semiweekly bulletins.

Standard & Poor's Corporation: *Standard Bond Reports*, looseleaf service with frequent revision.

———: *Standard Bond Reports: Convertible Bonds*, weekly.

———: *Earnings and Ratings Bond Guide*, monthly.

———: *Standard Corporation Records*, looseleaf with continuous updating.

Value Line Investment Survey: *Convertible Bond Service*.

Weekly Bond Buyer: weekly newspaper.

Chapter **25**

Selecting Bonds for Capital Gains

LEONARD W. ASCHER

CHARLES F. CONGDON

Bonds generally are considered income-type investments that offer yields with a high degree of safety. In the recent past they have filled this role, returning as much as 9 percent (in 1970–1971) on investments rated A and better by Moody's or Standard & Poor's. Moreover, once investors buy quality bonds for income, they can expect to receive that income without reduction, while depositors in savings accounts may expect banks to cut their interest payments if interest rates generally soften. Furthermore, bond investors can expect their bonds to rise in value as interest rates in the market decline, bringing them capital gains as a welcome fringe benefit to their protected income.

If investors are bold to the point of being speculators, they may buy bonds in the hope of selling them later at a handsome profit, or they may sell bonds short through their brokers, hoping to profit if bonds go down in price. To speed the action our investors turned speculators may even trade bonds on margin, magnifying their gains as much as fourfold. They may do this in the highest-grade bonds, which, like lesser securities, fluctuate in price.

BOND PRICES AND INTEREST RATES

Bond prices rise when interest rates fall and fall when interest rates rise in the bond market. An investor can make or lose money in such price changes, a risk that investment textbooks call the "interest rate risk." For example, had a bond speculator bought Pacific Gas and Electric Company 5 percent bonds due in 1989, rated AA by Standard & Poor's, in the week ended July 11, 1970, they could have been obtained at a price of 70. At that time, interest rates on 200 high-grade bonds as calculated by Moody's averaged 8.88 percent. Eight months later, in the week ended March 20, 1971, average interest rates had fallen to 7.88 percent, and bond prices generally had risen. Pacific Gas and Electric 5s responded by rising in price to 78, for a capital gain of 11.4 percent. Most bonds also rose in price as interest rates fell, but not at the same 11.4 percent rate of gain. Firestone AA 3¼s of 1977 could have been bought at 74 in July 1970 and sold in March 1971 for 80.5, for a gain of 8.8 percent. Yet both bonds behaved much as expected because of differences in their nominal interest rates and in their maturity dates. This points to another fact of bond investment: the degree of fluctuation in bond prices due to market interest rate changes depends upon each bond's interest rate, maturity, and quality and, of course, upon chance. Granted that chance can make a substantial difference in bond prices, as inspection of the New York Stock Exchange daily quotations will show, there is nevertheless a pattern to bond price changes that is related to interest rate changes in the market, a pattern that can be used deliberately to choose the best bond speculations available. To use this pattern speculators must understand *yield to maturity* and the vital role it plays in bond investment and bond prices in the market.

The Dominant Role of Yield to Maturity

Bonds seldom sell at their par value of $1,000. Although bonds are issued in denominations of $1,000, five bonds with a $5,000 face value are considered a "round lot" in the New York bond market. Quotations are given in percentages of par (100), with fractional prices stated in eighths, fourths, or halves, of a point.

Let us suppose that an investor buys a 5 percent bond due in twenty years for a price of 88½. Each year he or she receives $5 in interest, usually in two semiannual payments. At the end of twenty years the investor collects payment of 100 for the bond that cost 88½. The difference of 11.50, called "discount" in bond circles, is amortized, or spread over the life of the investment, adding to the bondholder's annual income. The total of current interest and amortized discount is expressed as a percentage of the value of the investment to produce a figure called "yield to maturity." The matter is complicated by the fact that the investor will be getting interest payments over the entire life of the investment, a stream of future dollars, and will receive a final payment of principal at maturity twenty years after buying the bond. To get a correct yield-to-maturity figure these future dollars should be corrected to present values, a problem that is nicely solved by using a bond values table (also called a bond basis book). There are several such publications (the most comprehensive costs approximately $300), sometimes available in general libraries or in brokerage offices. The price of the 5 percent bond due in twenty years will be found in the 5 percent section of the table in the twenty-year column, where the figure nearest to 88½ is 88.44. This indicates a yield to maturity of 6 percent.

Let us suppose that the going rate in the market should quickly fall by 1 percentage point, from 6 to 5 percent. The holder of an old 5 percent bond probably can now find a buyer for his bond at 100, bringing him a capital gain of 11.50, equivalent to 13 percent on the original commitment of 88½. Bonds tend to adjust in price; so yield to maturity will be comparable for bonds of equal quality and similar maturity. Borrowing corporations will be able to sell new bond issues with "coupon" (nominal interest) rates of 5 percent at par of 100. Big institutional investors, such as life insurance companies, emphasize yield to maturity in their bond selections, and it matters little to them whether they buy 4 percent bonds or 6 percent bonds as long as the bonds are priced to return the same income in the long run. Thus, institutional investors tend to buy on the basis of yield to maturity, and their demand helps to drive individual prices toward the point at which all bonds yield about 5 percent to maturity.

Let us consider another example. A 3 percent bond with thirty years to maturity is purchased at a price of 58½, for a yield to maturity of 6 percent. If interest rates plummet to 5 percent in the market, this 3 percent thirty-year bond should rise to a price that will yield 5 percent to maturity. The 3 percent section of the bond values table, thirty-year page, informs us that such a bond will be worth 69.09 at a

5 percent yield; so the holder probably would sell it for about 69, realizing a capital gain of 10.5 points, or 18 percent. The change in market interest rates that brought a 13 percent gain to the holder of the 5 percent twenty-year bond bestows an 18 percent gain on the 3 percent thirty-year bond. If these speculative purchases had been made on margin of 25 percent, the speculator in the 5 percent bond would gross 52 percent in a relatively short time, while the holder of the 3 percent bond would enjoy a 72 percent gain before commissions and taxes.

The Index of Interest Rate Risk

The behavior of the bonds in the foregoing examples suggests a tool for speculators to use in identifying bonds that carry the highest potential for capital gain. Such an instrument is the Index of Interest Rate Risk (IIRR), which shows the size of the capital gain on a bond if interest rates in the market fall by 1 percentage point and that of the capital loss if interest rates rise by 1 percentage point. Let us consider Philadelphia Electric Company 4½ percent bonds maturing in May 1994. On July 15, 1970, their price was quoted at 60½ in the New York bond market. At that price the yield to maturity would be 8.35 percent. Let us suppose that interest rates softened by 1 percentage point. The price of Philadelphia Electric 4⅛s of 1994 should rise to 68.20, at which price the bonds would yield 7.35 percent to maturity. The gain would be 12.7 percent. However, had interest rates in the market risen by 1 percentage point, to 9.35 percent, the bonds would have tumbled to 54, for a capital loss of 10.7 percent. These figures for gain and loss, 12.7 percent and 10.7 percent respectively, indicate the speculative potential of a bond. They may be used as an Index of Interest Rate Risk of plus 12.7 and minus 10.7 for the bond in question.

Other bonds will carry different IIRR values, indicating greater or smaller speculative possibilities. For example, the 2.75 percent bonds of the Philadelphia Electric Company due in December 1981 sold in April 1970 for 61.75. A fall of 1 percentage point should cause the bonds to rise in price, and the Index of Interest Rate Risk would be plus 9.4. The negative value would be minus 7.7. Obviously, a speculator focusing on capital gains would choose the 4⅛s of 1994 with their higher IIRR of 12.7 percent.

There is nothing magical in the 1 percent change in interest rate used for the Index of Interest Rate Risk. A change of ½ percent or 2 percent could be used, but 1 percent is convenient and works well. Speculators need not complete their speculation if interest rates fall exactly 1 percent; they may be constrained to sell if they fall only ½ percent, or they may be able to wait until they fall more than 1 percent. But whatever their decision, bonds with higher IIRR factors should outperform bonds with lower values.

Moreover, bond prices are unlikely to respond exactly as expected to interest rate changes because they are made by bond buyers and sellers in the market, and bonds sometimes behave better than expected and sometimes worse. But buyers seeking the best buys will bid up bond prices until they approximate general yields to maturity, causing bonds to act much as expected. A study of 235 bonds revealed that the relationship between expected bond prices and actual prices after a change of 1 percent in average interest showed a coefficient of correlation of .986 on a scale of 0 to 1.[1]

While the positive side of the IIRR may point to capital gains, the negative side should also be considered by conservative investors seeking to avoid risk. For them, a low negative index promises small price declines if the market should

---

[1]See Leonard W. Ascher, "Selecting Bonds for Capital Gains," *Financial Analysts Journal,* March–April 1971.

move downward, and these investors should prefer the Philadelphia Electric 2.75s of 1981 with their minus index of 7.7 over the 4½s of 1994 with their higher negative value of 10. Speculators too, should look at the negative side with a view to selling short bonds with a high negative IIRR when interest rates appear to be headed for a rise. A speculator selling short would choose the Philadelphia Electric 4½s of 1994 with their negative index of 10.6 over the 2.75s of 1981 with only minus 7.7. Should inflationary trends continue unchecked, interest rates may be expected to rise, probably substantially, bringing rich rewards on short sales, particularly on bonds with high negative IIRR values.

The Problem of Forecasting Interest Rates

The most difficult aspect of using the IIRR to speculate in bonds is the decision about the direction of interest rates, up or down. Fortunes and reputations have been lost by speculators and forecasters who have forecast falling interest rates, only to find the market going in a different direction. Operators are strictly on their own when forecasting interest rates, but once they arrive at a correct opinion, the IIRR will guide them to the bonds best suited to their purposes.

BOND ANALYSIS FOR CAPITAL GAINS

Although the IIRR is designed primarily for bond speculators, bond investors should not overlook capital gain and loss possibilities when analyzing bonds for investment. Together with such usual indicators as current yield, yield to maturity, maturity date, possibility of call, and quality rating, the IIRR should be considered by both speculators and investors. In Table 25-1, IIRR values are offered along with the usual measures used in bond analysis.

"Current yield," the interest rate divided by the price quotations on the bond, shows what investors can expect in income return on their dollars, but it also shows what income speculators can expect in addition to any capital gains that they hope to receive. When current yields are high, the contribution of income to the total speculative gain can be substantial. Furthermore, current income will pay for part or possibly all of the interest expense that investors must pay when they buy bonds on margin. In short selling of bonds, however, a high current yield will mean additional costs for the investors because they must pay the interest on the bonds borrowed to sell short. Current yields are therefore an important aspect of speculative decisions.

Yield to maturity is, of course, a major consideration to bond investors, but it also is of importance to speculators, as a measure of part of the gain they may expect in bond operations and also as a guide to special situations. For example, a bond not shown in Table 25-1, GMAC 5s of 1981, sold in July 1970 for 76, to yield 8.75 percent to maturity, or considerably above the return then available in the market on bonds of comparable quality. This suggested that the bond was underpriced. By mid-March 1971 these bonds had risen in price to 84, as interest rates fell by 1 percent in the market. The price expected was only 82.5, providing a more-than-expected gain. To put the matter succinctly, a bond with a yield to maturity that is higher than that of bonds of similar quality is likely to be a good speculation, because it may be undervalued in price even on the basis of currently prevailing interest rates.

Bond ratings should always be kept in mind by investors; they also should be important to speculators, because the highest-grade bonds respond reliably to changes in interest rates. Bonds of lower quality (less than BBB or Baa) are more responsive to business conditions, even to a point at which their prices will be dominated by the possibility of future default or even bankruptcy. There may be

TABLE 25-1 Bond Issues Ranked in Order of Index of Interest Rate Risk (Prices as of September 30, 1971)

Bond issue	Coupon rate	Maturity date	Rating (S&P)	Price	Current yield	Yield to maturity	Index of Interest Rate Risk (IIRR)
Southern Pacific Railway	2.75	Jan. 1, 1996	A	42.00	6.55	8.38	+14.5 −13.0
Baltimore Gas and Electric	3.00	July 15, 1989	AAA	55.00	5.45	7.68	+12.9 −11.0
AT&T*	8.75	Mar. 15, 2000	AAA	108.125	8.09	8.02	+12.2 −10.1
Pacific Telephone and Telegraph	3.125	Oct. 1, 1987	AAA	60.00	5.21	7.44	+11.9 −10.3
Philadelphia Electric	5.00	Oct. 1, 1989	AA	75.00	6.67	7.57	+11.8 −9.9
Niagara Mohawk Power	4.875	Sept. 1, 1987	AA	74.875	6.52	7.63	+11.1 −9.2
Household Finance	4.375	Nov. 1, 1987	A	67.25	6.50	8.04	+10.8 −9.3
Standard Oil of California	4.375	July 1, 1983	AAA	79.50	5.50	6.96	+9.2 −8.5

*Without warrants originally issued; callable after May 15, 1975.

promising opportunities for capital gains in low-grade bonds, as the researches of Hickman[2] show, but speculation in such bonds is a special enterprise, suitable for persons of extraordinary ability having access to information not easily available to nonprofessionals. All bonds shown in Table 25-1 are rated A or better.

Using the Index of Interest Rate Risk

The Index of Interest Rate Risk is, of course, the prime measure of speculative potential for bonds on the assumption of changes in general interest rates. It should pinpoint bonds most likely to rise or fall in price following interest rate decreases or increases. Certain bonds in Table 25-1 emerge as superior speculations when the IIRR is applied while others are obviously unexciting. The IIRR is best used in conjunction with the other analytical tools shown in Table 25-1.

Southern Pacific Railway 2.75 percent bonds of 1996 rate an acceptable A in quality, sell for 42 for a medium current yield of 6.55 percent per annum, and have a high yield to maturity of 8.38 percent. With an IIRR of plus 14.5 and minus 13.0, these bonds offer the greatest potential for gain or loss of any bond in the table. At a low price of 42, a call of the bonds is unlikely; so speculators may expect to keep their bonds. If the railroad paid off the bonds ahead of time, the redemption price of 100 would provide a magnificent gain of 58 points. These bonds appear to have unusual speculative possibilities.

Baltimore Gas and Electric 3s of 1989, with a rating of AAA and a price of 55, also have strong attractions. Although current yield is only 5.45 percent per annum, yield to maturity is an appealing 7.68 percent, while IIRR is a high plus 12.9 and minus 11.0. Unlikely to be called before maturity, these bonds are obviously one of the more promising speculations in the sample.

American Telephone and Telegraph 8.75s (without warrants) of 2000 carry a relatively high IIRR of plus 12.2 and minus 10.1. These bonds are rated highest-quality AAA and, priced above par at 108.125, will provide a high current yield of 8.09 percent and a yield to maturity of 8.02. All these apparent attractions, however, are negated by the call feature that permits the company to pay off the bonds as early as May 1, 1975, at 107, or less than the selling price at the date at which this chapter was written. There is little promise of capital gain here and high possibility of capital loss. Should interest rates fall, AT&T could borrow cheaply and call the bonds; should interest rates generally rise, the company would let the bonds run and the bondholders could expect the price of their bonds to fall. In this instance, the high negative value of 10.1 is the significant IIRR measure of these high-priced bonds. AT&T 8.75s are not a speculative vehicle.

The bonds in Table 25-1 are arranged in order of speculative potential as measured by the IIRR. Most are relatively high, although one, Standard Oil of California 4.375s of 1983, is included for contrast. Its IIRR of plus 9.2 should not excite speculators, but its low IIRR of minus 8.5 might comfort investors. With a relatively low current yield of 5.5 percent and a low yield to maturity of 6.96 percent, this bond must appeal to buyers seeking a special maturity date and very high quality.

The bonds in the table appear to exemplify the rule that distant-maturity, long-discount bonds offer the greatest speculative potential. Why then is it necessary to calculate and use the IIRR? Merely buy a long-term bond at a low price. Had that overly simple rule been followed when Commonwealth Edison 3s of 1999 (not shown in Table 25-1) were selling for 51 and Great Northern 3.125s of 2000 were selling at 41, speculators would have bought the Great Northern bonds with their

[2]Walter B. Hickman, *Bond Quality and Investor Experience,* Princeton University Press, Princeton, N.J., 1955.

longer maturity and lower price. Commonwealth Edison bonds, however, had a plus 16.7 and minus 13.3 IIRR, while the Great Northern bonds promised only plus 14.0 and minus 11.5, and thus were clearly inferior in capital gain potential. All quibbles over maturity and discounts may be resolved effectively by citing the IIRR figures for each bond.

Yield to Sale in Bond Speculation

Although the Index of Interest Rate Risk is a measure of potential price movement for bonds, it is only a rough measure because it makes no reference to the time required to realize speculative expectations, and it omits from consideration any contribution made by bond interest, which may be substantial, to the success of the operation. Furthermore, no allowance is made for the effect of income and capital gains taxes on the final net benefits. All these considerations make a substantial difference in the final results and should be taken into account by truly sophisticated bond managers. They need an overall measure of speculative success, comparable to investors' yield to maturity, for making speculative commitments or in reviewing existing bond portfolios. They may find such an indicator in "yield to sale."

Yield to sale may be approached through an example of bond speculation by a tax-free investor such as a pension fund. Let us suppose that a 3 percent thirty-year bond is available at 58½ for a yield to maturity of 6 percent and an IIRR of plus 18.1 and minus 14.3, indicating high speculative potential. If the purchaser must hold the bond for one year to realize expectations, the return per annum on price appreciation alone will be about 18 percent. In addition, a year's interest income of $3 will sweeten the deal, bringing overall return (yield to sale) to roughly 23 percent. If good fortune befalls the speculator within six months instead of a year, the capital gain will be about 18 percent for the half year, to which semiannual interest should be added to provide a total of about 19 percent for the half year, or roughly 38 percent on an annual basis. Turnover is a vital part of the speculative process, with the speculator striving to repeat these scores as often as possible; so successes must be calculated in terms of per annum results. Yield to sale does this.

Although the formula seems complex, it is no more difficult than the formula for yield to maturity. We begin with the gain realized from the rise in price resulting from a fall of 1 percent in interest rates. Thus, 3s of thirty-year maturity at 58½ should rise to 69.09 if interest rates in the market fall from 6 to 5 percent. To the 10.59 point gain should be added the interest income. If the holding period has been one year, $3 in interest should be added to 10.59, for a total of 13.59. The speculator put up 58.50 to buy the bond and sold it for 69.09; so the average value of the commitment has been 63.79 (69.09 + 58.50 ÷ 2). Divide 13.59 by 63.79 to arrive at 21 percent per annum in overall performance. Had the speculator been able to reach the goal in six months, receipts would have been 10.59 in gains and 1.50 in interest, for a total of 12.09. Dividing by 63.79 produces about 19 percent for the half year, or 38 percent per annum. The shorter the investor's holding period, the larger the gain per annum. Yield to sale should therefore be calculated and reported for a series of holding periods, as shown in Table 25-2.

This table, prepared with the aid of a computer, embodies a further refinement: correction has been made for the present value of future sums. Yield to sale so calculated is consistent with yield to maturity used in investment analysis. Yield to sale for bonds held to maturity is, in fact, yield to maturity. Should speculators be unable to sell out at a profit, they may hold the bonds while praying for a price rise until maturity arrives. Such disappointed speculators have thus been transformed into investors. Speculators hope to do better than investors, but to do so, they must

TABLE 25-2 Bond Issues Ranked by Yield to Sale*

Bond issue	Coupon rate	Maturity date	IIRR	Yields to sale, assuming holding periods of						
				3 months	6 months	9 months	12 months	24 months	36 months	48 months
Southern Pacific Railway	2.75	1996	+14.5	71.7	37.5	27.0	21.8	14.3	11.8	10.4
Baltimore Gas and Electric	3.00	1989	+12.9	62.6	33.1	23.9	19.4	12.8	10.6	9.4
AT&T	8.75	2000	+12.2	59.8	32.0	23.3	19.1	12.7	10.5	9.3
Pacific Telephone and Telegraph	3.125	1987	+11.9	58.6	31.1	22.6	18.4	12.2	10.1	9.0
Philadelphia Electric	5.00	1989	+11.8	56.6	30.3	22.0	18.0	12.0	10.0	8.9
Household Finance	4.375	1987	+10.8	54.7	29.7	21.8	18.0	12.2	10.2	9.2
Niagara Mohawk Power	4.875	1987	+11.1	53.4	28.9	21.2	17.4	11.7	9.8	8.8
Standard Oil of California	4.375	1983	+9.2	45.2	24.8	18.3	15.1	10.3	8.7	7.8

*Capital gains tax and income tax are disregarded.

give thought to the relentless passage of time, and yield to sale clearly reveals what may be expected for successive holding periods.

Using Yield to Sale in Bond Trading

Table 25-2 reports yields to sale for the eight bonds dealt with in Table 25-1. The order of presentation, however, is according to speculative performance on the assumption that the nontaxed speculators reach their goals within three months. Southern Pacific Railway bonds still lead the list with a yield to sale of 71.7 percent per annum for the three-month venture.

We note that Household Finance bonds have moved up in the ranking from next to last to sixth. If speculators must hold the bonds for longer than three months for a 1 percent fall in interest rates, their gains per annum will go down, but not all bonds will react in the same degree. For example, at the end of twenty-four months Household Finance bonds will pay off 12.2 percent per annum, a figure exceeded by only three other bonds and equaled by Pacific Telephone and Telegraph bonds. Should speculators be forced to hold their bonds in a lackluster market and wait four years to realize their expectations, those who purchased Household Finance bonds would be fourth in rank of speculative achievement. With Table 25-2 speculators or bond portfolio managers may see which bonds may be expected to return the best gains over any time periods that they may consider. Bond managers may decide to analyze their portfolios with special attention to yield to sale on the assumption that interest rates will fall by 1 percentage point in the market within twelve months' time. Using a computer, they can process a large number of bonds and receive a print-out that will report yield to maturity and yield to sale after twelve months (or any other interval), the bonds being ranked according to expected rates of gain. They may also process bonds that are not in their portfolios with a view to finding attractive replacements. Bond managers will, of course, consider all pertinent aspects of bond analysis, but yield to sale will apprise them of the relative benefits to be expected from the bonds selected. Yield to sale should be an important tool for sophisticated bond operators.

Yield to Sale for a Taxed Investor

Although some institutional investors may escape taxes, individuals and most institutional investors must pay burdensome income taxes on bond interest income and capital gains taxes on bond capital gains. The effect of taxes on bond speculations may vary among individual commitments because some produce a larger element of capital gains than others. Time of holding, too, is a factor, because on bonds held for longer than six months the tax rate may be cut in half. In any event, the effect of taxes may change the net benefits from various bonds so that the order of speculative preferences may be reversed.

Yields to sale after taxes may be calculated roughly by the same procedure illustrated for yields to sale for nontaxed investors. However, income tax must be deducted from interest income at the bondholder's income tax rate and capital gains tax from speculative appreciation at a different rate (a holding period of six months and one day is assumed). When we apply this formula to the 3 percent thirty-year bonds selling at 58½, the following results are produced for a bond held long enough to use the lower capital gains tax rates (an income tax rate of 40 percent and a capital gains tax rate of 20 percent are assumed). From the semiannual interest of $1.50 we deduct 60 cents in tax, to leave an aftertax return of 90 cents. From the capital gains of $10.59 we subtract $2.12, for an aftertax gain of $8.47. The overall aftertax benefit is $9.37. Since average investment in the bond must allow for the capital gains tax, $2.12 is deducted from expected selling price of 69.09, for a net selling price of 66.97. Averaging this with the purchase

TABLE 25-3 Bond Issues Ranked by Yield to Sale after Deduction of Income Tax at Rate of 40 Percent*

Bond issue	Coupon rate	Maturity date	IIRR	Yields to sale after income tax and holding periods of							
				3 months	6 months	9 months	12 months	24 months	36 months	48 months
Southern Pacific Railway	2.75	1996	+14.5	41.8	28.8	20.5	16.5	10.6	8.7	7.2
Baltimore Gas and Electric	3.00	1989	+12.9	36.6	25.3	18.2	14.7	9.5	7.8	6.5
AT&T	8.75	2000	+12.2	35.0	24.0	17.2	13.9	9.0	7.4	6.1
Pacific Telephone and Telegraph	3.125	1987	+11.9	34.3	23.8	17.1	13.9	9.0	7.5	6.2
Philadelphia Electric	5.00	1989	+11.8	33.1	22.9	16.5	13.3	8.7	7.1	5.9
Household Finance	4.375	1987	+10.8	32.0	22.4	16.3	13.3	8.9	7.4	6.2
Niagara Mohawk Power	4.875	1987	+11.1	31.3	21.8	15.8	12.8	8.5	7.0	5.9
Standard Oil of California	4.375	1983	+9.2	26.6	18.7	13.6	11.1	7.4	6.2	5.2

*Ranked in order of yield at the end of six months.

price of 58½ gives a value of 62.73. The overall benefit of 9.37 is divided by 62.73 to obtain a 15 percent rate of gain for six months, or a 30 percent yield to sale per annum on the expectation of a six-month holding period.

Computing yields to sale for one bond over a series of holding periods would be a chore by this method and a formidable task for a large portfolio of bonds—a task beyond the resources of most investors. Furthermore, correction should be made for present values of future sums. Such difficulties are taken in its stride by a computer that can calculate yields to sale for a long list of bonds and print out the results with the bonds ranked by relative yields to sale at any holding period. This has been done in Table 25-3. Most large bond operators have access to a computer for bond analysis projects.[3]

---

[3]A copy of the computer program described in this chapter is available from the College of Business Administration, University of Hawaii, 2404 Maile Way, Honolulu, Hawaii 96822.

Chapter **26**

How to Invest in Tax-exempt Securities

LEO BARNES

Apart from temporary occasions like the New York City bond scare of 1975, municipal, or tax-exempt, bonds have become increasingly popular with individual investors, corporations, and fully taxed investing institutions like banks. Their *key, fundamental advantage* is that investors, individual or corporate, whose top tax bracket is as low as 36 percent often find that tax-exempts can produce higher aftertax yields than most taxable investments, especially if the tax-exempts are also free of state and local as well as federal income taxes (see the comparisons in Table 26-1).

Other Advantages of Tax-Exempts

Tax-exempts have a number of other advantages:

1. In addition to high tax-free income, a tax advantage of municipals is that if taxpayers substitute sufficient tax-exempt interest for currently taxable investment income, *they may move down to a taxable-income level subject to lower surtax rates.*

2. There is continuing pressure in Congress to abolish all *future issues* of tax-exempts (existing tax-exempt bonds would not be affected). Instead of tax-exempt securities, state and local governments and agencies would issue taxable bonds at higher interest rates and receive a federal interest subsidy to pay for the difference between taxable and tax-exempt interest rates. Should such a tax reform be adopted, *existing issues of tax-exempts would acquire scarcity value, so that their prices would rise and their holders could, if they wished, realize capital gains on their sale.*

3. *Next to United States government bonds, tax-exempt state and local obligations have the best safety record of all types of investments.* For example, during the Depression of 1929–1932, the worst in American history, less than 2 percent of all tax-exempt issues in the United States defaulted, and most of these defaults were temporary. By contrast, about 6 percent of all utility bonds and about 16 percent of all railroad bonds were in default during that period.

Some Disadvantages of Tax-Exempts

Tax-exempt securities have several considerable minuses that should be evaluated before deciding that they are suitable for you:

1. *Like all bonds, tax-exempts fluctuate in price prior to maturity.* They respond to

changes in basic interest rates as well as to shifts in supply and demand for particular issues. You cannot be sure of getting your full principal back at any time, as you can with guaranteed fixed-asset investments like savings bonds and insured savings accounts.

2. *The future safety of some tax-exempts may not be as good as their historical record suggests.* That record applies primarily to general-obligation bonds, backed by the full taxing power of the issuer. Other varieties of tax-exempts, such as revenue bonds and, more recently, so-called moral-obligation agency bonds, carry higher risks. Increasing numbers of the almost 15,000 governmental units that have floated more than 100,000 tax-exempt issues face the twin dangers of unbalanced budgets and severe funding problems. In some cases, levels of taxation have reached the point of diminishing returns because of broad taxpayer exodus or increasing delinquency.

In addition, an increasing volume of moral-obligation issues, such as those of college dormitory authorities or urban development agencies, do not possess the complete taxing power security that lies behind "full faith and credit" general-obligation bonds. Further, estimates of future income from projects funded by revenue bonds are often inaccurate and overoptimistic, especially for the longer term. Conditions shift in a changing society, and what were once good revenue sources, such as college dormitories or certain toll roads, can become poor ones.

3. *High-pressure sales tactics by some tax-exempt bond dealers can be costly to investors.* Unscrupulous salespeople promote bonds of low-rated or nonrated little-known government units or agencies at enticingly high returns. Thus, it is important for investors in tax-exempts to deal only with reputable brokerage or tax-exempt bond firms, ones that will readily provide full printed information on issues, supporting revenues, risks, prices, and spreads. Never buy new issues of tax-exempts over the telephone without first checking a written prospectus.

4. *Marketability at satisfactory prices can be poor, especially for smaller lots.* As a general rule, holdings of less than $10,000 principal sum are considered small lots. Even a $10,000 block is often regarded as small, involving extra commissions, since institutions typically trade in much larger lots. Very few prices of tax-exempts are quoted in even the largest newspapers, and the seller is often at the mercy of the dealer or broker. Thus, the cost of selling a small lot of tax-exempt bonds could be as much as six months' to a year's income, not counting any decline in price. Therefore, in most cases it is better to own larger amounts of one higher-quality issue than smaller amounts of several different issues. Clearly, tax-exempts are not for investors who need or want full liquidity but rather for those who plan to hold their bonds until maturity or prior redemption.

5. *Tax-exempts are liable to much of the same erosion from inflation suffered by all fixed-asset holdings.* At an assumed inflation rate of 5 percent per year, a twenty-year tax-exempt bond would be worth at maturity only $377 of its original purchasing power. The corresponding figure for an 8 percent inflation rate is a depressing $215; and with two-digit inflation of 10 percent or more, the purchasing power loss is even more horrendous.

However, tax-exempts are somewhat superior to most taxable bonds as inflation hedges, to the extent that their high tax-free income is, in some years at least, higher than the rate of inflation. Thus, for an investor in the 50 percent top tax bracket, a 6 percent tax-free bond will offset a 5 percent annual inflation rate, while a 9 percent taxable bond will not. See also the discussion of stocks as inflation hedges in Chapter 5, Part 1.

Taxable versus Tax-exempt Yields

The aftertax advantage of a dollar of tax-exempt income over a dollar of fully taxable income is quite substantial, even for investors in a medium tax bracket. In addition, some tax-exempts are free of state and local as well as federal taxes.

The aftertax advantage of a dollar of tax-exempt income over a dollar of *favorably taxed long-term capital gain* is much less than that over a dollar of fully taxed dividends or interest, especially for taxpayers in the 55 percent and higher top tax brackets.

Table 26-1 shows the relative advantage of tax-exempt income over both fully

TABLE 26-1   Return Advantage of Tax-exempt Income over Dividends or Interest and Capital Gain

If your top federal tax rate percentage is:	To equal $1 in tax-exempt income, you would have to receive this much in:	
Percent	Dividends or interest*	Long-term capital gain†
20	$1.26	$1.11
22	1.28	1.12
25	1.33	1.14
27	1.36	1.15
28	1.39	1.16
31	1.44	1.18
32	1.47	1.19
35	1.54	1.21
36	1.56	1.22
39	1.64	1.24
40	1.66	1.25
41	1.69	1.26
42	1.72	1.27
42	1.78	1.28
45	1.82	1.29
46	1.86	1.30
48	*1.92*	1.32
50	2.00	1.33
52	2.08	1.35
53	2.13	1.36
55	2.22	1.38
56	2.27	1.39
58	2.38	1.41
59	2.44	1.42
60	2.50	*1.43*
61	2.56	1.44
62	2.63	1.45
63	2.70	1.46
64	2.78	1.47
66	2.94	1.49
67	3.03	1.50
68	3.13	1.52
69	3.23	1.53
70	3.33	1.54

*The dividend exclusion per investor is disregarded in this column.

†The capital gain tax rate is 50 percent of the rates shown in the first column, except for corporations with 48 percent top tax brackets, for which capital gain is 30 percent.

The appreciable corporate values for dividends and interest are italicized.

taxed investment income and favorably taxed long-term capital gain. It does this by stating how much (and, therefore, how much more) in dividends or interest and in capital gain you would have to receive to match $1 in tax-exempt income under top marginal tax brackets ranging from 20 to 70 percent.

Every investor should locate his or her spot in the table by noting the applicable top tax bracket and by learning to use the related figures for dividends or interest and capital gain. Similarly, the appropriate figure for any return that combines both fully taxable income and tax-favored capital gain, in any proportion, can easily be calculated from the table. In this way, each investor can readily prepare a tax-exempt–taxable return matrix for personal use.

For example: Your top tax bracket is 50 percent. Using the table, you note that, to match $1 in tax-exempt income, you would need $2 in fully taxable income but only about $1.33 in capital gains taxed at 25 percent (75 percent of $1.33 is $1). Thus, 2 and 1.33 are your key figures for calculating equivalent taxable returns at your top tax bracket of 50 percent.

Now you find that you have a choice among many tax-exempt issues, with different ratings and yields. You wish to compare their yields with the aftertax returns from taxable bonds, from capital gains on stocks or bonds, and from investments combining various proportions of both taxable income and tax-favored capital gains. Using your two key numbers, 2 and 1.33, you can easily do this by deriving your own taxable equivalent matrix, shown in Table 26-2 for investors in the 50 percent top tax bracket.

Here is how the figures are derived: To get the equivalent yield *a*, multiply each tax-exempt yield by your key number for income yield, or 2. To obtain the equivalent capital gain return *b*, multiply each tax-exempt yield by your key number for capital gain return, or 1.33. For any combination of fully taxable yield and capital gain return *c*, multiply your key number, 2, by the applicable income proportion percentage (from 10 to 90 percent). Next, multiply your key number, 1.33, by the applicable capital gain proportion percentage (from 90 to 10 percent). Finally, add the two previous products together.

Table 26-3 is a blank taxable equivalent matrix for your own use.

Federal and State Treatment of Tax-exempt Bonds

Holdings of tax-exempt bonds need not be shown on your federal tax return unless you have a realized capital gain or loss on such bonds. The interest you receive on tax-exempts is not even entered on your federal return. Of course, states require that income that is tax-exempt federally but taxable in the states be shown on state returns.

TABLE 26-2   Taxable Equivalent Matrix: 50 Percent Top Federal Tax Bracket*

	Percent								
Tax-exempt yield	5.0	5.5	6.0	6.5	7.0	7.5	8.0	8.5	9.0
(a) Equivalent fully taxed income yield	10.00	11.00	12.00	13.00	14.00	15.00	16.00	17.00	18.00
(b) Equivalent capital gain return	6.67	7.33	8.00	8.67	9.33	10.00	10.67	11.33	12.00
(c) EQUIVALENT RETURN: MIXED INCOME AND CAPITAL GAIN COMBINATIONS									
10 percent (a), 90 percent (b)	7.00	7.70	8.40	9.10	9.80	10.50	11.20	11.90	12.60
20 percent (a), 80 percent (b)	7.35	8.09	8.82	9.56	10.29	11.03	11.76	12.50	13.23
30 percent (a), 70 percent (b)	7.65	8.42	9.18	9.95	10.71	11.48	12.24	13.00	13.77
40 percent (a), 60 percent (b)	8.00	8.80	9.60	10.40	11.20	12.00	12.80	13.60	14.40
50 percent (a), 50 percent (b)	8.35	9.19	10.02	10.86	11.69	12.53	13.36	14.20	15.00
60 percent (a), 40 percent (b)	8.65	9.52	10.38	11.25	12.11	12.98	13.84	14.71	15.57
70 percent (a), 30 percent (b)	9.00	9.90	10.80	11.70	12.60	13.50	14.40	15.30	16.20
80 percent (a), 20 percent (b)	9.35	10.29	11.22	12.16	13.09	14.03	14.96	15.90	16.83
90 percent (a), 10 percent (b)	9.65	10.62	11.58	12.55	13.51	14.48	15.44	16.41	17.37

*Specific multipliers are 2 for (a) and 1.33 for (b).

TABLE 26-3   Taxable Equivalent Matrix:—Percent Top Federal Tax Bracket*

Tax-exempt yield	5.0	5.5	6.0	6.5	7.0	7.5	8.0	8.5	9.0

(a) Equivalent fully taxed income
yield
(b) Equivalent capital gain return

(c) EQUIVALENT RETURN: MIXED INCOME AND CAPITAL GAIN COMBINATIONS
10 percent (a), 90 percent (b)
  (10 percent ×   ) +
  (90 percent ×   ) = 1.
20 percent (a), 80 percent (b)
  (20 percent ×   ) +
  (80 percent ×   ) = 1.
30 percent (a), 70 percent (b)
  (30 percent ×   ) +
  (70 percent ×   ) = 1.
40 percent (a), 60 percent (b)
  (40 percent ×   ) +
  (60 percent ×   ) = 1.
50 percent (a), 50 percent (b)
  (50 percent ×   ) +
  (50 percent ×   ) = 1.
60 percent (a), 40 percent (b)
  (60 percent ×   ) +
  (40 percent ×   ) = 1.
70 percent (a), 30 percent (b)
  (70 percent ×   ) +
  (30 percent ×   ) = 1.
80 percent (a), 20 percent (b)
  (80 percent ×   ) +
  (20 percent ×   ) = 1.
90 percent (a), 10 percent (b)
  (90 percent ×   ) +
  (10 percent ×   ) = 1.

*My specific multipliers are _____ for (a) and _____ for (b).

Income from bonds of a state, city, county, or political subdivision, agency, or authority within a state are, for residents of that state, exempt from both state and local income taxes as well as from federal income taxes. Where such additional tax savings are available, broad geographical diversification of a tax-exempt portfolio outside one's own state is not desirable. However, where no state and local income taxes are in effect or in sight, such broader diversification is preferable.

Tax-exempt bonds of Puerto Rico, the Virgin Islands, and other United States territories are exempt from federal, state, and local income taxes no matter where their holders live.

Types of Tax-exempt Bonds

As of late 1976, there were more than $155 billion worth of outstanding tax-exempt bonds, with the total rising by about $5 billion per year. There are eight basic kinds of tax-exempt issues:

1. *General-obligation bonds.* These are backed by the full faith, credit, and taxing power of the state, county, city, or other governmental body issuing the bond. Other factors being equal, such bonds almost always get the highest ratings and sell at the lowest yields.

2. *Limited-tax bonds.* These are tax-exempt bonds backed by the full faith and credit of the issuer but not by its full taxing power. Only a particular tax or only

part of the receipts from a particular tax (for example, a sales tax) is pledged as backing.

3. *Special-tax or -assessment bonds.* These are issues secured by special levies on taxpayers, usually those in a neighborhood immediately benefiting from projects or improvements, such as schools, sewers, or local streets or roads.

4. *Revenue bonds.* These increasingly popular bonds are secured only by revenue from particular projects built or maintained by local government units or authorities, such as toll highways, bridges, tunnels, waterworks, utilities, sewers, and dormitories.

5. *Authority bonds.* Issued mostly for housing purposes, these can be general-obligation bonds, revenue bonds, or a combination of the two. When local housing authorities issue such bonds under contract with a federal government agency, these also are backed by the full faith and credit of the United States should the revenues of the housing project be insufficient to pay interest and amortization.

6. *Moral-obligation bonds.* These are a special type of authority bond used increasingly in the early 1970s by New York and other states. Here the backing of the bond is (1) the revenue from the authority project and (2) the moral obligation of the state or other government body. This moral-obligation technique was developed in New York State as a substitute for bonds backed by full faith and credit, which require prior approval by a voter referendum.

The first crucial test of moral-obligation bonds came in 1975, when the New York Urban Development Corporation defaulted because project revenues were thoroughly inadequate to meet interest obligations. Soon, however, a rescue operation that involved issuance of other moral-obligation bonds by another state agency was voted by the legislature. The investor lesson to be learned from this experience is that moral-obligation bonds should be evaluated strictly in terms of the covered project's ability to pay from its revenues. If that ability is lacking, the moral support is of dubious value. A sound revenue bond is preferable to a dubious moral-obligation issue.

7. *Industrial revenue or development bonds.* Most states seek to attract industry by permitting cities, other local units, and authorities to issue tax-exempt bonds to finance the construction of *privately operated* plants, facilities, and stores. These bonds are backed only by rents or other revenues from the privately operated facilities.

About $2 billion in industrial revenue bonds were outstanding at the end of 1967. Soon thereafter, Congress voted to eliminate tax exemption on all industrial bond issues of more than $1 million issued after April 30, 1968. So this technique is now available only for relatively small projects except in the case of pollution control bonds.

8. *Pollution control bonds.* These are tax-exempt bonds issued by state or local governments or authorities but financed and backed by the corporations using the pollution control facilities acquired with the bond proceeds. In practice, pollution control issues are tax-free corporate bonds. Their credit ratings depend on the financial strength of the companies involved, not of the issuing agencies.

For investors, pollution control bonds are attractive because of the high tax-free returns that are usually available. For the corporation financing them, the bonds are attractive because of the savings in interest that they provide over equal-quality taxable bonds. At 1976 interest rates, such savings range between 1.5 and 2.5 percent. Over the life of a twenty-year $10 million issue, the interest saving is about $3.5 to $4 million.

How Tax-exempt Bonds Are Issued and Traded

Most issues are offered in serial form. That is, specified portions of the total issue mature annually, typically over a period of twenty or even more years. Usually, bonds are issued in denominations of $5,000. However, small local assessment issues may come out in multiples of only $100, and some revenue bonds have standard units of as much as $100,000. The standard unit of sale is ten bonds, and any smaller number is an odd lot.

After issuance, tax-exempts are normally traded on a bid-and-asked basis. The dealer makes his profit by buying at lower prices and selling at higher ones. When you trade tax-exempts through a stockbroker, there will also be a commission to pay, but your total cost may be no higher, since presumably the broker will frequently have bought the bonds from bond buyers and dealers at lower prices than those available to individual sellers.

Typically, tax-exempts come in coupon or bearer form, so that title passes with delivery. However, for safety purposes, most tax-exempts may be registered for specified personal or corporate ownership, either as to principal only or as to both principal and interest.

Investments in tax-exempt bonds may also be made indirectly, via mutual funds specializing in them (see below, page 26-10).

How Tax-exempt Bonds May Be Insured against Loss

Since 1974 many tax-exempt bonds can be insured, at reasonable cost, by either their issuers or their owners. The insurers are specialized insurance companies or groups of insurance companies. The practical effect of either form of insurance is to raise the effective, de facto rating of an issue or of a portfolio to either AAA or AA. Such insurance is a noteworthy improvement in safety for investors in tax-exempt bonds. Here is how it works, first for issuing agencies and, second, for owners of larger tax-exempt bond portfolios.

The issuing authority obtains, prior to issuance, an insurance commitment from the insurer, for instance, the Municipal Bond Insurance Association (MBIA). The MBIA consists of Aetna Casualty and Surety Company (40 percent), St. Paul Fire and Marine Insurance Company (30 percent), Aetna Insurance Company (15 percent), and United States Fire Insurance Company (15 percent). These companies unconditionally and irrevocably guarantee, in the respective percentages shown, full and complete payment at the stipulated due dates of both principal and interest to the paying agent for the tax-exempt bonds. Standard & Poor's gives any new issue insured by MBIA its highest rating, AAA. New issues insured by the MGIC Indemnity Corporation have been uprated only to AA (as of 1976).

Such top ratings usually enables an issuer to save money through a lower rate of interest on the bonds. Thus, a revenue bond may be issued at the lower yield level of a general-obligation bond. It is hoped that this saving will exceed the cost of the insurance over the life of the bond issue.

One uncertainty is whether insurance payments in lieu of defaulted interest are exempt from income tax. Since such payments are being made by one or several insurance companies, not by a tax-exempt body, they could be considered taxable income. On the other hand, it is tax-exempt interest that is being insured, so that payments in lieu of such interest should also be deemed tax-exempt. The Internal Revenue Service in 1975 accepted the latter interpretation.

Owners of tax-exempt bond portfolios worth $50,000 or more may insure entire portfolios with a private insurance company, thereby increasing safety and peace of mind at a relatively low cost. Such insurance coverage was pioneered in 1974 by MGIC Indemnity Corporation, a subsidiary of MGIC Investment Corporation.

Portfolio insurance premiums are based on the interest rate and quality ratings of the bonds in the portfolio. Subject to the exclusions and restrictions stated below, low-rated as well as nonrated bonds can be covered provided a satisfactory weighted-average rating (for example, BBB) is maintained. In 1976 yearly insurance premiums ranged from less than 0.05 percent of the bond principal amount to a maximum of 0.35 percent. The policies are noncancelable and are automatically renewable on an annual basis. Bonds may be added to or sold from insured portfolios provided insurance is sought for the added bonds. However, all the bonds in a portfolio of tax-exempts need not be insured.

Under MGIC insurance policies, the following tax-exempts are not insurable: very short-term bonds and notes; units of outstanding municipal bond funds; and most unrated industrial revenue bonds, pollution control bonds, special-assessment issues, and real estate development bonds.

The two approaches to tax-exempt bond insurance are obviously in some competition with each other. To the extent that issuers insure their bonds to lower their interest costs, it is unnecessary for portfolio owners to carry bond insurance covering such issues. Conversely, to the degree that portfolio insurance is available to investors, they can properly ignore lower-yielding insured bonds in favor of higher-yielding, more risky bonds, not issuer-insured, and rely on their own portfolio insurance to achieve a high degree of safety.

From the larger investor's point of view, the latter alternative seems preferable. However, if your actual or potential tax-exempt portfolio is smaller than $50,000 and therefore not insurable, issuer insurance may be desirable. (Another alternative would be to invest in a tax-exempt bond fund that has insured its portfolio—a procedure that began in 1976.)

How to Select Tax-exempt Bonds

There are at least eight key factors that an investor should consider in selecting tax-free bonds:

1. *Bond coverage and ratings.* Various yardsticks are used to judge the capacity of a municipality or a government agency to pay its obligations. Essentially, they come down to tests of the adequacy of the taxes or revenues behind the bond, especially under the most adverse conceivable economic conditions. In effect, bonds should be evaluated on a depression basis.

General-obligation bonds are usually but not always rated higher than revenue bonds. The latter are often rated only after the agency involved has been operating long enough to demonstrate its probable earning power.

Some important questions to ask about *future* bond coverage are: (1) Will security for the bond be available for the entire life of the bond? (2) To what extent is the bond issue dependent on annual or periodic appropriations by the state (or territorial) legislature? (3) Does the bond issue fill an essential (or, at least, a highly popular) public service?

The leading statistical services, such as Standard & Poor's and Moody's, assign quality ratings for tax-exempts that are essentially similar to other bond ratings (see Chapter 24). Moody's *Manual of Governments and Municipals* provides statistical data and ratings for most tax-exempt issues. The larger municipal bond dealers also distribute weekly or periodic reports with detailed information on bond ratings, maturities, prices, and yields.

2. *Availability of insurance.* If you are committed to buying only bonds that are insured by their issuer or are insurable in your portfolio, availability of such insurance takes precedence over bond ratings.

3. *State and local taxation.* How states and localities tax bonds exempt from federal income taxes can be important. In states in which state income and intangible personal property taxes are appreciable, local tax-exempt issues that are exempt from these state taxes will usually be preferred to out-of-state issues subject to such taxes.

4. *Maturity date.* For bonds with the same rating, the shorter the maturity, the lower the yield and the greater the price stability (vice versa for longer maturities).

Unless you plan to invest in tax-exempts continuously and indefinitely, it is generally deemed prudent, in view of longer-term inflation prospects, to avoid maturities longer than ten to twelve years.

5. *Current price compared with par or call price.* In buying tax-exempts, as with other bonds, you usually have a choice between (*a*) older issues selling at discounts from par and call price and (*b*) more recent bonds selling at or close to par or call price. The latter yield more, but the former have greater long-term capital gain potential, since their prices rise as maturity nears. Thus, if your primary objective is maximum current tax-free income, avoid discount municipals. Your current tax-free yield will almost always be higher on comparably rated bonds selling at or close to par.

6. *Current yield.* Current yield, or the annual interest paid divided by the current price of the bond, is to be distinguished from yield to maturity, which is the annual rate of return on a bond if held to maturity, including any appreciation or depreciation to par from the current price. Generally, the higher the current yield, the greater the risk (ignoring insurance). However, from time to time research may uncover desirable bonds selling at some yield premium over other issues of equal quality because of temporary conditions or shifts in investor attitudes.

Then there are many tax-exempts that are not rated, usually because the issues are too small to capture institutional interest. Careful exploration of such issues may sometimes find higher yields without loss of quality. These issues may also be insurable, if their absence of ratings does not pull down the average rating of a portfolio below the level stipulated by the insurance company. Rated issues of smaller, less-known communities in *fast-growing areas* of the country may sometimes be available at attractive yields because institutional buyers tend to favor better-known localities.

7. *Yield to maturity.* On bonds selling below par, the yield to maturity is larger than either the current or the coupon yield because it includes the annualized capital gain to maturity. The reverse is true for bonds selling above par. The rate of return to maturity should be calculated *after* assumed capital gain taxes at maturity. Of course, the applicable tax rates at that future time are not known, and so it is customary to make calculations on the basis of current capital gain tax rates.

Discount tax-exempt bonds can be attractive to investors seeking long-term gain combined with tax-free income. However, as Table 26-1 shows, tax-free income is even more desirable than income taxed at capital gain rates. Thus, there is no advantage from lower-coupon tax-exempts selling at a discount *unless the aftertax value of the projected capital gain at maturity* (after deducting your probable capital gain tax liability at that time and discounting for the time value of the money interest income lost on the discount bond between now and maturity) *more than offsets the discount bond's lower current tax-free yield.*

8. *Marketability.* The more readily marketable tax-exempt issues are the general-obligation bonds of state and larger local governments and the revenue bonds of large and well-known issuers, such as the chief turnpike, port, or bridge authorities or local utility districts. Only these more widely traded issues are covered by even a small part of the financial press.

When to Buy Tax-exempt Bonds

Investors in very high tax brackets will be interested in tax-exempts virtually all the time for their superior tax-free income (check with the applicable taxable equivalent matrix). Middle-income investors should be somewhat more particular, expanding purchases of tax-exempts primarily when their returns are in a historically high range.

A broad decline in stock prices usually makes tax-exempts less attractive because it raises available yields on many stocks. So does any increase in taxable-bond prices or a general decline in interest rates, which reduces yields on tax-exempts.

In any event, there is rarely if ever any need to rush to buy municipal bonds. Careful research will usually pay off in higher returns.

Using Margin to Buy Tax-exempt Bonds

Buying tax-exempts on margin is a risky undertaking that is not suitable for the typical investor. Only when margin interest costs are unusually low should it even be considered. Above all, it must be constantly borne in mind that interest you pay on funds borrowed to buy, or even to carry previously purchased, tax-exempt issues is *not* deductible for income tax purposes.

Some investors borrow on stocks, taxable bonds, their homes, or other property that they already own and, after some time has elapsed, buy tax-exempts on a cash basis. In this way, the interest paid on the borrowed funds could be claimed to be tax-deductible. However, there is a real danger that the Internal Revenue Service will lump the several transactions together and thus disallow the claim of tax deductibility on the interest paid at least in part (for example, in proportion to the percentage of your total capital invested in tax-exempt bonds).

Buying Tax-exempt Bonds through Mutual Funds

A convenient way for busy investors to acquire a fully diversified portfolio of tax-exempt bonds is to invest in mutual funds specializing in tax-exempts. Until August 1976 such funds were exclusively closed-end-load institutions. This means that

1. The list of bonds in the fund is fixed at the inception of a particular fund series, and no new bonds are purchased during the life of the series, that is, until the maturity of the last remaining bond. The operation is thus thoroughly inflexible.

2. A sales charge, typically of 3½ to 4 percent, is levied at the time of purchase.

3. Shares of the fund cannot be redeemed at net asset value (NAV), but if a sale is desired, they must be sold in the market at prices that may be below or above NAV.

In August 1976, however, the Securities and Exchange Commission approved the public sale of *open-end* tax-exempt bond funds, in a form essentially similar to that of open-end stock and taxable bond funds (see Chapter 42). Thus, the newer open-end bond funds may, like any other open-end fund, be redeemed at any time at current NAV. Similarly, they can be either load or no-load funds and may or may not charge for redemption.

The spread of the open-end format to the tax-exempt area is a highly positive development that offers a worthwhile investment option for investors interested in tax-exempt income. Significantly, one of the first of such funds, the Fidelity Municipal Bond Fund, has no load charge and levies no redemption fee. It is hoped that this pattern will set a trend for this new investment medium.

Chapter **27**

Guaranteed Fixed-Asset Investments

STEPHEN FELDMAN

BACKGROUND

When individuals invest their money in stocks, bonds, real estate, or almost any other investment medium, they hope to receive a return on their investment. The possibility exists, however, that they will lose part or all of their original capital. If investors wish to avoid risking the loss of any of their investment dollars, they should place their money in investments for which the United States government or its agencies guarantee the return of the invested dollars. The federal government possesses the power to print money; therefore, it will never default on a loan, nor will it renege on its promises to insure repayments of any loans that it has guaranteed.

A bond issued by the federal government can certainly be redeemed for its face value at maturity. However, a rise in interest rates will cause the bond temporarily to decline in price. Investors who must liquidate their holdings before the final maturity date of a bond may incur a loss of their principal, even though ultimate repayment of the debt is guaranteed by the government. Although they were protected against the risk of default, they were still subject to a temporary decline in their principal precipitated by the interest rate risk.

The safest investments that can be made, ones that avoid even a temporary decline in the market value of the invested principal, are those that are *continuously guaranteed as to dollar principal* by the United States government or its agencies. Such a guarantee differs from the usual bond guarantee of repayment of principal at maturity because it also assures nonfluctuating prices at all times. One never takes a dollar loss on a government-guaranteed fixed-asset investment.

Investments that have such guarantees include savings accounts (in both savings and commercial banks), commercial bank certificates of deposit, accounts in federally insured savings and loan associations, and United States savings bonds and certificates.

Of course, investments that are free of both the risk of default and the interest rate risk will generally provide investors with a lower return than most other types of investments. During inflationary periods such low returns may confront investors with another very real, although somewhat more subtle, risk: the risk that the real value of their wealth may decline. If the annual aftertax return that individuals receive on their investments is less than the annual rate of inflation, they will have suffered a decline in the real value of their investments. For example, if $1 is placed in a 5 percent savings account by an individual in a 40 percent tax bracket, at the end of one year he or she will possess $1.03. However, if there was a 6 percent rate of inflation during that period, the $1.03 will be able to purchase only the same amount of goods that could have been purchased by approximately $.971 in the previous year, and the investor would have lost 2.9 percent of his real wealth.

The Right Time to Invest in Fixed Assets

During inflationary periods, investors should generally keep only a small portion of their funds in guaranteed fixed-asset investments. These investments may suffer a decline in their real value in such periods while other investments have traditionally offered attractive returns.

In periods of price stability, a larger portion of investors' capital should be placed in guaranteed fixed-asset investments. This practice is especially desirable for conservative investors who wish to avoid all risks.

In the rare periods of declining prices, it may be wise for investors to put a substantial portion of their money in guaranteed fixed-asset investments.

Types of Guaranteed Fixed-Asset Investments

Broadly speaking, there are three types of guaranteed fixed-asset investments. First, there is the fixed-price, fixed-yield investment for which both price and return on investment are fixed in advance throughout the life of the instrument. A prime example is the nonnegotiable certificate of deposit, for which both the principal sum and the interest return are specified (and usually guaranteed or insured, or both) to the set date of maturity. Second, there are fixed-price investments on which the yield can be raised but cannot be lowered. Government savings bonds are the outstanding examples. Although their yields are nominally fixed to maturity, they are not so in practice because the bonds are so quickly redeemable and exchangeable for higher-yield bonds. Therefore, whenever the government raises interest rates on new savings bonds, it invariably does the same for all outstanding bonds in the same series. Third, there are fixed-price investments on which the yield can be raised or lowered. Bank and savings and loan accounts are in this category. While principal sums are fixed and usually are insured, interest rates can be raised or lowered in any quarterly period in accordance with prevailing conditions in the money and credit markets.

SAVINGS ACCOUNTS

Individuals can have savings accounts in a savings bank or in a commercial bank. They can also have accounts on which interest is paid only on moneys that are left in the accounts until the end of the quarter or day-of-deposit-to-day-of-withdrawal accounts that pay interest on all moneys held in the accounts during the quarter as long as the accounts remain open with some minimum balance (usually $5) until the end of the quarter period. Generally, a commercial bank will pay a lower interest rate than a savings bank. (Congress has authorized certain regulatory agencies to impose specific ceilings on interest rates that commercial banks, mutual savings banks, and savings and loan associations may pay on various types of accounts.) There have been periods in which day-of-deposit-to-day-of-withdrawal accounts have paid the same interest rate as regular savings accounts. In these periods all investors should keep their money in the day-of-deposit accounts. At other times the regular savings accounts have paid ¼ percent more interest than the day-of-deposit accounts. During these periods funds that investors intend to keep in savings accounts for the entire quarter should be kept in regular savings accounts. However, funds that may be withdrawn for any reason during the quarter should be kept in day-of-deposit accounts.

Deposits and savings accounts are insured up to $40,000 per account. A person could literally invest millions of dollars in various savings banks ($40,000 in each bank) and have the entire amount insured by the federal government. There have been times (for example, early 1972) when savings banks' interest rates were higher than the interest rates on high-grade commercial paper and on Treasury notes. During such periods, savings accounts are an especially attractive place to put one's money.

The interest rates that savings banks pay are regulated by interest ceilings. However, many banks have attempted to pay higher effective rates than the law allows by using gimmicks such as gifts, frequent compounding, and paying interest on money for a longer period of time than the money is actually on deposit.

An individual who places $1,000 in a savings bank for one year and receives $50 in interest is receiving a 5 percent return on the investment. However, if the investor also receives a gift that is valued at $10, the effective return has been increased to 6 percent.

Another device used to boost the effective rate of interest is more frequent compounding. At one time, interest typically was compounded annually and then quarterly. Now, more and more institutions compound monthly and even daily. The differences in income resulting from monthly and daily compounding are slight, but investors should still take advantage of the added return. For example, 5 percent compounded annually becomes 5.13 percent when compounded daily.

When competition for savings deposits is rigorous, savings institutions use another technique to increase the effective rate that they pay above the legal ceiling: extra "grace period" interest. Some savings institutions pay interest retroactively to the start of an interest period or calendar month on deposits made shortly after the beginning of the month or period. Such front-end grace periods can run no longer than ten days. Many institutions also offer rear-end grace periods by permitting withdrawals during the last three days of a business period without any loss of interest.

Savings banks have been able to pay higher interest rates on longer-term savings certificates, usually issued for periods of two to five years.

COMMERCIAL BANK CERTIFICATES OF DEPOSIT AND CORPORATE COMMERCIAL PAPER

To meet competition, commercial banks have circumvented federal interest ceilings on their savings deposits by issuing certificates of deposit (CDs). CDs are unsecured promissory notes of a commercial bank. They are generally issued in minimum denominations of $100,000 and for a minimum period of thirty days. The first $40,000 of the CD is insured if the bank is a member of the Federal Deposit Insurance Corporation (FDIC). A bank is not obligated to redeem CDs before their maturity date, but they are negotiable and can easily be sold to a third party.

Commercial paper is an unsecured promissory note of a corporation other than a bank. It is usually sold in minimum denominations of $25,000. Generally, only the largest and most secure corporations can issue commercial paper, because it is unsecured and nonguaranteed and offers a comparatively low yield. However, Penn Central did have commercial paper outstanding when it entered bankruptcy. Commercial paper is always negotiable and is highly liquid. If you want to invest funds for a few days, you may wish to buy this type of paper. It can be purchased through a bank or a brokerage firm for a minimum fee.

ADDTIONAL ASPECTS

Government Insurance for Safety

Almost all banks subscribe to federal deposit insurance, under which individual checking accounts, savings accounts in both commercial and savings banks, and time deposits and certificates of deposit are insured for very quick payment (up to the limits specified below) in the event of financial trouble. The insurer is a permanent government agency, the Federal Deposit Insurance Corporation.

The maximum amount per depositor covered by FDIC insurance is $40,000. The protection limit is for a single depositor in any one insured bank (including all branches), regardless of the number of accounts the depositor has in the bank. Thus, if you have a checking account balance of $22,000, a savings account balance of $17,000, and certificates of deposit totaling $7,000 all in the same bank, you will be insured for only $40,000, not the full $46,000.

However, different members of the same family may have multiple accounts in the same bank, each insured up to the $40,000 maximum. Similarly, any one of a number of different special-purpose accounts (for example, joint owners with right of survivorship, administrator, partnership, executor, trustee, and guardian) will be treated as a single depositor and be separately insured up to the maximum limit per depositor. This option may be used to increase an investor's total insurance deposits in a single bank. Alternatively, an investor may have as many individual accounts as he or she wishes in different banks, and each will be insured.

Savings Deposits versus Time Deposits

Sums in checking accounts are demand deposits on which interest payments are forbidden by law. Other sums held in banks have generally been regarded as time deposits. However, in 1966 the Federal Reserve Board distinguished between two types of nondemand bank deposits. The term "savings deposit" was to be limited to sums on which a bank merely "reserves the right to require" (but in practice almost never does) thirty days' written notice before withdrawal. By contrast, "time deposits" are those for which a bank actually requires such notice by written contract. Federal Reserve requirements differ for each type of deposit.

SAVINGS AND LOAN ASSOCIATIONS

Savings and loan associations are institutions organized to lend money for housing in their immediate vicinity. You can borrow from savings and loan associations if you want to buy, build, improve, or refinance a house. Many of the associations' investments are in first mortgages on houses. They are therefore able to pay their members a somewhat higher rate of interest than savings banks, whose investments are more diversified.

There are more than 7,000 savings and loan associations in the United States. The majority are chartered by the state in which they are located; and laws, regulations, and practices thus vary from state to state. About 2,000 of the associations are chartered directly by the federal government. All operate under the same rules and are regulated and periodically examined by the Federal Home Loan Bank Board. Every account in federal savings and loan associations must be insured (up to $40,000) by the Federal Savings and Loan Insurance Corporation (FSLIC). State-chartered savings and loan associations may elect to join the FSLIC. A majority of them have done so.

FSLIC insurance is essentially similar, in maximum coverage and in its practical application to individual investors and the various types of multiple accounts they may set up, to FDIC insurance for depositors in commercial and mutual savings banks. Federally insured accounts, in either federally or state-chartered associations are highly safe and liquid investments.

Types of Savings and Loan Accounts

There are two types of savings and loan accounts:

1. *Savings share or passbook account.* This is the more popular of the two types. Earnings accumulate and compound unless investors specifically request that they be sent to them. Any amount, no matter how small, may be deposited at any time.

2. *Investment share or certificate account.* Here earnings are mailed to investors unless they specify that they are to be retained. Typically, certificates are issued only in multiples of $100.

In most savings and loan associations earnings are credited from the first of the month on funds received by the tenth (for mail depositors, the postmarked date is often honored as the date of receipt). Small sums can usually be withdrawn from savings and loan accounts on demand. Larger sums sometimes require reasonable notice (usually thirty days), in accordance with the regulations of the Federal Home Loan System.

Savings and Loan Brokers

If large sums are to be invested, the services of the savings and loan broker are particularly convenient. You can send one check to the broker, who will distribute your funds among the necessary number of insured associations. The objective of one-check convenience can also be achieved, but usually in a geographically more limited way, by dealing directly either with (1) a savings and loan company that owns and manages a number of insured associations or with (2) a central trustee for many different savings institutions, usually in the same state.

Choosing a Savings and Loan Association

Remember that not all savings and loan associations are federally insured. Some state-chartered associations, particularly in the West, are not. While funds in such institutions are usually quite safe, they lack the formal insurance protection of the FSLIC.

Of course, investors' funds should be committed only to capably managed and financially sound associations. The most recent balance sheets and income statements are usually available directly from savings and loan associations or from brokers. You will want to look with special care at the current figures and the trend for loan delinquencies and mortgage foreclosures. A listing of the 100 largest savings and loan associations in the United States, with their basic dividend rates, will be found in Moody's annual volume *Bank and Finance Manual.*

In recent years, some states have passed laws that allow savings and loan associations to become public corporations. When a savings and loan association becomes a public company, the earnings that have been retained by the association are the stockholders' equity of the new corporation. The ownership of these earnings and, therefore, of the stock in the corporation belongs to the depositors in the savings and loan association. Investors who have been keeping their savings in this particular association and have been receiving a fixed annual rate of interest may suddenly find that they receive a bonus of stock in the newly formed corporation. This stock may amount to as much as 10 percent or more of their accounts in the association.

In 1972 California became the first state to allow savings and loan associations to become stockholder corporations. Many investors, realizing how attractive this situation was (offering, as it did, an opportunity for sudden gain with absolutely no risk), would switch their savings from a mutual savings bank to a savings and loan association. To avoid this type of speculative appeal and reward their faithful depositors, most savings and loan associations that had the possibility of becoming public corporations in the mid-1970s established very early cutoff dates, often a year or more before the first savings and loan association in California became public, to determine those who would receive stock in the corporation. For example, to receive stock in the XYZ Federal Savings and Loan Association of New York, if this association becomes a corporation in late 1978 and issues stock, the investor must have had funds deposited with the association by some preestablished date, perhaps as far back as 1971 or 1972.

INTEREST RATE CEILINGS

Congress has authorized certain regulatory agencies to impose specific ceilings on the interest rates that commercial banks, mutual savings banks, and savings and loan associations may pay on various types of accounts. These ceilings are summarized below.

A mutual savings bank can pay 5¼ percent interest on a regular passbook account.

A certificate account with no minimum legal balance can earn 5¾ percent for 90 days to one year; 6½ percent for one year to 30 months; and 6¾ percent for 30 months or more. A certificate account with a $1,000 minimum balance can earn 7½ percent for four to six years and 7¾ percent for six years or more.

A federal savings and loan association can pay the same interest rates as a savings bank; however, a minimum balance of $1,000 is required on the 6½ percent, 6¾ percent, 7½ percent, and 7¾ percent accounts.

The savings banks and savings and loan association effectively increase their rates by compounding interest daily rather than annually. For example, a 5¼ percent account compounded daily yields 5.47 percent.

Commercial banks can pay 5 percent interest on a regular passbook account. A certificate account with no minimum legal balance can earn 5½ percent for 90 days to one year; 6 percent for one year to 30 months; and 6½ percent for 30 months and over. A certificate account with a minimum balance of $1,000 can earn 7¼ percent for four to six years and 7½ percent for six years or more.

For certificates of deposit of $100,000 or more there are no limitations on the interest rates that commercial banks or thrift institutions can pay. In Puerto Rico there are no limits on the interest that can be paid on accounts of $50,000 and over.

Tax Liabilities

Some savings institutions, in their competitive zeal, make exaggerated claims of how to get rich by depositing modest sums in them every month for thirty or forty years. They stress the power of compound interest, pointing out how, at 5 percent compounded annually, any sum will double in a little over fourteen years, quadruple in about twenty-eight years, and increase eightfold in a bit over forty-two years.

Such rosy projections usually ignore the eroding effect on interest credited to savings accounts of annual federal, state, and possibly local income taxes. Only in the case of federal savings bonds may taxes on interest be postponed for many years.

Tax Savings in Fixed-Asset Investments

Despite the facts presented in the preceding subsection, some small tax savings may be made in all types of fixed-asset investments. In particular, parents can save taxes by shifting some of their savings into accounts for their children in savings banks or savings and loan associations or by purchasing savings bonds in the children's names. The children's income will be taxed at a much lower rate.

UNITED STATES SAVINGS BONDS AND SAVINGS CERTIFICATES

Savings bonds, currently issued in only two series, E and H, can be bought from the federal government and sold back at any time only to the government, in both cases at prices exactly stipulated in advance. Almost any bank and many security brokers will sell you these bonds without any commission or service charge.

Series E bonds do not allow the investor to draw any current interest. Instead, they are sold at a 25 percent discount from par, and the investor receives profits from the stipulated rise in the price of the bond. The bonds have maturity dates 5 years from the first day of the month of purchase. A graduated interest yield that is only 4.5 percent in the first year imposes penalties on early cashing in the bonds. If held to maturity, these bonds pay a rate of 6.0 percent compounded semiannually.

The bonds may be registered in the name of one or two individuals. No single owner can buy more than $5,000 of E bonds (issue price) in one calendar year. In computing this limit, co-ownership bonds may be applied to the holdings of either or apportioned between them. For example, two persons may own a total of $10,000 issue price of Series E bonds in any one year. Bonds registered in beneficiary form are applied wholly to the owner. Series E bonds are redeemable at any time after sixty days from the issue date. Since bonds are issued as of the first day of the month of purchase, the waiting period for redemption may be as short as thirty-one days. On the other hand, the bonds may be held for as long as ten additional years after the initial maturity period. Furthermore, these bonds may be exchanged for an equivalent total of H bonds without paying any taxes at the time of the exchange. Any tax previously accrued on E bond interest will not be due until the H bonds are cashed.

Series H bonds are sold at their par values of $500, $1,000, and $5,000. They mature in ten years from the first day of the month of issue. The interest payments are mailed to the bondholder semiannually. H bonds provide an investment yield of approximately 6.0 percent per annum compounded semiannuly if they are held to maturity of ten years. The yield is 5.0 percent the first year, 5.8 percent for the next four years, and 6.5 percent for the next five years.

The bonds may be registered in the name of one or two individuals. The same purchase limits apply to Series H and Series E bonds, except that the ceiling with H bonds does not apply to H bonds received in exchange for E bonds.

The bonds are redeemable at par on the first day of any month after six months from the month of issue. One month's written notice is required before a bond can be redeemed. In addition to the general advantage of assured dollar stability of principal possessed by all government guaranteed investments, savings bonds have a number of special tax advantages.

Special Tax Advantages

1. Unlike corporate bonds or fixed-asset holdings, interest on United States savings bonds is exempt from all income taxes by any state or local authority. Such interest need not be reported on state or local returns.

2. The major tax advantage, however, goes to owners of savings bonds bought at a discount (Series E bonds). Investors in these bonds have the privilege of either (a) recording interest and paying tax on them annually or (b) postponing payment of the tax on the accrued interest until they redeem the bonds.

3. In addition, holders of maturing E bonds can elect to hold the bonds for as long as ten more years and postpone reporting or paying tax on the interest, both on amounts accrued in the original maturity period and on amounts accrued during the ten-year extension period, until redemption.

4. Owners of E bonds are now permitted to transfer to the equivalent amount of H bonds without paying any tax at the time of exchange. Any tax previously accrued on E bond interest will not be due until the H bonds are cashed. Such a tax-free trade could be desirable for persons who prefer to receive the semiannual interest payments made on H bonds. If holders could defer paying income taxes on the income they earn until they have retired, they will probably be in a lower income tax bracket and will pay this lower rate on the interest they earned for all the years that they had the bonds.

5. In any year, investors can switch from accumulating interest without reporting it to reporting it currently. If they do this, they must report all back accrued interest as income received in the current year. Similarly, with the permission of the Internal Revenue Service, they can switch from reporting currently to accumulating interest.

6. Parents of children under nineteen years of age who own savings bonds can save taxes by filing income tax returns for each child every year. By reporting the increased value of the bonds annually, they can prevent interest from being concentrated in the year that bonds mature or are redeemed. Parents may still claim each child as a dependent if they furnish more than half of the child's support. To get the full benefit of this tax saving, the child must be the sole owner of the bond, for if the child is merely a co-owner, he or she is entitled to only half the interest. The investor can get bonds reissued in a single ownership form by filing Form PD 1938 (obtainable at most places that sell savings bonds).

Disadvantages of Savings Bonds

In addition to the basic disadvantage of all fixed-value securities, that they lose purchasing power in an inflationary period, savings bonds have a special feature that may be disadvantageous. This is the fact that their yield over time is deliberately distorted to encourage holders to keep them to maturity and beyond. As short-term investments, savings bonds have yields far below those of savings and loan accounts and well below those of most savings deposits. For the same reason, whenever investors need additional capital for temporary use, it is generally preferable to liquidate other fixed-income assets rather than savings bonds even though their coupon, or listed, rate of return may be higher than on savings bonds.

CASH MANAGEMENT FUNDS

Cash management funds are open-end investment companies (mutual funds) whose objectives are current income and preservation of capital. In pursuit of these objectives some cash management funds invest only in short-term marketable securities of the United States government, certificates of deposit of large banks, commercial paper, and bankers' acceptances. In addition, many of these funds are no-load funds.

The funds are designed primarily as convenient alternatives to the direct investment of temporary cash balances in short-term United States government securities, certificates of deposit, bankers' acceptances, or commercial paper. They provide diversification, seek to employ idle cash at competitive yields, and are structured to reduce or eliminate the mechanical problems normally associated with investing directly in these money market instruments, such as scheduling maturities, investing in round lots, safeguarding receipts and deliveries of securities, reinvesting, and canvassing the market to obtain the best price when buying and selling.

The funds require a minimal initial deposit of between $1,000 and $5,000. In addition, many funds will accept additional deposits only in denominations of $1,000 and require a minimum balance of $1,000 in the account at all times.

An investor can buy or redeem shares in these funds at any time. In some cases redemptions can even be made over the telephone, and the fund will put the investor's check in the mail within twenty-four hours. It is also possible to call the fund to ascertain the yield that the fund is currently providing. The only risk of loss that the fund incurs is that one of the large banks in which it has purchased certificates of deposit could go bankrupt.

All funds pay a management fee to the group that manages the fund, and the fund itself has operating expenses. Some funds limit the management fee to 0.5 percent annually and operating expenses to 0.5 percent annually.

Cash management funds can provide an attractive investment vehicle, but an investor seeking almost total safety should follow the following steps:

1. Invest only in no-load funds.

2. Invest only in funds that invest exclusively in short-term United States government obligations, short-term obligations of government agencies that are guaranteed by the United States government, and certificates of deposit of large banks.

3. Invest in funds only when the annual management fee plus the annual operating expenses don't exceed 1 percent of the capital.

Chapter **28**

Federal Government and Government Agency Bills, Notes, and Bonds

STEPHEN FELDMAN

The federal government will never default on a loan. It has the power to tax its citizens to obtain the revenue necessary to operate the country and to repay its debts. Therefore, when an investor lends money to the federal government or makes a loan on which interest and principal repayments are guaranteed by the federal government, these loans are risk-free. As a consequence, such loans generally pay a lower rate of interest than is available from other securities with similar repayment terms. In January 1976, the total gross public debt of the United States government exceeded $595 billion.

TYPES OF SECURITIES

Individuals, corporations, and pension and retirement funds create a large and active market for obligations of the federal government. There are five principal types of United States Treasury securities of interest to individuals and institutions.

Treasury Bills

Treasury bills of the United States government are bearer obligations issued on a discount basis and redeemed at face value, without interest, on the date of maturity. Bills issued prior to March 5, 1970, are available in denominations ranging from $1,000 to $1 million. However, those dated March 5, 1970, and thereafter are issued in minimum denominations of $10,000. At present, the Treasury offers two new issues of bills each week for competitive bids; one issue matures in three months, and the other in six months. Tender offers are usually received by 1:30 P.M. (New York time) each Monday for settlement on the following Thursday. Noncompetitive tenders from $10,000 to $200,000 of each issue can be submitted without a stated price. Such bids are allotted in full at the average price of accepted competitive bids. Each month the Treasury offers, under the same general rules that apply to three-month and six-month bills, a series of bills with maturities of nine months and one year.

Treasury Notes

Treasury notes have maturities of one to seven years. They are issued in bearer or registered form, and interest is paid semiannually. A special kind of five-year note that pays only 1½ percent per year is issued each April and October in exchange for nonmarketable 2¾ percent investment Series B bonds of 1975–1980. Series B bonds must be converted to the special issue to become marketable.

Treasury Bonds

Treasury bonds, which are securities maturing in more than seven years, constitute the largest segment of the government's public debt. All bonds are available in registered or in bearer form, and the two forms are interchangeable. Interest is paid semiannually. Many of the bonds are callable at par five years before maturity on interest payment dates. To exercise the call option, however, the Treasury must give public notice four months before the call date.

Retirement Plan Bonds

In January 1963, the Treasury began issuing Retirement Plan bonds in accordance with provisions contained in the Self-Employed Individuals Tax Retirement Act of 1962. Obtainable only as part of bond purchase plans or pension and profit sharing plans, the bonds are sold at par in denominations of $50 to $1,000. Purchases in any one year may not exceed $5,000. Bond purchase plans meeting the requirements of the Tax Retirement Act are granted income tax advantages similar to those accorded pension and profit sharing plans. Self-employed individuals can deduct from taxable income up to $2,500 annually for contributions to their own retirement period. The bonds are not redeemable until the owner reaches the age of 59½ unless the owner dies or is disabled. Interest, together with the principal, is payable only upon redemption. At the time of redemption, a self-employed individual becomes liable for taxes on the interest earned and on the amount deducted from taxable income for the year in which the bond was purchased. Upon redemption of the bonds for pension or retirement funds, an employee is subject to income tax on interest and on any amount contributed by his or her employer to the purchase of the bonds.

Tax Anticipation Bills

From time to time the Treasury offers tax anticipation bills for bids on a competitive basis. The bills may be used at face value to pay the buyers' income taxes even though the maturity date is usually seven days after the tax payment date. Therefore, the yield is greater if buyers use the bills for tax payments instead of redeeming them for cash at maturity.

Income from all these Treasury securities is subject to federal income taxes but is exempt from all state and local income taxes. In addition, any gains on federal government obligations maturing in less than one year from the date of purchase are not considered capital gains. They are fully taxable at the federal level as ordinary income even if the issue is held for more than six months.

FEDERAL GOVERNMENT AGENCY SECURITIES

In addition to the direct government obligations described above, numerous bonds, notes, and certificates are issued by federal agencies as instrumentalities of the United States government. These agencies are established by acts of Congress, and the government maintains an interest in them by supervision and, in some cases, by capital ownership. Most of the credit activities of the agencies are financed by the sale of their own debt obligations to the public. Such securities are not guaranteed by the United States government (with the exception of Government National Mortgage Association participation certificates, on which the interest and principal are guaranteed), but they have achieved wide acceptance in the public market in recent years, since a default by a government agency would be disastrous to federal financing and is therefore highly unlikely.

Three agencies that are concerned with financing the agricultural industry are the Federal Intermediate Credit Banks, the Banks for Cooperatives, and the Federal Land Banks.

The twelve Federal Intermediate Credit (FIC) Banks lend to production credit associations and to other organizations that make loans to farmers. To raise money for the lending operations, those banks generally issue nine-month debentures between the fifteenth and twenty-fifth of each month for delivery on the first business day of the following month. In 1970 the banks decided to offer issues of intermediate-term maturity from time to time. The first of such offerings was of three years' maturity. Debentures maturing in less than six months may be used as collateral for advances from the Federal Reserve Banks at the discount window without interest rate penalties. Because of their eligibility for such Federal Reserve treatment, short-term FIC debentures may sometimes sell at a premium in relation to other agency securities with comparable maturities.

The twelve district Banks for Cooperatives, along with the Central Bank for Cooperatives, make loans to farmers' cooperatives. The banks are supervised by the Farm Credit Administration and are owned by the federal government and various farmers' cooperatives. To raise funds for their operations, the banks issue debentures, usually with maturities of six months.

The twelve Federal Land Banks offer long-term credit to farmers. The banks are supervised by the Farm Credit Administration and are owned by the Federal Land Bank Associations, which are composed of farmers who purchase stock in amounts equal to 5 percent of their borrowings. Funds are raised by sale of bonds, which frequently have slightly longer maturities than do those of the Federal Intermediate Credit Banks or the Banks for Cooperatives.

The Tennessee Valley Authority (TVA), a corporate agency of the United States government, was established to develop the Tennessee River and to assist in the development of other resources in the Tennessee Valley and adjacent areas. The TVA is authorized to sell bonds, notes, and other evidences of indebtedness to assist in financing its power program.

The Export-Import Bank is incorporated under the laws of the District of Columbia. Its president is a member of the National Advisory Council on International Monetary and Financial Policies. The general purpose of the Bank is to help finance and facilitate exports, imports, and the exchange of commodities between the United States and other nations. The lending authority of the Bank is controlled by Congress. To finance its operations, the Bank sells debentures and participation certificates.

The International Bank for Reconstruction and Development (World Bank) is an institution with the governments of 110 countries constituting its membership. Among its purposes are facilitating capital investment that will promote trade and improve living standards of member countries. The Bank guarantees and participates in loans and makes loans for productive purposes. It issues long-term debentures to finance its operations. The Inter-American Development Bank was established by the United States and twenty Central and South American governments, primarily to make long-term loans to finance projects for increasing the productive capacity of member countries. The Bank issues long-term debentures to finance its operations.

Under the Federal Home Loan Bank (FHLB) system, the eleven Federal Home Loan Banks advance home mortgage credit to member institutions, including some 5,000 savings and loan associations. The operations of the system are supervised by the Federal Home Loan Bank Board. Notes with maturities of one year or less and bonds with longer maturities are issued to raise funds.

Federal National Mortgage Association (FNMA or Fannie Mae), established in 1938, is by now well known in the mortgage finance field. Its primary function has been to buy (and, when money is plentiful, to sell) standard Federal Housing Administration (FHA)–insured and Veterans Administration (VA)–guaranteed mortgages made by private lenders. The purchases thus replenish the supply of capital in the housing market for additional housing loans.

For those unfamiliar with the way the mortgage market operates, a few facts will be helpful. The home buyer obtains his mortgage financing from a variety of mortgage lenders: banks, savings and loan associations, mortgage companies, and others. Some of these lenders, such as savings and loan institutions, savings banks, and insurance companies, not only make the original loan, as primary lenders, but also hold the mortgage as a long-term investment for their own portfolios. Others, such as mortgage companies and commercial banks, are largely primary lenders who sell their mortgages to long-term private investors (the secondary market) to replenish their funds and make additional primary loans. The ability of primary lenders to dispose of their mortgages to long-term investors determines to a large extent the volume of mortgage money available to home buyers. If loans cannot be sold on the private secondary market at a rate equal to demand, primary lenders soon find themselves short of capital and curtail their mortgage lending.

Fannie Mae was created to provide a supplementary secondary mortgage market for the then-new FHA-insured mortgages. Later, authority to purchase VA-guaranteed home loans under the GI Bill of Rights was added to its operation. Fannie Mae became the major factor in such financing after World War II because the private secondary market was unfamiliar with VA loans and reluctant to engage in an untried kind of financing.

FNMA's secondary market purchases of standard FHA and VA mortgages, by now generally accepted on the private market, were set up in a separate operation, based on the market rate and financed in large part through borrowing from the United States Treasury until 1954. The Housing Act of 1954 thoroughly recast this government secondary market. Standard FHA and VA mortgages were now generally accepted on the private market, and this original purchase function was set up separately, at market rates, as a supplement to the private secondary market. However, new types of government-backed financing, such as Urban Renewal Development and low-cost and cooperative housing, were entering the picture, and special help was needed for such financing. Fannie Mae was therefore rechartered with three separate functions: (1) the original support program for FHA and VA mortgage financing; (2) special assistance for the purchase of mortgages for these new types of financing; and (3) the management and liquidation of mortgages previously bought.

The regular secondary market operation of Fannie Mae continued to play an important role in financing the increasing need for mortgage funds in the years that followed and in balancing funds geographically between shortage areas and those with large supplies of investment money. The new special-assistance function was enlarged with the inauguration of new programs, such as new low-interest, 3 percent financing of low- and moderate-income rental housing and, more recently, interest subsidy financing of housing for lower-income families.

Housing Act of 1968 and the FNMA

In 1968 a basic legislative change was made. Under a new budget accounting concept proposed for the next fiscal year, Fannie Mae's expenditures for purchases of mortgages would have been carried as budget outlays even though the purchasing funds were obtained principally through borrowing from the public. Recognizing the adverse effect this would have on FNMA's response to home-financing demands, Congress enacted legislation to divide Fannie Mae into two continuing corporate entities.

One was a new Fannie Mae, which is a government-sponsored but privately owned corporation. The Department of Housing and Urban Development (HUD) continues to exercise control over the corporation's activities, such as its borrowing authority. In addition, the HUD Secretary may require that a reasonable portion of the mortgage purchases be related to the national goal of providing adequate housing for low- and moderate-income families.

The evolution of the new private organization was completed under the law after May 1, 1970. One-third of the outstanding stock is owned by mortgage and related business. The new private Fannie Mae has a board of directors made up of ten members elected by the stockholders and five appointed by the President of the United States. Fannie Mae, in its secondary market operations, buys mortgages at the market price, which includes a discount, or "points," that make the effective rate of return higher than the FHA rate. To finance this operation, FNMA may issue debentures, with the approval of the Secretary of the Treasury. These debentures which may be purchased by investors, generally provide a return slightly above that offered directly by the Treasury.

Government National Mortgage Association

With FNMA transformed into a separate private corporation for the normal secondary market operations, the 1968 act established the new Government National Mortgage Association (GNMA or Ginnie Mae). This corporation, which is part of HUD, assumed responsibilities for the remaining two functions of the 1954–1968 Fannie Mae.

Thus, Ginnie Mae operates in the following three areas, two of which are inherited from Fannie Mae and one of which is brand new: (1) the special-assistance function; (2) the management and liquidating of certain previously acquired mortgages, as well as the administration as trustee of the old Fannie Mae's Participation Certificate program; and (3) the mortgage-backed security program, a new function. The programs under which Ginnie Mae buys mortgages from private lenders are designated by Congress or the President, and the amount it can borrow from the Treasury for its purchases is determined by congressional authorization. All its programs involve mortgages that are not readily salable except at heavy discounts, either because of unconventional risks or because of low interest rates that cannot compete in yield with private mortgage investments.

Fannie Mae, in its secondary market operations, buys mortgages at the market price, which includes a discount that makes the effective rate of return higher than the FHA rate. Ginnie Mae, on the other hand, buys its special mortgages at par: the full amount of the outstanding balance of the mortgage. Its purchases are financed by borrowing from the Treasury. If its interest return on these mortgages is less than the government pays for the money it borrows, a net loss results. This loss may be paid for from the surplus funds, or an appropriation could be requested. Without this market for these special-program mortgages, private lenders would be unwilling to make loans for these special areas of housing needs.

Ginnie Mae's special-assistance operations suffer one restraint that is no longer a factor in the FNMA secondary market: its operations have a direct and often a substantial effect on the federal budget. Whereas FNMA obtains its funds for mortgage purchases from the private market, Ginnie Mae borrows its funds from the Treasury, and its mortgages become expenditures in the federal budget and add to the national debt. The extent of its dealings therefore is restricted at times because of overall budget and fiscal considerations.

A new system, known as the Tandem Plan, has been instituted jointly by GNMA and FNMA. It enables GNMA to meet certain special needs, particularly in the low-income housing field, without any substantial impact on the federal budget. The program links Ginnie Mae and Fannie Mae in tandem to provide a two-step arrangement for financing projects by nonprofit sponsors that furnish either low-rent supplements or interest subsidies for low-income families.

In the first step, Ginnie Mae issues a commitment to buy a mortgage upon completion of a project and to purchase the mortgage at par. Fannie Mae has agreed to purchase a certain amount of these mortgages at the market price. The second step involves the sale of the long-term mortgage by Ginnie Mae to Fannie Mae. Ginnie Mae's only cash outlay is the difference between the full amount of the mortgage, the par price, and the market price of Fannie Mae.

This difference constitutes only a small Ginnie Mae cash outlay in comparison with buying and retaining the mortgage. It has been estimated that Tandem Plan financing will provide as much as 30 times the financing possible under outright mortgage purchases, since the private funds of Fannie Mae replace government financing, thus reducing the amount of government expenditures.

Equally important is the fact that this arrangement is the means of financing much-needed lower-income housing that otherwise could not be undertaken. If these projects were to be financed by outside lenders, there would be a discount, a substantial charge, that nonprofit sponsors could not afford. Unlike other agency debentures, *the interest on and the principal amount of participation certificates are regarded as having the guarantee of the United States government.*

Ginnie Mae has developed a new program in which the investor can (1) receive an attractive yield, equivalent to that of mortgages; (2) avoid the extensive documentation required in the usual mortgage investment; (3) receive a steady cash flow of interest and amortization of principal each month; and (4) receive a guarantee by the Government National Mortgage Association bearing the full faith and credit of the United States.

This mortgage-backed security is designed to attract new sources of capital into housing, particularly the pension funds and state municipal retirement funds which do not have the mortgage departments that ordinarily would be needed to handle the complexities and voluminous documentation of a portfolio with mortgages. Now, a fund can make an equivalent mortgage investment by purchasing just one piece of paper.

Furthermore, it is possible for a fund to purchase a security of this type backed by mortgages in identifiable areas to encourage local home building. Under this program, an FHA-approved mortgagee obtains authority from GNMA to issue a certain amount of securities to be collateralized by a pool of specified amounts of FHA, VA, or Farmers Home Administration mortgages. The pool must be in a minimum amount of $2 million, and the mortgages cannot be more than twelve months old. The issuer services the mortgages and makes all payments due to the investor.

When the specified amount of mortgages has been accumulated in the pool, the mortgages are submitted to an approved custodian, usually a bank, where they are examined. After examination and appropriate certification, GNMA issues its guarantee of the mortgage-backed security or certificate, which is then sold to the investor. Mortgages are held in safekeeping by the custodian. The full faith and credit of the United States is pledged to the payment of all amounts that GNMA may be required to pay under the terms of its guarantee, and GNMA has complete authority to borrow from the Treasury to meet its obligations under the guarantee.

Mortgage-backed securities are issued and sold to mortgage bankers, banks, and thrift institutions throughout the country. If investors are unable to find an issue, they can write to GNMA, Department of Housing and Urban Development, Washington, D.C. 20410.

Taxes

As in the case of direct government obligations, income from issues of the Federal Home Loan Banks, Federal Land Banks, Federal Intermediate Credit Banks, and Banks for Cooperatives are exempt from state and local income taxes.

Chapter **29**

Investing in Preferred Stock

STEPHEN FELDMAN

Introduction

Preferred stock is often condemned as a cross between a common stock and a bond, with the disadvantages of both and the advantages of neither. Like a bond, a straight preferred ordinarily has none of the capital gain potential of common stock. Also, if general interest rates rise, the price of a preferred, since its yield is fixed, generally declines.

On the other hand, a preferred stock shares much of the common stock's risk, since the preferred dividend comes only after bond interest has been paid and, unlike the latter, is almost always deferrable. Furthermore, the issuing company is not required to redeem the preferred stock at a predetermined price and date, as is the case with a bond. Therefore, if a preferred stock declines in price, it can remain depressed indefinitely.

Since preferred stock typically yields very little if any more than bonds of equivalent quality, most nonconvertible preferred issues are relatively unattractive to individual investors. For persons investing primarily for income, it makes no sense to buy ordinary preferred stocks unless they can obtain a yield advantage over bonds that is great enough to compensate them for the additional incurred risk.

Preferreds for Corporate Investors. The basic reason why the yield differential for preferred stocks over bonds has virtually disappeared is the eagerness of *corporate investors* to purchase preferred issues because of their big tax advantage over bonds. Whereas individuals pay taxes on 100 percent of all dividend income after an exclusion of the first $100, corporations pay federal income taxes on only 15 percent of the dividends received from other United States corporations. This means that a corporation in the 48 percent tax bracket pays an effective tax rate of 7.2 percent on preferred dividends (48 percent times 15 percent). The same corporation would pay an effective tax rate of 48 percent on taxable bond interest.

Consequently, a corporation in the 48 percent bracket that invests $100,000 in preferred stock paying $10,000 annual dividends will pay taxes of $720 (15 percent of $10,000 equals $1,500 taxable income; 48 percent of $1,500 results in a tax of $720) and have a net aftertax profit of $9,280 for a return of 9.28 percent. If this corporation buys $100,000 in corporate bonds and receives $10,000 in interest, it will pay taxes of $4,800 and have an aftertax profit of $5,200, or 5.2 percent. Therefore, the corporation would much prefer the preferred stock even if it is somewhat more risky.

By contrast, nonconvertible preferred stock is not appealing to corporations as a method of financing, since dividends on preferred stock are not tax-deductible, while interest on corporate bonds is deductible. About the only advantage of a straight preferred stock over a bond for the issuing corporation is that dividends on preferred stock may be deferred, and the failure to pay such dividends need not lead to bankruptcy, whereas default on bond interest might do so.

For these reasons most corporations have stopped issuing straight preferred stocks. Major exceptions are public utilities and other regulated companies that are required to maintain minimum equity-debt ratios in their capital structure but wish to benefit their common shareholders by the leverage provided by preferred stock.

Special Features of Some Preferred Stocks.   All preferred stocks have a first claim on dividends before the common stock. A preferred stock with only that feature may be described as a "plain and simple" preferred. For the reasons given above, a plain preferred stock is generally unattractive. Therefore, additional features or gimmicks have often been added to plain preferred stocks to make them more enticing to investors. This has resulted in the following improvements or protective features for preferred stocks:

1. *Cumulative preferred stocks.* This is the basic protection for preferred stockholders. A plain preferred stock with only this feature added is called a "straight preferred." Almost all cumulative preferred stocks are fully cumulative. Any unpaid dividends accumulate and must be made up in full before any distributions can be paid to the common stockholders. A few cumulative preferred stocks (usually railroad issues) are cumulative only to the extent earned. This means that if the company does not earn all or part of its preferred dividend in any year, only the earned portion (if any) may be accumulated as a back dividend.

2. *Debt-free preferred stocks.* Other factors being roughly equal, the preferred stock of a debt-free company is usually more attractive than the preferred of a company with a sizable amount of bonds or other long-term debt. Since interest on bonds must be paid in bad times as well as good, the margin of safety for preferred stockholders in periods of recession is greater in debt-free companies. Of course, preferred stockholders usually have no assurance that their company will remain debt-free (sometimes, however, the stock certificate requires that a majority or even two-thirds of the preferred stock must approve new bond issues).

3. *Preferred stocks with sinking funds.* Here the company is required to set up an annual purchase fund to retire a stated percentage of the outstanding preferred stock at specified times at a specified price. In effect, the company is competing with you in buying up its stock. Therefore, such a preferred stock will usually tend to sell nearer its call price than a plain preferred of comparable quality.

4. *Noncallable preferred stocks.* Most preferred stocks can be called by the issuing company when it is advantageous to do so—for instance, when interest rates have dropped and the company can refinance itself at a lower cost. Occasionally, a noncallable preferred can be retired, but only by the approval of two-thirds of all stockholders (in such cases, the preferred stockholders may have several votes per share compared with the common stockholders). To win such a vote, a satisfactory offer to the preferred stockholders will be needed. However, some preferred stocks are truly noncallable and can be held by stockholders as long as desired. The only way that the issuing corporation can retire truly noncallable preferreds is to buy them up on the open market or to offer their holders a profitable exchange proposal, typically a substantially larger face amount of

subordinated debentures that would provide capital gains or higher income for the investor, plus worthwhile tax savings for the issuing company. Of course, noncallable preferreds don't have sinking funds, since theoretically they are "perpetuals" not to be retired.

Noncallable preferreds are especially attractive in recessionary periods of declining interest rates. In such periods, prices of bonds and preferred stocks rise as yields drop. But the price of a callable preferred stock that is not also convertible cannot rise very far above its call price because of the danger of capital loss through a call for redemption. By contrast, noncallable preferreds have no such price ceiling, and substantial capital gains are thus possible.

5. *Guaranteed stocks.* Here dividends are guaranteed by another company. See below, section "Guaranteed Stocks."

6. *Participating preferred stocks.* These are rather rare. A participating preferred may receive more than its stated rate of dividends in years when the company's earnings are exceptionally large. Instead of having all the additional earnings go to higher dividends on the common, a participating preferred shares in any such earnings over a specified amount per common share, typically on a fifty-fifty basis. Because of this extra potential on the upside, participating preferreds usually have less protection on the downside than typical preferred stocks. Thus they are generally noncumulative and callable. If they are cumulative, occasionally the company need not pay dividends even if earned.

Before investing in any of the participating preferreds, check the earnings record and probable earnings trend of the company carefully. If earnings are far below the point at which the preferred starts to get additional dividends, participation may be purely theoretical. On the other hand, the participation point sometimes is well below recent annual earnings per common share. In this case, the participating feature is well established, and the price of the preferred will usually reflect this fact.

7. *Convertible preferred stocks.* These are exchangeable at the owner's option into a specified number of shares of the related common stock at a stipulated price. This feature permits a preferred stock to participate in the capital gains potential of the related common. It thus offers a further advantage over the participating preferred stock.

8. *Convertible and participating preferred stocks.* Combining convertibility and participation represents the acme of improving attractiveness for preferred stocks, especially when the issue is also cumulative.

Preferreds with Special Yields

Cumulative Preferreds with Dividends in Arrears.   When a preferred has missed paying dividends, its quality is obviously deficient. The price of the stock drops, often sharply. Sometimes, however, the price decline is more severe than is justified by a company's future prospects. And here the investor looking for income or capital gain can step in profitably. The misfortune that caused the company to skip its preferred dividends may be only temporary, the management may have changed for the better, or the company may regularly skip preferred dividends at the bottom of its cycle and then make up for the lapse when its business improves. Whatever the reasons, you can almost always find a few speculative opportunities in preferred stocks with big windfall potentials in arrears.

Of course, when arrears have accumulated for many years and are very large, preferred stockholders will rarely recover in cash the full amount legally due them. Usually, a company whose earning power is recovering will offer to recapitalize, replacing the shares in arrears with another stock or bond—more attractive to shareholders in some respects but also almost always less restrictive for management. Alternatively, the company may make a tender to buy the shares in arrears at a discount from the amount legally due (call price plus accrued dividends). Such offers or tenders are frequently attractive enough to result in substantial gains.

If you are interested primarily in income, buying a preferred with back dividends can result in yields well over 10 percent as arrears are gradually or suddenly paid off. If you are interested primarily in capital gains, you should sell a preferred with arrears after an announcement of payment of the back dividend, after an offer to recapitalize, or after a tender to buy the shares, but before the ex-dividend or effective date. This procedure brings a double benefit:

1. From the general rise in the price of the stock, owing to the improvement in its earnings position

2. From the specific rise in the price of the stock after the special dividend or other corporate action has been announced

By selling just before the stock goes ex dividend, you will also gain all or almost all of the value of the dividend.

Guaranteed Stocks. A special form of preferred stock is guaranteed stock, the dividends of which are guaranteed by another corporation. Such stocks are mostly strategically located leased rail lines controlled by major railroads, although a few utility stocks also fall into this category. Most guaranteed issues were originally common stocks, but as guaranteed stocks they have in fact become preferred stocks. Indeed, Standard & Poor's rates the quality of guaranteed stocks in terms of its rating scale for bonds.

The main advantages of guaranteed stocks are two:

1. They provide relatively good income with high safety. Income from such stocks is virtually as secure as that from high-grade bonds, yet yields typically run from 30 to 50 percent higher.

2. Because of corporate tax savings that are possible, guarantors of guaranteed stocks are likely to make offers to exchange them for bonds at terms attractive to their holders.

Since very few shares of guaranteed stocks are available, they must be purchased carefully, in small quantities.

Things to Look for Before Buying Preferreds

When buying a preferred stock of whatever kind as a long-term investment, check the following:

1. *Full voting rights.* Preferred stockholders should not be deprived of a voice in the company.

2. *Restrictions on common dividends.* Adequate working-capital margins and a satisfactory surplus should be required before dividends on the common stock can be paid. This requirement helps protect preferred stockholders from a dip in earnings.

3. *Restrictions on new preferreds or bonds.* Management should be limited in its right to issue new preferred stocks or bonds. Usually, it is desirable that such issues be approved by at least two-thirds of the preferred stockholders.

4. Avoid buying new callable issues selling only slightly below their call prices. You can often get previously issued preferreds of equivalent quality, sometimes of the same company, selling at a much bigger discount from par.

5. On the other hand, in rare periods of low interest rates, beware of callable preferreds selling substantially above their call prices. If these are called, you face a certain capital loss.

How to Select Callable Preferreds

When a company with preferred stock accumulates a substantial surplus, there is pressure from both common and preferred stockholders to retire some or all of the preferreds. For the common stockholder who plans to keep his stock for a long time, retirement of the preferred means that he gets first call on earnings. His stock is then worth more, and he has the strong possibility of capital gain. For the preferred stockholder, the prospect of redemption tends to raise the market price of his stock to the level of the call price (usually par plus accrued dividends).

If you can spot a preferred stock that is likely to be partially or completely redeemed in the near future, you have an almost-certain chance of capital gain. This is doubly true if accrued dividends are involved. Even in a sharply declining bear market, such a stock will usually increase in price. However, finding such situations is very difficult.

You should know that all things being equal, if the volume of preferred stock outstanding is small relative to the common, the chance of redemption is greater because the cost is less. In addition, if the preferred stock is closely held by insiders, part of or close to management, the chances of eventual redemption are better, since the capital gains will go predominantly to the insider group.

If you are interested in capital gains on callable preferreds, seek (1) a stock selling well below its call price, (2) a relatively small amount of preferred outstanding, and (3) an issue held largely by management or groups close to it.

Convertible Preferred Stock

Investors who are evaluating convertible preferred stock would use criteria very similar to those used in evaluating convertible bonds. First, they would want to reassure themselves that the preferred stock meets the quality standards that they have established for this type of security. Second, the long-range outlook for interest rates should be fairly stable or down. Third, the minimum value of the preferred stock, if nonconvertible, should not be too far below the current selling price of the preferred stock. This difference is the maximum loss that the investor can incur even if the common stock drops drastically, provided that interest rates do not rise sharply and depress the value of the nonconvertible preferred. Also, the current price of the stock must not be too far below the conversion parity (say, a maximum of 20 percent). (For example, if a convertible preferred can be converted into ten shares of common stock and the preferred is selling for $120 per share, then the conversion parity price is $12 per share.)

Moreover, the potential price of the common stock must be well above the conversion parity. Finally, the current dividend yield on the preferred stock should compare favorably with the current dividend yield on the common stock.

Chapter 30
Real Estate Investments

PAUL F. WENDT

REAL ESTATE INVESTMENT CHARACTERISTICS

The size, value, and individuality of real estate assets are reflected in a wide variety of investment media, financing instruments, and legal forms of ownership that are applicable to the many different types of property. Legal and tax complexities associated with real estate ownership add to this basic lack of homogeneity, which has resulted in specialization of functions and compartmentalization of markets and real estate investment know-how. A specialist in "hot corners" for service stations in Los Angeles may have limited knowledge of other areas and profess ignorance of the investment characteristics of industrial, residential, or office building properties in that city.

The institutional structure of the real estate business is undergoing rapid changes with growing public interest in real estate investment. The large real estate firm, providing a department store range of appraisal, marketing, management, financing, and investment services, is evolving rapidly in response to demands from corporate and other large-scale owners of real estate. Leading firms have organized their own real estate investment trusts (REITs) and partnership syndicates.

Insurance companies, hailed by *Fortune* magazine as "the future largest landlords in America," have moved from a passive role as mortgage investors to become aggressive participants in real estate equity investment. Bank holding companies sponsor REITs; investment bankers have moved into asset management roles as they sell insurance, REITs, gold, cattle, and shares in limited partnership syndicates for petroleum exploration and real estate development. Manufacturing corporations organize real estate development and investment subsidiaries, while professional real estate promotors and others package limited partnership syndicates for high-income professionals seeking tax shelters and a retirement income.

The manifold types of property and real estate financing instruments and the diverse interests of various classes of investors have resulted in a smorgasbord of real estate investment opportunities. The uninitiated real estate investor must select investments with circumspection and obtain a quality of investment advice often difficult for the unwary to secure. Worse yet, the initiated may often have difficulty in differentiating between good and bad investment advice.

The simplest classification of real estate investments is by type of property. Unimproved land, apartments, commercial, industrial, and office buildings represent classes of real estate with distinguishing markets and investment characteristics. Even these classifications are much too broad, however, to reflect the important distinctions between farmland and vacant commercial or residential land or residential lots. Differences in investment characteristics between inner-city tenements and new "swinger" apartment complexes in the suburbs are as great as those between main street commercial properties, downtown department stores, and shopping centers or between downtown loft buildings and properties in modern industrial parks. It is useful at the outset to identify some of the important features distinguishing investments in land, apartments, and commercial and industrial structures. At this point, no attempt will be made to evaluate investments in these various types of real estate.

Vacant Land

Unimproved land is generally regarded as a speculation rather than as an investment because land alone seldom produces an income. Returns to the owner, therefore, are viewed as resulting from price appreciation. In this sense, unimproved land occupies a position similar to stocks that do not pay dividends. The carrying charges on land investment are high because of the necessity of paying local property taxes and interest with no offsetting cash inflow.

Vacant land can be regarded as having a life cycle leading to its development and ultimate redevelopment. Figure 30-1 represents a hypothetical life cycle of land values, reproduced from an article entitled "Land as a Growth Investment" published in the *Financial Analysts Journal* of July–August 1966. The essence of the investment or speculative appeal of vacant land obviously lies in the timing of purchases late in Stage I to take advantage of the presumed rapid rise in values during Stage II, the predeveloped period. The importance of timing is emphasized by the fact that, as a result of carrying charges and property taxes, vacant land ordinarily provides a negative income during Stages I and II. The risk in land investment results from the fact that the actual length of time represented for the stages in Fig. 30-1 is often indeterminate, leaving the landowner with the prospect of negative returns, often rising with property taxes, over a long period.

Investors searching for an attractive investment in undeveloped land will attempt to detect a discernible trend in land developments in a particular area or a specific event that may cause land to be developed in a region. The former case will often occur as people move from the inner city to the suburbs. Generally, the first suburban areas to be developed are the ones closest to the city. Gradually, the demand for property stretches farther and farther from the city. Certain sections of suburbia will become more prestigious, more desirable, and higher-priced than other sections. Possibly investors will notice that the "east side" or the "north shore" of a suburban community is most desirable. They may be able to determine which area on the east side or the north shore has not yet been developed but is just beyond the perimeter of development. That area may prove to be an attractive investment.

Sometimes a particular event, rather than gradual expansion, can greatly affect the value and price of real estate. The opening of Disney World in Florida caused a great increase in land values within a radius of approximately 75 or 100 miles. Investors who moved quickly after it was announced that Disney World would be built could have made a significant profit.

A further risk in land investment is associated with the problem of limited market absorption rates. Even though the sale prices of land may rise rapidly during the later period of predevelopment, as shown in Stage II, landowners often may find that only small portions of large landholdings can be absorbed by the market.

Professional land developers estimate returns on land investment by projecting absorption rates in terms of the numbers of acres or lots expected to be sold annually. The estimated net cash flows are then discounted after deducting development costs. Rising lot development standards and costs, added to rising

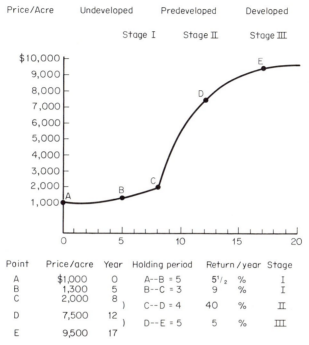

Point	Price/acre	Year	Holding period	Return/year	Stage
A	$1,000	0	A--B = 5	5½ %	I
B	1,300	5	B--C = 3	9 %	I
C	2,000	8	C--D = 4	40 %	II
D	7,500	12	D--E = 5	5 %	III
E	9,500	17			

Fig. 30-1 Theoretical land price increases according to stage of land development. [*Source: Financial Analysts Journal*]

property taxes, can often reduce sharply returns to landowners even during periods of rapid increases in lot sales prices.

Residential Income Property

Traditionally, rental housing has been regarded as a prime investment owing to the essential nature of the housing services provided, the relatively long economic life of properties, the potential efficiency in management, and the availability of attractive long-term financing and of an interest and depreciation tax shelter. Residential property accounts for the largest number and dollar value of real estate investments. According to the census of 1970, there were approximately 15 million dwelling units in structures with two or more dwellings per structure in the United States. On the basis of an estimated average of five dwellings per structure, there are approximately 3 million apartment properties. Since new multifamily units are being built at the rate of approximately 750,000 dwellings per year, it can be estimated that approximately 150,000 apartment properties are being added annually. These require real estate financing and investment funds in excess of $8 billion.

Commercial Property

Chain store properties under long-term leases in prime locations of large cities were gilt-edged commercial real estate investments during the first half of the twentieth century. The transportation crisis, the exodus of high-income groups to the suburbs, and the concomitant decline in the concentration of downtown shopping produced a major shift on the part of mortgage lenders and investors to suburban shopping center properties after World War II.

More than 1.5 million single retail units and 220,131 multiunit retail establishments reported sales of over $300 billion in 1967. If a multiplier of 6 times gross income is used, the value of the real estate involved in retailing approximated $1,800 billion. More than 360 shopping centers reported to the Urban Land Institute gross operating receipts of approximately $2 per square foot and net operating income before depreciation and financing charges ranging between 8.5 and 12 percent of capital costs. These shopping centers ranged in size from neighborhood centers of 50,000 square feet, requiring an average investment of from $500,000 to $750,000, to regional centers with more than 1 million square feet of space, requiring an average investment of $25 million. It is little wonder that regional shopping center investment is dominated by the large institutional investors. The rapid growth in the sales and profits of shopping centers has attracted many institutional real estate investors to such properties.

A large area of potential real estate investment remains for individual investors in existing and new retail areas, much of it involving single structures of 10,000 to 20,000 square feet that require a capital cost of approximately $15 to $20 per square foot. The estimated annual volume of new investments in retail and service facilities probably exceeds $1.5 billion.

Industrial Property

Most industrial real estate is owner-occupied. However, many industrial firms find it profitable to sell and lease back facilities, thereby releasing capital for other and presumably more profitable investments. Manufacturing firms spent more than $30 billion per annum on new plant and equipment from 1970 to 1972. Although a substantial proportion of this investment is financed directly by firms using the property, real estate investors do acquire significant dollar volumes of new and existing industrial real estate.

The factors to be taken into account in the investment analysis of industrial property are probably more numerous than for any other class of property. They include the location of raw materials, the labor supply, market distribution facilities, utilities, transportation, available sites for employee housing, the local tax structure, the financial rating of the corporation involved, and public controls over emissions and the environment.

The specialized nature of much industrial property makes it necessary for analysts to appraise the outlook for the industry as well as the position of the particular company within the industry. This task is less difficult, of course, in the case of warehousing and other general-purpose properties.

These factors account for the high degree of professional specialization in the marketing and investment valuation of industrial real estate. The diversity in the characteristics and techniques of investment analysis for different classes of property is matched by the variety of forms and methods of ownership.

Office Buildings

The post-World War II surge in government and service employment resulted in a tremendous increase in the demand for office space in the United States. Office buildings represent a volatile and high-valued category of real estate investment.

The annual volume of construction of new office buildings varies widely, while occupancy rates are extremely sensitive to changes in business conditions.

Time horizons for office building investment often span several business cycles. The long planning period required, the growing investment in headquarters office buildings for prestige purposes, and the sensitivity to mortgage market conditions add to cyclical instability in office building construction. "Competitive" office buildings (those not built for single occupancy by a large corporation) are usually financed with high loan-value ratios, frequently in combination with ground leases. The availability of depreciation and interest tax shelters is an important motivation for individual investment in office structures. Wealthy individuals often find the tax shelter features of office building investment particularly attractive, while many large construction and materials-manufacturing firms participate in office building investment.

The cyclical nature of office building construction and the rapid obsolescence of older office buildings force aggressive office building investors to engage in a game of musical chairs. Tenants will often rush to lease space in the newest and most prestigious office building, with the result that leases are canceled in older buildings, which suffer a loss in income and value. As rents gradually decline in the older structures and costs of construction and rentals in new buildings increase, the stage is set for a day of reckoning. Triggered by a cyclical decline in business expectations, corporate and other tenants may decide to continue present occupancy or to expand into older buildings in preference to signing long-term leases in new structures or risking a corporate investment in a prestigious headquarters office.

This chain of events may lead to a rapid increase in vacancies and vanishing cash flows for new office building investors. The long-planned office buildings still in the supply pipeline add to the evident overbuilding. Consequently, an extended period often must elapse before a new long cycle in office building construction gets under way. The intervening period is often one of stark adjustment and even foreclosure for the aggressive, highly leveraged equity investor.

For these reasons, office building investment is primarily for sophisticated high-income individuals or institutional investors. The investment decision requires specialized knowledge of construction, management, operating costs, complex multilayered financing instruments, and sophisticated cash-flow projection techniques. Public issues and private syndications of office building securities have in the past too frequently represented bailouts by disappointed or cash-poor entrepreneurs.

LEGAL INSTRUMENTS USED IN REAL ESTATE INVESTMENT

The real estate investor can choose from a wide range of investment instruments. Traditionally, the real estate mortgage has been the predominant instrument, reflecting the fact that real estate typically is financed with a high ratio of debt to value. The estimated flow of funds into real estate mortgages is summarized in Table 30-1. It can be observed that more than one-half of the estimated annual flow of $32 billion of mortgage funds for 1971 was used to finance single-family houses. However, the volume of multifamily and commercial mortgage funds exceeded $12 billion.

Total mortgage credit outstanding on multifamily and commercial properties is very large, and, as of mid-1971, was estimated to equal $148.5 billion, of which $121.9 billion was held by institutions and $26.6 billion by individuals and other holders.

Mortgage investments range widely in safety and regularity of income. A first-mortgage investment with a low ratio of debt to value on a property with an assured income often is a gilt-edged investment, equivalent to a high-grade bond. On the other hand, high loan-value ratios and unstable incomes frequently result in high-risk first-mortgage investments. Although second and third trust deeds or

TABLE 30-1   Financing Multifamily, Commercial, and Farm Mortgages
(In billions of dollars)

	1963	1964	1965	1966	1967	1968	1969	1970 (est.)	1971 (proj.)
USES (FUNDS RAISED)									
Multifamily mortgages*	3.2	4.6	3.6	3.1	3.6	3.4	4.9	5.6	7.6
Commercial mortgages	5.1	3.8	4.5	5.6	4.7	6.6	5.4	4.5	5.0
Farm mortgages	1.6	2.1	2.3	2.1	2.2	2.0	2.0	1.7	2.0
Total	9.9	10.5	10.3	11.0	10.5	12.0	12.3	11.8	14.6
SOURCES (FUNDS SUPPLIED)									
Savings institutions (contractual type)									
Life insurance companies	2.7	3.4	3.8	4.0	3.4	3.2	3.1	3.4	3.7
Private noninsured pension funds	.2	.3	.4	.3	.1	—	.2	—	—
State and local government retirement funds	.4	.5	.7	.8	.5	.4	.4	.4	.4
Total	3.3	4.2	4.9	5.1	4.0	3.6	3.7	3.8	4.1
Savings institutions (deposit type)									
Savings and loan associations	2.9	2.2	1.9	.9	1.5	2.1	1.8	3.2	4.9
Mutual savings banks	1.4	1.6	1.4	1.1	1.3	1.4	1.1	.7	1.0
Total	4.3	3.8	3.4	2.0	2.8	3.5	2.9	3.9	5.9
Total, savings institutions	7.6	8.0	8.3	7.1	6.8	7.1	6.6	7.7	10.0
Commercial banks	2.2	2.2	2.5	2.3	2.2	3.2	2.3	.7	1.0
Financial corporations	—	—	—	—	—	.1	1.1	1.4	1.4
Government									
United States government	−.1	—	—	.2	.1	.3	.7	.4	.5
Federally sponsored agencies	.3	.4	.6	.7	.7	.5	.6	.3	.5
State and local general funds	.2	.2	.2	.1	.1	.2	.2	.3	.3
Total	.4	.6	.8	1.0	.8	1.0	1.4	1.0	1.3
Residual (individuals and others)	−.3	−.3	−1.3	.6	.7	.6	.9	1.0	.9
Total	9.9	10.5	10.3	11.0	10.5	12.0	12.3	11.8	14.6
MEMORANDA									
Private multifamily housing starts									
Number (in thousands of units)	590	558	509	386	448	608	656	619	765
Average cost per unit (in thousands of dollars)	8.8	9.0	8.8	9.1	9.0	9.8	11.0	11.7	12.5
Construction outlays	5.2	5.0	4.5	3.5	4.0	6.0	7.2	7.2	9.6
Commercial construction put in place	5.0	5.4	6.7	6.9	7.0	8.3	10.1	10.4	10.0

*Comprises mortgages on residential structures of five or more units.
SOURCE: Bankers Trust Company, New York, *The Investment Outlook for 1971*, Table 9.

mortgages can be very risky investments when "unseasoned," they may assume greater attraction as prior liens are reduced and the owner's equity position assures a greater degree of safety for the junior mortgage holder.

The recent surge of interest in equity-participation mortgage loans has added to the diversity in mortgage investment opportunities. Among the more widely used forms of equity participation are the following:

1. The lender, in addition to receiving interest on the mortgage loan, receives a percentage of gross income as a bonus. This type of loan is particularly popular during periods of extreme scarcity of mortgage funds.

2. In a modification of this form of equity-participation loan, the lender receives a percentage of gross income in excess of a specified dollar amount. For example, the lender will receive 10 percent of the gross income above $200,000 per annum.

3. A third form of equity participation provides that the lender receive a percentage of a defined net income. This form is often employed in connection with leasehold improvement loans when the lender owns the land that is leased to the mortgagor upon the security of leasehold improvements. It is considered more attractive to the borrower since ground lease payments and mortgage interest are both deductible as expenses for tax purposes.

4. The joint-venture form provides a wide range of possible equity participation for the lender, who may also be a development partner in the property. In return for financial backing in providing construction and permanent mortgage financing, the lender often receives as much as 50 percent of the cash flow after debt service.

Most large institutional lenders regard the mortgage with fixed interest rates as an insufficiently responsive hedge against inflation. For that reason, many such lenders insist upon mortgages with variable interest rates or some form of equity participation. These investment forms may and often do resemble participating preferred stocks and debentures, which have been used in the securities markets for many years.

Supplying mortgage money is an important method of investing in real estate. Individual investors, however, may find this approach to be quite beyond their means. In addition, it may not offer the opportunity for capital appreciation that they desire. They may prefer to invest money in the form of equity and actually own the real estate. The most highly regarded equity investments are those carrying favorable mortgage terms. In such investments the income to the property is assured through the existence of a long-term lease with a prime tenant; there is a net lease, which means that the tenant pays the property tax on the property as well as any maintenance costs; and the income from the property is high enough to pay the interest and amortization on the mortgage and still provide a return for the investor.

A sell-leaseback arrangement may provide an especially safe form of equity investment. The major chain stores have been the most frequent users of this arrangement, under which the lease payments provide a minimum return to the purchaser of the property over the life of the lease. Many of these purchase-leaseback investments have investment characteristics similar to a corporate bond when the lessee has an AAA credit rating.

The range of risks represented by equity investment in real estate is influenced by the stability of the total returns to the property and by the debt-equity relationship. A high debt ratio, a thin equity interest, and a relatively unstable outlook for income to the property characterize a high-risk equity investment. Just as with corporate bonds, a high debt ratio may be justifiable if the income flow to the real estate is relatively certain and stable. In the absence of that stability, the real estate equity investor must be prepared to assume all the residual risks of the common stockholder in a corporation with a heavy bonded indebtedness.

Legal Forms of Ownership and Disposal of Real Estate

The principal legal forms of ownership used in real estate investment are the following:
1. Individual ownership
2. Partnership
3. Limited partnership
4. Corporation (financial and nonfinancial)
5. Real estate investment trust

Determination of the form of ownership depends upon the magnitude of the financial investment, other interests and assets of the investor, management considerations, and the investor's tax position. The bulk of small real estate investment holdings, including owner-occupied homes, are held by individuals in their own name or jointly between husband and wife. Tax implications of the form of holding real estate are so complex, varying geographically from state to state and over time with changes in laws, that an investor is usually advised to seek expert legal assistance in reaching any decisions.

Partnerships

The disadvantages of the general partnership as a vehicle for holding long-term investments are generally familiar to most businessmen. Although a partnership pays no income tax, the entity is usually dissolved on the death of a partner, each individual is fully liable for the debts of the partnership, and management responsibilities are often dispersed among the partners.

The limited partnership, composed of general and limited partners, overcomes many of these shortcomings. Limited partners ordinarily do not have control over the business and have only limited liability for debts of the partnership, up to the amount of their contribution to the partnership capital. Further, the death of a limited partner does not necessarily terminate the partnership, and provisions may be made for the transfer of the interest of the deceased partner to another or to others. The general partner, often referred to as the managing partner in this form of organization, has the basic management responsibility. The death of the general partner terminates the limited partnership, since the general partner does not have limited liability for debts of the partnership. These considerations and the importance of the role of the general partner have often resulted in the organization of limited partnerships with the general partner taking the form of a corporation. In this way, a corporation having unlimited life and limited capital assets assumes direction and management of the real estate investment. Everyone's liability is limited in this form of organization, and the limited partners still possess the tax advantages of a partnership.

Income to the limited partnership is reported individually by the partners and taxed at rates consistent with their other income and tax brackets. An information tax return must be filed with federal and state authorities.

Corporations

The corporate form has many advantages over the partnership as a vehicle for holding real estate investments, but its major disadvantage lies in the area of taxation. An individual or a member of a partnership may deduct operating losses on real estate as an offset to other income. Since many real estate investments show taxable losses, particularly in the early years of a new project, this advantage of tax loss offsets against other income is an important incentive.

However, operating losses by a corporation do not flow through to the individual stockholders. More important, operating profits are subject to the corporate income tax and, in addition, are subject to individual income taxation when received as dividends by the individual. In some circumstances (when the corporate tax rates are substantially below the individual's tax rates), there may be an advantage to the corporate holding form. The corporation may retain earnings, and eventually the stockholders may be able to take their profits through capital gains on the sale of their stock ownership.

The Subchapter S corporation is an organization of the corporate form in which the stockholders are taxed as in a partnership.

The many variations and legal pitfalls in corporate ownership reemphasize the importance of expert legal counsel in deciding upon the form of ownership in real estate.

Real Estate Investment Trusts

The REIT, established by the 1954 Internal Revenue Code, Section 856, is roughly similar to a closed-end investment company with a portfolio consisting of real estate investments. The principal advantage of the REIT, as compared with the corporate form of ownership, lies in the fact that if the REIT meets specific requirements, it will pay a corporate income tax *only on retained income.* There is no corporate tax liability if the REIT distributes all its income as dividends. Investors owning REIT shares have the advantages of limited liability, marketability of their shares, and perpetual life for the entity. In addition, they enjoy the advantage of flow-through of dividend income from the trust without corporate income tax liability. However, taxable losses to the REIT do not flow through to holders of its shares, as they do in limited partnerships.

The congressional objective in establishing the REIT medium was to equalize the investment choice between ownership of corporate securities through the investment company medium and investment in real estate mortgages and equities. However, to safeguard the real estate investor against unscrupulous promotion and specialization, Congress provided that the REIT should be a "passive" investor in real estate and, to that end, established a number of qualifications and safeguards. To qualify for tax exemption at least 75 percent of the value of the REIT's assets must be represented by real estate assets, cash, and government securities. Congress also established three limitations on the sources of income to the REIT to prevent its use as a speculative medium:

1. A REIT does not qualify for tax exemption if 30 percent or more of its gross income is composed of gains from the sale of real estate held less than four years or of securities held less than six months.

2. At least 90 percent of the REIT's gross income must be from dividends, interest, rents from real property, capital gains from securities or real property, or tax abatements or refunds.

3. At least 75 percent of the REIT's gross income must come directly from realty investments.

As a result of the combined limitations 2 and 3, at least 75 percent of the gross income of a REIT must come from real estate, and an additional 15 percent must come from either real estate or investment sources. A REIT is treated by the Internal Revenue Service as a corporation and is subject to corporate income tax rates unless it distributes 90 percent or more of its ordinary income. If all income is distributed, the REIT pays no federal income tax. It is required, however, to pay a corporate tax on retained income. The REIT pays a 25 percent tax on undistributed long-term capital gains. Dividends to shareholders designated as capital gains by the REIT are taxed at capital gains rates for the shareholders. Any distributions by a REIT other than from ordinary income or capital gains are treated by the IRS as a return of capital and reduce the original basis cost of the shares.

In addition to these federal requirements, a REIT must comply with the laws and qualifications specified by its state of incorporation and by each state in which shares are sold. The state of California issued specific regulations for REITs in 1962. The Midwest Securities Commissioners Association adopted a policy statement on real estate investment trusts that is generally followed by its member states and has also been adopted by the American Stock Exchange in considering applications for listing. This statement of policy includes limitations on the number of affiliated persons who can serve as trustees; restrictions upon dealing on their own account by trustees, officers, directors, and advisers; and limitations on management fees, expenses, leverage, and certain classes of investments.

REITs must also comply with regulations of the Securities and Exchange

Commission (SEC) with respect to registration, issuance of shares, and reports to stockholders. The SEC has adopted a special S-11 form for filings of real estate companies, including REITs, that contains special disclosure provisions relating to cash flow and other reporting and accounting procedures. These furnish important information for prospective investors.

TAX ASPECTS OF REAL ESTATE INVESTMENTS

The significant tax advantages offered by real estate have contributed to the growing public interest in real estate investments. The opportunities for tax shelters in real estate investments arise from several sources:

1. Investors can use accelerated depreciation on real property improvements and thus reduce taxable income.

2. Interest on debt is deductible as an expense before calculating taxable income.

3. Profits on the sale of real estate investments held for more than six months are taxable at capital gains rates.

4. The installment method may be used by the taxpayer, provided payments in the year of sale do not exceed 30 percent of the selling price. The opportunity to elect the installment sale method gives the taxpayer an opportunity to spread capital gains tax liability over a period of years.

5. Under some circumstances, an investor may effect a nontaxable exchange of a real estate investment for "like property" and postpone payment of the capital gains tax until the new property is sold. In such a case, the new property is considered substantially to be a continuation of the original investment and assumes the same basic cost.

The Tax Reform Act of 1969 effected changes in permitted depreciation methods, capital gains and losses, limitations on interest deduction, and the minimum tax. Although the changes are much too detailed for recapitulation here, the major changes can be summarized as follows:

1. New depreciable real property (other than new residential rental property) is no longer eligible for the double-declining-balance and the sum-of-the-years'-digits methods of accelerated depreciation.

2. New real property (other than residential) is eligible for the 150 percent declining-balance method of depreciation or for straight-line depreciation.

3. New residential real property is still eligible for 200 percent declining-balance depreciation. Used residential real property acquired after July 24, 1969, is eligible for 125 percent declining-balance depreciation if the remaining life of the property is twenty years or more. If the remaining life is less than twenty years, only straight-line depreciation may be used.

4. All other used real property acquired after July 24, 1969, is eligible only for the straight-line method of depreciation.

5. No changes were made in existing rules for depreciation of tangible personal property such as furniture. Thus, all accelerated methods are available for new furniture, and the 150 percent declining-balance method is available for used furniture.

6. The cost of rehabilitating low-income rental housing may be amortized over a sixty-month period, using no salvage value.

The 1969 Tax Reform Act also provided for 100 percent recapture of the excess of accelerated over straight-line depreciation if the property is sold within 8⅓ years and for declining percentages thereafter. After 16⅔ years, there is no recapture of excess depreciation on residential rental housing. The taxpayer was permitted to change from accelerated to straight-line depreciation without permission at any time after July 24, 1969.

Although the six-month holding period for long-term capital gains remained unchanged and the 25 percent rate on capital gains up to a maximum of $50,000 was retained for noncorporate taxpayers, the maximum long-term capital gains tax rates were increased for other noncorporate investors in three steps as shown below:

Year	Noncorporate Rate of Tax (Percent)
1970	29½
1971	32½
1972	35

Corporate capital gains rates were increased to 28 percent in 1970 and to 30 percent in 1971.

The 1969 act also limited the deductions for interest attributable to investment indebtedness. Beginning in 1972, taxpayers were allowed to deduct interest incurred for investment purposes only to the extent of the *sum* of the following:

1. The amount of $25,000 ($12,500 each in the case of a married individual filing separately)

2. Net investment income

3. The amount by which net long-term capital gains exceed net short-term capital losses for the taxable year

4. Half of the amount by which investment interest exceeds the sum of 1, 2, and 3

The effect of these limitations is to disallow a portion of interest expense for certain high-income taxpayers and to increase their federal income tax liabilities. However, disallowed interest can generally be carried over to succeeding taxable years, subject to limitations.

Another significant change in the Tax Reform Act of 1969 was the imposition of a minimum tax (in addition to all other income tax) on all taxpayers that employed various tax preferences after 1969. To force individuals and corporations benefiting from interest deductions, capital gains tax shelter, accelerated depreciation, depletion, and other preferences to pay a greater share of the tax burden, Congress imposed a 10 percent tax on certain tax preference items in excess of reported investment income.

Although the impact of this regulation varies widely with the circumstances of the individual investor and the details of tax computations are more complex than indicated above, the net effect of the tax preference limitations in the act are to reduce the potential tax shelter in real estate and in other investments as well for the high-income taxpayer. The magnitude of this reduction will be apparent from examination of Figs. 30-3 and 30-4.

The implications of the Tax Reform Act of 1969 for the real estate investor are highly important. They can be summarized as follows:

1. The advantages of the use of accelerated depreciation were substantially reduced for nonresidential property.

2. Investor interest would probably be attracted to residential properties because of the retention of accelerated depreciation for new residential construction.

3. The objectives of Congress were clearly to attract investor interest to the low-income housing field. However, unfavorable cost and income factors for rehabilitated and new low-income housing negated these benefits.

4. The excess recapture rules in the act and increased capital gains tax rates further encouraged high-income investors to use tax-free exchanges and installment sales methods to postpone tax liabilities.

5. The investment interest and tax preference limitations reduced the ability

of wealthy individuals to secure tax shelters in real estate and other investments. These provisions were partially offset in 1972 by the reduction in the maximum tax rate for individual taxpayers from 70 to 50 percent on earned income. These and other changes in the act had a limited impact on middle-income investors.

The Revenue Act of 1971 made only a few changes in the Tax Reform Act of 1969, primarily to clarify certain technical features of the 1969 act. The 1971 act, however, restored the full 7 percent investment credit with respect to depreciable personal property acquired after August 15, 1971, limiting eligible property to that having a useful life of three years or longer and allowing full credit only for property having a useful life of seven years.

The 1971 act also made significant technical amendments retroactive to 1970, further limiting the deductibility of "investment interest in connection with a property which is not leased." In 1971 the IRS also issued rulings that required a minimum percentage interest of the corporate general partner in a limited partnership syndicate if the syndicate was to be taxed as a partnership.

The significance to real estate investors of the foregoing brief review of recent tax legislation goes beyond the provisions of the laws. Further closing of so-called tax loopholes has been widely discussed in connection with tax reform legislation. Although it is difficult to anticipate the provisions of such legislation, most observers expect further limitations upon depreciation, interest, capital gains, and other forms of tax shelter available to real estate investors.

LEVERAGE IN REAL ESTATE INVESTMENT

Real estate investment has been described as the "art of using someone else's money to make money for oneself." There are many ways of achieving this aim. The principal financial instruments and techniques available for use by the equity investor are the following:

1. Mortgages or deeds of trust
2. Equity participations
3. Bonds and debentures
4. Subordination agreements
5. Ground leases
6. Property exchanges and installment sales
7. Syndications
8. Land contracts

Real estate mortgages and equity-participation agreements have been described above. The possible use of mortgage debt in combination with ground leases, subordination agreements, and other financial devices represents both the opportunity and the Achilles' heel of real estate investment.

As illustrated in Chapter 50, "Investing in Real Estate," the capitalized investment value of a project that cost $3 million to complete might equal $4 million. Under these circumstances, the developer-investor who receives a 75 percent loan commitment based upon the $4 million appraised value may be able to build without any outside equity capital or very much of his own working capital. Upon completion of the project, the bank making the construction loan is taken out by the "permanent" mortgage lender. The developer-investor is then able to pocket the net cash flow from the project in excess of required mortgage payments and federal taxes. The use of a ground lease permits the developer-investor to finance the land through a lease obligation and to take the lease payments as well as the depreciation on the total investment in improvements as expense items for tax purposes.

The sale of bonds or debentures to the public often offers another channel for the developer to incur debt to finance an investment. Title IV of the Housing Act of 1968, the New Communities Act, provides for a federal government guaranty of debentures issued by private developers investing in new towns. Special subsidies in the form of a write-down in land acquisition costs and absorption of the net project cost in urban redevelopment projects represent an additional potential subsidy for real estate development and investment in central cities.

The developer-investor in real estate can also take advantage of subordination agreements in land assembly for large investment projects. Under such agreements the landowner agrees to subordinate his or her interest to debt financing by the equity holder or purchaser of the land, subject to the equity investor's agreement to repay mortgage debt as the property is sold. This arrangement in effect provides the developer-investor with unencumbered land on consignment and reduces required capital investment.

For example, a developer-investor may desire to build twenty one-family homes on certain plots. The owner of these plots is willing to sell them at a price of $6,000 per plot (which may be above the going market price). To receive the desired price for the land, the owner may be willing to enter into a subordination agreement, under which the land is sold to the developer-investor. However, the owner is not paid for each plot until it is sold. Furthermore, if the developer borrows $20,000 from the bank to build a house on a plot, a claim of the landowner is subordinated to the claim of the bank. The developer has been able to borrow $20,000 from the bank because he or she already has the land valued at $6,000 and will build a house that can be sold for $34,000. The land and the money to build the house are obtained without any investment on the developer's part. Subsequently, when the house is sold for $34,000, the developer can repay $20,000 to the bank, pay $6,000 for the land, and have a profit of $8,000.

The syndication of investment properties may also increase potential leverage by attracting outside capital in the form of preferred stock, leaving management and control in the hands of the promoter-developer. The promoter is often able to exact a share in the equity for services in packaging and merchandising the deal. This, of course, reduces the potential returns for the cash investor.

For example, a promoter-developer may need $1 million to purchase and improve a particular piece of property. Finding that it is possible to get a mortgage of $800,000 if $200,000 in equity can be obtained, the developer forms a syndicate and sells 10 percent shares in it for $25,000. After selling eight shares to raise the $200,000, the developer retains 20 percent ownership in the syndicate as a fee for organizing the deal.

The sale of property by a developer-investor on "land contracts" or "real estate contracts" makes it possible for the seller to retain title to property and yet to continue as the owner of record during the period in which the buyer is making installment payments. Although the property may not be sold, the vendor can often have the advantage of using the recorded ownership interest as a basis for securing additional loan funds.

Property exchanges and installment sales are devices for postponing capital gains tax liabilities and can be regarded as interest-free loans by the federal government to the taxpayer. They offer a potential for pyramiding equities and minimizing cash outlays for taxes.

The vulnerability of these many devices for achieving a high degree of leverage in real estate investment derives from the danger that the income from the property will not be sufficient to permit payment of the interest charges on debt in addition to operating expenses, ground rent, and preferred dividends. Figure 30-2 illustrates the unhappy position in which the highly leveraged equity investor may be placed. Obviously, a reduction of only 2 percent in the gross rental income of $500,000 in this example or a similar increase in operating expenses and taxes would eliminate the equity return of $10,000 and place the investor's capital investment in serious jeopardy.

Wide choices of investment strategy are evident from this example. The rewards of excessively high leverage are balanced by the high degree of risk assumed. High-grade real estate investment properties can be just as speculative as volatile growth stocks if they are purchased on a thin margin of equity.

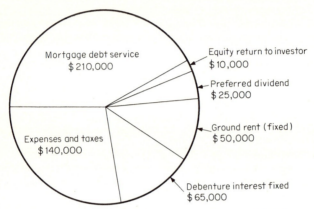

Fig. 30-2   Leverage unlimited. Gross rental income, $500,000.

YIELDS ON REAL ESTATE INVESTMENT

The yield on real estate investments is represented in a variety of ways to suit the needs and concerns of brokers, lenders, and equity investors of differing degrees of sophistication. The most widely used (although inaccurate) techniques express yield as a function only of the first or current year's income.

Real estate brokers often represent the yield on properties as

$$\text{Broker's yield} = \frac{\text{first year's net income before interest and depreciation}}{\text{purchase price}} \quad (1)$$

This approach assumes two things: (1) The property does not decrease in value, and depreciation therefore should not be considered. (2) The question of how the money is raised should be separated from the attractiveness of the property itself. The investment is deemed to be the purchase price of the property and not merely the equity invested, and the formula therefore does not consider the interest expense on the money that must be borrowed to buy the property.

In other circumstances, recognizing the importance of cash expendable income after mortgage service, the yield on real estate is represented as follows:

$$\text{Yield on equity after debt service} = \frac{\text{first year's cash spendable income after debt service}}{\text{cash down payment}} \quad (2)$$

This approach is concerned with the cash that investors receive from the investment each year as compared with the initial cash outlay. It is a somewhat simplistic but popular method of quickly evaluating potential real estate investments.

Recognition is often given to the so-called equity buildup resulting from loan payments on principal by adding back principal payments in the numerator of Equation 2, as follows:

$$\text{Yield on equity after mortgage interest} = \frac{\text{first year's cash spendable income} + \text{principal payments}}{\text{cash down payment}} \quad (3)$$

Most mortgages provide that the mortgagee must make constant annual payments to pay current interest and also pay off the principal over a stated number of years. For example, an investor who purchases property for $110,000 with $10,000 equity and a $100,000 mortgage with an interest rate of 8 percent may repay the mortgage with annual payments of $10,000. In the first year, $8,000 is the interest payment and $2,000 is a repayment of principal. In the second year, the interest is $7,840, and the principal repayment is $2,160. At the end of the mortgage, all the principal has been repaid, and the investor has clear title to the property without any liabilities. If the property could be sold for $130,000, the investor would receive net cash of $130,000 even though his original equity was only $10,000 and the increase in the property value was $20,000. Every time that a payment that decreased the principal of the mortgage was made, the investor's equity in the property increased. Therefore, in Equation 3 the profit is considered to be the cash inflow plus any payments that increase the investor's equity or decrease the outstanding principal on the mortgage.

In addition to giving recognition to the equity buildup, the investor may also want to consider the impact that the real estate transaction will have on his or her personal tax status. This can be accomplished by including the tax effect of owning the real estate in the numerator of Equation 3, as follows:

$$\text{Yield on equity after mortgage interest including tax savings} = \frac{\text{first-year cash spendable income} + \text{principal payments} + \text{tax effect}}{\text{cash down payment}} \quad (4)$$

The investor is allowed to deduct both the interest payments on the mortgage and the depreciation of the property in computing the income on the property for tax purposes. In the early years of the mortgage, most of the mortgage payments are for interest. Therefore, the investor may be able to deduct as much as 80 percent or more of the mortgage payments as well as the depreciation for tax purposes. It often occurs that the investor will have a positive cash flow on the property, although a loss will be shown for tax purposes. If the owner of the property is an individual or a partnership, the loss can flow through to reduce the personal income tax of the owner or partners. If the owner is in the 40 percent tax bracket and shows a tax loss of $5,000, $2,000 will be saved in taxes. Of course, in the later years of the mortgage, when most of the payment is for principal and not for interest, the tax advantage will be significantly reduced. The following example can be used to demonstrate different results that may be produced by each of the four equations above.

An investor is going to purchase a piece of property for $120,000 with a $20,000 cash outlay and an 8 percent twenty-year mortgage, with annual payments of $10,200. The property will be depreciated on a straight-line basis with a twenty-year life and no salvage value. The annual income from the building will be $17,200, and other cash expenses will be $5,000. The investor has a personal tax rate of 50 percent:

First Year

	Cash flow	Taxable income
Gross income	$17,200	$17,200
Cash expenses	5,000	5,000
Mortgage		
Interest	8,000	8,000
Principal	2,200	
Depreciation ($120,000 ÷ 20)		
Net cash flow	$ 2,000	
Net taxable income		($ 1,800)

$$(1) \text{ Broker's yield} \quad = \quad \frac{\$17,200 - 5,000}{\$120,000} \quad = 10.17\%$$

$$(2) \text{ Yield on equity} \atop \text{after debt vservice} \quad = \quad \frac{\$17,200 - 5,000 - 10,200}{\$20,000} \quad = 10.0\%$$

$$(3) \text{ Yield on equity after} \atop \text{mortgage interest} \quad = \quad \frac{\$17,200 - 5,000 - 8,000}{\$20,000} \quad = 21.0\%$$

$$(4) \text{ Yield on equity after} \atop \text{mortgage interest} \atop \text{including} \atop \text{tax savings} \quad = \quad \frac{\$17,200 - 5,000 - 8,000 + 900*}{\$20,000} \quad = 25.5\%$$

*50 percent tax savings on $1,800 taxable loss equals $900.

Many investors who are concerned primarily with the cash-flow aspects of a real estate investment will actually use a fifth approach. They calculate the cash return on their investment, as shown in Equation 2, and then determine what tax savings they will receive and how much cash they will realize upon the sale of the property after considering possible appreciation of the property plus the equity that has been built up and the capital gains tax involved. The possible return on this or any investment must then be weighed against the risks involved. A rental property with an AAA tenant with a long-term lease has a minimum amount of risk, whereas property that must be rented by the buyer would entail considerably more risk and warrant a higher return.

All the foregoing techniques represent shortcut approximations to the true cash yield to an investor, since they relate to one year's income only. A more sophisticated model for determining investment yield in real estate is presented in the author's book *Real Estate Investment Analysis and Taxation*.[1] Although the model reproduced below appears difficult to comprehend, the formulation is based upon present-value theories with wide application in security analysis and going-concern evaluations. The present-value formula determines the rate of discount that will equate all future net cash inflows to the original cash outlay. This rate is the true rate of return that investors will earn on their investments. The problem with this approach is the necessity to make future assumptions that are quite uncertain, such as the ultimate sales price for the property.

$$E = \sum_{t=1}^{n} \frac{R_t - I_t - A_t - T_t}{(1+r)^t} + \frac{P_n - GT - UM}{(1+r)^n} \tag{5}$$

where R_t = annual net income in period t
$\qquad I_t$ = interest paid on mortgage in period t

[1]McGraw-Hill Book Company, New York, 1969.

A_t = mortgage amortization in period t
T_t = income tax allowance in period t
P_n = sales price in period $t = n$
GT = capital gains tax
UM = unpaid mortgage
r = compound annual rate of return or yield
E = amount of original cash equity

Fortunately, this model has been adapted for use on the high-speed computer, making it possible to solve the equation for the rate of return on any investment in a few seconds. Furthermore, the more sophisticated programs provide a complete backup of loan amortization, depreciation, and cash-flow statements by years. As illustrated below, the model and the computer program can also be used to estimate investment values, given the investor's target equity yields. Rapid computational facility through use of computers makes it possible to analyze the rates of return on real estate investments, varying the assumptions concerning income, expense ratios, financing terms, depreciation options, holding periods, target yields, and the tax status of investors.

Figures 30-3 and 30-4, prepared by a leading West Coast realty firm, illustrate the variations in returns on land and income property investment under different sets of assumptions concerning tax status, holding periods, financing terms, and residual selling prices. It is apparent that the aftertax discounted cash-flow yields on land investment, shown in Fig. 30-3, generally increase as the debt leverage is increased. On an all-cash basis, shown as block 1, an investor in a 30 percent tax bracket would require an annual (simple, not compounded) appreciation rate over a five-year holding period of 25 percent per year to realize an aftertax yield of 12.5 percent. This assumes that annual expenses equal 2 percent of the year-end appreciated value. If the annual rate of appreciation in value is only 10 percent of the original purchase price, it can be seen in Fig. 30-3 that the investor in a 30 percent tax bracket would have a compound annual aftertax rate of return of only 5.12 percent for a five-year holding period on an all-cash basis.

An investment in land on an all-cash basis for a five-year holding period appears relatively unattractive unless a simple annual appreciation rate of 20 percent or more could be expected. The aftertax rate of return to the investor rises rapidly, however, when the assumed financial leverage is increased and high rates of appreciation are assumed to occur. There is no advantage, of course, in financial leverage unless a sufficiently high rate of appreciation in selling price offsets the interest costs associated with borrowing. The advantages of leverage increase as the tax bracket of the investor is assumed to rise from 30 to 70 percent. Explanation for this lies in the greater savings to the investor in a high tax bracket through deduction of interest payments.

The effect of the Tax Reform Act of 1969 upon the aftertax yields of investors in the 70 percent tax bracket can be seen by comparing the solid black lines in Figs. 30-3 and 30-4 with the open bars that indicate pre-1969 act yields. Although the effect of the Tax Reform Act was to reduce yields somewhat for the individual in a high tax bracket, the impact was not large when measured as a percentage decline in yields. Furthermore, it is apparent that the hypothetical yields shown for a five-year holding period would still be highly attractive to investors in all tax brackets.

The large percentage reduction (50 percent or more) in aftertax yields for a ten-year assumed holding period is evident for all tax brackets and is particularly notable for the high leverage assumed in panels in Fig. 30-3 identified as II, III, IV, and V. One explanation is connected with the method of calculating annual appreciation as a percentage (not compounded) of original cost. A constant 10 percent rate of appreciation based upon the assumed original land cost of $100,-

ANNUAL AFTER-TAX DISCOUNTED YIELD ON LAND INVESTMENT

EXHIBIT I ALL CASH.

EXHIBIT II 25% DOWN - 7.5% LOAN PAYABLE ANNUALLY, FULLY AMORTIZED IN 15 YEARS.

EXHIBIT III 15% DOWN - INT. ONLY FIRST 3 YEARS, 7.5% LOAN PAYABLE ANNUALLY, FULLY AMORTIZED OVER NEXT 15 YEARS.

EXHIBIT IV 5% DOWN - INT. ONLY FIRST 5 YEARS, 7.5% LOAN PAYABLE ANNUALLY, FULLY AMORTIZED OVER NEXT 15 YEARS.

EXHIBIT V 23 MONTHS PPI DOWN ($14,375): NO PYMT. FIRST YEAR, INT. ONLY AT 7.5% FOR NEXT 9 YEARS, INT. & EQUAL PRIN. NEXT 5 YEARS.

THE YIELDS ON THE OPEN BARS ARE BASED ON TAX LAWS EXISTING PRIOR TO 1969

30-20

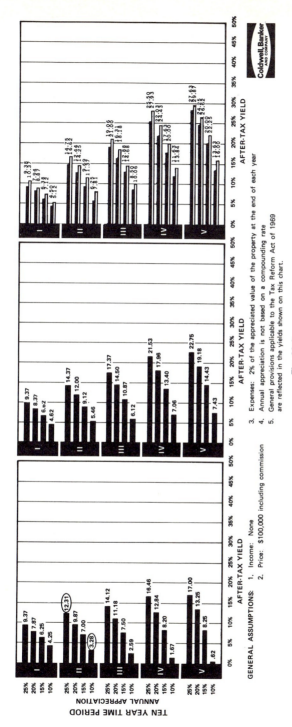

Fig. 30-3.

3. Expenses: 2% of the appreciated value of the property at the end of each year
4. Annual appreciation is not based on a compounding rate
5. General provisions applicable to the Tax Reform Act of 1969 are reflected in the yields shown on this chart.

GENERAL ASSUMPTIONS: 1. Income: None
2. Price: $100,000 including commission

ANNUAL AFTER-TAX DISCOUNTED YIELD ON HYPOTHETICAL INCOME PROPERTY INVESTMENT

EXHIBIT I
ALL CASH

EXHIBIT II
25% DOWN — 75% FIRST T.D., 9.5% INT. FULLY AMORTIZED IN 25 YEARS

EXHIBIT III
15% DOWN - 60% FIRST T.D., 9.5% INT. FULLY AMORTIZED IN 25 YEARS, 25% SECOND T.D., 10% INT. PAYABLE 1% PER MO. ALL DUE IN 10 YEARS.

EXHIBIT IV
10% DOWN - 75% FIRST T.D., 9.5% INT. FULLY AMORTIZED IN 25 YEARS, 15% SECOND T.D., 10% PAYABLE INT. ONLY. ALL DUE IN 5 YEARS.

EXHIBIT V
10% DOWN - 75% FIRST T.D., 9.5% INT. FULLY AMORTIZED IN 25 YEARS, 15% SECOND T.D., 10% INT. PAYABLE 1% PER MO. ALL DUE IN 5 YEARS.

THE YIELDS ON THE OPEN BARS ARE BASED ON TAX LAWS EXISTING PRIOR TO 1969

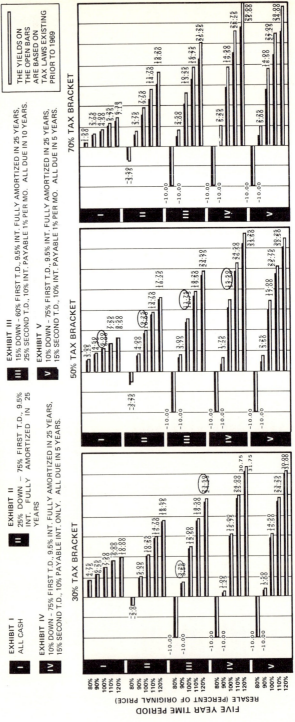

30-22

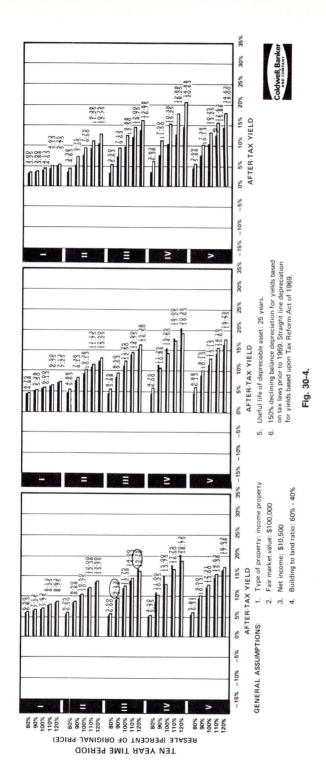

Fig. 30-4.

GENERAL ASSUMPTIONS:
1. Type of property: income property
2. Fair market value: $100,000
3. Net income: $10,500
4. Building to land ratio: 60% – 40%

5. Useful life of depreciable asset: 25 years.
6. 150% declining balance depreciation for yields based on tax laws prior to 1969. Straight line depreciation for yields based upon Tax Reform Act of 1969.

000 would represent $10,000 per annum.Under this assumption, the land would have an appreciated value of $150,000 at the end of five years and of $200,000 at the end of ten years. This represents a *compound annual rate* of increase of 8.5 percent per year for the five-year period but only 7 percent per year for the decade. The compound annual rate of increase for the last five years of the ten-year holding period is only approximately 5.75 percent. A constant absolute-dollar increase in value is equivalent to a declining percentage rate of increase. Furthermore, the present value of the constant increments of $10,000 is reduced as the holding period is increased. Expenses are assumed to be 2 percent of the *appreciated* value of the land. The investor is paying interest at the rate of 7.5 percent per annum plus 2 percent expenses, to carry an investment that is increasing only at a rate of 5.75 percent. The net result of a declining rate of increase in land value, rising expenses, and the longer waiting period involved is to reduce the aftertax rate of return to land investors in all tax brackets by approximately 50 percent when the property is held for ten years.

The conclusions for the prospective land investor can be substantiated by reexamination of Fig. 30-1. Land values must rise at rates above 10 percent per annum to provide an attractive return to an all-cash investor or to an investor who must pay interest costs of 7.5 percent plus taxes and other expenses to carry the investment. The losses in land investment are of course increased substantially when land values remain constant or even decline over long periods of time.

Figure 30-4 shows the variation in hypothetical aftertax yields on an income property assumed to cost $100,000 with a constant net income of $10,500. Again it can be observed that this property would represent a relatively unattractive investment on an all-cash basis for investors in all tax brackets. This emphasizes the fact that the principal advantage of real estate investment, in comparison with stocks, is derived from the tax shelter associated with leverage. It can be seen, however, that leverage works both ways, and, under the assumption of a decline in selling price over the five-year holding period, investors in all tax brackets would have experienced negative returns on their investment.

However, as the assumptions concerning sale price at the end of the five-year holding period are changed to reflect *appreciation in value,* the indicated rates of return to investors rise sharply. Income property is seen as relatively more attractive to the investor in high tax brackets in Fig. 30-4, even after allowing for the effect of the Tax Reform Act of 1969. Aftertax rates of return for a five-year holding period under the high-leverage financing of Plans IV and V are approximately 30 percent for investors in all tax brackets shown. It should be emphasized that the example illustrated makes no allowance for deduction of taxable losses against other taxable income. This option represents a strong inducement to many high-income taxpayers to purchase real estate investment property showing a negative taxable income.

The sharp reduction in yields for a ten-year assumed holding period, shown in Fig. 30-4, is due to the assumptions concerning resale prices and to the depreciation method assumed. A resale price of 120 percent of the original cost of $100,000 represents a 20 percent increment in value over a five-year holding period. The same total increase in selling price over an assumed ten-year holding period obviously represents no increase in value for the last five years in comparison with the first five years. A 20 percent increase in value over five years represents a compound annual rate of increase of 3.75 percent. The same increase in value over a ten-year period would represent a compound annual rate of increase of considerably less than half this amount.

The assumed use of straight-line depreciation in Fig. 30-4 implies that the property is nonresidential. This assumption eliminates the need for computing depreciation recapture. The returns for both five- and ten-year holding periods would be higher if the property were assumed to be eligible for 200 percent or 150 percent declining-balance depreciation.

The advantages of leverage depend upon the relationship between the rate of return on the investment on an all-cash basis and the interest costs assumed by the investor. The combination of low rates of return, high interest costs, and declining resale prices results in relatively low aftertax returns for investors in all tax brackets. Just as the investor in stocks must rely heavily upon market appreciation to realize high yields, so must the real estate investor look to future capital gains. The advantages to the real estate investor of a short-term holding period increases with the use of accelerated depreciation methods, since these permit higher retention of cash flows in the early years. As the holding period increases beyond eight years, the advantages of both depreciation and interest tax shelter tend to diminish rapidly, while income tax liabilities increase. This accounts for a typical holding period of less than ten years in most highly leveraged real estate investments.

DETERMINATION OF INVESTMENT VALUE

It has often been said that the appraised value of any parcel of real estate will vary with the purpose of the appraisal, the method of valuation employed, and the personality of the appraiser. The appraiser most frequently endeavors to ascertain what is called the "fair market value" of real estate. This represents a complex exercise in the application of skill and judgment to a wide variety of cost, market, and income data.

The determination of "investment value" represents a special case in valuation. Investors often know the cost or market price of a property and seek to determine what the property is worth to *them* as an investment. It should not be surprising, in view of the varying indicated rates of return on real estate illustrated in Figs. 30-3 and 30-4 and the different rates of return if alternative formulas are used, to find that the same property may have a different investment value for different individuals, depending upon their expectations, target yields, holding periods, and tax status.

Table 30-2, calculated by the author with the aid of the Real III computer program, shows the estimated values of a proposed shopping center for different investors on the basis of alternative target yields, holding periods, and expectations concerning future income, expenses, and resale prices. It can be seen that different individuals and institutions might have widely differing views concerning the investment value of this proposed shopping center.

The individual assumed to be in a 50 percent tax bracket and the life insurance company in a 30 percent bracket might be prepared to pay approximately $3 million for the proposed center if they both accept the assumption A forecasts and desire to hold the property for twenty years with an expected return of 10 percent. However, it can be seen that a modification of these stipulations to assumption B would imply that they would each be prepared to offer approximately $2 million for the property.

The market for investment real estate includes a wide variety of individuals and institutions with varying assumptions about the future and with differing yield objectives. It can be seen from Table 30-2 that an individual investor with a target yield of 15 percent on his or her equity investment would be justified in offering $2,198,220 for the proposed shopping center if he or she accepted assumption A, while under the less optimistic assumption B the investor might offer only $1,688,-358 for the property.

Figure 30-5 illustrates the sensitivity of cash-flow returns to changes in estimated future gross income, operating expenses, and sale prices. The rise in federal tax liabilities as the tax shelter from interest and depreciation declines gradually is also apparent under assumption A. The negative cash flows under assumption B after the fourteenth year of holding reflect the decline in net income and the assumed residual sale prices. This emphasizes once again that the failure of future growth in income to meet expectations has the same adverse effect upon real estate values and yields as in investment in growth stocks. Unfortunately, the problems of income forecasting are no easier for the average new real estate development

TABLE 30-2   Estimated Investment Values of a Proposed Shopping Center for Different Investors on the Basis of Alternative Target Yields and Holding Periods

Type of investor	Holding period (years)	Assumed target yields (percent)	Estimated investment value	
			Assumption A*	Assumption B†
Individual (50 percent	10	15	$2,198,220	$1,688,358
tax bracket)	10	12	2,367,446	1,788,546
	10	10	2,483,708	1,855,933
	20	15	2,321,392	1,664,011
	20	12	2,650,755	1,806,535
	20	10	2,910,538	1,913,095
Life insurance	10	15	2,305,750	1,796,775
company (30 percent	10	12	2,454,339	1,880,481
tax bracket)	10	10	2,556,101	1,936,206
	20	15	2,482,954	1,795,829
	20	12	2,779,290	1,914,806
	20	10	3,010,658	2,002,118

*Assumption A: Cost, $2 million; operating income for first year, $325,000, increasing 3 percent annually starting year 1; 5 percent vacancies; operating expenses, $75,000, increasing 3 percent annually. Building-land ratio, 80/20. Residual sale price, 6 times gross income after fourth year. Financing, 75 percent; 9 percent first mortgage, twenty-five years.

†Assumption B: Assumption change to zero growth in gross operating income and 5 percent increase in operating expenses. Residual sale price, 5 times gross income after fourth year.

project than for the "hot" issue in Wall Street. This accounts for the large yield spread between safe real estate investments secured by long-term leases to established tenants, with conservative loan-value ratios and the high pro-forma yields on new real estate development projects, with thin equities and uncertain future income and expense trends.

Miles Colean, an eminent authority on real estate, said many years ago:

> The facts are that, while a well-located, well-designed, well-built, and well-seasoned property may take on the aspect of a secure long-term investment, the creation of such a property is a venture of the most speculative sort, and even the operation of an established property is not without its hazards. The possibility of disastrous miscalculation is present at every turn. The site may prove less attractive than contemplated, or it may lose its appeal after some years of operation. The design may turn out to lack appeal or to become too soon obsolete. Building cost may have been underestimated and operating expense underestimated. The income expectancy may have been overestimated or prove insufficient to make up for the underestimate of expense. And if anything about the outlook is certain, it is that there are likely to be wide variations in income during the long period of the property's economic usefulness.

Thus, a real estate investment is appraised by an investor in the same manner as any other high-risk venture. The potential reward must overbalance the risk, and the opportunity for quick recapture of capital must be present. Otherwise, the investor will not consider the investment.

Many individual investors and some institutions lack the professional know-how and economic sophistication to employ the type of computer-assisted cash-flow analysis underlying the estimates in Table 30-2 and Figs. 30-3, 30-4, and 30-5. It is not surprising, therefore, that many investors rely upon shortcut analytical techniques and market sales of comparable properties to determine investment values.

The use of gross income multipliers is one of the most widely used techniques to determine the value of investment property. The gross multiplier represents the sale price for the subject or similar properties divided by the estimated or actual

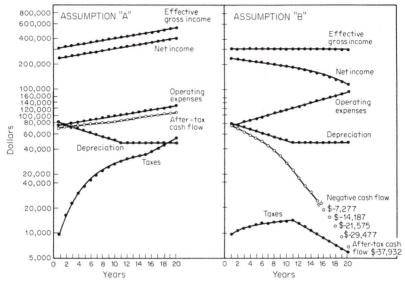

Fig. 30-5 Cash-flow analysis for proposed shopping center. See Table 30-2 for assumptions A and B.

gross income for the current year. The assumption in using this method is that the ratio of gross to net income and financing terms will be similar for similar classes of property and, therefore, that the before-tax cash flow to investors will be approximately the same in relation to the required equity investment.

The gross-multiplier technique is a variation of the comparable sales technique. Its advantage lies in the fact that the use of the multiplier (or its reciprocal, the ratio of gross income to sale price) permits the comparison of properties with varying levels of gross income and selling price.

Professor William M. Shenkel reported that the average selling price of apartment properties in Fort Lauderdale, Florida, in 1968 could be predicted with a relatively high degree of reliability by using a simple regression equation relating selling prices to gross income.[2] The equation of relationship revealed a simple coefficient of correlation between gross income and selling price of .97, indicating that 94 percent of the variation in selling prices of the sample properties was explained by differences in gross income. The equation resulting from Shenkel's analysis was:

$$\text{Value} = \$6,047 + 6.22 \times \text{gross income}$$

Table 30-3, reproduced from this study, shows an average difference of only 5.4

[2]"Cash Flow and Multiple Regression Techniques," *Journal of Property Management,* November–December 1969, pp. 264–276.

TABLE 30-3   A Comparison of Sales Prices and Computed Values of Forty-eight Apartment Buildings

Sale number	1968 sale price	Computed value	Difference between sale price and value	Percentage of sale price
1	$ 120,000	$ 110,930	−$ 9,070	7.6
2	125,000	121,612	−3,388	2.7
3	128,000	120,477	−7,523	5.9
4	135,000	125,304	−9,696	7.2
5	200,500	187,856	−12,644	6.3
6	240,000	217,332	−22,668	8.6
7	240,000	232,488	−7,512	3.1
8	245,000	236,650	−8,350	3.4
9	260,000	294,871	34,871	13.4
10	270,000	282,442	12,442	4.6
11	325,000	334,231	9,231	2.8
12	389,500	391,257	1,757	4.5
13	475,000	482,304	7,304	1.5
14	990,000	994,367	4,367	4.4
15	1,300,000	1,292,164	−7,836	.6
16	1,362,600	1,363,132	532	. . .*
17	180,000	177,578	−2,422	1.3
18	185,000	184,339	−661	.4
19	190,000	192,507	2,507	1.3
20	159,900	171,725	11,825	7.4
21	305,000	316,598	11,598	3.8
22	305,000	316,598	11,598	3.8
23	160,000	185,286	25,286	15.8
24	114,000	116,016	2,016	1.8
25	220,000	232,787	12,787	5.8
26	125,000	134,049	9,049	7.2
27	145,000	154,348	9,348	6.4
28	225,000	228,919	3,919	1.7
29	179,000	179,291	291	.2
30	204,000	196,821	−7,179	.4
31	183,500	182,539	−961	.5
32	110,000	88,864	−21,136	19.2
33	81,000	74,276	−6,724	.8
34	129,400	119,314	10,086	7.8
35	178,000	183,000	5,000	2.8
36	155,000	168,561	13,561	8.7
37	65,000	59,880	5,120	7.8
38	205,000	209,606	4,606	2.2
39	162,000	167,474	5,474	3.4
40	225,000	242,853	17,853	7.9
41	226,800	249,659	22,859	10.1
42	202,500	211,754	9,254	4.6
43	130,000	131,607	1,607	12.3
44	160,000	185,323	25,323	15.8

Sale number	1968 sale price	Computed value	Difference between sale price and value	Percentage of sale price
45	275,000	268,811	6,189	2.3
46	145,000	144,675	−325	.2
47	215,000	234,578	19,578	9.1
48	190,000	175,804	−14,196	7.4
Average				5.4

*Less than 0.1 percent.

percent between actual 1968 sales prices of forty-eight apartment properties and the computed value based upon this equation. The difference between the actual and computed sale prices exceeded 10 percent in only six of the forty-eight cases analyzed. Undoubtedly, this reflects individual differences in these particular properties from the rest of the sample and the expected variation in market sale prices that occurs in real estate. The range of gross multipliers will vary with the ratios of operating expenses to gross income for different types of property, with changes in financing terms and differences in regional business conditions and outlook, and with the age and condition of the properties.

The gross-multiplier technique is valuable as an appraisal tool and as a guide to the real estate investor. The addition of other variables and the application of multiple-regression techniques provides an even more refined method of determining investment values. The data requirements for use of the latter method are too severe for employment by the average investor.

The formulations for calculation of so-called net income, or broker's yield, that were illustrated earlier are also widely used. Net income multipliers, the reciprocals of broker's yield, are often used to estimate the value of an investment, as in the following illustration.

Comparable sale properties with net income of $100,000 have a sale price of $1 million:

$$\text{Broker's yield} = \frac{\text{first year's net income before interest and depreciation}}{\text{purchase price}}$$

$$\text{Broker's yield} = \frac{\$100,000}{\$1,000,000} = 10 \text{ percent}$$

$$\begin{array}{l}\text{Reciprocal of}\\ \text{10 percent}\end{array} = \text{net income multiplier} = {}^{100}\!/_{10} = 10$$

A prospective real estate investor who is offered a similar income property with a net income of $80,000 might conclude that it would have a value of 10 times $80,000, or $800,000.

Similarly, Equation 3, based on the first year's cash flow, can be used to estimate the capitalized value of the equity interest in a property. Adding the estimated debt to this equity value can provide a rough indication of investment value, as shown below.

Let us assume that a property shows net income before principal and interest and depreciation of $80,000, a mortgage on loan of $600,000, and interest payments of $60,000, leaving cash spendable income plus principal payments of $20,000 in the first year and a cash down payment of $150,000 using Equation 3:

$$\text{Yield on equity after interest} = \frac{\$20,000}{\$150,000} = 13.3 \text{ percent}$$

$$\text{Reciprocal of 13.3 percent} = \frac{100}{13.3} = 7.52 \text{ multiplier}$$

On the basis of this cash-flow multiplier, an investment property providing an annual before-tax cash flow of $20,000 per annum would have an indicated valuation for the equity investment of:

7.52 × $20,000	=	$150,400
Assumed debt		600,000
Indicated investment value of property		$750,400

As pointed out earlier, techniques based upon indicated before-tax cash flows for the first year only have serious shortcomings in comparison with more sophisticated approaches using estimated annual aftertax cash flows over an assumed holding period. However, these relatively crude techniques are widely used in real estate brokerage and can be justified as substitute methods for the real estate investor when estimation of future income and expenses is difficult. The real estate investor should recognize the hazards in projecting future cash flows based upon projections for one year only. It must be recognized, however, that long-term forecasts are equally hazardous, making estimates of investment value subject to a wide possible range of error.

A framework for the determination of investment value designed to narrow the margin of error is outlined below. It will be observed that some of the shortcut techniques discussed above are recommended as supplements to the projection and valuation of aftertax cash flows and residual sale prices at the conclusion of an assumed holding period.

Determination of Investment Value

Step A.   Obtain the following data:

1. Estimated total cost or market offering price of subject property.
2. Estimated future gross income and operating expenses, including property taxes.
3. Financing terms available on subject property.
4. Eligible depreciation methods for subject property.
5. Prevailing sale prices and gross income multipliers for similar properties.

Step B.   Estimate the following:

1. Investor's desired aftertax yield on subject investment.
2. Preferred or desired holding period of investment.
3. Annual cash flows during holding period after income taxes.
4. Residual sale proceeds of subject property at end of holding period after allowance for capital gains taxes.

Step C.   Estimate investment value:

1. Discount the estimated annual cash flows and residual sale proceeds over the holding period, using Equation 5. For short-term projections, this can be done by hand calculation. More complex long-term calculations require a computer.
2. Obtain comparable sale prices of similar properties in the market, making adjustments for noncomparability.
3. Multiply the estimated gross income for the subject property by observed gross income multipliers for similar properties.
4. Compare the above estimated values with current costs of replacement new for the subject property (to be used only if the subject property is new and has suffered little depreciation in value).

There is no implication that these separate approaches to the determination of investment value should result in the same figure. A wide difference between the estimate obtained under method 1, the discounted cash-flow technique, and the indicated value by method 2, comparable sales, or method 3, the gross-multiplier technique could be accounted for by (a) differences in the target equity yield between the individual investor and other buyers in the market; (b) differences in assumptions made by the individual investor concerning future income, expenses, or residual sale prices, or all three; or (*c*) differences in investors' tax brackets. Any of these or all in combination could explain variations in estimated investment values.

If investors' valuations arrived at by discounting estimated cash flows at their target yield rates and adding the value of debt are higher than the indicated going market prices for comparable properties, investors may conclude that either they are getting a bargain or that somewhere along the way they have been more optimistic than other investors. Fortunately, the use of computerized cash-flow models permits investors to test the sensitivity of their valuations to changing assumptions, as illustrated in Fig. 30-5. This process of trial and error may cause them to revise their estimates of investment value, or, alternatively, reaffirm their earlier analyses.

Investors will perform similar analyses in comparing their evaluations of an investment with the indicated value by use of the gross income multiplier. Obviously, if their valuations result in a higher gross income multiplier than that prevailing in the market for similar properties, they will find it necessary to justify the observed difference or to conclude that they have overvalued the property.

This analysis emphasizes the fact that real estate investment is an art and not a science. The computer can aid investors in reaching a decision, but the ultimate decision concerning investment value must be made by individuals, and the same property may have different values for different individual investors.

Costs are difficult for expert builders to estimate accurately and are even more elusive for real estate investors. Deductions from replacement costs to allow for depreciation range from indefensible presumptions to judgmental guesses about the difference between the value of a subject property and a new replacement. The larger the element of depreciation, the more unreliable will be an estimate of investment value based upon replacement cost new.

Chapter **31**

How to Select and Manage Real Property

Part 1 Selecting Real Property as an Investment

STEPHEN FELDMAN

Real estate investors will attempt to purchase property that will give them the highest possible return on their investment with the smallest amount of risk. In their efforts to select the appropriate piece of property they must determine in which state and which city they should invest at the current time, which neighborhood or which district within the area is most desirable for their purposes, and which particular piece of property they should buy. Of course, they must also determine whether this is the appropriate time to purchase any property and what type of property they desire (that is, residential or commercial).

REAL ESTATE MARKET ANALYSIS

In all types of markets, including real estate markets, the major factors involved are those related to supply, demand, and price. In most kinds of markets, price generally is merely a direct function of supply and demand. In real estate, however, price is viewed broadly to include taxes, interest rates, special charges, and other costs relating to the particular piece of property under consideration. Buyers can pay a higher direct price for property in a low-tax district, because the reduction in their tax payments can be added to their mortgage payment.

Real estate markets are inefficient and imperfect. There are no central exchanges to facilitate the purchase and sale of real estate, the product itself is not homogeneous, and supply-and-demand information is incomplete. Furthermore, real estate markets are affected by the seasons, with spring and fall usually representing the active periods.

Factors Conditioning Market Operation

The following are among the factors that condition the operation of real estate markets:

1. Each property is unique, since only one building can occupy a particular spot on the earth's surface. However, the degree of uniqueness varies. Row houses, town houses, and standardized detached houses in a large homogeneous neighborhood are virtually interchangeable. In contrast, every 25 or 50 feet of land may change in value in a central business district. Also, a special-purpose building may be suitable for use by only one tenant.

2. Some properties are parts of estates or are involved in litigation, with restrictions on sale or lease, and therefore cannot be sold or developed. Such properties, even though in desirable locations, are virtually out of the market.

3. Some owners have a sentimental attachment to their homes, farms, or other properties and refuse to sell for prices that reflect market conditions.

4. Some properties are leased for long periods and are not available for sublease or sale.

5. Buyers are often restricted to persons living in the city or neighborhood who are in a position to take advantage of bargains or the necessities of the seller.

6. Owners living outside a city frequently are not familiar with local developments that may increase or diminish the value of their properties.

7. Prices are affected by the terms and availability of financing.

8. Oral agreements are not binding as in stock market or grain market transactions, so that a seller or a buyer may not complete a transaction even though an obligation to pay a broker's commission may be incurred.

9. Whether the seller has a good title cannot be determined quickly as in the case of stocks or merchandise, and a period of time must elapse before the title can be passed.

10. Real estate cannot escape local taxes, as is often possible in the case of personal property.

11. The value of real property is often affected greatly by changes in local zoning laws.

12. The value of any specific property is affected by the character of the neighborhood and the economic outlook.

13. Buildings are not standardized commodities like automobiles. They may have hidden defects or exceptionally favorable features.

14. There is no machinery for selling short in real estate markets.

15. Although properties may turn over rapidly in periods of advancing prices, there may be long periods of low sales volume in times of stagnation and decline.

16. Residential real estate has been subject to rent control in time of emergency, which has checked the operation of normal market forces.

17. The value of real estate will be lowered by a high crime rate in the neighborhood. Property values depend on adequate police and fire protection.

18. Property values are affected by availability of water, sewer systems, utilities, and highways.[1]

In the short run the supply of real property of any type is fairly constant, and the major price determination factor is demand. The basic elements in demand are the terms and availability of financing and the income of the potential consumers of the real estate.

Analyzing Real Property

The main factors that investors should consider when they are analyzing a piece of real property as a potential investment are as follows:

1. Investors' expected return on their cash investment, including any antici-

---

[1] Arthur M. Weimer and Homer Hoyt, *Real Estate,* 5th ed., The Ronald Press Company, New York, 1960, pp. 256–257.

pated tax savings, is obviously the first and foremost consideration. Although the return will be affected by many other factors discussed below, investors should never become so involved with the analysis of property that they forget their primary objective. An area may be deteriorating or have a high vacancy rate, and taxes and financing may be high; however, if a strong tenant is willing to sign an attractive long-term lease on the property that provides a high expected return at the same time that the investor is receiving an effective tax shelter, this may be an attractive investment.

2. The general level of business activity affects real estate markets, especially for residential real estate, because when people are unemployed or fear becoming unemployed, they are less able or willing to purchase real property or to pay high rents. More important than the economy in general is the trend of local business conditions, which may in turn be influenced by general economic conditions. Of the many factors to be considered in studying local business conditions, the most important is the trend of employment and incomes. Income appears to be the primary factor in the demand for real estate. If local incomes are good and income prospects are favorable, the real estate market is likely to be active (unless there has just been a great surge of building). Even if no new residents are attracted to the area, higher incomes will mean an increase in the demand for housing. Heavier spending will also lead to a greater demand for commercial property.

3. The availability and the terms of the financing are always important considerations in any purchase of real property. In the recession of 1970–1971 real estate was often selling at very depressed and, therefore, attractive prices. However, it was often impossible to secure a mortgage that would have been necessary to consummate a purchase. If financing is not available, even the most attractive deals cannot be seen through to fruition. When financing is available, its terms are of paramount importance. Mortgage payments generally take one of two forms: (a) a constant annual payment each year during the life of the mortgage that is high enough to pay the annual interest and repay the principal during the life of the mortgage (almost all residential mortgages and many commercial mortgages take this form); and (b) payment of the interest annually and repayment of the principal at the expiration of the mortgage. This second type of mortgage is occasionally used for second mortgage on commercial property, especially if the mortgage is for a short time period, possibly five years.

An investor who finances real estate in a period of low interest rates will receive the advantage of a low interest charge for every year that the mortgage is in existance. At a later date if the property has increased in value and the investor wishes to secure a much higher mortgage on the property, the low interest charges on the original mortgage may make it possible to get a new mortgage with a "wraparound" and avoid any prepayment penalty on the old mortgage. Virtually all mortgages impose a rather severe penalty if the mortgage is prepaid. Therefore, if an investor has a $1 million mortgage on a piece of property and wishes to secure an additional $1 million, he or she cannot get a $2 million new first mortgage and repay the $1 million mortgage without being willing to pay a prepayment penalty. This penalty can be avoided only if the new mortgagor gives the investor $1 million in cash and assumes the mortgage payments on the original mortgage. This arrangement, which is called a *wraparound,* will be acceptable to the mortgagor only if the original mortgage had a lower rate of interest than the new mortgage.

4. Population data are another important consideration when evaluating real estate. Is the number of people in the community growing or declining? What is the median income level for a family in the community, and how wide are the deviations from this median? A growing community with a fairly high income level will demand more residential housing and more retail goods. If the population

continues to grow and the income level remains high, the value of both residential and commercial real estate will be increased.

5. The vacancy rate is one of the important indicators of real estate market conditions and trends. A surplus of vacant units will tend to retard price or rent increases even when demand is strong. Just what is meant by a surplus or deficit of vacant units cannot be defined exactly. The concept varies from one community to another and from one type of property to another. Normal vacancy for houses is usually considered as something less than 5 percent, and for apartments slightly over 5 percent; for business units it may run somewhat higher. However, these are only rules of thumb that vary from one place to another.

Whenever the supply of vacant units exceeds a normal percentage, the market tends to be depressed. Competition of owners and sellers seeking tenants and buyers forces prices and rents downward and restrains new construction. When vacancies are increasing, the market must be watched closely, for an unsound situation may be developing because of either declining demand or overbuilding. If an increasing amount of vacancy is not checked, a collapse of rents, prices, and market activity may result. A decline in the vacancy ratio, on the other hand, may be reflected in an upward movement of rents and prices; but market activity will be limited because demand for space cannot be translated into sales and leases until a supply of space is made available.

Information about vacancies in various types of properties is frequently collected by local real estate boards. At times the United States Postal Service conducts vacancy surveys in various cities. Often local public utility companies or departments will assemble data concerning vacancies, and the publishers of local directories may gather information of this type at periodic intervals. It is desirable that vacancy ratios be computed separately for different classes of property, for frequently one part of a market will have a shortage of space while another has a surplus.

6. Any persistent changes in market prices or rents upward or downward reflect basic market conditions. Sometimes these movements are of short duration, but if they persist for a year or more, it may usually be presumed that the trend will continue for a time.

On occasion, real estate brokers test the market by advertising a popular type of property at a very reasonable price or rental. They are then able to gauge market conditions by the number of responses received to the advertisement. Of special importance is the variation between listing and actual selling prices. Similarly, the difference between the rental rate asked and that finally paid is a reflection of the strength of the market.

The length of time new properties remain on the market before being sold or rented indicates the strength or weakness of demand. When long periods are required to dispose of property, the market is weakening. This assumes, of course, that prices have been set on a reasonably competitive basis.

Part 2 How to Manage Property

STEPHEN FELDMAN

One of the first questions that persons who own income-producing property must answer is whether they are going to manage the property themselves or hire professional managers to do the job. Investors who manage property themselves will save management fees, and they will be assured that the managers of the buildings have the best interests of the owners in mind at all times. An attempt will be made to minimize costs and maximize revenues, and the long-run value of the property will be considered when any decision is made. On the other hand, a professional management group is experienced in this field and may be able to do a more efficient job than owners can do. Furthermore, property management is a time-consuming and aggravating job for investors who have careers of their own to which they must devote their time and energy.

The chief professional organization in the property management field is the Institute of Real Estate Management. It was established in 1933 as an organization of management firms, but in 1938 it became a professional society of qualified individuals. Membership is limited to those who can meet stated experience, educational, and ethical standards and can successfully pass the designated examinations.

Whoever is ultimately designated as the manager of a piece of property will face problems that are unique to the management of real property. The durability of real estate necessitates managerial planning over longer periods of time than is necessary for many other types of business. Furthermore, real properties are economically inflexible; that is, once they have been improved, their uses are relatively fixed for long periods. Hence, to a large extent the manager is called upon to get as large a return as possible from relatively fixed resources.

Current expenses are only slightly more flexible than the basic investment. Many important operating expenses, such as taxes, insurance, and interest charges, are usually beyond the control of the property manager. Hence, a slight change in gross income usually means a considerably larger percentage change in net returns.

The fact that real properties are fixed in location means that the manager cannot move a property to those who desire its services; rather, they must be induced to come to it. For the same reason, the property cannot escape adverse developments affecting a city, a district, or a neighborhood. Working within the confines of these limitations, the real estate manager must attempt to maximize gross income, minimize expenses, and maintain or increase the resale value of the property.

PROPERTY MANAGEMENT FUNCTIONS

The functions performed by property managers include the general management processes of establishing objectives, planning to achieve them, organizing resources, and controlling operations. The property manager also performs the functions of (1) planning space, (2) marketing property services, (3) conserving the property and its surroundings, and (4) supervising the operation of the property, which will include, among other things, the maintenance of accurate records and accounts.[2] Figure 31-1 is an organization chart depicting the functional responsibilities of real estate managers.

Planning Space

If a manager has adequate information about the local market, his or her advice to the owner, architect, and builder will be of great value in planning a new building or in modernization and repair programs. A competent manager is able to give advice concerning the type of building accommodations most readily marketable,

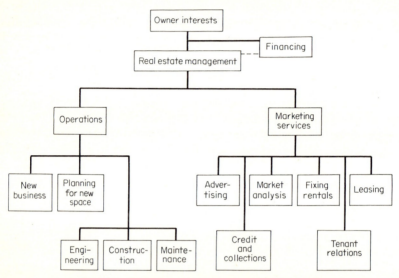

Fig. 31-1   Real estate management organization chart.

the competitive position of various types of properties in the market, and the many special requirements of prospective tenants. Also, the manager usually knows something of the most economical methods for arranging rooms, halls, and storage space.

In the case of older buildings, managers must accept the space available and utilize it as efficiently as possible. Sometimes it is possible to alter the arrangements of an older building, but whether this should be done depends on the possibilities of securing adequate return on the additional investment required.[3]

Establishing Rental Schedules

Once a building, regardless of type, has been constructed, the manager must fix a rental schedule and enter the market. Fixing a rental schedule calls for an accurate knowledge of such matters as the character of competing space, rents currently charged, the nature of the potential demand, the special requirements of prospective tenants, and the advantages and disadvantage of the location. First, a general level of rents is determined, and from it the manager is able to develop a rental schedule for the individual quarters. Specific rates, however, are determined by

[2]Ibid., p. 409.
[3]James C. Downs, Jr., *Principles of Real Estate Management,* 8th ed., Institute of Real Estate Management, Chicago, 1964, chap. V.

market conditions. If net income is to be maximized, rents must be adjusted carefully. For example, if rents are too low, all the space will be rented; but the total return will be less than what might be realized under a higher rental schedule. On the other hand, if rents are too high, the increase in the number of vacancies will reduce income. The determination of a rental schedule for a building is one of the basic functions of a manager, and to a large extent success or failure depends on the care with which this work is done. Moreover, the process of adjusting rental schedules is never complete: rents must follow the market, rising when the demand for space is strong and diminishing when demand falls off.

Concessions or special services provided by the owner may create a wide gap between the real and the nominal money rent. Thus, a rental may be set at $250 per month for an apartment, with a concession of one month's rent, which means that the real charge is $229.16 per month. Managers often make such arrangements instead of cutting rents, because they believe that when the market warrants a return to the old level, it will be easier to raise rents by eliminating concessions than by reinstating a schedule previously abandoned. The provision of special equipment and, in some cases, the payment of moving expenses to secure a tenant are other examples of concessions. These techniques are especially valuable in localities where all future rent increases are limited by law.

Selling Space

With the establishment of a rental schedule, it becomes necessary for the manager to secure tenants. If the building is new, it may be necessary to advertise and solicit tenants. A new building opens with a competitive advantage, for it usually makes available all the newest facilities. The opening of a new building, even a small structure, is always detrimental to existing buildings. When a large new office or apartment building is opened, the existing structures must face stiff competition. Tenants of existing buildings are made conscious of the advantages of the new building through advertising and systematic solicitation. If special concessions are offered by the new building or if rental schedules compare favorably with those of existing structures, there will be a tendency for tenants to move from their old quarters to the new building.

Leasing Practices

Contrary to popular belief, leases on residential property are usually more desirable for the tenant than for the owner. A lease ordinarily binds the owner and manager very effectively, because the property serves as security and guarantees performance of the terms of the contract. But unless the tenant is financially responsible and has assets that can be attached if the lease is broken, it is difficult to enforce a lease of this type. Furthermore, even if the tenant is financially responsible, the owner is obligated to mitigate damages by attempting to rent the property immediately; and it is often difficult to locate, serve, and get a judgment against a tenant. The manager should generally get one month's rent as security (two months if competitively possible and legal in the particular location) against damage and against the tenant's breaking the lease. Commercial leases with business firms provide the owner with considerably more protection because businesses generally possess greater financial responsibility than individuals do.

The rents fixed in a lease may be of several types: (1) a flat rate for the period covered; (2) a graded, or step-up, rental; (3) a percentage rental varying with the amount of the tenant's gross or net income; or (4) a rental adjusted by reappraisal of the property at certain times. Also, various combinations of these types may be worked out. For example, a lease on a business property might be drawn to provide for a minimum flat rent, plus a percentage of the tenant's gross business receipts if they exceed a certain stipulated amount. In the case of long-term leases, such an arrangement is often desirable to guard against important changes in the value of money.

Conservation of Property

The property manager is responsible for the maintenance of the property so that its economic life may be as long as possible. This means that a regular program for making repairs and replacements must be followed. The careful planning of repair programs over a period of time and the proper allowance for such work in the budgetary setup of the organization are important functions of good property management. In apartment house management it is usually safe to allocate one month's rent per year to normal repairs and decorations. Another 5 percent of the income is usually set aside for painting, roofing, renovation of heating equipment, and other types of repairs that need not be made every year but must be paid for over varying periods of time.

Insurance

The property manager may be responsible for placing insurance and paying for it regularly. Normally, fire insurance in an amount equal to approximately 80 percent of the replacement cost of buildings is carried (80 percent coinsurance). Sometime, in the case of large buildings, fire insurance is supplemented by use and occupancy insurance, that is, insurance against the loss of rent resulting from destruction of a building.

Public liability insurance typically is carried for all buildings. Boiler and plate glass insurance are necessary in some cases; and if rent collectors are employed, good practice requires that they be bonded. Insurance against theft, tornadoes, and other hazards is also carried by many management organizations. Good management often can effect substantial savings in insurance by eliminating various risks or by using coinsurance, thus securing the benefits of reduced insurance premiums.

Taxes and Other Fees

The payment of taxes and special assessments as well as local license and inspection fees requires careful and prompt attention by a property manager. In some instances, when the taxes on a building appear to be out of line with those on similar structures, management can effect savings by calling this fact to the attention of the proper tax officials. Errors are sometimes made by tax officials who may estimate the value of a building by its external appearance rather than by its earning power. This is especially true of large office buildings or apartment houses. The preparation and submission of accurate statistical materials to the proper tax officers, presenting data on earning power, is often a helpful method of attacking this problem. Problems of this type often arise in connection with older buildings which have been assessed at high values during years when their earning power was great but for which tax adjustments were not made as income-producing ability declined.

Section Six

Commodity Futures Trading

Chapter 32[1]

Mechanics of Commodity Futures Trading

RICHARD J. TEWELES

CHARLES V. HARLOW

HERBERT L. STONE

THE NATURE OF THE COMMODITIES CONTRACT[2]

Trading commodity futures is a skill, and no skill develops powerfully when one is wearing blinders. For that reason prospective traders must understand, insofar as possible, the nature of the environment in which they are to pit their skills against those of others who play the same game.

Regardless of whether the user of a futures contract is a hedger or a speculator, the common bond is the nature of the contract itself. That contract is a firm legal agreement between a buyer (or a seller) and an established commodity exchange or its clearinghouse in which the trader agrees to deliver or accept during a designated period a specified amount of a certain commodity that adheres to the particular quality and delivery conditions prescribed by the commodity exchange on which that commodity is traded. The contract, if allowed to run to its termination, is fulfilled by a cash payment on the delivery date based on the settlement price for that day in return for delivery of the commodity.

During the time that the contract is open, the trader must agree to a series of conditions with a qualified broker (or the clearinghouse if the trader is a member) that calls for an initial margin deposit, a prescribed margin level that protects the broker from possible losses resulting from adverse price movements, and the right to close out (offset) the contract at any time simply by properly instructing the

---

[1]Chapters 32, 33, 34, and 35 are drawn largely from Richard J. Teweles, Charles V. Harlow, and Herbert L. Stone, *The Commodity Futures Game*, McGraw-Hill Book Company, New York, 1974.

[2]The following discussion draws on Henry B. Arthur, "The Nature of Commodity Futures as an Economic and Business Instrument," *Food Research Institute Studies in Agricultural Economics, Trade, and Development*, vol. 11, no. 3, pp. 257–260.

broker to do so. The last condition is a bilateral one that permits the broker to close out the trader's position if margin is seriously impaired.

This basic commitment has several ramifications. Although the contract defines the quantity, quality, and location at which the commodity will be delivered, there are, as a rule, alternatives available to the seller that will permit delivery of a commodity with substantial deviations from the par specifications. The seller faces a scale of premiums or discounts in price because of such deviations, which might include different locations of delivery or variations in the unit weight of delivery or the deliverable grade. Deliveries must be made during the delivery month traded, but the actual day of the month is selected by the seller, who issues a notice of intention in the form of a warehouse receipt, shipping certificate, or bill of lading.

The trader holding a contract will be dealing most often through a futures commission merchant (broker) who is a member of an exchange and who will charge for his or her services a minimum commission set by the exchange. It is the member broker who is responsible for the fulfillment of the contract if he or she is a clearing member of the exchange. If the broker is not a clearing member, the trades must be cleared by a clearing member. The contracts themselves are subject to legal provisions and the rules of the various exchanges, such as the setting of hours and trading regulations and the daily trading limits beyond which a particular commodity cannot move.

There are, then, two major elements of the commitment assumed when a trader enters into a commodity futures contract. The first is a promise of actual delivery of the commodity at a designated date in a way that meets exchange specifications. The second is a promise to respond financially to daily price changes by payment, if necessary, of cash to a member broker, who must in turn respond to a call for cash from the clearinghouse, the operation of which is discussed below. This daily settlement process maintains the viability of the first promise of delivery, for if any trader wishes to cancel a commitment to accept or effect delivery of the actual commodity, he or she may merely enter the market and offset his or her present position. More than 98 percent of all futures contracts are settled by offset rather than by deliveries.

Until actual delivery a transaction in a commodity futures contract does not involve anything beyond the daily process of generating profits or losses against a good-faith margin deposit with a broker. No purchase or sale is required, and there is no debit balance; hence no interest is charged. All net balances are on the credit side and are marked to the market after each day's trading. The act of buying or selling occurs only after an intent to deliver occurs, when a specific buyer and seller are paired at the current settlement price.

MECHANICS OF TRADING

The list in Table 32-1 is not complete, but it does indicate the major commodity exchanges in the United States, typical commodities most actively traded on them, and pertinent contract and commission data concerning these commodities. From time to time changes occur in commissions, delivery months, opening times, closing times, and, of course, the list of commodities popularly traded. Most brokers will have updated information available, designated as "Contract Facts" or "Contract Information." There is no need for a customer to memorize the exact contract size of all commodities traded or the times at which the various exchanges open and close. He or she can refer to a copy of "Contract Information" and keep pertinent information in mind only for the positions in which he is currently interested.

Commodity prices appear on broker's quotation equipment and on the financial pages of newspapers much as common stock prices appear in the same places. In stock trading the unit of trading is usually 100 shares, and in bond trading it is five bonds. Commodities, however, trade in terms of contract units specified by the exchanges. For most grains and soybeans the unit of trading is 5,000 bushels. Traditionally, traders do not speak in terms of being long two contracts of corn, but rather of being long 10,000 bushels. The broker's board, quotation machines, and newspapers indicate the value of grains and soybeans in terms of dollars, cents, and eighths. Corn at $1.12½, for example, merely means that corn is valued at that price per bushel. It can be ascertained from "Contract Information" that a change of 1 cent per bushel on the standard contract of 5,000 bushels would represent a profit or loss to a corn trader of $50 on each contract. A change of ¼ cent is $12.50 on a 5,000-bushel contract.

Daily Trading Limits

To prevent extreme price changes in one day all exchanges limit the amount that prices are allowed to move daily. Basically there are two limitations. One restricts the amount that a price may move above or below the settlement price of the preceding day. This is usually called the "daily limit." The other is a restriction on the maximum range over which the price may move during one day. This is sometimes called the maximum permissible "daily range." Sometimes the daily limit and the daily range are the same, and sometimes the daily range is twice the limit. For example, in cattle the daily limit is 1 cent per pound, and the daily range is 2 cents. If cattle closed at 33.55 cents on one day, then 34.55 cents would be "limit up" and 32.55 cents "limit down." However, if the price moved up to 34.55 cents, it could trade all the way down to 32.55 cents because its permissible range is twice its limit. For orange juice, however, the daily limit and the daily range are both 3 cents per pound; therefore, if May orange juice closed at 44.70 cents and then traded up to 46.20 cents the next day, it could not then trade below 43.20 cents. Any amount of trading can take place at the limit, or the market can move down from limit up or up from limit down. Despite widespread misconception on this point, a market does not close because a daily price limit is reached; it merely cannot trade past that point. In the current month restrictions on limits may be modified to allow greater flexibility, and directors of an exchange can change limits under conditions deemed to be an emergency. Daily trading limits and ranges are indicated in Table 32-2. As in "Contract Information," there may be changes from time to time, and the trader is well advised to maintain current data, which are available from his or her broker.

Many traders who began by trading stocks are quite concerned about the possibility of being "frozen in" by an adverse limit move. It should be noted, however, that the alternative is an *unlimited* adverse move, which might provide far less comfort.

Taking a Position

When the account has been opened, the customer can take a position in one of the approximately forty commodities traded in futures markets. The procedure, as far as the customer is concerned, is almost exactly like trading a security. The customer gives an order to his or her registered representative, who transmits it to the representative's firm's wire room, from which it is sent to the exchange on which the selected commodity is traded. The report of the trade is then sent back to the office from which it originated and given to the customer. Orders may be placed by customers personally or by telephone, letter, or wire. Most of them are placed by telephone.

The broker is required to mail the customer a confirmation of the trade as promptly as possible. This is usually done on the day that the trade is made. A confirmation of a new position indicates the exchange on which it was made, the

TABLE 32-1 Contract Information

Commodity	Name of exchange	Exchange hours, CST	Usual par contract grade(s)	Delivery months*	Contract size	Prices quoted in	Minimum fluctuation	Dollar value of one tick	Dollar value of 1¢ move	Maximum daily limits above or below previous day's close — Cents	Maximum daily limits above or below previous day's close — Dollars	Round-turn commissions — Regular	Round-turn commissions — Day trade	Round-turn commissions — Spread
Wheat	Chicago Board of Trade	9:30 1:15	No. 2 soft red winter No. 2 hard red winter Nos 1, 2 northern spring	NUZHK	5,000 bu	¢/bu	$\frac{1}{4}$¢/bu	$12.50	$50	20¢/bu	1,000	$30.00	$20.00	$36.00
Corn	Chicago Board of Trade	9:30 1:15	No. 2 yellow	ZHKNU	5,000 bu	¢/bu	$\frac{1}{4}$¢/bu	12.50	50	10¢/bu	500	30.00	20.00	36.00
Oats	Chicago Board of Trade	9:30 1:15	No. 1 white No. 1, 2 heavy white No 3 extra-heavy white	ZHKNU	5,000 bu	¢/bu	$\frac{1}{4}$¢/bu	12.50	50	6¢/bu	300	25.00	17.00	36.00
Soybeans	Chicago Board of Trade	9:30 1:15	No. 2 yellow	XFHKNQU	5,000 bu	¢/bu	$\frac{1}{4}$¢/bu	12.50	50	20¢/bu	1,000	30.00	20.00	36.00
Soybean meal	Chicago Board of Trade	9:30 1:15	44% protein	VZFHKNQU	100 tons (2,000 lb/ton)	$/ton	10¢/ton	10.00	1	1,000¢/ ton	1,000	33.00	22.00	44.00
Soybean oil	Chicago Board of Trade	9:30 1:15	Regular; one grade	VZFHKNQU	60,000 lb (one tank car)	¢/lb	$\frac{1}{100}$¢/lb	6.00	600	1¢/lb	600	33.00	22.00	44.00
Broilers, iced	Chicago Board of Trade	9:15 1:05	USDA Grade A 2¼ to 3½ lb whole eviscerated	FHKMNQUX	28,000 lb (60- to 65-lb boxes)	¢/lb	$2\frac{5}{100}$¢/lb	7.00	280	2¢/lb	560	30.00	20.00	36.00
Silver	Chicago Board of Trade	9:00 1:25	0.999 fine	GJMQVZ	5,000 troy oz (5 bars)	¢/oz	$\frac{1}{10}$¢/oz	5.00	50	20¢/oz	1,000	30.00	15.00	32.00
Plywood	Chicago Board of Trade	10:00 1:00	½-in CDX; standard exterior 4 to 5 ply	FHKNUX	69,120 sq ft 36(60-piece units) (one boxcar load)	$/M sq ft	10¢/M sq ft	6.91	0.691	700¢/M sq ft	484	30.00	20.00	40.00
Stud lumber	Chicago Board of Trade	10:00 1:00	4 × 8s, group 1 8-ft 2 × 4s 10/15% utility	FHKNUX	100,000 board ft (two boxcar loads)	$/M board ft	10¢/M board ft	10.00	1	500¢/M board ft	500	33.00	22.00	44.00
Pork bellies	Chicago Mercantile Exchange	9:30 1:00	USDA seedless green—square cut—standard	GHKNQ	36,000 lb (12- to 14-lb bellies)	¢/lb	$2\frac{5}{100}$¢/lb	9.00	360	1.5¢/lb	540	45.00	27.00	48.00
Feeder cattle	Chicago Mercantile Exchange	9:05 12:40	USDA minimum 80% choice and maximum 20% good	HJKQUVZ	42,000 lb (650-lb average)	¢/lb	$2\frac{5}{100}$¢/lb	10.50	420	1¢/lb	420	40.00	25.00	43.00

Commodity	Exchange	Trading hours	Grade/description	Months	Contract size	Price quoted in	Min. fluctuation							
Cattle, live	Chicago Mercantile Exchange	9:05 / 12:40	USDA choice live steers	GJMQVZ	40,000 lb (1,050-lb average)	¢/lb	$2.5/100¢/lb$	10.00	400	1¢/lb	400	40.00	25.00	43.00
Hogs, live	Chicago Mercantile Exchange	9:20 / 12:50	USDA 1, 2, 3, 4 barrows and gilts	GJMNQVZ	80,000 lb (220-lb average)	¢/lb	$2.5/100¢/lb$	7.50	300	1.5¢/lb	450	35.00	22.00	38.00
Eggs, shell (fresh)	Chicago Mercantile Exchange	9:15 / 12:45	USDA extras 90% Grade A large white	All	22,500 doz (750 cases; one carload)	¢/doz	$5/100¢/doz$	11.15	225	2¢/doz	450	40.00	25.00	43.00
Milo	Chicago Mercantile Exchange	9:30 / 1:15	No. 2 yellow	NUZHK	400,000 lb (7,142.8 bu)	¢/cwt	$1/4¢/cwt$	10.00	40	15¢/cwt	600	30.00	20.00	33.00
Potatoes (Idaho Russet)	Chicago Mercantile Exchange	9:00 / 12:50	USDA No. 1 Size A 2-in diameter	FHJKX	50,000 lb (500 sacks)	¢/cwt	1¢/cwt	5.00	5	35¢/cwt	175	30.00	20.00	33.00
Lumber	Chicago Mercantile Exchange	9:00 / 1:05	Kiln- or air-dried random 2 × 4s hemlock—fir construction	FGHKNUX	100,000 board ft (two boxcar loads)	$/M board ft	10¢/M board ft	10.00	1	500¢/M board ft	500	40.00	25.00	43.00
Copper	New York Commodity Exchange (Comex)	8:45 / 1:10	Electrolytic ASTM standards	FHKNUVZ	25,000 lb	¢/lb	$5/100¢/lb$	12.50	250	5¢/lb	1,250	36.00	18.00	50.40
Mercury	Comex	8:50 / 1:30	99.9% pure	HKNUZ	10 flasks (76 lb each)	$/flask	$1/flask	10.00	0.10	500¢/flask	50	40.50	20.00	56.00
Silver	Comex	9:00 / 1:15	0.999 fine	FHKNUZ	10,000 troy oz (10 bars)	¢/oz	$1/10¢/oz$	10.00	100	20¢/oz	2,000	45.50	23.00	64.00
Potatoes (Maine or Idaho)	New York Mercantile Exchange	9:00 / 12:30	USDA No. 1 Size A 2-in diameter	FHJKX	50,000 lb (1,000 50-lb sacks)	$/cwt	1¢/cwt	5.00	5	50¢/cwt	250	30.00	15.00	32.00
Platinum	New York Mercantile Exchange	8:45 / 12:30	99.8% pure sheet or bar	FJNV	50 troy oz (1 sheet or bar)	$/oz	10¢/oz	5.00	0.50	1,000¢/oz	500	45.00	22.50	45.00
Silver coins	New York Mercantile Exchange	8:50 / 1:20	Dimes, halves, quarters pre-1965 United States	FJNV	$10,000 (10 bags)	$/bag	$1/bag	10.00	0.10	15,000 ¢/bag	1,500	35.00	17.50	35.00
Palladium	New York Mercantile Exchange	9:20 / 11:55	99.8% pure	HKMQUXZ	100 troy oz (4 sheets or ingots)	$/oz	5¢/oz	5.00	1	400¢/oz	400	40.00 / 52.00	20.00 / 26.00	40.00† / 54.00

(Continued)

TABLE 32-1 Contract Information (Continued)

Commodity	Name of exchange	Exchange hours, CST	Usual par contract grade(s)	Delivery months*	Contract size	Prices quoted in	Minimum fluctuation	Dollar value of one tick	Dollar value of 1¢ move	Maximum daily limits above or below previous day's close — Cents	— Dollars	Round-turn commissions — Regular	— Day trade	— Spread
Cotton No. 2	New York Cotton Exchange	9:30 2:00	U.S. middling 1 1/16-in white	FHKNVZ	50,000 lb (100 bales)	¢/lb	$\frac{1}{100}$¢/lb	5.00	500	2¢/lb	1,000	45.00 / 55.00	22.50 / 27.50	54.00† / 66.00
Frozen concentrated orange juice	New York Cotton Exchange	9:15 1:45	USDA Grade A Brix—51° 3% solids	FHKNUX	15,000 lb 4¶(55-gal drums)	¢/lb	$\frac{5}{100}$¢/lb	7.50	150	3¢/lb	450	45.00	25.00	54.00
Wool	New York Cotton Exchange	9:00 1:30	64s 2¾ in	HKNVZ	6,000 lb (clean weight)	¢/lb	$\frac{1}{10}$¢/lb	6.00	60	10¢/lb	600	50.00	27.00	60.00
Liquefied propane gas	New York Cotton Exchange	9:05 2:10	NGPA-HD-5	FKNUZ	100,000 gal (pipeline bulk)	¢/gal	$\frac{1}{100}$¢/gal	10.00	1,000	1¢/gal	1,000	40.50	20.00	45.00
Cocoa	New York Cocoa Exchange	9:00 2:00	Standard (beans)	HKNUZ	30,000 lb (200 bags)	¢/lb	$\frac{1}{10}$¢/lb	3.00	300	4¢/lb	1,200	60.00	30.00	70.00
Coffee (C)	New York Coffee and Sugar Exchange	9:30 1:45	Colombian (beans)	HKNUXZ	37,500 lb (250 bags)	¢/lb.	$\frac{1}{100}$¢/lb	3.75	375	2¢/lb	750	25.00 / 80.00	15.00 / 42.75	30.00† / 96.00
World sugar No. 11	New York Coffee and Sugar Exchange	9:00 2:00	Raw bulk 96% average polarization	FHKNUV	50 long tons (112,000 lb)	¢/lb	$\frac{1}{100}$¢/lb	11.20	1,120	1¢/lb	1,120	42.00 / 62.00	21.00 / 31.00	42.00† / 62.00

32-8

Commodity	Exchange	Hours	Grade	Months	Contract size	Price quote	Min. fluctuation			Daily limit				
Wheat	Kansas City Board of Trade	9:30 1:15	No. 2 hard red or hard yellow winter	NUZHK	5,000 bu	¢/bu	⅛¢/bu	6.25	50	25¢/bu	1,250	22.00	22.00	30.00
Rye	Winnipeg Commodity Exchange	9:30 1:15	Nos. 1, 2 Western Canadian	VZKN	1,000 bu 5,000 bu	¢/bu	⅛¢/bu	1.25 6.25	10 50	10¢/bu	100 500	4.50 22.50	4.50 22.50	9.00 45.00
Flaxseed	Winnipeg Commodity Exchange	9:30 1:15	No. 1, Western Canadian	VXZKN	1,000 bu 5,000 bu	¢/bu	⅛¢/bu	1.25 6.25	10 50	30¢/bu	300 1,500	5.50- 25.00	5.50 25.00	11.00 50.00
Rapeseed	Winnipeg Commodity Exchange	9:30 1:15	No. 1 Canadian	UXFHM Vancouver VXZKN Thunder Bay	1,000 bu 5,000 bu	¢/bu	⅛¢/bu	1.25 6.25	10 50	20¢/bu	200 1,00	5.50 25.00	5.50 25.00	11.00 50.00
Wheat	Minneapolis Grain Exchange	9:30 1:15	No. 2 northern spring U.S. 13.5% protein	NUZHK	5,000 bu	¢/bu	⅛¢/bu	6.25	50	20¢/bu	1,000	30.00	15.00	36.00

*Chicago Board of Trade Commodity month symbols for the current year listed in crop-year order when applicable:

January F March H May K July N September U November X
February G April J June M August Q October V December Z
Chicago Board of Trade commodity months symbols for subsequent years when needed:
January A March C May E July L September P November S
February B April D June I August O October R December T

†There are different commissions for different price levels.

NOTE: Similar information is available for all other futures not shown here, such as those traded on the International Money Market (IMM) and the London and other foreign exchanges.

SOURCE: Clayton Brokerage Company of St. Louis, Inc.

TABLE 32-2 Daily Trading Limits[a]

	Usual range above or below previous close	Usual range between high and low
GRAINS		
Oats (CBT)	6¢ per bu	12¢ per bu
Corn	10¢ per bu	20¢ per bu
Rye, Winnipeg	10¢ per bu	20¢ per bu
Grain sorghum; milo	15¢ per bu	30¢ per bu
Rapeseed, Winnipeg	20¢ per bu	40¢ per bu
Soybeans	20¢ per bu	40¢ per bu
Wheat (CBT, MGE)	20¢ per bu	40¢ per bu
Wheat (Kansas City)	25¢ per bu	50¢ per bu
Flaxseed, Winnipeg	30¢ per bu	60¢ per bu
METALS		
Copper (New York)	5¢ per lb[b]	10¢ per lb[b]
Mercury	$5 per flask[c]	$10 per flask[c]
Palladium	$4 per oz[d,e]	$8 per oz[d,e]
Platinum (New York)	$10 per oz[e]	$20 per oz[e]
Silver (CBT)	20¢ per oz[b]	40¢ per oz[b]
Silver (New York)	20¢ per oz[b]	40¢ per oz[b]
Silver Coins (CME)	$120 per bag[e]	$240 per bag[e]
Silver Coins (New York)	$150 per bag[e]	$300 per bag[e]
OTHERS		
Propane	1¢ per gal[e]	2¢ per gal[e]
Cattle	1¢ per lb	2¢ per lb
Soybean oil	1¢ per lb[b]	2¢ per lb[b]

Sugar No. 11	1¢ per lb[f]	2¢ per lb[f]
Sugar (London)	£10 per long ton[b]	£20 per long ton[b]
Hogs	1.5¢ per lb	3¢ per lb
Pork bellies	1.5¢ per lb	3¢ per lb
Broilers	2¢ per lb[b]	4¢ per lb[b]
Cocoa (New York)	2¢ per lb[b]	4¢ per lb[b]
Coffee (C)	2¢ per lb[b]	4¢ per lb[b]
Cotton No. 2	2¢ per lb[b]	4¢ per lb[b]
Eggs (shell)	2¢ per doz	4¢ per doz
Orange juice	3¢ per lb[b]	3¢ per lb[b]
Lumber	$5 per M board ft[b]	$10 per M board ft[b]
Wool	10¢ per lb[g]	20¢ per lb[b]
Potatoes (Maine)	50¢ per cwt[e]	$1.00 per cwt[e]
Soybean meal	$10 per ton[b]	$20 per ton[b]
Plywood (CBT)	$7 per M sq ft[b]	$14 per M sq ft[b]

[a] Price limitations are imposed by the various exchanges to prevent extreme price changes in any one day. When prices reach the trading limit, trading beyond that limit is stopped for that day. In nearly all markets the board of directors or governors has the power to change the limits in emergencies. In the current month the limitations are broadened in certain future contracts by permitting wider price changes, and in others by removing limitations entirely.
[b] Limit is removed from spot month on first notice day.
[c] Limit is removed from spot month on first day of delivery month.
[d] $5 and $10 per ounce above or below preceding close during spot month.
[e] Limit is removed from spot month on last trading day.
[f] Limit is removed from calendar month prior to delivery month.
[g] Limit is removed from spot month on eighth day of delivery month.

date, the price, and the size of the position. The confirmation of a position being liquidated contains the same information but in addition indicates the amount of profit or loss on the transaction and the total commission charged for entering and liquidating the position. This differs somewhat from a security confirmation of a closing transaction. Such a confirmation does not indicate the profit or loss because the broker may not have access to this information. A stock can be bought at one brokerage house, held for years, and then sold at another. Commodity positions are held for relatively brief periods and may not be readily transferred from one brokerage house to another. Commodity transactions indicate the entire round-turn commissions on the liquidating side, whereas security confirmations indicate one commission on the entry and another on the liquidation.

Liquidating a Position

A speculator who has established a long position may liquidate it in one of two ways: he or she may offset it with a sale or accept delivery of the commodity. One who has established a short position also has two possible routes to follow: he or she may cover the short position by buying or make delivery of the cash commodity if he or she has it in deliverable form and location or can acquire it. For virtually all speculators offset is the liquidation route chosen. Most do not want the cash commodity or have it available for delivery. Their purpose in being in the markets is to attempt to take advantage of price changes, not to deal in cash products.

If delivery is to become a factor, it is usually of greater concern to the speculator with a long position than to one with a short position because it is the latter who has the choice of whether to make delivery and when. Sometimes the holder of a long position holds his or her position into the delivery month, hoping that the amount of deliverable cash product is too small or too tightly held to make the risk of receipt of any great concern. In such a case the holder should become familiar with the rules of the exchange on which he or she is trading to appraise the odds of receiving early deliveries if any are made. Notices of delivery are posted on dates and at times specified by exchange rules. These notices are sometimes given to the long with the oldest position in terms of the date on which it was established and sometimes to the brokerage house with the oldest net long position. The latter circumstance might well mean that a trader with a long position held with a brokerage house which itself was net short could not get delivery at all. Considering the cost and trouble that an unwanted delivery can cause, a trader who is not highly sophisticated in commodity market operations might do well to liquidate long positions routinely before the first date on which notice of delivery is possible. These dates are available from any well-informed brokerage firm.

The trader who does choose to hold his or her position into a delivery month must also be aware of the last day of futures trading after which offset is impossible and delivery is the only route open. Some typical rules covering notice days and the last day of trading are indicated in Tables 32-3 and 32-4 respectively.

Types of Orders

A commodity may be bought or sold at the market, which means that the floor broker on the exchange must execute the order promptly at the most favorable price possible. A limit may be imposed by the customer, which precludes the floor broker from paying more on a buy order or selling for less on a sell order. This limit assures the trader of at least the price that he or she wants if the order is executed, but it means that he or she will run the risk of not getting the order executed at all if the floor broker finds it impossible to fill it at the specified limit. Unlike the trader of listed-security rounds lots, the commodity trader who sees the correct price of a commodity "sell through his or her limit" on the tape, board, or quotation machine cannot assume that his or her order has been filled. Because there are no floor specialists on the commodity exchanges, it is possible and often reasonable for a transaction to take place too far away from a floor broker to allow the broker to complete it. This is not considered "missing the market" unless there is some evidence of carelessness.

Stop orders are often confused with limit orders but are actually quite different.

TABLE 32-3   Notice Days

Commodity	Notice or first notice day
Sugar No. 11 (New York)	Fourteenth calendar day of month preceding delivery month[1]
Sugar (London)	Fifteenth calendar day before first day of delivery month[1]
Cocoa (New York)	Seven business days before first day of delivery month
Cotton No. 2 Propane Wool	Five business days before first day of delivery month[2]
Coffee (C)	Three business days before first day of delivery month
Copper Mercury (Comex) Silver	Two business days before first day of delivery month
Broilers Corn Oats (CBT) Plywood (CBT) Silver (CBT) Soybeans Soybean meal Soybean oil Stud lumber (CBT) Wheat (CBT; Kansas City; MGE)	Last business day before first business day of delivery month
Cocoa (London) Coffee (London) Eggs (shell) Grain sorghum; milo Pork bellies Silver coins (CME) Winnipeg grains	First business day of delivery month
Cattle Hogs	Monday, Tuesday, Wednesday, Thursday, business day on or after sixth calendar day of delivery month[3]
Lumber (CME) Orange juice[2] Palladium Platinum Potatoes (Maine) Silver coins (New York)	First business day after last trading day of delivery month

[1] Or business day immediately preceding.
[2] At least five business days prior to day of delivery.
[3] No holiday or business day prior thereto.

SOURCE: Clayton Brokerage Company of St. Louis, Inc.

TABLE 32-4   Last Day of Trading

Commodity	Last day of trading
Coffee (C)	Fifth calendar day before first day of delivery month[1]
Sugar No. 11 (New York) Sugar (London)	Last business day before first day of delivery month
Potatoes (Maine) Wool Cotton No. 2	Fifth business day of delivery month Eleventh last business day of delivery month Seventeenth last business day of delivery month
Palladium Platinum Silver coins (New York)	Fourteenth calendar day of delivery month[1]
Lumber (CME) Propane	Fifteenth calenday day of delivery month[1]
Orange juice	Tenth last business day of delivery month
Cattle Copper (New York)[2] Hogs[1] Mercury[2]	Twentieth calendar day of delivery month
Cocoa (New York) Corn Eggs (shell) Grain sorghum; milo Oats (CBT) Plywood (CBT) Soybeans Soybean meal Soybean oil Stud lumber (CBT) Wheat (Kansas city; CBT; MGE)	Eighth last business day of delivery month
Pork bellies Silver coins (CME)	Sixth last business day of delivery month
Broilers Silver (CBT; New York)	Fourth last business day of delivery month
Cocoa (London) Coffee (London) Winnipeg grains	Last business day of delivery month
London metals	Last business day prior to prompt date for delivery.

[1]Or business day immediately preceding.
[2]Or the full business day immediately thereafter.
SOURCE: Clayton Brokerage Company of St. Louis, Inc.

A "buy stop" instructs a broker to execute an order when the price of a commodity rises to a specified level above the current market. The difference between a buy limit order and a buy stop order is exemplified as follows. A customer is inclined to buy December sugar, which is then selling at a price of 5.43 cents per pound. He or she tells the broker to buy a contract at a price not to exceed 5.35 cents. This is a "buy limit." Another customer under the same circumstances tells the broker to buy a contract of December sugar but not until the price rises to at least 5.55 cents, at which point the order will be executed at the market. The buy limit order is usually placed below the current market and must be executed at the limit or better. The buy stop order is placed above the current market and may be executed at the price specified on the stop, above it, or below it, because it is executed at the market after the stop price is touched, at which point the stop is said to be "elected."

A "sell stop" instructs a broker to execute an order when the price falls to a given level, at which point it is to be executed at the market. Unlike a typical sell limit order, it is below the current market level and may be executed at a price at, above, or below the specified stop when it is elected.[3] A sell limit order may be used to establish a new position or to liquidate an old one. A buy limit may be used to establish a new long position or to liquidate an old short.

A stop order may be used to limit a loss, protect a profit, or establish a new position. In the first case a client may have bought sugar at 5.45 cents per pound and has instructed the broker to sell it if it falls to 5.37 cents in order to limit his or her loss to 8 points. In the second case the sugar may already have risen from 5.45 to 5.65 cents, and the customer places a sell stop at 5.53 cents because he or she wants to keep the position if the price continues to rise but does not want to lose back all the paper profit if the price declines. Some clients will raise their stops as the price advances in an effort to gain as much as possible from a major move, while making certain that they can probably lose back only a little of the gain. This device, frequently called a "trailing stop," has great appeal to new traders but works considerably better in theory than in practice. Many major price moves seem to have an uncanny tendency to elect all the trailing stops just before going into their accelerating phase. In the third case a client with no position believes that if the current price declines from 5.45 to 5.36 cents, it will continue to decline substantially. He or she would like to take a short position, although not until the price declines to that point. The client thereupon tells the broker to sell his or her contract of sugar at 5.36 cents stop. Buy stops are used for similar reasons: to limit a loss, to protect a profit on a short position, or to establish a new long position but only after the price begins to rise.

A somewhat more complex order is the stop limit. The client might instruct the broker not to buy sugar until it rises to 5.53 cents per pound and not to pay more than 5.55 cents. This is unlike the unlimited stop, which becomes a market order when the stop price has been touched. The limit price may be the same or different from the specified stop.

A "market-if-touched (MIT) order" is used somewhat like a limit order but with a minor difference. The limit order must be executed at the limit price or one more favorable to the client. The MIT order is executed at the market when the market has traded at the price specified on the order, and so it may be filled at that price, above it, or below it. This order is often used by chartists who believe that a particular price is at the extreme of a trading range and who want to take a position immediately if that price level is reached with no risk of missing the

[3]Some exchanges prohibit stop orders from time to time or allow only stop limit orders when they fear that stops might aggravate unusually volatile markets.

market. MIT orders are sometimes called "board orders." For example, a client with a long position in pork bellies at 45.60 cents per pound who preferred to take a profit on a limit order might say, "Sell my July pork bellies at 48.50 cents." This instructs the brokerage firm to sell the contract at 48.50 cents or more. The order may be entered for one day or a specified period or be open (good until canceled). Another client with a similar position who preferred MIT orders would instruct the broker to sell his or her position at the market whenever a transaction took place at 48.50 cents or higher.

Sometimes a customer may wish to take a position within a short time but would like the broker on the floor of the exchange to use personal judgment in the timing of the fill. The broker will do this if the order indicates that he or she is to fill it at the market but is to take his or her time and will not be responsible if by waiting too long or not waiting long enough the price is unsatisfactory to the customer. Such orders are marked "Take your time (TYT)," "not held," or both. Customers may also specify the time at which they wish their orders filled; that is, "on opening," "on close," or at a particular specified time.

"Alternative orders" provide for one of two possible executions: a customer may order 5,000 bushels of corn at $1.45 a bushel and 5,000 bushels of wheat at $2.56 a bushel but not want both. A far commoner example of the alternative order is the placing of an objective and a stop, with instructions to cancel one if the other is filled. For example, having bought one contract of soybean oil at 14.50 cents a pound, a customer may order the broker to sell the oil at either 14.95 or 14.25 cents stop, whichever occurs first, and then immediately cancel the remainder of the order to avoid inadvertently reversing his or her position. This second kind of alternative order is popular with the trader who has carefully determined his or her objective and maximum loss point for a position and prefers to enter the order rather than watch the market and have to hurry to place one order or another as the market approaches one of the two points. Such an order also helps overcome the temptation to overstay positions.

"Scale orders" are used to establish or liquidate positions as the market moves up or down. The sugar trader may instruct the broker to buy a contract of sugar at 5.45 cents and another contract each time the price drops 5 points from that level until he or she has accumulated six contracts. When the trader sells out the position, he or she may order the broker to sell one contract at 5.70 cents and another contract each time the price rises 5 points until the six contracts have been sold.

"Contingent orders" are filled by the broker after the price of another contract or even another commodity reaches a specified level; for example, "Sell one July pork bellies at the market when August bellies have sold at 32.60." This order is used when the customer believes that August bellies will set the tone of the market but that profits will be maximized in the July contract.

"Spreads" may be established at a fixed difference rather than at specified prices because the spreader is concerned only with the difference rather than with the level. The broker may therefore be ordered to "buy one July pork bellies and sell one February bellies at 80 points difference or more, premium February." Such an order could be used to establish a new spread position, which the trader believes will narrow, or to take the profit in a position at a narrower difference and be satisfied with the profit at 80 points' difference.

Daily Operating Statement

It is essential that traders be completely aware at all times of the status of their accounts. They must realize that it is the equity that is most important, not the closed profits and losses to date. Failure to accept this allows traders to convince themselves that they are ahead when they have taken some small profits but are keeping positions with large open losses in the hope that the markets will reverse and their losses will be recovered.

To avoid overextending an account traders should distinguish their gross power from their net power. "Gross power" is the capital (credit balance or ledger credit) in a commodity account increased or decreased by adjustments from all trades open at a particular time. The adjustments consist of margin requirements, commissions, and open profits or losses. Gross power can be used to margin new positions or can be withdrawn from the account. It is sometimes called "buying power" or "free credit." "Net power" is gross power adjusted by the risk in open trades. This risk may be measured by the loss that would be suffered if all trades open were stopped out.

A trader, for example, has an account with $5,000 and no open positions. For the moment, $5,000 is his or her gross power. Let us assume that the trader has bought two contracts of cotton at 31.25 cents a pound, which require a margin of $900 per contract, or $1,800 for the entire position. The commission expense for the transaction is $90. The trader's gross power is therefore reduced to $3,110. If cotton moves up 20 points a contract to 31.45 cents, the open profit of $200 can be added to gross power, which would then be $3,310. As far as the broker is concerned, this amount can be used for new positions or be withdrawn from the account. If a stop-loss order has been entered at 30.80 cents, it would be possible for each cotton contract to drop at least 65 points before it is sold. If the drop occurs, the value of the account would decline by $650. A cautious trader, therefore, would regard only $2,660 as really available for use. This is the trader's net power.

Traders use different devices to make certain that they are always aware of their equity. Some go to the length each day of withdrawing any excess created by improvement in their equity and depositing a check for the amount of the equity loss at the end of any day during which they suffer adversity. This makes them constantly aware that they are dealing in real money and not merely in debits and credits.

A somewhat simpler method, and one calculated to make traders more popular with their brokers, is to maintain a simple ledger sheet (see Exhibit 32-1). If the fluctuations in an account are alarmingly large or if a trader is overextended, this statement will make the danger clear before, rather than after, a margin call or sell-out notice is received.

Buying Power

Sometimes clients may wish to know how much is available for new trades or how much cash can be withdrawn from their accounts. This amount is called "buying power," "excess," "excess margin," or "gross power" and in either case would be the same at any given moment. To arrive at the figure it is necessary to subtract margin requirements on open positions from the equity in an account. This is just a way of saying that what is not being used is free to be utilized or withdrawn. The figure is computed by taking the credit balance, adjusting it by the open profit or loss, including commissions, on open positions to arrive at equity and then subtracting margin requirements to arrive at the buying power or free balance. A well-run brokerage firm should be able to provide its clients with their buying power, equity, and open profit or loss almost immediately on request.

The Monthly Statement

The monthly statements sent by brokers to their customers list the changes that took place in their accounts during the month. Such changes may result from the deposit or withdrawal of funds, the establishment or liquidation of positions, or changes in the prices of commodity positions held during the month and still held when the statement is mailed. Clients must be familiar with the following terms to have a reasonably good understanding of their statements.

"Credit or cash balance" represents the funds deposited into an account, modified by the realized profits or losses from positions that have been closed out. The credit balance is not affected by open positions even though they may represent

EXHIBIT 32-1   DAILY OPERATING STATEMENT
(Five weeks from _____ to _____)

	M	Tu	W	Th	F
Capital (includes unrealized gains and losses)	_____	_____	_____	_____	_____
Margin on open trades	_____	_____	_____	_____	_____
Gross power	_____	_____	_____	_____	_____
Risk on open trades	_____	_____	_____	_____	_____
Net power	_____	_____	_____	_____	_____
Additions and withdrawals	_____	_____	_____	_____	_____
	M	Tu	W	Th	F
Capital (includes unrealized gains and losses)	_____	_____	_____	_____	_____
Margin on open trades	_____	_____	_____	_____	_____
Gross power	_____	_____	_____	_____	_____
Risk on open trades	_____	_____	_____	_____	_____
Net power	_____	_____	_____	_____	_____
Additions and withdrawals	_____	_____	_____	_____	_____
	M	Tu	W	Th	F
Capital (includes unrealized gains and losses)	_____	_____	_____	_____	_____
Margin on open trades	_____	_____	_____	_____	_____
Gross power	_____	_____	_____	_____	_____
Risk on open trades	_____	_____	_____	_____	_____
Net power	_____	_____	_____	_____	_____
Additions and withdrawals	_____	_____	_____	_____	_____
	M	Tu	W	Th	F
Capital (includes unrealized gains and losses)	_____	_____	_____	_____	_____
Margin on open trades	_____	_____	_____	_____	_____
Gross power	_____	_____	_____	_____	_____
Risk on open trades	_____	_____	_____	_____	_____
Net power	_____	_____	_____	_____	_____
Additions and withdrawals	_____	_____	_____	_____	_____

paper profits or losses. The only way in which the original credit balance represented by the customer's deposit of margin may be affected is by an additional deposit, a withdrawal, or the closing out of a position at a profit or loss. The margin requirements established by the broker to support open positions do not appear on the statement but merely reduce the amount of the credit balance left free to take other positions.

"Equity" is the amount of money that the account would be worth if all open positions were liquidated. If there were no open positions in an account, credit balance and equity would be identical. If there were positions, equity would be determined by adding open profits less commissions to the credit balance and subtracting open losses plus commissions. A few firms indicate the net open profit or loss on statements to show their clients exactly where they stand. This plays havoc with the common practice of ignoring open losses in the hope that they will go away but is a desirable means of making certain that clients knows what they have. A statement that indicates the net open profit or loss is frequently called an "equity statement."

"Transfers of funds" made between a customer's regulated and unregulated commodity accounts are also shown on the monthly statement. Most brokers keep funds in the regulated account until the customer trades in a commodity not regulated by the Commodity Exchange Authority (CEA; now the Commodity Futures Trading Commission, or CFTC). A transfer will be indicated by a debit to the regulated account balanced by a credit in the unregulated account. The statement will show credit and open positions separately in the two types of account. Most firms give both on different parts of the same statement form. A few use separate statements. Transfers of funds within the accounts do not change the overall credit balance or equity but are just routine accounting entries to comply with federal regulations.

Regulatory Requirements

In addition to the rules of the various exchanges, traders may be concerned with some of the regulations imposed by the CFTC, which has many of the same functions relating to commodity exchanges and trading as the Securities and Exchange Commission (SEC) has to security exchanges and trading. Most of these regulations, some of which require certain capital and bookkeeping procedures, apply to brokerage houses, but sometimes an individual trader may be directly concerned. One of the commonest is that transactions in commodities regulated by the CFTC, as opposed to unregulated commodities, be accounted for separately. This is the reason why two monthly statements may be necessary and why most brokers encourage their clients to sign the "CFTC letter," or "authority to transfer funds." Unregulated commodities include those that trade on foreign exchanges not regulated by the CFTC, such as Winnipeg, and a few commodities of foreign origin, such as cocoa (cacao), silver, platinum, sugar, and coffee.

To provide accurate information on the activities of large and small traders, the CFTC requires large traders to file reports that can be compared with the number of open positions available from clearinghouses to arrive at a total of small positions. These reports are easily prepared and need be of no concern to the trader who chooses to comply. Some brokerage houses will help to prepare the forms or even perform the entire task if they are assured that a client is not trading elsewhere, which could lead to an inaccurate report. Current CFTC reportable positions are listed in Table 32-5. These reports are made on forms supplied by the Authority's regional offices. The CFTC has also set maximum limits, well above the specified reportable positions, that may be held by one person directly or indirectly through his or her control of other accounts. These limits are indicated in Table 32-6.

Tax Considerations

A commodity position in the futures market represents a contract to buy or sell and does not represent ownership of a commodity. The margin required by a broker may be viewed as a performance deposit and not as a payment in the usual sense of the word. When the contract is liquidated, the profit or loss merely represents the price difference from the level at which the contract was made, less the commission. There are those who quarrel with designations of commodity positions as "property," but they have been generally accepted as such and are considered to be capital assets. Although they are not regarded as securities (chiefly because they are seen as primary rather than secondary investments, hence do not depend on the performance of others), commodity contracts are subject in general to the same tax treatment as other capital assets including securities.

Commodity trading *does not* create the deductible interest expense that stock trading on margin does because no interest is charged on commodity accounts unless they are in deficit or are undermargined to the degree that the broker must

TABLE 32-5   Commodity Exchange Authority Reportable Portions*

Regulated commodities	Reportable position
Eggs (shell or frozen)	
Pork bellies	
Cattle	
Hogs	
Lumber	
Orange juice	25 contracts
Potatoes	
Soybean meal	
Soybean oil	
Wool	
Corn	
Grain sorghum, milo	
Oats	40 contracts
Soybeans	
Wheat	
Cotton	50 contracts

*The CFTC requires that reports be filed for each day on which a trade is made, for the day before, during, and one day after the following positions are reached by a person in the aggregate of all accounts which that person owns or controls.
SOURCE: Clayton Brokerage Company of St. Louis, Inc.

deposit his or her own funds with the clearinghouse, pending receiving adequate funds from the client, in which case he or she may charge interest.

No state or federal taxes are charged directly on transactions. The cost of a trade for tax purposes includes the commissions charged.

Holding-period rules are similar to those for securities: that is, transactions are considered to be first in, first out (FIFO) unless a different choice is specified on the orders given to the broker. For example, if a trader buys one contract of May potatoes at 4.52 cents a pound in January and a second contract at 5.53 cents in March, and then instructs the broker to sell one contract in April when the price is 5.80 cents, the transaction will be closed on the earlier purchase at 4.52 cents. If the client prefers to close the transaction against his or her later purchase at 5.53 cents, he or she may do so but must ask the broker specifically to use the later purchase before the sale is made. Reasons for such requests usually involve tax or morale motives. There is no problem with physical delivery of certificates because there are none. There is no provision in the commodity markets for short sales against the box.

Capital Gains Treatment.   The tax treatment of a commodity position depend on whether it was speculative or a hedge. Hedging carried on in day-to-day dealings of a business results in current operating expenses or credits and therefore in fully taxable operating profits and losses rather than capital gains or losses.[4]

[4]Henry B. Arthur, *Commodity Futures as a Business Management Tool,* Division of Research, Graduate School of Business Administration, Harvard University, Boston, 1971, p. 41.

TABLE 32-6   Commodity Futures Trading Commission Position Limits[a]

Commodity	Position limit	Daily position limit if different
Eggs (shell)	150 contracts[b]	
Pork bellies	250 contracts[c]	375 contracts[d]
Broilers		
Cattle		450 contracts
Cotton	300 contracts	
Plywood		
Stud lumber (BOT)		
Potatoes	350 contracts[e]	
Oats	400 contracts[f]	
Wheat	400 contracts[f]	
Soybean oil	540 contracts	
Grain sorghum	550 contracts[g]	
Corn	600 contracts	
Soybeans		
Soybean meal	720 contracts	
Hogs	750 contracts[h]	1,125 contracts[i]
Lumber (CME)	1,000 contracts[h]	2,000 contracts[j]
Silver		
Copper (Comex)	2,000 contracts[k]	
Mercury		

[a]Limits established by the CFTC on the positions that may be held or the daily trades made by a person in the aggregate of all accounts that he or she owns or controls in any one contract month or in all contracts combined. In addition, certain limits are imposed by some of the commodity exchanges.

[b]In addition to the limitations of 150 carlots on total net long or short positions, no person shall hold a net long or short position in excess of 100 carlots in the October egg future, 75 carlots in the November egg future, 50 carlots in the December egg future, or 50 carlots in the January egg future.

[c]150 contracts in February, March, July, and August; 200 contracts in May.

[d]225 contracts in February, March, July, and August; 300 contracts in May.

[e]150 carlots in March, April, May; 300 carlots in others.

[f]To the extent that the net position held or controlled by any one person in all futures in any one grain on any one market is shown to represent spreading in the same grain between markets, the limit on net position in all futures may be exceeded on such contract market, but in no case shall the excess result in a net position of more that 3 million bushels in all futures combined or more than 2 million bushels in any one future.

[g]825 net contracts in all months combined.

[h]300 contracts in any one contract month.

[i]450 contracts in any one contract month.

[j]600 contracts in any one contract month.

[k]4,000 net contracts in all months combined.

SOURCE: Clayton Brokerage Company of St. Louis, Inc.

Just where hedging ends and speculation begins is difficult to determine. There appears to be little question that bona fide hedges are benefited by lower margin requirements and that losses resulting from them are fully deductible and gains fully taxable as ordinary income. It is less clear, however, just what is "bona fide" and even what is a "hedge." The definitions used by the CFTC and Internal Revenue Service (IRS) differ materially.[5]

Speculative profits and losses have consistently been held to be long-term or short-term capital gains, depending on whether the positions were held for more or less than six months and whether they were long or short positions. The holding period of a commodity futures position begins on the day after acquisition and ends on the day on which it is liquidated. There is no settlement period of several days, as there is in securities, which may be important to the trader who liquidates a position during the last few trading days of the calendar year. If delivery of a cash commodity is taken, the holding period consists of the time that the futures contract was held added to the time that the cash commodity is held, because a commodity futures contract and the commodity delivered against it are usually considered to be substantially identical.

As in securities, all profits on speculative short positions are considered, with only rare exceptions, as short-term gains, regardless of how long the positions are held, in that short positions can hardly be considered capital assets. Of course, a long position is usually taken to liquidate the short position, but it is considered to be instantaneously liquidated.

In a closed-out loss reinstated by a similar position within thirty days of the date on which the loss was realized the law is not so obvious as it is in securities, in which such a loss is clearly not deductible. One Circuit Court of Appeals has ruled that wash sale rules apply, and another has ruled that they do not. The decisions have not been clearly reconciled. In practice, many commodity traders apparently assume that the rule does not apply because most commodity trades are quite short term and the government's revenue is unlikely to be materially affected in the long run.

Substantially Identical Nature of Different Commodity Contract Months.   Although a commodity futures contract and the commodity it represents are substantially identical with little doubt, it should be noted that there is some difference in court decisions concerning whether different contract months of the same commodity are substantially identical. This has important implications for those who trade spreads, whether motivated by speculation or by tax considerations. Ultimate settlement of this point, along with others, such as whether commodity futures and options (puts and calls) are securities, could have a drastic effect on the conduct of the commodity business. These questions are difficult to resolve but will undoubtedly be settled by the courts sooner or later.[6]

If different delivery months of the same commodity are not considered substantially identical, as is usually presumed by most traders and their tax consultants, then a trader who is long March cotton and short May cotton is able at the same time to realize a long-term gain on the March cotton if the position is held more than six months. If a trader is long with a substantial profit, which he or she is inclined to take, but needs only a short time more to be eligible for long-term capital gain treatment, he or she can sell another futures contract against the

---

[5]Thorough discussions can be found in the Commodity Exchange Act as Amended, Section 4a, and in the Internal Revenue Code of 1954. The latter is summarized in *Standard Federal Tax Reporter,* Code Volume, Commerce Clearing House, New York, Chicago, and Washington, 1969. See especially Code Sections 1221 and 1233.

[6]Laurence Goldfein and Lester Hochberg, "Use of Commodity Straddles Can Effect Impressive Tax Savings," *The Journal of Taxation,* December 1968, p. 342.

position without jeopardizing the holding period. There is no certainty, of course, that this procedure will ensure complete success. If the market should decline drastically, the profit on the long position would be replaced by a profit on the short side. Furthermore, the spread position itself involves the possibility of a loss on the difference and the certainty of greater commission expense. A spread of exactly the same commodity in the same delivery month on two different exchanges would certainly be considered substantially identical and therefore obviously offers no tax advantage.

Tax Spreads.   Much has been written about the possibility of using commodity spreads to convert short-term gains from any source into long-term gains, postponing one year's short-term gains to the next year, either in whole or in part, converting one year's short-term gain into a long-term gain the following year, or, possibly, transferring a gain from one entity to another. Such spreads are not easy to manage, and the IRS has a long, often successful record of attacking transactions whose obvious purpose is to secure a tax advantage rather than a profit. A trade may yield a tax advantage and no profit, but at least a profit should have been a reasonable possibility. Spread trading for tax purposes is no area for the amateur. A poor choice of spread positions or mismanagement of the positions chosen can result in losses to a client well beyond any possible tax savings. Many clients in this position may be considered unsophisticated in the commodity area, and the brokerage employee may be inexpert in taxes (and perhaps in commodities), with distinct adverse legal implications to the broker. A particular problem is caused when a short position is placed in the early month of a spread and a long position in the later month. This may result in a severe loss if a strong market in the nearby month gains substantially on the distant month. It is unlikely that an unusually strong market will cause a distant month to rise materially on the nearby month.

Aside from the difficulty of selecting and timing the trades, traders and their advisers should make certain of a high degree of probability that the commissions, interest loss on margin, and risk of loss on trades themselves are overcome by enough potential saving to justify the economic risk inherent in every trade, no matter how carefully conceived and executed.

Tax rules vary among individual speculators, among businesses that deal primarily or partly in commodities, and among dealers in commodities. Important changes are made in the rules as new court decisions are handed down. Investors or traders would do well to consult their tax advisers before making any important assumptions about their tax exposure.

Chapter **33**

The Fundamental and Technical Approaches

RICHARD J. TEWELES

CHARLES V. HARLOW

HERBERT L. STONE

THE FUNDAMENTAL APPROACH

In the long run conventional economic wisdom would conclude that the price of a commodity must ultimately reflect the equilibrium point of all the combined forces of supply and demand. Isolating, quantifying, and evaluating in some reasonable way the respective weight of each supply-and-demand factor is the job of fundamentalists.

Basic Market Factors

Total supply-and-demand balances for most commodities are analyzed on a crop year, not a calendar year, basis. For example, the season for wheat and oats begins on July 1 and ends on the following June 30. Comparable dates for corn and cocoa (cacao) are October 1 to September 30.

Generally, total supply includes the old-crop carry-over, new-crop production, and imports. Carry-over includes all unused stocks from all earlier seasons. Total demand is domestic consumption plus exports. Domestic usage may be broken down further, as in soybeans, for example, into the demand for meal and oil, which result from the bean-crushing operation, and seed requirements. In addition, supply-and-demand factors will include the levels of inventory and various external influences on production and consumption.

If substantial amounts of any commodity are owned by the government, are under government loan, or are desired by the government, allowance must be made for the possibility of increased or decreased supply or demand at some point in the future. If a substantial amount of any commodity is placed under loan, for practical purposes it is no longer part of the "free" supply. Similarly, if the strategic level of stocks of a given commodity by government standards is low, allowance must be made for a possible nonrecurring increase in demand.

For typical traders the planning horizon is such that most of the variables affecting supply are irrelevant. For some commodities, in some instances, therefore, analysis of supply may be much easier than that of demand. If the dominant short-run supply factors are "set in concrete," the number of variables involved in any analysis will be reduced along with the probability of wrong analysis. The use of many variables enables traders to explain past data but at the same time increases the probability of error in future analysis.

Basic market factors may result during a given crop year in total-supply shortage, total-supply surplus, free-supply shortage, or free-supply surplus. Innumerable combinations are possible within the components that make up the basic market factors. For example, traders may well examine the timing and extent of price moves in season in which a large crop follows a large crop, a large crop follows a small crop, a small crop follows a large crop, or a small crop follows a small crop. Of no small interest may be the size of the carry-over at the beginning of each season when associated with any of these combinations.

To all these basic factors must be added the critical component of *expectation*. Fundamentalists find that they are confronted not only with the factual relationships discussed above but with the compound relationships described by the demanding yet gossamer prefix *expected*. Hence the multiplicity of relationships increases dramatically. Supply factors double from carry-over, new-crop production, and imports to *expected* carry-over, *expected* new-crop production, and *expected* imports. Whereas fundamentalists once were required to reason as best they could concerning the combinational change that could occur among three dominant variables, there are now six variables, with the ensuing proliferation of possible outcomes. Demand for soybeans explodes from an analysis that includes the demand for oil and meal, the amount of beans crushed, and exports into the *expected* demand for oil, the *expected* demand for meal, the *expected* crush of beans, and the *expected* export figure.

Model Building

Figure 33-1 is a flow graph of the cocoa industry that illustrates the magnitude of the forces that affect the price of a particular commodity at any point in time. These relationships include hundreds of variables, some of which are quantifiable to some degree. Theoretically, if the flow chart is correct and all the factors that affect the price of cocoa have been included and weighted according to their dominance, a mathematical formula might be produced to explain the average price of cocoa for each crop year.

Because such an exercise would require many years to prepare if it could be done at all, simplification of these relationships appears to be a necessity. This simplification, referred to as "model building," attempts to reduce the number of variables from that approaching the infinite to a few dominant factors that retain the power of explanation.

As a simplification of reality, models have limitations recognized by good theory. A serious limitation is that many factors affecting the price structure must, by definition, be eliminated from consideration. Traders must develop sufficient insight into the supply-and-demand factors of a given commodity to be able to identify the *dominant* price-making influences at any point in the crop year. For example, with reference to Fig. 33-1, the planting of new cocoa trees will certainly have the effect of increasing the production of cocoa in the long run. The lag in such incremental supply, however, is approximately five years. The most sanguine fundamentalists would admit that the price of cocoa futures will reflect many other shorter-term influences in the meantime, such as figures that may indicate that cocoa users face a second year of reduced carry-over inventory levels. Therefore caution must be used in the selection of individual elements when models are constructed.

In eliminating so many factors from consideration in the interest of simplification, care should be exercised to ensure that such simplification not give way to contradiction of reality. For example, a case for sharply higher prices might be made for wheat futures if new-crop production fell below total estimated usage and if a simple two-variable model were constructed. However, let us assume that

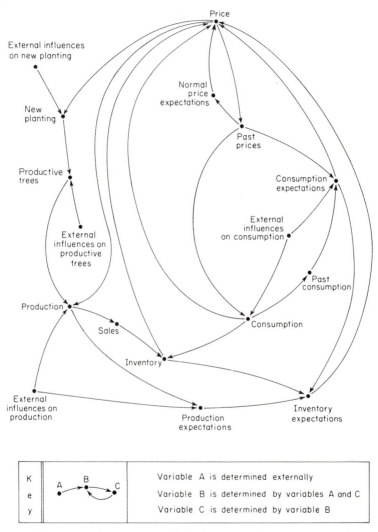

Fig. 33-1 Flow graph of the cocoa (cacao) industry structure. [*F. Helmut Weymar*, The Dynamics of the World Cocoa Market, *The M.I.T. Press, Cambridge, Mass., 1968, p. 2*]

wheat futures have fallen. If a less casual study inducted that old-crop carry-over had been at a twenty-year high, the model for supply would have to be expanded to include carry-over as well as new-crop production to avoid future contradictions.

Explaining versus Forecasting

Before proceeding to specific examples of explanatory and forecasting models, traders should be aware of the significant differences between the terms. One of the most insistent myths surrounding fundamental analysis in commodity futures is that *explaining* price changes is equivalent to *forecasting* price changes. On the contrary, an explanation is seldom equivalent to a prediction. In fact, explanation frequently requires only that the trader be equipped with 20/20 hindsight.

In an explanatory model the variables used to explain a price at a particular time are also measured at the same time and thus must be currently available with the prices they seek to explain. For example, let us assume that traders have found that the price of hogs is a function of the quantity of hogs available, the prices of substitutes (beef and veal, lamb and mutton, fish, and poultry), the income position of buyers, and consumer preference and that no further variables are necessary to explain past prices. Let us assume further that the proper quantities for all past years are absolutely known for all four of these variables and that they have been weighted properly. As magnificent as such a model of price behavior would be, it would enable traders only to *understand* past hog prices, not to *predict* future hog prices. The problem of turning explanatory variables into forecasting variables would still remain; for example, one determinant of the price for hogs, the quantity of hogs available, is reported quarterly in December, March, June, and September. Unfortunately no one has yet been able to forecast consistently the quantity of hogs before these reports are issued. If, as already discussed, the behavior of commodity futures prices is based partly on *expectations* and *changes in expectations,* it becomes a formidable task to predict price changes even if traders were given a perfect preview of the figures to be reported. Unless traders were also privy to accurate estimates of what figures were *expected,* they might still be unable to forecast the price changes that might follow the input of new information.

On the other hand, there are really only two general ways in which a forecasting model can be built. The first approach is to forecast the *next* hog quantity from a knowledge of past hog quantities. This simple extrapolative technique would have proven worth only if the explanatory variable, lagged for one three-month period, were found to have predictive value when estimating the quantity of hogs in the next report. For example, let us assume for a moment that traders had access to ten years of figures reflecting the quantity of hogs available as evidenced by the annual December report. It is now March, and the traders wish to forecast accurately the March quantity-of-hogs figure soon to be released. If their only source of information is the December hog quantity figure, they have an *explanatory* variable lagged by three months. If the pattern of December figures offers a significant clue over the years to the upcoming March figures, the traders can use this lagged explanatory variable to *predict* future variables. The published material to date, however, does not give the traders much encouragement in this regard.

The second method of forecasting isolates a variable that is predictive of hog quantities apart from past hog quantity figures. For example, the traders may find that quarterly changes in hog quantities are related to changes in the price of beef. However, for this information to be of forecasting rather than explanatory value, the prices of beef in the *present* period would have to correlate highly with the quantity of hogs available in a *future* period. Again research indicates that this approach to forecasting does not easily yield significant results.

Building an Explanatory Model

To date traders have been exposed to conceptual supply-and-demand analysis from which they gained an insight into basic economic relationships that can affect the pricing of commodities. The basic market factors intrinsic to each crop year were discussed, and the myriad possibilities that revolve around the factors themselves, as well as the expectations of those factors, were considered. The need to formulate a model that simplifies real-life complications while recognizing the limitations of such simplification leads traders to recognize the difference between explaining commodity futures prices and forecasting them.

TABLE 33-1   Miscellaneous Cocoa Data

Crop year	World production (before 1 percent weight loss)	World grind during crop year	World stocks, end of crop year	Ratio, actual carry-over stocks to grind	Crop year average price, New York spot Accra
	Thousands of long tons			Years	Costs per pound
1952–1953	798	787	168	0.214	33.6
1953–1954	776	770	166	0.216	55.4
1954–1955	802	690	269	0.390	43.0
1955–1956	843	785	319	0.406	29.3
1956–1957	896	895	310	0.346	26.6
1957–1958	771	890	183	0.206	42.9
1958–1959	908	842	240	0.285	38.4
1959–1960	1,039	897	371	0.414	30.7
1960–1961	1,173	999	533	0.534	24.2
1961–1962	1,124	1,089	556	0.511	21.9
1962–1963	1,158	1,149	553	0.481	23.4
1963–1964	1,216	1,158	598	0.516	24.3
1964–1965	1,482	1,274	791	0.620	19.0
1965–1966	1,205	1,378	605	0.439	22.5
1966–1967	1,333	1,364	561	0.411	26.9
1967–1968	1,333	1,387	492	0.354	30.4
1968–1969	1,225	1,348	356	0.264	44.5
1969–1970	1,413	1,335	420	0.315	37.9
1970–1971	1,479	1,372	512	0.373	30.1
1971–1972	1,548	1,499	545	0.364	28.2

SOURCE: As modified from F. Helmut Weymar, "Cocoa: The Effect of Inventories on Price Forecasting," *Commodity Yearbook,* Commodity Research Bureau, 1969, p. 16.

The ability to explain prices in any commodity necessarily precedes the ability to forecast prices. Perhaps the most rewarding way for fundamentalists to try to explain supply-and-demand factors is not only to simplify the countless variables into the more dominant factors, as discussed earlier, but to shorten the span of concentration from the entire crop year into more easily analyzed segments.

A particularly interesting area of concentration might be a discussion of the effect of inventory and inventory expectations on the price of cocoa (see Fig. 33-1). Many analysts agree that cocoa price levels are highly correlated with carry-over inventory levels.[1]

Table 33-1 provides basic information on supply, demand, and inventory and average price levels of cocoa for a number of years. Figure 33-2 graphs the yearly

[1]For an excellent comprehensive analysis of the economics of cocoa, see F. Helmut Weymar, *The Dynamics of the World Cocoa Market,* The M.I.T. Press, Cambridge, Mass., 1968. In the following discussion the authors draw as well on Dr. Weymar's article "Cocoa: The Effect of Inventories on Price Forecasting," *Commodity Yearbook,* Commodity Research Bureau, 1969, pp. 15–22. The latter was updated through private correspondence.

relation between the actual carry-over stocks (inventory) as a percentage of the world grind (consumption) and the average price of spot cocoa in New York.

Before examining this specific relationship, traders should understand why, in general, commodity price levels show a strong inverse relation to the ratio of carry-over inventories to the recent consumption rate. There are two basic reasons for

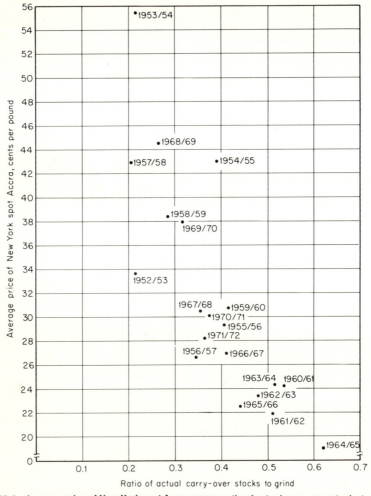

Fig. 33-2   Average price of New York spot Accra versus ratio of actual carry-over stocks to grind (years).

this phenomenon: (1) the need for prices to ration existing inventories if present levels are low and (2) the need to strike an equilibrium in the longer run between supply and demand.

Inventory Rationing. Inventory levels have an immediate impact on the relations between near and deferred contracts of the same commodity. An inverted market, in which the near futures are selling for premiums above deferred contracts, reflects the presence of relatively low levels of inventory. In a situation in which a manufacturing company's cocoa bean inventories are low, it faces real business risks. The company may have to change its production mix because it does not have on hand the amount or variety of cocoa beans it needs. Its vulnerability to strikes or transportation difficulties increases, and it may not be able to honor its shipping commitments. For these and other reasons there is a convenience yield that attaches to the holding of a minimum cocoa inventory in and of itself. This minimum inventory will be held even though a manufacturer may expect a decline in cash cocoa prices. On the other hand, if the cocoa bean inventory being carried is large in relation to the user's historical needs, any additional inventory not only will have no added value but will not be tolerated unless the costs of carrying excess inventory can be recovered. This recovery can take place either in an increase in the price of cocoa or by short hedging in the futures market at a premium sufficient to cover carrying costs.

Throughout this process it is price that is the rationing instrument. As inventory carry-over levels decrease, all other things remaining constant, nearby contracts increase their premiums over more distant futures, thereby forcing those who hold the inventory to bear an increasing penalty for not selling it in the cash market for a high price and replacing it with a lower-priced contract for delivery some months later. Conversely, when inventories are excessive, nearby prices will be battered in comparison with future contract prices, for potential storers of cocoa must be induced to carry substantial inventories.

Long-Run Equilibrium.   Obviously there are many long-term fluctuations in production and consumption that influence massive price changes in the price structure of cocoa. As always, expectations about these changes, both in their timing and in their impact, play an important part in generating a realistic price level. Yet a glance at Fig. 33-2 will confirm that whatever long-term price assessment is made in terms of production and consumption generally appears to be consistent with known current inventory levels. The reason for this seems to be that following a prolonged period of production surplus current inventories tend to be high, whereas subsequent to a series of short crops inventories fall to quite low levels. Thus, as Weymar notes, "The carry-over ratio alone explains major price movements reasonably well, both because it provides a measure of the near term need to ration or encourage inventory holding, and because it provides a good proxy for the market's assessment of the longer term supply-demand balance."[2]

Inventory Expectations.   Figure 33-2 confirms the general tendency for cocoa prices to vary in line with the ratio of carry-over inventories to the recent consumption rate. Traders must remember, however, that the price scale is quite large and that each grid on that scale represents 2 cents a pound, or $600 a contract. A miss of this dimension can represent as much as a 60 percent loss of a $1,000 margin requirement. For example, the carry-over inventory ratios for the 1952–1953, 1953–1954, and 1957–1958 crop years were almost the same, and, hypothetically, traders would have reason to expect that prices would ration supplies in a similar fashion. Yet average price levels for those years were 34, 57, and 44 cents, respectively. Clearly, such excessive scatter is disturbing to traders trying to explain these price levels.

This result has not been unanticipated. The reader will remember that model building presents disadvantages as well as advantages. The search for simplicity often eliminates factors that turn out to be dominant and demand recognition if a good explanatory model is to be built. As promising as the explanation is for cocoa prices given in Fig. 33-2, a dominant factor is missing. That factor, as might be surmised by now, is the variation in inventory *expectations*, which in many years

---

[2]F. Helmut Weymar, "Cocoa: The Effect of Inventories on Price Forecasting," *Commodity Yearbook*, Commodity Research Bureau, 1969, p. 21.

have differed significantly from the *actual* inventory carry-over figures eventually included in statistical records. The market never knows what world production and consumption will be for a given year until that reality is close to fulfillment.

The effect of including the expected carry-over ratio is illustrated in Fig. 33-3. The basis of computation is complex,[3] but it can be summarized briefly. At the

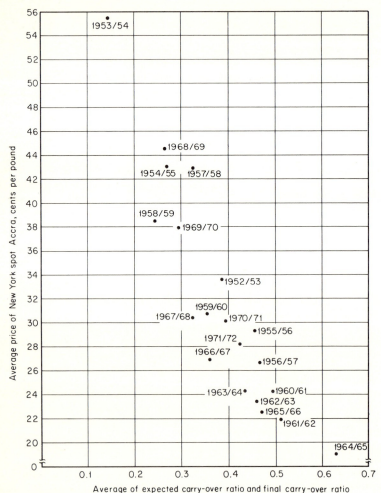

Fig. 33-3 Average price of New York spot Accra versus average of expected carry-over ratio and final carry-over ratio.

beginning of each crop year estimates of the new-crop production and consumption of cocoa are issued by Gill & Duffus, Ltd., in London. Because the carry-over stocks from the preceding year are known, a computation of the expected new-crop carry-over ratios can be made at that time. A year later, when the actual carry-over ratio is known, there are frequent mismatches between the expected and actual amounts. Figure 33-3 plots yearly average cocoa prices against the average

[3]See Appendix 4A in F. Helmut Weymar, *The Dynamics of the World Cocoa Market,* The M.I.T. Press, Cambridge, Mass., 1968, pp. 195–217.

for each year of the initial expected and *final* actual carry-over ratios. Justification for an averaging process is based on the fact that expectations tend to trend relatively smoothly to their actuality at the end of a given crop year. Certainly traders can appreciate that there is less scatter in Fig. 33-3 than in Fig. 33-2, which indicates a better fit and therefore a more satisfactory explanation of yearly average cocoa prices.

Toward a General Model of Prices.   Of course, not all commodities are similar to cocoa in that traders are able to isolate and quantify inventory adjustments as a promising approach to an explanation of price changes. There are futures markets for commodities without continuous inventories. Potatoes, for example, are produced seasonally, but most stocks are disposed of before June 1 each year. Other commodities such as live beef cattle and fresh eggs have no inventories at all in the usual sense. Traders must approach the basic market factors in these commodoties without the help of carry-over analysis.[4]

Lately interest has increased in the attempt to isolate and quantify factors that have a general explanatory effect, no matter what individual commodity is studied. The feasibility of an approach toward constructing a general model is gaining impetus because of the availability of the computer. A recent study, which utilized spectral analysis of six commodities (soybean oil, cottonseed oil, soybean meal, soybeans, rye, and wheat) used to monthly price changes over a nine-year period, concluded that in the long run prices were determined mainly by the prices of substitutable commodities, followed in importance by hedging and speculative activity, supply-and-demand components, and the business cycle.[5]

Building a Forecasting Model

The bridge from explaining past price changes to forecasting future price changes is not easily crossed. Many traders are sure that someone, somewhere, knows everything, in that this person is knowledgeable enough to list all the sets of supply-and-demand conditions that would cause *all* bull or bear markets. In reality, traders do extremely well to isolate, quantify, and evaluate any set of conditions *sufficient* to cause a particular bull or bear market, even if viewed retrospectively. The development of a forecasting model requires even more rigor.

There is no requirement that traders be omniscient to make money. It is enough that they isolate and quantify any set of sufficient conditions for bull and bear markets in the commodities that they are trading. Traders following this strategy will simply not trade a commodity (regardless of its price fluctuations, all of which are caused by sufficient conditions of which they are unaware) until they see the sufficient conditions that they have previously validated materialize. Then, and only then, will these traders take a position in the market.

Such a strategy is similar to that which might be followed by persons paid to predict fires. They might miss a great many fires caused by, say, chemical combinations of which they are completely unaware, but the specific knowledge that rags soaked with flammable fluids usually combust might be enough to earn them a generous living.

The purpose of the following discussion is to develop a basic understanding of some of the requirements for the construction of a successful forecasting model. To accomplish this the informal process with which the explanatory model dealt

---

[4]The recent emergence of futures markets for noninventory commodities is discussed by William G. Tomek and Roger W. Gray, "Temporal Relationships among Prices on Commodity Futures Markets: Their Allocative and Stabilizing Roles," *American Journal of Agricultural Economics,* vol. 52, no. 3, pp. 372–380, August 1970; and the ensuing "reply," vol. 53, no. 2, pp. 362–366, May 1971.

[5]Walter Labys and C. W. J. Granger, *Speculation, Hedging, and Commodity Price Forecasts,* D. C. Heath and Company, Boston, 1970, chap. 8.

must give way to an actual step-by-step statistical process. For example, let us assume that commodity analysts are attempting to isolate and quantify a supply-and-demand relationship in the soybean market that will have predictive value. Because inventory stocks were found to be an integral part in explaining cocoa price changes, the analysts similarly will decide to use the quantity of soybeans crushed and exported as a measure of the demand for a given period and the stocks of soybeans in all positions as an indicator of supply. Stocks in all positions are reported quarterly during the soybean crop year, which, for the purpose of this historical analysis, begins on October 1. Crush figures are available monthly, and export figures weekly. The earliest practical period, therefore, on which a meaningful comparison of usage and supply may be made is in January of each calendar year. Historically, the date of the "stocks-in-all-positions" report for soybeans has not varied significantly from January 24. At that time annual comparisons may be made between the size of the October–December crush plus exports and the stocks of beans in all positions.

In Fig. 33-4 the X axis represents the annual ratio of January 1 stocks of soybeans in all positions, divided by the previous quarter's usage. Since 1952 that ratio has been as low as 2.22 and as high as 3.38. The lower the figure, the higher the October–December usage of soybeans relative to the present supply. Plotted on the Y axis is the highest price reached by the July soybeans future between March 1 and the end of the July contract, measured against the Chicago equivalent of the loan price each year. For example, if the average farm loan price for soybeans in 1966 was \$2.50 a bushel, approximately 20 cents would be added to it to equal the Chicago equivalent. If the actual high reached by July soybeans on the Chicago Board of Trade from March 1 to the end of the contract was \$3.77¼, it may be said that July soybeans sold as high as \$1.07¼ above the Chicago equivalent of the loan price.

If there were a perfect linear relation between the variables X and Y, as shown in Fig. 33-4, the yearly dots would fall exactly on the regression line that serves to measure the historical average relation between the variables. The scatter about that regression line measures the "goodness of fit." Given the value of the January supply-and-demand factors that constitute the variable X, the "best" estimate of the high price in July beans is given by the Y' value of the regression line. This step may be accomplished graphically or by using the predictive equation $Y = 3.99 - 1.213X$,[6] which was computed by using the data from 1952 to 1972. As X becomes available on January 24 each year, the trader has only to solve for Y' to estimate the July high. The coefficient of determination r^2 is 0.55. This measures the proportion of change in Y that can be attributed to changes in X. The standard deviation $S_{y.x}$ of Y for any given X is 26.7 cents a bushel, which indicates that for any value X that becomes available on January 24 the July high price will be within 26.7 cents of the Y' value, as shown on the regression line approximately 68 percent of the time.

To date Fig. 33-4 has been constructed as a simple two-variable explanatory model that illustrates a principle with which traders are now familiar: prices tend to vary inversely to the ratio of inventories to the recent consumption rate. However, to achieve a *predictive* value from such a relationship a significant amount of the price rise in July soybeans in any given year must occur *after* January 24.

Certain conclusions are evident in a study of the relationships in Fig. 33-4. First, research indicates that the profit potential is poor when X is greater than 2.60. For most of these years the closing price of July soybeans on January 24 was not significantly below the high price reached in the subsequent March–July periods.

---

[6]This equation was determined by using the least-squares method, which is illustrated in any elementary statistics text.

There is no significant forecasting value to the model in these years. Second, when X is less than 2.60, the probability of a major bull market in soybeans in that crop year becomes high. The years 1954, 1956, 1961, 1965, 1966, 1971, and 1972 produced such a ratio. The trader in these years was faced with the possibility of sufficient conditions for a price rise of extraordinary amplitude. Because the

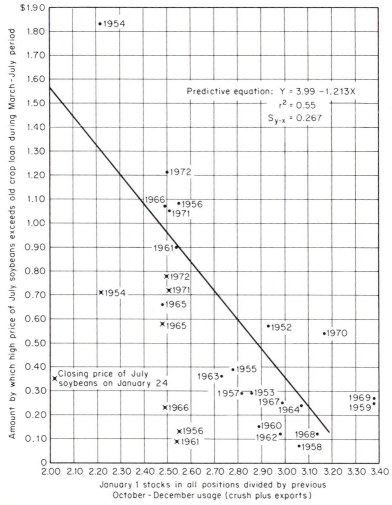

Fig. 33-4 Soybean supply (stocks in all positions, January 1) and demand [October–December crush plus exports (X)] versus price highs (Y) in March–July for July soybeans, 1952–1972.

stocks-in-all-positions report issued quarterly does not become available until about three weeks after the effective date, January 24 becomes the earliest practical date on which traders may take the position dictated by the predictive equation in Fig. 33-4.

Table 33-2 summarizes the results of instituting a long position on January 24 of each soybean crop year when X is less than 2.60. Column 2 gives the price of July soybeans versus the loan on January 24 of each crop year. Column 3 shows the March–July expected high price established by the predictive equation. The

TABLE 33-2   Results of Long Positions in July Soybeans Instituted on January 24 When X Is Less Than 2.60

Crop year (1)	Premium of January 24 price of July soybeans over Chicago equivalent of loan price (to nearest cent) (2)	Predictive equation price ($Y = 3.99 - 1.213X$) (3)	Equation profit potential (3) minus (2) (4)
1953–1954	$0.71	$1.30	$0.59
1955–1956	0.13	0.90	0.77
1960–1961	0.09	0.91	0.82
1964–1965	0.58	0.98	0.40
1965–1966	0.23	0.97	0.74
1970–1971	0.72	0.94	0.22
1971–1972	0.78	0.96	0.18
1972–1973*	1.98	1.09	−0.89

*Preliminary data for 1972–1973 present an interesting example of the dilemma faced by all traders using the fundamental approach. Following the January 24, 1973, stocks report, the premium of the price of July soybeans over the Chicago equivalent of the loan price was 89 cents *above* the average price expected by the predictive equation. Clearly, expectations of a bull market had pulled prices very high early in the crop year, and traders believing that prices could go even higher were faced with establishing a long position of more than $4 a bushel, a level rarely attained historically. The fact that July soybeans exceeded $6 a bushel in early March is one more illustration that historical relationships, although of immense help, do not guarantee traders a clear outline of Camelot.

potential profit is entered in column 4. By referring to Fig. 33-4, it may be seen that in each year except 1964–1965 the expected high price in July soybeans was equaled or exceeded in the given period. In the 1953–1954, 1955–1956, 1960–1961, and 1965–1966 seasons, the actual price on January 24 was more than 2 standard deviations removed from the regression line. For these years the trader could say with an extremely high probability (.95) of being correct that the price of July soybeans in the March–July period would be significantly higher than it was on January 24. The crop years 1970–1971 and 1971–1972 reflected a ratio of less than 2.60 on January 24, which called for 22-cent and 18-cent increases, respectively, in prices sometime between March and the end of the July contract. These expectations were exceeded in 1971 by 10 cents and in 1972 by 25 cents.

THE TECHNICAL APPROACH[7]

"Technical analysis" refers to a study of the market itself rather than of the external factors that affect the supply of and demand for a given commodity. The basic assumption underlying all technical analysis is that by studying statistics generated by the market it is possible to reach meaningful conclusions about future prices; that is, the way the market behaved yesterday may indicate how prices will behave today. Technicians do not believe that price fluctuations are random and unpredictable. They believe that if they study the transactions taking place, impending price movements will tip their hands.

Fundamentalists reason inductively, seeking to isolate and quantify dominant factors. By taking into consideration the expected supply and expected usage of a commodity, which includes such factors as carry-in, carry-out, production, exports, free supplies, substitutability, and a host of others, they try to deduce the

[7]James Alphier, research partner, Cambistics, Inc., Long Beach, Calif., is coauthor of this part of Chapter 33 with Teweles, Harlow, and Stone.

intrinsic value of the commodity. If the current price is substantially above or below this appraisal, appropriate action is taken in the futures market.

Technicians contend that this is a futile procedure. The factors that fundamentalists are examining are in many cases estimates subject to important revision. Furthermore, technicians assert that there are so many fundamental elements in play at any time that an important one can often be overlooked or those being analyzed may be weighted improperly. Even if all relevant supply-and-demand factors can be estimated with total accuracy, the technical analysts still believe that the result would be of only limited value in appraising prices.

Isaac Newton can be given credit for probably the best-known assumption on which most technicians operate: "A price trend once established is more likely to continue than to reverse." This is simply a restatement of Newton's first law of motion, applied to price action. If this concept is accepted as true, a successful trading strategy can be built on the simple principle of buying strength and selling weakness. The only problem remaining is the optimum way in which to carry it out. Several trend-following methods are presented below.

Moving Averages

An average is defined as "the quotient of any sum divided by the number of its terms." Thus a ten-day average of soybean closing prices is the sum of the last ten days' closings divided by 10. A moving average of prices is a progressive average in which the divisor number of items remains the same, but at periodic intervals (usually daily or weekly) a new item is added to the end of the series as, simultaneously, an item is dropped from the beginning.

If one is constructing a ten-day moving average of soybean closes, the average on the tenth day is the sum of days 1 through 10 divided by 10. On the eleventh day the eleventh day's close is added to the total, and the close of day 1 is subtracted. This new sum is then divided by 10. On day 12 the close of that day is added to the total, and the close of day 2 is subtracted. This total is divided by 10, and so on. Table 33-3 illustrates the computation of a ten-day moving average based on the closing prices of May 1961 soybeans.

TABLE 33-3   Computation of a Ten-Day Moving Average for a Typical May Soybeans Contract

Date	Close (cents)	Ten-day net change*	Ten-day total†	Ten-day average ‡
March 15	290.000			
March 16	291.500			
March 17	294.000			
March 20	290.500			
March 21	291.500			
March 22	300.500			
March 23	304.000			
March 24	204.500			
March 27	301.250			
March 28	305.250		2,973,000	297.30
March 29	297.750	+ 7.750	2,980,750	298.08
March 30	300.250	+ 8.750	2,989.500	298.95
April 3	300.500	+ 6.500	2,996.000	299.60
April 4	299.750	+ 9.250	3,005.250	300.53
April 5	302.250	+10.750	3,016.000	301.60

*Difference (plus or minus) between latest close and the tenth close, counting back.
†Sum of ten latest closes.
‡The ten-day-total column divided by 10. These figures in sequence make up the moving average.

Figure 33-5 shows a ten-week moving average of soybean closes. An examination of this chart will reveal the important properties of moving averages. The ten-week moving average smooths out the erratic week-to-week changes in actual prices and thereby indicates the underlying trend. Further, the moving average lags behind prices and crosses the current price only when a new direction is

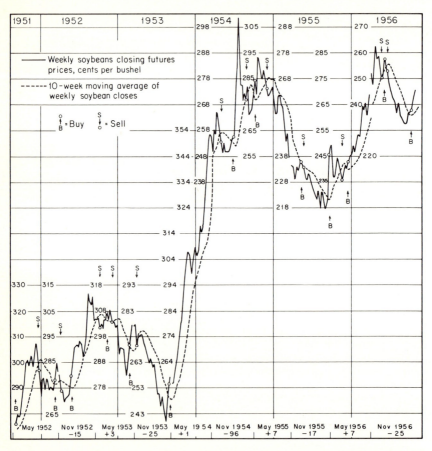

Fig. 33-5   May and November soybeans: weekly closing price versus ten-week moving average. Prices of contracts are adjusted to each other for continuity. [Guide to Commodity Price Forecasting, *Commodity Research Bureau, New York, 1965.*]

established. These same properties are characteristic of moving averages calculated for any time span.

Shown on the chart are "buy" and "sell" signals, given when price penetrates the ten-week moving average. Technicians acting on this signal are following the strategy of buying strength and selling weakness. They hope that the prevailing trend, like the buy signal of late 1953, will continue long enough and powerfully enough to compensate adequately for the kind of whipsaw losses that resulted from the first two signals of 1952.

There are countless systems that use moving averages,[8,9] but all are based on variations of just two factors:

1. The length of time used in computing the moving average. It is here that an important trade-off is involved. The shorter the length of time, the more sensitive the moving average will be to any change in trend. New trends will be acted on earlier and do not need much time to establish themselves. Traders pay for this sensitivity because the shorter the moving average's length, the greater the number of trades that will be made. This means greater commissions and a larger number of whipsaw losses. A longer period of time used to calculate the moving average will reduce the number of trades and the number of whipsaw losses but will signal new trends much later, often so late that the trend will be closer to completion than initiation.

2. The kind and amount of penetration required. In an effort to reduce false signals, many technicians demand more than just a simple penetration of the moving average. For instance, having the price in Fig. 33-5 penetrate the moving average by 5 cents before acting on any signal would eliminate several whipsaws. This strategy, however, is subject to the limitations described above. Too small an amount of penetration does little to reduce whipsaws and excess trades. Too large a penetration has the effect of cutting down profits on successful signals.

Swing Charts

Swing charts provide many of the trend-following properties of moving averages, but they are usually easier to calculate. Swing charts are similar to point-and-figure charts because the trader is interested in price movements of a certain minimum amount. Figure 33-6 is a chart of July 1971 platinum constructed by drawing in only those swings of 300 points or more. The key difference between the swing chart and a point-and-figure chart covering the same time period is that the swing chart shows the precise highs and lows and a point-and-figure chart is likely to show them to the nearest 20 or 50 points.

To carry out the basic trend-following strategy of buying strength and selling weakness traders buy when the top of a previous swing is penetrated on the upside and sell when the bottom of a previous swing is penetrated on the downside. These signals are shown on the chart.

The theory behind swing charting is that tops and bottoms in price become "important" if they are terminations of swings of some minimum amount. If they are later penetrated, a new trend is presumed to be in force. Traders who employ swing charts are following the age-old dictum "Take positions along the line of least resistance."

---

[8]A number of moving-average systems are presented in Garfield Drew, *New Methods for Profit in the Stock Market,* Metcalf Press, Boston, 1955; Curtiss Dahl, *Consistent Profits in the Commodity Futures Market,* Tri-State Offset Co., Cincinnati, Ohio, 1960, with 1961 addendum; C. W. Keltner, *How to Make Money in Commodities,* Keltner Statistical Service, Kansas City, Mo., 1960; Irving Levine, *Successful Commodity Speculation,* Levro Press, Newark, N.J., 1965; Robert Joel Taylor, "The Major Price Trend Directional Indicator," *Commodities Magazine,* April 1972. Dunn & Hargitt, P.O. Box 101, Lafayette, Ind., 47902, sells a computerized study of hypothetical trading in several commodities for a number of years in which most of the best-known moving-average trading systems are used.

[9]An increasingly popular form of moving average is one that has been exponentially smoothed. It is doubtful if exponential smoothing is an important improvement on the standard calculation of moving averages. One source on this as well as other smoothing methods is Robert Brown, *Smoothing, Forecasting & Prediction of Discrete Time Series,* Prentice-Hall, Inc., Englewood Cliffs, N.J., 1963. Brown's book particularly stresses the how-to aspect of smoothing procedures.

Any swing-charting method[10] is composed of just two elements: (1) the amount of the minimum swing to be charted and (2) the amount and type of penetration required when price penetrates a previous top or bottom. The same trade-off occurs here that occurs with moving-average methods. The smaller the amount of

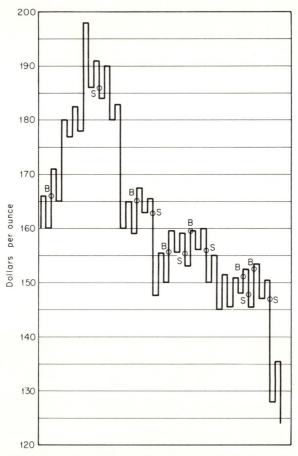

Fig. 33-6   July 1971 platinum 330-point swing chart. Buy and sell signals are shown for February–October 1971.

penetration required, the more quickly new trends are signaled and the more whipsaws that result. A larger required price penetration reduces whipsaw but also puts traders in later on the more successful signals. The choice of the amount of

[10]Keltner, op. cit.; William Dunnigan, *New Blueprints for Gains in Stocks and Grains*, privately published, San Francisco, Calif., 1956 (out of print but available from various specialty dealers); Richard Donchian, "Trend Following Methods in Commodity Price Analysis," in *Guide to Commodity Price Forecasting*, Commodity Research Bureau, New York, 1965, are comprehensive sources of information on swing charting as well as on moving-average and other trend-following techniques.

minimum price swing to be charted is analogous to the choice of the number of days to be used for a moving average.

Some technicians have constructed swing charts based not on price but on time.[11] Tops or bottoms that hold for some arbitrary number of days or weeks are defined as important. When they are penetrated, buy or sell signals are generated. The choice of the length of time during which a top or a bottom must stand and of the amount and type of penetration required make this kind of chart subject to the limitations of standard swing charts.

Advantages and Disadvantages of Using Trend-following Methods

Advantages.   (1) A trend-following technique is, by definition, objective. All the elements must be clearly defined before it can be put into practice. This means that traders can, if they have the facilities, determine how well any technique has worked in the past and define its important characteristics. Any number of variations can be back-checked in an attempt to optimize results. (2) Any trend-following method provides traders with a sizable part of their operating plans, with all the attendant benefits in terms of results and peace of mind. Because action points are so clearly defined, traders are not so likely to be beset by uncertainties. (3) Trend followers believe, along with many famous traders, that "the big swing makes the big money. If traders employ any trend-following method, it is impossible for a big move to occur without their participating in it.

Disadvantages.   (1) Traders who use trend-following methods begin with two counts against them. First, whipsaws are inevitable. One technician, himself an ardent trend-following advocate, indicates that 50 percent of all trades entered into by any such method will result in whipsaw losses.[12] Second, all signals acted on are late by definition. To compensate for these two liabilities, traders must realize substantial profits on the successful signals, and even during a normally active market this may be difficult to achieve. (2) A commodity moving within a trading range will provide trend followers with seemingly endless losses until a major trend is initiated. As long as there is no pronounced bias to the up or the down side, long positions will be taken on strength near the top of the range and short positions will be assumed on weakness near the bottom. Some cursory studies have indicated that commodity prices are without important trending characteristics for as much as 85 percent of the time.[13] If true, this consideration may present a formidable obstacle. (3) Optimum rules established for a trend-following method during one period may result in a poor performance during another. For example, appropriate rules for a moving-average system for trading 1960 world sugar, which had a range for the entire year of less than 100 points, would certainly not have been appropriate for the same commodity three years later. In 1963 world

---

[11]W. D. Gann, *How to Make Profits Trading in Commodities,* rev. ed., Lambert-Gann Publishing Co., Miami, Fla., 1951 (out of print but found in many big-city libraries), was probably the originator of this kind of swing chart. Gann covers the subject in greater detail in many of his commodity trading courses. A time factor is also used by many moving-average devotees; instead of requiring price to penetrate the moving average by a certain amount, traders require price to penetrate and then stay beyond the moving average by a certain number of days.

[12]Donchian, op. cit.

[13]This statement is made by John R. Hill in his course *Technical and Mathematical Analysis of the Commodity and Stock Markets,* Commodity Research Institute, 141 West Jackson, Room 855, Chicago, Ill. 60604, 1971. Most of the course is concerned with the presentation of graphical trading methods which assume that futures prices are usually without important trending characteristics. Such methods are antithetical to those used by trend followers.

sugar had a range of more than 900 points and often had a two-day range exceeding 100 points. To be used at all successfully, the elements of any trend-following method must be adjusted to both current and predicted volatility. Traders must be certain that their rules are not out of date for each commodity that they are following.[14]

[14]Houston Cox, *A Common Sense Approach to Commodity Trading,* Reynolds & Co., New York, 1968, presents a moving-average method that to some extent does adjust to current price volatility. A simpler but similar procedure is presented by Levine, op cit. Taylor, op. cit., adjusts the length of the moving average in relation to current volatility.

Chapter 34
Character-of-Market Analysis

RICHARD J. TEWELES

CHARLES V. HARLOW

HERBERT L. STONE

Traders using character-of-market methods operate on premises completely different from those of chartists or trend followers, both of whom have constructed a number of techniques based on the interpretation of price action. Those technicians who employ a character-of-market approach believe that a deceptive veneer has been painted over the true picture of supply and demand.

Character-of-market analysts seek statistical measurements of supply and demand that are independent of price or at least use price information much more subtly than chartists or trend followers. The important question asked by traders who use this approach to technical analysis is: What is the *quality* of a given move in price? The traders then try to commit their capital in line with price movements of good quality and to avoid, or even take an opposite position to, movements of poor quality.

Technicians have only three series of trading data to work with: price, volume, and open interest. Nevertheless, so many combinations and permutations of these data have been employed in character-of-market methods that we can touch on only the most illustrative and basic ones.

Oscillators

The term "oscillator" is given to a family of technical indicators based on measurement of price changes rather than price levels. The simplest type of oscillator is based upon the distance that the price of a commodity has traveled over a given period of time. For example, a ten-day oscillator is constructed by taking the price on the latest day and subtracting the price of the tenth previous trading day. The number obtained is either positive or negative, depending on whether the commodity has risen or fallen in the preceding ten days. The same procedure is followed during subsequent trading days.

The calculation of oscillators has often been carried to surprising complexity.[1] Some oscillators are specially smoothed, some are weighted, and some are modified in conjunction with one or more additional factors, such as volume. Sometimes all these options are used. Time periods employed for constructing oscillators can range from two or three days (even less if traders have access to intraday data) to several weeks or longer. The use of *any* oscillator, however, rests on one or both of these contentions:

1. A price rise or a price decline can become overextended if it gathers too much velocity. If the price of any commodity enjoys an unusual gain that is compacted into a short time span, the presumption is that buying is temporarily exhausted and part or all of the gain will be retraced. Such a market is said to be "overbought." The opposite kind of price action would lead to an "oversold" market. By constructing an oscillator a technician seeks to monitor excessive rates of price change that could lead to exhaustion and subsequent price reversals.

2. A price trend can simply peter out as it steadily loses momentum. In this case a price trend continues but generates less and less energy until it dies. A top is signaled when, for instance, the price continues to make new highs for the move but the oscillator moves from large positive numbers to small positive numbers. The reverse is true for a bottom. Used in this way, an oscillator is a tool for measuring the exhaustion of a price trend.

These two concepts are not mutually exclusive. Figure 34-1 shows the daily action of November 1970 eggs against a twenty-day price change oscillator. For this period levels in the oscillator above +300 (meaning that the price had advanced more than 300 points in the preceding twenty days) spotlighted markets that were overextended on the upside. Similarly, levels in the oscillator below −300 indicated that price had become oversold.

During this period the penetration of "trend lines," drawn across key tops or bottoms in the oscillator, indicated exhaustion in the current price trend. In line with this concept of exhaustion, it will also be noted that the oscillator can peak or bottom ahead of price in many instances, thus signaling possible reversal.

Advantages and Disadvantages of Using Oscillators

Advantages.   (1) Overbought or oversold signals generated from oscillators will usually work well in trading markets, which occur more frequently than trending markets. If there is no dominant trend, points of upside and downside exhaustion can, in theory at least, be identified with a fair degree of accuracy. (2) Signals of an overbought or oversold market can act as a valuable check on a trader's emotions. No matter how bullish a situation may appear, a high positive reading on the oscillator at the same time could be a sobering influence. The reverse is also true. (3) History is replete with examples of price trends that peaked or troughed, whereas accompanying rate-of-change oscillators showed a clear loss of momentum well in advance.

Disadvantages.   (1) Acting on overbought or oversold oscillator signals will lead to financial disaster in any market with a dominant price trend. During a powerful

---

[1] A potpourri of oscillator calculation and interpretation is to be found in the following: *Indicator Digest* Advisory Service, Palisades Park, N.J. 07650, in which many special studies have appeared over the last several years; Garfield Drew, *New Methods for Profit in the Stock Market*, Metcalf Press, Boston, 1955; Carl W. Floss, *Market Rhythm*, Investors Publishing Co., Detroit, 1955 (out of print but available from specialty dealers); James Waters and Larry Williams, "Measuring Market Momentum," *Commodities Magazine*, October 1972. H. M. Gartley, *Profits in the Stock Market*, H. M. Gartley, Inc., New York, 1935 (out of print but available from specialty dealers), gives highly detailed instructions on trading with price oscillators and discusses a number of possible predictive relationships mentioned by no other source.

bull or bear swing an oscillator will repeatedly move into overextended territory and will often stay there for a long time. This danger cannot be avoided because a trader who could consistently anticipate dominant price trends in advance would not be using an oscillator as a trading device. (2) Zones that represent overbought or oversold markets must be decided on the basis of history. If the commodity being followed suddenly becomes either more or less volatile, whether still in a trading range or not, previously determined zones will be worthless. All commodities do change their volatility over time. (3) Loss of momentum before key tops and

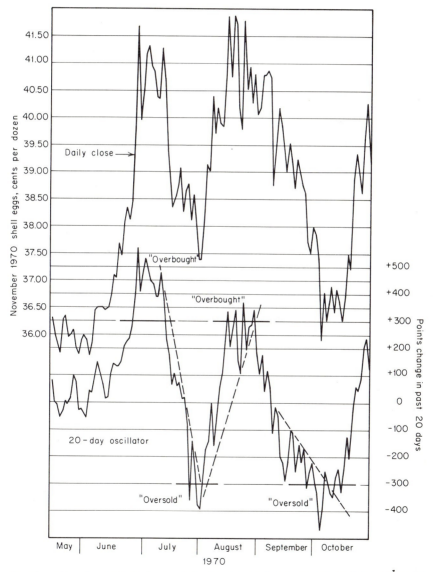

Fig. 34-1 November 1970 shell eggs daily close versus twenty-day net-change oscillator for May–October 1970.

bottoms are reached is well documented, but this phenomenon is much easier to see in retrospect. In Fig. 34-1 trend lines are drawn on the oscillator itself to determine loss of momentum. These trend lines could have been drawn in many other ways, and several of them would not have yielded satisfactory results. In practice, declining momentum will indicate a pause in the price trend or a reversal, and there is no way to tell which. Using this technique, analysts can often explain past price action, but they cannot easily predict future price changes.

Traditional Volume and Open-Interest Methods

"Volume" refers simply to the aggregate number of contracts or bushels of commodity futures traded in a given period; it is a measure of the combined futures market supply and demand for that period. "Open interest" is the total purchase or sale commitments outstanding. At any time, the purchase commitments or number of contracts long are equal to the sale commitments or number of contracts short. The different types of trades and their effects on the open interest are listed below. "Old" buyers are those who have outstanding long positions, whereas "old" sellers have outstanding short positions in the market. "New" buyers or sellers are those who are just entering the market to take a long or a short position.

Transaction	*Effect on Open Interest*
Purchases by old sellers from old buyers	Reduced
Purchases by old sellers from new sellers	Unchanged
Purchases by new buyers from old buyers	Unchanged
Purchases by new buyers from new sellers	Increased
Sales by old buyers to new buyers	Unchanged
Sales by old buyers to old sellers	Reduced
Sales by new sellers to old sellers	Unchanged
Sales by new sellers to new buyers	Increased

The open interest increases only when new purchases are offset by new sales. Decreases in open interest occur only when previous purchases are sold and are offset by the buying in of previously sold contracts. Since it is the effect on open interest that is reported and not the type of transaction, technicians interested in this aspect of market behavior must infer the latter from the former.

Volume and open-interest data are reported daily in newspapers and wire services. They are also printed and distributed at different intervals by the Commodity Futures Trading Commission (CFTC) and by various advisory services.[2] Most technicians use the totals for both the volume and open interest of a given commodity rather than the figures for individual contract months.

Significant changes in volume and open interest generally last from a few days to a month. These changes must be related to their respective seasonal patterns before a meaningful analysis may be undertaken. The seasonal changes are

[2]Edward B. Gotthelf, *The Commodex System,* Commodity Futures Forecast, 90 West Broadway, New York, N.Y. 10007, presents a completely mechanized system that converts traditional price-volume–open interest relationships into daily index numbers interpreted with objective rules. William Peter Hamilton, *The Stock Market Barometer,* Harper & Brothers, New York, 1922; Robert Rhea, *The Dow Theory,* Vail-Ballou Press, Binghamton, N.Y., 1932; Robert D. Edwards and John Magee, *Technical Analysis of Stock Trends,* John Magee, Inc., Springfield, Mass., 1948; and John R. Hill, *Technical and Mathematical Analysis of the Commodity and Stock Markets,* Commodity Research Institute, 141 West Jackson, Chicago, Ill. 60604, 1971, are all sources of interpretation of price-volume relations and generally follow the "classical" rules of devination. Two more complicated procedures for using volume data are "Quinn's Moving Volume Curve," found in Drew, op. cit., and the *Relative Volume Index,* Trend Way Advisory Service, P.O. Box 7184, Louisville, Ky. 40207. All but one of these sources refer to analysis of stocks, but the identical principles can be applied to commodities.

substantial for open interest, but seasonal changes in volume are not so wide or significant.

To illustrate the relevance of seasonal adjustments, let us consider the following example. Let us suppose that the total open interest in all soybean contracts amounts to 125 million bushels on October 15, when the May contract is selling at $2.75 a bushel. By November 15, May soybeans have risen to $2.86, and the open interest for all soybean contracts has increased to 137.5 million bushels. A quick judgment may conclude that prices have risen by 4 percent in the same period that open interest has increased by 10 percent. However, the seasonal rise from October 15 to November 15 is 14 percent. Although actual open interest increased by 10 percent, on a seasonally adjusted basis it really *decreased* for the period being examined. For a net increase of 10 percent to occur, open interest would have had to increase to 155 million bushels by November 15.

Because there is no measurable seasonal pattern for volume, technicians generally compare it with that of the immediate past; for example, if total soybean volume has hovered around 50 million bushels a day and suddenly increases in a week to 75 million bushels, a significant change may be occurring in the psychology of the market.

General rules have been formulated to indicate how significant net changes in open-interest and volume figures may be analyzed in conjunction with price analysis.[3]

The tendencies for volume alone may be summarized as follows:

1. When a major price advance is under way, volume tends to increase on rallies and to decrease on reactions.

2. Conversely, during a major price decline, volume tends to increase on down moves and decrease on rallies.

3. Volume expands sharply as bottoms and tops are approached.

Open interest, when compared with price action, tends to act in the following ways:

1. If prices advance and open interest advances more sharply than a seasonal analysis would suggest, aggressive new buying would seem to have taken place.

2. If prices advance and seasonally adjusted open interest declines, the advance has been fueled by short covering and might be regarded as technically weak.

3. If prices decline and aggressive new selling is taking place, the market may be considered technically weak.

4. If prices decline and open interest decreases beyond seasonal expectations, the decline has been fed by discouraged longs who have liquidated their unprofitable positions, leaving the market relatively strong technically.

A perhaps-oversimplified form of some of the relations among volume, open interest, and price is sometimes given as follows:

If prices are up and (1) volume and open interest are up, the market is strong; if prices are up and (2) volume and open interest are down, the market is weak. If prices are down and (1) volume and open interest are up, the market is weak; if prices are down and (2) volume and open interest are down, the market is strong.

The confidence level of such observations has not been statistically measured. One cursory study[4] found the following:

1. There was some forecasting value in blowoff action at major tops where prices advance sharply on high volume and a sharp drop in open interest.

[3]An advisory service that places much stress on analysis of open interest and presents rules of interpretation to its readers is John K. Hart, Commodity Trend Service, 518 Empire Building, Columbus, Ga. 31901.

[4]William Jiler, "Volume and Open Interest Analysis as an Aid to Price Forecasting," *Guide to Commodity Price Forecasting,* Commodity Research Bureau, Inc., New York, 1965, pp. 63–64.

2. Similarly, after a long decline when prices drop sharply on heavy volume and a sharp drop in open interest, a major bottom is possible.

3. Price moves away from consolidations tend to be greater if the consolidations period was marked by a buildup in open interest that was sharply higher than seasonal.

Advantages and Disadvantages of Using Traditional Volume and Open-Interest Methods

Advantages.   (1) The basic principles of interpreting volume and open interest appear to be quite logical. It seems reasonable that the expansion and contraction of volume and open interest compared with price action should yield worthwhile clues to the balance of supply and demand in the market. (2) The trader following volume and open-interest principles uses a three-dimensional model rather than the single-dimensional model found in other technical approaches. There are many other ways in which price action can be viewed, and many more shadings can be used to describe bullish or bearish behavior. (3) If the forecasting ability of volume and open interest is denied, there is still a significant amount of information to be obtained simply by monitoring such data. Traders know which contracts are most active, the size of the market in which they are dealing, and any important properties of trading activity.

Disadvantages.   (1) This type of analysis is replete with a number of ill-defined terms: "low volume," "increase in open interest," "decline of greater-than-seasonal expectation," and several others. To make use of this approach technicians must quantify their terms to avoid meaningless generalities. (2) General rules for volume and open-interest interpretation are well publicized. Application of these classical principles leads to the problem of the "self-fulfilling prophecy" discussed among the disadvantages of using price patterns. Volume and open-interest behavior that is clearly bullish or bearish can be discounted in the present price level as easily as other more familiar supply-and-demand factors. (3) The validity of these standard principles rests on unproven assertion. No publicly available studies that use volume and open-interest decision rules confirm their value in actual trading.

On-Balance Volume

The bulk of character-of-market analysis originates with the belief that big-moneyed traders consistently take positions prior to substantial price moves in any commodity. The big money is seen, for instance, as surreptitiously acquiring sizable long positions before price advances, well ahead of the "ignorant masses." This quiet buying is known as "accumulation." When the same interests are selling their longs and going short at the top of a rise before a large decline, their activity is called "distribution." Tracking the supposed clandestine flow of accumulation and distribution has led to the growth of countless technical methods over the years.

An old approach to measuring accumulation and distribution by the action of price and volume, which has enjoyed a popular renaissance since the early 1960s,[5] is currently known as "on-balance volume," or OBV. Easily calculated and graphed, OBV attempts to provide information on the quality of price movements by yielding a volume curve that can be compared directly with the price curve.

Table 34-1 illustrates a hypothetical OBV calculation. Each day's closing price is compared with the closing price of the preceding day. If the latest day has a higher closing price, *all* the volume of trading that day is assigned a plus sign. If the latest day's close is lower than that of the preceding day, all the volume is added to a

[5] Joseph Granville, *Granville's New Key to Stock Market Profits,* Prentice-Hall, Inc., Englewood Cliffs, N.J., 1963, has popularized this approach in recent years.

cumulative running total. This cumulative total is the OBV. The absolute level of the OBV curve is of no significance; the technician is interested only in the contour of this curve when it is compared with the contour of price, either graphically or in tabulated form.

The dominant theory behind OBV, as previously noted, assumes that large-scale accumulation or distribution can take place in the market. Because this activity would have to take place quietly, it is further assumed that worthwhile accumulation or distribution is carried out under cover of small net or deceptive price changes. The OBV curve is believed to illustrate the true state of affairs by showing whether volume of trading is highest during periods of rising or falling prices. When the bias in volume deviates significantly from the price curve, unusual activity is presumed to be taking place.

Under normal circumstances the OBV curve will move parallel to the price of the commodity under surveillance. As long as this relationship endures, traders using OBV will have no particular interest. However, when the OBV curve begins

TABLE 34-1   Computation of On-Balance Volume

Date	May cocoa daily closing price	Volume (number of contracts)	OBV (cumulative volume)
March 1	27.09	· · ·	· · ·
March 2	27.15	+3,000	+3,000
March 3	27.22	+2,500	+5,500
March 4	27.07	−800	+4,700
March 5	26.85	−1,200	+3,500
March 8	27.01	+2,500	+6,000

to diverge from price, notice is taken because many analysts believe that such divergence indicates accumulation or distribution. In Table 34-1, for instance, the price of cocoa dropped a nominal 8 points between March 1 and March 8. Yet the OBV record shows that 6,000 more contracts changed hands on days of rising price than they did on days of falling price. If this kind of behavior continued for a significant period of time, technicians would conclude that cocoa was being intensively accumulated. Moneyed interests would be presumed to be buying heavily, putting prices up for a day or so before quietly allowing them to drop on low activity until they moved again into a satisfactory buying area. In theory, this process would continue until accumulation was completed. Prices would then move much higher as the big money's analysis was proved correct and the "crowd" began to act on the now-favorable news developments affecting cocoa.

Figure 34-2 illustrates an actual example in which a daily OBV analysis spotlighted an impending break in pork bellies. During the period in late May 1967 labeled "1," prices moved to their final high above 43 cents, while several thousand more contracts changed hands at lower prices than changed hands at higher prices. The OBV curve peaked sixteen days before the price. Again in late June, during the period labeled "2," a 300-point rally raised prices well above the early June highs but left the OBV seriously lagging. These two marked divergences, presumably showing strong distribution, were followed by a sharp and sustained break in the market.

There are more sophisticated and complicated ways to calculate and use OBV,[6] but the basic principle of interpretation remains the same.

[6]David L. Markstein, *How to Chart Your Way to Stock Market Profits,* Parker Publishing Co., West Nyack, N.Y., 1966, advocates multiplying the amount of price change by the volume of trading. In 1972 R. F. Martel, *Charting Supply and Demand for Stock Analysis,* Martel & Co., 1505 Old Mill Road, Reading, Pa. 19610, presented a system that also attempts to quantify price-volume activity by means of a highly modified OBV curve.

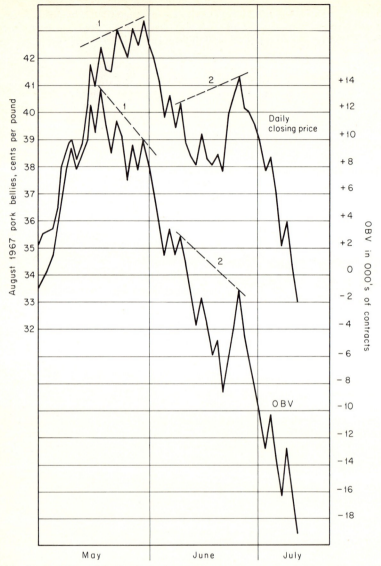

Fig. 34-2   August 1967 pork bellies daily close versus daily on-balance volume (OBV) for May–July 1967.

Advantages and Disadvantages of Using On-Balance Volume

Advantages.   (1) If there is, in fact, important money from intelligent sources that quietly assumes positions in advance of large price moves or if such substantial buying or selling takes place for any reason, it cannot help but leave a record in daily transactions. OBV pinpoints periods in which a substantial excess of volume takes place at higher or lower prices, thus giving technicians a lead for further study. (2) Whatever interpretation is used, OBV gives analysts information with which to quantify the volume of any price move. Even if traders are not looking for signals per se, the knowledge that the largest volume occurs on rising or falling prices, and how it compares with price, can be helpful in appraising market action.

Disadvantages. (1) Research to date indicates that the profit-making ability of large traders is impressive.[7] These studies have shown that large traders succeed mainly by trading on *short-run* price fluctuations. Such conclusions do not support the relatively longer-term accumulation-distribution thesis on which much of OBV analysis rests. (2) No objective rules of interpretation have ever been presented by advocates of OBV,[8] thus ensuring the impossibility of performing any tests that would determine whether the use of OBV would lead to nonrandom trading results. (3) On theoretical grounds the calculation of the most commonly used form of OBV is open to serious question. Each day's price change is determined by transactions on both the buying and the selling sides, and it does not seem reasonable to assign *all* the volume to the plus or the minus side simply because the close one day is higher or lower than the close of the preceding day. If pork bellies, for example, were up 130 points during the day but closed down 5 points, it would not seem proper to assign all the volume that day to the minus side. Calculation of basic OBV may be too simplistic.[9]

Armchair Tape Reading

In the late nineteenth century, when pools manipulated the stock and commodity markets, tape readers attempted to monitor the flow of inside money. They would watch every transaction on the tape and note the price and volume. If tape readers were shrewd enough, they might be able to deduce the action being taken by the pool and follow its lead.[10]

An important element of tape reading consisted of paying special attention to large blocks that appeared on the tape, as these were presumed to be the actual transactions of the pool. In later years, with the pools only a memory, the analysis of large transactions is still an integral part of tape reading. Tape-reading technicians believe that large transactions, by their very nature, represent important and farseeing money.

Some years ago a method was published[11] that enables a trader to "read the tape by proxy." It was designed solely to indicate when large transactions are appearing on the tape and thereby to provide a lead for further study. It is not presented here as a complete or proven indicator.

Each day the trader calculates a "resistance index" in the following way:

$$\frac{\text{Number of contracts traded}}{\text{High price} - \text{low price}}$$

[7]C. S. Rockwell, "Normal Backwardation, Forecasting, and the Returns to Speculators," *Food Research Institute Studies,* Supplement 7, 1967, pp. 107–130.

[8]Granville, op. cit., presented many objective collateral OBV calculations but failed to present a completely quantifiable set of decision-making rules.

[9]Two attempts to weight OBV more precisely in accordance with intraday price activity are David Bostian, *Intra-Day Intensity Index,* privately printed, Fort Benjamin Harrison, Ind., 1967; and Larry Williams, *The Secret of Selecting Stocks for Immediate and Substantial Gains,* Conceptual Management, Carmel Valley, Calif., 1973. These two variations are also open to criticism on theoretical grounds.

[10]Humphrey Neill, *Tape Reading and Market Tactics,* reprinted by Fraser Publishing Co., Wells, Vt., 1960; and Richard Wyckoff, *Studies in Tape Reading,* reprinted by Traders Press, New York, 1972, are sources of detailed instruction on tape reading. Edwin LeFevre, *Reminiscences of a Stock Operator,* reprinted by the American Research Council, New York, 1964, provides absorbing insights into tape reading from the legendary Jesse Livermore.

[11]Edwin H. Tomkins, *Systematic Stock Trading,* The Moore Guide, P.O. Box 42, Riverside, Ill. 60546, contains a complete discussion of his "resistance index." The author also discusses tape reading and short-term trading techniques.

This ratio measures the number of contracts that change hands in relation to the range for the day. When the ratio is unusually large, it may be presumed that unusually large transactions are crossing the tape. High ratios do not occur often, but they do stand out as "spikes" on the chart.

Figure 34-3 shows the daily closing prices of June 1971 live hogs graphed with a

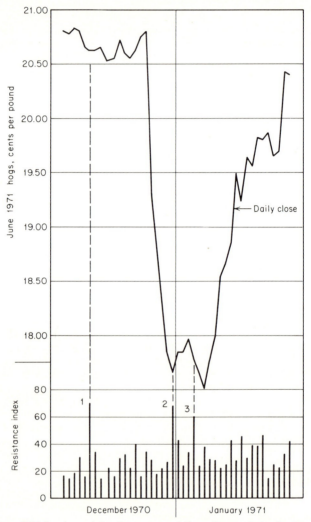

Fig. 34-3   June 1971 live hogs daily close versus daily resistance index for December 1970–January 1971.

daily resistance index. The three figures greater than 60 (meaning that 60 or more contracts changed hands per point of range in price) are numbered 1, 2, and 3. All three of these high-index days came close to advantageous buying or selling areas. Whether these days with unusually large tape transactions actually saw informed money taking a position in the market before a price reversal is an open question.

There is no question, however, that this technique can only be subjective and could not be used effectively without information from other sources or methods. Furthermore, price action and volume vary greatly over time. A large resistance index during one period may not be significant in another span of time, thus adding yet another interpretative problem.

Analysis of Open Interest to Determine Activities of Large and Small Traders

Another way to measure accumulation and distribution is the proposal made by many technical analysts to differentiate between "smart money" and "stupid money." Those making this differentiation believe that there are, essentially, two categories of traders, winners and losers. For example, in the stock market exchange specialists have often been identified as a winning group and odd lotters as a losing group. Techniques long in use with these and other series can be applied to commodities as well.[12] This approach attempts to focus on data showing the activities of winning and losing groups of traders and then suggests the following action:

1. Initiate positions opposite to those of the losing group when it shows a strong preference for one side of the market.

2. Initiate positions in line with those of the winning group when it shows a strong preference for one side of the market.

Twice monthly the United States government[13] provides a breakdown of the open interest in all regulated commodities. Both long and short positions are tabulated for three groups: bona fide hedgers, large traders with legally reportable positions, and the remaining portion of open interest, which consists of small traders with less than a reportable position. If it can be assumed that generally large traders are winners and small traders are losers over a reasonable period of time, it is possible to construct a number of technical indicators that might delineate the actions of these groups.

Figure 34-4 illustrates one of many gauges that could be constructed to measure the activity of large traders. The closing prices of December 1969 cattle are plotted at two-week intervals against a ratio that measures large-trader short positions as a percentage of the total open interest. When large-trader short positions are "low" (on this chart, below 6 percent), it might be assumed that they are strongly biased to the bullish side of the market and that prices therefore should rise. When they are "high" (9 percent or higher on this chart), an important degree of pessimism would be indicated and lower prices be expected to follow. It is surprising that although similar procedures have long been used to analyze stock prices and regular breakdowns of open interest have been supplied since 1923, this area of technical analysis has attracted almost no attention in the commodity field.

---

[12]In-depth discussions of techniques for handling odd-lot trading data are found in Drew, op. cit.; Garfield Drew, "A Clarification of the Odd-Lot Theory," *Financial Analysts Journal,* September–October 1967; Thomas J. Kewley and R. A. Stevenson, "The Odd-Lot Theory: A Reply," *Financial Analysts Journal,* January–February 1969; Stanley Kaish, "Odd Lot Profit and Loss Performance," *Financial Analysts Journal,* September–October 1969. Expositions of techniques for handling both specialist and odd-lot data are available from the Indicator Digest Advisory Service, op. cit.; Walter Heiby, *Stock Market Profits through Dynamic Synthesis,* Institute of Dynamic Synthesis, Chicago, Ill., 1965 (a supplement to this book explaining new techniques, "The New Dynamic Synthesis," was published in 1967); William X. Scheinman, *Why Most Investors Are Mostly Wrong Most of the Time,* Lancer Books, New York, 1970.

[13]Periodic reports on open interest are available from the Commodity Exchange Authority, Washington, 20250. Regional offices publish separate reports for commodities directly under their supervision. The CEA will furnish information on all reports available and on how to obtain them.

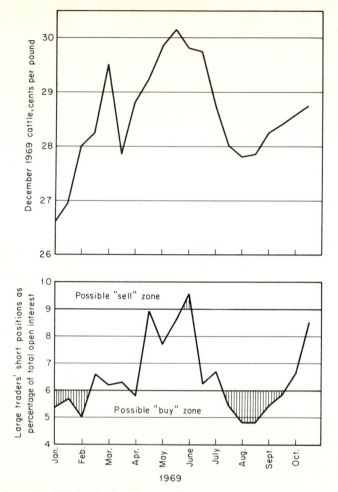

Fig. 34-4 December 1969 live beef cattle bimonthly closing price versus large traders' short positions as a percentage of total open interest for January–October 1969.

Because the total open interest is divided into six constituent parts, a great number of ratios or oscillators, or both, can be derived between these available series. It is also possible to play the large traders off against the small traders and isolate marked dichotomies of opinion. For example, a ratio of various large-trader positions to comparable small-trader positions would clearly pinpoint times of sharp disagreement between the two groups.[14]

[14]Roy E. Christian, *New Methods for Long Term Stock Market Forecasting,* Physicians' Market Letter, 1691 Wilshire Drive, Aptos, Calif. 95003, 1966 (there are also a supplement, *Long Term Study,* and several back letters), has discussed numerous means of using odd-lot, specialist, and other data that specifically employ the technique of measuring marked divergences of opinion between two groups of traders. The Physicians' Market Letter is defunct, but many of its studies are still available.

Advantages and Disadvantages of Using Open Interest To Reveal the Activities of Large and Small Traders

Advantages. (1) Similar techniques have been used with some success in the stock market for many years. The breakdown of open interest available on regulated commodities yields series of data that are highly analogous to those used in stock market analysis. (2) Whether or not traders construct operative technical indicators from the open-interest breakdown, knowledge of the current interplay between hedgers, large traders, and small traders can be helpful in explaining market action in any commodity. (3) This kind of analysis can become exceptionally intriguing when it is realized that little research has been published in this area. The six series of data available regularly have the potential of yielding large numbers of permutations and combinations in the form of ratios, rate-of-change oscillators, and other indices. Interesting new territory is offered to inquiring technical analysts.

Disadvantages. The work that has been done on the behavior of large and small traders argues against the value of open-interest breakdowns. Small traders, rather than acting consistently on the wrong side of the market, are better described as trading haphazardly. Large traders are consistent winners but are short-term–oriented as a group.[15] It might be concluded that there is no available information on stupid money, and that smart-money data are available but come too late and too infrequently to be helpful. (2) The biweekly report on open interest is available to the public with a time lag of two weeks or more, thereby reducing the effectiveness of using this information. (3) The reason that technical analysts have done so little work here is not that this area is obscure. Most commodity traders with even a rudimentary background in the stock market would see the possible relevance of open-interest data. Rather, this neglect might well indicate that the field is arid.

Contrary Opinion

> The supposedly stolid Dutch were overcome by the Tulip Craze, the volatile French had their Mississippi Bubble, while the sturdy English had their South Sea Bubble.
>
> As I read the account of these madnesses, I was tempted to shout, "This cannot have happened." Yet within my own lifetime I have seen similar deliriums in the Florida land boom of the 1920's and the stock market speculation that led to the 1929 crash. Something of the same crowd madness may have been at least partially responsible for Hitler's rise to power in Germany.
>
> These crowd madnesses recur so frequently in human history that they must reflect some deeply rooted trait of human nature . . . if his book showed how baseless are man's moods of wild hope, it also showed that man's moods of black despair are equally unfounded. Always in the past, no matter how black the outlook, things got better. . . . Whatever men attempt, they seem driven to try to overdo.[16]

With these words, Bernard Baruch explained how he related an account of the "madness of crowds"[17] written in 1841 to the extremes of psychology that he had observed in his own experience. His astute decision to sell his holdings in 1929 has been credited to his reading this book at an opportune time. Baruch apparently

---

[15]Rockwell, op. cit.

[16]Bernard Baruch, *Baruch: My Own Story,* Henry Holt and Company, Inc., New York, 1957, p. 219.

[17]Charles Mackay, *Extraordinary Popular Delusions and the Madness of Crowds,* L. C. Page & Company, London, 1932; reprinted from the 1841 edition. Several reprints of this book have since been published; it documents scores of occurrences in which people lost all semblance of reason and were dominated by mass psychology.

never attempted to utilize the lessons of history contained in McKay's book in any systematic way, but a stock market analyst named Humphrey Neill did ponder on the implications of swings in mass psychology. The result was a new way of thinking called "contrary opinion."[18]

Neill's contention was that crowd madness need not go to the point of making history before it could be detected and used to advantage. His belief was that any crowd, such as stock or commodity traders, could frequently be carried to extremes of action and opinion. Astute observers could recognize these extremes and act in a way opposite to the prevailing psychology to their own advantage. In other words, they would adopt a "contrary opinion." Neill attempted in his book to demonstrate that this phenomenon extends far beyond trading stocks or commodities.[19] However, only its use in practical commodity trading is considered here.

In market letters and boardroom talk the term "contrary opinion" appears frequently. Apparently most traders have come to believe that contrarians take positions opposite to the prevailing opinion almost as a reflex action. This popular notion is far too simple; true contrarians do more than merely lean against the current state of thinking.

Before money is committed to a trade, contrarians insist that certain basic elements be present. First, there must be a strong consensus about the future price or behavior of a commodity. This opinion must be almost unanimous—virtually taken for granted—before there is any chance that mass psychology has been carried to extremes. Examples of widely held opinions that would interest contrarians would be: "Beans are going much higher," "July cotton will go off the board weak," "February bellies will gain on the May," "Cocoa will take its lead from next month's purchase figures and not do much until then," and so on. Any of these opinions unfulfilled could represent a trading opportunity. Note that the opinion need not be only one of price direction. A normally popular commodity that has been unusually neglected is one example of a consensus that could provide contrarians with much food for thought.

A second and equally important prerequisite is that the strong bias of opinion be supported by "weak" reasons. In determining how strong or weak these supporting reasons are, contrarians differ sharply from fundamentalists. Traders using contrary opinion are not interested in how important facts are or even if they are true. The reasons behind an opinion are judged strong or weak only according to the manner in which they have been disseminated and the reaction they have produced.

To contrarians supporting reasons are weak if they have one or both of these characteristics:

1. *The facts have been widely publicized and well known for some time.* The presumption here is that any such facts are already discounted in the current price. For example, let us suppose that the great majority of traders are bearish on wheat. If such a position is popular because a coming bumper crop has been apparent for several weeks and prices have already dropped substantially, the question of how much risk remains on the downside may well be raised. If news of the impending record crop has generated most of the selling it warrants, any favorable developments will be a surprise to most traders.

This kind of well-publicized fact is especially weak if its realization is far in the

[18]Humphrey Neill, *The Art of Contrary Thinking*, The Caxton Printers, Caldwell, Ohio, 1960, is the definitive source of information on contrary opinion. Transcripts of various Contrary Opinion Foliage Forums held over the years are also available from Fraser Publishing Co., Wells, Vt.

[19]Neill, op. cit., contains an addendum in which he notes that popular expectations at the time of major world events were directly opposite to what actually occurred.

future. If, for example, the expected bumper crop is many months away from being harvested, a great many things could happen in the meantime (including the discovery that the crop is not nearly so large as the earlier estimates) to change the present bearish psychology sharply.

2. *The facts of the situation are not known but are only supposed.* This sort of situation can occur anywhere but is more common in international commodities that are unregulated, such as sugar, cocoa, copper, silver, and coffee. Opinion is formed on the basis of preliminary indications which have all been in agreement but for which no hard evidence is yet available. Cocoa may be regarded as an exceptionally bullish situation on the basis of preliminary crop estimates long before any solid facts are in on the crop size. Even if the crop is small, such expectations may already have been discounted in the current price. Other than extravagantly bullish news could find the market vulnerable to decline following the first factual reports.

If traders who use contrary opinion can find a situation in which there is a near-unanimous opinion supported by weak reasons, they have at least in theory, found a trade with high potential and low risk. The low risk comes from the probability that the factors that caused the consensus have been discounted. The high potential comes from the element of surprise that can be a dominating influence when mass psychology is carried to extremes and only one-sided news is expected. If the reason behind the crowd's opinion turns out to be entirely invalid, which has happened frequently in the past, contrarians gain a bonus.

Advantages and Disadvantages of Using Contrary Opinion

Advantages.   (1) More than almost any other technical approach, the premises behind contrary opinion are solidly logical. When strong feelings prevail toward a particular commodity, it is indisputable that conditions in that market are abnormal. Most known facts are likely to have been discounted completely or partly, offering little potential to traders who are following the lead of the majority. Of equal importance, such a market is extremely vulnerable to unexpected developments not in line with current thinking. (2) Even if a contrary-opinion approach is not used to signal trades, it can be valuable to traders who want to keep emotions in check. Watching for weak reasons behind strongly held opinions will keep traders from being carried away by the arguments of the moment and losing their perspective. (3) A contrary approach can often turn up important facts for both technicians and fundamentalists. Contrary opinion is more than a means of generating signals. It is a way of thinking that can be conceptually and practically useful. In the final analysis the success of contrary opinion depends completely on neglected facts coming to the fore. By directing attention away from popular thought patterns contrary opinion is one method whose primary purpose is to enable traders to think for themselves and possibly to unearth key factors on which trades may be based.

Disadvantages.   (1) Collecting an accurate sample of opinions can be most difficult. Many sources must be consulted to determine whether there is a strong consensus toward any commodity. Newspapers, brokerage house letters, private advisory letters, brokers themselves, their clients, and the signals currently being given by popular trading methods are only a few of the inputs needed to monitor a consensus situation that may be shaping up. It can be an arduous and sometimes almost-impossible task to uncover the prevailing psychology, even given a strong consensus. (2) Even if the state of prevailing opinion is known, the depth of that opinion may be hard to evaluate. One group of traders expecting plywood to "consolidate and retrace recent large gains during the next few weeks" is certainly not so bearish as others who expect a major collapse. Weighting these and other shades of opinion can be a perplexing problem.[20] (3) Although contrary opinion can provide traders with numerous psychological advantages, it can spawn at least one large psychological disadvantage. Used heavily, it can breed arrogance. (4) Points of extreme mass psychology in any commodity are quite infrequent. Even the most adept contrarians may have to wait a long time between trades. (5) The approach is not as precisely quantitative as is generally believed. Because of this, contrary opinion has not yet been put to an objective historical test to determine its validity and characteristics, as some other technical methods have. (6) It is much easier to initiate trades by following a contrary-opinion method than to know when or where to close them. In closing a trade, contrarians must rely heavily on other methods or personal judgment.

[20]One advisory service, Market Vane Commodity Letter, 431 East Green Street, Pasadena, Calif. 91101, attempts to weight the composite opinion of a number of brokerage house letters and to apply the results of this tabulated sample by suggesting positions opposite to strong consensuses.

Chapter **35**

Random-Walk Analysis and Spreads and Options

RICHARD J. TEWELES

CHARLES V. HARLOW

HERBERT L. STONE

RANDOM-WALK ANALYSIS

Although the fundamental laws of supply and demand have generally been accepted as determining the long-run price behavior of commodity futures prices, they have certainly failed in the short run to provide a similar insight. Most traders will agree that in the short run there is simply no significant correlation between fundamentals and prices; yet it is precisely in the short run that traders establish open profits and receive open losses.

Premises

Most discussions of short-run speculative price behavior take the "random-walk hypothesis" as their point of departure. This theory suggests that successive price *changes* in commodity markets are independent and that past prices are not a reliable indicator of future prices. One of the major premises of the random-walk theory is based on the concept of an "efficient market." An efficient market is defined as one in which there are large numbers of equally informed, actively competing people attempting to maximize profits. In such a market, at any moment in time, price reflects all available information, as well as those events *expected* to transpire in the foreseeable future. Holbrook Working was the first in the commodity futures field to offer a theory of expectations that rests on the premise that futures reflect *anticipated* changes in supply and demand rather than on their immediate values.[1]

In an efficient market actual prices approximate anticipated or intrinsic value. In a world of uncertainty intrinsic value is elusive. Disagreements will cause

[1]Holbrook Working, "A Theory of Anticipatory Prices." *American Economic Review Proceedings,* vol. 48, p. 191, May 1958.

random discrepancies between intrinsic value and actual prices. If the market is highly efficient, actual prices will move randomly about the intrinsic value.

Of course, intrinsic values change. Soybeans *do* moves from $2.85 to $3.50 a bushel, and there is nothing in the random-walk theory to suggest that superior intrinsic-value analysis is useless in an efficient market. Traders will always do well if they can identify long-run supply-and-demand changes before such expectations are reflected in actual price changes. On the average, however, competition will cause most of the effects of new information regarding intrinsic values to be reflected quickly in commodity prices. It is the random quality of new information and not changes in supply or demand that is responsible for the irregular behavior of futures prices. The duration and extent of such price adjustments will be random variables that will cause prices to overadjust, underadjust, sometimes precede the information, and sometimes follow it in a manner that successive price changes are independent. Such a market has come to be known as a random-walk market.

Behavior of Traders

If price changes are formed according to anticipations of supply and demand, it is important to analyze in greater depth the behavior of traders in response to news. In a *totally* efficient (hypothetical) market, when no new information is available, no new market position would be taken, and there would be no price changes. There would be established a general price equilibrium in which no trader who had the will to buy or sell had the power and no trader who had the power (one who held an open position or the funds to establish one) had the will. As new information emerged, all traders would analyze it. If a change in positions were dictated, those changes would be effected rapidly, and a new level of equilibrium would be established. In such a market traders would be successful only if they were better at analyzing and interpreting the information currently available to all traders because the history of equilibrium levels would tell them nothing about tomorrow's new input of information.

Moving from such an ideal market, we can analyze the aftermath of the input of new information on a more realistic market consisting of insiders and outsiders. The first group is made up of traders who by training or position learn about new developments quickly. The second group obtains new information only after the insiders have heard about it. Such a market would be less than strongly efficient.

As new information becomes available, a double response occurs: insiders react first, and outsiders' reactions follow. The first response is clear. If the new information is bullish, insider response would push prices higher. Conversely, if the new input is bearish, prices would fall. The later outsider response cannot be disposed of so simply. If the new information is bullish, prices could rise again, remain unchanged, or drop. The first possibility could occur if the demand by the outsiders exceeded the supply offered by the insiders at the higher price established by the insiders. The second possibility could occur if outsider demand were exactly offset by insider desire to sell at the higher price. The third possibility is that outsider demand could not offset some increased insider selling at a higher price. The second case reflects the most efficient market, that is, when insiders correctly predict subsequent outsider behavior. Even if this response is not always forthcoming and the insiders do not perfectly anticipate the outsiders, the insiders are as likely to overestimate as to underestimate the outsiders' response to market news. Thus on each input of bullish news traders could not establish a long position and expect prices to work higher, nor could they take a short position directly after the issuance of bearish news and have a high probability of profit.

The random-walk theorists agree that it is unlikely that their model describes the behavior of commodity price changes exactly. Yet they assert that although successive price changes may not be strictly independent, the amount of dependence is unimportant. If there is no such strategy, then a simple policy of buying and holding will equal the results from any sophisticated procedure for timing. Therefore, unless a trader can improve on the buy-and-hold policy, the independence assumption of the random-walk model is an adequate description of reality.

All this does *not* mean that short-term traders will not or cannot make money trading commodity futures; it *does* mean that, on the average, those traders will not beat a buy-and-hold strategy with information that they obtain from historical data.

SPREADS AND OPTIONS

Spreads and options may be considered by some to represent only a choice in a type of commodity position, but the subject is far broader than that and deserves separate and more elaborate treatment.

Most unsophisticated commodity traders are converted security traders who bring their habits with them. They are much more likely to be long the market than short and know little or nothing about spreads and options. Professional traders are at least as conversant with the short as the long side of the market and know considerably more about spreads and the concept of option trading.

Spreads

Spreads may represent a significant percentage of the open interest of a commodity and may be entered for either technical or fundamental reasons. The word *spread* has several meanings to commodity traders, but all imply a price difference. In its most general sense, the word applies to the difference between the cash and futures prices of the same commodity. In a more restricted sense, it refers to the difference in the prices of two contract months.

A spread also describes the actual position taken by traders who are simultaneously long one commodity contract and short another. They may hold equal but opposite positions in two different contracts of the same commodity, such as long 10,000 bushels of March wheat and short 10,000 bushels of May wheat. They may also have equal but opposite positions in two different but related commodities and still hold a spread position; for example, they could be long 10,000 bushels of corn and short 10,000 bushels of wheat or long 25,000 bushels of oats and short 25,000 bushels of corn. Opposite positions in unrelated commodities are not considered spreads. Traders may be long copper and short sugar, but these would be considered merely separate positions because there is little or no basic price relation between copper and sugar.

Historically, the terms "spread" and "straddle" had shades of difference, but they have since become interchangeable among commodity traders, and in practice the term spread is now more commonly used in the futures markets. There was once a tendency for traders to speak of spreads in connection with grain positions and straddles in connection with other commodities, such as cotton. The terms "spread position" and "hedge" are used interchangeably but incorrectly by some traders. A hedge refers to the concurrent holding of two opposite commodity positions, one in the cash, or spot, market and the other in the futures market. A spread position also refers to two concurrent and opposite positions, but both are in the futures markets. In its more general sense the term spread describes the price difference between the cash and futures markets in a hedged position. "Arbitrage" is a term related broadly to the others described here, but it generally suggests two positions entered simultaneously, or virtually so, one long and the other short, "locking in" a price difference so great that a profit is virtually assured. In the commodity markets this condition exists when a distant contract exceeds the price of the nearby contract by an amount exceeding the carrying charge, as in the example in the following subsection. Such opportunities also exist in the security markets when trading the same security on two different markets at two different prices or the same security in two forms, such as common stock against bonds or preferred stock convertible into the same common. Some also are able to take advantage of the price discrepancies that exist in foreign exchange.

Significance of Price Differences.   Most of the following discussion centers in the taking of a spread position, but it is worth noting how important the spread differences among the prices of various contract months are to the intelligent establishment of a position. Let us suppose that it is August and that traders believe that the price of wheat is likely to go up. They decide to establish a position of 10,000 bushels to take advantage of the expected price rise. They are aware that wheat is then trading for delivery in September, December, March, May, and July. How do they decide which to buy?

There are several factors to consider. One is the crop year that they believe presents the greater opportunity. The crop year for wheat begins on July 1. If the traders want to take their position in the forthcoming new crop, they have little choice, because the only new-crop contract trading in August is the July of the following year. If they believe the greater opportunity is offered in the current, or old, crop, they must choose among the September, December, March, and May contracts. One factor affecting this decision is the amount of time believed to be necessary for the expected upward price move to develop and the time when it is expected to begin. If the traders expect something to happen within a few days because of some near-term development, such as important export business, they could buy any of the old-crop contracts. They would probably lean toward the September delivery because less time is available for the tightness in wheat to be alleviated and it would best reflect a tight cash market.

If the traders expect to retain their position for some months, there is no point in considering September and no great attraction in the December contract. They can gain considerably more time by acquiring the March or May contracts. They have also gained the advantage of possible long-term capital gains on their tax returns if they should hold the position more than six months, which would not have been possible had they bought the September or December contracts. In addition, they save the commission that would be incurred if they bought an early contract and subsequently "rolled forward" into a later one.

The choice between the March and May contracts must still be made. Too many traders make this decision with little or no thought or, worse, for the wrong reasons. They may choose the March merely because they or their brokers have been keeping a chart of that contract and they have not followed the May, or they may buy the May because that contract happens to be on the quotation boards in the broker's office and the action on the March contract has not been followed. The decision would better be made logically on the current price difference, or spread, between the March and May prices.

To clarify this point, let us assume that the carrying charge on a bushel of wheat is 2¼ cents a month. That would be the actual cost of handling, storing, insuring, and financing 1 bushel for one month. The cost of carrying a bushel of wheat from the March contract into the May delivery would therefore be 4½ cents for the two-month period. It would be virtually impossible for May wheat to sell for significantly more than 4½ cents over the March delivery for any length of time. If it were to do so, it would become profitable for somebody to buy the March and sell the May at the unusually wide price difference. This activity is sometimes called arbitrage, and anyone engaged in it is called an "arbitrager." Arbitragers would be prepared, if necessary, to take delivery of the March wheat, hold the short May position as a hedge, and then deliver their cash wheat against the May contract during the month of May. More likely, the abnormal spread difference would dissolve sooner or later, and the arbitragers would take off both sides of their spread position and realize their profit. In either case they would be certain of a gain approximating at least the difference between the $4\frac{1}{2}$-cent normal carrying charge and the wider spread difference at which they had taken their position, unless there was a material short-run change in the carrying charge.

Because opportunities like this are so obvious to professional traders and profits in the real world are not so easily attained, the spread difference between March and May would almost certainly stop short of the $4\frac{1}{2}$-cent full carrying-charge difference. Yet if the spread difference was near the full carrying charge, it would be of considerable help to net-position traders trying to make intelligent decisions. At near the full carrying charge they would probably place their long position in the March rather than the May contract. Both contracts might go up equally, and they would realize the same gain in either one. Both might go down equally, and they would suffer the same loss in either one. If the spread difference changed, however, it would almost certainly do so either because March went up more than May or down less, and in both cases the traders would find the March contract the better alternative. March could not lose materially on May, but there is no limit to the amount it could gain on May in a strong market. Not only could it sell for more than May, but there is no $4\frac{1}{2}$-cent barrier to its premium. Because clocks run only one way, nobody has yet found a way to buy the May contract of a commodity, take delivery, and then redeliver it against the previous March contract. Premiums of nearby contracts over distant ones can get quite large in strong markets. When nearby contracts sell for more than distant contracts, the market is called "inverted." Traders must remember that risks in carrying-charge market spreads are limited; inverted market spreads are not.

If, with wheat at near a full carrying charge, traders believed that wheat was going to go down rather than up and they wanted to go short either March or May, their decision would be just as obvious. They would certainly go short the May contract rather than the March. Here again, the only way the spread difference would change materially would be for May to lose on March because March could not lose on May. With May providing the added attraction of two additional months for the trade to work profitably, the choice of March would be a poor one indeed.

There is a third type of trader who is alert to these price differences and who hopes to take advantage of them. This is the position spreader.

Spread Positions.   Position spreaders are less interested in the direction of price than in the difference between two prices. Rather than decide that a given contract price is too high or too low, they are interested in taking advantage of price differences that they consider abnormal. The possible positions open to these traders are intracommodity (or intercontract or interdelivery) spreads, intercommodity spreads, intermarket spreads, or a combination of them. The logic of those taking such positions is best made clear by examples.

Intracommodity Spreads.   Intracommodity spreaders try to take advantage of price differences that they believe are too wide or too narrow in the same commodity in the same market at the same time. They might note that May corn is selling for 4 cents over March and expect a strong market in corn to develop soon. If this should happen, they believe that not only would the general price level of corn go up but the March contract would gain on the May. If they are right, there is no limit to the amount that March could gain because it could not only close the prevailing discount but sell for more than May by a substantial amount. If they are wrong, there is little to lose because here, again, March cannot sell below the May for long by much more than the full carrying charge. Spread traders would take advantage of this opportunity by buying the March contract and selling an equal amount of the May against it. The position could be entered either by putting on both sides at the same time or by entering one at a time in order to try to establish a still more favorable difference. The latter procedure takes unusual skill and sometimes results in losing the opportunity observed in the first place.

When the spread has been established, spreaders merely have to wait for March to gain on May as much as they think it is going to and then take off (lift) their position. They do this by selling out their March contract and buying in their May. The removal of a spread position is often called "unwinding" or "back spreading." Here, again, the traders can take off both sides simultaneously by instructing the broker to remove the spread at the current market difference or at a difference of a fixed number of cents. They could also take off (lift) one side (leg) at a time and hope to improve their total profit by doing so. Like entering a spread one side at a time, removing it by lifting one leg at a time is not a good practice. Most traders seem to develop a peculiar knack for taking off the wrong side of their spreads first and then watching a profit achieved over a period of weeks dissolve in a few days or hours.

One of the most frequent questions asked by inexperienced traders is: Why spread in the first place? If traders like those described above think corn is going to go up, why not just buy the March? If the spreaders are correct in their analysis, they will make a profit on their March contract, lose on their May, and show a net profit on the difference because the March profit will exceed the May loss. It is obvious that they would have had a greater profit per contract if they had just bought the March. Their action in taking the spread, however, is not quite so foolish as it may appear. By taking the spread position they have reduced their investment. The margin on one contract, 5,000 bushels of March corn long against a short position of 5,000 May, may be only $500 for the entire position, compared with a margin requirement of $1,500 required for long March corn alone. If the price of March corn rises 15 cents and that of May 9 cents, the return on investment is greater on the spread than it would have been on the net position. The profit on the net March would have been $750 on a $1,500 investment, or 50 percent. The spread position results in a profit of $750 on the March and a loss of $450 on the May, but this represents a net gain of $300 on a $500 investment, or 60 percent. If the traders choose to be more aggressive, they can carry 15,000 bushels in a spread position for the same margin as a net position of 5,000 bushels.

It should also be noted that the analysis of the corn situation may have been wrong in the first place and that corn might go down and not up. In this case a net position in March corn could have been costly or even ruinous, whereas the spread position could hardly prove painful at all because March could not lose significantly on May. The cost of this insurance is not great because the commission on a 5,000-bushel spread position is only $36 versus $30 for a 5,000-bushel net position, and as we have seen, the funds needed to margin the position are much less. The spread traders have therefore increased their potential profit and reduced both their risk and their investment. It is even possible that the spreaders could be completely wrong in their analysis and still make money just because they spread. The price of corn could fall drastically, and the price level of May could lose on March simply because more net traders choose to sell it or have to sell it owing to pressure to liquidate. March, of course, still could not lose significantly on May because of the ever-present watchfulness of the arbitragers.

There is hardly any limit to the number of combinations open to intracommodity spreaders, but certain spreads do tend to be relatively popular, such as May potatoes against November, July soybeans against November, July cocoa against December, July flax against October, May wheat against July, and July sugar against October.

Intercommodity Spreads.   Some commodities are used for the same general purposes as others and therefore are interchangeable to a degree. The easier it is to substitute one for the other, the closer the relationship of their prices. Oats and corn are a case in point, as are hogs and cattle. If spreaders believe that the price relation between two commodities is unrealistic, they can sell the higher-priced, buy the lower-priced, wait for the relative price levels to approach normality, and then take their profit. The advantages of trading in this manner are similar to intracommodity spreads. The margin on cattle against hogs is usually about the same as it would be for either hogs or cattle taken alone. This is greater than in the case of the intracommodity spread, in which the margin on the spread is considerably less than it would be on one side alone. Unlike the intracommodity spread, however, there is seldom a commission reduction for spreads involving more than one commodity. Because drastic changes in the price levels of both commodities are likely to be similar, the risk of ruinous losses is considerably reduced at the cost of the opportunity to achieve windfall profits.

Among the more popular spreads of this kind are those involving soybeans and the products produced from soybeans, namely, soybean oil and soybean meal. Spreaders usually assume that crushers will find either oil or meal more profitable at a given time and that one of the product prices will be the stronger. If the current prices do not reflect the strength of one of the products adequately, spreaders can buy the product that they feel should be the stronger and sell the other against it. If they believe that the value of the two products combined is too low relative to the beans, they can sell one contract of beans and buy one contract each of soybean oil and soybean meal. This position is usually called a "reverse crush" because it is opposite to the position taken by soybean crushers, who are typically long beans, which they crush to be able to sell the products. A contract of oil plus one of meal does not exactly equal the amount of oil and meal that could actually be produced from the contract of 5,000 bushels of beans, but it is usually close enough to yield a profit if the beans prove to be selling too high on the products. If the traders think that beans will gain on the combined products, they can buy the beans and sell the products, just as crushers do. The establishment of such a position is sometimes called "putting on running time."

Popular intercommodity spreads include wheat versus corn, hogs versus bellies, domestic versus foreign sugar contracts, and oats versus corn. In the last-named case, traders frequently spread one contract of corn against two contracts of oats because they consider a contract of oats to be worth only about 56 percent of a contract of corn.

Intermarket Spreads.   Many commodities are traded on more than one market. Wheat is traded on the Chicago Board of Trade, the Kansas City Board of Trade, and the Minneapolis Grain Exchange. Chicago trades basically soft red winter wheat; Kansas City, hard red winter wheat; and Minneapolis, spring wheat. There is, however, a close relation among all these types, which are interchangeable for many purposes. In some cases the type trading on one exchange is actually deliverable against the type trading on another. All three basic types of wheat are deliverable on the Chicago Board of Trade. In this case the important limiting factors include the cost of transportation between cities as well as differences in the characteristics of the different types of wheat. If speculators believe that price differences are out of line between commodities trading in two cities, they sell the higher-priced contract and buy the lower-priced one. In spreads of this kind there is no commission advantage and seldom much, if any, margin advantage.

Popular positions include Winnipeg oats versus Chicago oats, New York cocoa or sugar against London cocoa or sugar, and Chicago versus Kansas City or Minneapolis wheat.

Combinations.   The fact that traders decide that Winnipeg oats are low on Chicago oats does not mean that they should be long December Winnipeg oats and short December Chicago oats. If they think that oats are too high on corn, it does not mean that they should be long March corn and short March oats. The fact that they chose both contracts in the same delivery month may indicate that they have not thought enough about their spread position. More often than not the nearby contract will gain on the distant contract in strong markets because of the influence of strong cash markets on the nearby futures contracts, and carrying charges will decrease or inversion will increase. In weak markets nearby contracts tend to lose on the distant contracts, and carrying charges will increase or inversion will decrease. The long side of a spread trade should probably be the contract that is lowest-priced in terms of the prevailing spread differences in the commodity, and the short side should probably be the contract that appears highest-priced at that time. For the best logical choice of both sides to be in the same delivery month would be sheer coincidence; yet this is the choice all too often made by spreaders who have given their positions only superficial thought.

Low-Risk Spreads.   Many traders contemplating speculation in commodity futures markets are in great fear of the risk involved. To reduce fear, many writers and speakers interested in attracting new commodity speculators are fond of discussing the "no-risk spread." The usual example given is an intracommodity spread trading at full carrying charge so that a trader could buy the nearby contract and sell the distant contract with virtually no risk at all except for a material change in the carrying charges. Actually, attractive opportunities of this kind are quite rare. Other traders will take spread positions before the contracts reach full carrying-charge difference, with the result that the spreads may never get there. The closer the actual prices approach the apparent ideal, the more likely it is that there is such extreme weakness in the nearby lower-priced contract that there is no reason for it to gain on the distant contract. The low-risk trade, therefore, may involve little risk but will have little potential. Traders who wait for full carrying-charge situations involving real potential may spend a long time waiting for a trade that will never be made successfully.

Tax Spreads.   Some advocate entering spread positions to achieve a tax advantage rather than to realize a profit. Purported advantages include the postponement of gains to another year or the conversion of short-term to long-term gains. The possibility is even advanced of converting a short-term gain in one year to a long-term gain in another.

Trading for tax advantages is a complex process and probably should not be attempted by traders acting without skilled professional advice. Not only is it quite difficult to accomplish the objective economically, but there is always the uncertainty that the government will allow the trade to be used for the purpose for which it was intended. Taxes were discussed briefly in Chapter 32, but a really detailed coverage of the subject is beyond the scope of this chapter and probably beyond that of some brokers and others who are sometimes too generous with advice in this complex and hazardous field.

Mistakes.   The most frequent mistake made by those who trade spread positions is establishing them for all the wrong reasons. A common example is that of net-position traders who have open losses that continue to get worse until they receive a margin call. They could, of course, solve their immediate problem by reducing or eliminating their position, but for some reason they regard a realized loss as something so much worse than an equity loss that they will do anything to avoid it. This error is so widespread and usually so disastrous that it is worth examining in some detail.

Let us presume that cocoa traders are convinced that the price of May cocoa at 31 cents a pound is such a bargain that it is worth the full use of their available trading capital of $5,000. The margin requirement for contract of 30,000 pounds of cocoa at the brokerage house of their choice is $1,200. They thereupon buy four contracts of May cocoa at 31 cents a pound and wait for great wealth to come their way. Unfortunately the news items concerning cocoa become unfavorable. Ghana announces that its crop looks better than had been expected. The Netherlands and Germany speak of decreased consumption, and suddenly May cocoa is 29 cents and "not acting well." The traders are convinced that this adversity is temporary, that the forthcoming rise will be bigger than ever, and wish that they could buy the cocoa now instead of when they did. Nevertheless, the broker's margin clerk, concerned only with numbers, points out that the open loss is $2,400 and that there is insufficient margin remaining to support four cocoa contracts.

The traders now have several choices. First, they could deposit additional funds, but they have none available for this purpose. Second, they could sell two cocoa contracts and keep the other two, but they do not like the prospect of having to make 400 points on each of two contracts to compensate for the 200 points they lost on each of the four. Third, they could admit that they were wrong about the cocoa market and get out of all four. This they find impossible to do because they would now have a realized loss of about $2,000 in addition to the necessity of admitting to themselves, their spouses, their broker, and their accountants that they are not particularly good traders. So they seek a way to postpone the inevitable by buying time. Accordingly, they order the broker to sell four contracts of July cocoa at its present price of 29.30 cents a pound. The margin requirement on a cocoa spread is only $400 compared with the $1,200 on a net long or short position; so the total margin requirement is reduced from $4,800 to $1,600. The equity in the account was reduced from $5,000 to $2,600 by the decline in May cocoa, and the margin call is satisfied.

On close examination it should be apparent that the traders have not really improved their position and may have made it worse. They have reduced their margin requirement from $4,800 to $1,600 but would have had no requirement at all if they had simply sold their May cocoa. Their new plan, if they have one, is probably to cover their short July position after cocoa stops going down and take their "profit." It should be clear, however, that their position will be no better than if they had just taken off their May cocoa and reinstated it. It is probable that the May will drop just as much as July if July goes down, and therefore their July closed profit will be equaled by an additional May open loss. The commission expense of trading the four July contracts is just the same as that incurred in taking off the four May. The moment the July short position is lifted, the margin requirement reverts to $4,800, and the traders have the same problem they had before because there has been no equity improvement. A common procedure for such people would be to take off July early one day and hope that May would rise enough by the close to overcome the margin call, which, of course, might happen. Because the trend of cocoa has been down, however, it is at least as likely that cocoa will go down during the day and make matters worse. In the end the traders might trade their July cocoa several times, paying commissions of about $200 every time they do until they have a margin call even on the spread position and their situation has become hopeless. At this point they will probably blame the cocoa exchange, their broker, or their bad luck, when actually they were guilty of overtrading, failing to take a loss quickly, and spreading for the wrong reasons. Aside from a rally in the May futures on the day they cover their July position, the only other way out of their predicament is an improvement in the spread itself resulting from May gaining materially on July, but in a bear market the reverse is more likely. The chances of spreading a bad position and then recovering by day-trading one side of the spread or by improvement of the spread itself are extremely slim ones.

A second serious error common among spreaders is choosing a spread in preference to a net position primarily to reduce margin and then putting on such a large spread position, just because the margin is low, that they ultimately take a greater risk and pay more in commissions than they would have paid with a net position. Such traders fail to realize that a spread provides some but not complete protection. Spreaders might consider a price difference warped and thereby offering an opportunity, but it might well become even more warped and result in a loss before it returns to normal, that is, if we assume that it was warped in the first place and did not merely reflect some condition overlooked by the spreaders.

Corn traders, for example, may regard May corn as cheap at $1.22 and consider the purchase of 5,000 bushels for an anticipated 6-cent gain, for which they would risk a 2-cent loss. The gain would give them a profit of $300 at the risk of a $100 loss. The required margin might be $400, and the round-turn commission $30. The $300 profit would be almost 75 percent of the margin deposited, but the traders conclude that they would do even better spreading because the broker will carry 5,000 May corn long against 5,000 December corn short for only $100. They believe that the expected 6-cent gain in May corn will result in its gaining 3 cents on December corn during the same time, which would represent a potential profit of $150 on the $100 margin, or a rate twice the 75 percent on the net position. The commission on the spread position would be $36 a contract compared with $30 on the net position; so the rate of net profit would still be materially higher.

This seems so attractive to the traders that they are reluctant to leave idle the remainder of the $400 margin that the net corn position would have required. They thereupon decide to utilize the same capital for the spread and put on four of the spreads, or 20,000 long May corn against 20,000 short December. If their trade succeeds, they will realize a gross profit of $600 less the total commission of $144 or $456 on the $400 margin. What they fail to consider is the possible adversity. It is unrealistic to assume that one could be prepared for a possible loss of less than 1 cent on a spread of this kind, which means that an unplanned loss caused by some unexpected event like a change in the corn loan could easily cause a loss of 2 cents or even more. A 2-cent loss on the spread would be $400 plus the $144 commission, which would more than wipe out the traders' capital. This is a far greater loss than could reasonably have been suffered on a net position. As a result, the apparently safer position with a smaller investment has become a far greater risk with an equal investment and a larger commission.

There is sometimes a temptation to establish a spread one leg at a time or to remove it one leg at a time. This has at least one clear disadvantage and usually two. The spread commission is lost. Instead of a corn spread, for example, costing the spread commission of $36, the customer must pay the full $30 for each side, or $60. Second, most traders have an uncanny ability to put on the wrong leg first or take off the wrong one first. This is so probably because most of them try to choose the exact moment that a market will turn, which is almost impossible to do. For example, let us suppose that the corn spread previously discussed has worked favorably and that May corn has gained the planned 3 cents on December. The traders could take off the spread at the prevailing difference and realize their profit. They could also cover their December short and allow the May to continue to rise. Instead, they will more often yield to the temptation to take off the May because it is the profitable side and stay short December, hoping that it will go down, overcome its paper loss, and allow them to show a profit on both legs of the spread. Actually, what seems to happen all too often is that the May side is taken off on a day when corn is strong, which very strength caused the spread to succeed. It is also taken off early in the day because the traders want as much time as possible for December to react. So corn continues strong, and the 3-cent profit that was realized over a period of months is lost in hours.

A mistake that is not quite so serious, but quite common, is the haphazard choosing of contract months. The traders could have timed their transaction by watching a chart indicating the difference between May and December corn, but at the moment of entry July might be a better choice than May or March better than December. The choice should be based on all pertinent factors, not on the casual choice of contracts on a spread chart or a broker's quotation board.

Options

Like so many terms in the financial field, "option" is used in more than one way in the commodity futures area. One, really a popular misnomer, applies to a designated futures month such as "the July option" for soybeans. Another, and more nearly correct form, has to do with the purchase of the right to buy or sell a commodity at a designated price during a designated future period. This is similar to the procedure used in stock, real estate, and personal services.

There are three basic forms of option applicable to the commodity markets. One is a "call," which is an option to buy a specified commodity at a specified price (the "striking price") for a designated period of time. The payment for this call is determined by market conditions such as the price level of the commodity, its expected price volatility, and the supply-and-demand conditions for the calls themselves. The payment is designated as the "premium." To profit by a position the price of the commodity must move up enough to cover the cost of the premium rather than merely the round-turn commission. Option traders nevertheless gain some advantages. Their loss is absolutely limited to the cost of their premium. Traders in the futures markets could enter a stop to limit their possible loss, but there is no assurance that the market will not sell through their stop or that they will not remove the stop, as is often the case. More important, option traders need not fear interim adversity. Regardless of adversity, they receive no margin calls and need only hope that they will achieve a satisfactory profit sooner or later during the period they have bought with their options.

A second popular form of option is the "put," which operates in much the same way as the call, with the same advantages and similar costs, except that buyers of puts have the right to sell a commodity contract at a set price over a specified period of time. They expect and hope that the price will decline.

The third type is a "straddle," or "double option." This gives buyers the right to buy or sell the commodity at a fixed price over a specified period of time or even both if the price moves over a range wide enough to yield them a profit on the upside and the downside. The straddle amounts to nothing more than a combination of a call and a put and, logically enough, costs approximately the same as a call and put combined would cost.

Usually the only options available are those that are written by underwriters in the London markets on sugar, copper, silver, or rubber. Intermittently, however, options written in the United States have been popular.

Trading in options (formerly often called "privileges") was carried on from time to time between the early 1860s and middle 1930s. There were many efforts by exchanges and state and federal governments to stop trading, but early rules and laws were largely ignored by those who were supposed to obey them and by those who should have enforced them, largely because the violations were so widespread that enforcement would have disrupted the entire commodity business.

The Commodity Exchange Authority (CEA) finally stopped trading in options on regulated commodities after 1936. The government was concerned about many aspects of options trading but especially about the artificial price movements caused by option traders' attempting to protect the options they had bought or sold. The volume of options traded became so large that it disrupted regular commodity trading on the exchanges, especially at the close of the markets, and was uncomfortably closer to a gambling practice than to a speculative activity.[2]

One flaw in the law prohibiting options proved to be its limitation to regulated commodities. About 1970 several firms took advantage of this loophole to begin trading in popular unregulated commodities such as silver, platinum, copper, silver coins, cocoa, sugar, and plywood. At about the same time the prices of many of these commodities became extremely volatile, which permitted option buyers to recover their premiums in unusually short times. Buyers of straddles could hardly lose and found themselves making important amounts of money within a few weeks or even days. Bernard Baruch's 2 and 2 still made 4, however, and with everyone winning losers had to be found. As long as new buyers of options entered the field faster than old ones left, there was no problem. In fact, the old ones were more anxious to reinvest in new options than they were to withdraw even their profits, much less their capital. From a short-term cash-flow point of view there was no immediate problem, but in 1973, as throughout history, the piper had to be paid. When regulatory bodies stopped trading "temporarily" and most of the public lost its confidence, liquidations equaled and finally exceeded new purchases of options, and the option companies could raise sufficient capital only by speculating successfully with the cash received for options quickly enough to pay off their underwriting obligations. The amount needed to be earned proved to be too great, the time available to earn it proved to be too short, and widespread failures of commodity option firms resulted.

The London options, which are written against actual cash commodities, underwritten by substantially capitalized companies, and realistically priced, remain popular among a small group of sophisticated traders. From time to time some American exchanges, particularly those in New York, move toward initiating option trading similar to that available in London. The Chicago Board of Trade began trading in stock options in April 1973, but theirs was more of an effort to attract business from the over-the-counter dealers' market in such options than an emulation of the old and largely discredited privilege markets.

Notes from a Trader

Spread trading is not so simple as taking net long or net short positions in a commodity. The advantages are sometimes so great, however, that it is well worth the necessary time and energy needed to master them. Most spread positions involve less risk than net positions and frequently less investment. The extra commissions incurred are usually a small consideration compared with the advantages. The avoidance of catastrophic losses is one of the greatest advantages of spread trading. Commodity markets sometimes have sudden, violent price movements. When one of these movements is in favor of a trader, a welcome windfall profit is realized, but when one is against the trader, he or she is no longer a commodity trader. Many speculators with experience in trading are happy to forgo the opportunity for such windfall profits if the equal chance for a disastrous loss can be avoided. Spreads accomplish this reduction of risk because what is lost on one side in an unusually large adverse move is frequently matched by an approximately equal gain on the other side. The cost of this insurance against disaster is quite low. For new traders spreads provide an opportunity to enter the commodity markets with minimum capital and risk.

If unregulated option trading revives, buyers should be as greatly concerned with the financial integrity of the underwriters as with the volatility of the underlying commodities relative to their price.

---

[2]Paul Mehl, *Trading in Privileges on the Chicago Board of Trade*, U.S. Department of Agriculture Circular No. 323, December 1934, pp. 75–78.

Section Seven

Special and Offbeat Investments

Chapter **36**
Investing in Gold

JOSEPH PETRITZ

During the Vietnam unpleasantness, a distressed little girl asked her mother: "What if someone held a war and nobody came?" More recently, she might have asked, "What if someone held a gold rush and nobody came?" The answer to the second question would be the easier. The United States had and hardly anyone did.

When President Ford announced on August 14, 1974, that ownership of gold by United States citizens would become legal on December 31, 1974, a wave of anticipatory speculation rolled around the world—speculation in gold itself, based on speculation about how much of the precious metal Americans might rush out to buy.

The London afternoon gold fix on the previous Monday (August 12) was $152.25 a troy ounce, and a week later it was $3 higher. The price backed and filled, but eventually, just before the magical New Year's Eve, it moved sharply up until the price in London grazed the $200 level, rising slightly above $200 on the Paris and Zurich markets.

Forecasts by reputed experts ranged from an eventual $500 an ounce or even higher to a pessimistic $100. Enough European speculators believed the former figure to run the price up at least to the $200 area, but a funny thing happened on their way to retirement to a life of ease.

As the time for gold ownership moved closer, United States media, inspired by the hurricane signals flown by the federal government and reputable financial institutions, laid down a barrage of caveats that cooled the enthusiasm of the vast majority of would-be gold buyers. By December 31, anticipation of a gold *rush* in the United States had been revised downward to a gold *stroll*.

But this first sampling of interest need not be taken as final. Many authorities anticipate growing public interest and participation as people learn more about the precious metal. There are several ways of investing in gold, some of which were legal through the years and others that were newly legalized. They vary in desirability as a hedge against inflation, as an investment, and as a store of value in a highly uncertain world. Each will be examined in turn as a guide to the affluent seeking a vehicle for preserving their wealth and possibly adding to it. These include:

- Ownership of gold bullion

- Ownership of gold coins, new or of numismatic value
- Purchase of bank, warehouse, or other gold paper
- Ownership of gold jewelry
- Purchase of gold-mining stocks
- Speculation on futures markets

Of these, only the futures markets generated substantial volume at the outset, as described later in this chapter.

THE MYSTIQUE OF GOLD

Any rational approach to ownership of gold, either actual or in the form of paper, requires some homework. Why do people believe in gold? Why has it excited emperors, peasants, and everyone in between through the centuries? Are gold prices truly established by the laws of supply and demand or by group psychology? Or by a mixture of both? Is gold accurately to be regarded as that "noble metal" or rather as that "barbarous relic"? The answer, to an extent, is in the eye of the beholder. Consider this statement:

> There is an old joke about gold: there are only two people in the world who really understand gold, and they disagree. The joke runs deep because it points to the fact that there are two radically different ways of understanding gold. The first is to construe gold as one more commodity of which there happens to be an ample supply. When one looks at gold in such terms, the puzzle is why is there such excitement about gold, and why do people *believe in gold*? The second method of interpreting the gold phenomenon is as an exercise in group psychodynamics. Here the issue is not whether the long-term supply of gold will exceed the demand, or whether the actual preferences that people have are rationally determined, but whether or not people will desire gold, and if so, how long will the desire last and how intense will it be? Economists are not capable of predicting or analyzing such questions because economic theory takes desires as a given, and does not purport to explain or predict the formation of such desires. On the assumption that an intense desire for an object whose primary use is as a support for mattresses is not a particularly natural appetite, it would seem to follow that the proper explanation of such passions lies within the realm of group psychology.[1]

SUPPLY AND DEMAND

What economists and other qualified persons *are* capable of understanding, if not necessarily interpreting in unison, are the powerful forces of supply and demand. As is true with any other commodity, prices do react to these primary forces. Supplies are obtained from the production of new gold or from private or official stockpiles. The aggregate consumption of gold reflects demand.

The following discussion about the supply and demand of gold, up to the heading "For and Against the Goldbug View," is extracted from a brochure published by the International Monetary Market Division of the Chicago Mercantile Exchange.[2]

Gold Production

> Two-thirds to three-quarters of the world's yearly production of gold comes from the Union of South Africa. Gold in South Africa tends to be found in thin seams, one to two miles or even more beneath the surface. This has meant that gold mining in South Africa has had to surmount significant technological obstacles and has had to be highly capitalized. To start a new mine in the 1890s cost about $2-million, but to start one in the 1970s costs closer to $200-million. In a recent year, nearly 80-million tons of rock were

[1]*The Rosenthal Report,* vol. 2, no. 8, Rosenthal & Company, Dec. 31, 1974.
[2]*Understanding Gold Futures Trading,* International Monetary Market Division of the Chicago Mercantile Exchange, Inc., October 1974.

extracted from the 46 South African mines, ground or "milled" to a fine powder, and passed through a cyanide solution to yield just under 1,000 tons of gold. That amount, however, was 74 percent of the non-Communist world's production for the year. Indeed, South Africa's share of production has grown so mightily and rapidly that it is now estimated that more than one-third of all the gold ever mined has come from South Africa. The production of the leading gold-mining countries is shown in Table 1 [Table 36-1].

It is predominantly in South Africa that a basic characteristic of the world's major gold-mining operation can be observed—cooperation. Through the Chamber of Mines of South Africa, established in 1889, the seven large gold-finance houses that have controlled South African gold production since the 1930s coordinate their overall operating policy, gold research, labor recruitment, refining, and marketing. Following

TABLE 36-1   Primary Gold Production
(In millions of troy ounces)

	1970	1971	1972	1973	1974*
Republic of South Africa	32.2	31.4	29.2	27.3	28.2
U.S.S.R.	6.5	6.7	6.9	7.1	7.4
Canada	2.4	2.2	2.1	1.9	2.2
United States	1.7	1.5	1.5	1.4	1.3
Ghana	.7	.7	.7	.7	.7
Australia	.6	.7	.8	.8	.7
Philippines	.6	.6	.6	.6	.6
Rhodesia	.5	.5	.5	.5	.5
Japan	.3	.3	.2	.2	.2
Colombia	.2	.2	.2	.2	.2
Other	1.8	1.7	1.6	1.5	1.3
World total	47.5	46.5	44.3	42.2	43.3

*Estimated.
SOURCE: Consolidated Gold Fields Limited.

the dictates of the Chamber of Mines, South African gold production is sold through the South African Reserve Bank.

The Chamber of Mines is trying to conserve South African gold resources. The impact of its conservation program on supply has been to promote the exploitation of lower-grade ore, and this decreases total gold production. Accordingly, even with higher prices, South African gold production has been declining since 1970, a trend also noticeable in Canada and the United States. Mine production in the non-Communist world is expected to continue this trend in 1974, slipping to about 1,075 tons. Despite falling gold-mine production, gold sales from South Africa increased considerably with 1973 sales of 788 tons because of a lower level of gold retention by the South African Reserve Bank.

The Soviet Union is the second-largest gold producer, although its exact position is unknown outside the U.S.S.R. A recent publication of Consolidated Gold Fields Limited suggests that Soviet gold production has climbed from approximately 244 metric tons in 1964 to 371 tons in 1973, with the 1973 figure being about 140 tons above other estimates. In addition to satisfying needs for foreign exchange arising from such problems as poor harvests, there has developed a tendency for the Russians to expand Free-World gold sales when gold prices are high and stop them when prices are low. It is estimated that 280 tons of Russian gold were sold in 1973 at an average price of $95 an ounce. Output in 1974 is forecast at 387 tons, of which 288 tons could be sold on the free markets if the Russians find the price attractive.

Canada and the United States also have experienced a production lag. However, in these countries much of the gold mined is a by-product of other metals, which are not necessarily responsive to gold-price changes. Canadian production is particularly being hampered by the declining availability of high-grade ores, and it is possible that its long-term yields may fall significantly. U.S. gold production peaked in 1915 and again in 1940 at nearly 5-million ounces a year. Since World War II, production has averaged about 1.7-million ounces a year.

In summary, the wise gold analyst will watch carefully trends in the production of gold in South Africa and the gold-selling policies followed by the South African Reserve Bank and the Soviet Union.

Gold Stocks

The near indestructibility of gold means that the vast majority of all the gold ever mined is still in existence. Some of it is held in jewelry, some in industrial use and equipment, some is hoarded, some is in government hands.

Official gold stocks are estimated at about 44,000 tons or one billion troy ounces. Of this, about one-fifth is held by the U.S. government and more than 70 percent of it is held by the world's developed countries. Much of this gold is used as a reserve asset in the International Monetary Fund's (IMF) Special Drawing Rights. As of November 13, 1973, the principal governments of the IMF can sell but not buy gold on the free market. Whether or not these governments will in fact sell their gold remains to be seen. Recent agreements allowing official gold reserves to be used as collateral to obtain loans for countries with balance-of-payments deficits suggest they may not be willing sellers.

Hoarding of gold is common in many countries. These holdings and the reserve assets of governments testify to the centuries-old usage of gold as the final standard of value in periods of turbulence, depression, inflation and unrest. Private hoards of gold are difficult to estimate, but figures commonly cited are 50,000 tons or 1.2-billion troy ounces of gold. As the data in Table 2 [Table 36-2] indicate, the movement of gold into hoarding, and into speculative and investment channels has tended to increase. Poor crop yields, with the resultant reduction in income, and increased demand for foreign exchange to pay for imports, led to some dishoarding in 1972 in some of the developing countries while there was a moderate 1973 profit-taking movement in some of these same countries. However, vastly increased oil revenues of the Arab states has resulted in their increased gold purchases, and their activity possibly could become a key factor in gold-price movements.

[*Greens Commodity Market Comments* for January 15, 1975, estimated that U.S.S.R. gold stocks are approximately 132 million ounces, as contrasted with the Consolidated Gold Fields estimate of 86.8 million ounces at the end of 1973 and the CIA estimate of between 70 million and 80 million ounces. The reason for the high Greens figure is the belief that the U.S.S.R., following World War II, confiscated bullion and gold coins from its own citizens and from the central banks and citizens of countries it occupied during the war. Furthermore, Greens expressed the conviction that unmined gold reserves in the Soviet Union are between 4 and 5 billion ounces, as against 1 to 1.5 billion ounces for South Africa and 3 billion ounces estimated to have been mined from the beginning of time.]

Estimating Gold Supply

The supply coming into the free market was about 12 percent greater in 1973 than in 1972; despite this increase, 1973 saw some of the most rapidly escalating gold prices in the history of mankind. Clearly, world production of gold responds only slowly to increased prices. The immediate response is to mine lower-grade ore, which tends to lower total gold production. High capital costs, lead times of seven to 10 years for new mine development, and technological hurdles in gold extraction imply that producers must be assured of long-term price strength before new mines will be developed.

Increased supply in the short term will tend to come from released reserves and dishoarding. Gold prices continuing in the high 1973 area probably would induce further reserve sales by South Africa and Russia as well as some private dishoarding. Calamities, such as crop failures, probably would stimulate more gold sales from developing countries. At late 1973 price levels, it was estimated that gold-fabricator usage would decline from 853 metric tons in 1973 to 725 tons in 1974. Since 1974 mine production in the non-Communist world is forecast at 1,075 tons, then 350 tons of production would be available for hoarding, speculation, and investment. Table 2 [Table 36-2] shows comparative figures for previous years. It is, therefore, the level of demand that will determine the amount of gold supplied to the free-world market, and that demand most likely will be motivated largely by monetary and emotional considerations.

Demand

The share of newly produced gold going into official reserves has been declining since 1965, and fabricator use of gold has slipped since 1972 while gold prices have risen to new highs. The demand pull that gold prices have experienced is caused by gold being increasingly acquired for investment, speculation, and hoarding.

Gold thus seems to be fulfilling its role as the barometer of international economic disturbances. The increased demand for gold is closely linked to the high levels of inflation that much of the world is experiencing.

TABLE 36-2   Gold Flows, 1968–1974

(In metric tons)

	1968	1969	1970	1971	1972	1973	1974*
Mine production in non-Communist world	1,245	1,252	1,273	1,236	1,182	1,120	1,075
Supply flow from Communist countries	−29	−15	-0-	60	220	280	. . .
Official purchases (minus) or sales	620	−90	−236	96	−151	6	. . .
Total supply to free market	1,836	1,147	1,037	1,392	1,251	1,406	. . .
Distribution of total supply Return to market (minus) or absorption							
Fabrication	1,227	1,205	1,381	1,391	1,350	853	725
Hoarding	72	60	88	80	−8	46	. . .
Speculation or investment	537	−118	−432	−79	−91	508	. . .

*Preliminary forecast.
SOURCE: *Gold, 1974,* Consolidated Gold Fields Limited.

Gold, Currencies, and the Inflationary Spiral

The worldwide acceleration of inflation in 1973 and 1974 resulted in vastly increased gold investment. With 1974 levels of inflation expected to be between 7 percent and 24 percent in the leading developed countries of the free world, inflation is a primary incentive for investors to move into gold. . . .

The legalization on December 31, 1974 of private gold ownership will make it possible for U.S. citizens and companies to use gold as an inflationary hedge. How good a hedge it will be remains to be seen. At one time, securities and real estate were generally regarded as inflation hedges, but these have been shown to be vulnerable in the face of tight money and restraints on prices, profits, and dividends. Corporate taxes being levied on inflated rather than real corporate incomes reinforce this trend. A broad economic program to fight inflation would not only use a restrictive monetary policy and high interest rates but also higher taxes on income. Without such a broad program, gold may be a realistic hedge against inflation.

Fabricator Demand

The pattern of gold demand has changed dramatically since 1973. Higher gold prices have meant higher costs for fabricators and, as Table 2 [Table 36-2] indicates, a smaller share of the total gold market. Total fabricator demand nevertheless remains strong. Net absorption of gold by jewelry manufacturers fell by 488 tons during 1973 whereas all other fabricator usage for gold was little affected. Total fabricator demand is shown in Table 3 [Table 36-3].

The largest use of gold is for fabrication of jewelry. In addition to its beauty and endurance, gold is prized in jewelry for its workability. In many developing countries of the world, gold jewelry for centuries has been a primary form of asset preservation and a long-term investment.

TABLE 36-3 Gold Fabrication by End Use

	1969 Metric tons	1969 Percent	1970 Metric tons	1970 Percent	1971 Metric tons	1971 Percent	1972 Metric tons	1972 Percent	1973 Metric tons	1973 Percent
Jewelry in advanced nations	502.3	41.7	500.1	36.2	551.7	39.6	700.1	51.9	419.0	49.1
Jewelry in developing nations*	403.9	33.5	562.5	40.7	507.0	36.4	292.6	21.7	86.2	10.1
Total, jewelry	906.2	75.2	1,062.6	76.9	1,058.7	76.1	992.7	73.5	505.2	59.2
Electronics	102.4	8.5	93.6	6.8	90.6	6.5	110.2	8.2	129.5	15.1
Dentistry*	64.6	5.4	63.9	4.6	70.0	5.0	72.5	5.4	72.7	8.5
Other industrial and decorative	63.1	5.2	61.9	4.5	68.2	4.9	71.2	5.3	71.0	8.3
Official coins	24.6	...	45.9	...	52.3	...	62.0	...	53.2	...
Fake coins, medals, and medallions	44.0	...	53.6	...	51.7	...	41.2	...	21.8	...
Total	1,204.9	100.0	1,381.5	100.0	1,391.5	100.0	1,349.8	100.0	853.4	100.0

*About 10 tons of the gold attributed to jewelry usage in developing countries probably is used in dental applications.
SOURCE: *Gold, 1974*, Consolidated Gold Fields Limited.

The second-largest use for gold is in electronics. Gold's excellent conductive capacity and resistance to corrosion make it ideal for a wide diversity of applications. It is significant that although reductions in the quantity of gold consumed per unit occurred in this type of usage, they were far outweighed by increases in the total units produced. The relatively high percentage of military usage in this sector tends further to limit the substitution of other metals. As Table 3 [Table 36-3] shows, there has been little change in the dental use of gold and a relatively small impact on official coinage, whereas higher gold prices seriously affected the large market in false coins, medals, and medallions.

Estimating Gold Demand

Numerous factors undoubtedly will influence the total demand picture for gold. Substitutions of other metals, if less expensive, will be attempted in some areas if consumer resistance to higher gold prices is widespread. War or the threat of war always increases gold demand. But these factors aside, gold demand should fundamentally reflect the monetary situation. Thus, wide fluctuations in foreign exchange rates and unstable financial institutions may engender further distrust of paper currencies. Uncontrolled, and perhaps uncontrollable inflation, fed by higher oil prices and growing balance-of-payments deficits, would continue to be reflected in demand for gold. Conversely, improvements in the monetary situation should result in reduced demand pressure for gold.

Means of attempting to measure demand for gold are necessarily general rather than precise because of the possible impact of investment, speculative, and hoarding demand. One of the measures that has been used is to emphasize gold's countercyclical tendency. Advocates of this approach compare gold trends to, particularly, stock-market trends in order to emphasize inverse relations between the two. Advocates of this approach find it consistent that the recent enormous increase in the demand for gold was in accord with deteriorating stock-market conditions.

Another "indicator" approach for measuring gold demand that can be used is to treat general commodity-price trends as indicators of gold-demand trends. Thus a significant upturn in commodity markets can be regarded as stimulating fears of inflation and so pushing gold demand.

FOR AND AGAINST THE GOLDBUG VIEW

So much for the supply-and-demand factors, as well as they can be known, that have such an important, if not ultimate, bearing on the price of gold. The interpretation of these factors is another matter. The goldbugs stoutly argue that gold is the ultimate store of value, the only commodity that will retain and increase its value. Less ardent observers believe that gold is a prudent investment only in times of great inflation.

Franz Pick, the seventy-six-year-old high priest of the goldbugs and a world-renowned currency authority,

> . . . is convinced that runaway inflation in the United States and other countries of the world will continue to eat away at the value of all currencies. And he is sure that the price of gold will climb much higher soon "because smart investors are running away from paper of any kind—bank notes, stocks, bonds, certificates of deposit, annuities, you name it." . . .
>
> On occasion, Pick has said that gold could soar to almost any price—$500 or $1,000 per ounce—"the sky's the limit," as long as world inflation persists.[3]

Another renowned currency authority, John Exter, a consultant on domestic and international money, pleads for a return to the gold standard. He told one audience that gold would be a good hedge in either inflation or deflation.

---

[3]*Esquire,* January 1975.

Speaking at the October 16, 1974, International Monetary Market's Monetary and Trade Outlook Conference in Chicago, Exter said:

> Money serves three functions. First, it is a means of payment; second, it is a standard of value—we quote prices in it; and third, it is a store of value.
>
> Scarcity and desirability are the keystones of store-of-value money. Paper standing on its own feet cannot serve as a good store of value; it is far too abundant. The only way to keep it scarce is to keep it freely convertible into some scarce commodity like gold at a fixed price.

Strongly advocating debt liquidation "of the deflationary kind," with less government intervention, so that market forces would be free to do the job, Exter had this advice for individuals:

> I suggest you go down the [inverted] pyramid [of debt] and remember gold is at its base as the enduring store-of-value money. . . .
>
> In my view, we are in the greatest rush out of paper into gold in all of history. If I am wrong about my forecast of deflation, and inflation continues to hyperinflate the dollar, the price of gold will go to infinity. But if I am right, the precise course of the gold price is more uncertain, though in the end I am confident that gold will be as good a hedge in deflation as in inflation.

Addressing the same gathering, Prof. Milton Friedman, the noted University of Chicago monetarist, questioned the value of gold as a store of value, saying that it is necessary to "look at the evidence over a long period, not just over a few years." Accordingly, he made his calculations to cover the period of 1929 to the present, allowing 3 percent a year in storage costs and lost interest and basing his findings on purchasing power rather than on the nominal price of gold. Gold bought in 1929 at $20.57 an ounce (illegally but without much difficulty) and sold in 1934 when President Roosevelt raised the official price to $35, would have brought "an 87 percent gain in purchasing power . . . you would have done very well." But gold bought in 1934 at $35 an ounce and held until 1968 (thirty-four years) would have resulted in the buyer's ending up with only 14 percent as much purchasing power as he started with. Professor Friedman stated:

> Six-sevenths of your wealth would have been eroded away by price increases of other goods and by storage costs over that period of time.
>
> Now we come to another brief bonanza. In 1968, suppose you had bought gold at $35 an ounce and held it until today (Oct. 16, 1974). Today the market price of gold is $150. You would have done very well, enormously well over that six-year period. Today, your purchasing power would be 2½ times as great as in 1968.
>
> Suppose, however, that you add the six years on to the prior 34 years . . . 1934 to 1974. At the end of that time, you would have ended up with 36 percent as much purchasing power as you had at the beginning.
>
> Suppose you had held it for the whole period 1929 to 1974. You bought it at its low dollar price and you are now holding it at its high. You would have lost one-third of your purchasing power. You would now have two-thirds as much as you started with.
>
> If you call that a good inflation hedge, I find it hard to follow that reasoning. Over the same period, stocks would have been a far better inflation hedge than gold. It isn't true for the past six years, but when I hear these goldbugs talk, they seem to be saying that all of American history is divided into two parts, 1492 to 1968 and 1968 to 1974. That doesn't seem to be a very sensible way to extrapolate the past.

Professor Friedman summarized his remarks by observing: "Gold has not been a reliable inflation hedge. There is nothing in the realm of theory or present empirical evidence to give you any reason to expect that it will in the future be any better an inflation hedge than it has been in the past." Nevertheless, those who have held gold from 1968 have little cause for complaint.

WHY THE 1975 GOLD BOOM FIZZLED

Before considering the various ways of investing in gold, it would be prudent to consider some of the factors that effectively quenched the anticipatory flames of desire for precious metal in the United States, preventing them from bursting into a conflagration before New Year's, 1975.

First were the "Buyer beware" signals hoisted by the Securities and Exchange Commission (SEC), the Treasury Department, the Federal Reserve Board, the Comptroller of the Currency, and the Federal Deposit Insurance Corporation, urging, among other things, that the seller's reputation be checked thoroughly with state or federal regulatory agencies as a precaution against fraud. An SEC bulletin warned of the old goldbrick ploy, mentioning one nervy assayer who conspired with a seller to certify that bars of almost pure lead were pure gold. A major refiner cautioned that technicians can produce goldbricks of gold-plated tungsten, which has a specific gravity close to gold's and is virtually indistinguishable from the real thing without sophisticated testing.

Federal agencies urged banks to refrain from buying and selling gold and forbade them to take positions in gold themselves, although they are permitted to act as depositories for gold. The Bank of America in San Francisco and the First National City Bank in New York, the nation's two largest banks, announced that they would not buy or sell gold, as did many other large banks. Some large institutions, however, along with some major brokerage houses, did open gold windows as an accommodation to their customers, but with firm caveats in their advertisements. Many persons, of course, had bought coins and jewelry in advance of December 31, 1974.

Probably the greatest deterrent to the purchase of gold bullion, gold coins, and even small souvenir wafers of gold was their price. Anticipating that Americans would buy from $1 billion to $3 billion worth of gold in 1975, European speculators drove the price up, as mentioned earlier, to the level of $200 an ounce by the close of 1974. This compared with a price of $35 an ounce that had existed officially from early 1934 to early 1968 in the United States. The price advanced somewhat with the establishment of the two-tier market in 1968. Under the two-tier system, central banks conducted their official transactions at the official price of $35. Free-market prices were whatever supply-and-demand conditions warranted on any given day. This halted the drain of official monetary stocks into speculative hands, and even in the free market prices went only as high as $44 before declining again to $35 in late 1969.

Then the picture changed abruptly, and prices began rising. Growing inflation and other factors accelerated the increase. When some central banks began redeeming their dollar holdings, they were effectively buying United States gold for $35 an ounce when, in fact, the free-market price was much higher and was climbing. This led to President Nixon's executive order of August 15, 1971, that closed the United States gold window and prompted the first of two devaluations of the dollar. Today no major currency can be redeemed for gold at the official price. Currencies are floating and are backed by a nation's economic net worth rather than by gold.

Meanwhile, even with its inflation-sparked price rise, gold was selling for only $90 an ounce late in 1973, which was still less than one-half the asking price when gold ownership became legal in the United States. By the end of January 1975, the price of gold established by the daily London fix had declined from its 1974 peak to as low as $169.50. The day well may come when astute investors will say "Now, the price is right" and start purchasing gold in anticipation of a rise in price that might more than offset the various negative factors recounted here. The goldbugs certainly believe this to be the case. By July 1976, however, the price had dropped as low as $107.75 and no buying stampede developed.

OWNERSHIP OF GOLD: SOME PRECAUTIONS

Among the ways in which it is possible to buy and sell gold are three in which outright ownership can be involved: (1) purchase of gold bullion in wafers weighing from ⅟₂₀ ounce to 10 ounces and in bars weighing from 25 ounces to 400 ounces; (2) in gold coins, including newly minted specie; and (3) in jewelry.

In all cases, it is imperative that the buyer know his seller. As the late Willie Sutton replied, when asked why he hadn't mended his ways and still persisted in robbing banks, "Because that's where the money is." Twelve-carat jewelry or bullion can be stamped "24 carat." A refiner's marks on a bar of bullion can be imitated. Money can be accepted by a mail-order bullion or coin operation, and a receipt returned showing that the goods are stored in the buyer's name when they are not. Where there is money or anything else of value, there is a Willie Sutton willing and frequently able to bilk a trusting someone else out of it.

There are, however, refiners, dealers in precious metals, brokerage firms, banks, coin dealers, and jewelers whose reputations are beyond reproach. The buyer should take the trouble to seek them out if they are not already known to him.

There are, additionally, four ways of participating in any rise in gold prices without taking possession of the metal itself. To be perfectly accurate, it should be pointed out that gold bullion, too, can be stored with the bank, brokerage house, refiner, or dealer from whom it is purchased without possession being taken, and there are both advantages and disadvantages to this, as will be pointed out later. Coins also can be left with the seller, if desired, with similar advantages and disadvantages. But gold-mining stocks, gold-owning mutual funds, warehouse receipts, and participation in futures markets do not require physical possession of the metal.

In both areas, the buyer should be aware of the overhanging influences above and beyond the bare statistics of supply and demand. These influences include the actions that may be taken by those who own gold.

For example, the Treasury Department, in a preconceived move to thwart the speculators and cool the gold fever that never came, announced on December 3, 1974, that it would auction off 2 million ounces of gold on January 6, 1975. In fact, only some 750,000 ounces actually were sold, with the sales price ranging from $153 to $175 an ounce. While this action barely caused a dent in the United States official gold reserves of 278 million ounces, the lack of interest exhibited by United States investors did depress the world price to $169 on January 6 from $200 a week earlier.

Another overhang is to be found in the plan of the IMF to sell some 25 million ounces of its gold at public auctions to be held over a period of four years, with the proceeds to go into a special trust fund that will finance loans to certain eligible developing countries. The plan calls for another 25 million ounces to go to its depositing member nations under a quota system at a price of SDR 35 per ounce. The auctions began in the spring of 1976, with the distribution to members scheduled to begin late in the year. The auctions were to be held about every six weeks. Like a fighter on the ropes, the price of gold was jolted by the original announcement of the IMF plans, belted again at the time of the initial auction in May, when it dipped to its lowest level in 30 months, and merely stung by the second auction in July. By then, some analysts agreed that the market had over-reacted to the plan and then had discounted future sales; prices began a slow climb.

Conversely, South Africa periodically holds gold off world markets to bring the price up to a more acceptable level. Striking miners in South Africa have rioted and, at some future time, could flood the mines, causing a sharp rise in price. The Soviet Union is not inclined to deplete its gold stocks but has done so when crop failures have made it necessary to go into world markets for grains. Conversely, the Arabs are expected to increase their gold holdings to maintain a percentage of their reserves in the metal as they receive more and more currencies for their oil.

The central banks could sell gold for paper currencies and then use those currencies to bolster their own sagging paper. And the hoarders, particularly in nations like France and India where gold hoarding has been a way of life for centuries, might decide that a truly rainy day had arrived and sell off substantial enough amounts of their holdings to cause a world price decline.

The goldbugs probably are right: the price of gold will rise. It probably will not rise at the 1968–1974 rate, during which many years of catching up had to be done. And history tells us that it will not rise in a straight line.

As the world got a feel for the United States' surprising indifference to gold after January 1, 1975, the price quickly declined by 15 percent, but there were up and down moves all the way. So the holder of gold should be prepared to take paper losses as the price rides its particular roller coaster, either up or down.

The question in the investor's mind should be whether the price is likely to ascend sufficiently to cover the costs of ownership, whether such ownership will indeed preserve his wealth and add to it, and if so, at a rate sufficient to outrun the pace of inflation. With these factors in mind, it is time to look at various possible types of gold ownership.

THE DIFFERENT FORMS OF GOLD

Gold Bullion

A person contemplating the purchase of gold bullion is confronted with several decisions, the most important of which is why he wants to own it in the first place. Then he must decide on the size he wants. Sizes run from a tiny $\frac{1}{20}$ ounce all the way up to 400-ounce bars with at least eight sizes in between.

The 1-ounce and smaller wafers, called "planchets," while not inexpensive, are not a very good investment but have found some favor as gifts and souvenirs. It should be borne in mind that the smaller the unit, the higher the cost per ounce. The cost per ounce of 100 one-ounce planchets will be far greater than for a single 100-ounce bar because of fabrication and packaging costs; and with the cost of the gold itself in the range of $175 to $200 per ounce, even a $\frac{1}{2}$-ounce piece of gold shouldn't be left lying around the house.

Those buying larger units must decide whether to take possession of the gold or leave it with the refiner, gold dealer, bank, brokerage house, or other seller for safekeeping. Storage costs are relatively low because of the small volume of space required, but insurance and necessary paper work can increase this cost significantly.

The advantage of such storage becomes clear in light of the fact that those who take possession of the metal and (1) keep it at home or (2) place it in a safety-deposit box leave themselves open to the likely need to have it reassayed when they try to sell it. Even if placed in a safety-deposit box, it immediately loses its guarantee of fineness (quality) once it has left the seller's hands. A reassay may cost anywhere from $30 to $100 per sample. Some sellers (for example, Engelhard Minerals & Chemical Corp. and the Deak-Perera group) will deliver ingots and coins in tamper-proof heat-sealed plastic envelopes to preserve their integrity, thereby solving that problem. If the gold is kept at home, however, there is the possibility of theft as well as the cost of insurance to consider.

What will the gold cost? As mentioned, smaller units will cost more per ounce than larger units. The latter will be priced in accordance with the day's London fix or the price for a nearby delivery month on a futures exchange. Added to the actual base price of gold will be the costs of manufacturing or processing, insurance, shipping, applicable sales taxes, transaction fees, and storage. All the costs involved could run the purchase price up as much as 20 percent. Buyers should ascertain what costs, in addition to the actual price of the gold bullion, are included. They also should insist on a written guarantee of fineness, and it should come from a reliable dealer.

In buying smaller units through retail outlets, it might be borne in mind that when the Japanese were first permitted to own gold in 1973, a fair-size gold rush developed, but it quieted down after a few months. When buyers of these small units began to return with them to the department stores where they'd bought them, they were told, albeit sweetly: "We sell gold; we do not buy gold."

Finally, it should be remembered that gold does not pay interest or dividends, interest must be paid on the money borrowed to buy it, and it is subject to taxes on any profits accruing from its later sale.

Gold Coins

It has been legal all along for United States citizens to own gold coins of numismatic value, and prices of coins followed the rising price of gold up the speculative ladder leading to the opening of United States gold bullion trading at the end of 1974, generally trading at a premium. In the past ten years, interest in gold coins has multiplied tenfold, as reflected in sales of $1 billion in 1974, up from $100 million a decade earlier. Some of this rise, of course, reflected inflated bullion prices. However, Edward Milas, owner of Chicago's Rare Coin Company of America, was quoted in March 1975 as saying, "Demand went to nil when private ownership of bullion became legal, and has stayed there." Other dealers reported a flat January with a miniboom immediately following. A Treasury official said at about the same time that he expected any future demand for gold to be satisfied in the coin market. Milas agreed, pointing to the ease with which coins can be sold back to dealers, giving the market liquidity. And, undoubtedly, some who bought at prices reflecting all-time high bullion prices, only to see bullion descend early in 1975, are holding their coins for later sale, hoping for more favorable conditions.

Investing in gold coins can be of two broad types. One would be to purchase authentic rare coins, just as one would purchase rare stamps or works of art, in the hope that the numismatic value of the coins would appreciate over a period of years. The other would be to purchase commemorative foreign coins, some of which bear dates around the turn of the century but are newly minted; limited-edition commemorative medallions and coins produced by private mints; and regularly circulated foreign gold coins.

The former, obviously, depend in value on their rareness and condition, rather than their gold content, and like a Rembrandt or a Stradivarius, carry a price tag infinitely greater than the modest value of the materials they're made of, with a good chance that their value will continue to increase. The latter should be bought only for the value of their gold content. For example, United States double eagles ($20 gold pieces) have been selling for far more than the value of their gold content even though they are not especially rare.

As with any other investment, several caveats are in order. For example, one highly regarded private United States mint came out with commemorative silver medallions depicting each of the presidents of the United States. Later, using the same dies, it reproduced the same work by the same designer in gold-plated silver. Finally, it offered a striking in gold from the same dies. This same "limited-edition" set was offered three times in three different forms, which speaks rather poorly for its exclusivity and value to collectors beyond the value of the metals used.

Limited-edition foreign coins sell for well above the value of their gold content in many cases; and if the price of gold should nose-dive, the buyer might be protected only by the face value of a particular coin if he chose to sell.

In any case, it is important to know the gold content of the coin and from this to calculate the premium the seller has imposed. The premium, as well as the price of the gold content, is subject to fluctuation, and it pays to shop around. For example, the South African Krugerrand weighs exactly 1 ounce, and its selling price is tied to the official price of gold. But if the price of gold is $180 an ounce and the krugerrand is selling for $195 at one dealer's, it may be selling for $190 or less at another dealer's. The price when the buyer resells to a dealer is likely to be correspondingly lower than the dealer's selling price. Further, the American Numismatic Association says that roughly one-third of the coins that it has studied are fakes of one kind or another and that perhaps as many as one-half of the coins sold are overpriced.

About Thanksgiving Day, 1974, the SEC filed fraud charges against three Utah coin dealers and one in Colorado, charging that together they had defrauded investors in gold and silver coins of more than $10 million by not delivering on orders they had taken. The SEC also investigated other so-called mints and exchanges.

Although some coins are harder to counterfeit than others, an accommodating cheater will be found if the price is right. A classic example concerned a coin dealer who, motivated by a photograph of a rare 1930 *O* half dollar, paid an upstanding collector $27,000 for it and later tried to sell it for $40,000 at a numismatic show. Someone casually rubbed his thumb across the mint mark, the *O*, and it popped off. It had been soldered on. Happily, the coin dealer got his money back.

The best course of action for the would-be coin buyer would be to do some library research in the field, subscribe to one or more sound numismatic periodicals, and establish a relationship with a highly reputable coin dealer. Fortunes have been made in coins, but not automatically.

Deposit Receipts

The deposit receipt concept calls for companies to buy large quantities of gold and store it, guaranteeing its fineness. Then they sell ownership of this gold in varying quantities, issuing receipts to the buyers to show that their share of the total pile is in storage in their names. One such fund, Dreyfus Gold Deposits, Inc., requires a minimum investment of $2,500, a 3 percent fee for buying and selling, and a 1½ percent annual maintenance fee.

Singularly, a Harris survey in January 1975 indicated: "A substantial 72 percent of the people in the gold market say they would 'feel more secure if they actually possessed the gold bars' and feel that being able to look at one's own gold bars is one of their reasons for buying gold in the first place." The flaws in this line of reasoning were expressed in the preceding subsection "Gold Bullion." Deposit receipts provide a relatively simple, clean way of participating in the gold market, as long as the buyer knows the seller to be ethical and financially sound.

Jewelry

Authentic antiques or other rare jewelry items, as is true of paintings or sculptures, may very well appreciate in value over the years to the extent of becoming a good investment. Those planning to go this route, however, should know what they are doing or rely on the judgment of an expert.

There are many excellent reasons for buying jewelry at retail, but return on investment is not among them. Walter Hoving, chairman of the board of Tiffany's, pointed out in a newspaper interview that gold jewelry reflects the cost of gold (from the mine to the retailer), the cost of design and craftsmanship, the jeweler's profit, and appropriate sales taxes. "If you have it melted down to separate its gold from the copper that was added to give it strength, you aren't going to be coming out ahead," he said.

Gold-Mining Stocks

The prudent investor will find that the normal precautions one takes before entering the stock market are multiplied when considering gold-mining shares.

Is gold mining a good industry to be in? That depends somewhat upon whether one is a goldbug or not. And if so, the kind of goldbug. Some regard gold as a hedge against inflation; others, as a hedge against deflation.

William O. Sumner is the San Francisco–based United States representative for James Capel & Co., a century-old London stock brokerage firm specializing in gold-mining shares. It is his opinion that United States citizens tend to regard such certificates as being highly speculative, while in truth he believes that it was the conservative element, concerned about the depreciation of paper money's value, that moved the price of gold up in recent years.

Another view is taken by Michael Levinson, vice president and a director of New York–based Dominick & Dominick, who has been into gold-mining shares, personally and for his customers, for some five years. He recommends bullion purchases as a hedge against inflation and mining shares as a hedge against deflation. He was on record in March 1975 as believing that the United States was taking the deflationary route and that mining shares eventually would be worth more than gold itself. A return to the gold standard, he asserts, would turn the situation around.

The prudent investor, too, having decided to get into gold-mining shares, will ask himself which are the best-managed companies with the best track record.

Sumner is partial to South African stocks, since "South Africa is the greatest gold-mining area in the world, producing 14 metric tons a week. And its companies mine gold exclusively, whereas most U.S. and Canadian mining companies produce gold as a by-product of other metals, notably copper. They are diversified into other types of mining, e.g., lead and zinc; and in some cases into wholly unrelated industries."

On the other hand, Sumner points out, South African mines have a life expectancy of only about thirty years and, under that nation's laws, there is only one mine to a company. When the mine is worked out, the company is disbanded. "So," he says, "the investor has bought stock in a hole in the ground, a wasting asset. Dividend yields will run from 8 to 14 percent, much higher than in the Northern Hemisphere, but half of that return should be regarded as a return of capital."

Sumner recommends two possible courses of action: (1) invest in a minimum of three different mining companies whose mines will "expire" over a staggered period of years or (2) buy stock in a mining finance house for a more conservative investment. These houses, he explains, finance, own part of, and manage from three to a dozen mining companies, thus spreading the risk. South African mines, by and large, are more profitable than their United States counterparts, chiefly because of cheap labor.

Levinson, on the other hand, has avoided South African shares principally because of the volatile political situation in that nation. He points out that United States and Canadian mining stocks have had an excellent recent performance record. "Mining shares," he says, "follow bullion prices in general, although not on a day-to-day basis. They also follow the stock market, but in reverse. When the market is rising, smart people will buy bullion to hedge against inflation. When it is dropping, they will buy mining shares as a hedge against deflation."

The International Investors Fund, which is heavily into gold-mining shares, performed exceptionally well during the 1972–1974 gold boom.

Another investment company (closed-end) heavily into gold is ASA Limited, formerly American–South African Investment, which showed a per-share net asset value increase to $78 at the end of November 1974 from $16.21 at the same time in 1970. Its policy is to invest 50 percent or more of its assets in common shares of companies conducting gold-mining and related activities in South Africa. ASA shares are listed on the New York Stock Exchange.

Gold Futures Contracts

The initial enthusiasm of the public for gold futures stands in sharp contrast to its indifference toward actual ownership of gold. It was unusual in the first place that five separate United States commodities exchanges would list futures contracts in the same commodity. And, from the opening bell on December 31, 1974, trading was much heavier than anticipated.

Normally, it takes a new commodity many weeks, even running into years, to mature on a futures exchange. But in gold's first year, nearly 900,000 contracts changed hands, with Chicago's International Monetary Market (IMM) (406,968) and New York's Commodity Exchange, Inc. (393,517) accounting for 800,000 of the aggregate. The Chicago Board of Trade, New York Mercantile Exchange, and Chicago's MidAmerica Commodity Exchange trailed. While this is still a relatively small volume total, as futures markets go, it is encouraging. It may take a couple of years for the real market to emerge, but initial volume and open commitments indicate that a liquid market (one that is easy to get into and out of) already exists, at least on the IMM and New York's Comex.

A futures market is an instrument used by producers, processors, and large users of commodities to lock in a price months in advance of their actual purchase or sale of a particular commodity. Such users are known as hedgers. They figure that they have enough normal risks of doing busines; so, in effect, they insure themselves against price risk by buying or selling futures contracts. Assuming the hedgers' price risk are the speculators, who try to calculate which way a particular market will move and buy if they believe it's going up and sell if they think it's going down.

The attractiveness of futures markets is found in the leverage they provide. The minimum security deposit required by the IMM for the gold contract, which consist of 100 troy ounces of 995 fine (pure) gold bullion, is $1,000 for a speculator. Many brokerage houses may ask the trader to put up more than $1,000. But let's say that the price of gold is quoted at $180 an ounce; then a margin deposit of $2,000, for example, would control $18,000 worth of the metal. If the market moves against the trader (goes down for someone who has bought or up for someone who has sold), additional security funds will be required, or the trader can liquidate his position at a relatively small loss.

Each $10 move on the IMM is worth $1,000 to the trader, and a trader who had bought one March contract for $2,000 on February 10, 1975, at $174 and sold it ten days later at $186.40 would have realized a profit of $1,240 on the $2,000 investment, less a nominal broker's commission of $45. Conversely, a trader who had gone short (sold) could have lost the total investment, plus the broker's commission. If this same trader had had the foresight to sell at $195 on opening day, December 31, 1974, and to buy back the contract at $165 on January 6, he or she would have realized a gain of $3,000, less the commission.

One secret to successful speculation is to place a stop-loss order when taking a position, thereby keeping losses to a minimum, and, at the same time, to permit gains to run until the market turns around. Even experienced speculators may have seven losing trades out of every ten, but by limiting losses and staying with winning positions many produce a most attractive bottom line.

Great leverage, of course, implies great risk; and commodities speculation is not for the fainthearted. Nor should anything but risk capital be used in this or any other type of speculation.

Only a relatively small number of futures contracts result in actual delivery, since they essentially are a pricing mechanism. But speculators who, perhaps, also happen to be goldbugs might buy one or more contracts for future delivery and then see the market go down. They might decide to take their loss in futures but also to take delivery of gold at its depressed price in the hope of seeing the metal increase in value at a later time. They would have to put up the full price of each contract they had bought: approximately $12,000 to $14,000 for each 100-ounce contract judged by July 1976 prices. The amount would be based on the settlement price on the futures exchange on the final day of trading for that contract month. Since cash and futures prices tend to move up and down together and to come together in the delivery month and since sellers pay all delivery costs, the speculators might be better off taking delivery on the futures market than making the same purchase in the cash market.

Although the risk is high in futures, the integrity of the contracts is above reproach. The IMM clearinghouse is the opposite party to every trade and guarantees contract fulfillment. Traders never need worry about the individuals who took the opposite side of their transactions. The IMM also has eight approved depositories for delivery and storage of gold bullion: five in New York and three in Chicago. They include the largest banks in those cities. Finally, starting on April 21, 1975, the Commodity Futures Trading Commission, established by Congress in 1974, became active. It oversees all United States commodity futures trading. With chances of fraud virtually eliminated, the trader's only concern need be with his or her own judgment.

Most major brokerage houses have commodities departments, and several have produced useful brochures for their customers and prospects. In addition, the International Monetary Market, 444 West Jackson Boulevard, Chicago, Illinois 60606, has two useful brochures that are available without charge on request.

Chapter 37

Art as an Investment

RICHARD H. RUSH

BACKGROUND

In 1960 an investor could have purchased a painting by Monet for $25,000 or $30,000. By 1976 this painting probably would have quintupled in value. In recent years, most works of art have risen steadily in value. There are exceptions to this generalization, particularly in the recession of 1970 and 1971. However, the major limitations of art as an investment medium are that paintings (a) do not provide current income for the investor, (2) are very illiquid investments, and (3) have large spreads between the selling price and the purchase price for the average investor. Even with these limitations, art can play an important role in the portfolio of many investors. This is true both because it has tended to rise in value in recent years and because the limited supply of paintings produced in a particular period or by a particular artist make art a good hedge against inflation. In addition, the "investment value" of a high-priced painting can be used as an excuse for putting a large sum of money into something that one wants in one's home simply because it is beautiful and adds to the richness of the family's life.

Art prices have risen rapidly during the past twenty-five years. For example, from 1950 to 1976 the price of eighteenth-century British portraits rose nearly 500 percent. Furthermore, many nineteenth-century British and American paintings increased in value by 1500 percent between 1960 and 1976. The rapidly increasing prices for fine art, apparent for decades, show few signs of weakening. One reason for this is that more Americans are art-conscious today than ever before. Before World War II there were about twenty art museums in the country; today there are about 10 times that number. But the overriding factor is that the available supply of art of the past cannot be replenished. Therefore, as a growing demand is paired with a constant supply, prices continue to rise.

HOW TO DETERMINE THE PRICE OF A PAINTING

The following questions must be considered by an individual before purchasing a painting for investment purposes:

1. *Who painted it?* This is obviously the starting point in determining the price or value of a painting. There is a definite market price for each artist whose works are traded in the international art market.

2. *Is the particular painting typical of the artist?* To have typical value the painting must in effect be a "signature of the artist." To one familiar with the works of the particular artist it must, without a great deal of study, be a Renoir or a Rembrandt or the work of whatever artist it is supposed to be. The more typical the painting is of the artist, generally the higher its value.

3. *When in the artist's painting life was the particular work done?* The earliest, most realistic Renoirs tend to bring less money than the later, more typically impressionist Renoirs. Van Gogh painted in three locations in the Netherlands before he went to France: The Hague, Drenthe, and Nuenen. While he was in the Netherlands, he painted in a somber manner in grays and browns. In Paris and in Arles he used a bright palette and a typically free brush stroke. There is no comparison between values of his paintings of the Dutch period and values of those of the French period. The latter paintings bring far more in the market. The same is true of Gauguin. Early in Gauguin's painting career he was an impressionist and not a highly distinguished one. His Tahitian paintings in warm tones are the ones most sought after and the ones that bring the largest sums.

4. *Does the painting have quality?* While this value-determining factor is placed fourth, it is of great importance, particularly in schools of art characterized by excellence of draftsmanship. A top-quality old master almost always brings a higher price by far than work by the same artist that is less well executed, and the best works bring disproportionately higher prices. Quality and its effect on buyers are instantly recognized in the viewing prior to painting sales. Most professional viewers, dealers included, agree on quality and on the elements of a painting that constitute quality.

5. *What is the condition of the painting?* The typical viewer finds this element hard to determine. For the knowledgeable buyer, however, repainting, overpainting, and other methods of repairing damages and overcleaning are not hard to discern. The ultraviolet light is of great help in determing where repairs have been made and where new paint has been applied. Condition may reduce the price and value of a painting to the vanishing point.

6. *What is the subject?* Religious subjects often reduce the price of a painting. In general, they lack popularity at present, particularly with certain segments of the buyer market. On the other hand, museums just as willingly buy religious paintings as others. Certain highly important Italian artists painted only religious subjects, and for these artists subject matter is less important. Ugly scenes are less in demand than pleasant ones. Landscapes are definitely preferred at the present time. In the case of the British portraitists, the subject is all-important. The portrait of a man wearing a black or a plum-colored coat is worth less than the portrait of a man wearing a crimson coat. In general, a portrait of a woman is worth much more than a portrait of a man, and a portrait of a child is worth the most. The value-determining elements of subject matter must be learned for each artist in whom a buyer is interested.

7. *What is the size of the painting?* A decade ago a very large painting was described as "oversize" and, in general, lacked the value of a smaller painting. Now large paintings have gone up in price relative to medium-size paintings. Very small paintings are worth disproportionately less than average-size paintings. What are most wanted on the present market are paintings of a size suitable for an apartment or a small house. This is the size of painting on which we quote and to which we refer throughout the chapter. It is a fairly standard commodity.

8. *What do the experts say?* If the painting is supposed to be a Rembrandt, what do the Rembrandt experts—Valentiner, Von Bode, Bredius, Friedländer—

say about the painting? If the painting is an Italian old master, what do Adolfo Venturi, Suida, Berenson, Pallucchini, Morassi, and Zeri, among others, say? For baroque Italian art, what does Manning say? Generally, the earlier the painting, the less its authorship can stand on its own feet and the more significant and value-giving is the expertise.

9. *What exhibitions was the painting in?* Was the painting ever shown in the National Gallery in Washington? In the Metropolitan Museum of Art? In the National Gallery in London? In the Louvre? Was it, if it is a Rubens, shown in the Rubens Exhibition in Brussels? The more significant the museum or the exhibition, the more authentic the painting and the higher its presumed quality. In general, collectors, dealers, and museums are anxious to exhibit their paintings, and the more prestigious the exhibition, the more valuable the exhibition is to the reputation of the painting.

10. *What is the pedigree of the painting?* Who owned the painting? Was it in the private collection of the director of the National Gallery in London? Was it in the collection of Charles I of England? Was it in the Erickson Collection? Was it once owned by the patron of Rembrandt, Jan Six? The person who owned a painting tends to establish its authenticity and quality. At least one expert buyer approved the painting enough to buy it and hang it.

11. *Is there a genuine signature?* Some artists like Renoir usually signed paintings. Cézanne, on the other hand, rarely signed his name to his works. Very often older paintings have falsified signatures. Very often these forgeries can be detected by an ultraviolet light. The paint in the signature stands out from the rest of the paint. Very often these added signatures are not expertly done by the forgers, and they frequently can be removed with a cleaning compound. Forged signatures are not as hard to detect as might be supposed.

12. *What is the price history of the artist?* This question is all-important in determining how much to pay. Here auction prices are of tremendous significance, and catalogs should be reviewed to determine price history and the present price level. However, only illustrated works in catalogs have much significance in determining price. Often unillustrated works have indeterminate quality, and in some cases they may not be by the artist to whom the paintings are attributed by the catalog. All catalog designations must be regarded with a degree of skepticism. Unless the potential buyer is intimately familiar with the artist whose work he is buying or has the help of an expert on the particular artist, it may be best to refrain from investing in art. It is easy to make a costly mistake.

13. *Who is selling the painting?* When a reputable auction gallery is selling the painting, it may stand behind its designation if some art authority subsequently questions the authenticity of the painting. In the field of impressionists and other later schools of art most first-rank auction houses will now take back a painting about which a serious question has been raised within a reasonable period of time. Sotheby, Parke-Bernet offers a five-year guarantee on the authenticity of authorship of most of its paintings. So will a large and important dealer, but even here a guarantee of both the authorship and the pedigree of the painting should be secured in writing before buying the painting. Lesser dealers often do not give guarantees. Neither do lesser auction houses. Generally the bigger and more reputable the gallery, the higher the price of a particular painting. A Third Avenue, New York, shop cannot get the same price for a Renoir that a large gallery can. On the other hand, the large gallery will often stand behind the painting's authorship and condition while the small gallery will not.

14. *Where and when is the painting offered for sale?* If the painting is offered for sale as a part of the Magnin Collection of impressionists at a well-advertised evening sale at Sotheby, Parke-Bernet in New York, the prices achieved are likely to be good, as in effect they were in the offering of this particular group of paint-

ings. Alternatively, if in the recession of 1970 a smaller New York gallery had offered these paintings in an afternoon sale, prices might well have been disappointing.

All factors considered, it is possible within limits to forecast the selling price of a particular painting at auction. It is very much easier to forecast the total realization of an entire collection, since a gross error in estimating the price of a particular painting tends to be canceled out. For a large collection of paintings it is entirely possible for a knowledgeable buyer to forecast total sales realization within 10 percent. For every painting traded on the international market there is, within limits, a market price as well as a price trend, and both elements are determinable.

THE PRICE HISTORY OF ART

A representative group of 125 artists was selected for the determination of the price trend of art. These were selected from among the major schools or types of art traded on the international market, since internationally traded art is what we are concerned with, and international art is the great investment medium. We shall not be discussing local artists or contemporary artists trying to make the grade or contemporaries with temporary popularity, perhaps under the impetus of dealer promotion. The chief means of determining price trends for these 125 artists was to record the prices of their paintings over a long period of time, from 1925 through 1976.

The most easily determined prices are auction prices, and the auction prices most used were those of the Parke-Bernet Galleries (now Sotheby, Parke-Bernet New York) in the United States, Sotheby's in London, and Christie's in London. These prices were supplemented by price recordings of a number of other auction houses in continental Europe. There were about 10,000 price recordings. The prices were further supplemented by a review of the smaller New York auctions over a period of twelve years (1960–1972), plus periodic dealer visits in New York and in other cities of the United States and annual visits to dealers in England, the Netherlands, Belgium, France, Germany, and Italy. Finally, the various schools of art studied were weighted according to the importance of their sales in the art market. The sales of French modern paintings, for instance, were weighted considerably heavier than those of the Central European expressionists simply because many more of the former were and are sold in the art market.

The Art Price Index[1] starts in 1925, and the price level of this year is arbitrarily made 100 percent. From this point the index rose to the peak of prosperity in 1929, when it reached 165. By the next year, the first year of the Depression, the index was back to its 1925 level of 100. By the year 1933, perhaps the trough of the Depression, the index had been halved and stood at 50. Two years later it had recovered to 71, and five years later, in 1940, it had recovered to 81. At the end of World War II it stood at 102. By 1950 it had gained 50 percent and stood at 150.

From this point art prices took off. Between 1950 and 1955 the index doubled, and by 1955 it had reached 290. The next five years saw the most phenomenal increase in art prices to date. The index by 1960 stood at 981; in five years it had tripled. The doubling from 1950 to 1955 and the tripling from 1955 to 1960 meant that in one decade art prices had increased to 600 percent of their original value.

The next decade saw a further rise in art prices in general, but not so extreme a

[1]The Art Price Index is based on auction prices at Parke-Bernet in New York and at Sotheby's and Christie's in London, the three leading auction houses in the two world centers of art and antiques. More than 10,000 individual price recordings were used to prepare the index.

rise as in the 1950s. For the decade ending in 1970 the Art Price Index tripled. The sixfold increase in the level of the index in the 1950s plus the tripling in the 1960s meant that in the twenty years ending in 1970 art prices in general increased 18 times. The following list illustrates the movement of the Art Price Index from 1925 to the present.

Year	Percent	Year	Percent
1925	100	1945	102
1929	165	1950	150
1930	100	1955	290
1933	50	1960	981
1935	71	1972	3,000
1940	81		

A Comparison with Stock Prices

A standard measure of price increase and investment value is stock prices. To a degree there is a parallel between painting prices and stock prices. If both painting prices and stock prices are arbitrarily placed at a level of 100 percent in 1925, there was a somewhat similar upward movement to the peak year 1929 in both series, but stock prices rose to more than twice the 1925 level. The drop into the trough of the Depression was of about a similar magnitude for both series. However, the Art Price Index constantly remained under the stock index for many years.

From the trough of the Depression both series moved upward in a generally similar pattern and continued the relationship, with art prices under stock prices, to 1950. Then an acceleration occurred in both art prices and stock prices; the degree of increase was about the same for both series. In the year 1957 stock prices took off at a tremendous rate. At this particular point, however, the Art Price Index for the first time passed the stock index and accelerated much more rapidly than did stock prices. At the end of the 1950s the art index stood far above the stock index, almost regardless of which stock index was used: the Dow Jones Industrial Average, the Standard & Poor's 500-Stock Index, or other indices of security price movements.

Let us next take a comparative look at what happened to art prices versus stock prices in the decade ending in 1970. The Dow Jones Industrial Average was far from doubling. The Standard & Poor's 500-Stock Index did a little better but still did not double in the decade. Art prices, on the other hand, tripled. Let us assume that 1960 was a base year and that we assign a value of 100 percent to the prices at that time. If we move forward to the spring of 1972, the Dow stood at 160, or 60 percent over its level in 1960. The Standard & Poor's 500-Stock Index was at the 182 level, or 82 percent over its level in 1960. The Art Price Index stood at 300. Its increase in twelve years had been 200 percent.

It is only fair to point out, of course, that dividends have been omitted from the comparison, and their inclusion would cause the stock averages to look very much better. In 1960 Moody's Composite Index of Common Stock Dividends stood at 3 percent. In 1965, too, the rate was 3 percent; in 1967, 3.4 percent; in 1968, 3.2 percent; in 1969, 3.4 percent; and in 1970, 4 percent. The rate of return is determined by yield based on price, so that the higher the price, the lower the dividend yield, and vice versa. For a decade we can pick up perhaps 40 percent in dividends to add to the stock price index (4 percent per year for ten years). Nevertheless, stock prices plus dividends did not equal or approach art price increases in this period.

Schools of Art and Their Price Movements

The one highly significant thing about price movements in art is that these movements are not homogeneous. They are a compilation of the individual movements of various types or schools of art. While certain schools may be increasing in price at a tremendous rate, other schools may be increasing at a much slower rate, and still others may be declining. In this respect art is like the stock market: at one time airlines may be moving up rapidly, and at the same time space age stocks may be moving up even faster, paced only by computers. At other times airlines may be moving down, while financial institutions may be moving upward

The same circumstances obtain for schools of art. Twenty-two schools of art have been traced for the entire period covered. In Tables 37-1 and 37-2 the price movements by schools of art are shown for the years 1950–1955 and 1955–1960.

TABLE 37-1   Prices by Schools of Art: 1955 as Compared with 1950 (1950 = 100 percent)

School	Percent of rise or fall
American moderns	300
European expressionists	290
Postimpressionists	220
Impressionists	138
Ten moderns (low-priced)	110
Eight moderns (medium-priced)	103
Italian painting to 1450	100
Italian primitives	94
Eighteenth-century British	94
Early-sixteenth-century Italian	67
Nineteenth-century American	63
Italian canal painters	50
Great moderns	40
Minor seventeenth-century Dutch	35
Barbizon painters	32
Flemish primitives	26
Great Venetians	23
Italian baroque	19
Major seventeenth-century Dutch	15
American old masters	−5
Nineteenth-century British	−10
Nineteenth-century Dutch	−20

Price Movements of the Various Schools of Art since 1960

Somewhere around 1960 the art market took on some of the characteristics of the stock market with respect to investor interest. Some schools of art became relatively unpopular, others experienced growth for the first time in years, and some began to boom. The art market overall and its movements had to be measured by a modified index. Flemish primitives of any consequence whatsoever, for example, virtually went off the market. If a painting could be purchased at all, it was a "school" piece rather than one by the master himself, a damaged or overpainted piece, or one so expensive that it was often sold privately after long negotiation. The same was true of all the early Italian schools of art. Genuine fine examples of the work of the great Venetians Titian, Tintoretto, and Veronese sold, when they did sell, at figures close to $1 million, and the famous Harewood Titian sold at auction in 1971 to J. Paul Getty for the equivalent of $4,032,000.

On the other hand, the new and rapidly rising school of abstract expressionists, typified by Jackson Pollock, the American drip artist, by Nicolas de Staël, and by Pierre Soulages, hit a peak around 1960, and movement upward from that peak proved to be a difficult accomplishment until the 1970s. This school of art was not included in the original Art Price Index because it was not in existence in the early years of the index, and abstract expressionism really came into its own in price in the 1950s. A good Jackson Pollock of a large size in 1960 might have brought as much as $125,000. It would bring the same figure a decade later. Soulages went into a temporary eclipse. Members of the Collectors' Club in the early 1960s offered several of the works of Soulages for sale at a sealed-bid auction. They were not in great demand. Soulages's prices have recovered somewhat, but there is still anything but a Soulages boom or a boom for Franz Kline, a somewhat similar abstract expressionist. On the other hand, Dubuffet is experi-

TABLE 37-2   Prices by Schools of Art: 1960 as Compared with 1955 (1955 = 100 percent)

School	Percent of rise or fall
Postimpressionists	754
Great moderns	557
European expressionists	307
Great Venetians	306
Eight moderns (medium-priced)	282
Ten moderns (low-priced)	195
Italian canal painters	161
Eighteenth-century British	148
Flemish primitives	127
Italian artists to 1450	100
Early-sixteenth-century Italian	100
American moderns	73
Major seventeenth-century Dutch	68
Impressionists	52
Nineteenth-century American	38
Minor seventeenth-century Dutch	30
Barbizon school	24
Italian primitives	21
Italian baroque	16
Nineteenth-century Dutch	0
American old masters	−5
Nineteenth-century British	−18

encing a price rise and has tended to rise since the 1960s, as has Willem de Kooning. The lesser abstract expressionists, particularly the Greek school of abstracts, tended to crash in the early 1960s. The postimpressionists Van Gogh, Gauguin, and Cézanne were at the relatively high price level of about $250,000 in 1960. By 1972 they had approximately tripled in price, to about the $750,000 level.

The great moderns Picasso, Matisse, Braque, and Léger could be bought for $50,000 or less at the beginning of the 1960s, and all, with the exception of Matisse, could at times be purchased for $30,000 or less. The price level of all these artists had approximately tripled by the early 1970s, and at times Picasso's prices far exceeded a multiplier of 3.

The Central European expressionists continued to be popular. In 1960 $15,000 would buy a fairly good expressionist painting. By the end of the decade prices had conservatively tripled, and at times Kandinsky reached a level of $150,000. Expressionist paintings, while subject to fad, were "in" paintings in the early 1970s.

The enormous rise of both postimpressionists and Central European expressionists in the 1960s and early 1970s could have been forecast by noting their phenomenal rise from 1950 to 1955 and from 1955 to 1960. The uptrend simply had to be projected. It should be pointed out, however, that the higher the price of a painting, the harder it is for that price to rise. There are fewer people willing or able to buy things that cost a great deal of money.

The eight medium-priced moderns are Chagall, Derain, Dufy, Modigliani, Rouault, Segonzac, Utrillo, and Vuillard. Their prices approximately tripled from 1960 on, but in a sense their popularity waned a little, and in the recession of 1970 there was apparently some forced selling of this school as well as some buyer resistance. An interesting thing happened within this medium-priced French modern school in the 1960s. Derain and Vuillard added immense luster to their works, which increased in price more than fivefold. They became a part of the most prestigious group of French modern paintings. Chagall too moved ahead in price in an approximately similar manner. While the rest moved upward, their degree of rise was by no means so great.

The low-priced moderns are De Chirico, Gris, Dali, Kisling, Lurçat, Marin, Miró, Rivera, Valat, and Laurencin. Overall these artists increased in price at least 5 times from 1960 to 1972. Diego Rivera, the Mexican artist, Dali, and De Chirico increased even more, and even a multiplier of 10 for these artists has considerable statistical logic behind it.

The Italian canal painters about doubled in price from 1960 to the early 1970s. Canaletto, Guardi, and Bellotto went from perhaps $50,000 to well over $100,000. Their works which are highly sought after, have a high degree of technical skill and beauty and extremely pleasing subject matter, mainly the Venetian Grand Canal.

In many ways the eighteenth-century British school was a disappointment with respect to price. From 1910 to 1930 this was *the* school of art to own; it was the school of wealthy Americans. On June 13, 1913, Romney's *Anne, Lady de la Pole* brought the equivalent of $206,850 in 1913 dollars. *Misses Breckford When Children,* by Romney, in July 1919 brought £54,600 ($273,000). When the collector Stotesbury bought Romney's *Captain Stables* at about this time, he paid $50,000 for it. When his estate sold the painting in 1944, it brought $5,500. This figure represented the average drop in the eighteenth-century British school of art of about 90 percent. *Captain Stables* was resold at the Parke-Bernet Galleries in New York in late 1970. It brough $35,000, in a remarkable recovery from the war and postwar low.

The leader of the school, Thomas Gainsborough, showed a similar price pattern, at least for his portraits. In 1959 *The Countess of Chesterfield,* a fine and large Gainsborough, brought the equivalent of $95,000. In the fall of 1970 a large and fine double portrait by Gainsborough brought $100,000. A Gainsborough landscape was, however, another thing. In 1960 *Mr. and Mrs. Robert Andrews in the Park at Auberies* ($27^1/_2$ by 47 inches) brought $364,000; the same figure would probably be achieved today. As for the minor eighteenth-century British portraitists, in the summer of 1971 a major London dealer offered for sale a large portrait of a mother and child by Beechey. The price was under $3,000. From 1960 to the early 1970s prices of the eighteenth-century British portraitists at best doubled, no more.

Let us look next at the French impressionists—Renoir, Degas, Monet, Manet, Sisley, and Pissarro, the painters of colorful and delightful landscapes as well as some portraits. Between 1960 and 1972 the prices of these artists, although not low in 1960, had risen by about 430 percent. These were average prices at the turn of the decade into the 1970s: Renoir, $225,000; Monet, 120,000; Degas, 250,000; Cassatt, 150,000; Sisley, 125,000; Pissarro, 120,000.

The seventeenth-century Dutch artists, both major and minor, moved sharply upward from 1960 to 1970. Before 1960 their rates of growth were approximately equal and anything but spectacular. As for the leaders, they were not in the greatest demand, not even Rembrandt, whose name is virtually synonymous with "old master." Vermeer was to all intents and purposes not on the market. Nevertheless, when a Vermeer did appear, even as late as 1960, it was not immediately snapped up as a great work of art worth in seven figures. The Vermeer level at that time was under $500,000. The finest work of Frans Hals, a portrait of a woman, could be purchased for $150,000. A portrait of a man could sometimes be purchased for $50,000. In the early 1960s a Rembrandt portrait could sometimes be purchased for about $100,000. However, by the end of the decade Vermeer, when obtainable, would command prices in the millions. A good Hals would bring $150,000, and a great Hals sold for about $3 million. Rembrandt had increased about 4 times in price and was continuing to rise.

The immense group of minor masters, predominantly landscapists from the Netherlands and Belgium (several thousand artists with many works continually on the market), rose about 10 times in value. In 1960 a good landscape by a minor Dutch artist like Claes (Nicolaes) Berchem, might have brought a few hundred dollars. In 1972 the same painting brought perhaps $2,500, or even more. Prices rose across the board for almost all Dutch and Flemish artists of the seventeenth century. The paintings were excellent in quality. They were in the collections of museums for the public to see and know. They were sought by museums and connoisseur collectors, and they were highly decorative and relatively small so that they could be hung in the modern home or apartment.

The Barbizon school of art, that pleasing nineteenth-century school of landscapists, increased in value but not spectacularly. This was a realistic school that preceded impressionism but was not characterized by the bright colors and the effects of outdoors of the impressionist paintings. Nevertheless, Corot, Daubigny, Diaz, Troyon, Théodore Rousseau, Millet, Jacque, François, and Harpignies approximately doubled in price.

In the nineteenth-century British school of art and in the corresponding Dutch school, the realistic painters, mostly landscapists, enjoyed a remarkable reversal of trend. From nothing or almost nothing in price in 1960, the works of these artists experienced a tenfold increase. In dollars, however, the increase was not quite so spectacular: a $100 painting rose to $1,000, still not a very high price. Moreover, many of the artists of this period could still be bought for little money, and the author, as recently as a couple of years ago, sat in a small auction house in London watching nineteenth-century landscapes and seascapes go for less than $25 to $50, although each was a well-executed and signed work.

About 10,000 British watercolors of the same period are sold in London alone every year. All the London auction houses, both large and small, sell such works of art. The artists range from J. M. W. Turner, Paul Sandby, and Thomas Girtin, whose watercolors range high in the five figures, to artists who can be purchased for the equivalent of $100 or less; all are qualified, highly decorative artists. One of the medium-priced watercolor artists whose works are available on the market fairly regularly is John Varley, who often painted water scenes; his works can be purchased for about $2,000. W. Russell Flint is another medium-priced English watercolorist; his paintings sell in the same price range as those of Varley, or perhaps a little higher. William Callow can often be purchased for prices in the neighborhood of $1,000. Thomas Rowlandson can be purchased in a price range from $1,500 to $5,000, while Francis Wheatley's prices run a little lower. One of the greatest watercolorists was Gainsborough, and his watercolors sometimes appear at prices ranging from $3,500 to $5,000, great buys from the point of view of artistic excellence.

An enormous school of art is the Italian baroque school, which flourished in the late sixteenth and the seventeenth centuries. In the 1960s critics' opinions of this school changed drastically. The school was not in vogue in the 1950s and had not been in vogue since the early 1800s, but in the 1960s it came back in force.

Museums set out to collect the school in earnest, and prices rose tremendously. In 1960 a list of the higher-priced baroque Italian artists was prepared as a kind of "target" collection. Many of the artists on the list painted landscapes, and all of them painted either landscapes or portraits. Thus one does not have the objection to this school of art that it is predominantly religious and thus lacks great acceptablility or universal appeal. The list included Pittoni, Guercino, Domenichino, Guido Reni, Strozzi, Piazzetta, Annibale Carracci, Castiglione, Magnasco, Salvator Rosa, and Sebastiano Ricci. Any artist on the list could have been purchased in 1960 for $10,000. Some could have been purchased for $7,500, and the whole list of eleven artists could have been bought for $100,000. The price for this target list of baroque artists in 1972 would have been about $600,000, with Pittoni, Ricci, and Reni at $80,000 to $90,000, Strozzi and Piazzetta at $30,000, and Magnasco at $25,000. The others ranged in price between $30,000 and $80,000.

In 1960 List 2 of lower-priced baroque Italian artists was prepared; it included Carlo Maratta, Gaulli, Baschenis, Zais, Batoni, Marieschi, Solimena, Pannini, François Didier Nomé (Monsù Desiderio), Giordano, Crespi, and Corrado Giaquinto. With the exception of Carlo Maratta, Giordano, Gaulli, and Batoni, all these artists produced excellent, beautiful, and highly decorative landscapes. In 1960 all twelve artists could have been purchased for a total of $48,000. In 1976 the same group would cost $290,000, representing a sixfold price increase. Nonetheless, the excellent landscapist Giuseppe Zais could be purchased for $10,000. So could Carlo Maratta, and for $15,000 works of the canal painter Marieschi and Solimena could be purchased. Many other baroque Italian artists are still priced under $10,000, and many can be acquired for less than $5,000.

Changes in Price of the American Schools of Art

Until the mid-1960s, American art rose in price as it had risen for at least a decade and a half, but it was by no means boom art. After 1965, however, the demand for American art of virtually all types and all periods burgeoned. Conservatively, prices of the entire group of schools included in the overall category "American art" increased fivefold in five years. At this point it would be of interest to discuss briefly the various segments of American art.

The American Old Master Portraitists.   American old master portraitists painted in roughly the same period of the eighteenth century as did the British portraitists. The Americans painted in the same general style as did the British portraitists and came under their influence. When they could afford to do so, the Americans went to England and studied under the great artists of the period. Often they stayed in England and there secured better commissions than they would have obtained had they returned home. The American artists were certainly able, but their art was patterned after the British portraitists of the period, who achieved a degree of excellence in portraiture never exceeded in any country in any era.

The preeminent American portraitist was John Singleton Copley. The most renowned American old master portraitist was Gilbert Stuart, whose fame grew overnight when he was commissioned to paint George Washington. Both artists have increased in price about tenfold in the last decade. In 1960, $15,000 would have purchased a good large Copley portrait of a man. The same portrait today would bring $150,000. The same price would have obtained for a Stuart Washington, of which there are about thirty originals in existence, all by the artist's hand. A good example of these thirty Stuarts would now bring $200,000 or more. In 1961 a large Gilbert Stuart of the period when he painted in Ireland was offered in London for $1,200. The same portrait today would sell for at least $12,000. American Gilbert Stuarts are treasured and should bring about $50,000. English Stuarts are a great deal cheaper, and some of the ugly women he painted might sell for less than $5,000. His Irish period is even less in demand, and examples might on occasion bring well under $5,000.

With Thomas Sully we move to the nineteenth century, but Sully is still classified as an American old master portraitist. In 1960 the Parke-Bernet Galleries in New York sold a Sully portrait of a young girl for $1,350, which was about the market price for one of his portraits at the time. At the end of the 1960s a Sully could be purchased for less than $5,000, but in 1970 an important Sully sold at a Washington auction for $28,000. On October 11, 1967, a small portrait of a mother and child by Benjamin West sold for $19,600 in London. The next year·a large painting was sold by the same London auction house, this one a West measuring 40½ by 57¼ inches, for the equivalent of $86,400. Smaller Wests, particularly religious ones, can be bought for less than $5,000 on the present market.

Another of the great American old master portraitists is Charles Willson Peale. In 1960 a Washington dealer discovered a Charles Willson Peale. He had purchased the painting as the work of an unknown for $150; it turned out to be a genuine Peale of William Harris Crawford, the Southern statesman. The dealer promptly sold the painting to the Atlanta Art Association for $5,000. Today the fair market price of this painting would be $50,000. Rembrandt Peale, one of Charles Willson Peale's sons, brings about $10,000 on the present market. A Joseph Blackburn brings about $40,000, and a John Neagle about $12,000 at the present time.

Western Art. Some of the most sought-after art of all periods and all countries by Americans today is Western art, the art of cowboys and Indians made famous by Frederic Remington and Charles Russell. Both artists painted in the latter nineteenth and early twentieth centuries.

At the beginning of the 1960s a Remington watercolor might sell in the neighborhood of $7,500, while an oil might bring $30,000. By the end of the decade watercolors had increased slightly, while Remington's oils had risen substantially. In December 1970 the Parke-Bernet Galleries sold a large oil for $105,000, and in April 1971 another large Remington brought $55,000. The price of Remingtons had tripled in the 1960s, most of the increase having taken place in the last half of the decade. In 1960 a Remington oil possibly would have sold for $30,000. At the same time an oil by Charles Russell might have brought $8,000. Subsequently, Russell began to approach Remington's prices. In 1968 two Russell watercolors were sold in London, one for $21,420 and the other for $27,720. In 1971 in Philadelphia a Russell watercolor sold for $41,000; two oils brought $75,000 and $90,000 respectively.

Charles Schreyvogel brings about $30,000 at the present time, and Catlin, Stanley, and Eastman all bring prices in the same general vicinity. In the medium-priced category are Edward Borein, at about $20,000, and Oscar Berninghaus, at $30,000. Henry F. Farny brings at least as much and often higher prices. So does Frank Tenney Johnson. Alfred Jacob Miller, on the other hand, while his oils are high in price, is in the $15,000 to $25,000 range for watercolors.

In the $15,000 to $25,000 range are Carl Bodmer, John Hauser, and Ernest Blumenschein. In the low-priced range (less than $10,000) are Carl Eytel, Charles Brinton Cox, H. Irving Marlatt, William R. Leigh, Carl Rungius, and Walter Ufer. Edwin Willard Deming, an excellent artist, has never been high in price, and at auction his paintings can sometimes be purchased for less than $1,000.

Thus, in the Western school of art there is something for everyone's pocketbook.

American Paintings of the Nineteenth and Early Twentieth Centuries. At the beginning of the 1960s a good Thomas Eakins, the realistic American painter who lived from 1844 to 1916, would bring about $15,000. In 1970 a large Eakins (79½ by 60 inches) of Cardinal Martinelli brought $130,000 at the Parke-Bernet Galleries. On December 10 of that year, the same gallery sold Eakins's *Cowboys in the Badlands* (32½ by 45½ inches), for $210,000. Most of the rise in Eakins and in this school of art in general took place after 1965.

The great portraitist James A. M. Whistler (1834–1903), who was also a great experimental artist, brought from about $4,500 to $5,000 in 1960. By the end of the decade his prices had increased nearly 6 times, and today his range is from $50,000 to $100,000. In November 1959, a good John Singer Sargent brought $6,250, an average Sargent price at the time. Sargent was a more brilliant portraitist than Whistler. On December 4, 1970, *Dr. Pozzi in His Home,* a good but not top-grade Sargent, brought $76,000.

Four of the typical landscape artists of the period are Winslow Homer, George Inness, Albert Bierstadt, and Thomas Moran. In 1960 a large Homer seascape would have brought about $125,000, and a yard scene, a typical Homer subject, would have brought $35,000. By 1970 a major Homer sold for from $350,000 to $500,000. In 1960 Inness was out of vogue, and his paintings, even large ones, could often be purchased for $1,000. In 1970 the Parke-Bernet Galleries sold Inness's *Homeward Bound* (26 by 36 inches) for $23,000, or about 7 times what the painting would have brought a decade earlier. Inness's best paintings will bring $40,000 to $50,000. As late as 1965 the prices of Bierstadt, the painter of the redwood country of California, were in the very low four-figure range. In 1970 his *Autumn Landscape with Deer* sold for $9,000. *Western Winter Landscape* brought the same price. The subject matter and the price history of Thomas Moran roughly parallel those of Bierstadt, but his prices tend to be lower.

In 1960 a good but small landscape by Jasper Cropsey could be purchased for $300. A decade later Cropsey had risen in price by 700 percent, with many small works selling in the $2,500 range. Two other Cropseys sold at auction at about the same time for $8,000 and $11,500 respectively. In 1960 a William Bradford landscape was in the not-wanted class. In 1965 his *Muir Glacier* was sold at auction in New York for $850, and in 1970 *Shipwreck off Nantucket* sold for $28,000. Even more striking is the rise in price of the artist Arthur F. Tait. In January 1965, a small Tait brought $550, while in April 1970 a similar Tait brought $6,000. In ten years the prices of this landscapist had risen almost 30 times.

A. H. Wyant brings about $10,000 per painting. The paintings of Martin J. Heade rose from $3,000 in 1965 to about $18,000 in 1970. Homer Martin's prices rose from about $1,000 to $4,000 in five years. Although these are the more spectacular examples, and some artists have achieved a high price level, there are literally hundreds of American landscapists of this period whose works can be purchased for less than $1,000.

American Impressionists, the Ten, and the Eight.   The leading American impressionist is Mary Cassatt, whose prices rose in the 1960s from $25,000 to the phenomenal level of $125,000 to $150,000. However, she is classified as a French impressionist rather than as an American one, since she lived in France and painted with the French impressionists.

The next most prominent American impressionist is Childe Hassam, who depicted rural New York, New England, and New York City. In the 1960s Hassam's prices at least quadrupled. In 1959 two of his best paintings sold for $5,500 and $8,750 respectively. In May 1970 his *East Hampton Elms in May* sold for $40,000. Yet small Hassam watercolors and even small paintings can at times be purchased for less than $10,000.

In 1960 all of the following artists could be purchased for less than $1,000, and some could be purchased for less than $500. Their approximate 1973 prices were as follows: Frank W. Benson, $4,000 to $5,000; Thomas W. Dewing, $4,000 to $5,000 (a fine Dewing, however, could bring $12,000); Gari Melchers, $6,000 to

$10,000; Robert Reid, still low in price (his top works, however, could bring $7,500); John Henry Twachtman, $7,500 to $12,000 (recently a major museum purchased an important Twachtman for $40,000); Henry Golden Dearth, still in the low range (about $1,200); Joseph R. De Camp, $3,000 to $5,000; Willard L. Metcalf, $10,000; Edward Simmons, still not in much demand (prices were low); and J. Alden Weir, $6,000 to $15,000.

The works of all ten of these artists are excellent in quality and highly decorative. Their level of prices places them within the reach of buyers who cannot touch many of the schools of art presently traded.

"The Eight" formed part of the Ashcan school, also known as the "revolutionary black gang." The subject matter of the paintings of this group is not always the most pleasant or the most universally accepted. The group often painted alleys, pool parlors, and other mundane and squalid scenes; yet they have gained enormous popularity in the United States, a popularity reflected in high prices.

1. *Maurice Prendergast.* He is a highly characteristic and stylized artist whose works are instantly recognizable. In 1960 his price level was about $30,000; now it exceeds $100,000.

2. *William Glackens.* He is the next-highest-priced artist in this group. Glackens's prices quadrupled in the past decade and are now at the $30,000 level.

3. *Robert Henri.* This artist is extremely colorful and impressionistic, and his works are experiencing a real vogue. His prices tripled between 1965 and 1976. Henri is a fine portraitist whose works are now in the $15,000 to $20,000 range.

4. *John Sloan.* In 1965 three of his portraits brought at auction $4,100, $1,750, and $3,400 respectively. His good portraits now bring about $25,000.

5. *Ernest Lawson.* The beauty and quality of Lawson's landscapes are hard to equal in the American school and perhaps in other schools as well. In 1965 three of his paintings brought at auction $3,500, $3,750, and $2,250 respectively. In 1972 his works brought $20,000 to $25,000. His favorite subject is High Bridge in New York, of which there are many renditions that frequently come on the market.

6. *Everett Shinn.* In 1965, $2,500 was a good price for a Shinn oil, many of which are of circus personnel. Some works brought in the neighborhood of $1,000. In 1976 a major oil by Shinn brought $25,000.

7. *George Luks.* George Luks was a master in capturing the atmosphere of New York. In 1950 his paintings brought less than $1,000, and often less than $500. In 1960 they brought $5,000, but by 1970 they had risen to 500 percent of that level.

8. *Arthur B. Davies.* In 1960 works of this artist, an excellent landscapist, could be purchased for about $1,000. Davies was the lowest-priced of the Eight. By 1976, however, his paintings sold for about $12,000. Occasionally auction houses realized lower prices, but $12,000 was the average retail price.

Taken as a whole, the group (the Ten and the Eight) experienced a rise in price of at least 1,000 percent between 1960 and 1976. If this school were traded more frequently on the international market, particularly in London, the degree of price rise would pull up materially the overall increase in art prices that took place in the last ten years.

Realistic Contemporary American Art.   Contemporary American artists include not only those who are living but those who were painting in the fairly recent past. The realistic contemporary school of American art, in contradistinction to the abstract school, is more photographic in quality. Yet this particular brand of realistic art is bold and experimental, it employs bright colors, it is to a considerable extent impressionistic, and some of the artists use abstract elements. A number of the artists in this school return to the subject matter and spirit of the Great Depression, which they capture exceedingly well.

Aaron Bohrod's *Landscape near Chicago* is typical of the subject matter and spirit of the Depression. The painting depicts a dilapidated house with a broken-down car standing in front of it. In the late 1960s Bohrod was selling for less than $1,000. By the early 1970s his prices were higher but not much higher, although his quality and subject matter are excellent. William Gropper's *The Senate* in the Museum of Modern Art in New York is of the same variety as Bohrod's paintings. This painting depicts a somewhat pompous windbag declaiming. Gropper's prices are very close to those of Bohrod, averaging a few thousand dollars. George Biddle is an artist of similar artistic skill and similar subject matter. His paintings also are in light demand, and his prices are perhaps only a little above those of Bohrod and Gropper.

Andrew Wyeth may well be the most respected, most beloved, and highest-priced American painter living today. Certainly he is the highest-priced realistic painter. His landscapes are artistic perfection and in tremendous demand. In 1960 his paintings sold for about $30,000. Today similar paintings are in the $100,000 range, although his lesser works and his watercolors sometimes sell at auction at a little over $10,000. N. C. Wyeth was the father of Andrew Wyeth. His typical scenes are landscapes and boats, in a strong, skillful style. In 1965 the Plaza Art Galleries in New York sold some of his large, important works in the $200 to $300 range. Today his prices are at about the $10,000 level.

Charles Burchfield definitely resembles the French moderns, Matisse in particular. He is a strong colorist and a landscapist. In 1960 his price level was about $750. In 1970 the Parke-Bernet Galleries sold his watercolor *Song of the Red Bird* (35¾ by 49½ inches) for $30,000. His smaller paintings sold in the same sale for $5,500 and $6,000. The price rise of this artist was phenomenal. Charles Demuth is a characteristic painter of New York scenes, and his watercolors are appearing more and more frequently on the market. In the late 1960s they sold in a range from $1,500 to $2,000. By the early 1970s they sold for about $15,000.

In the decade from 1960 to 1970 paintings by Georgia O'Keeffe quadrupled in price. At the beginning of the decade her works brought prices in the high four figures. Today $40,000 is not an unusual price for her paintings in pastel tones, many of them of leaves and flowers. Edward Hopper's landscapes are done with a good deal of dash and boldness and a free brush stroke. In the past decade his prices have quintupled. In a recent auction sale in New York two of his paintings brought $36,000 and $27,000 respectively. Reginald Marsh might be characterized as "the artist of Coney Island," and beach scenes with somewhat grotesque characters are typical of his works. His less important paintings in Chinese ink bring from $5,000 to $10,000, while his important oils bring from $50,000 to $60,000.

Eugene Speicher is one of the most accomplished of American portraitists of the modern school. He is particularly adept at portraits of women. In 1965 a small portrait of a woman was purchased for $175. In 1976, the same portrait would sell for about $2,000, still a low price for an artist of this quality. A large, important Speicher would cost about $10,000. Robert Brackman is the American artist who is closest to Speicher in subject matter, style, and quality. He is also closest in price. His portraits of women are superb. Occasionally his works go at auction at from $3,000 to $5,000. His prices have quintupled in five years, and they appear still to be low and rising. Leon Kroll, the landscapist of Riverside Drive, has seen his prices rise 10 times in ten years for these New York scenes; from a level of $500 they rose to $5,000. His much more wanted paintings of the French period tripled in price in the same years and are now at about the $15,000 to $20,000 level. In both types of paintings he is a contemporary leader. In 1960 Charles Sheeler, the painter of factory scenes, could be purchased for less than $5,000. By 1972 his paintings of the machine and factory age could be purchased for about $10,000.

In the past ten years paintings of this group of artists have increased in price about 5 times, with most of the rise taking place in the past five years.

The Modern French-American School.   Yasuo Kuniyoshi is typical of this group of painters. His works are extremely colorful, rather abstract, flattened, exaggerated, simplified in detail, and in bright colors. For many years he was in the $1,000 class. In 1972 a large Kuniyoshi was on the market for $35,000. Small paintings by this artist could sometimes be purchased at auction for less than $5,000.

Max Weber, certainly influenced by the French moderns, emphasizes composition and is somewhat abstract. His most wanted paintings are cubist. His oils of this type bring from about $25,000 to $50,000, and his cubist gouaches bring from $12,000 to $15,000. Louis Eilshemius's typical subject is a nude nymph in a landscape, perhaps by a waterfall. His paintings are in the $3,000 to $5,000 range. In a decade they have risen little in price; they are somewhat uninspired but competently executed. The reason for Eilshemius's low prices is that he produced a tremendous number of paintings, and many of them are on the market fairly regularly.

Overall the American schools of art have experienced a tremendous rise in price since 1960, and the greatest part of this rise took place after 1965. There seems to be no slackening in the rise in price of this entire category of art.

Factory Art

The increasing demand for art has created a new industry, the mass production of "original paintings." Usually each piece of art produced in these factories represents the labor of several specialists: one man sketches in a basic design in charcoal, another paints in the lakes and any other bodies of water, a third does the mountains and other pieces of landscape, and a fourth paints any living creatures. Humans are very rare. Then somebody signs the canvas to give it authenticity. This type of art is valueless from an investment viewpoint.

AUCTIONS VERSUS DEALERS

To a tremendously significant extent current, past, and future prices must be determined by reference to auction prices. These are public prices, available for inspection; dealer prices are not. Furthermore, the fact that auction houses sell the works of particular artists is a recognition of the market significance of the artists. Many artists are subjects of dealer promotion, some of it intense and costly, yet without auction prices it is not at all certain that dealer asking prices are not artificial. The auction proves the reality and permanence of the price of an artist, whether a living artist, a recent artist, or an old master.

The chief American auction house is the Parke-Bernet Galleries, now Sotheby, Parke-Bernet New York. The lesser auction houses in New York are still extremely important as a source of paintings and as an outlet for paintings offered for sale. However, their prices are generally unavailable and are not published, so that price trends in the United States can be determined only by reference to the priced catalogs of the Parke-Bernet Galleries. These catalogs are often available in libraries and art museums, including the Frick Art Reference Library and the Metropolitan Museum of Art in New York and the National Gallery in Washington. The standard commission for selling paintings by Sotheby, Parke-Bernet is 25 percent of the first $1,000 of the sale price, 20 percent of the next $4,000, and 15 percent of the next $10,000; and on that portion in excess of $15,000, the commission rate is 12.5 percent. For example, on $15,000 it is $2,550, or 17 percent.

Among other auction houses in New York that sell paintings are the following:
Plaza Art Galleries, Inc.

Coleman Auction Galleries
P.B. 84 (the lower-priced merchandise gallery of Sotheby, Parke-Bernet)
William J. Fischer, Inc.
Astor Galleries
Manhattan Galleries

There are two other major auction houses besides the Sotheby, Park-Bernet Galleries in New York: Sotheby's and Christie's, both in London. Price trends on internationally traded paintings can be drawn fairly accurately by reviewing the priced catalogs of these three establishments. There are other auction houses, notably in Paris, Rome, Munich, Vienna, and elsewhere, but these three houses handle most paintings available on the American market.

In general, auction prices are lower than retail prices, and dealers buy in great volume at auction and sell at retail at higher prices. The London auction market in particular is a dealer market. On the other hand, the auction houses sometimes secure the highest prices for certain paintings, notably impressionists, postimpressionists, and French moderns. As a rule, a great work of art can be sold at auction advantageously, for the auction house has the power to attract significant buyers, both private buyers and dealers, and handles publicity and advertising effectively.

At the other end of the scale are the secondary paintings, particularly secondary old master paintings. While you might offer such paintings to dealers directly for sale, the auction house is a good outlet. In general, dealers will not purchase secondary paintings at anything but rock-bottom prices because their market for such paintings is limited. Again the auction house has the power to bring in many potential buyers even for these paintings.

In general, the place to buy old master paintings is New York, and the widest selection of paintings is available at the Sotheby, Parke-Bernet Galleries, although most certainly not exclusively there. On the other hand, the place to sell old master paintings may well be London. There they tend to achieve higher prices, although transportation to London can be costly, and if the painting is not sold, return transportation is involved.

Dealers offer limited outlets for paintings except for the finest works in the greatest demand. Very often a dealer will accept a painting on consignment. Although in the end the dealer may secure a good price for the painting, paintings move slowly, and it may be years before a sale is made. The auction house, on the other hand, offers a certain sale within a reasonable period of time.

PROTECTING YOUR PURCHASE

An individual who is investing in art should always buy from a responsible dealer with an established reputation in the field. When buying a piece of art, it is common practice to have the dealer give detailed information on a bill of sale as to what has been purchased. This includes the name of the artist, the medium, the year in which the work was executed, and all other pertinent details. This is the investor's guarantee. It is also important for insurance purposes. The inexperienced purchaser should feel more secure in buying paintings from a member of the Art Dealers Association of America. To become a member of the association, a gallery must have been in business for five years and have a reputation for honesty and integrity in dealing with the general public, museums, artists, and other dealers.

Chapter **38**

Antique Furniture as an Investment

RICHARD H. RUSH

In 1958 a set of eight Italian chairs was purchased. Five of them had been made in the early part of the eighteenth century in Venice. They were painted a soft blue green with a floral design of pink and blue and green trailing leaf motifs. The paint was in excellent condition and had never been cleaned. Three of the chairs were reproductions made, perhaps, in the early years of the twentieth century to round out the set. They were of identical design and painted to match; only they were not antique. The set of eight chairs was purchased for $125 per chair.

At the present time, the five antique chairs are worth about $1,500 each, perhaps a little more. The reproduction chairs are worth about $150 each. The antiques are worth 10 times what the originals are worth, and they have risen more than 10 times in value in a decade and a half, while the reproductions have risen by a little more than 10 percent.

To be fair in making the price and price trend comparison between the antiques and the matching reproductions, we should say that the antiques at the time they were bought in 1958 were probably worth $150 per chair, while the reproductions were worth about $75. Thus, the reproductions have doubled in price in fourteen years, and the antiques have increased 10 times.

One can make a direct comparison of what happens to antique prices as compared with new furniture prices by visiting auction houses frequently or even just one time. In any event, this test was made: a group of secondhand furniture and a group of antique furniture were purchased in 1964. The next year, both groups were sold. The strictly secondhand furniture brought almost exactly what it had cost the year before. The antique furniture brought 248 percent of its 1964 price.

To compare prices of antique and nonantique furniture in another way, we can note prices at the same auction house at the same time, as the lesser auction houses (and often the leaders as well) handle both types of furniture at the same sale. Antiques virtually always bring high prices relative to secondhand furniture. Also, as a general rule, the auction house receives for secondhand furniture, no matter how fine or how new it is, from 10 to 20 percent of its new cost, rarely more.

DEFINING ANTIQUES

Before we proceed with a discussion of investing in antiques, it may be wise to define what is and what is not an antique. A collector of antiques, as opposed to an investor, may define an antique as a "man-made object of a kind that is no longer made and is valuable because of its age (usually 75 or 100 years or more) and historical implications." During World War II the Office of Price Administration issued a regulation concerning antiques that defined them in these terms:

> Antiques, for the purpose of this exemption, are (1) old objects such as furniture, tableware, household articles, etc.; which (2) tend to increase rather than decrease in value because of age; which (3) are purchased primarily because of their authenticity, age, rarity, style, etc. rather than for utility; and which (4) are commonly known and dealt in as antiques by the trade.

This definition is valid for the investor today, except for the date reference. Furniture made later than 1835 is not usually considered important by those who deal in antiques. For an investor, objects should be at least as old as the dates given below.[1]
Ceramics:
European, ca. 1830
Chinese export, ca. 1840
Staffordshire, ca. 1850
American ceramics, ca. 1890
Glass:
Blown-glass bottles and flasks, ca. 1860
Pressed glass, ca. 1840–1900
Opaque glass, ca. 1870–1890
Paperweights, ca. 1845–1860
Cut glass, ca. 1915
Art glass, ca. 1874–1933
Iridescent glass, ca. 1926
Silver:
American, ca. 1815–1830
European, ca. 1800
Pewter:
English, ca. 1750–1800
European, 1750–1790
Oriental, before 1750
American, before 1860
English britannia, before 1790
American britannia, before 1860
French Furniture:
Louis XIII, 1610–1643
Louis XIV, 1643–1715
Régence, 1715–1723
Louis XV, 1723–1774
Louis XVI, 1774–1793
Directoire, 1795–1799
Empire, 1804–1815
English Furniture:
Jacobean, 1608–1688
William and Mary, 1689–1702

---

[1]Edward J. Zegarowicz and George Sullivan, *Inflation-Proof Your Future*, Walker & Co., New York, 1971, pp. 102–104.

Queen Anne, 1702–1714
Chippendale, 1740–1779
Hepplewhite, 1780–1795
Adam, 1760–1793
Sheraton, 1790–1810
Regency, 1810–1820
American Furniture:
Pilgrim, 1650–1710
William and Mary, 1710–1725
Queen Anne, 1726–1750
Chippendale, 1760–1790
Hepplewhite, 1785–1800
Sheraton, 1795–1815
Duncan Phyfe, 1790–1847

According to the authors,

> There are dozens of other types and styles of antiques, but there are stable markets chiefly in those listed above. Shortages exist in every single one of these categories and prices are rising steadily.
>
> During the 1970's dealers found sharp price increases in fine authentic eighteenth-century American furniture. Some even predict it will become as highly prized as fine eighteenth-century French furniture was during the mid-1960's. Duncan Phyfe, in particular, is expected to spiral in value. Fine eighteenth-century English furniture may also show meaningful increases in value in the decade to come.
>
> Don't rush in. Pick a specialty. Study it carefully. What are its leading characteristics? Who were the foremost craftsmen? Bone up on the historical period involved. You should boast dealerlike knowledge before you enter the field.

CRITERIA FOR DETERMINING THE VALUE OF AN ANTIQUE

Antiques have market values that are determinable within certain limits. The factors that determine the value of any antique are fairly definite. They include style, maker, special characteristics, elaborateness, beauty, history, rarity, past public price, and original condition. Each of these factors will be explained with the use of examples.

Style Preferences

At the present time, Louis XV furniture stands at the style peak; it is in vogue and quite expensive. From a financial viewpoint, style is self-generating. The style trend increases demand; demand pushes up price; price increases bring in more investors. Then, simply because a piece of furniture is costly, it is sought out for purchase. It is an advertisement that the owner has wealth and also artistic discrimination. In 1938 no one wanted Louis XV antiques. They were out of style, and they had been going out of style all through the austerity period of the Depression, with its emphasis on functionalism and simple styles.

Louis XVI furniture has been coming into style since Louis XV became expensive, over a decade ago. Along with this furniture goes the very similar Adam furniture of England, which is highly decorative and in very short supply.

In the United States, American antique furniture is about as prestigious and about as high-priced as the most expensive French furniture. This furniture appeals to the real connoisseur and less to the "display artist." It is subdued but well constructed and of excellent, although conservative, design. The most preferred antiques of American origin are Queen Anne, followed by Chippendale. These two styles also predominate in England, but in England Chippendale appears to be preferred to Queen Anne and brings a higher price. In the late 1920s in England, Queen Anne furniture was by far the most highly preferred furniture.

The "coming-up" styles in both England and the United States are late-eighteenth-century and early-nineteenth-century Regency in England and the finer Hepplewhite and Sheraton in both England and the United States. Both of these styles are still moderately priced, as compared with other styles of furniture. In the same way, French Empire furniture is starting an upward style trend.

In continental Europe, Renaissance furniture and painted Italian furniture have been in demand for some time. These styles are less highly preferred in England and least in the United States, but they are increasing somewhat in preference.

In the present market, one piece of furniture stands out in buyer preference: the Louis XV bombé commode. Almost regardless of style and with the maker unknown, such pieces rarely sell for less than $20,000. In 1971 a pair of small bombé commodes was sold for the equivalent of $201,600; they went to J. Paul Getty.

Small tables of the Louis XV period are also in great demand, as are Louis XV fauteuils and bergères. French cylinder bureaus, fall-front desks, and settees are not in demand, and they bring relatively low prices.

In the United States the Chippendale bonnet-top or broken-arch highboy is in tremendous demand, and fine pieces of this type sell for $100,000 and up. Similarly priced are other Chippendale and American Queen Anne large case furniture. Armchairs are at a great premium, as are sets of chairs, whether Chippendale or Queen Anne.

In English furniture, large case furniture of the Chippendale era and large, superb, elaborately carved desks are in the $100,000-and-up class. If these pieces were made by Thomas Chippendale himself, they would be priced quite a bit higher.

In both England and the United States the simpler Chippendale chairs are relatively low-priced, and one chair of simple design is in very little demand. This rule applies to both American and English Chippendale furniture.

Furniture Maker

The most prestigious maker of any furniture made in the Western world is known simply as BVRB. For many years his name was not known, and he was simply called BURB. One scholar finally identified him as Bernard II van Riesenburgh. The two Getty commodes described above were by this great maker and are stamped with his initials. Similar important French makers are Dubois, Lacroix (RVLC), Oeben, Riesener, Jacob, Leleu, Tilliard, Gaudreau, and Joubert, all of the Louis XV era. In the Louis XVI era the leading makers were Riesener, Roentgen, Beneman, Weisweiler, the Jacob family, the Sené family, Vandercruse, Carlin, Topino, and Petit.

In America some of the greatest cabinetmakers were Goddard, Townsend, Bedlam, Haines, Gostelowe, Randolph, Affleck, McIntire, Seymour, Frothingham, and Aaron and Eliphalet Chapin, among others.

The identification of a piece of furniture as having been made by one of the leading furniture makers can easily double its value in the market.

Desirable and Undesirable Characteristics

Certain characteristics of a piece of furniture are considered good, and certain are considered poor; and these characteristics must be learned. Sometimes they represent sound thinking, and sometimes just style or fad.

For example, the straight up-and-down cabriole leg, the one that goes neither outward nor inward, is considered the best kind. A bonnet top or a broken-arch top on American furniture is considered much better than a flat top. In Chippendale furniture, ball-and-claw feet are preferred. In American furniture, ogee feet are preferred, as well as trifid feet; simple feet are the least preferred.

Elaborateness

In general, the simple is not preferred. The simple Chippendale chair is the least valuable chair. The elaborately pierced and carved splat on Chippendale chairs gives these chairs great value; so does the most intricate carving. On bombé commodes, marquetry and parquetry (inlay work) impart a good deal of value, as does fine lacquer.

Beauty

On American Sheraton tables, for example, slender legs are all-important: a very slender reeded leg gives the table maximum value; a medium leg means that the piece is worth less; a thick leg makes the piece much less preferred by collectors, and if the thick leg is without reeding, a good many Sheraton furniture collectors simply pass it by. In his excellent book *Fine Points of Furniture: Early American,*[2] Albert Sack illustrates pieces of furniture that are good and those that are considered bad.

Several French publications discuss the value-giving elements and value-detracting elements of French furniture, principally chairs and bombé commodes. These elements are tremendously important in determining values. Strange as it may seem, comfort to the sitter is one of the most important of all elements in determining the value of a Louis XV bergère or fauteuil. Strict ornamental value is important, but so is comfort.

History

Where did the piece come from? A few years ago, a pair of Renaissance Italian tables was offered for sale. They came from the William Randolph Hearst Collection, an important American collection of Renaissance furniture. This identification added, perhaps, 50 percent to the value of the two pieces. Similarly, a few years ago a Louis XV bureau was purchased in New York for a large sum of money. Under the piece was a painted number. This turned out to be an inventory number and was identified by the curator of the Louvre as being a Versailles Palace inventory number from the era of Louis XV. Immediately, the piece of furniture was worth twice its high purchase price.

Historical and aristocratic connections also add to value. A bed owned by Mme. Du Barry or a table owned by the late President Kennedy becomes more valuable than one owned by a "common man."

Rarity

As with any commodity, scarcity demands a higher price. An elaborate bonnet-top American highboy is a great rarity. It brings a price in six figures. So do small French tables with delicate legs. Over the years, these fragile pieces have been broken and have disappeared. As early as 1964 a French commode made by David Roentgen brought $176,000; not only was he a fine French ébéniste, but he was a rare one.

With rarity, however, must go vogue or style. Rarity alone will not give an antique high value; the item must be a style item, one that is in demand, and at the same time rare.

[2]Crown Publishers, Inc., New York, 1950.

Public Price

A high selling price for an item tends to bring an even higher price for it or for others like it by its maker or other makers of his kind. The fact that a pair of tables by BVRB brought $250,000 helps the entire market and market price for BVRB antiques. Once an item is known to be a money item, investors, as well as "conspicuous emulators," enter the market for it. Price trends that can be determined from public records of auctions are the best indication of what prices will be in both the immediate and the more distant future.

Original Condition

Although this value-giving element has been left for last, it might well have been placed somewhere near the top of the list, for it is extremely important.

These are the repairs and replacements that *damage values most seriously:*

1. Replacement of drawers or drawer fronts.
2. Additional carving and inlay work.
3. Reshaping of the splat on an English or American chair and piercing and recarving it.
4. New wooden seat.
5. Re-turning legs and bedposts.
6. Loss or replacement of bonnet or arched top on American pieces.
7. Making different shapes for table leaves or other shaped pieces or elements.
8. Changing the size or shape of a bureau or highboy.
9. Changing the shape of a sideboard or commode.
10. Different top on a bottom (as in a chest-on-chest or a chest-on-frame) or a new bottom or top. Such pieces are frequently found on the market today, and their value is problematic.

Below is a list of alterations that *damage value the least.* All antiques are damaged or worn to some extent after 150 or 200 years or more, and the following changes do not seriously hurt price. They are to be expected.

1. Surface stains and flyspecks.
2. Surface dents and cuts.
3. New runners for drawers.
4. New seat blocks.
5. Replacement of brass, particularly on American case furniture.
6. Filling in holes on American furniture where nobs were substituted for original brass in Victorian times and where original brass or replacement brass has now been replaced.
7. Small additions of wood where the original pieces came off or rotted away.
8. Warping if it is not too serious and particularly if it can be corrected by heating and pressing.

PRICES OF ANTIQUES

History of Antique Prices

The early 1920s saw the beginning of an antique boom. Beneath the boom or incipient boom lay a widespread interest in antiques and particularly in the value element of antiques. Emulation of the rich and their displays no doubt underlay the entire movement. J. Pierpont Morgan was the leader in this respect, and many of his purchases in the field of both art and antiques went on public display. Hearst, Widener, Frick, and others of the ultrarich apparently started the trend to antiques, and to a considerable extent the trend was to large, dark, and heavy antiques on the one hand and to refined American antiques on the other. The dark, heavy antiques were primarily Italian but also English Jacobean. The American antiques were generally of the later and more refined kinds, although there was also a boom in the very simple maple, cherry, and pine furniture of the farm and cottage. In the same period, there was a wave of patriotism in the United States, and early American "anything" was a preferred item.

Perhaps we can learn something about the future prices of antiques by their past history. To understand the price movements of antique furniture, let us use a scale called the Antique Price Index and assign 100 or 100 percent to the year 1925, four years before the great stock market crash of 1929.

In just one year, from 1925 to 1926, antique prices increased by 79 percent. By 1929 they were at a level of 270 percent, and there existed a mad rush to buy antiques and a preoccupation by many of the leading newspaper and magazine writers of the day with antiques and antique prices. A new phenomenon arose: the collector-dealer. Very often, laymen bought and sold antiques at a profit. This behavior has not been repeated to any degree since the 1920s.

Antique prices did not fall as rapidly as stock prices by any means, and by 1930 antique prices were not greatly off. As the Depression deepened, however, the antique business fell off, and by the depth of the Depression, in 1932, the Antique Price Index that we have constructed fell to 148.

The strange thing about this index is that it did not pick up as did most stock and industrial production indices and most price indices. By the year 1939 it was down to 66, and by the early war year of 1942 it had recovered only to 68. By the last war year it had risen to 175. People were fearful of holding money and anxious to get out of invaded or threatened areas, and they were buying antiques, thus moving their wealth. In addition, wartime incomes and a shortage of wartime furniture and everything else to buy made buyers turn to antiques.

The end of the war relaxed these stimulants. By 1950 the Antique Price Index had declined to 133. Five years later it was up to 202, by 1960 it had risen to 349, by 1965 it stood at 552, and in the early 1970s it was a little over 1,000.

The Antique Price Index was prepared by studying auction prices at Christie's and Sotheby's in London, Sotheby, Parke-Bernet New York, the Anderson Galleries, and the American Art Association in New York. Other auction prices were reviewed, and an annual survey of European antique dealers was conducted for many years.

In compiling the index, five years were spent in visiting a majority of auctions as well as the displays before sales. Since the lesser auction houses do not publish prices and rarely illustrate catalogs, one must visit the displays to examine what is offered for sale, for the descriptions in the catalogs may not accurately describe what is actually being offered for sale.

Antiques versus the Price of Art

Antique prices rose in the last half of the 1920s at a more rapid rate than did art prices. However, during the Depression they fell much later but kept on falling when art prices began to rise, especially after the war. Indeed, they declined until 1950, when they started their long upward climb.

If we make the index of both antique and art prices equal to 100 percent in the year 1950, we have an interesting comparison. By 1955 art prices had doubled; antique prices, on the other hand, had increased by only 50 percent. Between 1955 and 1960 art prices tripled; antique prices increased by a little over 50 percent. In the decade from 1950 to 1960 art prices increased 6 times in magnitude. Antique prices went up to 2½ times their 1950 base.

The performances of art and antique prices were very similar from 1960 to the early 1970s. Art prices tripled; antique prices increased by about 275 percent.

Antiques versus Stock Prices

Let us arbitrarily make the index equal to 100 percent in 1925 for both antique and stock prices, for comparative purposes. As indicated earlier, by 1926 antique prices had risen by 79 percent, and the index stood at 179. In the same one-year period, stock prices (Standard & Poor's 500-Stock Index) had risen by only 13 percent, with an index of 113.

By the year 1929 the Antique Price Index stood at the level of 270. Stock prices had accelerated into a wild boom, and the Standard & Poor's average stood at 233. However, this was still less than the Antique Price Index.

By 1932 the stock index had dropped to 62, but the Antique Price Index was well above this level, standing at 148. Antiques fared better in the Depression and were probably a better investment than were stocks.

Between 1932 and 1939, however, stocks advanced substantially better than did antiques. In 1939 the stock index stood at 108, but the antique index had declined to 66. This was not purely a depression-prosperity phenomenon. Antiques were out of style. Functionalism and simplicity had replaced ornamentation to a degree, and the wealthy and their trademarks were no longer in, partially because of the influence of the New Deal and a new emphasis on welfare, social security, and reform in general.

By the early part of World War II the stock index had declined to 78. On the other hand, the Antique Price Index had pulled up a few points to 68. By 1945, the last year of the war, stock prices had recovered to 136, but antique prices had recovered considerably more, to 175.

Five years later stocks had continued their recovery, and their index was at 165. The Antique Price Index, on the other hand, had declined to 133. People in the recovery period in which goods were again being manufactured for consumers did not emphasize antiques.

The year 1950 ushered in a new era in both antique and stock prices. The Great Boom had begun. Making the index equal to 100 percent in 1950 for both antiques and stocks for comparative purposes, we see that by 1955 the Antique Price Index was up to 150, but stock prices had risen to 220. By 1960 antique prices were at a level of 250, but stocks had risen to 304.

Again, let us begin with both the antique and the stock indices at 100 percent. By the year 1965 the rise in antique and stock prices was almost identical. By the spring of 1968, however, stock prices showed a slight decline, to 160, while antiques continued their rise to 225.

In many ways, 1968 was a critical year for stocks. Their index hit a high in December and then started on an interrupted decline. The year 1970 was a poor one in general, and the year 1971 saw five waves of rise and fall. For the period from 1960 to 1972 stock prices rose by only about 60 percent (from 100 in 1960), whereas antique prices increased about 3 times, from 100 to 275.

To be fair in our analysis, we must point out that stocks throw off an income in the form of dividends; antiques do not. Thus, we should add dividends to stock prices to form a comparison with antiques. The average dividend in this period was less than 3.5 percent, or less than 35 percent for the decade. Nevertheless, antique prices still pull ahead of the stock market (at least ahead of the overall stock market), and this comparison holds true regardless of which stock market index is used. The price movements of stocks and antiques are given in Table 38-1.

Beginning in 1969, however, antiques fell on periodic bad times. In the year 1970 the situation in antiques was critical in some cases. At auction in New York a large number of estates containing antiques came into the market. The antiques could not be held for orderly sale because executors wanted them moved as rapidly as possible. Thus, the Parke-Bernet low-priced gallery, P.B. 84, sold a tremendous volume of antiques and semiantiques at relatively low prices, as did other secondary galleries.

In England there was a critical period for many, if not most, antique dealers. Americans and American dealers were not buying. Numerous smaller antique dealers went out of business; many took large losses on their inventories. In Paris the situation was little better. The American buyer, an important element, was largely out of the market, and while prices of antiques in England and France did not decrease, sales were off.

By the end of 1971 the situation had improved greatly, and antiques were moving again. All through this period, the very finest items did not decrease in price or demand. They were moving constantly upward, and many museums and wealthy buyers did not stop their purchasing. In 1971, for example, two pieces of

TABLE 38-1   Price Movements of Stocks and Antiques

Year	Stocks (percent)	Antiques (percent)
1925	100	100
1926	113	179
1929	233	270
1932	62	148
1939	108	66
1942	78	68
1945	136	175
1950	165	133
1955	363	200
1960	561	332
1965	902	558
1968	897	759
1972	897	913

French furniture sold at record prices, $410,000 and $415,000, prices unheard of a few years earlier for any piece of furniture no matter how fine or how rare.

The lower-priced antiques continued to move, and their prices did not decline much, if at all. The middle-priced antiques, however, did suffer, as did middle-priced paintings. The middle-priced antique and art buyer was almost out of the market, particularly the corporate executive who now feared the loss of his or her job or who had already lost it. Nonetheless, by the fall of 1971 confidence had returned, and prices and sales of antique furniture picked up.

Although all of the items listed above comprise the family of items called antiques, we shall deal only with furniture in this chapter because furniture is generally the most popular and expensive of these items.

FIVE MOST SIGNIFICANT FURNITURE TYPES

It would be impossible to discuss all types of antiques in one brief chapter. Instead, we shall briefly discuss French, Italian, English, American, and Victorian furniture. Again, furniture has been chosen because it is the single most important antique item.

French

There are five major periods of French antique furniture: Louis XV, Louis XVI, French Directoire, Empire, and provincial.

The most prestigious of all furniture in the world today is French, and within this overall category the most preferred is *Louis XV*. This furniture is usually characterized by curves and by the double-carved cabriole leg. In the period from

1939 to 1976, Louis XV furniture increased more than 20 times in value and was among the world's most expensive antique furniture. In 1976 a good pair of bergères (armchairs with closed arms) or fauteuils (open armchairs) could be purchased for $20,000 to $25,000. Today, good small tables can be purchased for about $5,000, and because they are small and of apartment or small-house size, they are in constant demand.

Louis XVI furniture is characterized by straight lines and by straight classic legs. Prices of Louis XV furniture were so high in 1960 that demand turned to other items, such as the more plentiful and less expensive Louis XVI. Because of this increased demand, the prices of Louis XVI furniture rose by 400 percent in the 1960s; however, it is still priced well below Louis XV. At the present time, one oval-back side chair of good design and construction (but not the very best) can be purchased for about $1,000. In pairs, the price per chair goes up, as pairs are more desirable, more decorative, and more useful than single chairs. A pair might cost $2,500. Four chairs are even more desirable, and the larger the set, the higher the price per chair. A good commode of the Louis XVI period will cost about $10,000. A great commode like the David Roentgen commode sold at Sotheby's in 1964, brought $176,000.

The period of Louis XVI is followed by the *French Directory (Directoire).* This furniture is priced below Louis XVI. It is not as decorative or as well made, and it is considerably more austere. Although this furniture did more than double in price in the 1960s, it is still quite inexpensive. A Directoire commode, of somewhat simple design, can be purchased at the present time for about $2,500. Sometimes one in poor condition can be purchased from one of the lesser auctions for considerably less money and then restored. A good bergère should cost less than $500, as should a fauteuil. In sets, the price may be a little higher per chair.

From this type of furniture we move in time to *Empire* furniture made during the reign of the emperor Napoleon (1804–1815). This furniture is unique in that its entire style was decreed by Napoleon to glorify him and his military conquests. It is often elaborately decorated and frequently will have inlaid brass. The furniture is certainly well made, but it is heavy and perhaps as well suited to Napoleon's throne room as to the private home. It is, however, fairly plentiful. In 1960 Empire furniture was not preferred furniture, and its prices were relatively low. However, the price level of this furniture increased fourfold in the 1960s. The rise was substantial because 1960 prices were so low that a small dollar rise resulted in a large percentage rise.

In a Paris antique shop on the Left Bank, there has been an excellent set of eight Empire chairs for sale for some time, and the price is about $1,000 per chair. Single chairs, expecially side chairs, can be purchased for less than $500 per chair. Inlays of brass make the chairs more valuable. There is also a typical tripod table with a slate top that can often be purchased for $500 or less; there, too, brass inlays make the piece worth more.

A large amount of *provincial* French furniture is on the market. This furniture is usually not inlaid or lacquered. It is often heavy and of oak, dark in color, and not of the quality of finer French furniture. Provincial furniture originated in about 1715 and continued to be made at least to 1850, and so its age is rather indeterminate. Designs were changed very little over the decades. Often its design is Louis XV with curved legs, but drastically simpler than the genuine style. Prices for provincial furniture have never been very high in comparison with other furniture. Yet its prices more than doubled in the 1960s.

Italian

There are two distinct types of Italian furniture on the market today: *Renaissance* and *painted Italian.* There are two other types, but these do not appear in very great quantity, particularly in the United States. They are eighteenth-century natural wood furniture, based on Louis XV French furniture and of excellent design, and natural wood furniture of the same period but of very simple design. The latter category sometimes appears in large-city auctions. It also appears in rather large volume in the Italian market and sometimes in the London auctions.

Renaissance furniture is available at many auctions and in a number of dealerships throughout the United States. It is flat, straight in line, architectural, made of dark oak for the most part, and very heavy in weight and appearance. Much of it will not fit in smaller modern houses and apartments, although one or two pieces in a dwelling offer considerable ornamental interest. This was the furniture of William Randolph Hearst and J. P. Morgan.

If we go back to 1916, heyday of Renaissance furniture, we would find a sixteenth-century Tuscan center table going at the American Art Association in New York for $11,000. In the same year, one Dante chair sold at the same place for $5,500. These pieces were from the famous Volpi or Davanzati Palace sale.

In the late 1960s the Parke-Bernet Galleries in New York sold a top-grade gilded walnut cassone (chest) from sixteenth-century Florence for $2,400. It went to J. Paul Getty for his Italian palace. In the 1920s this chest might have brought 10 times this figure. Simpler items still do not bring high prices. In the disastrous season of 1970 in New York, P.B. 84 sold some excellent pieces at very low prices. An octagonal center table with lions' feet brought exactly $130. A fine early-Renaissance chair in old velvet brought $55, representing about a 90 percent drop from the peak of the 1920s. However, between 1960 and 1976 the average price of Renaissance furniture increased sharply.

There are essentially three types of pieces of Renaissance furniture that can readily be bought. The first is a credenza, or cabinet with drawers in the top and doors below that close over a cupboard. The second type is a chair, rather austere and not particularly comfortable. The third is the chest, or cassone, used to store things. These are ornamental but not very useful.

A fourth piece of furniture used to be plentiful and reasonable in price, but it is something of a rarity on the present market and is very high in price: the refectory table, similar to the once-popular library table found in American homes of a few decades ago. A refectory table of simple design, perhaps 6 feet long, would cost about $1,500. Very often these tables have elaborate replacements that can cut their value by as much as 75 percent. An elaborate and original table with excellent carving can bring up to $25,000. Early tables, as well as other early pieces of Renaissance furniture, bring much more than do pieces of the seventeenth century, which was the last century to turn out this type of furniture.

Large state chairs bring about $300 a chair. Some have period tapestry upholstery or antique velvet. They, too, are rather austere. Elaborate and finely carved credenzas can bring $10,000, while the simpler ones can be purchased for about $1,000.

Cassoni are probably the least wanted pieces of Renaissance furniture. The elaborate one described above brought only $2,400. Simpler ones can often be bought for $250 or even less, and their prices have not risen much in recent years.

The other main type of Italian furniture on the market is painted Italian furniture of the eighteenth century. This furniture is so different from the heavy dark Italian Renaissance furniture that it appeals to a completely different market. It is based on French furniture of the same period, Louis XV and Louis XVI, and is known in Italy by these French designations despite its Italian designation. The average price of this furniture increased by 4,000 percent between 1925 and 1976. An investor who bought $25,000 worth of the furniture in 1925 could be a millionaire today. In the 1960s alone, the price of this furniture increased by 350 percent.

Painted Italian furniture is highly decorative furniture, some of the most decorative ever created. It is lacquered in blues, greens, yellows, and other colors over shapely and relatively small bodies. On the basic color ground are painted pictures, vines, flowers, and other decorations. (Renaissance furniture is, for the most part, unpainted.)

Painted furniture is of several varieties. The highest-priced and the most highly preferred came from Venice in the early part of the eighteenth century. Fine furniture of this style was made all through the eighteenth century, but the earlier is perhaps the most highly priced. The dominant tone is green or blue green. Another type of painted furniture is that from Lucca. The typical Lucca color is yellow. Each area of Italy has its own variations of color and design.

The primary, value-determining factor in this furniture is the originality of the paint. A fine Venetian green commode with a shaped front and all-original paint will sell on the present market for $25,000 to $35,000. If one-fourth of the paint has had to be replaced, the value of the same piece would be, at most, $10,000 to $15,000. If half of the paint is a replacement, the value would be no more than $5,000. If none of the original paint remains, the value of the piece is problematic, and it is doubtful whether any collector of Italian furniture would want to own such a piece.

In London, in 1971, there was a set of twelve medium-blue chairs (not the most wanted color), which probably was partially restored. The set was offered for $30,000. Of course, the value per chair depended on the large size of the set; one chair alone might have sold for $1,000; a pair, for $3,000.

In the United States the demand for painted Italian furniture is low compared with the demand in the London antique market and very low compared with the market in Italy. Occasionally such furniture can be purchased at both large and small auction houses; however, its value in Italy can well be 10 times its value in New York or Washington.

In summary, Renaissance and painted Italian furniture have increased in price in the past decade by 325 percent. (All furniture of antique origin, for comparative purposes, has increased in price by 175 percent.) This is probably a result of the fact that Renaissance furniture was very inexpensive in 1960 and almost *had to rise* in price; painted Italian, being small and highly decorative, increased in price along with Louis XV and Louis XVI furniture simply because it made a welcome addition to the decor of any home.

English

English antique furniture is the most easily available furniture on the market today. It can be purchased readily in the United States and England, where it is sold or auctioned in almost every smaller city and in many towns. Virtually every auction house in the United States offers English antiques regularly, as do the antique shows that have proliferated all over the country in the past few years.

English antique furniture is both useful and decorative; its style underlies virtually all American antique furniture, but *the price of a comparable English piece is about 25 percent of the price of an American piece.*

In the years 1970 and 1971 the antique business in England was not good. Many dealers had to sell their antique furniture for less than they paid for it, and many were either forced out of business or simply closed up shop. The American recession and the decline of the American stock market had a direct effect on the English antique business. Many dealers throughout England depended on the American commercial buyer, the antique retailer or wholesaler. In 1970–1971 these buyers were noted by their absence from the English scene. Commodes could be purchased for $100 to $150, and chairs in sets for as low as $100 per chair, for example.

The earliest type of English furniture on the market in any volume is *Jacobean* furniture, which was made between 1608 and 1688. In many ways, it resembles the heavy, dark oak Renaissance furniture. It has risen in price in the past decade, but it is neither high in price nor as preferred as it once was. Like Renaissance furniture, it had its heyday in the decade of the teens and the twenties, thanks to the J. P. Morgan vogue. In the early 1970s, prices of Jacobean furniture were just a little bit higher than what they had been in 1929 and far lower than they had been in 1914. Amazingly, in the fall of 1970 a superb, richly carved Jacobean chair, with seventeenth-century tapestry, sold at P.B. 84 for $90. In the early 1970s, oak buffets could be purchased in the United States and England for less than $500 and often for $250. Oak chests, particularly the simple, less highly carved chests, would cost about the same price. A very elaborate refectory table, on the other hand, could well cost up to $5,000, while a simple one would cost less than $1,000.

William and Mary furniture is named after the English monarchs who ruled from 1689 to 1702. This, too, is large, heavy, dark, and somewhat awkward furniture. It is characterized by turned legs in the form of trumpets and similar bulbous shapes, X-shaped stretchers, finials, rectilinear shapes, and hooded tops. William and Mary serves as a transition from Jacobean to Queen Anne, a much-preferred style on today's market. The recent price history of William and Mary furniture is very much like that of Jacobean furniture. Since 1970, however, William and Mary has come into preference, and prices have been firming. Some recent prices for William and Mary are $1,000 for an excellent wing armchair covered with needlework; $500 for a good side chair; perhaps $750 for a gateleg table of small size; 750 for a settee; and $1,500 for a commode, a standard piece of William and Mary furniture. Prices of William and Mary furniture have not changed spectacularly since 1910.

Queen Anne furniture (1702–1714) is smaller and more graceful than William and Mary. A curved form and cabriole legs were used, and stretchers on the legs were eliminated; club and claw feet were used. Walnut, a more attractive wood than oak, became *the* wood of the Queen Anne period.

In London, in 1929, Queen Anne furniture posted the highest prices of all types of furniture sold, regardless of origin. On March 14, 1929, Christie's sold a walnut sofa and six chairs for the equivalent of $40,000. In the same year, another suite brought $50,000. Queen Anne furniture had increased 100 times in price between 1901 and 1929. However, between 1929 and 1960 it decreased in price by 30 percent. From 1960 through 1972 it increased by 50 percent, so that it was above its 1929 level. In the present market a good Queen Anne lowboy, an extremely popular item, can be purchased for $2,500. Large sets of sofas and chairs of elaborate design can, however, bring enormous prices, in the neighborhood of $15,000 to $25,000, particularly if covered in period tapestry. A fine pair of Queen Anne side chairs can bring $5,000, and a wing armchair $2,500.

Chippendale furniture (1740–1779) is universally accepted and universally in demand and at high prices. In this period, mahogany was *the* wood, and the ball-and-claw foot became characteristic of Chippendale furniture, particularly on the best pieces. The cabriole leg was also used, as was carving; the more carving, the more valuable the piece. Veneers were frequently used instead of solid woods.

Chippendale has steadily risen in price since the Depression. Between 1960 and 1972 the demand for this furniture increased, and its prices more than doubled.

Sets of fine Chippendale chairs are quite difficult to find, despite the fact that many sets were made. In a recent year a set of eight good Chippendale side chairs plus two armchairs was sold at Sotheby's in London for $14,560. A very simple set of Chippendale chairs, with little carving and with no ball-and-claw feet, might bring $5,000, but a pair of simple Chippendale chairs might bring only $500, and single chairs can often be secured. A wing armchair can bring $2,500. If the piece was actually made by Thomas Chippendale, the price skyrockets. In 1965 Christie's sold the famous Harewood desk by Thomas Chippendale for the equivalent of $120,540. Recently, a London dealer offered for sale a Chinese Chippendale (Chinese-style) gilt display cabinet for $126,000. A pair of carved and gilded open armchairs was offered by another London dealer for $15,000.

Hepplewhite flourished from 1770 to 1788. It is found on the market in England in great profusion and comes regularly onto the American market as well. It is generally much smaller than Chippendale and much less ornamented. It is graceful and uses straight-line classical design; mahogany is the dominant wood.

The price rise in this furniture from 1960 to the present time has been almost identical with that of Chippendale, even though the style is markedly different. Hepplewhite has recently reached the highest price levels in its entire history. It experienced very little boom in the 1920s, when it was not preferred, but then it didn't decline very much during the Depression. Like much other antique furniture, it hit a low point in 1939 and another low point in 1950.

Many kinds of useful and decorative pieces of Hepplewhite furniture are on the market. One particularly useful piece is the breakfront, which can be used as a bookcase or as a china cabinet. It is large and well designed, and it can often be purchased for around $2,500. Fairly recently, Parke-Bernet sold a magnificent but enormous breakfront (23 feet long). The buyer, a dealer, purchased it for $950, then didn't know what to do with it and offered it for resale at the same price; the moving cost was also enormous. The story is amusing but significant: buy an antique that is usable, by you or by someone else, or you can get stuck.

Sheraton furniture (1790–1810) is even more plentiful on the market, both in England and in the United States. It is small and well made, and it fits admirably into the small modern home. Its recent price rise has been somewhat similar to that of Hepplewhite, but not quite as great. To distinguish between Hepplewhite and Sheraton furniture, notice their top rails. The top rails of Hepplewhite furniture are frequently curved; the top rails of Sheraton furniture are usually straight across and flat. This is a usual distinguishing characteristic of the two styles of furniture, but there are many variations of design.

In the late 1960s, a set of six side chairs and two armchairs sold at Parke-Bernet in New York for $640. The set would bring little more today, as it is a relatively plain, average set of chairs. At about the same time, a settee and eight armchairs were sold in London. This was a more elaborate set and brought the equivalent of $1,904, still not a large sum as compared with the prices of other styles and periods of English furniture. Prices for finer pieces, however, are higher. A very fine set of four armchairs was sold at Parke-Bernet a little later for $2,700. There is even finer furniture of this style in satinwood with marquetry inlays. On the present market, a demilune commode of this style will bring at least $5,000.

The *Adam* style is earlier than Sheraton furniture but somewhat similar in quality. It was made between 1760 and 1793. It is not plentiful and very high-priced, particularly the gilded furniture that closely resembles Louis XVI French furniture. A fine Adam satinwood and marquetry semicircular commode was sold at Sotheby's at about the same time that the Sheraton commode of similar design was sold. It brought $16,800. Gilt wood and satinwood side tables often bring up to $5,000, and sets of gilded chairs of Louis XVI design bring up to $2,500.

Between 1950 and 1960 the price index of this furniture quadrupled, and by the early 1970s the index had almost quadrupled again. Between 1950 and 1976 the average price of this furniture increased by 1,500 percent. It is small, highly decorative, often-gilded furniture and is in short supply. For these reasons, its price is high and rising.

The last type of English furniture studied is *Regency* furniture, made between 1810 and 1820. This furniture experienced the highest rise in price of any type of

English furniture between 1960 and the present: 450 percent. The furniture was not in great demand in the 1920s and only came to be recorded in the auction market in the late 1930s. Regency furniture is simpler in form and decoration than its predecessors, Sheraton and Hepplewhite. Flat surfaces and very dark woods are used; at the same time, the furniture has a more massive quality and shows the influence of French Empire furniture. Brass, ormulu, and boulle work are used for decoration, and classic motifs are employed in design as well as decoration.

A Regency mahogany game table, 26½ inches long, was sold at Parke-Bernet in 1972 for $1,150. A more elaborate table, known as a sofa table, often brings up to $5,000. Regency drum tables bring about $1,500. Armchairs of rather simple design bring about $500 per chair, and elaborate ones can bring up to $1,500 each; they have incurvate arms and are highly ornamental in an elaborate and showy manner.

To summarize, English furniture increased in price by 150 percent from 1960 to 1972, whereas all antique furniture showed an increase of 175 percent. Regency and Adam furniture pulled the average English prices up, while all other English furniture lagged behind the average.

American

American styles of furniture are based almost entirely on English styles. Since England was the style leader in furniture from the seventeenth to the early nineteenth Century, American furniture makers were generally ten to fifteen years behind them.

American William and Mary is the earliest type of American furniture that can be found on the United States market in any volume. Earlier pieces of American furniture are totally different: they are austere, made of dark wood, in very short supply, and, if of good design, very high in price. Often, they are ornaments rather than pieces of usable furniture.

William and Mary furniture has never been preferred furniture, although it did increase in value by 50 percent between 1960 and 1972, and in the last few years there are signs that it may increase in value at a more rapid pace. Burl walnut and maple highboys come onto the market fairly frequently. In the early 1970s a piece of this furniture could be purchased for about $3,000. Lowboys of this era also come onto the market. These sell for $3,000 to $5,000, well under the cost of a comparable piece of Queen Anne.

The William and Mary period in America ran from 1710 to 1725. The *Queen Anne* period here ran from 1726 to 1750. This period furniture in America is possibly the most sought after of all American furniture, and only the next later style, Chippendale, can touch it in popularity and price.

The finest American Queen Anne pieces bring enormous prices. As early as 1966, Parke-Bernet sold a Queen Anne shell-carved walnut armchair that had been exhibited in the Metropolitan Museum of Art in 1963. It brought $27,500. In the same year, the same gallery sold a single side chair made in Philadelphia for $18,000. Simpler Queen Anne chairs might bring as low a price as $1,500 each, and an American Queen Anne tea table sold recently for $3,500 in New York at auction. There is a great deal of difference in price for Queen Anne furniture, the finer pieces bringing disproportionately high prices. Queen Anne furniture increased in price by 350 percent between 1960 and 1972.

Chippendale was the next American style, as it was in England. In America, the Chippendale period ran from 1760 to 1790. The early price history of Chippendale is very much like that of American Queen Anne. By 1960 this style of furniture was at a level of 4 times what it had been in 1925, but only one-third more than it had been in 1929. The price of this furniture increased by slightly more than 100 percent between 1960 and 1972.

The finest Chippendale pieces are, however, enormously high in price. In 1966 the Parke-Bernet Galleries sold a Chippendale wing armchair made in Philadelphia for $24,000, a price comparable to a Queen Anne armchair. In the same year, the same gallery sold six Chippendale side chairs, with fairly elaborate splats and carvings and ball-and-claw feet, for $27,000. A single Chippendale chair of simple design can be purchased for less than $500. A set of eight such chairs might bring $15,000. An elaborate New York Chippendale chair was recently for sale at $950. A set of eight such chairs can bring $25,000. The larger the set, the higher the price; a single side chair is not worth a great deal.

Although the present prices of Chippendale furniture may be high, this is by no means a new phenomenon. On April 24, 1929, well before the October crash of the stock market, the most notable sale of American antiques of all time was held at the American Art Association Galleries in New York: the Howard Reifsnyder sale. A Philadelphia Chippendale "sample" side chair made by Benjamin Randolph brought $15,000. A Philadelphia wing armchair by Randolph reached a price of $33,000. Four other chairs in the same sale brought $7,200, $8,700, $5,200, and $9,500 respectively. In the same sale, a chest-on-chest made in Philadelphia in about 1770 with ogee feet, a broken-arch top, and a carved basket of flowers brought $26,100. In the sale was included what is known as the Van Pelt highboy, a very elaborate chest; it brought $44,000.

The next period in American furniture is *Hepplewhite,* from 1785 to 1800. This furniture increased in price by 150 percent between 1960 and 1972. Unusual items even in this period of antiques have brought some rather high prices. In early January 1930, well after the stock market crash, the Philip Flayderman sale was held at the American-Anderson Galleries in New York. As part of the sale, there was offered an important tambour inlaid secretary made by the great maker named John Seymour about 1790; it brought $30,000. It probably would not achieve this price at auction today. In 1966 Parke-Bernet sold an inlaid mahogany tambour secretary (c. 1800) by John Seymour for $4,000 and a mahogany tester bedstead attributed to John Goddard for $5,250. However, lesser items brought lesser sums, just as they did even in the Flayderman sale in 1930, and these ultrafine pieces do not measure the market for Hepplewhite furniture. In 1972 a good sideboard with a serpentine shape might bring $2,500. A Pembroke table will be priced at $1,500. A bowfront chest may be priced at $2,000 or less, even if in light wood and inlaid, which is preferred. Lesser bureaus or chests can bring less than $1,000.

American Sheraton furniture has also moved rather unspectacularly in price since the base year of 1925. By early 1972 the price level was 2½ times the 1960 level, for a price rise of about the same magnitude as the American Hepplewhite increase.

In the summer of 1970, an excellent Salem, Massachusetts, Pembroke table, a small table with a shaped leaf on each side and with reeded legs, sold at the Weschler auction in Washington for $250, but the low price reflected the poor times. The table should now bring well over $1,000. A pair of American Sheraton chairs should bring about $1,500 to $2,000 for the pair, and large sets should bring more per chair. Sheraton side chairs are some of the most graceful and beautiful of all side chairs but are generally not elaborate in style. A drop-leaf breakfast table should bring about $2,000 on the present market; a worktable, about $1,000; a medium-sized dining table, about $2,500; and a sideboard, about $2,500. A sofa might bring $1,200, as sofas in almost all styles of antique furniture are not much in demand. In contrast, at the Flayderman sale of 1930 a good Sheraton sofa brought $6,000, a very high price.

A variation of American Sheraton furniture is *Duncan Phyfe* furniture, with its fine flat carving and reedings on legs and front rails. This furniture was the rage in the 1920s but has never reassumed the preeminent position it held at that time. Nonetheless, the price of this furniture tripled between 1960 and 1972.

Duncan Phyfe furniture does not appear on the market in any volume, and it is felt that dealers are quietly buying and stockpiling it in anticipation of a rise in price, which appears to be likely. A pair of lyre-back armchairs will bring $10,000 on the present market; so will a carved mahogany window seat, a typical Duncan Phyfe piece. A carved and inlaid card table will bring about $2,500, and a breakfast table about the same price; a sofa will bring about $3,000.

To summarize, all American furniture combined showed a rise in price of 175 percent between 1960 and 1972, which was just about the rise in antique furniture in general. American Queen Anne rose the most (350 percent), followed by Duncan Phyfe with a rise of 200 percent. The remainder rose less than the average for all American and for all antiques, regardless of origin or period.

Victorian

Victorian furniture, which was made from about 1830 to about 1900, roughly paralleled the reign of Queen Victoria (1837–1901) and is considered in a category of its own. It had never been the object of collecting by antique hunters and has never achieved great levels in price; however, there is definitely a growing interest in all things Victorian. Currently, Victorian is plentiful in both the United States and England.

Fifteen years ago, simple Victorian chairs could be purchased for $20 and settees for $75. Finer pieces of American Victorian furniture, made perhaps by the Belter factory in New York, would bring around $100. Fine tables of various sorts might bring $50. Today, simple Victorian pieces may bring $75 to $100 per chair; sofas, $150; and tables, $150. The finer Belter pieces and English Victorian pieces may bring upward of $1,500 apiece, particularly those with elaborate carvings. The percentage of price increase in the past decade or decade and a half has been great, but still no large sums of money are involved in the purchase of Victorian furniture. It can be expected, however, that as other antiques go up in price, demand will turn to Victorian pieces, particularly Belter pieces and fine copies of French, Louis XV pieces.

HOW TO PURCHASE ANTIQUE FURNITURE

The most reliable way to determine the values and the changes in values of antique furniture is to review the auction catalogs of the major auction houses. In most cases only they offer illustrations and publish prices received so that market price and market trends can be determined. These houses are Sotheby, Parke-Bernet New York; Sotheby's in London; and Christie's in London. A number of art and other libraries have sets of these catalogs, and they are available for inspection at the auction houses themselves. An individual can subscribe to only the furniture catalogs, the painting catalogs, or any other series of catalogs for the season covering a particular group of antiques or antiquities.

All auctions have displays in advance of sales, and bids can be left if the purchaser cannot be present in person. In addition to the above auction houses, the following houses handle sales of antiques in New York regularly:

Plaza Art Galleries, Inc.
Coleman Auction Galleries
P.B. 84 (Parke-Bernet's lower-priced auction gallery)
Manhattan Galleries
William J. Fischer, Inc.
Astor Galleries

Lubin Galleries
Lawner's Auctioneers
Cathedral Galleries
Tepper Galleries

Almost every medium-size and larger city in the United States has an auction house or a firm that auctions. O. Rundle Gilbert of Garrison, New York, conducts auction sales in the entire out-of-town New York area. In Philadelphia the Freeman Galleries handle a large volume of business, as do C. G. Sloan and the Weschler Galleries in Washington. Telephone books in each city generally list auction houses.

In addition, there is hardly a city in the country that does not have at least one antique dealer. It might appear that auction houses are the only place in which to buy antiques because they are a major source of merchandise for dealers, who must secure a markup on the items they buy at auction. Dealers should, however, always be visited, since they purchase privately, and their sales are not as subject to the intense competition that one finds at many auctions. Also, dealers, to some degree, provide a measure of authenticity or guarantee of what they sell. They generally do not like to be put in the position of selling someone a nonantique as a genuine antique, thus making themselves subject to suit. Then, too, dealers will usually take back an unwanted item, regardless of why it is unwanted, and allow the purchase price to be applied to another purchase. An auction house will generally not refund the money unless the catalog made a gross misstatement, which the buyer must demonstrate. The recourse of the auction buyer is simply to put the item back in the next auction and gamble that his or her loss will not be too great.

At the present time, England, including its smaller cities and towns, is the place to purchase English antiques. English dealers have plenty of antiques for sale, and in the past few years their sales have not been good. In the same way, Paris is now offering many fine antiques at not-too-high prices. American dealers and private buyers have not been shopping the English and French dealers, as they had prior to the recession of 1970. Now might be a good time to buy antiques, as these overstocks may not prevail.

There are a number of sources of information on antique furniture and other antiques. One of the best listings of books on antiques is by the Mid-America Book Company, Main Street, Leon, Iowa 50144. It is free.

The following list of books and brochures should be of help to you in learning about antiques and caring for them:

The Collector's Guide to Antique American Ceramics, Doubleday & Company, Inc.
The Collector's Guide to Antique American Glass, Doubleday & Company, Inc.
Helen Comstock, *The Concise Encyclopedia of American Antiques,* Hawthorn Books, Inc.
The Concise Encyclopedia of Antiques, compiled by *The Connoisseur*
Ralph and Terry Kovel, *The Complete Antiques Price List,* Crown Publishers, Inc.
Ralph and Terry Kovel, *Know Your Antiques,* Crown Publishers, Inc.
The Official Guide to Popular Antiques and Curios
Richard H. Rush, *Antiques as an Investment,* Prentice-Hall, Inc.
Richard H. Rush, *Investments You Can Live with and Enjoy,* Simon and Schuster Inc.
Philip Wilson, *The International Antiques Yearbook,* Walker & Co., New York

To learn how to care for your antiques, write to the American Association of State and Local History, 1315 Eighth Avenue South, Nashville, Tennessee 37203, for copies of these brochures (each is available at 50 cents):

No. 1 *Leather: Its Understanding and Care*

No. 2   *Caring for Your Collections: Textiles, China, Ceramics and Glass*
No. 5   *Storing Your Collections: Problems and Solutions*
No. 8   *Caring for Your Collections: Manuscripts and Related Material*
No. 9   *Safeguarding Works of Art: Transportation, Records and Insurance*
No. 10   *Caring for Your Collections: Conservation of Metals*
No. 40   *The Care of Antique Silver*
No. 47   *Caring for Clocks*
No. 50   *Insuring against Loss*

Finally, available periodicals include the following:

Antique Monthly, Box 440, Tuscaloosa, Alabama 35401; one year, twelve issues, $4

The Antique Trader, Dubuque, Iowa 52001; one year, fifty-two issues, $4

Antiques, 551 Fifth Avenue, New York, New York 10017; one year, twelve issues, $14; sample copy, $1.75

The Mid-Atlantic Antique Journal, P.O. Box 2092, Falls Church, Virginia 22042; one year, twenty-six issues, $4

Spinning Wheel, Exchange Place, Hanover, Pennsylvania 17331; one year, ten issues, $6; sample copy, 75 cents

Yankee, Yankee, Inc., Dublin, New Hampshire 03444; one year, twelve issues, $4; sample copy, 50 cents

SUMMARY

Antiques are as good an investment as many other strictly monetary investments. In the past decade antiques have tripled in value. The same cannot be said of a number of financial investments, including bonds and common stocks. Antiques have a further advantage: they look good in the home and are an advertisement of the owner's taste and wealth. Stocks and bonds do not have these advantages.

Antiques are not quite the investment that art is. In the past decade, art has increased a little more in value than have antiques, but art has had many more styles, artists, and individual pieces increase in value. In general, antiques have all marched steadily upward, but American realistic art, for example, has boomed since 1965; no style of antique furniture had equaled this boom.

Then, again, antiques do not provide any income (they furnish neither dividends nor interest), so that both art and antiques must, in a sense, be considered "dead" assets. They form the equity portion of one's investment portfolio, not the fixed-dollar-return portion, and without income-producing assets anyone's portfolio is deficient.

The market for stocks and bonds is immediate; the market for antiques is not. Neither is the market for art immediate. Sales of both art and antiques are usually possible only through public auction, and while auction prices for both art and antiques have been rising, and rising rapidly, there is no fixed or relatively fixed market price for anyone's work of art, and the price of a particular item when sold might be far from what is anticipated or needed by the owner. One should be able to determine the range in price for a particular item, however.

Finally, a disadvantage of antique furniture as an investment is that it is not an entirely trouble-free investment. Antiques must be repaired periodically; they are costly to move by truck and sometimes must be stored, which also is costly. Insurance is expensive on art and antiques. Proper humidity must be maintained to preserve them. The fact remains, however, that many antiques are beautiful, and some are, in fact, works of art that enrich one's home and one's life immeasurably.

Chapter 39
Scotch Whiskey

MAURICE L. SCHOENWALD

Scotch whiskey becomes more desirable and usually more valuable with age. It is not unique in this respect. Some wines, cheeses, and even meats improve with age. However, Scotch whiskey is different from wheat, cotton, diamonds, silver, gold, or pork bellies because these items are not affected by the aging process and can increase in price only from scarcity or inflation. Scotch receipts are not contracts or futures (see Chapter 32 for an explanation of these concepts).

Scotch investors buy existing barrels of Scotch whiskey in Her Majesty's bonded warehouses in Scotland and maintain title while the whiskey ages and changes intrinsically. When it is suitably aged and market conditions are appropriate, the whiskey still in Her Majesty's warehouse is sold to rectifiers or bottlers through a broker, it is hoped for a profit. It has always been necessary for the Scotch whiskey industry in Great Britain to finance a part of its inventory by selling the new fillings to individuals with capital and then to buy the whiskey back when it is suitably aged and salable. The whiskey industry in this respect has a unique problem. Probably even the giant International Business Machines Corporation would find it difficult to maintain and supply the capital to build and support a four-year inventory, but the whiskey industry must do more because of the aging requirements; a seven- to nine-year reserve of whiskey is normal.

Normal Investment

Investing in Scotch means purchasing warehouse receipts. Each receipt signifies that a certain type and quantity of whiskey is in the warehouse in Great Britain. In the traditional situation the investor purchases new fillings and holds them for at least three years and usually for four years. Some whiskeys are aged for ten, eleven, or twelve years or even longer. Trading units are about $2,500 each. Smaller units exist, but they are loaded with extra costs and are not profitable for the investor. During its four-year normal aging period, Scotch whiskey has often doubled in value. Of course, part of these profits is consumed by storage, insurance, and commissions.

At the end of the aging period, investors may sell warehouse receipts through a broker. However, if prices are strong, they may in a suitable market trade their holdings of aged whiskey for new zero-age whiskey of a greater quantity.

It would be nice if the relationship between old whiskey and new whiskey remained stable. But there are cycles in whiskey prices, and these cycles have made the purchase of Scotch whiskey a risky investment. Zero-age (new) grain Scotch, also known as new fillings, has on occasion increased in value by 400 percent or more in four years or decreased in value by 50 percent in the same period. It is said that one needs a strong wheelbarrow to carry whiskey; that is, investors should be able to afford to maintain their investments during adverse market conditions. Price depressions for mature goods have extended from 1968 to 1976.

Price Cycles and Market Developments

There have been two major cycles in the last twenty-five years. Production of Scotch whiskeys stopped during World War II, when facilities were converted to military use. The small carry-over of prewar production was insufficient to meet immediate postwar needs, which resulted in postwar shortages and a limited supply for a number of years. Between 1950 and 1957 consumption doubled. A limited supply of mature whiskey, combined with a quickly rising demand, pushed prices to abnormal heights. In 1956, for example, four-year-old grain prices reached a high of $8.40 per gallon, rising from $5.88 per gallon in the previous year (see Table 39-1). By 1959 prices receded and returned to more normal levels because greater production developed: four-year-old whiskey, for example, then sold at $4.48.

Early in the 1960s there developed a substantial trend toward the importing of bulk quantities of Scotch whiskey for bottling and labeling in the United States. Bottled Scotch imports in 1967 amounted to 28.1 million gallons; bulk imports were 9.3 million gallons. The five-year gain for bulk was 336 percent; the five-year gain for bottled Scotch, 30 percent. A great increase in wholesale prices developed during 1964–1965 because bulk importers, many of them not previously in the whiskey-importing business, began to bid strongly for supplies. In 1964 four-year old grain reached $5.60. Persons who had purchased that whiskey in 1960 had paid $1.40 for it. This high price encouraged the high level of production in 1965 and 1966.

The author believes that the cause for the price increase lay in the United States tariff regulations. Importing whiskey in bulk from the United Kingdom and rectifying, changing the proof, and bottling it in the United States resulted in substantial savings in import duties. The new bulk importers entered the market to exploit the tariff advantages and competed for goods with established bottlers. The established bottlers did not expect to lose their share of the market. There was a continuously growing market, and both groups assumed that they would control a large portion of it. The traditional bottlers and speculators overestimated their share of the growth and purchased too much, causing excess production during 1964–1965.

The result of the increased production was aggravated by a major credit squeeze in the United Kingdom from 1966 to 1968. A depression in prices of all ages of Scotch became significant during 1967 and 1968. The decline was accentuated by the fact that substantial volumes of whiskey were held on a margin basis, particularly in Switzerland. The decline in prices was intensified when Swiss stocks were forced on the market by the calling of margin. In 1969 and 1970 four-year-old Scotch began to have modest price increases as production declined. However, the price of four-year-old Scotch from 1967 to 1976 was lower than in any other period during the past twenty years. Overproduction in the mid 1960s has been the principal reason for the extended price decline.

In 1971 new grain was selling at comparatively low prices, and partially aged grain, which was in surplus, was selling at extremely low prices. In anticipation of a sharp increase in prices in the mid-1970s (due to a cutback in production in the late 1960s), some investors recommended purchasing partially aged grain and holding it for three or four additional years, hoping for an increase in the price of all Scotch whiskey of all ages. In this type of investment the Scotch does not increase in value intrinsically. Instead, the investors are depending on supply-and-demand changes to increase the price. Buying partially aged Scotch in this manner is an unorthodox and speculative venture, but it points out some of the possible investment opportunities that exist for investors in Scotch whiskey.

TABLE 39-1   Average Annual Prices of an Original Proof Gallon of Grain Scotch Whiskey, 1954–1972

Year	Zero-age	Four-year	Eight-year	Twelve-year
1954	$1.33	$5.88	$ 9.10	$11.83
1955	1.33	5.88	9.10	11.83
1956	1.75	8.40	10.36	13.46
1957	2.52	8.40	10.36	13.46
1958	3.22	5.72	10.36	13.46
1959	1.54	4.48	9.10	11.83
1960	1.40	4.20	7.56	9.82
1961	1.40	3.36	7.56	10.10
1962	1.68	3.43	7.56	10.10
1963	1.75	4.13	8.40	11.34
1964	1.89	5.60	10.36	13.98
1965	1.43	3.64	8.40	10.80
1966	1.40	3.15	7.56	11.34
1967	.98	1.26	3.76	6.00
1968	1.02	1.17	2.88	6.00
1969	1.08	1.47	4.26	6.00
1970	1.14	1.50	4.44	7.00
1971	1.15	1.10	2.40	9.00
1972	1.30	1.35	1.35	7.80
1973	1.56	1.56	1.39	1.86
1974	1.92	1.63	1.32	1.86
1975	2.16	1.31	1.21	1.12
1976	2.13	1.11	1.07	.96

Characteristics of the Commodity

Grain Scotch whiskeys are a neutral spirit; there are usually no important qualitative differences. Hence, traders need no special knowledge of the differences. Dealing in grain whiskey is similar to buying and selling cotton: it is not earmarked at this stage for pillowcases, sheets, or particular brands or labels. Most blenders consider grain whiskeys interchangeable; therefore, grain whiskeys could appear under any label of a blended whiskey.

Malt whiskeys are the source of taste in whiskey. Of the Scotch whiskey purchased at retail, 95 percent or more is a blend of grain and malt whiskey, while approximately 5 percent is pure malt. The proportion of malt in blends varies from 60 to 15 percent. Malts vary in quality. Zero-age malts can run from $1.92 to $2.64 or more per gallon. Some of the best malts are Glenfarclas, Smith's Glenlivet, and Glenfiddich.

The proportion of malts to grain in blends has been consistently *dropping*, giving rise to lighter whiskeys. This trend should continue to increase the demand for grain and decrease the demand for the more expensive, less required malt. Trading in malt because of variety in price differences requires sophistication and is not recommended for inexperienced investors.

There are huge qualitative differences among the more than 100 different malts, and consequently any form of meaningful price listings for malt is almost impossible. Investors in malts may be badly deceived unless they are aware of these qualitative distinctions. No regulatory system could effectively cope with this problem because of the unstructured nature of the industry and the large number of items involved. Therefore, when investing in malts, investors must achieve a high level of personal sophistication about the quality of the malts.

Investors should virtually never invest in a blend of whiskey, because it is extremely difficult to ascertain the quality of the blend. Furthermore, there is no readily available market for the resale of blended whiskey.

Investment Criteria

Scotch whiskey is traded in British sterling, and a rise or fall in the value of the pound will cause a concurrent increase or decrease in the value of the whiskey. The other factor that will affect prices is the supply of whiskey. For example, if production has been down, prices should ultimately rise.

Registration and Possible Fraud

Some United States brokers had believed for years that Scotch whiskey was a simple commodity and not subject to registration with the Securities and Exchange Commission (SEC). For a time the SEC accepted this view, and the broker of barrels of Scotch whiskey could obtain, in a proper case, a letter from the SEC that was in effect an exemption from registration and was characterized as a "no action" letter. Beginning in 1969 the SEC expressed the view that the sale of Scotch whiskey was subject to registration as a security. In 1973 it instituted proceedings against a number of firms to compel them to treat Scotch whiskey as an investment. The SEC was successful in these proceedings. Investors should not purchase Scotch whiskey until they have read the appropriate prospectus.

Insurance

A broker can easily arrange insurance for the investor in order to protect against (1) fire loss (at a cost of approximately ½ percent of value per annum); or (2) "all risks," including fire, except atomic radiation (at approximately ⅞ percent per annum). All-risks insurance includes insurance against excess evaporation.

Commissions and Storage

Various commissions are charged, and they are not regulated. Some brokers charge a straight 5 percent from the buyer or seller, while others charge a fixed cost per gallon. However, in some cases the commission is not shown but is buried in the price.

During the aging process, whiskey is stored in bonded warehouses licensed by the British Board of Customs and Excise. A resident customs officer at each warehouse checks each cask into and out of storage. He also takes periodic dippings to verify the alcohol content. Very strict security precautions, prescribed by the government, are maintained. The investor must pay all storage charges when they are due, and failure to pay these charges entitles the warehouse to place a lien on the owner's whiskey.

Scotch as Money for International Transfers

There were exceptional situations as in World War II, when Scotch whiskey was purchased and used by Americans as a form of currency. During the war, when Great Britain placed restrictions on the removal of currency from the United Kingdom, entities such as motion picture production companies used their earnings in the United Kingdom to purchase whiskey. They then exported the whiskey to the United States and sold it for United States dollars.

Scotch whiskey is still interesting from that point of view because it is imported into almost every country in the world. An owner of Scotch whiskey can probably convert it into local currency almost anywhere. In this respect, the ownership of Scotch whiskey has some resemblance to the ownership of silver, bullion, or diamonds.

Evaporation

The normal amount of evaporation over a four-year maturing period is approximately 11 percent (5 percent in the first year and 2 percent each year thereafter). When whiskey is purchased or sold, it is priced in terms of original proof gallons (OPG). Evaporation is assumed by the purchaser, and no deduction for evaporation need be made. The purchaser of any four-year-old whiskey assumes that a barrel contains 11 percent less whiskey than when filled. Evaporation therefore is not a concern in the price structure: the purchaser pays the going price per "evaporated gallon." Excess evaporation is covered by all-risks insurance, but claims for excessive evaporation are rare. However, if the investor holds the whiskey beyond the normal period of maturation, the risk of evaporation increases.

Taxes

Whiskey warehouses receipts in the hands of an investor are capital items and, as such, are subject to capital gain or loss treatment and are not taxable as ordinary income or loss. To be treated as a long-term capital item, the whiskey must be held for more than six months.

Section 4911 of the United States Internal Revenue Code imposes an interest equalization tax on securities. A purchase of whiskey by an American citizen is not subject to the interest equalization tax, because it is an acquisition other than a stock or a debt obligation.

American citizens residing in the United States are not subject to British taxes on these transactions. Insurance and storage when paid annually are deductible expenses. Expenses are deducted from the investor's ordinary income, while profits or losses on the sale are treated as capital items for tax purposes.

Sources of Market Data

Accrued Equities, Inc., 380 Lexington Ave., New York, N.Y., an active United States broker since 1960, periodically distributes a *Memorandum to Scotch Whiskey Investors* to its customers. Other brokers distribute market letters, but this is the only regularly distributed report of its kind in the United States. The *Memorandum* reports prices, market conditions, production data, and comments on other published reports from trade publications and brokers and makes its recommendations as to the purchase and sale of different ages of whiskey at different periods.

Harpers Wine and Spirit Gazette, Harpers Trade Journal, Ltd., 22 Cousin Lane, London, E.C. 4, reports on the industry, giving sources of price data or banks and brokers specializing in this trade. Lists of competing brokers appear in *Harpers;* about twenty competing brokers are listed.

Summary

The price history of Scotch whiskey portrays a commodity that offers a potentially high return for investors who are willing to accept the risk. Purchasers who are alert to production and consumption figures or who use a sophisticated broker can realize substantial earnings on a partially tax-sheltered basis. The only taxes are on the basis of long-term capital gains when received.

Whiskey should be of some interest to a migrant or to a resident of a country whose economics or currency or politics is or may be in trouble, since the whiskey is stored in the United Kingdom, a comparatively stable country. It is not an investment for those who need a quick turnover or fast speculative profits or a high degree of liquidity. However, an intelligent investment program can provide significant long-term profits.

BIBLIOGRAPHY

Business Week, New York, Feb. 17, 1973.

Daiches, David: *Scotch Whiskey: Its Past and Present,* The Macmillan Company, New York, 1969.

Market for New Fillings, Invergordon Distillers, Ashley House, 181–195 West George Street, Glasgow, Scotland, 1972.

National Association of Alcoholic Beverages Importers, Inc., *Annual Statistical Report,* 1025 Vermont Avenue, N.W., Washington, D.C. 20005, 1972.

The National Observer, Silver Spring, Md., March 1973.

"Personal Investment," *Fortune,* June 1964 (describing a normal period prior to the 1967 price drop).

Scotch Whiskey Report, Roger Mortimer & Co., 241 Salisbury House, London, E.C.2, England, 1972.

"Staggering Profits in Scotch," *Moneysworth,* May 29, 1972.

World Whiskey Market, Economic Associates, 34 Applebrooks, London, W.1, England, 1965–1976.

Chapter **40**

Investment in Rare Coins

STANLEY APFELBAUM

BACKGROUND

An increasing number of investors are entering the market for rare coins, and it is estimated that more than 8 million people in the United States now own, collect, or invest in rare coins. In 1950 perhaps only 250,000 people were interested in rare coins, and yet by 1985 the numismatic world is expected to comprise about 25 million persons.

The trend to coin investment is helped by modern methods of communication designed to meet the needs of investor-collectors; teletype services, weekly and monthly newspapers, and magazines are examples. Events such as numerous coin conventions and frequent auction sales of famous collections of coins are additional factors promoting interest. All these make a tremendous contribution to the spread of knowledge for those seeking information about price, rarity, and availability, and they tend to bring many new people into the field.

Coin collecting as a cultural hobby has been practiced for almost 2,000 years. Interest in coins is derived from man's natural appreciation of history, art, fine metalwork, and the intrinsic value concentrated in small desirable objects, to mention but a few of the more obvious attractions. Coin collectors have probably always been aware of the investment potential of their acquisitions. Now, however, with the continued acceleration of the coin market, this investment potential has become more apparent. As the interest and demand grow for coins, which are forever limited by the number issued in any one year, prices tend to rise.

A recently observed trend is the dramatically increasing number of *investors* (as distinguished from *collectors*) who are buying rare coins purely for appreciation and protection against every form of paper money debasement and devaluation.

Coin Information Sources

Weekly coin newspapers allow the investor to follow trends that are developing in the coin markets. In addition, you should find a reputable dealer who can provide you with good suggestions as to the future trend of prices of rare coins. However, you must be cautious with dealers who wish to sell you a coin or coins from their current inventories. If such an inventory is not large, dynamic, and of good quality, the limited choice possibly will inhibit your future profits.

You may choose to specialize in particular areas of numismatic investment. Reference works are available. For example, the popular collection and investment in United States silver dollars now has a new reference work, *The Comprehensive Catalogue and Encyclopedia of U.S. Morgan and Peace Silver Dollars,* that has been called second to none. This book contains information sufficient for the intelligent placement of funds in a highly specialized series of United States coins.

The Coin Market Versus the Stock Market

There are interesting similarities between investment in rare coins and the over-the-counter stock market, which is a true negotiated market, unlike the listed exchanges, which are primarily auction markets. One of the first similarities to be noted is the fact that rare coins are valued at a wholesale bid-and-asked basis. The national rare coin teletype system now numbers almost 200 dealers and makes quotations of rare coin prices readily available. Another similarity is the investor's opportunity to invest in multiple areas, the spectrum of investment reaching from the most speculative to the blue chip, from the $10 coin to the $100,000 coin, the contemporary brilliant uncirculated (BU) rolls of coins, and the superrare gold coins of extremely low mintage.

Among the many areas for investment in numismatics are United States gold coins, United States type coins (the collecting of one of each major type of coin minted by the United States since 1793), silver dollars, BU rolls, paper money, pattern coins, coin series (the complete series of Indian head cents, for example), coins minted at particular mints (such as the former United States mint at Carson City, Nevada), colonial coins, and Continental currency.

COIN VALUES

The three major factors that affect the price of a rare coin are the quality (condition) of the coin, the supply of the coin, and the coin's historical significance and attractiveness.

Quality of the Coin

The condition of the coin, which is often designated by its grading, is the most important factor in determining the coin's value. The value of a rare coin could often increase by as much as 100 percent if it were only one grade higher. It is unfortunate that there is no recognized uniform system of grading. However, there are generally accepted and workable vocabularies, albeit with minor variations.

The investor should own a grading guide. A standard volume by Martin R. Brown and John W. Dunn is *A Guide to the Grading of United States Coins. A Guide Book of United States Coins,* commonly called the "Red Book," sets forth a condensed grading guide that can be used to evaluate the condition of a rare coin, as shown in Table 40-1. This guide can be utilized by the unsophisticated collector but *never by either the investor or the dealer,* who must have a much more complex means of determining grades that fall just above and just below the grades listed in the table.

A grading practice to be aware of is that some unscrupulous dealers in coins continually handle "overgraded" material that is invariably advertised at cut-rate prices. The investor or collector should recognize that it would be impossible for material so priced to be anything but overgraded. It is the uninformed collector or investor who experiences the heartache and disappointment of great monetary loss when his or her portfolio is offered for sale and found to be overgraded.

Number of Coins

The second most important factor in determining a coin's value is the number of the particular coin that is available. A scarce coin will have a higher value than one that is more readily obtainable. For example, if one simply reviews United States proof set sales from 1936 to 1964, shown in Table 40-2, it is apparent that

TABLE 40-1   Red Book Grading System

Grade		Description
PF.	Proof	Coin with a mirrorlike surface, specially struck for coin collectors.
UNC.	Uncirculated	New. Regular mint striking, but never placed in circulation.
EX. FINE	Extremely fine	Slightly circulated, with some luster but faint evidence of wear.
V. FINE	Very fine	Shows enough wear on high spots to be noticeable. Still retains enough luster to be desirable.
F.	Fine	Obviously a circulated coin, but little wear. Mint luster gone. All letters and mottoes clear.
V.G.	Very good	Features clear and bold. Better than good, but not quite fine.
G.	Good	All of design, every feature, and legend must be plain, and date clear.
FAIR	Fair	Coin has sufficient design and letters to be easily identified. Excessive wear.

the sets that increased the most in value were the ones of which the fewest numbers were sold. Table 40-2 shows each year in which the United States government produced proof sets, together with their current values and the number of sets sold. As an illustration, note that in 1958 fewer sets were sold than in 1957 or 1959 and that, consequently, the price of a 1958 set is significantly above that of a 1957 or a 1959 set.

Another example of how the quantity of coins produced can affect the price of a coin can be seen when one evaluates the prices of uncirculated $3 gold pieces, shown in Table 40-3.

In 1933 by Presidential directive all citizens were required to return gold coins to the Treasury Department for remelting. However, there were certain loopholes in the request, unknown to most people. Because of these loopholes, collectible gold coins exist today. The value increases in the coins that were hoarded have been fantastic. An uncirculated $3 gold piece that could have been purchased from a collector in 1944 for $15 to $20 or in 1960 for $150 to $175, for example, sold in 1972 for about $850, and in 1976 for $2500.

Historical Significance

The third factor that affects the price of a coin is its historical significance and attractiveness. For example, a coin of beautiful design minted during the Civil War, will tend to be more valuable than a coin minted in the 1880s and showing a conventional home. However, this factor is considerably less important than the quality and supply of the coin.

HOW TO BUY AND SELL RARE COINS

The commonest question asked the coin adviser is: "When and to whom may I sell my rare coins when I desire to liquidate my investment?" The rare coin market has never been, and probably never will be, as liquid as the stock market. In the stock market investments may be liquidated even though the "bottom is dropping out."

TABLE 40-2   United States Proof Set Sales, 1936–1964

Year minted	Sets sold	Original price	1976 value
1936	3,837	$1.89	$1,475.00
1937	5,542	1.89	650.00
1938	8,045	1.89	320.00
1939	8,795	1.89	290.00
1940	11,246	1.89	210.00
1941	15,287	1.89	200.00
1942*	21,120	2.04	260.00
1950	51,386	2.10	170.00
1951	57,500	2.10	120.00
1952	81,980	2.10	75.00
1953	128,800	2.10	49.00
1954	233,300	2.10	25.00
1955	378,200	2.10	27.00
1956	669,384	2.10	11.00
1957	1,247,952	2.10	6.25
1958	875,652	2.10	11.00
1959	1,149,291	2.10	7.25
1960	1,691,602	2.10	6.25
1960	. . .†	2.10	20.00
1961	3,028,244	2.10	5.25
1962	3,218,019	2.10	5.25
1963	3,075,645	2.10	5.25
1964‡	3,950,762	2.10	5.50

*Sales discontinued during the remaining years of World War II and the early postwar years.
†Small date.
‡Last year of silver coinage.

In the rare coin market material may be liquidated at optimal value only if the sale is properly planned and presented through proper channels. Advantage will be taken of investors who attempt to dump their rare coin portfolios at a moment's notice.

Rare coins can be sold in the following five ways:

Rare Coin Auctions

The most highly recommended method of sale is a major auction. Here dealers and investors and collectors are pitted against each other to obtain material. The coins are cataloged by experts and pictured in words and photographs in a catalog meant to attract bidders. Taking into account the percentage for the auctioneer's services, it has been proved that realized prices upon auction are higher than prices obtainable by all other methods of sale. The only problem with this means of selling is that time is required for auction houses to present investors' material. These houses schedule four or five auctions per year at the most.

Coin Bourses or Conventions

National and local groups of coin dealers and collectors gather at coin conventions to trade information and coins and to provide bourses, where dealers from all over the United States can set up tables to exhibit and buy and sell their wares. At these conventions, rare coins of almost any quantity or value can be offered to an array of dealers for their bids. The material, of course, goes to the highest bidder. These conventions are usually attended by 50 to 200 dealers, each of whom is most interested in purchasing new material for inventory.

Rare Coin Magazines and Newspapers

In the weekly newspapers published within the coin field and in magazines published on a monthly basis, sellers can advertise their material to solicit bids.

TABLE 40-3 $3 Gold Pieces

Date and mint*	Quantity minted	1964 price, uncirculated	1973 price, uncirculated
1854	138,618	$ 245.	$ 700
1854 (D)	1,120	2,100.	4,000
1855 (S)	6,600	275.	900
1858	2,133	600.	1,400
1863	5,039	300.	750.
1865	1,165	500.	1,100
1869	2,525	275.	775
1874	41,820	230.	700
1880	1,036	400.	850
1889	2,429	315.	800

*D = Dahlonega, Ga.; S = San Francisco.
SOURCE: Records kept by Rare Gold Management, a subsidiary of First Coinvestors, Inc.

They can either list the available material in the advertisements or request that those interested send for a list of material. Hundreds of thousands of readers are reached in this manner.

Teletype System

By utilizing the teletype system through dealers who subscribe to it, sellers may offer their material to those on the system; sellers pay a fee for the service. The dealer will make a list of the material to be offered, publish it on the teletype machine, and take a commission as each piece is sold. The thing to guard against here is to employ a dealer who merely has "access" to the system; instead, sellers should utilize only dealers who actually have the teletype machines on their premises.

Coin Dealers

Nearly every town in the United States has coin dealers, but using the service of a dealer is by far the poorest way to liquidate one's investment. The investment is offered to a dealer whose capital is not known, whose interests may not coincide with those of the seller, and who may very well try to take full advantage of the fact that he or she is the only coin dealer in the area. This method should be avoided unless the dealer is well known for integrity and fair dealing in general.

Rare coins can be purchased through the same five sources through which they are sold. Once again, investors must exercise caution to avoid paying an excessive price for coins. They should carefully research their investment and pay only the going price of the coins.

COUNTERFEIT COINS

Fakers abound in every field of endeavor, whether it be medicine, the law, art, or the sciences. Certainly there are counterfeiters who try to swindle the unwary in the rare coin field, just as there are those who sell fake stocks or bonds. It therefore cannot be stressed too much that one must deal with a reliable purveyor of rare coins. The victims of counterfeiters in any field are invariably the greedy, the gullible, and the ignorant.

With the recent tremendous increase in the value of rare coins, old-fashioned counterfeit pieces that were crude and easily recognizable have given way to counterfeit coins that are difficult to recognize. Investors must be aware that fakes exist, but the occurrence of such coins should not be a reason to denigrate the entire rare coin investment area.

A counterfeit coin will always exhibit one or more flaws that the student of the particular series can spot. For example, the milling or reeding on the edge of a fake coin is seldom comparable to the original. The weight of a coin is a significant indication of authenticity. The entire appearance of a coin can also be an important way of determining if it is good. One should spend time noting the features of the original engraving and determine whether the questionable coin is in proper relief.

The Secret Service of the United States Treasury Department continually attempts to eliminate the counterfeiting or forging of American coins. Frequently, forged coins that enter the United States are brought by ignorant or greedy American citizens who have purchased them in foreign countries at bargain basement prices in the expectation of making a killing. If you are abroad, don't be lured into the same trap; otherwise you will probably suffer a financial loss.

WORLD EVENTS

The debasement of money and the introduction of fiat money usually begins slowly. This has been true historically and is even true for the United States. In 1964 the federal government claimed that silver coins would circulate together with cupronickel coins "for the forseeable future"; within approximately nine months all silver coins had disappeared. Today's young children may never see a silver coin unless it is produced by a coin collector, dealer, or investor.

For more than forty years the United States has been using "goldless" money. But the death of gold and silver coins is not yet accomplished. The governments of the world continue to ask or dictate that their citizens accept debased monies on an ever-increasing scale. But as citizens find that they can buy less with the moneys they have, they have begun to purchase more and more gold. And the return of interest to gold coins is echoed in the interest in rare coins in any metal.

In the light of these events and the mintage figures of rare coins produced by the United States as recorded in the Red Book, is it surprising that prices of rare coins increase at an average rate of twice the inflationary trend of the country?

SUMMARY

In summing up, we shall use a single illustration. Often we are asked: "The price of a silver trade dollar has risen, over the last few years, from $65 to $145. Why should we invest at the top of the market?" But consider that the original total mintage of these pieces was low, their average age is many years, their availability is about 10 percent of their original mintage, and, of that amount, only a very small percentage remains in the top grades. Is $145 too expensive for such a piece? Is $250, or $500?

In 1972 the average rare United States coin, taking into account ninety-four different series issued since 1793, rose by an average of 116 percent. Investing in coins may well offer one of the most profitable returns of any investment medium.

BIBLIOGRAPHY

Brown, Martin R., and John W. Dunn: *A Guide to the Grading of United States Coins,* 5th ed., illustrated, Western Publishing Company, Inc., Racine, Wis., 1969.

Forman, Harry J.: *How You Can Make Big Profits Investing in Coins,* Nummus Press, Flushing, N.Y., 1972.

Friedberg, Robert: *Gold Coins of the World,* 3d ed., Coin and Currency Institute, Inc., New York, N.Y., 1971.

Hoppe, Donald J.: *How to Invest in Gold Coins,* Arlington House, New Rochelle, N.Y., 1970.

Mallis, A. George, and Leroy Van Allen: *The Comprehensive Catalogue and Encyclopedia of U.S. Morgan and Peace Silver Dollars,* F.C.I. Press, Inc., Albertson, N.Y., 1976.

Money Talks, a numismatic anthology selected from *Calcoin News,* California State Numismatic Association, Hendricks Printing Company, Irvine, Calif., 1970.

Taxay, Don: *The U.S. Mint and Coinage,* Arco Publishing Company, Inc., New York, 1966.

Chapter 41
Stamps as an Investment

LEONA SELDOW

If you are contemplating an investment in stamps, proceed slowly; but if you enjoy the thrill of collecting, philately is a fascinating hobby that, if handled wisely, may lead to some increase in your investment. However, the possibility that you can protect yourself from the forces of inflation by investing in stamps is remote.

Books for the stamp collector[1] are replete with examples of tremendous gains to be made from an investment in particular stamps, but the mere fact that these examples are cited continually is an indication of the rarity of the occurrences. Edward J. Zegarowicz in his excellent book on the subject[2] tells of a collector who represented a syndicate of businessmen who paid $280,000, a record in the annals of stamp collecting, for a British Guiana 1856 1-cent magenta, a small octagon-shaped stamp that had been purchased by the seller in 1940 for $42,500. The gain was $237,500 over a period of thirty years. This particular purchase had fulfilled its purpose of serving as a hedge against inflation. The annual rate of return on a compound-interest basis was 6.3 percent before taxes, or 4.725 percent after a capital gains tax of 25 percent.

The rate of inflation during this period of time, based on the Consumer Price Index, was an average of 3.2 percent annually.[3] After taxes the investment in the magenta had bettered the inflation rate by 1.525 percent annually, and before taxes by 3.1 percent.

Determinants of Value: What Stamps to Buy

What should the hobbyist-investor look for when purchasing stamps? Just as the forces of supply and demand are what ultimately determine the value of other goods and services, so they do with stamps. The object is to ferret out the issues

[1]Two are Bill Gunston, *The Philatelist's Companion,* David & Charles, North Pomfret, Vt., 1975; and Kenneth R. Lake, *Stamps for Investment,* Stein and Day Incorporated, New York, 1971.

[2]Edward J. Zegarowicz with George Sullivan, *Stamps as an Investment,* Walker & Co., New York, 1971.

[3]The Consumer Price Index in 1941 was 44.1. It had risen to 116.3 by 1970 (1967 = 100). *Federal Reserve Bulletin,* May 1974, p. 59.

that, in the investor's opinion, will increase in value over a period of time because the demand for a given stamp will rise while the supply remains stationary or declines. There is a tendency for the existing supply of any issue to decline as the stamps may be used for postage and subsequently be destroyed, are hoarded by persons who will never part with them, or are in the possession of people who do not know how to care for them properly. The mishandling by the last-named group combined with incorrect storage practices can render stamps worthless.

In addition to scarcity, other criteria of value are the condition of the stamp, the shades of color, how well the design is centered, how the stamp is gummed, how it is canceled (lightly is best), and whether it is in mint or unused condition. "Mint" and "unused" are not synonymous terms. An unused stamp is a stamp that has not been used for postage but is not in perfect condition, while a stamp in mint condition is one that is in almost the same perfect condition in which it was when it was printed.

One of the country's leading stamp dealers[4] has set up four different classifications to describe the condition of stamps: (1) *superb,* a perfect stamp in the finest possible condition; (2) *very fine,* an above-average stamp in excellent condition; (3) *fine,* an attractive premium copy; and (4) *good,* a stamp in average condition, an item that may be off center or be somewhat heavily canceled but is undamaged.

In addition to the factors indicated above, the future worth of a particular stamp is determined in part by its appeal to collectors. To meet this test, the design of the stamp should be interesting, easily understood, and attractive to the eye.

The prudent investor is well advised to purchase carefully chosen, *single, expensive*[5] items, which will have a tendency to appreciate more rapidly with a greater degree of safety than will a multitude of smaller, cheaper items.

The country of origin affects the value of stamps in several ways. One of the most important influences on the stamp market is the popularity of collecting or investing within the country. Countries whose stamps are most often found in the top market brackets are generally those where collecting by both collectors and investors is enjoying a vogue, such as England and the United States. London and New York are the twin centers of the world's stamp market. Stamps of countries with a stable government and a sound currency will generally prove to be more valuable as an investment than those from countries where these conditions do not exist. The lack of stable governments and unsound money conditions in several South American countries has resulted in a sluggish market for their stamps. The stamps of Liechtenstein, Monaco, San Marino, and Vatican City, on the other hand, which are designed for the collectors' market, are suitable for investment. However, the stamps of some Eastern European countries, in which the cancellation is printed with the stamp, are likely to have little or no value to the investor.

The topic of a stamp may make it worth considering as an investment. A few topicals worthy of mention are stamps depicting the late President Kennedy, the late Martin Luther King, Jr., space exploration, and sports. Such stamps are likely to increase in value at a far greater rate than a similar stamp that carries the picture of a figure who is not internationally known.

Just as an investor in common stocks follows the stock market on a regular basis, so should the careful investor in stamps keep an eye on the stamp market week by week. The stamp collector should watch for indications of movement in the market for an issue before the collecting public creates a demand for a particular item.

[4]J. & H. Stolow of New York.
[5]Many owners of valuable collections are seldom interested in purchasing any item carrying a price tag less than $1,000.

What Not to Buy

Although United States commemoratives have no value for investment purposes, many people believe that they are a good investment and consequently purchase them for this purpose. But as great as is the number of people who collect them, the supply far exceeds the demand, for tens of millions of each issue are offered for sale.

There are countless stories of people who have diligently collected commemoratives through the years with the belief that the stamps would provide them with a much-sought-after hedge against inflation or furnish a nest egg for their heirs. However, when the "investor" attempted to liquidate or the heirs to sell at the time of the investor's death, they were shocked to find that the stamps would not bring even their face value. The post office will not redeem any stamps, and the only way that the face value could be realized would be for the stamps to be used as postage. The difficulty is that the principal users of large quantities of stamps generally use franking machines and consequently have little or no interest in stamps, for their use requires labor, a high-priced commodity in today's market. To compound the problem, stamps in a collection built over the years are of a smaller denomination than current first-class postal rates, and affixing such stamps to outgoing mail would require more labor than if stamps were purchased from the post office. Some direct-mail houses do use stamps rather than franking mail because they have found that their mail receives greater attention when stamps are affixed, but the additional labor required when using more than one stamp keeps them from acquiring any collector's stamps unless they are purchased at a discount. Large amounts of stamps must therefore be sold at a discount to realize any return *of* such an investment.[6] Obviously, there is no return *on* such an investment. There is actually a loss from two factors: (1) The money invested in the collection has produced no return through the years. (2) A careful collector will have paid insurance premiums to protect the collection from loss or damage by fortuitous events such as fire, water damage, theft, or burglary. Unfortunately, there is no way to protect the collection from loss in the marketplace.

Another area for the investor to avoid is stamps described by J. & H. Stolow as good. These may be creased, punched, heavily canceled, soiled or damaged in some way that makes the possibility of their increasing in value extremely doubtful if not impossible.

How to Buy Stamps

For the investor who does not wish to devote any time or effort to obtaining philatelic knowledge, it would be wise to cultivate an expert who can be trusted and permit such a person to buy and sell materials for him or her. If such an expert is not available, the uninformed collector-investor can benefit from the knowledge and experience of a reputable dealer. The dealer's prices, of course, include a percentage over the cost that the dealer pays to compensate for his or her expenses and profit. Because there are no standardized prices for stamps, it is wise to shop among various dealers. Under normal conditions, the prices charged by independent dealers will be slightly lower than those of stamp departments in department stores.[7]

---

[6]Mint sheets, adequately gummed, of United States issues, in quantities may be liquidated through the World Trade Corporation, Drawer 190, Evergreen, Colo. 80439, at a discount of from 10 to 15 percent.

[7]The American Stamp Dealers Association, 147 West 42d Street, New York, N.Y. 10036, has a list of dealers throughout the United States who are members of its organization.

Dealers who advertise in trade publications or elsewhere sometimes indicate in their advertisements that they will sell on approval. Such dealers are willing to forward, upon request, an assortment of stamps; stamps not meeting the needs or desires of the purchaser may be returned. This practice permits dealing with suppliers away from a collector-investor's home base and yet allows him or her the luxury of inspecting before buying. However, doing business in this fashion is costly, for it involves increased expenses for advertising, postage, and the losses involved for materials not returned as promised. Consequently, the prices charged may be satisfactory for collectors but are not advisable for investors. Normally the prices are so high that the possibility of any potential profit is negligible.

When the stamp collector-investor acquires some knowledge, he or she may be ready to use classified advertisements in the columns of philatelic trade publications, where offers of items may be found at worthwhile prices. Similar advertisements can also be found in many daily and Sunday newpapers, as in the Arts and Leisure section of the Sunday edition of *The New York Times.* These advertisements sometimes make it possible to develop contacts in faraway places that can be used to fill particular stamp needs. However, the investor should bear in mind that classified columns are generally not a stable source of supply and are better suited to the needs of the collector.

Still another source of supply is the auction. But the auction market is only for those with a sound knowledge of philately. The auction too is better suited to fill the needs of the collector than those of the investor.

To purchase a large number of stamps of any new issue, it is advisable to get in touch with the postal authorities of the issuing nation, who will accept international postal money orders in payment for such purchases.

Zegarowicz[8] points out in his book that arbitrage is common and often worthwhile for the investor, for by comparing United States catalog prices with prices in catalogs published in a stamp's country of origin, it is often possible to find a sleeper. He tells of a particular German stamp listed in *Scott's Standard Postage Stamp Catalog* at 42 cents, whereas *Michel Briesmarkenkatalog Europa,* published in West Germany and therefore a better reference work on German stamps, priced the stamp at 90 cents. Obviously, such a stamp would be a worthwhile item for an investor.

Since the early 1970s, the philatelic broker has become important. Such a person functions as an investment specialist in much the same way that a stock broker buys and sells marketable securities. Stamp brokers operate in several different ways. Some make lump-sum purchases, while others will agree to purchase as little as $10 worth of stamps monthly for their clients, with the understanding that the agreement may be canceled at will. Milton K. Ozaki is the best-known and largest of the philatelic brokers in the United States.[9]

Finally, an investor might decide on stamps that he or she believes are a sound investment and attempt to find and buy them whenever, wherever, and however they become available at the best prices possible.[10]

How to Sell Stamps

Value, as we have pointed out, is linked to the forces of supply and demand for any one stamp. However, the actual value of a particular stamp is only what it will bring in the marketplace, and this should be remembered when attempting to sell stamps.

The four ways in which an investor can liquidate his or her holdings are by selling

[8]Zegarowicz, op. cit.
[9]Ozaki's address is Drawer A, Evergreen, Colo. 80439.
[10]Gunston, op. cit., p. 213.

(1) to a collector, (2) to a retailer (a dealer), (3) to a wholesaler, or (4) through an auction market. Although the highest prices usually can be obtained by selling directly to collectors, selling costs can be high. In this case the seller must take on the role of a dealer, which means incurring the costs of advertising and the clerical expense of handling responses to the advertisements.

Small quantities of stamps (between five and ten items) can be sold to a retailer-dealer. However, if a large number of stamps is to be sold, it will be necessary to deal with a wholesaler even though prices in the wholesale market are likely to be approximately 40 percent of retail prices. You should not buy so many stamps that the services of a wholesaler will be needed when you wish to sell them. Selling at auction has two disadvantages: the auction firm's commission is 10 percent of the sales price, and the seller is required to accept the minimum or reserve price at which the collection is priced.

Stamp Catalogs

Stamp catalogs are valuable reference works for investors. They are one of the major sources used by average collector-investors in attempting to determine the value of the stamps in their collections or of those that they would like to acquire. However, the use of catalogs to determine values has limitations: (1) Although the prices indicated are the result of considerable research by the editors, the quoted prices are influenced by the editors' opinions, experiences, and prejudices, and the prices must therefore be considered subjective rather than objective determinations. This becomes obvious if you check different catalogs and find various prices for the same item. (2) Although catalog prices exert a strong pressure on the actual value of stamps, they are not definitive indicators of a stamp's true value. Often dealers expect to sell their stock at 50 percent of the listed price; that is, if a stamp lists for $1, it can probably be purchased for 50 cents, while a stamp listed for 50 cents can be bought for 25 cents. Sellers should bear in mind that the market price for any stamps in their collections are generally less than the catalog listing. The catalogs are normally a list of stamps of dealers together with prices at which they are prepared to sell, and these prices include the dealers' profit. Again, the condition, markings, and other criteria will influence the price that can be obtained for any particular stamp.

Other information that is included in catalogs pertains to the size of perforations, color, date of issue, quantity distributed, differences that may exist in color or perforations, and errors. A photographic representation of the stamp together with the catalog number is also included.

Words of Caution

Kenneth R. Lake, who has been involved in some phase of philately most of his adult life, cautions:

> Were stamp investment purely a hedge against inflation and a means of making profit, I would advise against it. But as an enjoyable hobby which can be made almost self-supporting, allied to sensible investment which should provide a worthwhile nest-egg, philately cannot be beaten.[11]

The pundits in the field[12] have several suggestions for the investor:

1. Buy only stamps about which you have knowledge. Do not get involved with stamps about which you know little regardless of how big a bargain they seem to be.

2. Be concerned with the condition of the stamps you buy. (Zegarowicz recommends buying only mint stamps.)

[11]Lake, op. cit., p. 15.
[12]Gunston, op. cit., pp. 38–39; Lake, op. cit., pp. 11, 173; Zegarowicz, op. cit., passim.

3. Before buying, attempt to have some knowledge of what the selling price might be.

4. Always remember that the value of a stamp is related to its country of issue, its scarcity, its topic, and the attractiveness of its design.

5. Irresponsible investment can have a catastrophic effect on an investor's bank account.

6. Keep up to date by reading philatelic magazines. Read the news pages, the tipster's column, and all the articles even if they are outside your special field. Study the advertisements to learn the prices quoted for materials offered. This is an excellent way to keep abreast of the market.

7. Join a specialist society. Regardless of how little you know, you will be welcome; this is an excellent way to become more knowledgeable. It is not wise to try to become a specialist in more than one or two areas.

8. Plan your collection. This will enable you to maximize your enjoyment as well as the return on your investment.

9. Do not buy an expensive item until you are very knowledgeable and are familiar with the stamp trade, retailers, auctions, and specialist societies and are able to judge the merits of your investment.

10. When the time comes to sell, determine in advance the price that you believe your item should bring. If you are not certain of the market value of a particular item, it may be wise to sell it at auction.

Stamp collecting is a wonderful hobby that almost anyone can enjoy. To be successful requires care, study, and shrewdness. If these qualities are cultivated, both the collection and the collector's pocketbook will gain.

Investment Companies

Chapter 42

Selecting Mutual Funds and Other Investing Institutions

LEO BARNES

If you are considering placing some or all of your investment dollars into mutual funds, closed-end investment companies, or other investing institutions, either for a regular personal investment program or for a tax-favored personal retirement plan, you have a choice among hundreds of institutions. Your big problem is "Which?" The logical means of arriving at a valid decision is a triple filtering process:

1. Which types of investing institutions are *eligible* for your consideration because they match your investment objectives?

2. Which of the investing institutions in these eligible categories are especially *suitable* for your needs because of appropriate size, reputation, diversification, bond-stock ratios, age and recession experience, low-cost, efficient operation, special features such as periodic investment and withdrawal plans, availability of capital insurance or investor plan completion insurance, or other criteria?

3. Which of the several suitable institutions are likely to be *best* for you in terms of probable performance, on the basis of the historical record and, more especially, of recent trends?

WHICH TYPES OF INVESTING INSTITUTIONS FIT YOUR BASIC INVESTMENT PURPOSES?

In considering their degree of diversification, bond-stock ratios, and primary investment targets, more than 1,000 mutual funds, closed-end investment companies, and other investing institutions can be classified in the following principal groups:

Fully Diversified Investing Institutions

1. *Conservative balanced institutions.* These have as their primary objective the preservation of capital and, as a secondary target, moderate growth and moderate income. Thus, their portfolios normally contain substantial proportions of bonds and preferred stocks as well as high-quality common stocks.

2. *Aggressive institutions.* These aim for near-term capital appreciation from

a diversified portfolio of relatively volatile stocks plus, in more and more cases, varying proportions of bonds. If investing institutions reduce their proportionate share of common stocks as market prices rise and increase their common stock ratios as market prices decline, they are described as "flexible" or "fully managed" rather than as "all common stock."

3. *Growth institutions.* The targets of growth institutions are longer-term growth of capital and larger future income, both at the probable expense of current income.

4. *Income institutions.* These institutions stress high current income above all other targets but normally do not neglect concomitant capital gains.

5. *High-performance institutions.* Responding to statistical findings that most institutions perform no better than what can be achieved by a completely random selection of listed common stocks, these institutions aim for very large capital gains and take greater risks in the hope of outperforming the market averages by wide margins. They try to achieve their goals by concentrating on more speculative growth or specialty issues, including "letter stock"; by employing leverage through the use of borrowed funds, options, and convertible securities; and, in the case of so-called hedge funds, by means of short sales so that profits can be made in declining or erratic markets as well as in rising ones.

Semidiversified Investing Institutions

6. *Economic area companies.* Usually mutual funds, these concentrate on relatively few industries, such as those connected with chemicals, energy, electronics, gold, real estate, or natural resources. Their prime objective is usually the long-term growth of capital, current income being secondary. The exception is real estate investment trusts, which stress high income.

7. *Regional investing institutions.* As their name implies, these institutions invest in companies active in a single state, region, or country, such as Texas, Florida, Canada, South Africa, or Japan, with the primary target of a long-term growth of capital.

8. *Special-situation institutions.* These institutions are similar in objective to performance companies, but they cannot diversify so widely, since the number of special situations at any given time is limited. Development or venture capital funds are also in this category.

9. *Tax shelter investing institutions.* These institutions operate primarily to achieve tax-favored income or capital gains or to defer such gains. Diversification is secondary. Tax-exempt bond funds, tax exchange funds, and investment companies with large tax loss carry-forwards are in this category.

10. *Money market institutions.* This investment alternative has been available only since 1972. There are now dozens of money market funds that invest in high-denomination money market instruments such as Treasury bills, bank acceptances, bank certificates of deposit, and higher grades of commercial paper. Average portfolio maturities range from less than one month to as long as eight or nine months, with a modal range of two or three months. The primary objectives of the funds are high short-term yield, calculated on a daily basis, with maximum liquidity and check-writing convenience, plus a very high degree of safety.

Which of the Listed Categories Are Satisfactory for You?

Almost every investor will be interested in at least several of the above categories of investing institutions because they are compatible with his or her investment targets. Thus, while conservative investors will of course be primarily interested in conservative investing institutions (category 1), they can also properly explore categories 3, 4, 7, 9, and 10. More enterprising investors have a somewhat wider choice; they will wish to investigate not only categories 2 and 3 but also categories 6, 7, 8, 9, and 10. Finally, speculative investors can seek fulfillment among investing institutions in categories 5, 6, 8, 9, and 10.

WHICH ELIGIBLE INVESTING INSTITUTIONS ARE MOST SUITABLE FOR YOU?

Having decided, at least temporarily, which general types of investing institution you are ready to consider, the next problem is: Of the numerous institutions within these categories that are compatible with objectives, which are most suitable for you? Among the main tests of suitability are the following:

1. *Relative size.* The size of an investing institution such as a mutual fund has pluses and minuses. The big plus factor is that the greater the assets of the institution, the smaller usually is the percentage of each investor's total investment that goes for investment management. From this point of view, you should have very special reasons for putting your money in an investing institution that is working with less than $15 to $20 million in assets.

Over some such basic minimum (which should be adjusted for future inflation), size remains an important factor to evaluate. Greater size is often the tribute of investors to management success. However, excessive size is undesirable and will usually boomerang. A very large institution may become so unwieldy that it loses liquidity and suffers in performance as compared with an equally competent smaller fund.

As explored further below, large institutions may have such substantial holdings in particular securities that they cannot sell them out quickly without the costly consequence of dropping prices. This loss of agility for very large institutions makes it hard for them to match or beat the market averages. Thus, ironically, relative ultimate failure becomes the almost inevitable outcome of greater initial success.

Therefore, if your primary target is maximum portfolio performance, you should avoid the giant institutions unless they split the funds under their financial control through multiple or competitive management devices, as described below. When the assets of the particular fund in which your money is invested rise to around $100 million, it is time to start exploring alternatives because the fund's potential for maximum performance will probably be declining.

2. *Liquidity and marketability of securities.* In line with the criterion of size, an investing institution will usually strive for maximum feasible liquidity and marketability for its investments so that it may rectify its investment mistakes promptly without the additional price deterioration that results from inadequate markets. For example, almost all the investments of mutual funds and other investment companies, bank trust funds, insurance company variable annuities, and the like should be the securities of large companies that have active listed or over-the-counter markets.

Such marketability for an investing institution's securities is to be distinguished from *investors'* liquidity, which, as in the case of most mutual funds, can be excellent even though some of a particular fund's holdings may be of poor marketability.

3. *Risk exposure level.* Investors should be able to assign a *relative risk rank* to the particular fund into which their dollars are to go. Marketability is one element of market risk. As indicated below, a number of other types of investment risk must also be carefully noted and evaluated. They range from business cycle and financial risks to foreign and moral risks. It is feasible to assign an estimated *combined risk percentage rank* to any investing institution portfolio, and the desired maximum level of risk can then be used as an absolute filter.

4. *Recession and bear market experience.* Most investing institutions have been created or developed since World War II, many of them since 1960 and some since 1970. The younger the institution, the more limited its recession and bear market experience. If you are a very conservative investor concerned above all with preservation of capital and safety of income, you may wish to limit your choice of investing institutions to those whose portfolio managers have performed relatively well (that is, less poorly) in the seven bear markets during the thirty years from the end of World War II to 1975, those of 1946–1949, 1957, 1960, 1962, 1966, 1970, and 1973–1974.

Increasingly, services specializing in mutual funds and other investing institutions, as well as periodicals like *Forbes,* are rating the institutions specifically on such bear market performance. You should have very special and important reasons for investing in an institution that fails such a test—above all, truly exceptional performance in strong markets that substantially offsets a poor record in bear markets. Similarly, recently created investing institutions might well be avoided until they have established a satisfactory bear market performance record.

5. *Identity, reputation, and caliber of present management.* Who are the managers? What is their reputation and record? Are the present investment managers of an institution responsible for its past performance record, or are they merely newcomers trying to uphold a tradition?

6. *Investor portfolio flexibility.* Increasingly, mutual fund managements are broadening available exchange privileges so that investors may shift, at any time, all or part of their holdings in any fund under the same overall management into one or more of other related funds. Such a switch can be accomplished whenever an investor believes that it is desirable under current market conditions. This exchange privilege is available either at no cost or for a nominal service charge.

In other words, more and more mutual fund managements now conceive of their services as providing a "family" of funds. Included may be as many as five to eight funds (occasionally more), ranging from aggressive stock funds, through various types of balanced stock-bond, income, and bond funds, to short-term money market funds.

Some bank trust departments have similar exchange privileges, though often with less flexibility, in that portfolio shifts may be made without charge or at nominal cost only on specified occasions, perhaps once a year. Sometimes real estate pooled funds or mortgage trusts are also available from banks for exchange purposes.

The portfolio flexibility provided by exchange privileges is particularly valuable for investors who have confidence in their ability to time major market moves but lack the time or ability to handle their own portfolios, as explained below.

7. *Acquisition and redemption costs.* These costs are relevant and important in translating an institution's portfolio or management performance into final investor results. Obviously, if two investing institutions have closely similar portfolio performance for a five-year period but one is a load fund with an 8 or 9 percent sales charge and the other a no-load fund, the latter will show superior investor results. Redemption costs are also worth considering; no-load funds often impose them, while almost all load funds do not. Of course, these are much smaller than acquisition costs, and may be only hypothetical.

8. *Institutional operating expenses.* Similar considerations apply to operating costs. While minor differences in operating cost ratios are not very important, the fact that such ratios are larger than average for an institution of a given type and size may be a clue to management's carelessness with investors' money.

9. *Reinvestment options and cost.* This is still another cost that can reduce investor results as compared with management performance. For reinvestment

purposes, realized capital gains are usually treated differently from income dividends, especially by mutual funds with a sales charge. Almost all funds reinvest capital gain distributions without cost, but many charge the regular sales load for reinvesting income dividends (in most cases, since dividends are relatively small, this will be the maximum charge).

Automatic capital gain reinvestment may be especially important to investors who do not need maximum investment returns for current living expenses. The availability of such a plan may make them choose a mutual fund rather than an otherwise equally eligible closed-end investment company or a bank trust fund without such a plan. Similarly, a no-cost dividend reinvestment policy may move an investor to select one eligible mutual fund rather than another with a slightly better performance record.

10. *Accumulation plan availability, features, and costs.* These criteria may be of decisive importance to investors who plan to dollar-average by regularly and systematically investing relatively small amounts.

11. *Withdrawal plan availability and costs.* Investors systematically planning for retirement may wish to restrict their investments to institutions that provide regular automatic withdrawals on a monthly or quarterly basis at nominal cost.

12. *Life insurance availability.* When combined with periodic investment plans, life insurance is known as "plan completion insurance." In contrast to the usual policies, such insurance does not guarantee the investor's estate any specific sum of money. Instead, it provides cash to complete, immediately after the investor's death, the unfinished portions of a periodic investment plan. Thus, the value of the shares delivered to the estate may be more or less than the total amount invested, depending on market prices at the time of the investor's death.

13. *Availability of capital protection insurance.* In 1974 insurance by private insurance companies against capital and interest loss became available on individual tax-exempt bonds and on investor portfolios of such bonds (see Chapter 26). The next year such protection was sometimes extended to a few tax-exempt bond funds and occasionally to taxable bond funds. The cost is relatively low for bonds and bond funds, and conservative investors may find such a safety feature very desirable or essential.

What the insurance does is to guarantee that all bond income will be paid when due and that bond principal will be paid at maturity rather than at the time of any default. If tax-exempt income is in default, the replacement insurance payment is also considered to be tax-exempt.

A related but quite different type of insurance is now increasingly available on some stock mutual funds, but only over an investment period of at least ten years, during which all capital gain distributions and income dividends must be reinvested as received. The insurance premium is about 0.7 percent per year over the ten-year period.

Although this may seem to be insurance of one's capital, it really is not. Nor does it insure an investor's income. All this insurance does is to guarantee that provided the investor reinvests all capital gain distributions and income dividends, the value of his or her principal at the end of the investing period (say, ten years) will be the same as or more than the original investment, plus the cost of the insurance.

On such terms, of course, this insurance is hardly a bargain. The value of your original capital could drop as much as 40 percent in ten years, and yet you could not collect a cent of insurance if, as is more than likely, your reinvested capital gain distributions and income dividends, compounded at only 4 percent per year, made up this 40 percent capital loss. Over a ten-year period, you probably would do better by investing the cost of the insurance yourself in almost any type of mutual fund and letting it compound.

Mandatory versus Optional Investing Institution Features

You should use the preceding thirteen point checklist as a filter for preparing a list of desired investing institution features that are *musts* for you and another list of such features that are desirable but *optional* for you. Use the first list to locate and identify all the investing institutions you can that possess all your required features. For example, you might discover a total of twelve mutual funds, closed-end investment companies, and bank trust funds that have all your "must" requirements. You could then easily note which and how many of your desired optional features these twelve institutions also possess. All this information will be helpful in your final choice, as explored below.

WHICH OF THE SUITABLE INVESTING INSTITUTIONS SHOULD YOU FINALLY CHOOSE?

You, the investor, are now ready for the last step in selecting one or several investing institutions. Remaining are the institutions that have survived our previous double screening: (1) In terms of your investment objectives, you have discarded as ineligible several types or categories of investing institutions. (2) From among the eligible institutions in the acceptable categories, you have eliminated those that are unsuitable for special reasons, such as size, bear market experience, risk exposure, or portfolio flexibility.

You now face the problem of choosing among the suitable remaining investing institutions. This is done by a third and final filtering procedure, based mostly on the actual past performance record and the probable future performance of the rival institutions.

Your Selection Target: Diversify among the Best

Much time and effort have been spent in defining the statistically ideal investing institution. All kinds of tests and standards have been developed over the past few decades. Nonetheless, very probably you will not be able to decide among suitable candidates with anything like slide rule accuracy. Here are some reasons:

1. *Quite a number of different tests of excellence have been advanced and recommended over the years.* An institution that is near the top of the list on one test will not do so well on another, especially when somewhat different time or base periods are involved.

2. *Past superiority does not always imply, let alone guarantee, future success.* Moreover, the question of the appropriate time period is always troublesome. Should it be three years, five years, ten years, or some other period? Also, to what extent should improving performance in more recent years offset lower average performance for a longer period? Perhaps one investment management can learn from the past investment performance of other, more successful managements.

3. *There are structural differences in different types of investing institutions, such as mutual funds and closed-end investment companies.* These make statistical comparisons among them difficult or misleading or produce different investor results with identical management performance, as explained below.

All in all, the best you can hope to do when checking the statistical records of a number of suitable investing institutions is to filter out the *obviously poorer performers.* You will then have left a few suitable candidates with comparatively good records. These should be put to the final tests described below.

For all stock and stock-bond investing institutions, the following tests are recommended:

1. *Management performance* (defined below) for all remaining candidates should be derived and compared for the past ten-, five-, three-, and one-year

periods. The purpose of these multiple overlapping periods is to find any long-term trend of improvement or deterioration. Recent superior results for individual institutions merit somewhat greater weight than more remote superiority.

2. What about so-called *risk-adjusted performance?* This concept was popular in the early 1970s on the ground that only institutions in the same risk class (typically defined in terms of relative market volatility, or beta) can properly be compared with one another. For reasons presented earlier in the *Handbook* (see Chapter 3), we are not especially impressed with this approach. We recommend instead that market risk be taken into account in two more practical ways:

a. The investing institutions to be compared should be arranged by category, as outlined in the section "Which Types of Investing Institutions Fit Your Basic Investment Purposes"—for example, diversified stock investing institutions, diversified balanced stock-bond institutions, diversified income institutions. semidiversified institutions, and so on. This simple procedure enables us to compare performance for institutions that have the same investment targets.

b. Another useful way of evaluating the impact of market downside risk is to compare the management performance of investing institutions separately in bear markets and in bull markets. This procedure will clarify and supplement the overall management performance results for the four time periods recommended in paragraph 1. It is helpful to rank such performance in down or up markets by quintiles, or 20 percent groups, roughly equivalent to the grades of A, B, C, and D.

3. If *income yield* is important for investors, as for income stock or bond mutual funds, the longer-term average and the latest dividend or interest yields, or both, should be compared.

4. Finally, the problem of *management continuity and responsibility* for past performance of an investing institution, described in the section "Which Eligible Investing Institutions Are Most Suitable for You?" should be explored. If a new management is not responsible for the reported past performance, this performance must either be downgraded or be disregarded completely in evaluating the present management. To put it another way, the reliability of past performance statistics is weakened whenever there has been a substantial or complete change of institutional management.

Distinguishing between Management Performance and Investor Results

While closely related, the *performance* of an investing institution's management may be somewhat different from the *results* for any investor in that institution. Results are naturally of paramount interest to the investor.

Most commonly, identical management performance by two mutual funds can lead to different investor results because of big differences in sales charges or in capital gain and income dividend reinvestment policies. Such differences are particularly important when comparing equally competent managements of a load mutual fund and a no-load fund. Similarly, identical management performance by two closed-end investment companies could produce different investor results because of varying prevailing discounts from or premiums over net asset value or because of the impact of leverage in one of the companies, as described below.

Management performance can be defined or specified in various ways. A major source of variation is the treatment of capital gains and income distributions. Statistically, both can be treated as cash payouts to investors that are not reinvested, as transactions that result in immediate reinvestment, or as being invested only annually, at the end of the fiscal year. Alternatively, in each of these procedures capital gains alone can be treated as reinvested while all income distributions are treated as cash to their recipients.

Theoretically, almost all of these options have some validity. Pragmatically, however, since most capital gain distributions are automatically reinvested as soon as they are received while most income distributions are taken in cash, the following seems to be the preferred definition of management performance:

For investing institutions that do not employ leverage, management performance represents the change, over a specified period, in net asset value per share or unit, *plus* (1) all capital distributions per share or unit, regarded as having been taken in shares (in effect, reinvested immediately on the data of payment), and (2) all income dividends per share treated as cash and not reinvested.

For investing institutions employing leverage (those which have preferred stock, bonds, or other debt prior to the common stock or invest in part in leverage instruments such as warrants or options), the computation of management performance should be based on total assets rather than on net asset value per common share. This is done to eliminate the effects of leverage, which is considered as either improving or worsening management performance. Leverage makes prices and asset values per share rise or fall faster and further than they do for nonleveraged investing institutions.

What about a Fund of Funds as the Performance Answer?

A "fund of funds" is a mutual fund that invests only in shares of other mutual funds, presumably those with superior performance records and prospects. In other words, the fund pursues our investment objective of diversifying with the best.

If a fund of funds is successful in this pursuit, it would be a good investment, provided investor results are not diminished by the double sales charge that could result from a load fund of funds investing in other mutual funds. Thus, if we assume approximately equal management performance, a no-load fund of no-load funds would produce investor results superior to those of a load fund of load funds.

The historical record of the few funds of funds in operation is a mixed one, illustrating once again that above-average past performance is no assurance of equally good future achievement.

What about Index Funds as a Pragmatic Performance Compromise?

Another simplified way of investing that was gaining popularity in 1976 is the "index fund." As its name implies, such a fund invests in the stocks making up a stock market average or in an appropriate smaller surrogate list of stocks that closely match's the average's performance. Such an achievement apparently would satisfy many investors (including institutions) who have failed to keep pace with the market averages in recent years.

Of course, the investor results for an index fund would be somewhat below those of the related market average because of the fund's load charges and operating expenses, both of which should be very low. Nonetheless, such results might be deemed satisfactory by some investors who may not have the time or the patience to select investing institutions in the manner here recommended.

For a more complete discussion of index funds, see Chapter 57.

Selection Criteria for Taxable and Tax-exempt Bond Funds

For high-quality bond funds, whether taxable or tax-exempt, satisfactory yield, not capital gain, is the primary investment target. Once again, it is investor results—the net yield to investors after all charges, expenses, and special fees, as for insurance—that is the central figure for investors.

However, some safety-conscious investors will also wish to relate the reported or calculated net yields for the current year and the past two or three years to the *quality ratings* of the bonds in the funds. Presumably, and normally, a larger number of low-rated bonds in a fund will raise its average yield. To evaluate the adequacy of a fund's yield as related to its quality or safety, the *weighted-average rating* of all the bonds in the fund must be calculated or estimated.

A few bond funds specialize in discount bonds of all qualities or in low-rated bonds only. For these, capital gain as well as unusually high income is an investment target. Accordingly, their evaluation would resemble that of a stock fund or a bond-stock fund rather than that of a high-grade bond fund.

For additional details on taxable bond funds, see Chapter 45; on tax-exempt bond funds, see Chapter 26.

What about Money Market Funds?

Selection criteria for these popular short-term funds are essentially similar to those for longer-term high-grade bond funds, primary stress being placed on income and safety. There may be incomparabilities in the yield figures for different money market funds because of somewhat different methods of computation, but these should be relatively minor. However, be suspicious of any money market fund that reports a current yield much higher than that of other funds with similar portfolios: the difference may be more statistical than real.

Similarly, if questions of safety are involved, it is necessary to compare the proportions in which the different money market funds under consideration are invested in (1) federal government securities, (2) bank instrumentalities, and (3) commercial paper. For some conservative investors, a large proportion of federal government securities may be deemed more important than a slightly higher effective yield. Efforts may also be made to gauge the quality of a particular fund's choices of bank securities and commercial paper, primarily in terms of the size and reputation of the banks and business firms involved.

For additional details on money market funds, see Chapter 27.

Timing Option of Portfolio Exchange Flexibility within One Investing Institution

Investors who believe that they have the ability to time major equity and bond market moves with some degree of success, even though they do not have the time or expertise to select individual securities effectively, may be attracted by the exchange option discussed above. Such a concentration on timing rather than security selection and portfolio management, combined with the use of the exchange privilege to operate a very low-cost formula plan, can be an extremely useful option for knowledgeable and alert but busy investors. Considerable sums in commission costs could be saved in shifting from equities to bonds or cash equivalents in a money market fund, or vice versa, thus improving overall investor results.

Chapter **43**

Diversified Closed-End Investment Companies

MARK HANNA

A closed-end investment company raises its initial capital by selling its stocks or bonds. It proceeds to invest this capital in other securities to achieve its stated objective of income or capital gain, or both. The distinguishing feature of a closed-end company is that its own securities, stocks and bonds, are traded in the open market like any other corporate issues. Thus, at any given time the value of its common stock may be above or below the value of the securities held in its investment portfolio (the so-called net asset value). Moreover, unless the company offers a new security issued to the public, which is an infrequent occurrence, its capitalization remains static.

A closed-end company that meets the specifications of the law will qualify as a diversified investment company and receive certain tax advantages. The legal specifications as well as the tax implications are similar for closed-end and open-end diversified companies (see Chapter 42).

The passage of the Investment Company Act of 1940 resulted in the growth of open-end investment companies, or mutuals. A mutual fund is a management company that offers for sale or has outstanding any redeemable security of which it is an issuer. (The act defines a closed-end company as any investment company that is not an open-end company.) The salient fact about investment companies after 1940 is that open-end companies grew explosively with the assistance of a hoard of salesmen, while the older type of investment company was eclipsed. Mutual funds' assets have grown from less than $450 million in 1940 to more than $50 billion at the end of 1975, for an increase of more than 11,000 percent, while closed-end companies' assets increased from about $614 million to almost $7 billion, or by more than 1,000 percent. Put another way, the growth in mutuals was more than 10 times as large as the growth in closed-end funds. The discrepancy had been considerably greater in 1970, but the burgeoning growth of closed-end funds in the early seventies swelled their assets.

GROWTH DETERRENTS FOR CLOSED-END FUNDS

Why did open-end funds come to dominate the field of diversified investment companies? Was their growth basically a function of superior merchandising, or do closed-ends have an inherent drawback that no reasonable amount of merchandising could overcome? Certainly, no one can doubt that funds basically are sold to the public rather than bought by the public. Although this circumstance is less applicable to investment company shares than to life insurance, it is still an important determinant of relative growth rates.

The fact that commissions are much greater for selling open-end than for selling closed-end shares leads to a lopsided effort in favor of open-end shares even among customers' men who function primarily as security salesmen and not as fund salesmen. And, of course, an army of fund salesmen sell nothing but mutual funds, while there is not even a platoon of closed-end salesmen. Commissions for mutual fund salesmen run about 9 percent, whereas there is no more than the regular exchange commission for listed closed-end shares. Unquestionably, for day-to-day sales the commission structure has favored mutual fund salesmen.

However, this comparison is not the complete story. The point at issue is not just the commission on transactions of outstanding closed-end shares but the commission on new issues. It's through new issues that growth in fund assets can occur, not through transactions that transfer existing shares from old to new owners. Relatively large commissions are allowed by the exchanges on primary issues. Therefore, if a new closed-end investment company is issuing shares of stock to the public for the first time, the commission would be quite large, and the broker would be motivated to sell these securities.

The real problem, then, lies elsewhere: the commission differential is not the cause of the paucity of new issues of closed-end fund shares. That paucity is caused by two factors. First, instead of buying new shares in a closed-end investment company and paying a high commission, the investor can purchase shares in an existing closed-end fund and pay only the normal brokerage commission. Therefore, the investor will prefer to purchase existing shares in a fund rather than buy stock being offered for the first time. Second, an existing fund could attempt to sell shares by offering the new shares at a discount from the prevailing market price. However, this will dilute the net asset value (NAV) per share of common stock, to the dissatisfaction of the old stockholders.

For example, if a fund had 100,000 shares of stock outstanding and net assets of $800,000, then the NAV per share would be $8. If this fund issued an additional 100,000 shares at a price of $7 per share (plus brokerage commissions), it would have 200,000 shares with net assets of $1.5 million, for an NAV per share of $7.50. The old stockholders would not like having their shares diluted.

While the problem of capital expansion is difficult even if the market price of the shares of closed-ends is the same as the NAV, the problem of issuing new equity is compounded by the fact that generally the market price is considerably less than the NAV for closed-ends. This combination of factors—a market price typically well below the NAV and the circumstance that new issues must be sold (net to the fund) at an even greater discount below the market price—means that a new issue has a very substantial diluting impact upon the NAV.

If, for example, the stock of a fund with an NAV of $10 is selling in the market for $8 per share and the management of the fund wishes to sell additional stock, the new stock must be sold at a discount from the $8 per share, and this will have a substantial diluting impact upon the NAV of $10.

This same type of dilution occurs when shareholders are allowed to take dividends or capital gain distributions, or both, in stock, since they usually are permitted to do so at the market values of the stock. A further drawback in this case is that measures of investment performance usually make no adjustment for the value of the *implicit* rights. Thus, the dilution impact is not offset by adding back the value of the implicit rights, as would be the case if one were measuring NAV performance and *explicit* rights were used.

For example, if a fund has an NAV of $10, the market price of its stock is $8 per share, and the stockholders can use dividends or capital gains to buy additional stock at $8 per share, then the NAV will be diluted. However, the published measures of investment performance often don't make allowances for this type of dilution, and an investor reading these performance measures may be led to believe that the NAV has declined because of poor asset management.

The impact upon the NAV through time can be substantial. The total effect depends upon the size of the dividends and capital gain distributions and the size of the market price discount below the NAV.

Since closed-ends funds face potential dilution of the NAV if rights are used to allow stockholders to subscribe at prices well below the NAV, one possible solution might be a continuous policy of starting new closed-end funds by preexisting managements. Stock in the new funds could be sold at, say, 9 percent commission on an over-the-counter basis and subsequently listed. These funds would have to have some unique appeal to offset the fact that alternative closed-ends would be available at discounts. This generalized alternative is not a great problem in view of the success of load mutual funds in raising capital despite the existence of alternative no-load mutual funds.

An inescapable fact is that closed-ends simply have not been imaginative in their packaging of funds. Mutuals have led in innovating ways to make funds more attractive. The Closed-End Investment Company Association has not been nearly so active as its mutual fund counterpart. In fact, as Richard Fishbein pointed out in an earlier article in 1964, the Closed-End Investment Company Association did not even have a permanent address, and this was still true in 1970.[1]

Another inescapable fact, however, is that, even with greatly increased merchandising effort, the discount problem would be a powerful inherent deterrent to the equity financing of closed-end funds.

Would financing with more debt and preferred stock be a means of increasing the assets of closed-ends? Again the overriding fact is that the inability or, at least, the difficulty of raising equity capital places a ceiling on leverage financing unless a fund is willing to increase the degree of leverage. However, most closed-ends have not even maintained their leverage, much less increased it. They allowed their leverage to decline drastically by not replacing bonds in their capital structure as they matured, despite the fact that the market value of their equity rose drastically, as did their interest coverage. These funds could have used debt and preferred stock financing to increase their asset growth without increasing leverage merely by keeping the degree of leverage constant as equity increased through reinvestments as well as from the upward trend in prices after World War II.

Let us assume, for example, that a fund had $1 million in assets and $400,000 in debt. Therefore, the net asset value was $600,000, and the debt-equity ratio was 66.67 percent ($400,000 divided by $600,000). If the market value of the assets increased by $300,000, the fund could borrow an additional $200,000 and still maintain a debt-equity ratio of 66.67 percent; it would then have $1.5 million in total assets and $600,000 in debt. More than likely, however, if the leverage had not been reduced so much, the discount might not have closed so much, a fact that facilitated much equity financing in the late 1960s when discounts actually were transformed to premiums in many cases.

Investors who buy stock in a fund with a relatively high degree of leverage are

---

[1] Richard Fishbein, "Closed-End Investment Companies," *Financial Analysts Journal,* vol. 26, p. 72, March–April 1970.

accepting additional risk, but they have a chance for higher profits. However, it appears that the additional risk will cause the stock to sell at a larger discount from the NAV.

Moreover, in the early part of the post-World War II period considerable stigma was attached to leveraged funds. This stigma was removed in the latter part of the period as memories of the Great Depression receded; some funds did increase their leverage in the late 1960s. In fact, a renaissance of leverage emerged with the founding of dual-purpose funds, which initially met with a good reception (see Chapter 44).

In summary, then, the growth of the closed-ends has been inhibited by the fact that the shares of such funds as a rule sell at a discount below net asset value. Whether this discount could have been overcome by a stepped-up improved merchandising effort is debatable. It probably could not. At any rate, the existence of sizable discounts has been the historical norm for diversified closed-end investment companies, although some closed-ends of a specialized nature often have sold at premiums.

DISADVANTAGES AND ADVANTAGES OF CLOSED-END FUNDS

Disadvantages for Investors

The chief disadvantage of closed-ends is the destablizing effect of *changes* in the size of the discount. If investors were faced with very stable discounts expressed as a percentage of market price below the NAV, the discount would be a decided advantage. They would receive a higher return from their investment than if they had to pay the NAV without incurring any greater risk. The market price would rise or decline by the same percentage as the NAV. For example, let us assume that the market price for a particular fund is always 10 percent below its NAV. If the NAV declines from $20 to $16, for a drop of 20 percent, the market price would decline from $18 to $14.40, for a similar drop of 20 percent.

But since the market prices of closed-ends are not tied in any fixed relationship to their NAVs, as is the case with mutuals, they are likely to fluctuate with greater variance than their NAVs. Historically, the discount has widened in bear markets and narrowed in bull markets. The discount, then, is a disadvantage. Risk-averting investors would buy closed-end shares only if they received a rate of return greater than the return if the fund had been open-ended. Of course, that additional return is obtained by paying less for the fund shares than their NAV, that is, through the discount mechanism.

One writer holds that the variability of the NAV and the potentially heightened variability of the market price about the NAV are of little concern to typical fund investors since they are notoriously long-term investors: "The exposure to unpredictable market forces upon liquidation of the shares is usually of minor importance over the life of the investment."[2] However, the author disagrees with such an analysis. In the first place, with redemptions currently exceeding purchases of mutual funds, one wonders about the accuracy of the assumption about the length of investment in funds. Of more importance, however, many long-term investors are not unconcerned with the liquidity of their investments. But even if we grant that they are less concerned with liquidity, long-term investors are surely interested in the potential impact of changing discounts on their long-term rate of return.

For example, let us suppose that one buys shares in a closed-end fund when the

---

[2]Eugene J. Pratt, "Myths Associated with Closed-End Investment Companies," *Financial Analysts Journal*, vol. 22, p. 81, July–August 1966.

NAV is $100 and liquidates them ten years later when the NAV is $130. Let's suppose further that a 10 percent premium existed at the time of purchase, that a bear market ensued for eight years, and that stocks had only recently moved onto higher ground. If the recent discount is 25 percent, the impact on our long-term investor's rate of return is of no small consequence. Instead of having a long-term capital gain of 30 percent over the ten years, the investor has an 11.4 percent loss.

Of course, one could argue that the opposite situation, in which our investor bought at a sizable discount in a bear market and sold out at a premium, might just as well happen. However, it appears that most long-term investors fear disappointment and losses more than they appreciate windfalls. Thus, the argument that closed-end fund shares are not inherently worth less than comparable open-end shares because long-term investors are not concerned with shifting discounts does not appear to be valid.

Advantages for Investors

One advantage for investors whose risk preferences allow for the use of leverage is that closed-ends can supply such leverage, whereas open-ends can at most use limited amounts of bank borrowing. Investors would prefer to use fund leverage instead of their own leverage because of the limited liability to the investor in a fund. However, we should recall that the bulk of closed-ends have no leverage, and those few funds that do generally have heavy offsetting fixed-income assets in their portfolios.

Some argue that the discount itself adds to the leverage. This is unquestionably true with respect to *income* leverage: investors have more money (NAV) working for them in the portfolio of a closed-end fund than the price paid for the stock, even in the case of funds without leveraged capital structures. This is one of the major advantages of investing in a closed-end fund at a discount.

The impact of the discount on capital gain leverage is questionable. Leverage is added when the discount is bound to narrow, as for a closed-end fund converting to an open-end fund or in case of liquidation. But these events are quite unpredictable. It is true that there is, in addition, a tendency for the discount to narrow in bull markets. Thus, *average* discounts narrowed greatly in 1946 and 1968. Yet for some closed-ends in those years peaks occurred without an unusual decline in discounts. However, investors lucky enough to predict a bull market are likely to enjoy greater profits in closed-ends than in open-ends, as most discounts are likely to narrow substantially.

Closed-ends do have an advantage over the mutuals in that they need not be concerned with the impact of portfolio composition upon potential buyers of the fund shares; only rarely do they offer new shares to the public. Besides not having to tailor their portfolios to meet the fads of the day, closed-ends need not consider potential share liquidations, as mutuals must. Therefore, they can hold less liquid or less marketable securities.

This freedom from redemption was a tremendous advantage for closed-end companies in the early 1970s, when almost all open-end mutual funds were losing more shares through redemption than they were gaining in new sales. For this reason, too, the new bond investment companies that came into existence after 1970 were overwhelmingly closed-end rather than in the traditional open-end form (see Chapter 45). Investors pay the same commission when they buy and sell stock in a closed-end company as they do when they trade securities in other companies. This commission is much lower than the commission (8½ percent) charged when they purchase shares in open-end load funds, but it is, of course, much higher than the zero commission charged on purchases of no-loads.

Finally, if a closed-end fund selling at a discount were to convert into a mutual fund (load or no-load) or if it were to liquidate, investors in this fund would receive an immediate capital gain. This potential windfall profit always exists for a closed-end fund selling at a discount. Quite a number of closed-end funds did so convert in the 1960s and early 1970s. Closed-ends remain prime takeover targets for subsequent conversion to mutual funds or outright liquidation.

POSSIBLE REASONS FOR THE DISCOUNT

Unrealized Capital Gains

Discounts vary from fund to fund simultaneously (cross-sectional discount variability) and for funds in general through time (time-series discount variability). One reason often suggested for the former variability, which could also affect the latter type, is the proportion of unrealized capital gain (UCG) to the NAV of the fund. As a fund shifts stocks in its portfolio or converts stock to cash for various purposes, these capital gains will be realized and tax liabilities will arise. Thus, it is argued, each dollar of today's NAV has less value to the extent that it contains a potential future capital gain tax liability. It has been suggested that the discount reflects the present value of such future tax payments. Eugene J. Pratt claims that the investment community generally accepts the view that unrealized capital gain is the major cause of the discount.[3] He goes on to express the belief that this generally held view is baseless.

One of Pratt's arguments is that the tax liability potential is unimportant if realized capital gains are paid out in small amounts. That, however, is not a satisfactory argument since the present value of even small amounts can be consequential. His basic argument, however, treats the case of massive capital gain distributions in the immediate future. Here he holds that the sizable tax liability should have no present negative impact upon value.

Pratt correctly points out that a capital gain distribution by the fund has two effects: a tax liability to investors arises immediately, but it is offset by a rise in the investors' cost basis equal to the distribution. Thus, if investors were to sell out simultaneously, an equal offsetting capital loss would occur. There would then be a tax saving on the loss equal to the tax on the gain.

However, investors usually would not sell out until quite some time in the future. Thus, once we take into consideration the time value of money, the present value of the future tax saving is likely to be less than the present value of the immediate tax payments required on the capital gain distributions.

Therefore, while Pratt rightly points out the incorrectness of the generally held view that the discount on closed-ends reflects the present value of future tax payments (as presently existing gains become realized), he should also have pointed out that the discount might reasonably reflect the *difference* between the present value of such future tax payments and the even more distant offsetting future tax savings.

Recognition of Management Value

A large number of widely publicized studies have produced considerable evidence that funds have not performed well relative to the market if risk is considered. Perhaps investors have long since held the view that fund managers are nonproductive; then the discount might represent the present value of the future fees managers will extract from the fund assets. Professor Frank Jen, who suggested this possible explanation, also holds that if this view were the cause of the discount, it would follow that superior performance should be rewarded with premiums.

[3] Ibid., p. 79.

If indeed this discounting process were the basic explanation, we would expect the discount to decline in prosperous periods when the time value of money increases and to increase in recessions when interest rates decrease. Of course, this role of the time value of money would be important no matter what negative future possibility the discount is believed to reflect.

Market-Level Influence

Prosperity itself, apart from its association with the time value of money, evidently has some impact upon the size of the discount. It has been suggested that the confidence bred by prosperity leads to higher valuations of the NAV by closed-end fund buyers, thereby narrowing discounts. Thus, if we use the stock market level as a reflection of prosperity, discounts widened greatly in the bear market from 1946 to 1949 and then narrowed generally as the market advanced in the bull market that ended in 1960. However, *since 1960 this relationship has been much more erratic and unreliable.*

Compensation for Extra Risk

It has been pointed out that the discount is probably a function of the added risk to closed-end investors stemming from the fact that the share price has a greater variability than the NAV. Of course, the variability of the NAV itself would also likely be a prime determinant of the size of the discount. Funds with greater NAV variance would probably have greater share price variability, and investors would require an additional return to compensate them for this extra risk. They, of course, receive this return by paying less for the stock, which would lead us to expect larger discounts among funds with greater NAV variance.

Other Determinants

There are, of course, other possible determinants of the discount. Among them might be such factors as whether a fund has a consistent capital gain distribution policy (a policy of relatively large distributions or a policy of retaining its distributions) and the size of the management fee. It is interesting to note that all the factors that might cause the discount also exist in open-end funds, and these securities can never be purchased at a discount.

Chapter **44**

Dual-Purpose Funds

GEORGE S. JOHNSTON

What They Are

Dual-purpose investment companies first appeared in the United States in the spring of 1967, although such companies had existed in England for at least two years prior to that time. Seven companies were started with cash, and two began with an exchange of securities. Seven were listed on the New York Stock Exchange, and two traded over the counter. The funds and their assets are shown in Table 44-1.

Dual-purpose funds are closed-end investment companies with two classes of shares, income shares and capital shares. Each class was issued separately and is traded separately. In their basic form, the funds were structured with an equivalent number of shares of each class that are sold at equal net asset values. The *income shareholders* receive all the income produced by the fund, and the capital shareholders thus receive no income. At a stipulated date, the income shares are redeemed at a price related to original net asset value, and the *capital shareholders* are entitled to the assets remaining in the fund. The capital shareholders thus receive the benefit of all capital appreciation accrued during the lifetime of the income shares.

Whom They Are For

Dual-purpose funds were designed specifically to provide professional management and diversified equity portfolios for investors who are able to characterize their investment objectives as either (1) solely capital appreciation or (2) solely income. Although these objectives seem conflicting, in a properly structured dual-purpose fund each class of shares complements the other, and their relationship gives the fund the opportunity to provide more of what each seeks in exchange for what he does not seek.

For investors who can categorize their objectives realistically in this fashion, a security whose return combines income and capital appreciation is inefficient to the extent that part of the return is in a form which, for maximum benefit, must be converted into the preferred form, often at some expense or with the assumption of undesired risk. For example, investors with substantial assets and a high-income

TABLE 44-1   Dual-Purpose Funds

Company and life*	Capital shares		Income shares		
	Initial net assets (in thousands)	Initial net asset value	Initial net asset value	Redemption price	Cumulative dividend
American Dual-Vest (1967–1979)	$43,211	$ 13.80	$ 13.80	$ 15.00	$ 0.84
Federated Dual-Exchange Fund† (1967–1979)	34,132	25.00‡	25.00‡	25.00‡	1.3175
Gemini Fund (1967–1984)	36,435	11.00	11.00	11.00	0.56
Hemisphere Fund (1967–1985)	32,142	11.44	11.44	11.44	0.625
Income & Capital Shares (1967–1982)	27,633	9.15	9.15	10.00	0.50
Leverage Fund of Boston (1967–1982)	54,900	13.725	13.725	13.725	0.75
Putnam Duo-Fund (1967–1983)	27,460	9.12	18.24	19.75	0.908
Scudder Duo-Vest (1967–1982)	99,835	9.15	9.15	9.15	0.64
Scudder Duo-Vest Exchange Fund† (1967–1983)	37,366	500.00	500.00	500.00	30.00

*Life of company until redemption of income shares.
†Fund organized by tax-free exchange of low-cost securities.
‡Adjusted for 20-to-1 split on Mar. 15, 1968.
§Increases over life of shares.

tax bracket may seek only to enhance their capital. If such an investor purchases a stock that appreciates by 12 percent during the ensuing year and pays dividends amounting to 3 percent on cost, he or she has a 15 percent annual rate of return before taxes. The 3 percent dividend, however, must be declared on the investor's tax return as current income, high taxes paid on it, and the remainder invested in pursuit of his or her goal. The investor probably would have preferred the return to be all in the form of capital appreciation.

At the other extreme, a typical charitable foundation requires generous current income and growing future income but is unable to spend capital or to assume large risks. It might purchase an income stock with an attractive dividend and the potential of some dividend growth and capital appreciation. By way of example, the stock pays cash dividends amounting to 5 percent and appreciates by 3 percent in a year's time, producing a total annual return of 8 percent. This investor presumably would have preferred the entire 8 percent return in the form of income provided risk and other factors were the same.

A dual-purpose fund permits each class of investor to achieve its separate goals without the capital investor's having to resort to high-risk stocks or the income investor's having to select fixed-income bonds or high-payout equities that may promise little or nothing in the way of growing yield. The dual investment goals are achieved by a partnership in which each partner initially contributes equal amounts of capital and from which each receives a specialized return based on twice the capital invested by him or her.

How They Work

One of the lessons of past investment experience is that stocks with growing earnings will produce not only capital growth but also, in time, greater income. In fact, common stocks generally regarded as growth securities often have impressive records of consistent dividend increases. The problem with these issues from the standpoint of an income-oriented investor is that although they produce rapidly *growing* income, their *current* yield is usually considerably below average.

The dual-purpose form accommodates participation in these types of issues by income shareholders because they are receiving income derived from the capital shareholders' investment as well as their own. Clearly, capital shareholders may also stand to benefit from investment in securities with above-average growth in earnings. The objectives of both are thus met effectively through the purchase of securities that promise growing earnings and dividends. *A dual-purpose fund, in other words, does not require a dual portfolio.*

The income shares of all dual-purpose funds have a stated cumulative dividend privilege payable over the life of the shares. This dividend represents a minimum expectable payout, not a maximum, since all income in each year is paid to the income shareholders. To the extent that the total cumulative amount to which income shareholders are entitled is not paid prior to redemption, the capital shareholders compensate the income shareholders for the amount owed at that time. The lives of the income shares vary among the different funds from twelve to eighteen years from the original offering date. Redemption prices also vary. Some funds redeem income shares at original net asset value, while other promise to pay a stated premium above this figure.

After the redemption of the income shares, the capital shareholders have the right to redeem their shares at net asset value. They will thus receive at that time the benefit of any capital appreciation earned on the *total capital:* their initial investment and the investment of the income shareholders.

Realized capital gains through the years are reinvested by the funds after paying capital gains taxes at the prevailing corporate capital gains tax rate. In any year in which this occurs, the capital shareholders report their proportionate gain in their individual tax returns, take a credit for the tax paid on their behalf, and increase the cost basis of their shares by the difference between the two.

A meaningful measure of net asset value for the income shares at any time is thus the redemption price. The net asset value of the capital shares is whatever is left: total net asset value less the net asset value of the income shares, less any dividend arrearage.

Why They Are Unique

Dual-purpose fund shares have characteristics that make them incomparable with other available investment vehicles. The income shares, for example, have a fixed lifetime, a stated dividend privilege, and initial asset coverage of 200 percent—features of fixed-income securities. At the same time, they provide the potential of *growing* income, a feature of common stocks. The income shares thus might be dubbed "cost-of-living bonds."

The capital shares have a potential for growth superior to that of a regular portfolio of similar securities through the assured use of someone else's capital for a long-term period. They also have an ultimate right of redemption at net asset value, which shares of conventional closed-end investment companies do not have. The capital shares are often described as "50 percent margin accounts," but there is this difference: the "loan" is not callable for a number of years.

Because the shareholders of each class contributed equal amounts of capital and receive a specialized return based on twice the capital invested by them, they are receiving *more* of the specialized kind of return they want than they could obtain from alternative forms of investment with comparable risk-opportunity relationships.

Where They Are, Have Been, and Are Going

If net asset values reflect the investment judgments of the funds' managers, market values reflect the investment judgments of the funds' shareholders. As with other closed-end investment companies, market values are influenced by the normal forces of supply and demand as well as by net asset values. Thus, usually the price of income shares of the various funds logically is somewhat in line with current return and stated dividend. By contrast, the capital shares typically sell at substantial discounts.

To some extent, these appraisals may well involve incomplete understandings by investors and ineffective missionary work by the funds. The discounts for the respective funds, moreover, do not seem to have a consistent relationship with funds' relative performance.

The historical asset value record clearly indicates that the leverage factor is at work on the downside as well as on the upside. It also leads to the obvious conclusion that if an advance of stock prices can be predicted, capital shares of dual-purpose funds should represent attractive investment vehicles, and if a decline can be predicted, these shares should represent relatively unattractive vehicles but an excellent short-sale medium.

To the extent that stock prices are expected to rise over a period as long as the lifetime of the income shares, it seems reasonable to expect that dual-fund capital shares, given the same horizon, will respond favorably. Finally, the disparity in past results among the various funds suggests that specific selection, as is always the case, must take into account the abilities and accomplishments of individual managers.

The discounts from net asset values at which the capital shares often sell alter their fundamental risk-opportunity ratios. The leverage increases proportionately to the extent that the capital shares decline in price below the net asset value and declines proportionately whenever the capital shares sell above the net asset value

TABLE 44-2   Illustration of Effect of Major Market Discount on a Dual-Purpose Fund's Capital Shares

Assumed changes in unit value by Mar. 31, 1982 (percent)	Assumed final unit value	Assumed final capital share asset value	Percentage gain or loss from $8 per share
+200	$60.45	$51.30	+541
+100	40.30	31.15	+289
+50	30.22	21.07	+163
+20	24.18	15.03	+88
No change	20.15	11.00	+37
−20	16.12	6.97	−14
−30	14.10	4.95	−38
−50	10.07	0.92	−88

NOTE: Market price, $8 per capital share. Asset value, $11 per capital share (which does not reflect income arrearages). Unit value, $20.15 (which does not reflect accumulated income). A unit is one income share and one capital share combined.

per share. Similarly, leverage is decreased if the total value of the fund rises and is increased if the total value falls.

Along these lines, Table 44-2 indicates that, for example, if the current net asset value of the capital shares is $11, the market price is $8, and the unit net asset value (capital share net asset value plus income share net asset value) is $20.15, a 35 percent gain from the present market price would be attained over the period until redemption even if the net assets of the fund itself showed no gain. If the fund as a whole declined by 20 percent, the decline in capital share net asset value would be 14 percent. If the fund appreciated by 20 percent, the gain to the capital shareholder would be 88 percent.

On paper, at least, it would seem that the two classes of stock taken together should sell at a price closer to net asset value than shares of closed-end funds with comparable portfolios, if only for the reason that the latter have no fixed and stated right of redemption. Moreover, the fact that each class can be purchased separately to meet precisely the specialized purposes of their owners should represent a "value added."

In determining a meaningful valuation of dual-purpose fund shares, we cannot easily apply the methods used in analyzing conventional securities. However, some basic mathematical relationships may help. Table 44-3 indicates that if capital shares are selling at a 20 percent discount from the net asset value and if thirteen years remain until the income shares are to be redeemed, a 5 percent annual growth rate of the fund's portfolio will produce a 10 percent annual rate of return for the capital shareholder. If an investor believes that the fund's portfolio will

TABLE 44-3   Rate of Return of Capital Shares over Thirteen Years (Market Value at a 20 Percent Discount from Current Net Asset Value)

Dividend arrearages*	Selected rates of growth in net asset value (percent)				
	5	6	7	8	9
None	10.0	11.4	12.7	14.1	15.4
5	9.9	11.3	12.7	14.0	15.3
10	9.7	11.2	12.5	13.9	15.2
15	9.5	11.0	12.4	13.8	15.1

*Expressed as a percentage of the redemption value of income shares.

grow at a rate in excess of 5 percent a year, the capital shares are undervalued. The table translates other assumptions on the annual growth rate of the fund's porfolio into the annual experience of capital shares currently priced at a 20 percent discount from the net asset value. Note that the existence of dividend arrearages has a negligible effect on the final results.

Another way of formulating guidelines for valuation is to hypothesize a dual-purpose experience over an extended period in the past. Table 44-4 summarizes the capital and income experience of the Dow Jones Industrial Average for five fifteen-year periods both on an actual basis and on the basis of a restructuring of the DJIA in dual-purpose form. As indicated, an average of the results of the five

TABLE 44-4   Dow Jones Industrial Average in Dual-Purpose Form

Periods ending December 31	Open	Close	Percentage change	Percentage change, hypothetical capital shares	Capital shares compound annual percentage rate of return
1951–1966	269.23	785.69	191.8	383.6	11.1
1952–1967	291.90	905.11	210.1	420.20	11.6
1953–1968	280.90	943.75	236.0	472.0	12.3
1954–1969	404.39	800.36	97.9	195.8	7.5
1955–1970	488.40	838.92	71.8	143.6	6.1
Average, all periods			161.5	323.0	9.7

Inclusive years	Dividends over period	Opening price	Average percent yield for hypothetical income shares
1952–1966	338.50	269.23	14.2
1953–1967	353.21	291.90	13.8
1954–1968	368.44	280.90	14.7
1955–1969	384.87	404.39	10.6
1956–1970	394.82	488.40	9.0
Average, all periods			12.5

fifteen-year periods produces a 323 percent change for the hypothetical capital shareholder, or an average annual compound rate of return of 9.7 percent— *available to taxable investors at favorably taxed capital gain rates.* The average annual yield for the hypothetical income shareholder for the five fifteen-year periods is 12.5 percent—*fully available to nontaxable investors.*

This analysis should be viewed with the skepticism appropriate for any hindsight assessment, but it does indicate how the dual-purpose interrelationships operate on an ordinary portfolio over various and sometimes-difficult investment time periods. A proper valuation of dual-purpose fund shares in the future should start from this theoretical premise.

A key conclusion would seem to be that *a dual-purpose fund committed to the index fund technique* (see Chapter 57), and thus assured of performance matching that of an overall market index, *would make an ideal investment medium.*

However, in practice (through 1975, in any event), the management performance of the capital shares of most dual funds has been disappointing. Thus, from the inception of the funds in 1967 through the end of 1975, the Dow Jones Industrial Average rose only fractionally, by about 1 percent. By contrast, the total net asset values of the dual funds, despite a substantial rise in 1975, declined by more than 20 percent over the eight-year period. Only one fund, Gemini, had managed to show an increase in net asset value since its 1967 launching.

In sharp contrast, the income shares of the seven major dual funds were fulfilling their high-income role in truly excellent fashion. At the end of 1975, they were providing a *current* yield ranging from 9 to 10.4 percent, and since all the income shares were selling below their redemption prices, their yields to date of redemption were even higher than their current yields, in a range of 10.8 to 15.1 percent.

Chapter 45
Taxable Bond Funds

CARL E. ANDERSEN

LEO BARNES

A taxable bond fund is an investment company that invests in taxable corporate and government bonds, usually nonconvertible, and sometimes in other taxable debt vehicles. In other respects, it is similar to an investment company that invests in stocks. It is governed by the same laws, operates in much the same manner, and is taxed or not taxed on the same basis. Of course, bonds are quite different from stocks, and the main purpose of the analysis that follows is to help investors who wish to invest in bonds to choose the bond funds most suitable for their needs. For some overall principles and considerations, see also Chapter 42, "Selecting Mutual Funds and Other Investing Institutions."

Open-End versus Closed-End Bond Funds

As in the case of stock investment companies, taxable bond investment companies may be either open-end mutual funds or closed-end investment companies. This is not the case for *tax-exempt* bond funds, which up to 1976 are legally allowed to be only closed-end companies.

Prior to 1970 bond investment companies were almost entirely open-end mutual funds, with a load charge; typically they were part of a family of mutual funds run by a single management company, consisting mainly of a variety of stock and balanced mutual funds. However, with the sharp rise in mutual fund redemptions after 1969, the special advantage of the closed-end form, which excludes redemptions, led to the formation of many new closed-end bond investment companies, designed to capitalize on investor disillusionment with stocks and stock mutual funds, and to the virtual exclusion of open-end bond funds.

Two other advantages of the closed-end form were also of interest to bond fund managements:

1. The use of leverage through borrowed money is permissible with a closed-end investment vehicle but not with an open-end fund. Thus, closed-end bond funds can vigorously pursue capital gains with the help of leverage, as explained below.

2. The standard, relatively low stock commission rates are applicable to the purchase and sale of closed-end bond funds on the stock exchanges or over the counter. This advantage over load bond mutual funds (but not, of course, over no-load bond funds) is discussed in greater detail below.

Variations in Quality, Risk, and Yield among Bond Funds

Lower-quality bonds pay higher interest rates than better-quality bonds because the investor in such bonds incurs a greater degree of risk. A study by Braddock Hickman, published in 1958 under the sponsorship of the National Bureau of Economic Research, concluded that large investors who purchase a large portfolio of well-diversified high-yield–high-risk bonds would have received a return, after allowing for losses, that exceeded the yield on a portfolio of high-quality issues. This was true because the income received from the average bond in the high-yield–high-risk portfolio was significantly higher than the yield on the average bond in the low-yield–low-risk portfolio. The higher income more than compensated for the larger number of defaults that occurred in the high-risk portfolio.

Many investors, however, may not have enough funds to invest in a highly diversified portfolio. They may be able to invest in only one, two, or three different bonds. If one of these were to default, they would suffer severe financial hardship. It would, therefore, be prudent for them to invest only in high-quality bonds even though they would not be getting the highest possible return. By contrast, investing in a bond fund provides investors with the safety advantages of diversification, so that they may benefit from the higher income available from a large number of lower-quality bonds. Of course, available bond funds provide a broad range of quality and safety, from AAA ratings to nonrated, highly speculative discount bonds.

Capital Gains from Regular Bond Funds

Conservative bond funds concentrate on achieving the maximum income available from the bond quality level they require. More aggressive nonconvertible bond funds also aim at both short- and long-term capital gains in the expectation of adding 3 to 4 percent per year to their investors' income return. The resulting total return of 10, 11, or 12 percent would make such bond funds quite competitive with stock funds in long-term average return.

If an aggressive bond fund's timing is fairly successful, short-term capital gains can be increased by rapid turnover and the use of borrowed funds for leverage. On the other hand, if management timing is below average, losses will be mutiplied by such tactics and techniques.

A safer way of achieving capital gains and usually tax-favored long-term gains is to invest in older low-coupon bonds selling at considerable discounts from par. Of course, current income yields are lower on such bonds, in many cases (particularly on top-rated bonds) fully offsetting the eventual capital gain at bond maturity, especially if the time value of money is taken into account. However, for lower-quality bonds, the combination of relatively high current income and eventual tax-favored capital gain *may* provide a higher total combined *aftertax* return than that available from a high-yielding bond of equivalent quality selling at or close to par. This would be especially true for investors with substantial accumulated carry-forward long-term capital losses, against which long-term bond capital gains could be offset tax-free. The whole operation is obviously hazardous, however, since an investor's capital gain tax rate at some future maturity date is not known in advance. Indeed, it is conceivable that the entire capital gain tax advantage might be eliminated by Congress prior to the maturity date.

All in all, the historical record of the more aggressive bond funds since their inception does not lend much support to the hope of regular, consistent capital gains from a bond fund portfolio. Investors in such funds should therefore focus primarily on maximum current bond income, any additional capital gain being regarded as pleasurable serendipity.

Capital Gains from Convertible Bond Funds

By contrast, recurrent capital gains on a fairly regular basis are a more definite possibility with a *convertible* bond fund. So too, of course, are current capital losses when stock markets are in retreat.

Convertible closed-end bond funds are the most volatile type of bond investment company available to investors. The price movements of these funds' convertible bond holdings largely reflect those of related common stocks, particularly if leverage is employed. For this reason, convertible bond funds usually sell at larger discounts from net asset value than nonconvertible bond funds do.

Of course, it is feasible and desirable for a convertible bond fund to switch substantially or completely to nonconvertible bonds whenever its management believes that the stock market trend is down. Such a shift will reduce volatility and risk, but it is usually difficult to accomplish without taking some losses.

Buying, Selling, and Operating Costs of Bond Funds

Such costs vary considerably from fund to fund, especially when one compares regular-load, low-load, and no-load mutual bond funds with closed-end bond funds purchased and sold at prevailing stock commission rates for varying amounts of shares. In addition, all types of funds have expenses for operations and for management fees that, combined, typically range from less than ½ percent to about 1½ percent. These expenses will be reflected in reduced income yields.

Accordingly, bond investors who confine their investments to high-quality issues, say, AAA, AA, and A and their equivalents, will almost always be as well or better off by buying such bonds directly rather than through a load bond fund. The picture is, of course, quite different for a *no-load* bond fund. For more speculative bond investors, the benefits of diversification from a bond fund offset, at least in part, a load fund's higher sales costs. And again, these benefits are usually available at lowest cost from a no-load bond fund. In all cases, bond investors should keep constantly in mind the basic distinction between the *management performance* of bond funds and their *investor results,* as explained in Chapter 42.

Income Advantages of Closed-End Bond Funds Selling at a Discount

Not only may closed-end bond funds be purchased at relatively low stock commission costs, but they may also be especially attractive for income if they can be purchased at well below their net asset value per share. For example, let us suppose that the net asset value per share of such a fund is $10 but that its shares are trading at $8.50. If the fund is earning at 8 percent return on the dollars it invests, it will be earning 80 cents per share. However, an investor who paid $8.50 per share will receive a return of 9.4 percent (80 cents divided by $8.50).

There is also, of course, a chance for capital gain if the prevailing discount on a bond fund shrinks or disappears, but there is a corresponding danger of capital loss if the discount at the date of purchase has increased by the time that the investor wishes to sell. So the main, bird-in-hand benefit of the discount is in terms of recurrent realized income, not essentially in a hypothetical capital gain.

Bond Funds as Keogh Plan and IRA Retirement Vehicles

Most types of bond funds can be excellent vehicles for self-employed investors with Keogh retirement plans or for employees who have set up their own investment retirement accounts (IRAs). Such funds usually provide a somewhat higher return than most savings banks and are quite safe over a long-term period. However, investors must be prepared for temporary reductions in prices and net asset values during periods of rising interest rates. See also the discussion of Keogh Plans and IRAs in Chapter 63.

Chapter 46
Venture Capital Investments

KENNETH W. RIND

Venture capital is the organized financing of relatively new enterprises to achieve substantial capital gains. Such young companies are chosen because of their potential for considerable growth due to advanced technology, new products or services, or other valuable innovations. A high level of risk is implied by the term "venture capital" and is implicit in this type of investment, since certain ingredients necessary for success are missing and must be added later.

Venture investments can be divided into several classes, usually called "first round," "second round," "third round," and so on, or "first stage," "second stage," "third stage," and so on. A first-round investment of *seed capital* is made in a "start-up," a company just being organized. Such first-stage financing provides at least enough capital so that a meaningful milestone may be achieved, a process that can take from six months to two years and usually requires from $150,000 to more than $1 million. On the assumption of first-round success, second-round money for working capital will be sought at a "step-up," or higher price, to permit the company to obtain a sizable backlog. At the next stage, the company may raise third-round venture money for expansion of facilities, or it may *go public*, since by then it will have a limited record of sales and earnings.

Later financings by other than public investors are called "private placements." These are not generally considered venture capital investments even when they contain a large measure of risk, because they are made on the basis of a historical record of sales and earnings.

Two types of venture capital investments do not fall under the previous definition. In a "buy-out," the venture capitalist helps a management team to purchase a going concern from a family or a division from a company, partially with the leverage of borrowed funds. In a "turnaround," a venture group will help to purchase management control in the hope of adding the capabilities necessary to convert a losing company into a profitable one.

Venture capital is concerned primarily with technological companies, but such investments can be made in any potentially rapid-growth area in which a small group with intelligence and drive can compete with larger firms.

Most new enterprises require varied types of assistance in their early days.

Generally, the venture capitalist will provide help and guidance to the portfolio company throughout its unsettled stages, which may last from three to seven years. Investment in a single company may range from $150,000 to $7 million, with most venture capitalists in the United States favoring $500,000 to $1 million as a customary commitment. The majority of rapid-growth companies in the United States were financed originally by venture capital, and it has proved to be an important force in keeping industry competitive in many technological areas.

Because relatively large sums are involved, venture capital is not generally suitable for individuals making direct investments. Although some companies have been started with small sums advanced by relatives or friends, the prognosis for this type of investment is not favorable.

While there are vehicles through which individuals can participate in publicly traded venture capital pools managed by professionals (a small number of closed-end funds and many small-business investment companies, or SBICs), the most successful venture capital groups are private ones. This is true because the flexibility and rapid decision making required in working with small companies are hampered by the governmental regulation of public investing groups. However, an astute investor should be aware of the activities of the publicly traded organizations. A well-timed investment in a venture capital fund just before a public offering for one of its successful private investments can be very rewarding. Additionally, an investment in a newly public company that is still being nurtured and guided by a successful venture capital group can provide the investor with the opportunity to benefit from the substantial increase in the odds for success enjoyed by a company involved with such a group.

History of Venture Capital

It is not possible to say exactly when venture capital originated in the United States, since pools of domestic and European investors in the nineteenth and early twentieth centuries were involved in backing various new industries such as railroads, steel, oil, and glass. A turning point came in 1911, when a group of wealthy individuals merged three weak companies (International Time Recording Company, Tabulating Machine Company, and Computing Scale Co.) into a single entity to manufacture and market office equipment. They were wise enough to recruit Thomas Watson as president of the firm in 1914, and in 1924 its name was changed to International Business Machines (IBM).

However, the modern venture capital era is generally thought of as beginning after World War II. It was given much of its impetus by Laurance Rockefeller, who even prior to that time had helped to finance Eastern Airlines, in 1938, and McDonnell-Douglas, in 1939. In the early postwar period, venture capital investments were concentrated in a few wealthy family groups, many of which had originally made their fortunes in earlier ventures. Among these were the Rockefellers (Standard Oil), the Phippses (Carnegie Steel), the Rosenwalds (Sears), the Pitcairns (Pittsburgh Plate Glass), and the Whitneys (John Hay Whitney and his sister, Joan Whitney Payson, heirs of the Vanderbilt shipping fortune).

The formation of American Research & Development (AR&D) in 1946 was an important event because this was the first venture organization open to public investment. In its first eleven years it financed more than 100 companies and made 35 times its investment. Later, other groups were formed to invest pooled moneys in ventures. Draper, Gaither & Anderson and Davis & Rock, which reportedly made 20 times its investment in seven years, were notable examples on the West Coast.

Early Corporate Successes

In the early 1950s, typical ventures required considerably less funding than they do today since, at the inception, the entrepreneurs could obtain government research and development contracts to support themselves. A number of non-profit research groups associated with universities were able to obtain venture capital and prosper in a "for profit" environment. These include Itek, in reconnaisance; GCA, in geophysics; Tracor, in undersea warfare; and Conductron, now part of McDonnell-Douglas, which began operations in radar signal processing.

A number of successful organizations were formed by large groups of people leaving the major computer companies. Examples of this are Control Data Corporation, founded in 1958 by people from Univac; Scientific Data Systems, now part of Xerox, founded in 1964 by people from Packard-Bell, in which an investment of $257,000 became worth $60 million; and Mohawk Data Sciences, founded in 1965 by people from Univac, which has achieved a leading place in the peripheral equipment field.

Several other venture capital investments used the concept of gathering a number of smaller technological companies under a single corporate wing. Litton Industries, founded in 1952, and Teledyne, founded in 1961, began in this manner.

Fitting in none of these categories were such venture capital–backed companies as Digital Equipment, Raychem, and Memorex, which all provided their initial investors with returns of more than 100 to 1. AR&D's $70,000 investment in Digital Equipment became worth more than $500 million.

A Securities and Exchange Commission (SEC) study of public offerings of venture capital–backed companies between January 1967 and March 1970 showed that, on the average, a company went public at about 7 times the price twelve months after the investment. During this period, several venture capital groups could point to average appreciation in their portfolios of 30 to 40 percent per year.

Later Venture Capital Sponsors

Drawn by these large gains, many new groups entered the venture capital field in the 1960s and early 1970s. Small-business investment companies (SBICs) were authorized by the Small Business Investment Act of 1958. They are corporations, licensed by the Small Business Administration (SBA), an independent government agency, that are provided with tax incentives and government loans of as much as $35 million (up to four times the initial capital) to make equity-type investments in small businesses. An SBIC may not invest more than 20 percent of its initial capital in a single company.

More than 800 SBICs have been licensed, and by 1970 they had invested more than $1.8 billion in 15,000 small companies. More than 50 of them have raised public money, but more than half merged, failed, or were converted into operating companies. The seven largest SBICs had an average annual appreciation of more than 40 percent during a six-year period in the 1960s. However, more recent records have been decidedly negative. Greater Washington, one of the major SBICs, created a holding company and joined the New York Stock Exchange in 1969.

In the late 1960s and early 1970s, a number of new closed-end public venture funds were formed, among them Inventure Capital, Fund of Letters, Value Line Development Capital, Diebold Venture Capital, Price Capital, and Source Capital. Insurance companies, banks, mutual funds, university endowment funds, and new private pools, some of them using money from foreign investors (including the Rothschilds), became involved in venture capital. Investment bankers, such as Oppenheimer & Co., also gathered pools of capital for this purpose.

Among the participating insurance companies are Aetna, Allstate (Sears), CNA, Connecticut General, John Hancock, Massachusetts Mutual, Paul Revere, and Prudential. Other financial companies include American Express, Boothe Computer, CIT, Talcott, and Transamerica. The banks include Bankers Trust, Bank of America, Chase Manhattan, Continental Illinois, First National Bank of Boston, First National Bank of Chicago, First National City Bank, Irving Trust, Marine Midland, Morgan Guaranty, and Wells Fargo.

Corporations, too, have become active in venture capital. Some, such as DuPont, Ford, and Exxon, entered the field to obtain a window on technology of interest to them. Others, like California Computer, Data Products, Electronic Memories, General Electric, and Mohawk Data Sciences had the intention of either marketing the products developed or of subsequently acquiring the entire firm. Still others, such as Singer, became venturers for purely financial reasons, although generally they did so with the expectation that they would be able to offer assistance to the young firm by providing it with management skills.

In addition to the companies previously mentioned, venture capital investments have been made by Alcoa, Allen-Bradley, American Broadcasting, Boise Cascade, Borden Chemical, Champion Paper, Coca-Cola, Control Data, Corning, D. H. Baldwin, Dow Chemical, Emerson Electric, FMC, General Mills, Harris Intertype, Hercules, Illinois Central, International Paper, LTV, Mobil Oil, Motorola, North American Phillips, Northrop, Pillsbury, Recognition Equipment, Signal Companies, Sprague, United Shoe Machinery (USM), Universal Oil Products, and University Computing.

In all, about 125 SBICs (including 21 public and 34 bank-owned SBICs) with about $1 billion in capital and about 350 other organizations with about $2 billion in committed capital (including funds) are active venture capitalists. An SEC study of 784 venture capital transactions during the period from January 1965 to September 1969 showed that investments totaled $765 million, consisting of about $350 million by institutions, $277 million by venture capital organizations, and $138 million by securities firms. It is estimated that total venture capital investments of from $300 million to $800 million in about 1,000 companies were made annually by professional groups during this period. This compares roughly in size with new public offerings for companies having net worth of less than $5 million.

From 1969 to 1972 approximately forty venture capital companies with committed assets of almost $500 million announced their formation. A number of the most important investors formed the National Venture Capital Association to provide a centralized means of communicating with the government, the securities industry, and the public.

Requirements for Venture Capital Success

Special analytical and judgmental abilities and a considerable outlay of time are necessary for success in venture capital. A venture capital organization must be large enough to support a proper staff for investigation and assistance. It must have additional capital available for its investments if they require it, since unforeseen problems are frequently encountered.

In general, the earlier informal venture capital partnerships did not anticipate the extensive efforts required by the general partners and have now been dissolved. The investing organization must be willing to devote a large amount of time and effort to guiding the entrepreneurs and assisting them in areas in which they are deficient. Thus, the ability to establish a good working relationship with each company's management is imperative. Because technology is such an important consideration in venture capital, most venture capital groups include a scientist or an engineer to assess proposals and maintain better rapport after investing. Financial and negotiating skills are also required.

Most venture capital groups are small, consisting of fewer than ten people, usually at a ratio of 1 person per 5 investments. Various organizational forms have been utilized, but the limited partnership is most popular for private organizations. The general partners who manage the investments generally take a fee of 15 to 20 percent of the profits, plus up to 5 percent of the assets each year for expenses.

Past experience has taught successful venture capital groups to look for certain features in potential investments. Most important is a leader of a complete management team who has the drive and wholehearted commitment to build a major company. Coupled with this dedication must be flexibility and realism to enable the leader to change direction when required. Unique capabilities that can lead to several products having a large market are also important, although some companies have done well on the basis of a single product by building a marketing organization able to distribute the results of others' development work. If a company has several capabilities, however, it must be careful that it does not squander its resources by diversifying too far afield.

Successful venture capitalists expect the entrepreneurs to provide a complete, persuasive business plan of strategy including financial, personnel, and other resources required, as well as attainable milestones. They also find it useful to coinvest with knowledgeable partners, so that the heavy work burden can be shared and any problems which arise can be attacked from several angles simultaneously.

There are, in addition, several things that successful venture capitalists have learned to avoid. Among them are the following:

1. Investments are not to be made in pure research. Specific product goals permit the investor to monitor the company's progress.

2. Nobody should find the venture's equity structure unfair. Room is left for options to middle management and for assuring the reward of extraordinary effort inside the founding group.

3. Insufficient financing can seriously hamper a company's operations. Enough funds must be provided to eliminate the need for management to be involved continually in money-raising activities.

4. The number of investments must be limited, so as not to overload the venture capitalist's resources and thus prevent early awareness of problems in portfolio companies.

5. Hasty commitments are always to be avoided. Typically, the business plans of more than 100 companies are investigated for every investment made.

Certain standard procedures are followed by all professional venture capitalists. It is of primary importance that venture capitalists be assured of a proper flow of good proposals by demonstrating that they are good venture partners. Candidate sources are, in addition to the entrepreneurs themselves, other venturing groups, bank loan officers, investment bankers, and finders. Successful venture capitalists are sought out by all these groups.

All proposals received must be screened, and only a select few are chosen for more intensive examination. Screening proposals for preliminary interest is followed by lengthy investigations, which may take from three to eight weeks of actual work time spread over a period of months. Since management is most important, an exhaustive investigation of the people involved must be made by questioning former employers, competitors, and knowledgeable industry figures. Checks are made with present and potential customers and users of competitors' products or services. Consultants are utilized. Opinions of industry associations are sought.

All the underlying assumptions of the business plan must be investigated. Is there really a demand for the product? Will new products make the old ones obsolete? Can the people involved manufacture the product at a satisfactory price?

A detailed investigation of the willingness of the marketplace to accept a new product or service is mandatory. In this regard, an interesting study was made by *Industrial Research*, a magazine that gives awards each year to the 100 most interesting new scientific developments. In following up the results from the award winners of the preceding five years, the magazine found that in one year, 1970, some 43 percent of the winners had not sold any of their products!

Additional factors investigated include backgrounds of other investors, industry trends, and compliance with securities laws. If all seems well, the financial arrangements must be negotiated. If the proposal is rejected, an effort is frequently made to explain why and to suggest other investors who might be interested.

Afterward, the venture capitalist generally helps the corporation to formulate business strategy, recruit and evaluate the skills of potential management personnel, institute proper management controls and planning procedures, choose legal and accounting firms, and decide on management compensation. The capitalist's role includes acting as a sounding board for new ideas and providing information on the industry, potential customers, and competitors. The venture capitalist is expected to assist in all financial relationships and negotiations, such as bank borrowing, contracts, acquisitions, and decisions with respect to public and private offerings of securities.

A great deal of time is spent with problems that arise in portfolio companies. As competition develops, interpersonal relationships degenerate, and everything takes longer than expected, the venture capitalist must sometimes assume an active role rather than a consultative position in the venture.

How to Make Money from Venture Capital

Investing in a venture capital fund to be offered to the public for the first time is generally not a good idea. Usually such funds carry investments at cost or at a discount from the quoted public market price because of reduced liquidity. Further, the fund's shares typically will sell at a discount from net asset value after such discounts. This double discounting is difficult to surmount.

From the preceding discussion, however, it is clear that young companies that have been able to attract professional venture capital groups have certain advantages as investments for others. The individual investor can feel reasonably sure that the company has been investigated in some detail and meets most of the criteria previously mentioned. In addition, the company will have become accustomed to good planning and reporting and will continue to benefit from the advice and assistance of seasoned businessmen who are prepared to assume roles as active as necessary to solve any problems.

While such assistance is obviously worth a premium to the investor, often companies selling at only slight markups from prices paid by venture capitalists can be found. Since professional venture capitalists will permit public offering of their companies' securities only when they believe in the viability of those investments, such companies should be sought out by the individuals willing to invest in speculative companies. Conversely, a lack of sophisticated venture capital backing is a danger sign, since a very good correlation can be made between corporate failure and lack of professional backers.

Additionally, while the record of publicly traded organizations investing in venture capital has not been completely encouraging, many of these groups have made outstanding investments. A public organization's report to its stockholders may be an invaluable source of information to the sophisticated investor. Careful reading may reveal the likelihood that one of its star investments will be going public or will be substantially marked up in valuation for other reasons. Private investments are usually carried at cost even though the public offering price could be a factor of 10 to 100 times higher. A substantial increase in the value of a single investment will frequently cause a large markup in the asset value of the investing organization. Alternatively, the shares of the newly public company may be spun off to the parent's shareholders, providing them with worthwhile capital gains.

It may also be possible, since most venture capital companies sell at varying discounts from net asset value, to use the psychology of the market toward this type of investment. However, it is clear that blind investment in such groups without regard to their discounts has been an unsatisfactory investment policy in the past.

Investors should also find it worthwhile to note the business areas in which venture capitalists are investing. To at least some extent a judgment has been made that these are areas in which small companies can successfully build large corporations. Thus, a survey of venture capitalists in the late 1960s and early 1970s would show that the most popular areas for investment at that time were medical products, communications, services, environmental controls, leisure, automation, electronics, peripheral equipment, computers, construction, power sources, and office equipment.

Although it is not recommended that individual investors make venture capital investments by themselves, some investors may choose to disregard our advice. In that case they should familiarize themselves with the various complex SEC regulations. Regulations regarding the liquidity of such investments, for example, will hamper their ability to sell their shares in such investments even after a public offering. On the other hand, individuals may be intrigued by the tax advantages of properly structured venture investments. These factors are too complex to be discussed in detail, but in any case good legal advice is required by any investors contemplating private investments.

One magazine that keeps abreast of the activities of professional venture capitalists is *SBIC / Venture Capital,* published by S. M. Rubel and Company of Chicago, Illinois. It should provide the alert investor with the background information needed to take advantage of the investment approaches discussed here.

A CASE STUDY OF A VENTURE CAPITAL SUCCESS

The following is the hypothetical financing history of a fully successful venture:

A first-round investment of $750,000 is made by the venture capital group in return for 75 percent of the equity, giving the company a $1 million valuation. The entrepreneurs, on the other hand, might invest only $50,000 for their 25 percent. A year later, after a prototype has been developed, $1.5 million is raised for 33⅓ percent of the company. (The step-up in price is 3 times.) Third-stage financing might occur when the company has a $10 million backlog and expects $15 million of shipments with $1.5 million of earnings. This could be at $4 million for 25 percent of the company, or a step-up of 8 times the original price.

After dilution from options, the first-round investors would own about 25 percent of the company, which probably would be valued at more than $30 million in a public offering, indicating an appreciation of 10 times the initial investment. Subsequent private investment, which would be termed private placements even though some venture capital groups might participate, could be made for various reasons.

The venture capital organization will typically recover its investment and a profit through taking dividends, a merger, selling its interest to others in a public offering, or spinning off its holdings to its shareholders or partners.

Section Nine

Tax Planning and Shelters

Chapter **47**

Defining Short- and Long-Term Tax Policies

ROBERT E. DIEFENBACH

IMPORTANCE OF TAX PLANNING

For most individuals and institutions income taxes represent a significant cost of living and doing business. Avoiding unnecessary tax costs should therefore play an important role in most investment planning. Moreover, unlike reductions in business costs or increases in income, which are diluted by taxes, the avoidance of tax costs represents net aftertax savings. An investor in the 50 percent tax bracket, for example, gains twice as much benefit from a tax saving as from an increase in ordinary income of the same amount.

Tax savings have the important quality of being relatively certain in the year in which they are realized. Unlike investment decisions, the effectiveness of which depends in varying degrees upon correctly forecasting events and conditions, decisions that are effective in avoiding current taxes depend only upon knowledge of the tax laws.

The avoidance of tax costs, however, becomes less certain when longer-range planning is involved. Tax laws have changed and will continue to change. Investments that must depend entirely upon favorable long-range tax consequences to produce an acceptable return should be scrutinized carefully. In recent years the benefits obtainable from many "tax shelter" investments have been reduced or eliminated through changes in the laws. Such changes represent a trend that can be expected to continue.

Although the avoidance of tax costs is an important consideration in asset management, it is rarely the dominant consideration. This statement is particularly true in the timing of purchases and sales. Transactions should be governed by their investment merits, favorable tax consequences being regarded as an additional benefit. Many poor investment decisions are made with the excuse that they were implemented for tax purposes. The fact that the outcome of investment decisions is uncertain does not relieve investors of the burden of bringing their best judgment to bear upon these decisions.

The weight that should be given to tax considerations depends upon the investors' marginal tax rate, or tax bracket. The effective marginal tax rate for investors is the percentage of each dollar of additional ordinary investment income that they must pay out in taxes to the various governmental authorities having taxing authority over that income. The higher that rate is, the more important tax considerations become in investment planning.

Tax considerations basically affect two areas of investment policy: (1) the type of investments selected and (2) the timing of purchases and sales. These are discussed more fully below.

ORDINARY INCOME, CAPITAL GAINS, AND TAX-FREE INCOME

Ordinary Income

For individuals the sources of ordinary investment income include dividends on common and preferred stocks, interest on corporate and federal obligations, loans, and mortgages, and rental receipts. The maximum marginal federal income tax rate on such income under the Tax Reform Act of 1976 is 70 percent. A lower maximum rate of 50 percent applies to so-called earned taxable income, which includes wages, salaries, professional fees, and other compensation for personal services. A $100 exclusion is permitted for dividend income, which serves to lower the effective tax rate on such income for small investors.

Increasing Importance of State and Local Taxes.   State and local income taxes are becoming increasingly significant in the investor's total tax picture. As of January 1, 1976, almost 90 percent of the fifty states and the District of Columbia imposed income taxes of some type. In addition, income taxes are imposed by many major cities.

Calculating a Total Marginal Tax Rate.   To determine the effective marginal income tax rate on fully taxable income the marginal income tax rate applicable to the investor's taxable income at each level of government must be included in the calculation. Most states do not permit a deduction for other income taxes paid. In these states the investor's effective marginal income tax rate may be calculated by using the following formula: $T = L + S + F (1 - S - L)$, where T represents the investor's marginal income tax rate and L, S, and F represent the applicable marginal income tax rates for local, state, and federal governments, respectively, all expressed in dollars per dollar of taxable income. An investor living in New York City, for example, with sufficient taxable income to place him or her in the tax brackets of 70 percent for federal, 15 percent for state, and 3½ percent for city income taxes, would have an effective marginal income tax rate of $T = 0.035 + 0.15 + 0.70 (1 - 0.15 - 0.035) = 0.756$, or 75.6 percent.

In states that permit all or a portion of federal income taxes to be taken as a deduction from state taxable income, the net effect of the state income tax tends to become less significant in the higher federal income tax brackets. The following formula may be used to approximate the investor's effective marginal income tax rate if federal income taxes are fully deductible from state taxable income: $T = F + (1 - F) (S - FS + L)$.

Consideration of Future Income Levels.   For long-term investment planning, it is necessary to consider expected future effective income tax rates as well as current rates. Career advancement and inflation are the major factors leading to projections of higher future income levels, while anticipation of retirement is generally the dominant consideration in projecting lower levels of income. At best such projections can be based only upon rough estimates, but in comparing the aftertax return expected from alternative investments over a period of years, some attempt should be made to use the most realistic information available. Projecting the future marginal income tax rate on a given level of income is even more subject to uncertainty. The most reasonable procedure, however, is to assume that current tax rates will persist unless there is some reason, such as legislation in the process of enactment, to believe otherwise. Corrective action in the form of adjustments to investment planning can and should be taken if material changes are made in the tax laws.

Corporate Taxation.   Corporations pay federal income taxes of 20 to 22 percent on the first $50,000 of net taxable income and 48 percent on net taxable income above $50,000. If a corporation owns common or preferred stock in another corporation and receives the dividends on this stock, 85 percent of the dividends received are excluded from the taxable income of the corporation. For example, a corporation in the 48 percent marginal tax bracket that receives $20,000 in dividend income pays federal income taxes of $1,440 (15 percent of $20,000 = $3,000 × 48 percent = $1,440). Therefore, corporate executives are motivated to invest excess corporate funds in the stock of other corporations that pay high dividends.

Treatment of Long-Term Capital Gains

In general, long-term capital gains for individuals are gains realized upon the sale of investments held for more than one year (nine months in 1977).

Computing the Tax.   Prior to 1971 federal tax laws provided for alternative computations of the tax on all net long-term capital gains. Taxpayers had the option of reducing capital gains by 50 percent, adding it to their other income, and computing the total tax in the regular way or of adding a 25 percent tax on the long-term capital gains to the tax on their other income computed as if it were their only income. This option remains available for net capital gains up to $50,000. However, beginning in 1972 the law provided that for gains in excess of $50,000 individuals' only option is to reduce capital gains by 50 percent and add them to their other income. Long-term capital gains are thus subject to an increased maximum effective tax rate of 35 percent before a possible additional tax on "preference items."

Capital Gains as a Tax Preference Item.   Since 1971 the 50 percent deduction permitted for long-term capital gains has been considered an "item of tax preference." The amount of all such tax preference income in excess of the amount of regular federal income tax payable in a given year plus an exemption of $10,000 or one-half of regular taxes paid, whichever is greater, is taxable at a rate of 15 percent. The effect of this minimum 15 percent tax on preference items has been to raise the maximum effective marginal federal tax rate on long-term capital gains to 37.25 percent.

The following example will illustrate the computation of the minimum 15 percent tax on items of tax preference. Let us assume that an investor has net long-term capital gains in excess of net short-term losses of $200,000 but no other tax preference items and that his or her total federal income tax before computing the minimum tax on preference items is $50,000. Since the investor will have included only $100,000 of the long-term gains in determining the tax, the remaining $100,000 becomes an item of tax preference. From this amount the investor deducts an exclusion of $25,000 (one-half of regular taxes of $50,000; the $10,000 minimum exemption does not apply) and also the $50,000 of income taxes due before computing the minimum tax. His or her minimum tax is 10 percent of the remaining $25,000, or $2,500, bringing the total tax to $52,500.

The maximum marginal federal tax rate on long-term capital gains applies to investors in the top (70 percent) tax bracket whose tax preference items exceed their tax plus $10,000 or one-half of regular taxes paid, whichever is greater. For these investors the tax on each additional $100 of long-term capital gains amounts to $35 (70 percent of $50) plus a minimum tax of $2.25 (15 percent of $50—$35), bringing the total additional tax to $37.25, or 37.25 percent.

Income Averaging.   The tax position of investors with long-term capital gains is somewhat eased, although further complicated, by income averaging. If taxable income in any year, including the taxable 50 percent of long-term capital gains, exceeds 120 percent of average taxable income for the four preceding years, taxpayers can elect to be taxed as if one-fifth of the excess had been received in the current year and each of the four preceding years.

Thus, for example, if an investor who already had taxable income in 1976 of $50,000 found it desirable to realize a $200,000 long-term capital gain and his or her average annual taxable income for the four-year period 1972–1975 was $45,000, he could treat $96,000 ($50,000 + $100,000 − 1.2 × $45,000) as if one-fifth, or $19,200, had been earned in each of the years 1972 through 1976 on top of an average income base of $54,000 (1.2 × $45,000). If the investor did not use income averaging, the 1976 tax on a taxable income of $150,000 (assuming that he or she was married and filing a joint return) would have been $76,980. By taking advantage of income averaging, however, the investor would pay a tax on 1976 taxable income of $73,200 ($54,000 + $19,200) plus the difference between the tax on $73,200 and the tax on $54,000 at 1976 rates for each of the four previous years. The total 1976 tax computed on this basis would have been $70,920, representing a saving of $6,060.

To employ income averaging, investors must have been citizens or residents of the United States during each of the five years used in the averaging period and must include as taxable income in each of these years all income earned outside the United States. In addition, investors must compute their average income for the four-year base period in a manner consistent with their current status (single, married and filing jointly, head of household, and so on), and the amount of income to be averaged over the five-year period must exceed $3,000.

Offsetting Losses against Gains.   For federal income tax purposes capital gains and losses are combined, or "netted out," in the following manner. First, short-term capital losses are deducted from short-term capital gains to produce net short-term capital gains or losses. Second, long-term capital losses are deducted from long-term capital gains to produce net long-term capital gains or losses. Third, net short-term gains or losses are combined with net long-term gains or losses to determine the taxpayer's net gain or loss position for the taxable year.

If there is an excess of net short-term gains over net long-term losses, this excess must be added to ordinary income. Similarly, if there is an excess of net short-term losses over net long-term gains, this excess is deductible from ordinary income. If there is an excess of net long-term gains over net short-term losses, 50 percent of this excess is added to ordinary income. And if there is an excess of long-term losses over net short-term gains, 50 percent of this excess is deductible from ordinary income.

If a taxpayer has both net short-term gains and net long-term gains or both net short-term losses and net long-term losses, the short-term portion is added to or deducted from ordinary income, while only 50 percent of the long-term portion is added to or deducted from ordinary income.

Since long-term capital losses are deductible from short-term capital gains on a dollar-for-dollar basis but are only 50 percent deductible from other ordinary income, it is clearly advantageous to offset net short-term capital gains with long-term capital losses when it is feasible to do so. Conversely, it is advantageous to defer realizing long-term capital gains, when feasible, if the realization of such long-term gains would result in offsetting net short-term losses.

Carrying Forward Capital Losses.   The maximum net capital loss deduction that may be taken in any year is $1,000 ($500 for married persons filing separately). This deduction consists, first, of any net short-term capital loss up to the $1,000 maximum and, second, of 50 percent of any net long-term capital loss available to make up the $1,000 total. Losses not utilized in any year may be carried forward to reduce capital gains or ordinary income in future years for an unlimited period until the amount has been fully utilized.

Losses carried forward retain their original status. Unutilized short-term capital losses thus are deductible from future capital gains or ordinary income on a dollar-for-dollar basis, while unutilized long-term capital losses are fully deductible from future capital gains but only 50 percent deductible from future ordinary income. Because prior to 1970 long-term capital losses were fully deductible from ordinary income, any unutilized capital losses incurred prior to 1970 remain fully deductible, up to the maximum of $1,000 ($500 for married persons filing separate returns), from both capital gains and ordinary income.

Treatment by State and Local Governments.   Although treatment varies considerably among state and local governments, many state governments conform their treatment of capital gains and losses to federal tax law by using taxable federal income as the state tax base. A majority of the states make use of this approach, and the number is likely to increase over the years because of the inherent economies in tax return auditing.

Certain states, however, tax long-term capital gains at the same rate as ordinary investment income. Connecticut and Massachusetts are in this category.

Tax-free Investment Income

Interest on the obligations of state and local governments and their agencies, the category of investments generally referred to as municipal bonds, is the only form of investment income that is completely exempt from federal income taxes. The interest on obligations of a state and the interest on obligations of local governments and agencies within that state are generally also exempt from income taxes imposed by that state. However, the interest on obligations of local governments is generally not exempt from any income taxes imposed by such governments.

The tax-exempt status of interest on municipal bonds has been repeatedly called into question by legislators in recent years. The question is a complex one, having to do with constitutional law, and directly affects the financing costs of state and local governments. However, the privilege conferred upon wealthy investors and certain financial institutions by this tax-exempt status has been increasingly regarded as a social inequity. For this reason it is by no means certain that municipal bonds will maintain their tax-exempt status indefinitely. However, most authorities believe it unlikely that any change in the federal income tax law affecting the tax-exempt status of municipal bonds would be made retroactive to apply to outstanding securities.

Tax-free Dividends.   In contrast to interest on municipal bonds, so-called tax-free dividends, which are treated as a return of capital to the investor for tax purposes, are not in fact entirely free of taxes. Such dividends may be all or partially free of taxation when received if the company making the distribution has no accumulated earnings and either no taxable earnings in the current year or earnings that are less than the amount of the dividend distribution. This situation can arise from the sale of assets at a loss or from heavy noncash charges against income created by allowances for depletion or depreciation of assets. In the case of depletion and depreciation, the charges permitted for tax purposes may be greater than those judged by management to be adequate in reporting to stockholders. When this situation occurs, a company's dividends may be entirely or partially tax-free even though the company reports a profit to its stockholders.

In some cases the manner of reporting to stockholders may be determined by regulatory accounting requirements rather than by management judgments. Western Union Corporation is a case in point. For the year 1971 Western Union reported consolidated net income of $13.7 million and year-end retained earnings of $131.2 million. However, both the $5.8 million of dividends paid on the company's preferred stocks (including the preferred stock of the telegraph company subsidiary) and the $13.8 million of dividends paid on common stock during 1971 were wholly tax-free to stockholders. Western Union at end of 1971 had an accumulated operating deficit of approximately $24 million for income tax purposes and no taxable income for the year. The Federal Communications Commission (FCC) requires that the telegraph company use straight-line depreciation for rate-making purposes, whereas accelerated depreciation is used in determining taxable income. Furthermore, the FCC requires that a portion of interest charges, social security taxes, and pension costs be capitalized as plant and equipment or as preacquisition costs and written off over a period of years. Even research and development expenditures are capitalized for rate-making and reporting purposes and amortized over an eight-year period. As a result, the company did not have any taxable income before 1976, and dividends on the preferred and common stocks were tax-free in the interim.

Since the tax status of a company's dividends often changes from year to year, it is important for investors to understand the accounting treatment that gives rise to a tax-free dividend in each specific case in order to make reasonable projections with respect to the tax status of future dividends. Corporations paying dividends that are wholly or partially tax-free enclose tax information applicable to each dividend with the divident payment.

Upon receipt of a tax-free dividend, representing as it does a return of capital, an investor is required to write down the cost of the stock upon which the dividend was paid by the amount of the tax-free distribution. If the stock is sold at some future time, therefore, the investor will, in effect, pay a tax on this "tax-free" dividend as a capital gain, except to the extent that the price realized from the sale has declined as a result of the dividend. Thus, if the price of the stock should decline by the exact amount of the dividend, the investor pays no tax because he or she has realized no gain as a result of the dividend. For example, if an investor purchases stock in a company at a price of $20 per share and the company pays a tax-free dividend of $1 per share, the investor must lower his or her cost basis to $19 per share. If the stock is sold ultimately for $21 per share, the investor has a capital gain of $2 per share; if it is sold ultimately for $19 per share, he or she has neither a gain nor a loss on the sale.

Other Sources of Tax-free Income.   There are additional sources of investment income, somewhat less readily available to the investor than tax-free corporate dividends, that may be wholly or partially tax-free. These may be developed through the ownership, either individually or in partnership with others, of assets against which heavy depreciation or depletion charges are permitted for income tax purposes. Such assets include improved real estate, equipment leased to business, oil and gas properties, and mining operations. As in the case of tax-free corporate dividends, the tax benefit results from deferring the payment of taxes and from obtaining long-term capital gains treatment for this income when it is realized upon the ultimate disposition of the assets. By continuously rolling over or accumulating this type of investment, many investors are able to defer a major portion of their tax burden indefinitely. However, since 1970 the tax benefit has been reduced by the minimum 10 percent tax on items of tax preference, which, in addition to long-term capital gains as discussed above, include such items as the excess of interest paid to purchase or carry property held for investment over the net taxable income generated by the property, the amount of accelerated depreciation taken on property, depletion, and certain amortization allowances.

Disadvantages of Tax-free Income.   One disadvantage to many investors of tax-exempt interest and the various other forms of tax-free income results from the progressively graduated income tax rate schedule for individuals and the wide variation in the income tax structure for corporations, particularly financial institutions. The effect of these wide differences in tax rates may make a given investment relatively more valuable to other investors and therefore provide a lower aftertax rate of return to most individuals than fully taxed income. The following example will illustrate this point more clearly.

For an investor in a 50 percent tax bracket, a tax-free yield of 5 percent is equivalent to a taxable yield of 10 percent. Therefore, he or she would earn an equivalent return on a tax-exempt bond selling at $1,000 and paying $50 per year in interest and on a fully taxable bond selling for $1,000 and paying $100 per year in interest. Consequently, if the tax-exempt bond began to fall in price below $1,000 while the taxable bond remained at a price of $1,000, the investor in a 50 percent tax bracket would purchase the tax-exempt bond and drive the price back to $1,000. The investor in a 30 percent bracket would receive an aftertax return of 5 percent on the tax-exempt bond; however, he or she would receive an aftertax return of 7 percent on the taxable bond. Obviously, the presence of other investors in higher tax brackets makes it unwise for this investor to purchase tax-exempts.

Tax-free dividends representing a return of capital can present further disadvantages. The future of a corporation with no retained earnings and no taxable current income is generally less predictable than that of a tax-paying corporation with a consistent earnings record and a significant earned surplus. There is little benefit to be derived from obtaining tax-free income for a period at the cost of a substantial loss in capital. Such investments, therefore, warrant more than the usual amount of scrutiny.

Measuring the Aftertax Value of Investment Returns

To make a meaningful comparison of the returns from alternative investments it is necessary to adjust all such returns to an aftertax basis. Table 47-1 compares the effect of federal marginal income tax rates on the net value to the investor of the three basic types of investment return discussed above.

TAX CONSIDERATIONS IN THE SELECTION OF INVESTMENTS

Taxes are only one factor to be taken into consideration when selecting investments. Other factors are investors' dependence upon a regular flow of investment income, the minimum return they require from their investments, and their ability or need to undertake risk.

Common Stocks

The investment return offered by common stocks consists of dividend income and the opportunity to realize capital gains. Investors' judgment of the relative value to be placed upon current dividend return, expected future dividend return, and expected return from capital appreciation should begin with the adjustment of these current and expected returns to an aftertax basis.

Common stocks of corporations that reinvest a large proportion or all of their earnings and therefore pay out a relatively small proportion in dividends or no dividends whatsoever to common stockholders often present the most likely opportunities for capital gains. A policy of paying minimal or no dividends by a company that is generating profits and cash can reflect either the opportunity for a high return on new investment capital within the corporation's business or heavy capital demands generated by rapidly growing markets for the corporation's products or services. Since corporate earnings distributed to stockholders are in effect taxed twice, once at the corporate income tax rate and again at the investor's personal income tax rate, investors in the higher tax brackets should emphasize the opportunity for capital appreciation rather than dividend income in their selection of common stocks.

Common stocks with current dividend rates that result in a high dividend yield on the price of the stock often sell at such apparently generous yields because of the presence of a substantial amount of risk or a minimum expectation of future

TABLE 47-1   Aftertax Values of $1 Additional Taxable Income for Selected Tax Brackets

Marginal tax rate (percent)	Dividends or interest	Long-term capital gains	
		$50,000 or less	Over $50,000*
14	$0.86	$0.93	. . .
15	0.85	0.925	. . .
16	0.84	0.92	. . .
17	0.83	0.915	. . .
19	0.82	0.905	. . .
22	0.78	0.89	. . .
25	0.75	0.875	. . .
27	0.73	0.865	. . .
28	0.72	0.86	. . .
31	0.69	0.845	. . .
32	0.68	0.84	. . .
36	0.64	0.82	$0.82
38	0.62	0.81	0.81
39	0.61	0.805	0.805
42	0.58	0.79	0.79
45	0.55	0.775	0.775
48	0.52	0.76	0.76
50	0.50	0.75	0.75
53	0.47	0.75	0.735
55	0.45	0.75	0.725
58	0.42	0.75	0.71
60	0.40	0.75	0.70
62	0.38	0.75	0.69
64	0.36	0.75	0.68
66	0.34	0.75	0.67
68	0.32	0.75	0.66
69	0.31	0.75	0.655
70	0.30	0.75	0.65

*If not subject to minimum tax. If the minimum tax is applicable, the calculations are variable, depending on the amount of regular taxes paid (see above, page 47-5).

growth. Individual investors must compete in the market for investments with a number of tax-exempt institutions, such as pension funds, churches, colleges, and charitable foundations. For these institutions a dollar of dividend income is worth as much after taxes as a dollar of long-term capital gain. In addition, there are many financial corporations which, although taxable in varying degrees, benefit from an 85 percent deduction on intercorporate dividends. Because dividend income is worth more after taxes to a very substantial pool of capital than to most individual investors, the price the individual investor must pay for substantial dividend income is often uneconomically high on an aftertax basis. Nevertheless, investors must judge for themselves each specific investment alternative examined. Securities markets are not completely rational, and there have been a number of periods in which the opportunity for growth has commanded a premium in the market that could not be justified or sustained.

Fixed-Income Securities

Fixed-income securities such as bonds or preferred stocks offer interest or dividend income and, except for convertible issues, limited opportunity for capital gains. The interest on corporate bonds, commercial paper, and obligations of the federal government is normally fully taxable as ordinary income. Since the capital gain opportunities offered by bonds are limited and the interest is fully taxable, corporate bonds, except for convertible issues or bonds at a deep discount, have little to recommend them in the investment program of individual investors desiring long-term capital gains. Long-term obligations of the federal government are similarly inappropriate unless purchased at a substantial discount. Short-term federal obligations, however, can be considered an alternative to savings accounts for the liquid portion of investors' assets. High-grade commercial paper serves a similar function but only for large investors.

High-grade taxable bonds purchased at sufficiently deep discounts so that appreciation when held to maturity will provide a major portion of the total return are suitable for capital gain–oriented portfolios. The maturity dates of such bonds can be selected to provide for relatively constant annual realization of capital gains over an extended period. Furthermore, these types of investments are desirable because the long-term capital gains are predetermined and subject to only a minimal amount of risk.

Municipal bonds are appropriate longer-term fixed-income investments for individual investors provided their tax brackets are high enough to offset the yield differential between municipal bonds and fully taxable securities of similar quality. For large investors in the higher tax brackets a portfolio of municipal bonds maturing within one year can provide relatively attractive aftertax returns for the liquid portion of investment assets.

Nonconvertible preferred stocks generally provide relatively unattractive after-tax returns for individual investors when risk is taken into consideration. Corporations receive an 85 percent exclusion on preferred dividends, and they therefore bid for the available preferred stock and drive down the yields. In addition, the opportunity for capital gains in preferred stocks is limited, further reducing their attractiveness.

TAX CONSIDERATIONS IN THE TIMING OF PURCHASES AND SALES

Tax policies with respect to buying and selling assets affect two areas of investment decision. The first of these areas is the average rate of investment portfolio turnover, and the second concerns the decision to hold or switch individual assets.

Nontax Considerations Affecting Turnover Policy

The rate of turnover in an investment portfolio will naturally fluctuate from year to year and should not be subjected to rigid policies. Nevertheless, it is possible to draw some general guidelines on turnover that follow from investors' situations and objectives.

To begin with, investment turnover is a function of investors' time horizons. An investor who selects assets on the basis of their long-term appreciation potential can be expected to have a lower portfolio turnover rate than one who hopes to take advantage of short-term market swings on a trading basis. A five-year time horizon, for example, meaning that the investor typically evaluates investment alternatives on the basis of their expected return over a five-year period, suggests that the average holding period will be about five years. Some investments will be sold earlier because of changing prospects or a reevaluation of original expectations, and some will be held longer if they are believed to offer further potential. But the average holding period can be expected to approximate five years, which in turn implies that the average portfolio turnover rate will be approximately 20 percent. The average time horizon employed by any investor may be determined largely by a wide variety of nontax considerations, such as a psychological preference for short-term trading as against holding for the long term, the amount of time the investor is able or willing to devote to investment management, or the possession of specialized knowledge in certain fields, such as real estate, petroleum exploration, or commodity trading. The turnover of investment assets may, in addition, be dictated by the investor's cash-flow requirements.

Lastly, investment turnover can be affected to an important degree by changing economic, social, or market conditions that cause significant changes in the prospects for a given industry or an entire class of investment assets. Policies with respect to investment turnover must be sufficiently flexible to be responsive to such changes.

Tax Considerations and Turnover Policy

The capital gains tax on realized profits represents a transaction cost in the same way that transfer taxes and brokerage commissions are transaction costs. Unlike transfer taxes and commissions, however, the capital gains tax rate is a function of investors' income tax brackets. In general, therefore, the higher investors' income tax brackets, the more they should lean toward a policy of low portfolio turnover through emphasis on longer-term investments. Capital gains taxes on portfolios with high turnover can lead to persistent erosion of capital. It is significant that studies of the pretax investment returns on mutual funds show no relationship between portfolio turnover and investment performance. To the extent that this is true, *aftertax* investment returns are reduced by high portfolio turnover rates. Although consistently above-average investment performance is clearly a function of the effectiveness of asset management, in practice it has not been demonstrated that the effectiveness of asset management is a function of portfolio activity.

The Hold-or-Switch Decision

The decision to continue to hold an investment asset or to dispose of it and acquire another asset is basic to all asset management. Unless assets are exchanged outright, the decision to switch is often visualized as two decisions, one involving the relative attractiveness of cash compared with the investment held and the other involving the relative attractiveness of an alternative investment to cash. This concept of switching assets creates a need to be right twice in the minds of investors. If an investor can dispose of an investment held at a profit, he or she has already been right once and therefore is often better prepared psychologically to switch than if he or she must admit having been wrong once by disposing of an asset at a loss.

Some successful traders in commodity and securities markets advocate a policy of cutting losses short and letting profits run. There is, on the other hand, much statistical evidence to support the thesis that in efficient markets, such as the New York Stock Exchange, future price performance is completely unrelated to past price performance. Proponents of this thesis would decree that the hold-or-switch decision, at least from the investment standpoint, be made without regard to the existence of gain or loss. A reluctance to sell at a loss combined with an eagerness to take profits, however, is compatible with neither of the above approaches.

Furthermore, the capital gains tax tends to tilt the balance in favor of taking losses and letting profits run.

Net short-term losses are deductible for income tax purposes from both ordinary income and capital gains on a dollar-for-dollar basis, whereas only 50 percent of net long-term losses are deductible from ordinary income. For this reason it is advantageous from the tax standpoint to take losses promptly. Similarly, because net short-term gains are taxable as ordinary income and net long-term gains are taxable at reduced rates as described above, it is advantageous from the tax standpoint not to realize gains until they qualify as long-term.

Capital gains taxes remain as a restraint upon switching out of investments when disposition would result in the realization of long-term gains. However, the impact of the taxes is less than in the case of short-term gains, and the availability of offsetting losses often can reduce or eliminate this capital gains tax restraint in a given situation.

Switch with No Repurchase Expectation. When no future repurchase of the investment to be sold is contemplated, the restraint imposed by the capital gains tax upon realizing long-term gains is relatively minor. Future repurchase is usually not anticipated, for example, in the case of real estate, mining, or oil properties or in the case of the common stocks of companies in industries for which the long-term outlook is judged to be unpromising. In such cases the capital gains tax restraint upon switching can be expressed by $B > A/(1 - TG)$. In this formula A represents the future proportionate change in price expected for an investment currently held, B represents the proportionate change in price expected for an alternative investment over the same period, T represents the investor's effective marginal capital gains tax rate, and G represents the proportion of unrealized gain present in the current market price of the investment currently held. The aftertax differential in dividend return or interest yield between the two alternative investments over the period considered is assumed to be insignificant.

For example, if an investor in the 25 percent capital gains tax bracket ($T = 0.25$) holds a stock for which he or she paid $20 per share currently selling at $50 [$G = (50-20)/50 = 0.6$] and which is expected to increase in price to $60 in two years [$A = (60-50)/50 = 0.2$], the investor can justify selling that stock to purchase an investment with an expected appreciation greater than $0.2/(1 - 0.25 \times 0.6) = 0.235$, or 23.5 percent, over the same period. Since the appreciation required from the alternative investment is not substantially greater than the 20 percent gain expected from the present holding, the capital gains tax does not impose a very severe restraint upon the switch decision in this situation.

Temporary Switching. The above formula applies, as has been stated, in cases in which no repurchase of the investment to be sold is contemplated. In many investment situations, however, such as attempting to take advantage of price swings in the stocks of cyclical industries or selling a stock believed to be temporarily overpriced in the anticipation of obtaining a better short-term performance elsewhere, the future repurchase of the asset to be sold must be considered in the hold-or-switch decision. In these situations the capital gains tax must be regarded as a more severe restraint upon asset management.

Attempting to quantify the amount of restraint to be imposed upon a hold-or-switch decision in cases in which an investor desires to repurchase an investment currently held at some future date involves a fairly complex calculation. The investor must pay a capital gains tax on any profit that he or she currently has in the stock, as well as brokerage commissions and transfer taxes. Unless the investor believes that the stock will decline very significantly in price before resuming its upward movement or the cash is needed immediately for an outstanding short-term investment opportunity, it generally does not pay to sell a stock on which there is an unrealized gain with the intention of repurchasing it at a later date.

TAX ASPECTS OF INVESTMENT COMPANIES

Regulated versus Nonregulated Companies

An investment company may be either regulated or nonregulated. A nonregulated company is taxed like any other corporation. However, the overwhelming majority of investment companies are regulated.

If a company is regulated, it is taxed only on the amounts not paid out to its stockholders, and the usual corporate tax rates apply to these amounts (the 85 percent intercorporate dividend credit does not apply, however). Stockholders receiving dividends from such companies pay their full personal rate on the portion representing interest, dividends, and net short-term capital gains and pay the appropriate capital gains tax on the portion representing net long-term capital gains. The investment company must inform the taxpayer of the proportionate shares of each dividend represented by the various sources of income.

If the company retains capital gains and pays a tax thereon, the stockholder is entitled to a credit if he or she would have paid a lower tax had all the income been distributed. The investor can also raise the cost basis of his or her stock by the aftertax amount of the retained capital gain. For example, if the investor paid $50 for the stock and the company subsequently realizes a capital gain of $2 per share, paying a 50-cent capital gains tax and retaining $1.50 net after tax, the investor considers his or her stock to have cost $51.50 for purposes of calculating the tax liability when the stock ultimately is sold. Furthermore, if the stockholder would have paid a tax of 40 cents on a capital gain of $2, he or she would receive a tax credit of 10 cents (50 cents − 40 cents).

Unrealized Gains and Losses

When net unrealized gains represent a significant portion of the assets of an investment company, they may be the result of an excellent historical investment performance or merely of a very low rate of portfolio turnover. Conversely, if an investment company's net assets contain little or no unrealized gain, the cause may be either a lackluster investment performance or a relatively high turnover rate. The presence of a substantial net unrealized loss, on the other hand, is generally the result of an unsuccessful investment performance in some past period.

Impact on Capital Gains Distributions.   Substantial unrealized appreciation in an investment company portfolio represents an assurance to the shareholder that, given a reasonably stable turnover policy, management has considerable flexibility in maintaining a fairly consistent annual payout of capital gains. If, on the other hand, unrealized appreciation is minimal or nonexistent, the annual payout of capital gains to shareholders can be expected to fluctuate considerably. In the special case in which an investment company has a substantial net unrealized loss and an accumulated deficit, no capital gains distributions are to be expected. In fact, the company will normally elect unregulated status and be taxed as an operating corporation to permit distribution of dividend income to be tax-free to shareholders as a return of capital.

Tax Effect of Portfolio Gains.   Some investors may be concerned that they are buying into a tax liability if they purchase shares in a regulated investment company with a portfolio containing net realized or unrealized gains. This concern has sometimes been cited as a factor contributing to the discount from net asset values at which many closed-end investment companies sell in the market.[1] In actuality, however, such concern is largely unfounded.

Distribution of Gains.   Capital gains realized on sales of portfolio securities in the

---

[1]See, for example, Eugene J. Pratt, "Myths Associated with Closed-End Investment Company Discounts," *Financial Analysts Journal,* July–August 1966, p. 79.

normal course of operations are generally distributed to stockholders near the end of the year in which the gains are realized. In this case investors would pay a tax on the distribution at the long-term capital gains rate. However, the total amount of unrealized gain in the portfolio of the investment company has little direct bearing on the amount of such distribution in any year. Let us assume, for example, that an investor with an effective long-term capital gains tax rate of 25 percent were to purchase the shares of an investment company at a price of $50 per share and that their net asset value is $50 per share, of which $40 represents unrealized gain. (The existence of a market premium or discount on the shares is immaterial from the tax standpoint.) If the investment company realizes and distributes capital gains in the amount of $4 per share, the investor would owe a tax of $1 on this distribution. The asset value and, normally, also the price of the investment company shares would decline by the amount of the distribution. If the investor should then sell his or her shares, a $4 capital loss would result, exactly offsetting the $4 gain realized upon receipt of the distribution. (If the investment company had realized and elected to distribute an unusual gain—for example, $10 per share—the investor would probably find it advantageous from a tax standpoint to sell his or her shares either prior to the distribution or immediately thereafter to avoid a capital gains tax payment on what would in this case amount to a return of capital.)

An investor who purchases shares in an investment company with unrealized capital gains will, in effect, be prepaying his or her taxes if the company realizes and distributes capital gains. However, regardless of whether the investment company has total unrealized gains or losses, the ultimate total taxes that the investor must pay will not be affected.

Retention of Gains.   When realized gains are retained by a regulated investment company, the capital gains tax is paid by the company at the corporate capital gains tax rate on behalf of the shareholders. The shareholders then obtain a credit for this tax payment against their personal income taxes and increase the cost basis of their shares by the amount of aftertax gain retained by the company. Using the example above, if the investment company realized and elects to retain an unusual capital gain of $10 per share, it would pay a capital gains tax (currently at a rate of 30 percent) of $3 on behalf of its shareholders. The net asset value, and presumably the price, of the shares would decline by $3, the amount of the tax. The investor would write up the cost of his or her shares by $7, the amount of retained gain. He or she would obtain a net tax credit of 50 cents (the $3 paid on his or her behalf by the investment company less a personal tax liability of $2.50). If the investor should then sell the shares, his or her tax credits would be equal to the loss sustained on the transaction, as follows:

Original cost of shares	$50.00		$50.00
Write-up	7.00		
Adjusted tax cost of shares	$57.00		
Selling price	47.00		47.00
Tax loss	$10.00	Actual loss	$ 3.00
Value of tax loss at 25 percent	2.50		
Tax credit	0.50		
Total tax credits	$ 3.00		

Liquidation.   In the event of complete liquidation of an investment company, the amount of net assets represented by unrealized gain is of no concern to investors. Their tax basis remains the price at which they purchased the shares. If the company in the example above liquidated its entire portfolio at market and distributed the total proceeds of $50 per share to its shareholders, it would pay no tax and investors who purchased shares at a price of $50 would also pay no tax since they would realize no gain on the transaction.

Possible Effect of Unrealized Gains.   Investors who purchased shares in a regulated investment company, whether it be a mutual fund or a closed-end company, therefore do not acquire someone else's tax liability merely because unrealized gains comprise a portion of net assets. However, the amount of unrealized gains in the portfolio of an investment company may affect management's investment policy and therefore should not be ignored.

A large proportion of unrealized gains, for example, may act as a constraint upon turnover and perpetuate a very conservative policy with respect to switching holdings. Conversely, the absence of unrealized gains may put pressure upon management to trade aggressively in an attempt to realize gains for distribution to shareholders.

Chapter 48
Introduction to Tax-sheltered Investments

RALPH POLIMENI

The Sixteenth Amendment to the United States Constitution states that taxes may be levied on income from whatever source derived. It would appear that all dollars or goods received by individuals as income are subject to federal income taxes, but over the years Congress has granted special deductions for certain items and exluded some income from taxation. Items that receive special tax treatment are commonly known as "tax loopholes" or, technically speaking, "tax shelters." If tax shelters are properly used, they can substantially reduce or, in some cases, completely eliminate an individual's taxable income.

Broadly defined, a tax shelter is any legal method of tax avoidance available to individuals that is designed to protect them from the full impact of regular income tax rates. This, in effect, constitutes any deduction that individuals may take on their tax returns.

This chapter will deal with a specialized area of tax shelters called "tax-sheltered investments." a tax-sheltered investment either generates income that is tax-free (for example, interest on municipal bonds) or provides substantial tax deductions (for example, depreciation of buildings) that, when effectively utilized, serve to offset ordinary income and thereby reduce taxable income. A tax-sheltered investment is also undertaken to generate a regular income or to realize a profit upon termination of the investment, or both.

Development of Tax-sheltered Investments

Contrary to popular belief, most tax-sheltered investments did not develop because of errors or omissions in the federal tax laws that were capitalized upon by prudent tax attorneys or accountants. Instead, most tax-sheltered investments were created by Congress specifically to stimulate investment in certain sectors of the economy and so to achieve desired economic and social goals. Thus, the government created specific tax-sheltered investments to foster investment in desired areas by allowing these investments to be eligible for certain tax preferences. Inasmuch as most tax-sheltered investments are highly speculative, the government supports the concept that an additional incentive is necessary to funnel investment capital into desired areas.

Therefore, while investors are promoting their own financial position, they are also helping to carry out national economic goals. For instance, with the increasing need for larger amounts of energy, the exploration for additional oil reserves has become a necessity. To stimulate individual investors to put their funds in oil exploration, the federal government provides large tax advantages for oil-drilling investments.

Another example is a real estate investor who receives the benefits of deductions for interest payments, property taxes, depreciation, and possibly capital gains treatment. At the same time the government is able to stimulate economic growth in suburban areas.

Objectives of Tax-sheltered Investments

When considering tax-sheltered investments, investors must set forth certain objectives. Although objectives will vary with each investor, some general objectives are applicable to all investors. Investors should strive to attain the following general goals:

1. A tax-sheltered investment that is economically sound to withstand varying economic conditions.

2. A tax-sheltered investment that is relatively safe from changes in tax laws that may adversely affect the desirability of the investment. This objective may make it necessary to research proposed tax legislation or to limit investments to areas that correspond with national economic needs.

3. A tax-sheltered investment that allows investors to attain maximum leverage on the equity invested.

4. A tax-sheltered investment that will generate income of a rate best suited to the investor's tax-planning needs.

5. A tax-sheltered investment that will either appreciate in value or generate a growth of income to provide for a hedge against inflation.

6. A tax-sheltered investment that will complement an investor's present financial portfolio.

Planning for Tax-sheltered Investments

With proper planning, investors can benefit from tax-sheltered investments in the attainment of lower income taxes and, to some extent, in the avoidance of other taxes such as estate taxes. Proper planning dictates that only sound business investments be undertaken as tax shelters. Careful planning and detailed investigation of various tax-sheltered investments are necessary to safeguard the original equity capital invested and, it is hoped, to generate at least a reasonable return on the investments. The relevant criteria to be considered when planning for non-sheltered investments (degree of risk, liquidity factors, and earning potential) are likewise applicable to tax-sheltered investments. Since tax-sheltered investments are very speculative, the need for careful analysis and investigation before capital is invested cannot be overemphasized.

An individual's future investment plans should also be considered when contemplating a tax-sheltered investment. The possibility of future changes in the investor's cash flow and tax bracket will directly affect the desirability of the investment.

The prospective investor should also review the various tax-sheltered investments available to select the type of investment that will best suit his or her needs. It should be kept in mind that what may be a good tax-sheltered investment for one person may prove to be a disaster for another.

It should also be noted that tax-sheltered investments are not geared for individuals who cannot afford the risk and the often-substantial capital deemed necessary for such a venture. Most authorities on tax-sheltered investments agree that investors should be in at least the 50 percent tax bracket to benefit effectively from a tax-sheltered investment. Their position is based on the fact that such investments were intended originally to act as an incentive to encourage speculative investment. The higher an investor's tax bracket, the more he or she has to benefit from a tax-sheltered investment and the less to lose. For example, an investor in the 50 percent tax bracket who invests $20,000 is gambling with only $10,000 of his or her own resources because if the entire investment should be lost, the investor can claim the $20,000 as a tax loss (if it meets specific criteria). When the loss is applied against the investor's other earned income, there will be a $10,000 tax saving.

For example, let us assume that the individual's other taxable earned income before the $20,000 loss is $500,000. Since the maximum tax on earned income is 50 percent, the tax would be $250,000. However, if the loss of $20,000 is deducted from the taxable income of $500,000, the taxable income becomes $480,000, and 50 percent of this sum is $240,000. The tax has thus been reduced by $10,000. When the $10,000 in tax savings is deducted from the $20,000 originally invested, the actual loss is $10,000.

In effect, the government (more appropriately, the American taxpayers) will share 50 percent of the investor's losses. In many cases, if the investor should turn a profit on the investment, he or she will be subject to only a capital gains tax of 25 percent. Thus the higher the tax bracket, the less an investor is actually gambling with his or her own resources and the more attractive a tax-sheltered investment becomes.

On the basis of the above example, American taxpayers would bear 50 percent of the investor's losses and share only 25 percent of the gains. Obviously, the investor receives the better deal.

Evaluation of Tax-sheltered Investments

Choosing the appropriate tax-sheltered investment is a complex task. The fact that each tax-shelter carries with it certain advantages and certain disadvantages generally leads to the conclusion that no one shelter will completely meet an individual's needs. A reasonable solution may require a trade-off. That is, the individual would proceed to choose two shelters that complement each other. An investor may wish to choose a shelter with short-range benefits but long-term drawbacks and, concurrently, another shelter that would serve his or her long-range goals but lack immediate benefits.

General guidelines to follow in evaluating different types of tax-sheltered investments are presented to aid the investor in selecting an appropriate shelter for his or her needs.

Tax Considerations.   The amount and type of taxes to which a particular tax-sheltered investment is subject should be determined. The following questions may be considered:

1. Is income from the tax-sheltered investment considered ordinary income (dividends from corporations), tax-free income (interest from municipal bonds), or income subject to capital gains treatment (sale or exchange of capital items)?

2. Can any losses from the investment be offset against the investor's other ordinary income?

3. What tax deductions are available under the tax shelter?

4. How large will the tax deductions be?

5. Will deductions be constant, or will they decrease over the years?

6. Does the tax-sheltered investment generate any tax preference items (for example, is it subject to a 15 percent minimum tax above a $10,000 exemption, or one-half of the taxpayer's regular income)?

The estate tax is another tax to be considered seriously when evaluating alternative shelters. Some shelters are specifically vulnerable to estate taxes. When planning alternative tax shelters for an estate, it may be best to select those whose tax consequence is a long-term capital gain. The reason is that capital gains or losses to an estate receive the same tax treatment as capital gains or losses to an individual.

Most investment prospectusus will provide a section on the specific tax ramifications of the tax shelter. This section should be carefully read and thoroughly understood before an investment is undertaken.

Time Factors.   Some of the more effective tax shelters do not provide immediate economic benefits in terms of aftertax income but instead offer long-term benefits. An investor should be cognizant of the variation in timing benefits that different tax shelters offer and seek a shelter that supports his or her present income objectives.

Legal Ramifications.   The potential investor should view tax-sheltered investments from a legal standpoint, since they may be subject to legislative changes or judicial interpretations. A prime legal ramification to be considered is the shelter's degree of social usefulness. Generally speaking, the more socially useful a shelter is, the less vulnerable it is to legislative changes. A shelter dealing with the exploration and refining of petroleum exemplifies a socially useful tax haven that will probably be around until a substitute for oil is developed.

There are many variables that can weaken the protection provided by the social usefulness of a shelter. One such variable is popularity. Tax shelters that become increasingly popular with the financial community may also become increasingly vulnerable to change, since such shelters draw congressional attention and public criticism. Of course, if these tax shelters have sufficient political power to back them, investors can generally expect Congress to place only minor limitations upon them.

An investor should strive for rapid liquidity of benefits if a particular tax shelter appears to offer solid benefits but also to be legally vulnerable to legislative change. Grandfather clauses would not inhibit legislation that would provide for a minimum taxable income, thus affecting the tax advantages in many sheltered investments such as oil or cattle. If the investor is not concerned with immediate economic benefits but is willing to derive benefits at some future period, he or she should consider only shelters that are fairly invulnerable to legislative changes.

Alternative Shelters.   A tax shelter should always be compared with an alternative shelter that appears to have similar economic potential. It is also conceivable to consider a comparison between a sheltered investment and a nonsheltered investment.

Possibility of Additional Investment.   Some types of tax shelters require investors continually to increase their investments to reap potential benefits. As a consequence, investors may be required to make much larger investments than they originally anticipated.

A prospective investor should take into consideration the ramifications of death when a constantly escalating investment is involved. If the investor should venture into this type of shelter, it is suggested that some of the sheltered income be directed into insurance so that after his or her death sufficient resources will be available (via the proceeds of the insurance policy) to maintain any anticipated additional investment required. Failure to provide adequate resources for additional investment may force an early liquidation of the tax-sheltered investment and, in many cases, result in a penalty or a loss.

Detailed Evaluation.   When evaluating a prospective investment, the investor should take into consideration all his or her other invested shelters. The individual's tax bracket depends upon what deductions or sheltered investments he or she may have in the particular year.

It is also necessary to consider items of tax preference both in the year of investment and in the year of liquidation. The minimum tax on preference items was introduced by the 1969 Tax Reform Act and increased by the 1976 Tax Reform Act. The tax preference legislation provided for a 15 percent tax on tax preference income with an exemption allowed to individuals (filing joint returns) equal to the greater of $10,000 ($5,000 in case of a married individual filing separately) or one-half of the taxpayer's regular income tax, in addition to an allowance for the usual federal income tax liability. Preference income is derived from several areas including capital gains, accelerated depreciation, depletion costs, bad debts, and excess amortization. It is possible for the minimum tax on preference items to dilute the benefits received by many tax shelters. For example, if an investor had $60,000 in tax preference income and reduced it by the $10,000 exemption along with a $15,000 tax liability, he or she would be liable to the government for an additional $5,250 in taxes.

Tax preference income		$60,000
Tax preference exemption	$10,000	
Federal income tax liability	15,000	25,000
Excess tax preference income		$35,000
15 percent tax rate		.15
Tax preference liability		$ 5,250

Choosing the Right Investment

The investor must measure the specific shelter in the light of his or her entire sheltered investment program. The question is whether the shelter is in balance with the present investment portfolio. Achieving this balance can be a complex matter, and the investor must thoroughly understand his or her overall financial situation. Evaluation should also include a review of tangible assets, working capital, and reserve requirements of the investor's present investment program. The important point to remember is that the existing program must be considered. The tax-sheltered investments should be regarded as an extra incentive to the prior determination of total investment program objectives.

Investment Control

The potential investor must be able to devote the time required to measure the actual performance against the projections. If the performances do not correspond with projections, the variances may have been caused by tax law changes, fluctuating economic conditions, or a variable with the investment program itself. The problem of managing property acquired through investment may have to be handled professionally. If the investor is unable to budget his or her time for the proper management of such property, this function should be delegated to another individual.

Tax Shelter Pitfalls

Many pitfalls can await the prospective investor who is negligent in seeking economically sound investments that involve tax savings. Therefore, accounting and legal consultation is highly advisable before the investor commits his or her resources. This point cannot be overemphasized.

Some of the more common pitfalls that may prevent an investor from achieving his or her goals are discussed below.

1. *Tax penalties.* The investor should be wary of an investment that has no business purpose. In such a case, the Internal Revenue Service (IRS) may disallow any deductions on the ground that the investment is a nonbusiness venture. If an

investment is declared to be nonbusiness in nature, the investor will also lose any deductions taken on prior returns and become subject to an interest penalty on the understated amount of tax liability from prior years. This situation is common with complicated corporate reorganizations that involve transfers of stocks and operating assets between several entities.

2. *Liquidity levels of shelters.* An important point for the investor to keep in mind is whether he or she is in a financial position to handle *low-liquidity shelters.* Such shelters cannot be turned rapidly into cash or may be converted into cash only after incurring a penalty or loss. Real estate investments are a prime example of a low-liquidity shelter. Once the initial investment has been made on a promising piece of real estate, it may require a long holding period before it can be liquidated at the desired rate of return. Therefore, when engaging in low-liquidity tax-sheltered investments, the investor should make certain that he or she has enough resources on hand to provide for future contingencies.

3. *Timing elements.* The investor should obtain whatever accounting and legal consultation is needed early enough to permit sufficient lead time. Tax-sheltered investments require lengthy research and investigation to cover the complex questions that inevitably arise. The consultant must become thoroughly familiar with the investor's needs so that the correct type of investment to fit his or her financial resources and investment goals can be determined. After these needs have been determined, considerable time may be required to find the appropriate investment and judge its quality.

4. *Internal Revenue Service rulings.* The investor is warned against conceivable misinterpretation of IRS rulings and court decisions. It is advisable that tax and legal consultation be fully utilized so that the investor avoids risking the possibility of retroactive as well as potential negative effects on the particular tax-sheltered investment chosen.

5. *Promoter's approach.* A thorough investigation should be undertaken to determine the selected promoter's integrity and credibility. One of the simplest and most effective means of investigation is to check the promoter's past experience and success in prior projects. In addition, it is advisable for the investor to recheck with outside experts the information received from the promoter. Such a check serves as a control and as a protective measure for the investor, for it is his or her capital resources that are being utilized.

An investor should beware of promoters who speak only of the marvelous tax benefits of the proposed investment, "neglecting" to mention that they reserve for themselves most of the equity in the investment. Obviously, the investor would forfeit economic gains merely to acquire tax benefits.

6. *Excessive interest rates.* The investor is interested ultimately in leverage maximization. However, should the investor be negligent, it is conceivable that he or she might be vulnerable to excessive interest rates, which in turn would unnecessarily reduce the investment's potential profitability. This topic is discussed in greater detail below in the paragraph "Excess investment interest."

7. *Contingencies.* All contingencies relating to long-range tax-sheltered investments should be investigated. Since the investor's income is a critical factor in the attractiveness of most tax-sheltered investments, any changes anticipated in the investor's income such as the feasibility of early retirement, a bonus decrease, or other possible losses in income cannot be overlooked. A change in income resulting in a lower tax bracket can significantly alter the benefits resulting from a specific tax-sheltered investment. Therefore, an anticipated drop in income level may require changing an individual's investment portfolio.

8. *Statutory risks.* The investor should be watchful for risks (for example, depreciation recapture provisions) that may turn the benefits of future capital gains into ordinary income. If this should be the case, the investor would want to

avoid such tax shelters. It is recommended that the investor keep abreast of contingent statutory changes and attempt to anticipate how these changes would affect the shelter in question.

Moreover, future statutory changes may have adverse effects on present sheltered investments. The Tax Reform Acts of 1969 and 1976 are prime examples of changes in the tax laws. The acts were aimed at reducing the tax benefits of tax-sheltered investments.

The 1969 act brought about three major changes:

1. *Maximum tax on earned income.* The act introduced a descending progression of maximum marginal tax rates on earned income. Prior to 1971 the rate was 70 percent, but beginning in 1972 the rate was limited to a 50 percent maximum. The purpose of the congressional cut-back was to discourage the utilization of tax-sheltered investments. Nevertheless, individuals with high levels of income can still utilize tax-sheltered investments effectively to reduce their tax liability.

2. *Minimum tax on preference items.* The 10 percent minimum tax on preference items is applicable to total tax preference items in excess of allowable exemptions. The point is that the minimum tax does not take effect with any one preference item but is a combination of tax preference items. The investor is also allowed a seven-year additional exemption carry-forward of the amount if regular income taxes exceed total preference items over $30,000.

3. *Excess investment interest.* There is an automatic limitation on the amount of investment interest that may be deducted in any one year. The limitation is $25,000, but the investment interest subject to this provision is so-called excess interest. Excess interest is defined as the amount of interest that exceeds the investor's investment income and long-term capital gains by more than $25,000. That amount of excess interest still qualifies for a 50 percent deduction rather than the usual full amount. This limitation affects mainly tax-sheltered investments in which highly leveraged situations prevail and borrowing is an important factor, as in real estate and equipment leasing.

Congress, after several years of deliberation, in 1976 enacted one of the most comprehensive tax reform acts in twenty years. Like the Tax Reform Act of 1969, a major purpose of the Tax Reform Act of 1976 was to restrict the advantages of tax shelters. The areas of the 1976 act that have an important effect on tax shelters are as follows:

1. A major objective of the 1976 act was to limit severely leveraged tax shelters. The loss on certain activities cannot exceed the total amount that the investor is at risk in each activity at the close of the taxable year. The at-risk rule limits risk to the extent of the cash, the adjusted basis of other property contributed, and any amount borrowed for which the investor has personal liability for payment from his or her personal assets. Thus, limited partners in highly leveraged investments are limited to the amount of loss that they are allowed to take in the following activities: (*a*) farming (farming operations involving trees other than fruit and nut trees are excluded); (*b*) exploiting and exploring for oil and gas resources; (*c*) producing, distributing, or holding motion picture films or video tapes; and (*d*) equipment leasing.

2. Prepaid interest must be deducted over the period of the loan instead of when cash payment is made.

3. A limitation of $2,000 is imposed on the amount of additional first-year depreciation that a partnership can pass through to its partners.

4. Fees incurred in the syndication of a partnership must be capitalized; organization fees may be amortized over a five-year period.

5. Retroactive allocations of partnership income or loss to prior periods before a partner entered the partnership are not allowed.

6. An individual's minimum tax on tax preference items has been increased

from 10 to 15 percent, reduced by an exemption equal to the greater of $10,000 or one-half of regular income taxes.

7. The maximum tax of 50 percent on earned income still applies, however; when individuals are engaged in a trade or business in which both personal services and capital are material income-producing factors, a reasonable amount (not to exceed 30 percent) of an individual's share of the net profits from the trade or business may be treated as earned income.

Even though the 1976 Tax Reform Act further reduced the potential of sheltering income, opportunities still exist to shelter income. Some of them are as follows:

1. The at-risk rule, which severely limits the tax benefit of highly leveraged shelters, does not apply to real estate transactions.

2. Intangible drilling cost deductions are still available for oil and gas investments; however, part of the intangible drilling cost now constitutes a preference item.

3. As long as the investor is not considered to be a part of a syndicated partnership or joint venture, he or she may still deduct farm losses.

Some of the many pitfalls that investors may encounter when dealing in tax-sheltered investments have been discussed. They have been presented to encourage caution on the part of investors before they commit themselves and their resources. For a discussion of tax-sheltered investments in cattle, real estate, oil and gas, and equipment leasing, see Chapters 49, 50, 51, and 52.

BIBLIOGRAPHY

Berman, Daniel S., and Sheldon Schwartz: *Tax Saving Opportunities in Real Estate Deals,* Prentice-Hall, Inc., Englewood Cliffs, N.J., 1971.

Commerce Clearing House, Inc.: "Tax Reform Bill of 1976," *Standard Federal Tax Reports,* vol. 63, no. 42, September 1976.

Chapman, W. E.: "Real Estate Tax Incentives," *National Tax Journal,* September 1973.

Drollinger, William C.: *Tax Shelters and Tax-Free Income for Everyone,* Epic Publications, Ann Arbor, Mich., 1972.

Fass, P. M., "Motion Pictures as a Tax Shelter: A Current Analysis of the Technique and Problems," *The Journal of Taxation,* March 1974.

Silbert, Gerald: *Tax Sheltered Investments,* Practising Law Institute, New York, 1972.

Gordon, M.: "More Tax Shelters: Weighing the Rewards and Risks in Schemes to Balk the IRS," *Barron's,* October 1973.

Hellerstein, Jerome R.: *Taxes, Loopholes and Morals,* McGraw-Hill Book Company, New York, 1963.

Hershman, A.: "New Tax Shelter In 370s," *Dun's,* October 1973.

Schreiber, Irving: *Tax Savings in Investments,* Panel Publishers, Inc., New York, 1969.

"Tax Shelters: The Action Is in Oil and Real Estate," *Business Week,* Dec. 22, 1973.

Chapter 49

Investing in Cattle

RALPH POLIMENI

A new breed of farmers, commonly known as tax farmers, has evolved in recent years. These new farmers rarely if ever become involved in the actual production of farm goods. Their ranks are composed of doctors, attorneys, accountants, motion picture stars, and members of other professions. However dissimilar these professionals may seem, they share a similar objective: to decrease their tax burden through tax deductions via cattle investments. The typical investor in cattle is usually in the 50 percent tax bracket. Anything short of this tax bracket doesn't produce tax savings sufficient to outweigh the inherent risks of beef cattle production.

There are two main methods of beef cattle production, cattle feeding and cattle breeding. The discussion in this chapter will stress cattle feeding because the two-year holding period for long-term capital gains on a breeding program does not make cattle breeding as attractive a tax shelter as cattle feeding. A brief discussion of how breeding works is presented at the end of the chapter. It should be noted that most of the general risks, advantages, and considerations inherent in the cattle-feeding business can also be applied to cattle breeding. A potential investor in cattle breeding should study the information presented in the cattle-feeding section to get a fuller perspective of the cattle industry.

FEEDING

Most cattle earmarked for eventual slaughter are acquired from breeders. The breeders use approved seed stock and hope to bring forth the better genetic factors inherent in the cattle. The average calf is weaned at about eight months of age, when it usually weighs about 500 pounds. Within three years from birth the average calf grows to a weight of about 1,000 pounds. Approximately two-thirds of the cattle grown in the United States are grain-fed on feeder lots for at least half a year before they are sold as slaughter cattle

Feedlots

The ability of the feedlot operator is a very important variable in determining whether an investment in breeding cattle will be profitable. An agent for the investor will usually enter into an agreement with a feedlot to fatten the feeder cattle that the investor has bought from a breeder. The buying of the cattle may even be arranged through the feedlot. The cattle are then boarded at the feedlot for about six months, during which they gain an average of 2 pounds a day. When the desired weight is reached or the price is right, the fattened cattle are shipped to market for slaughter. The freight charges both in and out of the feedlot are usually paid by the investor, as are all the expenses incurred while his or her cattle are at the feedlot. The investor's profits are computed by market price less expenses. It is important for small investors to remember that they can never feed or board their cattle as cheaply themselves as on a central feedlot. The overhead of the lot is being spread over many more cattle than just those owned by particular investors, thus lowering the price per head. The buying of large amounts of grain also helps to lower prices for investors.

It is of the utmost importance that the feedlot operator be capable and reputable. Good records are important to enable the operator to determine which grains bring the best gains and in what way expenses should be allocated. The investor is sent periodic reports on the current status of his or her investment. More and more feedlots are switching to computerized records and statistical testing to find the best ways to run the lots.

Many feedlots are merging with others to form huge multiple-owner feedlots. There are many advantages to this form of lot, not the least of which is the availability of large amounts of capital needed to run the feedlots more profitably.

Tax Considerations

Tax deferral was a key factor in the tax advantage in cattle feeding. The 1976 Tax Reform Act requires that farming operations classified as farming syndicates may deduct only expenses for feed, fertilizer, and other supplies relating to the farm when they are used or consumed. Prior to the 1976 act, a farmer was permitted to use the cash method of accounting and deduct preproductive expenses currently. The result of the 1976 act is that farming syndicates must use the accrual basis of accounting and capitalize preproductive expenses. A farming syndicate is defined as a partnership or other enterprise (other than a corporation, unless the corporation elects to be treated as a small business corporation) that engages in farming which at any time offers for sale any interest required to be registered with a federal or state agency having authority to regulate the offering of such securities for sale. Also, if more than 35 percent of the losses of the enterprise is allocable to limited partners or entrepreneurs, the farming operation is considered a farming syndicate.

Investing in a cattle tax shelter is still available in transactions structured to avoid being considered part of a syndicated partnership or joint venture. When a feedlot operation is not considered a farming syndicate, ordinary income may be offset by paying food and interest costs in advance and deducting the payment in the period of purchase rather than in the period to be benefited. The method of accounting that allows costs to be deducted when they are paid instead of when they have expired is called the cash basis of accounting. It enables the investor to receive benefits from the tax savings. Under a partnership all items of income, deductions, credits, or losses are apportioned among the limited partners.

To illustrate this point, let us assume that the investor is an unmarried male physician with no dependents earning $70,000 a year. After deducting his business expenses and various other miscellaneous items, he has a taxable income of $50,000 at the time that he enters into the cattle deal. If he didn't invest in cattle, his federal tax would be $20,190. Once involved with cattle, the investor deducts food, maintenance, shelter, interest, transportation, management fees, and other costs involved in the feeder enterprise. Let us assume that these costs amount to

$15,000. This lowers the doctor's taxable income to $35,000 on which the federal tax liability is $11,790. There is thus an immediate tax saving of $8,400. The following year, when the cattle are finally sold, the sales figure is reduced by the amount remaining on the loan that initially bought the cattle (leverage up to 90 percent is available) plus added expenses in the second year. Subtracting the feeder's share of any profits leaves the investor with a smaller taxable income from cattle than the sales price would reflect. If the investor is still in a high tax bracket, another cattle feeder program can be entered into to lower the taxable income in the second and third years. The cattle deal is usually entered into during the last part of the investor's taxable year.

Losses from the cattle business are deductible against the investor's nonfarm income. As will be seen, additional risks may be encountered when losses are deducted.

A pitfall that the investor must guard against in offsetting farm losses against nonfarm income is the "hobby" versus profit motive. The IRS has ruled that losses can be deducted only if the investor is in the business to make a profit. An investor is deemed to be in a business for profit if a profit has been made in any two of the preceding five years. This requirement can be overcome by the taxpayer if he or she can prove to the IRS that the purpose of entering the cattle business was to make money, not just to offset nonfarm income. In the breeding of cattle, it may take more than ten years to raise a breeding herd to a level at which it will make a significant profit in two of five years.

Feeder programs, as opposed to breeder programs, are not subject to minimum tax on tax preference items. Moreover, deductions for depreciation are not allowed in a cattle feeder business, and depreciation recapture provisions therefore do not apply.

General Advantages

Cattle have advantages over other forms of investment that enhance their value as a possible business venture. An investor in need of cash can move his or her cattle to market in a day or two and have them sold within a week. It would take a little longer if the investor were trying to get a particular price for the cattle, but usually the demand is greater than the supply. If the investor needs cash but doesn't want to sell the cattle, possibly because of a poor market or the loss of tax benefits, he or she can go to a bank and get nearly 90 percent value by using the cattle as collateral. The investor thus obtains the needed cash without risking the loss of tax benefits that the sale of the cattle would entail. He or she would get the additional bonus of being able to write off the interest on the loan, which would not be allowed in other methods of investment.

Cattle investment may be considered a secure investment for a number of reasons. In a feeder program the investor may find that possible loss is guaranteed to be no more than a certain amount.

Although the net earnings in cattle are no higher than the average return in common stocks (usually 3 to 5 percent), the leverage is much higher than in the stock market. The maximum margin in the stock market is approximately 50 percent, whereas financing of nearly 90 percent can easily be found in the cattle industry.

Both cattle feeding and cattle breeding can be used as deterrents to the imposition of the 70 percent penalty tax on a personal holding company. The situation inherent in a personal holding company is found to exist when a corporation is formed with five or fewer members owning more than 50 percent of the capital stock and derives 60 percent or more of its income from interest, dividends, and rents. The 70 percent tax is imposed if the income from the corporation is not distributed to the shareholders. The corporation usually does not wish to distribute its income because the individual shareholders would then be subject to tax on the income received. To combat this situation, what is needed is income that is considered nonpersonal. This income must be large enough to reduce the total personal holding income of the corporation to less than 60 percent.

Let us assume that a small investment company has $10,000 in dividend income, $5,000 in interest income, and $5,000 in rental income. For the cattle business to eliminate the need for the personal holding company tax of 70 percent, adjusted gross income of at least $13,500 must be received to reduce the total personal holding company income to less than 60 percent.

General Risks

Although very astute prospective investors are being convinced of the advantages of cattle feeding, the disadvantages are sometimes glossed over by its promoters. When considering cattle, investors are generally not as knowledgeable as they would be in areas such as stocks and mutual funds. This being the case, they must rely on information received from those around them. The possibility of being "babes in the woods" in any area of investment could be disastrous. Even if investors are informed of the uncertainties of the investment, being so far removed from this type of business, they have no real way of understanding these risks.

There are also risks with respect to the cattle themselves. The death rate of cattle runs to an industry average of 2 percent despite inoculations and other safeguards used by feedlot operators. What appears to be a small percentage may amount to a loss of many thousands of dollars when we consider that each head of beef cattle weighs from 800 to 1,200 pounds at the time of sale. The loss from the death of cattle is usually suffered by the investor rather than by the operator unless the investor has had the foresight to arrange for insurance against the loss of his or her herd.

Another problem is that costs involved in cattle feeding have risen amazingly. Prices for all types of grain have risen to many times the previous level, and some items that were free now cost the feedlot operator thousands of dollars a year.

Cattle are a commodity and are thus subject to the whims of the marketplace. The price of grain, the amount of imports, the number of cattle, and other factors cause the price of cattle to fluctuate as much as 5 percent a day. An individual in the cattle business on a short-term basis can be caught in a squeeze of falling prices for as long as a few months. Low prices may force an investor to keep the herd for a longer period than planned (in anticipation of future price rises), and the extra cost of feeding and maintaining it will decrease possible profits, possibly below the break-even point. The sharp price fluctuations are somewhat reduced for an investor who stays in the business for a longer time, usually five years. It is hoped that the fluctuations of price will average out over this period.

Still another drawback to cattle investing is that the terms of partnership agreements are usually quite restrictive for the investor. The promoter, or general partner, is usually able to withdraw from the program at any time, while in most cases the investor is unable to do so without incurring a financial loss.

The fees built into the program are often paid directly to the general partners. In a recent prospectus, for example, the general partner got $6.25 per head of cattle plus one-third of all "net" profits over $10. In addition, a 10 percent commission was paid to the underwriter of the deal, which was a subsidiary of the general partner. These sums added up to more than 12 percent in commissions; by any standard, this created a high break-even point.

Some management agreements do not charge a flat fee but ask for a share of the profits. As an example, one of the large management groups charges 10 percent of the profits in any single year regardless of whether the whole five-year plan makes a profit. The 10 percent in profit years might be enough to make the whole five-year plan unprofitable.

The method of financing the cattle-breeding business is still another risk to be confronted. In a typical cattle deal the investor uses about $25,000 of his or her own money, along with $50,000 of bank-financed funds. This procedure increases by 3 times the possible profits to be made in the deal, minus interest. This type of financing seems to be the only way that the purported large profits of the business can be made. The problem, of course, is that even after an investor loses his or her own money, he or she is still responsible for the loan of $50,000. Still another problem is that, as a result of downward fluctuations of cattle prices for a few months or more, the bank may require the investor to put in more cash to keep from losing the whole investment.

After all these other risks have been considered, the nontax farm income of the investor must be examined. If the investor's income tax bracket is not high enough, he or she will not make enough through tax savings to warrant the risks in a cattle program. As shown in Chapter 48, a 50 percent tax bracket is usually the minimum required to make a cattle deal profitable for an investor.

BREEDING

The upgrading of the standard of living has been closely correlated with the increased demand for beef cattle. The rapid increase in the consumption of beef has been partially met by the cattlemen's need to enlarge their herds and increase their productivity.

The rising cost of feed for the cattle has caused an increase in their wholesale and retail prices. These price increases have usually been passed on to consumers, who have sometimes boycotted meat in their neighborhood supermarkets. Such boycotts are one way in which consumer demand for meat has been slowed, but it has by no means been stopped.

The easy financing of a cattle-breeding enterprise has attracted potential investors. Many banks and institutions offer up to 90 percent financing on cattle, thus enabling an investor to get a $100,000 deal in cattle for an initial cash outlay of only $10,000 in equity.

Many herds are sold to investors under a management agreement that specifies charges for managing the herd. The investor is thus divorced from any active participation in the maintenance of the herd. Most agreements also provide that management handle the sale of the herd and employ correct record-keeping methods. Status reports are sent to investors to keep them informed of the progress of the investment. Management agreements are especially useful for investors who have no practical knowledge of the cattle industry. In this way an "expert in the field" can handle the day-to-day processing of the investment while the investors' interest is held to the bottom line after sale. All management fees are deductible expenses of the operation. In the larger feedlots, there are usually full-time managers to handle any unexpected contingencies.

Cattle-breeding programs specialize either in raising male calves for slaughter and female calves for reproduction or in the genetic upgrading of a purebred herd. A purebred herd is usually more expensive and more difficult to sell than one from a cattle-feeding program.

Tax Considerations

Cattle breeding entails a number of tax considerations:

1. Cattle herds are entitled to an investment tax credit (as of 1976 limited to one per herd). The 1971 Revenue Act allowed a farmer to take advantage of the

investment tax credit for the first time. A credit of 7 percent can be taken in the first year that the livestock is placed in use by the taxpayer. The full credit of 7 percent is allowed if the useful life of the animal is seven years or more; two-thirds of full credit, if five to six years; and one-third, if three to four years. Certain limitations may apply to the maximum credit if the taxpayer is not the original owner. Cattle must be "new property" to be eligible for the investment credit. An item is considered new property if its original use commences with the investor. For example, a newborn calf is considered new property if the female was not used previously as a dairy animal.

2. Livestock held for breeding purposes will be eligible for capital gains treatment if it is held for more than two years. The cattle must be "property used in the trade and business" of the taxpayer and not subject to ordinary income treatment under the excess deductions account and the depreciation recapture provisions. Net losses on livestock are considered ordinary losses and are deductible in full. The losses are not subject to the limitations on the deductibility of capital losses. Section 1251 of the Internal Revenue Code requires the taxpayer to set up an excess deductions account in which "net farm loss" exceeding $25,000 in one taxable year must be recorded. The account can be reduced by "net farm income" in subsequent years but will be raised by further farm losses exceeding $25,000. Certain other kinds of ordinary income can reduce the excess deductions account. When the cattle are sold, any gain that under ordinary circumstances would be considered a capital gain will be taxed as ordinary income to the amount in the account, and all amounts above this sum will be considered a capital gain.

Capital gains also apply to calves that are born into the herd. They have a zero tax basis, whereas cattle that were purchased have a tax base equal to the original purchase price less any depreciation taken to the date of sale.

3. Purchased cows are allowed depreciation. Depreciation on cows purchased after 1969 is recaptured and treated as ordinary income to the extent of the profit received on the cattle sold. Calves born to the herd are not subject to depreciation because no expenditure is involved.

A first owner of an animal is allowed to take accelerated depreciation. A fast tax write-off is possible because the Revenue Act of 1971 permits investors to use 20 percent shorter lives of cattle when computing the depreciation rates. Investors other than original owners are limited to the 150 percent declining-balance method or straight-line depreciation. Salvage value must be deducted from the purchase price to determine the depreciation base. In cattle the salvage value is the value of cattle after they have outlived their usefulness.

Cattle purchased after 1969 are subject to depreciation recapture, which means that any gain, to the extent of the depreciation taken, is taxed as ordinary income and is not eligible for capital gains treatment. For example, let us assume that in 1976 an investor sold breeding cattle purchased in 1973 and realized a gain of $50,000. If the investor had previously taken a $20,000 depreciation deduction on the herd, he or she would have been eligible to treat only $30,000 as a capital gain. The remaining $20,000, the amount equal to the depreciation deduction, would have been treated as ordinary income.

4. All management business expenses are deductible against ordinary income. So are normal breeding expenses such as grain, medicines, and shelter for the cattle. The deduction is made in the year of purchase rather than in the year of benefit. The benefits of a breeding program are similar to those of a feeding program, except for the ones mentioned previously in this chapter. An added benefit is obtained through a management agreement whereby the investor pays only 6 percent commission of the sale of his or her cattle rather than the usual 10 percent for a sale through a cattle broker.

5. A loss resulting from the operation of a breeder herd is deductible against nonfarm or noncattle income. As stated in the section on feeding, the hobby versus profit motive must be fully explored.

6. The portion saved by capital gains is considered a tax preference item and is therefore subject to a 15 percent minimum tax above the $10,000 exemption (or one-half of the taxpayer's regular income tax).

Risks

Cattle breeding exposes investors to a number of risks:

1. One of the risks inherent in the breeding of cattle as opposed to feeding is that breeding cattle may be hard to dispose of when the investor wishes to sell them. Feeder cattle can be disposed of at any time, but since the demand is smaller for breeding cattle and their price is greater, it may be harder to sell the herd and get a particular price at any given time. The lessened demand lowers the premium prices that have been received.

2. Another risk in a breeding program is that although the company usually guarantees that the cattle will be bred and be fertile, it does not guarantee their progeny. If the offspring are not fertile, they must be culled and sold at rates substantially lower than the price that they would normally bring.

3. Liens can be disastrous to an investor in cattle. In many Midwestern states, an individual who furnishes food, shelter, or other services to livestock has a lien on the cattle to the extent of the services delivered. If the management agent defaults on bills to produce or service suppliers, the suppliers can foreclose on the lien and force the sale of the cattle.

This circumstance reemphasizes the need for care in choosing a management agent. Since state laws differ, a prospective investor would be wise to check the laws in the particular state in which he or she plans to do business.

Chapter 50

Investing in Real Estate

RALPH POLIMENI

The1976 Tax Reform Act did not apply the at-risk rule to real estate transactions (under this rule an investor is not allowed to deduct losses related to a venture in excess of the amount for which he or she is economically at risk in the venture). Thus real estate investments may still provide attractive tax shelters.

Real estate investments permit considerable financial leverage and substantial tax benefits. In many cases, the investor need provide only a small percentage of the total cost of the property and finance the balance by securing a mortgage, using the real estate acquired as collateral.

BENEFITS

Substantial tax benefits may be derived from real estate investments through deductions for interest payments on mortgages, property taxes, and depreciation on buildings and fixtures. Capital gains treatment on qualifying assets may also be available.

Other benefits of tax-sheltered real estate investments include the following:

1. Property values may be appreciated by repairs, which, in turn, are tax-deductible. To illustrate, let us assume that an apartment house requires a new roof. A tax-deductible revitalization of the roof would also result in an appreciation of the apartment house.

2. Gains realized from property appreciation may be eligible for capital gains treatment. Let us assume that investment property was purchased on January 1, 1976, for $50,000 and sold on November 15, 1976, for $75,000. The $25,000 profit may be treated as a long-term capital gain and thus be taxed at a lower rate than ordinary income.

3. Some losses resulting from the sale of property may be eligible for treatment as ordinary losses. That is, losses can be used to offset ordinary income. For example, let us assume that a physician has taxable income of $60,000 for the year 1976 and also incurred a $15,000 loss on the sale of property. This $15,000 loss may be used to offset the physician's ordinary income. Taxable income is therefore reduced to $45,000.

4. Real estate investments may generate tax-free income. This is possible

when depreciation charges are large enough to offset revenue received from rental income and when the cash inflow exceeds the cash outflow. For example, let us assume that the investor's yearly expense payments (interest on mortgage, taxes, maintenance, and so on) amount to $5,000 (cash outflow) and that the yearly rental income from the investment is $6,500 (cash inflow). The investor thus receives $1,500 in cash every year in excess of expenses. Let us further assume that the investor's yearly deduction allowable for depreciation is $2,000 (a noncash deduction requiring no cash outflow). Therefore, instead of showing $1,500 as income from the investment the investor would declare a $500 loss ($1,500 excess cash revenue over cash expenses less the $2,000 noncash depreciation deduction).

Capital Gains and Nontaxable Exchanges

Capital gains are special tax treatments applicable to investment assets that meet specific criteria. Generally, the asset in question must be a capital asset (principal capital assets are investment property and property held for personal use). The investor is also required to retain the property for more than six months (nine months in 1977 and twelve months in 1978 and subsequent years). Capital gains are generated when the asset meets these criteria and is sold at a price above its adjusted tax basis.

If an investor wishes to defer gains on real estate to a future period, he or she may consider a nontaxable exchange. A nontaxable exchange consists of a reciprocal transfer of one piece of business property for another. Through this transaction, the investor in effect has continued the investment in the original asset. Accordingly, the investor is not taxed on the gain from the exchange, which is measured by the excess value of the property received over the adjusted basis of property given. For tax purposes, the newly acquired property bears the tax basis of the old property. It should be noted that the unrealized gain on the exchange is not permanently deferred because the investor is subject to a higher gain or a smaller loss when the new asset is disposed of.

The Tax Reform Act of 1969 introduced provisions relating to the treatment of capital gains. One change affected the 25 percent alternative tax rate for individuals. The 25 percent tax rate may be applied only to capital gains up to and including $50,000 a year. Gains exceeding $50,000 are eligible for the 50 percent capital gains deduction.

Depreciation and Real Estate

The deduction for depreciation on buildings and man-made structures purchased in conjunction with land adds to the attractiveness of real estate investments. Depreciation may be defined as the wearing out or decline in the value of an asset through use or obsolescence. Accountants define depreciation as the allocation of an asset's cost over its estimated useful life. The annual depreciation charge set by accountants does not necessarily coincide with the physical decline in the value of an asset. This is true because the major objective of charging depreciation is not to reflect the market value of an asset but to spread its cost over the periods in which revenue is generated. This procedure is aimed at producing a proper matching of expenses with revenue for a particular period.

Separation and Eligibility of Assets. An asset's eligibility for the depreciation deduction depends upon two elements. The first is that the property be utilized in business or trade, and the second is that the property be held for income production (that is, the property must be purchased with the initial intention ultimately to realize a gain on its use). Prior to acquisition, the property need not have been held for income production.

Depreciation cannot be taken on personal assets used for other than business purposes (a personal residence or an automobile not used in business). However, if a personal residence is converted into a business office, the property becomes eligible for depreciation.

Generally, an asset must have a finite life (eventually be used up) to qualify for the depreciation deduction. Assets that may be considered eligible for the depreciation deduction are grouped into the following general categories:

1. Assets that are permanent and tangible in nature; for example, office furniture, fixtures, buildings, and equipment.

2. Intangible assets (copyrights and patents) if they have a limited useful life. Intangible assets must also be used in conjunction with business or income-producing property to be eligible for depreciation. Technically speaking, depreciation of intangible assets is referred to as amortization.

3. Assets utilized in farming operations; for example, buildings and other equipment used on the farm. In addition, dairy animals are depreciable to the extent that they are not included in a farmer's inventory.

4. Idle assets of a business also are depreciated despite the fact that they are not being utilized.

The cost of an asset to the investor plus installation generally is the dollar amount to be used as a basis for computing the depreciation charge. Special tax rulings (which are outside the scope of this discussion) govern the basis of depreciation when an asset is acquired through a donation, gift, or bequest.

Land is not depreciable, since it has an infinite life. Even when it is used for business purposes, it is not eligible for depreciation.

Lastly, the investor should be reminded that the depreciation deduction is considered an ordinary deduction. In other words, depreciation is deducted against ordinary income when computing taxable income.

Internal Revenue Code Rulings on Depreciation Methods.   The taxpayer may select the method of computing depreciation as long as the method chosen appears to be sound. The depreciation method selected should be applied consistently from period to period. A discussion of the depreciation methods available follows:

Straight-Line Depreciation.   The straight-line method of computing depreciation is the simplest and most widely utilized. It allocates equal portions of the cost of an asset over its estimated useful life. Any salvage value that the asset may have reduces its depreciable value. Thus, the asset's cost minus any salvage value equals depreciable value. The depreciable value is then divided by the asset's estimated useful life to arrive at the periodic deduction.

Declining-Balance Depreciation.   The declining-balance method of depreciation allocates the greatest amount of depreciation to the early years of an asset's life and successively smaller amounts to the later years. This is economically beneficial because the payment of taxes is deferred to a later period, thus providing more funds for current operations.

During the first half of the asset's life, expenses (that is, depreciation) are increased, and taxable income and federal taxes are reduced. Naturally, the reverse occurs in the later years of the asset's life; expenses decrease, causing taxable income and federal taxes to increase. However, this disadvantage is partially offset because as most assets get older, they require additional maintenance and repair, the costs of which are tax-deductible. Salvage value is not considered when depreciation is computed by using the declining-balance method. Nevertheless, the Internal Revenue Code states that no asset can be depreciated beyond its salvage value.

The declining-balance method allowed by the Internal Revenue Service (IRS) depends upon the asset. The *double-declining-balance method* can be applied to new assets that have useful lives of at least three years. Under this method the rate applied may be double that of the straight-line method (it must not exceed 200 percent).

The 150 percent declining-balance method is applicable to used assets having useful lives of at least three years. The rate established is applied toward the undepreciated cost (asset cost less depreciation already taken). However, the IRS places limitations on the declining-balance method. Regulations state that this method cannot be utilized for an asset possessed by a donee, transferee, or vendor.

Sum-of-the-Years'-Digits Depreciation.   The *sum-of-the-years'-digits* method is another accelerated-depreciation method in common use. Under this method of computing depreciation, a fraction is developed. The numerator represents the asset's remaining useful life and the denominator the sum of the years estimated to be the asset's useful life. The fraction is multiplied by the asset's value to determine the deduction. The limitations stated for the declining-balance method are applicable to the sum-of-the-years'-digits method.

The 1969 Tax Reform Act and Depreciation.   The Tax Reform Act of 1969 defined the types of assets eligible for rapid depreciation and set guidelines pertaining to depreciation methods for different types of property:

1. Additions of certified pollution control devices on structures made after 1968 and in existence before 1969 may be depreciated under the straight-line method over sixty months, depending on the useful life.

2. Rehabilitation of existing low-income rental properties made after July 1969 and before 1975 that exceeds $3,000 per dwelling unit over a period of two consecutive taxable years may be depreciated under the straight-line method over sixty months without regard for salvage value.

The different categories of properties were defined in the Tax Reform Act. The special rules regarding depreciation methods were applied in the following areas:

1. *New residential rental real estate.* Rules in this category apply to the construction of new apartment housing. All methods of depreciation may be used for new residential rental property. The decision is at the discretion of the apartment house owner.

2. *Used residential real estate.* Rules in this category apply to the purchase of an existing apartment house. If the used property has a remaining useful life of at least twenty years, straight-line depreciation and the 125 percent declining-balance method are permitted.

3. *New real estate.* Rules in this category apply to property that has been constructed for purposes other than that of residential income. An office building or a factory is an example of this type of real estate. Investors with real estate belonging to this category may elect to use the 125 percent or the 150 percent declining-balance method.

Depreciation Recapture.   Some tax benefits previously received can be recaptured when certain events occur. This situation exists when part or all of a gain on the sale of a depreciable asset is treated as ordinary income instead of as a capital gain (to the extent that the gain equals a deduction for past depreciation). Any gain over and above the prior depreciation deducted will be eligible for capital gain treatment. The type of property, the date on which the property was acquired, and the time period during which it has been held will dictate which provision of the capital gain treatment will prevail.

Any excess depreciation taken in previous periods will also be subject to recapture. Excess depreciation is defined as the difference between the amount actually deducted after December 31, 1963, by an accelerated-depreciation method and the amount that would have been deducted under the straight-line method. The 1969 Tax Reform Act required that depreciation in excess of straight-line depreciation on commercial property be recaptured. The act extended this provision to apply also to residential real estate (post-1975). Moreover, if a property is held for less than twelve months, all depreciation (including straight-line depreciation) must be recaptured as ordinary income. The following is an example of depreciation recapture.

Let us assume that an apartment building was purchased on December 31, 1974, for $28,000 and was sold on January 2, 1976, for $30,000. The adjusted basis (cost of property plus capital improvements less depreciation) of the building was $25,000, and the depreciation deduction for the year 1975 was $3,000. Thus the recomputed tax basis is $28,000, as follows:

Sale price, January 2, 1976	$30,000
Adjusted basis	25,000
Gain	$ 5,000
Recomputed basis (cost of $25,000 plus depreciation of $3,000)	$28,000
Adjusted basis	25,000
Ordinary income	$ 3,000
Capital gain income	2,000
Total gain	$ 5,000

CLASSIFICATION OF REAL ESTATE FOR TAX PURPOSES

For purposes of taxation, real estate investments have been subdivided into categories. Four groupings exist, each of which serves a different purpose for the investor:

1. *Residential realty.* The sale of residential realty may result in either a taxable capital gain or a nondeductible loss. An example of residential realty is the personal dwelling of an investor.

2. *Business property.* A new gain from the exchange or sale of business property is offset by losses from similar transactions. Only the excess gain is treated as a capital gain, while a net loss is treated as an ordinary loss. An example of business property is an office building or a factory.

3. *Real estate dealers.* Property held by real estate dealers is not eligible for capital gains treatment. This is so because property held by dealers is deemed to be property held as "inventory" for the continuation of the dealers' trade and business. Any gain or loss from a transaction of a real estate dealer is held to be an ordinary gain or loss. A dealer, however, can avoid the ordinary income provisions by segregating part of his property into an "investment" account. If this property is not held for sale in the normal course of the dealer's business, capital gains treatment can be used when the investment is finally terminated.

4. *Investment realty.* This is considered a capital asset. Capital gain treatment (whether short-term or long-term) is employed as if the investment were in the area of stocks or securities.

Tax Preference Items

The introduction of tax preference items in the 1969 Tax Reform Act significantly affected real estate investment tax shelters. The major effects of the act are in the following areas:

1. *Accelerated depreciation.* The excess depreciation taken on personal property in previous periods is considered a tax preference item. As stated above, excess depreciation is the difference between the depreciation allowed under the

accelerated method and that which would be allowed under a straight-line method.

2. *Capital gains.* Tax preference for noncorporate taxpayers is applied to half of the excess long-term capital gains over net short-term losses. The corporate structure is subject to three-eighths of the excess of net corporate long-term gains over net short-term losses.

Analysis of the 1969 and 1976 Tax Reform Acts

The Tax Reform Act of 1969 supports new residential rental properties. This support is reflected in the fact that owners of new rental properties are entitled to utilize the fastest methods (200 percent declining-balance and sum-of-the-years'-digits methods) of depreciation.

The effects that the Tax Reform Acts of 1969 and 1976 had upon investment in real estate can be summarized for the following major areas:

1. A limited use of accelerated depreciation was applied to new construction other than new residential property after July 25, 1969. Subsequent to July 24, 1969, used property (other than residential) was limited to straight-line depreciation.

2. Rules for the recapture of excess depreciation were introduced to close some of the loopholes in that area of the law.

3. The government saw the need for the rehabilitation of housing and thus introduced fast write-offs for rehabilitated houses.

4. There is a limitation of $25,000 on the amount of deductions allowable on investment interest.

5. A minimum tax of 15 percent was levied on tax preference income (reduced by $10,000 or one-half of the taxpayer's regular income tax).

6. The amount of net capital losses that may be offset against income was limited to $1,000 (increased to $2,000 in taxable years beginning in 1977 and to $3,000 in taxable years beginning in 1978 and thereafter).

7. The sale of low- and moderate-income housing became tax-free.

8. A new two-year limit was set on the time allowed for replacement of property that was subject to an involuntary conversion.

9. The installation of pollution control devices could be used to claim a fast write-off.

Group Ownership of Real Estate

If an investor wants to invest in group ownership, he or she has three choices: a real estate investment trust (REIT), a mortgage investment trust (MIT), or a real estate syndication (RES). Generally speaking, one of the major benefits of group ownership is that it enables an individual to invest without having to manage the investment. This presupposes that the investor is a limited partner in the investment. If the group desires, it can employ a professional manager to handle its affairs. In addition, potential risk is lowered by the diversification of properties.

Forms of Group Ownership

Real Estate Investment Trusts (REITs). An amendment to the 1960 Internal Revenue Code created .the REIT. The general operation is similar to that of mutual funds, as the IRS intended in its amendment. The amendment gave the investor in a REIT benefits similar to those involved in mutual funds. In a REIT the use of a professional investment council and the pooling of group assets makes the possibility of large profits accessible to the group. The risk to the individual is lowered as a result of the purchase of diversified properties. Normally, REITs are not taxable if more than 90 percent of the ordinary income is distributed to the shareholders. Thus, the investor is taxed personally on the profits and avoids double taxation.

As compared with industrial corporations, REITs are highly leveraged. Since investors are dealing with high mortgages and low down payments, the prime consideration is cash flow rather than the price-earnings ratio. The cash flow is received as a result of net income plus depreciation. Depreciation does not cause a cash outflow, and it reduces the tax liability of the REIT.

REIT shares are certificates of beneficial interest, not stock certificates. They are not as easily transferable as shares in mutual funds because the daily price of a share is not readily determined. However, most REIT shares are quite marketable, and some are listed on regional and national stock exchanges. Thus, the price of shares is affected by market conditions.

The small investor is afforded the same advantages as a large investor in a REIT, insofar as it permits the smaller investor to pool his or her assets without being subjected to double taxation prevalent in the corporate form. A major tax disadvantage in the REIT is that losses in excess of trust income cannot be used by the investor to offset other income. For example, let us assume that a REIT has a net loss of $1 per share and that an investor owns 1,000 shares. That investor cannot deduct the $1,000 loss from his or her other personal income for tax purposes.

The 1976 Tax Reform Act brought about a number of changes to REITs. One significant change allows a REIT to correct violations of the income and distribution requirements that, prior to the act, would have resulted in a loss of qualification. Other changes are:

1. Gross income and distributions, beginning in taxable years after 1979, will be increased from 90 to 95 percent.

2. REITs are now permitted to organize as corporations and are allowed to deduct net operating loss carryforwards for a period of eight years.

3. A REIT election status that has been terminated (because the REIT has failed to meet all qualification requirements) may be reinstated when the reasons for the termination have been corrected.

The trust must have at lease 100 owners. The various types of REIT emphasize short-term obligations, long-term obligations, or a combination of both.

Mortgage Investment Trusts (MITs).   This form of organization deals in real estate mortgages. The trust invests its own capital, as well as borrowing from a bank at the prevailing rate, and in turn loans the capital at a higher rate. The MIT will normally manage every facet of the real estate enterprise. There is no cash flow from depreciation; instead, the MIT members receive cash from amortization charged off against interest earned.

Real Estate Syndication (RES).   The RES is the commonest form of group ownership. A limited partnership is usually preferred to a general partnership because each limited partner is liable only for his or her investment (limited liability), and a general partner has unlimited liability. Losses not exceeding a partner's interest (partner's capital contribution plus his or her share of partnership profits) may be used to offset ordinary income. The major benefit of the limited partnership is the fact that it limits taxation to each partner rather than to the partnership, thus lowering taxes. To avoid being taxed as a corporation, some limited partnerships can obtain an advance ruling on their tax status from the IRS. A limited partnership must have at least one general partner who manages the venture, leaving the other partners with no voice in the operation of the business.

SECOND-HOME INVESTMENTS

A homeowner is allowed to deduct only the interest payments on his or her mortgage and paid real estate taxes, whereas a homeowner who rents a second home all year is also allowed to deduct, besides interest and real estate taxes, repairs and maintenance, heat, utilities, water, and, most important of all, depreciation. The depreciation deduction is a key factor in making the renting of a home desirable.

It must be remembered that depreciation is not a cash outflow and therefore does not use existing funds. If the homeowner is able to generate rental income (cash inflows) from renting his or her home that will at least equal the cash outflows (mortgage payments, taxes, repairs, utilities, and so on) plus a small excess of inflows to provide a margin of safety, the venture should be beneficial to the homeowner for the following reasons:

1. Each mortgage payment will increase the homeowner's equity in the home. Thus, the tenant is paying the mortgage for the homeowner.

2. Most homes will appreciate in value as time progresses, and the owner will therefore find the value of the property increasing.

3. When the mortgage is paid off, the homeowner should be receiving a greater net cash inflow.

4. The deduction allowed for depreciation will in most cases generate an ordinary loss for the rental venture that can be used to offset the investor's other ordinary income.

For example, let us assume that an individual buys a three-family house for $90,000 and rents the three apartments for $250 each. The annual cash outflows are as follows:

Mortgage payments (including interest and taxes)	$7,000
Maintenance and utilities	1,500
Total annual cash outflow	$8,500

Cash inflow (rents)	$9,000 ($250 × 3 × 12)
Cash outflow	8,500
Excess cash inflow	$ 500

The tax-deductible items are as follows:

Interest on mortgage and taxes (the part of the mortgage payment going to repay principal is not tax-deductible)	$6,000
Maintenance and utilities	1,500
Tax-deductible items	$7,500

Without the deduction for depreciation, the investor would have to report $1,500 as ordinary income ($9,000 in income less $7,500 in expenses).

In computing depreciation, the value of the land and the estimated salvage value of the building must be deducted from the total cost of $90,000. Let us assume that the land and salvage value amount to $24,000 and that the building has a remaining life of thirty years. Under straight-line depreciation, the annual deduction would be $2,200 ($66,000 depreciable amount divided by 30 years). Now, instead of the investor reporting an income of $1,500, he or she would, after deducting depreciation, report a $700 loss that could be offset against his or her ordinary income. It should be stressed that these figures are hypothetical and that the merits of each venture will depend upon the individual situation.

There are many possible problems that may develop in assuming a landlord status. A few of them follow:

1. Being a landlord can be time-consuming, especially if the building rented is in poor condition and constantly in need of repairs.

2. As a building gets older, it requires more repairs and upkeep and may generate a need for greater cash outflows.

3. The loss of a tenant will substantially reduce the amount of cash inflows and may require additional cash outflows to paint and recondition the vacated apartment to make it attractive to a new tenant.

4. Rising fuel prices and property taxes may tip the balance of cash flows and require the landlord to put in additional funds.

5. Neighborhoods change, and the building, instead of appreciating in value, may decline.

6. Mortgage payments will remain the same over the years, but the amount allotted to interest payments will decrease while the proportion going to principal repayments will increase. The amount of the mortgage payment eligible for deduction will thus decrease each year because interest is tax-deductible, whereas repayment of principal is not.

7. If the building is sold, any gain realized will be subject to depreciation recapture.

8. There is a $25,000 limitation on the amount of interest that is tax-deductible.

COOPERATIVES AND CONDOMINIUMS

Lately much has been heard about the purchase of cooperatives and condominiums. Both these investments can be used to increase an investor's tax savings. The primary difference between a co-op and a condominium is that in a condominium there is direct ownership of individual apartments, while in a co-op the corporation owns the buildings, and each tenant owns shares in the corporation.

A co-op is easily formed. The first step is for the owner of an apartment house to set up a corporation with bylaws and charter applicable to a cooperative. In some states a specified percentage of the tenants in an apartment house must agree to the change to a co-op. If we assume that this has been accomplished, the owner then sells the apartment house to the corporation, which in turn sells shares of stock to the cooperating tenants. With the shares of stock in the co-op the tenant receives a proprietary lease that sets forth the stockholders' rights and limitations and the maintenance charges per share necessary to cover the corporation's expenses. There is a certain amount of protection for all stockholders in the corporation because the lease usually includes a provision which states that the tenant cannot sublet or assign his or her lease without the consent of the co-op's board of directors.

The tax saving inherent in a housing co-op is quite significant when compared with stocks and other investments subject to tax. As with most other tax shelters, the higher the bracket of the investor, the higher the tax saving. In a co-op situation the rent paid to the corporation, besides reducing the tenant's tax, builds equity in the investment by reducing the corporation's mortgage.

However, there are requirements to which both the shareholders and the corporation must adhere. To be a bona fide co-op, the corporation must derive at least 80 percent of its gross income from shareholders. The stockholders, for their part, must receive no dividends that are not from corporate earnings and profits and can take no deductions that are not in direct proportion to the number of shares held in the corporation. A co-op is one of the few corporations in which a shareholder can pay a lump sum for maintenance, interest, overhead, taxes, and so on and still be able to allocate the payment among interest, taxes, and so on and deduct these on his or her individual tax returns. (Usually interest must be paid separately to be deductible.)

The shareholder is entitled to deduct a proportional share of all the expenses—taxes, interest, and maintenance—that are incurred by the corporation. If the shareholder is renting his or her apartment to another person, he or she can then deduct depreciation on the apartment. Depreciation is also allowed as a deduction when the apartment is used solely for business purposes. The depreciation is calculated by figuring the pro-rata share of the corporation's total depreciation expense. If only part of the apartment is rented or used for business, the amount of depreciation is reduced by the percentage for personal use.

Buying a co-op is treated for tax purposes like buying another house. The IRS has ruled that if, after the sale of his or her principal residence, a person reinvests in another house or co-op within a specified period of time, the gain is postponed.

To form a condominium, the owners of the property being considered must declare, in the form of a deed, that a condominium is wanted by all parties. The deed is then binding on the original as well as future owners. It should be noted that another unanimous decision can restore the building to its original status. After the deed has been executed, the owners of the apartment building may sell the individual apartments as if they were one-family houses. Also, as with one-family houses, taxes are assessed on an individual basis for each unit. The individual owner has a proportional share of the common elements of the building. These include the lobby, elevators, stairs, pool (if any), land, and other items of a similar nature.

Since each apartment is a separate entity, the mortgage and taxes are paid by the owner of each apartment. As with a one-family house, the purchaser of a condominium can arrange for a mortgage. A pro-rata share of the worth of the apartment determines the amount of maintenance attributable to each owner. As long as an individual owns an apartment, he or she is responsible for his or her share of the maintenance of the common elements.

There are tax deductions that make it quite advantageous for an investor in the 50 percent bracket or higher to purchase a condominium for purposes of rental. The monthly maintenance charges, interest, and taxes are all deductible. If the individual is an original owner of the building, he or she can take advantage of accelerated-depreciation methods. These can be either the sum-of-the-years'-digits method or the 200 percent declining-balance method. By using one of these methods, the owner of the apartment can receive rental income in cash while reporting a loss for tax purposes when the deduction for depreciation is included.

Although there are many positive attributes to owning a condominium, the purchaser may find unforeseen drawbacks. There might be a considerable rise in maintenance charges each year, as well as a mandatory membership fee for a possible pool or attached golf course. Lack of demand for rentals should also be considered.

Chapter **51**

Investing
in Oil and Gas

RALPH POLIMENI

Since oil and gas provide approximately three-fourths of United States energy requirements, it is not surprising that Congress has provided tax incentives to foster a search for new supplies. Encouragement is directed not only at many of the largest oil companies but also at individuals seeking to invest money and minimize tax dollars.

In recent years domestic production of oil has not been able to satisfy our growing consumption, thereby forcing the United States increasingly to rely upon imported supplies. Until recently the United States never experienced the effects of a peacetime fuel shortage; consumption patterns continued to move upward, while oil reserves lagged behind. Even with projections that an impending scarcity of petroleum products was imminent, little positive action was undertaken. It wasn't until we came face to face with the shutoff of supplies from the Middle East that we fully recognized the gravity of the problem. Thus began the so-called energy crisis. It may actually have been a blessing in disguise. If not for the sequence of events that led to the energy crisis, the United States might well have continued its increasing reliance on imported oil supplies. In addition, the energy crisis served to illustrate the economic importance of developing domestic oil reserves to the point of independence.

The United States is faced with an economic rather than a physical problem: we have vast amounts of oil reserves available in Alaska and in offshore drilling. The problem lies with the rate at which we can develop these resourses economically. The federal government, acting as a catalyst, can promote further development of our oil and gas resources. In the past, it has acted by providing several tax incentives. Now the government may find it necessary also to relax several of its environmental restrictions. By relaxing environmental restrictions (perhaps unfortunately), vast new areas of petroleum resources will become more economically feasible. The construction of the Alaska oil pipeline, once halted by environmental objections, is under way. Environmentalists will probably make other concessions on the basis of projected needs, thereby increasing the number of economically attractive prospects for oil investors.

TAX CONSIDERATION OF OIL AND GAS INVESTMENTS

Three basic tax advantages are available to the oil and gas investor:

1. A tax deduction may be taken for intangible drilling and development costs in the year in which the expenditure is made.

2. There is a capital gain advantage as a result of the sale of oil and gas investment property that has been held for more than six months.

Intangible Drilling and Development Costs

One of the most attractive features of an oil and gas investment is the deduction of intangible drilling and development costs. These intangible costs are amounts without salvage value that are expended in the process of drilling a well. Such items include amounts paid to the drilling contractor, services, wages, fuel repairs, supplies, core analysis, electric logging, and other nonsalvageable costs.

Since a considerable degree of risk is involved in drilling for oil, most drilling programs attempt to minimize the risk by undertaking several drilling operations. If a particular well is determined to be a nonproducer, all the costs of drilling it are deductible. As a net result, the average drilling program can be expected to provide the investor with a deduction equal to 80 percent of his initial investment. This 80 percent deduction can be applied against other types of income and is deductible in the year in which the drilling contract is paid.

The costs in a producing well that are not immediately deductible are the producing properties and tangible equipment costs. These costs are capitalized and are deducted through depletion or depreciation. The leasehold costs of producing property, or acreage costs, are deducted through the allowance for depletion. Costs that have not been recovered by depletion when the property is abandoned are deductible as a loss. The costs of salvageable tangible equipment are recovered through depreciation and salvage value.

Recapture of Intangible Drilling Costs for Oil and Gas Wells

After December 31, 1975, amounts deducted for intangible drilling expenses on productive wells must be recaptured upon the disposition of the oil or gas property by treating these amounts as ordinary income to the extent that they exceed the amounts that would be allowed if the intangible expenses were capitalized and the costs amortized over the useful life of the wells.

Depletion Allowance

When an oil and gas program proves to be productive, the investors are entitled to a deduction for depletion on the income derived from the production and sale of the oil or gas. Thus, a portion of the gross income from the sale of oil or gas is received tax-free by the investors as a result of the depletion allowance. The investors are entitled to choose the greater of either percentage depletion or cost depletion in determining this allowance. Usually percentage depletion is more advantageous, except during the initial year of operation or in years in which operational and program costs are extremely high in relation to income.

Cost Depletion.   Cost depletion is a method whereby the capitalized costs of the oil-producing property are recovered over its productive life. The amount deductible each year is determined by multiplying a ratio of the estimated unrecovered reserves to a current year's production by the undepleted costs of the property. If total depletion deductions exceed total leasehold or property costs, the cost depletion method is not allowed.

Percentage Depletion.   Percentage depletion was formerly more commonly used than cost depletion to arrive at the depletion deduction. After January 1, 1975, however, the 22 percent depletion allowance for oil and gas wells was repealed except for (1) natural gas sold under a fixed contract, (2) regulated natural gas, (3) geothermal deposits considered to be a gas well that are within the United States or a possession of the United States, and (4) royalty owners and independent producers. Thus the use of percentage depletion was severely curtailed and is no longer available to most investors.

When the use of percentage depletion is allowed, it is computed by multiplying the gross income of each producing property by 22 percent. The amount deductible is limited to 50 percent of taxable income before the depletion deduction. As a result, in years in which drilling costs are high, the 50 percent limitation on net income would usually dictate the use of cost depletion.

An important advantage of percentage depletion is its complete independence from capitalized costs of property. The advantages of tax-free income from the percentage depletion deduction are allowed even after all property costs have been recovered. In regard to this point, it should be remembered that percentage depletion is a tax preference item.

The example below illustrates the use of percentage depletion. In year 1 the 50 percent limitation restricts the amount of depletion deduction, while in year 2 the full 22 percent deduction is allowed.

		Year 1		Year 2
Gross income		$10,000		$10,000
Operating expenses	$1,000		$1,000	
Depreciation	1,000		1,000	
Drilling expenses	4,000	6,000	...	2,000
Net Income		$ 4,000		$ 8,000
22 percent of gross income		$ 2,200		$ 2,200
50 percent of net income		2,000		4,000
Depletion deduction allowed		$ 2,000		$ 2,200

A noteworthy feature is that the proportion of *net income* that is tax-free usually exceeds 22 percent. The 22 percent depletion deduction is taken on the gross income. Therefore, when applied to net income, the actual dollar amount of the deduction is greater than 22 percent of net income. In year 2 of the example the depletion allowance is 27.5 percent ($2,200 ÷ $8,000) of net income. As a result, only 72.5 percent of net income is taxable.

Capital Gains

If an investor decides to sell his or her interest in oil and gas properties after holding them for more than six months, the aggregate net gain or loss from the sales is treated as a capital gain or loss. In most situations a portion of the gain from the sale will probably be taxed as ordinary income because of the depreciation recapture provisions of the Internal Revenue Code.

Other Tax Aspects

Increasing the Deduction. In some drilling programs emphasis is placed on achieving the largest possible deduction for the investor. One way of increasing the deduction is through the leasing of tangible equipment. Normally, tangible equipment is capitalized and depreciated. However, if the equipment is leased rather than purchased, the cost of the leased equipment can be considered an intangible deduction.

For the high–percentage-bracket taxpayer, a drilling program offering a 100 percent first-year deduction can be very rewarding. For example, an investor in the 60 percent tax bracket with a 100 percent deduction on a $10,000 oil investment would save $6,000 in taxes while the investment would cost only $4,000 in aftertax dollars. Should the investor recover the initial pretax investment, he or she would realize a 150 percent profit ($4,000 aftertax dollars × 150 percent = $10,000 recovery of initial investment) on his investment. Thus, the large first-year deduction has a significant effect in determining the subsequent profitability of the investment.

Year-End Tax Planning. The Internal Revenue Service has provided the oil investor with a valuable year-end tax planning device. It has allowed the time of payment to be determined by the time when the drilling contract is paid rather than when the expenses actually occur. Therefore, payments for drilling contracts can become an intricate part of year-end tax planning even though the actual costs are not incurred until the following year.

Certain conditions must be met to take advantage of year-end tax planning. The main criteria are:

1. There must be a valid business reason for the prepayment.

2. The contract must contain an obligation for the investor to make the cash payment in the year he or she took the deduction.

3. The contract must contain an irrevocable obligation on the part of the operator to drill a well on a specific leasehold.

In summary the basic tax advantages are:

1. Intangible drilling and development costs are immediately deductible.

2. The costs incurred in the drilling of a nonproducing well (dry well) are entirely deductible.

3. The percentage depletion or cost depletion allowance is allowed on income from the production and sale of the oil or gas.

4. Any gain from the sale of oil and gas properties is subject, in most cases, to long-term capital gains.

SELECTING A PROGRAM

In choosing an appropriate oil and gas investment program both tax and nontax factors must be considered. Since various programs may emphasize certain tax aspects over others, it is essential that the individual merits of each program coincide with the investor's financial needs. Similarly, the nontax aspects such as risk, liquidity, and program structure require careful consideration.

There are several programs by which the investor can take advantage of the tax benefits available from oil and gas investments. Most programs are in the form of either joint ventures or limited partnerships. Although the programs vary greatly in structure and benefits, they usually offer the entire range of tax benefits discussed above. An investment in an oil royalty, on the other hand, offers more limited tax benefits. Royalties are usually regarded as a nonoperating interest without operating costs. Therefore, royalty owners are not permitted to deduct intangible drilling costs.

Selecting the correct program for your individual needs is by no means easy. Several variables must be considered, and a vast amount of investigation is necessary. Each oil investment program can be divided into two main components, the organizational structure and the drilling program. The organizational structure will determine such variables as personal liability, liquidity, risk spreading, and the availability to the investor of specific tax benefits. The drilling program will primarily determine the degree of risk for the entire program.

Organizational Structures of Tax-sheltered Oil and Gas Investments

One of the first criteria to consider when making an oil investment is whether you want a public or a private drilling program. As a general rule, public drilling programs are more expensive than comparable private programs because of the additional costs of going public. Public programs, however, are better documented and easier to research; therefore, they are often safer investments. If an investor is able to receive firsthand information on a private program, he or she may be in a more advantageous position than an individual investing in a public program. An important point to remember is that the same tax and investment considerations apply to both private and public drilling programs.

There are three basic ways in which an investor can participate in tax-sheltered oil and gas investments. There are also numerous variations of these alternatives, which account for the uniqueness of each oil investment program. The three basic means of investment are:

1. The purchase of a royalty interest
2. Participation in a joint venture
3. Investment in a limited partnership

Royalty Interests.   Royalties in an oil or gas program are nonoperating interests that entitle the owners to shares of the total production. Since these are considered nonoperating interests, owners of royalties are free from the costs of development and production. Accordingly, royalty owners are not allowed a deduction for intangible drilling and development costs, but they can take advantage of the percentage depletion allowance. In each year in which they receive income from their proprotionate share of the oil produced, up to 22 percent of the gross proceeds (the percentage allowed depends on the average daily production) are tax-free, subject to a limitation of 65 percent of the taxpayer's taxable income. In addition to percentage depletion, royalty owners are entitled to long-term capital gains treatment if they sell their royalties after holding them for more than six months.

A full royalty usually represents one-eighth of the total oil or gas produced. Frequently, royalties are divided into smaller increments and sold as fractions of a full share. They can usually be purchased either from the owner of the oil interest or through a securities salesman who deals in oil and gas.

The types and costs of oil royalties vary greatly. The least expensive and riskiest is the nonproducing royalty. Such royalties are purchased before drilling has occurred. In effect, nonproducing royalties are gambles. The degree of risk and the price on such royalties is determined by the location of the well and its proximity to known reserves. Should a sizable oil find result, the value of the royalties would appreciate considerably. At that point, holders of the royalties could either sell their interest for a substantial gain or hold the royalties, thereby deferring income over the life of the well.

Investments in producing royalties involve less risk since the oil reserve is already known to exist. The only degree of uncertainty lies in the determination of the amount of remaining oil reserves, but current technology has been able to provide fairly accurate estimates for investment purposes. As a result, producing royalties are often sound investments that serve to defer income over several years and provide a hedge against inflation.

Joint Ventures.   In an attempt to take full advantage of the tax benefits allowed in an oil investment, the investors or sponsors of the program sometimes form a joint venture. By forming a joint venture, several investors can divide shares of the lease among themselves. Each share, referred to as a "working interest," represents the individual's portion of the total investment.

The joint venture is organized solely for the specified program and terminates upon completion of the business activity. For income tax purposes it is treated as a partnership except in filing its first-year tax returns. In the first year an election may be held to permit each partner to treat his or her share of income and expenses as though he or she owned a business. Therefore, the large first-year intangible drilling and development costs are deductible on each partner's individual tax return.

In most joint ventures, investors pay for both intangible and tangible costs of the program. As a result, only a portion of their investment is deductible as intangible drilling costs. The deductible portion will usually vary between 70 and 80 percent of the investment. The remainder of the investment is capitalized and is eligible for depreciation deductions over the remaining years.

There are two main drawbacks to joint ventures. The first is that joint ventures involve unlimited liability. In the event of unfortunate or unforseeable circumstances, the investor (partner) in a joint venture can be held liable to an amount greater than his or her initial capital contribution. Second, joint ventures do not provide the flexibility characteristic of limited partnerships.

Limited Partnerships.   Limited partnerships have become a popular means of investment in oil and gas for individual investors. The reason for their popularity is that they offer first-year deductions usually in excess of 90 percent as well as limited liability to investors.

The limited partnership is characterized by a "functional split" between tangible and intangible costs. The terms of the partnership usually call for the limited partners (investors) to pay for all the intangible costs whereas the general partner (sponsor) pays all the tangible or capitalized costs. With this type of arrangement the limited partners may deduct their entire capital contribution. The general partner is entitled to the depreciation benefits on the capitalized costs. Income from the operation is divided between the general and limited partners in accordance with the terms stipulated in the partnership contract. The general partner will usually receive between 35 and 50 percent of the income, the remaining income being divided among the limited investors.

There are a few potential dangers that investors should be aware of before entering a limited partnership. If the limited partnership takes on too many characteristics of a corporation, it may be taxed as a corporation. If that should occur, the limited partners would not be allowed the deduction for intangible costs.

Consideration should be given to the fact that the general partner incurs no costs unless a productive well is found and developed. Because of this unique situation, the general partner may tend to concentrate on higher-risk drilling. In this type of drilling the intangible costs incurred greatly exceed the tangible costs, thus favoring the general partner. The reverse is true if the program concentrates on low-risk drilling. Therefore, diversity of the types of property drilled is an important consideration in a limited partnership.

Types of Drilling Programs

There are three major areas for investment in oil and gas programs:
1. A producing well
2. An offset well (drilling near a producing well)
3. A wildcat well (exploratory drilling)

Some programs concentrate on only one of these areas, but most use some combination of the three types to attain a diversified investment program.

Producing Wells.   A producing well is a low-risk investment for investors interested primarily in substantially increasing their income flow. Usually programs of this type are set up as joint ventures; they offer a good return on investment along with a high cash flow. The producing well is usually purchased from a wildcatter who is interested only in finding the oil, not in production.

The amount and accessibility of the reserves are the major factors that determine the value of a producing well. If the investors' estimate of the reserves in a well is overstated and, as a result, they overpay, they are likely to realize little if any gain. It must also be remembered that investments in producing wells are long-term investments. Therefore, the expected future income stream should be discounted to its present value to calculate the anticipated return on an investment. The partnership for a producing well terminates when the production ceases; an average life of ten to fifteen years can be expected.

Benefits from a producing well are twofold. First, income is provided on a partially tax-free basis over a considerable length of time. Second, the degree of risk from a producing well is considerably less than that from other types of oil investments. As in most situations, however, the lower risk usually yields a lower return. The degree of risk that investors are willing to assume is related directly to the amount of return that they can anticipate.

Offset Wells. Drilling near producing wells, or offset drilling, is considered an intermediate risk for investors. The chances of hitting oil are good. In offset drilling three out of four wells drilled on proven grounds are successful, although the size of the find may be limited. The offset well is drawing from a reservoir that has already been tapped by existing wells, and the high operating costs often exceed income when the well is a limited producer.

An offset drilling program offers investors the two major tax benefits associated with an oil investment, the intangible drilling deduction and the depletion allowance. Consequently, these programs attract investors looking for an immediate deduction against current income and a modest income flow in later years.

Offset drilling is often used in multiple write-off programs. When exploratory drilling has been successful, additional wells are drilled nearby to assure maximum utilization of the reserve. The additional drilling occurs after the first year to allow deductions not only during the first year of the program but in any year in which an additional well is drilled. Additional funds are obtained by a combination of borrowing and assessing the limited partners. It is important to determine beforehand whether assessments for additional drilling are optional. If such assessments are mandatory, investors should have additional liquid assets available. If they do not, they should consider another program.

Wildcat Wells. Exploratory drilling, or wildcatting, is the riskiest type of oil exploration. Essentially, it involves drilling for oil in unexplored areas or on unproven grounds. Investors interested in this type of program usually seek the large first-year deductions characteristic of wildcatting programs.

Many wildcatting programs require interested investors to be in at least the 50 percent income tax bracket. Actually, those in the highest tax brackets will realize the smallest losses if the drilling proves unsuccessful (they will also realize the largest gains if the drilling is successful). Investors in high tax brackes can recover a substantial portion of their pretax investment during the initial year as a deduction. They are also in a better position to sustain a loss than those in a lower income bracket.

In wildcatting, it is not uncommon to find a ratio of dry wells to successful wells of approximately 9 to 1. The probability of discovering a reserve of substantial size or what would be considered large is about 1,000 to 1. Therefore, to lower the risks most programs extend their exploration over a large number of wells, thus increasing their chances for a strike.

Wildcat investors have the option to sell their interests after oil has been discovered or to maintain their interest to receive the income from production. Since most wildcatters are interested in the intangible deductions and long-term capital gains, they often sell their interests to those who want to invest in producing wells.

CHANGING LEGISLATION

Oil investors must be aware that the tax benefits granted them are subject to change. For instance, the 1969 Tax Reform Act reduced the percentage depletion allowance from 27.5 percent to 22 percent, and tax preference treatment was applied to capital gains and percentage depletion. Percentage depletion was virtually eliminated for most investors as of January 1975. The 1976 Tax Reform Act required that amounts deducted for intangible drilling expenses on a productive well must be recaptured upon the disposition of the oil or gas property. Therefore, prospective investors should give careful consideration to proposed legislation at the time of investment.

CHECKLIST FOR OIL AND GAS TAX-SHELTERED INVESTMENTS

In selecting the most suitable oil and gas investment program for your needs, you should consider the following factors:

Personal Liability.   Most programs are either joint ventures or limited partnerships. When possible, choose a limited partnership because your risk is limited to your capital contribution. Joint ventures have unlimited liability.

Management.   Select a program whose management has proved itself by experience and past success. The size of the program should be within management's capabilities.

Diversification.   Greater diversification usually means lower risk. The more wells and types of wells (wildcat or offset) drilled, the greater the diversification. The amount of diversification is limited by the assets available to the program. If a program is too large, however, the size of your interest tends to be very small. That can be an unattractive feature if you decide to sell.

Liquidity.   Most oil investments are not considered liquid, although they may be marketable. The timing factor is very important to a successful sale of an oil investment. Some programs offer a buy-back provision for investors who want to sell before the end of the program. However, most buy-back provisions impose a penalty that tends to weigh heavily against sellers.

Changing Legislation.   Changing tax legislation can significantly alter the complexion of your tax-sheltered investment. Before investing money in any investment, investigate pending changes in the tax laws.

Assessments.   Many programs seek multiple deductions by developing offset wells in later years. In doing so, some programs assess investors to raise additional capital. Determine beforehand whether assessments in your program are mandatory or optional.

Risk.   Some programs involve considerably greater risk than others. Investment in producing wells involves the least risk, and investment in wildcat drilling the greatest risk. High-risk programs should be left to those in high tax brackets.

Conflicts of Interest.   Often the arrangement in a limited partnership agreement presents a conflict of interest between the general partner and the limited partner. The conflict results from the functional split between tangible and intangible costs. Carefully analyze the contract arrangement of a program for potential conflicts.

Government Regulation.   Consider possible government restrictions that can affect the profit potential of your oil investment. They can limit the amount of production, put a ceiling on prices and profits, and restrict the industry by environmental laws.

Leverage.   Leverage is usually not available in oil investments. When a loan is available, it must be a third-party nonrecourse loan against proven existing reserves.

Chapter **52**

Equipment Leasing as a Tax Shelter

EDWARD J. LANDAU

MARTIN RICHARDS

Over the last decade the leasing of equipment has become a multibillion dollar enterprise. Billions of dollars' worth of trucks, bulldozers, microscopes, computers, jet planes, oil tankers, fishing boats, and other types of equipment are leased annually in the United States. Most leases are standard financial arrangements between the manufacturer or a leasing company and the end user of the equipment, but a few leasing transactions are structured as tax shelters for high-income individuals.

The user of the equipment normally decides to lease equipment for such business reasons as the unavailability of sufficient cash to make the purchase, the inability to borrow the full purchase price of the equipment, or the adverse effect that the borrowing may have on the company's available credit lines. An investor will enter into an equipment-leasing arrangement for the primary purpose of obtaining immediate tax deductions that can be used to offset other income.

This chapter focuses on leverage lease shelters because from the tax standpoint they are the most advantageous type of equipment lease transaction. It will briefly describe a leverage lease shelter, set out the economics, discuss the tax ramifications, and attempt to point out some of the pitfalls.

Before proceeding, however, it should be emphasized that this chapter is written for business people, not tax lawyers, and some of the intricacies involved in leverage leasing will either be ignored or be mentioned only cursorily. Further, since each taxpayer's situation is unique, the reader is cautioned not to make any shelter investments without first consulting his or her tax lawyer or accountant.

Leverage Lease Shelters: Structure

The usual leverage lease shelter consists of (1) a limited partnership, (2) a promoter, (3) one or more investors, (4) a bank or other financing institution, and (5) a lessee.

The limited partnership in this situation has only one general partner and one or more limited partners. The general partner, who is financially liable for the acts of the partnership, is a corporation that has been funded either with a minimal amount of cash or, in the more sophisticated shelters, merely with demand notes of the promoter. The limited partners are the investors, whose exposure ordinarily is limited to their investment.

The promoter is generally otherwise involved in the sale, leasing, and servicing of the type of equipment that the partnership will acquire. Usually the promoter will own 100 percent of the general partner and will have a contract with the partnership to maintain all the equipment under lease.

Leveraging is created by the partnership's borrowing up to 80 percent of the purchase price of the equipment pursuant to banking arrangements negotiated by the promoter before the formation of the partnership. The bank will secure its loan with a lien on both the equipment and the lease rental payments.

The lessee is the user of the equipment.

Taxation of the Limited Partnership

A partnership, whether limited or general, is not subject to federal income tax, but each partner must report his or her share of the taxable income or loss of the partnership whether or not any property or money has been distributed to him or her during the year.

The amount of partnership "losses" that may be used by an investor to offset other income is limited to the investor's basis in the partnership. Initially, the investor's basis is the amount of the individual's contribution of money or property to the partnership. This basis is subsequently increased or decreased by the individual's share of the venture's gain or loss. Any money or property distributed to the partner will reduce his or her basis, but never below zero, and any additional contribution of money or property will increase this basis.

Partnership losses are passed to the investor, but since their deductibility is limited to the investor's basis, the key is to increase the basis without additional risk to the investor. Regulations of the Internal Revenue Service (IRS) permit a partner's basis to be increased by his or her share of the increase in partnership liabilities, provided that no partner has any personal liability for the debt. Furthermore, a partner's share of a limited partnership's nonrecourse debt is the same percentage as his or her share of the partnership profits. This method of basis step-up is illustrated by the following example:

A limited partnership is formed with three limited partners and one general partner. Each partner contributes $50,000 in cash to the partnership, and each will receive 25 percent of the profits and the losses. The partnership purchases equipment for $1 million by investing $200,000 of its money and by borrowing the balance ($800,000) from a bank on a nonrecourse basis. Each partner is now able to increase his or her partnership basis by $200,000 (25 percent of the bank loan), and each will therefore be able to deduct up to $250,000 of partnership "losses" against his or her other income.

All this seems quite simple, but the IRS has frequently taken the position that even though the organization is a valid partnership under state law, it will be treated as a corporation for tax purposes. This disastrous consequence can be avoided if the partnership has no more than one of the following "corporate characteristics": limited liability, free transferability of interest, continuity of life, and centralized management.

1. *Limited liability.* The IRS position is that if the sole general partner is a corporation and the total contributions to the partnership are less than $2.5 million, the net worth of the general partner must at all times be at least $250,000 or 15 percent of the total contributions, whichever is less. If partnership contributions are $2.5 million or more, the general partner's net worth must at all times be at least 10 percent of the total contributions. These net worth requirements are applied separately for each limited partnership in which the general partner

has an interest. In computing the general partner's net worth, notes and interests in the limited partnership are excluded. Moreover, the limited partners may not own more than 20 percent of the stock of the general partner or any of its affiliates.

Even though the general partner meets the net worth requirements at inception, there is no assurance that it will meet them in the future. Consequently, the investor should obtain a representation that the general partner will continue to satisfy this requirement at all times.

2. *Free transferability of interest.* Generally free transferability will not be present if the partnership agreement specifically provides that a limited partner may not transfer his or her interest without the written consent of the general partner.

3. *Continuity of life.* State law and the partnership agreement usually provide that the substitution or withdrawal of the general partner will terminate the partnership unless all the limited partners agree to a change. This will result in the partnership's not having the corporate characteristic of continuity of life.

4. *Centralization of management.* All shelter limited partnerships are, almost by definition, centrally managed by the general partner because the limited partners who own substantially all the interests in the partnership allow the general partner to make all management decisions. As a practical matter, therefore, a limited partnership will be taxed as a corporation if it runs afoul of any of the first three prohibitions.

The IRS has ruled that a venture can obtain an advance ruling of partnership tax status if (1) the general partner will have at least a 1 percent interest in all material tax items of the partnership, (2) a creditor who makes a nonrecourse loan to the partnership will have no interest in the venture other than as a creditor, and (3) the total of losses claimed by the partners for the first two years of operation will not exceed the amount of money invested in the partnership. Since it is deductions, fast and large, that most investors look for when they become limited partners, the requirement set forth in point 3 makes it difficult for a leverage shelter to qualify for an advance ruling.

Deductions

The principal deductions generated by an equipment-leasing shelter are *depreciation* of the equipment and *interest payments* on bank loans.

Depreciation. Three factors are essential to the computation of the depreciation of a piece of equipment: basis, useful life, and salvage value. The "basis" of a purchased asset is its out-of-pocket cost plus any liens against the property. The "useful life" is the length of time over which the asset will be employed in the taxpayer's trade or business, and "salvage value" is the asset's estimated fair market value when it is no longer used by the taxpayer.

A taxpayer may choose any reasonable method in computing depreciation. Some of the more common methods are (1) straight-line, (2) double-declining-balance, and (3) the sum-of-the-years'-digits. The double-declining-balance rate, which initially is twice the straight-line rate, may be used for most new tangible assets. Although no salvage value need be taken into account when using this method, it usually does not permit an asset to be fully depreciated by the end of its useful life. Accordingly, it may be advantageous for a taxpayer to elect to change from the double-declining-balance method to the straight-line method after a number of years.

The example in the accompanying table illustrates the depreciation deductions allowable under each method when applied to a piece of equipment with a five-year useful life that was purchased on January 1 for $100,000. It is assumed also that the equipment has a salvage value of $20,000, which the taxpayer elects to reduce to $10,000.

Allowable Depreciation*

Year	Straight-line	Double-declining-balance	Sum-of-the-years'-digits†
1	$18,000	$40,000	$30,000
2	18,000	24,000	24,000
3	18,000	14,000	18,000
4	18,000	8,640	12,000
5	18,000	3,360	6,000
Salvage value after five years	$10,000	$10,000	$10,000

*Although the basis of property cannot be reduced below its salvage value, a taxpayer may elect to reduce the salvage value of property having at least a three-year useful life by an amount not exceeding 10 percent of its original depreciation basis.

†One commentator has indicated that to maximize the depreciation deduction "the 200% declining balance method should be used for the first two years with a change to the sum of the years'-digits method in the third year." This may be done without IRS consent if the taxpayer uses the asset depreciation range system. Commerce Clearing House, Inc., *Depreciation Guide 1973,* paragraph 124, 1973.

In addition to the usual depreciation deductions a limited partner can, if the partnership makes the election, obtain an additional depreciation deduction for certain kinds of property acquired by the partnership during the year. This deduction is generally limited to 20 percent of the cost of the property, up to $4,000, and is available only if the purchased property has a useful life of six years or more. The deduction, of course, reduces the basis of the property for purposes of the depreciation methods discussed above.

The Internal Revenue Code also permits the use of an asset depreciaiton range system that is based on a broad industry classification of useful lives. This procedure was established to end arguments between taxpayers and IRS agents on the useful life of various types of property. It may be elected annually and covers all eligible assets placed in service by the partnership during the taxable year. The system's advantage is that an asset may be treated as having a useful life 20 percent below or above its actual useful life. Depreciation is then computed over the selected period.

Interest.   Under the terms of most leverage lease arrangements, the lending institution will receive one year's prepayment of interest. This expense will be passed through to the partners in the same manner as any other expense. It must be noted, however, that some loans provide for the prepayment of two or three years' interest in the first year. The IRS has ruled that a deduction will be denied for any prepayment that extends more than twelve months beyond the current taxable year, and proper deductibility of two or three years' interest in one year thus is highly doubtful.

Investment Credit

The investment credit, like any other tax credit, is a dollar-for-dollar reduction in the amount of tax due. It applies primarily to tangible personal property having a useful life of three or more years and is a percentage of the asset's cost. If the property has a useful life of seven or more years, the percentage is 7 percent; if it has a useful life of five to seven years, the percentage is two-thirds of 7 percent; and if it has a useful life of three to five years, the percentage is one-third of 7 percent.[1]

Although generally available to most corporations, the investment credit is available to individual limited partners of a lessor partnership only if (1) the term of the lease including options to renew is less than 50 percent of the equipment's useful life and (2) for the first twelve months of the lease the unreimbursed ordinary business expenses of the partnership relating to the property exceed 15 percent of the lease rental payments. Ordinary business expenses for these purposes do not include depreciation, interest, or taxes.

The investment credit is one of the primary incentives for becoming a limited partner. Consequently the promoter's attorney will attempt to draft leases that will satisfy these requirements, despite the fact that they were enacted specifically to prevent this type of abuse.

A very recent revenue ruling provides that a lease for slightly less than one-half of the equipment's useful life, containing a provision to the effect that shortly before the end of the lease term the parties may negotiate another lease, does not violate the 50 percent-of-useful-life requirement.

The second requirement for obtaining the investment credit may be satisfied by having a contract between the promoter and the partnership, whereby the promoter or the manufacturer will maintain all the partnership's equipment for a fee. This fee cannot be guaranteed and must be based on the amount of servicing performed during the year. If the money paid for servicing during the first twelve months exceeds 15 percent of the rental payments, the business expense test will be met. However, because there is no valid way of predetermining service cost, an investor can never be sure in advance that he or she will be able to obtain the investment credit.

Allocation of Partnership Deductions

Deductions will be allocated to the partners in the proportion in which they share in profits and losses unless the partnership agreement provides otherwise. Some of the speculative shelters have attempted to make the investment more attractive by allocating all the depreciation deductions to the limited partners. The permissibility of this type of allocation has not been finally determined. Accordingly, any discussion of such allocations is well beyond the scope of this chapter, other than to mention that unless the allocation has economic significance apart from the tax consequences, it will probably be disallowed.

A Numerical Explanation

The following simplified example will illustrate some of the above principles that are involved in a typical leverage lease transaction:

1. A limited partnership is formed on January 1, 1975. Each of the four limited partners contributes $42,500, and the general corporate partner contributes $30,000.

2. Profits and losses are allocated in the proportion of 96 percent to the limited partners, to be divided equally among them, and 4 percent to the general partner.

3. On January 1 the partnership acquires a piece of equipment with a seven-year useful life for $1 million, of which $200,000 is paid from the partnership account and $800,000 borrowed from a bank. The loan is payable in equal monthly installments over a seven-year period with interest at approximately 14 percent per annum.

---

[1] The amount of the credit has generally been increased to 10 percent for property placed in service on or after January 22, 1975, and before January 1, 1977.

4. Simultaneously, the partnership enters into a contract leasing the equipment to a company. Under the lease the company must make constant payments of $16,400 per month for a seven-year period.

5. There is no third-party service contract, since the purpose of such an arrangement is to make money for the promoter and give the investor an uncertain chance of obtaining the investment credit. Therefore, the excess of the

TABLE 52-1   Computation of Partnership's Taxable Income or Loss*

Calendar year	Rental income	Depreciation†	Interest‡	Administration expense§	Total expense	Partnership income (loss)
1	$ 196,800	$ 285,714	$118,720	$ 2,500	$ 406,934	$(210,134)
2	196,800	204,081	100,566	2,500	307,147	(110,347)
3	196,800	145,773	82,426	2,500	230,699	(33,899)
4	196,800	104,123	64,276	2,500	170,899	25,901
5	196,800	86,769¶	46,126	2,500	135,395	61,405
6	196,800	86,770	27,976	2,500	117,246	79,554
7	196,800	86,770	9,831	2,500	99,101	97,699
Total	$1,377,600	$1,000,000	$449,921	$17,500	$1,467,421	($ 89,821)

*All computations are rounded off to even dollar amounts.

†Using the double-declining-balance method, disregarding the additional first-year depreciation deduction for these purposes, since it amounts to only $4,000, and assuming salvage value of less than 10 percent of the cost, thus eliminating it from the calculation.

‡Interest at 14.09 percent on an $800,000 borrowing.

§Consisting of the fee paid to the general partner for keeping partnership records.

¶Switching to straight-line depreciation.

NOTE: Most shelters provide for a substantial amount of start-up costs, which represent attorneys' and accountants' fees and other miscellaneous charges. The IRS usually takes the position that such costs must be amortized over the term of the lease. These fees have not been included in this example.

Some transactions are arranged with 15 percent partnership equity rather than the 20 percent set forth in this example.

It has been assumed that the taxpayer pays sufficient taxes and has no other preference items so that he or she will not be in a preference tax situation with respect to the excess of the double-declining-balance method of depreciation deduction over the amount of depreciation that would obtain if the straight-line method were used.

double-declining-balance depreciation over the straight-line depreciation will be a preference item. However, because the rental income exceeds the related business expense, the interest will not be considered excess investment interest.

Tables 52-1 and 52-2 set forth the effect of the transaction to the partnership and to an individual limited partner.

The Investor

This chapter has so far discussed the taxation of the partnership and its deductions. It does not necessarily follow, however, that all partnership deductions can be effectively utilized by the individual investor, and it is therefore crucial to understand how these deductions affect the investor's tax position.

Since earned income is currently taxed at a maximum federal rate of 50 percent and unearned income at rates up to 70 percent, a tax shelter is most advantageous to a high-salaried individual having significant amounts of unearned income, because most shelter deductions fall first against unearned income.[2] For example,

[2]Rarely is it worthwhile for an individual in a tax bracket of less than 50 percent to invest in a tax shelter.

if a married individual has $160,000 of earned taxable income and $30,000 of dividend and interest income, the $30,000 is taxable at a rate of approximately 68 percent, and $30,000 of shelter deductions would create an effective saving of 68 percent of $30,000, for a net in-pocket saving of $20,400.

Tax Preferences. The Tax Reform Act of 1969 provided for a new category

TABLE 52-2 Computation of a Limited Partner's Share of Gain or Loss and Cash Flow (24 Percent of the Partnership's)*

Calendar year	Each limited partner's share of income (loss) for tax purposes	Income taxes saved in 70 percent bracket	Each limited partner's share of cash distribution†	Net cash flow
1	$(50,432)	$35,302‡	$ 3,778	$39,080
2	(26,483)	18,538	3,778	22,316
3	(8,136)	5,695	3,778	9,473
4	6,216	(4,351)	3,778	(573)
5	14,737	(10,316)	3,778	(6,538)
6	19,093	(13,364)	3,778	(9,586)
7	23,448	(16,414)	3,778	(12,636)
Total	$(21,557)	$15,090	$26,446	$41,536§

*All computations are rounded off to even dollar amounts.

†24 percent of the excess of cash receipts ($196,800) over cash expended for administration expenses ($2,500) plus $178,560 to repay the bank loan together with interest.

‡Since the excess of the double-declining-balance rate of depreciation over the straight-line rate is approximately $35,714 and since this amount exceeds $30,000, the individual's taxes on earnings subject to the maximum rate of 50 percent will be increased. This is not reflected in the example because no assumptions have been made as to the individual's tax picture. However, if a married individual filing a joint return had $200,000 of earned taxable income, $100,000 of dividend and interest income, and, after deductions, $240,000 of taxable income for 1973, his or her tax would increase by $1,143 as a result of the excess depreciation over the straight-line rate. If the investor was not in a maximum tax position, the excess of preference depreciation would not affect the tax due.

§If we assume that the residual value of the equipment is 20 percent of the initial investment or that the lessee is given a 20 percent purchase option, the partnership will receive $200,000 on the sale of the equipment. Each limited partner will receive a cash distribution of $42,500 when the partnership is liquidated. However, since the partnership's basis in the property is zero, the limited partner's share of the $200,000 gain will be $48,000 (24 percent of the partnership profits). In general, with a tax rate at 70 percent, taxes will be $33,600 and result in an additional net cash flow of $8,900. Thus after the entire transaction has been completed, the limited partner will have a net cash gain of $41,536 plus $8,900, or $50,436, less the original investment of $42,500, for a final net cash gain of $7,964.

called "tax preference items." This category includes one-half of the excess of long-term capital gains over capital losses, the spread on the exercise of a qualified stock option, and, if the property involved is subject to a "net lease," the yearly excess of accelerated depreciation over the straight-line rate. Since a net lease arises if the lessor's ordinary business expenses relating to the equipment are less than 15 percent of the yearly rental income, there can be no advance assurance that a sufficient amount of expenses will be incurred to avoid the net lease problem.

Indeed, to the extent that preference items exceed only $30,000, they reduce an individual's "earned income" that is subject to the 50 percent "maximum tax." This has a substantial effect on the taxes owed and is one of the major drawbacks to a shelter. Its effects should be carefully assessed by each taxpayer before he or she invests in a shelter. For example, if a married individual filing a joint return has $200,000 of earned taxable income, $100,000 of dividends and interest, and after deductions $240,000 of taxable income, his or her tax would increase by $1,143 if the accelerated depreciation from the shelter investment was $35,714 more than depreciation would have been under the straight-line method (see footnote ‡ to Table 52-2).

Excess Investment Interest.   In addition to tax preference items, the investor must be aware of the limit on the deductibility of investment interest. Excess investment interest is basically the amount of investment interest that exceeds the sum of (1) $25,000, (2) net investment income, (3) the excess of deductions attributable to net lease property over the income from such property, (4) the taxpayer's net long-term capital gain, and (5) one-half of the excess of investment interest over items 2 through 4. Net investment income is generally the excess of such items as interest, dividends, rents, and royalties, plus depreciation recapture on the sale of an asset over investment expenses.

Usually $25,000 plus the amount of dividends received will be sufficient to permit the interest deduction if the leased property is not subject to a net lease. If the property is subject to a net lease, the investor will probably avoid loss of a current interest deduction if the rental income exceeds the business and interest deductions attributable to the property. The individual's accountant should, however, make the computation.

Lease or Sale.[3]   Throughout the chapter we have assumed that the agreement between the partnership and the user of the equipment is a lease. However, just as a partnership may be taxable as a corporation, a lease may be a conditional-sale agreement. The IRS's position is that a "lease" transaction will be considered a sale if:

1. The agreement is not structured as a lease.
2. The payments are applied specifically to an interest that the "lessee" will ultimately acquire in the property.
3. The "lessee" will acquire title on payment of a specified number of "rental" payments.
4. The "rent" is very high for a short period and relates directly to the purchase price of the equipment.
5. The "rental" payments greatly exceed the current fair rental value of the equipment.
6. The property may be acquired at a nominal option price in relation to the expected fair value of the property at the time when the option is to be exercised, or the option price is very small in relation to the total "rental payments."
7. Some portion of the payments are designated interest or are readily recognizable as such.
8. The total "rental" payments and option price approximate the purchase price of the equipment plus interest and carrying charges.

The effect of an agreement's being considered a conditional sale would be disastrous to the investor. Consequently, it is imperative that the opinion of the

---

[3]The IRS has indicated that for advance-ruling purposes a leverage lease arrangement must satisfy the following criteria to be recognized: (1) The lessor must have an equity investment of at least 28 percent of the value of the property, and this must be maintained during the lease term. (2) The value of the property at the end of the lease must be at least 20 percent of the leased property's original cost and have a useful life of the longer of one year or 20 percent of the originally estimated useful life. (3) The lessee may not have the right to purchase the property at less than its fair market value, nor can it pay any part of the property's cost or lend money to the lessor to acquire property. (4) The lessor must be able to show an intention to earn a profit from the transaction, aside from the available tax benefits.

partnership's counsel include an unqualified statement that the leases will in fact be leases for tax purposes.

Termination

Although the reader may now believe that he or she is somewhat familiar with equipment shelters, he or she must not overlook the fact that losses generated in the first few years generally become gains about halfway through the lease. Therefore, the investor will want to get out of the partnership at the crossover point, because from then on the investor's cash flow may never equal the taxes due on his or her share of the partnership income.

There are many ways of disposing of a limited partnership interest, but this discussion will focus on the consequences of a sale or a complete termination of the partnership and on the effect of a gift of the partnership interest to charity.

Sale of a Partnership Interest. A gain or loss on the sale of a partnership interest is treated as a gain or loss from the sale of a capital asset, except to the extent of "unrealized receivables" and "substantially appreciated inventory." Gain, of course, is the difference between a partner's basis (which has probably been reduced to zero by the partnership's "losses") and the amount realized (the money received plus the selling limited partner's share of nonrecourse partnership liabilities). Unrealized receivables include the amount of depreciation recapture that would be allocable to the partner if the partnership sold all its assets.

Therefore, because the partner's basis in the partnership is probably very low and his or her allocable share of depreciation recapture high, most if not all of the gain recognized on the sale of the partnership interest will be ordinary income and a preference item. Since the amount of cash paid for the interest will be equal to the fair market value of the partner's share of the partnership assets minus the partner's allocable share of the nonrecourse debt, the cash received may be substantially less than the tax due from the sale. Also, if the full investment credit was initially taken and the interest is sold within a seven-year period, a portion of the investment credit will be recaptured.

Termination of the Partnership. On termination of a partnership its assets will be sold and the proceeds usually distributed in the following order: payment to creditors in the order provided by state law, repayment of any partner's loans to the partnership, payment to the limited partners of the balances in their capital accounts, repayment to the general partner of any balance in its capital account, and the excess to the partners in the proportion in which they share in partnership profits.

The partners will naturally be required to recognize gain or loss on the sale of the partnership's assets. Gain (loss) will be the difference between the partnership's basis in the assets and the amount realized, which includes any liability to which the property is subject. To the extent that there is gain, it will be allocated to each partner in the same proportion as any other gain. Moreover, since the bank loan will be repaid before any cash is distributed to the partners, the partners will probably have a larger tax liability than the cash received.

If the partnership is terminated after all loans have been repaid, the residual value of the equipment will determine whether the cash received will cover the tax liability (see footnote § to Table 52-2 for a numerical example). This residual value is the key element that makes equipment shelters more advantageous than most other shelters.

Charitable Contribution of a Partnership Interest. After all loans have been repaid, the amount of any charitable contribution is the value of the property reduced by any ordinary income that would result on its sale. A gift to charity at this point would have little value because the partner's basis in the partnership interest is probably close to zero, and, as a result of the depreciation recapture provisions, the gain that would be recognized on a sale would be ordinary income.

Prior to repayment of loans, a gift of a limited partner's interest within seven years from the date on which the property was put to use will result in the recapture of part of the investment credit if the full credit was initially taken by the partner. The contribution will be considered a sale of the interest to the extent of the partner's share of partnership debt with the result that the partner may have taxable income. Indeed, the limitations on the amount of the charitable deduction must be reviewed especially with regard to any ordinary income that would be recognized on the sale of the interest, since the value of the charitable contribution must be reduced by any ordinary income element in the property.

Summary

This chapter has attempted to give the reader an insight into the tax effects of a leverage lease equipment tax shelter. It has indicated how a partnership is taxed and the kinds of the deductions available, including the different depreciation methods, additional first-year depreciation, and interest. It has focused on the investment credit and pointed out its pitfalls, as well as such troublesome areas as preference items, excess investment interest, and the characterization of the transaction as a lease or a sale.

It should be apparent that an equipment-leasing shelter, aside from its income potential (which is usually small), is merely a method of changing the year in which income is taxed, for deductions in the early years become gains in later years. The primary advantage is limited to individuals who can expect their income to fall off in a few years because of retirement or because the present year is an exceptionally high-income year. Of course, an individual who is constantly in a high tax bracket can continue to defer tax by purchasing an interest in a new tax shelter in the year that the crossover point to gain is reached in the prior shelter. However, the deferred tax must eventually be reckoned with.

No mention has been made of the effect of state or local taxes or of Section 183, which disallows certain deductions if a transaction is not entered into for profit, and these factors must be considered. Finally, we want to reemphasize that an individual's tax picture is unique and therefore should be reviewed at least annually by a competent tax adviser.

The Tax Reform Act of 1976 radically changed all tax shelters including equipment leasing. It is still too early to interpret fully all the implications of these changes, and the investor should rely on his or her own tax experts and not solely on this chapter while making investments discussed in the chapter.

BIBLIOGRAPHY

Calkins, Hugh, and Kenneth E. Updergraft, Jr.: "Tax Shelters," *The Tax Lawyer,* vol. 26, no. 3, American Bar Association, Spring, 1973.
Commerce Clearing House, Inc.: *Standard Federal Tax Reports,* vol. 60, no. 42, Sept. 11, 1973.
"Guideline Rules on Equipment Leasing," *The CPA Journal,* vol. XLIV, no. 9, New York State Society of Certified Public Accountants, September 1974.
Income Tax Regulations: Pertinent Revenue Rulings, Revenue Procedures, and Technical Information Releases, as amended through July 1974.
Internal Revenue Code of 1954, as amended.
Livsey, Robert C.: "Limited Partnerships: How Far Can IRS Go in Limiting Their Use in Tax Shelters," *The Journal of Taxation,* vol. 39, no. 2, Tax Research Group, Ltd., August 1973.

Schmidt, Henry W., and Richard G. Larsen: "Leverage Leasing: Tax Factors That Contribute to Its Attractiveness," *The Journal of Taxation,* vol. 41, no. 4, Tax Research Group, Ltd., October 1974.

Stine, Gordon T.: "Ship and Equipment Leasing as a Tax Shelter," *New York University Institute on Federal Taxation,* vol. 1, Matthew Bender & Co., Inc., New York, 1973.

Tannenbaum, Donald M.: "Leverage Shelter Operations: Oil & Gas, Motion Pictures and Other Theatrical Shelters," *New York University Institute on Federal Taxation,* vol. 1, Matthew Bender, & Co. Inc., New York, 1973.

Willis, Arthur B.: Willis on Partnership Taxation, McGraw-Hill Book Company, New York, 1971.

Section Ten

Policies and Strategies for Portfolio Management

INTRODUCTION

In this section we explore appropriate available policies and strategies for effective portfolio management by both individual and institutional investors. First, in Chapter 53, Dr. Keith V. Smith elucidates some underlying theoretical principles of central portfolio decisions and provides us with basic concepts and definitions of portfolio risk, return, and efficiency. In Chapter 54 he performs similar functions for portfolio diversification and concentration in their several aspects.

In Chapter 55, Dr. Lemont K. Richardson goes on to analyze key concepts and principles of portfolio decision making, primarily in terms of their practical applications in the investment environment expected for the balance of the 1970s. Next Dr. Leo Barnes explores in Chapter 56, chiefly from the practitioner's operational point of view, the special factors to be stressed in managing an individual's investment portfolio. In the following Chapter 57 he performs a similar task for institutional portfolio management.

Finally, in Chapter 58, Rudolf Hauser concludes this section with a thorough case study illustrating how some of the theories and recommended practices presented in the preceding chapters have (and have not) been applied in recent years by one major type of institutional investor, state and local government pension funds.

Chapter **53**

Determining Efficient Portfolios: Basic Principles of Portfolio Decision Making[1]

KEITH V. SMITH

The first nine sections of the *Handbook* deal with wealth management and the process of investing from the viewpoint of individual investment opportunities. In Section Ten we consider wealth and investment management from the viewpoint of the entire portfolio of securities and other investment assets that are held. The major theme of this section is that a portfolio is more than just the sum of its individual components and that relationships between these components therefore must be considered for us to understand the properties of the aggregate portfolio.

To illustrate this central theme, we shall consider several scenarios. A retired couple sells ten corporate bonds of General Electric Company to pay for a cruise to Europe. As part of their investment program to provide college education for their children, a young married couple purchases fifty common shares of Exxon Corporation. A professor directs his university to invest $100 of his monthly salary in a variable annuity plan that is managed by the trust department of a local commercial bank. The portfolio manager of a large mutual fund allocates $500,-000 to the purchase of mobile home stocks. Four medical professionals pool their capital and construct a medical building in which they will house their respective practices.

All these scenarios feature the purchase or sale of a single investment asset. Also inherent in each scenario is the idea of either immediate or future consumption by the individual or individuals involved. In other words, investing is the use of nonconsumed current wealth with the hope of providing for greater wealth and hence greater consumption at some future date. And as we shall see, portfolio decision making by an individual rather closely parallels his or her consumption decision making.

Presumably, each investment decision reflected in the scenarios was based on

[1]Much of the material in Chapters 53 and 54 is also treated in *Essentials of Investments* by Keith V. Smith and David K. Eiteman, Richard D. Irwin, Inc., Homewood, Ill., 1974.

certain characteristics or attributes of the particular asset. For example, the individual or individuals might have considered the income generated by the asset, the expected growth in market value of the asset, and the degree of safety inherent in owning that asset. Such characteristics, however, do not really provide a complete or proper perspective for making that decision. Rather, each decision should have been made relative to the total portfolio of the individual or individuals involved. For example, the couple should have evaluated the common stock of Exxon relative to their other investment holdings. And the professor's investment in a variable annuity is only one part of his total portfolio. This means that the characteristics or attributes of individual assets must somehow be combined to obtain the corresponding characteristics for the entire portfolio. Each portfolio thus becomes a distinct entity with measurable characteristics. Furthermore, it becomes necessary to consider the interrelationships between assets to assess fully the aggregate characteristics of the portfolio.

Chapters 55, 56, 57, and 58 in Section Ten consider the unique problems of portfolio management by both individuals and certain types of institutional investors. To provide a proper perspective for those chapters, Chapters 53 and 54 include a review of certain concepts and guidelines germane to portfolio decision making overall. Although a few formulas and graphs will be needed to make the basic levels of portfolio decision making fully understandable, the presentation will be kept as simple as possible, and illustrations will be used in lieu of mathematical rigor. Before proceeding to develop a portfolio perspective, however, it is appropriate to consider the scope of portfolio decision making.

Scope of Portfolio Decision Making

Portfolio decisions are made by both individuals and institutions. As should be inferred from the foregoing scenarios, virtually all individuals and households must make at least some portfolio decisions. Even if an individual spends all of his or her income on immediate consumption, a portfolio decision is made on the individual's behalf when certain funds are invested as part of his or her retirement. Most individuals also are able to save at least some part of their income. No matter whether these funds are placed in savings, bonds, stocks, or real estate, the individuals are adding to their portfolios of investments. In some cases, the individuals themselves make the investment decisions directly. In other cases, they allocate their savings to institutional portfolios, and a professional money manager makes the investment decisions on their behalf. Examples of institutional investment opportunities include mutual funds, pension funds, trust funds, and insurance companies.

To appreciate the vast scope of portfolio decision making, it is useful to examine selected aggregate statistics for recent years. Table 53-1, for example, includes the financial assets of households for the period 1967–1971. During the years 1968–1971, the total holdings of financial assets by households ranged from $1.8 to $2.1 trillion. We see further that the largest single holding is common and preferred stock, followed by savings accounts and pension fund reserves. In Table 53-1 as well as in other tables, holdings of stocks are reported in market values. The largest growth in holdings over the period 1967–1971 is for corporate bonds, although they represent one of the smallest categories on an absolute basis.

It is also useful to examine the flow of funds into investment assets as well as the dollar holdings by individuals and institutions. The sources and uses of long-term investment funds for 1967–1971 are shown in Table 53-2. Funds from a variety of different institutions are seen to have flowed foremost to real estate mortgages and then to corporate and government bonds. The major sources of funds during that period were savings institutions, commercial banks, and life insurance companies.

TABLE 53-1   Financial Assets of Households, 1967–1971
(Billions of dollars)

Asset	1967	1968	1969	1970	1971
Currency and demand deposits	$ 104.1	$ 116.7	$ 120.4	$ 126.5	$ 134.9
Savings accounts	341.5	371.8	377.8	422.4	496.0
Life insurance reserves	115.4	120.0	125.0	130.3	137.0
Pension fund reserves	185.2	206.2	216.8	237.4	268.1
Government bonds	126.6	130.9	149.8	147.8	129.4
Corporate bonds	16.8	21.7	27.4	39.8	47.0
Common and preferred stock	709.9	821.7	727.2	715.4	823.6
Mutual fund shares	44.7	52.7	48.3	47.6	55.0
Mortgages	36.6	38.4	40.2	42.5	44.9
Other assets	22.5	27.0	34.3	34.6	34.0
Total holdings	$1,703.4	$1,907.1	$1,867.3	$1,944.3	$2,169.9

SOURCE: *National Fact Book of Mutual Savings Banking,* 1972, Table 58.

After remaining fairly constant in the years 1967–1969, the total flow of investment funds increased to $67.8 billion in 1970 and to $102.9 billion in 1971.

It is difficult to estimate the total investment holdings of all types of investment assets by individuals and institutions. The relative holdings of common and preferred stock listed on the New York Stock Exchange for both individuals and institutions are included in Table 53-3. Five major categories of institutional portfolios are reflected in the table. The first category consists of life and nonlife insurance companies. The second category includes corporate and governmental pension funds. Mutual funds and other investment companies comprise a third category. Personal and common trust funds are included collectively as a fourth category. And the fifth category consist of foundations and educational endowments. We see that these institutions collectively accounted for approximately one-

TABLE 53-2   Sources and Uses of Long-Term Investment Funds, 1967–1971
(Billions of dollars)

	1967	1968	1969	1970	1971
Uses of funds					
Government bonds	$ 8.8	$ 9.9	$ 8.5	$12.2	$ 21.0
Corporate bonds	14.7	12.9	12.1	20.2	19.1
Common and preferred stock	2.3	−0.9	3.4	5.9	11.1
Mortgages	22.9	27.4	27.8	26.4	48.3
Other*	3.9	5.7	7.0	3.1	3.4
Total uses	$52.6	$55.0	$58.8	$67.8	$102.9
Sources of funds					
Life insurance companies	$ 7.7	$ 7.7	$ 5.5	$ 5.9	$ 9.5
Nonlife insurance companies	3.0	2.6	2.6	3.9	5.1
Corporate pension funds	5.9	5.4	6.2	6.8	7.1
Governmental retirement funds	4.5	4.2	4.8	6.6	7.9
Savings institutions	12.9	14.0	13.0	14.2	34.2
Commercial banks	16.3	19.5	11.0	15.8	25.8
Mutual funds	1.5	1.9	2.7	1.8	0.8
Other†	0.8	(0.3)	13.0	12.8	12.5
Total sources	$52.6	$55.0	$58.8	$67.8	$102.9

*Includes foreign securities and term loans.
†Includes individuals, business corporations, and other investor groups.
SOURCE: Bankers Trust Company, *Bankers Trust Investment Outlook for 1972,* Table 2.

TABLE 53-3   Annual Holdings of New York Stock Exchange Common and Preferred Stock, 1967–1971   (Market value in billions of dollars)

Portfolio	1967	1968	1969	1970	1971
Life insurance companies	$ 10.9	$ 13.2	$ 13.7	$ 15.4	$ 20.5
Nonlife insurance companies	13.0	14.6	13.3	13.2	15.5
Corporate pension funds	51.1	61.5	61.4	67.1	86.8
Governmental retirement funds	2.8	4.1	5.8	8.0	11.3
Mutual funds	42.8	50.9	45.1	43.9	52.5
Other investment companies	8.2	8.2	6.6	6.2	7.1
Trust funds	79.8	88.4	84.2	83.2	91.5
Foundations	15.6	17.5	15.7	15.9	18.6
Educational endowments	7.8	8.1	7.9	8.0	8.9
Total institutional holdings	$232.0	$266.5	$253.7	$260.9	$312.7
Individuals and other*	592.8	708.4	607.7	591.2	689.3
Total holdings	$824.8	$974.9	$861.4	$852.1	$1,002.0

*Includes minor holdings by foreign investors and savings institutions.

SOURCE: Securities and Exchange Commission, *Release No. 2582,* Statistical Series, April 1972, Table 4.

third of total stockholdings during the years 1967–1971. The three largest holdings of stock during 1971 by institutional investors were trust funds, corporate pension funds, and mutual funds. By far the greatest growth in stockholdings during the 1967–1971 period occurred in corporate pension funds and governmental retirement funds.

In the late 1960s and early 1970s the importance of institutional investors increased relative to individual investors. Not only did institutional holdings increase, but so did the volume of institutional transactions as compared with individual transactions. At present, it is estimated that institutional trading accounts for over two-thirds of the total volume generated, at least on the organized security exchanges. Contributing to this situation is the increased portfolio turnover by institutional investors, as shown in Table 53-4. Overall turnover grew from 24.7 percent in 1967 to 30.9 percent in 1971, or by just about one-fourth. Mutual funds continued to be the most active among the institutional portfolios represented in the table, although increased turnover occurred for all four types during the 1967–1971 period.

In later chapters of Section Ten, special attention will be given to the investment problems of individuals and also certain of the institutional portfolios that have been identified. Before doing this, however, we shall proceed to examine the problems of portfolio decision making in greater detail.

TABLE 53-4   Annual Turnover Rates for Selected Institutional Investors, 1967–1971
(In percentages)

	1967	1968	1969	1970	1971
Life insurance companies	18.2	26.8	29.4	27.8	30.9
Nonlife insurance companies	9.7	16.0	26.7	28.1	22.7
Corporate pension funds	17.2	18.7	21.3	20.5	22.4
Mutual funds	40.7	48.4	51.0	45.6	48.2
Total selected institutions	24.7	29.4	32.4	29.8	30.9

NOTE: Turnover rate equals the average of purchases and sales for the year divided by the average value of total holdings at the beginning and at the end of the year.

SOURCE: Securities and Exchange Commission, *Release No. 2582,* Statistical Series, April 1972, Table 3.

Economics of Portfolio Decision Making

Deciding upon a portfolio of investment assets is similar in many respects to other decisions made by an individual. To show this, we shall briefly review the standard *theory of consumer choice* among two commodities, as illustrated in the top panel of Fig. 53-1. Let us suppose that an individual is trying to decide how to spend a portion of his or her monthly income on leisure activities during the coming

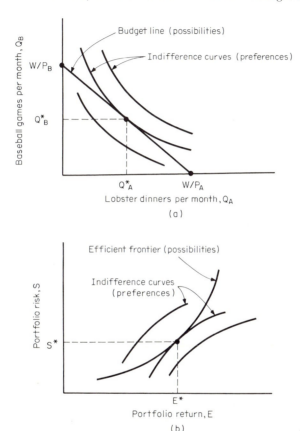

Fig. 53-1 Comparison of consumer choice (a) and portfolio choice (b).

month and that he or she is limiting attention to major league baseball games and lobster dinners at an outstanding seafood restaurant. Commodity A represents lobster dinners, while Commodity B represents baseball games. The quantities of lobster dinners and baseball games are represented by Q_A and Q_B, respectively, while P_A and P_B are their respective prices. The individual is faced with the decision of how to spend a monthly allotment of W dollars on lobster dinners and baseball games, of both of which he or she never seems to get enough.

We see in the top panel of Fig. 53-1 that the optimal consumption decision, designated by $(A_A^*, A_B^*$ is found by combining two distinctly different types of information. First, the locus of consumption *possibilities* is given by the straight line $W = P_A Q_A + P_B Q_B$, where income W and prices P_A and P_B are given and where Q_A and Q_B are the choice variables of the individual. The possibilities line, commonly referred to as the "budget line," represents the maximum opportunities available in the markets for lobster dinners and baseball games. Second, the locus of investor *preferences* is given by a series of indifference curves that are convex to the origin in the commodity space. Each indifference curve represents the locus of quantities, of lobster dinners and baseball games per month about which the individual consumer is indifferent. As one moves upward or to the right, or both, in the diagram, each indifference curve represents a higher level of satisfaction to the individual.

The solution of the problem of consumer choice (Q_A^*, Q_B^*) can be seen to occur at the tangency of the budget line and the highest attainable indifference curve. That is, the individual selects for the month that combination of lobster dinners and baseball games that affords him or her the highest possible level of satisfaction, given the resources that he or she is willing to devote to lobster and baseball. At the optimal solution, the marginal rate of substitution between lobster and baseball is just equal to the slope of the budget line. It is important to note that the optimal quantities of lobster dinners and baseball games, Q_A^* and Q_B^*, are found by combining two types of information: possibilities and preferences. Information about preferences is found by talking with individuals about their preferences for various combinations of commodities, while information about possibilities is obtained by examining the markets for those commodities.

The *theory of portfolio choice* is similar in many respects, but there are important distinctions. First, the objects of choice are not commodities or services that may be consumed but portfolios of investment assets that, it is hoped, will provide for greater consumption at later dates. Second, possibilities and preferences are defined on certain attributes of those investments and portfolios rather than on the investments and portfolios themselves. By far the most popular treatment of portfolio choice, as shown in the bottom panel of Fig. 53-1, is based on return and risk as the two attributes on which investors are presumed to select investment assets and hence construct portfolios. For now we designate return by E and risk by S.

The shapes of the curves differ from those in consumer choice because risk is an undesirable attribute as opposed to return, which is a desirable attribute to investors. As a result, the family of indifference curves is concave to the origin, while the portfolio possibilities curve is convex to the origin. The possibilities curve is often referred to as the "efficient curve" or the "efficient frontier." Each portfolio along the efficient frontier, including the optimal solution, has by definition the highest possible return for that level of risk or the lowest possible risk for that level of return. Optimal solution of portfolio choice, designated by (E^*, S^*), is seen to be at the tangency of the portfolio possibilities curve with the highest attainable indifference curve. As with consumer choice, the solution of portfolio choice is found by bringing together information about portfolio possibilities (based on a study of investment assets and their attributes) and information about the preferences of investors.

Many of the properties of efficient portfolios, the assumptions about investor behavior, and the implications of portfolio theory are embedded in the problem of portfolio choice as illustrated in the bottom panel of Fig. 53-1. Before we can fully understand the richness of portfolio theory and the importance of proper portfolio decisions, it is necessary to show how the attributes of investment assets, particularly return and risk, can be combined to obtain the corresponding attributes of portfolios.

Asset Return

What is the return on an investment asset? For a savings account it is the rate paid by the savings institution, while for a government or corporate bond it is the yield to maturity. In both instances, the periodic payment to an investor and the repayment of principal represent legal obligations on the part of the savings institution, the issuing government, or the issuing corporation. Although there is some chance that the investor may not receive either the periodic payments or the principal repayment, the chances are typically quite high that he or she will receive the full return on his or her investment. Moreover, it is important to note that periodic payments to investors should be adjusted for the taxes (regular income or capital gains taxes) that become due when those payments are received. That is, return on an investment asset should always be considered on an aftertax basis. Henceforth, we shall assume that all returns are defined on an aftertax basis.

For common stock and other riskier investment assets such as real estate, the periodic and terminal payments do not represent legal obligations on the part of the issuing organization. In view of this uncertainty, there is no straightforward measure of return to the investor. Return may be quite high, or it may be nonexistent. A common procedure in cases of uncertainty is to specify the *expected return* of the investment asset. Informally, this may be a "guesstimate" of the return expected by the investor. Formally, expected return is taken as the mean value of the probability distribution about investment return, which is treated as a random variable having several possible outcomes. To calculate expected return, each possible return is multiplied by the probability of that return, and the weighted returns are added over all possible outcomes. For example, if there are equal chances of a 7 percent or a 12 percent aftertax return on a certain investment, the expected return is just $(0.50) (7 \text{ percent}) + (0.50) (12 \text{ percent}) = 9.5 \text{ percent}$. If the odds are 3 to 1 in favor of the higher return, expected return is just $(0.25) (7 \text{ percent}) + (0.75) (12 \text{ percent}) = 10.75 \text{ percent}$. Expected return is conceptually appealing since it is a measure of central tendency for the underlying probability distribution, but it does require the investor, his or her broker, an investment adviser, or someone else to specify that probability distribution. In any event, the investor's particular tax status should be used to convert possible returns to the appropriate aftertax basis.

As a further illustration, let us consider that the common shares of Company A are being analyzed as a potential investment. Three possible outcomes for per-share return are projected, and the calculation of expected return proceeds as follows:

Possible Outcome, k	Return, R_k	Probability, Π_k	Weighted Return, $\Pi_k R_k$
1	$5\% = .05$	.25	.0125
2	$13\% = .13$	.50	.0650
3	$17\% = .17$	.25	.0425

Expected security return $E_A = .1200 \ (12\%)$

By multiplying each possible return R_k by its associated probability Π_k and summing all three possible outcomes, we see that the expected return is 12 percent for the common stock of Company A.

The suggested measure of asset return, therefore, is the mean value of an entire probability distribution for the attribute. Alternative probability distributions are illustrated in Fig. 53-2. For Company A, the three possible outcomes are shown with dots. The dashed curve represents a possible probability distribution defined over many possible outcomes. The expected return of 12 percent for Company A is shown to be the mean or average value of the entire probability distribution. A similar expected return of 12 percent is indicated in Fig. 53-2 for Companies X, Y, and Z even though the underlying probability distributions are distinctly different. For example, the range of outcomes is greater for Company X but less for

Company Y. And unlike the other three distributions, which exhibit symmetry, the probability distribution for Company Z is positively skewed to the right, which means that there is a small chance of a high return from that security. Although the entire probability distribution of possible aftertax returns is of interest to an investor, a common practice is to focus on mean value as a measure of asset return.

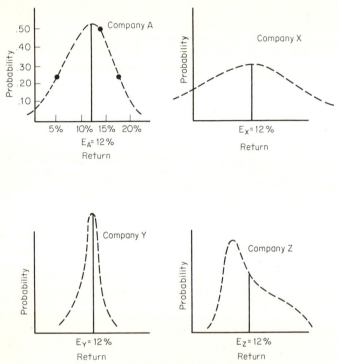

Fig. 53-2   Probability distributions.

Portfolio Return

For the young married couple who bought fifty shares of Exxon Corporation, that particular new holding is only one of the three securities that they own. And the variable annuity of the professor is just a part of a total portfolio, since he and his wife also own shares of a large mutual fund plus a small trust fund set up at the death of her parents. In addition, they have a savings account that they maintain as a cash reserve. The expected return for their portfolio, for that of the young married couple, or for any portfolio is logically measured as a weighted average of the expected returns on all the assets in the particular portfolio. The weights in such an average should be based on the relative market values of the individual assets. This procedure is applicable even if the individual assets are themselves portfolios. For example, all four of the assets held by the professor and his wife are portfolios.

To illustrate the suggested procedure, we calculate expected return for the portfolio of the professor and his wife to be 7.57 percent, as shown in the accompanying table.

Return on Illustrative Portfolio

Investment asset	Market value	Relative weight	Expected asset return (percent)	Weighted return
Savings account	$ 3,700	.203	5.0	.0101
Mutual fund	4,300	.236	9.2	.0217
Trust fund	9,000	.495	8.0	.0396
Variable annuity	1,200	.066	6.5	.0043
Total	$18,200	1.000		.0757 (7.57%)

In this calculation, the relative weights are found by dividing each individual market value by $18,200, which is the aggregate market value of the portfolio at present. Of the component returns, only that of the savings account is known with reasonable certainty. All the others are expected returns whose estimates perhaps are based on the experience of similar investments in recent years. Obviously, the professor and his wife could increase their expected portfolio return by shifting dollars out of savings and into any of the other three types of investments. A maximum expected return of 9.2 percent would be achieved by allocating their entire investment wealth to the mutual fund. This, of course, would be a riskier portfolio since it would consist of only a single investment asset.

Asset Risk

What is the risk of owning a common share of Exxon, a corporate bond of General Electric, or a share of some mutural fund? Although many possible responses might be made to this question, most would focus on the chances that the individual actually will receive a return on his or her investment. To some, this concept of risk is implemented with a qualitative assignment such as high-risk, moderate-risk, low-risk, or risk-free. Bond and stock ratings, for example, include qualitative assessments of the risk inherent in such investment assets.

To others, the concept of risk is best expressed with a quantitative measure that somehow expresses the variability of possible returns. For a virtually risk-free asset (such as a United States Treasury bill) whose return outcome is certain, risk may be taken to be zero; for other investment assets whose possible return is not certain, a numerical assignment for risk must be made. Variance or standard deviation of the probability distribution of return is a frequent choice, because it reflects the entire dispersion of possible outcomes, usually measured about mean asset return. To some, possible outcomes below mean return would seem to be the essence of risk, with possible outcomes above mean return being desirable. To others, upside variability should be included because it is just another dimension of uncertainty associated with the holding of an investment asset. This controversy has led to the suggested use of semivariance or minimum possible return as more suitable risk measures because they ignore upside deviations from mean return. These alternative measures unfortunately do not readily lend themselves to tractable solutions of portfolio choice. Accordingly, we shall continue to discuss risk in terms of total dispersion about mean return, even though the resulting risk measure may not be conceptually acceptable to all investors.

An illustration of how variance and standard deviation are calculated is shown in the table at the top of page 53-12.

Variance of return is seen to be the sum of squared deviations from the expected return $E_A = 12$ percent, each weighted by the probability Π_k of that particular outcome. For Company A, variance $S_A^2 = .0019$. Standard deviation of return is the square root of variance; hence, $S_A = 4.4$ percent. Since standard deviation of

Company A Common Stock

Outcome k	Return R_k	Probability Π_k	Weighted $\Pi_k R_k$	Deviation $R_k - E_A$	Squared $(R_k - E_A)^2$	Weighted $\Pi_k (R_k - E_A)^2$
1	.05	.25	.0125	−.070	.004900	.001225
2	.13	.50	.0650	.010	.000100	.000050
3	.17	.25	.0425	.050	.002500	.000652

Expected return E_A = .1200 (12%)

Variance $S_A{}^2$ = .001900
Standard deviation S_A = .044 (4.4%)

return is expressed in the same units as expected return, we shall work with standard deviation rather than variance even though they are directly related.

Another common stock being considered for inclusion in the portfolio is that of Company B. Its probability distribution of return, plus expected return and standard deviation of return are calculated as shown in the accompanying table.

Company B Common Stock

Outcome k	Return R_k	Probability Π_k	Weighted $\Pi_k R_k$	Deviation $R_k - E_B$	Squared $(R_k - E_B)^2$	Weighted $\Pi_k (R_k - E_B)^2$
1	.06	.25	.0150	−.030	.000900	.000225
2	.09	.50	.0450	.000	.000000	.000000
3	.12	.25	.0300	.030	.000900	.000225

Expected return E_B = .0900 (9%)

Variance S_2 = .000450
Standard deviation S_B = .021

In comparing the common stocks of Companies A and B, we see that Company A has both a higher expected return and a higher level of risk, as measured by the standard deviation of return. These two cases illustrate a central feature of investment assets, namely, that higher return generally is accompanied by higher risk. This feature would appear to hold true regardless of how security risk is being measured, and it should not be restricted to the expected return and standard deviation model illustrated here.

In Fig. 53-3, we see a comparison of the probability distribution, the expected returns, and the standard deviations of returns for the common stocks of Companies A and B. We also note that the probability distribution for Company B is symmetrical about the expected return while that for Company A is not. We have yet to see, however, the full implications of holding several investment assets together in a portfolio. To do this, we must proceed from asset risk to portfolio risk.

Portfolio Risk

To explain and illustrate portfolio risk, we must determine the relative holdings of each asset to be included in the portfolio. We know from the prior discussion that the expected return on a portfolio is just a weighted average of the expected return of the component members of the portfolio. For possible portfolios of the common stocks of Company A and Company B, we see in the table on page 53-13 that portfolio return varies from 9 to 12 percent.

An equal investment in Company A and Company B results in an expected return of 10.5 percent. For simplicity, we shall consider such an equal-investment portfolio to illustrate portfolio risk.

Portfolios of Company A and Company B Common Stocks

Portfolio holdings	Expected portfolio return
100% A	$(100\%)(12.0\%) = 12.0\%$
80% A and 20% B	$(80\%)(12.0\%) + (20\%)(9.0\%) = 11.4\%$
60% A and 40% B	$(60\%)(12.0\%) + (40\%)(9.0\%) = 10.8\%$
50% A and 50% B	$(50\%)(12.0\%) + (50\%)(9.0\%) = 10.5\%$
40% A and 60% B	$(40\%)(12.0\%) + (60\%)(9.0\%) = 10.2\%$
20% A and 80% B	$(20\%)(12.0\%) + (80\%)(9.0\%) = 9.6\%$
100% B	$(100\%)(9.0\%) = 9\%$

Unfortunately, calculating a measure of portfolio risk is not as straightforward as that for return. The reason is that we must somehow determine how the uncertainty of Company A common stock is related, if at all, to the uncertainty of Company B common stock. In other words, we again measure risk as the uncertainty associated with possible outcomes, except that now we are interested in possible returns to the entire portfolio. One way of interrelating the returns of two different assets is to relate their possible outcomes to states of the world or of the economic environment in which asset returns materialize. We shall consider three extreme cases that span the range of possibilities.

In case 1 we assume that there are three possible states of the economy during the subsequent period over which asset returns will materialize. The three states are termed "optimistic," "neutral," and "pessimistic." Outcomes for securities are related to these states of the economy. Furthermore, we assume in case 1 that the

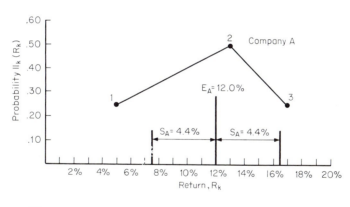

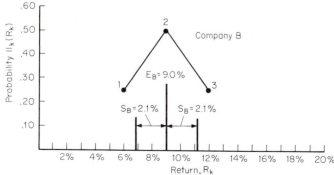

Fig. 53-3 Comparison of risk and return for two common stocks.

returns of Company A and Company B common stocks are directly related; that is, both stocks experience their highest returns (17 percent and 12 percent respectively) when economic prospects are optimistic and their lowest returns (5 percent and 6 percent respectively) when economic prospects are pessimistic. Examples of case 1 include firms within a given industry, such as the automobile, steel, or housing industry, that is tied to major developments in the economy.

Calculation of expected return and standard deviation of return for a portfolio is handled in a manner similar to that for individual securities, as shown in the accompanying table on page 53-15.

Notice that in this calculation probabilities Π_k are associated with states of the economy. Portfolio outcomes R_k are equal mixes of the respective returns on Company A common stock and Company B common stock. From there the calculation procedure exactly follows that used for individual assets. We see that expected portfolio return $E = 10.5$ percent is accompanied by standard deviation $S = 3.2$ percent.

In case 2 we assume that the returns of Company A and Company B common stocks move in opposite directions to each other relative to the three states of the economy. Although there are few if any real-world examples of case 2, it is useful as an extreme case. The calculation, shown in the accompanying table on page 53-15, proceeds as before.

We see that expected portfolio return $E = 10.5$ percent remains the same but that standard deviation of portfolio return is only $S = 1.2$ percent. The reason for this reduction in risk is that the highest return for Company A occurs with the lowest return for Company B. This causes the range of portfolio outcomes (8.5 percent to 11.5 percent) to be much smaller than the range (5.5 percent to 14.5 percent) for case 1, in which the two returns move together. This is the essence of why *diversification* leads to reduced risk and why the tenets of portfolio theory are of great importance to all investors.

Between the extremes of case 1 and case 2 are situations in which the returns of two assets do not move together perfectly. Case 3, in fact, deals with the situation in which the return of Company A common stock is completely independent of the return of Company B common stock. There are numerous examples of firms in dissimilar industries, such as aerospace and retailing or shoes and shipbuilding, that approximate case 3. In this case there are no longer only three states of the economy with which possible outcomes are associated. If each asset has three outcomes, then there are nine (3 × 3) possible outcomes for portfolios consisting of Company A and Company B common stocks. For each of these nine possible outcomes, the probability of that outcome Π_k is the product of the probability Π_k (A) of Company A common stock return and the probability Π_k (B) of Company B common stock return. Once the portfolio outcomes R_k (again an equal-investment mix) and their associated probabilities Π_k are determined, the calculation of return and risk for the portfolio proceeds as before. As seen in the accompanying calculation for case 3 on page 53-16, expected portfolio return $E = 10.5$ percent is again the same, while standard deviation $S = 2.4$ percent is between the extremes of cases 1 and 2.

The results of combining Company A common stock with Company B common stock can now be summarized. In Fig. 53-3, the expected return and standard deviation of return for the two stocks were illustrated. Now in Fig. 53-4 we plot those individual values along with expected portfolio return and standard deviation of portfolio return for the three cases. Since we have illustrated the combination of two securities equally held into a portfolio, we see that all three cases occur at a level of expected portfolio return equal to 10.5 percent, which is just halfway between the respective expected returns of Company A and Company B. The level of risk, as measured by standard deviation, depends on the degree of

Equal (50 Percent) Investment in Company A and Company B Common Stock for Case 1

State of economy	Probability Π_k	Outcome of A (percent)	Outcome of B (percent)	Portfolio outcome, R_k (percent)	Weighted $\Pi_k R_k$	Deviation $R_k - E$	Squared $(R_k - E)^2$	Weighted $\Pi_k (R_k - E)^2$
Optimistic	.25	17	12	14.5	.03625	.0400	.001600	.000400
Neutral	.50	13	9	11.0	.05500	.0050	.000025	.000013
Pessimistic	.25	5	6	5.5	.01375	−.0500	.002500	.000625
				Expected portfolio return $E = .10500$ (10.5%)			Variance $S^2 = .001038$ Standard deviation $S = .032$ (3.2%)	

Equal (50 Percent) Investment in Company A and Company B Common Stock for Case 2

State of economy	Probability Π_k	Outcome of A (percent)	Outcome of B (percent)	Portfolio outcome, R_k (percent)	Weighted $\Pi_k R_k$	Deviation $R_k - E$	Squared $(R_k - E)^2$	Weighted $\Pi_k (R_k - E)^2$
Optimistic	.25	17	6	11.5	.02875	.0100	.000100	.000025
Neutral	.50	13	9	11.0	.05500	.0050	.000025	.000013
Pessimistic	.25	5	12	8.5	.02125	−.0200	.000400	.000100
				Expected portfolio return $E = .10500$ (10.5%)			Variance $S^2 = .000138$ Standard deviation $S = .012$ (1.2%)	

Equal (50 Percent) Investment in Company A and Company B Common Stock for Case 3

Possibility	Outcome $R_k (A)$ (percent)	Probability $\Pi_k (A)$	Outcome $R_k (B)$ (percent)	Probability $\Pi_k (B)$	Portfolio outcome R_k (percent)	Joint probability Π_k	Weighted $\Pi_k R_k$	Deviation $R_k - E$	Squared $(R_k - E)^2$	Weighted $\Pi_k (R_k - E)^2$
1	17	.25	12	.25	14.5	.0625	.00906	.0400	.001600	.000100
2	17	.25	9	.50	13.0	.1250	.01625	.0250	.000625	.000078
3	17	.25	6	.25	11.5	.0675	.00718	.0100	.000100	.000007
4	13	.50	12	.25	12.5	.1250	.01563	.0200	.000400	.000050
5	13	.50	9	.50	11.0	.2500	.02750	.0050	.000025	.000006
6	13	.50	6	.25	9.5	.1250	.01188	-.0100	.000100	.000013
7	5	.25	12	.25	8.5	.0625	.00531	-.0200	.000400	.000025
8	5	.25	9	.50	7.0	.1250	.00875	-.0350	.001225	.000153
9	5	.25	6	.25	5.5	.0625	.00344	-.0500	.002500	.000156

Expected portfolio return E = .10500 (10.5%)

Variance S^2 = .000588

Standard Deviation S = .024 (2.4%)

interrelation between those two returns. For case 1, we recall that the two returns move together exactly; this is referred to as "perfect positive correlation." For this case, we also see in Fig. 53-3 that the level of portfolio risk is also just halfway between the respective risk levels of Companies A and B. For Case 2 the two returns move in exactly opposite directions; this is referred to as "perfect negative correlation." The result of finding two securities so related is a portfolio risk level considerably below that of either individual security or asset. For the intermediate case 3 with independent returns, we see a modest reduction in portfolio risk. The dashed lines in Fig. 53-4 indicate the loci of portfolio return and risk values for

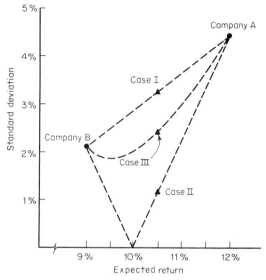

Fig. 53-4   Portfolios of two equally held investment assets.

other-than-equal investments in the two common stocks. As seen in case 2, it is possible to obtain a *riskless* return by properly combining two assets whose returns have perfect negative correlation. It can be shown that an investor would invest the fraction $S_B/(S_A + S_B)$ = 32.3 percent of his or her wealth in Company A common stock and the corresponding fraction $S_A/(S_A + S_B)$ = 67.7 percent of his or her wealth in Company B common stock to achieve the risk-free return $E_A S_B/(S_A + S_B) + E_B S_A/(S_A + S_B)$ = 9.97 percent.

For portfolios consisting of only two assets, such as Company A common stock and Company B common stock, we can write specific equations for portfolio return

$$E = X_A E_A + X_B E_B \tag{1}$$

and portfolio risk

$$S^2 = X_A^2 S_A^2 + X_B^2 S_B^2 + 2X_A X_B S_A S_B C_{AB} \tag{2}$$

where X_A and X_B are the relative proportions of investment wealth allocated to the two assets, and C_{AB} is the correlation coefficient that measures the degree of association between the returns of the two assets. We know that correlation coefficients vary between minus unity as in case 2 (perfect negative correlation) and plus unity as in case 1 (perfect positive correlation). For independent returns, the correlation coefficient is zero, and the last term of equation 2 disappears. The first two terms in equation 2 have to do with the riskiness (variance) inherent in

Company A stock and Company B stock respectively, while the third term has to do with the interrelationship of return between the two stocks. The covariance of return between the stocks of Company A and Company B is simply $S_A S_B C_{AB}$. As C_{AB} decreases, therefore, portfolio risk as measured by variance of portfolio return decreases. This is why diversifification is aided if we can find pairs of investment assets whose returns are independent or tend *not* to move together.

If a third asset, Company G common stock, were added to the portfolio, the relevant equations would become

$$E = X_A E_A + X_B E_B + X_G E_G \tag{3}$$

$$S^2 = X_A^2 S_A^2 + X_B^2 S_B^2 + X_G^2 S_G^2 + 2X_A X_B S_A S_B C_{AB} \\ + 2X_A X_G S_A S_G C_{AG} + 2X_B X_G S_B S_G C_{BG} \tag{4}$$

Here we note that there are three variance terms and three covariance terms. These basic expressions for the return and risk of the portfolio can easily be extended for a universe of any size. For a universe of four assets, there would be six covariance terms, one for each pair of assets in the universe. Hence, as the number of assets in the portfolio increases, the number of covariance terms in the expression for portfolio risk increases at a faster rate. This is demonstrated in the accompanying tabulation.

Number of Securities	Number of Covariance Terms
2	1
3	3
4	6
5	10
6	15
7	21
8	28
9	36
10	45
15	105
20	190
25	300
50	1,225
75	2,775
100	4,950

Obviously, as the number of securities increases beyond twenty or so, the number of covariance terms that must be estimated becomes prohibitive.

Efficient Portfolios

As more and more assets are considered, opportunities for larger portfolio return or smaller portfolio risk become available. An efficient portfolio was defined above as having the highest possible return for a given level of risk, or the lowest possible risk for a given level of return, from among a given universe of investment opportunities. The problem of portfolio decision making, in fact, is to select an efficient portfolio that, as shown in Fig. 53-1, allows the investor to attain the highest level of satisfaction as defined in terms of return and risk.

The combination of several assets into portfolios is illustrated graphically in Fig. 53-5. The closed area represents the locus of feasible portfolios in terms of the two attributes, return and risk. The large dots represent a universe of seven invest- ment assets. Along with Company A and Company B, we also have the common stocks of Companies D, F, G, H, and J. The triangles in Fig. 53-5 represent a few of the many portfolios that can be constructed from this particular universe. Portfolios along the heavy curve comprise the efficient frontier. Each coefficient

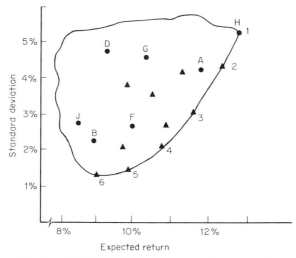

Fig. 53-5   **Efficient frontier from a universe of seven assets.**

portfolio is defined by its expected return E and standard deviation S. It is also defined by its composition, that is, by the relative proportions of assets that are held. For the six portfolios identified as being efficient in Fig. 53-5, the composition might be as shown in the accompanying table.

Composition of Efficient Portfolios
   (in percentages)

Efficient portfolio	A	B	D	F	G	H	J	Total
1	. . .	. . .	. . .	. . .	. . .	100	. . .	100
2	. . .	. . .	. . .	. . .	21	79	. . .	100
3	26	. . .	. . .	. . .	28	46	. . .	100
4	29	. . .	. . .	18	32	21	. . .	100
5	36	11	. . .	10	40	3	. . .	100
6	31	27	. . .	9	33	. . .	. . .	100

   The first efficient portfolio has the highest expected return, without regard to risk, that can be achieved from the universe of investment opportunities. It consists of the single stock, Company H, that has the highest expected return among the seven members of the universe. The second most efficient portfolio consists of 79 percent Company H and 21 percent Company G. Moving down the efficient frontier, additional assets enter into efficient frontiers to reduce risk. At each point, of course, the proportions must total 100 percent. We notice that certain stocks, Company D and Company J, never appear in an efficient frontier. The sixth efficient frontier, consisting of only four assets, has the lowest level of risk that can be achieved. In other words, it is possible to obtain the maximum benefits of diversification without having to invest in a large number of individual assets. Further discussion of diversification is deferred to Chapter 54.

Portfolio Decision Making in Perspective

We have seen how portfolio theory suggests that individual assets should be combined into portfolios to achieve desired levels of return and risk. Before proceeding to further discussion of portfolio management by both individuals and institutions, it is well to add perspective to the particular approach to portfolio decision making that has been covered thus far in Chapter 53. First, the suggested approach is based on only two attributes, expected return and variance (or standard deviation) of return. These are the first two moments of the probability distribution defined on either asset return or portfolio return. The particular model that has been discussed and illustrated is sometimes referred to as the "mean-variance model" since mean and variance are used to measure the two attributes of most importance to investors.

Inputs to the mean-variance model include (1) expected return for each asset in the universe of investment opportunities being considered, (2) the standard deviation of return for each asset, and (3) the correlation coefficient (or covariance) between each pair of investment assets. We have seen that for a large universe of assets the number of required inputs can become very large. Moreover, there are alternative procedures for obtaining these inputs, such as an objective extrapolation of historical data, subjective estimates of investment analysts, or perhaps a combination of those two extremes. Although further elaboration of these alternative procedures will not be made here, we shall consider in Chapter 54 a simplifying method of generating the inputs needed for the mean-variance portfolio model.

Output of the mean-variance model is the efficient frontier of portfolios. Each efficient portfolio is characterized by its expected return, the standard deviation of that return, and the proportional composition of the portfolio. The proportional composition, as has been illustrated, indicates which assets of those in the universe should be held in the portfolio and how much of the available wealth should be allocated to each.

Following this, the choice of a specific portfolio along the efficient frontier depends on the preferences of the investor for portfolio return and portfolio risk as measured by expected return and variance of return respectively. It was emphasized above that portfolio decision making is accomplished by bringing together information on possibilities and information on preferences. Much of this chapter has dealt with providing information on possibilities through the concept of an efficient frontier. Less has been said about the subsequent step of choosing a particular efficient portfolio because in each case that choice depends on the individualized preferences of the investor.

Finally, it should be emphasized that this approach to maximizing return, minimizing risk, and thereby constructing portfolios of investment assets is a useful means of thinking about portfolio decision making, despite disagreement over appropriate risk measures and despite difficulties in generating all the inputs needed for calculating efficient portfolios. Moreover, the suggested approach to portfolio decision making is not simple. Although similar complexity has caused wide gaps between theory and practice in many fields, the gap in the field of investments has narrowed substantially in recent years. Today return-risk trade-offs, the rationale of diversification, and, to some degree, the concept of efficiency are well established in the language of professional money managers. In addition, certain aspects of portfolio theory, especially in the area of performance measurement, are widely used in practice today.

BIBLIOGRAPHY

Francis, J. C., and S. H. Archer: *Portfolio Analysis,* Prentice-Hall, Inc., Englewood Cliffs, N.J., 1971.
Levy, Haim, and Marshall Sarnat, *Investment and Portfolio Analysis,* John Wiley & Sons, Inc., New York 1972.

H. M. Markowitz: *Portfolio Selection: Efficient Diversification of Investments,* John Wiley & Sons, Inc., New York, 1959.

W. F. Sharpe: *Portfolio Theory and Capital Markets,* McGraw-Hill Book Company, New York, 1970.

K. V. Smith: *Portfolio Management,* Holt, Rinehart and Winston, Inc., New York, 1971.

———and D. K. Eiteman: *Essentials of Investing,* Richard D. Irwin, Inc., Homewood, Ill., 1974.

Chapter **54**

Security, Industry, and Portfolio Diversification

KEITH V. SMITH

Nature of Diversification

Inherent in a discussion of portfolio decision making and efficient portfolios is the concept of diversification. Many decision makers may appear to focus only on the relative merits of individual investment opportunities, but the concept of diversification is applicable only if investors take a portfolio perspective of their investment holdings. Although diversification was mentioned in Chapter 53, it is well to take a closer look here at both the nature and the scope of diversification as well as at its implications for both individual and institutional portfolios. We begin with a more detailed examination of the nature of diversification.

Probably the commonest definition of diversification is that it somehow has to do with risk reduction. Indeed, we saw in Chapter 53 that as one moves down the efficient frontier of investment opportunities, additional assets enter into portfolios to achieve lower portfolio risk as measured by the variance of portfolio return about mean or expected return. Risks can be reduced by adding assets because the high returns of some assets offset the low returns of others and thereby decrease the range of possible portfolio outcomes. But this can happen only if the high returns of all assets do not occur together and the low returns of all assets do not occur together. The correlation coefficient between the returns of two assets has been shown to be a convenient means of measuring this effect. Hence, diversification to reduce risk is accomplished when assets whose returns are less than perfectly positively correlated are combined into portfolios. Pairs of assets whose returns are independent or are negatively correlated offer greater opportunities for risk reduction than asset returns that are positively correlated.

The mean-variance model for portfolio choice includes a broader definition of diversification than just risk reduction, for as stated in Chapter 53, an efficient portfolio is one that simultaneously has the lowest risk for a given level of return or the highest return for a given level of risk. By definition, therefore, "efficient diversification" has to do with both risk reduction and return enhancement. Presented graphically, as in Fig. 53-5, the efficiency of diversification for a given portfolio is measured by the closeness with which that portfolio approaches the efficient frontier and not merely by its vertical coordinate.

Other forms of diversification are also mentioned in the literature of investments. For example, diversification may be examined by the nature of the companies that issue securities, such as blue-chip firms, cyclical firms, or growth firms. Another dimension of diversification may comprise the industries represented in the portfolio, such as utilities, chemicals, oils, manufacturing, and drugs. Industry diversification is particularly popular because much of the research done by brokers and other institutions is organized about industries. Yet another focus on diversification is obtained by type of assets, such as government bonds, corporate bonds, preferred stock, common stock, real estate, and others. Finally, for certain institutional portfolios that have fixed payout commitments over time, such as pension funds and insurance companies, diversification by maturity of bonds may be an important property. In all these approaches, the common theme is to reduce risk by selecting dissimilar assets for the portfolio.

Scope of Diversification

The extent of diversification by individuals and institutions varies considerably. Several constraints cause differences in the level of diversification. For certain types of institutional investors, legal constraints force minimum levels of diversification. For example, an investment company must have at least 75 percent of its total assets invested in securities to qualify as "diversified" under the Investment Company Act of 1940. Moreover, no more than 5 percent of an investment company's diversified assets can be invested in a given security, and no single holding can exceed 10 percent of the voting stock of a corporation. The 5 percent limitation necessarily ensures that a diversified investment company must hold at least twenty different securities, while the 10 percent limitation may cause larger investment companies to hold even larger numbers of securities.

Related to the legal constraints faced by institutions are marketability constraints that also may force minimum levels of diversification. If an investment company has assets of $250 million and attempts to hold, say, twenty-five securities, each position would have a market value of $1 million. At an average price of $50 per share, this would necessitate a block of 20,000 shares. To buy or sell such a large block in a single transaction, would likely have a pronounced effect on the price of the transaction, pushing the price upward if shares are being purchased or downward if they are being sold. We saw in Chapter 53 that turnover rates for institutional investors have increased in recent years. Thus, institutions are virtually forced to have larger numbers of securities in their portfolios to minimize these "costs" of marketability.

Although there are no legal constraints on the maximum level of diversification by an institution, practical considerations may influence the number of different securities that are held. First, the resources necessary to analyze and monitor a large number of different issues may be limited. Whether economic and security analyses are done internally by an institution or acquired externally from brokers or other sources, the size of the institutional portfolio may place a practical limit to diversification. Second, an institution that specializes in investments within certain industries or certain types of technology may be limited in the number of different issues that may be held. Third, and perhaps more important, as the number of issues held becomes larger and larger, it becomes more and more difficult for an institution to perform better than the market, simply because a large diversified portfolio begins to resemble the market. And since increased attention has been given to performance in recent years, there are definite limits to diversification for portfolios with a heavy emphasis on performance.

Among the institutional investors mentioned in Chapter 53, we have more comprehensive data on mutual funds since their holdings are a matter of public record. The accompanying table reveals the size and growth of the mutual fund industry over thirty years. Included are funds belonging to the Investment Company Institute. The total assets under management at the end of 1971 exceeded

$55 billion. Average assets per mutual fund exceeded $200 million in the mid-1950s, but dropped to $140 million by the end of 1971.

The average number of securities held by these mutual funds was abour 55 at the end of 1971. The number of holdings ranged from a few issues for small and specialized funds to a high of 536 issues held by Investors Mutual Fund, which also had the largest total assets ($2.8 billion) under management at the end of 1971. Other funds with high levels of diversification included Axe-Houghton Fund B with 395 issues, Investors Stock Fund with 242 issues, and Value Line Special Fund with 233 issues. If we assume equal investment in each issue, the average holding among the 392 mutual funds would be $141 million divided by 55 issues, or $2.6 million. And at an average price of $50 per share, this average holding would amount to $2.6 million divided by $50, or 52,000 shares.

Diversification by individuals is a completely different picture, both in the

Growth of the Mutual Fund Industry

Year-end	Number of funds	Total assets (millions)	Average assets (millions)
1940	68	$ 447	$ 6.6
1945	73	1,284	17.6
1950	98	2,531	25.8
1955	125	7,837	62.7
1960	161	17,026	105.8
1965	170	35,220	207.1
1967	204	44,701	219.1
1969	269	48,291	179.5
1971	392	55,045	140.4

constraints involved and in the resulting levels of security holdings. There are no legal constraints for individuals, and marketability is not a problem except in rare instances of privately held securities. Constraints of capital, time, knowledge, and information do exist for individual investors, and these tend to cause maximum levels of diversification. The primary constraint for most individuals is simply that they can allocate only a small amount of capital to investments. In addition, they are normally limited in the time that they can devote to their investments as well as in the knowledge they have of various investment opportunities. Although an individual certainly should best know his or her own objectives and constraints, he or she may not be able to combine these with information about investment opportunities in order to make reasonable investment decisions. And the inability of the individual to obtain timely information may itself prove to be a constraint that limits the diversification of his or her portfolio. In contrast, brokerage fees and indivisibilities of shares are likely to be the major constraints that result in minimum levels of diversification. An investor normally cannot buy fractional shares of a security (except as part of monthly investment programs), while odd-lot differentials increase the costs of buying less than round lots.

As with institutions, we do not have complete data on the investment holdings of individuals. It is possible to estimate the average holdings of common stocks listed on the New York Stock Exchange (NYSE). At the end of 1971 the total holdings of common stock by individuals were $689 billion (see Table 53-3 in Chapter 53), while the holdings of NYSE stocks by individuals was $475 billion. It was also estimated that there were 18.3 million shareholders of NYSE stocks. Hence, the average holding per individual was $475 billion divided by 18.3 million, or $25,900. Because the distribution of such holdings certainly is positively skewed toward larger average holdings, one would expect the median holding per individual to be considerably smaller than the average holding. If we assume that individuals buy only round lots of stocks having an average price of $50 per share, the average number of different issues held by an individual would be $25,900 divided by $5,000, or 5.2 stocks. This figure is consistent with the New York Stock Exchange shareholders' survey, which reports that investors have an average of fewer than four stocks in their portfolios.

Market Model for Analyzing Diversification

We have seen that differing constraints lead to rather different patterns of diversification for individual and institutional investors. Individuals on the average hold small numbers of securities, while institutional portfolios on the average consist of many different issues. Although we would expect different patterns of diversification for these two classes of investors, it is not yet clear what constitutes an appropriate level of diversification. Is a portfolio of 5 common stocks held by an individual properly diversified, or does diversification require the holding of 100 or more issues as for a mutual fund? To analyze further the question of proper diversification for a portfolio, it is useful to review a "market model" that has received considerable attention in recent years.

As mentioned before, the risk-reduction definition of diversification is based on the premise that not all asset returns will move together. Accordingly, it is of interest to have a bench mark of comparison against which to measure the return of an individual asset or the respective returns of pairs of assets. The overall security market provides just such a bench mark. By relating the return of each asset in the universe to the return of the market, it is possible to derive the interrelationship between the returns of pairs of assets. It is also possible to decompose the measure of risk for an asset or a portfolio into two important components, only one of which can be reduced by proper diversification.

Of interest are the returns of investment assets, together with the interrelationships between pairs of asset returns, for some future period. Because of the difficulties of estimating such returns and interrelationships, it is not uncommon practice first to examine the returns and interrelationships that have been experienced in the past. In many instances, past returns may bear little resemblance to what logically is expected in the future. In other instances, patterns of returns over past horizons may be considered reasonably indicative of future returns. In all instances, however, it is likely that past returns and interrelationships would be examined prior to making future estimates. In what follows, we shall use historical returns as a basis for estimating future returns, but with the clear realization that this procedure may not always be appropriate.

As an illustration, let us suppose that annual returns for two assets, the common stocks of Company G and Company H, plus the return for a leading stock market index over a recent ten-year horizon were as shown in the accompanying table.

Annual Returns of Common Stocks of Companies G and H and of a Market Index

Year	Return on company G R_G (percent)	Return on company H R_H (percent)	Return on market R_M (percent)
1	7	1	4
2	9	5	9
3	-2	-12	-3
4	5	14	7
5	10	24	13
6	1	8	2
7	8	8	10
8	2	2	-2
9	16	20	18
10	13	18	12

The market model is a linear relationship between asset return and market return, as shown for each of the two companies in Fig. 54-1. For each company the ten pairs of returns have been plotted, and a "free-hand fit line" has been drawn through the set of 10 points. This line is sometimes referred to as the "characteristic line" for the asset or portfolio. It reveals the historical, and hence anticipated, relationship of asset or portfolio return to market return.

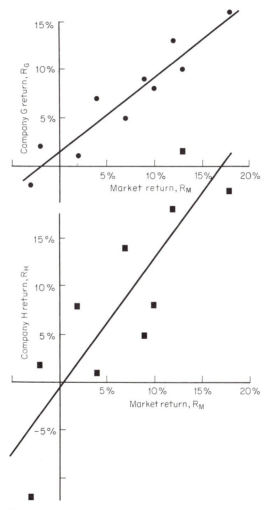

Fig. 54-1 Characteristic lines for two common stocks.

For Company G, the market model thus can be written as

$$R_G = A_G + B_G R_M + e_G \tag{1}$$

while for Company H, the market model is

$$R_H = A_H + B_H R_M + e_H \tag{2}$$

The respective intercepts, A_G and A_H, indicate the levels of return achieved by

Companies G and H when market return is zero. Other things being equal, it is desirable for a common stock to have a high value of the intercept term. Conversely, the respective slopes, B_G and B_H, indicate the responsiveness of asset return for Companies G and H to market return. The slope term is also referred to as "volatility," or "beta," in the literature of investments. When market return is high, it is desirable for volatility to be large, but when market return is low, lower volatility is desirable. The other terms, e_G and e_H, are random error terms that have zero expected values and finite residual variances Q_G^2 and Q_H^2 respectively.

By using the ten years of return data for Company G, Company H, and the market, the parameters shown in the accompanying table were estimated. We note that Company G has the largest intercept term, while Company H has the largest slope term. The average return of Company H was somewhat higher than the return of Company G over the decade, but its variability of return was almost twice as large as that for Company G. Residual standard deviation, as measured by Q_G and Q_H, concerns the way in which the individual observations are spread out

Parameters of Companies G and H and the Market

	Company G	Company H	Market
Average asset return	6.9%	8.8%	7.0%
Asset standard deviation	5.3%	10.1%	6.4%
Intercept term	1.4%	−0.5%	. . .
Slope term	0.77	1.32	. . .
Residual standard deviation	1.7%	5.5%	. . .
Coefficient of determination	0.89	0.70	. . .

about the characteristic line. We see that $Q_H > Q_G$ as expected from observing the two plots in Fig. 54-1. Finally, we see that goodness of fit, as measured by the coefficient of determination (the percentage of explained variation), is higher for Company G than for Company H.

Systematic and Nonsystematic Risk

Again, there is some evidence that historical returns as summarized by characteristic lines are likely to be experienced in the future for many assets. That being the case, Equations 1 and 2 can be used to discuss future returns of Company G and Company H, given different levels of market return. For instance, let us consider Company G. The return on that particular common stock is viewed, as before, as a random variable subject to some underlying but unspecified probability distribution. Similarly, market return is itself a random variable. Expected asset return for the next period is given by

$$E_G = A_B + B_G E(R_M) \tag{3}$$

where $E(R_M)$ is the expected return on the market. The only difference between Equations 1 and 3 is that the former involves random variables, while the latter involves the expected values of those variables.

The variance of asset return for Company G is given by

$$S_G^2 = B_G^2 S^2(R_M) + Q_G^2 \tag{4}$$

where $S^2(R_M)$ is the variance of market return. The corresponding equations for Company H are

$$E_H = A_H + B_H E(R_M) \tag{5}$$

and

$$S_H^2 = B_H^2 S^2(R_M) + Q_H^2 \tag{6}$$

Equations 4 and 6 are very important relationships in that, under the linear model assumption, total asset risk is seen to consist of two components. The first component is termed "systematic risk," since it depends on market risk $S^2(R_M)$ and the responsiveness of asset returns to market return as measured by the respective volatilities B_G and B_H. The second component is termed "nonsystematic risk," since it is unique to individual assets and does not depend on the market.

A breakdown of total asset risk into the systematic and nonsystematic components permits a better understanding of the role of diversification in portfolio decision making. As individual assets are combined into portfolios, nonsystematic risk can be reduced, but the systematic risk inherent in the market remains. To see this, let us consider a portfolio consisting of only the two securities already examined, the common stocks of Company G and Company H. We have seen, in Equations 3 and 4 of Chapter 53, how expected portfolio returns and portfolio variance depend upon the individual asset returns, standard deviations, and correlation coefficients. Under the market model assumption, expected portfolio return becomes

$$E = X_G A_G + X_H A_H + [X_G B_G + X_H B_H]E(R_M) \tag{7}$$

while portfolio variance is given by

$$S^2 = X_G^2 Q_G^2 + X_H^2 Q_H^2 + [X_G B_G + X_H B_H]^2 S^2(R_M) \tag{8}$$

The bracketed quantity in each equation is seen to be an average of asset volatilities weighted by asset proportions and hence is often referred to as "portfolio volatility." It may be thought of as a weighted-average response to the market by the assets held in the portfolio. The first two terms in Equations 7 and 8 are unique to the stocks of Company G and Company H, while the third term in each case depends on portfolio volatility and information about the market.

To illustrate how individual assets contribute to the total portfolio, we need estimates of market return and risk as well as the proportional holdings of the assets in the portfolio. The average return of the market and the variance of market return over a past period can be used as estimates of market return and risk respectively. From the prior calculations, we would have market return $E(R_M)$ = 7.0 percent and market risk $S(R_M)$ = 6.4 percent. And under the assumption of an equal investment portfolio, we would have $X_G = X_H = 0.5$.

Portfolio volatility under these assumptions becomes $X_G B_G + X_H B_H = (0.5)$ $(0.77) + (0.5) (1.32) = 1.045$; expected portfolio return by using Equation 7 becomes $E = (0.5) (1.4 \text{ percent}) + (0.5) (-0.5 \text{ percent}) + (1.045) (7.0 \text{ percent}) = 7.77$ percent; and portfolio variance by using Equation 8 becomes $S^2 = (0.5)^2 (1.7 \text{ percent})^2 + (0.5)^2 (5.5 \text{ percent})^2 + (1.045)^2 (6.4 \text{ percent})^2 = 53.01$. Standard deviation is just the square root of this variance, or 7.28 percent. An equal-investment portfolio of Company G common stock and Company H common stock would thus have an expected return of 7.77 percent and an associated risk level of 7.28 percent.

By using Equation 8, it is also possible to decompose total portfolio risk into the systematic risk and nonsystematic risk components as shown in the accompanying table. We see that nonsystematic risk accounts for 1.4 + 14.3 = 15.7 percent of the

Portfolio Risk Components

Risk component	Variation	Percentage of total
Nonsystematic, Company G	0.72	1.4
Nonsystematic, Company H	7.56	14.3
Systematic	44.73	84.3
Total	53.01	100.0

total variation in portfolio return. For only two securities in the portfolio, this is a rather low level of nonsystematic risk. It can be explained by the high correlations of both Company G and Company H with the market.

Practical Levels of Diversification

If additional assets were added to the portfolio and similar calculations performed, we might expect both nonsystematic and total risk to decrease and also the relative percentage of nonsystematic risk to decrease. To demonstrate this phenomenon, let us suppose that the common stock of Company I is added to the portfolio and that equal proportions $X_G = X_H = X_I = 0.33$ are thus set for a three-asset portfolio. The parameters of the characteristic line for Company I are intercept $A_I = 0.07$ percent, slope $B_I = 1.10$, and residual variance $Q_I = 5.0$ percent. The expected return for Company I common stock is $E_I = A_I + B_I E(R_M) = 0.07$ percent + $(1.10)(7.0$ percent$) = 7.77$ percent, which is just the value of portfolio return for an equal investment in Companies G and H.

Expected portfolio return and portfolio variance for a portfolio of these three securities would be given by

$$E = X_G A_G + X_H A_H + X_I A_I + [X_G B_G + X_H B_H + X_I B_I]E(R_M) \qquad (9)$$

and

$$S^2 = X_G^2 Q_g^2 + X_H^2 Q_H^2 + X_I^2 Q_I^2 + [X_G B_G + X_H B_H + X_I B_I]^2 S^2(R_M) \qquad (10)$$

respectively. Substituting appropriate values gives a portfolio volatility of (0.33) $(0.77) + (0.33)(1.32) + (0.33)(1.10) = 1.063$, which is slightly higher than before. Not surprisingly, expected portfolio return remains at the same level, $E = (0.33)$ $(1.4$ percent$) + (0.33)(-0.5$ percent$) + (0.33)(0.07$ percent$) + (1.063)(7.0$ percent$) = 7.77$ percent. Conversely, the breakdown of portfolio variance can be summarized as in the accompanying table. The standard deviation of return for this portfolio is just the square root, or 7.25 percent.

Thus, portfolio risk is reduced by diversification while keeping expected return at the same level. The percentage of total risk attributed to Company G and Company H is reduced. Moreover, nonsystematic risk for the portfolio is only 0.6 + 6.3 + 5.2 = 12.1 percent in this three-security equal-investment example, as opposed to 25.1 percent in the previous two-security example.

We can generalize the result of this illustration. As additional securities are added to the portfolio, total risk will decrease, as will the percentage of nonsystematic risk to total risk. The absolute level of systematic risk may increase or decrease, depending on whether portfolio volatility increases or decreases, but the relative amount of systematic risk will increase. This is why systematic risk is viewed as the critical component of risk for a well-diversified portfolio.

For a large mutual fund or other institutional portfolio with numerous holdings, virtually all risk would be expected to be systematic risk. It is sometimes stated that systematic risk cannot be avoided. This is not necessarily true, as it can be reduced by lowering the value of portfolio volatility. If the bracketed quantity in Equation 8 or Equation 10 were zero, systematic risk would itself disappear. This would be

Portfolio Variance

Risk component	Variation	Percentage of total
Nonsystematic, Company G	0.31	0.6
Nonsystematic, Company H	3.29	6.3
Nonsystematic, Company I	2.72	5.2
Systematic	46.28	87.9
Total	52.60	100.0

possible if each asset had zero volatility or if the weighted average or portfolio volatility were zero. Zero portfolio volatility would be described by a perfectly horizontal characteristic line, and there would be no responsiveness of portfolio return to market return. A well-diversified portfolio with a horizontal characteristic line, in fact, would be tantamount to a risk-free portfolio. This would not be expected in practice, where, as increasing numbers of securities are held, portfolio volatility instead approaches unity, and systematic risk approaches market risk.

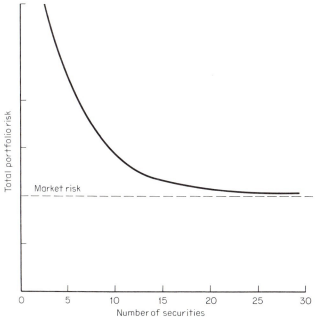

Fig. 54-2   Effective limits of diversification.

Although the effect of diversification has now been demonstrated, the practical limits of diversification have not. We recall that, on the average, individual investors hold four or five securities, while at least one type of institutional investor, mutual funds, hold somewhat more than fifty securities. It has been of interest to researchers to try to determine the level of diversification beyond which additional securities do little to reduce total risk. The finding of the research seems to be that a portfolio of ten or fifteen securities is apt to provide the greater part of attainable diversification. The finding is best seen in Fig. 54-2 by an illustrative curve that plots total portfolio risk as a function of the number of equal-investment securities in the portfolio. The important bend in the curve occurs between ten and fifteen securities, thus suggesting that range as a practical level of diversification.

Diversification by Industry

Earlier in this chapter, diversification by industry was mentioned as one possible definition of diversification. Casual observations of the investment literature and the practices of certain institutions reveal the popularity of an industry approach to investments. Financial commentators report that the aerospace industry is depressed or that the housing industry is booming. Investment research departments of banks, insurance companies, and other institutions assign individuals to become expert analysts in one or more industries. If we assume that security returns within a given industry are highly correlated and thus more or less move together, a useful view of portfolio diversification is obtained through the industries that are represented rather than through the individual securities.

It is interesting to illustrate the broader concept of efficient diversification by using industries instead of securities. Standard & Poor's Corporation provides a classification of more than eighty industries, each of which can be treated as an individual investment opportunity. Stock price indices for this set of industries constitute a data base that can be used to study industry diversification. At any point, expectations for asset returns and interrelationships among returns over some future period can be used to determine efficient portfolios of industries. Because there are many fewer industries than individual securities, an industry analysis of that type is a useful means of narrowing the scope of more detailed security analyses.

The industries in the accompanying table appeared in efficient portfolios calculated at the end of each year from 1966 to 1971. In these portfolio analyses, expectations for industry returns at the end of each year are based solely on historical returns over the preceding ten quarters. As such, the suggested findings do not necessarily represent the industries that might have been chosen if expected returns had been based on the subjective thinking of professional security analysts.

Nevertheless, it is interesting to examine the patterns of diversification that did result. First, only twenty-seven industries among those identified by Standard & Poor's Corporation appear in efficient portfolios at least once during the 1966–1971 period. Second, the number of industries in any single year ranges from three (1970) to ten (1968). These levels of industry diversification are not inconsistent with the practical level of diversification (ten to fifteen securities) suggested by Fig. 54-2, because efficient diversification is a broader concept that involves expected portfolio return as well as total portfolio risk. Third, it is noted that portfolio holdings change rather drastically from year to year, thus reflecting changes in expectations for different industries. Mobile home builders and pollution control are the two industries appearing most frequently in efficient portfolios over the six-year period. Fourth, some of the suggested industries, such as office and building equipment, pollution control, real estate, and truckers, have indeed been popular in recent years. Others, which have not been as popular, undoubtedly appear in efficient portfolios to a greater degree for their interrelationships with other industries than for their individual merits. This is truly the essence of efficient portfolio construction and diversification.

Diversification in Perspective

Diversification has been shown to be a central feature of portfolio decision making. Moreover, we commonly observe diversification being practiced by both individuals and institutions. For each of these two major types of investors, certain constraints have been identified that influence the minimum and maximum levels of diversification. Institutional portfolios have been seen to contain fifty or more securities on the average, while individual portfolios contain only about five securities on the average. If an investigation of diversification were expanded to assets other than securities, average numbers of holdings would increase for individuals and institutions that are not confined to security investments.

The market model, which assumes a linear relationship between security return and market return, has been proposed as a means of examining the necessary but cumbersome interrelationships between pairs of securities. This model has also been shown to be a useful framework for decomposing total risk as measured by variability of security or asset return into two components. Nonsystematic risk is the component of total risk for a security that is not explained by the market model. Systematic risk is the component of total risk that is related to the risk inherent in the market itself. Systematic risk also depends on security volatility, which is defined as the responsiveness of security return to market return.

The expected return and risk of a portfolio can be expressed in terms of the

Industries in Efficient Portfolios

Industry	1966	1967	1968	1969	1970	1971
Banks			X			
Beverages: brewers				X		X
Beverages: soft drinks						X
Building materials: heating and plumbing			X			
Coal: bituminous					X	
Containers: metal and glass	X					
Containers: paper			X			
Cosmetics		X		X		
Electronics	X	X				
Gold mining		X	X			
Home furnishings			X			
Hotel and motel		X				
Lead and zinc				X		
Mobile home builders		X	X	X		X
Motion pictures	X	X				
Office and building equipment		X				
Oil: integrated international			X			
Pollution control	X			X	X	
Radio broadcasters	X					
Real estate			X			
Retail stores: food chains			X			
Retail stores: variety chains				X		
Savings and loan associations			X	X		
Soap						X
Tobacco: cigarettes					X	X
Truckers						X
Toy manufacturers		X				

expected return and risk of its member securities. Furthermore, the total risk of a portfolio includes both nonsystematic and systematic risk components, just as each member security does. If the returns of all member securities were perfectly positively correlated, there would be no advantage to diversification in reducing risk. If security returns are less than perfectly positively correlated, however, diversification does succeed in reducing risk. We have seen that as securities are added to the portfolio, total risk decreases, as does the percentage that nonsystematic risk bears to total risk. Systematic risk may increase or decrease, depending on how portfolio volatility changes. Portfolio volatility is just a weighted average of security volatilities, each weight being the proportional dollar holdings of a security in the portfolio. It is also the slope of the characteristic line for the entire portfolio.

There are practical levels of diversification. As increasing numbers of securities are added to the portfolio, the percentage of nonsystematic risk decreases and, in fact, approaches zero in the limiting case. At the same time, portfolio volatility approaches unity, and systematic risk for the portfolio approaches market risk. It would take a very large number of holdings for these diversification effects to be achieved completely. Fortunately, the majority of the diversification effects can be achieved with a portfolio consisting of only ten to fifteen securities. Until this practical level of diversification is achieved for a portfolio, there are significant gains in risk reduction from adding a greater number of securities. Once the practical level is achieved, however, further gains are minimal. Ironically, the practical level of diversification includes a greater number of securities than are held by individuals on the average but a smaller number than are held on the average by institutions. This finding does not point to irrationality on the part of either individual or institutional investors as much as it highlights the various constraints that have been identified for the two types of investors.

Finally, it should be emphasized that deciding on a proper level of diversification for a portfolio is only one part of portfolio decision making. Indeed, the broader concept of efficient diversification requires enhancement of return along with reduction of risk, and this is not an easy task. Diversification by industry, a common practice especially among institutions, can be viewed as a useful procedure for ensuring that maximum gains in risk reduction are achieved with a limited number of industry holdings. Once an efficient combination of industries has been identified, particular securities must be chosen from each industry.

Chapter **55**

Policies for Portfolio Decision Making

LEMONT K. RICHARDSON

This chapter of the *Handbook* discusses the basic concepts and principles of portfolio decision making and considers their practical application in the investment environment expected to prevail in the years ahead.

The discussion is divided into two parts. The first part reviews the leading mathematically and scientifically oriented concepts and principles of portfolio management. It opens with an appraisal of the concept of portfolio efficiency and the attributes of efficient portfolios. The strategic importance of portfolio diversification in minimizing risk is then considered from the standpoint of the degree of diversification required to reduce risk to an acceptable level. The discussion concludes with a critical review of the various techniques for measuring risk, with particular emphasis upon "beta."

The second part of this chapter is devoted to a review of what might be considered the traditional, commonsense principles of portfolio decision making. The basic merits of adopting a highly aggressive investment approach, that is, of favoring common stocks over bonds and other conservative fixed-income investments, are first examined in the context of recent and prospective yield relationships prevailing in the markets. Procedures for appraising the worth of such special investment features as equity "kickers" and call protection on fixed-income securities are considered next. The discussion concludes with a detailed evaluation of the strategic importance of timing in achieving above-average portfolio results. These are compared with the practical long-term implications of alternative investment strategies, such as straightforward dollar averaging, that obviate the need to exercise judgment about timing in portfolio management.

LEADING SCIENTIFICALLY ORIENTED PRINCIPLES OF PORTFOLIO MANAGEMENT

The business of security selection and portfolio management long was considered an art. Individual investors and professional portfolio managers achieving above-average performance results were thought to possess uncanny abilities with respect to the selection of specific investments and the timing of their investment decisions. An overriding consideration in the appraisal of an investor's or portfolio's performance results, however, was the risk factor: Was the level of performance achieved worth the risks involved? Could exposure to risk be scaled down without sacrificing future performance results? Was the assumption of high risks essential to assure the attainment of above-average performance results? How could risk be systematically measured?

As the investment world became increasingly performance-oriented during the second half of the 1960s, now referred to as the "go-go" years, efforts to provide quantitative and rational, that is, scientific, answers to the foregoing risk-related questions commanded considerable attention. The origins of a substantial part of this scientific effort can be traced to the writings of Harry M. Markowitz, who in 1952, as a University of Chicago economics graduate student, was among the first to demonstrate how the theory of games (probability theory) could be applied in the selection of individual stocks and portfolio management.

Concept of Portfolio Efficiency

In 1959 Markowitz published a monograph entitled *Portfolio Selection: Efficient Diversification of Investments,* which represented an expansion of his original thoughts as a graduate student. This monograph is the basic primer on portfolio efficiency and, in some respects, gave fresh recognition to the strategic importance of the function of portfolio analysis and management.

Early in his book Markowtiz said, "Portfolio analysis begins where security analysis leaves off." The securities analysts identified stocks that offered the promise of high expected returns (as measured by cash dividends plus market appreciation due to growth in earnings, an increase in price-earnings multiples, or a combination of the two) based on market, economic, political, and numerous other factors and trends. The task of the portfolio manager was to select from the long list of candidate stocks compiled by the securities analysts those stocks that (1) best suited such basic investment objectives of the portfolio as liquidity and income growth and (2) offered a high "expected rate of return" consistent with the manager's basic investment objectives, plus a reasonable degree of certainty that the expected rate of return would be realized. Markowitz summed up the functions of the portfolio manager as follows:

1. Careful selection of the combination of likely return and risk that best suits the manager's particular needs

2. Determination or structuring of a portfolio that would provide this combination of risk and return.

Markowitz also accepted the basic tenets of the "risk-reward theory" (discussed in Chapter 2 of the *Handbook*), indicating that high expected returns on individual stocks and entire portfolios typically were associated with an unacceptably high degree of uncertainty. "If safety is of extreme importance," he observed, "'likely return' must be sacrificed to decrease uncertainty. If a greater degree of uncertainty can be borne, a greater level of likely return can be obtained." On balance, however, Markowitz felt that most rational investors preferred certainty to uncertainty.

Markowitz defined an efficient portfolio as one in which the expected rate of return was maximized and the risk minimized. If two portfolios, A and B, both offered the same expected return of 10 percent but A had lower uncertainty of return than B, then portfolio A would be more efficient than B. The expected rate of return, as posited by Markowitz, represented the weighted average of the possible future portfolio returns, each such return being weighted by its corresponding probability of occurrence. Risk or uncertainty represented the degree of dispersion in the possible future returns, as measured by the standard deviation around the weighted-average expected return. Variability in portfolio rates of return (or portfolio market values, in the final analysis), therefore, was the yardstick of risk measurement in Markowitz's concept of portfolio efficiency. Since publication of Markowitz's pioneering study in 1959, variability in rates of return and market values has grown to become the accepted standard of risk measurement in most academic and practical discourses on investment theory and portfolio management.

Illustrations of Portfolio Efficiency

The concept of portfolio efficiency, as originally defined by Markowitz and expanded by others, can be further illustrated by reference to two portfolio extremes taken from the entire spectrum of portfolio asset combinations available in the market. The time horizon is six months and one day, just long enough to establish long-term capital gains.

At one extreme would be the efficient portfolio selected by the investor or portfolio manager who placed the highest premium on safety of principal and was completely averse to risk. Such a portfolio would consist almost entirely of Treasury bills. The probability that the actual return or actual value of this Treasury bill portfolio would deviate from the expected return six months later is virtually nil. Although the actual return on this portfolio would be quite low, usually in a range of 5 to 6 percent, the risk-averse investor would be satisfied because no other combination of securities could provide the *same expected return* with *less uncertainty*. For an investor willing to accept a very low return in exchange for zero uncertainty, a portfolio consisting entirely of Treasury bills would meet all the requirements of an efficient portfolio.

At the other end of the spectrum, an efficient portfolio that satisfied the requirements of a high-risk–oriented investor probably would consist of a single asset, such as the common stock of a young, highly leveraged company in a high-technology industry, that offered the highest possible expected rate of return imaginable but also was characterized by a high probability of substantial loss ranging all the way up to a 100 percent loss if certain events didn't turn out as anticipated. This single-asset portfolio also would satisfy all the attributes of efficiency because, in the judgment of the high risk taker, no other combination of securities with *less uncertainty* could offer the *same expected return*.

Security Selection and Portfolio Efficiency

There is a general consensus that efficient portfolios are characterized by a high degree of diversification. "Don't put all your eggs in one basket" is a traditional saying. By investing in many different types of assets (for example, mortgage bonds, leases, convertible subordinated debentures, preferred stocks, and common stocks) and by holding a broad list of different investments within each of these asset categories, the portfolio manager will minimize the chance that the value of his or her portfolio will be adversely affected by sudden, unforeseen events in one sector of the economy or one segment of the securities markets. Although diversification may not eliminate risk completely, it certainly helps to reduce it.

The foregoing is a highly simplified exposition of risk minimization through diversification. Markowitz and others who have contributed to the body of literature on portfolio efficiency have stressed, in addition, that minimizing investment risk through portfolio diversification depends importantly on what types of securities are selected. Markowitz pointed out, for example, that if the returns on all securities tended to move up and down in unison, that is, if their movements were perfectly correlated, "diversification could do nothing to eliminate risk." As an illustration, a portfolio consisting of the common stocks of thirty electronics companies probably would be riskier than a portfolio consisting solely of the stocks of ten companies in ten different industries. Markowitz gives an even more extreme example to demonstrate his point: "One hundred securities whose returns rise and fall in near unison afford little more protection than the uncertain return of a single security."

So far, so good. The proponents of portfolio efficiency make an important contribution to our body of knowledge concerning investment management when they say that to reduce risk it is essential to select securities whose returns are not highly correlated, on the basis of either past experience or expectations concerning the future. The important consideration in investment selection, therefore, when the portfolio manager sits back to ponder a particular security recommended by his or her staff of securities analysts, is the relation between the expected return on that security and the expected returns on all other securities in the portfolio.

In this regard, Markowitz argued that in portfolios consisting of a large number of securities the addition of one more security affected the overall variability or risk characteristic of the portfolio, not according to the magnitude of the security's own variability, "but according to the sum of all its covariances with the other securities in the portfolio." In nontechnical terms, what Markowitz really meant was that, in appraising the extent to which the addition of one more security to a large diversified portfolio would affect the risk characteristic of the portfolio, it was not enough to consider only the variability of that security. It also was necessary to consider the relationship of that security's variability to the variability of *all* other securities in the portfolio.

Using covariance analysis, Markowitz showed how the addition of a risky security, that is, one with a highly volatile expected return, to a given portfolio could, by lessening the overall variability in expected return, give a more conservative cast to that portfolio than would be obtained by the addition of a completely riskless security! In these circumstances, a particular security could be very appropriate for one portfolio but entirely inappropriate for another, depending upon their respective composition and investment objectives. The basic problem of portfolio management, according to Markowitz, is to "pick securities so that their average covariance is small." The portfolio manager, he concluded, must think in terms of "selecting a portfolio as a whole, not securities per se."

Unfortunately, Markowitz's concepts are so complicated and costly in practice that they have little practical application in day-to-day investment decision making and portfolio management. Relatively few sophisticated professional portfolio managers have seen fit to operate according to the precise principles laid down by Markowitz, as outlined above.

Portfolio Diversification and Risk Reduction

Although diversification is an important consideration for all types of investors, substantial investors have a greater ability to achieve such diversification almost automatically by spreading their holdings within and across different asset categories. Smaller investors typically do not enjoy this flexibility. On balance, therefore, the significance of diversification is inversely related to the size and mix of an individual investor's financial asset holdings.

"Risk" is a term with widely varying common meanings. Broadly speaking, for us risk denotes the investor's uncertainty concerning the rate of return to be realized on a given investment. To many individual investors, the crucial questions concerning risk are (1) the probability of absolute loss of capital and (2) the probability of earning a return (as measured by dividends plus capital gains) below that afforded by alternative investment opportunities. Either of these eventualities may arise because of a general decline in the market or because some or all of an investor's portfolio holdings may fall on bad times.

Practically speaking, portfolio diversification cannot protect investors against general market-related risks (such as a sharp decline in common stock prices relative to bond prices in anticipation of a major recession or a war) but only against risk associated with a particular security or industry group. If diversification were carried to the point at which all securities available in the market were represented in a portfolio (and appropriately weighted), the risk characteristics of that portfolio would be exactly equivalent to those of the general market. In these circumstances, the important question is the extent to which portfolio diversification aids in reducing nonmarket risks.

More specifically, what is the effect of increasing the number of separate issues held in a common stock portfolio on the portfolio's rate of return compared with that of the general market? Is the dispersion in portfolio rates of return relative to the market materially reduced as portfolio size (that is, the number of separate issues held) is increased? These questions can be answered by examining the extent to which the returns or investment performance of selected investment portfolios, representing varying degrees of diversification, varies from the general market return.

A 1970 study by Lawrence Fisher and James Lorie provided, for the first time, some quantitative bench marks for measuring the effectiveness of portfolio diversification in reducing investment risk. The focus of the Fisher-Lorie study was on the determination of the dispersion of the rates of return among "unmanaged" portfolios of varying size (in terms of the number of separate stocks held) around the general market return. In making this determination, Fisher and Lorie computed rates of return, as measured by the ratio of the terminal value to original cost, for large numbers of unmanaged portfolios consisting of specified numbers of individual stocks, ranging from 1 to 128 issues, selected randomly from all stocks listed on the New York Stock Exchange (NYSE). Corresponding rates of return were computed for all stocks listed on the NYSE to indicate the general market return. These rates of return were computed for nonoverlapping periods of one year, five years, ten years, and twenty years from 1926 through 1965.

A major finding of the Fisher-Lorie study was that randomly selected, unmanaged portfolios need to include *at least eight separate issues* to reduce investment risk (as measured by the dispersion of rates of return around the general market return) to a reasonably acceptable level. The reduction in risk was very significant as the number of separate stocks held in a portfolio increased from one to eight. As additional stocks were added, the reduction in risk was much more modest.

The Fisher-Lorie study also found that the holding period, that is, the investor's time horizon, had some bearing on investment risk. The longer a stock portfolio was held, the more effective portfolio diversification became in reducing the level of investment risk.

Portfolio diversification, therefore, helps importantly to reduce investment risk by minimizing the impact of nonmarket factors (the chance that the market prices of certain stocks may plunge sharply because of unforeseen economic or political developments) on the overall performance of the investor's portfolio relative to the general market. As noted previously, however, portfolio diversification cannot reduce the investor's exposure to general market-related risks.

One final note of caution should be sounded regarding portfolio diversification and risk reduction, particularly for the benefit of individual investors. The quantitative studies that support the theory that increasing portfolio diversification helps to reduce investment risk are based on comparisons of the performance of *randomly* selected stock portfolios with that of the general market. In contrast, the individual investor, operating on his or her own, may be tempted to select stocks in a highly emotional and biased fashion in response to the often-irresistible lure of current investment fads and favorites, such as hot electronics stocks during the early 1960s, conglomerates during the late 1960s, and fast-food restaurant chains and amusement park operators during the early 1970s. Achieving portfolio diversification along these lines could pyramid risks and produce disastrous results.

It should not be inferred from this cautionary note that individual investors, in managing their own portfolios, should abandon all efforts to analyze individual stocks and their respective industry trends and to make systematic selections in favor of throwing darts at the list of NYSE stocks. Stock selection should proceed on a rational basis, focusing on strongly capitalized and favorably situated companies in a broad cross section of industries. This is what investing is all about.

Computer Invasion of the Money Management Field and the Beta Factor

Markowitz's novel approaches to security selection and portfolio management, which are derivatives of his concept of portfolio efficiency, ultimately paved the way for a major penetration of the field of portfolio management by computer applications specialists. This penetration proceeded gradually during most of the 1960s and then spread with the speed of a brush fire in the period after the savage bear market of 1969–1970.

By the early 1970s many large institutional investors were placing substantial reliance on computer techniques in measuring the risk characteristics of individual securities and the investment performance of their portfolios and portfolio managers. In addition, more than fifty large brokerage firms and banks were selling computer measurement services of this type, either on a fee basis or for "soft dollars," that is, in consideration for brokerage commissions, pension management fees, or compensating deposit balances received from their customers.

The proliferation of these new computer services in the aftermath of the bear market of 1969–1970 can be attributed in large measure to a growing concern among institutional investors about the dual problem of investment performance and performance measurement. The bear market of 1969–1970, which brought an abrupt but temporary end to performance-oriented investment thinking, caused many institutional investors, including the directors of mutual funds and pension fund trustees, to ask whether their portfolio managers were taking excessive risks to achieve certain actual or expected levels of performance.

Symptomatic of this concern was an article entitled "What Price Performance?" in the July 5, 1971, *Barron's*. The author, Dr. Robert A. Levy, president of a computer services company (and a *Handbook* contributor), affirmed that, during the late 1960s, the portfolio managers of many mutual funds had taken "excessive risks" in their quest for performance "by barreling into letter stock, companies with small capitalizations and outfits with sexy names and limited prospects." In the circumstances, the author felt the need of a new performance yardstick that would take account of both performance and risk, that is, measure performance on a risk-adjusted basis.

A performance-versus-risk litany began to appear in the nation's financial press and academic journals on finance at the end of 1970 and in early 1971. This soon became popularly known as the "beta revolution," because many of the articles on the subject and services offered by brokerage firms and banks made specific reference to beta factors, beta coefficients, and portfolio betas.

In October 1971, for example, the Wells Fargo Bank in San Francisco announced a new investment technology service that used "portfolios betas" to control uncertainty and risk in common stock portfolios. An advertisement in *The Wall Street Journal* describing this new service said: "Modern capital theory tells us that returns on well diversified funds have different levels of uncertainty because of different levels of responsiveness to changes in the market. This relative responsiveness can be controlled by using a number called the 'Portfolio Beta.'"

The beta factor, or beta coefficient, is a highly simplified measure of risk, the origins of which can be traced to Markowitz's basic treatise on portfolio efficiency. In brief, beta factors describe the risk characteristics of individual securities and entire portfolios in terms of the sensitivity of their respective values or rates of return, or both, to fluctuations in the general stock market price level and rate of return. Two important things to know are: (1) To what extent do price movements and investment returns of individual stocks and portfolios over time correlate with changes in the general stock market, that is, can be explained or predicted in terms of the stock market as a whole? (2) How much of their respective price and rate of return variability is not explainable by general market factors? (Since price performance importantly affects the rate-of-return performance of individual stocks and portfolios, the rest of our beta factor discussion will refer solely to the use of beta factors in measuring portfolio risk in terms of rate-of-return variability.)

If the return on a stock or a portfolio is the same as the general market return, the beta factor is 1. A risky portfolio will have a high beta coefficient, generally substantially greater than 1, that is, one in which a given market return (positive or negative) will be associated with a much larger (positive or negative) return on the portfolio. A relatively risk-free portfolio will have a low beta factor, generally substantially less than 1.

Calculation of beta coefficients for all stocks that enjoy an active investment following and for every professionally managed stock portfolio in existence, the beta advocates felt, would provide the most accurate, unbiased answers to the nagging problems of performance measurement. If a portfolio outperformed the market, was it because the manager took excessive risks, that is, risks greater than those attending the market as a whole, or was the performance attributable to the manager's superior ability to select specific stocks that outperformed all other investments of similar risk?

In addition to appraising investment performance after the fact, application of beta concepts, the beta supporters argued, would enable portfolio managers to make appropriate adjustments in their holdings to maximize profits or minimize losses on the basis of their expectations concerning prospective changes in the general level of stock prices.

For example, if a portfolio manager expected the market to advance sharply and his or her existing portfolio had a low "beta" factor, he or she could enhance performance during the expected market advance by switching from low- to high-beta stocks and, in general, increasing the overall volatility of the portfolio relative to the market. Conversely, if the portfolio manager expected the market to decline, he or she could minimize the impact of this decline on the value of the portfolio by switching from high- to low-beta stocks and, in general, decreasing the overall volatility of his or her portfolio.

Postmortem on Portfolio Efficiency and Beta Factors

At this point, some readers might conclude that there is no great art or mystique to investing and portfolio management. All one need do is to turn to some computer service that has calculated the betas for every publicly traded stock and has the programming wherewithal, backed up by the requisite data bank, to calculate the betas for any conceivable combination of securities. Also essential is the means to perform all the other elaborate statistical tests prescribed by the disciples of portfolio efficiency in order to determine the combination of securities, including the specific dollar amounts to invest in each security, that would, for a given level of expected return, entail less risk (that is, variability relative to the general market return) than any other combination of securities available.

At first glance, the arguments and methodology of the beta advocates and disciples of portfolio efficiency are compelling. But when one stops to reflect on the logic underlying these concepts, a different conclusion is warranted. Both concepts are based on the supposition that investment risk consists solely of, and is measured by, variability in the market values or rates of return, or both, of specific stocks and entire portfolios relative to the general market.

At this juncture, the reader should recall the limitations of the variability standards of risk measurement discussed in Chapter 3. The evidence there presented suggested that a definition of investment risk based on variability in market values and rates of return not only was highly arbitrary and misleading but had no practical value in day-to-day investment decision making and appraisal of prospective investment performance. The only real value of the variability standards, it was concluded, was in measuring investment risk after the fact, and even here their application is of quite limited value, for reasons that are now discussed.

It is common sense to recognize that the risk characteristics of specific stocks and entire portfolios can and do change with the passage of time, reflecting, for example, the impact of dramatic technological and political events on the prospective earning power and financial integrity of individual companies and entire industries, either for better or for worse. The earnings outlook for Anaconda and Kennecott in 1970 and beyond, most investment analysts concurred, was materially affected by the confiscation of their Chilean mining properties in that year. Similarly, Polaroid's long-range earning power could be adversely affected if Eastman Kodak (or some other competitor) successfully challenged its heretofore-dominant position in the instant camera and film market. Again, since the final months of 1973 the long-term earnings outlook for companies in energy-intensive industries has become clouded as a result of the energy crisis. Finally, changes in the level of management competence also can affect the prospective earnings trend and stock market performance of individual companies.

The prospective investment performance of investment companies and pension funds can be greatly affected by shifts in basic investment policy, changes in the postures and attitudes of the portfolio managers, or a combination of both. For example, many portfolio managers who may have been willing to take greater-than-average risks during the second half of the 1960s to achieve performance adopted a strong preference for risk aversion following the bear markets of 1969–1970 and 1973–1974.

The foregoing actual and hypothetical examples of how risk characteristics change with the passage of time could be expanded almost indefinitely, bringing in subtle and less clear-cut examples. In the circumstances, securities analysts and portfolio managers who appraised the investment risks of specific stocks and entire portfolios in terms of their respective betas would, in effect, be making decisions and recommendations on the basis of risk relationships that were no longer valid.

The implications of investment decisions made in this manner are revealed by the results of a number of quantitative studies of the relationships between the previously demonstrated risk characteristics of large numbers of common stocks and their subsequent realized rates of return. The principal findings of these quantitative studies, discussed below, appear to be damaging to the cause of the beta advocates. In general, they tend to refute the views that stocks and portfolios with high betas are riskier than those with low betas and that risky investments tend to provide, on the average, higher returns than low-risk investments.

In June 1971, at a time when the beta cult was gaining considerable momentum,

Dr. Walter A. Morton published a study comparing the relationship between the previously demonstrated risk characteristics of 400 of the 425 stocks in Standard & Poor's Industrial Stock Index and their subsequent, actual realized rates of return. The risk characteristics of each stock were based on its past price volatility relative to the general stock market during the period 1956–1965, and the rate of return on each stock was calculated for the period 1966–1968 by averaging the rates of return that would have resulted from six different buy and sell decisions during this two-year period. The results of the Morton study (discussed in greater detail in Chapter 3) indicated no significant statistical relationship between risk taken and return realized. High-risk and low-risk stocks alike provided high as well as low returns. In simple terms, Dr. Morton demonstrated that high-risk stocks could not consistently be relied on to produce higher-than-average returns.

In June 1973, the editors of *Fortune* published the results of a virtually parallel study, comparing the relationship between the demonstrated risk characteristics and the actual realized rates of return on 840 of the 1,000 stocks in *Fortune*'s first and second lists of 500 industrial companies. The risk characteristics of each stock were denoted by beta coefficients calculated by the Merrill Lynch beta measurement service from market price movements during the five-year period ending in December 1971. The rates of return were calculated for the year 1972 and reflected dividends plus or minus market price change. In general, 1972 was an up year for the stock market; the rate of return on Standard & Poor's Composite Index of 500 stocks was 18 percent. It would be logical to expect, therefore, that stocks with high betas would outperform the market during 1972. The results of the *Fortune* study indicated almost the reverse. Stocks with high betas generated the lowest average returns in 1972, while stocks with low betas provided the highest average returns. In other words, the *Fortune* study indicated a strong *inverse* relation between risks taken and returns actually realized by investors during 1972.

The foregoing theoretical discussion and quantitative evidence suggest the need for a critical reappraisal of the practical worth of the application of betas and the principles of the risk-reward theory in investment decision making and portfolio management. Continued primary reliance by professional investment managers on betas and other mathematical techniques that essentially predict the future in terms of the past could dull the initiative for continued scrutiny and evaluation of all relevant factors that affect the level and trend of earnings of specific companies and industries, and, in the final analysis, their market valuations and effective investment returns. This dulling of the analytical function in investment management, coupled with adherence to the dictates of the risk-reward theory, could produce very indifferent results in the long run.

COMMONSENSE CONSIDERATIONS IN INVESTMENT DECISION MAKING AND PORTFOLIO MANAGEMENT

From time to time since the early 1960s, the investment policies and investment performance of certain types of institutional investors have been subject to severe criticism. Professors associated with the Wharton School, for example, have made mutual funds a favorite whipping boy, pointing out, in their various studies, that professionally managed mutual funds have achieved, on the average, essentially the same level of performance as the stock market as a whole. Such Wharton School findings conveyed the impression that individual investors, on the average, could do about as well as the professionally managed funds simply by buying stocks on a random basis, that is, by throwing darts at the list of NYSE stocks published in *The Wall Street Journal*. These studies also raised questions about the proper level of management fees and acquisition costs paid by investors for such average results.

Merits of Buying Common Stocks in the Light of Prevailing Yields on Fixed-Income Investment Alternatives

In February 1967, McGeorge Bundy, president of the Ford Foundation, in discussing the growing financial needs of American colleges and universities, shook his finger at the investment performance of their endowment funds. He said:

> It is far from clear that trustees have reason to be proud of their performance in making money for their college. We recognize the risks of unconventional investing, but the true test of performance in the handling of money is the record of achievement, not the opinion of the respectable. We have the preliminary impression that over the long run caution has cost our colleges and universities much more than imprudence or excessive risk-taking.

Bundy pointed out that an improvement of only 1 percent in the annual investment return on higher education endowment funds would provide colleges and universities with an additional $120 million a year, an amount of capital more than twice the size of the Ford Foundation's annual budget for education and research.

These pronouncements were reflective of the mounting conviction among numerous investment experts and observers that the prudent man rule of fiduciary obligation, with its emphasis on income and preservation of capital, might not be valid for trusteed endowment and pension funds with virtually perpetual investment horizons. Buttressing this conviction was the recognition of the vast structural changes in the American economy since the early 1930s, which minimized the possibility of another great depression, financial collapse, and prolonged period of stagnation. In these circumstances, these investment experts urged that long-term institutional investors should accelerate the transition from fixed-income investments to equities. In the spring of 1970, one such expert recommended that bonds should be held "only as needed for permanent defensive reserves" and suggested that, as a rough rule of thumb, this defensive reserve be limited to no more than 10 percent of the entire portfolio.

Many long-term institutional investors might, with some justification, have felt offended by the exhortations of the investment experts "to get out of bonds and into stocks," because it represented a course of action that they had been pursuing for some time. Data published annually in the Federal Reserve Board's flow-of-funds accounts confirms a continuing absolute and relative shift from fixed-income securities to common stocks since the early 1960s in the portfolios of private pension funds, state and local government retirement funds, life insurance companies, and other major institutional investors.

The tilt toward equities by the portfolio managers of state and local government retirement funds and life insurance companies since 1960 is most interesting. The management philosophy of these funds traditionally has been regarded as highly conservative and fixed-income–oriented. Yet, between 1960 and 1971 the common stockholdings of state and local government retirement funds increased more than twentyfold, from a relatively low base of $400 million to $11.2 billion. Private pension funds during the same period increased their equity holdings slightly more than 5 times, to $86.6 billion. Life insurance companies expanded their holdings of common stocks roughly 4 times, to $20.5 billion. At year-end 1971, common stocks comprised 67 percent of the total financial assets held by private pension funds, 17 percent of state and local government retirement system financial assets, and 10 percent of life insurance industry financial assets. At year-end 1960, these common stock percentages had been 43, 2 and 4 percent respectively. In 1972, an up market for common stocks, these three groups of institutions were substantial net buyers of equities.

If allowance is made for purchases by institutional investors in recent years of convertible subordinated debentures and other fixed-income investments with equity "kickers" (such as mortgage loans providing for participation by the lender in the gross income or net profits of the mortgaged property), the absolute and relative increases in the equity asset positions of private pension plans, state and local government retirement funds, and life insurance companies are probably substantially greater than indicated above.

That the exhortations of some investment experts to large institutional investors "to get out of bonds and into stocks" are largely gratuitous, in that they endorse something already taking place, is only a minor point. A more basic criticism is the fact that proposals to accelerate the shift from bonds to stocks appear to be based on the questionable premise that higher investment returns are assured by such an assumption of greater risks. Although past investment experience can be cited to support the general proposition that common stocks, on the average, do provide higher returns than bonds, the investment decision maker should recognize that this proposition may not be quite as valid in the future. Since the late 1960s a fundamental change has occurred in the relationship between promised maturity yields on high-grade fixed-income investments and expected yields on common stocks.

From 1970 through 1975 promised maturity yields on new-issue and seasoned high-grade corporate bonds averaged almost 8 percent; in addition, new corporate bond issues offered call protection of five years and longer. (At times in both 1970 and 1975 new high-grade corporate bond flotations sold at yields averaging more than 8.8 percent.) Bond maturity yields of this magnitude are quite substantial compared with historical experience. Elaborate statistical studies have shown that historical rates of return on common stock investments since the mid-1920s, as measured by cash dividends and market appreciation, have averaged about 9 percent per year.

Given these comparative returns, both the propriety and the timing of the investment experts' recommendation that long-term investors continue to shift from bonds to common stocks are subject to serious question. The apparent near parity in prospective bond and common stock returns raises the important question of whether long-term investors will be adequately compensated for the increase in investment risks implicit in a further shift from bonds to common stocks, even under the most generous assumptions of the future rate of growth in common stock earnings and dividends. Maturity yields of 8 percent or more on high-grade corporate bonds establish the basic opportunity cost standard for all types of rational investors, professional as well as individual. The basic issue confronting these investors, therefore, is whether the expected investment returns on common stocks in general and on specific issues will provide a sufficient premium over and above their basic 8 percent opportunity cost standard to compensate for the obviously greater risks of common stocks. (This premium or yield differential can be referred to as the "risk premium requirement.") Only after this decision has been made can the investment experts or portfolio technicians, or both, be called in to render advice about the attributes of an efficient portfolio, the selection of individual issues, and the amounts to invest in each issue that would assure portfolio efficiency.

Determination of the Risk Premium Requirement

Investors' rate-of-return expectations on common stocks probably are influenced to a large extent by their posture toward risk. Investors who are averse to risk tend to have lower rate-of-return expectations, while risk-oriented investors tend to operate on the basis of fairly high rate-of-return expectations. In the investment decision-making process, however, all rational investors make assumptions, implicit or explicit, as to the earnings and dividend growth rates (and, therefore, expected rates of return) on specific common stocks. Common stocks simply are not purchased on the basis of *current* earnings and dividends.

On this premise, the current market price of common stock represents the discounted present value of an expected future stream of payments. The expected rate of return on a common stock (or an entire stock portfolio, for that matter) therefore can be expressed as the discount rate, that is, the interest rate, that equates both the prospective dividend income stream and prospective market price at the end of some holding period with the current market price, that is, the investor's cost basis. (The time period involved may be one year, five years, ten years, or an infinite number of years.)

One formula expresses both the expected and actual realized rate of return for any common stock by the following simple equation:

$$I = \frac{D}{P} + G$$

where
   I = annual rate of return
   D = current annual cash dividend
   P = current market price
   G = expected annual rate of growth in dividends or earnings, or both

With the additional assumptions that both the stock's price-earnings and dividend-payout ratios remain constant, the growth rate factor G in this equation also expresses the rate of appreciation in the market value of a stock. For stocks that pay no cash dividends or for which the likelihood of dividend payments is minimal, the only way that an investor can realize a return is through market appreciation, and this is a function of earnings growth.

As an example, let us take a stock for $50 ($P$), selling at 10 times its annual per-share net earnings of $5 and paying an annual cash dividend of $2.50 ($D$), based on a 50 percent payout of earnings, to yield 5 percent (D/P). If earnings per share rise at an annual rate of 6 percent (G) over ten years to $8.96 in the tenth year and the price-earnings ratio remains constant at 10 times earnings, this stock will have a market value ten years hence of about $90, representing an 80 percent gain over the investor's original cost of $50. Meanwhile, the investor's annual cash dividend income stream on this stock will rise steadily at the rate of 6 percent a year from $2.50 in the first year to $4.48 in the tenth year, based on continuation of the 50 percent earnings payout. If the investor sells his or her stock at the end of the tenth year, the combined return over this ten-year holding period, giving effect to both the 80 percent appreciation in the value of the stock and the stream of annual dividend payments, will amount to about $75. This combined-return figure of $75 represents a 150 percent profit to the investor on his or her original cost basis of $50, or a simple annual rate of return of 15 percent averaged over the ten-year period. Compounded annually, the rate of return is roughly 11 percent (5 percent in dividends plus 6 percent in annual appreciation).

The foregoing example represents a practical illustration of the strategic factors that an investor should consider in appraising the expected rate of return on any common stock investment: the cash dividend yield and growth rate in earnings and dividends that are required to make the stock attractive relative to alternative investment opportunities. Obviously, higher growth rates would have to be assumed for stocks with relatively low or zero dividend yields than for stocks with high dividend yields.

Also, when bond maturity yields are high or are rising, investor expectations of common stock earnings and dividend growth rates must become increasingly sanguine to justify commitments in equities rather than in fixed-income securities. When high-grade corporate bonds provide maturity yields of 7.5 percent or more, which has been the case almost continuously since 1970, common stocks with current annual dividend yields of 5 percent would have to offer the prospect of realizing long-term earnings and dividend growth rates of more than at least 2.5 percent a year to provide the common stock investor with an effective rate of return just equal to the bond investment alternative. But since common stocks are generally viewed as being riskier than bonds, an annual earnings growth rate substantially higher than 2.5 percent would be required to justify the purchase of common stocks vis-à-vis high-grade bonds. Just how much more is a function of the return differential or risk premium requirement needed to compensate for the greater risks involved.

Investor determination of risk premiums tends to be highly subjective, and the opinions of professional investment managers differ widely concerning the differential in expected rates of return required to justify the purchase of common stocks instead of high-grade bonds. On the basis of the historical common stock and corporate bond rate-of-return studies cited in Section One of the *Handbook*, the differential between realized rates of return on common stocks and high-grade corporate bonds since the mid-1920s appears to have averaged about 4 percentage points in favor of common stocks. During this period, common stock returns averaged about 9 percent per year, and high-grade corporate bond yields about 5 percent. This 4 percentage point yield differential may be viewed as a proxy for the investor's minimum risk premium requirement needed to justify the purchase of common stocks instead of high-grade corporate bonds.

On this evidence, purchases of common stocks with current dividend yields of only 5 percent when high-grade corporate bond yields average a relatively low 7.5 percent would have to be justified on the basis of minimum earnings and dividend growth rate assumptions of 6.5 percent a year. A current dividend yield of 5 percent plus a 6.5 percent growth factor would provide the common stock investor with an effective annual rate of return of 11.5 percent, as shown by the following basic common stock rate-of-return equation:

$$I = \frac{D}{P} + G \quad \text{or} \quad 5 \text{ percent} + 6.5 \text{ percent} = 11.5 \text{ percent}$$

This is 4 percentage points more (the minimum risk premium requirement) than the 7.5 percent yield on high-grade bonds. Any growth rate assumption of less than 6.5 percent would not offer a sufficient risk premium to justify purchase of the common stock in question.

Hazards of Common Stock Growth Rate Assumptions

Professional investment managers and individual investors are constantly making assumptions, implicit or explicit, about the growth rates of both specific common stocks and common stocks in general. A decision to purchase a high-quality growth stock with a current dividend yield of 3 percent or less, instead of an electric utility stock yielding 7 percent or more or a high-grade corporate bond yielding 7.5 percent or more, obviously must be based on some assessment of the future earnings or dividend growth rates, or both, of the high-quality growth stock and, therefore, of its projected effective rate of return vis-à-vis the electric utility stock and high-grade bond investment alternatives.

The lower the current dividend yield, the higher the growth rate assumption needed to justify the purchase decision. In the case of stocks with current dividend yields of 5 percent, a minimum growth rate assumption of 6.5 percent would have to be made to provide an effective rate of return fully competitive, in terms of the basic risk premium requirement, with the 7.5 percent maturity yields generally available on high-grade corporate bonds since 1970.

The basic question, therefore, is: *What are the risks and hazards involved in the common stock growth rate assumptions made by investors?* More specifically, how reasonable is a 6.5 percent annual growth rate assumption for common stock earnings and dividends in terms of the historical record and in light of our present knowledge about the future?

Since the mid-1920s common stock per-share earnings have risen at a rate of about 4 percent compounded annually. The gross national product (GNP) has grown at a rate of slightly more than 5 percent compounded annually during this period. (Both of these growth rates are in current dollars and therefore reflect the effects of inflation. If we adjust for inflation, which has averaged close to 3 percent annually since the mid-1920s, the real growth rates for corporate earnings and the GNP would be materially lower.)

During the balance of the 1970s and early 1980s, the GNP could grow at a slightly faster rate than it did during either the 1926–1970 or the 1950–1970 periods, principally as a result of an acceleration in the rate of increase in the labor force and a faster rate of inflation. However, prospects for an acceleration in the rate of growth in corporate earnings, either in the aggregate or on a per-share basis, are less certain. It is a simple fact of life that a profit growth projection for any company or group of companies much beyond two years is exceedingly perilous. In *The General Theory of Employment, Interest and Money,* John Maynard Keynes expressed great skepticism about the practical worth of the long-term earnings forecasts and the influence on the markets of the people who claimed to have this predictive power. Keynes said:

> Our knowledge of the factors which will govern the yield of an investment some years hence is usually very slight and often negligible. If we speak frankly, we have to admit that our basis of knowledge for estimating the yield ten years hence of a railway, a copper mine, a textile factory . . . amounts to little and sometimes to nothing; or even five years hence. In fact, those who seriously attempt to make any such estimate are often so much in the minority that their behavior does not govern the market.

Some investment experts, however, apparently are not deterred by the hazards and limitations of making long-term earnings and dividends forecasts. For example, in an article in the March–April 1970 issue of the *Financial Analysts Journal,* one such expert, Charles D. Ellis, projected the dividends and yields on utility stock portfolios twelve, twenty-four, thirty-six, and even ninety-six years hence to demonstrate the ultimate cash income advantages of a utility common stock portfolio yielding 4 percent and growing at a rate of 6 percent annually over a bond portfolio yielding 6.5 percent to maturity. Ellis also stressed the difficulty of predicting bond interest rates even twenty years hence, saying that most bonds currently held in any portfolio "will have matured or been called in 20 years and will be replaced with other bonds at presently unknown interest rates." Bond interest rates, he concluded, could trend higher or lower, but the utility portfolio dividend income stream "will surely trend higher, and only the rate of increase is uncertain." It is reasonable to assume that the long-term dividend growth projections by Ellis, as well as similar equity-oriented growth projections by other investment experts who favor getting out of bonds and into equities, will have little demonstrable impact on the day-to-day investment decisions of practical-minded investors.

It may be worth noting, moreover, that in the years since Ellis made his growth projections of the dividend yields on a utility common stock portfolio, relatively few utility companies have been able to attain per-share e·rnings and dividend growth rates of 6 percent per year, the growth rate Ellis used to demonstrate the ultimate cash income advantages of a utility common stock portfolio over a bond portfolio. Many electric utilities, in particular, evidenced little or no per-share earnings growth from 1970 to 1975; and the market values of their common shares often declined, providing investors with negative returns during this period.

TABLE 55-1   United States Inflation, 1965–1975

Year	Consumer price index (1967=100)	Wholesale price index (1967=100)	Percent change from previous year	
			Consumer price index	Wholesale price index
1965	94.5	96.6	1.7	2.0
1966	97.2	99.8	2.9	3.3
1967	100.0	100.0	2.9	0.2
1968	104.2	102.5	4.2	2.5
1969	109.8	106.5	5.4	3.9
1970	116.3	110.4	5.9	3.7
1971	121.3	113.9	4.3	3.2
1972	125.3	119.1	3.3	4.6
1973	133.1	134.7	6.2	13.1
1974	147.7	160.1	11.0	18.9
1975	161.2	174.9	9.1	9.2

SOURCE: U.S. Bureau of Labor Statistics.

The foregoing considerations, on balance, should serve to persuade all rational investment decision makers to pause and reexamine the basic merits of shifting from bonds and other high-yield fixed-income investments to equities. This cautionary note, however, should not be construed as a blanket disavowal of all equity investment opportunities for the foreseeable future but simply as an affirmation of the view that investors in the future will have to exercise considerably greater diligence in making additional equity commitments than in the past.

Appraising the Worth of Special Investment Features

The period since 1965 has been characterized by two notable factors: (1) a sharp acceleration in the rate of general price and wage inflation in the United States economy and (2) pronounced cyclical swings in interest rates. The dimensions of the United States inflation problem are summarized in Table 55-1.

Throughout these periodic swings in interest rates and a generally high rate of inflation, private investors had to ponder a number of special investment factors to a much greater extent than ever before. It is appropriate to refer to these factors not so much from the standpoint of whether investors during the period beginning in 1965 did, in fact, make correct decisions but rather as to how they should weigh these factors in the future.

Equity-Participation Privileges

On those occasions beginning in 1965 when interest rates surged sharply higher, opportunities for investors to purchase so-called equity-participation securities also increased. In fact, the shortage of new investment funds relative to demand often enabled large institutional investors to insist on equity participation as a condition of financing. Equity-participation securities include not only traditional subordinated debentures convertible into common stock at specified prices in the future but also mortgage loans, notes, and debentures with equity kickers attached, enabling the lenders to participate in the prospective profits or revenue growth of the company or venture being financed.

Purchase of equity-participation securities invariably involves the explicit sacrifice of higher current or maturity yields obtainable on straight debt and preferred issues in exchange for expected higher effective yields obtainable through the exercise of the equity-participation privilege. In early 1972, for example, investment-grade industrial companies sold long-term convertible debentures at effective interest costs, as measured by the coupon rates, ranging between 4.5 and 5.75 percent. In contrast, the interest costs on new investment-grade straight corporate bond offerings at the same time ranged between 6.75 and 7.6 percent, indicating a yield advantage of approximately 2 full percentage points in favor of the straight debt offerings.

What the investor must determine, therefore, is the prospective worth of the equity-participation feature in terms of (1) the forgone opportunity to earn a higher interest income return on a straight debt issue and (2) the greater risks that are a function not only of a possible step-down in credit quality from a senior to a subordinated creditor position but also of the interplay of the many factors affecting the level and trend of earnings of the company or venture offering the equity participation.

It would be a waste of effort to build a mathematical model to assist the investment decision maker in determining whether a straight debt issue yielding 7.5 percent to maturity is a better deal than one yielding only 5.5 percent plus the opportunity to participate in an uncertain stream of future profits. Each situation must be considered on its own merits in the light of present knowledge about the future. It would be helpful, moreover, to have empirical evidence of the extent, if any, to which actual trade-offs in the past between higher-yield straight debt and lower-yield equity-participation debt issues had actually enhanced realized portfolio yields.

Coupon, Maturity, Yield, and Call Protection

As a result of the pronounced cyclical swings in interest rates since the mid-1960s, investors also have had to give continuing, careful consideration to each of the multiple factors affecting the investment yields on bonds. For bonds of the same general quality rating, these factors include the interest coupon, the number of years to maturity, future changes in the level of interest rates, and the call protection features, if any. Interest coupons on outstanding high-grade corporate bonds, which denote their annual interest income expressed as a percentage of par, range from a low of about 3 percent to a high of 10 percent or more. Maturities on these issues range from less than five years to about forty years at the most.

The range of investment alternatives currently available to the bond investor in a given category of credit quality is therefore quite substantial. For some bond investors, however, the array of investment alternatives may be limited by portfolio liquidity requirements. But liquidity considerations aside, the bond investor may purchase any of the following:

- Low-coupon bonds with short to long maturities
- High-coupon bonds with short to long maturities
- Short maturities with low to high coupons
- Intermediate maturities with low to high coupons
- Long maturities with low to high coupons

The important decision facing the bond investor is what course of action to follow, given his or her expectations of future changes in the level of interest rates.

During periods of *rising* interest rates, prices of low-coupon bonds will decline proportionately more than will those of high-coupon bonds in the same maturity range; and, in the case of bonds having the same coupon rate, longer-term maturity obligations will experience sharper relative price declines than will short maturities. Conversely, during periods of *declining* interest rates, prices of low-coupon bonds will rise proportionately more than will those of high-coupon bonds in the same maturity range; and among bonds having identical coupon rates, longer-term maturities will experience greater relative price increases than will short maturities. Over the entire interest rate cycle, accordingly, bond price volatility is *directly* proportional to the length of maturity and *inversely* proportional to the coupon rate.

Long-term low-coupon issues, therefore, have the greatest price volatility, while short-term high-coupon obligations have the lowest price volatility. The longer a bond's maturity, the greater the impact of a change in market interest rates on the present value of the bond's coupon income stream. The lower a bond's coupon rate, the greater the impact of a change in market interest rates on the present value of the bond's discount, that is, the difference between the bond's present market price and its par value payable in a lump sum at maturity. For low-coupon deep-discount bonds, payment of the discount at maturity can represent a sizable portion of the bondholder's effective annual return, depending on the time to maturity.

In these circumstances, if higher interest rates are expected in the foreseeable future, bond investors should refrain from purchasing long-term low-coupon bonds. Instead, they should temporarily "park" their funds in short-term investments until market interest rates reach their peak. On the other hand, if bond buyers harbor any reservations about their ability or the ability of their credit market experts to spot interest rate peaks, they should consider going into long-term high-coupon bonds. As Sidney Homer and Martin L. Leibowitz, two sophisticated students of the bond market, point out in their monograph *Inside the Yield Book* (1972), investors who purchase long-term high-coupon bonds during a period of rising interest rates benefit by being able to reinvest their high-coupon income at rising interest rates.

If bond investors think market interest rates have reached a cyclical peak and are about to decline for some time to come, they should favor long-term low-coupon issues over high-coupon obligations, provided the differential in maturity yields is not too great in favor of the high-coupon bonds and the risk that the high-coupon bonds may be called is real. In these circumstances, long-term low-coupon bonds will offer the double-barreled advantage of (1) greater capital gains, that is, price appreciation as the large discount is gradually reduced as maturity comes closer, and (2) virtually complete call protection to maturity by virtue of the bonds' deep discount from par. Again, if bond investors have any reservations about their own projections of the interest rate outlook, they should give serious consideration to the long-term high-coupon bond alternative.

Finally, bond investors need to give careful consideration to the cost or worth of call protection. Not all bonds can be bought with complete assurance that they can be held to maturity, so that bondholders will be able to realize the yield to maturity shown in the yield book on the basis of the original cost, coupon rate, and number of years to maturity. (The maturity yield for any bond shown in the yield book assumes that the bond's coupon income is regularly reinvested and compounds at a rate exactly equal to the yield to maturity.)

During periods of sharply declining interest rates, holders of high-coupon bonds face the real risk that their bonds may be called for redemption by issuers determined to replace their high-cost loans with lower-cost (lower-coupon) loans. The option to call rests solely with the corporate bond issuer, subject to the provisions of the loan agreement.

If bonds are called, bondholders lose the opportunity to realize the bonds' promised yield to maturity; instead, they realize only the yield to call date, which for high-coupon bonds is generally less than the yield to maturity. In addition, bondholders are confronted with the unhappy task of searching for an alternative bond investment that will provide a yield competitive with the former promised maturity yield on their called bonds. Since bond calls are most apt to occur during periods of declining interest rates, maturity yields on the available replacement bonds seldom equal the former promised maturity yield on the called bonds.

Bond investors have three decision options with respect to the call risk problem:

1. They can purchase low-coupon deep-discount bonds that will assure them virtually complete call protection until maturity.

2. They can purchase high-coupon bonds, specifying the most restrictive call provisions, that is, the highest call price and greatest number of years to call.

3. They can purchase high-coupon bonds offering no call protection whatsoever.

The maturity yields shown in the yield book will be highest for the third bond purchase option, but there the risk of call also will be greatest. The maturity yields shown for the first bond purchase option will be the lowest, but the call risk will be virtually nil. The maturity yields and call risk of the second bond purchase option will fall somewhere between the first and third options. Generally speaking, therefore, maturity yields on bonds are inversely proportional to their call protection: the greater the call protection, the lower the maturity yield.

Bond investors' expectations concerning the future level and trend of interest rates (plus some yield calculations) will largely determine which decision is appropriate for dealing with the call risk problem. For example, *if it is expected that interest rates will continue to rise in the foreseeable future,* the third decision option is obviously the appropriate one. The risk of call diminishes as interest rates rise, and investors will be able to reinvest their high-coupon income at these higher rates, thereby increasing their total return.

On the expectation that interest rates are at or near their cyclical peaks and will decline, the third decision option is completely inappropriate because the risk of call will escalate. Accordingly, bond investors must choose between the first and second options. This choice should be based upon an appraisal of the following: (*a*) the yield to maturity and yield to call on the high-coupon call-protected bond (the second option) and (*b*) the yield to maturity on the high-coupon call-protected bond (the first option).

If the price of the high-coupon call-protected bond is at or near the call price, it is reasonable to assume that the yield to call will represent the minimum yield obtainable on this bond. Although the maturity yield still may be higher than the yield to call at this price, the bond is a potential candidate for redemption; and if the price continues to rise with a further easing in credit conditions, the risk of call probably will materialize, thereby wiping out all chances of realizing the full yield to maturity. If, in these circumstances, the maturity yield on a low-coupon deep-discount bond was equal to, or even slightly lower than, the yield to call on the potentially callable high-coupon bond, *the purchase of the low-coupon bond would provide more effective protection against the risks of call,* given the background of a probable or anticipated decline in interest rates.

Timing of Investment Decisions

Without question, timing is a crucial factor affecting investment performance. The famous Fisher-Lorie study of common stock rates of return during the period from 1926 through 1965 clearly demonstrates the importance of timing in achieving superior investment results. This study showed that the investor who bought common stocks in January 1926 and sold them in December 1928 would have realized an effective compounded annual rate of return of 23.9 percent (reinvestment of dividends and no capital gains taxes are assumed), whereas the investor who bought in December 1928 and sold in December 1930 would have experienced a negative annual rate of return of 31.7 percent, or a substantial capital loss. The investor who bought stocks in December 1935 and sold in December 1936 would have realized an annual return of 6.3 percent, but if he or she sold at the end of 1937, he or she would have experienced a negative annual return of 10.9 percent. The investor who bought in December 1960 and sold in December 1963 would have realized an annual return of 10.4 percent, but one who bought in December 1961 and sold in December 1963 would have had an annual return of only 2 percent. The years since 1965, the terminal year in the Fisher-Lorie study, show an even greater range in performance results.

This wide range, however, has been overshadowed by other findings of the Fisher-Lorie study, notably that common stocks yielded positive returns in more than 90 percent of the 820 total possible overlapping investment time periods in the forty-year time span (1926–1965) covered by the study and that the average annual rate of return realized, that is, the modal or most frequent rate of return, for all 820 of these overlapping investment periods was 8.8 percent. These findings have supported the view that investors will nearly always profit by buying common stocks and that, over the broad sweep of time, they will, on the average, earn materially higher rates of return on common stocks than on bonds and other fixed-income investments. Several large brokerage houses widely publicized the results of the Fisher-Lorie study of common stock rates of return, distributing condensed versions to current and prospective customers and discussing the results in investment seminars.

However, drawing conclusions with respect to appropriate investment strategies for the future on the basis of past results averaged over long periods of time is exceedingly perilous. Long-term averages invariably tend to show favorable results, such as respectable rates of growth in employment, incomes, and personal wealth and positive yields on common stocks and bonds, and conceal all sorts of calamities.

Thus, investors holding corporate bonds and common stocks bought before 1930 would have had a significant percentage of their portfolio (in terms of both number of separate issues and original book value) in default at one time or another during the early 1930s. In numerous instances during this period, state regulatory agencies compelled banks and insurance companies subject to their jurisdiction to dump their holdings in enterprises that had gone into bankruptcy, thereby forcing these institutions to realize substantial losses and preventing them from realizing positive yields on such investments during the ensuing economic recovery to general prosperity.

Equally significant, even if less well documented, is the collective experience of the vast multitude of individual investors during the Depression years. How many people who bought securities during the final stages of the bull market of the late 1920s sold out at or near the bottom of the market during the early 1930s because they (1) were convinced that prosperity would never return, (2) couldn't meet brokers' calls for additional margin, or (3) had to raise cash to buy groceries and meet mortgage payments? On the other hand, how many individuals aggressively bought securities at the bottom of the market during 1932–1933, when the future appeared the bleakest but the subsequent returns would have been the greatest?

Since the Great Depression, the bond and stock markets have gone through numerous cycles, creating opportunities to buy and sell at very attractive prices.

Within these broad market cycles there have been even greater ups and downs in the market values of securities of companies in specific industries such as electronics during the late 1950s to early 1960s, land developers during the early 1960s, conglomerate organizations during the mid-1960s to late 1960s, and fast-food chain and amusement park operators during the late 1960s to early 1970s.

Investors who consistently bought at or near the market lows and sold at or near the highs and, even more important, bought and sold the industry fads and favorites at the right times clearly would have done amazingly well. But such consistency in performance is seldom if ever achieved.

The simple fact of the matter is that no one individual nor any organization of professional investment experts can lay claim to having the ability to anticipate, unfailingly, the highs and lows of the bond and stock markets. If any one professional investment organization possessed such clairvoyance, that organization would consistently outperform all its competitors year in and year out; but rankings on the annual investment performances ladder—for growth funds, balanced funds, income funds, closed-end funds, and so on—tend to change rather dramatically from one year to the next and over the broad sweep of time. Numerous mutual fund managers did achieve outstanding performance results during the go-go years of 1965–1969, but the performance records of many of the same managers since 1970 have been nothing short of disastrous. As a result, some of these former high-performance achievers have left the investment business entirely and are now remembered only by those unfortunate investors who got burned by betting that these achievers could extend their performance records to infinity and by the occasional financial reporter interested in doing a new and fresh chronicle of the famous go-go period.

Individual investors and professional investment managers must make continuing judgments as to timing—to buy stocks and sell bonds, to buy bonds and sell stocks, to hold cash or its equivalent. These judgments should be based on their expectations concerning changes in (1) the general business outlook and, therefore, the level and trend of interest rates and corporate profits and (2) the level and trend of common stock prices in general and of prices of specific equity securities.

The making of such judgments could be avoided forever by (1) holding liquid assets in the form of savings accounts, Treasury bills, and finance paper or (2) pursuing a policy of dollar averaging on a regular monthly or quarterly basis and dividing one's purchases equally between a broad list of fixed-income investments and common stocks. However, neither of these two judgment-avoiding approaches would appear to offer sufficiently high annual yields to augment real capital values in an environment likely to be characterized by an annual rate of inflation of 4 to 6 percent and corresponding depreciation in the value of money.

What conclusions should be drawn from the foregoing discussion? A primary conclusion is that substitutes for the exercise of informed judgment in the timing of investment decisions are not likely to produce above-average investment results. No mathematical formulas or sets of hard-and-fast rules are available to assist the investment decision maker in determining whether now is the time to buy or sell specific equity securities, to switch from high-coupon to low-coupon deep-discount bonds or from short to long maturities, to accelerate the switch from bonds to stocks, or to favor high current yields over low yields and high growth. Any decision with respect to the timing of each of these and numerous other investment alternatives, including the respective longer-term implications of each decision alternative, must be considered on its own merits and in light of present knowledge about the future. This is what portfolio management is all about.

Chapter 56
Special Factors in Managing Individual Portfolios

LEO BARNES

This chapter is intended for the use both of individuals managing their own investments and of investment managers handling individual accounts. The materials sometimes overlap, but where this is the case, the relevant applicable portion can readily be selected by each type of user.

Portfolio management is a continuous process of investment selection, elimination, efficient combination, and upgrading. For individuals and individual accounts, its procedures can conveniently be divided into four major tasks:

1. Determining rational individual investment and tax requirements, capacities, and targets.

2. Establishing continuing but changing eligible lists for each investor by means of investment "filters" that (a) embody relevant legal and institutional restraints, (b) delimit suitable investment areas or categories in terms of task 1, and (c) reduce eligible lists to manageable size through "valuation" filters applied to current markets.

3. Selecting the most efficient and rewarding available portfolios from such eligible lists through the use of valuation and technical filters.

4. Continuing systematic supervision and upgrading of the selected portfolios for maximum aftertax holding-period return.

RATIONAL INDIVIDUAL INVESTMENT AND TAX REQUIREMENTS, CAPACITIES, AND TARGETS

Traditionally, seven major investment targets, most of them interrelated and overlapping, have been conveniently grouped in three sets of investment approaches:

Conservative. (1) Preservation of capital; (2) safe present and future income, including tax-exempt income.

Enterprising or aggressive. (3) Growth of capital; (4) above-average current income; (5) rising future income; (6) special tax shelters.

Speculative. (7) Maximum capital gains, preferable tax-favored long-term gains but fully taxed short-term gains if necessary.

What are the main differences among these three approaches? They can probably best be defined in terms of *acceptable risk levels* (*see* Section One and Chapter 52 of this section). The conservative investor demands safety more than any given level of return. The primary goal is preservation of capital and, only after it is assured, a very safe and stable income. Portfolio turnover is low, and holding periods are long.

The enterprising or aggressive investor will take larger risks for the *probability* of a greater *long-term* total aftertax return from tax-favored capital growth plus income. Such an investor will often cash in capital gains soon after the end of the long-term holding period and will sometimes sell to realize losses before they become long-term.

The speculative investor will take the highest risks to achieve relatively few tax-favored maximum capital gains, usually at the price of numerous capital losses, which he or she tries to limit by using stop-loss techniques. Such an investor will buy, sell, and sell short most frequently, often deliberately ignoring long-term holding periods.

It is entirely feasible for some investors to combine two or even all three of these basic approaches. If they do so, it is probably desirable to separate the funds involved into distinct investment programs, even utilizing different investment advisers or brokers for each program.

For all types of investors, capital growth or income targets may be stated initially in nominal dollar and percentage terms. However, it is also useful to adjust such dollar totals and rates for estimated prospective inflation and income taxes and thus to derive *real* postinflation and aftertax return expectations.

Which Target Is Primary: Income or Capital Gain?

Both conservative and aggressive investors must next either assign relative weights to, or make a clear-cut choice between, capital gain and income-oriented investment targets. Such a choice involves three major considerations.

First, if income from investments is required for current living expenses, the assurance of such income needs logically and practically comes before hopes for capital gain. In such cases (and, in today's inflationary world, they are numerous and increasing), the investor's budget requirements for assured current and future income from investments must be carefully spelled out and provided for.

This can be done either on a *minimum* or on an *optimum* basis. In minimum terms, how much annual income does the investor need from investment sources to get along? In optimum terms, how much investment income is desired for a more comfortable or even a luxurious scale of living? Under either approach, a *yearly expense budget* for the individual or family must be established. Then, from such a budget target, total available or projected annual noninvestment income from employment or other family resources is subtracted. The remaining sum is the level of yearly investment income required to meet the established yearly expense budget.

The next consideration is the investor's need for *current capital liquidity*. Psychological factors are important here and are similar to the factors treated below in the discussion of possible loss of principal. The primary financial factor to be considered is the magnitude and timing of major future monetary responsibilities that will definitely or probably require the consumption of capital. The most usual example is college education for one's children; a less important situation might be a major anniversary vacation or celebration. If the size of such future expenditures is relatively large, more conservative capital-preserving investments are obviously preferable to speculative or cyclical ones.

Ideally, what could be utilized here are a long-term income projection and a long-term balance sheet for each investor. Estimated future financial responsibilities could thus be matched with anticipated future income and savings, including securities, real estate, other investments, pensions, profit sharing, and social security. Estimates should be made on an aftertax basis at liberally projected marginal or top income and capital gain rates. The perennial danger that capital gain tax rates may be raised, perhaps to ordinary income levels, should be borne in mind in estimating future capital requirements. Similarly, reserves for possible investment losses and errors should be generous. The adequacy of an investor's life, health, and disability insurance totals is also relevant here, and outlays may need to be increased before investments are made.

Although each investor is unique, future requirements and resources follow common age and family patterns. They tend to be similar for young families, for families in the middle years, for individuals and couples approaching retirement, and for retired investors.

A third basic question that must be answered in choosing between capital gain and income targets is each investor's *capacity to risk permanent loss of principal,* as opposed to the risk of temporary paper losses in intermediate market declines or in longer-term bear markets. Frequently, the decisive factor is not the size of the capital sum involved but the investor's psychology, temperament, and general philosophy of life. Financially and logically, persons of substantial wealth are best able to risk the permanent loss of part of their capital, whereas investors with relatively small monetary stakes can ill afford such losses. In actual practice, however, the larger one's fortune, the more conservative and careful one is apt to be in trying to preserve it; while the smaller.the capital sum involved, the greater is the likelihood that investors will have the impulse to take a speculative flier in the hope of increasing their capital significantly.

Importance of Aftertax Decisions

Careful estimation of aftertax investment results is more than ever a necessity for investors and investment managers. Here are some of the reasons:

1. Income tax and capital gain rates, especially in the upper-income brackets, are very likely to continue at high, possibly even rising levels.

2. Increasing state and local income taxation is probable in many areas of the country, thanks to inflation and more restrictive tax-exempt bond markets.

3. Concurrently, historically high yields on many tax-exempt issues (in response to higher investment risks and other market shifts) have made municipal bonds realistic alternative investment instruments for increasing numbers of investors in middle-income tax brackets.

4. Tax shelters and tax preferences (as for capital gains) are being subjected to continual legislative attack and frequent legislative change.

In such a turbulent tax environment, it is the net aftertax return on various investment alternatives that is decisive for investors. Investment decisions made solely on the basis of pretax returns often are erroneous. Investors should also remember that every dollar of taxes saved is worth much more than a dollar of income or capital gain, since it is net after taxes, and that the higher one's tax rates, the greater the income (or pretax) value of a given amount of tax savings.

Calculating net aftertax returns is more complicated than it may seem because state and local income taxes are almost invariably deductible from taxable income for federal tax calculations. How to make the necessary adjustments for state and local income taxes is explained in Section Nine.

The end products of such adjustments are two total or combined marginal tax rates for every investor subject to state or local taxes, or both, as well as to federal income taxes: (1) the higher combined rate applicable to fully taxed income, including investment income; and (2) the lower combined rate applicable to tax-favored capital gains from investments. In addition, (3) the relatively few investors who sometimes (usually for safety reasons) purchase municipal bonds, the income from which is exempt from federal taxes but is taxable at state or local levels, or both, would have a third marginal tax rate, applicable only to out-of-state tax-exempt income.

To illustrate these three kinds of marginal tax rates, let us take as an example Investor A, whose current top or marginal federal income tax rate is 48 percent. This investor is also subject to a state top income tax rate of 15 percent and a city top income tax rate of 4 percent. Corresponding marginal capital gain tax rates are presumed to be half of the ordinary income rates, or 24 percent federal, 7.5 percent state, and 2 percent city. These tax rates add up to 67 percent for ordinary income and 33.5 percent for capital gain. However, the effective state and local tax rates are reduced by the 48 percent federal tax saving applicable to them. In the case of Investor A, the combined effective marginal tax rate is 48 percent plus 7.8 percent (52 percent of 15 percent) and 2.08 percent (52 percent of 4 percent), or 57.88 percent, rather than 67 percent. Correspondingly, the combined effective rate on capital gains would be 28.94 percent, not 33.5 percent. (If Investor A had invested in municipal bonds of issuers taxable in his or her state, the effective marginal rate for such issues would be the simple sum of the state and local rates, reduced by A's marginal federal rate, or a total of 9.88 percent, rather than 19 percent.)

Each investor should carefully note and remember the two (or three) combined effective top marginal tax rates applicable in any given year. So should the professional investment manager handling individual accounts. From such rates, the applicable relative aftertax investment returns from various types of investments can readily be calculated.

According to the above example, here is what Investor A would net after all income taxes on $100 from four possible types of return:

1. Fully taxed investment income (from stocks, bonds, or other investments): $42.12 ($100 minus $57.88 in taxes). The index is 100.0.

2. Tax-favored capital gains: $71.06 ($100 minus $28.94 in taxes). The index is 168.7.

3. Municipal bonds taxable by state and local governments: $90.12 ($100 minus $9.88 in taxes). The index is 214.0.

4. Totally tax free municipal bonds: $100. The index is 237.4.

These key figures and indices can be used by Investor A to derive net aftertax returns from any number of specific investments belonging to the four categories, provided the applicable tax rates are unchanged. However, if Investor A becomes subject to higher or lower tax rates, the effective rates must be recalculated as illustrated above. Table 56-1 provides a convenient form of work sheet for such calculations.

ESTABLISHING CONTINUING ELIGIBLE LISTS FOR EACH INVESTOR

After each investor's rational income, capital gain, and risk requirements are determined, the next major phase of portfolio construction and management is the establishment of appropriate tests, criteria, or investment filters by which some investments are selected as eligible for particular portfolios while other possible investments are rejected.

Investment filters can be conveniently classified as *absolute, semiabsolute,* and *relative.* "Let us make a portfolio of 10 common stocks with the highest projected return in a list of 100 stocks" is an example of the use of a relative filter. No specific payoff requirement has been set; in a down market, the return of the ten best

TABLE 56-1   My Net Marginal Aftertax Return from Alternative Investments

Type of investment	A. Current pretax return			B. Net percent of return retained by me*			Net aftertax return		
	Income	Capital gain	Total	Income	Capital gain	Total	Income	Capital gain	Total
1. Savings bank, day-to-day									
2. Savings bank, term certificate									
3. Treasury note									
4. Federal government bond, long-term									
5. AAA corporate bond									
6. BBB corporate bond									
7. Residential mortgage									
8. Tax-exempt bond									
9. Tax-exempt bond, locally taxed									
10. Common stock A									
11. Common stock B									
12. Common stock C									

*To be calculated as described in "Importance of Aftertax Decisions."

stocks might be negative. By contrast, "Let us invest only in stocks for which the expected rate of return is 12 percent" illustrates the use of an absolute filter.

A semiabsolute filter is intermediate between these two examples but considerably closer to the absolute filter. "Let us invest only in stocks for which the expected rate of return is at least 5 percent more than the current yield on AAA bonds" is an example of using a filter that is not completely absolute, completely relative, or completely variable. But it is obviously closer to an absolute filter than to a relative one, and we therefore designate it as semiabsolute.

For investing institutions handling individual accounts, some kinds of investment filters are mandatory because of the legal requirements of federal or state governments. Other filters may be virtually mandatory because they are the product of long-established institutional practices or experience.

Larger Investment Universe versus Smaller Eligible List

Rationally, every investor should select his or her current portfolio from larger investment groupings. It is useful to classify these groupings as (1) the entire investment cosmos (all possible investments for all investors); (2) a particular investor's investment universe or group of areas; (3) the investor's current eligible list, from which a current portfolio is selected. How does one go from group 1 to group 2 or from group 2 to group 3?

The transition from group 1 to group 2 is usually relatively simple. Almost all investors confine their investments to a relatively small number of particular investment areas with which they are familiar. In approximate order of conservatism, the principal accepted areas include (a) savings and savings and loan accounts; (b) federal government and federal agency bonds and notes; (c) tax-exempt municipal and revenue bonds; (d) corporate bonds; (e) common stocks; (f) preferred stocks; (g) convertible bonds and preferreds; (h) mutual funds of various types; (i) closed-end investment companies; (j) listed and over-the-counter options: (k) commodities and futures; (l) real estate; and (m) a variety of special offbeat investments, such as tax shelters, art, and antiques. (All these areas are discussed and analyzed in detail in various sections of the *Handbook*.)

Few if any investors can effectively "cover the waterfront." They should accordingly select from the dozen or so major areas listed above a smaller number that appeal to them in terms of their basic requirements and their investing capacities. Commonly, areas a through i, which include the traditional types of securities, will be of primary interest to most investors. They will be utilized almost exclusively in this section of the *Handbook* as illustrative material.

It is entirely appropriate for each investor to note specifically the investment areas to which he or she proposes to pay attention. Are all of them really necessary to meet his or her objectives? A proper answer to this question is important, because concentrating on or specializing in a few areas will usually be more rewarding than dabbling in a wider range of potential investment areas.

The next problem is the transition from general areas of investment to specific *eligible lists*. Why should an investor have specific eligible lists as well as a specific portfolio? The answer is that such a dual procedure will usually produce superior portfolios, because two sets of filters, not just one, are being utilized, the first for establishing good eligible investments and the second for selecting, at any given time, the best or most suitable of the good eligibles.

We discuss below appropriate procedures for drawing up eligible lists for funds, stocks, mutual funds, and other investment media. It should always be borne in mind that the smaller the number of specific investments in your portfolio, the smaller need be your eligible list for the portfolio and the higher and more rigorous your standards should be for admitting investments to the list. An eligible list of 1,000 securities may be appropriate for a mutual fund portfolio of 200 securities but not for an individual investor's portfolio of a dozen or a score of stocks.

Use of Investment Media Other Than Securities

There are a number of investment areas other than stocks and bonds in which returns are frequently larger and risks often no greater. However, their liquidity and marketability are usually inferior to those of securities. A great variety of such investments are analyzed in detail in other sections of the *Handbook*. In utilizing these sections for portfolio management, the investor should seek to establish and to *formalize in writing* the requirements or filters deemed appropriate for each investment medium, in much the same way that we do in the following pages for stocks and bonds. You will find that the material in these *Handbook* sections has been prepared to facilitate the establishment of such requirements.

Moral, Social, or Political Factors as Filters

Much has been said and written in recent years about the social and moral responsibilities of business, beyond the applicable legal requirements, in such areas as environmental protection, equal opportunities for women and minorities, and various aspects of politics and international relations, such as trading with Communist nations or the Arab-Israeli dispute. To what extent do or should such matters play a role in investment selection and portfolio management?

To some degree, they are already involved automatically through their impact on corporate sales and profits. If racial or sexual discrimination is unpopular among consumers and investors, the company that practices such discrimination will lose sales and profits and suffer lower price-earnings multiples. Such a fact would then be *financial* reality fully relevant to the choice of the company involved for your eligible list or your portfolio. Thus, the appropriate question here would seem to be whether a moral or social issue should be considered by investors on an *ethical* as well as on a financial basis.

Obviously, if an individual investor or an institutional investor like a church or a university has strong convictions on moral, social, or political issues, these can readily be embodied in appropriate investment filters. "No securities of companies involved in specified disapproved activities" is a simple form of game rule that can easily be carried out at the *primary level* of the companies involved.

For example, if one is both a teetotaler and a prohibitionist, one can very simply avoid the securities of liquor companies. But what about major suppliers of such companies, or retailers who sell liquor in one relatively small department, or a conglomerate for which liquor represents only 5 or 10 percent of total sales? Should securities of such firms be excluded too? Clearly, if one's moral standards are very stringent, it may become difficult to construct a portfolio providing a satisfactory rate of return.

Thus, from the point of view of investment efficiency, it is probably wise to avoid this issue completely and to draw a moral line only with respect to *illegal* activities. Then, if moral commitments are embodied in law, as they frequently have been in recent years, they will automatically be taken into account, equally for all affected firms, by investment and portfolio managers.

Ultimately, however, this is a matter of individual choice. If an investor wishes to apply and enforce certain moral, social, or political scruples beyond the requirements of law, these desires can and should be respected, even at the price of some loss in portfolio performance. Of course, the portfolio manager should take care to emphasize this risk and to disclaim in advance any responsibility for poorer performance.

Eligibility List Requirements for Bonds

A summary of the usual major considerations for bond eligibility follows (see Section Four for additional details on bonds). In view of the large number of bond issues available, individual investors should keep their eligible list standards very high.

1. *Minimum quality rating.* The customary institutional requirements permit investment only in bonds that are (or would be) rated BBB or better by Standard & Poor's or the equivalent in other rating systems. Such a minimum rating requirement automatically excludes the vast majority of convertible debentures. Departure from this basic institutional standard by individual investors should be undertaken only after the most careful estimation that the additional probable return is worth the additional risk. This may be the case when the yield spread between BBB-rated bonds and lower-quality issues are abnormally large, as they may be near the bottom of bear markets.

2. *Other institutional eligibility requirements.* In addition to minimum ratings, institutions often have additional minimum size and quality requirements for bonds. Issue size requirements are established for purposes of liquidity and resale. The chief example of additional quality restrictions is recent default by an issuer. Some institutions are forbidden by law to purchase the bonds of an issuer in default during the prior decade even if the current bond rating is satisfactory.

In addition, many institutional bond buyers make more detailed qualitative analyses of individual bond issues before including them in their eligible lists. Such analyses, which stress income and capital coverage ratios, duplicate in large measure the work of the several rating agencies and are therefore unnecessary for individual investors who restrict their bond investments (as they should) to rated issues.

3. *Yield.* Minimum yield requirements for bonds are best set by individual investors in terms of their investment alternatives. Thus, you could specify that otherwise-suitable bonds would not be eligible for purchase if their *current* yields fell below those of bank certificates of deposit of appropriate duration, either longer-term (five to seven years) or shorter-term (one to two years). Alternatively, available mortgage rates on insured mortgages could be used as a yardstick.

4. *Maturity ranges.* In view of economic uncertainties and the impact of chronic inflation, investors may wish to restrict their bond holdings to short (one to two years) and intermediate (five to ten years) maturities in order to limit price volatility. On the other hand, taxable bond investors interested in capital gains may wish to try to benefit from the large price swings available from long-term bonds as interest rates fluctuate.

5. *Callability protection.* Noncallability for at least five years for bonds selling near or above par, especially bonds issued at unusually high yields, is a sensible eligibility standard. When bonds are purchased in the secondary market, the duration of remaining noncallability should be carefully checked.

6. *Convertibility.* Taxable individual and institutional investors are sometimes interested in convertible bonds because of the possible additional tax-favored capital gains if the related common stock advances. The eligibility questions to be answered are (a) how much current income yield is to be sacrificed as the price for convertibility and (b) how much lower a quality rating for the convertible is acceptable. Individual investors can usually safely accept ratings below BBB for convertible bonds if the nonconvertible bonds of the company involved are rated BBB or higher. Taxable institutions with legal rating restrictions, however, cannot do so.

Eligibility List Requirements for Stocks

These requirements can be of almost endless variety and include all three types of filters, absolute, semiabsolute, and relative. As in the case of bonds, the greater the number of filters an investor utilizes, the smaller the resulting eligible list. Similarly, the tougher the standards employed in any filter, the smaller the list.

Investors may utilize either *multiple* eligible lists (one list per major filter such as income yield, safety, value, growth, or technical strength) or a much smaller *single* unified list that embodies the net outcome of all accepted filters. It may be useful to regard the former as the preliminary eligible lists and the latter as the final eligible list. Alternatively, an investor may wish to maintain only preliminary eligible lists and construct a portfolio directly from them.

As you consider the following detailed assembly of filters commonly used to establish stock eligible lists, you may find it useful to note for special attention the filters that most strongly interest or appeal to you.

1. *Listing.* This is a traditional conservative eligibility requirement. It can mean listing on any regulated stock exchange, but in practice it refers almost always only to the New York and American Stock Exchanges or even to the New York Stock Exchange alone. This filter is not recommended to individual investors, primarily because it serves no useful function for them. The reduction in the number of eligible stocks still leaves thousands of issues to be evaluated, and numerous promising unlisted companies with above-average profit potentials are automatically excluded. And, of course, this filter will become obsolete if separate exchanges are abandoned and replaced by a single, nationwide unified trading list.

2. *Consistent profitability.* This absolute filter sharply limits common stock investment to companies that have been invariably profitable for specified time periods, usually the last ten, fifteen, or twenty years. The longer the time span, the smaller the eligible list because greater numbers of recessions will be included. Even the ten-year period includes the deepest recession since the 1930s, that of 1973–1975, as well as the sharp recession of 1969–1970.

Of course, if you wish to work with an extremely small eligible list, you may consider using a filter of companies that are at least twenty-five years old and have never shown a loss. Even in this case, however, almost always one or two such companies will probably turn sour, emphasizing the basic point that it is future, not past, profitability with which investors should be primarily concerned.

3. *Rising profitability.* This is another absolute filter focused on companies whose annual profits per share tend to rise year after year, say, for each of the past five years or for at least four of the past five years. If 1974 and 1975 are included, this can be a very rigorous filter and may leave the investor with too small an eligible list to be effective.

4. *Consistent, regular dividends.* With rising or even uninterrupted profitability a very difficult test to pass in recent years, uninterrupted dividend-paying ability becomes an attractive filter, particularly for investors requiring or desiring regular investment income. Companies that pay dividends through thick and thin clearly have something going for their shareholders. As in the case of profits, the required time period may be ten, twenty, or more years. The longer the time, of course, the fewer companies surviving to make the eligible list.

5. *Rising dividend payments.* This absolute filter closely corresponds to filter 3 (rising profitability) and, like filter 4, is useful primarily for income investors. Some companies with low dividend payout ratios pride themselves on being able to raise their dividends by a relatively small percentage each year, even though earnings may remain level or decline slightly in some years. As with filter 3, the eligible list may be too small to be useful.

6. *Minimum quality rating.* Quality ratings are not as widely used for common

stocks as they are for bonds or preferred stocks. However, they are available for many leading stocks from the major investment services like Standard & Poor's and Moody's and can be usefully employed as a common stock eligibility filter for these stocks by safety-conscious investors. Portfolios could be limited to stocks from the top three or four ratings, for example, A+, A, and A− in Standard & Poor's earnings and dividend rankings. Using such a filter reduces one's stock universe from thousands to hundreds.

7. *Minimum risk.* If stocks are not quality-rated by the service or investors desire to measure risk more specifically themselves, various risk filters may be employed. One standard aspect of risk is price volatility, customarily indicated by a stock's beta factor, which is available for hundreds of leading stocks from many services.

But, as indicated in Chapter 3, average combined upside and downside volatility over a period of years is a poor measure of the various sources of capital loss to which an investment in common stocks may be exposed. The broader concept of risk as the danger of partial or total loss of one's investment or income therefrom, or both, provides the most comprehensive approach to risk analysis and the use of risk filters to establish eligible lists.

There are at least a dozen specific sources or categories of risk with which stocks and many other investments can be, and often are, threatened. They are discussed briefly below, so that investors may use some or all of them as eligible list filters. You may also wish to consult Chapter 3 for a more comprehensive treatment of risk.

a. *Business and business cycle risk.* Is a stock highly susceptible to business cycle patterns, either general patterns for business as a whole or specific cycles of its own?

b. *Financial risk.* This risk is related to category *a* but can be independent of it. A company can go bankrupt, even though business is good, if it is overloaded with debt, if it must refund a big debt issue in tight capital markets, or if its financial management of inventories, accounts receivable, and other aspects of its business is inept.

c. *Downside market price risk.* This risk is equivalent to *downside* beta (upside beta per se is not a risk but a benefit). Investors may wish to study a stock's downside volatility in greater detail than a simple combined beta factor figure. This may be done first by exploring a stock's price behavior in previous market downturns and then by trying to answer the question of whether the company's exposure to the other types of risk in this checklist makes it more or less vulnerable in the current period.

d. *Marketability risk.* The risk of a common stock, real property, or other investment may be substantially increased because of poor marketability, which prevents sale at a satisfactory price.

e. *Inflation risk.* The impact of above-normal inflation varies for different companies. Some may be able to raise their prices to match rising costs, while others may not. Companies with moderate debt leverage may be helped, while those with no debt or excessive debt may be hurt. If an investor suspects that a particularly inflationary period lies ahead, this type of risk should be carefully explored.

f. *Interest rate risk.* Rising interest rates often accompany mounting inflation but may occur independently of it. Companies with substantial and recurrent debt requirements (notoriously in housing and other types of building) are particularly susceptible to this type of risk.

g. *Domestic political risk.* Companies that do business with federal, state, or local governmental bodies are subject to this source of risk. A political change may mean a switch in government policy, and even if there is no policy change, either administrative or legislative personnel shifts may alter business opportunities.

h. *Domestic social risk.* In recent years companies have found themselves open to injury by various social pressure groups, such as consumer or environmentalist organizations or groups with a domestic or foreign political orientation. The activities of these groups may hurt company sales, curtail sources of supply, or raise business costs.

i. *Devaluation risk.* Companies with substantial foreign sales are most susceptible to this potential danger (either from the United States or from foreign countries), and it should be carefully explored.

j. *Economic, political, and social foreign risk.* This category involves all the other risks from abroad that multinational companies and other firms with substantial foreign sales constantly face, ranging from restriction of activities, through punitive taxation, to outright confiscation.

k. *Statistical and accounting risk.* "Figures don't lie, but liars figure." The accounting procedures of many firms, while legal and receiving the certification of accountants, may not be as conservative or as solid as may be considered desirable. Not all profit dollars are equally sound. Some companies seek to maximize or exaggerate earnings per share for stock market gains, while others take a more conservative, longer-term point of view. Investors may wish to screen out the former.

l. *Moral risk.* Such management risk is very hard to detect or anticipate but must be explored in some cases, particularly for smaller and lesser-known companies. This exploration involves the study of the background and prior affiliations and connections of a company's top management personnel.

After all or most of the preceding dozen categories of risk have been explored, it is possible to assign to any company an estimated *combined risk rank,* which could be used as a filter. Ranks could range from 1 to 5, from 10 to 100, and so on. Alternatively, this comprehensive risk analysis could be used in an absolute filter, with the discovery of any serious risk eliminating a company from one's eligible list.

8. *Other fundamental value filters.* These filters can be used effectively to narrow the field of eligible issues. For example, an investor could insist on a minimum required yield for a stock to be eligible, say, 6 or 8 percent, or on some maximum price-earnings ratio, say, 12 or 15 times earnings per share, or on both these filters. These and similar tests are simple absolute filters by which investors can reduce eligible lists to manageable proportions.

It is also feasible to utilize more sophisticated or more complex fundamental filters, usually semiabsolute or relative rather than absolute, to establish eligible lists. Thus, a value investor's eligible list could consist of all issues that are currently "fairly" or "prudently" priced in terms of the selected fundamental standards. (See Section Three for additional details.)

As an alternative, various investment services publish on a regular basis eligible or "master" lists, based on fundamental analysis or filters, that may be used for this purpose. For example, the Value Line Investment Survey every week updates two eligible lists of 100 stocks each, one a list of stocks with the highest current dividend yields of more than 1,500 regularly covered stocks in the survey and the other a list of 100 stocks with the greatest long-term appreciation potential (three to five years) from their current price. Quite a number of different value portfolios might be constructed from the data furnished in these two Value Line eligible lists (see below, "Value Line Relative Portfolio Procedures").

9. *Technically oriented filters.* Somewhat more unusual in drawing up formal eligible lists is the use of purely technical filters to produce lists consisting only of

technically strong common stocks. (More customarily, technical indicators are used to pick actual portfolios from an eligible list determined by fundamental factors, but there is no reason why the reverse could not also be adopted.) Thus, a technically oriented investor might say: "I am interested only in technically attractive stocks. From a list of such eligible issues, I shall then go on to select my portfolio in terms of each stock's fundamentals."

In this way, the Value Line, in addition to publishing two weekly lists of 100 stocks each that are attractive for their yields or long-term potentials, releases a weekly list of 100 stocks that seem technically strong for maximum performance in the next twelve months. The historical performance record of this list of the technically strongest stocks is well above average.

10. *Authoritarian filters.* Another feasible approach to eligible lists is to derive them on the basis of how esteemed authorities are investing, either individually or en masse. Thus, the 100 stocks most favored by institutional investors would be an eminently respectable eligible list from which individuals could effectively select a portfolio of 5 to 15 issues. Similarly, the choices of a respected investment service or adviser could serve a similar function.

Another somewhat more cumbersome authoritarian device is to follow the lead of corporate insiders, the officers and directors of major United States corporations, and construct a portfolio consisting only of companies in which the insiders have been buying stock on balance. A number of investment services provide up-to-date information on such insider decisions, which can often produce above-average profits.

11. *Special-situation filters.* Such filters would be used by investors interested largely or exclusively in special situations. The various special-situation approaches that can be used to establish such eligible list filters are described in detail in Chapter 16.

12. *Stock market indices as eligible lists.* This can be a very effective portfolio device for individual investors and also for institutional investors (see Chapter 57). Why not confine one's eligible equity investments either to the thirty blue-chip stocks in the Dow Jones Industrial Average or to the sixty-five stocks in the Dow Jones Combined Average? By trying to select the ten or fifteen better-performing stocks in either of the indices and by investing in the appropriate relative proportions (as determined by the weighting methods used for the index), investors should be able to outperform these widely used market averages by a worthwhile amount.

For individuals, either of the two Dow Jones averages would seem to provide a more suitable eligible list than other larger indices, such as the comprehensive Standard & Poor's 500-Stock Index. However, it would be entirely feasible to select the 50 or 75 or 100 largest (most heavily capitalized) companies in the S&P 500 and to utilize this selected portion as an eligible list. Alternatively, the selection from such a larger index might be done on an industry basis for broader diversification, the largest company in each industry normally being selected for the eligible list.

Common Stock Eligible List Appraisal Review

Some conscientious investors may wish to draw up their eligible lists on the basis of their own tailor-made, rigorous terms, perhaps including specific filters not referred to above. As an aid to such investors, there follows a detailed summary of various possible specific filters, arranged by categories of investment requirements, which, in combination with our preceding analysis, may generate useful ideas for additional practical filters.

Basic Growth Potential

Appraisals should include minimum earnings growth requirements in terms of factors like the following:

1. Average annual percentage gain in total and per-share earnings, before and after taxes, for (*a*) the past five years, (*b*) the latest fiscal year, and (*c*) the latest interim period available.

2. Projected average annual percentage gain in total and per-share earnings, before and after taxes, for the next three to five years.

3. Longer-term industry or industries growth outlook.

Special Growth Factors to Be Reviewed

Special contributions to earnings growth may be required in one or more of the following areas: (1) research and development; (2) plant and equipment improvement and expansion; (3) new products ready for market; (4) new markets; (5) mergers and acquisitions; (6) management capabilities (aggressiveness, replacement depth, and so on).

Value and Growth Evaluations

Growth potentials and special factors, plus other value considerations, must be evaluated in terms of current market and economic conditions and the financial strength of the companies involved. The following should be reviewed for each eligible list candidate: (1) debt-equity ratio trend for the past five years; (2) ratio of annual cash flow (earnings plus depreciation) to debt due in the next twelve months; (3) trends in dividends per share and payout ratios for the past five years; (4) profit-sales ratio trend for the past five years; (5) percent-earned-on-equity and percent-earned-on-total-capital trends for the past five years for earnings both before and after taxes; (6) price-earnings ratio high-low range and average for 1963–1972 and since 1973; (7) historically warranted current price range, based on factor 6; (8) current price, related to factor 7 and other value, price-earnings, and dividend yield factors.

Evaluation of Current Technical Position

A variety of technical approaches are discussed in Chapter 19. In evaluating eligible list candidates, it is helpful to concentrate on the following technically oriented information: (1) industry relative strength; (2) company relative strength; (3) chartists' ratings and evaluations; (4) technical ratings of other services; (5) approximate major six-month profit-taking dates; (6) corporate insiders' buying or selling on balance; (7) mutual funds' and other institutions' buying or selling on balance; (8) stock exchange specialists' buying or selling on balance; and (9) latest monthly short position, up or down.

Conclusion: A Filter Checklist

As a result of the preceding analysis, each investor should be ready and able to complete a checklist in the following format: "My eligible list for common stocks will be developed by using the following filters: 1, 2, 3, 4, and so on."

Mutual Funds and Investment Companies as Eligible Investments

Many investors decide to achieve a useful combination of return, safety, and diversification by investing in several mutual funds or closed-end investment companies, or both. In such cases, the relevant eligible list would consist of funds or investment companies that meet these objectives (presumably fully diversified stock and stock-bond funds or companies). The list could include the entire roster of such funds or companies. Better would be a narrower selection from such a large list, such as the ten funds or companies with the best five- or ten-year records, the ten best of the largest funds or of the medium-size funds, or a list chosen by means of some other criterion. The selection of mutual funds and investment companies is discussed in Chapter 42.

Pruning and Updating Eligible Lists

Eligible lists may begin to become obsolete almost as soon as they have been completed. Profitable companies turn unprofitable, firms that have never reduced their dividends suddenly do so, and so on. Ideally, investment eligible lists will be changed as soon as such events occur. In practice, even with computerization it often takes weeks or months before eligible lists are revised.

One major advantage of using eligible lists prepared by investment services is that revisions are made frequently without any effort on the investor's part (the Value Line lists are revised each week, so that old eligible lists need only be discarded and replaced by current ones).

In any event, it seems a sensible precaution for individual investors to revise their eligible lists at least quarterly and preferably monthly. Such revisions will often lead to corresponding changes in portfolios.

SELECTING THE MOST EFFICIENT AND REWARDING PORTFOLIOS FROM ELIGIBLE LISTS

The most decisive step in portfolio management is, of course, the final selection of an initial working portfolio from each investor's eligible list. Ideally, this process involves the effective utilization of additional filters designed to achieve the investor's safety, income, shorter-term capital gain, and long-term appreciation targets, in line with the respective absolute or relative weight assigned by the investor to each target. In practice, portfolio selection is frequently much simpler than this ideal formulation. In the analysis that follows, we try to achieve a pragmatic combination of the practical with the ideal.

Bond-Stock (Debt-Equity) Ratio Decision

The first portfolio question an investor must answer is: At this time, what proportion of my total investment funds should be in equities (stocks, real estate, commodities, and so on), and what proportion in debt or priorities (bonds, mortgages, money market mutual funds, and so on)? The answer will determine the size of each of these two major portfolio divisions, which in turn will be relevant to the related questions, discussed below, of the number of issues and the degree of other diversification called for in the portfolio.

The techniques for making this basic decision are treated elsewhere in the *Handbook*. They involve the investor's basic attitude toward risk, estimates of current and prospective returns from available equities and priorities, and economic and financial timing considerations (see Sections One and Two).

For illustrative and discussion purposes, let us assume in the following subsections that, unless otherwise specifically indicated, the investor has opted for stocks and bonds and has set an initial stock-bond ratio of 75 to 25 percent.

Diversification Needs of Individuals' Bond Portfolios

The key rule for bond diversification is that the lower the quality of the issues involved, the higher the risk and the greater the desirable diversification. If an investor's debt investments are exclusively in government bonds or federally insured bank deposits, diversification is more a matter of investor convenience, in terms of the availability of funds and desired maturity dates, than of portfolio necessity. For many investors, one or two bonds or bank accounts will often suffice. At the other extreme, if the bonds that one has selected for maximum return are rated B or BB or the equivalent, they have a considerable element of risk and should be diversified in much the same way that stocks are diversified, as described below.

Diversification Needs of Individuals' Stock Portfolios

There is an inherent conflict between two primary investor goals: (1) to *concentrate* holdings for maximum or above-average return and (2) to *diversify* holdings for minimum or below-average risk (see the analysis of Keith V. Smith in Chapter 53). How can these conflicting purposes be reconciled in practice? For most individual investors, the answer can only be to keep diversification to the necessary minimum and to avoid diversification for diversification's sake. By contrast, very large institutional investors are often compelled to diversify into 100 or more stocks because of both legal ownership restrictions and the need for market liquidity. For most individuals, neither of these factors is relevant.

Individual investors also have the option of limiting risk by means of stop-loss techniques, which prevent or limit losses by requiring sales of securities when their prices drop by a stipulated percentage (typically 10 or 12 percent) below their latest high point. The adoption of such techniques by individual investors reduces the need for diversification and permits them to "diversify only among the best."

Specifically, most individual investors would have higher portfolio returns with little increase in overall risk if they limited the maximum number of issues in their stock portfolios to between 10 and 20. This means that one is choosing one's top 10 or 20 stocks rather than one's top 50 or 100, and it seems plausible that for most investors, their favorite 10 stocks will outperform their favorite 50 or 100.

Even with a large individual stock portfolio (of, say, $1 million), holdings of single issues need not exceed $50,000 to $100,000 to maintain a portfolio of ten to twenty issues. In current markets, holdings of this size do not mean any great loss of liquidity with large listed companies. To be sure, some special situations and smaller companies may require smaller individual holdings, but these could be offset by somewhat larger holdings than $50,000 or $100,000 for other more liquid situations.

To lower risk, the ten to twenty securities in an individual's portfolio should be diversified into about five to ten industries, preferably with *differing economic cycles of sales and profits*. This requirement increases safety because it reduces "covariance," or closely similar stock price movements among an investor's holdings (see Chapter 53).

Constructing Simple Portfolios Geared to a Single Primary Investment Target

Many small portfolios are set up rather simply in terms of the investor's *predominant* investment target only: yield, safety or quality, short-run but tax-favored capital gain, or long-term appreciation. Given such a single target, five to ten stocks in different industries are selected by the broker or investment adviser from a master list or lists to achieve that objective.

This procedure may satisfy the investor and produce tolerably adequate results, but it is hardly professional portfolio management. Whenever the investor's need is not assured investment income, the goal of portfolio management should be maximum total holding-period return after taxes. The achievement of that more complex goal calls for the satisfaction of several investment targets rather than just a primary one.

Constructing Complex Portfolios with Multiple Investor Requirements

It is accurate and useful to classify investor requirements in four categories: (1) safety or quality; (2) income yield; (3) price reasonableness, or "value," frequently based on projected future growth and assumed to be reflected in longer-term price appreciation; and (4) short- or intermediate-term technical strength leading to capital gains (tax-favored long-term gains, it is hoped, but short-term gains if necessary).

These four requirements are usually in conflict: the more we have of one of them, the less we obtain of the others. Only at or very near the bottom of a bear market, as in November 1974, do we find ideal common stock investments: a high-quality stock having an excellent yield, selling at a very reasonable price, and showing considerable technical strength. At other times, investors and their advisors must choose the optimum, but less than perfect, available combination of characteristics that fulfill their objectives.

As in the process of setting up eligible lists from the larger security universe, described above, such a choice is made by using additional standards or filters. Once again, these can be absolute, semiabsolute, or relative. Let us examine first the purely relative approach.

Value Line Relative Portfolio Procedures

Perhaps the most sophisticated example of such a relative approach is the one utilized by the Value Line Investment Survey for many years up to 1973. In this formulation, each of the four key investment requirements or targets enumerated above is ranked by each investor in order of importance, from 1, or most important, to 4, or least important. As the second step in the procedure, the four ranks are weighted with numerical weights of 11 for rank 1, 6 for rank 2, 2 for rank 3, and 1 for rank 4. These four weights are designed to add up to 20 (11 + 6 + 2 + 1) for the ultimate purpose of achieving a maximum score of 100 as described below.

The third step in this relative approach deals with stocks rather than with investor targets. It is the derivation of relative weighted ranks for the performance of each of the more than 1,500 stocks in the Value Line's equity universe, in terms of the degree to which each such stock is estimated to fulfill each of the same four basic investment characteristics or targets: safety, yield, long-term price appreciation, and intermediate-term technical strength or price performance.

The five Value Line ranks applicable to each of these characteristics are designated by the roman numerals I (best), II, III, IV, and V (worst) to distinguish them from the investor's ranks of 1, 2, 3, and 4. The relative weights assigned to these five ranks range from 5 (for I, or best) down to 1 (for V, or worst). Should investors disagree with the Value Line analysts' judgment, they can assign the same ranks and weights in their own fashion.

We thus arrive at the fourth and final step in our relative procedure, the combining of each investor's ranked and weighted target requirements with the ranked and weighted manner in which each stock is estimated to fulfill those requirements. This coalescence is achieved by simple multiplication and addition. Investors multiply the relative weights for their four desired stock targets by the relative weights assigned to each stock by the Value Line (or the investor) for the same four characteristics. Then the sum of the four multiplications becomes the total score for each stock, showing its relative total desirability in terms of each investor's weighted requirements.

We may summarize this sophisticated relative evaluation procedure as follows:

1. *Stock characteristics or investor requirements.* Safety, yield, long-term price appreciation, intermediate-term relative strength.

2. *Investor ranks (and weights) for the requirements (highest to lowest).* 1 (11), 2 (6), 3 (2), 4 (1).

3. *Adviser ranks (and weights) for the stock characteristics (highest to lowest).* I (5), II (4), III (3), IV (2), V (1).

4. *Possible range of scores for any single stock characteristic as an investor requirement.* These individual scores are derived from the multiplication of the weights in parentheses in steps 2 and 3. Thus, the maximum possible score for a single characteristic would be 55—(11) × (5); the minimum possible score would be 1—(1) × (1).

5. *Possible range of scores for all four stock characteristics as investor requirements.* These total scores are derived by adding the products as derived in step 4. Thus, the maximum possible score for an individual stock in terms of all four investor requirements would be 100 (55 + 30 + 10 + 5), while the minimum score would be 20 (11 + 6 + 2 + 1).

The foregoing procedure is obviously a very elegant formulation, but the evidence seems to be that most investors did not find it particularly useful in practice. They simply were not convinced that a stock with a total score of, say, 69 was necessarily superior for their requirements to a stock with a score of 67 or 65. Basically, the reason for such investor reluctance to adhere to this system would seem to be that most investors have, or wish to have, at least *one or two absolute or semiabsolute standards rather than only relative ones.* In particular, as we have seen, investors want absolute standards for income yield and safety or quality below which they will not go no matter how overwhelmingly attractive a particular stock may be in fundamental value or technical strength.

This fact was recognized by the Value Line editorial directors in 1973, when its portfolio selection system was drastically changed to require the use of absolute filters for income and safety. At the same time, the Value Line editors were forced to conclude that their stock rankings of fundamental value for long-term price appreciation did not successfully correlate with actual stock price movements over either the intermediate or the longer term. By contrast, however, they confirmed that, over the preceding decade, their estimates of stocks' price performance for the next twelve months, which involved some technical factors, did correlate very favorably with the actual twelve month results.

Value Line Shift to More Absolute Standards

Accordingly, the Value Line in mid-1973 changed its recommended portfolio procedures to eliminate completely its fundamantal-value filter. This filter was replaced by a semiabsolute filter: any given stock's relative market volatility as measured by its beta factor (see Chapter 3).

Here is how this new volatility filter is to be applied: (1) If investors are bullish on the general market, they should buy more volatile stocks so that their total portfolios will have average betas of 1.10 or higher. (2) If investors are uncertain about the direction of the market, they should buy and hold stocks of average volatility so that their total portfolios will have average betas of .90 to 1.10. (3) If investors are bearish about the general market, they should concentrate on stocks with below-average volatility so that their total portfolios will have average betas of less than .90.

All in all, the Value Line shifted from a system of using all relative filters for the four major desired investor requirements or targets to one of utilizing two absolute filters (income yield and quality), one relative filter (projected price performance in the next twelve months), and one semiabsolute filter (market volatility as measured by beta).

Useful Conclusions on Portfolio Methodology

We have devoted much attention to the evolution of the Value Line portfolio methodology in order to reach a number of useful conclusions:

1. The Value Line shift toward *absolute filters* confirms that wherever such filters are applicable, they are almost always to be *preferred to relative filters*. If one can be firmly absolute, there is no need to be weakly relative.

2. The Value Line change of methodology confirms the *probable futility of long-term projections and forecasts* for portfolio management. The thousands of projections of three to five years made in the past by highly educated and factually informed Value Line analysts have not been successful in outperforming the market at large. It would appear that the world, the economy, and the stock market offer too many unpredictable surprises to permit useful-for-making-money forecasts beyond the next six to twelve months, a time span for which technical analysis seems superior to fundamental valuation.

3. Thus, the Value Line experience accentuates the *importance of technical analysis* for successful portfolio management. In contrast to the indifferent market performance of its fundamental-valuation methodology, the Value Line's technically oriented filter—probable market performance in the next twelve months—has been demonstrated to produce results that are notably superior to the market averages since 1965.

Continuing Role of Fundamental Analysis

Many subscribers to the Value Line Investment Survey were dismayed by the statistical findings summarized above and were very reluctant to discard fundamental analysis because of those findings. Nor did the Value Line itself discard fundamental analysis despite its poor empirical results, any more than business firms or economists reject economic and financial forecasting just because it frequently proves to be erroneous.

For many if not most investors, this reluctance to give up fundamental analysis is sound, because such analysis can add *a dimension of safety and psychological security* to investment and portfolio management. A portfolio of "prudently" priced stocks that shows moderate technical strength is, for many investors, more satisfactory and acceptable than a portfolio of stocks that are "imprudently" overpriced but show considerable technical strength (as most overpriced stocks do in the initial phases of their overvaluation). A prudently valued stock is worthwhile for many investors even though it may not achieve maximum capital gains, because its risk is less and the reliability of its dividend yield and overall quality rank is reinforced. It is thus quite proper and useful to utilize various prudent value and growth filters in selecting stocks for your portfolio from the appropriate eligible lists.

How to Use Multiple Filters with Multiple Eligible Lists to Combine Requirements

We now return to our four basic investor requirements to demonstrate how a combination of four filters can be employed to select the most efficient stocks for your portfolio. The task can become complicated even with the simplest approach, and the assistance of a computer can be very helpful.

Let us suppose that, by the use of appropriate selected filters, you have developed the following four eligible lists of stocks from which you wish to derive a portfolio of twenty stocks:

1. 100 stocks that meet your absolute *quality* or *safety* filter, all rated A+ or higher by Standard & Poor's (or the equivalent by some other reputable service).

2. 75 stocks that have passed your absolute *income* filter, say a current dividend yield of 6.5 percent.

3. 100 stocks that have been recommended as *prudent values* by an investment advisory service whose record and reputation are respected, none of which sells at more than 10 times current earnings per share.

4. Finally, you have a list of 60 stocks that show *strong technical momentum patterns* for the intermediate term (six months to one year), prepared by a favored technically oriented service.

How do you construct a portfolio from these four lists? First, your absolute quality and income filters must be utilized, since they are mandatory. Each of the twenty stocks in your portfolio must be on both list 1 and list 2. You would also very much like them to be on lists 3 and 4, and if you can find (by inspection or by means of a computer) twenty stocks that are on all four lists, most of your portfolio problems will have been solved. However, quite probably you will be unable to find such a set of twenty stocks and will therefore have to settle for lower-than-optimum relative ratings for value and technical strength for the twenty stocks that best meet your absolute standards for safety and income before going on to fulfill your diversification requirements, as discussed above.

Depending on the relative priorities among investor requirements, many variations of this portfolio treatment are possible and likely. Thus, if you have no minimum income requirement and are interested above all in tax-favored capital gain, your primary filters will be your technical eligible list 4, as modified by your absolute quality or safety requirements from list 1 (say, B+ or higher ratings by Standard & Poor's or the equivalent). Your attitude toward your fundamental-value list 3 will probably be quite flexible, ranging from complete indifference to curiosity about the extent to which the fundamental rankings are in step with the technical ones. You may then perhaps note the income returns that will result from your prior portfolio selections but will not make any changes as a result of your findings. Finally, the portfolio diversification requirements previously described may be considered briefly but not with any great conviction. From the safety standpoint, there probably will be inadequate diversification in the selected portfolio, since technical strength tends to run in industry groupings. This will not bother you, since your primary investment goal is technically oriented performance.

Choosing a Portfolio from a Single Unified Eligible List

If your common stock eligibles have already been filtered down to a single smaller eligible list that fulfills all your filtered requirements of safety, yield, growth, value, and technical strength, stock portfolio selection becomes the relatively simple task of selecting the best from the good. Your eligible list should show for each stock on it the score for each requirement. Then your selection will be made in terms of the relative primacy or priority of your investment targets.

If maximum income is your first priority, you naturally will choose the highest-yielding stocks from your single eligible list. If maximum holding-period return is your primary target, you will concentrate largely or exclusively on relative technical strength. If longer-term price appreciation is your top goal, you will focus on issues with the strongest earnings growth patterns, and so on.

Multiple Eligible Lists or a Single Unified Eligible List?

The answer to this question is largely a matter of personal preference of when filters are to be used and of how quickly a portfolio is to be selected from among eligible candidates. If speed in final selection is psychologically important to you, a single unified eligible list will be preferred. Many investors, however, will prefer to skip one filtering procedure and go directly from three, four, or more eligible lists for different investment target to their selected portfolio. The total time required will usually be somewhat shorter.

Selecting Bonds from Bond Eligible Lists

Here again, available selection procedures for achieving a portfolio of suitable bonds range from very simple to quite complicated methods.

1. *Bonds for maximum current yield.* If you invest in bonds exclusively for high current yield and are not systematically striving to increase your total return by seeking capital gains, your selection procedure is simplicity itself. Just pick from your bond eligible list the number of bonds you wish to hold (for diversification reasons) with the highest current yields. Normally, such high-yielding bonds will be selling at or close to par. It will almost aways be desirable to avoid short- and intermediate-term bonds quoted more than fractionally above par because if interest rates should rise, you might not be able to recover from the resulting price declines before maturity.

As stressed above, taxable investors should make their yield comparisons on an aftertax basis. Frequently, tax-exempt bonds of suitable quality will then be the preferred alternative.

2. *Shorter-term discount bonds for maximum aftertax return to maturity.* Older bonds selling in the 60s, 70s, and 80s sometimes offer bond investors who do not require maximum current income the probability of somewhat larger aftertax returns, combining fully taxed income and tax-favored capital gain, over holding periods extending to or beyond the maturity dates ⸱ ⸱ the bonds.

The uncertainties in this procedure must be stressed. A higher return is not a sure thing. Buying bonds for $850 each today and receiving $1,000 per bond five or six years from now for a capital gain of $150 per bond does not necessarily mean a greater total return after taxes than buying equal-quality bonds selling at par and providing a higher current return. Thanks largely to the influence of professional bond buyers and traders, aftertax bond returns, adjusted for the time value of money, tend to equalize themselves at any given quality level.

Investors must make the appropriate calculations in each case on an aftertax basis by using their own applicable tax rates. This procedure is not as simple as it may seem, because it requires projecting your probable future tax rates for both ordinary income and capital gain. Such rates depend not only on your and your spouse's future income but also on possible legislative changes at the national, state, or local level.

All this is quite difficult to predict more than a year or so in advance. In particular, there is perennial pressure from tax reformers to reduce or eliminate the aftertax advantage of capital gain. If such reforms are enacted prior to the maturity of discount bonds, their aftertax-return advantage could disappear and even turn into a loss.

Bear in mind, too, that the capital gain portion of your return is not received until a later date, at or near bond maturity. Because of the time value of money, funds received at that time are worth less than the same dollar amount received currently even if there were absolutely no price inflation between now and then. If you add the impact of probable continued inflation, the real aftertax return, discounted to present value, is further reduced.

3. *More sophisticated techniques for bond capital gains.* Professional bond investors, including bond mutual funds and other institutional investors, seek to make additional capital gains in bonds by taking advantage of projected *interest rate changes* resulting from economic, financial, and money market developments. If you wish to emulate these professionals, here are some of the basic underlying principles involved in the three main situations:

a. Differences in bond maturities. As the general level of interest rates moves up or down, prices of long-term bonds fluctuate more than those of intermediate- or short-term bonds on both the upside and the downside. This greater variability is due not only to the time value of money but also to the greater risks attaching to longer maturities. A greater number of unfavorable market developments can occur over a longer period, especially under inflationary conditions.

b. Differences in coupon yields. The lower the coupon yield of a bond, the greater the probable price change in response to interest rate changes. This is largely a reflection of the time value of money. As noted above, the return on lower-coupon bonds usually involves some capital gain to be realized at or near a future maturity. By contrast, any larger return from a high-coupon bond is normally quickly received, starting at the next semiannual payment date.

c. Differences in yield spreads among bonds of different quality, tax status, and call provisions. Such yield spreads vary with economic and market conditions. Thus, if the business cycle has turned toward recession, riskier lower-quality bonds will usually provide a greater yield advantage in comparison with higher-quality bonds than they do in periods of prosperity. As an example of market influences, when the federal government is operating at a larger-than-usual deficit, its need for bond market funds is greater, and the normal yield spread between government issues and high-grade corporates in favor of the latter will narrow. Similarly, major changes in tax-exempt markets, as in the hectic years 1974 and 1975, will increase or decrease tax-exempt yield differentials after taxes. Of course, when bonds with varying tax positions are compared, differences in yield spreads should be figured on an aftertax basis.

Finally, call provisions can be important if interest rates are expected to drop, with resulting price increases toward or above call levels. In such an event, bonds that are subject to near-term call are less attractive than bonds protected against call and will sell at relatively lower prices, considering their coupon and maturity.

Portfolio of Mutual Funds as a Possible Ideal

In theory, an ideal portfolio management arrangement would be the exclusive use of various types of eligible mutual funds and closed-end investment companies, utilizing different mixtures and proportions of the eligible funds or companies as economic and market conditions change. In this way, the selection of specific securities is in the hands of outside experts, while the individual investor devotes full attention to the problems of overall investment timing and the appropriate portfolio mix at any given time.

Thus, in the first stages of a bull market, an investor following this procedure would be fully invested only in aggressive stock funds or closed-end companies with high average betas, or volatility. (When we refer below to mutual funds, closed-end investment companies are meant to be included when appropriate.) As the bull market advances and bond interest rates rise, investments would be shifted increasingly to all-stock funds with below-average betas (if there are any such), stock-bond funds, convertible bond funds, and special-situation funds. Finally, if and as a bear market develops, the investor's assets would be switched to all-bond funds, money market funds, and, perhaps, speculative leveraged funds that engage in short selling (if any can be found with a decent performance record).

Such periodic shifts could be explored and made every month or once a quarter. They could be achieved at minimum cost in two ways. First, there are a number of mutual fund managements with a broad gamut of funds that allow investors to shift among the funds either without cost or for a nominal service charge. Alternatively (or in combination with the first procedure), an investor could include in his or her eligible list an array of different types of no-load mutual funds, which can be bought without cost and sold either without cost or for a relatively small sales charge (see Chapter 42).

CONTINUING PORTFOLIO CONTROL AND IMPROVEMENT FOR HIGHER RETURN AND LOWER RISK

After investors have selected initial portfolios that are most efficient for them in terms of their investment objectives, the task of portfolio management becomes a process of continuing control and improvement. The twin targets are, of course, to maximize return and minimize risks, usually given the same set of investor constraints employed to construct the initial portfolio but sometimes with new constraints developed by experience or compelled by changed investor circumstances.

In this subsection we analyze ways in which portfolio returns can be improved by (1) timely selling, switching, and upgrading; (2) taking advantage of leverage and other volatility factors; (3) profiting from bear markets through short sales and the purchase of puts; (4) increasing portfolio income through the systematic writing or sale of options; and (5) making the most of personal or specially available superior abilities, or "substrategies."

When and How Often to Sell, Switch, and Upgrade

Ideally, if investment switches could be made without buying and selling costs and without tax penalties, portfolio management could be virtually continuous. Changes could be made at hourly or even shorter intervals to increase return or lower risk. A computer would have to be utilized for maximum results from such continuous turnover, but computer programs can be and have been developed for this purpose.

In the real world, only tax-exempt institutions can escape tax penalties, while larger institutions have much lower transaction costs than medium-size or smaller individual investors. Thus, large tax-exempt institutions can take advantage of both tax exemption and minimum transaction costs to turn over their portfolios more frequently for maximum return. In fact, institutional turnover increased markedly in the 1960s and early 1970s as institutions responded to this apparent opportunity. By contrast, individuals incur relatively heavy tax penalties for taking profits frequently, and high commission costs further reduce their aftertax rates of return.

These differing *time horizons* for tax-exempt institutions and individuals have become upsetting and injurious to the stock market. Institutions discovered to their dismay that when they tried to sell more frequently, too few individual investors were available to buy. This resulted in higher stock market volatility and price instability, which tended to make millions of individual investors forsake the stock market. This development in turn not only further reduced common stock marketability but also prevented institutions from realizing the theoretical gains from more frequent turnover. Indeed, *relative* institutional performance (that is, performance in comparison with a broad market average) has *declined* since 1962, and at an increasing rate, largely because of this misfit. In the words of Charles D. Ellis, institutional investing has become a "loser's game."[1]

The point of all this is that theoretical gains from short time horizons or holding

---

[1]"The Loser's Game," *Financial Analysts Journal*, July–August 1975, pp. 19 ff.

periods and rapid turnover are illusory in today's markets. Longer time horizons that encourage maximum investor participation in the stock market would seem to be more effective in practice.[2]

It is up to each investor to determine the appropriate time horizons and holding periods for (1) loss situations, (2) systematic periodic upgrading of portfolios, and (3) gain situations. These three types of cases are arranged in the order of the definiteness with which positive and widely applicable recommendations can be made, from the most to the least definite.

Losses Should Usually Be Taken Quickly

Accepting losses *fast* is a basic rule of successful personal portfolio management. This acceptance should be almost automatic. Investors probably lose more money by letting paper losses build up to justify their original judgment, however belatedly, than they do through any other investment error. Take a loss as soon as it is clear that the original estimate of the situation is not working out. You need not wait until you have long-term alternative use for the money, since the funds can be put in interest-bearing short-term investments that are instantly available.

The first step in handling losses properly begins as soon as a security is bought. You should clearly indicate in writing, for easy future referral, the *maximum loss* you are willing to take before admitting that a mistake has been made by you or some other security analyst. For example, let us suppose that a stock is bought at 40 in the belief that it is worth and should rise to 50 in the year ahead. Instead of rising, it drops to 38, then to 36, and then to 34. At what point should you admit that the original buy decision was wrong? If you are like many investors, you will decide to review the situation before selling. Perhaps the original decision is still correct, and you have been the victim of a general but temporary market decline. It is hard to avoid wishful thinking in making such a review, and the soundest advice is to be extremely skeptical and thus to favor the sell side.

On the other hand, more and more investors are discovering the benefits of cutting potential losses by systematically placing *stop-loss* orders under the purchase price after each common stock purchase. They never cancel such orders but let the market decide the wisdom of the original purchase. This practice has much to recommend it.

The price at which a stop-loss order is set should be determined by the relative volatility of the stock involved. A stock's beta is a satisfactory initial measure of such volatility. For a stock with a low beta, the stop-loss point could be 10 percent under the purchase price; for one with an average beta, the stop-loss spread could be 12 or 13 percent; and for one with a high beta, 15 or 16 percent. Such losses are large and sometimes unnecessary, but they protect investors against even more severe bear market declines. And if the sold stock is replaced by another, a general market recovery will mean price appreciation for the substitute issue that may fully offset the loss or even show a net gain.

There is also an important tax saving for individual investors in cutting losses while they are still short-term for tax purposes. Short-term losses can be used in full to offset short-term gains and up to $1,000 in fully taxed ordinary income. By contrast, $2 in long-term losses is needed to offset $1 of ordinary income. Accordingly, a week or two before any remaining loss situation in your portfolio is slated to become long-term, it becomes an urgent candidate for immediate sale. You should have to make very few such decisions.

---

[2]Similarly, tax law changes that would reward longer holding periods, such as declining capital gain tax rates in proportion to length of holding periods, would appear to be probably effective in reducing market instability and thereby increasing average investor return.

Frequent Systematic Upgrading Produces Higher Returns

The preceding conclusions on loss situations have been quite positive and highly probable. Similarly firm conclusions apply also to systematic portfolio upgrading but at a slightly lower order of probability.

Systematic overall portfolio upgrading is desirable at least every six months *regardless of market conditions* and as an entirely distinct and separate operation from realizing losses or gains on individual stocks. Here is how such systematic upgrading should be handled. The price changes for the past six months for each stock or other equity security in your portfolio should be reviewed and noted. Then, for an average portfolio of about twenty stocks, the two or three stocks that show the poorest price performance for this period should be sold. For larger portfolios of more than twenty-five stocks, the poorest-performing 10 to 15 percent of the holdings could be eliminated at six-month intervals.

Such systematic semiannual portfolio reviews may well make you appreciate some of your better holdings more than ever. Indeed, you may conclude that you would do better in the future by reducing the number of your holdings from, say, twenty to seventeen or from ten to eight by reinvesting the proceeds from the sale of your weaker holdings in your better securities. But always bear in mind the need for adequate diversification, as discussed above.

How to Decide Whether to Hold or to Cash in Profit Situations

Your answer to the key question of how frequently profits should be realized depends on many factors besides current market conditions and future prospects for your holdings. Also involved are your age, your tax bracket and the resulting impact of capital gain taxes (the higher the bracket, the greater the impact), the nearness of the date on which heavily taxed short-term profits become less heavily taxed long-term ones, and, finally, the availability of offsetting losses for tax purposes.

In addition, your answer to this question is related to your basic personal approach to timing investment purchases and sales. Thus, if you invest largely or exclusively for long-term appreciation, you may operate on the assumption that "good stocks are made to keep and not to sell" and take profits only when a formerly good company turns sour. Most investors know of cases in which stocks have been held in a family for generations, with each succeeding generation much richer than the preceding one. However, the statistical evidence is quite strong that succeeding generations would have been even richer had they and their ancestors taken profits more frequently. Even moderately successful timing pays off (see Section Two).

The practical choice for most investors is whether (1) to sell on a broad scale only when the peak of a bull market is thought to be near or at hand or (2) to sell and switch more frequently than that to improve annual rates of return. Of course, if your primary target is quick capital gain, you should be ready and willing to take profits as soon as feasible after the required holding period. On the other hand, if you are committed to a formula timing plan, it will give you overall selling signals, although the choice of *what* to sell is still up to you.

When investors in their seventies or older are liable to heavy capital gain taxes, they should be more responsive to letting paper capital gains on sound companies continue to ride even if some temporary price weakness is in view. As long as unrealized capital gains at the time of the investor's death in large measure escape heavy taxation, this policy is sound. However, there is almost unceasing pressure in Congress to impose capital gain taxes at death, and the current prospects for such legislation should be carefully watched by older investors and their investment managers.

To help you make up your own mind on whether to take profits only in terms of major bull and bear market swings or to take them more frequently and systematically, you will want to review the following key arguments on both sides.

Arguments for Major-Cycle Profit Taking Only

The reasons for this choice all add up to the conclusion that you will usually lose or make less money over the long run through frequent or periodic selling and switching. The three key arguments are:

1. *Frequent selling and switching tend to turn your attention away from your basic investment goals.* You may be tempted to take profits on your more successful investments and hold on to your less successful ones. Thus, your portfolio is apt to show quality deterioration over the longer term.

2. *Capital gain taxes on realized profits lead to steady erosion of your capital.* Such erosion occurs in moderate amounts at lower tax levels and in greater totals at or near the maximum 35 percent capital gain tax ceiling. For example, if you are a rich investor subject to the 35 percent rate and your $100,000 investment in a stock has doubled to $200,000 for a capital gain of $100,000, the federal government takes 35 percent of your gain, or $35,000, and state and local governments may take additional sums. So your capital remaining is not $200,000 but about $160,000 or less taking into account commissions and transfer taxes.

Thus, you now face the problem of finding investments for $160,000 with as good a profit potential as the $200,000 in stock you sold. This means finding one or more stocks worth $200,000 but selling for about $160,000, which is far from easy. The higher your capital gain tax rate, the bigger the bargain you must find to replace the investment in which you "took a profit."

3. *Buying and selling commissions and transfer taxes must also be paid.* These usually add 4 to 6 percent or even more to the cost of switching from one stock to another, and such costs are more apt to rise than to decline.

Arguments for More Frequent or for Periodic Profit Taking

These arguments (and there are more of them) add up to the position that you will come out ahead over the longer term by taking profits frequently or periodically rather than only at or near bull market peaks. The eight key points of this side of the case are the following:

1. *By taking profits periodically you can benefit from stock market swings.* You benefit especially from wide bull and bear market swings and possibly from smaller intermediate price swings as well. It would be a pity not to make the most of such fluctuations.

2. *New buying opportunities are usually available when or soon after you take a profit.* At almost any time, there are some stocks that are relatively undervalued and some industry groups that are performing better than the averages. Moreover, in sharply declining markets bonds or cash equivalents are better holdings than stocks.

3. *Spectacular price gains are often followed by equally sensational declines.* In such cases, trying to save capital gain taxes is an illusion.

4. *In other cases, spectacular price gains are followed by much slower advances.* In such instances, avoiding or postponing capital gain taxes may cost you more than you save because you will be forgoing profits from other investments with superior gain potentials.

5. *Normal market price swings usually enable investors to offset capital erosion resulting from taxes and buying and selling costs.* Table 56-2 shows the impact of long-

term capital gains taxes on selling and rebuying securities on which capital gains have been realized. Note that even at the top capital gain rate of 35 percent, if you were to double your investment before the capital gain tax (as in our earlier illustration), a market decline of less than 18 percent would permit you to restore your capital position. At the 25 percent rate, the needed decline is only 12.5 percent. Both spreads are well within the normal range of yearly or intermediate price fluctuations for most stocks.

6. *Unless you hold an appreciated asset until death or give it away as an approved*

TABLE 56-2 Impact of Long-Term Capital Gain Taxes on the Sale and Repurchase of Securities and Other Assets

IF your capital gain on the security or other asset is:	AND if your net effective combined capital gain tax rate (federal, state, and local)* is:							
	16%	18%	21%	25%	30%	35%	40%	45%
	Then you can repurchase the security or other asset without loss from tax erosion if, after you sell it, it declines by the appropriate percentage shown below from your selling price:†							
10%	1.5%	1.6%	1.9%	2.3%	2.7%	3.2%	3.6%	4.1%
20	2.7	3.0	3.5	4.2	5.0	5.8	6.7	7.5
25	3.2	3.6	4.2	5.0	6.0	7.0	8.0	9.0
30	3.7	4.2	4.8	5.8	6.9	8.1	9.2	10.4
40	4.6	5.1	6.0	7.1	8.6	10.0	11.4	12.9
50	5.3	6.0	7.0	8.3	10.0	11.7	13.3	15.0
60	6.0	6.8	7.9	9.4	11.3	13.1	15.0	16.9
70	6.6	7.4	8.6	10.3	12.4	14.4	16.5	18.5
75	6.9	7.7	9.0	10.8	12.9	15.0	17.1	19.3
80	7.1	8.0	9.3	11.1	13.3	15.6	17.8	20.0
90	7.6	8.5	9.9	11.8	14.2	16.6	18.9	21.3
100	8.0	9.0	10.5	12.5	15.0	17.5	20.0	22.5
125	8.9	10.0	11.7	13.9	16.7	19.4	22.2	25.0
150	9.6	10.8	12.6	15.0	18.0	21.0	24.0	27.0
175	10.2	11.4	13.4	15.9	19.1	22.3	25.5	28.6
200	10.7	12.0	14.0	16.7	20.0	23.3	26.7	30.0
250	11.4	12.9	15.0	17.9	21.4	25.0	28.6	32.1
300	12.0	13.5	15.8	18.8	22.5	26.3	30.0	33.8
400	12.8	14.4	16.8	20.0	24.0	28.0	32.0	36.0
500	13.3	15.0	17.5	20.8	25.0	29.2	33.3	37.5
600	13.7	15.4	18.0	21.4	25.7	30.0	34.3	38.6
700	14.0	15.8	18.4	21.9	26.3	30.5	35.0	39.4
800	14.2	16.0	18.7	22.2	26.7	31.1	35.6	40.0
900	14.4	16.2	18.9	22.5	27.0	31.5	36.0	40.5
1000	14.5	16.4	19.1	22.7	27.3	31.8	36.4	40.9

*The tax rates shown above combine federal capital gain tax rates up to a maximum of 35 percent (as of 1976) with possible additional and varying state and local capital gain taxes, *adjusted*, however, for the federal tax deduction made available by these additional taxes.

For example, investors with a top federal income tax rate of 50 percent are liable to federal capital gain taxes at 25 percent. If they are also subject to a state capital gain tax of, say, 7.5 percent and a local capital gain tax of 2.5 percent, their *effective* additional tax rate for both the state and the local tax is 5 to 7.5 percent plus 2.5 percent minus a 5 percent federal deduction (at the 50 percent top income tax rate). Accordingly, their net effective combined tax rate in the table would be 30 percent (25 percent federal plus 5 percent state and local).

†This table does not take into account the commission costs of either selling or repurchasing securities or other assets, nor does it consider the possible loss of income while an investor is out of a security or asset, which may or may not be fully offset by income from other interim investments.

charitable donation, you do not escape capital erosion by holding a stock indefinitely—you merely postpone it.

7. *Payment of a capital gain tax on the sale of securities results in a higher tax basis on your new securities.* As a result, your *future* tax liability may be correspondingly reduced. Indeed, from the tax standpoint, it is often preferable to pay relatively small capital gain taxes frequently than to pay a larger tax all at one time. By so doing, your *average* tax rate for the entire period could be lower. In addition, you will be freer to make your investment decisions primarily in investment terms rather than for tax reasons.

8. *In the mixed markets of most years, capital losses are usually available against which capital gains can be taken (and thus investment switches made) at little or no tax cost.* To the extent that this occurs, fears of tax erosion are illusory.

To sum up, the eight arguments presented above favor (1) concentrating on the combined probable future total return potential of your investments as compared with available alternatives and (2) paying relatively little attention to the impact of the long-term capital gain tax, which usually can only be postponed and not avoided.

Which Profitable Holdings Should Be Sold Periodically?

The problem of selecting profitable holdings for sale inevitably involves some form of *ranking*. We must sell the securities deemed to have less remaining profit potential than others, either for the visible future or for some specified period.

Such ranking procedures can be and have been intuitive, approximate, or relatively precise. About the first type, little can be communicated. So we are left with the practical choice of (1) being admittedly approximate, on the ground that we cannot usefully predict future stock prices, or (2) being systematically precise, in the expectation or hope that system and precision will be able to improve portfolio performance by worthwhile amounts. There is both theoretical and statistical evidence that such improvement is feasible.

First, here are some brief comments about the approximate approach still used by many investors. Stocks to be sold can be described or specified as (1) those that are greatly *overpriced*, or (2) those that have reached the *investor's price objective*, and (3) those that are judged to have *less future profit potential than other securities* on the investor's eligible list. Criterion 3 seems to be the most useful and decisive of these. There is no point in switching out of supposedly overpriced stocks or securities that have reached a specified target price unless you are fairly sure that there are other available stocks, bonds, or other investments on your eligible list that will do better than these candidates for sale. Accordingly, this judgment should be the decisive test in the approximate approach: If Stock A is sold, which eligible investment will provide a better future return?

Usefulness of Systematic Performance Rankings for All Eligible Securities

Clearly, criterion 3 could be used most effectively if all the securities in the investor's eligible list could be usefully ranked in the order of estimated probable price performance over some uniform holding period or time horizon such as six months, one year, or two years. Thus, if there were 100 securities on your eligible list, the ideal procedure would be to rank them in order of probable price performance from 1 (best) to 100 (poorest). Of course, such precision is unattainable in practice, and a *group* ranking system must be used. The eligible securities would be ranked in, say, three to five groups. As we have seen, this is the procedure employed by the Value Line Investment Survey, with great statistical success.

Given such proven superior statistical results, it would seem logical that all investors and profolio managers utilize the general Value Line methodology or a close approximation of it unless they have a system that can be statistically demonstrated to have even better results over a corresponding time period. As of 1976, no such system is publicly available.

Value Line Portfolio Technique for Utilizing Price Performance Ranks

The Value Line ranks more than 1,500 stocks for probable price performance in the year ahead in five balanced but equal groups, as follows: (1) the top 100 stocks, group 1; (2) the next 300, group 2; (3) the average middle majority of 750 or more stocks, group 3; (4) the next 300, below average, or group 4; and the bottom 100, group 5. The portfolio strategy recommended by the Value Line is as follows:

1. Buy only stocks ranked 1 (highest).
2. Hold such stocks as long as they continue to be ranked 1 or 2 (above average).
3. As soon as a stock drops to rank 3 (average) or below, sell it and switch to another eligible stock ranked 1 (highest).

Such a strategy would usually result in a complete portfolio turnover about once a year. However, the cost of such a turnover in double commissions and transfer taxes would be far more than made up by superior results.

It is difficult to disagree with the *logic* of the Value Line technique, although investors may not always see eye to eye on the specific rankings of individual securities by the Value Line. The only modification that may be appropriate is with respect to recommendation 3. A switch to another eligible stock ranked 1 may not be desirable near market peaks, when high-yielding bonds may temporarily provide a larger return than that of even the 100 best stocks with the top ranking of 1.

The proven superiority of the precise Value Line ranking system would seem to make older intuitive or approximate portfolio switching techniques obsolete. *It is accordingly recommended that at least the logic of the Value Line approach be adopted and utilized for any other method of ranking securities in a portfolio.*

Improving Portfolio Results by Utilizing Volatility and Leverage

If an investor or portfolio manager can keep in tune with the major direction of the relevant investment market (stocks, real estate, commodities, and so on) most of the time, rates of return can be substantially improved by the judicious use of different kinds of investment volatility and corporate and investor leverage. However, since investment risk is also increased simultaneously by such procedures, their use should also be accompanied by measures designed to minimize risk, discussed below.

Volatility and leverage are different but closely related financial forces. "Volatility" can be defined as the rate of variability in either the price or the rate of return of an investment. As we have seen, it is essential to try to distinguish between an investment's upside and downside volatilities whenever possible. In either case, the volatility of any investment results from general market forces, overall economic and business cycle conditions, the profitability of a company's operations, and the degree of leverage in its capital structure (capitalization leverage).

The proportions of an investment's volatility that result from these different factors will vary from one situation to another. Here are some of the main points about volatility to keep in mind:

1. The market forces affecting volatility include not only the general level and direction of investment prices but also the floating supply of a stock or other

investment and its volume of trading. These may change considerably over a period of time because of insider purchases or sales and market fads or fashions in industries or in individual stocks.

2. The unique business cycle sensitivity of a company is a special factor affecting volatility that should be considered and evaluated in addition to overall economic conditions. As a typical example, stocks of machine tool companies are normally much more volatile than those of food companies.

3. The capital structure of a corporation affects its volatility through what is known as "capitalization leverage." Here, leverage is effective because preferred stock, bonds, or other borrowed funds, which constitute a firm's "prior capitalization," have priority claims on earnings before the common stock. At any given time, however, the total of these prior claims is fixed in amount; it does not go up when earnings advance or go down when earnings decline. As a result, any increase or decrease in earnings above the fixed charges on prior capitalization has a multiplied effect on the earnings left over for the common stock and, it is hoped, on the price of that stock. Of course, earnings leverage is much more certain than price leverage; earnings may rise or fall while a stock moves in the opposite way or not at all.

The degree of earnings leverage varies directly with the relative amount of debt and other prior capitalization. The greater the total prior capitalization, the greater the leverage.

Common stocks of companies with sound capitalization leverage are attractive instruments for investors seeking long-term growth and inflation protection. Such leverage is usually a clue to a firm's determination to expand its operations at a rate higher than its own available cash flow would permit.

4. A company's volatility can also be affected by "operating leverage." This is the use by a company of its fixed or overhead costs as a lever to enable it to convert a relatively small change in sales into a relatively large change in earnings. Operating leverage becomes particularly interesting to investors as revenues approach a firm's break-even point.

A combination of high fixed costs (for plant, equipment, machinery, and relatively permanent executive and administrative personnel) and low variable costs (for materials and production workers) results in maximum operating leverage, that is, the greatest percentage change in profits as sales revenues advance or decline. Thus, extensive automation implies considerable operating leverage because of relatively high fixed overhead costs and relatively low variable labor costs. Consequently, profits for a highly automated firm will increase rapidly once its output rises above its relatively high break-even point.

But the reverse is also true. A highly automated firm typically needs a substantial volume of sales to support its relatively high fixed costs and resulting high break-even point. If its sales drop below the break-even point, its losses will be relatively larger. In other words, operating leverage works both ways. A less highly automated firm, with lower operating leverage but more flexible variable costs, could show a profit at lower levels of capacity.

Investor Leverage with Borrowed Funds

We turn now to *leverage that investors can make for themselves.* There are a great variety of ways in which borrowed funds may be used to increase the profit potentials (and the risks) of investing. Most of these specialized techniques are examined in detail in the treatment of specific investment areas in various sections of the *Handbook.*

Using borrowed funds is most advantageous when money and credit are plentiful. It is least desirable under tight money conditions. When money is cheap, margin requirements (and usually stock prices) are almost always relatively low.

Thus, the risk of capital loss is relatively small, and the chances of accelerated capital gain by the use of borrowed funds is relatively great. By contrast, expensive credit typically reflects peak boom conditions, in which both stock prices and margin requirements are relatively high. Here the chances of capital gain are reduced while the risks of loss are increased.

Similarly, if you borrow from a bank on your securities, bear in mind that, under very tight credit conditions, such loans are often among the first not to be renewed when the bank is short of lendable funds. This may compel you to sell securities at undesirable prices or at inconvenient times.

To sum up, if you buy or are thinking of buying with borrowed funds, there is an easy-to-apply risk yardstick. *Debt is safest when it is most feasible and increasingly dangerous as it becomes less feasible.* An excellent operating rule is to keep your current debt position at or below prevailing Federal Reserve Board margin requirements, even though you need not legally do so on previously acquired holdings. In addition, try to make certain that the securities you hold on borrowed funds have sufficient marketability to be sold quickly with minimum loss if you decide or need to sell them.

To determine your security buying power and cash withdrawal capacities under current or varying margin requirements, use the following three key formulas:

(1) Current equity = market value of securities held − debit balance (or + credit balance).

(2) Excess margin, current cash withdrawal capacity, or cash buying power = current equity − required margin.

(3) Marginable security buying power = excess margin ÷ margin requirement percentage.

Investor Leverage with Special Instruments

The important difference in this type of leverage, which relies primarily on warrants, calls, puts, and other options (discussed in Chapters 22 and 23) is that no money need be borrowed to achieve the desired leverage effects. *The instrument itself has the leverage built in.* A relatively small investment controls a potentially large profit swing, with no theoretical limit on the upside and with the downside risk limited at most to the total cost of the leverage instrument. This loss is extremely large as a percentage of the funds invested if the entire value of the leverage instrument is wiped out (as in the case of an unexercised call or put) but is still comparatively small in absolute terms. The loss will usually be less if the leverage instrument has residual value, as for a warrant.

Maximum Results by Combining Different Types of Leverage

In practice, it is often possible to utilize two, three, or even four varieties of leverage at the same time. Thus, purchase of a listed warrant could be combined with a corporation's capitalization and operating leverage to achieve triple leverage. If the listed warrant can be bought on margin, quadruple leverage results.

More usually, the investor can buy on margin the common stock of a company with capitalization leverage for double leverage. If the company also benefits from operating leverage, triple leverage will be achieved.

Improving Portfolio Results by Selling Short and Writing Options

In addition to (1) taking timely profits and losses, (2) systematic upgrading, and (3) the successful use of volatility, leverage, and leverage instruments, it is feasible for investors to improve portfolio returns by the proper employment of two other techniques: (4) maximizing return in bear markets by means of selling short and buying puts and (5) increasing portfolio income through the systematic selling of options.

Profiting from Selling Short. Short selling is a way of making money when stock prices are going down. It usually consists in selling a security (or commodity) that you do not own but have borrowed. You sell the stock first and buy it later in anticipation of a decline in its price. Your profit results from selling the originally borrowed stock at a higher price than you pay later when you buy the stock and return it. If such a gain is made, it is always short-term for tax purposes and is fully taxed as ordinary income even if the short sale was held for more than six months.

Most investors regard short selling as a highly risky operation. However, in the highly volatile, two-way markets of recent years, it would appear to be a useful means of hedging against downside risk.

Basic Precautions for Short Sellers. The following six dos and don'ts are the lessons of experience in selecting stocks for short sales:

1. Avoid selling short against the market trend, especially the intermediate trend, unless you have very special information about a stock. Short selling is better if the major trend is also down.

Since short selling is usually a short-term affair, it is important to utilize technical rather than value standards to determine the market trend. In other words, it is often dangerous to sell a stock short merely because it seems grossly overvalued by reasonable standards derived from past performance.

2. Despite this recommended reliance on technical methods, be particular about selling short against the *business* trend. In choosing short-sale candidates, it is usually safer to select companies and industries with poor business prospects for at least the year ahead.

3. Avoid stocks that are closely held or that have only a small number of shares outstanding. You may be caught in a short squeeze and thus have to pay a very high price when you buy to terminate the short sale.

4. Except in very special situations, when selling short shun stocks that pay substantial dividends, since these go to the lender of the stock.

5. For this reason, warrants, which are highly volatile and do not pay dividends, are good short-selling instruments.

6. Always protect your short position with a stop-loss order.

Writing Options for Higher Portfolio Income. Most investors who use calls, puts, and other options are on the buying side. But for every buyer of an option, there is a seller, or writer. Sellers are usually stock exchange firms or larger individual and institutional investors who wish to increase the income from their portfolios by a worthwhile amount. Such writers sell call options on securities that they own and would be willing to sell at prices somewhat above the current market, and they sell put options on securities that they would be willing to buy at prices somewhat below the current market.

Writing puts and calls as a fairly continuous source of additional income is particularly attractive when stock yields are low and capital gains hard to come by. With the listing of options since 1973, option writing has become more popular and feasible for greater numbers of investors.

How much you can currently get for selling an option depends partly on supply and demand. Thus, in weak markets and particularly in confirmed bear markets, writers will be more reluctant to sell puts, and puts on volatile stocks will tend to command larger premiums. On the other side, in rising markets and particularly in confirmed bull markets, writers will be more reluctant to sell calls, which will then command larger premiums, especially on volatile issues.

In general, you should favor selling calls on stocks that you believe will not rise high enough during the life of the options to make their exercise profitable.

Similarly, you should favor selling puts on stocks that you believe will not fall appreciably during the option period. In both cases, if you are correct, the option won't be exercised, and you will net the entire premium.

Sales of puts and calls should be systematically staggered over many months. It is wise to avoid selling too many options at one time and for closely bunched expiration dates because you may have to buy or sell more of your stocks than you planned to do if many of these options are exercised by their purchasers. A standard working rule is that no more than 20 percent of the value of options sold should expire in any one month.

Improving Portfolio Results with Personal or Special Substrategies

This miscellaneous subsection is designed to exploit the special contacts and abilities of many individual investors, investment analysts, and portfolio managers. For example, if an investor happens to be a chemist or a physician (or is a close relative of a friend of such a person), he or she may be in a position, a little before other investment analysts, to get in on the ground floor of a new drug therapy procedure that will greatly enhance the profits of a particular drug company.

Similarly, some investors, through personal or family connections, may have regular private access to significant corporate information before it is made public. While the private dissemination of such information may be in violation of Securities and Exchange Commission rules, it is often inadvertent or unavoidable.

Another source of above-average gain may be a connection with a competent special-situations analyst (see Chapter 16), with an arbitrage specialist who can guarantee an account a small but sure profit on a very short-term investment for a high annual rate of return, or with an investment analyst who is outstandingly knowledgeable in a particular field.

Investors and portfolio managers should be constantly on the lookout for such special chances to improve portfolio results. These opportunities have been grouped under the designation "substrategies."

Minimizing Risk of Loss with Stop Orders, Formula Plans, and Hedging Techniques

Reducing portfolio risk is the other side of the coin that calls for increasing portfolio returns. The latter takes advantage of *upside* volatility, while the former tries to avoid or minimize the disadvantage of *downside* volatility.

Stop Orders to Limit Losses.   In our discussion above of the desirability of taking losses promptly, we referred to the use of stop orders. In what follows the techniques involved are described in greater detail.

A stop order (also called a "stop-loss order") is either (1) an order to sell (or sell short) a security at the *highest* price obtainable if its market price falls to or below a price that you specify or (2) an order to buy a security at the *lowest* price obtainable if its price rises to or above a price that you specify. Here we are thinking primarily in terms of definition 1.

A stop order has the following four uses:

1. *To limit loss when you buy.* For example, you buy 100 shares of a stock at 25. You wish to limit your possible loss to about $300; so you place a stop order to sell at 22. If you have made a mistake and the price of the stock drops to 22, your stop order becomes a market order. Your broker will then sell your stock at the best price he or she can, usually somewhat below the 22 limit.

2. *To assure a minimum profit.* Again you buy 100 shares of a stock at 25. This time your judgment is right, and the stock rises to 35. You would like to be sure of a profit of at least $750; so you place a stop order to sell at 33. Should the stock drop back to 33, you will be sold out at a price as close to 33 as is feasible.

3. *To provide continuous profit protection.* The technique described in paragraph 2 can be used in a series of steps, going up on stock purchases and down on short sales, thus providing a continuous sliding-scale guarantee of a profit. This protective stop-order technique has been called "dangling stop-loss insurance." It is systematically applied in the investment timing procedure known as automatic trend following, which is analyzed in Chapter 9.

4. *To limit short-sale losses.* Continuing with the same example, let us suppose that you now think that your stock at 35 has outpaced the general market and is due for a relapse. You therefore sell it short at that price. You would like to limit your possible loss to about $300; so you place a stop order to buy at 38, at which point you will be bought out of your short sale if the stock moves against your expectations.

We have already noted that the key question of where to set the trigger on a stop order depends on the volatility of a stock as well as on its expected market behavior. In addition to the use of beta factor figures, it is helpful to study either line or point-and-figure charts of a stock before reaching a decision on a suitable stop point.

Despite a number of practical difficulties involved in executing stop orders, many careful investors and market traders enjoy the peace of mind that such orders provide. They recognize the basic truth that most investors will not quickly close out a position that has gone against them unless the transaction is carried out automatically for them by means of a stop order.

Stop orders are not always available on all stocks. Therefore, other means of limiting losses, particularly the hedging techniques discussed below, may have to be used in such cases.

Formula Plans to Cut Volatility.   Formula plans are another device that reduces risk by limiting volatility. However, most such plans curtail upside as well as downside volatility, thereby reducing return as well as risk. A detailed analysis of various types of formula plans will be found in Chapter 9.

Hedging Techniques to Minimize Capital Loss.   Options, warrants, and convertible securities may be employed as hedging instruments to limit losses and also to achieve small but highly probable net gains from the combined purchase-hedge operation. A brief summary follows (more details will be found in Chapters 21, 22, and 23).

Puts to Protect against Capital Loss.   You can protect yourself against capital loss by purchasing a put on a stock that you buy or own. If the stock declines in price, you can get out at the cost of the put because, through the put, you have a buyer at the original higher price. If the stock goes up, you have lost only the cost of the put. If you wish to achieve a long-term gain by using this procedure, you must buy a put good for more than six months under the special tax rules governing puts.

Stop orders may also be used for this purpose, usually at little if any cost and with no problems about long-term gain. Thus, they would seem to be preferable to puts for protecting yourself against capital loss.

Hedging Uses of Warrants.   Warrants can be used as a hedging device in at least two ways:

1. When the stock market is high, you may feel uneasy about being heavily invested in common stocks, but you are not sure that the bull market is over. In this situation, a broad warrant hedge is in order. You can shift 50 percent or more of your investment funds into bonds or cash equivalents and invest the remainder in fast-moving warrants. If the market continues to rise, the portion of your funds invested in warrants could show as much capital gain as if you had kept all your funds in common stocks. However, if you use this technique, it is important that you employ stop orders to limit losses on the warrants if the market reverses to the downside.

2. More speculative investors may also hedge systematically by buying warrants and selling short the related common stock at the same time. If the stock goes up, they will profit because the warrants should rise proportionately more than the stock. If the stock goes down, they may still profit whenever the total loss on the warrants is less than the gain on the short sale.

Hedging Uses of Convertible Bonds or Convertible Preferred Stocks.   Instead of warrants, convertible securities may be used for hedging purposes, thus combining income and capital gain from the purchase of the convertible and the simultaneous short sale of the related common stock.

Chapter **57**

Special Factors in Managing Institutional Portfolios

LEO BARNES

Most portions of the preceding chapters of Section Ten are fully or largely applicable (with appropriate modifications) to institutional as well as individual portfolio management. In this chapter we go on to analyze the special characteristics of most institutional investors. Our primary purpose is to explore the practical significance of these special features, both general and particular, in achieving optimal institutional portfolio performance.

In dealing with the special characteristics that are applicable to all or almost all institutional investors, we attempt to distinguish among factors involving (1) basic long-term portfolio *policies*, (2) intermediate and shorter-term portfolio *strategies*, and (3) day-to-day and week-to-week portfolio *operations*.

INSTITUTIONAL INVESTORS: THEIR SPECIAL CHARACTERISTICS

In comparing institutional with individual investors, the following distinctive features are well known and need only a brief summary:

1. *Longer life span and longer investment horizons.* Most institutional investors are perpetual, far outlasting mortal individuals. Their investment goals and related time horizons are thus usually long term rather than intermediate or short-term.

2. *Large relative size.* A portfolio of $100 million is small on the institutional scale. Portfolios of $500 million are increasingly common, and there are growing numbers of institutions with $1 billion or more in assets.

3. *Rapid growth.* Institutional portfolios have been growing much more rapidly on the average than have individual portfolios. This is true not only because greater numbers of individuals are turning their funds over to institutions, but also because some types of institutions, notably private and public pension funds, have been expanding continuously thanks to substantial periodic contributions with only minor concomitant distributions.

4. *Greater portfolio activity.* Not only has institutional security turnover been rising in the 1960s and early 1970s, but large current capital inflows have compelled more frequent investment and portfolio decisions to buy and to sell. This

greater portfolio activity calls for maximum professional and technical competence.

5. *Greater illiquidity.* This feature is a major result of institutional size. Despite lower institutional commission costs, large holdings of single investments cannot be sold as quickly or as cheaply as can smaller individual holdings. (The true total transaction costs of institutions are discussed below in the subsection "The Portfolio Mix.") Such relative illiquidity is still another reason for longer institutional time horizons.

6. *Different or special tax or tax-exempt status.* Most types of institutional investors are tax-exempt, and to a large degree their portfolio decisions can be made independently of tax considerations. In particular, for such institutions a dollar of ordinary income from interest or dividends is just as valuable as a dollar of capital gain and usually a lot less risky. Such tax exemption is one factor contributing to more rapid institutional portfolio turnover. Other institutional investors such as mutual funds or insurance companies operate under tax rules and regulations quite different from those applying to individuals, and these differences have a decisive impact on their portfolio operations.

IMPACT OF SPECIAL INSTITUTIONAL CHARACTERISTICS ON PORTFOLIO POLICIES

The six distinctive general institutional features outlined above have important implications for at least six key portfolio policies of most institutional investors: (1) the nature of individual portfolio holdings; (2) the portfolio mix among equities, priorities, and cash equivalents; (3) the time pattern of portfolio return; (4) the amount of portfolio volatility; (5) the level of portfolio risk; and (6) the degree of portfolio diversification and concentration.

Blue-Chip Nature of Most Institutional Holdings

The large portfolios of most institutions call for correspondingly large holdings of single issues. Liquidity needs demand that these large individual holdings be highly marketable. Thus, most institutions cannot rationally make substantial investments in smaller unlisted growth companies with limited marketability however alluring their promise of long-term return.

Of course, there is one type of exception to this general position. It occurs when portfolio management has made a specific policy decision to invest in a very special company in the justified expectation that, within the institution's time horizon, it will have become a larger listed company with satisfactory marketability—a Xerox or a Polaroid in the bud.

The Portfolio Mix: Stocks, Bonds, and Cash

The choice of an optimum portfolio mix among stocks, bonds, cash, and cash equivalents is probably the single most important decision of the portfolio manager. Such a decision has two main aspects: (*a*) What is the appropriate central or long-term average mix for any given portfolio? (*b*) Should this mix be changed from time to time, and if so, when and within what ranges? Let us first examine the latter problem.

The long-view time horizons and the large size of most institutional portfolio holdings would seem to be strong arguments against the high cost of periodic back-and-forth shifts of portfolio ratios of stocks to bonds or cash. An illustration of this principle is the relatively poor performance of many institutional portfolios in the decade from 1965 through 1974. Undoubtedly, one reason for such institutional underperformance often was the cost of excessively high institutional turnover.

The cost of turnover for institutional investors can legitimately be construed to include not only the relatively low institutional brokerage charges but also some or all of the cost of gradually selling out a big position, typically at lower and lower prices, and gradually buying a large block of replacement stock or stocks, typically at higher and higher prices. Obviously, such costs cannot be specified as precisely as commission costs; they vary from stock to stock, from time to time, from institution to institution, and from market to market.

However, over the long run, it has been estimated that the total round-trip cost of a large institution's turnover, including brokerage commissions, probably averages 10 percent or more of initial stock market value per trip. Even perfect or near-perfect timing of both major and intermediate market moves and of most individual stock moves (a combined prospect that seems unattainable in practice) would only somewhat reduce, not eliminate, such considerable institutional turnover costs.

The central implication of this analysis is that if turnover costs are not to fritter away performance results, the stock-bond-cash portfolio mix of large institutions investing for the long run, as well as the specific securities comprising such a mix, should be held relatively stable over long periods of time.

Let us now turn to the problem of determining the appropriate common stock ratio range in a large institutional portfolio. All studies of very long-term stock and bond performance show that, over a period of many years, listed common stocks have higher returns than high-grade bonds. Thus, there has been a strong initial statistical presumption in favor of a relatively high proportion of equities for institutional investors with long time horizons.

However, as stressed in our discussion of inflation risks in Chapter 5, such a conclusion would seem to be invalid for prolonged periods of above-average inflation like 1968–1975, especially when, as in many of those years, inflation occurs during recessionary times as well as booms. In such periods, even though bond prices may be declining as interest rates rise, common stock prices are often apt to be declining to an even greater extent. As a result, with interest yields far above dividend yields, bonds provide higher and safer cash returns than stocks.

Statistical evidence in support of this view is provided in a study by Frank C. McLaughlin for the investment counsel firm of Thorndike, Doran, Paine & Lewis, published in 1975, which shows the following:

1. Since 1950 bond yields have increased dramatically, while stock *earnings yields* (and, of course, the related dividend yields) have declined even more dramatically, until the bear market of 1973–1974. Comparing the data for the S&P 500-Stock Index and for new issues of high-grade corporate bonds, yields on bonds rose from 2.75 percent in 1950 to 7 percent in 1968 and to a range of 9 to 10 percent in 1974. By contrast, earnings yields dropped from a high of 17 percent in 1950 to 5.5 percent in 1968, stayed in the range of 5 to 7 percent from 1969 to 1973; soared above 13 percent at the end of the 1973–1974 bear market, and finally dropped back to a range of 8 to 9 percent in 1975.

2. As a result of these relative shifts, *since 1970 portfolios of high-grade bonds would have provided a higher total return than the S&P 500-Stock Index in almost every one of the twenty-two successive three-year periods ending with each calendar quarter through June 1975.* (Very similar comparative results would have been obtained if three-month Treasury bills or insured savings accounts had been used instead of high-grade bonds.) However, because United States inflation rates have retreated from the horrendous 10 or 11 percent of 1974, the preceding evidence, which is based on data for only the previous twenty-six years, may not be decisive for the later 1970s and early 1980s. It is therefore advisable to turn to other available studies, covering longer time periods than twenty-six years, for additional evidence on relative stock-bond returns and risks.

These studies show that the longer the time periods covered, the better the overall results for stocks as compared with bonds. Similarly, they also show that the longer the investment *time horizons* chosen within the total time period covered by a study, the better do stocks perform. Thus, another study by Thorndike, Doran, Paine & Lewis surveyed the 103-year period from 1872 through 1974. It found that by utilizing an investment time horizon of fifteen years there was not even one fifteen-year period within these 103 years that showed a negative return on a broad stock market index like the Cowles All Stocks Index (used before 1926) or the S&P 500-Stock Index (used since 1926). However, if the time horizon is reduced from fifteen to seven years, the chances of a loss in total equity return rise from zero to 4 percent, or 1 in 25. And if the investment time horizon is dropped to one year, the chances of a loss soar from 4 to 31 percent, or almost 1 in 3. Over the whole 103-year period, the average total annual return on stocks was 9.4 percent, or more than twice the average total return on high-grade bonds.

Of course, just as a 26-year test period may be too short for useful future projections, so may one of 103 years be too long. Let us therefore look at studies covering time periods falling between these two ranges, for which the results are so disparate.

Quite a number of studies, covering periods from the mid-1920s up through the 1960s and early 1970s, have been made. These years include the great bull market of the 1920s, the crash and Depression of the 1930s, World War II, and the postwar periods of boom and bust. And as might be expected, the results for this intermediate period are much more favorable for stocks than those for the shorter 1950–1975 period, but somewhat less favorable for stocks than the very long 103-year period. Here is what two of the more recent of such studies, covering the forty-eight years from 1927 through 1974, reveal:

1. A 1975 study by Professors Richard S. Bower and Kenneth J. McPartlin of Dartmouth utilized an extremely long time horizon of thirty-five years and assumed repeated annual investments of equal amounts either in high-grade bonds or in a conservative diversified stock portfolio. They found that, over several overlapping thirty-five-year periods from 1927 to 1974, investors who dollar-averaged in stocks would have earned more than investors who dollar-averaged in bonds for every such period.[1] Unfortunately, thirty-five years is much too long a time horizon to be of use to even the most conservative institution.

2. This impracticality is remedied in another historical study covering the 1927–1974 period, by Robert A. Levy, president of Computer Directions Advisors and a contributor to the *Handbook.* Dr. Levy utilized institutionally relevant ten-year periods for three types of portfolios, with the following results:

a. An *all-stock* portfolio consisting of the S&P 500 would have earned 5 percent or more in 84 percent of the ten-year periods from 1927 through 1974 and 10 percent or more in 46 percent of such ten-year periods. It would have lost money in 8 percent of such periods.[2]

b. An *all-bond* portfolio, using only AAA bonds, would have earned 5 percent

[1]Note that this thirty-five-year period is much longer than the fifteen-year time horizon used in the study for Thorndike et al., for which, based on 1872–1974 experience, the chance of a negative return from stocks in any fifteen-year period within those 103 years was also zero.

[2]Observe the significant difference between the Levy findings for ten-year periods going back to 1927 and the findings of Thorndike et al. for seven-year periods going back to 1872. The chance of loss in common stocks for the former, at 8 percent, is exactly twice as high as for the latter. By all logic, for identical time periods the chance of loss in common stocks for ten-year periods should be *less* than their chance of loss for seven-year periods. The only rational explanation would seem to be that the fifty-five-year period from 1872 through 1926 was more favorable for stocks than the forty-eight-year period from 1927 through 1974.

or more in only 18 percent of the ten-year periods from 1927 through 1974, but it would have lost money in none of such periods.

c. A *mixed stock-bond* portfolio (75 percent from the portfolio in paragraph *a* and 25 percent from the portfolio in paragraph *b*) would also have earned 5 percent or more in 84 percent of the ten-year periods from 1927 through 1974 and 10 percent or more in 39 percent of such ten-year periods, but like the all-bond portfolio, it would have lost money in none of such periods.

Clearly, the Levy findings would seem to highlight the attractiveness, for many institutional investors, of a stock-bond ratio of 75 to 25 percent. There appears to be the same chance of moderate gain as in an all-stock portfolio plus the same chance of no loss as in an all-bond portfolio. The only penalty is the smaller chance of earning a larger gain of 10 percent or more as compared with the all-stock portfolio.

In addition to Levy's significant historical findings, some practical considerations suggest that institutional caution is the better part of valor and that it would be wiser to include some high-yielding bonds in current portfolios. One such pragmatic factor is the reality of sales targets for institutions like mutual funds, for which performance scores are kept on an annual and even a quarterly basis. Below-average mutual fund performance over such shorter time horizons may lead to lower sales and higher redemptions in magnitudes unacceptable to management.

Another factor suggesting a somewhat larger proportion of bonds in institutional protfolios than has recently been deemed desirable is the fiduciary responsibility requirement of the Employee Retirement Income Security Act of 1974 (ERISA). While legally applicable only to employee benefit plans, this and related requirements are, because of overlapping managements, also having an impact on the portfolio strategies of other types of institutions.

Which Stock-Bond Ratios Work Best?

There are few definitive historical clues to which stock-bond ratio is most effective over the long run: 80/20, 75/25, 60/40, 50/50, and so on. As would be expected, statistical results vary from period to period and from year to year. Thus, for the relatively short five-year span from 1970 to 1975, it did not seem to make much difference which such ratio was chosen. Results were about the same in the end for almost all commonly used proportions.

However, the longer-term superiority of common stock returns over bond yields would seem to imply higher rather than lower stock ratios for long-term institutional investors. Another answer might be a modified variable-ratio formula plan, under which bond proportions are increased moderately as bond yields rise relative to stock yields (see the discussion on formula plans in Chapter 9).

**Time Pattern of Portfolio and Individual Security
Returns**

An institution's normal time horizon is the crucial factor in determining the favored time pattern for its portfolio return. Of course, institutions with high stock-bond ratios have relatively little actual control over future rates of return for their entire portfolios, which are in large measure the product of stock market and economic behavior. However, they may be able to influence somewhat their total portfolio return patterns by appropriate strategic decisions on individual stocks, bonds, and other types of investments.

Thus, institutions with longer-than-average time horizons could prudently invest in a number of developing long-term growth situations, with much higher returns in more remote future years expected to more than offset lower returns in earlier years. A major historical example is the securities of uranium producers, which were purchased by some institutions and other investors in the 1950s and 1960s in the expectation of major profits later in the 1970s (which are usually being realized). Of course, if such germinal long-term investments can be made with consistently favorable results year after year, an ideal pattern of return will be achieved.

On the other hand, some institutions may have uncharacteristically short time horizons for special reasons. An example would be the endowment fund of a college with a large current deficit. Here, at least temporarily, the institutional pressures may stress maximum short-term performance, emphasizing larger current income and a greater amount of realized capital gains.

Level of Portfolio Volatility

The lesson of United States stock market history, at least up to 1968, and of bond market history through 1975 would seem to be that the greater the recorded volatility of a *large* group of *listed* securities, the larger the average annual rate of total return (income plus capital gain). Institutions with large portfolios and long time horizons can take advantage of this probability by investing in *adequately diversified* groups of more rather than less volatile listed stocks or bonds, or both. Moreover, if upside volatility is distinguished statistically from downside volatility, superior results can be obtained by concentration on issues with relatively high *net upside volatility*.

Level of Portfolio Risk

The *Handbook* has repeatedly stressed that downside volatility is just one component of investment risk. So the acceptance of a high level of portfolio volatility combined with optimum diversification does not imply a similar generous or relaxed attitude toward the many other types of investment risk. To the contrary, these should be screened out of a portfolio to the maximum feasible extent both in the establishment of institutional eligible lists and in the final selection of securities from such lists (the procedures are summarized in Chapter 56). In practice, a low-risk portfolio will probably turn out to have a relatively high level of net upside volatility.

Required Degree of Portfolio Diversification or Concentration

A rule of minimum required diversification is as applicable to institutional investors as it is to individuals. However, the appropriate levels of diversification are normally significantly greater for institutions. This is due to such factors as (1) greater portfolio size, (2) legal and institutional diversification requirements, (3) problems of liquidity and marketability, and (4) the institutional ability to take advantage of higher stock volatility through greater diversification.

Because of such considerations, 100 or more stocks may be needed for large institutional portfolios rather than the 15 to 20 recommended for most individual portfolios. A $500 million portfolio consisting of 100 stocks would mean an average issue size of $5 million. This figure would double to $10 million for a $1 billion portfolio. Both totals are usually feasible in terms of marketability for either acquisition or sale.

The rule of minimum required diversification works differently for institutions that reject the high-volatility approach previously discussed. Despite the historical evidence, quite a number of conservatively oriented institutions have never accepted that approach. Still other institutions have become much more conservative since the collapse of "go-go" investing in the late 1960s. Both groups prefer to invest in lower-volatility high-quality stocks, plus high-yielding bonds of satisfactory or required quality.

The diversification needs of such institutional investors are much smaller than those of institutions utilizing the high-volatility approach, because overall portfolio risk has been reduced by the selection of higher-quality securities. It is therefore feasible and desirable to rely on a smaller number of issues that, it is hoped, will provide above-average returns. In such cases, maximum diversification would be inefficient.

There is also a small group of institutional portfolios that favor concentration on a relatively few "exceptional companies" and thus reject even moderate diversification. In effect, they regard themselves as special-situation funds, seeking maximum returns from a handful of high-performance growth situations. Their antidiversification philosophy is: "Carefully select a few choice eggs for your basket and watch that basket carefully." Such a philosophy is fine if and while it works, but it can result in large losses if mistakes are made and substantial individual holdings must promptly be liquidated.

Available diversification strategies are discussed in detail by Keith V. Smith in Chapter 54.

IMPLICATIONS OF SPECIAL INSTITUTIONAL CHARACTERISTICS ON PORTFOLIO STRATEGY

Portfolio strategies try to relate policy to reality. They involve those major decisions by portfolio managers that are crucial for the success or failure of given portfolio policies—judgments on the probable future direction of the economy, interest rates, and stock, bond, and other investment prices in general, on relative major investment and industry group performance, and on timely special-situation or great-company opportunities.

Strategic Management by Committees or by Executives?

Such judgments and decisions are made either by institutional executive or advisory committees or by individual portfolio managers. For optimum results, recent experience suggests that strategic and, of course, operational decisions are usually better made by full-time professional portfolio managers or several such managers than by investment advisory committees meeting once a month or even once a week. However, such committees may be very effectively utilized, first, in establishing or changing basic portfolio policies and, second, in reviewing and evaluating the strategies and operations of the portfolio executive or executives.

Single, Multiple, or Competitive Management for Large Institutions?

Are several portfolio managers better than one for very large institutions? Is rewarding competitive portfolio achievement effective or desirable? These questions arise because of the large size of many institutional portfolios, which makes it feasible to try to take advantage of plural management. One very large portfolio can be split up into two, three, or four smaller but still relatively large subportfolios, each under the supervision of a different portfolio manager.

Usually, these several managers will operate under the same basic portfolio policies, as established by the investing institution's directors or executive. However, it is also possible to have flexible alternative investment policies for the different subportfolios, so that one could be an all-stock growth fund, another a fund stressing income, still another a balanced stock-bond fund, and so on, either as permanent policy or as a policy response to current conditions.

Sometimes such multiple management of subportfolios is also made financially competitive management, with superior results appropriately rewarded, either by larger management fees for a given portfolio or by a bigger subportfolio for future management, resulting in larger future management fees. Of course, the basic purpose of transferring portfolio assets to more successful management is not so much to reward the manager as to improve overall future results for the investing institution.

Thus, many alternative management options are available for institutions. Which techniques are to be preferred on the basis of the available evidence? Here are some probable conclusions:

1. The greater efficiency and flexibility of multiple management of very large institutional portfolios make such management attractive. Two or three good portfolio managers handling somewhat smaller portfolios are apt to outperform one good portfolio manager handling a giant portfolio. Perhaps the major danger is costly excessive turnover of portfolios, particularly when such a program is begun, as each manager strives to tailor his holdings to his or her special convictions. The cost of such turnover could completely eliminate the benefits of investment superiority.

2. When we compare rewards through management fees geared to results and rewards from the shifting of assets to more successful managements, we find that the latter has not worked as well in practice as it promises in theory. In addition to the excessive turnover that this practice frequently engenders, any performance superiority often tends to be trivial and short-lived. As a result, all that happens is that a small percentage of an institution's assets is juggled back and forth among the several portfolio managers. Thus, management fees geared to results would seem to be the superior incentive. Of course, higher manager salaries are another alternative but one that would not seem to be as efficient as a performance bonus.

3. As for the choice of a single unified investment policy or multiple investment policies for plural subportfolios, statistical evidence is lacking. However, the dangers of excessive and expensive turnover would seem to be more likely with the multiple than with the unified approach, which therefore is to be favored unless new statistical evidence on results suggests the reverse.

Successful Portfolio Strategy Makes the Most of Major Changes in the Investment Environment

Logically, institutional portfolio strategy should succeed more often than individual portfolio strategy because of its broader and deeper management base. Large institutions have the facilities to evaluate systematically and take prompt advantage of significant economic, financial, industry, and market changes. This circumstance should enable them to increase the number and magnitude of their winning investments and reduce the number and magnitude of their losing investments. Similarly, it seems plausible that portfolio shifts and adjustments subsequent to initial selections, if they are based on generally correct major strategic decisions, will turn out better on the average than separate, isolated, or impulsive changes.

All in all, if three-fourths of an institution's investment gains typically come from the best one-fourth of its portfolio, while three-fourths of its losses come from the worst one-fourth, sound portfolio strategy could plausibly set a target of increasing the top gain area to one-third while reducing the maximum loss area to one-sixth.

Index Fund Approach as a Useful Strategic Tool

Despite the evident logic of the preceding paragraph, it is a significant fact that many institutional investors, while undoubtedly performing better than most individual investors, have in recent years failed to keep up with the popular averages, especially with the fast-moving Standard & Poor's 500-Stock Index. One estimate, by Charles D. Ellis in 1975, is that, over the preceding decade, fully 85 percent of professionally managed portfolios failed to match the cost-free and turnover-free performance of the S&P 500.

Such institutional performance has been widely regarded as disappointing and inadequate. An increasingly popular proposed method of improving institutional performance, so that it at least matches that of an index like the S&P 500, is to have a portfolio that always exactly duplicates the composition and relative proportions or weights of the chosen index—in effect, an index fund.[3]

The widespread adoption of this technique would have some very curious and serious consequences. Thus, if, say, even one-tenth of all institutional investors successfully aped the S&P 500 and thereby outperformed many other institutional investors, there would be a rush of institutional imitators jumping on the index fund bandwagon. Institutions' widespread purchases of the same major index stocks and their concomitant avoidance of all other stocks would obviously tend to boost the performance of the S&P 500-Stock Index and depress the performance of the rest of the market.

Naturally, this would induce an increasing number of institutions to adopt the index fund technique and encourage individual investors to shift their assets to the various index funds, thus reinforcing and widening the performance gap between the S&P 500 and the rest of the market. Most traditional security analysis and portfolio management would become unnecessary, and many financial analysts, executives, and supporting personnel would lose their jobs.

Thus, the ultimate logical outcome of the index fund approach would be to turn over the essentially uniform operations of all the many index funds that had come into operation to the single company that could handle them most efficiently and at the lowest cost: Standard & Poor's (probably by that time it would have changed its name to Standard & Good).

Of course, another and more worthy consequence of the index fund approach could well be the counterdevelopment of funds and other institutional investors that claimed or aimed for performance *superior* to that of a broad market index like the S&P 500. And, ironically, perhaps the simplest way to achieve at least a small margin of superiority over an index or an index fund would be to utilize the latter as an initial strategic tool. For the same type of analysis that enables one to construct an index fund that exactly matches the performance of an index can logically be extended to construct a *"near-index" fund that, more often than not, could outperform that index.*

For example, the stocks in an institutional portfolio could be classified and arranged in exactly the same industry breakdown used for a market index like the S&P 500-Stock Index. Then, the relative proportions of holdings in each industry for both the portfolio and the index could readily be compared and the differences noted. Each such difference, plus or minus, would then have to be fully justified by the portfolio manager, with appropriate statistical and other evidence, to show specifically how it contributed to portfolio performance superior to that of the index.

By thus focusing on specific portfolio differences and adjustments that could fairly quickly result in superior performance as compared with the index standard, the probability of success would seem to be significantly greater than for a more generalized portfolio effort that ignored the index. Deviations from the index and its industry distribution pattern could be made one at a time and only after the most careful analysis of both fundamental and technical factors.

---

[3]It should be noted that even if this index technique were completely successful and the investment performance of institutional portfolios exactly equaled that of a market index like the S&P 500, the *results for investors* would still be below the index performance because institutions have operating and administrative expenses that an index, of course, does not incur.

In this way, a judgment that proved erroneous could be quickly reversed without too much damage to portfolio results, while the implications of the error might be successfully used in future adjustments of the index fund.

In making comparisons of portfolios with indices, it is useful to use more than one index. Three or four market indices are usually enough, and one of them should be an *unweighted* index, like that of the Value Line Investment Survey. Such an unweighted index is useful as an indication of how the typical individual investor is faring. The S&P 500 and the Dow Jones averages are more indicative of how listed blue-chip stocks are doing. When institutions also invest in stocks that are not listed on the New York Stock Exchange, the American Stock Exchange Index or the NASDAQ indices can also be useful. See Chapter 2 for an explanation of the construction and behavior of these various market indices.

IMPLICATIONS OF SPECIAL INSTITUTIONAL CHARACTERISTICS ON CURRENT PORTFOLIO OPERATIONS

As the preceding discussion of indices and index fund analysis suggests, institutional portfolio policies and strategies require continual, systematic portfolio analysis and evaluation for optimum implementation. Ready institutional access to computer facilities gives them a notable analytical edge over individual investors, who usually lack such access.

How Special Computer Programs Can Help Performance

In addition to the standard analytical programs that are available from computer companies or programming firms, each institutional investor should try, with the help of its programmers and programming advisers, to develop special programs that can be used rapidly and effectively to improve portfolio performance.

Any special analytical technique that has been developed by an institution in the course of its portfolio operations should be promptly computerized. A fruitful methodology developed in recent years that can often be helpful in this connection is "decile analysis." In this approach, any desired characteristic of a company or its stock is arranged and ranked in 10 percent groups, both for the companies in any given or proposed portfolio and in some reference group of companies such as the Standard & Poor's stock indices, the institution's master eligible list, or even all listed stocks or all stocks in a computer bank.

For example, let us suppose that a portfolio manager is stressing rapid growth in company profitability at relatively reasonable stock prices. What is desired is relatively rapid growth in the rate of return on a company's total capital over the past five years but only if the stock is available at a reasonable price (relative to current price-earnings ratios for some standard reference list or index). A decile analysis of both characteristics is run off by computer for, say, the S&P 500-Stock Index and the institution's current eligible list.

What is wanted are companies in the higher decile ranks for profitability but in the lower decile ranks for price-earnings ratios. It is hoped the institution's eligible list has more such companies than the S&P reference list and that some candidates for purchase or further investigation turn up. Alternatively, some companies on the S&P list but not on the eligible list might be discovered to be interesting in terms of the dual starting requirement, and they are explored for possible inclusion in the eligible list.

Similar analyses can be made of the concentration or diversification, in terms of deciles, of any investment characteristic that is interesting at any given time: earnings growth, yield, volatility, labor and other costs, and profit margins. More complex decile analyses would involve various useful or profitable *combinations* of desired company and stock characteristics.

Take Full Advantage of Brokers' Research

This advice is perhaps at the other end of the spectrum from decile analysis by an institution's computer. There is no good reason why institutional investors should not make the most of the research facilities and output of the brokers who execute their orders, which may generate commissions from a large institution to the tune of hundreds of thousands or millions of dollars per year.

Traditionally findings of brokers' research go to the institution's own security analysts, who then exercise a sort of veto power, so that if they do not agree with the brokers' findings, these are not passed on to the institution's portfolio manager. By contrast, a more recent approach has the brokers' recommendations going directly and exclusively to the portfolio manager, who can thus compare them with the in-house recommendations. Perhaps the most suitable procedure is a combination of the two practices. This would hurt nobody's feelings and encourage joint discussion of brokers' recommendations by the security analysts and the portfolio manager.

FROM GENERAL PRINCIPLES TO DETAILED RULES
FOR PARTICULAR INSTITUTIONS

The generalized description of and principles for institutional portfolio policies, strategies, and operating procedures provided in the preceding subsections are in practice flexibly adjusted to different types of institutional investors' characteristics and needs. These special characteristics of individual institutions can be analyzed most efficiently under five main headings:

1. What is the institution's primary purpose, its reason for existence? In particular, is it primarily beneficiary-oriented or sales- and profit-oriented, or some mixture of both?

2. Precisely how is the institution compensated for portfolio management, and how are its portfolio results measured?

3. What legal requirements on policies, strategies, and operations apply to the institution at federal, state, and local levels?

4. How are the institution and its clients or beneficiaries taxed on income, other payments, and realized capital gains at federal, state, and local levels?

5. Are any other special institutional constraints, specific or intangible, relevant to current portfolio operations?

Clarifying and Specifying Institutional Purposes and Beneficiaries

Institutional investors can be viewed as primarily self-oriented or as primarily beneficiary-oriented. In most cases, of course, such orientations overlap; so the accent here is on the *primary* purpose.

Thus, a mutual fund is typically run for the maximum profitability of its management company and the latter's stockholders. But to achieve this primary target it tries very hard to enrich the investors in its shares.

By contrast, a nonprofit college endowment fund aims primarily to improve the lot of its college beneficiary through successful investing. To the extent that it succeeds, however, it will also usually increase the income and wealth of the endowment fund's investment management through higher compensation.

As a third example, let us take a tax-exempt corporate pension plan. Its beneficiaries are primarily the workers and executives participating in the plan, who are promised given levels of retirement benefits. Therefore, the initial target of the pension fund's portfolio management is to achieve the level of return needed to provide those retirement benefits in the future. However, there are often additional pressures from the corporate sponsor of the pension plan for better investment performance than the minimum required rate of return in order to reduce future corporate contributions to the pension plan. And, of course, if these two investment targets are met, the pension fund's investment adviser will also benefit from higher compensation.

As a final contrasting example, let us consider a private charitable foundation or trust set up by a wealthy individual for tax and estate purposes as well as for charity and with no rigid annual commitment to charitable beneficiaries. In this case, the target of maximum near-term performance may be nonexistent except as a matter of professional self-esteem for the managers of the foundation's investments.

Given the possibilities of such mixed purposes, an institutional investor must carefully specify and rank its several investment purposes, beneficiaries, and resulting targets.

Fulfilling Federal, State, and Local Legal Requirements

Compliance with various federal, state, and local legal requirements obviously affect institutional portfolio operations very specifically and immediately and on a priority basis. If one can invest only in listed companies with a ten-year record of uninterrupted dividends, this requirement clearly must be one's first portfolio filter. Similarly, an institution's diversification rules frequently will be determined largely by laws covering ownership in, and voting control of, individual companies. In the case of investment companies, of course, diversification is substantially influenced by the eligibility requirements for federal tax exemption.

If the laws of several or many different states apply to an institutional investor and are in disagreement, each must be observed for operations and sales within each state's jurisdiction. Sometimes, however, it is feasible to take the most stringent or restrictive state requirement and use it to set a single policy for an institution's nationwide activities. For example, the maximum state diversification requirement frequently becomes a portfolio manager's national norm.

For private employee pension funds in particular, the requirements of the Employee Retirement Security Act are detailed and complex and must, of course, be fulfilled before other optional portfolio policies and strategies can be implemented. In particular, ERISA's provisions on fiduciary responsibility and personal liability, on diversification, and on bond valuation (bonds may be valued at amortized cost in calculating pension contributions) have led many pension fund managements to increase their holdings of bonds and real estate and reduce common stock ratios.

Impact of Tax Differentials and Exemptions on Portfolio Management

Federal, state, and local provisions for the taxation of income, realized capital gains, and payments and distributions from capital, by both institutions themselves and their customers or beneficiaries, have an important if not a major influence on portfolio management. Notably, institutions for which both income and capital gain are completely tax-free for themselves and their beneficiaries have the enviable option, when interest rates are high, of being able to choose assured high-level income rather than seek potential but hypothetical capital gain.

Much the same is true for institutions such as pension and profit sharing funds in which, although future distributions to beneficiaries are taxable in part to the latter under often-complicated rules, income and realized capital gains can both be accumulated tax-free by these funds prior to such asset distributions.

On the other hand, institutional investors such as mutual funds that, from the tax point of view, are essentially conduits for their shareholders, should at all times bear clearly in mind the various tax positions of the latter when making portfolio decisions. It may sometimes be the case, especially for large diversified funds, that these several shareholder tax positions effectively cancel each other out, so that portfolio decisions may be made only on investment considerations. But such a position should not automatically be assumed to apply.

Adjusting to Other Special Institutional and Psychological Constraints

Finally, certain institutional and psychological constraints, involving the institution itself, its personnel, and its clients, from quite specific postures to more subtle prejudices and other intangibles, have some impact on portfolio procedures. These usually involve some resistance to new ideas and perhaps may be summarized in the single term "tradition." These possible constraints should certainly be subjected to critical analysis from time to time, in an effort to determine whether they are still appropriate, valid, or effective. At the other end of the scale, there are particular strategies or substrategies (see Chapter 56) which are special to an institution, which can improve portfolio results, and which should certainly be maximized.

Keeping Institutional Portfolio Rules Usable and Current

Both the general and the specific principles and factors explored and analyzed in this chapter should terminate in a carefully written and edited set of portfolio procedures, rules, and guidelines for each institutional investor. Every effort should be made to keep such guides fully updated, completely current, and revised as necessary, with a looseleaf or other revisable binder to hold them. They should become the indispensible "bible" for an institution's portfolio managers.

Chapter **58**

Case Study: The Investment Management of State and Local Government Pension Funds

RUDOLF HAUSER

THE NATURE OF GOVERNMENT PENSION PLANS

The average life expectancy at birth in the United States in 1930 was almost sixty years; in 1975 it was more than seventy-one years. At age sixty-five, a man is now expected to live more than thirteen years, and a woman more than seventeen years. Because of the absolute level of and steady growth in real income in the United States, society has come to demand paid retirement as a right. Yet, in the face of the rising length of the retirement period and a decline of more than 60 percent in the purchasing power of the dollar since 1947, it has been almost impossible for most persons to have saved adequate sums to provide for a comfortable or even, in some cases, a subsistence standard of living in their twilight years. This problem has been met partially by the introduction of pension benefits by government and industry and by the steady expansion of the social security program.

Growth and Magnitude of Government Pension Plans

The earliest government retirement programs can be traced to the military retirement system and to the informal plans for teachers, police, and firemen in the latter part of the nineteenth century. Several formal state and local government retirement plans were established in the first third of the twentieth century. The civil service retirement system for federal government civilian employees was instituted in 1920. The mid-1930s and early 1940s saw the start of a rapid growth in the number of teacher and general employee retirement systems. Since 1972 more than 2,300 separate systems have been administered by state and local governments.

These plans play an important role in the United States economy. As of 1975 it is estimated there were about 11 million members in state and local systems, with more than 1.5 million receiving benefits. The federally administered civilian systems (excluding social security) had close to 5 million additional members, with more than 1.4 million receiving benefits. In the fiscal 1974–1975 period, state and local government systems' benefits and withdrawal payments were $7.5 billion, government contributions were $9.1 billion, and employee contributions were $4.5 billion. The system's cash and security holdings totaled $98.1 billion.

Financial assets of state and local government retirement funds grew at an 11.8 percent compound annual rate over the twelve years ending in fiscal 1974–1975, reflecting the rapid growth of the number of government employees, their salaries, and the liberalization of pension benefits. Over the most recent five years this growth was slightly faster, at a 12.3 percent rate. These trends are generally expected to continue, although at a much more subdued rate. The author would not be surprised to see the funds' assets swell to about $150 billion by 1980.

Nature of the Benefits Provided by Government Pension Plans

In most of the existing plans, both the employer government and the employees contribute. A few plans use a money purchase approach, in which benefits are determined solely by the contributions to and earnings of the system rather than by benefit formulas; some plans use this purchase approach for employee contributions only.

The commonest method is to pay benefits according to a predetermined formula, most frequently a monthly amount equal to a certain percentage, such as 1.5 or 2 percent, of final average salary times the number of years of service. Final average salary is usually defined as the last five years, the best five years in ten, and so on, although some systems use longer periods, and some, such as the New York City police and teachers, retire employees based on their last year's salary. Naturally, there are many variations among these formulas, including differences in the percentage for length of service and varying percentage rates for different salary levels (to integrate plans with social security and so on). Only a few plans base benefits on career earnings rather than on final average salary.

The increasing use of benefits based on final average salary has protected many government workers against both rising prices and increases in the standard of living during their working years but has not afforded them full protection from the ravages of inflation during their retirement years. To solve this problem, some retirement systems have enacted automatic increases in retiree benefits at a fixed percentage per annum (for example, the employees' retirement system of the state of Hawaii) or of the change in the Consumer Price Index up to a specified percentage (for example, the Colorado Public Employees' Retirement Association). However, it is ad hoc increases from time to time that have been used most frequently to help retired members.

Some systems have created variable annuities into which employees may voluntarily place all or some of their contributions. The federal civil service system provides for increases during retirement based on changes in the Consumer Price Index. In some cases these increases are financed by a higher employee contribution rate, and in others increases are payable only out of earnings in excess of some assumed rate. However, the increases often are financed by the taxpayer. It might be noted that well over half of state and local government employees are also covered by social security.

In addition to retirement payments, most governments also provide death and disability benefits. Members leaving the system are entitled to withdraw their contributions, usually with some credited interest. Vesting of retirement benefits is generally provided after five to twenty years of service. Benefits not related to separation from service, such as health benefits, also are offered, and on occasion they are administered by those responsible for the retirement benefits.

To provide for future benefits in a systematic way that (1) matches costs with services purchased, (2) avoids future excessive drains on a government's resources, and (3) provides greater assurance that benefits can be paid, government retirement plans are supposed to be funded in advance of payments. Such funding must consider both current and past service costs. These past costs relate to credited service before the inception of the plan and increased benefit rates applied to service credited previously at lower rates.

Although many systems, particularly in the western United States, provide for amortization of past service costs over a reasonable number of years, the funding policies of many others are inadequate. This can be quite costly to future generations of taxpayers, as some systems have already learned. For example, efforts to fund current and past liabilities raised the planned employer contributions to Detroit's policemen and firemen retirement system for the 1972–1973 fiscal year to more than 55 percent of the planned payroll.

INVESTMENT POLICIES OF STATE AND LOCAL GOVERNMENT PENSION FUNDS

Safety of Principal

Given this historical and statistical background, let us examine the investment needs and limitations of state and local government retirement systems. Except for money purchase plans, the employer governments are liable for a specified level of benefits, which must be met if necessary out of future taxes. Because of this taxing power, employees have some security beyond the plan's assets. However, many communities do decline in size or wealth, or both, and future taxpayers may refuse or be unable to tax themselves at rates sufficiently high to make up for possible investment losses in pension fund assets or for inadequate funding. Failure to achieve the actuarially assumed rate of return would obviously increase future contribution requirements. Hence, there is a definite need not only for a reasonably adequate level of funding but also for a prudent investment policy giving full consideration to the requirement of *safety of principal*.

Rate of Return

A *high rate of return* is also an important consideration. Investment returns help reduce the employer's contribution burden. With the cost of government services and tax burdens rising so rapidly, any relief on the cost side is most welcome. More important, liberalization of benefit formulas over time, increased salaries (most plans calculate benefits on final pay bases), and ad hoc or other adjustments for cost-of-living increases tend to escalate pension funding needs above initial actuarial assumptions. Investment earnings in excess of actuarially assumed rates help to overcome these additional costs to some extent.

Plan members are also aided when greater investment earnings are directly reflected in variable annuities and money purchase plans and indirectly in other plans, because higher earnings may increase legislators' receptivity to increasing benefit levels. This suggests that although extremely risky investments should not be undertaken, most funds can and should shoulder risks beyond those encountered in the highest-grade corporate and government obligations.

Liquidity

Most pension funds' assets will continue to grow far into the foreseeable future, and most benefits to be paid are of a fairly predictable and gradual nature. Although death benefit payments and withdrawals can create large one-time withdrawal needs, the probable levels seldom would necessitate any significant *liquidity* need except in very small systems. Consequently, these pension funds normally have only a small need for liquidity and probably would not have to sell large amounts of assets at temporarily depressed prices. This circumstance greatly enhances their ability to purchase assets that may undergo considerable cyclical fluctuation but entail only modest risk on a long-term basis. Naturally, some cash and very liquid assets must be retained, but in most funds less than 5 percent of assets is probably sufficient for this purpose. Some liquidity in less conservative assets is also desirable to give the fund a certain amount of flexibility for switching investments. This latter need is greater for larger funds having $1 billion or more in assets than for a small fund with assets of only a few million dollars.

Use of Tax-exempt Bonds

Like their private counterparts, state and local government pension funds are *not subject to any tax liability;* so they need not consider the tax consequences of their investment policies. This circumstance would appear to make investments in municipal securities normally undesirable. Nonetheless, it is argued that the retirement fund should not be looked at separately from its employer government and that purchase of the sponsor government's securities would reduce the taxpayers' interest costs. This is an entirely valid point of view because the taxpayer bears the ultimate burden of all government costs.

If state and municipal bonds were sold directly to the pension fund, underwriting expenses would be eliminated, and the government would increase its income tax revenues to the extent that local investors might have fewer locally tax-exempt issues to buy than they desire to hold. However, it is unlikely that all tax-exempt bonds sold to the public would have been purchased by local investors; and, more important, the typical local income tax rates (assuming there even is an income tax) are such that the added revenues raised on other issues held by local investors in lieu of the desired local municipal bonds would likely be less than the interest differential between municipal and corporate issues. Hence, one must conclude that municipals are basically an unattractive investment for state and local government pension funds.

The financial difficulties experienced by New York City in 1975 raised some new questions with regard to investment in the parent government's securities. After many years of trying to reduce their holdings of municipal securities, the New York City retirement funds found themselves forced to agree to purchase $2.5 billion of Municipal Assistance Corporation bonds as part of a plan to keep New York City from going technically bankrupt. Whereas the funds had just recently sold a package of municipals to enable them to invest in corporate bonds, they now had to sell packages of corporate bonds so that they could bail out the city by investing in tax-exempts. (Of course, on the other side, it should be noted that the interest rates on the new tax-exempts were relatively high.)

What is involved here is a conflict of interest between the active working membership and those already retired or about to be retired. If a private corporation seems as if it might not survive, the retirees and those with large vested benefits would clearly feel more secure if they had an adequately funded pension fund invested elsewhere than in their own company's securities. One would think that those in similar positions would feel the same about a municipal retirement system. But the younger active employees might be far more willing to risk sacrificing an uncertain and distant benefit in order to reduce the risk of more immediate layoffs, wage freezes, and pay cuts.

When the possibility of such a conflict might arise, there is much to be said for a money purchase approach and a procedure for each employee to decide what should be done with his or her own share of the fund. This is not the sort of moral predicament in which trustees of such a fund should have to find themselves. Nor should the fund have to keep a special highly liquid reserve just to be able to bail out the blunders of the local government at very short notice.

Nevertheless, the investment manager of a state or local government retirement fund might do well to keep an eye on the fiscal affairs of the employer government and the related political situation in order to be able to appraise the chances of being placed in a situation similar to that of the New York funds and to be ready to adjust his or her investment strategy and liquidity needs accordingly. The evolution of fiscal difficulties might range from cutbacks of contributions to the funds of varying magnitudes to the greater extreme evidenced in New York. Purchase of the parent's securities under adverse circumstances could invite income tax problems for plan members. Such problems were avoided in the New York case only through special federal legislation.

Other Policy Factors

Stability of income is not an important investment consideration for most pension funds because their goals are long term, disbursements are predictable and gradual, and usually contributions are larger than disbursements. Hence the emphasis should be on total return, including both realized and unrealized capital gains on common stock transactions.

One of the major differences between private and public pension funds is that the latter's investments are governed by somewhat *stricter specific state government regulations.* The public funds' dependence on legislators for investment rules further complicates the matter by adding political considerations. Far more significant is the fact that the laws often severely limit the choice of investments.

A related factor is the sophistication and talents of the *decision makers* and the size and quality of their *investment staffs.* Often the boards of trustees, which have ultimate responsibility for investment decisions, are composed of political figures and employee members who have limited financial backgrounds. The problem is particularly acute for smaller funds. Often such small funds are run on a part-time basis by a government official who has little investment expertise. Even the larger systems frequently lack the staff necessary to run an aggressive investment operation. There is also a question of whether governments are willing to provide competitive pay structures for investment personnel.

To counter these disadvantages, many systems use outside professional consultants. However, the consultants' advice is usually subject to approval by system officials or the board of trustees before action can be taken, although there has been a recent trend toward allowing outside managers greater discretion. Furthermore, the systems have often been unwilling to pay fees that would justify intensive efforts on the consultants' part.

These management limitations decrease the ability of many of the retirement systems to assume a level of risk that would otherwise be justified. In addition, the limited size of many systems reduces their ability to diversify and lowers the level of risk that they can undertake on any specific investment in order to obtain an acceptable overall risk level.

HOW STATE AND LOCAL GOVERNMENT RETIREMENT SYSTEMS HAVE CONDUCTED THEIR INVESTMENT OPERATIONS

Given the preceding investment criteria, it may be of interest to review how state and local government retirement funds conducted their operations in the past. During the 1950s government officials and fund managers were still mindful of the financial failures of the 1930s. They emphasized safety of principal, as evidenced by the breakdown of their financial assets in fiscal 1957. At that time, fully 39.9 percent of assets were invested in federal government securities, and another 25.8 percent were invested in state and local government securities. A modest 26.3 percent of assets were invested in corporate bonds, while stocks accounted for a paltry 1.4 percent of the total.

However, as confidence in the federal government's ability to avoid major recessions grew, as governmental employee costs rose rapidly, and as corporate pension funds set an example by establishing more aggressive investment policies in the 1950s, an effort was begun to reduce government issue holdings in favor of higher-yielding corporate bonds. It became increasingly evident to the decision makers that the tax-exempt feature of municipals offered no benefit to these retirement funds. After peaking at $4,403 million at the end of fiscal 1961, these holdings fell to $728 million by the end of fiscal 1975 through maturities and outright sales. Federal government holdings reached a peak by year-end of fiscal 1965 and had been reduced by $3,938 million by the end of fiscal 1973. There was a sharp reversal of this trend in 1974–1975, but 66 percent of the federal government securities held at the end of fiscal 1975 were in generally more attractive agency issues.

Most of the increases in the first half of the 1960s were in corporate bonds and mortgages. From the end of fiscal 1960 to year-end of fiscal 1965, holdings of corporate bonds rose from 32.9 percent of assets to 47.5 percent, and mortgages increased from 6.4 percent of assets to 10.6 percent. During this period stockholdings rose only from 2.1 percent of assets to 4.5 percent. The move toward greater corporate bondholdings continued, although at a slightly more subdued pace, with corporate bonds comprising 56.2 percent of assets at the end of fiscal 1971. Since then, the relationship of corporate bonds to total assets has been relatively steady, falling slightly to 54.7 percent of the total at the end of fiscal 1975. The relative importance of mortgage holdings increased hardly at all through fiscal 1971 but fell sharply thereafter, from 11.2 percent of assets at the end of fiscal 1971 to 7.5 percent at the end of fiscal 1975. The most dramatic shift was the increase in corporate stockholdings to 22.2 percent of assets at the end of fiscal 1975. Highlights of the changing composition of assets since 1959 are shown in Table 58-1.

The changes spotlighted in the table were made possible by *amendments in the applicable laws* governing investments and a more aggressive attitude on the part of fund managers. California exemplifies the difficulty and lengthiness of the battles to change the laws. A study prepared by Moody's for the state in 1960 recommended the purchase of equities. It was not until 1964 that the electorate had a chance to vote on, and to defeat, the necessary constitutional amendment. The necessary constitutional amendments for the public employees' and teachers' systems were not passed until 1966 and 1970 respectively.

The main objection to more liberal investment policy has usually centered in excessive risk. The opposition has also used fears of improprieties, desires to help local governments, housing, and industry, and concerns about efforts to control private companies as negative arguments. The necessary changes were often made only because of the need to increase return in the face of escalating pension costs.

MORE RECENT STATE AND LOCAL GOVERNMENT RETIREMENT FUND INVESTMENT POLICIES

The laws governing state and local government investment policy in 1976 range from the very conservative to prudent man legislation. At one extreme is a state such as West Virginia, which allows its West Virginia state retirement and trust funds to invest only in securities of the United States and its agencies, general-obligation state banks, International Bank for Reconstruction and Development (World Bank) bonds, and corporate bonds rated at least AA by two national rating services. On the other hand, states like Idaho, Connecticut, and Maine have a full prudent man rule. Basically, the prudent man rule states that investments should be made and managed by persons exercising "the judgment and care under the circumstances then prevailing, which men of prudence, discretion, and intelligence exercise in the management of their own affairs, not in regard to speculation but in regard to the permanent disposition of their funds, considering the probable income as well as the probable safety of their capital." Miami also has a

TABLE 58-1   Changing Composition of State and Local Government Retirement Fund Assets

Fiscal years ended in the twelve months ending in June	Total cash and security holdings (in millions)	As percent of total cash and security holdings				
		Federal government securities	State and local government securities	Corporate bonds	Corporate stock	Mortgages
1959	$16,340	33.9	25.3	30.6	1.8	5.2
1960	18,539	32.1	23.4	32.9	2.1	6.4
1961	20,875	28.7	21.1	35.8	2.3	8.2
1962	23,294	26.2	17.4	40.9	3.0	8.8
1963	25,629	25.1	13.8	44.1	3.4	9.5
1964	28,639	24.3	10.8	46.6	3.9	9.8
1965	31,814	23.2	8.6	47.5	4.5	10.6
1966	35,262	20.0	7.2	50.1	5.2	11.7
1967	39,265	16.9	6.2	51.6	6.1	12.3
1968	43,681	14.0	5.4	53.4	7.6	12.1
1969	48,876	11.9	4.9	54.7	10.1	11.3
1970	54,918	9.4	3.9	54.9	12.6	12.0
1971	61,605	7.2	3.3	56.2	15.4	11.2
1972	68,760	5.4	3.5	55.1	18.3	10.2
1973	78,417	4.4	1.9	55.3	21.8	8.7
1974	87,488	6.1	1.0	54.8	22.4	7.6
1975	98,064	6.7	0.7	54.7	22.2	7.5

NOTE: Cash and deposits and other assets are not shown; therefore, indicated percentages do not total 100 percent.
SOURCE: U.S. Bureau of the Census.

prudent man rule, and some systems, such as those of Colorado, Kansas, and Oregon, have a prudent man rule with limits on the amount of stock or certain other assets that can be held.

In some states, the rules governing life insurance or fire and casualty insurance company investments apply to state and local government pension funds, and in others the rules governing mutual savings banks are in force. Often these rules apply with modifications. Other states, such as Arizona, Illinois, Minnesota, Ohio, and Pennsylvania, have detailed laws governing legal investments and limits thereon designed specifically for the pension funds.

In terms of actual policy, one can go from a state such as Idaho, which had about 70 percent of its assets in common stock and most of the remainder in corporate bonds in 1975, to a system like that of Wyoming, which at that time had over a third of its assets in United States government securities and all the rest in corporate bonds. Some systems manage their portfolios actively, and others devote little effort to their investments. Some now let outside consultants manage their common stock portfolios.

The remainder of this chapter is devoted to a summary of current policies by type of assets, a discussion of the increasing use of outside managers, and some comments on the directions state and local government investment policy should take.

Government Securities

Very few systems are increasing their positions in state and municipal bonds, and most are reducing their holdings as these mature and through outright sale before maturity. For example, in 1972, before New York City's fiscal crisis, its retirement systems sold $194 million (face amount) of New York City bonds through the novel approach of a sealed auction. In the 1950s, New York's policy had been to sell all its municipal bonds to its pension funds; as a result, the pension funds run by the comptroller's office still had 4.8 percent of their assets invested in such bonds as of June 30, 1974, compared with 57.7 percent in June 1962 and 16.2 percent in June 1972. In many cases the more marketable bonds have already been sold. The proceeds of such sales are usually reinvested in higher-yielding corporate bonds.

Most systems also continue to reduce their holdings of Treasury issues, although some systems may find Treasury bills an appropriate medium in which to invest temporarily idle funds. Some systems have found government agency securities to be more attractive, and such issues now exceed the amount of Treasury issues held. These securities provide higher yields than Treasury issues of comparable maturities and are of high quality. Some also provide good call protection.

The relevant investment laws usually permit unlimited acquisition of all securities issued directly by the Treasury and its agencies. Restrictions on municipals sometimes require that the issuer not have been in default for the last ten or so years, although this proviso sometimes applies only to out-of-state bonds. To invest in municipals outside the state, the issuing city is often required to have a certain population level. Revenue bonds are not always permitted. A few states allow investments only in municipal bonds of their own states, others allow investment in bonds issued by other states but not by their political subdivisions, and some allow purchase of specified revenue bonds in the home states but not in other states. These restrictions reflect attempts to lower local government borrowing costs and to help the local economy.

Fully insured deposits in savings and loan or mutual savings bank accounts located within a state are also frequently permissible. Many systems also are permitted to invest up to a specified maximum percentage of assets in Canadian government bonds and in bonds of the World Bank, the Inter-American Development Bank, and the Asian Development Bank.

Corporate Debt Obligations

Corporate debt is the most important investment medium for most state and local government systems today. Most such investments are very conservative; very few have a rating below Baa, and most are rated A or better. Indeed, fifteen states permit the state-administered systems to invest only in corporate bonds rated A or higher by one or two national rating services; and two, South Carolina and West Virginia, require an Aa or Aaa rating. (Some of these restrictions further reflect the desire to help local economies. South Carolina corporations, for example, need have only an A rating in that state, while in North Dakota the rating requirement does not apply to firms within the state.) Of states with laws specifying rating requirements, only California, South Dakota, and Vermont permit ratings as low as Baa. Other states not using ratings employ different quality-imposing criteria, such as interest coverage ratios, indicate that laws governing insurance companies or savings banks apply, or use prudent man rules. The point is that all these systems have by and large been limited to a relatively conservative bond investment policy.

In their book *The Role of Private Placements in Corporate Finance,*[1] Eli Shapiro and

[1] Harvard University Press, Cambridge, Mass., 1972.

Charles R. Wolf report on a questionnaire they sent to various state and local government retirement systems. Of the $3.3 billion in corporate bonds held in 1967 by the twenty reporting funds, only 1 percent were rated Baa, 8.2 percent were nonrated, 57.4 percent were rated Aaa or Aa, and 33.4 percent carried an A rating. State and local government retirement systems have been active in the private placement market, but their high quality standards have restricted them to issues of larger corporations rather than those of newly emerging companies.

The Shapiro-Wolf study showed that thirty of forty-five funds responding to their questionnaire made private placements in 1967 versus only six in 1960. The issues that the funds buy usually have standard provisions and very rarely have equity kickers. In addition to adhering to high quality standards, they are further restricted by a lack of adequate personnel to investigate thoroughly and negotiate more complex and risky private placements. The retirement systems often prefer larger private placements in which other investors participate. In addition to higher yield, such private deals often offer good call protection. Purchases of publicly issued bonds are made directly from selling syndicates and also in the aftermarket.

In the past, most systems took a buy-and-hold approach to their long-term corporate bond purchases. More recently, however, the larger and better-managed pension funds, like their private counterparts, have come to realize that they may often increase their return by trading, that is, by selling their low-coupon bonds for higher-coupon bonds offering a greater investment return.

Thus, the New York City and New York State retirement systems increased their bond-switching program after legislation enacted in 1970 allowed them to amortize losses on sales over a twenty-year period. For example, in the fiscal year ending June 30, 1974, the New York City retirement systems switched $268 million (principal amount) of bonds into other corporate issues offering a higher return. The significance of this trading should not be exaggerated: the New York City system held a total of $3,930 million of corporate bonds at the end of fiscal 1974.

Because of the high-quality restrictions on bonds, very few systems have used convertible bonds to any great extent. Among the exceptions are the Hawaii employees' retirement system and the Michigan public school employees' retirement fund, which had 7.9 and 7.3 percent, respectively, of their assets invested in convertible debentures as of June 30, 1971. Sometimes convertible issues are considered together with stocks in setting limits on the percentage of funds investable in equities.

Mortgage and Real Estate Investments

As noted above, mortgage investments have become quite common among state and local government retirement systems, with a good number of systems holding 20 percent or more of their assets in this form. The most frequent type of investment allowed is in Federal Housing Administration (FHA)–insured or Veterans Administration (VA)–guaranteed mortgages. Some states, such as Mississippi, New Mexico, and North Carolina, have permitted such investments only for mortgages in the home state. Generally, however, these investments can be made anywhere in the United States.

Permission to invest in conventional mortgages is less frequent and sometimes more closely restricted geographically. Most systems seem to concentrate their holdings in local residential mortgages.

The small staffs and small sizes of many of these systems leave them little choice on mortgages. By concentrating on insured mortgages, they gain both a high degree of safety with a higher return than that obtainable on government bonds and, in some periods, on high-grade corporate bonds. (Return comparisons should be made after adjustment for the servicing cost and amortized acquisition costs on mortgages.) They also have a long-term investment with some liquidity provided through the gradual amortization of the loans.

The New York systems are a notable exception to this pattern. By law, the state and city systems may invest only in mortgages with an unpaid principal of $250,000 or more at the time of purchase. These mortgages can be conventional or insured, can cover property anywhere in the United States, and can equal up to 75 percent of the value of real property improved by a building. The New York City retirement systems hold conventional mortgages on garden apartments, apartment buildings, shopping centers, and office buildings. One mortgage on an office building was for $59 million. With total assets of more than $7 billion, such an investment approach is feasible. In addition to being considered by the system's own mortgage staff, all acquisitions are ruled on by a three-man mortgage advisory committee, whose members are drawn from the mutual savings banking and life insurance industries.

Some systems, such as those in New York, may acquire certain real estate investments directly. In practice, however, most of the real estate held appears to be used by state or local governments. Some real estate may also be owned by certain funds under sales and leaseback arrangements when the corporations leasing the real estate have bonds that would qualify for investment. For example, the Ohio public employees' retirement system may make such agreements if the lessor is rated A or better by a standard rating service.

Preferred Stock Investments

Preferred stock sometimes is included with common stocks under legal investment limits and sometimes is handled separately. Certain laws have standards based on ratios of available earnings to fixed charges; some laws require that the particular corporation's bonds qualify for investment. Very few systems have invested more than a minimal amount of their assets in preferred stocks. Straight preferreds are often attractive to corporations because corporations can exclude 85 percent of the dividends when calculating their taxes, but this feature is of no benefit to tax-exempt pension funds.

Common Stock Investments

Common stock still represents only a modest portion of total state and local government retirement fund investments, but it is gaining ground rapidly. The primary obstacle often is the *legal constraint* on the amount of common stock that can be held. As noted before, some systems may hold no stock, and an increasing number are switching to prudent man rules. The great majority have limits typically ranging from 10 to 50 percent of assets. Among the larger states the limits are as follows: California public employees, 25 percent; Illinois, 33⅓ percent; New York, 30 percent; Ohio, 35 percent, and Wisconsin (fixed funds), 35 percent.[2] In some cases, these limits include preferred stock and convertible bondholdings. Sometimes further limits are placed on the amount of stock purchasable in a single year. For example, the Michigan systems can invest up to 25 percent in common stock, but only a maximum of 5 percent of assets per year on a cumulative basis and an absolute limit of 8 percent in any one year.

The applicable laws often place additional restrictions on common stock purchases. Holdings in individual companies are often limited to a specified percentage of the system's assets. Reflecting fears of excessive control of any corporation, some laws also limit the percentage of a company's stock that can be held;

[2]SOURCE: Securities Industry Association, *State and Local Pension Funds,* New York, 1972.

frequently this is 5 percent, but sometimes it may be as high as 10 percent and as low as 1 percent. A 5 percent limit does have the advantage of preventing a portfolio manager from holding too much of a company's stock when things go wrong and it becomes difficult to sell large blocks of stock.

Quality restrictions are also quite common. These may require that the company have paid dividends on the stock for the preceding five or ten years and that these dividends have been covered by earnings over the period in question. In some cases, the bonds of the company in question must qualify, and in others the stock must have been rated in the three highest rating classifications by a stock-rating service.

Many systems can buy only common stock traded on a registered securities exchange, with typical exceptions for the stocks of banks and insurance companies with $20 million or $50 million of capital. In a few cases the company's assets must exceed a set minimum. Minnesota and New Mexico have a $10 million minimum-asset level, but California requires $100 million. The quality standards most frequently encountered are those applying to dividends and listing. In some states the laws governing the regulation of local mutual savings banks or insurance companies apply.

In practice, most state and local government retirement funds pursue a conservative policy in their common stock investments. They tend to hold large numbers of high-quality, well-known stocks. Most systems concentrate their holdings among leading companies in growing and more stable industries. Although there is a high incidence of holdings in the leading automobile and chemical companies, most systems have invested only a small portion of their common holdings in the more cyclical industries. The emphasis is on high visibility and rising earnings. Like the holdings of the private pension funds, their largest holdings are often in glamour growth stocks. Holdings in stable moderate-growth areas like banking and food stocks are also very common.

However, some systems have emphasized utility and other stocks that provide greater current income. This practice was more common in the past, but systems such as the Virginia supplemental retirement system and the various retirement systems of the state of New Jersey, which formerly concentrated very heavily in utility stocks, have turned away from that group and shown greater interest in growth stocks.

Many systems have opted for holdings of a very large number of stocks, with some of the larger systems having more than 100 common stocks in their portfolios. But some of these systems, such as the Minnesota retirement funds, have embarked on programs to reduce the number of stocks held.

Turnover of common stockholdings tends to be quite low (usually under 10 percent per annum). This reflects the emphasis on long-term holdings, the general conservatism of the portfolio managers, and the fact that the bulk of the common stockholdings were acquired relatively recently. Nonetheless, a few systems do have a higher turnover rate more typical of other institutional investors, and the overall trend of turnover is likely to increase somewhat as the average age of holdings lengthens. At times greater attention to the need to sell stockholdings might be advantageous.

Some systems have followed a policy of regularly investing a given dollar amount or percentage of cash flow in common stocks, resulting in at least an approximation of dollar cost averaging. Other systems are somewhat more flexible in their stock-buying policies. Most managers of these government pension funds probably do not take an aggressive approach to market timing and concentrate instead on the purchase of securities that they believe will be attractive for the long term.

During the 1973–1974 bear market period, as in 1969–1970, state and local retirement systems at first continued to invest a large portion of their net cash flow in common stocks. There was quite a lag before they started to react to the market nosedive of those two years. The quarterly survey of large systems by the Bureau of the Census shows that the increase in stockholdings as a percentage of the increase in cash and security holdings declined from 43.4 percent in 1973 to 28 percent in the first half of 1974 and to 18.5 percent in the second half of 1974. Although the market staged a sharp recovery in the first half of 1975, these funds experienced a further reduction in the ratio to 16.8 percent.

Undoubtedly, the steepness of the bear market (a decline of almost 50 percent from the peak in January 1973 to the trough in October 1974, as measured by the Standard & Poor's 500-Stock Index) may have raised some concerns about the desirability of large investments in common stocks on the part of fund managers.

Evidence of renewed interest in stocks was given by an increase in the ratio to 28.3 percent in the second half of 1975. However, by the first quarter of 1976 the ratio had reversed again and declined to 19.6 percent. Quite obviously, considerable caution persists among retirement system managers.

Use of Professional Outside Management

Some state and local government retirement systems manage their funds without the use of outside professional investment advisers. Examples are the New Jersey and Wisconsin systems. Many of the smaller systems also must forgo outside help because of the limitations of their assets and budgets. Most of the medium-size and larger systems do use outside help on an advisory basis for either all their assets or just their common stock investments.

Investment advisory recommendations usually must be approved by the board of trustees or administrative officers of the systems. Some systems handle the actual executions directly; others have the advisers handle them.

A far more interesting trend is that some systems are now utilizing discretionary managers or multimanagers, or both. In a full discretionary management arrangement, such as those used by the public employees' retirement system of Oregon and the Virginia supplemental retirement system, the administrator of the system and board of trustees need decide only how much money should go into equities and how much of it each manager should get.

In a multimanagement system on a nondiscretionary basis, such as those used by the New York City teachers' variable annuity program and the New York City retirement funds, decisions also must be made on whether the adviser's stock recommendations are satisfactory. Even here, more streamlined procedures are being used. The New York City teachers' program has a three-man investment finance committee that can approve a decision within twenty-four hours if necessary. The Arizona, Connecticut, Delaware, Hawaii, Illinois, Kansas, and Maine systems, along with the New York State common retirement fund, also use multimanagers or advisers; and the trend is spreading steadily.

This trend is increasing the importance of the art of selecting and evaluating investment managers. Most systems make their initial management selections very carefully. The process starts with a list of potential advisers, which may be compiled with the aid of an outside consultant. Sometimes consultants are used to assist in the selection process and for continuous help in evaluation thereafter. Those selected are invited to answer questionnaires that will aid in the selection process. The list is then culled, and the remaining advisers are further examined through personal presentations to the board of trustees, visits to their offices, interviews with the prospective portfolio manager, and so on.

Among the questions considered are whether the organization properly understands the investment needs of the fund, the quality of the management the portfolio will receive, the persons who will make the portfolio decisions, the manager's investment philosophy and methods, and the past record of performance. Often an attempt is made to achieve some diversification in the selection of managers by choosing competent firms that use different investment approaches.

Once a manager has been selected, performance is reviewed frequently. Such reviews examine the reasons behind actions taken, the record of performance on a risk-adjusted basis, and results in comparison with those of similar funds. Most funds review their advisers' performance over a number of years before any move is made to replace managers. Cash-flow allocations are determined on the basis of past performance and evaluations of how well the managers will be able to perform in the anticipated market environment, given their investment philosophy.

Investment advisers and managers often are given authority to allocate *commissions* for trading ability and research, but in other cases the funds make these decisions. Far too often commission business can be given only to brokerage firms with offices in the applicable state, or such firms must be accorded preference. However, other systems realize the value of commissions in buying outside research and investment performance evaluation services.

HOW SHOULD STATE AND LOCAL GOVERNMENT RETIREMENT FUND INVESTMENTS BE MANAGED?

Obtain a Fund Large Enough to Manage

One of the first responsibilities of a state or local government retirement fund's board of trustees is to ensure that the fund is run by competent investment managers. The many remaining small local funds should attempt to pool their assets with those of the larger state-administered funds in their respective states. Many local funds have already done so, as is evident by the fact that in the twelve months ending June 30, 1975, $2,623 million of the $6,597 million in government contributions to state-administered systems came from local governments. North Carolina has set up a separate local governmental employees' retirement system for this purpose. Such pooling relieves local governments of responsibility for investments.

When several smaller systems exist within a state or a city, it might be wise to consolidate the investment management in one organization. Examples of this approach are the State Board of Investment in Minnesota and the Division of Investment in New Jersey. The deputy treasurer for investments runs all seven of Connecticut's retirement funds, and the office of the comptroller runs all five of New York City's retirement funds. (However, New York City's teachers' variable annuity is run directly by the Teachers' Retirement Board.)

It is possible to pool the local systems in a state in their entirety (conglomeration) and thereby provide the following advantages: uniform benefits, ability to obtain greater investment diversification, lower risk of adverse mortality experience, and an end to the "leapfrogging" of benefits that occurs when employees in one system can point to more advantageous benefits in a neighboring system.

Decide on the Basic Investment Needs of the Fund

Having obtained a sufficiently large pool of assets to justify the expense of proper investment management, the next step is to analyze the needs of the fund and to select competent professional management. It would be advisable for the board of trustees to include people from outside financial institutions, such as banks, insurance companies, and savings banks, who could provide some investment knowledge, or to include such people on separate advisory committees. As noted in the subsection "Mortgage and Real Estate Investments," the New York City systems appear to have made excellent use of such outside talent.

The needs of the funds and a general investment policy must be determined, because this information is required before an intelligent search for an investment adviser can be made. Actuarial consultants should be employed to determine an adequate level of funding and to provide projections of cash flows. With this information the board can assess its future liquidity needs, its exposure to rising inflation, and the level of risk that it can safely assume. A broad investment policy can thus be outlined.

A system having a growing number of active members, possessing a high ratio of active to retired members, and operating in a sound and growing community can afford to take a relatively aggressive investment stance. By contrast, a fund in a city with a slowly growing or declining level of government employment, with a low ratio of active to retired members, and with a deteriorating economic environment may have to undertake a very conservative approach, with relatively high primary and secondary liquidity reserves and rather low investment in common stocks and private placements. In essence, the greater the probability that contributions will continue to exceed benefit payments far into the future, the larger the system, and the more competent its investment management. the greater is the level of acceptable risk and the less the need for liquidity.

Obtain Competent Investment Management

Systems with sufficient assets may elect to employ their own investment staffs, relying on their own expertise and brokerage house research. Nonetheless, like other conservative institutions in the past, they may find it politically difficult to pay salaries attractive enough to entice topnotch investment people, or they may fear other political difficulties if they attempt such direct management. These large funds, along with many medium- and smaller-size ones, might find it most advantageous to employ one or more outside managers. The use of carefully selected discretionary managers who clearly understand the needs of their clients would usually be the best approach.

However, because many states have laws requiring the board of trustees to make the final investment decisions, this procedure may not always be possible. In such cases, efforts should be made to streamline the decision procedures. Small sub-committees of the board, whose members could be consulted by telephone, could facilitate rapid decision making. However, this is not to say that all decisions need be made in haste. Larger funds might find the use of multimanagers desirable. One fund official or group should be responsible for monitoring the results frequently, preferably monthly, and measuring them against other funds and indices. This official or group should also see how the results were obtained. Unsatisfactory managers should be replaced by new ones.

Such judgments should take into account both investment results (measured over an adequate period of time such as a few years) and the care with which the manager has applied a policy consistent with the funds' objectives. (A high performance level might be quite unsatisfactory if excessive risk had been taken in violation of stated policy.) The subsection "Use of Professional Outside Manage-ment" should be consulted for further ideas on choosing a manager.

Bond and mortgage investments would often be managed internally even when outside stock advisers are utilized. However, medium- and larger-size funds with large bond portfolios might find aggressive outside bond advisers useful in improving overall return if their own staffs lack personnel skilled in bond trading. Systems with assets too small to justify the expense of outside professional manage-ment might find mutual funds, particularly no-load funds, an adequate alternative for the stock portion of their assets. They could use a committee of civic-minded local bankers and others to help select such funds. (Seattle is one city that has used mutual funds in its retirement system.) Very small systems might just consider purchasing a mix of fixed and variable annuities from life insurance companies for their members.

Risk versus Return and Other Investment Policy Decisions

The next important question relates to the level of acceptable risk, the portfolio mix, and other investment policy considerations.

Liquidity needs based on probability analysis of cash-outflow needs relative to cash inflows must be considered first. They can be provided through short-term money market instruments and bonds that mature when such liquidity is needed. The primary liquidity reserve should be large enough to cover the largest probable cash-flow imbalances. Secondary liquidity reserves should be large enough to cover any probable cash-flow imbalances over the next few years, even considering the probability of such events as a cutback in government contributions because of a tight budget situation, a wave of early retirements from the system, or even a need to bail out the parent government when it can no longer sell its securities publicly. Normally, liquidity needs would be quite modest.

The tax-exempt nature of these funds makes investment in municipal bonds and straight preferred stock generally undesirable. *Primary emphasis* should be placed on achieving the best return possible for a given level of risk, irrespective of objectives of helping local industry, housing, or brokerage firms. For most funds the projected increase in active members, the growth envisioned in the community, and the rise assumed in the level of benefits and wages suggest that investment policy should be modestly aggressive, avoiding a policy in which the entire portfolio is vulnerable to a permanent decline in value. There is no reason why the funds should be less aggressive than private noninsured pension funds and life insurance companies of comparable size.

However, a fund in a declining community, in which future cash outflow for benefits very possibly may exceed contributions and dependable interest and dividend income, must pursue a far more cautious investment policy. Most larger systems' portfolios could include some conventional mortgages and stocks of smaller secondary but well-managed and adequately financed companies with good long-term prospects. More important are careful, competent investment management, an adequate level of diversification (particularly among the riskier assets), and a modest overall risk level in the total portfolio. Both current income and realized and unrealized capital gains and losses should be considered in determining investment return.

Some thoughts on the *actuarial rate-of-return assumption* are also in order here. Too low an assumed rate will result in larger current contributions than are necessary to achieve planned benefit levels and may produce greater employee pressure for higher benefits if actual investment results significantly exceed that assumed rate. Retirees might also receive lower monthly annuities than their own contributions would justly entitle them to.

Too large a rate assumption, on the other hand, may create political difficulties when the return is not met, delude governments into thinking they can afford overly generous benefit levels, necessitate increased contributions in the future to make up investment deficiencies, and encourage the portfolio manager to take excessive risks to achieve the return assumption.

The assumed actuarial return should be based on reasonable long-term assumptions, taking account of the desired risk level, the actual long-term experience, the return on present holdings, and a conservative estimate of long-term prospects. It must never be based on some historically high return on stocks realized over a period of only a few years or on historically high coupons on recent new-issue bond offerings. Although most public retirement funds have used modest actuarial return assumptions, some private funds have switched to questionably high rates in the last few years. It is a lot easier and pleasanter to be able to raise the actuarial rate in the future than it is to be forced to lower it.

Business Risk and Portfolio Policy

Two big risks are the effects of declines in the overall economy or in particular regions or industries (business and financial risk) and price level changes (including interest rate risk). A clearer comprehension of the workings of the economic system (including a better understanding of the effects of monetary policy on the economy), combined with the government's strong determination to avoid excessive unemployment, makes another prolonged depression in the United States unlikely.

However, the economy is now more vulnerable to major recessions than it was before 1971, as evidenced by the 1973–1975 recession. Thus, although the economic risks of today suggest a more cautious policy toward equity investment than might have been desirable in the early 1960s, a much higher level of common stock investment than the recent average (22 percent) of large state and local government retirement funds would seem reasonable for most funds, given their ability to ride through even prolonged periods of economic decline without being forced to sell their stocks.

Because investment performance is usually reflected fairly rapidly in variable annuity payments, the total pension payments of such persons should be backed partially by fixed-income securities to avoid excessive declines in the payments on which the recipients may be dependent to maintain their standard of living. (Such fixed income may be provided in part by social security payments.) Total fixed payments, along with the level of variable payments likely after a severe decline (as judged by past experience), should be adequate to keep retirees from facing severe hardships.

The risk of more permanent changes and even the extremes of temporary changes can be partially guarded against by proper diversification. This requires the purchase of securities that would not all be adversely affected by the same occurrences. It is generally realized that this means that not all stocks should be as sensitive to a rise in interest rates or to a decline in the economy as other stocks are. But even the purchase of only high-quality, high–price-earnings growth stocks in various industries could be risky if investors decided that the high multiples were no longer warranted relative to other investment opportunities. (These growth stocks often tend to move together.)

A more serious long-term risk would relate to changes in the social, political, and economic structure that would have the effect of reducing the real return on investment. Although such major changes have often been considered unlikely, the risk of these changes cannot be entirely ignored, particularly as they could increase greatly in an inflationary environment when business may be viewed as a convenient scapegoat for society's problems. Some observers have commented on the decline of property rights in the United States and voiced fears that this trend might continue.

Section Eleven
Retirement Planning

Chapter **59**

How to Use Insurance
for a Richer Retirement

MARK R. GREENE

The Life Insurance Concept

Life insurance is a method by which a group of people may cooperate to even out
the burden of loss resulting from the premature deaths of members of the group.
The insurer collects contributions from each member, invests these contributions,
and guarantees their safety and some minimum interest return. The insurer then
distributes benefits to the estates of those members who die. Life insurance is a
means of making sure that when one is accumulating property to provide certain
benefits for someone else, usually a member of one's family, these plans will be
realized whether one dies prematurely or lives to a ripe old age.

Life insurance is a method of creating an estate. It has been said that people
have two main types of estates: (1) the present, or actual, estate; and (2) the future,
or potential, estate. The present estate consists of property that one has already
accumulated, while the potential estate refers to property that one will normally
accumulate in the future to provide financial security for one's dependents *if one
lives long enough*. If the individual dies prematurely, the potential estate is never
realized. Life insurance, thus, is a way of creating an actual estate for the benefit of
dependents if the worker does not live to realize his or her potential estate. The
individual may use life insurance policies as a savings medium as well as to provide
death protection. If he or she does not die prematurely, these savings are available
for his or her old age or for possible distributions to dependents. To accomplish
these objectives, however, the proper types of insurance contracts must be elected.
This does not mean that the insured must "die to win."

Major Classes of Contracts

There are three main types of life insurance contracts: those aimed at protection,
those aimed at savings, and those offering a blend of savings and protection.

Term insurance is aimed entirely at protection and contains no savings element.
When you buy term insurance, you buy pure protection and nothing else. When
someone buys a fire insurance policy, he or she will collect nothing from the
company unless there is a fire; the policy will be worthless when the time for which
it has been written has expired. Exactly the same sort of situation exists for a
person who buys term insurance from a life insurance company. If the person dies
within the term for which he or she is insured, the company will pay his or her

beneficiary the face amount of the policy, but if the person is still alive at the expiration of the time for which the policy was written, the policy is of no value.

Term insurance is usually employed for temporary needs. Thus if a person has a mortgage obligation for twenty years, a decreasing term insurance policy lasting exactly twenty years may be purchased. At the end of this period, the mortgage has been repaid, and the life insurance policy expires. In the meantime, the policyholder has the security that if he or she should die before the mortgage has been repaid, the proceeds will be available to the beneficiary either to repay the mortgage or to use the funds for other purposes. Because term insurance policies expire at a certain point in time and almost always do not run beyond age sixty-five or seventy, they cannot be used to fulfill needs that run throughout a person's life. In this sense, term insurance policies are said to be temporary.

Whole life insurance contains a savings element but emphasizes primarily the protection element. Whole life policies are designed for lifetime needs. Premiums may be arranged to extend for the entire lifetime of the insured, or they may be shortened so that the policy is paid up in a shorter period, such as within ten or twenty years or at age sixty-five. Examples of lifetime needs are funds for retirement income to a spouse and funds to take care of the last expenses that will occur at death: funeral expenses, estate taxes, current debts, court costs. Whole life insurance contracts are set up so that a level premium is paid no matter how old one becomes, and the policy is in force throughout life.

Endowment or retirement contracts emphasize mainly the savings element. They are also temporary in that they expire at the end of a certain period, such as ten or twenty years or at age sixty-five. In these policies a person saves a stated sum of money over a stated period of years. The insured has the protection that if he or she should die before the period expires, the insurance company will complete the savings program for him or her. Endowments are ordinarily purchased with a specific savings goal in mind, such as to provide a retirement fund. If the insured dies, the fund will be available for his or her beneficiary.

Life insurance policies have many variants; in fact, insurance companies constantly try to devise new contracts that meet the needs of certain people better than the older forms. The family income policy, the modified life policy, and the multiple protection policy are examples of policies combining whole life and term policies.

A twenty-year *family income policy* provides that if the policyholder dies within twenty years after the policy has been taken out, his or her beneficiary will receive a stipulated annual income for the rest of the twenty years. At the end of the twentieth year, the beneficiary receives, in addition, the face value of the policy or its equivalent in the form of income. A *modified life policy* starts as term insurance and then after a stated period, usually five years, automatically changes to whole life at a higher premium. During the first five years, the low term premium rate prevails. The basic purpose of modified life is to provide permanent insurance for young people who are not yet in a position to pay for it. The *multiple protection policy* uses term insurance to provide double or triple the face amount of a permanent type of policy such as ordinary life for a set period ranging from five to twenty years.

For any life insurance policy, the greater the savings element, the greater the premium. For example, typical annual rates per $1,000 of insurance for a forty-year-old male might be as follows: term to age sixty-five, $13; ordinary life, $22; twenty-year endowment, $44.

Merits of Saving through Insurance

Life insurance proceeds become available to beneficiaries in two ways: (1) through the accumulation of cash values in the policy and (2) as death proceeds for the benefit of others. The policy provides several ways in which these funds may be employed. Before discussing these, let us consider some of the advantages of saving money through the medium of life insurance.

1. Life insurance lends itself to a regular, consistent savings plan. Since it may be purchased in any denomination to fit the savings budget of individuals with varying incomes, it meets the psychological needs of most savers for a regular savings plan. It has a semicompulsory flavor. Experience has shown that individuals are reluctant to give up a life insurance savings plan even if their income drops or unemployment strikes. As premiums come due, they are regarded as any other bill and tend to be paid regularly. If an individual is saving through a mutual fund or through monthly deposits at a savings bank, he or she may well omit payments. However, the individual usually thinks twice before permitting his or her life insurance policy to lapse.

2. The investment element in the life insurance contract is safe. Even in the worst economic depression ever experienced in the United States, that of 1929–1932, almost no savers in life insurance lost money. A few life insurance companies went bankrupt, but their obligations were assumed by other insurers.

3. The investment element in life insurance is liquid. This means that for all practical purposes the savings element is available in cash to the insured through borrowing whenever he or she needs it.

When an individual borrows the savings element from his or her insurance policy, the insurer regards the transaction as any other investment that it might make and charges the insured interest, usually at a relatively low rate. While the saver is using these funds, however, his or her policy is being credited with interest and dividends earned by the insurer. The net cost of the loan, therefore, may only be 1 or 2 percent. See also discussion below in the subsection "Loan Provisions."

4. The rate of return in life insurance is reasonable, considering the liquidity and safety of the investment. Currently life insurance companies earn approximately 5 percent on their investments. This approximates the return to policyholders on the investments if their policies contain an investment element. It should be noted that policyholders do not earn 5 percent on the total premiums they pay, because part of the premiums is devoted to pure insurance protection and only the other part constitutes the savings element.

Use of Life Insurance Proceeds

Five options (with some insurers, more than five) are available to the insured in accepting the proceeds of life insurance. These options are available not only to the policyholders if they live to retirement but also to their beneficiaries, who may wish to use the proceeds as a retirement income. The five methods are (1) a lump-sum option, (2) a fixed monthly amount of income, (3) income divided equally over a fixed period of time, (4) a life income option, (5) an interest option, and, with some insurers, (6) variable-annuity options.

Lump-Sum Option.   Taking life insurance proceeds in a lump sum is not really an income option. However, the lump sum can be converted to an income option by depositing the lump sum in a savings and loan association or in some other investment medium and drawing an annual income from it. In some cases the lump sum is deposited with a trustee who manages the money in various investments that produce an income either to the policyholder or to the beneficiary. See below, subsection "Use of Trustees."

Fixed-Amount Option.   All life insurance companies permit the insured to receive the proceeds of their insurance in a fixed monthly income according to their needs at the particular time. For example, let us suppose that an insured person wishes to receive $100 a month for as long as the insurance proceeds last. Let us assume that the insured has $10,000 of insurance proceeds. Under normal interest assumptions (approximately 2.5 percent), the insurer will continue to pay $100 a month for ten years and eight months. If there are only $5,000 of proceeds, the insured's income will continue for four years and seven months. If the proceeds are $20,000, the $100 monthly income will continue for thirty-four years and two months, and so on.

Fixed-Period Option. In some cases the insured may wish to spread the available proceeds of life insurance over a definite period of years. For example, a person may wish to retire early, say, at age fifty-five. Realizing that social security will not begin until age sixty-two, he or she may wish to cash in his or her life insurance and have it paid as an income for a period of seven years. If there are $10,000 of insurance proceeds settled under the seven-year fixed-period option, the insured will receive $140.25 a month. If the insured wishes to retire at age fifty and needs an income for twelve years, $10,000 of insurance proceeds would provide him or her with $91.56 a month for twelve years.

Life Income Option. In many cases the insured will wish to accept the life insurance proceeds under a life income option, sometimes known as an "annuity option." Under this option both the principal and interest earnings are liquidated so that the insured is guaranteed a lifetime income. The annuity option has been called the opposite of life insurance because it distributes the estate in an orderly way to the insured individual while he or she is alive instead of accumulating the estate, the objective in life insurance.

There are several possible arrangements, according to the type of refund feature the insured wishes: (1) If the policyholder elects to use the life insurance proceeds in a life annuity with no refund at death, he or she will be guaranteed an income for life. However, if the insured dies right after the income begins, the entire principal sum is "lost," and his or her heirs will not receive any benefits. (2) If the insured has dependents or wishes to leave funds to others, he or she may elect a refund feature, such as ten years certain. Under this option the insurer guarantees ten years of payments to someone and life income to the annuitant. If the policyholder selects this option and dies five years afterward, the insurer will continue the income to his or her beneficiaries for five more years. On the other hand, if the insured lives for eleven years and then dies, there is no refund to any beneficiary. (3) If the insured selects a refund annuity, the insurer simply refunds any unpaid installments to the beneficiary. For example, under the refund option, if an insured spends $15,000 for an annuity paying $100 a month at age sixty-five and dies after having received payments that reduced the principal by $5,000, the remaining $10,000 may be refunded to the beneficiary either in a lump sum or in installments.

Another type of life income option is known as the "joint and last survivorship option." It is perhaps one of the most useful of all of the life income options because it guarantees an income to two persons, usually husband and wife, as long as either shall live. The income to the survivor may be the same amount that was paid to the insured during his or her life, or it may be reduced to two-thirds or one-half of the amount paid to the insured.

Sample incomes under various options for one major insurer are given here for a male aged sixty-five. The figures are shown in monthly life incomes for each $1,000 of proceeds.

	Income
Straight life annuity	$6.75
Life income, ten years certain	$6.16
Life income, twenty years certain	$4.94
Life income on an installment refund	$5.57
Joint and last survivorship (two-thirds to the survivor)	$5.72

Thus, it may be seen that if the insured has $10,000 of life insurance cash value, he could receive $67.50 a month for life as a retirement income with no refund at death. If he selects the joint and last survivorship annuity and his wife is the same age, they would receive together $57.20 a month as long as either lives, but upon the death of one the survivor would receive two-thirds of this sum, or approximately $39 per month.

It may be observed that the typical life insurance settlement options are based upon conservative interest assumptions. In the above case the interest assumption was 2.5 percent. Proportionately larger amounts will be paid if insurers supplement the interest return with dividend income. A major advantage of the life income option is that the insured can not outlive his or her income. Another advantage is that he or she has no investment worries in old age. The insurer guarantees the principal and a minimum interest rate and, in addition, will pay a dividend supplement according to the excess amount over the guaranteed interest that it is earning on its investments.

Interest Option.   If the insured or his or her beneficiary elects the interest option, the insurer keeps the proceeds of the policy and pays out an interest income equal to some minimum rate. Excess payments are made if investment earnings permit. The principal remains intact and can ultimately be withdrawn.

Variable-Annuity Options.   One of the disadvantages of the settlement options is lack of protection against inflation. A relatively fixed return is paid upon the investment element in life insurance. If the cost of living doubles, the amount of income selected by the annuitant remains the same. To help overcome this problem, many life insurers are now offering variable-annuity options. Under these options the proceeds of life insurance may be handled quite differently from a fixed-settlement option. Instead of the funds being invested in the regular investments of the insurer (bonds, mortgages, and other fixed-income investments), they are invested in common stocks. The annuity is expressed in units, in a manner similar to the shares of a mutual fund. The annuitant thus is guaranteed so many units for life under one of the options discussed above, such as life only, life with ten years certain, joint and last survivorship, and so on. The value of the unit changes periodically according to changes in the value of the common stock portfolio in which the funds are invested.

The details of the variable annuity are somewhat complex, but the general way in which it operates may be described simply. Let us assume that the insured has saved $50,000 for retirement. (The savings need not have been made in a life insurance company.) At age sixty-five the insured pays the life insurer $50,000 for a variable annuity. The $50,000 is converted into units each worth some dollar amount, say, $1. In this case, the life insurer converts the 50,000 units into a life annuity of approximately 3,333 units per year on a straight life annuity basis (this assumes that the average life expectancy at age sixty-five for a male is fifteen years). The first year the insured receives $3,333 as an annuity. Now let us assume that the value of the stock market portfolio rises by 10 percent by the second year. Each unit is now worth $1.10; therefore, the insured would receive $3,666 during the second year.

The variable-annuity idea depends upon the assumption that the stock market is a reasonable protection against inflation and that it also assists the insured to maintain his or her standard of living during retirement. The insured is spared the problems of making investment decisions during the retirement years. The insured accepts the investment risk that the value of his or her stock portfolio, which backs up the variable annuity, will decline. However, if the general price level also declines equally, the value of the savings in terms of purchasing power would remain constant. Of course, there is no guarantee that changes in the Consumer Price Index will be exactly parallel to changes in the variable annuity.

As a matter of fact, over short periods consumer prices and stock prices very often move in opposite directions. It is only over a reasonably long period that there is a rough correlation between the two indices.

It has been pointed out that the variable annuity attempts to provide funds for a retirement income with a varying dollar value but a *constant purchasing power.* The regular annuities discussed above provide an income with a fixed dollar value but with varying purchasing power. The purchasor of a fixed annuity assumes that it is more desirable for a retired person to have an income whose amount is fixed in dollars but whose real value fluctuates.

As with other annuities, the variable annuity provides an income that the insured cannot outlive. The insurer assumes the mortality risk that as time goes on annuitants as a group live longer than expected. Thus, the number of units received by the variable annuitant remains constant throughout life.

The variable annuity is relatively new in the United States, but by 1970 approximately 500,000 persons in the United States were covered by variable annuities, compared with 1.5 million persons covered by regular fixed-dollar annuities. The number of individuals covered by variable annuities appears to be growing at a rate of about 25 percent annually.[1] Although the variable-annuity concept is too new to have built up a lengthy financial history over several business cycles, there is some convincing evidence that demonstrates the potential value of variable annuities in assisting the long-term saver without undue risk and that this income is likely to be greater than that which would have been built up under conventional methods.

Perhaps the most extensive study of stock market performance in recent years was made by Lawrence Fisher and James H. Lorie of the University of Chicago.[2] They demonstrated that if an investor had purchased all stocks listed on the New York Stock Exchange (NYSE) and held them for thirty-five years (the period 1926–1960), his or her net annual return after all taxes and commissions upon the sale of the portfolio would have been 8.2 percent compounded annually.[3] Thus, if an investor had put $10,000 in all the stocks on the NYSE in 1926, he or she would have received the sum of approximately $178,000 in 1960 after taxes and commissions. On the other hand, a $10,000 investment earning 5 percent compounded over the same period would have yielded the saver only $57,340. Of course, there is no guarantee that the stock market will continue to outperform other investments in the future.

The first and oldest variable-annuity plan was formed in 1950 by the College Retirement Equities Fund (CREF). The initial value of the unit was $10. By December 31, 1970, the unit had reached a value of $39, and by December 31, 1971, it had risen to $46.21. The value of the accumulation unit in CREF reached its peak in November 1968 at $47.67. Its low point was in August 1953, when the unit fell to $9.35. The compound rate-of-return equivalent to an increase in value from $10 to $39 over a twenty-year period is about 7 percent, considerably greater than the compound rate of inflation of about 2 percent during this period. During the twenty-year period 1950–1970, the Standard & Poor's Composite Index of stock market prices rose slightly faster than the CREF accumulation unit, or at an annual compound rate of 7.4 percent. The gross national product, which is one

[1]Institute of Life Insurance, *Life Insurance Fact Book,* New York, 1971, p. 55.
[2]Lawrence Fisher and James H. Lorie, *Rates of Return on Investments in Common Stock,* University of Chicago Center for Research in Security Prices, Chicago, 1963.
[3]This figure is adjusted for the federal income taxes of an investor who was in the $10,000 income bracket in 1960, was married, and had standard deductions. It is assumed that the investor reinvested all dividends over the years after paying income taxes on them as they were paid out.

measure of living standards, increased at a compound annual rate of about 4 percent during the period 1950–1970, expressed in constant 1958 dollars.

Another variable-annuity plan with a history long enough for evaluation is that offered by the Variable Annuity Life Insurance Company (VALIC). VALIC was formed as a company in Washington in 1955. After several years of difficulties during which the legal and regulatory status of the variable annuity was being decided, the company finally increased its capitalization, and in 1967 it was merged with the American General Insurance Company of Texas. A history of its monthly payments to annuitants over the period from March 1959 to March 1969 is shown in Table 59-1. These payments are compared with the payments that

TABLE 59-1   Monthly Variable Annuity Payments of CREF and VALIC, 1959–1969

		CREF	VALIC	CREF-VALIC ratio
March	1959	$100.00	$100.00	1.0
June	1959		102.86	
September	1959		103.98	
December	1959		98.67	
March	1960	101.00	98.06	1.03
June	1960		97.58	
September	1960		98.05	
December	1960		96.63	
March	1961	119.00	109.72	1.08
June	1961		117.68	
September	1961		115.95	
December	1961		119.57	
March	1962	119.00	117.05	1.02
June	1962		108.89	
September	1962		93.62	
December	1962		90.04	
March	1963	103.00	103.75	1.0
June	1963		108.14	
September	1963		107.73	
December	1963		111.46	
March	1964	120.00	115.84	1.03
June	1964		117.00	
September	1964		121.31	
December	1964		122.41	
March	1965	128.00	127.68	1.0
June	1965		129.97	
September	1965		122.05	
December	1965		130.54	
March	1966	138.00	130.85	1.05
June	1966		129.13	
September	1966		119.39	
December	1966		115.45	
March	1967	145.00	124.30	1.17
June	1967		136.24	
September	1967		135.94	
December	1967		133.61	
March	1968	136.00	132.06	1.03
June	1968		141.22	
September	1968		148.88	
December	1968		160.13	
March	1969	148.00	162.48	.91

SOURCE: VALIC, prospectus describing group variable retirement annuity contracts, May 9, 1969. CREF payments have been calculated from annual reports of the company. Data are rounded.

would have been paid by CREF, whose operations were described above. It will be observed that CREF's annuity is changed only once each year, whereas VALIC's annuity changes quarterly. The records of CREF and VALIC are similar, with CREF's performance slightly exceeding VALIC's in most years of the period except for 1969.

Limitations of Settlement Options

Two of the major disadvantages of using life insurance settlement options are the relative inflexibility that characterizes them and the limited rate of return paid on funds invested.

1. Once a settlement option has been elected and the income is being collected by either the insured or his or her beneficiary, the amount or timing of the payments cannot generally be altered unless advance provisions to do so have been agreed upon. For example, many insurers will not allow a widow or widower to receive in one lump sum, at her or his election, the commuted value of part or all of the payments due under income settlement options.

Generally the insured may not arrange that, for example, if his or her spouse remarries, the settlement option is changed so that other parties, such as children, receive the proceeds. Settlement options other than a lump sum are not usually available to corporations or partnerships. Fixed or limited installments may not be made payable beyond thirty years after the death of the insured. Interest may not accumulate under the interest option beyond the children of a beneficiary.

Contingent beneficiaries may be named in life insurance, but no mode of settlement may be used beyond the first contingent beneficiary. Thus, the insured may not use the fixed-amount option to provide for his or her spouse and, upon his or her death, for a child and, if the child dies, for a nephew. If the child dies, any settlement must be paid in cash to any other beneficiary. Furthermore, if the spouse dies before the child, the child may not choose a settlement option.

2. The rate of return available to the insured under settlement options is conservative. Most insurers guarantee only about 4 percent interest on the funds employed to pay settlement options. Excess interest, if any, is usually added to the monthly payments. The insured or his or her beneficiary drawing income settlements may not usually count on a rate of return larger than the current earnings rate of the life insurer, which in recent years has averaged slightly more than 5 percent.

Use of Trustees

To help circumvent some of the inflexibilities and limited rates of return characterizing life insurance settlement options, many insureds designate a trustee to receive the proceeds of life insurance in a lump sum. The trustee, who is usually a member of a trust department in a banking institution, may be given as much or as little discretion in distributing the proceeds as may be deemed advisable. For example, the trustee may be instructed to pay to the beneficiary a monthly income sufficient to enable him or her to maintain a "reasonable standard of living." Any contingency such as the remarriage of a spouse or the incompetence of a beneficiary child can be provided for. In the meantime, the trustee may invest the proceeds according to the "prudent man rule," which means that the trustee has broad flexibility in selecting securities for investment, including common stocks or real estate. Many authorities believe that the trust arrangement is superior to settlement options, particularly if the amounts involved are substantial enough to cause estate tax problems. This is generally the case if the total estate equals or exceeds $200,000. However, trustees charge a fee for money management, whereas no extra charge is made by life insurers in connection with settlement options. Trustees' fees must be weighed against the value of their services in each case.

Life Insurance in Retirement Years

There are many reasons for carrying life insurance beyond retirement and into old age. Among the needs for continuing protection are (1) funds to meet funeral expenses, current debts, taxes, and estate settlement costs; (2) funds to provide an income for a dependent spouse, parent, or child; (3) funds for gifts to charities; and (4) funds to equalize bequests to various beneficiaries.

To use life insurance for these continuing needs, contracts of a permanent type, such as whole life insurance, must be used. Normally these contracts must be taken out before the insured retires, since poor health or high premiums may prohibit its use at advanced ages. Life insurance is a commodity one must purchase "when one doesn't need it," that is, when the insured is in good health.

Estate clearance costs are much larger than is commonly supposed. Even on relatively small estates of $100,000, estate taxes alone may cause a shrinkage of between 12 and 15 percent. For larger estates, say, $500,000, estate taxes may cause a shrinkage of between 20 and 33 percent.[4] Depending upon the insured's life-style, other estate costs may run into substantial amounts.

Life insurance permits one to cover these expenses with "fractional dollars." For example, if a retired person estimates that estate settlement costs will be $10,000, he or she may maintain an ordinary life insurance contract that has been taken out at a younger age for this need. If the policy had been taken out, say, at age forty, the insured would have been paying in about $275 annually. If we divide $10,000 by $275, we see that it would take thirty-six years before the sum of all premiums would equal the death proceeds. If the insured dies before age seventy-six, the policy will reimburse his or her estate by more than has been paid in the premiums. This calculation ignores the interest that could have been earned on the premiums in a separate investment. If interest at 5 percent is considered to have been earned on the $275 premium, it would still have taken twenty-one years before the sum of all the premiums would have equaled the proceeds of the $10,000 policy.

Many retired persons still have dependents. On the average, husbands predecease their wives by about six years. Life insurance proceeds can be used to supplement the income to the wife if other resources are insufficient. Social security income or an employer's retirement pension alone may not amount to enough income to permit the wife to live comfortably or in the style to which she has become accustomed. If an obligation exists for the care of an aged parent, life insurance can guarantee that funds will be available to meet this obligation if the insured predeceases the parent.

Life insurance is an ideal vehicle to fund gifts to charities or to other groups such as one's church, university, or club. Even relatively small sums applied to a life insurance policy can provide a relatively large gift.

Life insurance can also be employed to equalize bequests. For example, a parent might have his or her entire estate invested in a business that he or she wishes to leave to a son, but if this is done, nothing would be left for a daughter. Rather than leave the business in joint ownership to the son and daughter, the parent can provide for the daughter through life insurance in an amount sufficient to equalize the inheritance.

Claims by Creditors

One substantial but often unappreciated benefit of life insurance as a vehicle for financial security is that it may be insulated from the claims of creditors. If a retired person wishes to employ most of his or her funds for a business operation

---

[4]*Advanced Underwriting Service,* vol. 1, sec. 1, p. 17. Estimated by Research and Review Service in a study covering 72,630 estates.

but wants to avoid jeopardizing his or her family's financial security in case the business fails, he or she may use life insurance in the knowledge that business creditors may not attach either the cash values or the proceeds of the policies to satisfy claims. (This assumes that the insured has not deliberately paid up the insurance policies with funds that would otherwise have been available for the claims of creditors with an intent to defraud them.)

Provisions can also be incorporated in life insurance under the so-called spend-thrift trust clause, under which the creditors of beneficiaries may not attach the proceeds of life insurance to satisfy claims that the beneficiary may have incurred. This clause enables the insured to guarantee that no matter how indiscreet the beneficiary may be (say, because of financial inexperience), he or she will continue to receive the benefits of life insurance proceeds.

Loan Provisions

One of the advantages of permanent life insurance is that the cash values of the policy are always available to the insured as a loan or, in case of policy lapse, as cash surrender values. Loans are available at predetermined interest rates, usually 5 or 6 percent. They need not be repaid. If the insured elects not to repay, interest accumulations and the loan principal are subtracted from the death proceeds if the insured dies.

Interest and dividends continue to accumulate free of federal income taxes on the policy cash value even though the insured may be borrowing on the policy. The interest on the policy loan is usually deductible for federal income taxes except under certain circumstances.[5] The net financial effect of borrowing is often to produce a gain for the policyholder.

Disability Income and Waiver of Premium Riders

One may purchase a rider to a life insurance contract providing certain health insurance benefits. The disability income rider, for example, usually provides $10 per month for each $1,000 of the policy face amount to an insured who becomes permanently and totally disabled. Such a rider usually expires at about age sixty-five, however, and is thus not available for retired persons unless the disability was incurred prior to a certain age, such as age sixty. In this event, the disabled insured may draw a lifetime income under the life insurance policy, and at his or her death the full proceeds of the policy unreduced for disability income payments are paid to beneficiaries. At age forty a disability income rider paying $10 a month for each $1,000 of face amount costs approximately $8 annually. At age forty-five the same rider costs about $10 annually.

Almost always coupled with the disability income rider is the "waiver of premium rider," under which the insured is excused from all premium payments under the policy as long as he or she is permanently and totally disabled. Usually there is a waiting period of six months until a disability is deemed permanent. Such a rider is valuable because it guarantees that disability will not cause the insured to lose life insurance protection. Statistics reveal that the probability of total and permanent disability actually exceeds the probability of premature death at most ages. Depending on the type of contract and age of issue, the waiver

---

[5]These circumstances occur mainly when the insured has taken out insurance with the intent of borrowing the cash value on a regular basis to help pay premiums. Under current federal tax regulations, a policyholder may deduct the interest costs of a life insurance loan if no portion of the four annual premiums in the first seven years of a policy is obtained to finance single-premium policies or policies in which a substantial number of the premiums are either prepaid or deposited under a premium deposit plan. Thus the tax advantage referred to is available on policies at least four years old on which no loans have previously been taken.

premium rider may cost between 50 cents and $1 per $1,000 for ages under forty. At age forty-five the rate may approximate $1.40 per $1,000 of face amount, and at age fifty $2.

Insurability Riders

Some life insurance policies are written with what have become known as "insurability riders." Under the terms of these endorsements an individual is permitted to buy additional insurance at specified periods in his or her life up to certain limits. For example, he or she may be able to buy an amount of insurance equal to the original face of the policy. This must be done on some anniversary date, such as every three or every five years. In effect, the insurability rider is an option to buy additional insurance. It does not constitute insurance itself but is only an option to buy.

Variable Life Insurance

There has been proposed a new type of life insurance in which the amount of protection given to the insured varies with changes in the Consumer Price Index or in the stock market. The idea is to provide automatic adjustments to keep life insurance protection in line with changes in the cost of living. For further information, see Chapter 61.

Nonforfeiture Options

All state laws require that life insurance contain what are known as "nonforfeiture options." There are three types: (1) cash surrender option, (2) extended-term option, and (3) paid-up insurance of a reduced-amount option. The cash surrender option is simply the right of the insured to receive the cash value in a lump sum if he or she decides to let the policy lapse. Each policy contains a table showing exactly what this cash value is. Obviously the nonforfeiture options apply only to policies that have some cash value, that is, permanent insurance contracts.

The extended-term option should not be overlooked. Under this option, if the premium of a policy is not paid, the insurer uses the accumulated cash value to buy additional term insurance equal to the policy amount and extend it for as many months and years as possible at the premium applicable to the age that the insured has attained. For example, an individual may have a cash value of $250 in a policy by the time he or she has reached age forty-five. Let us assume that he or she lapses the policy by not paying the premium but makes no other demand on the insurance company for the return of the cash value. At age forty-five the $250 of cash value in the policy will extend coverage for about twenty-five years and ten months. A table in the policy indicates the exact period. A policy may have been allowed to lapse inadvertently and, no claim being made upon it, may be "good" for a great many years. Certainly retired persons should realize that old insurance policies may potentially have value under the extended-term option. They should be investigated carefully to see whether they are still in force.

The paid-up insurance of a reduced-amount option is the third nonforfeiture option. Let us assume that the policy has a $10,000 contract with $5,000 of cash value at age sixty-five. Rather than lapse the policy and take the cash surrender value, the insured may apply the $5,000 to a paid-up policy of, say, $8,000. Under this contract no further premiums need be paid. If the insured dies, $8,000 is paid to his or her beneficiary. The $8,000 policy still has a cash value of about $5,000. If a retired person has been paying on insurance for a good many years and desires to stop paying premiums, this may be a potentially valuable option. If the retiree needs the cash value, he or she can borrow on the contract under favorable conditions as outlined before. In the meantime he or she pays no federal income taxes on the accumulating interest or dividends and has life insurance protection as well.

Agency Commissions

Typically, the life insurance agent selling policies to individuals receives commissions as his or her main source of income. (An exception is made for the beginning agent, who receives an allowance of a regular dollar amount, often in the form of an advance against future commissions.) Such a commission varies according to the type of policy sold. For example, it is usually about 50 percent of the first year's premium in the case of ordinary life insurance, plus a 5 percent renewal commission for ten years. In the case of term plans, the commission is much smaller, averaging about 30 to 35 percent or less of the first year's premium. It is obvious that the typical life insurance agent has less incentive to push term policies than ordinary life policies. Not only does the ordinary life policy have a larger premium than a term policy, but it also carries a greater commission rate. In many cases this commission income structure works to the disadvantage of the buyer of life insurance, who may actually need term insurance, rather than ordinary life, for his or her particular needs. Yet the agent is not likely to present term insurance in as favorable a light as he or she does ordinary life.

This commission structure applies to life insurers chartered in the state of New York. For insurers chartered in other states and not operating in New York the commissions paid on life insurance are generally higher, sometimes reaching 100 percent or more of the first annual premium. New York has more restrictive limits on the amounts that can be paid for the acquisition of new life insurance business than is true of most other states.

No agents' commissions are allowed on policies converted to paid-up status, purchased through reinstating an old policy, or purchased through the application of dividends on existing insurance. Agents' commissions on policies issued to groups such as employee groups are much lower than those on individual policies, ranging from 7 to 12 percent of annual premiums on a scale graded according to size. The larger the group premium paid, the lower the commissions. It is clear that in the end consumers pay all the costs of the product that they purchase, including life insurance agency commissions. Thus, they may reduce their costs if they can buy group insurance, convert existing insurance to new forms, reinstate old policies rather than purchase new ones, or use dividends to purchase insurance rather than take them in cash and buy new or additional coverage from an agent. In interpreting these comments, we must realize that factors other than agents' commissions are involved in the cost of life insurance and that the agent performs services other than selling in earning his or her commission.

Various Sources of Life Insurance

Life insurance is available from several institutions, including (1) mutual insurers, (2) stock insurers, (3) fraternals, (4) savings banks in certain states, (5) insurers owned and operated by the state and federal governments, (6) insurers of retirement and group life insurance plans, and (7) privately owned "direct writing" insurers using no agents. Although space does not permit a full description of each of these sources and an analysis of their operations, each will be described briefly.

Mutual Insurers.   About 65 percent of all life insurance is sold through insurers legally owned by their own policyholders, that is, by mutual insurers. Usually mutuals offer premiums higher than other types of insurance (this type of insurance is called "participating insurance"), and they expect to pay back dividends to the policyholders of any funds not needed for the operation of their businesses. These dividends are not taxable income to the recipient but are considered the return on an overcharge in the original premium. The amount of the dividend is only estimated, never guaranteed. The insured has various options in the use of the dividends, such as purchasing additional insurance, accumulating the dividends with the insurer at interest, or receiving them in cash each year.

Stock Insurers.   Stock insurers are organized as profit-making corporations and are owned by their stockholders. Profits, if any, are owned by stockholders. Stock insurers may offer both participating coverage and nonparticipating insurance (life insurance not receiving dividends). However, studies have revealed that mutual insurers do not necessarily offer insurance at a net cost below that of stock insurers. In practice, the operations of stock and mutual insurers are quite similar. Initially, however, nonparticipating life insurance involves a lower cash outlay for the insured than does participating insurance.

Fraternals.   In many states fraternal organizations are chartered to offer life insurance to their members. Such life insurance is offered at cost to the membership and is nonprofit in nature. Therefore, it is usually much less expensive than insurance issued by insurance companies. Fraternals account for a very small proportion of the total life insurance in force.

Savings Bank Life Insurance.   One may purchase life insurance through savings banks in a few states, such as New York, Massachusetts, and Connecticut. These banks sell over the counter and do not employ individual agents. Although savings bank life insurance is less expensive than agency-sold contracts, it has grown relatively slowly. This may be true because an insurance salesman is the catalyst that causes many individuals to purchase insurance.

Governmental Insurers.   The federal government and at least one state government (that of Wisconsin) offer programs of life insurance. The largest life insurance program is offered through the social security system, under which survivors of covered workers receive life insurance benefits in the form of burial allowances and income to dependents. Under this program widows and children of deceased insured workers receive income allowances until the youngest child is eighteen (in some cases until age twenty-three if the child is attending an approved institution of higher education). In addition, the widow receives an old-age allowance beginning as early as age sixty. The costs of the program are shared equally by employee and employer through payroll taxes.

The United States government administers several programs of life insurance for war veterans. Special programs have been set up for veterans of World War I (United States government life insurance), World War II (national service life insurance), and the Korean and Vietnam conflicts. These programs are financed largely from general tax revenues, although the veterans holding some policies in some cases pay premiums to finance a portion of the costs.

Retirement Plans and Group Life Plans.   Many retirement plans offered by private employers contain an element of life insurance, in that if an employee dies after a certain period of service, the surviving spouse receives a pension based upon the retirement contributions of both employee and employer. Often such benefits are administered by a commercial insurer or a trustee. In many cases the retirement plan is doubled with a plan of group life insurance paid for by the employer (in some cases, contributed to by the employee).

Life insurance benefits offered through the facilities of payroll deductions (pensions and group life insurance) have been growing in importance for many years. A significant reason for this growth is the cost saving made possible through the group plan. Not only are agency commissions greatly reduced, but the costs of collecting premiums, paying claims, conducting medical examinations, and handling inquiries are lower than those applicable to individually issued contracts. Furthermore, an individual employee may receive up to $50,000 of protection under current income tax regulations without paying any income taxes on the value of the benefits received. At the same time, the employing firm may deduct the cost of such benefits on its federal income tax return.

Direct Writers.   Some life insurance is offered directly to the public through commercial insurers that employ no agents. The cost of agency commissions is thereby eliminated. Examples of such direct writing companies are the Teachers

Insurance and Annuity Association (TIAA) and the Government Employees Insurance Company (GEICO). All business is transacted through the mails. Where necessary, independent persons such as medical doctors are employed to perform certain services.

Conclusion.   The rational and informed investor will generally prefer to purchase insurance only after careful investigation of the insurer's financial stability, the quality of service offered, and the costs of the policy. Comparisons among insurers usually reveal wide differences in these basic factors.

Chapter **60**

Combined Insurance and Stock Investments

STEPHEN FELDMAN

THE NEED

Insurance premium funding programs were created originally to solve a basic problem faced by the head of virtually every family: how, with limited funds, to build an adequate retirement, or "living," estate while at the same time protecting loved ones with enough insurance coverage to provide a "death" estate in the event of premature death or income protection in the event of prolonged disability.

Insurance premium funding programs apply the simple principle of leverage to personal financial planning. Leverage increases the overall financial risk involved in any kind of equity investing, but it puts more dollars to work than would otherwise be possible. This is how it operates: First, the individual puts *all* the dollars he or she has available into a mutual fund investment. This investment then serves as collateral for a series of loans that pay the premiums on an insurance policy. This method puts all available funds to work for possible capital growth. It is hoped that the eventual investment appreciation will cover interest charges and return a profit as well.

This concept can be applied to the fulfillment of all personal insurance needs: life, disability, income protection, and various forms of property and casualty coverages. However, most personal insurance premium funding programs still hinge on the essential need for life insurance protection and the natural hesitancy to accept this protection as just another pure expense.

Insurance premium funding may also be utilized by a company that wants to establish pension and profit sharing plans or provide insurance protection against the loss of a partner, major stockholder, or key employee while keeping all cash contributions actively employed in an investment in common stock. Insurance premium funding is also used to establish retirement benefits (through Keogh plans) or provide overhead expense protection (through a disability policy) for individuals who are self-employed.

Split-Dollar Plan

For twenty-five years financial planners have attempted to answer the dual needs of their clients for life insurance protection and retirement income with a product known as the "split-dollar plan." Under a split-dollar arrangement, an individual enters a program for the coordinated purchase of mutual fund shares and life insurance protection. Although in theory emphasis could be placed in varying degrees on one or the other, in practice split-dollar plans have divided contributions equally between equities and insurance.

In spite of its popularity, it has now become obvious that the split-dollar plan does not give proper consideration to two very important economic factors, continuing inflation and increasing life-spans. Fixed-dollar cash-value life insurance benefits available for retirement purposes are likely to be worth less than the actual investment in the policy. Furthermore, the "insured" is far more likely to survive the maturity date of his or her policy and live far longer afterward, with increased cash requirements.

Insurance premium funding recognizes the likelihood that an individual will live to enjoy a long retirement. At the same time it permits him or her to provide adequately for his or her family in the event of death or disability. A minimum initial investment in a program, for example, may be $750. This amount is invested entirely in mutual fund shares. A loan against the shares pays the $300 premium on a whole life policy that provides a typical thirty-five-year-old man with $22,428 in insurance protection, a forty-five-year-old man with $15,393 in insurance protection, or a fifty-five-year-old man with $10,559 in insurance protection. This man may elect to purchase additional insurance protection, but his annual premium must amount to no more than 40 percent of his mutual fund investment. In other words, his investment in mutual funds must always remain at least 2.5 times the amount of his premium.

After the initial $750 purchase, the investor will buy additional mutual fund shares on a dollar-cost-averaging basis each month, according to a formula designed to raise the equity to a point above the minimum collateral requirement by the time that the next premium becomes due. Employing the same $750 in a 50:50 split-dollar arrangement would reduce the equity investment by one-half. However, it would increase the life insurance policy by 25 percent, from $300 to $375. Splitting the dollar to purchase the same $300 policy results in a 40 percent reduction in equity investment ($450). Insurance premium funding leverages the equity portion of the $300–$450 split-dollar plan by 60 percent.

The advantage of insurance premium funding over the split-dollar plan for any particular ten-year period depends essentially on whether the capital appreciation of the mutual fund shares exceeds the interest that must be paid on the loans for the life insurance premiums. If the shares fail to appreciate sufficiently, the result would be a financial loss.

Going It Alone

Of course, an individual may choose to do it himself or herself, entering neither an insurance premium funding program nor a split-dollar arrangement but making mutual fund investments and insurance purchases separately. The most negative feature of this decision is the absence of any built-in incentive for regular reinvestment in equities.

Do-it-yourself programs are also difficult from a practical standpoint. Personal loans with payout periods as long as ten years are virtually unheard of; interest charges on these loans, in all likelihood, would exceed the established rates of a formal program. And going it alone will definitely consume time and effort that an individual may not be able to afford. The major advantage for the individual who establishes his or her own program is that he or she can invest in a no-load mutual fund and save the sales fee of approximately 8.5 percent on all the money invested. In contrast, the insurance premium funding program offers (1) insurance protection, (2) moderate interest charges, and (3) a regular investment program. Moreover, an individual need not sacrifice versatility to participate in insurance premium funding. Most funding companies offer a wide range of choices among mutual funds and insurance policies.

HOW THE PROGRAM WORKS

All insurance premium funding programs work in essentially the same way. First, the mutual fund is selected, and the investor purchases the required number of shares, pledging them as collateral for a loan to pay the insurance premiums. At the end of the ten-year program, the participant repays the loan principal plus the accumulated interest. He or she can do this in several ways:

1. The investor may employ outside cash resources.
2. If the policy is a whole life contract, the investor may apply its cash value against the loan.
3. The investor also may choose to redeem the appropriate number of mutual fund shares.
4. The investor may combine any of these possibilities. After the loan is paid, the remaining shares may be carried forward for the establishment of a new program, if desired.

The objective, of course, is that income dividends, capital gains distributions, and market appreciation over the period of the program will be greater than the interest costs on the borrowed capital.

Dollar Cost Averaging

A common question is: How does the participant know when to make his or her investments? The power consistently to outguess the market is beyond the reach of even the sharpest investment professionals. In general, stock prices have gone up over the long term, but individual issues have always tended to rise and fall along the way. So inexperienced investors cannot count on a get-in-and-get-out system to help them reach their investment goals, especially if, like most people, they have neither the time, the training, nor the access to information needed for sound investment decisions.

But time can be made to work for the individual. Dollar cost averaging is a method of investing in common stocks or mutual funds that enables an individual to buy shares over a period of time at a *cost* per share that is lower than the average *price* per share during the same period.

In short, individual investors can pay lower-than-average prices for shares whether they buy when the market is up, down, or mixed. This means that their breakeven points are lower, and they can reach a profit sooner. For a more detailed explanation of this topic, see Chapter 9.

Collateral Requirements

Federal Reserve Board requirements dated June 1972 state that every time a new premium loan is made, the mutual fund shares securing the loan (the shares are usually purchased at the same time) must have a collateral ratio of $250 for each $100 borrowed. After that, the value of the fund shares cannot fall below 135 percent of the total outstanding loan. Most companies inform participants if the value of their shares falls near the 135 percent mark, say, at 150 percent. This gives the individuals time to evaluate their current financial status and take appropriate steps.

In most programs dividend income and capital gains distributions are automatically reinvested in additional mutual fund shares. If the value of the shares exceeds the 2.5:1 ratio established by the Federal Reserve Board, the excess shares may be released to the participant.

Preventing a Program's Liquidation

The client has several ways to prevent the liquidation of his or her program should the value of the mutual fund investment fall toward the collateral limit:

1. The client may increase his or her investment by buying additional mutual fund shares in a lump sum.

2. The client may repay all or a portion of the loan from outside sources.

3. The client may pay the premiums directly to the insurance company, obviating the need to increase the collateral for the time being.

4. The client may opt to divide the annual premium into two, three, or four smaller payments spread out during the year. This prevents the loan balance from building up heavily at any one point during the year.

Selecting the Right Mutual Fund

Companies offering insurance premium funding programs differ widely in the number and type of mutual funds they offer in connection with their programs. Some companies accept a list of mutual funds that may extend into the hundreds. Others restrict their programs to permit the use of only a few, usually nationally known funds or funds managed by the companies themselves.

The mutual fund should be one whose objectives closely parallel those of the individual investor. Generally speaking, the appropriate fund is not, on one hand, an aggressive high-risk fund, nor is it, on the other, a conservative income fund. In a down market, most of the aggressive or speculative funds suffer heavily, thus increasing the possibility that the client's fund shares will fall to the collateral limits. However, a conservative income fund generally will not produce enough capital gains to fund a program. So the best type of mutual fund is a relatively conservative growth fund with a history of performing well in an up market, albeit less well than an aggressive fund, but also with a history of preserving assets in a down market.

There are very good reasons why insurance premium funding programs uniformly employ mutual fund shares as their investment medium.

Liquidity.   First of all, there is liquidity. You can readily redeem shares for cash, and you don't have to look for a buyer. The fund will buy back your shares on any business day at the current net asset value per share. This figure is published daily in every major newspaper. Of course, the value of the shares on redemption may be more or less than the participant's cost, depending upon the market value of the portfolio's securities at redemption.

Diversification.   Second is the ability to spread risk across a diversified investment portfolio. The average investor cannot hope to diversify his or her securities holdings over more than a very few companies, but diversification is a basic principle of fund investing. Mutual funds reduce risk by spreading investments over many securities. At any given time, most mutual funds own stock in tens, even hundreds, of companies.

Professional Management.   Third is the factor of professional management at a relatively low cost. Intelligent management is vital to any investment program. So, the ultimate benefit to any participant in an investment program is the fact that his or her money is in the hands of full-time investment professionals. Fund managers are trained, experienced, and motivated to put the fund's efforts to work in a manner best suited to meet the fund's stated objectives, and they do all this at a cost that is reasonably low when spread over hundreds or thousands of investors. Fees charged by fund managers vary but are closely regulated by federal authorities.

Investment Objectives.   Fourth and really inseparable from the third factor is the importance of coordinating the mutual fund's investment policy with the financial objectives of the participant in a funding program. Every participant should have a clearly defined investment goal. Each mutual fund has a stated objective that is clearly outlined in the fund's prospectus. This prospectus should be read carefully before purchasing shares of any mutual fund.

Administration and Supervision.   Fifth is the factor of relatively easy administration and supervision. Mutual funds supply every shareholder with a year-end tax statement. This statement tells you the amount to include in your tax return and the portion, if any, that should be reported as a capital gain.

Costs

Interest on premium loans varies, but in most cases the interest charged is equal to the effective prime interest rate when each *new* loan is made, plus 2 or 3 percentage points. In addition, three specific fees may be charged to the investor. First, frequently an "open-account" fee is paid to the fund when the insurance premium funding program is started. Second, a normal insurance commission is paid from premium payments. (For a discussion of insurance commissions, see Chapter 59.) Finally, sales charges are included in the prices paid for the mutual fund shares. These charges are generally 8.5 percent of the invested funds.

For illustrative purposes, in a minimum ten-year personal funding program the participant will make a cash investment of $8,250 ($1,500 the first year and $750 for each of the succeeding nine years). For the decade ending December 31, 1976, interest charges on the premium loan would have amounted to $1,496, mutual funds sales charges to approximately $810, insurance commissions to $300, and other fees to $140. Total charges would have come to approximately $2,746. It is hoped that these charges would have been more than offset by appreciation, reinvested dividends, and capital gain distributions taken in shares during the same period.

VERSATILITY OF INSURANCE

Insurance for Individuals

The advisability of making provision for a personal living estate and a death estate simultaneously is obvious. Providing for a death estate traditionally has reduced the amount available to provide for retirement, but funding programs offer a different alternative. Many types of insurance can be funded. Some companies offer only whole life with its related cash-value accumulation; others offer only term insurance, which provides pure death protection without the accumulation of cash values. Some offer a combination of these two basic forms. Others offer clients more advanced products, such as deposit term insurance.

There is also logic in the funding of disability plans. Like death, disability cuts off the flow of income to one's family. Also like death, it is less a probability than a possibility during the income-earning years. The head of family will most likely maintain his or her income until normal retirement without significant interruption. Nevertheless, if disability does stop income, the results can be disastrous. So, if after funding life insurance needs, one still has dollars available to add to the investment program, it makes sense to leverage them to provide the additional insurance protection against disability. In fact, over the course of a funding program, a participant may build up surplus shares (above the minimum 2.5 times the loan balance) that will allow him or her to add disability coverage without increasing the size of the periodic mutual fund investments.

An individual also may fund his or her other insurance expenses, deferring them for ten years while having the opportunity to realize enough appreciation to reduce or eliminate the expense entirely. However, this is hardly the life-or-death issue that brought the concept of insurance premium funding into being. Since available investment dollars are limited (and keeping in mind the requirement that share collateral remain 2.5 times the premium loan balance), a client normally should consider this option only after he or she has taken care of life insurance and income protection needs.

Insurance for Businesses

Businesses, especially small and medium-size companies, can apply insurance premium funding to their special needs just as individuals can. The operation and even the survival of a partnership or a closely held corporation can be threatened when a partner or a principal stockholder dies. Buy-and-sell agreements, secured by various life insurance policies, can be executed to face up to this possibility. Normally, however, these policies are bought with "dead" dollars, and the only way in which survivors win is by losing, that is, by suffering the loss of one of the principals. Insurance premium funding can offer the possibility of making a profit while the insured is still alive to enjoy it. It can offer (1) a possible capital gain to offset all or part of the cost of insurance protection, (2) a built-in inflation hedge that may provide more dollars at payout time to compensate for the decline in dollar value, and (3) capital accumulation that can be used to fund a supplemental pension or deferred compensation plan.

However, to use insurance premium funding, a company must have excess funds to invest in mutual funds as well as funds for insurance premiums.

Profit sharing plans, corporate pension plans, and Keogh retirement plans for individuals who are self-employed can also utilize the principles of insurance premium funding if enough excess funds are available. The company is technically the program participant in each instance, and individual life insurance policies are issued to each medically qualified eligible employee including owner-employees. Payments under the plans would be made at the established dates either from the respective life insurance policies or from the mutual fund account, or from both. Simultaneously, the employer has the opportunity for capital appreciation from the mutual fund account.

Insurance for Charitable Organizations

A recent application of the insurance premium funding concept has been its use as a vehicle for tax-deductible charitable contributions. An individual simply sets up an insurance premium funding program as he or she normally would, then names a church, school, hospital, or other charitable organization as the beneficiary of the life insurance policy.

The individual retains the mutual fund shares, and the charity receives the life insurance cash values or, in the event of death, the face value of the policy. The entire amount of the loan for the life insurance premiums is considered a charitable contribution and is therefore tax-deductible each year. The interest on the loan also generates a tax deduction when it is paid.

Flexibility

Insurance premium funding programs may usually be altered to adapt to changing circumstances. For instance, a participant may surrender his or her policy and continue the mutual fund investment by paying the premium loan and continuing the mutual fund investment program, or he or she may stop the mutual fund investment and continue the insurance by paying off the loan and then paying the premium directly to the insurance company. In most cases, an individual may also change the mutual fund shares in his or her collateral account to shares of a different fund.

If the program is terminated for any reason before the end of the period, the premium loan becomes due. If an individual chooses to redeem a portion of his or her mutual fund shares to make a payment, the shares not required to pay the premium loan remain in the investment account. At the end of ten years, a participant may (1) pay off the loan and terminate the program, (2) pay off the loan and start a new program, (3) delay payment of the loan and continue the same program for another five years.

Today there can even be a guarantee against loss of the mutual fund investment if the client wishes such assurance. One feature is in the form of a rider to funded insurance policies. It guarantees that at the end of the program the client may trade in his or her mutual fund shares for a ten-year annuity that returns more than he or she paid for the shares, regardless of what those shares are worth when the time comes to cash them in.

The price of the insurance policy, which is owned in full by the participant, is the same as if the policy had been bought separately. This policy remains in effect, at the same premium rates, even after the program has been terminated.

Participants have no personal liability to repay the loan if the value of the mutual fund shares is insufficient to cover the premium loans. Since the loan is a nonrecourse loan, the company can look only to the mutual fund shares for repayment. It cannot ask a participant to repay the premium loan from any other personal property or insurance cash values.

Chapter 61
Variable Life Insurance

FRANK J. FABOZZI

Life insurance offers an investor the quickest means of creating an estate for his or her dependents in the event of his or her death. One of the shortcomings in purchasing a fixed-benefit life insurance policy is that the benefits are not protected against inflation. As a result, what may appear to be adequate financial protection at a given point in time may not be adequate in later years.[1]

At this writing, some life insurance companies are putting together a life insurance package aimed at overcoming this drawback. Such policies, to be known as "variable life insurance," will be sold only as whole life policies. Although only one insurance company has sold variable insurance contracts to the general public at this time, several life insurance companies have filed prospectuses with the Securities and Exchange Commission (SEC) to sell such contracts.[2] The final package that these companies will be permitted to market will depend upon legislative and SEC action. Here we shall discuss the main elements of the proposed variable life insurance package.

Elements of Variable Life Insurance

The potential policyholders of variable life insurance will pay fixed annual premiums similar to those paid by holders of fixed-benefit life insurance policies. A portion of the premiums paid will be used by the life insurance company to set up a common stock portfolio.[3] Based upon the performance of the common stock

---

[1]Life insurance is sometimes purchased in conjunction with a buy-out arrangement involving a closed corporation or partnership. However, as the value of the assets of the concern appreciate in value because of inflation, proceeds realized from a fixed-benefit policy may be insufficient for the purchase of the deceased's share by the survivors. This is another example of the inadequate financial protection that results from the use of fixed-benefit life insurance policies during periods of inflation.

[2]Such policies are sold in Canada, Great Britain, and the Netherlands. In the United States these policies have been sold to employers with qualified pension funds. Aetna, Equitable, and New York Life have played a leading role in fostering the development of the variable life concept in the United States.

[3]Policies with variable premiums may be offered sometime in the future. Such policies are known as "Dutch-type," or unit, contracts.

portfolio, death benefits can fluctuate, but minimum benefits are guaranteed. Hence, the death benefits cannot fluctuate below this minimum. To the extent that, in the long run, a carefully selected portfolio of common stock is a good hedge against inflation, variable life insurance will serve as such a hedge.

A potential policyholder would have to sacrifice two things when buying a variable life insurance policy instead of a comparable fixed-benefit policy. First, although the annual premium will be fixed, it will be higher than that for a comparable fixed-benefit policy. As of the writing of this chapter, the differential in premiums has not been determined.

The second sacrifice that a variable life insurance policyholder will make involves the cash, or surrender, value of the policy. With a fixed-benefit policy a certain cash value is guaranteed. Under a variable life policy, the policyholder must be prepared to accept the risk that the cash value at any given time will be less than the guaranteed cash value under a corresponding fixed-benefit policy because of fluctuations in the market price of the stocks held in the portfolio of the insurance company. Since the amount that an investor can borrow against a life insurance policy depends upon the cash value of the policy at the time, the policyholder of variable life insurance is not guaranteed a minimum amount. As a consequence, during recessionary periods when the investor may find it necessary either to borrow against or to surrender his or her policy, less might be available because of the probable simultaneous decline in stock prices.

Comparison of Variable Life Insurance and Mutual Fund Shares

Because the value of a variable life insurance policy depends upon the performance of the common stock portfolio held, variable life insurance may appear to resemble mutual funds. (In fact, it is this similarity that funds cite as a reason for SEC regulation of variable life insurance.) However, in terms of providing financial protection the two diverge. That is, funds do not guarantee the estate of an investor a specified sum of money. Even if an investor couples his or her payments for a fund with the plan completion life insurance package offered by most funds, financial protection still is not obtained. That is, the plan provides that the investor's contractual obligation with the fund will be completed; yet the value of the shares delivered to the estate will depend upon the market value at the time.

From the point of view of an investment vehicle the two also diverge. The value of a share of a mutual fund will vary at the same rate as the market value of the securities in the fund's portfolio. Per contra, the value of a variable life policy will not vary at the same rate as the underlying portfolio of securities.[4] How closely the value of the policy will in fact reflect changes in the portfolio established for the benefit of policyholders will depend upon the type of policy purchased.

Selecting an Insurer

The process of selecting a life insurance company from which to purchase a policy will no longer be a casual decision if an investor decides to purchase a variable life policy. The final decision as to which insurer to choose will have many ramifications for the investor. The investor's decision should be based on the results of an investigation of two key factors.

First, the investor must be aware of the previous investment performance of the company just as he or she would be in selecting an investment company. In particular, to minimize the risk concerning the cash value and borrowing value of

---

[4]Only a portion of the premiums paid by all policyholders is set aside in a reserve account. Any return earned on the securities in this account will be distributed over all policyholders. Hence, the increase in the face value of an individual's policy will be less than the gain earned on the reserve account.

a variable life policy, careful examination of investment performance during bear markets is warranted.

Since many policy features of variable life contracts will probably not be uniform, the investor must also examine the provisions of the policy offered by the insurer. Policy variations will affect the rate at which potential death benefits vary with the market performance of the underlying portfolio, the rate at which the cash value accumulates, and the degree to which an investor can borrow against the policy.

For example, for the face value of a policy to increase by only 3 percent per annum for the first ten years, the average annual rate of return that must be realized on the gross investment will vary. For an increase of 3 percent, one insurer has estimated that a 9.1 percent average annual rate of return will be required on the gross investment, while another insurer has estimated that a 23 percent average annual rate of return must be achieved. In some policies death benefits will be more responsive to changes in the underlying market portfolio than the accumulated cash value during the first twenty-five to thirty years of the policy, while with other policies offered the opposite situation will be realized. It is therefore imperative that the investor study in detail the provisions of different policies offered by competitive insurers, or by the same insurer if it offers more than one policy, in relation to his or her needs.

Regulation of Variable Life Insurance Policies

Because the value of a variable life policy depends upon the performance of an equity-based portfolio, there was a controversy over who should regulate the sale of variable life insurance contracts, for such policies are both a stock investment plan and a life insurance plan. Because of the stock investment feature, the SEC can regulate variable life insurance, if it so desires, under the same rules that control the sale of securities. On the other hand, since the transaction is a sale of life insurance, it can be regulated by state insurance departments that regulate other types of insurance.

On ancient maps, the unexplored fringes of the world bore the notation "Here be monsters." The SEC's slow and indecisive action with respect to variable life policies exhibited an analogous fear of the unknown. On January 31, 1973, the SEC ruled that variable life policies would be regulated by the state insurance departments. It thus exempted variable life contracts from the stringent rules of the Investment Company Act of 1940. However, the SEC did require that companies selling such policies register them with the SEC prior to public sale and that adequate disclosure with respect to financial information as required by the Securities Act of 1933 be provided to the public.[5] Because mutual funds are regulated under the 1940 Investment Company Act, they have argued that the same agency should regulate variable life contracts, which will offer strong competition for their securities.[6] In September 1973, a proposed amendment to the previous ruling was issued by the SEC. The exemption of variable life insurance

---

[5]The question of proper disclosure leads to further complications. The SEC is not quite sure what should be included. It has been suggested that a prospectus should include some kind of estimated projection concerning the kind of return that a potential policyholder might expect to be earned on the reserve account. This would provide a key input into an investor's decision on the insurer from which to purchase a policy if such estimates are determined in a reasonable manner. Nevertheless, projections are not permitted under the Securities Act. Recently, the American Institute of Certified Public Accountants has sanctioned projections in the annual reports of corporations. The SEC has not taken a stand on such matters at the time of this writing.

[6]There is nothing to prevent mutual funds from entering the variable life market. Several mutual funds are flirting with this idea.

from federal regulation would be conditional upon the individual states' providing equal protection for consumers similar to that provided for in the 1940 act. The final decision reversed the previous ruling and now requires regulation by both the SEC and the state insurance departments.

Some Unresolved Questions

Because of the nature of variable life insurance, several questions still remain unanswered. The first unresolved question is how the Internal Revenue Service (IRS) will treat the payment of death benefits to the beneficiary of a variable life policy. Death benefits from a fixed-benefit policy are exempt from federal income tax. However, death benefits from variable life insurance include capital gains from the common stock portfolio as well as dividends. Will such benefits still be exempt from federal income tax? As yet, the IRS has not stated its position. There is also a question of whether the IRS can even make such an administrative decision or whether the tax question in this case must be settled through legislation. The final decision will obviously be important for potential policyholders considering variable life insurance as part of their estate planning.

Second, what is the most effective method of dealing with certain policy provisions such as grace periods, reinstatement, and nonforfeiture? For example, for a fixed-benefit policy a premium paid within the grace period is treated as if it were paid on the due date in determining the liability of the company to the policyholder with respect to policy benefits and cash value.[7] It is not plausible to extend this provision to variable life policies, since the company's liability to the policyholder may fluctuate between the due date and the date on which the premium is actually paid. Thus, it is possible for a policyholder who pays his or her premium within the grace period to obtain a special gain as the result of stock price movements during this period.

Conclusion

As to whether an investor should purchase variable life insurance as opposed to fixed-benefit insurance, both of which provide the beneficiary with guaranteed death benefits, the decision will depend upon whether the investor believes that in the long run the investment performance of a common stock portfolio will be better than the investment performance of a portfolio consisting of fixed-income assets such as bonds and mortgages, for this will result in larger death benefits and cash values under a variable policy than under a comparable fixed-benefit life insurance policy. The potential increase in the value of the policy will provide the needed hedge against inflation. The investor's decision will also depend upon whether he or she is prepared to accept the risk that at any time the cash value of a variable life policy will be less than the guaranteed cash value under a similar fixed-benefit life insurance policy.

---

[7]The actuarial procedure for determining the liability of the insurance company to a variable life policyholder will probably be similar to the procedure utilized to ascertain such liabilities with variable annuities.

Chapter **62**
Professional Corporations

JOEL KAUFFMAN

The corporate form seems to offer some tax and other advantages, primarily in the pension area, for self-employed professionals. For this reason alone, the following information should be considered by all practicing professionals who have reached a stage at which a significant portion of their incomes are being paid for federal income taxes.

After a long history of fighting the concept of professional corporations, the Internal Revenue Service (IRS) has conceded that where state law permits, professional practitioners may practice as professional service organizations and that such organizations will be treated as corporations for federal tax purposes. However, some states do not permit all professions to incorporate. Furthermore, the form of permitted organizations varies with individual laws. Therefore, before proceeding an individual must determine whether his or her profession may incorporate under the laws of the state of his or her domicile and what, if any, obligations incorporation entails.

By and large, there is no fixed rule to determine whether a particular professional will benefit by incorporation. In general, if an organization is treated as a corporation for tax purposes, its members will be allowed to reap the fringe benefits presently allowed to corporate employees. On the other hand, corporate tax status carries with it the specter of double taxation of profits: the payment of a corporate income tax on profits and a second payment of individual income tax by individual shareholders if distributions to them are held to be dividends. Subchapter 5 corporations (small corporations that meet certain standards) avoid the problem of double taxation. However, they are excluded from qualifying as professional corporations.

The more obvious benefits that accrue in practicing as a professional corporation are the same as those that traditionally have accrued to any business enterprise utilizing the corporate form. These benefits should be compared with those of the Keogh plan. First, let us consider the tax benefits.

Tax Benefits

There are five types of tax benefits to be derived from professional corporations.

1. Certain amounts paid by the corporation to qualified profit sharing, pension, or thrift plans[1] are currently deductible by the professional corporation.

[1]Under the provisions of the Internal Revenue Code.

However, they are not currently taxable to a stockholder-employee. In general, an amount equal to 25 percent of the annual compensation of employees (without the $7,500 limit that exists under the Keogh plan) may be deducted in this way.

2. The income earned on the assets of a qualified pension fund is not subject to current tax. This means that the full amounts paid in by the corporate employer or employee will earn income and be compounded without being reduced by the payment of income tax.

3. A participant may usually make a voluntary contribution to a qualified thrift plan of an amount up to 10 percent of his or her compensation. Amounts so paid will be allowed to compound in the manner set forth in paragraph 2.

4. Lump-sum distributions made to participants at retirement, disability, termination, or death are taxed at reduced rates. Furthermore, if such a distribution is paid as a result of the death of a participant who was employed by the corporation at the time of death, it may pass to beneficiaries without being subject to a federal estate tax.

5. Periodic payments made to a retired participant are taxed under the annuity tax provisions, which may result in a lesser tax liability.

Professional Corporation versus Keogh Plan

To judge the extent of the aforementioned benefits, they should be compared with those available to self-employed individuals under a Keogh plan. Comparison will usually indicate that the limitations of a Keogh plan make it less desirable than a corporate retirement plan. Briefly, these limitations are as follows:

1. A limitation of $7,500 on annual deductions for each employee paid to a qualified pension plan.

2. The requirement that all employees be granted immediate vesting rights in a pension plan as opposed to the requirement that a corporate plan vest within a reasonable waiting period.

3. Under a Keogh plan all employees must be admitted to participation after three years' employment, while the requirement for a corporate plan is merely that participation be granted on nondiscriminatory basis.

4. Lump-sum death payments are subject to the federal estate tax. With a corporate plan a federal estate tax may be avoided.

In addition to the benefits set forth above, a corporation may provide a number of insurance benefits for stockholder-employees without subjecting them to income tax. These benefits include:

1. Group term life insurance up to a maximum face amount of $50,000.

2. Group medical insurance, hospitalization, accident, and health plans.

3. A payment of up to $5,000 may be made to the beneficiaries of a deceased corporate employee that will not be subject to federal income or estate tax.

4. A medical reimbursement plan providing for the payment of all medical and dental expenses of key employees and their dependents may be provided by the corporation.

Nontax Benefits

In general, the corporate form is traditionally held to provide various nontax benefits. The extent to which these benefits apply to a professional practice corporation are probably minimal because of the nature of the service provided and the many limitations set forth in the professional corporation statutes of the various states. The extent to which these benefits are available may be determined by reference to the proper state statute:

1. *Continuity of existence.* A partnership comes to an end upon the death or insanity of any partner. For all intents and purposes the life of a corporation is indeterminate.

2. *Ease of transferability of interest.* It is usually easier to transfer stock than to transfer an interest in a professional partnership practice.

3. *Limitation of liability.* A corporate stockholder is normally liable for losses only to the extent of his or her investment, while a sole practitioner or a partner has unlimited liability for a loss or claim.

Costs of Incorporation

Incorporation will usually result in additional annual costs as well as the initial cost of organization. These costs may include:

1. Additional clerical and bookkeeping costs
2. Additional state and local special corporate taxes such as franchise and corporate income taxes
3. Increases in the cost of malpractice insurance as a result of utilizing a professional practice corporation
4. Payroll taxes and other expenses, such as workmen's compensation insurance, applicable to salaries paid to employee-stockholders
5. Trustee fees for pension and other employee trusts

An important caveat to be observed is that if a corporation has a profit above the payment of salaries and fringe benefits, it will be liable for the payment of corporate income tax. However, this problem can be minimized by arranging to pay out all or practically all amounts earned in the form of salaries and fringe benefits.

Conclusion

Professional people today face an ever-increasing tax burden, which makes it virtually mandatory that they explore all avenues available for minimizing taxes. Often, practicing in a corporate form provides a simple vehicle for achieving substantial income and estate tax savings. It behooves the prudent practitioner to analyze carefully his or her situation in conjunction with qualified tax counsel to determine whether the advantages of incorporation outweigh its disadvantages in his or her particular situation.

Chapter **63**
Retirement Planning

PETER A. DICKINSON

No matter how much or how little money you will have in retirement, you must make adjustments and do some long-range planning. Your retirement income will, of course, decrease, but so will your expenses, and your way of life will be altered. At age sixty-five, the average man can expect to live about fourteen more years, and the average woman about seventeen more years. You'll have to take into account that inflation will probably increase prices; so the sooner you begin planning, the greater your chances will be for a comfortable, successful retirement.

Financial experts say that to be reasonably comfortable a retired person or couple needs an annual income equal to about 67 percent of preretirement aftertax income. In many cases, pension plans plus social security will give retirees only about 40 to 60 percent of the average sum that they were earning in their last years on the job. A report to the White House Conference on Aging predicts that only two-fifths to one-half of the elderly in 1980 are expected actually to have incomes from private group pensions.

No one spending pattern can suit everyone, but for the "average" retired couple the Bureau of Labor Statistics budget breaks down this way:

	Percent
Housing	35
Food	26
Transportation	9
Clothing and personal care	9
Medical care	8
Gifts and contributions	6
Other expenses (recreation, reading, and so on)	6

TAX EXEMPTIONS

Personal Exemption

If you were sixty-five or older at the end of the tax year (December 31), you can claim an additional $750 exemption (you already have one $750 exemption). If your spouse was also sixty-five or older and does not file a separate return, you may claim an additional $750 exemption for him or her as well. Thus, if you and your spouse are sixty-five or older, you are allowed four exemptions, totaling $3,000. You may take another $750 exemption if either of you is blind.

Retirement Income Credit

If you are retired or are sixty-five or older, you may be entitled to a credit against your tax of up to 15 percent of retirement income. If you are under age sixty-five, "retirement income" includes only taxable income received from a pension or an annuity of a public retirement system for retired federal, state, or local government employees.

If you are sixty-five or older, retirement income includes taxable income from salaries, interest, dividends, and certain rents as well as pensions and annuities. The maximum amount on which the credit is computed is $2,500 for single persons and for married persons filing joint returns where one spouse only is sixty-five or older, and to $3,750 for couples filing jointly where both spouses meet the age requirement.

Only half of such income above $7,500 is subtracted for single persons and half of income above $10,000 for couples in figuring the credit. Taxpayers over age seventy-two will receive credit for all their earnings, but social security and other tax-exempt pension benefits and annuities is subtracted from the base.

The retirement income credit is the most complicated tax you'll have to compute in retirement. Examples and specific information are furnished in *Tax Benefits for Older Americans,* published by the Internal Revenue Service (IRS Publication No. 554).

Medical Tax Deduction

If you itemize deductions, you may deduct certain medical and dental expenses that you paid for yourself, your spouse, and dependents for which you were not reimbursed. Such expenses are deductible, however, only to the extent that they exceed 3 percent of your adjusted gross income. Medicines and drugs may be added or included in your medical expenses *only* to the extent that they exceed 1 percent of your adjusted gross income. Half of the premium paid for medical insurance, up to a yearly maximum of $150, may be deducted without regard to the 3 percent limitation. This is true for all individuals regardless of age.

The monthly payment for medical insurance under the Medicare program qualifies as a deductible medical expense. However, your tax payments for Medicare hospital insurance, which are deducted from wages, don't qualify as a deductible medical expense.

Sale of Residence

If you have owned and used a residence for five of the last eight years and are sixty-five or older, you may exclude from gross income any gain made if the adjusted sales price is $35,000 or less. If the adjusted sales price is greater than $35,000, the amount of capital gain that can be excluded is in the same ratio that $35,000 bears to the adjusted sales price. For example, if the adjusted sales price is $70,000, you can exclude one-half of the gain.

The adjusted sales price is the amount that you realize from the sale after commissions and other selling expenses, minus fixing-up expenses. If you trade your old residence for a different residence, the transaction is treated as a sale and a purchase. Gain on the old residence may qualify for exclusion from gross income.

For example, you are sixty-eight years old and meet the requirements listed above. During the year you sold your residence for $22,000, which had a basis of $16,000. You paid $1,700 for commissions and other selling expenses and also paid $400 for painting and other fixing-up expenses in connection with the sale. The amount that you realized was $20,300 ($22,000 less $1,700), and therefore you had a gain of $20,300 minus $16,000, or $4,300. Your *adjusted sales price,* however, is only $19,000 ($20,300 amount realized, less $400 fixing-up expenses). Since the adjusted sales price is not more than $35,000, you may elect to exclude the entire gain of $4,300.

You can use this election only *once in a lifetime.* If you or your spouse individually or jointly have made the election, neither of you can make it again.

Nontaxable Income

Payments that need not be reported as taxable income include social security benefits; railroad retirement benefits; Veterans Administration pensions and insurance proceeds to veterans or their families and disability retirement pay; public assistance benefits; gifts, bequests, and inheritances; life insurance proceeds resulting from the death of the insured (in some cases); certain pension and annuity income; and dividend income of $100 per person or $200 per couple.

With respect to pension and annuity income, usually the employee pays no taxes on the portion of the benefits that he or she provides, especially if his or her entire investment will be received in payments within the first three years. If costs cannot be recovered this quickly, the investment is divided by the expected total return, calculated in terms of the contract's duration or the individual's life expectancy. For example, for an annuity or pension benefit costing $10,000 that is expected to return $14,000, some 71 percent of each payment would be nontaxable. You can get further information or help by sending for IRS Publication No. 575.

State Exemptions

Most states have some form of personal or property tax relief for persons over age sixty. In some instances this relief may take the form of a "circuit breaker" that gives the elderly a tax rebate or reduction when property taxes reach a certain percentage of family income.

Usually, you must apply for these exemptions through your local city or county office. As these laws are constantly changing, be sure that you ask what tax relief provisions you may be entitled to. In some cases states have strict residence requirements for eligibility; so it doesn't always pay to move to a "retirement state" with the expectation that you may be entitled immediately to tax relief.

For information, write to the state tax board or state unit on aging, usually located in the state capital, or send for a copy of *Tax Facts for Older Americans,* free from the American Association of Retired Persons, 1909 K Street NW, Washington, D.C. 20006.

SETTING FINANCIAL GOALS

The best way to see if your income will meet your expenses is to draw up a work sheet. Under the heading "Estimated Monthly Income" include:

Company pension
Social security
Savings accounts
Bonds and preferred stocks
Common stocks and investment trusts
Life insurance (endowment or annuity)
Real estate
All other sources

Under "Estimated Monthly Expenses" include:
  Housing (include rent or payments, utilities, furnishings, and house operation)
  Food and beverages
  Clothing (include cleaning and other upkeep)
  Medical care (include cost of any health insurance or service)
  Transportation (all types)
  Taxes
  Savings, insurance, and investments
  Personal and miscellaneous
  Make some provision for flexible items and any debts and allow at least three months' expenses for emergencies. Two areas in which retired people can reduce costs are medical expenses and insurance.
  1. *Medical expenses.* Be sure to sign up for Part A (hospital) and Part B (medical) of Medicare. Also, consider taking out a low-cost policy to fill some of the gaps in Medicare. For a list of firms selling these policies, write to Health Insurance Institute, 277 Park Avenue, New York, New York 10017.
  2. *Insurance.* Determine how much insurance you actually are buying or already own. You may find that there is little difference between the face value and the cash value of your policy. You can take the cash value in a lump sum or in installments, or you can convert your policy into an annuity. Or you can convert your policy into a paid-up one of lower face value.

RETIREMENT INCOME

These are the primary sources of retirees' income:

Sources	Percent
Earnings	30
Social security	26
Income from assets	25
Public pensions	6
Private pensions	5
Public assistance	3
Veterans' benefits	3
Other	2

  Are you surprised to see that *earnings* account for the largest portion of income for persons sixty-five and older? Dr. Eric Pfeiffer and Glenn C. Davis, of the Duke University Center for the Study of Aging, asked 500 subjects aged forty-six to seventy-one if they would work if they didn't need to earn a living. The results were as follows: 90 percent of the men and 82 percent of the women said "Yes." Of the men in the age group from sixty-two to seventy-one, 97 percent said that they would still work.
  Why this work fixation? The authors of this study, *The Use of Leisure in Middle Life,* emphasize that we live in a work-oriented, not a leisure-oriented, culture. They back up this statement with another finding: when they asked subjects whether their work or their leisure activities were more satisfying, more than half indicated that they derived greater satisfaction from their work.

Working Full or Part Time

Beyond making money, many retirees work for other reasons. For instance, working gives you something to retire to, may improve your health, allows you to maintain status, and gives you a chance to develop new interests. Working also helps structure your life. Regular hours, meetings, and even deadlines help regulate life and stimulate living. They get you out from underfoot and endow you with a sense of purpose.

A study, *The Working Retired,* by Dr. Gerda G. Fillenbaum of Duke University, shows that (1) the working retired tend to be among leaders in their occupation and exhibit status characteristics, (2) before retirement they had made plans to continue working, and (3) they viewed the past favorably and had confidence in their abilities.

There are many ways to return to work. For instance, Roger M. Blough, who retired as chairman of the United States Steel Corporation, rejoined the law firm where he got his start and is currently practicing law as an active partner.

One factor to take into account is that under the terms of the social security amendments, you can earn up to $3,000 annually (or $250 a month) and still draw full social security benefits. Over that amount, you lose $1 for every $2 that you earn. If you continue working after age sixty-five, your social security benefits will be increased by 1 percent for each year that you defer receiving benefits.

If you have money to invest and are willing to work hard, you might investigate opportunities in franchising. Among franchise opportunities are automotive products and services, auto rentals, building services and products, candy shops, car washes, cosmetics, credit and collection services, doughnut shops, employment agencies and personnel, restaurants, health aids and services, home services and equipment, ice cream stores, laundry and dry-cleaning stores, motels, paint stores, rental services, sports and recreation, and travel. You can get a pamphlet entitled *Advice for Persons Considering a Franchise Business* by sending 10 cents to the Government Printing Office, Washington, D.C. 20402. Michael Haider, former chief executive of Standard Oil Company of New Jersey (now Exxon Corporation), James M. Roche, former chairman of General Motors, William McChesney Martin, retired Chairman of the Board of Governors of the Federal Reserve System, and Ernest L. Molloy, chief executive of R. H. Macy, still serve on various directorships, boards, and committees. Many other executives are engaged as consultants or work in service fields or fields classed as "managerial" or "proprietary."

If you're looking for a past-retirement position, get in touch with a temporary personnel agency. One such agency is Mature Temps, which is endorsed by the American Association of Retired Persons and has offices in eleven cities including Los Angeles, San Francisco, Chicago, New York, Boston, East Orange, New Jersey, Philadelphia, Plymouth, Pennsylvania, Baltimore, Washington, and Atlanta.

Social Security

Social security benefits will be an important source of income for most retirees. However, these payments are not automatic; you must apply for them. Social security officials advise that you file benefit claims three months before you plan to retire to allow ample time to be informed of and to gather the required claim-supporting proofs. When you file for benefits, you should bring a birth or baptismal certificate, a copy of your last federal income tax return or a withholding tax statement, and your social security card.

The amount of payment is computed from your average earnings under social security laws. The more regularly you work under social security and the higher your earnings, the higher your benefit will be. The "average" monthly check for a retired worker in 1976 was $218 a month, and the maximum benefit was $287.30

a month. The new law calls for a comparable benefit increase whenever the Consumer Price Index rises by 3 percent or more in a year, reflected in benefits payable beginning in July of each new year.

To receive monthly cash payments for yourself and your family or for your survivors to get payments in case of your death, you must first have credit for a certain amount of work under social security. This credit may have been earned at any time after 1936.

Most employees get credit for a quarter year's work if they are paid $50 or more in covered wages in a three-month calendar quarter. Four quarters are counted for any full year in which a person has $400 or more in self-employment income. A worker who receives farm wages gets credit for a quarter year's work for each $100 of covered wages that he or she has in a year up to $400.

You can be either fully or currently insured, depending on the total amount of credit that you have for work under social security and the amount that you have in the last three years. Just how much credit you must have to be fully insured depends upon the year in which you reach sixty-five if you are a man and sixty-two if you are a woman.

For further information, get in touch with your local social security office, or write to the Social Security Administration in Baltimore. Be sure to ask for its booklet *How to Estimate Your Retirement Check,* and review Fig. 63-1.

Medicare Benefits.   Medicare offers free hospital benefits to persons sixty-five and older and optional medical benefits for $7.20 a month (July 1, 1976). As of January 1, 1977, the hospital insurance program pays the cost of covered services for the following hospital and posthospital care:

- The first sixty days in a hospital (except for the first $124) and all but $31 per day for an additional thirty days for each spell of illness.
- A lifetime reserve of sixty additional hospital days if you need more than ninety days of hospital care in the same benefit period. Hospital insurance pays all covered services except for $62 a day.
- Up to twenty days in an extended-care facility and all but $15.50 per day for an additional eighty days of each spell of illness. These services will be provided only after a hospital stay of at least three days.
- Up to 100 home health visits by nurses or other health workers in the 365 days following your release from a hospital or extended-care facility.

If you sign up for optional medical benefits under Medicare, you agree to pay a premium of $7.20 monthly. The medical insurance will pay 80 percent of the reasonable charges for the following services after the first $60 in each calendar year:

- Physicians' and surgeons' services.
- Home health services even if you have not been in a hospital (up to 100 visits a year).
- A number of medical and health services, such as diagnostic tests, surgical dressings and splints, and rental of medical equipment.
- Outpatient services, such as physical therapy, diagnostic tests or treatment, and certain services by podiatrists.

Benefits have been steadily expanded. Among new provisions are coverage for medical equipment needed in your home, provisions for doctors' unpaid but itemized bills to be sent directly to Medicare for payment, and chiropractic services. However, Medicare will pay only about 50 percent of your medical bills, and it still contains major gaps, including payment for private nursing care and out-of-hospital drugs. You may want to consider getting policies, such as those offered by Blue Cross/Shield, Aetna Life, Mutual of Omaha and other private insurers, to fill these gaps.

Pension and Profit Sharing Plans

Besides social security, some retirees can count on retirement income from some of the following sources:

1. *Pension plans.* The four major types of pension plans are (*a*) a flat benefit per month; (*b*) a service-related benefit plan, under which a certain benefit is paid for each year of service; (*c*) a compensation-related benefit plan, under which a certain percentage of regular salary is paid; and (*d*) a pay-and-service combination, such as 1 or 2 percent of an annual average salary multiplied by the number of years worked.

2. *Profit sharing.* Profit sharing plans usually take the form of a current distribution plan under which a certain amount is paid to the employee quarterly, semiannually, or yearly. A more popular form is the deferred distribution plan, in which an employee's share of company profits is put into an investment fund and distributed later.

3. *Thrift or savings plans.* Employees save a certain amount of each pay installment, and employers contribute to the fund, often matching or paying a percentage of the employees' savings.

These and other retirement plans are sometimes coupled with a limited continuation of other benefits, such as health and survivor insurance, that the employees enjoyed during their working years.

How to Evaluate Your Pension Plan.   If you are covered by a pension plan, ask these questions:

1. Does your plan allow the sponsoring organization to make amendments or discontinue the plan? If so, what about your previously acquired rights?

2. Are your payments guaranteed for life? Can you name a beneficiary? What would your beneficiary receive?

3. Are your payments matched or more than matched by your company?

4. Would your beneficiary get a lump sum or monthly payments if you died before retirement?

5. Is there any control over how your pension funds are handled or invested?

6. Will you get back what you have contributed if you leave the company? If so, will you get interest or part of your employer's contribution? Is your pension transferable?

These questions are important, because critics of the United States pension system such as Sen. Jacob Javits of New York and consumer advocate Ralph Nader say that hundreds of thousands, perhaps millions, of persons who were or are members of private pension plans will never see a pension check. In addition, a report by the Senate Committee on Labor and Public Welfare states that, in a group of plans with $10 million in assets, only 5 percent of the employees who left the plans since 1950 have ever received a penny in benefits.

Provisions of the Employee Benefit Security Act.   The Employee Benefit Security Act of 1974 alleviates some of these problems. Under the act persons now in a plan will be assured of some pension after a reasonable length of service, will be able to change jobs and still retain some benefits, and will have the option of providing some benefits for survivors. Those not in a pension plan will be able to establish *individual retirement accounts,* and *self-employed persons* will be able to set aside even more tax-free money in a pension plan.

Under the provisions of the 1974 act, workers may be admitted to a plan when they reach twenty-five years of age or have one year of service, whichever is later. Plans already in existence that provide 100 percent vesting immediately on starting work can require three years of employment with the company before participa-

You need work credits

Before you can get a social security retirement check, you need to have credit for a certain amount of work under social security. The chart below shows how much credit you need.

If you reach 62 in	You need this much credit for work
1975	6 years
1976	6¼
1977	6½
1978	6¾
1979	7
1981	7½
1983	8

No one ever needs more than 10 years of work.

If you stop working under social security before you have this much credit, you can't get retirement benefits. But the credit you've earned will stay on your record, and you can add to it if you return to work in a job covered by social security. (You can request a statement of your social security earnings at any time. You can get the request form at any social security office.)

Who can get checks

A retired worker can get full monthly checks at 65. So can his wife 65 or older and his dependent children. Reduced payments can start as early as 62.

3

Here's how to estimate the amount

Follow the directions below and you'll find out the approximate amount of the monthly checks you'll get from social security after you retire.

Step 1

Your retirement check is based on your average earnings over a period of years. Based on the year you were born, pick the number of years you need to count from the following chart:

Year you were born	Men	Women
1909	18 years	15 years
1910	19	16
1911	19	17
1912	19	18
1913	19	19
1914	20	20
1915	21	21
1916	22	22
1917	23	23
1918	24	24

Write the number of years here _____

Step 2

Fill in the worksheet on the next page. Column "A" shows maximum earnings covered by social security. In Column "B," list your earnings beginning with 1951. Write "0" for a year of no earnings. If you earned more than the maximum in any year, list only the maximum. Estimate your earnings for future years, including any years you plan to work past 65. Stop with the year *before* you retire.

4

Worksheet

Year	A	B
1951	$3,600	$
1952	3,600	
1953	3,600	
1954	3,600	
1955	4,200	
1956	4,200	
1957	4,200	
1958	4,200	
1959	4,800	
1960	4,800	
1961	4,800	
1962	4,800	
1963	4,800	
1964	4,800	
1965	4,800	
1966	6,600	
1967	6,600	
1968	7,800	
1969	7,800	
1970	7,800	
1971	7,800	
1972	9,000	
1973	10,800	
1974	13,200	
1975	14,100	
1976	15,300	
1977	15,300*	
1978	15,300*	
1979	15,300*	
1980	15,300*	
TOTAL		$

* The maximum amount of annual earnings that count for social security will rise automatically in future years as earnings levels increase. Because of this, the base in 1977 and later may be higher than $15,300.

5

Step 3

Cross off your list the years of your *lowest* earnings until the number of years left is the same as your answer to Step 1. (You may have to leave some years of "0" earnings on your list.)

Step 4

Add up the earnings for the years left on your list. Write this figure in the space marked TOTAL at the bottom of the worksheet and here. $ _____

Step 5

Divide this total by the number you wrote for Step 1. The result is your average yearly earnings covered by social security. Write the figure here. $ _____

Then turn the leaflet over.

6

Step 6

Look at the benefit chart on the next page. Under the heading, "For Workers," find the average yearly earnings figure *closest* to your own. Look over to the column listing your age at retirement to see about how much you can expect to get. Write the figure here. $_____

Step 7

If you have an eligible wife or child, or both, look under the heading "For Dependents" to find about how much they can get, based on the same average yearly earnings you used to figure your check. Write the amount of any dependents' benefits here. $_____

Step 8

Finally, add the figures you wrote for Steps 6 and 7 to see about how much your total family retirement benefit will be under social security. Write the figure here. $_____

The total cannot exceed the amount in the "Family benefits" column.

7

Monthly retirement benefits

Average yearly earnings	For Workers				For Dependents[1]				Family[2] benefits
	Retirement at 65	at 64	at 63	at 62	Wife at 65 or child	Wife at 64	Wife at 63	Wife at 62	
$923 or less	$101.40	$94.70	$87.90	$81.20	$50.70	$46.50	$42.30	$38.10	$152.20
1,150	123.60	115.40	107.20	98.90	61.80	56.70	51.50	46.40	185.40
1,500	150.10	140.10	130.10	120.10	75.10	68.90	62.60	56.40	225.20
2,000	169.80	158.50	147.20	135.90	84.90	77.90	70.80	63.70	254.70
2,500	189.80	177.20	164.50	151.90	94.90	87.00	79.10	71.20	284.70
3,000	209.70	195.80	181.80	167.80	104.90	96.20	87.50	78.70	320.60
3,500	227.30	212.20	197.00	181.90	113.70	104.30	94.80	85.30	368.70
4,000	246.80	230.40	213.90	197.50	123.40	113.20	102.90	92.60	421.80
4,500	266.70	249.00	231.20	213.40	133.40	122.30	111.20	100.10	474.80
4,750	277.70	259.20	240.70	222.20	138.90	127.40	115.80	104.20	504.10
5,000	286.10	267.10	248.00	228.90	143.10	131.20	119.30	107.40	528.10
5,250	296.70	277.00	257.20	237.40	148.40	136.10	123.70	111.30	554.60
5,500	304.70	284.40	264.10	243.80	152.40	139.70	127.00	114.30	566.60
5,750	314.90	294.00	273.00	252.00	157.50	144.40	131.30	118.20	581.30
6,000	323.40	301.90	280.30	258.80	161.70	148.30	134.80	121.30	593.30
6,250	331.50	309.40	287.30	265.20	165.80	152.00	138.20	124.40	605.40
6,500	341.70	319.00	296.20	273.40	170.90	156.70	142.50	128.20	619.90
6,750	351.50	328.10	304.70	281.20	175.80	161.20	146.50	131.90	632.60
7,000	362.40	338.30	314.10	290.00	181.20	166.10	151.00	135.90	645.80
7,250	373.30	348.50	323.60	298.70	186.70	171.30	155.70	140.10	659.20
7,500	384.20	358.60	333.00	307.40	192.10	176.10	160.10	144.10	673.10
7,750	395.20	369.60	343.20	316.80	197.60	181.20	164.70	148.20	691.60
8,000	402.00	375.20	348.40	321.60	201.00	184.30	167.50	150.80	703.60

[1] If a woman is eligible for both a worker's benefit and a wife's benefit, the check actually payable is limited to the larger of the two.

[2] Worker 65 or older, wife under 65 and one or more children.

8

9

A word about maximum benefits

Some people think that if they've always earned the maximum amount covered by social security they will get the highest benefits shown on the chart. This isn't so. For people reaching 65 in 1976, maximum monthly benefits are $364 for a man and $378.80 for a woman. The reason is that the maximum amount of earnings covered by social security was lower in past years than it is now. Those years of lower limits must be counted in with the higher ones of recent years to figure your *average* earnings and thus the amount of your monthly retirement check.

For more information

If, after reading this leaflet, you still have questions about your social security benefits, call any social security office. The people there will be glad to help you.

U.S. Department of
Health, Education, and Welfare
Social Security Administration
DHEW Publication No. (SSA) 76-10047
November 1975
☆ U.S. Government Printing Office 1975: 621-011/38

Fig. 63-1 How to compute your social security benefits. *Social Security Administration*

tion rights are granted. In addition, a company can bar pension rights to a worker who upon being hired is within five years of retirement.

Employers with pension plans have the following three options for vesting (accrued retirement credits that the company cannot revoke):

1. Each participant is vested for at least 25 percent of his or her accrued benefits from the employer's contributions after five years of service, plus an additional 5 percent for each of the next five years of service and an additional 10 percent for each succeeding year. Thus, a worker would be entitled to 50 percent of his or her pension after ten years and 100 percent after fifteen years.

2. An employee with ten years of service would have full pension rights (vesting) after not more than ten years' additional service.

3. Under the "rule of forty-five," a worker is entitled to at least 50 percent of vesting when the sum of his or her years of service and age total forty-five. Vesting would increase by 10 percent for each additional year. The rule applies only after an initial five-year period of service, but full vesting is assured after fifteen years of employment regardless of age.

The company also has three options on which to base a pension:

1. The company could give benefit rights at a rate of 2.5 percent a year for ten years and $3^{1}/_{3}$ percent thereafter.

2. The company could allot pension rights at a flat 3 percent a year.

3. The company might gear its plan to the workers' proportional time with the company.

To assure that pension money will be available, the 1974 act tightened financing, insurance, fiduciary, and disclosure standards. It states that formal pension plans must be directed by a fiscally responsible group qualified by the federal government, such as an insurance company or a trust. The act also created a new agency, the Pension Benefit Guarantee Corporation, which insures pensions up to $750 monthly. Companies and unions pay premiums of from 50 cents to $1 per worker per year.

Persons controlling pension fund assets must operate in a prudent manner and must diversify their assets. Also, pension plans must give annual accountings of their actions to beneficiaries, the Department of Labor, and, in some cases, the Social Security Administration. A worker must be given a summary of the plan's major provisions "written so as to be understandable by the average plan participant." At the worker's request, he or she must also be given an accounting of the plan's financial condition. Every worker covered by a plan is entitled to notice in writing if his or her claim for benefits is denied, with the specific reasons for the denial included; the worker may also bring suit in a federal court to recover benefits wrongfully denied.

Individual Retirement Accounts. Workers who do not participate in either company or union pension plans now may contribute up to 15 percent of their annual incomes or $1,500 a year, whichever is less, to a special retirement account. Taxes on both contributions and earnings will be deferred until the worker starts drawing out the money but not before age 59½. Contributions must be made either in a special United States Treasury bond paying 6 percent interest, special annuities that do not start paying out until age 59½, or a trust run by an insurance company or a bank. There is a 10 percent penalty if the money in an individual retirement account is drawn out before age 59½, and the money *must* start to be withdrawn by age 70½.

Self-employed Pension Plans: Keogh Retirement Plan. Retirement plans for corporation employees are an accepted feature of contemporary life. For some time corporations have been able to set aside tax-free dollars to provide retirement funds for their employees. Until recently, however, the self-employed business or professional person has had no such plan available.

In 1962 Congress passed the Keogh Act, or Self-employed Individuals Tax Retirement Act. Since that date the law has been amended to broaden the tax benefits, and a 1974 revision allows the self-employed individual to contribute each year up to $7,500 or 15 percent of earned income, whichever is less. Earned income is basically compensation for personal services; in general, it is computed after deducting business expenses.

The new law also allows a person to put the first $750 he or she earns as a self-employed person into a tax-free pension plan, even though this sum is 100 percent of his or her earned income. This might be attractive for someone who moonlights in his or her own business. In other words, a self-employed person can put as much as $750 into a pension plan if he or she earns between $750 and $5,000 ($750 is 15 percent of $5,000), plus 15 percent of all earned income in excess of $5,000.

As a self-employed person, you will realize three principal advantages under the Keogh plan.

1. Within the legal limits described above, you may deduct for tax purposes 100 percent of the regular contributions that you put into the plan for yourself and your employees.

2. It is not necessary to pay income taxes on earnings in your retirement fund as long as the money remains in the fund. Furthermore, there is a compounding effect. For example, if you are in a 50 percent tax bracket and you invest $1,000 at 8 percent (4 percent after taxes), it will take approximately eighteen years to double your money. However, if you could invest the $1,000 in a tax-free pension fund at 8 percent, you would double your money in approximately nine years.

3. You pay income taxes on this money only when you withdraw it from the plan. At that time presumably you will be retired and in a lower tax bracket. However, even if you are still in a high tax bracket, the funds have already accrued on a tax-free basis.

However, if you should withdraw funds from the plan before you are 59½ years of age, you will pay a 10 percent penalty plus the ordinary income tax on the money withdrawn.

A major disadvantage of the Keogh plan is that if you are a self-employed person who is also an employer (for example, a physician who employs a nurse), you must establish a similar plan for all eligible employees. An eligible employee is defined as a full-time employee who has three years or more of service. A full-time employee is defined as one who works more than twenty hours a week and more than five months a year. If you contribute 15 percent of your earned income to the plan, you must contribute 15 percent of the earned income of each eligible employee. If you wish, you can choose a lower percentage rate for yourself and your employees.

Additional voluntary contributions may be made by each participant-employer and employees up to 10 percent of earned income (maximum, $2,500) if at least one employee is covered by the plan. Voluntary additions may be withdrawn at any time without penalty, although earnings thereon can be taken out only when normal retirement benefits commence. Voluntary additions are not tax-deductible, but the earnings are free from tax until retirement.

Mechanics of the Keogh Plan. If a self-employed person is establishing a new plan, he or she can join one already approved (through many mutual funds, commercial banks, savings banks, savings and loan associations, and insurance companies) or establish his or her own approved plan. It is perfectly legal to have more than one Keogh plan. For example, you may wish to have one plan with a mutual fund and another with a savings bank. However, your annual maximum contributions are still subject to the same limitations.

It is not possible to borrow against a Keogh plan, and contributions cannot be attached or garnisheed by creditors. One thing to remember is that the law covers only earned income for personal services rendered. Rent, dividends, and interest income cannot be included. The accompanying work sheet will enable you to compute your annual tax savings by using a Keogh plan.

WORK SHEET

Yourself	*Example*	*Your Figures*
1. Earned income	$50,000	_____
2. Contributions for yourself (up to 15 percent of item 1 or $7,500, whichever is less)	$ 7,500	_____
3. Your tax bracket	50%	_____
4. Tax saving on your contribution (item 3 times item 2)	$ 3,750	_____
Employees		
5. Total annual salaries of your eligible employees	$15,000	_____
6. Contribution percentage of compensation (item 2 divided by item 1)	15%	_____
7. Amount of contribution for your employees (item 6 times item 5)		_____
8. Tax saving on contribution for your employees (item 7 times item 3)	$ 1,125	_____
9. Net cost of employee contribution (item 7 minus item 8)	$ 1,125	_____
Summary		
10. Tax saving on your contribution (item 4)	$ 3,750	_____
11. Net cost of employees (item 7 minus item 8)	$ 1,125	_____
12. Your net tax saving (item 10 minus item 11)	$ 2,625	_____

Benefits are paid upon retirement, but not before age 59½ or later than age 70½, or upon permanent disability, or upon death (to named beneficiaries). In case of termination of employment of an employee, the value of the employee's account is applied to purchase a deferred nontransferable life annuity that will commence payment at the employee's normal retirement date. You may elect to receive your own retirement benefits in annuity form, in a lump sum, or by monthly checks drawn from your fund account.

Early Retirement

A U.S. Department of Labor study of private pension plans covering 20 million workers showed that almost 90 percent of these workers could qualify for some type of early retirement, and Social Security Administration figures showed that more than 7 million workers had retired before age sixty-five, or more than 50 percent of all retired workers then collecting benefits.

Why the impetus for early retirement programs? For one thing, government (federal, state, or local), which employs 1 out of 6 civilians, along with the military, allows persons to retire after twenty or thirty years of service, in some cases regardless of age. Many private companies are finding it desirable to offer special incentives to retire older workers, especially if they are less productive than younger ones, and thus make room for those coming up from the bottom.

Moreover, many companies are providing liberalized early retirement benefits. Liberalization generally takes one of three forms:

1. Cash pension benefits are reduced for each year that an employee is under age sixty-five, but the reduction is less than in standard actuarial plans.

2. Benefits normally available at age sixty-five are paid in full earlier, provided specific age and length-of-service requirements have been met.

3. Regular early-retirement payments are supplemented until age sixty-five, when full social security benefits are available.

Some companies use two of these liberalized forms, and they are more common when pension plans are negotiated with unions.

In a typical pension plan, a worker who selects early retirement receives a reduced benefit that is calculated to give him or her the same amount of money, stretched over a longer period, that he or she would have received by waiting until age sixty-five. If we assume that an employee would collect a $500 monthly pension at sixty-five, his or her payments would be reduced as shown in the accompanying table..

Relationship between Monthly Pension and Retirement Age   *(Monthly Pension of $500 at Sixty-five)*

Age at retirement	Monthly pension
64	$459
63	$423
62	$391
61	$362
60	$335
59	$312
58	$291
57	$271
56	$254
55	$238

Also to be taken into account is the fact that while social security benefits are available at age sixty-two, they are permanently reduced by five-ninths of 1 percent for each month in which they are received under age sixty-five. So the amount received by a person who retires at sixty-two is 80 percent of his or her full benefits. Early retirement may entail an additional risk if prices continue to rise because of inflation.

Deferred Profit Sharing Plans

In some cases, employees belong to profit sharing plans that give cash or deferred payments, or a combination of the two, on termination or retirement. Some of these plans have a contributory feature, with employees committing a certain amount of each check to their profit sharing accounts in addition to the contribution made from profits by the employer. Company contributions in the most successful deferred plans have on the average amounted to 8 to 15 percent of employees' base pay. Benefits in cash plans have fallen in about the same range.

As taxable income, cash plans are simple. Employees pay regular income taxes on the money they receive. If a deferred plan qualifies under IRS rules for tax-sheltered status, a profit sharing trust fund provides the following advantages:

1. The employers' contributions (up to 15 percent of covered pay) are deductible as business expenses.

2. The employee member is not taxed on his or her share of the company's contribution until he or she actually receives the money. If the employee gets the

money in a lump sum on retirement or termination of employment, his or her effective tax is usually lower than regular income tax. If the employee receives his or her profit sharing over a period of years under an installment or annuity arrangement, he or she pays taxes only on funds received each year and not at all on any portion that was the employee's own contribution to the fund. If the employee dies, the portion of the profit sharing account that was contributed by the company is excluded from federal estate tax.

3. The money put into the plan is invested. There is no tax on the earnings from the investment, and there is no capital gains tax if investments such as securities or land are sold at a profit. Neither are earnings on an employee's contributions to a fund taxed.

To qualify for tax shelter status, a profit sharing fund must be primarily a deferred one, permanent, and in writing, and it must be for the exclusive benefit of employees. It must cover about 70 percent of employees, and eligibility must not favor officers, stockholders, or higher-level employees. Its benefits and contribution formulas also must not be discriminatory, and it must have a prescribed formula for allocating profits and distributing funds. Companies considering starting a plan can get information and planning assistance from the Council of Profit Sharing Industries, 20 North Wacker Drive, Chicago, Illinois 60606.

HOW TO MANAGE MONEY IN RETIREMENT

There may come a time in retirement when you lack the desire to manage your money or feel unable to do so. If this time arrives, you can make many arrangements, including those described below.

Banking Services for Seniors

Trust departments of commercial banks offer a wide range of services to help manage your money. When you visit the trust officer, he or she will ask you to fill out a special form detailing your assets and liabilities to determine the net value of your potential estate. Net value includes real estate, stocks and bonds, savings, mortgages and notes held, life insurance, business interests, personal property such as automobiles and household furnishings, and expected retirement income. After subtracting liabilities and possible expenses, the bank's trust department can determine the best way to manage your money now and after the death of the breadwinner. Examples of possible ways follow.

1. *Custodian account.* In this arrangement, you appoint the bank your custodian, and the bank holds your stocks and bonds, collects dividends and interest, and collects any other income that you wish handled for you. The bank will pay your utility and other bills, income taxes, and property taxes or handle almost any other financial details for you.

Special services of a custodian account could include presenting securities for payment when they are called ahead of their maturity or when bonds are due or securities must be delivered. The account would also keep a record of security transactions, maintain a record of assets, and perform other services of a financial secretary for a monthly fee.

2. *Investment management account.* The procedures and benefits of this type of account are much the same as for a custodian account, except that the bank will be responsible for investment advice and will distribute your assets over various securities, collect your dividends, and even provide a certain amount of cash regularly.

3. *Living trust.* In a custodian or an investment management account, you give the bank limited power of attorney to sign your name under certain circum-

stances, but you may reach a point at which you wish to give the bank complete discretionary power to handle all your finances to provide for you and your heirs. In this case you could establish a living trust. Your attorney draws up an agreement that appoints the bank the trustee of your estate to serve in your place if you become incapacitated. A living trust can be drawn up to provide maximum flexibility, free your assets from probate court account and inventory, and make provisions for contingencies. In the case of separate assets, the husband can be trustee of one trust and his wife the trustee of another. Then they can act as substitutes for each other's trust in case of death or mental incompetence.

Trusts may also be set up in wills to provide added security and flexibility, afford greater protection of property, and save on taxes. Trusts are either beneficiary-controlled or trustee-controlled. Here are the benefits of each:

1. *Beneficiary-controlled trust.* In this form your spouse can control the property but have someone else manage it. Your spouse can get the income for life and can withdraw the principal at any time, paying taxes as if the trust was an outright bequest. When your spouse dies, the principal is taxed as part of his or her estate, subject to certain "previously taxed property" adjustments.

2. *Trustee-controlled trust.* In this form of trust your spouse gets the income but not the principal unless the trustees decide that he or she needs it for comfort or support. Since the principal is not withdrawn, no part of the trust can be taxed a second time at his or her death—an advantage for that part of your estate that doesn't qualify for a marital deduction.

Here are two other forms of trusts you might want to consider. Your lawyer or banker can help you set them up.

1. *Life insurance trust.* This trust would make necessary cash available to your executor to settle your estate and give your family an added source of income. By giving discretionary power to the trustee, you can make the principal available to your family whenever it needs money.

2. *Pilot trust.* This trust would cover any supplemental property passing under the will, any deferred benefits, and any proceeds from life insurance, both ordinary and group. The pilot trust then becomes the testamentary vehicle and can provide for two trusts, marital and nonmarital. The spouse could receive income currently from both trusts; under the marital trust he or she could have full power of appointment during his or her life as well as by will. Under the nonmarital trust, the principal could pass at your spouse's death to your spouse's children.

Mutual Fund Withdrawal Plans

If you have a mutual fund, you might be able to withdraw regular amounts or a fixed percentage after the fund has reached a prescribed minimum, usually $10,000. You can arrange to withdraw the sum from income from shares or from a combination of income and capital (by liquidating shares). Some funds will adjust the sum according to current prices to avoid selling off too many shares when prices drop. As an illustration, in a well-managed fund that earns approximately 8 percent per annum, you could withdraw $1,000 per year for twenty years before you would exhaust the principal (of $10,000) and income.

Income from Annuities

Annuities were discussed in Chapter 59, but we'd like to point out some special features here.

1. *Income increases with age.* The older you are when you buy an annuity, the more income (interest plus some principal) you would get. At age sixty-five a man might get around $7 a month for every $1,000 of annuity; at age seventy the

monthly sum would increase to around $9 per $1,000. As a rule, women would get income at about a five-year-lower rate than men because of their longer life expectancy.

2. *The more frequent the income payments, the greater the purchase price.* An annuity paying $10 a month will cost slightly more than an annuity paying $120 a year, for when you pay $10 a month instead of $120 at the end of a year, the company loses some interest on its investments. Thus, it raises the purchase price. In addition, if the annuity is paid monthly rather than annually (at the end of the year), in the year in which the annuitant dies he or she will receive monthly payments that would not have been paid if only one payment per year were received. Also, it costs the company more to send out twelve checks a year instead of one check. Thus, the company would raise the price of the annuity if a monthly check were required.

Most insurance companies have limits on minimum purchase prices and annuity payments. Usually, you must buy at least $1,000 worth of annuity and get payments of at least $10.

Taxes on Annuities and Pensions

Generally, you are not taxed on contributions that you have made to an annuity or a pension and on which you have paid taxes. If your entire investment is received in payments within the first three years, the amount up to your investment is tax-free, but all amounts exceeding your investment in the plan are included in your income.

If payments are stretched over a longer period of time, your costs are prorated over the entire life of the contract, according to an exclusion ratio. Your investment is divided by the expected total return, which is calculated in terms of the contract's duration or your life expectancy. Thus, on an annuity costing $10,000 that is expected to return $14,000, some 71 percent of each payment would be nontaxable.

For further information on taxes on annuities and pensions, send for Publication No. 575, *Tax Information on Pensions and Annuities,* available from local offices of the Internal Revenue Service.

Too Old or Too Ill?

There may come a time when you feel too old or ill to manage your money. Perhaps friends or relatives believe that you may need help in managing your affairs. If that time comes, here are some other arrangements that you can make.

Trusts.   As discussed above, you could put your assets into a trust account and have your bank invest your money or pay your bills. Under a typical plan, $50,000 might be invested in a common stock account and, for an annual fee of a few hundred dollars, yield around $200 monthly out of earnings. The principal would be left intact for emergencies. For a somewhat higher fee, the trustee could arrange for automatic payment of some bills and even to make arrangements for emergency health care and so on.

Lifetime Care.   You can put most of your assets into a life care arrangement in which you are guaranteed room, board, and medical care for life. Fees are based upon actuarial tables of life expectancy upon age of entry. Housing alone starts at around $25,000, and you might pay an additional $300 a month or more per person for meals and medical care (see also below, subsection "Life Care Residence").

Social Security Payments.   If you are unable to manage your own affairs, the Social Security Administration will mail your check to a qualified individual. You can get further information from local social security offices.

Railroad Retirement.   If an annuitant has been declared incompetent, his or her check will be sent to the court-appointed representative or one selected by the

Railroad Retirement Board. To initiate such proceedings, check with a Railroad Retirement Board district office.

Federal Employees Retirement Program.   The Civil Service Commission will conduct an investigation to judge whether a payee is incapable of handling his or her own affairs. For information, write to the Bureau of Retirement, Insurance, and Occupational Health, Civil Service Commission, Washington, D.C. 20415.

Private Pension Plans.   Practices vary, but most plans have arrangements for some qualified person to receive the check of someone who is too old or too ill to manage his or her affairs. Check with individual employers.

Conservatorship or Guardianship.   In about one-third of the states and the District of Columbia, a person may petition the court for the appointment of a conservatorship or guardianship. Under these plans you can create two kinds of protection, estate care and personal care.

The conservator or guardian *of the estate* handles all the ward's personal or real property and money. The conservator or guardian decides what to spend, how to spend it, and what investments to make. He or she also collects any money due, pays bills, and keeps a record of all transactions.

A conservator or guardian *of the person* is responsible for the physical care and welfare of his or her ward. He or she may choose where that ward will live and may arrange for necessary medical and nursing care. All the bills incurred by the individual are turned over to the conservator of the estate; in some cases, the same person may be the conservator of the estate and of the person.

Most states allow any relative or a friend of the relative (other than a creditor) to petition the court for appointment as a guardian or conservator. The extent of inadequacy to determine need varies. In roughly half of the states it is necessary only to prove that the person is unable to manage his or her affairs. In the remaining states proof must establish that the incapacitated person is "mentally incompetent" or a "spendthrift" according to the testimony of his or her doctor, other witnesses, or the person concerned.

If an institution such as a bank acts as the conservator or guardian, it will charge a management fee, possibly $300 or more annually for a $50,000 estate. An individual serving as a conservator or guardian must be bonded and usually must pay legal and accounting fees to satisfy the court. The individual conservator or guardian is paid a fee for his or her services and is usually reimbursed for use of a car or other transportation needed to perform official duties.

If you feel that you or a friend or relative needs a conservator or guardian, check with an attorney in your state to see what procedures you must follow to establish this legal relationship.

LOCATION AND HOUSING IN RETIREMENT

Location

While most people retire in the same or general area in which they live, many of us dream of retiring in some warmer climate that is good for the health and easy on the pocketbook. Unfortunately, most of these dreams are unrealistic. Even in the so-called sunshine states you can find wide variations in costs, climate, availability of housing, and services. For instance, Arizona has three distinct climatic zones: (1) the dry, flat, desert south, where temperatures can range 30 degrees daily in winter and summer; (2) the central mountain region, with a four-season climate; and (3) the high plateau northern region, with extreme temperatures in winter and summer. Costs can run from expensive, in areas around Phoenix and Tucson, to moderate, in some of the smaller mountain towns. Areas that might be touted for their "healthy environment" might be marred by pollution or dust storms, and low taxes in some areas could be offset by other higher taxes or reduced services.

Here are about the only other generalizations that you can make about conditions in various regions:

1. *Cost of living.* Using an index of 100 for the average retirement costs in all United States cities, the Bureau of Labor Statistics rated metropolitan areas at 104 and nonmetropolitan areas at 89. The Northeast had the highest index rating, with Hartford, Connecticut, leading with a rating of 113 and Portland, Maine, low with 103. In the North Central area, the region of Chicago and Northwestern Indiana was high at 103, and Green Bay, Wisconsin, low at 98; nonmetropolitan areas were 92. In the South, the region of Washington and nearby Virginia and Maryland was highest with 105, and Baton Rouge low at 91; nonmetropolitan areas were 83. In the West, Honolulu was high at 113, and Denver and Bakersfield, California, low at 98; nonmetropolitan areas were 93.

2. *Taxes.* Generally, taxes were highest in the Northeast and lowest in the North Central states. Taxes were generally higher in the West than in the South. However, most states have homestead tax exemptions and property tax exemptions for seniors. *These states usually have strict residency requirement before you can become eligible for exemptions.* Be sure to inquire at state units on aging before you move for tax reasons. Also, some lower taxes might be offset by other higher taxes or extra costs for services. Remember that you get what you pay for in taxes. If you want certain services or protection, they'll cost about the same wherever you live.

3. *Health care.* The availability of hospital beds and doctors tends to reflect the general population trend. Thus, you'll find the largest number of hospital beds (general medical and surgical plus nursing homes) in the Northeast, with 9 per 1,000 population. There are 7.5 beds per 1,000 in the North Central states, 7.4 in the South, and 6.2 in the West. However, both the North Central states and the South have more general hospital beds but fewer nursing home beds than the Northeast.

Your Choice of Retirement Housing

If you do decide to sell your present house and move to a new location, remember that you have certain tax advantages in selling your present residence if you are sixty-five or older (if the house is jointly owned, one of the owners must be over sixty-five). Some housing choices you might want to consider are discussed below.

Retirement Villages or Adult Communities. The original "retirement villages" were built in outlying areas of the sunshine states (Florida, Arizona, and California). These communities usually sold single-family units to couples over age sixty and usually restricted children under age eighteen. However, in past years as more and more of these communities have been built near major metropolitan areas, especially in the Northeast, they have lowered their age to "forty-eight and older," they offer a wider variety of housing (garden apartments, co-ops, condominiums), and they are now called "adult communities."

Most of these communities stress "active retirement living" and feature various recreational facilities (golf, tennis, bowling) and hobby and craft shops. Housing ranges from around $15,000 in Florida to more than $50,000 in the Northeast. You may pay extra for the use of recreational facilities—a special point to watch if the builder originally subsidizes the facilities and then turns them over to the residents. In this case, you might find your cost for these facilities much higher than you originally anticipated.

If you move into an adult community and are preparing to pay around $25,000 (and more) for your housing, you should add an extra $100 to $200 per month for sewers, water, electricity, taxes, insurance, and recreation.

Condominiums and Cooperatives. Condominiums and co-ops are becoming increasingly popular, so much so that some areas have declared a building moratorium on them. When you buy into a condominium you get title to your unit, and you usually have all the tax advantages of owning a single-family house. You also enter into joint ownership of the common grounds of the condominium and are generally assessed a monthly fee to maintain and operate the property.

You can deduct all payments for interest and taxes on your unit, but the IRS has clamped down on some of the special tax shelter provisions. For instance, the IRS now allows total deductions only up to the amount of any rental income (many owners rent out their units during part of the year). Under the old rule, the IRS would allow you to deduct other expenses (maintenance, utilities, depreciation) if you rented your unit for a certain length of time.

In a co-op you become a shareholder in an association that owns the building and grounds, and you only have the "right" to occupy one of the units. The mortgage payments and other expenses are included in your monthly fee. You usually can deduct your share of property taxes and mortgage interest charges. However, if you want to sell your equity in your unit, you may find that your new buyer may have to be approved by unanimous vote of the other shareholders, and if anyone defaults on his or her payments, the other owners may have to assume the burden.

The fact is that most condominiums and co-ops have elaborate contracts that bear upon your pocketbook and personal freedom (in some cases, there are restrictions on willing or selling your unit; in other instances, there are restrictions on activities). That is why it is so important to have your lawyer look over these conditions:

1. What services are included, and what are the charges? Are charges subject to change? If so, under what conditions?

2. Are there any restrictions on your personal life or in selling, renting, or willing your property? In some cases, the board of directors or management may have a "private" set of conditions as to persons to whom you will be allowed to rent or sell (often based on racial or religious grounds).

3. What rights and responsibilities do you have for the common grounds (including recreational areas)? Are charges subject to change if the management turns over facilities to residents?

4. If you rent for a trial period, can you get your money back if you decide not to buy? If you do decide to buy, will the rent money be applied to the purchase price?

Condominium and cooperative housing costs from a minimum of $15,000 to well over $100,000. Your monthly maintenance fees might run from $50 up; so be certain to know exactly what you are buying.

Retirement Hotels and Residence Clubs.   If you like congenial hotel or club living, you might investigate these possibilities. Many of these hotels and clubs are former resort facilities that have been refurbished to more or less their former glory.

These facilities offer what you would usually expect from a hotel or a club: room and board and the use of facilities. However, you might have to share toilet facilities, and you might not always have the variety of food you like. While some hotels have arrangements with nearby doctors and hospital facilities, you might find yourself on your own if you need medical care.

Most of these hotels and clubs are located in resort areas of Florida, Mississippi, Louisiana, Texas, Arizona, and California. However, as with much retirement housing, hotels are opening up in most major metropolitan areas (many hotels sold at auction end up as retirement hotels). Rates run as low as $150 a person for a shared room to over $350 a month for a suite. Most hotels offer a trial period before they'll accept you (and vice versa). Be sure to ask for and take this trial period before signing up for any long-term arrangement.

Life Care Residences.   Many churches, unions, and fraternal orders have built life care residences (usually high-rise apartment buildings) where you can get room, board, and medical care for life. While you must be in good physical and mental condition before you move in (you must have either a medical examination or a statement from your doctor), these residences usually cater to people in their seventies and eighties. Also, you may have to be placed on a waiting list, where you could remain for months or years before you become eligible. And while many such church, union, and fraternal housing is nonprofit and supposedly open to other than members of the sponsoring organization, residents are predominantly members of the group.

Entrance fees run from around $15,000 to $100,000 for the housing unit alone. Monthly fees (for meals, medical care, and recreation) generally run around $300 and can exceed $800 for two. In some cases (usually in church-sponsored housing) you may have to turn over all your assets to the facility. But if you are unable to meet your monthly payments, the difference is usually made up out of benevolent funds or other forms of aid.

Life care housing is "forever"; so make sure that it suits you physically, psychologically, sociologically, and financially. Find out as much as you can about the sponsoring organization and about their services and medical care. Look over the buildings, facilities, availability of services, and recreation to see if this is what you need and want—forever. In many cases life care housing for a couple could cost $100,000 or more. Balance this against what it would cost you to remain in your present situation. But face this fact: *at some point, you and your spouse will probably need nursing care.* Is your present housing suitable or adaptable to that care? Do your insurance policies (besides Medicare) provide for long-term nursing care? If not, you may find that life care housing might be a bargain. Most life care residences offer a trial period with a full or partial refund after a certain stage. Be sure to ask about the trial period.

Finally, *check any life care contract with your lawyer.* This will probably be the most important contract you sign: make sure you can live with it—forever.

Buying Land and Building Your Own Retirement Housing

Many retirees prefer to buy their own housing site and to build their own housing units. While buying raw land for investment or retirement housing can be a good investment, some people are enticed into buying investment or retirement acreage without seeing it.

This land, usually located in the West or in Florida, is frequently advertised in newspapers in the Northeast. Often the down payment and monthly payments are so low that it hardly seems worthwhile investigating the site. But too often the site turns out to be far out in the desert or deep under water.

To protect you, the federal government has an Interstate Land Sales Full Disclosure Act which requires that subdivisions of fifty or more lots cannot be sold until a statement has been filed with the Secretary of Housing and Urban Development (HUD) that describes the ownership of the land, the state of its title, its physical nature, the availability of roads and utilities, and so on. HUD approves the document after checking that no important facts have been omitted. If the law is violated, either the buyer or the government could take the seller to a state or federal court.

The law doesn't authorize the federal government to judge the quality, value, use, or zoning of the land. Its purpose is to give the buyer true information so that he or she can base a decision on fact. If you do not receive the federal property report forty-eight hours in advance of signing the contract, you have forty-eight hours in which to change your mind. *Don't sign any contract that contains a waiver of these rights.*

If you're tempted to buy land for possible retirement use, make sure that it is near enough to needed facilities (hospitals, fire stations, police protection, shopping) so that you won't get stuck if you build or will have a long wait if you want to sell.

Retirement Overseas

If you feel adventurous, you might want to investigate retirement overseas or south of the border. The most popular retirement countries are Italy, Canada, the Philippines, Greece, Mexico, Germany, Great Britain, and Spain.

However, you might find some unexpected problems in retiring overseas. In the first place, while you can usually get social security checks mailed to most places (except Iron Curtain countries), you may find that mails and cashing services are not reliable. In addition, Medicare may not cover you outside the United States or its possessions. The best way to find out is to send for the booklet *Social Security Benefits outside the United States,* available free from local social security offices (ask for SSA Publication No. 609).

You might find that unless you speak the language, you can be isolated in a strange land (this might be a serious problem in an emergency). Then, consider the purity or reliability of water and electricity. You may have to take special precautions or get some sort of converter to adapt these to your needs. Also, can you own title to the land or the house, and can you sell it or will it to whomever you wish? What about medical facilities, doctors, specialists? Are these services available when you need them?

As with any other housing, you should investigate the area, talk with the residents, and check with bankers and lawyers (and your lawyer) before you make a move overseas. Also, think how far you may be from friends and family. Could you visit them if you became homesick or if there was a family emergency?

Conclusion

When it comes to housing costs, it's not usually *where* you live that determines what you pay, but *how* you live. If you live in an area where the taxes are low, you'll usually find that you pay other higher taxes or costs in compensation. If you want certain comforts, facilities, or services, you'll find that you will have to pay for them in one way or another.

So about the only way in which you can save money on living costs is to *change your way of living.* Housing is basically shelter, but it can dictate your way of life. Similarly, your way of life can dictate your housing costs. If you want to live as you do now, it will probably cost you just as much, no matter where you live.

Appendix

State Agencies on Aging

Alabama

Commission on Aging
740 Madison Avenue
Montgomery, Alabama 36104

Alaska

Office of Aging
Department of Health and Social Services
Pouch H
Juneau, Alaska 99801

American Samoa

Department of Manpower Resources
Governor of American Samoa
Pago Pago, American Samoa 96920

Arizona

Division for Aging
State Department of Public Welfare
543 E. McDowell Street
Phoenix, Arizona 85004

Arkansas

Office on Aging
4313 West Markhan
Hendrix Hall
P.O. Box 2179
Little Rock, Arkansas 72203

California

Department on Aging
918 J Street
Sacramento, California 95814

Colorado

Division of Services for the Aging
Department of Social Services
1575 Sherman Street
Denver, Colorado 80203

Connecticut

Department on Aging
90 Washington Street, Room 312
Hartford, Connecticut 06115

Delaware

Bureau of Aging
Division of Social Services
Department of Health and Social Services
2413 Lancaster Avenue
Wilmington, Delaware 19805

District of Columbia

Office of Services to the Aged
Department of Human Resources
1329 E Street N.W.
Washington, D.C. 20004

Florida

Program Office of Aging
1323 Winewood Boulevard
Tallahassee, Florida 32301

Georgia

Department of Human Resources
Office of Aging, Suite 301
618 Pomade Leon
Atlanta, Georgia 30308

Guam

Office of Aging
Department of Public Health and Social
 Services
P.O. Box 2816
Agana, Guam 96813

Hawaii

Commission on Aging
1149 Bethel Street
Honolulu, Hawaii 96813

Idaho

Office on Aging
Capitol Annex No. 3
506 North Fifth Street, Room 100
Boise, Idaho 83720

Illinois

Office of Services for Aging
Department of Public Aid
State Office Building
618 East Washington Street
Springfield, Illinois 62706

Indiana

Commission on the Aging and the Aged
Graphic Arts Building
215 North Senate Avenue
Indianapolis, Indiana 46202

Iowa

Commission on Aging
415 West 10th Street
Des Moines, Iowa 50309

Kansas

Division of Services for the Aging
Department of Social Welfare
State Office Building
Topeka, Kansas 66612

Kentucky

Commission on Aging
403 Walling Street
Frankfort, Kentucky 40601

Louisiana

Commission on Aging
P.O. Box 44282
Capitol Station
Baton Rouge, Louisiana 70804

Maine

Services for Aging
Community Services Unit
Department of Health and Welfare
State House
Augusta, Maine 04333

Maryland

Commission on Aging
State Office Building
301 West Preston Street
Baltimore, Maryland 21201

Massachusetts

Executive Office of Elder Affairs
Department of Elder Affairs
120 Boylston Street
Boston, Massachusetts 02109

Michigan

Commission on Aging
Department of Social Services
3500 North Loyan Street
Lansing, Michigan 48913

Minnesota

Governor's Citizens Council on Aging
Suite 204
Metro Square Building
St. Paul, Minnesota 55101

Mississippi

Council on Aging
P.O. Box 5136
Fondren Station
2906 North State Street
Jackson, Mississippi 39216

Missouri

Office of Aging
Department of Community Affairs
P.O. Box 570
Jefferson City, Missouri 65101

Montana

Commission on Aging
Department of Social Services
P.O. Box 1723
Helena, Montana 59601

Nebraska

Commission on Aging
State House Station 94784
Lincoln, Nebraska 68509

Nevada

Division of Aging Services
Department of Health, Welfare, and
 Rehabilitation
505 E. King Street
Carson City, Nevada 89710

New Hampshire

Council on Aging
P.O. Box 786
14 Depot Street
Concord, New Hampshire 03301

New Jersey

Division on Aging
Department of CommunityAffairs
P.O. Box 2768
363 West State Street
Trenton, New Jersey 08625

New Mexico

State Commission on Aging
408 Galisteo Street
Santa Fe, New Mexico 87501

New York

Office for the Aging
New York State Executive Department
855 Central Avenue
Albany, New York 12206

North Carolina

Governor's Coordinating Council on Aging
Administration Building
213 Hillsborough
Raleigh, North Carolina 27603

North Dakota

Aging Services
Social Services Board
State Capital Building
Bismarck, North Dakota 58505

Ohio

Division of Administration on Aging
Department of Mental Health and Mental
 Retardation
34 North High
Columbus, Ohio 43215

Oklahoma

Special Unit on Aging
Department of Institutions, Social and
 Rehabilitation Services
P.O. Box 25352
Capitol Station
Oklahoma City, Oklahoma 73125

Oregon

State Program on Aging
318 Public Service Building
Salem, Oregon 97310

Pennsylvania

Bureau for the Aging
Office of Adult Programs
Department of Public Welfare
510 House and Welfare Building
Harrisburg, Pennsylvania 17120

Puerto Rico

Gericulture Commission
Department of Social Services
Apartado 11697
Santurce, Puerto Rico 00910

Rhode Island

Division of Services for the Aging
Department of Community Affairs
150 Washington Street
Providence, Rhode Island 02903

South Carolina

Commission on Aging
915 Main Street
Columbia, South Carolina 29201

South Dakota

Programs on Aging
State Office Building
Pierre, South Dakota 57501

Tennessee

Commission on Aging
Capitol Towers
306 Gay Street
Nashville, Tennessee 37219

Texas

Governor's Committee on Aging
Southwest Towers
211 East 7th Street
Austin, Texas 78711

Trust Territory of the Pacific Islands

Division of Community Development
Department of Public Affairs
Government of the Trust Territory of the
  Pacific Islands
Saipan, Mariana Islands 06950

Utah

Division on Aging
345 South East
Salt Lake City, Utah 84102

Vermont

Office on Aging
Department of Human Services
81 Riva Street
Montpelier, Vermont 05602

Virginia

Gerontology Planning Section
Division of State Planning and Community
  Affairs
830 East Main Street
Richmond, Virginia 23219

Virgin Islands

Commission on Aging
P.O. Box 539
Charlotte Amalie
St. Thomas, Virgin Islands 00801

Washington

Office on Aging
Department of Social and Health Services
Mail Strip 43-3
Olympia, Washington 98504

West Virginia

Commission on Aging
State Capitol, Room 420–26
1800 Washington Street East
Charleston, West Virginia 25305

Wisconsin

Division on Aging
Department of Health and Social Service
Room 686, 1 West Wilson Street
Madison, Wisconsin 53702

Wyoming

Adult Services
Department of Health and Social Services
Division of Public Assistance and Social
  Services
Hathaway Building
Cheyenne, Wyoming 82002

Administration on Aging: Regional Offices

*Region I (Connecticut, Maine, Massachusetts,
  New Hampshire, Rhode Island, Vermont)*

J. F. Kennedy Federal Building
Government Center
Boston, Massachusetts 02203

*Region II (New Jersey, New York, Puerto Rico,
  Virgin Islands)*

26 Federal Plaza
New York, New York 10007

*Region III (Delaware, District of Columbia,
  Maryland, Pennsylvania, Virginia, West
  Virginia)*

P.O. Box 13716
Philadelphia, Pennsylvania 19101

*Region IV (Alabama, Florida, Georgia, Kentucky,
  Mississippi, North Carolina, South Carolina,
  Tennessee)*

50 Seventh Street, NE, Room 404
Atlanta, Georgia 30323

*Region V (Illinois: Indiana, Michigan,
  Minnesota, Ohio, Wisconsin)*

15th Floor
300 South Wacker Drive
Chicago, Illinois 60606

*Region VI (Arkansas, Louisiana, New Mexico,
  Oklahoma, Texas)*

1507 Pacific Avenue
Dallas, Texas 75201

Region VII (Iowa, Kansas, Missouri, Nebraska)

601 East Twelfth Street
Kansas City, Missouri 64106

Region VIII (Colorado, Montana, North Dakota, South Dakota, Utah, Wyoming)

Nineteenth and Stout Streets, Room 9017
Federal Office Building
Denver, Colorado 80202

Region IX (Arizona, California, Hawaii, Nevada, Samoa, Guam, Trust Territory of the Pacific Islands)

50 Fulton Street, Room 204
Federal Office Building
San Francisco, Calfironia 94102

Region X (Alaska, Idaho, Oregon, Washington)

Mail Strip 630
Arcade Building
Seattle, Washington 98101

Source: U.S. Department of Health, Education, and Welfare, Social and Rehabilitation Service, Administration on Aging, Washington, D.C. 20201.

BIBLIOGRAPHY

Brotman, Herman B.: "The Fastest Growing Minority," *Family Economics Review,* U.S. Department of Agriculture, March 1972.
Chen, Yung-Ping: "Background Paper on Income," White House Conference on Aging, Government Printing Office, Washington, 1972.
Consumer Views, First National City Bank, New York, October 1971.
Donelson, Kenneth, and Irene Donelson: "When You Need a Lawyer," Doubleday & Company, Inc., Garden City, N.Y., 1964.
Doone, C. Russell, and Charles W. Hurell: *Investment Trusts and Funds from the Investors' Viewpoint,* American Institute for Economic Research, Great Barrington, Mass., March 1972.
The Family Banker, Continental Illinois National Bank and Trust Company of Chicago, various issues, 1971–1972.
Financing a Trillion-Dollar Economy, Merrill Lynch, Pierce, Fenner & Smith, New York, April 1970.
A Guide to Budgeting for the Retired Couple, Home and Garden Bulletin No. 194, U.S. Department of Agriculture, 1972.
Harwood, E. C.: *The Harvest Years Financial Plan,* American Institute for Economic Research, Great Barrington, Mass., November 1971.
How to Take Care of Financial Details, American Trust Company, 1970.
It's Your Credit, Manage It Wisely, Money Management Institute, Household Finance Corporation, New York, 1970.
Reaching Your Financial Goals, Money Management Institute, Household Finance Corporation, New York, 1971.
Robbins, Ira S.: "Background Paper on Housing," White House Conference on Aging, Government Printing Office, Washington, 1972.
Small, Samuel: *Starting a Business after Fifty,* Pilot Books, New York, 1970.
Social Security and Medicare booklets, Social Security Administration local offices.
Tax Facts for Older Americans, American Association of Retired Persons, Washington, annually.
Your Retirement, Institute of Life Insurance, rev., New York, January 1973.

Section Twelve

Estate Planning

D. LARRY CRUMBLEY, EDITOR

ROBERT KATZ, CONSULTING EDITOR

Chapter **64**

Maximizing Your Estate for the Rest of Your Life

D. LARRY CRUMBLEY

EDWARD E. MILAM

There has been a steady but creeping inflationary spiral in the United States since the early 1930s. Moreover, in recent years the country has experienced rampant inflation of as much as 5 or 6 percent per year. Inflation is a silent tax increase on everyone. However, for the retired person who has accumulated some wealth, inflation can be the severest tax increase possible. A man may have built up what he considers to be a rather large estate at the time of his retirement. He may intend to live comfortably off the income derived from the assets in the estate and leave all these assets to his heirs. However, if he should live fourteen years after his retirement and during this time there is an inflation averaging 5 percent per year, the real value of his savings and other fixed-dollar assets in his estate will have decreased by almost 50 percent. Some of his assets, such as stocks and real estate, may have increased in value during the inflation. However, as these assets increase in value, they are subject to higher estate taxes. This is true even though their real value, deflated for inflation, may actually have declined.

As assets increase in value, more and more individuals are encountering a little-known tax called the federal estate tax. Whereas only the rich once had to pay this tax, average middle America may now be caught by this tax trap.

Legally an estate is created upon the death of an individual. The laws of every state in the Union dictate that upon a person's death his or her property must be held intact for a period of time. It is necessary that this property be administered for the benefit of the heirs and creditors. Thus an estate is a creation of law. The estate is a new and distinct entity and should not be confused with the decedent, the executor of the estate, or the beneficiaries. This estate is composed of the sum of the values of all property to the extent of the decedent's interest in such property at the time of his or her death.

In addition to being subjected to administration, the estate is faced with the burdens of federal and state taxation. To minimize these taxes and to control the administration of property, individuals should seek methods or plans more effectively to provide for their beneficiaries and to accomplish their objectives. It seems fruitless for an individual to work his or her entire life to build up an estate for his or her heirs and then have this estate confiscated by various governmental bodies through the lack of adequate planning. The drafting and implementation of such plans are known as estate planning.

History of Estate Planning

Even though estate planning has become popular only in recent years, it is not new. The Code of Hammurabi gave early Babylonians the right to dispose of their property at time of death. This code provided for both testate and intestate succession. The early common law of England placed burdens on the holding of legal title to land. Death taxes, trusts, and wills existed under the English feudal system. As early as the fifteenth century there were estate planners who devised ingenious techniques to aid their clients. The estate planner of that time was interested primarily in determining ways in which his client could transfer legal title of his land to his beneficiaries and avoid the burdens incident to the descent of land.[1]

For all practical purposes estate planning in the United States evolved only in the twentieth century. The tax statutes of the late nineteenth and twentieth centuries aroused tremendous interest in estate planning. In 1913 the Sixteenth Amendment authorized the enactment of a federal income tax, and in 1915 estate tax statutes were enacted. These were followed by the enactment of gift tax laws in 1932. Meanwhile, toward the end of the nineteenth century, the individual states had begun passing state inheritance laws and taxes. The simultaneous development of estate planning and the enactment of tax laws in the United States gave many people the misconception that estate planning and tax planning are synonymous.

Necessity of Estate Planning as Part of Personal Finance

Since estate planning is a relatively new development in the United States, many people do not understand its purposes or know who needs it. Estate planning applies to anyone with income or property. It may be even more important to the small estate owner than to the large owner because the waste of a single asset in a small estate could prevent the accomplishment of the owner's objectives and bring hardship to his or her family. In other words, everyone who owns assets needs an estate plan. This plan might be reflected by a simple will or by a complex arrangement consisting of several of the planning devices or tools available to the estate owner.

ESTATE-PLANNING PROCESS

Because there are differences in people's objectives, attitudes, temperaments, and net assets, an estate plan should be designed to meet an individual's specific needs. Since estate planning differs for every individual, many uncertainties confront anyone who attempts to develop such a plan. However, the estate-planning *process* is basically the same for each case.

For purposes of analysis, the estate-planning process can be broken into five steps:
1. Gathering the facts
2. Evaluating the obstacles of estate impairment

[1]Lawrence J. Ackerman, "Estate Planning Principles," in D. W. Gregg (ed.), *Life and Health Insurance Handbook*, Richard D. Irwin, Inc., Homewood, Ill., 1959, p. 494; William J. Bowe, *Estate Planning and Taxation*, chartered life underwriters' ed., Dennis and Co., Inc., Buffalo, N.Y., 1964, pp. 1–2.

3. Designing the plan
4. Implementing the plan
5. Reviewing the plan[2]

Each of these steps is briefly discussed in the following subsections.

Gathering the Facts

The first step in the estate-planning process is getting the facts, for these will serve as the basis for all other procedures. Gathering the facts may seem to be a simple task. In many cases, however, the most challenging part of the estate-planning process is the attempt to obtain all the necessary information. The facts needed can be classified in four categories: (1) domicile, (2) property, (3) beneficiaries, and (4) the individual's objectives.

1. Domicile is an important factor since it determines the law that will govern the validity of the will and its provisions. Domicile determines how title to property is held: community property versus separate property and joint tenancy versus a tenancy in common. Because of the significant differences that exist between the laws of various states, the domicile of the estate owner must be determined before plans are formulated.

2. A complete inventory of all the taxpayer's assets and liabilities should be gathered. Detailed information regarding all business and personal assets and liabilities should be obtained. Such data would include information about insurance policies, powers of appointment, property owned separately and jointly, business interests, retirement and death benefits, claims under wills and trusts, and rights in future interest. In addition, full information about the estate owner's obligations must be secured. These data would include information about personal debts, business debts, accrued taxes, mortgages, leases, installment contracts, and all other debts including contingent liabilities.

Special problems concerning an estate owner's business interests often arise in the analysis of his or her property, especially when such interests amount to a large portion of the estate. These interests may be held in the form of sole proprietorships, partnerships, stock in a closely held corporation, or any combination of these. If this is the case, there is a problem of valuation. Such interests must be properly valued for estate tax purposes in accordance with the Internal Revenue Code and Regulations. Another problem is determination of the ability of the business to produce income for the benefit of the taxpayer's heirs after his or her death or retirement. Even though the business is the chief source of a taxpayer's income and wealth and will continue to be so as long as he or she actively manages its affairs, it may not continue to be profitable in the absence of the taxpayer. At death, this business interest becomes an investment of an estate, and it is valuable only if it continues to be profitable. Thus, care must be used in an evaluation of business interests.

3. Facts concerning the beneficiaries of the estate owner must be gathered and accumulated by the owner or by his or her estate-planning team.[3] These facts include the names and birth dates of the estate owner and all his or her beneficiaries. At this time the owner's responsibility to his or her family should be evaluated.

---

[2]Several authors have referred to the estate-planning process and the involved nature of each step. See H. W. B. Manning, "Estate Planning for Three Stages of Individual's Life," *Commercial and Financial Chronicle,* vol. XCVIII, pp. 9, 13, July 4, 1963. See also Ackerman, op. cit., p. 495; Irving Pfeffer, "The Nature and Scope of Estate Planning," *California Management Review,* vol. IX, pp. 24–29, Fall, 1966; William H. Hoffman, Jr., *Effective Estate Planning Procedures for Minimizing Taxes,* Prentice-Hall, Inc., Englewood Cliffs, N.J., 1968, p. 2.

[3]An estate-planning team is often composed of an attorney, a certified public accountant, a trust officer, and a life insurance underwriter.

Such personal information as the character of the estate owner's spouse and other heirs and their business abilities should be considered. A taxpayer's state of health, the wealth now available to the heirs, their financial needs, and the attitudes of individual beneficiaries toward each other are important.

In summary, an estate owner should obtain data about the health, wealth, education, character, and living needs of all his or her beneficiaries.[4]

4. The last classification of facts is the determination of the objectives of the estate owner. This is often the most difficult phase of gathering the facts. An estate owner's attitude about the financial maintenance and security of his or her family must be formulated. Many people feel that their heirs should have complete and unrestricted freedom to use the assets left to them, while others fear to entrust substantial amounts of money in lump sums to their beneficiaries.

In addition to gathering the facts, an estate owner must determine and evaluate his or her currently existing estate plan. Whether the estate owner is aware of it or not, he or she has an estate plan, which may have been developed consciously or accidentally. Therefore, a taxpayer must accumulate information concerning all gifts, trusts, wills, and reversionary interest that he or she has created or possesses.[5]

The task of gathering the facts may seem tedious and dull, but it is often the most challenging and important part of the estate-planning process. Many times estate owners have not made a thorough analysis of their estates and often are surprised at the results. Such an analysis is necessary to lay a firm foundation for the rest of the estate-planning process.

Evaluating the Obstacles Causing Estate Impairment

The second phase of the estate-planning process is an evaluation of the obstacles that could impair the value of the estate. An estate owner and the members of his or her estate-planning team must be aware of the many forces that can shrink the value of the estate and deny the estate owner the attainment of his or her objectives. Some of the more obvious of these impairments are the cost of the last illness, funeral expenses, estate administration expenses, and the federal estate tax. Consideration must be given to all debts of the estate owner, including the current unpaid bills, as well as debts of greater magnitude and longer duration such as mortgages, installment contracts, and business obligations. Attention must also be directed toward unpaid income and property taxes as well as state inheritance taxes. These are just a few of the more obvious obstacles of impairment.

According to Pfeffer, four classes of risk are encountered in estate conservation problems. These are *business, investment, legal* and *tax risks.*[6]

The management of any business is subject to a wide spectrum of risks, and competent managerial personnel must have the ability to operate the firm successfully. Some relevant questions for estate planning are (1) whether management has the technical ability and training to continue profitable operation of the firm, (2) whether there are heirs or key employees who have the aptitude, temperament, and capacity to be potential successors to the management, and (3) whether additional capital contributions will be necessary to maintain the current level of earnings.[7] Moreover, any evaluation of business risks must include an analysis of the current and future economic climate and its influence upon the business. In addition, there are important insurable business hazards to be considered. These include legal liability, property damage, theft, surety bonds, and life, accident, and health risks.

[4]Hoffman op. cit., p. 3.
[5]Ackerman, op. cit., p. 498.
[6]Pfeffer, op. cit., p. 26.
[7]Ackerman, op. cit., pp. 497–498.

If a taxpayer's business interests are closely held, special problems arise. These include problems of valuation and liquidity. To analyze effectively the business risks of a closely held firm, the estate owner and his or her estate-planning team should be thoroughly familiar with the taxpayer's particular business as well as with the economy in general. In valuing the business interests for estate-planning purposes several factors must be considered. These include the nature and history of the business, conditions in the specific industry as well as the general economic outlook, the financial condition of the organization, the book value of the taxpayer's interests, past earnings, current earnings as well as potential earning ability, dividend policy, and the value of goodwill and other intangibles. To determine whether the business can serve as a source of liquidity for the estate, an analysis of the firm's cash flow must be conducted.[8]

Portfolio management is concerned with investment risks.[9] If the estate owner has significant investments, he or she must analyze these holdings with respect to the investment risks and take steps to prevent impairment of the estate by these risks. Such steps would include diversification of various kinds and the selection of securities on the basis of their relative invulnerability to the risks.[10]

The estate owner must define the goals to be achieved with his or her investments. For example, he or she may desire a high current income with a minimum amount of risk or seek growth and capital gains even at the price of additional risk. Earlier sections of the *Handbook* discuss goal selection for the investor, choosing individual stocks to accomplish these goals, and portfolio management.

Another type of risk in estate planning is legal risk, which arises from the failure of the estate owner and the estate-planning team to execute properly the appropriate documents essential in carrying out the owner's objectives. All wills, trusts, contracts, and titles to property must be valid and be properly executed. These instruments should be prepared by a competent lawyer and reviewed periodically to assure that they are still in accordance with the estate owner's desires. Estate plans that are developed in an atmosphere of ill-defined objectives, procrastination, poorly drawn legal documents, and uncoordinated planning result in designs that are unstable and open to attack. Much of the ultimate frustration in the legal aspects of estate planning can be avoided by consulting an attorney who is well versed in preventive law.[11]

Another risk encountered in estate conservation is the tax risk. This risk often causes the greatest stress and frequently is the risk responsible for the estate owner's seeking estate-planning assistance. Poor tax planning or no planning at all can seriously deplete the value of an estate. Many factors having significant tax consequences must be evaluated. These include the differential tax treatment of ordinary income and capital gains, of the transference of community property versus separate property, of estates held in joint tenancy rather than in common, and of gifts in contemplation of death versus valid gifts. Another factor having significant tax consequences is the successive taxation of estates when surviving heirs die shortly after the death of the estate owner.[12] An evaluation of the tax risks calls for a high degree of skill in the estate-planning process. For the estate-planning team to be effective, at least one member must be thoroughly familiar with the basic provisions of the federal estate and gift tax laws and have an understanding of those sections of the Internal Revenue Code that govern the

[8]D. Larry Crumbley and P. Michael Davis, *Organizing, Operating, and Terminating Subchapter S Corporations: Taxation and Accounting,* Lawyers and Judges Publishing Company, 1974.
[9]For a useful classification of these risks, see Donald E. Vaughn, *Survey of Investments,* Holt, Rinehart and Winston, Inc., New York, 1967, p. 49.
[10]Pfeffer, op. cit., pp. 26–27.
[11]Ibid., p. 27.
[12]Ibid., p. 27.

taxing of income of fiduciaries. Such knowledge is necessary so that effective tax planning can be carried out during the taxpayer's lifetime and be continued throughout the administration of his or her estate.

Some member of the estate-planning team should be familiar with the interrelationships between the federal estate and fiduciary income tax laws. When properly handled, many of these interrelationships concerning tax elections by the administrator can produce significant overall tax savings for the beneficiaries of the estate. For instance, the value of the assets as shown on the estate tax return may determine some of the basis of these assets to the beneficiaries for income tax purposes under the fresh start provision for appreciation prior to 1976. There are many other interrelationships between the two taxes that must be considered by the administrator and the tax adviser.

Tax planning not only is very important in estate planning but also is necessary in post-mortem planning. During this time many decisions that have significant effects upon the conservation of the estate are made. A proper analysis of the alternatives could result in significant tax savings and help preserve the taxpayer's estate.

Several other factors that cause impairment of the estate should be considered by the members of the estate-planning team. One of the most important is the liquidity of the estate. Many estates are burdened with debts and obligations; the estate must pay the cost of the last illness, funeral expenses, estate administration expenses, and federal and state taxes and also honor the decedent's cash bequests. Since there must be sufficient liquid assets to meet these requirements, the liquidity needs of the taxpayer's estate should be determined. Using the information obtained during the fact-gathering process as a guide, the members of the estate-planning team should be able to make rough estimates of these costs. These estimates will help determine the estate cash requirements and serve as additional background information for the preparation of the estate plan. If the estate is burdened with a shortage of liquid assets, income-producing assets may have to be sold, possibly for less than their real value, to meet these needs. The dilution of income-producing assets may have significant adverse effects upon the decedent's survivors.

Another force of impairment that demands consideration is the instability of the values of the estate property. Changes in consumer preference, obsolescence, or improper management of the estate's assets could severely shrink the value of the estate. Consideration should be given to the possibility of prolonged and expensive illness or disability, loss of income, and legal liability of the estate owner. Insurance should be acquired to help reduce the burden in case any of these possibilities occur.[13]

Certainly the members of the estate-planning team must analyze all the factors that could shrink or deplete the value of the taxpayer's estate. However, this evaluation of risks is only one step in the estate-planning process. There are several other steps that are just as important and must be performed during the planning process.

Designing the Plan

Designing the plan is the next step in the estate-planning process. No meaningful plan can be drawn until all the facts have been gathered and the objectives of the estate owner determined. This plan must be based upon the facts and at the same time give life to the owner's objectives. It should be as simple and as flexible as possible and still accomplish its objectives.[14]

[13]Ackerman, op. cit., pp. 494–495.
[14]Ackerman, op. cit., p. 498.

A variety of tools will help accomplish the objectives of the estate owner. Through analyzing various combinations of these methods of transfer, the ultimate plan is developed. The plan should be tested and the consequences evaluated. No attempt is made here to mention all the available vehicles of transfer, but a few are discussed for illustrative purposes.

The will is a key vehicle of transfer, and its preparation is often the first step taken by estate owners in planning the disposition of their estates. Some useful devices attached to this vehicle are the marital deduction and marital deduction trusts. The basic consideration in using the marital deduction is the favorable tax consequence. The costs of this tax saving, however, may be a compromise of one's objectives, a possible deferred increase in transfer costs, or a loss of control of an asset.[15] If the marital deduction is used, the estate planner must observe the appropriate sections and provisions of the Internal Revenue Code and Regulations.

Under certain conditions and limitations, the estates of citizens and residents of the United States are allowed a marital deduction of up to 50 percent of the adjusted gross estate or $250,000, whichever is greater. The purpose of the deduction is to eliminate the tax advantages held by persons domiciled in community property states. The federal statutes provided all taxpayers with the tax treatment previously available only to residents of community property states. For tax purposes Congress made the community property system applicable to the other states. For a more detailed explanation of the concept, see the subsection "Taxable Estate."

Trusts provide another means of transfer. Inter vivos and testamentary, revocable and irrevocable, and funded and unfunded trusts may be used by the estate planner. Some important advantages are derived from the fact that trusts are based on the concepts of property arrangement and property settlement. The main purpose of the trust device is to serve as a means of preserving and administering property for the benefit of the beneficiaries.

Because the trust permits considerable flexibility in the disposition of property, it is one of the most valuable tools in estate planning. The trust device provides the flexibility needed to achieve nontax estate objectives, such as relieving other family members of responsibility, obtaining confident management of the property, and providing discretion in income and principal distributions. Of perhaps equal significance in many instances are the income and estate tax economies obtainable through the use of trusts.

Trusts are formed for many purposes. In fact, a trust may be created to achieve any desired objective as long as that objective is not illegal or contrary to any policy or rule of law. Some of the commoner types of trusts, classified as to purpose, include insurance trusts, educational trusts, support trusts, charitable trusts, and marital deduction trusts.

When a trust is created, it is only natural and proper that it be planned so as to maximize the use of the available favorable tax provisions. However, the purpose of its establishment ordinarily is not merely to save taxes. The saving of taxes is only one reason for the creation of trusts: the primary reason should be the process of providing an orderly and sensible disposition of the trust property according to the desires of the estate owner.

Another means of transfer is life insurance. Often life insurance is the only practical way of guaranteeing that sufficient cash will be available to meet the financial costs of death. The use of life insurance has many advantages. In many states its use provides savings in estate taxes. Also, insurance proceeds can be removed from the probate estate, thus reducing probate and administration costs. Often the most important use of life insurance in estate planning is to meet the

---

[15]Ibid., p. 499.

obligations of the estate, thus preventing the forced sale of income-producing assets. In essence, the use of insurance in the estate plan will be determined by the needs for liquidity, flexibility, tax minimization, investment, and the requirements of family income.[16]

Private annuities represent another important vehicle of transfer, but the risks involved must be carefully considered. In such a contract, the annuitant transfers property other than cash to the obligor in return for the latter's unsecured promise to make periodic payments of money to the annuitant for a specific period of time. The period is usually the life of the annuitant. Thus the major risk to the annuitant is the obligor's failure to make the required payments.

The private annuity offers several tax advantages. First, since it is a valid sales contract, the property is removed from the obligor's estate. Second, each payment is broken into three portions: an excluded portion, an ordinary income portion, and a capital gain or loss portion. This confers on the annuitant the additional advantages of spreading any gain from the sale of such property over a period of several years for income tax purposes. In essence, it gives the annuitant a deferment for payment of the income taxes associated with the transfer.

For example, let us assume that Taxpayer X, a sixty-year-old female, owns rental property with a fair market value of $100,000 and an adjusted basis of $50,000. She transfers this property to her son, Taxpayer Y, for Y's legally enforceable promise to make periodic annual payments to her for the remainder of her life. The agreement is effective on January 1, 1974, and the first payment is due on December 31, 1974.

The basis of X's property ($50,000) must be compared with the present value of the annuity to determine X's capital gain. To prevent gift tax consequences, the present value of the annuity must equal the fair market value of the transferred rental property of $100,000. The present value of the annuity is determined by tables in the Regulations [Section 20.2031-10 and Section 1.101-2(e)(1), (iii)(b)(3)]. Table A(2) of Regulation 20.2031-10 indicates that the *present worth* of an annuity for a sixty-year-old female is 10.5376. To prevent a gift tax, the present value of the annuity must equal $100,000; thus the annual payments are determined by dividing $100,000 by 10.5376. This indicates an annual payment of $9,489.82 for the life of Taxpayer X. The excess of the fair market value of the annuity received over the basis of the rental property transferred represents capital gain ($100,000 minus $50,000 equals a $50,000 realized capital gain). See Section 1.1001-1(e)(1) of the Regulations.

Taxpayer X's tax effects are as follows. For income tax purposes the annuity falls under Internal Revenue Code Section 72 and Revenue Ruling 69-74. The annual payment of $9,489.82 is divided into three portions: capital gain, exclusion, and ordinary annuity income. The computation and application of these three items follow:

1. $201,184 expected return [annual proceeds of $9,489.82 multiplied by 21.2 years, X's life expectancy (Table 1, Regulation Section 1.72-9)]

2. $50,000 (investment in the contract) divided by $201,184 (expected return) results in an exlusion ratio of 24.9 percent

3. Annual proceeds, $9,489.82

4. Exclusion, $2,362.97 (24.9 percent of $9,489.82)

5. Capital gain income, $2,358.49 ($50,000 divided by 21.2 years, X's life expectancy)

6. Ordinary annuity income, $4,768.36 (item 3 minus the total of items 4 and 5, or $9,489.82 minus $4,721.46 equals $4,768. 36)

The exclusion ratio of 24.9 percent remains constant throughout the contract.

---

[16]Ibid., pp. 499–500.

However, after the capital gain of $50,000 has been fully reported, subsequent amounts received must be reported as ordinary income.

For estate tax purposes the full value of the rental property ($100,000) is removed from Taxpayer X's gross estate. The property has been legally transferred for a consideration that upon X's death retains no value because the annual payments cease with her death.

Another effective vehicle of transfer in estate planning is the use of lifetime gifts; they eliminate all probate and administration expenses on the property transferred. Nontaxable gifts reduce estate taxes because the gift property and the amount of income that would have accumulated from the property are both removed from the transferrer's gross estate. Often the use of a gift provides savings in income taxes because the income that is generated by the asset given as a gift is shifted from the high income tax bracket of the transferrer into the lower income bracket of the transferee. Of course, the use of gifts produces many advantages other than taxes. Gifts may be employed to preserve control of a business within the family or to serve the specific desires of the estate owner for his or her children. Like all other devices, gifts have their costs; the most significant cost of making a gift is the complete loss of control of the asset.[17] Lifetime gifts are discussed in greater detail in the section "Federal Gift Tax."

Before lifetime gifts are made, it must be remembered that under certain circumstances the gift property may later be included in the donor's gross estate even though the gifts were made during his or her lifetime. Any transfers of property by the decedent without adequate and full consideration and made within three years of death are made in *contemplation of death,* and such property is thus included in the gross estate of the decedent. For example, if a man gives $20,000 to his daughter and dies two years later, this gift will be considered as having been given in contemplation of death and would be included in computing the gross estate of the deceased along with gift taxes paid on the transfer. Likewise, the relinquishment of a power over property transferred during life or the exercise or release of a power of appointment within three years of death is deemed to have been made in contemplation of death.[18]

The vehicles of transfer discussed here are only a few of those available to the estate owner. During the designing and before the implementation of an estate plan, the advantages and disadvantages of these methods of transfers must be evaluated. The vehicles that help accomplish the estate owner's objectives should be incorporated in the estate plan.

Implementation of the Plan

Before the estate plan becomes effective, the appropriate legal documents must be executed. The necessity for careful planning and execution of the documents cannot be overemphasized. Faulty execution is a sure way of invalidating the entire efforts of any estate plan.

The legal documents must be reviewed periodically to ascertain that they continue to express the estate owner's objectives. A periodic review of financial status and family relationships should be conducted to determine whether there have been any changes that necessitate revision of the estate plan. Also, the plan should be reviewed in the light of any changes or potential changes in the legal or tax aspects of the environment. Such a review could bring about a modification in the plan that would produce significant benefits to the estate owner, while neglect of such a review could be very costly.

[17]See D. Larry Crumbley, *A Practical Guide to Preparing a Federal Gift Tax Return,* Lawyers and Judges Publishing Company, 1976.
[18]IRC, Sec. 2035.

PROBATE

Probate is a legal and bureaucratic process that takes place after an individual dies, enabling him or her to pass on property to the legal heirs as specified in his or her will. Probate may drag on for years before the heirs actually receive possession of the decedent's assets.

The delay during probate occurs because the assets come under the jurisdiction of the probate court. The will must be found and read to determine who the executor is and who are named as the heirs. However, the heirs do not inherit the money immediately. The decedent may have specified in his or her will who the heirs are and how the estate should be disposed of. But the law states that no one other than a judge can legally say who the heirs are, that someone was not illegally omitted, and that all the taxes and debts of the deceased have been paid and the creditors satisfied. The taxes include income taxes, federal estate taxes, and state inheritance taxes. Furthermore, legal fees must be paid before the heirs can receive any income or capital from the estate.

Until the assets have been distributed, the executor named in the will takes over the administration of the estate. If an executor was not named, the court appoints an administrator. It is the executor's job to choose the probate attorney, take an inventory of all the assets, pay all just claims, establish a separate trustee account to receive all the income and pay all the expenses, keep adequate records of all transactions, arrange for the estate to be appraised, file and pay the appropriate taxes, make a final accounting of his or her stewardship to the heirs, get a final decree of distribution from the court, obtain a release from the heirs of their distributive shares, and change the ownership from the deceased to the new owners.

The executor's first job is to appoint a probate attorney. However, even after the attorney has been appointed, the executor is still the person in charge of the estate. The attorney must follow the instructions of the executor, who has the power to dismiss the attorney at any time. The executor's next responsibility is to take an inventory of all the assets.

The court must be petitioned for a hearing on the will, and all possible heirs and creditors must be notified that the testator has died. After this step has been taken, there should be a petition for the appointment of an inheritance tax appraiser, who in most states is a local official. The appraisal process can often be time-consuming.

Once the estate has been appraised, the executor must complete and file a state inheritance tax return. If the appraisal has been disputed, there may be a long and expensive fight that ultimately ends in the courts. Under the Federal Tax Law prior to the enactment of the 1976 Tax Reform Act, a Federal Estate Tax Return had to be filed for all estates in excess of $60,000. The 1976 Tax Reform Act provides that no estate tax return will be required for a decedent dying in 1977 unless his gross estate exceeds $120,000. For subsequent years the filing requirements are as follows; $134,000 for 1978; $147,000 for 1979; $161,000 for 1980; and $175,000 for 1981 and thereafter.

Once all death taxes and claims against the estate have been paid, the executor must prepare a final accounting of his or her stewardship to the heirs. In small estates the heirs may sign a waiver of accounting, but in larger estates the accounting may be a complicated and lengthy process.

After the judge has been satisfied that everything is in order, he or she signs the final decree of distribution. The heirs sign a receipt for having received their distributive shares, and that is the end of the probate process.

As the reader can readily see, this process can be time-consuming and costly. In the event of hardship, the executor can employ two methods to secure funds for the heirs while the estate is in probate. The first approach is usually utilized by dependents of the deceased. A petition can be made to the courts asking that a monthly family allowance be paid to the dependent or dependents. According to the size of the estate and the normal living standard of the dependent, the judge will set an amount and allow the executor to pay the dependent a monthly income. The second method is a partial distribution. Once enough time has elapsed to determine that the will is not going to be contested and that all claims against the estate have been paid, a petition can be filed with the court to allow the executor to pay a lump sum to the heirs from the available assets.

Avoiding Probate

Property that will pass by will is called a "probate asset," and property that will pass by operation of law is called a "nonprobate asset." The way in which property is owned is the determining factor, and probate may be avoided by correct ownership. Assets owned in any of the nine following ways will not go through probate.

1. Joint tenancy with right of survivorship. This type of ownership is often used between husband and wife. When title is held in this manner and one of the parties dies, the surviving tenant automatically inherits the property. There are two major disadvantages to using this form of ownership. First, it is not possible for either spouse to leave any of these assets to any other party. Second, it may be desirable for tax purposes for the assets to be left in a trust (the advantages of trusts are discussed in Chapter 66).

2. A living trust (discussed in Chapter 66) is a nonprobate asset. Title to the property passes directly to the successor trustee.

3. Designating a life insurance beneficiary. This is very convenient because the insured can name not only one beneficiary, but contingent beneficiaries as well, in the event that the first beneficiary dies before the death of the insured. The insurance proceeds go directly to the beneficiary, and probate is avoided. However, a beneficiary designation could be undesirable if the proceeds of the policy might be needed by an executor of the estate to pay death taxes and other administration costs. This problem could occur if most of the estate consisted of nonliquid assets such as a private company or real estate.

4. Designating a pension plan, profit sharing plan, or deferred compensation plan beneficiary. These plans are similar to insurance policies in that they can be payable to a beneficiary rather than to the estate. Once again, the liquid position of the estate must be a consideration.

5. Joint tenancy as a matter of convenience. This is a joint tenancy with right of survivorship when the joint tenants are not spouses. It may be used by a parent and a child. This ownership avoids probate, but since one of the tenants originally owns all the property and continues to receive all the income, the asset is 100 percent taxable in his or her estate.

6. United States government bonds held in co-ownership form are nonprobate assets.

7. Tenants by the entirety. This form of joint tenancy can be used only by a husband and wife and apply only to real estate. The advantage of this type of ownership is that the property cannot be attached by a creditor of either the husband or the wife alone.

8. In some states, a husband and wife can claim their home as a homestead. The home is protected from seizure as a result of a judgment's being obtained against either or both of the joint tenants because of an unpaid debt. A lien can be obtained on the home, but the property cannot be taken away from the owners to satisfy the lien. The Internal Revenue Service (IRS) and the holder of the mortgage on the property are the only two creditors that can take the home.

9. Gifts in contemplation of death are taxed in the estate, but they are nonprobate assets.

FEDERAL ESTATE TAXES

To be effective in estate planning, the estate owner must know the basic provisions of the federal estate and gift tax laws. For years after 1976 a new unified schedule of tax rates apply to cumulative transfers during life and at death. He or she must also have an understanding of the sections of the Internal Revenue Code that govern the taxing of income of fiduciaries. This knowledge is necessary so that effective tax planning can be carried out during the taxpayer's lifetime and be continued throughout the administration of his or her estate.

The estate owner must be familiar with the interrelationships of the federal estate and fiduciary income tax laws. When properly handled, many of the interrelationships concerning tax elections by the administrator can produce significant overall tax savings to the beneficiaries of the estate.

Basically, the gross estate includes all property owned in whole or in part by the decedent at the time of his or her death. The value of such property is limited to the extent of the decedent's interest in the property. The gross estate may also include property in which the decedent did not have an interest at death. This would include property in which the decedent had a general power of appointment, gifts made in contemplation of death, property owned jointly by the decedent and others, dower or curtesy of a surviving spouse, revocable transfers made by the decedent, proceeds of certain insurance policies on the decedent's life, and annuities. Thus, the decedent's gross estate for federal estate taxes could be very different from the estate for probate purposes.

To determine the decedent's taxable estate, certain deductions are subtracted from the gross estate. Some of the allowable deductions include funeral and administrative expenses, debts of the decedent, taxes, casualty losses, charitable contributions, and a marital deduction for bequest to the spouse.

For example, let us assume that a person leaves a gross estate valued at $500,000. If the decedent has allowable deductions, including the marital deduction, of $270,000, the net taxable estate is $230,000. Under prior law the decedent's estate would also have been entitled to an exemption of $60,000, which would have further reduced the taxable estate. The 1976 Tax Reform Act replaced the exemption with a unified credit which directly reduces the gross estate tax.

The appropriate estate tax rates are applied to the taxable estate to obtain the gross estate tax. However, to determine the net estate tax payable, certain authorized credits are subtracted from the gross estate tax. Among them are credits for state death taxes paid, gift taxes, a tax on prior transfer, and foreign death taxes, in addition to any unused unified credit.

Before one can understand the interrelationships between federal estate taxes and income taxes of fiduciaries, a knowledge of the estate tax laws is essential. The following subsections present a discussion of the federal estate taxes.

Nature of the Tax

The unified federal estate and gift tax is an excise tax on the privilege of transferring property at the time of a person's death as well as on lifetime gifts. It is not a property tax or a tax on the right of the beneficiary to receive the property. Unlike the rates of an inheritance tax, the rates of the estate tax do not depend upon the relationship of the beneficiaries to the decedent. The amount of the tax is calculated by applying the progressive estate tax rates to the taxable estate.

The estate tax laws apply not only to every citizen and resident of the United States who dies leaving property but also to any nonresident alien who dies leaving property located within the country. However, the application of federal estate taxes differs between persons who are citizens or residents and those who are nonresidents and not citizens. This subsection is concerned with the statutes governing the taxing of estates of United States citizens and residents. To determine who is a resident of the United States for the purpose of estate taxes, the term "residence" is considered to mean the person's domicile.

GROSS ESTATE

Before making any kind of analysis of the amount of estate tax to be paid on his or her death, an individual must know what will be included in the gross estate and how these assets will be valued. Without a knowledge of these two things, he or she is helpless in estimating the potential estate tax.

All property, including real or personal, tangible or intangible property, owned in whole or in part by the decedent at the time of his or her death, is included in the gross estate to the extent of the value of his or her interest in such property. Until July 1, 1964, the gross estate did not include any real property located outside the United States, but the law was amended to include such property of all decedents dying after that date. Since the gross estate includes the value of the decedent's interest in all property owned at death, ownership is an important factor in determining the gross estate. Normally, local property law controls the issue of ownership for tax purposes.

Even though the decedent's gross estate is composed of a wide variety of property owned by him or her, it is not limited to owned property. The gross estate also includes certain other property in which the interest of the decedent is considered to be substantially equivalent to ownership, although the decedent held no legal interest in the property at the time of his or her death. Such other property includes the following:

1. *Dower or curtesy interests.* (Dower is the provision of the law that entitles the widow to a life estate of a certain portion of the real estate of her husband; curtesy provides the same privilege to the husband from his wife's estate.) The gross estate shall include the value of all property passing to the surviving spouse as dower or curtesy or by virtue of a statute creating an estate in lieu of dower or curtesy. The nature and extent of dower and curtesy are determined by the laws of the specific state. However, state law does not determine the tax status of the interest under the federal statute.[19]

2. *Transactions in contemplation of death.* Any transfers of property by the decedent without adequate and full consideration and made within three years of death are in contemplation of death, and thus the property is included in the gross estate of the decedent. The gift must be "grossed-up." In essence, both the gift and any gift tax liability attributable to the transfer must be included in the gross estate. Likewise, the relinquishment of a power over property transferred during the decedent's lifetime or the exercise or release of a power of appointment within three years before death is deemed to have been made in contemplation of death.[20]

If this provision were not in the law, an estate owner could transfer his or her entire property without subjecting it to estate taxes simply by making gifts to his or her beneficiaries. Any transfers made for adequate and full consideration, like any transfers made more than three years before death, are not deemed to be transfers in contemplation of death and are not included in the gross estate.

Under prior tax law, gifts made within three years of death rested on a rebuttable presumption that such gifts were made in contemplation of death. This presumption could be rebutted by showing that the decedent's dominant motive at the time of the transfer was one associated with life. The 1976 Tax Reform Act eliminated all questions of motive by including in the estate *all* gifts made after December 31, 1976, and within three years of death.

[19]IRC, Sec. 2034.
[20]IRC, Sec. 2035.

3. *Transfers with retained life estate.* Included in the gross estate is the value of all property or property interest transferred by a decedent, by trust or otherwise, if he or she retained for life, or for any period not ascertainable without reference to his or her death, or for a period that does not in fact end before death:

a. The possession, right to income, or other enjoyment of the property.

b. The right, either alone or in conjunction with any other person, to designate who shall possess or enjoy the property or the income therefrom.[21]

According to Regulation 20.2036-1, the use, possession, right to the income, or other enjoyment of the property is considered as having been retained by the decedent if it is to be applied to the discharge of any of his or her legal obligations including an obligation during his or her lifetime to support a dependent. The phrase "right . . . to designate the person or persons who shall possess or enjoy the transferred property or the income therefrom" does not apply to a power held solely by a person other than the decedent. But if the decedent reserved the unrestricted power to remove a trustee at any time and appoint himself or herself as trustee, the decedent is considered as having the powers of the trustee.

4. *Transfers taking effect at death.* The decedent's gross estate must include the value of any interest in property transferred by the decedent in any way, except for an adequate and full consideration in money or money's worth, if all the following conditions are met:

a. Possession or enjoyment of the property could, through ownership of the interest, have been obtained only by surviving the decedent.

b. The decedent has retained a reversionary interest in the transferred property by the expressed terms of the instrument of transfer, and the value of such interest immediately before the death of the decedent exceeds 5 percent of the value of the transferred property.

For the purposes of this section, the term "reversionary interest" includes a possibility that property transferred by the decedent may return to the decedent or to his or her estate or may be subject to a power of disposition by him or her. This term does not include rights to income only. The value of such reversionary interest is determined by the usual methods of valuation including the use of mortality tables and actuarial principles.[22]

5. *Revocable transfers.* Property transferred during life is includable in the decedent's gross estate if at death the enjoyment of the property is subject to change through the exercise of a power to alter, amend, revoke, or terminate by the decedent either alone or in conjunction with another person.[23] However, according to Regulation 20.2038-1, this section does not apply:

a. To the extent that the transfer was for adequate and full consideration in money or money's worth.

b. If the decedent's power could be exercised only with the consent of all parties having an interest in the transferred property.

c. To a power held solely by a person other than the decedent.

6. *Annuities.* The gross estate includes the value of an annuity or other payment receivable by a beneficiary by reason of surviving the decedent under any form of contract or agreement, including employment plans and agreements (except life insurance contracts) when the value of the annuity or other payment is attributable to contributions made by the decedent or his or her employer if

a. The payment or annuity was payable to the decedent.

b. The decedent possessed the right to receive such payment either alone or in conjunction with another for his or her life or for any period not ascertainable

---

[21]IRC, Sec. 2036.
[22]IRC, Sec. 2037.
[23]IRC, Sec. 2038.

without reference to his or her death, or for any period which does not in fact end before death.[24]

The amount included in the gross estate is limited to that part of the value of the annuity receivable under such a contract that is proportionate to the part of the purchase price contributed by the decedent. For this purpose, any contribution made by the decedent's employer or former employer for reason of his or her employment shall be considered as having been contributed by the decedent. However, the value of annuities or other benefits receivable by a beneficiary (other than the estate) under certain "qualified" employee benefit plans is excluded. This exclusion applies only to the benefits attributable to the employee's contributions.[25] Further, for estates of decedents dying after 1976, *lump-sum* distributions from all qualified retirement plans are included in the gross estate.

7. *Joint interest.* A decedent's gross estate includes the value of property held jointly at the decedent's death by the decedent and another person or persons with the right of survivorship. Jointly owned property is includable in the gross estate except to the extent that the property or its acquisition cost is traceable to the survivor. Thus, any property acquired jointly by the decedent and another joint owner through a gift or other device is included in the gross estate only to the extent of the decedent's fractional share of such property.[26]

Regulation 20.2040-1 applies this section to all classes of property, whether real or personal, regardless of when the joint interest was created. The section has no application to property held as tenants in common. In the case of community property, only the decedent's interest in such property is included in his or her gross estate. In most states this interest is one-half.

This section also covers property held by the decedent and spouse jointly, as well as property held by them as tenants by the entirety, as long as the interest was created before January 1, 1977. The 1976 Tax Reform Act changes the rule for joint tenancies created after 1976 where the joint tenants are husband and wife. Under the new law, only one-half of the value of property owned jointly is included in the decedent's gross estate. This rule applies, regardless of which spouse furnished the consideration, so long as the following requirements are met:

a. Either or both of the spouses must have created the joint interest.

b. If the property involved is personal property, the creation of the joint interest must have been a completed gift for gift tax purposes.

c. If the property involved is real property, the donor must have elected to treat the creation of the joint interest as a taxable gift at the time the interest was created.

d. The joint tenants are only the decedent and his or her spouse.

8. *Power of appointment.* The value of all property over which the decedent possessed a general power of appointment at the time of his or her death is includable in the gross estate. A general power of appointment is one under which the holder has the right to dispose of the property in favor of himself or herself, his or her estate or creditors, or the estate's creditors. There are some exceptions to this definition of a general power of appointment:

a. If the holder's right to consume or invade the property is limited by an ascertainable standard relating to his or her needs for health, maintenance, support, or education, the power is not considered to be a general power of appointment.

b. A power created on or before October 21, 1942, which is exercisable by the decedent only in conjunction with another person.

[24]IRC, Sec. 2039(a).
[25]IRC, Sec. 2039(b), (c).
[26]IRC, Sec. 2040.

c. A power created after October 21, 1942, which is exercisable by the decedent only in conjunction with the creator of the power or with a person having substantial interest in the property subject to the power and in which the interest is adverse to the exercise of the power in the decedent's favor.

For example, let us assume that the decedent and A were trustees of a trust under which the income was to be paid to the decedent for life and the remainder to A. Under the terms of the trust, the trustees had power to distribute the corpus to the decedent. Since A's interest is substantially adverse to the exercise of the power in favor of the decedent, the decedent does not have a general power of appointment. Thus, the property would *not* be included in his or her gross estate.

If the power may be exercised in favor of both the decedent and the persons whose consent the decedent must have, the power is general to the extent of the decedent's fractional interest in it.[27] For example, let us assume that under the terms of a trust the decedent, B, and C hold an unlimited power jointly to appoint the income or corpus, or both, among a group of people, including themselves. If upon the decedent's death the power does not pass to B and C jointly, then B and C are not considered to have an interest adverse to the exercise of the power in favor of the decedent. Therefore, the decedent is considered to possess a general power of appointment over one-third of the property subject to the power, and that one-third of the property must be included in his or her gross estate.

With a general power of appointment over property, the donee has almost as much authority over the property as he or she would have as legal owners of the property. Thus, without the provisions of this section a person could easily prevent the application of estate taxes to his or her estate by disposing of legal title to the property but holding a general power of appointment over it.

9. *Proceeds of life insurance.* Proceeds of insurance on the decedent's life receivable by or for the benefit of the estate or by other beneficiaries are included in the gross estate of the decedent. For estate tax purposes, life insurance comprises not only the common forms of insurance but certain other types of policies including accident insurance, war risk insurance, and group insurance. When the proceeds of a life insurance policy are payable to named beneficiaries, special rules apply. *The proceeds of such a policy are included in the gross estate only if the decedent possessed at his or her death any incidents of ownership in the policy or certain reversionary interest.* The term "incidents of ownership" include the following powers: to change the beneficiary, to borrow from the insurer the cash surrender value of the policy, and to cancel or assign the policy. The term "reversionary interest" includes the possibility that the policy or the proceeds of the policy may return to the decedent or to his or her estate. For the proceeds of the policy to be included in the decedent's gross estate, the value of such reversionary interest must exceed 5 percent of the value of the policy immediately before the decedent's death. The value of the reversionary interest is determined by the usual methods of valuation including the use of mortality tables and actuarial principles.[28]

10. *Transfers for insufficient consideration.* Transfers that are subject to estate tax as transfers in contemplation of death, transfers taking effect at death, transfers subject to a general power of appointment, or transfers with retained life estate, if made during the decedent's lifetime for a consideration, are taxable only to the extent that the consideration is deemed inadequate. The amount included in the gross estate is the excess of the fair market value of the property transferred over the value of the consideration received by the decedent.[29] For example, let us assume that a man sold a piece of property valued at $60,000 to his daughter for

[27]IRC, Sec. 2041.
[28]IRC, Sec. 2042.
[29]IRC, Sec. 2043.

$15,000 and dies one year later. In effect, he gave her a gift of $45,000 in contemplation of death, and this $45,000 would be included in the value of the estate along with gift taxes paid on the transfer.

Section 2033 of the Internal Revenue Code requires the inclusion in the decedent's estate of a wide variety of property interests owned by him or her on the date of death. Regulation 20.2033-1 and numerous court cases have applied this section to many specific items of property interest. According to this regulation, property subject to homestead or other exemptions under local law must be included in the gross estate. Notes or other claims held by the decedent should be included even though they are canceled by his or her will. Accrued interest and rents are includable even though they are not collected until after his death, and under certain circumstances dividends payable to the decedent also are included. Bonds, notes, bills, and certificates of indebtedness of the federal government or its agencies, which are exempt from other taxes, are subject to the estate tax and are included in the decedent's gross estate. The tax treatment of many other particular property interests is covered, and some of these interests are discussed in the following paragraphs.

As a general rule, income, dividends, interest, compensation, and other items accrued at the time of the decedent's death should be included in the gross estate. However, this rule does not apply if any of these types of payments are made only as a matter of grace.[30] The following accruals have been held to be includable in a decedent's estate:

1. Executor's fees accrued at the date of the decedent's death[31]
2. Accrued interest on the decedent's capital investment in a partnership[32]
3. Accrued interest on Series G bonds even though they were held for less than six months[33]
4. Dividends[34]
5. A bonus[35]
6. Partnership profits[36]

For estate tax purposes, dividends accrue at the stockholder-of-record date. Thus dividends, which are payable to the decedent or to his or her estate because on or before the date of death the decedent was the stockholder of record, constitute a part of the gross estate. If the record date is after the date of death, the dividends are not included in the gross estate. This rule applies no matter how the gross estate is valued. However, if the record date is after the valuation date and the stock is selling ex dividend on the valuation date, the dividend is added to the quotation to obtain the includable value of the stock.[37]

Any bonus paid to the decedent's estate or to a named beneficiary may be subject to tax as an accrual. However, the bonus is not included if the employer is under no obligation to make the payment.[38]

Like any other accrual, partnership profits to the date of death of the decedent

---

[30]*Maas Exec. (Sakas) et al. v. Higgins,* 312 U.S. 443 (1941), 61S. Ct. 631, 85 L. Ed. 940, 25 AFTR 1177.

[31]*Est. of G. Percy McGlue,* 41 BTA 1199 (1940).

[32]*Est. of John F. Degener,* 26 BTA 185 (1932).

[33]*Est. of Willis L. King, Jr.* (Mellon Nat. Bank & Trust Co.), 18 TC 414 (1949).

[34]Revenue Ruling 54-399, 1954-2 CB 279; *Estate of George McNaught Lockie v. Commissioner,* 21 TC 64 (1952).

[35]*Est. of Leonard B. McKitterick;* 42 BTA 130 (1940), dismissed (2 Cir.; 1941).

[36]*Bull, Exec. v. U.S.* (1935), 295 U.S. 247, 55 S. Ct. 695 (1935), 15 AFTR 1069, rev'g (1934) 6 F. Supp. 141, 13 AFTR 262 (1934).

[37]Revenue Ruling 54-399, 1954-2 CB 279; *Estate of George McNaught Lockie v. Commissioner,* 21 TC 64 (1952).

[38]*Est. of Leonard B. McKitterick;* 42 BTA 130 (1940), dismissed (2 Cir.; 1941).

are included in the gross estate.[39] In some instances profits accruing after the partner's death are included in the gross estate.[40] If there is a partnership agreement which provides that the deceased partner's estate is to share in the profits for a definite period of time after death, such profits accruing to the estate are included in the gross estate.[41]

Any property owned as a tenancy in common is included in the decedent's gross estate to the extent of his or her fractional interest in such property.[42] Even cemetery lots are included in the decedent's gross estate under certain circumstances. If any part of a cemetery lot not designed for the interment of the decedent and the members of his or her family has a salable value, that salable value is included in the gross estate.[43]

All valid and enforceable claims or choses in action owned by the decedent are included in his or her gross estate. The following types of claims and choses in action are includable: right to executor's commissions,[44] contingent-fee legal services,[45] debts due the decedent,[46] claims against a partner,[47] computed value of claim for advance,[48] and others. Any notes held by the decedent are included in the gross estate unless the obligations end on his or her death.[49]

Depending upon the nature of the payment, death benefits provided for in pension or profit sharing plans may or may not be included in the decedent's gross estate. Even though the decedent had the right to appoint his or her share of the fund to his or her beneficiaries, the proceeds paid from such a trust fund are not necessarily included in the gross estate if the decedent did not have a vested interest in the fund.[50] If the decedent had an enforceable vested interest in such a fund, the proceeds paid from that fund to his or her beneficiaries are included in the gross estate.[51]

Cases, revenue rulings, and income tax Regulations apply Section 2033 of the Internal Revenue Code to many other miscellaneous items of property and property interest. These are too numerous to discuss or even to list, but most of the more important ones have been covered.

In attempting to determine whether a particular property interest should be included in the gross estate, the same tests are applied to all types of property and property interest. Basically three questions must be answered:

    1. What types of property are includable in a decedent's estate?

    2. Did the decedent have an interest in such property sufficient to warrant inclusion in his or her estate of the value of the interest involved?

    3. If the decedent had an interest, did he or she still possess it at death, and to what extent?[52]

The answers to these questions are quite important to the estate owner because they govern the taxability of his or her property. Normally there is no problem

---

[39]*Bull. Exec. v. U.S.* 1935), 295 U.S. 247, 55 S. Ct. 695 (1935), 15 AFTR 1069, rev'g (1934) 6 F. Supp. 141, 13 AFTR 262 (1934).

[40]*Est. of George Wood,* 26 BTA 533 (1932); *Est. of John F. Degener,* 26 BTA 185 (1932).

[41]Revenue Ruling 66-20, 1966-1 CB 214.

[42]*Harvey, Exr. v. U.S.,* 185 F. 2d 463 (7 Cir.; 1950).

[43]Reg. 20.2033-1(b).

[44]*Est. of G. Perry McGlue,* 41 BTA 1199 (1940).

[45]Revenue Ruling 55-123, CB 1955-1, p. 443.

[46]*Est. of Hiram F. Hammer,* 10 BTA 43 (1928).

[47]*Isaac W. Baldwin Est.,* 59, 203 P-H Memo TC.

[48]*Est. of Theodore O. Hamlin* (Lincoln Rochester Tr. Co.), 9 TC 676 (1947).

[49]*Comm. v. Austin,* 73 F. 2d 483, 43 AFTR 748 (1934).

[50]*Hammer v. Glenn,* 212 F. 2d 483 (6 Cir.; 1954), 43 AFTR 748.

[51]*Est. of Charles B. Wolf,* 29 TC 441 (1957), 3 AFTR 2d 1797.

[52]*Federal Estate and Gift Taxes Explained,* Commerce Clearing House, Inc., Chicago, 1967, p. 30.

with the first question. Code Section 2033 is quite broad and requires the inclusion in the gross estate of practically all property in which the decedent had an interest. There are very few exceptions to this rule. For example, even property that passes by state law as dower or curtesy is included in the gross estate. However, one exception to this very general rule occurs when payments are received by a decedent's family under the Social Security Act.

Question 2 is really a question of property law. The governing factors depend largely on common-law and statutory rights, and normally the issues are determined by the application of property law to the facts.

The third question presents most of the difficulties for the estate owner. To resolve this question, it is necessary to gather information concerning the duration of the decedent's interest in property and interests that had begun to accrue at his or her death but had not come into his or her possession. Certain general conclusions may be drawn from the cases in which these issues were decided. Basically these conclusions are as follows:

1. If the interest comes into existence prior to the decedent's death and does not pass with his or her death, the property must be included in the gross estate.

2. Vested remainders are included in the gross estate.

3. A life interest is not included in the gross estate.

4. Contingent remainders that are defeated by the decedent's death are not included in the gross estate.[53]

As we have seen in the preceding discussion, in which many cases, revenue rulings, and income tax regulations were cited, these tests hold up. By answering these three questions with reference to any particular property or property interest, the estate owner can determine whether that property must be included in the gross estate.

Valuation

After the estate owner has determined which items of property will be included in the gross estate, he or she must decide how these items will be valued for estate tax purposes. These assets will be valued at their fair market value at the date of death or on the alternate valuation date. But what is the fair market value?

For estate tax purposes, fair market value is defined as the price at which the property would change hands between a willing buyer and a willing seller, neither being under any compulsion to buy or sell and both having knowledge of all relevant facts. The fair market value is never determined by a forced-sale price. Neither is it to be determined by the sale price of the item in a market other than that in which the item is most commonly sold to the public, taking into account the location of the item. Therefore, if a particular item of property is normally retailed, the fair market value of the item to be included in the decedent's gross estate is the price at which the item or a comparable item would be sold at retail.[54]

In determining the fair market value of any item of property, all the relevant facts and elements of value as of the valuation date must be considered. The following paragraphs discuss the normal means of valuing particular types of property.

Stocks and bonds are included in a decedent's gross estate at their fair market value per share or bond on the valuation date. This fair market value is the mean value between the highest and lowest selling prices on the date of valuation. When there are sales on dates within a reasonable period of time both before and after the valuation date but no sale on the valuation date, the fair market is the weighted average of the means between the highest and lowest sales on the nearest dates

[53]Ibid., pp. 30–31.
[54]Reg. 20.2031-1(b).

both before and after the valuation date. This average should be weighted inversely by the respective numbers of trading days between the valuation date and the nearest selling dates. If there are no actual sales within a reasonable period of time of the valuation date, the fair market is considered to be the mean between the bona fide bid-and-asked prices on the date of valuation.

If it can be established that the value of such stocks and bonds determined on the basis of selling prices or bid-and-asked prices does not reflect the fair market value, other relevant facts and elements must be considered in determining the fair market value. For example, if the block of stock was so large in relation to actual sales on the existing market that it could not be liquidated in a reasonable time without depressing the market or if the block represents a controlling interest, then the price at which other lots change hands may have little relation to the true market value.[55]

If no actual sales prices or bona fide bid-and-asked prices exist, other factors must be considered in determining the fair market value. In the case of bonds, the soundness of the security, the interest yield, the date of maturity, and other relevant factors must be considered. The factors to consider in the case of shares of stock are the company's net worth, prospective earnings, dividend-paying capacity, and other relevant factors. Some of the other factors are the goodwill of the business, the economic outlook of the industry, the company's position within the industry, and its management.[56]

There is no theoretical standard or general formula for valuing the stock of closely held corporations. The factors to be considered in determining the value of such stock vary with the particular facts involved. The weight to be given to any factor depends upon the specific circumstances of that case. The following fundamental factors should receive careful analysis in each situation:

1. The nature and history of the business
2. The economic outlook in general and the condition and outlook of the specific industry in particular
3. The book value of the stock and the financial condition of the business
4. The earning capacity of the company
5. The dividend-paying capacity
6. Whether the enterprise has goodwill or other intangibles of value
7. Other sales of stock and the size of the block to be valued
8. The market price of actively traded stocks of corporations engaged in the same or a similar business[57]

The fair market value of a decedent's interest in any business is the net amount that a willing buyer would pay a willing seller for such interests, neither being under any compulsion to buy or to sell and both having a reasonable knowledge of all the facts. A fair appraisal should be made of the business's earning capacity and of all its assets including goodwill. These factors should be considered in determining its net value.[58] However, the value of a business interest may be fixed at a mutual buy-and-sell agreement. For such an agreement to be effective for estate tax purposes, it must bind the estate to sell, either by giving the survivors an option or by binding all parties, and the price must not be so grossly inadequate as to make the agreement a "mere gratuitous promise."[59] Several techniques are discussed below under the heading "Section 303 Redemption," involving estates that are composed of stock in closely held corporations.

---

[55]Reg. 20.2031-2(a)–(e).
[56]Reg. 20.2031(f).
[57]Revenue Ruling 59-60, 1959-1 CB 237.
[58]Reg. 20.2031-3.
[59]Revenue Ruling 59-60, 1959-1 CB 237. For example, see D. Larry Crumbley, "Buy and Sell Agreements for Subchapter S Corporations," *Trusts and Estates,* vol. 108, pp. 17–21, January 1969.

All cash belonging to the decedent, including that in the possession of others and that deposited in banks, is included in the gross estate. His or her bank account may be reduced by valid and bona fide checks outstanding on the date of death but subsequently honored by the bank.[60] The fair market value of any secured or unsecured note held by the decedent is presumed to be principal of the note plus interest accrued to the date of death. Under certain circumstances the executor may establish that the value of the note is something less or is even worthless.[61]

Generally, the fair market value of the decedent's household and personal effects is considered to be the price that a willing buyer would pay to a willing seller. There should be a room-to-room itemization of these articles. A separate value should be listed for each item; however, all articles in a room worth $100 or less may be grouped. Instead of making such an itemized list, the executor may under the penalties of perjury submit a written statement containing the aggregate value of the property as appraised by a competent appraiser. However, if these household and personal effects include any articles having an artistic or intrinsic value of more than $3,000, the appraisal of an expert must be filed with the estate tax return. Before the executor may sell or distribute any of the household or personal effects in advance of an investigation by an officer of the IRS, he must give the district director notice of such action accompanied by an appraisal of such property.[62]

The fair market value of annuities, life estates, terms for years, remainders, and reversions is their present value. The Regulations provide tables to be used in calculating the present value of such interest.[63] The value of a contract for the payment of an annuity or an insurance policy on the life of another person is the price for which such a contract could be acquired on the date of the decedent's death from a company regularly engaged in the selling of contracts of that character. If further premiums are to be paid on a life insurance policy on the life of another person, the value of such a policy may be approximated by adding to the interpolated terminal reserve at the date of the decedent's death the proportionate part of the gross premium last paid before the decedent's death that covers the period extending beyond that date.[64]

The Tax Reform Act of 1976 set up special rules for the valuation of real property used for farming or in a closely held business. Under prior law, the fair market value of such real property was determined according to its "highest and best use." The act provides that fair market value can be determined according to its "actual use" if the following conditions are met:

a. The adjusted value of the real and personal property used in the business must comprise at least 50 percent of the adjusted value of the decedent's gross estate.

b. The adjusted value of the real property itself must be at least 25 percent of the adjusted value of the decedent's gross estate.

c. In no event may this alternate valuation reduce the gross estate by more than $500,000.

However, if within fifteen years after the death of the decedent the heir sells or transfers the property to nonfamily members or the property ceases to be used in the business, the estate tax benefits are recaptured. This recapture is not triggered by the death of the heir without converting the property to nonqualified use.

This special valuation procedure is available to estates of decedents dying after 1976.

[60]Reg. 20.2031-5.
[61]Reg. 20.2031-4.
[62]Reg. 20.2031-6.
[63]Reg. 20.2031-7.
[64]Reg. 20.2031-8.

Section 303 Redemption

Often the major asset of an estate is stock in a closely held corporation. When this situation occurs, an administrator should not overlook a Section 303 redemption, which provides an opportunity to take assets out of the corporation at little or no tax cost. Under this valuable section an estate or the heirs of the stockholders of a corporation may withdraw cash or property from the corporation without paying a dividend tax on an amount equal to the sum of federal and estate death taxes and funeral and administrative expenses.

An administrator must be sure that four basic requirements are met before a redemption can be treated as a distribution to pay death taxes:

1. Any redeemed stock must be included in determining the gross estate of the deceased shareholder.

2. The value for federal tax purposes of all the stock of the corporation that is included in determining the value of the decedent's gross estate must be more than 50 percent of the adjusted gross estate (gross estate less expenses, debts, and losses).

3. The amount that can be distributed without dividend treatment is limited to the sum of the death taxes (estate, inheritance, legacy, and succession taxes and any interest thereon) and funeral and administration expenses allowable as a deduction to the estate under Section 2053 or Section 2106.

4. The redemption may take place over a period of time extending as long as fifteen years, where an election has been made to pay the tax in installments, as discussed below. However, for any redemption made more than four years after the decedent's death, capital gain treatment is limited to a distribution which is the lesser of:

a. The amount of the qualifying death taxes, funeral, and administrative expenses which are unpaid immediately before the distribution; or

b. The aggregate of these amounts which are paid within one year after the distribution.

5. The capital gains treatment will apply only to the extent that the redeeming stockholder's interest in the decedent's estate is reduced by the payment of estate taxes, funeral and administrative expenses.

Even the limitation of $4\frac{1}{2}$ years may be circumvented by having the corporation issue notes to redeem the stock. If such notes are not payable during the stipulated time limitation, Section 303 treatment may still not be lost if (1) the ability to pay for the stock existed at the time that the stock was redeemed by the corporation, (2) the notes have a fair market value at the time of issuance equal to their face value, (3) they bear at least 4 percent interest, (4) they do not represent equity, and (5) all payments are made on time.[65] Thus, a corporation may conserve working capital by extending its payout beyond the time limitation. From the point of view of the shareholder, if the price of the redeemed stock rises above its valuation for estate tax purposes, he or she should try to spread out the gain by using the installment tax method.

Although the redemption proceeds need not be in the form of cash, noncash redemptions may not be desirable since funds are most often needed to pay federal and state death taxes and administration costs. However, any property distributions do not actually have to be used to pay death costs.

Installment Payments of Estate Taxes

A complement to Section 303 is the relief provision of Section 6166A that permits an executor to elect to pay the estate tax in yearly installments over a period as long as

---

[65]Revenue Ruling 65-289, 1965-2 CB 86; Revenue Ruling 67-425, 1967-2 CB 134.

ten years. To qualify for installment payments, interest in the corporation must meet two tests:

1. The value of the interest in the corporation must equal at least 35 percent of the gross value of the estate or at least 50 percent of the taxable estate of the stockholder.

2. The corporation must have ten or fewer shareholders, or 20 percent or more of the value of the voting stock of the corporation must be included in the decedent's gross estate.

If these requirements are satisfied, the executor may elect to pay the estate tax over a ten-year period, in annual installments for two to ten years. This relief election must be made when the estate tax return is filed, accompanied by the first installment payment. Interest on the postponed tax is paid at the rate of 4 percent per year (this rate may be compared with today's market). Since an executor is unlikely to distribute all assets while there is still an outstanding debt, this election requires an estate to remain open for ten years.

An immediate acceleration of the entire estate tax occurs if any of the following transpires:

1. There is a disposition of 50 percent of the interest in the corporation.

2. Any installments are not paid when due.

3. Aggregate withdrawals of money or property from the corporation equal 50 percent of its value.

4. The undistributed net income remaining in the estate after the fourth installment is not applied in toto for payment of the outstanding tax.

The 1976 Tax Reform Act further liberalized these rules by enacting Section 6166, which provides an alternative fifteen-year extension. To qualify for this fifteen-year extension, interest in the corporation must meet two tests:

1. The value of the interest in the corporation must equal at least 65 percent of the decedent's adjusted gross estate.

2. The corporation must have fifteen or fewer shareholders, or 20 percent or more of the value of the voting stock of the corporation must be included in the decedent's gross estate.

If these requirements are satisfied, the entire tax attributable to the qualifying stock interest is deferred for five years and then paid off in ten equal annual installments. Interest is payable annually at a rate of 4 percent on the tax attributable to the first $1 million in value of the business, and at the standard rate on the balance. This election requires an estate to remain open for fifteen years.

An immediate acceleration of the entire estate tax occurs if any of the following transpires:

1. There is a disposition of $33\frac{1}{3}$ percent of the interest in the corporation.

2. Any installments are not paid when due.

3. Aggregate withdrawals of money or property from the corporation equal $33\frac{1}{3}$ percent of its value.

4. The undistributed net income in the estate after the due date for the first installment is not applied in toto for payment of the outstanding tax.

Another relief provision is available to a shareholder of a corporation. Under Section 6161, if an executor can show reasonable cause, the district director will extend the time for payment of the estate tax up to ten years.

Alternate Valuation Date

All property and property interest belonging to the decedent on the date of his or her death must be included in his gross estate. These items of property are valued at their fair market value. Now the question arises: Fair market value at what date? Here the executor must make a decision; he or she may elect to value the estate either at the date of decedent's death or as of the date six months from date of death. This latter date is referred to as the "alternate valuation date."

If the alternate valuation date is to be used, the executor must make such an election in the estate tax return. In no case may such an election be made or a previous election changed after the due date of the estate tax return. Also, such an election, if made, applies to all the property of the gross estate and cannot be applied to only a portion of the property. This election is not effective for any purposes unless the value of the gross estate exceeds the limits necessary for the filing of an estate tax return.[66]

When the executor elects to use the alternate valuation date, the value of the gross estate is determined by valuing all the property included in the gross estate as follows:

1. Any property distributed, sold, exchanged, or otherwise disposed of within six months after the decedent's death must be valued as of the date on which it is disposed of.

2. Any property not distributed, sold, exchanged, or otherwise disposed of within six months after the decedent's death must be valued as of the date six months after the decedent's death.

3. Any property, interest, or estate that is affected by a mere lapse of time must be valued as of the date of the decedent's death. However, it must be adjusted for any change in value not due to a mere lapse of time as of the date six months after the decedent's death or as of the date of its disposition, whichever occurs first.[67]

Of course, the purpose of the alternate valuation date is to permit a reduction in estate taxes if there has been a shrinkage in the aggregate value of the estate property. Under prior law, the basis of property acquired from a decedent was "stepped up" to the valuation of that property on the estate tax return. Therefore it was advantageous, under certain circumstances, to elect the *higher* value for estate tax purposes because savings in later income taxes, resulting from the stepped-up basis in the hands of the heir, could bring about an overall tax savings. The 1976 Tax Reform Act provides that the basis of property received from a decedent who died after December 31, 1976, is to be the same basis as the decedent's basis immediately before his death. However, to soften the immediate impact of this, a "fresh start" rule adds to the decedent's basis the appreciation in value attributable to the period the decedent held the property before January 1, 1977.

TAXABLE ESTATE

The taxable estate is determined by subtracting from the gross estate all allowable deductions as follows:

1. A deduction is granted to the extent allowable under local law for funeral expenses. Funeral expenses include a reasonable expenditure for a tombstone, monument, and burial lot for either the decedent or his or her family, future upkeep of the lot, and the cost of transportation of the person bringing the body to the place of burial.[68]

2. All reasonable and necessary expenses incurred in the administration of the decedent's estate are deductible from the gross estate. The administration of the estate includes the collection of the assets, the payment of debts, and the distribution of property to the proper beneficiaries.

The three types of administrative expenses are executor's commissions, attorney's fees, and miscellaneous expenses. A deduction for executor's commissions is

---

[66]Reg. 20.2032-1(b).
[67]IRC Sec. 2032.
[68]IRC, Sec. 2053; Reg. 20.2053-2.

allowed to the extent that such an amount has actually been paid or for an amount which at the time of the filing of the estate tax return may reasonably be expected to be paid, but no deduction is allowed if the commission will not be collected. Attorney fees actually paid or reasonably expected to be paid are deductible. These fees do not include charges incurred by beneficiaries incident to litigation as to their respective interests. Miscellaneous administrative expenses include court costs, surrogates' fees, accountants' fees, appraisers' fees, and clerk hire. All expenses necessarily incurred in preserving and distributing the estate, including the cost of storing or maintaining property of the estate when immediate distribution to the beneficiaries is impossible, are deductible.[69]

3. A deduction is allowed for all bona fide and legally enforceable claims against the estate for debts incurred by the decedent, to the extent that these are paid from property included in the gross estate. Thus, any income or gift taxes owned at the date of death would be deductible under this provision. Also, a deduction is allowed from the decedent's gross estate for the full unpaid amount of a mortgage or other indebtedness in respect of any property included in his or her gross estate at its full fair market value. This deduction would include an amount for interest accrued to the date of the decedent's death.[70]

4. The value of the gross estate is reduced by any losses arising from fire, storms, thefts, or other casualty incurred during the settlement of the estate. The amount of this deduction is limited to losses not compensated for by insurance or otherwise.

5. Any bequest, legacy, or devise made to qualified religious, charitable, scientific, and educational organizations or to the United States, any state, or political subdivision is deductible. In contrast to the treatment of charitable deductions for income tax purposes, there are no percentage limitations for estate tax purposes, nor must payment be made to domestic organizations.[71]

6. Under certain conditions and limitations, the estates of citizens and residents of the United States are allowed a marital deduction of up to 50 percent of the adjusted gross estate or $250,000, whichever is greater. The purpose of the deduction is to eliminate the tax advantages held by persons domiciled in community property states. These statutes provided all taxpayers with the tax treatment that formerly was possible only for persons domiciled in community property states. For tax purposes, Congress made the community property system applicable to all the states.

Thus, a marital deduction is allowed for the value of all property passing outright to the surviving spouse. This deduction is limited to 50 percent of the value of the adjusted gross estate or $250,000, whichever is greater. The adjusted gross estate is found by subtracting from the entire value of the gross estate the aggregate amount of the deductions allowed for funeral expenses, administrative expenses, debts of the decedents, and casualty and theft losses.[72]

For example, let us assume that Dick Gordon's estate consists of the following property and obligations:

Cash	$ 50,000
Business property	450,000
Stocks	400,000
Funeral and administrative expenses	40,000
Debts of the decedent	30,550

[69]IRC, Sec. 2053; Reg. 20.2053-3.
[70]IRC, Sec. 2053; Reg. 20.2053-6, 20.2053-7.
[71]IRC, Sec. 2055.
[72]IRC, Sec. 2056.

According to his will, the cash and stocks pass to his wife and the business property to his son. Thus,

Gross estate	$900,000
Deductions under Sections 2053 and 2054	70,550
Adjusted gross estate	$829,450
Marital deductions (limited to 50 percent of the adjusted gross estate)	414,725
Other deductions	60,000
Taxable estate	$354,725

Transfers that qualify for the marital deduction include property interest taken by the surviving spouse according to the will, under the laws of intestacy, by gifts in contemplation of death, by rights of survivorship by the entirety or as joint tenants, and as a beneficiary of life insurance. Normally, to qualify for the marital deduction, the property must pass outright. If the surviving spouse receives a terminable interest in the property, it does not qualify for the marital deduction. A terminable interest is an interest that will terminate or fail after a certain period of time, upon the happening of some contingency, or upon the failure of some event to occur.[73]

There are three exceptions to the terminable-interest rule whereby property passing to the surviving spouse, which would otherwise be considered terminable interest and thus be nondeductible, may still qualify for the marital deduction:

1. Property passing to the surviving spouse with the only condition being that the spouse survives by a period not to exceed six months and in fact does survive by such a period.[74]

2. Property passing from the decedent either in trust or as a legal life estate when the surviving spouse has a general power of appointment and is entitled to all the income from such property. This income must be paid to the spouse at least annually.[75]

3. Life insurance or annuity payments held by the insurer with a general power of appointment held by the surviving spouse. If the proceeds are payable in installments, the installments or interest must be paid to the surviving spouse at least annually.[76]

To secure the maximum marital deduction, many wills contain a formula bequest expressed in terms of 50 percent of the adjusted gross estate or the maximum allowable marital deduction (for example, one-half of the adjusted gross estate or an amount that will equal the maximum marital deduction available under the Internal Revenue Code). The exact form of a marital-bequest clause can have important consequences on the property distributed to the beneficiaries of the decedent; thus, careful consideration must be given to the drafting of such a clause.

For example, if a husband dies leaving his half of a joint estate to his surviving spouse, the entire estate, both his half and her half, will be taxed when she ultimately dies. In effect, the husband's half of the estate is being taxed twice. However, if the second spouse dies within a ten-year period from the death of the first spouse, the estate tax would be reduced.

If the second spouse died less than two years after her husband's death, 100 percent of the husband's estate would not have been taxed again. The amount of credit against the first estate is progressively reduced to zero over a period of ten years according to the following schedule:

[73]IRC, Sec. 2056(b).
[74]IRC, Sec. 2056(b)-5.
[75]IRC, Sec. 2056(b)-5.
[76]IRC, Sec. 2056(b)-6.

Period of Time Exceeding	Period of Time Not Exceeding	Percent of Credit Allowance (Percent)
. . .	2 years	100
2 years	4 years	80
4 years	6 years	60
6 years	8 years	40
8 years	10 years	20
10 years	. . .	None

DETERMINATION OF TAX

Once the taxable estate has been determined the "adjusted taxable gifts" (all taxable gifts made after December 31, 1976, not included in the estate) are added thereto. The sum represents cumulative lifetime and deathtime transfers taxable under the unified rate schedule enacted by the 1976 Tax Reform Act. The unified rates, applied to estates and gifts, range from 18 percent on the first $10,000 to 70 percent on the entire taxable estate or gift in excess of $5 million. From the tax computed at these rates, there is allowed a subtraction of the gift tax payable with respect to all gifts made after December 31, 1976 (including gifts included in the estate). The resulting tax is then subject to a further reduction by a unified credit, which replaces both the $60,000 estate tax exemption and the $30,000 lifetime–gift tax exemption allowed under prior law. (Note that any part of the unified credit which was used to offset gift taxes during the decedent's lifetime is not available to offset estate taxes.) While an exemption reduces the tax base, a credit reduces the tax directly. The following schedule sets forth the unified credit allowed each year and the equivalent exemption:

Year	Unified Credit	Equivalent Exemption
1977	$30,000	$120,666
1978	34,000	134,000
1979	38,000	147,333
1980	42,500	161,563
1981 and thereafter	47,000	175,625

In addition to the unified credit, the estate tax is subject to reduction by other credits allowed on account of other taxes. The major credits allowed as deductions from the gross estate tax payable in calculating the net estate tax payable are credits for state death taxes, a credit for tax on prior transfers, and a credit for foreign death taxes.

A credit is allowed against the federal estate tax for the amount of any estate, inheritance, legacy, or succession taxes actually paid to any state, territory, or the District of Columbia in respect of any property included in the decedent's gross estate. If the decedent's taxable estate does not exceed $40,000, no credit is allowed for state death taxes. If the taxable estate exceeds $40,000, the credit is limited by the table in Part (b) of Section 2011 of the Internal Revenue Code.[77]

The credit for state death taxes is limited to taxes that actually were paid. The credit must be claimed within four years after the filing of the estate tax return for the decedent's estate unless a petition has been filed with the Tax Court or an extension of time for payment of the tax or a deficiency has been granted.

Since the credit for state death taxes is limited to the amount of taxes actually paid, it is necessary to provide the IRS with the required information in full. Such information is especially important if a deposit has been made with the state as

[77]IRC, Sec. 2011.

security for payment of the state tax or if discounts or refunds may be allowed by the state. The information to be furnished to the district director should disclose the total amount of tax imposed by the state, the amount of any discount allowed, the total amount actually paid in cash, and the identity of the property with respect to which the state tax has been paid or is to be paid.[78]

A credit is allowed against the estate tax for all or a part of the tax paid with respect to the transfer of property to the decedent by someone who died within ten years before or two years after his or her death. The credit for tax on prior transfers is allowed only for prior estate taxes, not for gift taxes. Also, within limits the credit is allowed for more than two successive decedents. If the transferer died within two years before or after the present decedent's death, the credit allowed for the tax is 100 percent of the maximum amount allowable. If the transferer predeceased the decedent by more than two years, the credit allowable is reduced by 20 percent for each full two years by which the death of the transferer preceded that of the present decedent.[79]

The credit for tax on prior transfers is limited to the smaller of the following:

1. *The amount of the estate tax of the transferer's estate pertaining to the transfer.* Thus the credit is limited to an amount that bears the same ratio to the transferer's adjusted federal estate tax as the value of the transferred property bears to the transferrer's adjusted taxable estate.

2. *The amount by which the estate tax of the present decedent, determined without regard to a credit on prior transfers, exceeds the estate tax for the present decedent's estate, determined by excluding from the gross estate the net value of the transfer.*[80]

Since many other countries levy death taxes on the transfer by nonresident aliens of property situated within their boundaries, the estates of many United States citizens are subjected to double taxation. For this reason, the United States government has entered into estate tax conventions with a number of foreign countries to provide relief from such double taxation.

As a protection against double taxation, the estate is allowed a credit against the federal estate tax for any inheritance, estate, legacy, or succession tax paid to a foreign country and its political subdivisions on any property included in the decedent's gross estate. The credit for foreign death taxes is limited to the smaller of the following amounts:

1. The amount of the foreign death tax attributable to such property situated in the country imposing the tax and included in the decedent's gross estate.

2. The amount of the federal estate tax attributable to such property.[81]

For example, let us assume that a foreign country taxes a person's estate $12,000 for property owned in that country. If the amount of federal estate tax attributable to that property is $15,000, then $12,000 will be deducted from the taxes that the estate must pay. However, if the federal estate tax attributable to the property is $10,000, then only this $10,000 will be deducted from the taxes that the estate must pay.

For the credit to be allowed, the taxpayer must establish to the satisfaction of the IRS the amount of taxes actually paid to the foreign country, the amount and date of each payment, and the description and value of the property on which such taxes were imposed. He or she may also have to submit other information necessary for the verification and computation of the credit. To be allowed, this credit must be applied for within four years after the filing of the estate tax return.[82]

---

[78]Reg. 20.2011-1(b)(2).
[79]IRC, Sec. 2013.
[80]Reg. 20.2013-2, 20.2013-3.
[81]IRC, Sec. 2014.
[82]IRC, Sec. 2014(d), (e).

ESTATE-PLANNING TIPS

It is quite evident that the federal estate tax laws are complicated and involved. Nevertheless, the estate owner must have a firm understanding of these laws and be aware of their interrelationships with the income tax laws. Even though the estate owner must consider the impact of taxes on his or her plan, he or she must not limit estate planning to tax planning. The objective of the estate plan should be to maximize the use of the taxpayer's assets and not merely to minimize taxes. However, there are several simple tips that should help an estate owner to reduce the total tax burden:

1. The estate owner should keep accurate inventories of assets and investments. He or she should make certain that another person knows the location of his or her will, assets, and inventory sheets.

2. A spouse probably should leave approximately one-half of the adjusted gross estate or $250,000, whichever is greater, to the surviving spouse to obtain the maximum marital deduction. However, since the marital deduction is limited, there are no major *tax* benefits in giving the spouse more than the maximum.

3. A taxable estate should not be closed until at least six months after the date of the decedent's death. Only then can an administrator determine whether the alternate valuation date should be elected.

4. An excellent way to reduce an individual's estate tax liability is to reduce the gross estate by a systematic program of lifetime giving. Succeeding subsections discuss ways in which a portion of an estate can be transferred without incurring a gift tax.

5. Because of the advantage of a fresh start step-up in basis to the heirs of a decedent, an individual may wish to retain any noncash property that has substantially increased in value before 1977. Although such a tax plan maximizes the estate tax, it does eliminate any potential income tax that would have been payable if the assets had been sold before death.

6. A listing of bond and securities market quotations for December 31, 1976, is essential.

7. Do not forget to file any applicable state inheritance tax returns.

8. There may be savings in administrative costs and taxes if certain assets are sold immediately prior to death. Such "sales in contemplation of death" remove the capital gain tax paid on the sales from the gross estate. This technique may be beneficial since the tax add-on to basis does not include the amount of the transfer tax applicable to any carry-over basis.

FEDERAL GIFT TAX

A systematic program of lifetime giving may reduce an individual's federal estate tax liability as well as his or her income tax payments. Such a program is especially beneficial as the value of the taxpayer's assets increase as he or she grows older. If an estate owner plans to leave assets to his or her children, he or she may wish to make gifts while still living. If the estate surpasses the taxable levels, the owner may wish to consider reducing the value of the estate by making lifetime gifts. If the taxpayer is in a high income tax bracket and has children or other relatives (possibly in lower income tax brackets) to whom he or she would like to make gifts, savings in both income tax and estate tax may be obtained by giving some assets to them. If they would receive the assets eventually in any case and the taxpayer has no real financial need now, he or she may wish to gain the tax benefits and at the same time see his or her relatives enjoy the use of those assets during the taxpayer's lifetime.

Since making gifts is an obvious method of avoiding the onerous estate tax at death, the federal government has enacted a tax on gift transfers to close part of this escape route. However, an estate owner can still make gifts without incurring this tax. He or she is allowed to make tax-free gifts of $3,000 to *each* person during *each* year. Further, if both spouses consent on the gift tax return to split their gifts, all gifts *to third parties* are considered as having been made one-half by each spouse. Thus, a husband and wife can give $6,000 per year per donee without incurring a gift tax. Prior to the enactment of the 1976 Tax Reform Act an individual could give an additional $30,000 in tax-free gifts at any time during his or her life. This $30,000 exemption and the $60,000 estate tax exemption were both replaced by the unified tax credit. In addition, under prior law the gift tax rates were only 75 percent of estate tax rates. Moreover, assets moved from the highest estate tax bracket were taxed at the lowest gift tax bracket. Therefore, even though the individual exceeded the tax-free limits, there were still advantages to making life-time gifts. The Tax Reform Act removed these advantages by providing a single unified rate schedule for both estate and gift taxes and a unified credit (set forth above).

For all gifts except qualified charitable transfers made after 1970, gift tax returns and payments must be made on a quarterly basis. Both the gift tax return and the payment are due by the fifteenth day of the second month following the close of the calendar quarter as follows:

Calendar Quarter	Due Date
March 31, 1976	May 15, 1976
June 30, 1976	August 15, 1976
September 30, 1976	November 15, 1976
December 31, 1976	February 15, 1977

For years after 1976, a gift tax return does not have to be filed until the first quarter in which the total cumulative taxable gifts made during the calendar years exceed $25,000. Of course, if the total gifts are less than $25,000, only one return should be filed for the year.

For tax years beginning after 1976, quarterly gift tax returns are required only when taxable gifts, in any particular year, exceed $25,000.

The first $3,000 of gifts of *present* interest to any one donee during a calendar year are excluded in determining the taxable gifts of a donor, but this annual exclusion can never be greater than the value of the interest. A present-interest gift occurs when the donee has an immediate right to use, possession, or enjoyment of the gift property. The donee must have more than a mere vested right to such property.

There is no $3,000 annual exclusion for gifts of *future* interest. A future-interest gift is one that is limited to commence in use, possession, or enjoyment. For example, a man may give a gift to a spouse for her lifetime, the property to pass to her son at her death. The gift to the son is a gift of future interest since he does not have the immediate right to the use, possession, or enjoyment of the gift property.

In determining the $3,000 annual exclusion per donee, the exclusion is applied in the order in which gifts are made, for years before 1977. For example, let us assume that a taxpayer gives his son $3,000 on February 14, 1976. No gift tax return would be required on May 15 if this was the only gift. If, however, the taxpayer gives his son $3,000 again on October 17 of the same year (and no split-gift election is made), a gift tax return would have to be filed, and any tax liability would have to be paid by November 15, 1976. It is not exactly clear when an exclusion for a present interest is allowed. Regulation 25.2503-3(b) states that the annual exclusion applies to a present interest in any income if any exists and if its value can be determined. In

Rosen,[83] a donor was allowed an annual exclusion even when the assets placed in a trust consisted of shares of stock that had never paid a dividend and it was unlikely that any dividend would be paid in the near future. The IRS has taken the position that it will not follow the *Rosen* decision if a trust stipulates that all income must be paid to the beneficiary but allows the corpus to be invested in non-income-producing property.[84]

The accompanying table reflects the federal unified estate and gift tax rates in effect for all years after 1976.

Federal Unified Estate and Gift Tax Rate Schedule

If the amount with respect to which the tentative tax to be computed is:	The tentative tax is:
Not over $10,000	18 percent of such amount.
Over $10,000 but not over $20,000	$1,800, plus 20 percent of the excess of such amount over $10,000.
Over $20,000 but not over $40,000	$3,800, plus 22 percent of the excess of such amount over $20,000.
Over $40,000 but not over $60,000	$8,200, plus 24 percent of the excess of such amount over $40,000.
Over $60,000 but not over $80.000	$13,000, plus 26 percent of the excess of such amount over $60,000.
Over $80,000 but not over $100,000	$18,200, plus 28 percent of the excess of such amount over $80,000.
Over $100,000 but not over $150.000	$23,800, plus 30 percent of the excess of such amount over $100,000.
Over $150,000 but not over $250,000	$38,800, plus 32 percent of the excess of such amount over $150,000.
Over $250,000 but not over $500,000	$70,800, plus 34 percent of the excess of such amount over $250.000.
Over $500,000 but not over $750,000	$155,800, plus 37 percent of the excess of such amount over $500,000.
Over $750,000 but not over $1,000,000	$248,300, plus 39 percent of the excess of such amount over $750,000.
Over $1,000,000 but not over $1,250,000	$345,800, plus 41 percent of the excess of such amount over $1,000,000.
Over $1,250,000 but not over $1,500,000	$448,300, plus 43 percent of the excess of such amount over $1,250,000.
Over $1,500,000 but not over $2,000.000	$555,800, plus 45 percent of the excess of such amount over $1,500,000.
Over $2,000,000 but not over $2,500,000	$780,800, plus 49 percent of the excess of such amount over $2,000,000.
Over $2,500,000 but not over $3,000,000	$1,025,800, plus 53 percent of the excess of such amount over $2,500,000.
Over $3,000,000 but not over $3,500,000	$1,290,800, plus 57 percent of the excess of such amount over $3,000,000.
Over $3,500,000 but not over $4,000,000	$1,575,800, plus 61 percent of the excess of such amount over $3,500,000.
Over $4,000,000 but not over $4,500,000	$1,880.800, plus 65 percent of the excess of such amount over $4,000,000.
Over $4,500,000 but not over $5,000,000	$2,205,800, plus 69 percent of the excess of such amount over $4,500,000.
Over $5,000,000	$2,550,800, plus 70 percent of the excess of such amount over $5,000,000.

NOTE: The tentative tax applies to the sum of (1) the amount of the taxable estate and (2) the amount of the adjusted taxable gifts.

[83]22 AFTR 2d 6019 (CA-4, 1968).
[84]Revenue Ruling 69-344, 1969-1 CB 225.

Gifts to Minors

Gifts made to minors can be an effective estate-planning tool. One very important exception to the future-interest rule is a transfer under the Uniform Gifts to Minors Act. In the typical situation, an estate irrevocably transfers securities, cash, or life insurance to a minor by registering the property in the name of the custodian designated by the donor. To be certain that the property will not be included in the donor's estate, the donor or his or her spouse should not be the custodian. Revenue Ruling 59-357[85] indicates that if the donor is the custodian and dies before the donee reaches the age of twenty-one, the custodial property will be included in the donor's gross estate.

Estate tax benefits are not the only advantage of a gift to a minor. There are income tax advantages, although these were reduced by the Revenue Act of 1971. Previously, a taxpayer could transfer securities to a dependent with a substantial part of the income being shielded from tax because of the availability of the low-income allowance and his or her personal exemption. However, after 1971 such allowances as well as the standard deduction are limited by the amount of earned income for a taxpayer who is the dependent of another. Nevertheless, since the dependent's tax bracket is substantially lower than the donor's, there is still a tax saving. Regardless of the relationship of the donor or of the custodian to the donee, if income from the gift property is used to discharge the donor's support obligation, the income is taxed to the donor.

Gifts of stock in closely held corporations may be a useful tool for family income splitting, but any gift should be bona fide, and the donor should not retain any interest in the transferred stock. The Commissioner of Internal Revenue may use the general principles of *Gregory* or *Knetsch,* in which the transfer of the property did not have economic reality. For example, in one case a father gave 25 percent of a Subchapter S corporation to each of his two minor sons. Although he filed a gift tax return, he paid no gift tax and waited a year before he typed the mother's name in as the custodian. The donor prepared and signed tax returns for the children and paid the sons' tax liabilities from his own funds. Custodian bank accounts were not established for the donees until several years later. The Tax Court held that the stock transfers had "no economic reality" and were thereby not bona fide.[86] Of course, gifts other than shares of stock must also have economic reality.

A recent court case illustrates a sale-and-leaseback technique that can be employed advantageously by many professionals and businessmen in using a guardianship to split income among children (*Brooke,* CA-9, July 26, 1972). In the facts of the court case, a physician gave his children, aged six to fourteen, his business real estate, including his own medical building. The state probate court appointed the physician the guardian for the children, and he paid himself (as guardian for his children) the reasonable rental value of his medical office. These rent payments were used to pay for the children's health, insurance, and education. As might be expected, the IRS asserted that the real estate transfer lacked a business purpose and, therefore, that the physician could not obtain a tax deduction for the rental payments.

The court disagreed with the IRS. It accepted the following nontax motives as sufficient business purposes for the transfers: the physician's desire to provide for the health and education of his children, avoidance of friction with partners in his medical practice, withdrawal of his assets from the threat of malpractice suits, and

[85] 1959-2 CB 212.
[86] *Duarte,* 44 TC 193 (1965); *Beirne,* 52 TC 210 (1969). For a more complete discussion, see Crumbley and Davis, op. cit., pp. 53, 215–217.

reduction of the ethical conflict arising from a physician's being the landlord for a pharmacy.

In the same court case the IRS also sought to tax the physician on the income he used for education and other expenses of his children. This is the typical ploy of the IRS when funds of a trust are used to discharge the legal obligation of a parent to support his children. Again the court declined to go along, opining that the items involved were over and above the support that state law required of the father.

A businessman can possibly split income from his business operations by giving his children his business real estate, including his business office. Obviously he must have nontax reasons for such transfers and must document the reasons. He can lease the business establishment from his children. The children would be taxed on the rental income (at lower tax rates), and the businessman could deduct such rental payments as an ordinary and necessary business expense. Warning: for federal estate tax purposes, the fact that the father is the custodian of the property would cause the property to be included in his gross estate if the father died before his children reached age twenty-one. Thus, it may be wise to appoint someone else, possibly the mother, as the custodian.

Split-Gift Election

Under the tax laws, split-gift election can be quite effective for an estate owner. The consent of the spouses to treat a gift by either as a split gift must be made on a calendar quarter basis. For example, if a gift by a taxpayer in April is to be treated as a split gift, consent by the taxpayer and his or her spouse to treat the gift in this way must be obtained no later than the date on which the gift tax return is filed (that is, August 15 of the same year).

Statute of Limitations.   There is an advantage for a donor to pay a small gift tax liability, say, $1, if the donor gives a gift for which valuation is important. This situation occurs because a gift tax must be paid to start the statute of limitations running. The filing of a nontaxable gift tax return is not sufficient. Thus, a payment of a nominal gift tax today may avoid valuation headaches in the future.

Charitable Gifts

To avoid disrupting existing patterns of giving to charitable organizations, donors are *not* forced to file on a quarterly basis qualified charitable transfers. Instead, they are required to report charitable transfers on the fourth-quarter return or at such earlier time as they may be required to file a return for a noncharitable gift.

A "qualified charitable transfer" is defined as a transfer for which a deduction is allowable under Section 2522 for the full amount of the gift. For example, if a donor gives outright securities to a qualified charitable organization, he or she is entitled to a charitable deduction and need not file a special return for such gift.

But let us suppose that the donor transfers property in trust to a son for life, allowing the son to receive the income from the property and giving the principal (initial investment) to a charitable organization after the son's death. This gift would not be a qualified charitable transfer, since a gift tax charitable deduction is not allowable in an amount equal to the full amount transferred. Thus, the donor must file a return reporting the entire gift to the split-interest trust by the fifteenth day of the second month following the end of the calendar quarter. The taxpayer may have to pay a gift tax for the interest transferred to the son.

Shifting the Gift Tax to the Donee

The donor has the primary obligation to pay any gift tax on a transfer. However, for any number of reasons the donor may wish the donee to pay the gift tax liability. For example, a donor may not wish to pay a gift tax on a gift that he or she gives to someone else. Or the donor may not have sufficient liquid assets to pay a potential gift tax. Further, a donee may be forced to pay a gift tax as a result of nonpayment by the donor. The federal government has a ten-year lien on gift property on which gift taxes have not been paid. One technique recently approved by the IRS[87] permits a donor to shift the payment of the gift tax to the donee. At the same time the donee pays a tax on a smaller "net gift," not the full fair market value of the gift.

If a donee by agreement or by implication obligates himself to pay any gift tax as a condition of the transfer, the fair market value of the gift property is reduced by any gift taxes paid by the donee to arrive at the taxable gift. It does not matter whether the donee assumes personal liability for the gift tax or receives the property subject to the gift tax. Of course, since the amount of the taxable gift and the gift tax are mutually dependent variables, an algebraic formula or trial-and-error computations are necessary to determine the gift tax liability.

The procedure for determining the taxable gift and the gift tax may be broken into three steps as follows:

1. By the trial-and-error method, or "eyeballing," determine the gift tax bracket into which the net gift falls. This step should never require more than two or three calculations.

2. Compute a tentative tax based upon the taxable gift without considering the gift tax that is to be deducted from the taxable gift.

3. Divide this tentative tax by 1 plus the marginal tax rate for the selected tax bracket.

For example, let us assume that an estate owner, having made no gifts in preceding years, makes a gift having a fair market value of $120,000 to a donee who has agreed to pay the gift tax resulting therefrom:

Step 1. After the $3,000 annual exclusion is deducted, the net gift of $117,000 will fall within the $100,000–$150,000 unified tax bracket.

Step 2. The tentative tax on $117,000 is $28,900.

Step 3. Divide the tentative tax by 1 plus the marginal tax rate to obtain true tax:

$$\text{True tax} = \frac{\text{tentative tax}}{1 + \text{marginal tax rate}} = \frac{\$28,900}{1 + .3} = \$22,230.77$$

Thus, the taxable gift is $94,769.23 ($117,000 minus $22,230.77), and the gift tax liability is $22,230.77 before the unified credit.

Regrettably, the applicable revenue ruling does not clear up another problem encountered in a net gift situation. The IRS position in a number of cases has been that the donor has a taxable gain for *income tax purposes,* since a net gift is actually part sale and part gift. Although this ruling is concerned only with the gift tax and not the income tax consequences of a transfer, it does view this particular transaction "as a gift in part and a sale in part." However, some of the more recent court cases indicate that the Commissioner is wrong.[88]

To Give or Not to Give

There is no special and precise formula that can be used to indicate when and if a taxpayer should make a gift. Each taxpayer must be given individual attention, emphasis being placed on tax and nontax factors. But a combination of the annual

[87]Revenue Ruling 71-232, IRB 1971-21.

[88]*Turner,* 49 TC 356 (1968), affirmed, 23 AFTR 2d 69-1352 (CA-6: 1969); *Estate of Morgan,* 37 TC 981 (1962), affirmed, 11 AFTR 2d 1231 (CA-6; 1963), cert. den. For a more complete discussion, see D. Larry Crumbley and W. Eugene Seago, "Proper Planning Shifts Gift Tax to Donee," *Trusts and Estates,* vol. 111, pp. 358–360, May 1972.

exclusion, the specific exemption, and the gift-splitting election allows a potential donor to transfer a great deal of property to family members and thereby escape the federal estate tax. For example, a husband and wife could together transfer $360,000 of tax-free gifts to their three sons and their sons' wives over a ten-year period without using up any of their unified estate and gift tax credit. (Keep in mind that the equivalent exemption for 1977 is $120,667; this amount could also be given tax-free.) The calculation of this tax-free amount is as follows:

$$\begin{array}{r} \$6,\!000 \text{ annual exclusion} \times 6 = \ \ \$ \ 36,\!000 \text{ per year} \\ \times \ \ \ \ \ \ 10 \text{ years} \\ \hline \text{Tax-free gifts} \qquad\qquad\qquad \$360,\!000 \end{array}$$

This illustration should clearly demonstrate the advantages of planned and systematic inter vivos giving by an estate owner.

There are certain key factors that the estate owner and his or her advisers should consider in deciding whether or not to give.

1. *Taxpayers should consider the present value of money.* If a potential gift tax is involved, the donor will have lost the use of this money for the rest of his or her life. Use compound interest tables to determine the true economic loss. For example, suppose that a taxpayer is considering a $100,000 gift that would result in a gift tax of $15,525. Estimate the taxpayer's remaining life from the government's longevity tables. Thus, if the taxpayer has only five remaining years of life expectancy and the gift tax is compounded at 6 percent, the probable true economic loss is approximately $20,786, not $15,525.

This is true because the $15,525 gift tax is paid immediately. If it were not paid to the government and were invested to earn 6 percent after taxes, in five years it would grow to $20,786. If we estimate that the taxpayer will live for ten years rather than the normal five years and use a compound interest rate of 6 percent, the true economic loss is approximately $27,800, not $15,525.[89]

The estate owner should also consider the fact that often the money may be of more use and have more value to the donee than to the donor. This may be an extremely important nonquantitative factor in deciding whether a gift should be given.

In our discussion we have used a 6 percent aftertax rate of return. An estate owner must determine what rate of return after taxes he or she can receive without assuming any risk. The lower the rate of return, the less important the immediate tax payment becomes, and this tends to cause the immediate gift to appear more attractive.

2. *The income position of both the taxpayer and the potential donee should be considered.* If the donor is in a high tax bracket, there can be a significant income tax saving if income-producing property is given to a donee in a lower tax bracket. Also, there may be state and estate income tax savings if the property is transferred.

3. *It is important to bear in mind that there is a fresh start step-up in basis of any appreciated property if such property is included in the gross estate.* Thus, if the estate is highly appreciated and the taxpayer is fairly old, it may be advantageous for the beneficiaries to receive this step-up in basis for appreciation up to December 31, 1976, via the estate rather than a carry-over of the original low basis under a gift transaction.

4. *Taxpayers should consider any applicable state inheritance taxes (for example, New York has graduated rates of from 2 to 21 percent) and state gift taxes.* A greater number of

[89]D. Larry Crumbley, "Introducing Probabilities and Present Value Analysis into Taxation," *Accounting Review*, vol. 47, pp. 173–174, January 1972.

states have inheritance taxes than have gift taxes. Since these state estate taxes may exceed the federal credit for state inheritance taxes, a lifetime gift can avoid these taxes.

5. *An estate owner should consider a program of lifetime giving to minimize the tax on his or her estate.* A man and his wife with three married children can give them $432,000 tax-free in a twelve-year period. The couple can give $6,000 per year tax-free to each of their children and to each of the children's wives or husbands. This is equivalent to $36,000 per year, or $432,000 over a twelve-year period.

Other Estate-planning Suggestions

Additional significant gift tax–planning suggestions are summarized below:

1. The split-gift provision for husband and wife is a very valuable tax-planning tool. Once the election has been made, however, it applies to all applicable gifts of both spouses in the calendar quarter in question.

2. Where the donor's spouse has made only nominal gifts in the past, the split-gift election should probably not be made if the other spouse has made substantial gifts. That is, the more generous donor may be in a much higher gift tax bracket. By splitting the gift, the total gift tax liability may be increased.

3. The split-gift election must normally be made before the filing deadline of the tax return. If no returns have been filed, the election period is extended. However, as soon as a return without the consent has been filed and the filing deadline has passed, no election can be made.

4. The 1976 Tax Reform Act has liberalized the marital deduction for gifts. An unlimited deduction is allowed for the first $100,000 of lifetime gifts to a spouse. The next $100,000 is fully taxed, and an additional marital deduction of 50 percent of all transfers in excess of $200,000 is allowed. Under prior law the marital deduction was 50 percent of all such gifts, regardless of the amount of the gifts involved.

5. Gifts to a spouse may be advantageous if they fall within the annual exclusion. However, if a gift tax must be paid and there is a chance that the donee spouse will die first, with the gift property reverting to the donor, the donor is back in his or her original position but minus gift taxes paid.

6. IRS agents scrutinize closely blockage discounts that are applied to transfers of shares of stock. An estate owner should be prepared to prove any discount taken.

7. If a donor transfers property subject to a liability that he or she does not intend to pay, then the donor should state such intentions in writing at the time of the gift.

8. An estate owner in a high income tax bracket may wish to give income-producing property to a donee in a lower tax bracket.

9. A gift of property and subsequent leaseback is a valuable tax-planning tool. One family member in a high tax bracket can give the property to a family member in a lower tax bracket. If the property is leased back to the donor in an arm's-length transaction, the donor can obtain a rental expense deduction and the donee will report rental income. The overall result is a family net income tax saving.

10. A husband should consider giving up all "incidents of ownership" in insurance policies. If his wife owns all the insurance policies insuring his life, none of the policies will be included in his gross estate. The husband should likewise be the owner of policies on his wife's life. Only the value of the policy on the date of the gift is included in "taxable gifts."

11. A donor must be careful if gifts are made by check near the end of the year. If the donee holds a check until the following year, the annual exclusion applies to that year. The taxpayer has lost the annual exclusion for that donee for this year, and any other gifts to the donee in the following year would be taxable.

12. If a short-term trust is established primarily to provide funds for a child's college education, the trust instrument should not indicate that the trust income is designed specifically for educational purposes. Although some states have taken the position that a father has no duty to supply his minor child with a college education, other states provide that the father is obligated to do so under certain circumstances. If the taxpayer lives in the latter type of state, any funds used by the child for an education could be taxable to his father.

13. Since a donee can increase the basis of gift property by part of the gift taxes paid by the donor, the donee should retain adequate records to substantiate the donor's basis, the fair market value of the property at the date of the gift, and the amount of gift tax paid. The donee should retain such information as long as he or she retains the gift property.

Philanthropy Can Be Rewarding

Motivated by social, moral, or economic reasons, many individuals combine tax savings with philanthropy. Private philanthropy performs a special and important role in the United States. It provides for areas into which government cannot or should not venture, such as religion, and it initiates thought and action, experiments with new and untried ventures, and dissents from prevailing attitudes, and acts quickly and flexibly. It enriches the pluralism of our social order.[90] Since the Tax Reform Act of 1969 drastically affected almost all areas of charitable contributions, this subsection is devoted exclusively to the new and old provisions with respect to such contributions and to the significant tax savings that can result from properly planned transactions.

Although a charitable deduction was rejected by the House of Representatives in 1913, when the federal income tax was adopted, such a deduction was included four years later in the War Revenue Act of 1917. The deduction was adopted so that the high wartime tax rates would not shrink charitable contributions.[91] Currently, contributions to certain qualified organizations are deductible from adjusted gross income by taxpayers. Since they are deductible from adjusted gross income, a taxpayer should make charitable contributions only in years in which he or she has enough itemized deductions to exceed his or her standard deduction; otherwise, the contributions will be wasted. As the tax code expanded, this deductibility feature was applied to the estate and trust area, the federal estate tax, the federal gift tax, and the corporate tax area.

The following organizations among others generally are qualified charitable organizations: a church or association of churches, a college or university, a hospital, governmental units, certain private foundations, a chest, trust, fund, or foundation organized and operated exclusively for religious, charitable, scientific, literary, or educational purposes or for the prevention of cruelty to children or animals, and other organizations that are exempted from taxation under Section 501(a) of the Internal Revenue Code.[92] Donations to individuals and to foreign charities (except where a treaty allows it) do not qualify.

The Tax Reform Act of 1969 did not affect income tax returns on which the standard deduction is utilized or on which all the contributions are made in cash to qualified charities within the old 20 percent and 30 percent limitations. However, the 30 percent limitation has been increased to 50 percent, and the list of eligible organizations qualifying for this 50 percent limitation has been expanded to include certain private foundations.

[90]*Treasury Department Report on Private Foundations,* House Committee on Ways and Means, 89th Cong., 1st Sess., Feb. 2, 1965, p. 5.

[91]*Congressional Record,* 65th Cong., 1st Sess., 1917, p. 7628.

[92]IRC, Sec. 170(e); Reg. 1.170A(c).

To appreciate these limitations, an individual must understand that there are two types of charitable organizations, public charities and private charities. Gifts to public charities qualify for the 50 percent ceiling; for such public charities an individual can deduct up to 50 percent of his or her "contribution base," and contributions in excess of this ceiling can be carried over for the succeeding five tax years.[93] A person's contribution base is his or her adjusted gross income, disregarding any net operating loss carry-back.[94] The charities qualifying for the 50 percent ceiling include most churches, the American Red Cross, the United Fund, the Boy Scouts of America, the Salvation Army, and many other well-known charities. When in doubt, the taxpayer should ask the potential charitable organization if contributions to it qualify for a deduction or consult IRS Publication No. 78, *Cumulative List: Organizations Described in Section 170(c) of the Internal Revenue Code of 1954.* Merely because an organization is tax-exempt does not automatically mean that it is a qualified charity.

All qualified charities that are not 50 percent charities are 20 percent charities. These 20 percent charities are private foundations or organizations (for example, the Crumbley Foundation) but not private operating foundations. Gifts to 20 percent charities are deductible up to the lesser of 20 percent of the taxpayer's contribution base *or* 50 percent of his or her contribution base *minus* contributions to 50 percent charities (including carry-overs of such contributions and with no reduction for the 30 percent ceiling on appreciated property).[95] For example, if a person contributes 38 percent of his or her contribution base to a 50 percent charity (for example, a church), his or her contributions to 20 percent charities are deductible only up to 12 percent of the contribution base. Furthermore, the taxpayer is *not* allowed to carry over any excess gifts to 20 percent charities.

Contribution of Appreciated Property

There are three new sets of tax rules for all contributions of appreciated property (that is, all property which would give rise to any gain if sold, such as stocks, real estate, stamp collection, and antiques):

1. Ordinary income–type property
2. Tangible personal capital gain property and contributions of capital gain property to certain private foundations
3. Appreciated capital gain property

Property whose appreciation would not be *all* long-term capital gain to the contributor if he or she sold it at its fair market value on the date on which it was contributed falls into the first category of ordinary income–type property. For a charitable contribution of any property that gives rise to any ordinary income appreciation on disposition, the property's fair market value on the date of contribution is reduced by the amount of the ordinary income appreciation to determine the deductible amount.[96] Inventory, Section 306 stock, letters, and memorandums given by a person who prepared them or for whom they were prepared, and works of art donated by the artist who created them fall within this category.

For example, let us suppose that you purchased AT&T stock for $2,500 and contributed the stock to a church four months later when it was worth $4,000. Since the $1,500 of appreciation is a short-term gain, your charitable deduction is

[93]IRC, Sec. 170(b)(1)(A).
[94]IRC, Sec. 170(b)(1)(F).
[95]IRC, Sec. 170(b)(1)(B).
[96]IRC, Sec. 170(e); Reg. 1.170A-4(a)(1).

only $2,500 ($4,000 minus $1,500). If, however, the stock was held at least six months and one day and then contributed to the church, this transaction would fall within the third category, and there would be no reduction in the appreciation.

It should be noted that the 1976 Tax Reform Act increases the holding period necessary to qualify a capital asset for long-term capital gain or loss treatment. For taxable years beginning in 1977, the holding period increases to "more than nine months." For taxable years beginning after 1977, the holding period increases to "more than one year."

There may be situations in which there is part capital gain and part ordinary income (for example, recapturable property). If depreciable personal property subject to recapture is contributed to a charity, the deduction is limited to the fair market value of the property reduced by that portion of the gain that would be treated as recaptured ordinary income. Let us suppose that a taxpayer has held for more than six months depreciable personal property which has a fair market value of $10,000 but a tax basis of only $5,000 and on which $4,000 of recapturable depreciation has been taken. A contribution of this property would result in a $6,000 deduction ($10,000 minus $4,000).

Obviously an individual should give gifts other than short-term and ordinary-income property to charities whenever possible. An individual will often be better off by leaving this type of property to a charity in his or her will. The individual's spouse will get a marital deduction based on the assets' market value; however, the property will be removed from the estate before the estate tax is computed.

Into the second category fall two types of transactions. First, if the asset contributed is tangible personal property, then to qualify for the full deduction its utilization by the charity must be directly related to the exempt function of the charity. If the utilization is not directly related to the exempt function of the charity, the deduction is limited to cost plus 50 percent of the appreciation for noncorporate donors. The percentage becomes 37.5 percent for corporate donors.[97] For example, a painting (not created by the taxpayer) has a cost basis of $2,500 and a gain fair market value of $4,000. The painting is held for three years and then given to a church, which sells it to use the proceeds. Since the painting is not directly related to the exempt function of the church, the deduction would be limited to the cost of $2,500 plus one-half of the appreciation, or $750, for a total deduction of $3,250. However, if the painting is donated to a museum to be used for display purposes, the donor is entitled to a $4,000 deduction.

Thus, whether a contribution to a charity is for an "unrelated use" or a "directly related use" is very important to a taxpayer. The term "unrelated use" means a use that is unrelated to the purpose or function constituting the basis of the charitable organization's tax exemption.[98] For example, if a stamp collection contributed to an educational institution is used by that organization for educational purposes by being placed in its library for display and study by the students, the use is not an unrelated use. But if the collection is sold and the proceeds are used by the organization for educational purposes, the use of the property is an unrelated use. If a collection is contributed to a charitable organization or a governmental unit, the use of the collection is not an unrelated use if the donee sells or otherwise disposes of only an insubstantial portion of the collection. Obviously, potential donors of appreciated tangible personal property must match the item of property to be given with an appropriate charity.

What proof of use should a taxpayer maintain? The taxpayer may establish that the contributed property is not in fact put to an unrelated use by the charity or that,

---

[97]IRC, Sec. 170(e)(1)(B)(ii).
[98]Reg. 1.170 A-4(b)(3)(i).

at the time of the contribution, it is reasonable to anticipate that the property will not be put to an unrelated use by the charity.[99] For example, in the case of a gift of stamps to a museum, if the donated stamps are of a general type normally retained by such a museum, it is reasonable for the taxpayer to anticipate (unless he or she has actual knowledge to the contrary) that the stamps will not be put to an unrelated use by the museum, whether or not the stamps are later sold or exchanged by the charity.

If a taxpayer makes a charitable contribution of appreciated property and claims a deduction in excess of $200, he or she must attach to the tax return the following information:[100]

1. The name and address of the organization to which the contribution was made.

2. The date of the actual contribution.

3. A detailed description of the property along with the conditions of the property.

4. The manner of acquisition (for example, purchase, gift, or inheritance).

5. The fair market value of the property along with the method utilized in determining this value. If there was an appraisal, a copy of the signed report of the appraiser should be included.

6. The cost or adjusted basis of the property.

7. If the deduction is reduced by any of the appreciation, the reduced amount.

8. Any agreement or understanding between the taxpayer and the charity.

9. The total amount claimed as a deduction for the following year.

Any deduction for a charitable contribution must be substantiated, when required by the district director, by a statement from the organization to which the contribution was made indicating whether the organization is a domestic organization, the name and address of the contributor, the amount of the contribution, the date of actual receipt of the contribution, and such other information as the district director may deem necessary. When the property has a fair market value in excess of $200 at the time of receipt, such a statement shall also indicate for each such item its location if it is retained by the organization, the amount received by the organization of any sale of the property and the date of sale, or, in case of any other disposition of the property, the method of disposition. The statement should indicate the use of the property by the organization and whether it is employed for a purpose or function constituting the basis for the charity's exemption from income tax under Internal Revenue Code Section 501 or, in the case of a governmental unit, whether it is employed exclusively for public purposes.[101]

A second type of transaction will cause a one-half reduction in the appreciation of appreciated property. If capital gain property is given to a private foundation which is not a private operating foundation or a community foundation and which does not make qualifying distributions equal to the amount of such contributions within 2½ months after the close of the year, the deduction is limited to the property's fair market volume minus one-half of the appreciation.[102]

A third category involves the contribution to a charity of appreciated capital gain property that is directly related to the charity's exempt function. Capital gain property is a capital asset which, if sold at the time contributed, would give rise only to long-term capital gain.[103] Property used in a trade or business, coins,

[99]Reg. 1.170 A-4(b)(3)(ii).
[100]Reg. 1.170 A-1(a)(2)(ii).
[101]Reg. 1.170 A-1(a)(2)(iii).
[102]IRC, Sec. 170(e)(1)(B)(ii).
[103]IRC, Sec. 170(b)(1)(a).

stamps, antiques, art works, and so on qualify as capital gain property. When a taxpayer contributes such property to a qualified charity, his or her deduction ceiling is reduced to 30 percent for such property rather than to the normal 50 percent, unless the taxpayer makes a special election to reduce the amount of the contribution. In other words, the total amount of contribution of capital gain property considered for deduction purposes for any tax year cannot exceed 30 percent of the taxpayer's contribution base (generally adjusted gross income). When an individual makes a special election, his or her deduction ceiling remains at 50 percent along with a 50 percent carry-over, but he or she may deduct only the capital gain property's basis plus one-half of any appreciation.[104]

For example, let us assume that Chuck Charitable, who has a $10,000 adjusted gross income, makes a charitable contribution of part of his antique collection to a museum for display purposes during 1976. The portion of the collection contributed has a basis of $2,000 but is valued at $10,000 on the date of contribution. Under the general rule he has made a contribution of $10,000. During 1976 Chuck may deduct $3,000 (30 percent times $10,000) and has a contribution carry-over of $7,000 (but subject to the 30 percent carry-over rule). On the other hand, if Chuck so desires, he may elect to have his contribution be $6,000 ($2,000 basis plus 50 percent of $8,000 appreciation). Here he could deduct $5,000 during 1976 (50 percent times $10,000) with a contribution carry-over of $1,000 (subject to the 50 percent carry-over rule).

A taxpayer probably will not wish to elect the 50 percent rule if he or she makes a contribution of highly appreciated capital gain property. Of course, a taxpayer who owns property worth substantially less than its cost basis should sell it and then contribute the proceeds to the charity.

If a person contributes any property to a charitable organization and pays an appraisal fee to someone to determine the fair market value of the property, the appraisal expenses are deductible from his or her adjusted gross income, provided he or she itemizes deductions.[105]

Comprehensive Example

A more comprehensive example should help to illustrate these three major sets of rules. Let us assume that Chuck Charitable on July 1, 1976, makes the charitable contributions shown in Table 64-1, all of which, except for the stocks, are made to a church. After the applicable adjustments have been made, the amount of charitable contribution allowed by Chuck Charitable (before any ceiling limitations) is as shown in Table 64-2.

If we assume that the donor in the preceding sample, instead of an individual, was a corporation, the amount of charitable contributions allowed (before the 5 percent limitation) would be as shown in Table 64-3.

Unlimited Deduction

Before the Tax Reform Act of 1969, taxpayers who met certain conditions could take an unlimited charitable deduction. Basically, the taxpayer could take the full amount of his or her charitable donations if for eight of the ten preceding tax years contributions plus income taxes exceeded 90 percent of taxable income. This unlimited deduction was gradually reduced so that in tax years after 1974 the

---

[104]IRC, Sec. 170(b)(1)(D)(iii).
[105]Revenue Ruling 67-461, IRB 1967-52, 12.

TABLE 64-1

Property	Fair-market value	Adjusted basis	Recognized gain if sold
Ordinary-income property	$ 50,000	$35,000	$15,000
Property which, if sold, would produce long-term capital gain			
Stock held more than six months contributed to:			
A church	25,000	21,000	4,000
A private foundation not described in Section 170(b)(1)(E)	15,000	10,000	5,000
Tangible personal property held more than six months (put to unrelated use by church)	12,000	6,000	6,000
Total	$102,000	$72,000	$30,000

TABLE 64-2

Property	Fair-market value	Reduction	Contribution allowed
Ordinary-income property	$ 50,000	$15,000	$35,000
Property which, if sold, would produce long-term capital gain			
Stock contributed to			
The church	25,000	. . .	25,000
The private foundation	15,000	2,500	12,500
Tangible personal property	12,000	3,000	9,000
Total	$102,000	$20,500	$81,500

TABLE 64-3

Property	Fair-market value	Reduction	Contribution allowed
Ordinary-income property	$ 50,000	$15,000	$35,000
Property which, if sold, would produce long-term capital gain			
Stock contributed to			
The church	25,000	. . .	25,000
The private foundation	15,000	3,125	11,875
Tangible personal property	12,000	3,750	8,250
Total	$102,000	$21,875	$80,125

maximum deduction per year was 50 percent. During these transitional years, the
following maximum deductions were allowed:[106]

Year	Percent
1970	80
1971	74
1972	68
1973	62
1974	56

Bargain Sale

A bargain sale may be an excellent technique to minimize a donor's out-of-pocket
cost. Before the Tax Reform Act of 1969 an individual could sell appreciated
property at cost to a charity and end up with his or her investment back without
any tax plus a charitable deduction for any appreciation. Now, however, the donor
must allocate his or her cost basis between the part of the property that he or she
sold and the part that is a gift.[107] Therefore, he or she has a taxable gain on the
bargain sale but still has *minimized the out-of-pocket cost of the charitable gift.* However,
if a donor wishes to give the charity the largest benefit, he or she should make an
ordinary gift to the selected charity.

For example, Cherry Charitable sells her coin collection worth $10,000, which
she has held a number of years, to a museum for her cost of $4,000. She must
allocate 60 percent of her cost ($2,400) to the portion given and 40 percent
($1,600) to the portion sold. If she is in the 50 percent tax bracket, her $6,000 gift
($10,000 minus $4,000) saves her $3,000 in taxes, and she recovers her $4,000
investment, for a nice total of $7,000. If we assume further that she does not have
capital gains in excess of $50,000, she will pay a tax of no more than $600 on her
$2,400 long-term capital gain (25 percent times $2,400). Her net return thus is
$6,400, and her favorite charity has $6,000 more in its coffers.

Let us suppose that Cherry makes an outright gift of the coins to the museum. If
the coins are directly related to the exempt function of the museum, the $10,000
gift saves her $5,000, and the museum gets the full $10,000 tax basis.

Nondeductibles

No deduction is allowed for the contribution of services. For example, if an
individual donates his or her services to a nonprofit organization, the cost of the
time is not deductible. However, unreimbursed expenditures, such as outlays for
transportation or lodging, made incidentally to the rendering of services to a
qualified organization are deductible as contributions.[108] The standard mileage
rate for computing the cost of operating an automobile in rendering gratuitous
service to a qualifying organization is 6 cents per mile. Parking fees and tolls
attributable to such travel are separately deductible.[109]

An individual who gives a charity a right to use his or her property can no
longer take a charitable deduction for the rental or other value of such a right.
Before the Tax Reform Act of 1969 this technique was available, but no charitable
contribution deduction is now allowed for the contribution of a mere right to use
property.[110]

---

[106]Reg. 1.170A(b)(1)(C); Reg. 1.170A(f)(6)(B).
[107]Reg. 1.170A-4(c)(2).
[108]Revenue Ruling 57-327, 1957-2 CB 155.
[109]Revenue Ruling 70-24, IRB, 1970-41, 58.
[110]IRC, Sec. 170(f)(3).

Future Interest in Property

A transfer of a future interest in property to a charity may *not* be deducted as a charitable contribution until all intervening interest in and right to the possession or enjoyment of the property have expired.[111] Thus, except for a remainder interest in a residence or farm and a certain remainder interest in a trust, no deduction is allowed for a gift in the future. Let us suppose that an individual conveys by deed of gift to a museum title to an art collection in 1975 but reserves the right to the use, possession, and enjoyment of the collection during his or her lifetime. At the time of the gift the value of the collection is $40,000. Since the contribution consists of a future interest in tangible personal property in which the taxpayer has retained an intervening interest, no contribution is considered to have been made in 1975. Let us assume that the taxpayer relinquishes all his or her rights to the use, possession, and enjoyment of the art collection and delivers it to the museum in 1976, when the collection is worth $45,000. In this case the taxpayer is treated as having made a charitable contribution of $45,000 in 1976.

If a charitable gift exceeds $3,000 or is a future-interest gift, the transfer must eventually be reported on a gift tax return. But when the charitable gift is reported, the taxpayer is allowed a deduction *on the gift tax return,* in a "wash" effect. There is no percentage limitation as to the amount deductible on the gift tax return. A donor is not forced to file on a quarterly basis his or her qualified charitable transfers. Instead, he or she is required to file a return for a noncharitable gift.

Corporate Deduction

An individual who owns a business under a corporate structure may also have his or her corporation make charitable gifts. A corporation is allowed to deduct as charitable contributions up to 5 percent of its taxable income computed without regard to:
1. The deduction for charitable contributions
2. The dividend-paid deductions on certain preferred stock of utilities
3. The Western Hemisphere Trade Corporation deduction
4. Any net operating loss carry-back
5. Any capital loss carry-back[112]

Any excess contribution in any one year may be carried over and shall be deductible for each of the given succeeding tax years in order of time.[113] If the corporation is in the 48 percent tax bracket, approximately one-half of any contributions is, in effect, contributed by the federal government.

[111]Reg. 1.170A-5.
[112]Reg. 1.170-3(a).
[113]Reg. 1.170 A(d)(2)(A).

Chapter **65**

Charitable Remainder Interests in Trust

TERENCE E. SMOLEV

The 1969 Tax Reform Act restricted the use of charitable remainder trusts to two basic types, the annuity trust and the unitrust. These two forms of trusts together with the gift annuity and the pooled income fund are now the only ways in which property other than a residence or a farm can be given to a charity in the future while the taxpayer obtains a current income tax deduction.

To the high-bracket taxpayer unitrusts, annuity trusts, the pooled income fund, and the gift annuity provide generous tax benefits. These benefits will be discussed in this chapter.

CHARITABLE REMAINDER UNITRUST

The Internal Revenue Code[1] defines a charitable remainder unitrust as a trust from which a *fixed percentage* (at least 5 percent) of the net fair market value of its assets, valued annually, is to be paid, at least annually, to one or more persons for their lives or for a term of years not exceeding twenty years. The individuals receiving payments must have been living at the creation of the trust. Upon the death of the last income beneficiary or upon the expiration of the term of years, the trust must terminate and the corpus be distributed to the charitable remainderman.

Unitrust Variations

The "standard" unitrust requires that the fixed percentage (not less than 5 percent) of the net fair market value of the assets, valued annually, be paid regardless of whether the trust has earned sufficient income for the payment. This type of trust contemplates invasion of corpus.

There are two variations of the standard unitrust: (1) the income or fixed-percentage, whichever is lower; and (2) the income or fixed-percentage, whichever is lower, with deficiencies paid in later years.

[1] IRC, Sec. 664(d)(2).

Net-Income Variation

The Internal Revenue Code permits a trust document to provide for the payment of income only from a trust if the income is less than the fixed percentage.[2] In years when income is greater than the fixed percentage, only the amount of the fixed percentage is paid out.

Net-Income-plus-Deficiencies Variation

It is possible to provide for the net-income–variation type of unitrust to permit amounts in excess of the fixed percentage to be paid in years in which income exceeds the fixed percentage. However, such excess income paid out is limited to the amount of accumulated deficiencies existing from years when income was less than the fixed percentage.

Unitrusts and Tax Planning

An interesting method of tax planning involves the use of unitrusts. A taxpayer with an income in a high bracket does not want additional income in his or her years of high tax rates. However, the taxpayer does want deductions that will give him or her lower taxes and possibly more spendable cash. A unitrust of the net-income-with-payment-of-deficiencies variety may be useful to such a taxpayer. If the trustee knows that the donor does not need or want additional income in certain future years, it may decide to invest the unitrust assets in low-yield, high-growth securities in those years. When the donor falls into a lower tax bracket, the trustee may decide to sell out the low-yield investments and reinvest the funds in higher-yield securities to pay the fixed percentage plus the accumulated deficiencies. This plan has the effect of moving taxable income from high tax years to low tax years. Also, since a unitrust is a tax-exempt trust,[3] there is no tax on the sale of trust securities, thus allowing the low-yield, high-growth securities to be transferred into high-yield securities without the loss of corpus that would normally result from payment of a capital gains tax.

Another interesting tax-planning use of a unitrust is found in estate planning. If a donor retains the income interest in a unitrust, upon his or her death the estate will include the value of the trust corpus for federal estate tax purposes.[4] This increases the adjusted gross estate, which in turn increases the allowable marital deduction (see Chapter 64) without increasing the estate tax, since the amount that the charity receives is a deductible item in computing the tax.[5]

For example, Mr. X may have an adjusted gross estate of $400,000, not including the $100,000 fair market value of a unitrust in which he has a life interest. Therefore, his total adjusted gross estate is $500,000. He will get a $250,000 marital deduction as well as a $100,000 charitable deduction, leaving him with a taxable estate of $150,000. If the gift had been given outright during his lifetime, his adjusted gross estate would have been $400,000, and after the marital deduction his taxable estate would have been $200,000.

Unitrust Example

D, a male who will be fifty years old on April 15, 1976, transfers $100,000 to a charitable remainder unitrust on January 1, 1976. The trust instrument requires that the trust pay to D at the end of each taxable year of the trust 5 percent of the fair market value of the trust assets as of the beginning of each taxable year of the trust. The present value of the remainder interest of $100,000 is $37,816, based

[2]IRC, Sec. 664(d)(3)(A).
[3]IRC, Sec. 664(c).
[4]IRC, Sec. 2036.
[5]IRC, Sec. 2055.

on government tables.[6] This is true because a fifty-year-old man is expected to live for many years, and the correct value of $100,000 to be received at the end of his period of life expectancy is $37,816.

If we assume that D is in the 50 percent tax bracket, his charitable deduction of $37,816 saves him taxes of $18,908. Thus the actual cost of his gift is $100,000 minus $18,908, or $81,092. In the first year of the unitrust, D would receive 5 percent of $100,000, or $5,000, a 5 percent rate of return. However, if we compute his rate of return on his actual cost of $81,092, it is actually in excess of 6 percent.

If instead of cash D had transferred appreciated securities with a fair market value of $100,000 and a cost basis of $60,000, he would have saved more than $10,000 in capital gains tax, which would have had to be paid if the securities had been sold rather than given. Therefore, his actual cost of the gift is reduced, and his rate of return would be in excess of 7 persent.

The rate of return may be even higher and the actual cost lower, depending upon tax laws in effect in the donor's state of residence as well as the type of property gift.

CHARITABLE REMAINDER ANNUITY TRUST

The Internal Revenue Code[7] defines a charitable remainder annuity trust as a trust from which a *fixed dollar amount* (which is at least 5 percent of the initial net fair market value of all property placed in trust) is to be paid, at least annually, to one or more individuals for their lives or for a period of years not exceeding twenty years. The individuals receiving payments must have been alive at the creation of the trust. Upon the death of the last income beneficiary or upon the expiration of the term of years, the trust must terminate and the corpus be distributed to the charitable remainderman.

Annuity Trust Versus Unitrust

There are the following important differences between annuity trusts and unitrusts.

1. The charitable remainder annuity trust pays a fixed dollar amount each year regardless of the corpus growth, inflation, or deflation. Unitrusts, on the other hand, pay an amount that varies with the corpus value. As the corpus value increases, payments to the income beneficiary also increase.

2. A donor cannot add corpus to an annuity trust but can do so to a unitrust. Continuing gifts are thus easier to make with unitrusts since new trust instruments need not be drawn for each transfer.[8]

3. Neither the annuity trust nor the unitrust permits invasion of corpus for the benefit of any beneficiary.[9]

The trustee cannot be prohibited from investing in a manner that would produce income or gain currently in either a unitrust or an annuity trust.[10] Distributions to beneficiaries are treated as having the following characteristics in the hands of the recipients for either the unitrust or the annuity trust.[11]

1. As ordinary income to the extent of the sum of the trust's ordinary income for the taxable year of the trust and its undistributed ordinary income for prior years.

[6]Reg. Sec. 1.664-4(b)(5).
[7]IRC, Sec. 664(d)(1).
[8]Reg., Sec. 1.664-2(b); Reg., Sec. 1.664-3(b).
[9]Reg., Sec. 1.664-2(a)(4); Reg., Sec. 1.664-3(a)(4).
[10]Reg., Sec. 1.664-1(a)(3).
[11]IRC, Sec. 664(b); Reg., Sec. 1.664-1(d).

2. As capital gain to the extent of the trust's undistributed capital gains. Short-term capital gains are considered to be distributed first, then long-term capital gains.

3. As other income to the extent of the sum of the trust's other income for the taxable year and its undistributed other income for prior years.

4. As a distribution of trust corpus.

Annuity Trust Example

D, a male who will be fifty years old on April 15, 1976, transfers $100,000 to a charitable remainder annuity trust on January 1, 1976. The trust instrument requires that the trust pay $5,000 to D at the end of each taxable year of the trust. The present value of the remainder interest is $43,335.50, based on government tables.[12]

If we assume that D is in the 50 percent tax bracket, his charitable deduction of $43,335.50 saves him taxes of $21,667.75. Thus the actual cost of his gift is $78,332.25. D will be receiving a 5 percent return on his annuity trust investment of $100,000. However, if we compute the rate of return on his actual cost of $78,332.25, it is actually in excess of 6 percent. If D had transferred appreciated securities rather than cash, his actual rate of return would have been even greater.

POOLED INCOME FUND

A pooled income fund is a trust to which each donor transfers property, contributing an irrevocable remainder interest in such property to or for the use of a charitable organization and retaining an income interest for the life of one or more beneficiaries living at the time of the transfer. The property transferred is commingled with property transferred by other donors. The income beneficiaries are entitled to their pro-rata share of fund income. Upon the death of an income beneficiary, his or her pro-rata interest in the fund is severed and used by the charitable organization for its charitable purposes.[13]

The pooled income fund is generally maintained by charitable organizations to provide a means for a donor to make a gift while retaining a life interest (or giving the life interest to another) when the donor cannot afford to make a large-enough gift in unitrust or annuity trust form.

The donor to a pooled fund receives a charitable deduction for the value of the remainder interest left to charity. This value, as with unitrusts and annuity trusts, is based on government tables.

GIFT ANNUITY

The gift annuity provides for an irrevocable transfer of cash or property to a charitable organization in return for a promise by the charity to pay a fixed dollar amount annually for the donor's life.

The gift annuity should be contrasted with the charitable remainder annuity trust, which also pays a fixed dollar amount. There are several differences between the two. Probably the most important difference is that the charitable organization's entire assets are fully liable for the payment of a gift annuity, whereas only the individual annuity trust's assets are liable for payments. Thus if the gift annuity payments exceed the amount of the original gift, the charity must continue to make payments out of other assets. On the other hand, if an annuity trust's assets are fully depleted, the trust terminates and the beneficiary does not receive any additional payments.

[12]Reg., Sec. 20.2031-10.
[13]IRC Sec. 642(c)(5).

Other differences are as follows:

1. A portion of every gift annuity payment is nontaxable as a return of capital. Annuity trust payments may be fully taxable, partly taxable, or nontaxable, depending upon the form of investment by the trust.

2. Gift annuity payments depend upon the annuitant's age at the time of the gift. Annuity trust payments are set by agreement without regard to the beneficiary's age.

3. Donors incur capital gains tax when funding gift annuities with appreciated property. There is no capital gains tax upon the funding of an annuity trust with appreciated property.

4. Payments to a beneficiary are taxed differently if made from a gift annuity instead of from an annuity trust. The characterization of distributions to beneficiaries from a gift annuity differs from that of an annuity trust as outlined above.

Chapter **66**

Trusts and Their Uses in Family Financial Planning

P. MICHAEL DAVIS

What Is a Trust?

In his *Handbook of the Law of Trusts,* George G. Bogert has defined a trust as "a fiduciary relationship in which one person is the holder of the title to property, subject to an equitable obligation to keep or use the property for benefit of another."[1] It is appropriate to explore the meaning of the terms used in this definition, since an understanding of them will be central to the discussion that follows.

The term "fiduciary" suggests a relationship based upon trust and confidence. The person who creates the trust is called the "settlor" or "grantor." Trusts normally have assets, which may consist of any property or property rights. Among the commoner types of assets held by trusts are real estate, stocks and bonds, and life insurance policies. Trusts may even have ownership interests in business enterprises operated either as sole proprietorships or as partnerships. The entity that holds title to the property is called a "trustee." The trustee may be an individual or a corporation. Corporate trustees are usually trust departments of commercial banks or independent trust companies. The person or organization for which trust property is held is called a "beneficiary." Trusts are most often governed by official documents. The document that establishes how the trust property is to be managed as well as the rights and duties of the various parties is called a "trust instrument."

Why Use Trusts?

Trusts are highly useful devices in overall family financial planning. An individual may be able to accomplish personal goals through the use of trusts that otherwise would not be possible by reason of death, incapacity, or change of financial circumstances. The trust may be used to ensure that the individual's desires are carried out after his or her death. Trusts may also be used to provide security for those who are left behind, such as aged parents, the spouse of the deceased, and dependent children.

[1]George G. Bogert, *Handbook of the Law of Trusts,* 4th ed., West Publishing Co., St. Paul, 1963, p. 1.

Expert managerial guidance may be ensured through the use of a trust. The corporate trustee has investment skills that should produce a greater rate of return on trust property. Inexperienced beneficiaries may cause assets to be squandered in the absence of guidance.

Significant tax savings may result from the proper use of trusts. Individuals are liable for the payment of personal income taxes during their lifetimes. Death brings forth liability for federal estate and state death taxes. Gift tax considerations may have a significant role to play in the decision to give away property before death. Trusts can greatly simplify probate problems and can facilitate savings of estate taxes as well as of administrative costs.

Planning for Life as Well as for after Death

It is indeed unfortunate that so many people attach such a narrow meaning to the term "estate planning." Notions of wills, estate taxes, and distributions to beneficiaries at death are vividly portrayed with all sorts of adverse consequences. Admittedly, these are important aspects of estate planning that should not be overlooked. However, the lifetime goals of the individual are also significant for estate planning. It is this aspect of estate planning that is most often overlooked. Trusts have a significant role to play in the "living" aspect of estate planning. For example, trusts may be used to accumulate funds for children's education or for retirement.

Tax Saving Is Not the Only Goal

Matters of taxation are highly significant aspects of estate planning. There is, however, a danger that the saving of taxes will overshadow other major estate-planning objectives to the extent that the personal goals and desires of the individual are lost in the shuffle. As a practical matter, an estate plan that does not give adequate consideration to both the individual's predeath and afterdeath goals is incomplete. It should be noted that tax aspects will be considered throughout this chapter.

Purpose of This Chapter

The purpose of this chapter is to examine trusts and determine how they can help to fulfill family financial planning goals. Sound financial planning must start with the recognition of goals. To encourage thought along these lines, the following subsection is devoted to a consideration of some of the commoner goals of financial planning. Thus, it is appropriate to explore how trusts can be utilized in realizing these goals. Of necessity, the analysis is limited to the commoner types of trusts.

The following discussion is designed to stimulate thought and action with a view to effective planning. However, a little knowledge can be dangerous in the hands of a layman. The information contained in this chapter is no substitute for the advice of professionals in the estate-planning field. Therefore, after the individual has formulated a tentative set of financial goals, he or she is urged to consult an attorney, certified public accountant, or trust officer. Each of these professionals is skilled in certain aspects of financial planning. The combined efforts of the individual's attorney and trust officer are necessary to help complete a set of planning goals and to make arrangements for their implementation. The certified public accountant is especially helpful when business interests are to be considered.

FAMILY FINANCIAL PLANNING GOALS

Each family unit is unique. In some cases, the head of the family must make provision for aged parents as well as for a spouse and children. The age and general state of health of the various family members are also important. Moreover, the size of the estate has significance, for assets may be insufficient to permit all goals to be fulfilled. Regardless of the wealth involved, the plan should take into consideration, to as great an extent as possible, the personal goals and desires of the individual.

An individual may use a trust for one or more of the following reasons: conservation of assets, maximization of income, provision for retirement, support for spouse and dependents after death, minimization of administrative costs, minimization of taxes, continuation of a family business, or planning in the event of marital breakup.

Conservation of Assets

The individual may wish to consolidate his or her asset position by transferring some savings to a trust on a year-by-year basis. In this manner a sizable estate can be accumulated during the working years. Not only can retirement be provided for, but a source of wealth can be established for the individual's heirs.

The head of the family may be concerned about his or her estate after death. If the estate is dissipated too quickly by the heirs, the funds may not be adequate to fulfill his or her wish for support. A trust may be established to hold and manage assets for benefit of spouse and children after the head of the household is no longer around to fulfill this obligation.

Maximization of Income

An individual with a sizable liquid estate may desire the highest possible return on his or her wealth but not wish to become involved in its management. Through a trust, authority to manage assets can be delegated to a corporate trustee and thus relieve the individual of the necessity to follow the market. Trust departments of banks can manage investment portfolios with a view to accomplishing the individual's investment goals. If the estate is too small to justify portfolio management in its own right, shares may be purchased in the trustee corporation's common trust fund.

The investor may want to exercise control over investment changes in his or her portfolio but have no interest in clipping coupons and depositing dividend checks. An agency account with a trust department may be the appropriate vehicle to accomplish this investment goal.

Provision for Retirement

Changes in our society have made early retirement a worthwhile goal and one that can be fostered by timely financial planning. The income from an investment trust may be accumulated for retirement. Upon retirement the monthly remittance could be one-twelfth of the anticipated annual income. If this arrangement produces insufficient income, the trust principal could be systematically depleted.

For example, an individual may have accumulated $100,000 in an investment trust at retirement. The trust can generate $7,800 per year ($650 per month) in income. If the individual needs $800 per month to live in retirement, the trust principal can be depleted each month by $150 ($800 minus $650). However, as the principal is depleted, the future income that the trust can generate is reduced, and larger amounts of principal must be withdrawn continually to make up the same monthly total.

Planning for retirement must include consideration of social security, pension, profit sharing, and insurance settlement options. The reader is urged to consult Section Eleven of the *Handbook* for coverage of these points.

Support for Spouse and Dependents after Death

The well-being of the spouse and children in event of the head of household's death is a prime concern. Such a contingency should be given adequate consideration in planning for financial security. Trusts may have a significant role to play in achieving this goal.

Trusts may be established by will. These are called "testamentary trusts." Trusts may also be established by agreement with the trustee. Trusts of this type are called "living or inter vivos trusts."

Under the terms of either a will or an agreement, a trust may be directed to hold property for the benefit of the spouse and children. The income from this property may be payable to the spouse for life, the principal being distributed to the children when the youngest reaches age twenty-five.

Minimization of Administrative Costs

Probate is considered a dirty word. It is that process whereby the will is made official by filing it with a court having jurisdiction over such matters. Probate involves proving that the will is authentic and that it is the maker's most recent one. Probate is also an administrative proceeding whereby the affairs of the deceased are concluded in accordance with his or her will, if there is one. If the deceased has not made a will, he or she is said to have died intestate, and his or her property will be disposed of in accordance with the state's law of descent and distribution.

Probate is expensive. Lawyers must be paid to settle the estate, and the process could last many years. If property is located in more than one state, problems are compounded, and so is the expense of winding up the estate. Since administrative costs are usually based upon a percentage of the estate, costs can be reduced by disposing of assets before death. The phrase "avoiding probate" suggests planning one's estate so that most property is given away or placed in trust before death.[2] A living trust can thus help reduce administrative costs, with the result that a greater estate is available to one's heirs.

Minimization of Taxes

No one wants to pay taxes, and tax minimization is a significant financial planning goal. The planning process involves giving adequate consideration to income, estate, and gift taxes.

Federal income tax rates are progressive. The rates for a married person filing a joint return rise from 14 percent on the first $1,000 of taxable income to 70 percent on taxable income in excess of $200,000. Each taxable entity is subjected to progressive taxation. Therefore, a trust can be used to take income out of higher brackets. The trust will pay tax on its taxable income, presumedly at a lower rate.

The trust creates a separate entity for income tax purposes that is entitled to its own personal exemptions as well as to the benefits of lower tax rates because of the progressive nature of the tax. For example, let us assume that an individual with a taxable income of $100,000 creates a trust that has a taxable income of $10,000. The trust will pay a relatively low tax rate on its first $10,000 of taxable income. If the trust did not exist and the individual had taxable income of $110,000, he or she would pay the highest tax rate on the marginal $10,000. However, this advantage applies only if the trust accumulates the income. If the income is distributed to a beneficiary, then the beneficiary, and not the trust, pays the income tax on the income.

Estate and gift taxes should be considered together. The estate tax is a tax on the value of one's eastate at death. Except for gifts given in contemplation of death, the estate tax cannot be levied if no estate remains to be taxed. A trust may also be used to remove assets from an estate before death in order to avoid estate tax liability.

The gift tax represents an attempt to close a very big escape hatch in the estate tax. In the process of giving an estate away, liability for gift taxes will likely be

---

[2]The reader is urged to consider Norman F. Dacey, *How to Avoid Probate*, Crown Publishers, Inc., New York, 1966.

incurred. With the adoption of the 1976 Tax Reform Act, estate and gifts are taxed at a unified rate ranging from 18 percent on the first $10,000 of the taxable estate or gift to 70 percent on the taxable estate or gift in excess of $5 million. Therefore, overall estate and gift taxes will be the same regardless of whether the transfer is inter vivos or testamentary. (For a more detailed discussion of estate and gift taxes see Chapter 64, "Maximizing Your Estate for the Rest of Your Life.")

Continuation of a Family Business

An individual may own a small but successful business that he or she desires to leave to his or her children when they are ready to assume control. Voting stock could be placed in trust for benefit of the children until they reach a specified age. Proper management can thus be assured. The children can obtain valuable business experience during this period as employees of the business.

Planning in the Event of Marital Breakup

Marriage is not as permanent as it used to be. Dissolution of the family unit brings forth a host of financial problems. Provision must be made for alimony and child support payments. A prudent man will want to fulfill these requirements with as little impact as possible upon present and future earning capacity. His wife desires a settlement that will satisfy her needs and those of the children without the necessity of additional litigation. She also wants the settlement process to be as painless as possible.

Trusts can help a man to meet his alimony and child support requirements. An irrevocable trust can be established with the income payable monthly to the wife as alimony and child support. Upon the remarriage or death of the wife, the trust principal could be held for the benefit of the children, with the income payable to them. If the children are of sufficient age, the trust assets could be distributed to them. This plan should appeal to both husband and wife. Each will appreciate the automatic nature of this settlement. Needless to say, this settlement option is not available to an individual who cannot afford to part with sufficient assets to generate the level of income required.

Conflicting Goals

Thus far discussion has centered in suggesting possible goals and objectives for family financial planning. Goals are personal, and therefore no list should be considered complete. The purpose of this discussion has been to cause the reader to consider his or her own goals.

It is highly unlikely that all goals can be fulfilled. Some goals may conflict with other goals. As a practical matter, there may be insufficient assets to fund each goal properly. Then the problem becomes one of selecting the more important goals and allocating scarce resources to their fulfillment.

Trusts to Fulfill Family Financial Planning Goals

The rest of the discussion considers various types of trusts that can be used to fulfill family financial planning goals. Trusts can be divided into three basic types: (1) testamentary trusts, (2) irrevocable living trusts, and (3) special-purpose revocable trusts and other types of agreements. Other applications have evolved from these basic types.

TESTAMENTARY TRUSTS

Attributes and Applications

Testamentary trusts are created by will to commence at the death of the testator. In his or her will the testator directs the establishment of a trust and may specify the property that is to enter the trust. The trustee is directed to hold and invest property for the benefit of certain persons, with the assets of the trust to be distributed to other persons at a specified time.

Testamentary trusts can be used to keep a family unit together. Shelter as well as income for living expenses must be provided. The family residence may be placed in trust for the benefit of the spouse and children for as long as it is needed. If the home is no longer needed or proves to be too costly to maintain, the trustee may be directed to sell the property and invest the proceeds with a view to purchasing smaller facilities. The cost of maintaining the home could be paid by the trustee.

A trust of this nature frees the spouse from day-to-day management responsibilities and provides safety for trust assets. If the testator elects not to use the trust device, the estate would probably be divided between spouse and children. As a practical matter, one larger trust is probably more efficient than several smaller ones. Flexibility is an important feature, for it would be most difficult for the testator to divide the property so as to consider the special needs of his or her heirs.

If the spouse should die before the children reach majority, the trust can provide funds for their support and education. In the absence of a trust of this nature, property of the deceased parents would be placed in guardianship for benefit of minor children. Such guardianship comes to an end when a child reaches age twenty-one, which may be too early. The recent movement to a majority at age eighteen will have no implications for this area of estate planning. The adult status of eighteen-year-olds is a function of state statutes that specifically allow for such privileges at age eighteen. The Uniform Gift to Minors Act governs some of these transactions, and it expressly states that an adult is one who has attained the age of twenty-one and that a minor is a person who has not yet attained the age of twenty-one [KRS 385.011(1), (2)]. Moreover, the trust for minors is a creature of federal statute, and age twenty-one is expressly stated [IRC 2503(c)].

Advantages and Limitations

The testamentary trust can be a highly useful estate-planning device when it is applied to the proper set of circumstances. It allows the individual full ownership and control of his or her property until he or she dies. This type of flexibility may appeal to some people. Also, since the testamentary trust does not function until the death of the testator, administrative costs during his or her lifetime are virtually eliminated.

A great deal of publicity centers in the death of a prominent citizen and the probate of his or her will. Testamentary trusts are thus given public notice and may subject the heirs to all sorts of pressure from outsiders. The living trust avoids such problems because it is in operation before the death of the individual.

Tax Considerations

Prior to the 1976 Tax Reform Act, testamentary trusts were of limited value to a large estate, inasmuch as such trusts did not remove assets from the gross estate of the grantor because they did not become operable until the decedent's death. On the other hand, inter vivos trusts, where the grantor divested himself or herself of dominion and control over the property, were effective to remove the assets from the grantor's estate. Even though the inter vivos trusts were subject to a gift tax, an overall savings was accomplished because the gift tax rates were lower than the estate tax rates. The reform act put both lifetime and deathtime transfers on an equal basis.

However, if sizable fortunes have been amassed, testamentary trusts can help to avoid future estate tax levies against the property. In the absence of an estate plan, the estate is passed on to the heirs of the deceased. These heirs will actually own the property. Each time that the property is passed to another generation, an estate tax levy takes place. Successive levies of estate taxes can be partially avoided by giving children only life estates. Trust assets will not be subject to the estate tax upon the death of the children because no property is transmitted to others when the child dies. Thus the life estate is extinguished by death. Although the testamentary trust offers no estate tax advantages at the grantor, it does offer estate tax advantages for one future generation so long as the total transfers, per child, do not exceed $250,000.

Testamentary trusts also offer advantages for small estates. Proper use of the marital deduction may completely eliminate the taxable estate. The marital deduction is discussed in Chapter 64. Briefly, it allows the deceased to leave a spouse up to 50 percent of the adjusted gross estate or $250,000, whichever is greater, to reduce the taxable estate accordingly. This tax treatment is available without the use of testamentary trusts. However, the testamentary trust does provide a useful vehicle whereby maximum advantage may be taken of the marital deduction.

Thus, there are limitations to the use of testamentary trusts. Some limitations can be overcome through the use of living trusts, and this type has advantages of its own. Living trusts can often be used to accomplish estate-planning goals with greater benefit to all.

IRREVOCABLE LIVING TRUSTS

Attributes and Applications

The irrevocable living trust comes into being when the grantor transfers forever property to a trustee to be held for the benefit of another person or institution. The irrevocable feature prevents the grantor from changing his or her mind. However, such a trust may be irrevocable for only a period of years, after which it may be revoked by the grantor. The specific provisions should be clearly spelled out in the trust instrument. The grantor may retain power to amend an irrevocable trust. This power suggests that assets may be added to the trust and beneficiaries' shares changed. However, the retention of too many powers may cause principal tax benefits to be lost.

A number of benefits accrue through the use of living trusts. For example, a father may wish to supplement the income of his son or daughter. However, he does not want to put his child in the position of having to manage his or her portfolio. Also he wishes to minimize his own income and estate tax liability as much as possible. The estate-planning wishes of the father can be accomplished through the use of an irrevocable living trust.

Advantages and Limitations

The chief limitation of this type of trust is the fact that it cannot be revoked by the grantor at his or her will. The grantor would therefore be well advised to think twice before entering into an agreement of this nature.

There are many advantages to an irrevocable living trust. If the trust reflects the individual's estate-planning goals, he or she may observe the manner in which the trustee will be carrying out his or her wishes. The ability to observe the level of income that the trust generates should influence a decision to add property to the trust. The use of this type of trust is also a good way to test the corporate trustee if other similar trusts are contemplated.

Irrevocable living trusts remove property from an individual's estate before death. In addition to the tax consequences discussed below, this feature eases administrative problems and reduces costs. A greater degree of privacy is fostered for the heirs, because dispositions of property in trust are not a matter of public record.

Tax Considerations

Considerations of taxation contribute greatly to the desirability of a living trust. In the absence of the trust, the grantor would have taxable income to the extent that it is earned by the investments. However, for income tax purposes the trust creates a separate entity that is entitled to its own personal exemptions and also benefits from lower tax rates because of the progressive nature of the federal income tax. If the trust is required to accumulate income, this income is taxable to the trust, but if it is required to distribute income, the income so distributed is included in the taxable income of the beneficiary who receives it. It is generally accepted that both the trust and its beneficiaries are in lower tax brackets than the grantor of the trust. The degree of control that the grantor exercises becomes critical to the manner in which the trust is to be taxed. For example, if the trust is revocable, its income is taxed to the grantor without any income tax benefit.

Estate taxes may be saved by the use of an irrevocable living trust. Because the grantor has parted permanently with the trust assets, they are not included in the grantor's gross estate. Under the law prior to the 1976 Tax Reform Act, a grantor could create a trust which provided income for life to be paid to his or her child, with the remainder to be paid to the grantor's grandchild, upon his or her child's death. When the child died, no part of the trust was included in his or her estate because all they had was a mere "life estate." In addition, the child did not make a transfer of the remainder interest which would cause such property to be included in his or her estate. The 1976 Tax Reform Act changed this result by imposing a tax on the "generation-skipping trust" upon the child's death. The tax, although imposed upon the trust assets, is computed by adding the value of the trust to the child's taxable estate and computing the additional estate tax. A limited exclusion is provided for "generation-skipping trusts" in favor of the grantor's grandchildren, to the extent that the total transfers per child of the grantors do not exceed $250,000. Therefore, a grantor with three children could create up to $750,000 of generation-skipping trusts, which would not be taxed to his children's estates, regardless of the number of grandchildren he or she has.

Under the unified tax structure for estate and gifts there is no longer an overall tax advantage to inter vivos trusts over testamentary trusts. Taking into account the fact that gifts tax is paid years before the estate tax, the present value of the money must be considered, as explained in Chapter 64. This makes the lifetime gift more expensive than the testamentary gift. However, this additional expense should be weighed against income tax savings, probate, and administrative expense savings.

REVOCABLE LIVING TRUSTS

Attributes and Applications

As stated above, the issue of revocability is significant. The chief characteristic of the revocable living trust is the fact that the grantor has the right to revoke it; because of this feature, most tax benefits from the trust are lost. Thus, a grantor will elect this type of trust for business rather than tax considerations.

For example, a business executive may wish to accumulate a separate estate to provide for a more satisfactory retirement and yet does not want to become involved in problems of portfolio management. The corporate trustee is in position to provide the desired management and investment services. Moreover, the individual may wish to test the effectiveness of the trustee before proceeding with his or her estate planning. The individual may not be able to afford to divest himself or herself of wealth before death, and yet he or she may want the benefit of a trust that is already in operation as a part of the estate plan. Used in conjunction with a will directing that the balance of the estate be added to the trust upon his or her death, the revocable living trust can be a highly useful estate-planning device.

Advantages and Limitations

The principal advantages of this type of trust are readily apparent from the above discussion. An additional advantage could be that use of the trust simplifies the estate settlement procedure. Benefits of the trust would continue to be available to the deceased's spouse without interruption.

The chief disadvantages to this trust lie in the tax area. It may be, however, that a grantor of moderate wealth simply cannot afford to take advantage of the various tax benefits resulting from the irrevocability feature, because he or she may feel the need to have his or her funds available at all times. However, there is more to estate planning than tax planning, and if this trust can help to fulfill the grantor's planning objective, it should be given every consideration.

Tax Considerations

This type of living trust has little impact upon the total federal income tax picture because it is revocable. While the grantor is alive, the trust income is included in his or her taxable income. After death the income is taxable to trust beneficiaries. Thus, from a federal income tax point of view, there is no benefit in the use of a revocable living trust.

The assets of the revocable living trust are included fully in the grantor's gross estate. This fact suggests that no estate tax benefits are to be obtained from the trust. However, if the terms of the trust provide that the income is to be paid to the spouse for life and the assets are thereafter to be distributed to the grantor's children, the trust principal is not included in the spouse's gross estate. Thus, the trust has the effect of avoiding one levy of estate tax.

The grantor does not have gift tax liability when the trust is established because no gift has been made. However, payment of the income to a person other than the grantor may create taxable gifts to the extent of the distributed income.

SHORT-TERM TRUSTS

The short-term trust provides many of the features of an irrevocable trust, except that it is irrevocable for a minimum of ten years. Thus, if the grantor can divest himself or herself of property for at least ten years, he or she may receive many tax benefits and still regain the assets upon termination of the trust. As a practical matter, most of the benefits of this trust are in the tax area.

An individual of considerable wealth may wish to assist his daughter and her husband with gifts of money. He may continue to do this as he has done in the past. If possible, he would like tax benefits to flow from these gifts. The father can establish a short-term trust for a period of at least ten years. When the term expires, the trust principal reverts to the grantor.

The short-term trust has other applications. For example, it can be used to accumulate funds for children's college educations. It can also be used to support an aged parent or merely to amass funds.

Tax Considerations

As has been suggested, the chief benefits of the short-term trust are due to the favorable income tax situation that it generates. The most important single benefit is the ability of this trust to remove taxable income from the high bracket of the grantor and cause it to be taxed in the much lower bracket of the trust or beneficiaries. If the income is accumulated, it is taxed to the trust. However, if the trustee is required to distribute trust income to beneficiaries, the income is taxed to the beneficiaries who receive it. There can be substantial tax savings over the life of the trust.

There may be estate tax consequences to the grantor. If the grantor should die while the short-term trust is in existence (that is, before the principal has been returned to him or her), the estate is subject to tax, though only upon the date-of-death value of the reversionary interest that the grantor had retained. Because money has a time value, the closer the date of death to the end of the trust, the greater the reversionary interest (the value of the grantor's interest) for tax purposes. Regulation 20.2031-7(d) provides tables to assist in this valuation.

The establishment of a short-term trust also has gift tax consequences. The value of the gift is determined by reference to the duration of the trust. The trust constitutes a complete transfer for gift tax purposes only for the value of the property after the value of the grantor's retained reversionary interest has been subtracted. For example, for gift tax purposes the value of the gift of a short-term trust is about 45 percent of the trust principal (this amount is determined from a Treasury valuation table).

TRUSTS FOR MINORS

Attributes and Applications

The trust for minors is a modification of the basic living trust model. It is also called a Section 2503(c) trust.[3] This trust is irrevocable. The income from it may be used to support a minor child, or it may be accumulated for the child for distribution when he or she reaches age twenty-one. This trust may be used to build up a separate estate for a minor child and to provide a degree of security for the child if something should happen to his or her parents.

Advantages and Limitations

Most of the advantages of this type of trust lie in the tax area. The chief disadvantage is that the Internal Revenue Code specifies that to receive the tax advantage all principal and income must be distributed to the beneficiary at twenty-one, when he or she may not be ready to manage a vast sum of money. As discussed below, the advantage of this trust is the fact that the annual gift tax exclusion can be used.

Tax Considerations

The trust for minors provides the income tax advantages common to many other trusts. As a separate entity for tax purposes, the trust is taxable on the income that it accumulates, but the income that the trust distributes is taxable to the beneficiaries. The income splitting thus achieved causes some income to be taxed in a much lower bracket.

The trust helps to reduce estate taxes because the principal is removed from the grantor's estate. It will, however, be a part of the minor's estate; no skip-a-generation benefits are available.

Most problems occur in the gift tax area. As a general rule, the $3,000 gift tax exclusion applies only to a gift of a present interest as opposed to a gift of a future

[3]Section 2503(c) of the Internal Revenue Code sets forth the basic rules for this type of trust.

interest.[4] The gift of a present interest, such as a cash or property gift that is made available, benefits the donee immediately. However, the gift of a future interest has no immediate benefit to the donee, for it is not really available until sometime in the future. An exception to this rule is provided by Section 2503(c) of the Internal Revenue Code, in that a trust for minors can generate a gift tax exclusion for the donor under certain circumstances. The code is rather specific in stating that such gifts are not gifts of a future interest if trust assets are to be used for the benefit of the minor before he or she reaches age twenty-one. To the extent that trust assets have not been used for benefit of the minor before he or she becomes twenty-one, they must be distributed to him or her on that date. If the minor does not live to age twenty-one, the trust must become a part of his or her estate.[5]

Thus, the donor faces a real dilemma: he or she must choose between causing the trust to continue after the beneficiary reaches age twenty-one and the annual exclusion for gift tax purposes. If the gift tax exclusion is significant to the overall estate plan, the donor must be satisfied with the fact that the trust principal and any accumulated income will be made available to the donee when he or she becomes twenty-one. However, if the donor has already used the $3,000 annual exclusion, this consideration is not a factor.[6]

The Regulations provide an exception to the distribution requirement, in that the donee may elect to extend the term of the trust upon attaining the age of twenty-one.[7] The effectiveness of this provision depends on the influence that the donor and the trustee are able to exert upon the donee, who may be encouraged not to withdraw the trust at the age of twenty-one. If the donor can rely upon the donee's good judgment, objections to the trust for minors are substantially diminished.

ALIMONY TRUSTS

Attributes and Applications

The trust to pay alimony is an adaptation of the basic living trust model. In most cases, this type of trust is irrevocable. In the negotiations surrounding a divorce, both husband and wife want to maximize their economic positions. At issue are division of property (property settlement), provision for periodic payments to the spouse (alimony), and provision for periodic payments to the spouse for benefit of children (child support). To settle his financial responsibilities to his wife and children, the husband may create an irrevocable living trust for their benefit. The income from the trust will be used to satisfy the alimony and child support requirements. Upon the death or remarriage of the wife, the trust would continue to pay an income for support of the children if they are under age twenty-one. At some point, the trust principal would be paid to the children. If there are no children, the trust principal could revert to the grantor upon the death or remarriage of his wife.

Advantages and Limitations

The alimony trust is advantageous for both husband and wife, in that it firmly establishes support and maintenance requirements. The wife is assured that

---

[4]IRC, Section 2503(b); Reg. 25.2503-3(a).

[5]IRC, Sec. 2503(c).

[6]Section 2503(b) allows the donor a $3,000 annual exclusion for gift tax purposes for each donee. Thus, if the donee has already received $3,000 from the donor in question, the donor has used his or her exclusion, and the exclusion is no longer available.

[7]Reg. 25.2503-4(b)(2).

Advantages and Limitations

The chief advantages of irrevocable life insurance trusts lie in their ability to save tax dollars. In addition, an trust is so that proceeds will be used for the ... professional management is provided in many jurisdiction if the estate has been established, the insured no longer has the right to change his or her ...

Tax Considerations

The insurance trust can be used to shift taxable income from the high tax bracket ... one's spouse purchase the insurance and name the children as beneficiaries. Upon the death of the insured, the usual rules of trust taxation apply. Trust income is taxed to the trust if accumulated and to beneficiaries if distributed.

Irrevocable insurance trusts also create estate tax advantages. Placing the insurance in trust has the effect of permanently removing the proceeds from the insured's estate. If the spouse of the insured is an income beneficiary only, a second estate tax levy is avoided.

Placing insurance in trust constitutes a taxable gift. However, the value of the gift is the replacement value of the insurance rather than its maturity value. In the case of the unfunded trust, a taxable gift is given when premiums are paid by the insured. Because the payment of insurance is a gift of a future interest, the $3,000 annual exclusion does not apply.

ACCUMULATION TRUSTS

Attributes and Applications

A trust that accumulates rather than distributes its income is called an "accumulation trust." Both living and testamentary trusts can be accumulation trusts. Although the trust may accumulate funds for any purpose, the principal purpose and advantage appear to be the saving of federal income tax dollars. In estate planning, heavy emphasis is placed upon the avoidance of estate taxes. However, when a sizable estate is involved and the plan is to run for many years, the federal income tax may take a larger amount than does the estate tax. The accumulation trust, then, attempts to minimize the impact of the federal income tax.

Tax Considerations

Because of the progressive nature of the federal income tax, substantial income taxes can be saved by spreading income over a number of tax-paying entities. This discussion has stressed the fact that the entity that receives income will be taxed on it. It has been noted in each case that income distributed to beneficiaries is included in their taxable income but that income retained in the trust is taxed to the trust. The principle of the accumulation trust is to cause the trust to be taxed in ... feature is lost.

Maximum use of the marital deduction often results in the establishment of two trusts. One is a marital deduction trust, and the other is a residuary trust. The usual plan calls for the income from both trusts to be owned by the wife. However, maximum emphasis on the accumulation feature suggests that the trustee be allowed to make all distributions from the marital deduction trust. The wife would be taxed on the income of the marital deduction trust but not on principal that she might withdraw. The residuary trust would be taxed on its income. Thus, the income is split between two taxable entities, the residuary trust and the wife, with a considerable saving of federal income taxes.

For example, let us assume that a man dies and his wife receives two $100,000 trusts, a marital trust and a residual trust. The total income of the two trusts may be $16,000 per year. The wife receives the entire $16,000 from the marital trust. Of this, part would be income from the trust and part a withdrawal of principal. The wife is taxed only on the income portion. The income received by the residuary trust is taxed at a lower rate to that trust. The entire $200,000 remains intact, as the amount withdrawn is equivalent only to the income.

This plan also reduces estate taxes at the wife's death. If the wife has consumed her marital trust, the gross estate at her death will be reduced. She was only an income beneficiary of the residuary trust, and therefore the principal of that trust will never enter her estate.

Income splitting can similarly be achieved through the use of trusts for children as well as other short-term trusts. Much of this advantage was removed by the Tax Reform Act of 1969, which established an unlimited throwback rule.[9] The throwback rule causes the distribution to be taxed as it would have been in the year that the income was earned.

However, the 1976 Tax Reform Act restored the pre-1969 rule that distributions of income accumulated by a domestic trust before a beneficiary's birth or while he or she is under age twenty-one are not considered to be accumulation distributions and therefore are not subject to the throwback rule.

The throwback rule still applies to all other trusts. For example, let us assume that in a particular year the effective tax rate on trust income is 20 percent but that the effective tax rate of the beneficiary is 50 percent. Instead of having the income taxed to the beneficiary at the rate of 50 percent, the trust elects to accumulate it and pay tax at the rate of 20 percent. One could assume that because the trust has already been taxed on the income, distributions of that income would be tax-free to beneficiaries. The function of the throwback rule is to cause the beneficiary to be taxed on the distribution in the year when the distribution actually takes place but at the higher rate that he or she would have had to pay if the distribution had been made in the earlier year at his or her then-higher rate. In effect, the distribution is thrown back to the year in which the income was earned by the trust so that it may be taxed as if it had been included in the beneficiary's taxable income for that year. If the beneficiary is in a higher bracket in the later year, however, the throwback rule will cause the distribution to be taxed at a lower rate and entitle the beneficiary to a refund. The mechanics of this calculation are extremely complex.[10] Nevertheless, accumulation trusts can postpone taxation and thus result in benefits from the time value of money.

SPRAY, OR SPRINKLING, TRUSTS

Attributes and Applications

A spray, or sprinkling, trust may be either a testamentary trust or a living trust. Most testamentary trusts give a lifetime income to the spouse and the remainder to

[9]IRC, Secs. 665-669.
[10]P. Michael Davis and Frederick W. Whiteside, *A Practical Guide to Preparing a Fiduciary Income Tax Return,* Lawyers & Judges Publishing Co., Tucson, Ariz., 1976.

the children of the deceased. It may be that the spouse or a particular child does not need the income in any given year. If income is paid to high-bracket beneficiaries, most of it is consumed by additional taxes. Moreover, if income is distributed to those who have no need for it, their estates will be swelled and higher estate taxes result.

Under the terms of a sprinkling trust, the trustee has the power to apportion benefits to certain classes of beneficiaries on the basis of individual need. Because those with the greatest need are to be found in the lower tax brackets, substantial income tax saving can result.

Advantages and Limitations

The principal nontax advantage of the sprinkling trust is its extreme flexibility to cope with the needs of the beneficiaries. This is true whether the need is of an emergency nature, such as illness, or of an investment nature, such as capital to start a new business. Another nontax advantage is the fact that beneficiaries cannot spend their money until it is allocated to them. Because the will is not specific as to amounts, creditors are unable to attach an individual's share of the trust. Moreover, the interest cannot be made collateral for a loan.

There are also limitations to the use of a sprinkling provision. In the first place, it may sometimes reward worthlessness and create family hostility. Careful selection of the trustee should overcome problems of this nature. Second, the principal beneficiary, usually the grantor's spouse, may feel less secure because the trust does not provide a specific amount. This objective may be overcome by a provision that allows sprinkling with funds that are not needed by the principal beneficiary.

Tax Considerations

As suggested above, the principal benefits of sprinkling trusts lie in the tax area. Income taxes are saved because taxable benefits are allocated on a need basis and individuals in need are usually in the lower tax brackets. Estate taxes also are minimized because distributions are not allowed to accumulate in the estates of those who already have sizable estates. There are no significant gift tax consequences.

CONCLUSION

In this chapter, the role of trusts in family financial planning has been considered. First, it is necessary to develop a set of planning goals. Having formulated these goals, the various kinds of trusts that can be used to fulfill these goals should be explored.

The major purpose of the chapter has been to stimulate thought with a view toward meaningful planning for the future. With personal goals in mind and a general knowledge of trusts, the individual is in a better position to discuss his or her problems with a professional estate planner.

Chapter **67**

Life Insurance Alternatives in Estate Planning

MARK R. GREENE

MAXIMIZING ESTATE VALUES

As mentioned in earlier chapters, life insurance may play an important role in tax planning for an estate both before and after the death of the owner.

This subsection presents examples of how life insurance can be used as an effective instrument of good estate planning.

Proper Selection of Life Insurance Contracts

Because of variations in the savings element, some life insurance policies are far more expensive and offer less estate protection than others do. Maximum estate protection in life insurance in the event of premature death can be achieved through term policies. However, if the insured does not die early, the best life insurance contract might be one emphasizing savings. Often the best contract is one that offers a blend of savings and protection.

If $1,000 a year is placed in a term-to-sixty-five contract at age forty, it will provide about $71,000 worth of death protection. The same $1,000 placed in an ordinary life contract at age forty provides only $43,000 worth of death protection. The difference is due to the fact that at age sixty-five the ordinary life contract has a considerable cash value, whereas the term policy will expire with no cash value. The differences between the two contracts illustrate the necessity of selecting policies for specific needs.

Some individuals prefer to purchase term insurance and invest the difference in other securities. Since the life insurance policy may be expected to yield only approximately 5 percent on the investment element, the insured may reason that if he or she can earn an additional amount on a "side" investment, his or her estate value will be maximized. Such a technique is known as the "buy term and invest the difference" plan.

An example will be useful in clarifying this technique. If the premium for ordinary life insurance is $25 and the premium for twenty-year term insurance is $7, it would pay to buy term insurance for $1,000 and place the $18 difference in comparable investments elsewhere. In the end a greater cash value will be obtained than if the entire $25 had been used to purchase a $1,000 ordinary life policy.

Table 67-1 gives a more detailed analysis of this argument. In terms of two $10,000 policies, column 1 lists the dividends estimated (but not guaranteed) for a $10,000 ordinary life policy whose gross annual premium is $248.70. Column 2 shows the annual net payments after dividends (dividends are estimated, not guaranteed); dividends are assumed to be used to reduce premium payments. Column 3 shows the accumulated net payments for the policy over the twenty-year period. The total paid by the end of this period is $3,759.40. Column 4 shows the guaranteed cash values under the policy for each year. At the end of the twenty years, the guaranteed cash value is $3,720. Column 5 shows the cumulative net cost of the policy: the difference between the amounts in columns 3 and 4, or the cumulative difference between net premium payments and cash values. By the end of the period, the policyholder has paid in only $39.40 more than his or her guaranteed cash value. Column 6 shows the net insurance protection for each year. This amount is the difference between $10,000, the face amount of the policy, and the guaranteed cash value in column 4. If the insured dies during the twenty years, his or her estate receives $10,000, which is made up of the net insurance protection and the cash value.

Now let us assume that the insured decides that he or she will be financially better off by purchasing term insurance for the protection element and investing separately the difference in premiums between term insurance and ordinary life insurance. To secure a proper comparison, term insurance must be bought each year in the amounts shown in column 6. If the estate owner purchases $10,000 of term insurance, the estate, in case of death, will amount to $10,000 plus what has been saved on the side. The total amount so provided will exceed the estate created by the ordinary life policy, and the comparison will not be accurate.

Column 7 shows the term premium per $1,000 for the net insurance protection needed. Column 8, which results from multiplying column 6 by column 7, shows the total premium for the term insurance plan. Although the term insurance premium per $1,000 almost triples over the twenty-year period because of age increases, the total premium outlay is slightly less than double because the net amount of insurance purchased declines steadily. By the end of the period, a total of $1,639.81 has been expended on the term insurance plan to provide the same net insurance protection as that provided by the ordinary life plan.

Column 9, which gives the difference between the cost of the term plan and the ordinary life premium, is determined by subtracting each item in column 8 from the corresponding item in column 2. It is this sum that is available for separate investment. Column 10 shows how this investment will accumulate at an assumed interest rate of 7 percent. By comparing column 10 with column 4, we see that the ordinary life cash values in column 4 accumulate somewhat more slowly than the separate investment in column 10. The insured has earned only slightly more than 4 percent on the net investment element in his or her ordinary life contract, and he or she has not earned 4 percent on the entire premium expenditures, since a substantial sum had to go to provide the pure insurance protection.

The insured who elected the plan of investing the difference and earned 7 percent has done better than he or she would have done under the ordinary life plan. However, the accumulation under the ordinary life plan is tax-free, but under the separate plan it is not. Thus, the 7 percent return on a separate investment (if we assume that the insured could earn this amount) is reduced by the amount of income taxes payable by the saver. Under these assumptions, if the saver is in the 40 percent income tax bracket (federal and state taxes combined), he or she would have earned 4.2 percent after taxes on the separate investment (7 percent minus 40 percent of 7 percent). This is approximately equal to the return that the insured would have realized with an ordinary life plan. The higher the tax bracket, the greater the net advantage of the ordinary life plan. The saver also

TABLE 67-1 Ordinary Life Plan versus Decreasing Term and a Separate Investment of the "Difference" in Premiums

Policy year	Dividend (1)	Annual net payment (2)*	Total net payments (3)	Cash value (4)	Cumulative net cost (5)	Net insurance protection (6)†	Term premium per $1,000 (7)	Total term premium for net protection (8)	Net payment for ordinary life less cost of pure term insurance (9)‡	Accumulation of column 9 at 7 percent (10)
1	$ 21.00	$227.70	$ 227.70	$ 80.00	$147.70	$9,920.00	$ 6.36	$ 63.09	$ 164.61	$ 176.13
2	24.80	223.90	451.60	300.00	151.60	9,700.00	6.56	63.63	160.27	359.95
3	28.60	220.10	671.70	530.00	141.70	9,470.00	6.79	64.30	155.80	551.83
4	32.40	216.30	888.00	700.00	188.00	9,300.00	7.05	65.57	150.73	751.74
5	36.50	212.20	1,100.20	880.00	220.20	9,120.00	7.34	66.94	145.26	959.79
6	40.50	208.20	1,308.40	1,070.00	238.40	8,930.00	7.66	68.40	139.80	1,176.56
7	44.60	204.10	1,512.50	1,250.00	262.50	8,750.00	8.02	70.18	133.92	1,402.21
8	48.70	200.00	1,712.50	1,430.00	282.50	8,570.00	8.42	72.16	127.84	1,637.15
9	52.90	195.80	1,908.30	1,620.00	288.30	8,380.00	8.86	74.25	121.55	1,881.81
10	57.20	191.50	2,099.80	1,810.00	289.80	8,190.00	9.34	76.49	115.01	2,136.59
11	61.50	187.20	2,287.00	2,000.00	287.00	8,000.00	9.88	79.04	108.16	2,401.89
12	65.90	182.80	2,469.80	2,190.00	279.80	7,810.00	10.49	81.93	100.87	2,677.96
13	70.70	178.00	2,647.80	2,380.00	267.80	7,620.00	11.17	85.12	92.88	2,964.80
14	75.30	173.40	2,821.20	2,570.00	251.20	7,430.00	11.92	88.57	84.83	3,263.11
15	80.40	168.30	2,989.50	2,760.00	229.50	7,240.00	12.74	92.24	76.06	3,572.91
16	85.40	163.30	3,152.80	2,950.00	202.80	7,050.00	13.66	96.30	67.00	3,894.70
17	90.30	158.40	3,311.20	3,140.00	171.20	6,860.00	14.68	100.70	57.70	4,229.06
18	94.90	153.80	3,465.00	3,340.00	125.00	6,660.00	15.81	105.29	48.51	4,576.99
19	99.40	149.30	3,614.30	3,530.00	84.30	6,470.00	17.04	110.25	39.05	4,939.16
20	103.60	145.10	3,759.40	3,720.00	39.40	6,280.00	18.37	115.36	29.74	5,316.72
Total	$1,214.60							$1,639.81	$2,119.59	

*$248.70 gross premium of ordinary life plan at age thirty-five; $10,000 face amount, less contemplated dividends in column 1.

†$10,000 less column 4.

‡Represents the difference between column 2 and column 8. This column then is the amount available for outside investment, the insured enjoying the same net protection as he or she enjoys with the ordinary life plan.

SOURCE: Adapted from materials furnished by the Standard Insurance Company, Portland, Oreg., and appearing in Mark R. Greene, *Risk and Insurance*, 2d ed., South-Western Publishing Company, Incorporated, Cincinnati, 1968, p. 608.

runs the risk of (1) not maintaining his or her savings on a regular basis, (2) not finding outlets for savings in convenient denominations so that full interest is earned and compounded regularly on all savings, and (3) losing part of the principal through mistakes in investment judgment. In addition, the saver is denied use of the settlement options available in the ordinary life policy for the ultimate disposition of cash values. The saver also has the option, under the ordinary life plan, of continuing his or her insurance protection indefinitely, while under the other plan the insurer may not usually obtain protection past age sixty-five.

Therefore, the return on the life insurance investment is reasonable when we consider the safety and liquidity of principal that it provides. However, the dividend schedules are not guaranteed, and the return may not be as high as is often assumed. Since the element of insurance protection must be paid from the premium, we should not fall into the error of assuming that the entire premium is available for investment and represents savings. Likewise, we should not assume that the cost of the insurance protection is measured by the net cost figure, such as $39.40 in column 5 of Table 67-1. The net cost in that example is $1,639.81, the total of column 8, or 44 percent of the total net premiums of $3,759.40.

Conclusion.   In the above example, it was demonstrated that an individual would have had to earn 7 percent on his or her taxable separate investment to equal the ordinary life performance. Although it may be necessary to take investment risks that are greater than the risk of the ordinary life policy, many investors are able to exceed this amount. In view of the potential gains, these risks will appear minimal to many investors.

Borrowing Cash Values to Maximize Estate Values

In the preceding example, it was assumed that the estate owner would simply purchase term insurance and use the difference between the ordinary life premium and the term insurance premium to invest elsewhere, presumably at a rate higher than that obtainable in the life insurance policy. In recent years, many individuals have taken advantage of the life insurance and loan provisions in an advantageous way and without additional risk. This technique is accomplished by borrowing on cash values in the existing permanent life insurance contract at relatively low insurance policy interest rates and reinvesting the proceeds elsewhere, such as in bonds and mortgages guaranteed by the United States government that pay interest rates higher than the rate that must be paid by borrowing on the cash values in the life insurance contract. This procedure has been especially valuable for individuals in high income tax brackets who have relatively large sums of money tied up in cash values of insurance.

An illustration of the potential savings on such transactions is presented in Table 67-2. In this example, the insured earns 48 percent more money on his or her outside relatively risk-free investment than he or she does by keeping the funds in the life insurance policy. To maintain estate protection during the period of this borrowing, many insureds purchase term insurance in the amount of the loan so as to preserve the original amount of coverage. In the event of their death under these conditions the beneficiaries not only receive the original estate protection but gain the additional value of the cash borrowed from the policy and reinvested.

Use of Dividends to Purchase Life Insurance

Most life insurance policies are known as "participating"; that is, an overcharge is made in the premium to permit dividends to be paid to the policyholder. The dividend provides the insurer with a margin of safety for fluctuations in expenses, interest earnings, and other costs. In general, the dividends may amount to between 15 and 20 percent of the gross premium in participating policies. The dividends are not subject to income taxes but are in reality the return of an overcharge in the premiums.

These dividends may be paid in cash, applied to reduce premiums, used to purchase paid-up additional amounts of coverage, or held by the company to accumulate with interest and be available to the insured upon demand. In some

TABLE 67-2   Hypothetical Example Showing Income Tax Advantage to Policyholder in Borrowing on Life Insurance and Reinvesting in the Open Market at a Higher Return

ASSUMPTIONS

1. Married taxpayer is in a 36 percent tax bracket applicable to a taxable income level of between $24,000 and $28,000.

2. Taxpayer borrows $5,000 at 5 percent on a life insurance policy which he or she has held for at least four years and on which he or she has not previously borrowed in order to pay any premiums.

3. Taxpayer reinvests $5,000 at 8 percent in a bond investment with safety comparable to that of the life insurance policy. (Investment acquisition expense is ignored.)

4. The taxpayer is currently being credited annually in the life insurance policy at a rate of 4 percent, made up of guaranteed interest plus dividends (not guaranteed), all tax-sheltered.

5. Calculations ignore federal or state income taxes, if any, that may be due when policyholder ultimately surrenders the policy.

CALCULATIONS

Gross interest return on the bond (0.08 × $5,000)		$400
Less federal income tax (0.36 × $400)*		−144
Aftertax return on outside investment		$256
Earnings in the policy (0.04 × $5,000)	$200	
Less cost of policy loan interest (0.05 × $5,000)	−250	
Net cost of loan	−$ 50	
Plus tax savings on other income because of ability to deduct policy loan interest (0.36 × $250)*	+90	
Aftertax gain from policy loan transaction	$ 40	+40
Total aftertax return		$296
Difference between earnings ($200) on cash value in life insurance policy and net earnings on outside investment ($296), or net dollar gain by the transaction		$ 96
Percent increase in annual return ($96 ÷ 200)		48%

*Certain federal income tax regulations must be met before interest on life insurance loans is deductible.

cases the estate owner will allow dividends to be used to buy additional level-premium insurance or additional term insurance. Dividends are credited at the end of each policy year, and interest credited to these accumulations is subject to federal income tax.

One way to increase effective estate protection is to use the dividends to purchase either paid-up additions or new coverage on a level-premium basis. One of the advantages of using this method is that the initial loading charges are minimized. No agent's commission, for example, is levied upon such purchases. The cash values of the additional insurance purchased are still available to the insured in case funds are needed for emergencies. Dividends, therefore, represent a useful alternative for maximizing estate values. A new policy with inflation protection is treated in Chapter 61, "Variable Life Insurance."

Proving the Claim

Some of the provisions of life insurance should be noted at this point because failure to observe them may cause difficulty in having the policy proceeds paid into the estate for distribution. Clauses that should be mentioned specifically are (1) the misstatement-of-age clause, (2) the incontestable clause, and (3) the suicide clause.

Misstatement-of-Age Clause.   Under the wording of this clause, which is found in every life insurance policy, the insurance company demands proof of age at the time of the insured's death. If this age differs from that stated in the policy, the amount of insurance proceeds is adjusted accordingly. For example, if an insured was thirty years old when he or she took out a policy but stated that his or her age was twenty-five and this is discovered upon the insured's death at age sixty-five, the insurance company will reduce the proceeds to the amount that would have been purchased had the true age of thirty been stated at the time when the policy was taken out. For this reason it is a good idea to make sure that birth certificates or other records that will prove the insured's age beyond doubt are easily available. In the absence of such proof, it is not uncommon for an insurance company to use evidence such as that found in a coroner's report. The coroner's report may or may not contain an accurate estimate of the age; and if the age is overstated, the beneficiary may suffer delays in obtaining payment or be required to accept a reduced settlement.

Incontestable Clause.   If an individual dies within two years of taking out a life insurance policy and the original statement on the application is found to contain material errors or misstatements, the insurer may successfully resist a claim for payment. After two years have expired, the incontestable clause provides that no misstatement, even a fraudulent misstatement, may void the insurance. For example, an individual may state that he or she has not seen a doctor in five years but in fact has been under continuous treatment for a serious disease. If this insured dies before two years are up and the insurer discovers this misstatement, his or her policy proceeds may not be paid (although premiums may be refunded) even if the cause of death of the insured had nothing to do with the misstatements.

Suicide Clause.   All life insurance policies contain clauses to the effect that if an individual is found to have committed suicide within one year or two years of the date on which the policy was taken out, the proceeds will not be paid. It is not uncommon for deaths under mysterious circumstances to be construed as suicide by the insurer, particularly in the case of new policies under which the two-year suicide clause has not run out. Obviously, suicide notes are strong evidence that a suicide has taken place and would deprive the beneficiary of insurance proceeds that might have been received if the suicide note had not been left. Beneficiaries who are convicted of murdering the insured may not collect, but the insurer must still pay the policy proceeds to the estate.

Nonforfeiture Options

It is clear that proper selection of a nonforfeiture option will affect the size of the life insurance estate (these options are explained in Chapter 59). Use of the extended term option will provide the maximum amount of death proceeds. If the nonforfeiture option of "paid-up policy of a reduced amount" is employed, obviously a smaller sum will be paid from the life insurance policy than would have been paid under the extended term option. The cash or loan value option in effect cancels all insurance protection. Therefore, if an individual wishes to maximize his or her estate size through life insurance, the extended term option should be employed.

LIFE INSURANCE IN MEETING ESTATE SETTLEMENT COSTS

Estate settlement costs can be substantial. Since estate costs generally must be settled in cash, life insurance proceeds make ideal vehicles through which these costs may be met. Examples of various estate settlement costs are as follows:

	Percent
Cost of estate administration	4–5
Current debts	4–6
Federal and state estate taxes	

Federal Taxable Estate *after Deducting $60,000 Exemption*	*Percent*
0–$5,000	3
$5,000–$10,000	7
$10,000–$20,000	11
$40,000–$50,000	22
$100,000–$250,000	30
$250,000–$500,000	32
$1,000,000–$1,250,000	39

Under present federal law, estate taxes gradually increase to a maximum of 77 percent on estates reaching a value of $10 million.

TAX TREATMENT OF LIFE INSURANCE

Under present law, life insurance itself enters the estate for tax purposes. However, it is possible to avoid this tax by ascertaining that someone other than the insured has all the incidents of ownership of the policy. The insured must not make his or her estate the beneficiary. Thus, it is possible to transfer ownership of a life insurance policy to a spouse or a child; when the insured dies, the proceeds will not be considered as being in the estate and hence will not be taxable. The insured may continue to pay the premiums on the policy. However, if death occurs within three years of transferring ownership of life insurance, tax regulations provide that the proceeds of the policy may be brought back into the estate for estate tax purposes under the "gifts in contemplation of death" rule.[1] We should remember that gifts of life insurance are subject to gift taxes, which are about three-fourths of the estate tax rates.

If a person transfers the ownership of a life insurance policy to a spouse, who then dies, the value of the policy is taxed in the spouse's estate before it can be inherited by the insured or by any other person.

Other Tax Advantages of Life Insurance in Estate Planning

Besides the avoidance of estate taxes, there are several other advantages in the use of life insurance to minimize estate transfer costs. These may be enumerated briefly as follows:

1. No federal income taxes are levied on the increases in cash value that may be attributed to interest and dividends. The same rule applies to state income taxes. Thus, if an estate owner is in the 40 percent tax bracket, a 5 percent earning in life insurance is equivalent to more than 8 percent of earnings in taxable investments.

2. No income tax is levied upon the death proceeds of life insurance under most circumstances. This is the case because the life insurance is designed to indemnify a person with an insurable interest in the life of the insured for his or her loss. Thus, life insurance proceeds are not considered income for the beneficiary, but rather a reimbursement for his or her loss and hence are not taxable for federal income taxes.

3. Life insurance receives a tax advantage if the insured holds the policy until retirement and cashes it in. In realizing the gain, the procedure is to subtract from

[1]IRS, Revenue Ruling 67-463.

the insured's total investment in the contract the cash value that he or she withdraws. The total investment, however, consists of the sum of all the premiums paid for the life insurance (not premiums paid for waiver of premium or disability income riders). Since the life insurance premiums include an element for death protection as well as for savings, normally the sum of all the premiums will approximately equal the proceeds withdrawn. Consequently, almost no income taxes are generally due when life insurance policies are cashed in. In effect, the insured has received a deduction for the amount of his or her insurance premium that has been attributed to the protection element. For example, let us suppose that a person takes out a $50,000 ordinary life policy at age thirty-five for $24 per $1,000. By age sixty-five he or she will have paid in $36,000. The guaranteed cash value of this contract at that time is about $32,000. Although the insured has enjoyed interest earnings on the policy during its life, no income tax is due because the cost basis ($36,000) is less than the cash value.

4. When a retired person selects one of the annuity options and outlives his or her life expectancy, the remaining amounts paid to him or her are *essentially* tax-free. This benefit may be illustrated with an example. Let us assume that the cost of the contract is $12,500. The next step is to determine the expected return on the annuity. If we assume that the $12,500 produces an annuity of $100 a month for life and that the person's life expectancy is fifteen years, the expected return is $18,000. The next step is to find the portion of the $100 a month that may be excluded. This exclusion is calculated by dividing the cost of the annuity by the expected return: in this case, $12,500 divided by $18,000, or approximately 69.4 percent. The annuitant may exclude 69.4 percent of each $100 received throughout his or her life tax-free. The remaining 30.6 percent is fully taxable as ordinary income. Now if the insured lives beyond the fifteen years, his or her normal life expectancy, this same favorable tax treatment continues even though he or she has fully recovered the $12,500 capital.

This outcome may be compared with the situation that would exist if the person had invested the $12,500 in a bond paying 5 or 6 percent. At 6 percent, for example, his or her investment would produce interest of $750, which would be fully taxable.

5. Another tax advantage of life insurance for aged persons is that under current tax law an employer may give $5,000 tax-free to the widow of a deceased employee.[2] The $5,000 is tax-deductible to the employer, so that the net cost to the employer is considerably less than $5,000. The $5,000 may be funded through a life insurance policy, premiums on which are *not* tax deductible. This procedure is especially suitable for small business people desiring to help their employees' families in times of stress.

PROVIDING LIQUIDITY IN THE ESTATE

A perplexing estate problem is recovering in cash for one's heirs money that is invested in a business. A person may have worked for many years building up a business that involves most of his or her life savings. The values thus accumulated, however, may have little market value upon his or her death. Creditors may be unwilling to continue to extend credit to a firm whose owner and chief manager has just died. Much of the goodwill of the business may be lost, since many of the best customers of the firm may have dealt with it because of personal relationships with the owner. Potential competitors may see an opportunity to buy out the business but may not be inclined to pay its fair market value to the insured's estate. The owner's heirs may not be interested or able to carry on the business or, if they

[2]IRC, Sec. 101(b).

do so, be able to earn the return that has been possible in the past. In other words, there are many ways in which the death of the owner will cause a rather substantial loss to the beneficiaries unless proper plans have been made. Life insurance can be of material assistance in helping to reduce these losses.

The major instrument through which business estates may be preserved is prior agreement, often called a "buy-and-sell agreement," in which the business is valued according to a certain formula. For example, the formula may state that the business will be valued at some multiple of the average net earnings as defined in the preceding five years. Let us suppose that a business has been earning an average of $50,000 a year for ten years and that the multiple agreed upon is 10. In this event, the business would be valued at $500,000 for purposes of the estate valuation.

The owner may now make arrangements with a potential buyer to purchase the business upon the death of the owner. The funds for the purchase may come from life insurance taken out on the insured by the buyer. Upon the owner's death, the buyer is required to use the life insurance proceeds to purchase the owner's interest from his or her heirs. In this way, the heirs receive the cash, the buyer receives the business, and the business may be continued in the manner originally planned.

The buyer may own a life insurance policy or may secure funds for the purchase either by borrowing or from other sources. In some cases, the potential buyer is a key employee of the firm.

Since the life insurance proceeds as well as the policy itself are the property of the buyer, no additional amount of life insurance proceeds enters the owner's estate for estate tax purposes. One advantage of the arrangement, aside from the increased liquidity that it gives to the owner's heirs, is the additional incentive that it may give to a key employee to work hard and see that the business succeeds. Life insurance arrangements similar to that described above are also known as "business continuation agreements." Under the federal estate tax law, buy-and-sell agreements funded by life insurance have been accepted in valuing the business for estate tax purposes (it is assumed that these agreements reasonably express the fair market value of the business interest). Thus, another uncertainty, the size of the estate tax, is removed in financial planning.

If the business is owned not by a single individual but by a partnership, similar arrangements may be made. For instance, if there are only two or three partners, each partner may buy insurance on the life of the others in an amount sufficient to buy the deceased partner's share of the business. To take a simple example, let us suppose that there is a business whose value is determined to be $500,000 according to a formula similar to that described above. This business is owned equally by two partners, A and B. In a business continuation agreement, each partner takes out $250,000 of life insurance on the life of the other. In the event of either partner's death, the surviving partner is bound by contract to purchase the interest of the deceased partner. In that way, the deceased partner's family's estate is maximized and is available immediately in the form of cash.

In the event that one partner is not insurable or is at an advanced age at which insurance becomes too expensive to purchase, other funding techniques may be arranged. For example, the younger partner may make advance arrangements for purchasing the senior partner's interest through periodic payments after the senior partner's death and may sign a note to that effect.

If there are more than two or three partners, an agreement known as an "entity arrangement" has been used successfully. Under this arrangement, the partnership itself, as an entity, owns the insurance. There is an agreement that if one of the partners dies, the proceeds of the insurance on this person's life will be used to retire his or her interests. The partnership owns and pays for the insurance. Since the life insurance proceeds increase the assets of the partnership upon the death of one of the partners, that partner's interest is thereby increased in the proportion of the business that he or she owns. Let us assume that there is a four-member partnership, each partner owning one-fourth of a business worth $500,000. The partnership has insured each partner for $125,000. Upon the death of one of the partners, the net value of the partnership is not $500,000 but rather $625,000. The deceased partner's interest is now worth one-fourth of $625,000, or $156,250. To handle this problem, the other partners may purchase additional insurance to meet the obligation, or a note may be signed for the additional amount.

One of the objections to the entity agreement is that each partner is in effect paying premiums to purchase his or her own interest, an interest that he or she already owns. However, this appears to be a relatively modest price to pay for the advantages accrued to a partner's family in making his or her estate larger and more liquid than it would otherwise be.

KEY-EMPLOYEE INSURANCE

One of the important elements of building up a successful estate and in preserving it is the development and training of key employees within the person's business firm. It is common to insure the lives of key individuals in such a way that the value of the business and hence of the estate is not diminished if one of these employees should die. A key employee may be an inventor, a star salesman, a superb organizer, or an astute financier. In any event, the sudden loss of such key persons may cause a considerable financial loss to the corporation. Many corporations insure their presidents for several million dollars. In the event of the death of the key individual, the corporation may be indemnified for his or her loss through life insurance. The proceeds for the indemnity are usually spent to retrain an additional person or to restore a loss of customers that may have been attributable to loss of the key employee, to reconstitute the inventive work that the person may have accomplished, or for other purposes.

Split Funding Arrangements

A variation of key-employee insurance has been known as a "split funding arrangement." Under this arrangement the employer and the employee share the policy premium, with the employer paying an amount equal to the accumulating cash values in the policy. To protect his or her interests the employer takes a lien on the cash value accumulating in the contract. The employer or the employee may own the policy, but the employee is the beneficiary.

Let us assume that the initial premium for a $50,000 contract is $1,000 annually. Initially the employee pays the entire $1,000, because the contract will have little or no cash value. After a few years, however, the cash value has risen, for example, to $5,000, and each year the increase in the cash value exceeds the $1,000 premium because of the accumulating interest. After a certain point is reached, the employee no longer is required to pay any premium; the employer pays the entire premium and takes as security the cash values in the contract. The pure amount of protection declines each year as the amount of cash value rises. Table 67-3 indicates how the arrangement would work. It may be observed that under this arrangement the employee gets a substantial amount of pure protection insurance for his or her estate at relatively little personal outlay.

However, the Internal Revenue Service (IRS) will not allow the employee to receive an unlimited amount of term insurance on a tax-free basis. Let us assume that the maximum amount of term insurance coverage of an employee, using government tables, costs less than $600. As long as the value of the term insurance in the contract is less than this amount, there will be no income tax. However, as the cost of term insurance rises above the $600, the employee will be required to pay income tax on the value of the insurance in excess of that amount allowed by IRS Regulations. Since the employee's income tax rate is always less than 100 percent, however, he or she pays only a fraction of the total cost. Thus, under such a plan the employee would receive term insurance at a cost considerably less than the total cost that he or she would have had to pay on a contract bought individually.

TABLE 67-3   Hypothetical Example of Split Funding to Maximize Estate Protection   ($50,000 Ordinary Life Policy)

Policy year	Annual premium (1)	Paid by employer (2)	Paid by employee (3)	Cash value (4)	Estate protection ($50,000 − column 4) (5)
1	$1,000	0	$1,000	0	$50,000
2	1,000	$ 300	700	$ 300	49,700
3	1,000	400	600	700	49,300
.	.	.	.	.	.
.	.	.	.	.	.
.	.	.	.	.	.
10	1,000	1,000	0	5,000	45,000

NOTE: Data are hypothetical but are reasonably representative of typical split funding plans. The estate protection to the employee may in some cases exceed the amount shown in column 5 because of accumulating dividends.

ESTATE TAXATION OF LIFE INSURANCE AND ANNUITIES

Reference has been made to the estate and income tax situation applying to both life insurance and annuities. It should be pointed out that much of an individual's life insurance may be in the form of group life insurance purchased entirely by his or her employer. The employee may make arrangements to keep the proceeds of such life insurance out of his or her estate for estate tax purposes under most circumstances. For example, it has been held that if an employee assigns his or her group life policy to a beneficiary, this is not an "incident of ownership" under Internal Revenue Code Section 2042, and hence the proceeds of the policy escape estate taxation in the estate of the decedent. Although the subject is rather complicated and is changing constantly, it may be said that it is generally possible to minimize estate taxation of life insurance proceeds if proper professional and legal advice is obtained beforehand.

In general, the value of an annuity purchased individually that has payments continuing to some named beneficiary is taxable in the estate of the insured. Internal Revenue Code Section 2039(B) provides that the amount of such an annuity that is includable in the decedent's gross estate is proportional only to the purchase price contributed by the decedent. In other words, if someone else has purchased the annuity, the value of any remaining annuity payments to a beneficiary is not considered as a part of the decedent's estate and thus escapes estate taxation. Thus, that portion of an annuity paid for by an employer escapes estate taxation in the decedent's estate.

Under present regulations the amount of life insurance paid by an employer on behalf of an employee under $50,000 escapes federal estate and income taxation.

If the employer provides more than $50,000 of life insurance to an employee, its value for income tax purposes to the employee is determined according to government tax tables.[3] In general, the type of insurance that qualifies for tax exemption is term insurance.

MARITAL DEDUCTION AND USE OF TESTAMENTARY TRUSTS

Under federal law a husband may give up to one-half of his total estate to his wife, either during his lifetime or by will.[4] The advantage of such procedure is to reduce estate taxation.

Under a testamentary trust one-half of the husband's estate may be left to the wife to qualify for the marital deduction; the other half may be left for the benefit of the children. The wife may receive the advantage of the children's estate by being able to receive income and even principal payments from it. However, unless she has complete power over its ultimate disposition (called "power of appointment"), the trust does not qualify as being in her estate for estate tax purposes. Thus, as explained in Chapter 66, when the wife dies, the estate is not taxed a second time. If proper legal arrangements are made, the wife may have the advantage of using all the property that the married couple has accumulated while still keeping the estate tax to a minimum.

Although testamentary trusts must be set up by attorneys and all the legal details and requirements in the state of residence must be met, it is well worth the time and trouble to investigate this concept as a way to maximize estate values for all the family and other beneficiaries.

TAX-SHELTERED ANNUITIES

Another way in which some employees may maximize their estate values is through tax-free accumulation of savings under various plans. Examples of such plans are (1) tax-sheltered annuity plans permitted under Sections 403(b) and 501(c)(3) of the Internal Revenue Code for educational and other similar organizations, (2) Keogh plans for the self-employed, and (3) voluntary additional salary reduction plans under normal corporate qualified pension programs.

Under each of these arrangements, a person may in effect save money in a retirement savings plan and avoid the federal income tax that would otherwise be levied if the money was taken as ordinary income in the year in which it was earned. In effect, this means that the individual has received an interest-free loan from the government on the funds that otherwise would have been due in taxes.

Tax-sheltered annuities may be variable or fixed. A person who has accumulated a significant tax-sheltered annuity is freed from the problem of having to accumulate other income-producing property to leave to his or her family when he or she dies. Thus, an annuity plan may be considered part of an estate *accumulation* plan as well as an orderly and scientific *distribution* of an estate. The use of life insurance and annuities together thus makes an ideal combination for estate planning.

VESTING

An additional comment should be made about the security of corporate pension plans and other private plans. A vested plan is one in which an employee has an

[3]IRS, Reg. 1.79-3(d)(2).
[4]IRS, Sec. 2053, 2054.

irrevocable interest in the employer's contribution to a pension plan. Because of delayed vesting, many individuals are deprived of their pensions. This is true because an employee may leave his or her company before a certain period of years has expired. For example, if a plan has a ten-year vesting period and the individual leaves his or her employer after nine years, he or she receives no benefit of the employer's contributions to the pension plan. In all cases, of course, the employee receives his or her own contributions to the plan, plus any profits that have been earned on these contributions. But if the employee leaves before vesting has occurred, he or she gets no benefit from the employer's contribution. (If the benefits do not vest within five years, the employer does not get a tax deduction until the actual vesting occurs.) It is entirely possible for an employee to change jobs two or three times in his or her career, each time leaving immediately prior to the vesting period. In this event, no private pension would be due, and he or she would be forced to retire upon social security alone. Needless to say, under these circumstances, the employee would accumulate very little of an estate in the form of pension plans. It is possible that within the next few years Congress will pass laws that will offer greater security for private pension plans. This passage will obviously have a substantial effect on estate planning, since it will be unnecessary for an individual to accumulate nearly as much private savings as he or she would otherwise have to accumulate to guarantee financial security in old age.

BIBLIOGRAPHY

Greene, Mark R.: *Risk and Insurance,* 3d ed., South Western Publishing Company, Incorporated, Cincinnati, 1973.

Gregg, David W. (ed.): *Life and Health Insurance Handbook,* 2d ed., Richard D. Irwin, Inc., Homewood, Ill., 1964.

Guilfoyle, A. F., and Kenneth T. Schachleiter: *Tax Facts on Life Insurance,* National Underwriter Company, Cincinnati, annually.

Insurance and Risk Management for Small Business, 2d ed., Small Business Administration, Washington, 1970.

Mehr, Robert I.: *Life Insurance Theory and Practice,* 4th ed., Business Publications, Austin, Texas, 1970.

White, Edwin H. (ed.): *Fundamentals of Federal Income and Estate and Gift Taxes,* 11th ed., The Research and Review Service of America, Inc., Indianapolis, 1965.

Chapter **68**

The XYZ of Wills

JAMES TURLEY

Importance of Having a Will

"For now you can be steward no longer" (Luke 16:2). With this biblical admonition we take up the discussion of wills.

An individual may have amassed great wealth during his or her lifetime. To control the disposition of this wealth the grim certainty of his or her demise must be faced. It is not pleasant, and for that reason all too many men and women die intestate (without a will). The fortune that was so laboriously attained will no longer be the individual's to guide or to care for. To avoid this problem, the individual must plan and determine who is to have the economic benefit, who is to manage the assets, and just how his management will achieve the desired results for his or her heirs.

The vehicle for accomplishing this purpose is the will. Even if an individual does not prepare a formal will, he or she does have a will of sorts. The state in which he or she lives has descent and distribution laws or laws directed to intestacy, the state of dying without a will. The individual might not like the provisions of the law, but these will be attached to his or her estate, like it or not, unless he or she comes to grips with the matter and builds his or her own will.

The following discussion is not intended to be a detailed text on the subject of wills but rather a digest of the topic that will give the reader an appreciation of what wills entail.

History of Wills

The history of wills is long and involved. It has been said that family ownership preceded individual ownership. In the case of family ownership there was no need for an arrangement for the succession of property. The family's living members used the property. A member of the family or even the head of the family may have died, but the family continued to make use of the assets that "belonged" to it. As individual rights developed, they came to be distinguished from family property, and hence rules of succession became necessary. It must be understood, too, that the right to own property personally or even to use it existed only at the pleasure of the sovereign (that is, the head of a family, the chieftain of a tribe, or the king of a nation). Thus the right to pass property on emanated from the sovereign, required his permission, and usually was a great exception to the norm.

The earliest wills go back to Egypt. One of the earliest-known examples was the will of Wa, which was drawn somewhere around 2900 B.C. In that testament Wa purported to dispose of his property among members of his family and to grant freedom to certain of his slaves. He recognized in the will that it was made with the knowledge and consent of the Pharaoh.

One element stands out in the early discussions of wills: there is no inherent right to make one. Further, in the United States there is no constitutional right to make a will. The right exists purely by local statute. Since a will is a statutory creature, the laws regarding it must be followed to the letter.

Types of Wills

At this point it might be well to set aside some misconceptions regarding wills by describing several types of ineffective wills:

1. The informal writing out of a document which expresses your intent regarding the disposition of your property, signing it, and then having a notary affix his or her signature and seal does not constitute a will in most jurisdictions in the United States. While such an instrument may have some validity in Europe, in the United States it is all but ineffective.

2. Where a valid will does exist, the practice of striking out certain provisions and inserting new ones does not constitute a valid adjustment to an otherwise valid instrument. Quite to the contrary, it will act to destroy an otherwise effective document.

3. Unique instruments, the nuncupative will and the holographic will, have limited use in the United States. The former is an oral will that is declared before witnesses and is subsequently reduced to writing. The latter is written in the testator's own hand. Some jurisdictions permit a holographic will but require that it be found with the testator's important documents and that it be dated and signed. No formal attestation or witnessing is required.

There is one other type of will that departs from the norm, the Louisiana Mystic Will. The mystic, or closed, will is written, signed, and sealed up by the testator and placed before witnesses, and a notarized statement wherein the testator declares that the envelope contains his or her last will and testament is made. This written endorsement is signed by him or her and by the witnesses.

These three types of wills are rarely used today and should not be indulged in even as a bit of whimsy.

4. Joint and mutual wills. A single document, designed to serve as the wills of two persons, under which the survivor takes the property of the first to die and the combined assets pass in a designated manner on the survivor's death. In some instances, the will is backed up by a contract. Should the survivor revoke the will and execute a new one, the beneficiaries under the revoked joint or mutual will could not compel its probate but would have a cause of action against the survivor's estate by reason of the contract.

Joint or mutual wills are not recommended, for they usually create difficulty for both the executor and the family; further, the tax consequences of such a will seldom if ever favor the estate. Marital deductions have been impaired, and questions have arisen regarding the tax treatment of jointly owned property that otherwise would never come up. This form of will is mentioned only to acknowledge its troublesome existence and to caution against its use.

5. A libelous will is one used by a testator to make a last derogatory comment on the character of persons for whom he or she has an intense dislike. Here are two instances that boomeranged. A mother, who felt that her son-in-law had set her daughter against her, developed a virulent hatred for both and so stated in her will in violent and uncouth language. She naturally left them out of her dispositive plan. The daughter and son-in-law brought suit against the executor for testamentary libel and recovered. Had the mother remained silent, they would have received nothing. In another case, a wife stated in her will that her husband had abandoned her, left her destitute, refused to support her, and besides did not love her. Here too the party so attacked sued his wife's executor for testamentary libel and recovered.

Intestacy and Testacy

No one really dies completely intestate, for if you have not taken the precaution of having your will prepared by your own attorney, the state has a ready-made will for you. The likelihood that such an arrangement will meet your family's requirements is small indeed. For example, if a man dies intestate leaving a wife and a single child, in some states each takes 50 percent; if the man dies with more than one child, the wife takes one-third, and the remaining two-thirds is divided among the surviving children. In other jurisdictions, the surviving spouse and children share pro rata. Think then of the decedent with ten children. The surviving spouse and each child receive one-eleventh of the late lamented's estate. One wonders how long the departed will be lamented and how soon it will be before bitter recrimination sets in.

Too, there is the situation of the farmer with a devoted and hardworking wife and a son who at best could be called a wastrel. The farmer did not want to make a will for fear that his son would break it; so he went to the county seat and put his farm and homestead in his wife's name. Now his wife would be certain to have it all. Only one thing went wrong: his wife died shortly thereafter in an accident and had no will. The local law of intestacy provided that all the surviving husband could take was a right of curtesy (that is, a right to use the land but with the title vested in the son). The cries about the courthouse were pitiful to hear.

The foregoing case brings out the point that both husband and wife should have wills. The legislatures of the various states did not set out to create difficulty. They attempted to create the best legislation possible to deal with the problems at hand. To be considered were principles of guardianship of minor children, rights of relatives, management of the estate's assets, and protection of creditors. Of necessity, the legislation had to be general or broad in nature, but inherent in such legislation is a neutrality. The laws vary from state to state, but a general pattern is discernible. Seldom does a surviving spouse get more than 50 percent if a child or children survive. If the children are minors, the surviving spouse does not even have a free hand in utilizing their funds for them. The use of a minor's funds is restricted until he or she attain majority. Even when the parent is the guardian, bonds must be posted; periodic accountings as well as a judicial proceeding are necessary to get approval of acts already performed. The parent or guardian must go into court for approval to expend moneys. All these things cost money, and it all comes from the estate. Should a guardian die during the course of the minority, there must be an accounting, which is burdensome, and a new guardian must be appointed.

Intestacy is expensive, since the bond that must be posted is a charge on the estate. Also, the administrator is limited in his or her actions by the laws of the jurisdiction in which he or she functions. To sell property, compromise claims, and distribute assets, the administrator may have to resort to judicial authorization. Again, the costs of such a proceeding are borne by the estate.

The appointment of the administrator whose function it is to administer an intestate estate is decreed by law. Usually the lot falls to the surviving spouse, and if the spouse is unable or unwilling to serve, then to a child. It does not take long to conjure up the difficulties. Sometimes two or more children are appointed, and this gives rise to a new set of troubles: the children may not see eye to eye, they may be hostile to each other, and the internecine bickering spills over to the surrogate's court. There are instances, too, in which no relative can be found to serve and the court has appointed the principal creditor of the estate as its administrator. The creditor's prime concern is settling his or her score, and under these conditions the quality of administration is generally not very good.

The intestacy laws were never drawn to achieve tax economies. To avoid the unnecessary impact of state and federal taxes, a will is essential.

The law of most jurisdictions calls for a will to be in writing, dated, signed at the end, and witnessed. Some jurisdictions may require the addition of an "attestation" clause, in which the subscribing witnesses state that the testator did make, publish, and declare the foregoing instrument to be his or her last will and testament and that the testator knew the contents thereof and requested the witnesses to witness his or her signature and then to sign as witnesses in his or her presence and in the presence of each other.

These are the purely legal requirements; unfortunately, they do no more than to assure that the instrument was properly executed. Many properly executed wills have created havoc beyond comprehension. It is to the avoidance of this havoc and unnecessary travail that the balance of this chapter is directed.

PREPARATION OF A WILL

Every strong structure rests on a firm, well-constructed foundation and is built to the requirements of the occupant. A will is no different. The foundation is a thoroughly prepared estate analysis followed by an estate plan. They must of necessity be unique, tailored to the testator's individual needs. With the analysis and the plan completed, the next step is the drafting of the will and any ancillary documents such as inter vivos (living) trusts, term trusts (those for a period of years), insurance trusts, designed to hold policies of insurance during the lifetime of the insured and to receive the proceeds of the policy on the insured's death, deferred-compensation contracts, stock purchase or redemption agreements, options, and business continuation agreements. In some instances, it may be necessary to prepare prenuptial agreements. The consideration of gifts should also be considered. If a family enterprise is involved, the method of succession should be thoroughly explored.

The first step in the preparation of a will is the selection of the personnel with whom to work. Not every attorney is a specialist in this field, and you would do well to consult one. Family counsel may always bring in a specialist to assist him. Remember, any expense in this area is money well spent for it will save much later. Your banking institution will in all probability have a trust department with trained personnel ready to assist you and work with counsel. Although bank trust people do not practice law, they have great depth of experience in the field of estate and trust administration and can offer suggestions that will ease administation.

The next step is to analyze the family, the assets, and your thinking. It is absolutely essential that you be frank with counsel. The estate program rests on a tripod of information: people, property, and plan. The tripod rests on the ground of tax and administrative law; these are counsel's responsibility. The tripod itself is your responsibility. You must tell counsel of the persons to be considered: spouse, children, grandchildren, parents, brothers, and sisters, along with the ages of each, any illnesses—physical or mental—that should be taken into consideration, and personality traits that have a bearing (kleptomania, improvidence, lack of judgment, etc.). In short, the attorney or analyst must know your family as well as or better than you do. It might be mentioned here that having the addresses of these persons will greatly speed administration, so they too should be furnished counsel.

After the people involved have been considered, the assets must be reviewed. What and where are they? How are they owned (in one name or jointly with spouse, member of family, or business associate)? Joint ownership has many pitfalls. In one unfortunate instance, a highly successful real estate operator entered into a course of business conduct that suited him and his associate well. He was the money man, and the associate was the guiding genius. All the property was owned in joint name with right of survivorship. No one had told the associates to do this; they just did it. As time went on, the relationship deteriorated until each was looking at the other with suspicion. The money man was shocked to learn that under the ownership arrangement the entire value of the property would be taxed in his estate but that the property itself would pass to the associate.

There are other ownership problems. Is a co-tenancy involved, and, if so, with whom? Where is the property located: locally, out of the state, abroad, in an Iron Curtain country? Are there any problems concerning the property? Is it subject to some existing agreement such as a stock restriction? If it is real estate, is a condemnation proceeding or an eminent domain action pending? Is the property in an area of increasing or decreasing value? If closely held corporations are involved, who are the associates, and what if any resolution of rights among the parties has been developed?

A rarely revealed item is the interfamily loan, in which one member of the family lends another funds, permits his stock to be hypothecated to back up a loan, or has signed as a co-maker on a note. In the event of death, the executor is charged with amassing the assets, and calling a family loan can be embarrassing. The hypothecated stocks may be tied up for an inordinate length of time, and, as a co-maker on a loan, the estate is liable if the surviving family member should default.

The final leg of the tripod is the plan. Just what would you like to see happen? How would you like to have the members of the family cared for after you pass on? Wills are blueprints for living; all too often they are some ghastly joke. What you set forth in your will will govern your family's well-being for many years to come; hence it must be carefully thought out. You must think in terms of the surviving spouse living alone and the possibility of remarriage. You must think of schooling for minors and adult children whose education is not complete. You must think of medical emergencies, weddings, and tragedies, along with the possibility of simultaneous death, which would then necessitate guardianship for minor children. Unless your counselor has walked you through the above steps your will will be every bit as blind and ill fitting as the laws descent and distribution. And there is a good possibility that intestacy would be a boon. A will can be an excellent document, in fact, a model of draftsmanship. In one instance a man's estate, over $350,000, was jointly owned with his wife: the policies of insurance owned by him on his life were made payable to his wife. All the will controlled was his personal effects. There was also a situation in which a man gave fine asset information and the will was drawn accordingly—here too an excellent document. When questioned closely he admitted that he used the property but it actually belonged to his wife!

Therefore, begin by making a list of your family members, whether or not they are to be considered, and to what extent they are to be considered. If they are to be left out, say so and why. List ages, health, and propensities in the following way:

Relatives	Age	Data
Self: Martin O'Day	67	Health excellent
Wife: Sally	52	Hypertension
Son: John	40	Attorney, well off
Daughter-in-law: Polly	35	Good health
Grandchild: Rose	11	Child model
Daughter: Helen	30	Single, schoolteacher
Brother: Joseph	70	Heart trouble
Parents deceased		
Wife's mother: Sue Adler	75	I support her
Wife's father deceased		
Wife's sister: Maude	50	Dental technician, self-supporting

The asset structure often dictates the mechanics of distributing the estate as specified in the will. Jointly owned property does not pass under a will but rather by operation of law. Insurance proceeds do not pass under a will, unless the estate is the beneficiary, but rather by contract as set forth in the beneficiary designation. A cash-flow chart should be prepared to determine which assets should best be used to fund the various bequests. Unless this is done, the will at best is a beautiful essay.

In the estate illustrated, the assets are so arranged that there is an inadvertent overuse of the marital deduction (one-half of the adjusted gross estate). In addition, the illustrated estate will require adjustment to render it "administratably efficient." Here we have Martin O'Day, a resident of New York State, with a substantial estate. But as it stands, this estate has inherent major problems.

Assets Schedule

Property	Martin O'Day	Sally O'Day	Joint assets
Residence			$ 65,000
Household effects			20,000
Personal effects	$ 5,000	$ 25,000	
Insurance	150,000 p/w*	20,000 p/m†	
Summer home, Maine	15,000		
Summer home's furnishings			5,000
Fishing and hunting equipment	5,000		
O'Day Coffee Co., Inc., New York, 60 percent of stock	400,000		
O'Day Laundermat, Newark, N.J., 51 percent of stock		65,000	
Marketable securities			150,000
Savings	20,000	7,500	40,000
Checking	6,500	1,200	3,300
Savings certificate			50,000
Car	1,500	4,000	
Real estate syndication, Florida			10,000
Totals	$603,000	$122,700	$343,300
Grand total			$1,069,100

*p/w = payable to wife.
†p/m = payable to mother.

First, there are the combined federal and New York State estate taxes, which would approximate $117,000 by using the full marital deduction. Second, there is the cost of administration, which includes last debts, funeral expenses, executor's commissions, and attorney's fees. These should total between 6 and 8 percent. In Martin O'Day's estate, they would approximate $57,000. Thus, we have a total quick cash requirement of almost $175,000.

Reviewing the asset structure, we see that O'Day's testamentary assets, those passing under his will, include only $26,550 in liquid assets. To be sure, his wife will receive $150,000 of insurance proceeds. But will they be available to the estate? One should not count on a beneficiary's cooperation. Cash is nice and clean and uncomplicated; most people understand it. A loan to an estate against estate assets, the principal one being a company whose guiding genius has just died, is quite another matter.

The beneficiary might well become uncooperative through fear or misunderstanding. So the executor may have to look to the jointly owned property for the needed liquidity, and that is not under his jurisdiction. If the will provides for the testamentary estate to pay all taxes, it might well be that the closely held business would have to be liquidated or sold.

Too, the closely held corporation probably has no dividend record. How can one fund a trust with such an asset? Who is going to run the company? Are dividends going to be available? If not, how will the beneficiary or the trustee be paid? If dividends are to be declared, will the asset be deemed underproductive and a sale required?

Definitions of Key Terms

Adjusted Gross Estate.   The gross estate less last debts, funeral expenses, attorney's fees, and executor's commissions.

Administrator.   One who administers the estate of a decedent who has died intestate (without a will).

Administrator c/t/a/.   Administrator *cum testamento annexo* (with the will annexed). Where the executor appointed does not act for any reason and where there is no successor executor nominated in the will or none who qualifies, the court appoints an administrator to carry out the terms of the will.

Draftsman.   Attorney who composes the will for the testator.

Executor.   One who administers an estate under a will.

Fiduciary.   One standing in a position of trust (an executor, trustee, or guardian).

Gross Estate.   The testator's total worth.

Guardian.   One who acts as the guardian of the person or the property of a minor.

Nontestamentary Estate.   Assets that pass outside the will, by operation of law or by contract (insurance proceeds, jointly owned property, deferred compensation contracts, pension death benefits, and so on).

Probate.   The act of proving the validity of a will, sometimes, in error, taken to mean the administration of an estate. You cannot avoid probate unless you die intestate. Probate proves that the will offered was the testator's, that he was under no duress at the time of its execution, that he was sane, and that he knew the nature and extent of his assets and his natural objects of bounty.

Special Guardian; Guardian *ad litem;* Next Friend.   Person appointed by the court to protect the interests of a minor at the time of probate, during administration, and on interim or final accountings.

Taxable Estate.   Assets in one's estate subject to estate or inheritance taxes in one or more jurisdictions.

Testamentary Estate.   Assets that pass under a will.

Testator.   One who executes (signs) a will.

Trust.   An arrangement in which assets called the "trust res," "corpus," or "principal," are held by the trustee, who has "naked legal title to the property" but no beneficial interest, for the use and benefit of another called the "beneficiary." The beneficiary may have a right to income for life or for a term of years, at the end of which the trust res as then constituted could revert to the one establishing the trust, called the "grantor" or "settlor," or pass to one called the "remainderman." Such reversion or payout terminates the trust.

Trustee.   One who administers a trust under a will or an instrument made during the lifetime of the grantor.

Contents of the Will

The first thing that a will does is to clear the air. The introductory statement revokes all other wills and codicils and declares the following statements to be one's last will and testament.

While it is unnecessary, the second declaration usually directs that all the last debts and funeral expenses be paid. Whether or not you make this pious statement, be assured that the creditors will be paid. A rather disturbing thought for many is that one's estate does not belong to one's heirs. It belongs to the creditors, and only after they have been satisfied and taxes paid are the heirs considered.

The third item that is almost standard is to make a bequest of one's residence to his or her surviving spouse. While in many instances the family place is jointly owned by husband and wife with right of survivorship, this bequest is confirmatory in nature so that, on the chance that there is some alteration in the method of ownership, the disposition of the home is effected. Too, this bequest usually provides that the policies of title and fire insurance follow the gift. In some states this is provided by statute, but in others it is not.

Household effects usually but not always, follow the gift of the home. If there is a deviation in mind, the will permits one to spell it out in detail. Again, if possible, insurance should follow the chattel.

The will gives you a chance to choose your beneficiaries and to limit those who are to receive under your will. You can specify who gets what or how much and how. You can even make conditional bequests, although most courts are unsympathetic to them.

Tangible personal property can present a problem. Here too the will gives you the opportunity to express yourself. Not only can you make certain that grandfather's heirloom watch that so proudly graces your waistcoat will pass to your eldest son, but you can also provide that, in the event that he should predecease you, it would pass to your younger son or to some other appreciative member of the family. If none survives to take the watch, then you could provide for a charitable gift or a sale and direction as to how the proceeds of that sale are to be utilized.

Perhaps one of the commonest devices for handling personalty is the "coward's way out": provide that the executor divide the objects among the surviving parties in as nearly even shares as possible and that the executor's decision be final and binding on all. Piously, too, the executor is usually charged with the burden of considering the preferences of the legatees insofar as possible.

Too, the testator may provide that, if the legatee does not survive, the gift will lapse and fall back into the general estate. Sometimes the testator will provide that a fine object be left to a specific person and when the time comes to put the will into play, lo and behold the object has been sold or given away. This is known as ademption, and unfortunately the legatee is disappointed.

With home and household effects as well as one's personalty distributed, we turn to the bulk of the estate, usually composed of stocks, bonds, insurance (sometimes made payable to the estate), cash, fringe benefits from the decedent's company, a closely held business, joint ventures, real estate syndications, and so on. Usually the first problem is just how the spouse is to be cared for. Depending on the size and composition of the testator's assets the required or desired property may be left outright to the spouse, in trust for the spouse's benefit, or partly of each.

The trust area is one of great difficulty. Few draftsmen really check the assets available for the trust's funding to see if they are suitable for inclusion in a trust fund. Cash and marketable securities are fine, proceeds of insurance policies are excellent, but undeveloped land in West Pennsyltucky is not. Nor is stock in a closely held business of the testator's own company necessarily acceptable. You have to look at the dividend record. Remember that a trust holds the stock or other property for the use and benefit of the beneficiaries. The trustee depends on the income produced by such property to "benefit" the beneficiaries and to pay himself or herself. If there is nonproducing or underproducing property, the trustee may be forced to sell even though the property may not lend itself to ready sale. It is essential that the testator and his or her advisers check the anticipated corpus of the trust to ascertain if it will really yield the benefits that the instrument calls upon it to deliver.

Real property, except in certain situations, does not lend itself to the role of principal trust asset. Even realty corporations, the stock of which could conceivably be sold to raise the moneys to meet withdrawal requirements, are not very satisfactory, for there is seldom a ready market for a minority interest. Also, if too much stock is sold, control may be jeopardized.

Again, a testator knows that some undeveloped land that he has been holding is very likely to increase in value and feels that a trust is the right vehicle. The difficulty here is that the trustee must maintain this property. There are taxes and insurance to be paid each year, and assessments may be levied against the land. Where is the money to come from if that property is the sole asset?

However, such a bequest in trust is sometimes appropriate. For example, if the testator's spouse is independently wealthy or if other assets are more than enough to meet the spouse's needs, such a trust is proper and even desirable. In a rare device called an "estate trust" the surviving spouse takes nothing during his or her lifetime, and everything accumulates; then at the spouse's death the entire corpus plus all accumulations is paid to his or her estate. Even in such an extreme case, the draftsman should be very careful and point out to the testator that things can change and hence suggest that the trust contain an escape hatch which provides that if the surviving spouse ever is in need, the trustee is authorized and directed to alter course and pay income to the spouse. In the event that the property comprising the trust corpus is nonproductive or underproductive, the trustee is authorized to sell it on the direction of the surviving spouse and replace it with income-producing property.

The beautiful part of a will is that a business executive can build it just as he or she would make a business or market projection. He or she can provide for exigencies that may not develop until the future, if ever; but the safeguard is there.

With a will a person not only has the ability to designate those who are to benefit and how but can go further by setting forth detailed guidelines for executor and trustee. When a question arises in the administration of an estate, the administrator looks at the will to see if the question is answered. If it is, there is no problem; if it is not, counsel must be called in and the surrogate's court construes the document. This construction proceeding is costly and time-consuming. Usually, it could have been avoided by a lucid instrument that provided guidelines.

If you establish a marital trust (that portion which will pass to the spouse and qualify for the federal estate tax marital deduction), you can provide that the income be paid annually, semiannually, quarterly, or monthly. You can even provide that if the income is insufficient to meet the demands of the situation, the trustee may apply principal on your spouse's behalf even to the exhaustion of the fund if required. In addition, you can provide for principal to be available over and above income for a spouse's "comfort, well-being, and support." You can direct that the trustee be generous rather than niggardly in making determinations regarding the application of funds. The power of appointment must, of course, be broad enough to comply with the provision of the federal tax law that permits the marital deduction (that is, that the spouse may leave the unused portion to whomsoever the spouse chooses including the spouse's estate and creditors of the estate).

Residuary Trust

The residuary trust presents a real challenge to the draftsman, for it is in this trust that the testator tries to cover all bases. Many times the assets available just do not permit the accomplishment of the testator's desires, and the plan must be trimmed. One must look back at the cash-flow chart and see if the financial muscle is available.

Many testators try to have a residuary trust care for the wife and children and even a dependent parent. This plan is frequently overly ambitious, and guidelines become imperative. It is helpful if divisions in the form of percentages are set forth. Perhaps the testator might want the spouse to have first call on the income and principal; if so, this should be clearly stated.

In the directions given in the will, one must be careful not to be too specific. For example, one might provide for college and graduate school for a child, and the child might want to go into business instead. Moneys provided for education would not then be available for starting a business. The obvious answer is to generalize the language, permitting graduate education, vocational training, or the establishment of a business, or all of these. Moreover, in making such an application, the trustee could be authorized to support that which would normally be beyond a "banker's risk."

Avoiding Challenges of the Will

Many testators take a very dim view of having their wills challenged and so make use of an "*in terrorem* clause." Such a provision is designed to discourage opposition to the probate of a will by causing the contesting party to forfeit any benefits he or she might have under the will. Some jurisdictions have legislation that prevents a person from attacking a will unless he or she can benefit specifically from the challenge. By the simple device of providing in the will that in the event of a challenge the beneficiary (challenger) is changed and another takes his place, the testator may make it illegal for the person to mount a challenge.

Simultaneous Death

Many married people are concerned that they are going to die together in an automobile accident or plane crash. In these days of great mobility when husband and wife frequently travel together, this is frequently a possibility. Often, whole families travel or vacation together, and this too should be considered in the plan. To preserve the maximum marital deduction, the husband usually provides that in the event of a simultaneous death his wife will be presumed to have survived him. This provision presupposes that the wife has relatively few assets in her own name. Again one must go back to the asset structure and examine what happens taxwise under each of the following circumstances:

1. Husband predeceases wife.
2. Wife predeceases husband.
3. Husband and wife die simultaneously.
4. The testator and a beneficiary other than the spouse die simultaneously.

It might well be that husband and wife have almost equal estates. In such a case, an equalization provision may be desirable, so that the spouse with the larger estate would give to the lesser estate only enough to produce two estates of equal size. Each estate must be individually programmed, and the tax and administration expenses carefully estimated before the draftsman puts pen to paper. There are no shortcuts.

Family Problems

A situation sometimes arises in which one spouse loves the other dearly but has no such tender sentiments for the spouse's family. If the spouse has a will, it may well provide for his or her family. This is not what the first spouse desires; yet he or she wants the marital deduction. Here only partial success is possible. Provision can be made that, in the event of a simultaneous death, the spouse deemed to have survived will receive the maximum marital deduction and that the balance of the assets will go elsewhere.

Unhappy Marriages

Sometimes a marriage may not be very successful. It has not ended in a divorce, but the dislike of the two parties is more than noticeable. Here each would like to cut the other off completely. In most jurisdictions this is not possible. Indeed the legislatures have seen fit in many states to spell out the minimum that one spouse can leave to another. If the testator leaves less than the required amount to the spouse, the surviving spouse has a "right of election" against the will. In many instances the spouse, if shortchanged under the will, can come in and carve out the legal share of the estate; those assets are forever lost to the children or other members of the testator's family. Under a proper will provision the challenging spouse can be limited to a few dollars outright and a life interest in the balance. Hence, at the surviving spouse's passing, the funds would be available for carrying out the testator's intentions once again.

Federal and State Taxes

The tax clauses under a will should not be treated lightly. Taxes are going to be paid—you can rest assured of that—but how? Are they to be apportioned against each beneficiary? What about that insurance policy on your life payable to wife, child, partner, corporation, etc.? If you own it, it will be part of your taxable estate. The jointly owned property? This too is part of your taxable estate, and usually the whole value, not half, is taxed in your estate. Then any living trust you may have established, if it is revocable or you have retained a lifetime economic interest in it, will be taxed in your estate. Deferred compensation contracts and many more items will be in your taxable estate. BUT these items are not necessarily included in your testamentary estate, i.e., those assets passing under your will.

Now you must consider whether or not the testamentary estate is to bear the tax burden or only part of it. If it is, what part of the testamentary estate carries the load? Is it to be borne as an expense of administration, or will the burden be picked up by the residuary estate? In most jurisdictions, if the will does not provide for tax payments, the tax burden will be apportioned among all beneficiaries.

Forgiving a Family Debt

If you are going to forgive a family debt, do so by all means, but make specific reference to its size, date of creation, and terms. If the debt is a no-interest loan, say so. Remember that if there is a record of the debt anywhere, it will be included in your estate, and your executor or administrator has a duty to collect it. Also, the debt is an item that is subject to estate tax.

The Executor: His Rights, Duties, and Responsibilities

The so-called boiler plate in a will consists of provisions setting forth the rights and duties granted to or imposed upon the administrator of an estate so that he or she may successfully carry out the duties and requirements imposed upon him or her by the will and by the laws of the jurisdiction in which the executor is called upon to function. Many testators become annoyed by the pages of powers granted and ask counsel if they are necessary. The answer is almost always "Yes." The testator must be certain that whenever he dies, the will would provide adequate tools for his or her executor. Laws vary from state to state, and if the will is silent, the executor must prove that the law of wills and estates where the testament was executed granted the authority in question (asking the court to take judicial notice of the laws of a sister jurisdiction). This takes time and costs money, a good deal more than a few extra pages in a will. The more complex the estate, the more detailed the powers must be.

In choosing your executor or trustee, get one who is responsible financially. Select an appointee who will be able to be on the scene day and night, who will not sicken, die, or take vacations—in short, one who will be permanent. Finally, you want the benefits of your estate to inure to the good of your heirs and not be dissipated in unnecessary constructions proceedings, litigation, or sloppy administration. The fiduciary should be able to achieve every possible economy for your estate. If all these considerations are taken into account, it is usually advisable to select a corporate fiduciary. Banks and trust companies are eminently well equipped to perform these functions.

BECOMING TESTATE

And now the last act, executing the will. A will is a statutory creature and must be accomplished in keeping with the laws of the testator's jurisdiction. The following are generally required:

1. A statement that you make, publish, and declare the instrument before you as your last will and testament.

2. A statement that you are familiar with its contents, having read it over.

3. A statement that you ask the witnesses (usually three, rarely fewer than two) to witness your signature.

4. You date and sign the last page; this is optional. Some attorneys have every page signed or initialed at the end.

5. You request the witnesses to sign as witnesses and do so in your presence and the presence of each other. Some wills have the attestation clause following the testator's signature, and the witnesses sign after the said clause, it having been read to them aloud. In an alternative procedure the witnesses sign below and to the left of the testator's signature, after which follows the attestation clause. They then sign again and write their home addresses.

You are now testate. The will now needs a home, and the testator's safe-deposit box is not the place. Most banks have will safekeeping boxes and will keep a will there at no charge, if favored with a fiduciary appointment. Attorneys will accommodate their clients by keeping the original in their firm's safe or safe-deposit box. Whatever you do, keep it where it can be reached if needed. On death, your own safe-deposit box is sealed. If the will is kept in the house, it can easily be lost, but you should have a conformed copy for your personal file for ready reference.

The will should be reviewed, preferably every three years and certainly every five. In fact, whenever anything that affects your dispositive thinking occurs, you should review your will.

In a chapter such as this, only highlights have been touched: most specific statutes, tax laws, or regulations, as well as case law, have been deliberately omitted. The field is specialized in the extreme. You should not move without a group of specialists at your side: the attorney-draftsman, the accountant, your trustman, and your life underwriter. Remember that the will is you in totality, all your holdings for all your family, with all your thought for the rest of their lives. Remember, too, you will die but your will will live.

Index

Soviet Union, gold production in, **36**-5 to **36**-6, **36**-13

Soybean meal or oil:
CFTC position limit for, **32**-21
contract information on, **32**-6
daily trading limit on, **32**-11
last day of trading for, **32**-14
notice day for, **32**-13

Soybeans:
CFTC position limit for, **32**-21
contract information on, **32**-6
daily trading limits for, **32**-10
forecasting model for, **33**-10 to **33**-12
last day of trading, **32**-14
moving averages for, **33**-13 to **33**-14
notice day for, **32**-13

Special situations, **16**-1 to **16**-15
balance sheet analysis in, **16**-14
convertibles in, **16**-15
earnings valuation in, **16**-12 to **16**-14
external, **16**-9 to **16**-10
extraordinary stock market undervaluation or overvaluation, **16**-10 to **16**-12
filters for, individual-portfolio eligible lists, **56**-12
internal: acquisitions and mergers, **16**-2 to **16**-3
cash and cash equivalents, companies well supplied with, **16**-9
management-initiated litigation, companies that may benefit from, **16**-9
other ways of improving stock liquidity and marketability, **16**-8 to **16**-9
recapitalizations, **16**-5
reorganizations and asset conversions, **16**-5
repurchases by companies of their own stock, **16**-6 to **16**-7
residual stubs and liquidations, **16**-6
spin-offs, **16**-3 to **16**-5
stock splits or large stock dividends, **16**-7 to **16**-8
tender offers and fights for control, **16**-6
internal factors versus external factors in, **16**-1 to **16**-2
measuring gain or loss potentials of, **16**-2
options in, **16**-15
technical analysis and timing in, **16**-14 to **16**-15

Speculative activity, indicators of excessive, **8**-5 to **8**-6

Spendthrift trust clause, **59**-12
Spin-offs, profiting from, **16**-3 to **16**-5
Split-dollar plan, **60**-2
Split funding arrangements, **67**-10 to **67**-11
Split-gift election, **64**-35
Splits, stock (*see* Stock splits)
Spray trusts, **64**-14 to **64**-15
Spread orders, **23**-14, **32**-16
Spread positions, **35**-5
Spreads:
appeal of, **23**-16
calendar, **23**-16 to **23**-17

Spreads (*Cont.*):
in commodity futures trading, **35**-3 to **35**-11
combinations, **35**-8
intercommodity spreads, **35**-7
intermarket spreads, **35**-7
intracommodity spreads, **35**-5 to **35**-6
low-risk, **35**-8
tax considerations, **32**-23, **35**-8
margin rules for, **23**-12 to **23**-13
price, **23**-18 to **23**-19

Sprinkel, Beryl, **9**-12, **9**-20
Sprinkling trusts, **66**-14 to **66**-15
Stamp brokers, **41**-4
Stamp catalogues, **41**-5
Stamps, **41**-1 to **41**-6
Standard & Poor's, bond ratings by, **24**-3, **24**-15 to **24**-16
insurance and, **26**-7
municipal bonds, **26**-8
Standard & Poor's 500-Stock Index:
Antique Price Index and, **38**-8
art prices and, **37**-5
computation of, **2**-2 to **2**-3
money supply related to, **9**-13
Standard & Poor's 425 Industrial Stock Index, **2**-16, **8**-12
as inflation hedge, **5**-12 to **5**-15
1960–1973 price changes in, **2**-18 to **2**-19, **2**-21
Standard & Poor's Rails as inflation hedge, **5**-12 to **5**-15
Standard & Poor's Utilities as inflation hedge, **5**-12 to **5**-15
Standard Oil of California, bond issues of, **25**-5, **25**-6, **25**-8, **25**-10
State agencies on aging, **63**-21 to **63**-24
State gift taxes, **64**-37 to **64**-38
State government bonds (*see* Municipal and state bonds)
State income taxes, municipal bonds and, **26**-5, **26**-8
State inheritance taxes:
estate planning and, **64**-4
gifts and, **64**-37 to **64**-38
wills and, **68**-10
State pension funds (*see* Pension funds)
Stigler, George J., **15**-10
Stock-bond ratio (*see* Bond-stock ratio)
Stock exchanges (*see* Exchanges, securities)
Stock insurers, **59**-15
Stock Investors' Confidence Index, **8**-12
Stock market (*see* Bear market; Bull market; Overextended market; *and entries below*)
Stock market bottoms, long-lead indicators for forecasting, **7**-12 to **7**-14
Stock market cycles (*see* Stock market trends)
Stock market indicators:
arithmetic average of price relatives, **2**-5 to **2**-7
combination link relatives, **2**-7
comparative performances of, **2**-7 to **2**-8
consensus approach to, **8**-26 to **8**-29
in correlation and regression analysis, **3**-8, **3**-9